Metaphysical Themes 1274–1671

Metaphysical Themes
1274–1671

ROBERT PASNAU

CLARENDON PRESS · OXFORD

UNIVERSITY PRESS

Great Clarendon Street, Oxford ox2 6dp

Oxford University Press is a department of the University of Oxford.
It furthers the University's objective of excellence in research, scholarship,
and education by publishing worldwide.

Oxford is a registered trade mark of Oxford University Press
in the UK and in certain other countries

British Library Cataloguing in Publication Data
Data available

Library of Congress Cataloging in Publication Data
Data available

ISBN 978–0–19–956791–1

ISBN 978–0–19–967448–0 (pbk)

For Kim,
without whom this might have been a better book,
while yet everything else would have been so much worse.

CONTENTS

The most ancient opinions are often returned to as if new, and many delight in resurrecting them because—having been forgotten—they seem to say new and marvelous things. And so it is that the young listen to them with pleasure, because it is natural for what is new and marvelous to delight the senses.

Buridan, *In De an.* III.11

But Aristotle, that supreme dictator of human wisdom, what did he think about this?

Vanini, *De admirandis* dial. 2, p. 7

There is nothing more seditious and pernicious than a new doctrine.

Morin, *Refutation* p. 3

History neglects nearly all these particulars, and cannot do otherwise; the infinity would overwhelm it.

Hugo, *Les Misérables* I.3.1

1

Introduction

1.1. Four Centuries

The present study seeks to learn something about the metaphysics of substance in light of four rich but for the most part neglected centuries of philosophy, running from the late medieval period to the early modern era. At no period in the history of philosophy, other than perhaps our own, have metaphysical problems received the sort of sustained attention they received during the later Middle Ages, and never has a whole philosophical tradition come crashing down as quickly and completely as did scholastic philosophy in the seventeenth century. My hope is to understand the nature of the late medieval project, and the reasons for its demise.

The very first thing that must be done, in pursuing such a project, is to find a better way to talk about these four centuries. Apart from the ever growing absurdity of referring to the seventeenth century as the modern era, the labels 'medieval' and 'modern' carry connotations that I wish to eschew, and make assumptions that I do not wish to take for granted. It is, moreover, entirely a matter of taste and perspective regarding when one wants to situate the start and close of the "classical era," the "Middle Ages," the "Renaissance," or "modernity." For William Ockham, near the start of the fourteenth century, the moderns were his flat-footed contemporaries, whose views he demolished; a century later, the *via moderna* was Ockhamism. For Kenelm Digby, in 1644, the moderns are recent scholastic authors; forty-nine years later, Locke takes "the Corpuscularians" to be the moderns, and to have "possessed the Schools" in place of "the Peripateticks." Ours is still a different perspective. One might like to follow Hobsbawm's suggestion that, for 80 percent of humanity, the Middle Ages ended only in the 1950s. Given my own rather more parochial historical interests, I tend to think of modernity as coming in the late twelfth century, with Averroes's magisterial commentaries on Aristotle. With respect to all such judgments, there can be no fact of the matter.[1]

---

[1] I might as well confess from the start that I aspire, perhaps quixotically, to nothing less than a reform our philosophical usage of the term 'modern.' Although it is admittedly useful to have a ready label for seventeenth- and eighteenth-century philosophy, we can perfectly well talk about it this era in just those terms: as the philosophy of a certain century. Moreover, by retaining 'modern' to talk about truly modern thought—beginning *circa* 1900—we gain something much more valuable: a handy way of talking about this more recent transformation in philosophy, without having to resort to the misleading label 'analytic philosophy,' which in turn leads to the pernicious distinction between

In what follows, I set aside all such talk of modernity, renaissances, and middle ages. My subject is simply four centuries in the history of philosophy. Naturally, I have had to pick and choose. In many areas, where seventeenth-century philosophy was largely barren, it would have been a tedious and depressing exercise to watch the insights of the scholastic era fall into neglect and disrepute. For this reason, I have set aside language, logic, and natural theology, and instead focused on that area where the contrast among views is most striking and illuminating: the domain of metaphysics. It is, however, no part of my agenda to decide on winners and losers, advances and retreats. If nothing else, the diversity and complexity of views precludes any such global pronouncements. We can speak in general of the *scholastics*, referring to those philosophers from the thirteenth century well into the seventeenth (and beyond) who taught philosophy and theology in a university setting, in accord with a common Aristotelian method, vocabulary, and set of assumptions. It will very quickly become apparent as we proceed, however, that scholastic philosophers agree among themselves no more than does any group of philosophers from any historical period. The superficial similarities of style and vocabulary conceal enormous differences of doctrine, just as great as those that divide philosophers today.[2]

The variety of philosophy during the seventeenth century is better known, but even so it gets understated by our selective attention on a handful of the most original and interesting thinkers—Descartes, Hobbes, Spinoza, Locke, Leibniz. There are of course tremendous differences even among these thinkers, but these are as of nothing when compared to the full spectrum of seventeenth-century views, all the way from Spinozistic monism to the most doctrinaire and conservative scholasticism, and all points in between. Needless to say, I have not managed to cover all points in between, neither for the seventeenth nor for any century. It would in fact be quite impossible to cover

the "analytic" philosophers and that grab-bag of modern historical figures who are not analytic and so get called "continental" philosophers.

On the moderns, see Ockham, *Quod.* V.22 (*Opera theol.* IX:564–5): "moderni ponant quod in omni praedicamento sunt multa ordinabilia secundum superius et inferius, . . . et dicunt quod istis abstractis semper correspondent decem parvae res distinctae primo . . .". For the *via moderna*, see e.g. Gilbert, "Ockham, Wyclif'; Gabriel, "Via Antiqua"; Courtenay, "Antiqui and Moderni."

Digby invokes the moderns at *Two Treatises* I.6.1: "it will not be amiss to express what we mean when we reject qualities, and how, in some sense, we are content to admit them. According to that description that Philosophers ordinarily do make of them (and especially the modern), we can by no means give way to them." See also Locke, *Some Thoughts*, sec. 193: "Only this may be said, that the Modern Corpuscularians talk, in most things, more intelligibly than the Peripateticks, who possessed the Schools immediately before them."

On the beginnings of modernity, see Hobsbawm, *Age of Extremes*, p. 288. Compare Johnson, *The Birth of the Modern*, whose dates are 1815–30, Himmelfarb, *The Roads to Modernity*, which focuses on the late eighteenth century, and Barzun, *From Dawn to Decadence*, who shares my predilection for the twelfth century: "if any renaissance ever did occur, it was in the twelfth century, leading to the high medieval civilization of the thirteenth" (p. 47). Walter Map, the twelfth-century English courtier, argued that the span of human life ensures that the scope of 'modernity' will be roughly a century (*De nugis curialium* I.30).

[2] The term; *scholasticus*; in its present sense, is in common use from the sixteenth century on: see e.g. Fonseca, *In Meta.* VII.1.1 (II:200bB); Vasquez, *In Summam theol.* 3a 194.2 n. 11; Suárez, *Disp. meta.* 50.5.3: "hanc opinionem nullus fere Scholasticorum secutus est . . ."; Scipion Dupleix, *Metaphys.* II.3.1. Something like its present usage can be found in Dietrich of Freiberg (*circa* 1280): "Cuius rei consideratio [de natura accidentium] non modicam ingerit difficultatem scholastice inquirentibus, compugnantibus ad invicem rationibus ad rationes et auctoritatibus ad auctoritates . . ." (*De accidentibus* 1.2 [*Opera* III:55]). It appears even before the era I recognize as scholastic, in Peter Lombard in the twelfth century: "De hoc enim sancti doctores subobscure locuti sunt, atque scholastici doctores varia senserunt" (*Sent.* II.30.6.1). The term itself appears frequently in Augustine in the late fourth century (see *Confessions* VI.9.14 etc.). For a detailed investigation, see Quinto, *Scholastica*.

it all, even in a lifetime. The human mind tends to suppose that what it does not know about does not exist, and for our four centuries this fallacy is especially misleading. The almost unknown era of philosophy between 1400 and 1600 gave rise to vast quantities of material, much of which still survives. Although the fifteenth century is practically *terra incognita* to modern scholars, we have more philosophical texts from that century than from the previous two centuries combined, and more studies of Aristotle from the sixteenth century than we have from the whole prior history of Latin Aristotelianism, all the way back to Boethius.[3]

This vast and disparate material complicates any attempt to generalize not only about the relative merits of the different periods, but also about the extent to which developments in the seventeenth century can be regarded as novel. There is no temptation greater, for the medievalist, than the urge to hold a text triumphantly aloft and announce to the world that an allegedly modern idea had already been had, back in the year 1283. Although, as will be clear already, I am sympathetic to scholastic thought, I have tried to resist such triumphal moments. Indeed, from a certain vantage point it seems clear enough that post-scholastic thought represents a radical inversion of the prevailing Aristotelian paradigm, turning inside-out the characteristic scholastic conceptions of form, matter, and substance. If these seventeenth-century ideas were not exactly new—having been anticipated not just by scholastic authors but also by Islamic and ancient Greek thinkers as well—they were nevertheless pursued with a sophistication and thoroughness that makes that century well worth the massive amount of attention it has received from historians of philosophy. Even so, as we will see in many domains, much of what is most interesting about seventeenth-century metaphysics flows quite naturally from scholastic thought, and looks much less original when considered in that light. I have accordingly come to think of the progress of ideas over these four centuries as analogous to the famous Necker Cube, the different faces of which assume a greater or lesser prominence depending on how one looks at it.

The chapters that follow work through various fundamental metaphysical issues, sometimes focusing more on scholastic thought, sometimes on the seventeenth century. Although the organization is not chronological, it may be helpful to know from the start something about the scope of my research. I begin with the first challenges to what I call classical scholasticism, the scholasticism of Bonaventure and Thomas Aquinas among others. Both died in 1274, a date that furnishes the book's nominal starting point. Those classical authors naturally disagree on many fronts, but here I treat that period largely as background, and pick up the debate with the first generation of critics of classical scholasticism—especially Peter John Olivi (who began his magnum opus *circa* 1274), John Duns Scotus, and, later, William Ockham. From there I pick and choose among various scholastic authors of the fourteenth through

---

[3] For the proliferation of philosophy texts in the fifteenth and sixteenth centuries, see Schmitt, "Towards a History" p. 9. On the varieties of seventeenth-century philosophy, see Mercer, "Vitality," Schmitt, *Aristotle and the Renaissance*, and Ariew, "Modernity," which begins: "There is very little content to the concept of Modernity except as a term of contrast with Antiquity and the Middle Ages, and what is signified as "modern" changes, depending upon the specific contrast one wishes to make" (p. 114). For reflections on Descartes as a "modern" philosopher, see Sorell, "Descartes's Modernity." For a powerful argument against dividing up our four centuries into medieval–Renaissance–modern, see Schmitt, "Recent Trends." For a recent example of my strategy of thinking of the period simply in terms of a series of centuries, see Perler, "Introduction."

sixteenth century, and then begin to track the rise of post-scholastic, non-academic philosophy—philosophers working outside the university context, who often mounted the most thoroughgoing challenges to the scholastic tradition. I stop in the seventeenth century with what I see as the end of the first stage of developments in post-scholastic philosophy: on the continent, with Descartes and Gassendi, and in England, with Boyle and Locke. The first drafts of Locke's *Essay Concerning Human Understanding*, dating from 1671, furnish the nominal closing date of this study. Although it would not be until December 1689 that Locke finally published the *Essay*, many of his central ideas date from those initial drafts, and I believe that the overall character of his thought was largely fixed around this time. Insisting on this admittedly somewhat artificial terminus has the considerable advantage of allowing me to exclude what I regard as a second generation of post-scholastic thought, arriving after 1671—in particular, Spinoza, Malebranche, and Leibniz, to say nothing of Berkeley and, still later, Hume. I discuss these figures only in passing. Of course there is inevitably something arbitrary about such decisions regarding where to start and stop, and I hope these lines of demarcation will not be taken too seriously. The truth, if you like, is that I pursued the issues as far as I could.

In terms of *historical* influence, the most prominent philosophical trends during this period are scholastic Aristotelianism and the rise of the mechanical philosophy. The first remained dominant within the universities for the entirety of our period, and the second brought about a philosophical and scientific revolution that began outside the universities but ultimately conquered all. In my view, these two trends are also the most *philosophically* interesting developments during this period. This is not an assumption I made from the start; it is the conclusion of a great deal of research. Readers whose interests lie elsewhere—aficionados of humanism, or the wild and wooly ideas of Renaissance Platonism—will want to find another guide to these centuries.[4] Even where my interest is greatest, however, my enthusiasm is not unalloyed. Scholastic authors were bound by threat of ecclesiastical censure to a rigid orthodoxy, even in many philosophical domains (Ch. 20). This gives their work, at least superficially, a veneer of stultifying conformity that, among many lesser figures, in truth goes all the way down to the core. When seventeenth-century authors were able to break free from this imposed orthodoxy, wide vistas opened up, but the path most often taken was a dry and barren reductivism (§14.2, §19.7). This would eventually be replaced by more philosophically interesting and scientifically fruitful theories, at the hands of figures like Leibniz and Newton, but it would take most of the seventeenth century to achieve such results. These later developments are, to my mind, the second-generation fruits of the metaphysically reductive tendencies of the earlier seventeenth century. Scholastic philosophy first had to be destroyed, before anything else could be built in its place.

---

[4] On the humanists, Hankins writes that "the humanist movement called for a radical change in the conception of what philosophy was and what it was for. For humanists philosophy was demoted to the position of one branch of literature among several. The emphasis was placed on moral philosophy, the only part of philosophy deemed useful to human life. Metaphysics, psychology and natural philosophy were neglected when not openly mocked for their obscurity and triviality. Logic was subordinated to rhetoric and reshaped to serve the purpose of persuasion" ("Humanism" p. 45). He goes on to say, on the next page, that "it did not produce great philosophers."

On Aristotelianism remaining "the predominant philosophical tradition," see Bianchi, "Continuity and Change" pp. 49–50, and the data he offers there.

Even so, that process of destruction, like the collision of atoms at high speed, is in many ways the most illuminating place to conduct research.

1.2. The Metaphysics of Substance

The subject of this book is four centuries of debate over metaphysics, in our modern sense of that term. Although we now think of metaphysics differently from how the field was defined during our period, I will not attempt, here or later, to grapple with the question of what metaphysics is or was taken to be. Instead, I will take for granted our current sense of what a metaphysical question is, and I will pursue such questions over a range of historical contexts, including not just treatises on metaphysics, or commentaries on Aristotle's *Metaphysics*, but also works on logic, physics, biology, psychology, and theology.

I do not try to survey all of metaphysics, but confine my attention to the metaphysics of substance. This is to say that I take as my principal focus various questions concerning the unity, persistence, and change of those features of reality—substances—that we regard as existing in the most proper sense. Within this broad field, my principal interest is material substance, and accordingly my starting point, in Part I, is the thesis that all change requires an enduring material substratum of change. This leads, in Part II, to a discussion of how matter, suitably informed, yields the substance itself—the dog, cat, or stone that comes into existence, endures through various sorts of changes, and ultimately goes out of existence. Part III then takes up the general character of the properties or accidents that come and go while that substance persists, and parts IV and V consider the two principal kinds or categories of such properties—Quantity and Quality. Finally, with all these ingredients in mind, Part VI turns to the question of how substances persist as unified beings through time.

If this study shows nothing else, I think that it shows how little we yet understand these issues. Even with respect to what is most central to the Aristotelian project—prime matter (Chs. 2–3), sensible qualities (Chs. 21–2), and substantial forms (Chs. 24–5)—we have a woefully poor understanding of what exactly the scholastics thought. The situation becomes even worse when we turn to more peripheral issues such as modes (Ch. 13), successive entities (Ch. 18), powers (Ch. 23), and integral parts (Ch. 26). And these are as nothing compared to the really obscure problems of metaphysics during our period, such as the nature of inherence (Ch. 11), extension (Chs. 14–16), location (Ch. 17), and persistence (Chs. 28–30). It is emblematic of the poverty of our knowledge in these areas that even with regard to our topic's central organizing concept—substance—scholars have labored under the most grievous misunderstandings, even with respect to the canonical figures of the seventeenth century (Chs. 6–9).

Most authors during our period worked under rigid ideological constraints that made certain theses impossible—on pain of death—to maintain. One can nevertheless find, on most topics, an extremely wide range of views. Even on so fundamental a question as how substances persist through time, one finds authors taking seriously theses that run the full gamut of possibilities, from the view that nothing truly persists, and that instead all entities are *entia successiva* (Ch. 18), to the opposite extreme that all entities are permanent (Ch. 28). It is, moreover, not just in the seventeenth century that such views emerge; they are indeed discussed in detail, as we will see, all the way back in the fourteenth century.

At the same time, there is a great deal of commonality among authors. Everyone during our four centuries accepts the reality of substances, as the things that exist in the most proper sense. Everyone accepts that there are permanent, enduring entities—that not everything is successive (Ch. 18). Nearly everyone accepts a distinction between material and immaterial entities (Ch. 16). Nearly everyone accepts that everything that exists is particular (§5.3, §27.4), and is located at a particular time and place (Chs. 16–17). These are points of agreement among both scholastic and post-scholastic authors.

Despite the enforced orthodoxy of much of scholastic thought, and despite the tedious reductionism of much of post-scholastic thought, these four centuries mark some of the highest points in the history of philosophical thought. When studied in conjunction they put on display what is perhaps the fundamental issue in metaphysics: the choice one faces between either pursuing ontological parsimony or vindicating our ordinary ways of conceiving the world. The usual program of the Aristotelian scholastics is to pursue the second at the expense of the first, and so one finds among the Aristotelians a vast and exotic ontology of actualities and potentialities, all designed to allow us to make sense of the world as it seems to be—a world of extended, finite substances, cohering and enduring through time, variously colored and shaped, capable of interacting in complex ways with other substances. The usual post-scholastic program, in contrast, pursues parsimony at the expense of explanatory adequacy, and so dismantles large segments of the Aristotelian framework. The result is an austerely reductive ontology of bodies in motion—an ontology that makes it nearly impossible to account for much of our commonsense worldview of enduring substances. Such choices create the principal tension that motivates this study.

1.3. Metaphysical Parts

Suppose, at least for a while, that there are enduring substances of familiar sorts—dogs, cats, stones, and the like. Suppose these substances come into existence at a time, exist for some time, and then go out of existence. Eventually, we will be in a position to reconsider this hypothesis (Chs. 18, 28–30), but let us start, at least for now, the way a good Aristotelian should. A good Aristotelian believes that the common wisdom of the folk is not to be despised. This means, in the domain of metaphysics, taking seriously the notion that what exist most properly are the ordinary, enduring substances of everyday experience.[5] This substance-based ontology lies at the foundation of scholastic metaphysics. To study the decline of scholasticism in the seventeenth century is, in no small part, to witness the collapse of this foundation. In the chapters to come, a ready way to gauge this book's progress toward its conclusion will be to measure how much of that substance ontology still remains intact.

---

[5] For Aristotle's use of the received opinions of others (ἔνδοξα), see *Topics* I.1. See also *Meta.* VII.3, 1029a33–34: "Since it is agreed that there are some substances among sensible things, we should look first among these. For it is an advantage to advance toward that which is more intelligible."

In order to explore this substance-based ontology, and eventually to test its cogency, we should consider what such substances are composed of. A natural answer to that question—and one that should by no means be despised—is that a plant, say, is composed of branches, leaves, parts of leaves, and so on. These are the *integral parts* of a substance; set them aside for now. It is not perfectly evident that a substance has any other kinds of parts. But suppose we could show that something about a substance changes independently of its integral parts, or endures after all its integral parts have ceased to exist, or simply cannot be explained in terms of its integral parts. Then we would have reason to suspect there are constituents of substances that are not any of its integral parts. These are what I will call the *metaphysical parts* of a substance. To call them parts at all is potentially misleading, in that such parts are utterly different from integral parts. But this is the customary Aristotelian usage, reflecting the idea that such entities do indeed belong to the substance, without being identical to the substance. The term 'metaphysical' is my label, one that seems apt inasmuch as such parts can be identified not by the usual empirical methods, but only by abstract, metaphysical arguments—arguments whose very abstruseness makes them vulnerable to dismissal if not derision.[6]

The Aristotelian tradition recognizes two main kinds of metaphysical parts: form and matter. If there is one overarching tendency that characterizes the seventeenth-century critique of scholasticism, it is the tendency to reject metaphysical parts in favor of an analysis solely in terms of integral parts. On this rests the rejection of substantial forms, real accidents, and unactualized prime matter. Out of this arise the characteristic disputes of the post-scholastic era, over the mind–body problem, causality, substance, identity over time, and the appearance–reality gap—issues brought to the forefront of philosophical discussion in the seventeenth century because of the immense difficulty in dealing with these matters without appealing to metaphysical parts. These problems remain with us today. Although we now tend to speak not of form and matter but instead of properties, functions, dispositions, and the like, the issues are much the same.

---

[6] The term 'metaphysical parts' is not scholastic. Scholastic authors do regularly speak of integral or (often equivalently) quantitative parts, which are standardly contrasted with essential (or qualitative) parts. See, e.g., Ockham, *Tract. de corp. Christi* 12 (*Opera theol.* X:112–13); Aquinas, *Summa theol.* 1a 8.2 ad 3: "Est autem duplex pars: scilicet pars essentiae, ut forma et materia dicuntur partes compositi, et genus et differentia partes speciei, et etiam pars quantitatis, in quam scilicet dividitur aliqua quantitas." Metaphysical parts, on my usage, include not only these essential parts, but also accidental forms and perhaps other accidental, metaphysical entities (if there be others). McMullin, "Matter as Principle," considers at length the status of such parts (which he calls "M-Principles") in Aristotle and in twentieth-century philosophy. The fundamental source for the scholastic distinction between kinds of parts is Aristotle, *Meta.* V.25, 1023b12–25, which explicitly speaks of form and matter as parts. For a fine recent overview, see Arlig, "Mereology" and also Clemenson, *Descartes' Theory of Ideas* p. 17. For a late scholastic treatment, see Goclenius, *Lexicon* pp. 788–99. For a survey of Scotistic usages, see Fernández García, *Lexicon* pp. 464–5. See also Burley's brief treatise, *De toto et parte*, and Buridan, *Summulae* 6.4.4, which discusses integral parts in detail.

The distinction endures into the seventeenth century, but not always intact. Locke, for instance, seems not quite to grasp it when he remarks: "integral parts, in all the writers I have met with, besides [his adversary], are contra-distinguished to essential; and signify such parts, as the thing can be without, but without them will not be so complete and entire as with them" (*Second Vindication* sec. XII, p. 246). He thus goes on to treat the head as an essential rather than integral part of the body. Leibniz, without using the language of parts, gets at something like the distinction I wish to draw in his early letter to Thomasius: "Nam etsi utraque explicatio et scholasticorum et recentiorum esset possibilis, ex duabus tamen possibilibus hypothesibus semper eligenda est clarior et intelligibilior, qualis haud dubie est hypothesis recentiorum, quae nulla entia incorporalia in mediis corporibus sibi fingit, sed praeter magnitudinem, figuram et motum assumit nihil" (*Phil. Schriften* IV:164–5; tr. Loemker p. 95).

It is indeed hard to think of any problem in philosophy more profound and far-ranging than the status of metaphysical parts.

It will be useful to have a shorthand expression for talking about the movement away from metaphysical parts, toward a theory couched entirely in terms of integral parts. I will therefore deploy the term 'corpuscularian' to refer to theories that postulate only integral parts within bodies, rejecting all metaphysical parts. I will also use the closely related term 'mechanistic,' but for a different thesis: that the causal relationships between bodies can be explained entirely in terms of local motions produced through contact. Both of these terms date from the seventeenth century, and have been used more or less loosely since that time in something like the way I will use them. Throughout this volume, I will use these terms more precisely than usual, in accord with the definitions just given, so as to be able to refer directly to these two sets of fundamental issues.[7]

The great forerunner of corpuscularianism was the Presocratic atomist Democritus, whose views were familiar throughout the scholastic era thanks to Aristotle's detailed reports. Albert the Great remarked back in the middle of the thirteenth century that there was something right about Democritus's appeal to atoms: in analyzing any body, such as a piece of flesh, there is a point at which one cannot divide further without that body ceasing to be the kind of thing it is, with its characteristic operations. If these are what atoms are, then Democritus is right to say that they compose all bodies. That is, "he did not err, if he was thinking of quantitative, physical composition. He did err, however, in that he did not see the first essential composition, which is of form and matter. For a minimal part of flesh is composed of matter and form" (*In Gen. et cor.* I.1.12). Albert was not particularly well informed about the atomist project, but what matters for now is the way he criticizes Democritus. Atoms cannot be basic entities, according to Albert, because they themselves are subject to another, more fundamental, metaphysical sort of composition, that of form and matter. Hence "quantitative, physical composition" is not ultimate.

Later authors commonly made this same point in the context of the four Aristotelian elements—Earth, Air, Fire, Water (§21.2). Giles of Rome, a generation after Albert,

---

[7] On the term 'corpuscularian,' see Boyle, *Certain Physiological Essays* (*Works* II:87) and *Excellency and Grounds of the Corpuscular or Mechanical Philosophy* (*Works* VIII:103–4; Stewart pp. 138–9): "When I speak of the *Corpuscular* or *Mechanical* Philosophy,...I plead only for such a philosophy as reaches but to things purely corporeal...." For the details, see *Origin*, passim, which he describes as "an introduction into the elements of the Corpuscularian philosophy" (p. 4). See also Locke, *Essay* IV.3.16: "I have here instanced in [≈ invoked] the corpuscularian hypothesis, as that which is thought to go farthest in an intelligible explication of the qualities of bodies, and I fear the weakness of human understanding is scarce able to substitute another which will afford us a fuller and clearer discovery of the necessary connection and coexistence of the powers which are to be observed united in several sorts of them." Later authors recognized Boyle as having coined the term 'corpuscular' in this sense—see, e.g., Leibniz, *Confessio naturae* pt. I (*Phil. Schriften* IV:106; tr. Loemker p. 110).

For a typical statement of what I am calling *mechanism*, see Boyle's *Excellency*: "the *Mechanical* Philosopher being satisfied that one part of matter can act upon another but by virtue of local motion, or the effects and consequences of local motion" (*Works* VIII:109; Stewart p. 145). See also Locke: "The next thing to be considered is how bodies operate one upon another, and that is manifestly by impulse, the only way which we can conceive bodies operate in us" (*Essay* II.8.11). And see Thomas Sprat in 1667: "generation, corruption, alteration, and all the vicissitudes of nature are nothing else but the effects arising from the meeting of little bodies of differing figures, magnitudes, and velocities" (*History of the Royal Society* p. 312).

For an extended recent overview of the rise of corpuscularianism and mechanism in the seventeenth century, see Gaukroger, *Emergence of a Scientific Culture* ch. 8.

traced the levels of composition from the whole human body down to hands and feet, and then to flesh and bones, and then to the four elements. Just as those higher levels are not fundamental, "so nor is a human body composed firstly, absolutely, and unconditionally out of the four elements, because such elements are resolved into matter and form. Therefore matter is prior in the composition of a mixed body to the so-called elements" (*In Gen. et cor.* II, f. 248rb). Hence although one might be tempted to take at face value the Aristotelian doctrine of the four elements as *basic*, in fact these are "elements" only relatively speaking. The most basic Aristotelian elements are form and matter.[8]

Although the paradigm cases of integral and metaphysical parts are easily enough distinguished—limbs, organs, left half, right half, as contrasted with form and prime matter—it is less obvious how to give a general account of the distinction. I suggested above that metaphysical parts can be so-called because our grasp of them depends on abstract, metaphysical arguments, whereas integral parts can be grasped empirically. But this cannot be the criterion for the distinction. Most obviously, it cannot be right for integral parts at the microscopic level. The debate over atomism, even when viewed in its narrowest, least interesting guise, as a debate over the divisibility of bodies (§5.4), is every bit as metaphysical as is any debate over metaphysical parts. Nor will this serve as a criterion even at the macroscopic level, because even there the status of a body's integral parts turns on extremely difficult metaphysical questions (Ch. 26).

It also helps not at all to mark the integral–metaphysical distinction in terms of materiality versus immateriality, or concreteness versus abstractness. Although there might at first glance seem something immaterial about metaphysical parts, that characterization hardly fits prime matter, a paradigmatically metaphysical part. And inasmuch as forms inhere in prime matter, they are to that extent *material* forms, and fundamentally a part of the physical, material world. When scholastic authors distinguish between the material and the immaterial, they intend a distinction that cuts across the different sorts of forms, so that some forms—in particular, the human soul—are immaterial, whereas most others are material (§16.1). Metaphysical parts also do not seem to be especially abstract. Like integral parts, metaphysical parts are located in time and space, and have causal powers. Indeed, I will be arguing that one of the most important tendencies of later scholastic metaphysics is to conceive of metaphysical parts in increasingly concrete, physical terms, not just as formal or material causes, but also as efficient causes. When Aristotelianism comes under attack in the seventeenth century, it is almost always conceived of in these terms, as a physical hypothesis about the causal structure of the natural world (see esp. §6.1, §10.5, §24.3).

But pointing to materiality gets us into the right neighborhood for drawing the distinction. What we want to say is not that the integral parts of a body are its *material* parts, but that they are the parts of a body that are themselves *bodies*. Metaphysical parts, in contrast, are not bodies but are instead the ingredients of bodies. This further entails that, for the Aristotelian, integral parts are always themselves composed out of further metaphysical parts—in particular, out of form and matter.

---

[8] For Giles of Rome on hylomorphic composition as ultimate, see also *In Gen. et cor.* II, ff. 242rb–243ra. Similar discussions appear in a trio of later *Gen. et cor.* commentaries: Nicole Oresme (II.3), Albert of Saxony (II.3), and Marsilius of Inghen (II.3).

The great question that animates philosophical disputes during our four centuries is just how many metaphysical entities must be postulated. If one focuses on the paradigm cases—prime matter, substantial form, and real accidents—then the answer we now associate with the seventeenth century is *zero*. René Descartes was not the first but he was the most influential proponent of this view. Writing in 1638, he invited a correspondent to "compare my assumptions with the assumptions of others: that is, compare all their real qualities, their substantial forms, their elements, and almost infinitely many other such things, with my single assumption that all bodies are composed of various parts" (II:200). In place of this near infinity of metaphysical parts, Descartes offers mere bodies and their parts—their integral parts, that is. This same reductionist program was already in place in his early, unpublished *The World* (1629–33):

If you find it strange that in explaining these elements I do not use the qualities called Hot, Cold, Wet and Dry—as the philosophers do—I shall say to you that these qualities themselves seem to me to need explanation. Indeed, unless I am mistaken, not only these four qualities but also all the other [qualities], and even all the [substantial] forms of inanimate bodies, can be explained without the need to suppose for their effect any other thing in their matter besides the motion, size, shape, and arrangement of its parts. (XI:25–6)

Ultimately, Descartes would not limit his rejection of substantial forms to the case of inanimate bodies (line 4), but would famously include the forms of living bodies: souls. The reductive strategy, however, remained the same: in place of the obscure metaphysical parts of the scholastics, Descartes put an account of the body's integral parts, variously shaped and variously moved, according to the laws of nature.

Corpuscularianism is practically definitive of seventeenth-century thought, at least in its main current, appearing in various forms in Francis Bacon, Isaac Beeckman, Sebastian Basso, Galileo, Pierre Gassendi, Kenelm Digby, Henry More, Walter Charleton, Robert Boyle, Locke, Newton, and Leibniz—among many others. We will have many occasions, in the chapters that follow, to consider the strategy in its variations and intricacies. One general historical puzzle that arises for our four centuries, however, is why this view became so commonplace during the seventeenth century and yet was practically undefended before then. As we will in Chapter 19, the view *had* been defended, in particular by Nicholas of Autrecourt in the 1330s. It was, however, condemned in 1347, and subsequently forbidden among later scholastics. Only once the Church's authority had weakened in the seventeenth century could these unspeakable ideas, bottled up for centuries, burst onto the scene, generating a ferment of philosophical activity that makes it not entirely ridiculous to speak, even now, of this period as the dawn of modern philosophy.

All the same, even if the scholastics were unable to give the sorts of answers characteristic of the seventeenth century, they nevertheless almost always asked the same questions. The corpuscularian strategy, in particular, was on the table from early in the fourteenth century, in large part because of the influence of William Ockham. As we will see, Ockham held a more-or-less orthodox scholastic view with respect to prime matter (Chs. 2–3), substantial form (Chs. 24–5), and qualities (Ch. 19). But Ockham took the startling view that these were the only sorts of metaphysical parts. His fame and notoriety among later scholastics arose in large part from his powerful and persistent attempts to eliminate from his ontology every vestige of metaphysical commitment that could not be reduced to one of these kinds of entities. Ockham deploys over and over (esp. §14.3, §19.2) the following test in assessing the proper degree of ontological commitment: for any new characteristic that we might ascribe to a given body, consider whether that new claim can be accounted for solely in virtue of facts about the spatial location of that body and its integral parts. If such facts are sufficient to account for the claim in question, then it is superfluous to introduce any further ontological items. Ockham regards this kind of argument as decisive against the reality of a great many alleged entities, and it is this that drives his famous Razor. Although he by no means counts as a corpuscularian, he brings into play the sort of argument that would be invoked throughout the seventeenth century against all kinds of metaphysical parts. As will become steadily more apparent, the seventeenth-century rejection of scholasticism grows naturally out of trends that date back to the beginning of the fourteenth century.

Usually, in discussing the metaphysics of substance, I will tacitly set to one side the extensive ontology of immaterial entities—souls, angels, and God—that nearly all parties to the debate accept, no matter how reductively corpuscularian their views otherwise are. The most notable exception to this consensus was Hobbes, the most thoroughgoing corpuscularian of all the figures under discussion. On his austere picture, the only things there are—the only things in the universe—are bodies (§16.2). To say that bodies are subject to accidents is just to say that those bodies move about and act on other bodies. Any supposedly spiritual substance, such as an angel or even God, must itself be a body.

Hobbes's unqualified corpuscularianism is exceptional, both in its rejection of immaterial entities and in the rigor with which he applied it to bodies (§7.1, §10.2, §28.4). More often, corpuscularianism comes in degrees. Would-be corpuscularians nearly always find themselves obliged to appeal to metaphysical parts at one point or another in their attempts to explain reality. This is true even for Descartes, whose ontology includes not just substances but also modes (§13.5)—thus the passage quoted above concludes by invoking the reality not just of matter but also of "the motion, size, shape, and arrangement of its parts." Postulating modes further leads Descartes to a conception of substance as something surprisingly indeterminate and metaphysical (§13.7). As we will see repeatedly, much of what is interesting in seventeenth-century philosophy comes not from attempts to give corpuscularian accounts of various physical phenomena, but from the way corpuscularian philosophers felt forced to diverge from the strictly corpuscularian at various junctures, in order to save some vestige of the commonsense ontology of substance defended by the scholastics. Much of what follows will be devoted to studying these episodes, and attempting to determine, in individual cases, whether and why the corpuscularian philosophy had to be compromised.

1.4. Sources

Four centuries may look like too much territory to cover in anything other than a superficial way. It is, however, essential to my purposes to try. If one picks up the story only from the end of the sixteenth century, one can give a passable account of which scholastic authors directly influenced which post-scholastic authors. There is little doubt, for instance, that most of what Locke knew about scholasticism came from minor textbook authors from around the start of the seventeenth century. One can learn quite a lot, then, by comparing these textbooks to later figures like Locke, and many recent scholars have done just this. The approach is of limited value, however, if one wants not just to connect the historical dots, but also to understand the philosophical issues. Late scholastic textbooks are wholly dependent on earlier scholastic material, and the ideas in these later textbooks, superficially sketched for the edification of an undergraduate audience, cannot be adequately appreciated apart from those traditions. To understand these traditions in turn requires going back all the way to the late thirteenth and early fourteenth centuries. It is here that one finds the original and most powerful statements of the various scholastic ideas that ground the mainstream of philosophical thought all the way until nearly the end of our period. Compared to this earlier material, the later textbooks are as shadows on a cave wall.

As I visualize the terrain of this study, it takes the rough shape of two plateaus divided by a trough. The plateaus—those periods of greatest philosophical flourishing— correspond to the initial and final hundred years of our period, leaving the trough in between for the two hundred intervening years. Such is my provisional impression, but the reader should keep in mind, here and on every page to come, just how vast a corpus of material is extant from these four centuries, and just how little of it, in absolute terms, I have managed to read.

To read these texts means, in most cases, to read them in Latin, and usually to read them in centuries-old editions, if not in manuscript. Almost none of the works I will be talking about have been translated into English or any other modern language. Most have not been edited in modern times, and indeed I suspect that some have not been read at all, by anyone, in centuries. It is perhaps no wonder, then, that scholars have almost never attempted to tell the sort of continuous story I am purporting to offer, across the entirety of this period. Accordingly, I have for the most part not had the benefit of a well-developed secondary literature. Many of the topics that I discuss have received almost no attention from modern scholars, and often I have had to construct my own taxonomy of positions and attendant nomenclature.

I have not, however, been without helps of various sorts. One feature of the scholastic period that makes it more tractable is the scholarly, reference-laden nature of these writings. Then as now, university professors cite their sources, and talk about the views of others, often at great length. So even if I have read only a fraction of philosophical texts from our four centuries, I have read enough to know which works were generally regarded as the most important, and I have managed to read those. One can also learn a great deal about the scholastics from reading their seventeenth-century critics. Although I will periodically complain that one or another criticism is misguided, I think in general that the famous figures of the seventeenth century get their scholastic forebears largely right, and that indeed they know this material better than we know it today. After all, they grew up with it. For this reason, just as I hope to shed light on seventeenth-century thought by considering its scholastic context, so I hope to illuminate scholastic thought by considering its ultimate rejection. One of the best ways to appreciate the Aristotelian approach to metaphysics is to consider why it was abandoned, and what came of that.

The first-generation critics of scholasticism—Bacon, Descartes, Hobbes, etc.—were not professors, and their writings are popular today in part just because they are not scholarly. They rarely mention scholastic authors by name, and it is usually impossible to know exactly which sources might have been influential on them. In the chapters that follow I almost never engage in speculation regarding which scholastic texts an author like Descartes or Locke might have had foremost in mind. Although such historical detective work may afford a veneer of scholarly precision, it can in fact be nothing more than speculation, and is accordingly of negligible value for my purposes. The most important avenue for understanding the historical context of post-scholastic thought is not to look for direct lines of influence between one text and another, but simply to understand the spectrum of scholastic views that would have been broadly familiar to anyone in the seventeenth century with a tolerably good philosophical education. As modest a goal as that may seem, it has never come anywhere close to being realized, in any area of scholastic thought.

This is not to deny, of course, that there has been some excellent scholarly work done on the history of metaphysics over these four centuries. Such work is scarce for the scholastic era, and especially the later scholastic era. But when one manages to cross the great Sahara of the fifteenth and sixteenth centuries into the era of the mechanical philosophers, there suddenly appears on the horizon a magnificent oasis, in the form of a massive, highly sophisticated secondary literature on every aspect of the period. Readers making the journey with me will perhaps come to share my puzzlement over why this oasis appears when and where it does, since it accompanies at most a modest increase in the philosophical sophistication or interest of the primary texts. Even so, weary travelers must take refuge where they can, without complaint. So although the main focus of my attention is on the texts themselves, I have tried to learn as much as I could from this brilliant body of scholarship on later seventeenth-century authors, especially Descartes and Locke. I try to indicate all of this—the scholarly lacunae, my debts, and my areas of disagreement—in the notes. These notes are, however, very much intended for specialists. The main text is written with the hope and expectation that most readers will ignore the fine print.

Readers at all familiar with the recent flourishing of interest in metaphysics will recognize that I owe a significant debt to this body of work as well. Indeed, without the example set by this literature, it is hard to imagine my having written this book—both hard to imagine my understanding the issues well enough to have written it, and hard to imagine my thinking it worth the many years of effort. This is a debt, however, that I do not spend any time acknowledging in the pages that follow, and quite deliberately so. Although there is undoubtedly much to be learned by comparing the metaphysics of my four centuries with metaphysics today, there is also a considerable risk in so doing. As soon as one begins to apply modern templates to older texts, one forecloses the possibility of finding those texts to be doing things that do not simply, boringly, anticipate modern ideas, but actually do something interestingly new. So although each and every chapter to come is tacitly indebted to recent work in philosophy, I have kept that material out of the text, both for my sake and for the reader's. If others think this material worth bringing into dialogue with contemporary debates, I will be very glad, but I see that as a further step best left for others.

Taking all of these resources together gives us not just 400 years of work on metaphysics, but over 700—stretching from the thirteenth century all the way into the twenty-first, taking into account not just the scholastics and their first generation of critics, but also the subsequent ways in which readers have understood these four centuries of thought. In looking closely at the original sources, and then the many subsequent iterations of interpretation, my impression is not of a field coalescing around some increasingly well-defined truth, or fluctuating between two well-defined alternatives. Instead, the history of philosophy appears to me to display much the same pattern that Harold Bloom has found to characterize the history of poetry—a pattern of ongoing traditions occasionally punctuated by innovations, where the innovations turn out, on close inspection, to be often a product of misinterpretation. Scholastic authors misinterpret other scholastic authors; their critics misinterpret them all the more. Modern scholars misinterpret the scholastics and their critics. Throughout, even when philosophers are not trying to do something new, the obscurities of our subject often ensure that we do so anyway, unwittingly. As the chapters to come will show repeatedly, many of the important metaphysical ideas of our period—the defining character of substance (§6.2), the idea of a substratum (§9.1), the nature of immateriality (§16.3), the notion of a power (§23.5)—are in fact a product of one of these episodes of Bloomian Interpretation. Such episodes are indeed so rife, for so much of the history of philosophy, that with respect to that history we might well be said to be living in a dark ages of our own.

PART I

MATTER

2

Substratum

2.1. The Surprising Consensus

We should begin with those parts, or elements, that are most basic. But which are those? Albert of Saxony, the influential fourteenth-century natural philosopher, writes that "on one possible description, an element is what is found last when bodies are taken apart, and what is found first when bodies are generated" (*In Gen. et cor.* II.3). If this is how we understand *element*, then the truly first element of bodies is prime matter: it is presupposed by generation and exists after corruption. If the vulgar masses think of earth, air, and so on as the primary elements (Ch. 21), this is only because "the vulgar do not perceive that prime matter is prior." These are Albert's conclusions, but they are conclusions that would be widely accepted across our four centuries. Hence, in considering the constituents of material substance, it seems reasonable to begin with prime matter.[1]

In view of the notorious obscurity of the doctrine of prime matter, this might seem a difficult place to begin, and an unlikely place to find consensus. Jacob Zabarella, the great sixteenth-century Paduan scholastic, opens his treatise on the subject with the forbidding remark that "nothing in the natural world seems to be more obscure and difficult to grasp than the prime matter of things" (*De rebus naturalibus*, Prima materia I.1, col. 133). Be that as it may, this is a topic on which scholastic and post-scholastic authors share a surprising amount of common ground. Franco Burgersdijk, an early seventeenth-century scholastic,[2] writes:

All seem to have granted to Aristotle that the generation and corruption of natural things requires contraries and matter, or a common subject for the contraries. . . . All have judged by unanimous consensus that matter is . . . the first subject from which natural things are composed, and into which, when they expire, they are ultimately dissolved. (*Collegium Physicum* II.3–4, pp. 13–14)

---

[1] Albert of Saxony's account of prime matter as elemental is also found in Nicole Oresme, *In Gen. et cor.* II.3 (p. 199), and in Marsilius of Inghen, who remarks that "strictissime, . . . nihil est elementum nisi materia prima" (*In Gen. et cor.* II.3, f. 102ra). Albert and Marsilius are probably both following Nicole in their commentaries, as they often do.

[2] On Burgersdijk, see the studies in Bos and Krop, *Franco Burgersdijk*.

Authors less sympathetic to scholasticism reach the same conclusion. Gerard and Arnold Boate, in their *solida confutatio* of Aristotelian natural philosophy from 1641, acknowledge that "no sane person denies . . . that some preexisting matter is required in all generation." This thesis, "the most certain of all things," is one that "no one has ever called into controversy" (*Phil. naturalis* I.2.1, p. 12). Jean Chrysostome Magnen, later in that same decade, confidently holds that "no one will deny that prime matter should certainly be postulated" (*Democritus reviviscens* 1.1, p. 58). Walter Charleton, a few years later, describes it as "unanimously confessed by all" that there must be a material substratum composing all bodies and enduring through change (*Physiologia* II.1.1.3).

Naturally, proponents of corpuscularianism did not endorse the scholastics' *metaphysical* construal of prime matter. Burgersdijk, after describing the consensus, goes on to remark that "what this subject or matter is, and what the contraries are, and how many, and of what sort they are, and whether they ought to be called the principles and elements of natural things—there has almost never been more diversity in views about a thing than there is about this." Charleton prefaces his above-quoted remark with the cautionary note that "what is the general matter of all concretions . . . has been by more disputed than determined, in all academies." The young Leibniz tells his former teacher Thomasius in 1669 that "nothing is more true than Aristotle's view of primary matter," but immediately goes on to remark that what is at issue is whether this and other Aristotelian theories "can be explained by size, shape, and motion."[3] For the strict corpuscularian, on my terminology (§1.3), prime matter would have to be accounted for in terms of a thing's integral parts. Atomists in particular had no difficulty in postulating some sort of analogue to prime matter, inasmuch as they could appeal to a homogeneous stuff that endured through all change. I will take up the difference between corpuscularian and metaphysical prime matter in the following two chapters, after here focusing on their areas of agreement.

The hostility of seventeenth-century corpuscularians toward scholasticism is such that one might reasonably be inclined to doubt whether—despite the superficial expressions of agreement—there is in fact any substantive common ground here. In fact, however, there are two very interesting and significant theses that nearly everyone in our period accepts. First, there is the *substratum thesis*:

All natural change requires a substratum that endures through the change.

Second, there is the *conservation thesis*:

Prime matter is naturally conserved through all change.

In effect, the proponent of these two theses is staking out the commonsensical middle ground between two radical views. On one extreme is the view that nothing ever goes out of existence; on the other extreme lies the view that nothing ever endures. As we will see in the final part of this study, there were authors during our period who were tempted by one or the other of these radical extremes. Even so, the consensus, throughout our four centuries, was that something in between ought to be said: that

---

[3] *Phil. Schriften* IV:164 (tr. Loemker pp. 94–5). Leibniz, it should be said, remarks in the same passage that the doctrine of substantial forms is also certain. This is a far more idiosyncratic perspective, as we will see in Ch. 24.

there is an enduring core to material things that persists through all change, but that such change is itself perfectly real.[4]

The degree of consensus over these two theses is remarkable, given that neither seems self-evident. As we will see below, the two theses are close to being mutually entailing, but they often seem to have been regarded as independently motivated. Let us, then, consider them in turn.

2.2. The Substratum Thesis

An Aristotelian, proceeding under the assumption that there are enduring complex substances, will want to distinguish between cases of change to an enduring substance and cases of change from one substance to another. Changes of the first kind are traditionally called *alterations*, and changes of the second kind are called *substantial changes*, when one substance is *corrupted* and a new one *generated*. (Strictly, 'alteration' refers only to *qualitative* change, but a somewhat broader usage will be useful here.) If we consider only alteration, then the substratum thesis thus restricted (call this special case S^A) becomes self-evident, because the substratum will just be the substance. The controversial case, then, is the case of substantial change (S^{GC}). Why not allow, when one substance is corrupted and a new one generated, that there might be an ontological rift that goes, as it were, all the way down? Why, for instance, when a dog is corrupted, and a dog-corpse is generated, must there be any part of the dog that continues to exist as a part of the dog-corpse? Why couldn't the situation be as shown below, with

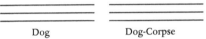

Dog   Dog-Corpse

nothing to bridge the rift between one substance and the next? (Ignore for now the question of what the depicted strata represent, exactly, and whether a corpse is indeed a substance.) The gap in the schema does not denote that any time must elapse between the dog's corruption and the corpse's generation; let it be instantaneous. The question is whether anything must endure through that instant of death.

That something must endure—that the picture must instead be as shown below,

Dog   Dog-Corpse

where the bottom line represents prime matter—might seem to be one of those dogmas of scholastic metaphysics that post-scholastic authors would gladly rid

---

[4] In the seventeenth century, the doctrine of an enduring material substratum can be found in anti-Aristotelians such as Basso, *Phil. nat.* De forma I, intentio 1; Hobbes (note 18 below); Boyle, *Possibility of the Resurrection* (VIII:308; Stewart pp. 202–3); Henry More, *Ench. meta.* 9.1–2. Newton writes, in an unpublished manuscript: "Ex materia quadam communi formas et texturas varias induente res omnes oriri et in eandem per privationem formarum et texturarum resolvi docent omnes" (McGuire, "Transmutation" p. 76).

The consensus over the substratum and conservation theses is perhaps so universal as to make these doctrines all but invisible to modern scholars. One of the few to discuss these issues is Des Chene, who writes that "in the sixteenth and seventeenth centuries, at least, the substrate argument was unchallenged" (*Physiologia* p. 59). In contrast to my view, however, Des Chene regards the thesis as "almost anodyne."

themselves of. In fact, though, I have found no one who rejects the substratum thesis. One quick explanation for this consensus would be that everyone is using *generation* and *corruption* as technical terms, to cover precisely the case where a thing comes to exist out of preexisting matter, or goes out of existence while its matter endures.[5] But although scholastic authors do often use the terms in these technical senses, and sometimes do defend S^{GC} on these narrow, definitional grounds, there was a consensus that the technical usage is warranted just because we have independent grounds for thinking that S^{GC} is true. That is, the technical use of 'generation' and 'corruption' was warranted by a prior confidence in the thought that all natural coming into and going out of existence will involve enduring matter.

Why this confidence? By far the most common argument in favor of the substratum thesis appeals to the *ex nihilo* principle, that *nothing is made from nothing*. Aristotle had said that its denial was the thesis that, "more than any other, had preoccupied and alarmed the earliest philosophers" (*Gen. et cor.* I.3 317b29–30), and he repeatedly invokes the doctrine as one that is almost universally accepted.[6] The Jesuit Benedictus Pererius,[7] in his superb treatise on natural philosophy, *De communibus principiis* (1562), offers this as the first of a series of arguments in support of prime matter: "Nothing is made from nothing, and everything is made out of something, and from something, and is made [to be] something. Indeed, not anything can be made out of anything, but out of a certain, definite subject" (V.4, p. 281). Gassendi, in his defense of corpuscularian prime matter, draws on Epicurus and Lucretius to make the same argument.[8]

---

[5] The quick argument for substratum by technical definition is offered by Albert of Saxony, *In Phys.* I.14 (p. 199): "Secunda conclusio: nihil potest generari ex nihilo. Probatur: nam hoc ex quid nominis generationis implicat contradictionem; sed a nullo potest fieri quod fieri implicat contradictionem; ergo etc." (Albert treats the *ex nihilo* principle as essentially equivalent to the substratum thesis.) Ockham, in contrast, explicitly rules out this sort of argument by definition (*Summula* I.11, *Opera phil.* VI:187).

[6] Aristotle cites the *ex nihilo* principle as almost universally accepted at *Phys.* I.4, 187a27–29 and *Meta.* XI.6, 1062b23–24, and endorses it himself, when properly understood, at *Phys.* I.8, 191b13. He appeals to it as the basis for the substratum thesis at *Meta.* VII.7, 1032b30–1033a1: "Therefore, as is said, it is impossible that anything should come about if nothing were present before. So it seems that some part will be present of necessity in what comes about, since the matter is a part, and since it is present in what comes about and becomes that." At *Physics* I.7, 190a33–b5, Aristotle usefully distinguishes between S^A and S^{GC}: "Now in all cases other than substance it is plain that there must be something underlying (ὑποκεῖσθαί τι), namely, that which becomes. For when a thing comes to be of such a quantity or quality or in such a relation or place, something underlying is always presupposed, since substance alone is not predicated of another underlying thing, but everything else of substance. But that substances, too—the things that are without qualification—come to be from some underlying thing, will appear on examination. For there is always something that underlies, from which proceeds that which comes to be; for instance, plants and animals from seed." The passage does not state the substratum thesis quite as clearly as it might, because it does not expressly say that the subject "from which" a thing comes will endure in the new thing. Although translating ὑποκείμενον literally, by "something underlying," seems to suggest as much, the word might also be rendered by "subject," which removes the implication. And the concluding example, of seeds becoming plants and animals, does not seem to support the substratum doctrine. Averroes, however, goes to some length to show that the case of a seed becoming a living thing points toward an enduring substratum just as much as does the case of a white thing becoming black (*In Phys.* I.62, f. 18rb). See also *Gen. et Cor.* II.1 329a24–b3 and *Physics* I.9 192a29–34 (discussed in §2.5).

[7] For more information on Pererius, see Blum, "Benedictus Pererius."

[8] Gassendi appeals to the *ex nihilo* principle as follows: "Caeterum et quia Materia in rerum successione et generationum corruptionumque serie, est semper omni forma prior, omni forma posterior, tamquam praevia, socia, et superstes cuilibet formae, sumpta exinde fuit Effati illius occasio, quod Satyricus expressit illo carmine, *De nihilo nihil, in nihilum nil posse reverti*" (*Syntagma* II.I.3.1, I:232ab). He goes on to cite Aristotle's appeal to it, and then Epicurus's, and then at great length, Lucretius's. See also *Syntagma* II.1.3.5 (I:259b): "Cum natura nihil ex nihilo faciat, redigatve in

What exactly is the argument? The *ex nihilo* principle is subject to various interpretations, some of which are too weak to yield the substratum thesis, and some of which are too strong to be plausibly defended. As ordinarily understood—what I will call its *weak reading*—the principle requires a thing to be brought into existence through some preexisting materials. To do otherwise, to make something where before there was nothing, is what (speaking strictly) is called *creation*. Only God can do that (or do its contrary, *annihilation*). Yet even if we accept that creation, so defined, is not naturally possible, this by itself will not get us the substratum thesis. To rule out my making bread *ex nihilo* implies only that I need certain ingredients. I cannot make bread out of nothing and moreover, as Pererius implies above, I cannot make bread out of just anything—I need "certain, definite" ingredients. Still, this weak reading of the *ex nihilo* doctrine does not yield the substratum thesis, because it does not imply that those ingredients (or any part of them) must themselves endure through the baking process, and continue to exist in the final product. (I assume that ordinary language is neutral on the question of whether an *ingredient* continues to exist within the final product.) To get the endurance result, we need a stronger reading of the *ex nihilo* doctrine. Perhaps the doctrine requires not just that there be some preexisting ingredients (any old ingredients); perhaps it requires the very ingredients that constitute the thing generated. But this is liable to be too strong. Aristotle, for instance, had speculated (*Phys.* I.4, 187a27–b7) that this sort of understanding of the *ex nihilo* principle is what led Anaxagoras to the strange view that anything generated must have already preexisted in the constituent materials. For Anaxagoras there would be bread—perhaps too small to be seen—in the ingredients used to bake the bread, and so on, for everything that there is. Surely this is not how we want to understand the *ex nihilo* doctrine.

What we want, of course, is the idea that *something* of the final product must have been in the ingredients—not the bread itself, but something underlying the bread which also underlay the ingredients. This is what Pererius is gesturing toward when he remarks that "everything is made out of (*ex*) something, and from (*ab*) something, and is made [to be] something." Although the passage might be clearer (it alludes to an important text on this subject from Aristotle [*Meta.* VII.8, 1033a24–27]), the idea seems reasonably clear: that there must be ingredients, *and* something from those ingredients must be a constituent in what is made, *and* the thing made will (in part) be what the ingredients (in part) were. This *strong ex nihilo* principle does yield the substratum thesis. But we still have not seen anything like an argument for either principle. In general, it is easy to find authors appealing to the *ex nihilo* principle in defense of prime matter, but hard to find anyone who spells things out. In other cases, we will see how bedrock scholastic theses that were taken for granted by early scholastic authors are subsequently given a more sustained defense later on, as the opposition

---

nihilum, oportet quidpiam superesse in Concretionum dissolutione quod inexsolubile, intransmutabileque sit." Diogenes Laertius's *Lives*—the most important source during the latter part of our period for information on ancient atomism—ascribes the *ex nihilo* principle not just to Epicurus (X.38–9) but also to Democritus (IX.44).

For other appeals to the *ex nihilo* principle as the grounds for the substratum thesis see Coimbra, *In Phys.* I.9.1.1, arg. 2 (p. 150); Eustachius a Sancto Paulo, *Summa* III.1.1.2.2 (II:120); Albert of Saxony, *In Phys.* I.14 obj. 1 (p. 190): "si non [possibile sit aliquid fieri de novo, nullo subiecto praesupposito], hoc maxime esset propter hoc quod ex nihilo nihil fit"; pseudo-Marsilius of Inghen, *In Phys.* I.17. Magnen puts the *ex nihilo* principle first among a long list of principles: "Ex nihilo nihil fit: hoc est, agentia naturalia exigunt subjectum ut agant, et materiam circa quam versentur" (*Democritus reviviscens* disp. 1, pp. 54–5).

to scholasticism grew. But because the doctrine of prime matter was never challenged, it rarely received a sustained defense.

2.3. Arguments for the *Ex nihilo* Principle

One of the most thorough discussions of the substratum thesis comes near the start of our period, in Ockham's brilliant *Summula philosophiae naturalis* (*c.*1320). The very first question of Book I asks how it can be established that form and matter compose natural bodies. He offers in effect the same argument as Pererius above, fleshed out over twenty-five lines so as to establish that the enduring thing (call it 'matter') must be only a part of the thing generated, and that therefore there must also be something new in the thing generated (call it 'form'). But then—and this is the sort of thing that makes the book brilliant—Ockham immediately adds:

This argument is based on the principle *ex nihilo nihil fit*, which the philosophers held to be a principle granted by everyone and on that basis to be known. For this reason no philosopher insisted on a proof of it. Yet this not withstanding, I will show dialectically (*persuadebo*) that nothing is made from nothing. (I.1, *Opera phil.* VI:156–7)

In setting out to give a merely dialectical argument, he takes for granted that the principle cannot be proved demonstratively (that is, from necessary first principles, showing the reason why it is true). Instead, he will show that the principle is *almost* certainly true, by appealing to experience. But before offering his argument, he makes a crucial clarifying remark about what exactly the principle means:

Something is said to be made *ex nihilo* when some necessary effect presupposes nothing as a part or a subject of that effect—no matter how much it presupposes something as an efficient cause. (I.1, VI:157)

So the *ex nihilo* doctrine does not rule out a thing's having an efficient cause—obviously, since otherwise not even God could make something *ex nihilo*. But it rules out more than a lack of ingredients, as on the weak reading of the principle; it further rules out the case where those ingredients do not constitute a "part or subject" of the thing generated. No wonder, then, that Ockham stresses that the argument for prime matter (via the substratum thesis) is grounded on the *ex nihilo* principle. On his strong reading of that principle, it turns out to be equivalent to the substratum thesis. And so no wonder, too, that others would appeal to the *ex nihilo* principle in arguing for the substratum thesis without offering any account of how the entailment goes. The one principle entails the other because they are the *same* principle.[9]

Before looking at Ockham's rather subtle argument from experience for the *ex nihilo* principle, and so for the substratum thesis, we might consider a much more straightforward argument from experience. This argument makes the simple inductive claim that we always see new things being composed of preexisting matter; therefore we can

---

[9] Ockham is quite clear on the identity between the substratum thesis and the *ex nihilo* principle, remarking: "Probare igitur quod nihil potest fieri nisi aliquid ei praesupponatur tamquam pars vel subiectum eius, est probare quod ex nihilo nihil fit" (*Summula* I.1, *Opera phil.* VI:157). For a very detailed analysis of the different senses of the *ex nihilo* principle, see Buridan, *In Phys.* I.15 (f. 18v).

conclude that this principle holds universally. Such an argument for the substratum thesis was commonplace, but it is given a particularly striking formulation by John Buridan, lecturing in the mid-fourteenth century:

The second conclusion is that it is necessary for everything that is naturally made to be made from a preceding subject or in a preceding subject (for a form is not made integrally *from* a preceding subject but rather *in* it). Yet I do not believe that this conclusion is demonstrable, but merely declarable through an induction in which no counter-instance is found. This is how Aristotle proves that conclusion ... (*In Phys.* I.15, f. 18vb)

Like Ockham, then, Buridan thinks no demonstration of the substratum thesis is possible. But Buridan's discussion is particularly interesting because he thinks the best we can do is a simple induction from our experience of change. He thinks that this is how Aristotle argues (at *Phys.* I.7, 190a33–b11), and he thinks that in general this is the method of reasoning one must use in the natural sciences. Thus he immediately continues:

and such induction should be regarded as a principle of natural science. For otherwise you could not prove that every fire is hot, that all rhubarb is purgative of bile, that every magnet attracts iron. Such inductions are not demonstrations, because they do not conclude on account of their   3 form, since it is not possible to make an induction from all cases. ... Through such an induction the intellect, if it does not see a counter-instance or counter-argument, is compelled by its natural inclination to the truth to concede the universal proposition. Moreover, he who is not   6 willing to grant such declarations in the natural and moral sciences is not worthy to play a significant role in them. (Ibid.)

Inductive arguments are not formally valid (lines 3–4), but they play a critical role in the natural science. Why should we accept them? Buridan's interesting answer is that (a) science would collapse without them, and (b) the intellect is "compelled" (*cogitur*) to accept them. He goes out of his way to make these claims about induction for two reasons. First, he is concerned with the claims of a skeptical movement in Paris, championed especially by Nicholas of Autrecourt (esp. §28.2), that rejected large swaths of Aristotelian doctrine on the grounds that it could not be proved. Second, Buridan's position here is rather delicate. He wants to claim that the substratum thesis cannot be demonstrated, and at the same time he wants to show that we have good reasons to endorse the thesis, but without going too far and showing that it is absolutely impossible for a thing to be made *ex nihilo*. Aristotle and Averroes did take that further step, and argue that creation *ex nihilo* is impossible, even for God, and that hence the world has always existed (*Phys.* VIII.1–2). As a Christian, teaching in a Christian university, Buridan is obliged to teach in accord with the faith, and so restrict the substratum thesis to cases of natural change. Hence he needs to stress that the inductive method is a principle of "natural science," thereby leaving room for his conclusion that the *ex nihilo* principle can be violated by God.

We might question the prospects for this sort of partial generalization, one that makes an induction from observed cases in order to reach a conclusion that holds generally (in natural cases) but not universally (inasmuch as it allows supernatural exceptions). For now, however, I want to consider a more basic assumption that Buridan makes: that we are in a realm where observation can play any role at all.

He takes it as a given that we can observe, at least in some cases of substantial change, that the substratum thesis holds. In fact, however, this is surely a case where observation offers no help at all. What we *see* occurring, through substantial change, is some amount of sensible continuity: more-or-less the same bulk, with more-or-less the same sensible qualities, seems to endure. But it is a further substantive step, a step that requires metaphysical rather than empirical argument, to show that these constant appearances are supported by some ongoing substratum. An enduring subject of change is simply never observed.

Zabarella, recognizing this point, would later propose a somewhat more sophisticated inductive argument. He acknowledges that in cases of substantial change we never observe an enduring substratum. So the inductive argument we have to make (and that he finds Aristotle making in *Phys.* I) goes from S^A to S^{GC}—that is, from there being an enduring subject of accidental change to there being an enduring subject of substantial change:

We see that wax goes from being without [a certain] shape to taking on a shape, and that water goes from being cold to being made hot. The subject of the generation of air from water is not likewise apparent, since it is insensible and hidden. Instead, the water seems entirely to pass away, and the whole substance of the air seems to be generated from no preexisting matter. So Aristotle, from the case of accidental change, led us to recognize that the same is the case for substantial generation. (*De rebus nat.*, Prima materia I.3, col. 136)

The inductive move here is rather dubious: why should we think that the case of accidental change shows anything about the need for a substratum in substantial change? Zabarella is well aware of the difficulties; he characterizes the argument as "a weak dialectical proof." Again, however, there is a more fundamental worry about whether the issue admits of *any* empirical treatment. Although Zabarella is quite clear that instances of S^{GC} cannot be observed—indeed he overstates the case by claiming (lines 3–4) that we seem to observe the contrary of S^{GC}—he still assumes that we can observe instances of S^A. Strictly speaking, however, even this much is not subject to observation. What we observe, in cases of accidental change, is an ongoing continuity in sensible qualities, together with some discontinuity in sensible qualities—for instance, a soft, warm, pale yellowish mass of stuff takes on a rounded shape. We customarily give a name—say, wax—to that mass, and think of it as enduring. But although we have been assuming for the sake of argument that there are such enduring substances, and stipulated that 'alteration' refers to any change made to an enduring substance, we in fact never observe that such alteration actually occurs. This is a metaphysical claim, and requires metaphysical argumentation (see Chs. 7, 18, 28–30). Hence even Zabarella's more careful inductive argument fails.[10]

---

[10] For other examples of Buridan's brand of straightforward inductive argument for the substratum thesis, see Eustachius, *Summa* III.1.1.2.2 (II:120), pseudo-Marsilius of Inghen, *In Phys.* I.17 (f. 16vb), and Albert of Saxony, *In Phys.* I.14 (pp. 197–8). Albert's discussion contains remarks on induction that are very similar to Buridan's. The complaint that induction would be a valid form of argument only if it could, impossibly, be based on observation of every case, would be restated in the seventeenth century as a criticism of Aristotelian method by Gassendi, *Exercitationes* II.5.5. Pseudo-Marsilius, like Buridan, stresses that we can have no demonstrative knowledge of prime matter: "Tertia conclusio: quod nullus processus quo devenimus in notitiam primae materiae est demonstrativus. Patet quia non potest demonstrari quin omnia fuissent ab aeterno, vel etiam quin omnia generentur secundum se tota" (*In Phys.* I.20, f. 19rb). Zabarella's

Since this is an issue we will encounter repeatedly in the chapters ahead, it bears emphasis here. Questions of identity over time—whether a thing endures, or is succeeded in time by something new and perhaps qualitatively quite similar—are metaphysical questions that can never be decisively settled by observation. One might, in an anti-metaphysical mood, decide that observation is our best guide to these matters. Perhaps, but in that case the point to make is that our evidence about identity over time is, in Zabarella's words, weakly dialectical rather than demonstrative. This is true not just for matter and substance, but even for the sensible qualities themselves. We may observe continuity in a sensible quality, such as a color, but whether in fact we are observing the same enduring quality, or a sequence of numerically distinct qualities, is not a question that can be settled by observation. We do not have to wait until Hume to see this last point made explicit. One of the liveliest areas of scholastic dispute, with regard to identity over time, concerns whether the accidental forms of a substance endure through its corruption. It was often argued that, even if the dog corpse seems to have the same color and feel as the living dog did, in fact none of the dog's accidental forms endure beyond its death. The sensible qualities of the dog corpse may be exactly like those of the living dog, but they are not numerically the same (§6.3 and §25.3). In general, then, it is vital to distinguish empirical questions from metaphysical questions. This is especially vital when discussing scholastic philosophy, because one of the most distinct features of the period—especially in contrast with the corpuscularianism of the seventeenth century—is its commitment to metaphysical arguments that go beyond the strictly empirical evidence. To conflate these is to take the first step toward dismissing scholastic philosophy.

If observation misleads even in the question of whether sensible qualities endure, then it can hardly be a guide to the more obscure case of an enduring material substratum. We need a better argument, then, in support of the strong *ex nihilo* principle and the equivalent substratum thesis. Let us return to Ockham. His argument begins by distinguishing between accidental change and substantial change, and describes the latter as a case where one thing is made through the destruction of something else. The question then is whether or not something of the thing destroyed remains in what is generated:

Either (i) that which is destroyed is totally destroyed, so that nothing of it remains in the generated fire, or (ii) something from it remains in the generated fire (which is what one has to say if it remains, since it cannot remain anywhere else). 3

If one says the second [= ii], that something remains in the generated fire, then it is certain that what remains is not the fire itself, for then that fire would exist before its generation. Therefore it is part of the fire, and we have the intended conclusion, that the generated fire 6 presupposes something as a part.

If, on the other hand, nothing of what is destroyed remains [= i], then the fire could have been made regardless of whether the other thing was or was not destroyed. The opposite of this 9 is clear from experience. Proof of the inference [at lines 8–9]: every effect can sufficiently be made by its causes when they are disposed in the proper way and brought close and there is no intervening impediment nor any stronger countervailing agent. But the thing's being destroyed 12

discussion of the inductive argument for the substratum thesis particularly stresses that it is *a posteriori* in the Aristotelian sense of arguing from effects, "absque ulla ex natura rei ducta ratione."

is not, according to you, a cause of the fire's being produced, nor is there an intervening impediment, nor a stronger countervailing agent. Therefore it can be made regardless of whether the thing was or was not destroyed—which appears false to the senses. (*Summula* I.1,   15 *Opera phil.* VI:157–8)

The last paragraph is the critical part. Here Ockham makes the inference (lines 8–9) that the denial of the substratum thesis leads to the false result that when a thing is generated from certain ingredients, those ingredients might just as well survive apart from the thing that has been made. Ockham regards this whole proof as merely dialectical because he has no way of proving that this *is* a false result, other than by appealing to our everyday experience. But if this is indeed the weakest link, then we will surely want to accept the argument. After all, it seems an obvious dictate of experience that when I make bread, the eggs and flour *cannot* survive—unless they survive within the bread, which is of course the result Ockham is after (at the level of prime matter). Consuming the ingredients is utterly necessary for making the bread. So here, for a change, is an argument where the experiential data does seem relevant to the intended metaphysical conclusion.

The crucial inference of lines 8–9 is equivalent to the following claim: that to explain why there are no ingredients left over after a thing is made one must postulate that those ingredients endure as the substratum of the newly made thing. Ockham's proof of this claim (lines 10–15) rests on a brief analysis of causation, where 'cause' is understood in a broad Aristotelian sense. Suppose we grant, as it seems we must, that the ingredients are among the causes that must be "disposed in the proper way" and "brought close" (line 11). According to the substratum thesis, those ingredients continue to exist within the new effect. If one denies that, and holds instead that the ingredients go out of existence, then one needs some account of why this must be. Their destruction looks, absurdly, like a further and quite unnecessary step in the causal process, since Ockham's opponent ("you" at line 13) must grant that the ingredients' destruction is not itself a cause. Why not, then, just skip the step where the eggs and flour are destroyed? It looks as if the opponent of the substratum thesis could have his bread and keep his eggs and flour too, baking loaf after loaf without ever needing to buy more ingredients. The only way Ockham sees to avoid this absurd result is to insist that the eggs and flour (or, to be precise, the prime matter beneath the eggs and flour) endures as the bread's substratum.

It seems to me this argument has a certain intuitive pull, but might nevertheless be evaded by a determined opponent. To be sure, it is not possible to make bread without somehow using the ingredients. But it still seems an open question whether we should think of *any* of those ingredients as persisting within the bread, or whether they might instead *all* be destroyed (all the way down to the most basic material level) when the bread comes into existence. If we postulate such complete discontinuity, then Ockham is quite right to demand some account of why the ingredients have to be destroyed. But perhaps this is just a brute law: that the making of one thing requires the destruction of the ingredients. This seems no more unmotivated or mysterious than the substratum thesis itself, which simply sets forth a different sort of brute law. In answer to Ockham's argument, then, we would say that although the destruction of the ingredients does not play a causal role in the generation of the effect, it is a necessary side-effect of the process.

Yet even if Ockham's argument is not decisive, arguments of this general form seem to have been widely accepted by later scholastic authors. Almost no one seems to think it possible that the ingredients might play a causal role and yet be wholly destroyed during the process of generation.[11] Some authors suggest that the most the ingredients' destruction could accomplish would be to open up empty space for the new substance to squeeze into. (Suárez wryly remarks that, if that were their only role, they might instead just move out of the way.)[12] The force of the intuition that the ingredients must partly endure is indeed so strong that it seems there must be some deeper motivation here. This deeper motivation can be found, I believe, in an argument that goes back to John Duns Scotus.

2.4. The Causal Simultaneity Argument: Scotus

Scotus is one of those rare philosophers whose principal achievement lies not in proposing novel theories but rather in offering deep and original arguments for common theories. In his *Lectura* (*circa* 1298), Scotus sets out to prove the existence of prime matter in the usual way, by invoking the Aristotelian idea of a substratum for change. But Scotus immediately introduces an objection of the sort we have been considering here: that the ingredients in substantial change might play a role in bringing about a new substance, but then wholly go out of existence at the instant of change. In reply, Scotus exploits the temporal details of the situation to argue that what has been destroyed cannot play a causal role:

On the contrary, that which is to be corrupted is prior to the generated things' being made— prior both in origin and execution. Therefore if, at that instant at which the agent generates, nothing of what is corrupted remains, then the agent presupposes nothing for its action. But

---

[11] I have found only a few instances of anything like dissent from the substratum thesis and the *ex nihilo* principle. First, Averroes speaks of "moderni" who hold that "generatio fuit ex non ente" (*In Phys.* I.60, f. 17vb). He regards this as so incredible, though, that it leads him into a discussion of how people can become accustomed to say or do almost anything, no matter how self-evidently wrong or bad, if they are set a bad enough example. He seems to despair of breaking this habit in any way other than by frequently repeating the correct view of the matter. I do not know who these "moderni" are.

Second, according to Cross (*Physics of Duns Scotus* p. 259), William of Ware accepts the substratum thesis, but only on the basis of faith. As far as natural reason can show, it might be possible for creatures to create—that is, to bring a thing into existence *ex nihilo*. Ware, that is to say, evidently questions more than the substratum thesis: he questions whether any prior ingredients are necessary at all. And he goes beyond merely claiming there are no demonstrative arguments for substratum. Evidently, he thinks there are not even effective dialectical arguments. (Scotus recites Ware's view at *Ord.* IV.1.1 n. 27; the Wadding edition cites Ware, *Sent.* II.1.6, which exists only in manuscript, and which I have not consulted.)

Third, and most explicitly, Nathanael Carpenter holds the contrary of the substratum thesis, contending that "omnia fiunt ex nihilo" (*Phil. libera* I.4). He defends this claim at some length against what he describes as the "opinio communis" that things arise *ex nihilo* only if created by God. His most telling argument observes that if there is something that remains through substantial change, then the enduring substratum would overlap with the newly generated thing, and "sic haberet duas distinctas essentias, et sic una res esset duae res, quod absurdum" (p. 77). In effect, this sort of objection to an enduring substratum just is an objection to scholastic metaphysical parts, which precisely require treating one thing as a composite of multiple overlapping things.

[12] For the idea that wholly destroyed ingredients might do nothing more than open up new space, see Albert of Saxony, *In Phys.* I.14 (p. 194); pseudo-Marsilius, *In Phys.* I.17 (f. 16va); Suárez, *Disp. meta.* 13.1.6.

since that action is its entirely complete action, it follows that the agent, by its entirely complete action, will generate *ex nihilo*. (*Lectura* II.12 n. 13)

Scotus's language is not as clear as it might be, but his point is tolerably clear (and gets further clarified over the following three paragraphs of the text). When one thing is corrupted and another is generated, the corruption comes first: there is no temporal overlap. But now consider the instant of generation. That which is corrupted is, *ex hypothesi*, no longer around at all. So the agent that brings about the new substance cannot be relying on those corrupted ingredients, because the ingredients are not there. And it is not as if one can say that the agent does not need those ingredients *now*, but needed them earlier. For now is the moment that counts; this is the moment where the new substance comes into existence, where the agent's "entirely complete action" (line 4) is taking place. So if the agent does not need those ingredients now, it never needs those ingredients. As Scotus puts it two paragraphs later, "the agent according to you has the whole effect within its own active power, because it presupposes nothing of that [corrupted thing] at the instant of generation."[13]

This strikes me as a powerful argument in favor of the substratum thesis, provided one is willing to grant the crucial but unstated assumption: that causal relata must be contemporaneous. What Scotus requires here, for the argument to go through, is that *a* can be the immediate cause of *b*'s coming to exist at some instant only if *a* also exists at

---

[13]   Here is the surrounding context to Scotus's main argument, as quoted in the main text. First Scotus raises an objection (n. 12): "Ad hanc rationem dicitur a quibusdam quod agens naturale agit in passum corrumpendum, et illud passum corrumpendum praesupponit in quod agat; sed in instanti corruptionis non praesupponit, sed tunc totum vertitur in totum, ex I *De generatione* [317a22]." He then makes the reply translated in the main text (n. 13): "Contra: prius naturaliter est corrumpendum quam genitum fiat, et prius in originando et exsequendo; igitur si in isto instanti nihil corrumpendi manet in quo generans generat, nihil praesupponet suae actioni; et cum illa actio sit actio sua perfectissima, sequitur quod actione sua perfectissima generans generabit ex nihilo, quod est contra propositionem acceptam quod 'omne agens naturale praesupponit passum in quod agat.'" He then considers the reply to this that generation *ex nihilo* can mean either from nothing at all, or from ingredients that are wholly destroyed, and that only the first is naturally impossible (n. 14). To this he replies (n. 15): "Contra: agens quod habet in virtute sua totum effectum, non minus potest producere amoto quocumque quo posito magis debilitatur virtus eius quam fortificetur; sed per te generans habet in virtute sua activa totum effectum, quia nihil eius praesupponit in instanti generationis. . . ." He then goes on to show that if the agent already has its complete causal efficacy at that instant, without the ingredients, then it would be counterproductive ("debilitating" rather than "fortifying") for those ingredients to have been destroyed. Very similar but less well developed discussions can be found in *Rep.* II.12 n. 3 and *In Meta.* VII.5 n. 9, where 'non' should be omitted from the first sentence. The *Ordinatio* as printed in the modern critical edition does not include distinction 12 of book two.

Ockham's argument in *Summula* I.1 looks very much like a crisper and clearer version of Scotus's, but with the crucial temporal component omitted. It is easy to believe that Ockham got the basic argument from Scotus, but hard to see how he could have left out the most important bit. Intriguingly, though, the version of Scotus's argument printed in the old edition of *Ordinatio* II.12.1 (Wadding VI.2:665) does for some reason omit the temporal element, and instead tries to run the argument without any appeal to the instant of generation. It is tempting, then, to suppose that Ockham's source for the argument was this version of Scotus's *Sentences* lectures.

Gregory of Rimini argues along lines similar to Ockham's, and also seems simply to take for granted that the ingredients cannot be a cause. He offers the barest hint of the crucial temporal component of the argument, remarking "esto quod lignum quod fuit corruptum, quando ignis ille fuit genitus, *non fuisset ibi*, adhuc [istud generans] sufficiens fuisset producere illum ignem. Nam constat quod illud lignum non fuit causa efficiens nec totalis nec partialis huius ignis. . ." (*Sent.* II.12.1, V:248). The highlighted *ibi* clause is temporal: the wood does not exist at the time when the fire is produced. In the seventeenth century, the argument appears in Dabillon, *Physique* I.3.1, p. 97: "et si le bois perit tout à fait lors que le feu est engendré, il ne contribue aucunement à sa production. Pourquoi donc le feu ne se fait il pas aussi bien du marbre que du bois?"

Walter Chatton, *Rep.* II.12.1 (III:283) states the argument more clearly than Scotus, albeit briefly, but presumably Scotus is his source: "Teneo tamen conclusionem communem quod materia est in entibus. Et probo persuadendo, quia efficaciter probari non potest, ut dixi. . . . Item, causa realis pro illo [instanti] quo causat, est; sed effectus causatur a passo in instanti quo capit esse, et hoc causatione reali; ergo non praecorrumpitur productioni effectus."

that instant. This is why Scotus insists that the thing corrupted is prior to the thing generated, and no longer exists at the instant of generation. If it is indeed completely non-existent at that instant, and if causation requires temporal overlap, then the ingredients cannot play any direct causal role. But it seems implausible to think that the ingredients play some sort of prior, indirect role in the process, before their corruption. Hence the denial of the substratum thesis entails the seemingly absurd consequence that one never makes something new out of prior ingredients. All generation would be *ex nihilo* in the strong sense of being literally from nothing.

The causal simultaneity thesis looks intuitively plausible, although of course it might be (and has been) questioned. The thesis does come up for sporadic treatment among scholastic authors, but I know of no satisfying treatments of the subject.[14] Still, although this discussion has to stop where its sources run out, we can see a kind of satisfying coherence in how things stand. A plausible defense of the substratum thesis can be mounted if one postulates at the start a certain minimal amount of overlap: the temporal overlapping of cause and effect. Unsurprisingly, to get a result, such as the substratum thesis, that makes a claim about temporal overlap, it helps to build some kind of overlap requirement into the premises. One still needs a few more non-trivial assumptions: in particular, that nothing can be made naturally without some kind of raw material, and that such raw material is a kind of cause of the new thing that is made. Moreover, Scotus's argument leaves untouched the character of this enduring raw material. Still, this is the best argument I have found for believing in an enduring substratum for change.

2.5. The Conservation Thesis

The substratum thesis seems to tells us only that, for any given natural change, there must be some enduring subject. Perhaps there is a different subject for different kinds of changes, and perhaps what endures through one kind of change will be corrupted by another kind. The conservation thesis seems to add something more to this picture: that there is a single, most basic substrate that endures through every material change, something we call prime matter. In fact, however, given a couple of very weak assumptions, the substratum thesis entails conservation. Aristotle long ago proved this, and scholastic authors commonly rehearse the argument. Suppose, contrary to conservation, that our best candidate for prime matter (call it M_1) naturally came into existence anew. Then, by the substratum thesis, there would have to be some preexisting subject (call it M_2) out of which prime matter came, and which endures as the subject of M_1. M_2 cannot be M_1, since *ex hypothesi* M_1 newly exists. Hence M_2 must be a part of M_1. But in that case M_1 is not the best candidate for prime matter after all; M_2 is a

---

[14] Scotus argues for the simultaneity of cause and effect at *In Meta.* V.2, but I cannot see that the discussion makes much progress. Oresme's discussion at *In Phys.* II.8 is more worthwhile. It is worth keeping in mind that, to be effective in the present context, the causal simultaneity thesis must extend beyond efficient causality, to cover material causality as well. Would it extend to final causality? That may seem unlikely, given the nature of final causes, but there was a lively scholastic dispute over the proper understanding of final causes, and on some accounts simultaneity would hold even there. See Pasnau, "Final Causes." The topic of causal simultaneity comes up again in §18.3 below, where Wyclif argues against the thesis.

better candidate. Could M_2 itself have previously come into existence through some natural process? Perhaps, but then we can run the argument again, and at some point we will arrive at the permanent substratum, M_n, which is the real prime matter. An analogous argument holds for the possibility of prime matter's going out of existence. Hence, given the substratum thesis, it is incoherent to reject the conservation thesis. The argument does make a couple of assumptions, unstated by Aristotle, that are familiar from other sorts of foundation-seeking arguments: (a) there can be no infinite regress of underlying subjects; (b) underlying subjects cannot run in a circle, level-wise, such that, for instance, M_2 is the substratum for M_1 and M_1 the substratum for M_2. With these assumptions in place, the argument is decisive.[15]

Conservation obviously entails the substratum thesis—or at least it does so within the material realm. The standard, although not universal, assumption of our period is that there are aspects of the created world that do not contain prime matter, and so are immaterial (Ch. 16). But since such entities—angels and rational souls—are not subject to generation and corruption, they are not relevant here anyway. In general, moreover, the two theses must be limited to cases of natural change. Conservation does not preclude matter's being divinely created or annihilated, and the substratum thesis does not apply to creation and annihilation. Authors from our four centuries unanimously endorse the Christian doctrine that matter was created by God, before which time there was no material world at all. Given these restrictions, however, and a few plausible assumptions, the substratum and conservation theses are mutually entailing.

Despite the fact that the conservation thesis can be derived from the substratum thesis, authors often seem to be committed to conservation in its own right, as if it were self-evident. This is particularly clear in seventeenth-century authors, who eagerly endorse the thesis quite apart from its Aristotelian framework. The idea appears in the earliest corpuscularian philosophers, such as Nicholas Hill's *Philosophia Epicurea Democritiana* (1601), which holds that "there is no multiplication of matter," just the continual rearrangement of the primary stuff (n. 504). (The obscurity of Hill's book inspired Mersenne to remark that "one would have to transcribe it, if one wanted to convey its reveries" [*L'impiété* ch. 10, p. 239].) The doomed Giulio Cesare Vanini (executed for heresy in 1619) insisted on a similar point: "If celestial matter is unchangeable, our matter too of its essence is perpetual and immutable. For it itself is never

---

[15] Aristotle's argument from substratum to conservation is at *Physics* I.9 192a29–34: "If matter came to be, something must have existed as a primary subject from which it should come and which should persist in it; but this is its own very nature, so that it will be before coming to be. (For I call *matter* the primary subject of each thing, from which it comes to be, and which persists in it, not accidentally.) On the other hand, if matter ceases to be it will ultimately pass into that [primary subject], so that it will have ceased to be before ceasing to be." Surprisingly, Irwin and Fine go out of their way to remark in a footnote to this passage that it establishes only the substratum and not the conservation thesis. In their words, "it does not show that there is some matter that never comes to be or perishes" (Aristotle, *Selections* p. 94n). It seems to me clear, though, that the passage establishes precisely that, and moreover shows that Aristotle is unambiguously committed to the substratum thesis.

Use of the argument is commonplace among scholastic authors, sometimes being ascribed to Aristotle and sometimes not. Ockham ascribes it to Aristotle at *Summula* I.11 (VI:187) and *In Phys.* I.18.7 (IV:205–6), and Aquinas's commentary likewise spells it out clearly (*In Phys.* I.15.139). Suárez rehearses the argument (*Disp. meta.* 13.1.4), without crediting it to Aristotle. Magnen, too, appeals to it, in showing that the ingenerability and incorruptibility of prime matter follows from its status as the first subject of any body (*Democritus reviviscens*, p. 59). For an example of someone questioning the no-circularity assumption, see D. C. Williams, "Form and Matter" pp. 514–15, who claims that matter can be the substratum for form, and form the substratum for matter. But Williams rejects the substratum thesis quite generally.

corrupted, but rather what is made from it is corrupted" (*Amphitheatrum* exerc. 5, p. 26).[16] Seventeenth-century authors were encouraged in these pronouncements by the renewed attention that Epicurus's writings were receiving (§5.2). His two most basic physical doctrines were the *ex nihilo* principle—"nothing comes into being out of what is not"—and a very strong version of the conservation principle: "the totality of things was always such as it is now, and always will be." Gassendi had highlighted these ideas, and they come to be a commonplace of seventeenth-century thought.[17]

Authors who defend the conservation thesis often claim in the same breath that prime matter is completely inalterable. This is a further claim, which I will set aside. Focusing solely on conservation, we might consider how Hobbes tries to defend it, independently of the substratum thesis. Hobbes treats conservation as a conceptual truth, in the sense that he takes its denial to be inconceivable:

When we say that an animal, a tree, or any other named body is generated or destroyed, even though these are bodies, it should not be thought that a body has been made from non-body, or non-body from body, but a non-animal from an animal, a non-tree from a tree, and so forth.   3
That is, those accidents on account of which we name one thing an animal, another a tree, and another something else are generated and destroyed, and consequently those names that applied to them before no longer apply. But that magnitude on account of which we name   6
something a body is neither generated nor destroyed. For even if we can feign in our mind that a point swells up to a huge bulk and then contracts down to a point—this is to imagine something's being made from nothing (*ex nihilo*), and nothing's being made from something—still we   9
cannot comprehend with our mind *how* this could be done in nature. And therefore philosophers, not permitted to abandon natural reason, suppose that a body can neither be generated nor destroyed, but only appear to us in one way and then another, under different images, and   12
consequently be named in one way and then another. Thus what is now called a human being is later called non-human, but what is now called a body should not later be called a non-body. It is clear, however, that all other accidents beyond magnitude or extension can be generated and   15
destroyed. When a white thing is made black, for instance, the whiteness that existed no longer exists, and a blackness that did not exist is produced. Therefore bodies and the accidents under which they variously appear have this difference: that bodies are things, and not generated,   18
whereas accidents are generated, but are not things. (*De corpore* 8.20)

---

[16]   Here are some of Hill's statements in favor of the conservation thesis: "Materia prima hylaea, physica, est prima hypostasis passive ..." (*Philosophia* n. 29); "Prima corpuscula sunt vere solida, impenetrabilia, inalterabilia, multiformis, divinae actioni in natura terminos ponentia" (n. 116); "Nec materiae, nec formae substantialis aliqua est multiplicatio; generatio vero nihil est aliud quam anaxagorica homogeneorum collectio, et actuatio ad sensum" (n. 504).

For Vanini, see also *De admirandis* dialogue 2 (p. 10): "Alex[ander]. At merito, ni fallor, objiciam Coeli materiam nulli esse corruptioni obnoxiam, nostri vero quam plurimis. I[ulius] C[aesar]. Istud vero pernego, ipsa enim nunquam corrumpitur, sed id quod ex ipsa fit."

[17]   For Epicurus's commitment to the substratum and conservation theses, see *Letter to Herodotus* 38–39 [tr. Long and Sedley, sec. 4A]. For Gassendi's treatment, see *Syntagma* II.I.3.1 (I:232–3) and *Epicuri Syntagma* pt. II sec. 1 chs. 17–18 (pp. 62–7) [tr. Stanley, *History* pp. 870–1]. The most strident statement of the conservation thesis that I have found occurs in Charleton, *Physiologia* II.1.1.9: "... Annihilation and Creation are terms not to be found in the dictionary of nature, but proper only to omnipotence: nor is there any sober man who does not understand the common material of things to be constantly the same, through the whole flux of time, or the duration of the world, so as that from the creation therefore by the *fiat* of God, no one particle of it can perish, or vanish into nothing, until the total dissolution of nature, by the same metaphysical power, nor any one particle of new matter be superadded thereto, without miracle. The energy of Nature is definite and prescribed, nor is she commissioned with any other efficacy than what extends to the molding of old matter into new figures; and so the noblest attribute we can allow her is that of a *translator*."

Much here needs to be set aside for now. The concluding remark that accidents are not things (line 19) will be the subject of discussion later (§7.1, §10.2). We must likewise set aside the suggestion that changes in species are simply nominal changes (§27.5, §28.4, §29.4). For our purposes, the crucial part of the passage occurs at lines 6–14, where it is said that "we cannot comprehend" (lines 8–10) how a body could be naturally generated or destroyed. Even there, more is going on than we can presently handle, because Hobbes is speaking not of matter but of body, which he takes to include (or perhaps consist of) magnitude and extension. Hence Hobbes claims not just that a body cannot come into or go out of existence, but also that it cannot undergo any change in size. As we will see in Chapter 4, this sort of linkage between body and extension is common in the seventeenth century, but was generally rejected by scholastic authors, who thought of extension as an accidental property of a given bit of matter, one that might be increased or decreased, or perhaps even lost entirely. For present purposes, we can set aside the fact that most scholastics are talking about prime matter shorn of extension, whereas Hobbes's prime matter is body, which has extension. If Hobbes thinks that bodies cannot undergo change in extension, he thinks *a fortiori* that bodies cannot go into or out of existence. This is where Hobbes and scholastic philosophers are on common ground, and to this extent they each endorse the conservation thesis.

Hobbes thinks the denial of conservation is inconceivable. Evidently, what he really objects to is the denial of the *ex nihilo* principle (lines 8–9), which is not surprising given how tightly bound this principle is to the substratum thesis and so in turn to the conservation thesis. But we should again ask of Hobbes, as we did of others, why he insists on this principle. He allows that we might "feign in our mind" (line 9) that there might be nothing, then some matter swelling up, and then swelling down into nothing again. What he insists on is that "we cannot comprehend with our mind *how* this could be done in nature" (lines 9–10). The point, I take it, is that we might be able to form a mental image of the *ex nihilo* principle's being violated, but that we cannot conceive of *how* such a violation could happen. This seems a helpful distinction to draw. In effect, Hobbes is asking us to distinguish between two sorts of conceivability, one of which does not track possibility whereas the other does. Let us grant, at least for the sake of argument, that if we cannot conceive of *how* something happens, we have at least prima facie evidence against its being naturally possible. If Hobbes can show that violating the *ex nihilo* principle is in this sense inconceivable, he will have made a strong case for the conservation thesis.[18]

Is Hobbes entitled to his inconceivability claim? One might think that his case rests on his austere brand of corpuscularianism (§7.1), according to which the only things

---

[18] Hobbes himself endorses treating extended body, shorn of accidents, as equivalent to prime matter: "Quid ergo est [materia prima]? Merum nomen; non tamen frustra usurpatum; significat enim corpus considerari sine consideratione cuiuscumque formae et cuiuscumque accidentis, excepta solummodo magnitudine sive extensione et aptitudine ad formam et accidenta recipienda; ita ut si quoties opus est uti hac voce, *Corpus generaliter sumptum*, utamur hac materia prima recte fecerimus" (*De corpore* 8.24). See also *De mundo* 7.2: "idem [primam materiam] agnoscunt Philosophi illi qui omnia conflari ex atomis putant, nam atomos eas faciunt homogeneas, et solis figuris inter se differentes, tanquam illas atomos materiam illam unicam esse dicerent, quam Aristoteles vocabat primam."

Regarding Hobbes's distinction between mere imagining and conceiving, see his Third Objections, VII:178: "Differentia magna est inter imaginari, hoc est, ideam aliquam habere, et mente concipere, hoc est, ratiocinando colligere rem aliquam esse, vel rem aliquam existere." See §16.2 for further discussion of Hobbes's theory of body, as well as Leijenhorst, *Mechanisation* pp. 145–55.

that exist are bodies and their integral parts. But although this certainly puts Hobbes in quite different territory, compared to scholastic proponents of the permanence thesis, it is not clear that this territory is any more hospitable to a defense of the permanence thesis. After all, corpuscularianism does not, in and of itself, say anything about the conditions under which bodies endure. It would be quite open to a corpuscularian account to suppose that everything that exists routinely goes in and out of existence. To block that sort of view, Hobbes needs some further argument.

So far as I can see, that further argument is simply the brute claim that generation *ex nihilo*, as well as corruption *in nihilum*, are inconceivable. But this, when unsupported by any further argument, looks plausible only when the *ex nihilo* principle is given the weak reading described in §2.2, as the principle that a thing can come into existence naturally only on the basis of some prior ingredients. It is easy to see how the denial of that principle might look inconceivable. As stressed earlier, however, the weak principle does not yield the substratum or conservation theses, because it does not block the possibility of the ingredients' being completely destroyed in the process of generation and replaced by something entirely new. What Hobbes needs is the inconceivability of this last sort of scenario—that is, he needs to insist on the strong *ex nihilo* principle. But it is not at all clear why the denial of that principle is inconceivable.

Hobbes's attempt to defend the conservation thesis looks rather feeble in comparison with the best scholastic efforts, like those of Scotus or even Ockham. So far as I can find, other post-scholastic authors have even less to say in this regard: they treat substratum and conservation as axiomatic, but without explaining why. This will not be the last time that we find a surprising amount of agreement running throughout our four centuries. For although in many respects seventeenth-century thought turns scholastic philosophy inside-out, that transformation was in part accomplished in just the way the phrase suggests: by taking familiar conceptual tools and redeploying them. The substratum and conservation theses were two such tools. It should not be surprising, moreover, that there was agreement in these particular areas. The doctrine of prime matter makes its appearance in Aristotle, after all, precisely in order to accommodate various aspects of Presocratic thought, especially atomism. Given the renewed seventeenth-century interest in those ancient ideas (§5.2), it is natural that they would find some measure of common ground with Aristotelians over the idea of an enduring substratum of change.

That there is common ground here has important consequences for metaphysics throughout our period. In endorsing not just the weak *ex nihilo* principle (that everything comes from something) but also the strong principle (that in everything new, something of the old must endure), authors have to face the question of just what that enduring stuff is. The logic of the strong principle, moreover, exerts a constant pressure toward ascribing a greater and greater reality to the substratum. For when the substratum thesis is grounded on the idea that the ingredients must endure through the change, if they are to play a causal role, then it is natural to suppose that quite a lot of the ingredients must endure: not just some bare, abstract, potential stuff, but actualized bodies, with extension and qualities of their own. For if the ingredients that survive are not stuff of a certain kind, then what work are those ingredients doing? The remainder of Part I will take up this issue of what the substratum of change is, but the issues spill over into subsequent discussions as well. As we will see in §6.3, the same sorts of considerations that lead to postulating an enduring substratum also suggest that this substratum should be the subject of (at least some) accidents. And once one starts down that road, it becomes tempting to suppose that the enduring substratum is in fact the substance—that what exists, most basically, are not dogs and cats and stones, but the enduring stuff out of which complex aggregates are constituted. Eventually, we will see this line of thought culminate in the idea that nothing really goes out of existence, and that generation and corruption are an illusion (Ch. 28). In this way, the substratum thesis, innocuous as it seems to philosophers throughout our period, in fact contains the seeds of the ideas that would undermine the commonsense ontology it was initially intended to preserve.

3

Theories of Prime Matter

3.1. The Paradox of Pure Potentiality

The general consensus over the need for an enduring substratum through material change leaves wide open the character of such a substratum. Here I begin to consider the two rival camps, corpuscular and metaphysical. As one might expect from a topic as obscure as prime matter, there are a bewildering variety of views—so many, and so diverse, that it is not easy to draw a firm line distinguishing the metaphysical scholastic approach from the corpuscular approach characteristic of the seventeenth century. One of the most intricate and interesting disputes concerns whether prime matter is extended. This will be the topic of the following chapter. First, we should consider the issue that lies at the heart of the dispute: the alleged potentiality of Aristotelian prime matter.

Stock characterizations of Aristotelian prime matter focus on its potentiality for receiving form. According to Eustachius a Sancto Paulo, author of an elementary seventeenth-century textbook on scholastic philosophy, "everyone says that prime matter, considered in itself, is free of all forms and at the same time is open to all forms—or, that matter is in potentiality to all forms" (*Summa* III.1.1.2.3, II:120). Franco Burgersdijk, another seventeenth-century textbook author, offers almost exactly the same definition: "Matter is free of and open to all forms, and so is called pure potentiality" (*Collegium physicum* II.13, p. 21). So much was fairly uncontroversial, but yet to say anything more was rather difficult. For a somewhat fuller, but still characteristic treatment, we might look at what seems to be a mid-fourteenth-century Parisian set of questions on the *Physics*, published under the name "Johannes Marsilius of Inghen," but not in fact authored by Marsilius of Inghen. Pseudo-Marsilius lists six "conditions" of Aristotelian prime matter (*In Phys.* I.20):

1. It is pure potentiality.
2. It is cognizable by analogy to form.
3. It is perpetual.
4. It is unformed.
5. It is one in all bodies.
6. It is the principle of every natural change.

These conditions, as pseudo-Marsilius understands them, are general enough to have been accepted by almost all scholastic authors. Two of them, (3) and (6), plainly hold as well for corpuscular prime matter, as we saw in the previous chapter, and we can set them aside here. By (5), pseudo-Marsilius means only that prime matter is the same *in kind* everywhere, something that would also be generally accepted by corpuscularian authors (but see the following section for some complications). Even (2) matches closely with corpuscularian views, despite its reference to "form," since the force of (2) is that prime matter cannot be perceived, and so must be inferred from what can be perceived. Corpuscularian authors would have to acknowledge the same. (On matter's obscurity, see §7.2.) In short—going just by pseudo-Marsilius's list—the varieties of prime matter over our four centuries share four characteristics, which we might abbreviate as their being perpetual, basic, uniform, and hidden. This leaves just (1) and (4) as candidates for distinguishing metaphysical, scholastic prime matter.[1]

Pseudo-Marsilius offers various interpretations of both (1) and (4), but he ultimately arrives at the view that (1) should be understood as making the same claim as (4), that prime matter is unformed. With this, we are back at the textbook account of prime matter as "free of and open to all forms." But what does it mean to be free of form? According to pseudo-Marsilius, this means "it does not have any form of its own as an essential part of itself." William Ockham had reached a similar conclusion, that prime matter "is in potentiality to all substantial forms, having none that necessarily and always exists in it" (*Summula* I.9, VI:179). These formulations go to the heart of the difference between scholastic prime matter and corpuscular prime matter. For corpuscularian authors, as we will see below, prime matter always has some sort of well-defined character. Although thoroughgoing corpuscularians will not speak of *forms* inhering by nature in their prime matter, they nevertheless give it certain features, such as shape and size. Scholastic prime matter is by nature characterless—it is as close to a bare substratum as one can get while still having a substratum. This brings us right up against the central paradox of scholastic prime matter. By common consensus, forms are what give a thing its nature, or more generally its properties and characteristics. Yet, also by common consensus, prime matter is that which underlies all forms and so is of itself free of those forms. So how can prime matter be real—that is, how can it exist—without having some character? Surely nothing can exist without existing in some way or another.

Scholastic treatments of this paradox must steer between two unacceptable outcomes. If they give prime matter some kind of character, as it seems they must, then they face the risk of turning prime matter into the actual substratum of corpuscularian theory. If, fearing this result, they stress the pure potentiality of prime matter, they then risk the suggestion that such matter does not actually exist at all—not just because

---

[1]   Pseudo-Marsilius describes the unformed character of prime matter as follows: "Secundo modo intelligitur conditio quod materia prima sit *informis*—id est, quod non habeat aliquam formam propriam tanquam partem essentialem sui" (*In Phys.* I.20; f. 19vb). Compare his almost identical account of what *pura potentia* means (f. 19ra): "Tertio modo dicitur ens in *pura potentia*: non quia non sit presentialiter: sed quia non est actu forma vel formam habens quam sibi determinat a natura, et isto modo materia prima dicitur ens in pura potentia." On the question of authorship, see Dewender, "Einige Bemerkungen."

Another useful scholastic attempt to characterize prime matter can be found in Johannes Magirus, *Physiologia* I.2.2, who lists four "proprietates": ungenerated, uncorrupted, unformed but suited to be informed, and desiring natural forms.

existence is a kind of actuality (a point that might perhaps be finessed), but more fundamentally because a thing can exist only by existing in a certain way. Thomas Aquinas's famous insistence that matter is *pure potentiality* has led one recent commentator to see in it "the complete rejection of matter as any kind of stuff having independent ontological status." If this were right, Aquinas would be fundamentally at odds with the overwhelming consensus of later scholastic and seventeenth-century thought. But it is not easy to see how prime matter can exist, short of understanding it in corpuscular terms.[2]

There was a considerable scholastic debate over Aquinas's highly austere conception of matter as pure potentiality, a doctrine that would become one of the defining tenets of Thomism. Although the debate is important, it has to be understood in a broader context, as an issue that arises only after various other questions have been resolved. The first questions to ask—the central questions of the previous chapter—are whether the substratum and conservation theses are true. If one decides that they are, then the next question is whether that permanent substratum should be understood in metaphysical or corpuscular terms. To embrace the first is to treat matter as somehow less than fully actualized, and so in potentiality for form, a doctrine that might reasonably be thought to lie at the heart of any Aristotelian metaphysics. Once one goes that far, the question then arises of whether matter is, in its own right, purely potential, or whether it admits of some sort of intrinsic actuality. Here the paradox of prime matter is particularly virulent: if matter is the subject of form, then it seems as if it ought to be free of all form, and so free of all actuality; but yet it seems that nothing real could be completely unformed. Rejecting the austere view of the Thomists, André Dabillon, a mid-seventeenth-century follower of Ockham, remarked that "matter and form are real substantial beings that exist actually in nature: for the things that compose an actual being actually exist—otherwise, the substantial whole would be composed of nothing" (*Physique* I.3.2, p. 103).

Despite remarks such as that, scholastic authors from the fourteenth century onward standardly accept as a stock phrase the characterization of prime matter as pure potentiality. "All the philosophers seem to agree on this," says Suárez (*Disp. meta.* 13.5.1), and indeed one does find the expression even in Ockham, whose conception of matter is radically different from that of the Thomists (§4.4).[3] The crucial issue, then, is

---

[2] One way to finesse the question of existence as actuality is to distinguish between two kinds of actuality, one pertaining to existence, which prime matter has, and then another kind that prime matter lacks (see, e.g., Ockham, *Summula* I.10, *Opera phil.* VI:182; Marsilius, *Abbrev. in Phys.* I, f. 4vb; Suárez, *Disp. meta.* 13.4.9). Another, bolder strategy is to deny that prime matter has existence in its own right; instead, it gets existence in the way it gets all actuality, through form. Aquinas is the leading advocate of this latter strategy (e.g., *Quod.* III.1.1); see also Zabarella, *De rebus nat.*, De prima materia II.4, col. 186. For a very clear, critical discussion of that approach, see Pererius, *De communibus principiis* V.13, pp. 309–13.

I myself am responsible for the suggestion that Aquinas's prime matter might entirely lack ontological status (*Thomas Aquinas on Human Nature* p. 131). My research into later scholastic thought in one respect tends to undermine this interpretation, since there seems to be *no one* who thinks that prime matter does not really exist. In another respect, however, the later history lends some support to my interpretation, since a near consensus develops that Aquinas's view is unacceptable because it has the consequence that prime matter would not really exist. My proposal—which I am still inclined to endorse, or at any rate not ready to give up—amounts to embracing that consequence as one that he intended.

[3] For recent discussions of the pure potentiality thesis, as first put forward by Aquinas and then criticized by Ghent, Scotus, and Ockham, see Adams, *William Ockham* II:633–47; Cross, *Physics of Duns Scotus* pp. 17–26; Wippel, *Metaphysical*

not the phrase itself, but how matter, in its potentiality, is understood. Most scholastic authors—even many of those, like the later Jesuits, who are generally sympathetic to Aquinas—reject the Thomistic approach, insisting that matter must have some measure of actuality. To keep their view distinctively Aristotelian—that is, to avoid treating prime matter in corpuscularian fashion, as fully actualized stuff—these authors need some account of what it means for matter to be real, and yet in some sense merely potential. A way down this narrow path was suggested by Averroes, whose twelfth-century commentaries on virtually the whole Aristotelian corpus became by far the most important scholastic guide to the interpretation of Aristotle. Averroes offered this cryptic remark with regard to prime matter: *est quasi medium inter non-esse simpliciter et esse in actu*—"prime matter falls halfway, as it were, between complete non-existence and actual existence" (*In Phys.* I.70).[4] This remark particularly resonated with Latin authors because it unknowingly echoed a remark of Augustine's: "I sooner judged that what lacks all form does not exist, than thought of something in between form and nothing, neither formed nor nothing, unformed and next to nothing" (*Confessions* XII.6).

It was, to say the least, not easy to see how such suggestions might be spelled out. What in the world does it mean to exist "halfway"? The usual first step toward an adequate account was to stress that prime matter has incomplete existence, in the sense that it cannot exist on its own, without some form. Even this much was not entirely uncontroversial. Although everyone agreed that prime matter could not *naturally* exist on its own, there was dispute over whether this was *logically* possible—whether, in other words, God could make prime matter exist without form. Aquinas's very rigorous insistence on prime matter's pure potentiality led him to deny that this was within God's power (§10.3), but even some who wanted to agree with Aquinas about the pure potentiality doctrine (such as the Coimbran commentators of the late sixteenth century) were not prepared to deny God's ability to bring about prime matter without form.[5] (What makes Aquinas's position especially hard to defend is that form

---

Thought of Thomas, ch. 9. For the sixteenth-century Jesuit debate, see Des Chene, "Descartes and Coimbra" as well as *Physiologia* pp. 81–97.

The phrase "pure potentiality" is commonly endorsed by scholastic authors, even if the author's view is in fact much closer to Scotus's than to Aquinas's. Thus Burgersdijk uses the phrase, as quoted in the main text, but then immediately goes on to say that "materia actu suam habet essentiam atque existentiam substantialem distinctam ab essentia atque existentia formae, quam si non haberet, non video quomodo corporum constitutionem posset ingredi, immo quomodo posset dici capax formarum et non potius purum nihil." Suárez remarks that "non est enim nobis negandum quin materia sit pura potentia, cum in ea assertione philosophi omnes convenire videantur" (*Disp. meta.* 13.5.1), but he goes on to ascribe to it quite a bit of actuality. See too Scheibler, *Metaphys.* I.22.15.5 (pp. 301–2). For Ockham, see *Summula* I.10 (VI:182): "primo modo accipiendo actum, dicendum est quod materia est in potentia ad omnem actum substantialem et nullum actum habet de se, sed est pura potentia. ..." One exception is Pererius, *De communibus principiis* V.13 (p. 321): "illa pura potentia aut est nihil aut aliquod ens; si nihil, ergo similiter materia nihil est; si ens, non igitur iam est pura potentia." On Jesuit allegiance to Aquinas, see §20.2.

[4] Buridan remarks that Averroes's "quasi medium" remark "non est propria locutio ... sed hoc dicitur ad talem sensum quia nec ipsa nihil est nec ipsa hoc aliquid in actu nec etiam ipsa est aliquis actus formalis, etc." (*In Phys.* I.20 ad 4, f. 25ra). For another attempt to make sense of Averroes's dictum, see Burley, *De formis* p. 14.

[5] For a negative answer to the question of whether God could make prime matter without form, see Aquinas, *Quod.* III.1.1; Capreolus, *Defensiones* II.13.1.1 (IV:18–19); Cajetan, *In De ente* q. 9. For an affirmative answer, see Scotus, *Ordinatio* II.12.2 (VI.2:680–98); Boethius of Dacia, *In Gen. et cor.* I.19; Gregory of Rimini, *Sent.* II.12.2.3 (V:285–88); Gabriel Biel, *Sent.* II.12.1; John Major, *Sent.* II.12.1 and *In Phys.* I.7.2; Coimbra, *In Phys.* I.9.6; Eustachius a Sancto Paulo, *Summa* III.1.1.2.4 (II:123). The negative answer was reported to have been censured in 1277, although it does not appear on Tempier's famous list of 219 censured articles (see Thijssen, *Censure and Heresy*, p. 53). For recent discussion, see Des Chene, *Physiologia*, pp. 124–34.

and matter are supposed to be really distinct, and a real distinction is often thought to require two-way separability. But separability is a much more complicated matter than is generally realized [§13.6].) Regardless of whether prime matter is logically or merely naturally dependent on form, the fundamental problem remains untouched: how can prime matter exist without having any sort of character, or how can it have some character without coming to look like the fully actual substratum of the corpuscularians? Invoking prime matter's incompleteness, in the sense of its dependence, helps to distinguish it from the fully actual integral parts of corpuscularianism, but, as Parts II–III of this study will show, there are many Aristotelian metaphysical parts that are incomplete in just this same way. So we have not learned anything distinctive about prime matter.

How might the paradox of prime matter be dissolved? The most promising strategy I have seen attempts to explain prime matter's incompleteness in terms of its indeterminateness. This idea gets advanced with particular force by Peter Auriol, a highly creative but little studied theologian active at Paris in the second decade of the fourteenth century:

Prime matter has no essence, nor a nature that is determinate, distinct, and actual. Instead, it is pure potential, and determinable, so that it is indeterminately and indistinctly a material thing. And in this way it is the matter of everything generable and corruptible, so that it is not determinately any of the beings in the world—such as stone, earth, and so forth—but it can be determined so as to be stone, earth, and so forth. (*Sent.* II.12.1.1, II:151bA)

This all by itself is not an especially creative idea—indeed, Auriol quotes Averroes as appealing to the indeterminacy of matter—but it does provide some insight into the mysterious character(lessness) of prime matter. On this account, it is not that prime matter has no character, but that its character is such as to be susceptible to determination in whatever way a material thing might exist. Such determinability is itself a kind of positive character, and gives us reason to think of prime matter as a genuine being. It seems best to think of this state not as a kind of halfway existence, but as a full-fledged form of existence that is attenuated only insofar as it is dependent on some further actuality, to be made determinate.[6]

---

[6] Auriol's discussion of the indeterminacy of prime matter is extremely complex. After stating the theory in article one, he goes into a long and complex discussion in article two concerning how such indeterminacy is compatible with prime matter's being a positive being. In the passage quoted in the main text, Auriol characterizes prime matter as having no essence, but later he is willing to say, when pressed, that "materia habet quidditatem suo modo: est enim formabile purum et possibile" (*Sent.* II.12.1.7, II:173bC). Elsewhere he helpfully distinguishes between two senses of incomplete being: one sense that implies being "in gradu parvo et diminuto," and another sense "quia est inchoativum alicuius completae rationis" (II:172bD). Prime matter is incomplete in the first sense, but it is the second sense, he says, that really captures its character. Auriol returns to the topic of prime matter as indeterminate at *Sent.* II.12.1.7 (II:172bCF, 173bAC), and again at *Sent.* II.12.2.1 (II:174–80). An interesting and very distinctive feature of Auriol's view here is that he wants to make substantial form indeterminate in just the way that prime matter is, so that these two indeterminate entities give rise to a determinate composite substance (see Ch. 11 note 18).

The Rome edition of article three of Auriol's *Sent.* II.12.1 mislabels it as article two, and is subsequently one off on the numbering of articles 4–7. I cite the articles by their proper number, ignoring the misprint.

Prime matter's indeterminacy is a familiar notion. Aristotle, for instance, had remarked: "By matter I mean that which in itself is neither a particular thing nor of a certain quantity nor assigned to any other of the categories by which being is determined" (*Meta.* VII.3 1029a20–21). (We will see Glanvill mock this text in §3.3.) Plotinus had also put great weight on the indeterminacy of prime matter, holding that "matter is essentially indefiniteness" (*Enneads* II.4.15). Much later, Suárez conceives of this in spatial terms: to inform matter is "replere—ut sic dicam—illud vacuum quod erat in potentialitate materiae" (*In De an.* disp. 2 q. 4, p. 254).

This sort of picture of prime matter gives us a way to understand debates over its nature. Authors who disagree over whether prime matter has extension, for instance, can be understood to be disagreeing over just how indeterminate prime matter is. Could it, for instance, exist entirely at an extensionless point? For the authors who are most strict about the indeterminateness of matter, this is a possibility. Albert of Saxony expresses his commitment to this sort of view by taking prime matter to possess "infinite passivity," which is to say that it is susceptible to undergoing anything that some active power can bring about. So—this is his example—if God can make one body be in two places at once, then that body's matter will not stand in the way. There is nothing in the nature of prime matter that prevents it from having two locations at once. At this point, further paradox looms, when one reflects on the prospect that prime matter might be open to *everything*. If it is open to bi-location, then it is hard to see what it would not be open to. But if it is open to everything, then it once again becomes unclear whether prime matter can be said to have any positive nature at all, and equally unclear what it contributes to material substances, beyond being simply a *very bare* substratum.[7]

Before pressing these issues any farther, it will be useful to characterize corpuscularian theories of prime matter.

3.2. Corpuscular Prime Matter

For the corpuscularian, given how I understand that doctrine (§1.3), prime matter must be one or more of the integral parts of the body undergoing change. Perhaps this is what Giulio Cesare Vanini has in mind when he remarks that "the whole of prime matter, considered as prime matter, is nothing other than its parts" (*Amphitheatrum* exerc. 5, p. 28). Since experience does not directly acquaint us with any such enduring substratum of physical parts, the corpuscularian must posit an invisible realm of incorruptible corpuscles. Many seventeenth-century authors make it quite clear that the motivation for this postulate falls directly out of their dual commitments to corpuscularianism and the substratum thesis of the previous chapter. Thus Gassendi, setting out Epicurus's views as his own, explains:

The first argument by which Epicurus contends it necessary to postulate atoms is the same as that by which Aristotle proves there is in things an ingenerable and incorruptible prime matter from which, preexisting, all things are generated, and into which surviving remnant all things are ultimately dissolved. For Epicurus contends that atoms are matter of this sort—

[7] Albert of Saxony characterizes matter's infinite passivity as follows: "Tunc sit ista conclusio: materia prima est passibilitatis infinitae, hoc est est sic passiva quod nullo modo activa.... Ex hoc sequitur, si prima causa posset facere idem corpus simul esse in diversis locis, quod materia prima posset hoc pati. Patet ex hoc quod cuiuslibet materia est passiva, cuius prima causa est productiva" (*In Phys.* I.16, pp. 218–19).

The alchemist Jean d'Espagnet offers a colorful account of the philosophical theory of prime matter. Here is the 1651 translation of his *Enchyridion physicae restitutae* (1623): "The Philosophers did believe a first matter to be an elder birth to the Elements, but this, as it was but scarce apprehended by them, so was it as briefly, and as it were in the clouds and obscurely handled by them, they made it void of qualities and accidents, yet the first subject of them without quantity, yet by which all things have their dimensions, endowed with simplicity, yet capable of contraries, without the reach of sensible knowledge, yet the basis of sensibles, drawn out through all places, yet unperceivable; covetous of all forms, tenacious of none, the root of all bodies, yet not sensible but conceivable only by an act of the intellect: lastly, nothing in act, all things in aptitude. So have they laid a fancy for the foundation of nature" (p. 13).

immutable, or free from birth and destruction. The difference is only that he wants the natural decomposition to stop at unbreakable corpuscles, whereas Aristotle does not have any way to describe the matter at which the decomposition ultimately arrives. (*Syntagma* II.1.3.5, I:259b)   6

The argument to which Gassendi refers (lines 1–2) is the one described at the start of §2.5, based on the strong *ex nihilo* principle.

Set aside for now the final gibe at the Aristotelian view—that "Aristotle does not have any way to describe" the matter he postulates (lines 6–7)—and consider Gassendi's own positive proposal, that the enduring substratum be identified as "unbreakable corpuscles," or, for short, atoms. Gassendi was the best-known and most influential advocate of atomism in the seventeenth century, but there were many others, before and after him (§5.2). Decades before Gassendi, Isaac Beeckman wrote in his *Journal* (in 1620) that "the whole essence will signify for me the whole corporeity of the atoms, which is prime matter" (II:86). To be sure, not everyone was happy to use the label 'prime matter' in connection with these enduring, unbreakable corpuscles. In their condemned Parisian broadsheet of 1624 (§19.6), Antoine de Villon and Etienne de Clave offer this as the first of fourteen propositions:

Prime matter, which the Peripatetics set forth as the subject principle of change, whether it has existence of itself, or from form, is utterly fictitious and clearly has been thought up by Aristotle without any foundation.

Still, in their final proposition, they endorse the doctrine of atomism, as a conclusion entailed by their previous thirteen propositions. And with that they have their permanent substratum of change.[8]

Whether or not this sort of permanent substratum should be known as prime matter is simply a terminological question, calling for a strategic decision about whether to highlight the continuities or the discontinuities between scholastic and post-scholastic thought. If one wants to keep fixed the precise meaning of scholastic technical terminology, then the result—as with Villon and de Clave—will usually be a categorical rejection of the scholastic theory. If, on the other hand, one is willing to use the terminology more flexibly, so as to capture some worthwhile vestige of Aristotelian thought, then often the terminology can be retained, as Gassendi retains the terminology of prime matter. (The most prominent example of this sort of flexible, conciliatory usage is Locke's retention of the distinction between primary and secondary qualities [§21.1].)

Given that the enduring substratum of Gassendi and other post-scholastic authors will not be pure potentiality, just what sort of actuality should be ascribed to it? To be sure, as the next chapter will consider, it will be extended. But what else? Here there was little agreement. Atomism is the most common version of corpuscular prime matter, but it is not the only option. Indeed, atomism neither entails nor is entailed by the combination of corpuscularianism and the substratum thesis. Those two theses

---

[8] The 1624 Parisian broadsheet is reproduced in Kahn, "Entre atomism" p. 246, and also transcribed in Launoy, *De varia fortuna* pp. 205–11. "I. Materia prima, quam pro principio transmutationis subiectivo constituunt Peripatetici, sive existentiam habeat a se, sive a forma, commentitia prorsus est, et sine ullo plane fundamento ab Aristotele excogitata. . . . XIV. Ex his omnibus manifestissimum est ignoranter, aut potius malitiose irrisa, et sugillata ab Aristotele duo antiquorum dicta, omnia scilicet esse in omnibus, et omnia componi ex atomis seu indivisibilibus." For an English translation, along with extensive discussion of the historical context, see Garber, "Defending Aristotle."

together do yield the result that bodies must have some enduring integral part. But atomism does not entail endurance, and the endurance of integral parts does not entail atomism. First, atomism does not yield endurance, because atomism requires only that there be a stopping point in the physical division of bodies (§5.4). That is, the atomists are very clear that their central claim—the claim that defines the theory—is that there is a point at which bodies become too small to be naturally broken into smaller pieces. Here is Gassendi:

Note that one speaks here of the Ἄτομον not as the vulgar think (and even some of the learned have supposed), as what lacks parts and is free of all magnitude and so is nothing other than a mathematical point, but as something that is so solid and, so to speak, hard and compact as to leave no room for division, separation, and cutting. That is, there is no force in nature that can divide it. (*Syntagma* II.1.3.5, I:256b)

From this it does not follow that atoms are incorruptible (let alone that they are ingenerable). For although it is not naturally possible to divide an atom into smaller pieces, it might yet be possible to make an atom go out of existence. Here would be one way of doing so: suppose, as some atomists do, that atoms are individuated by their shapes. Then suppose that, even if atoms cannot be divided, they can be flattened or bent or otherwise changed with regard to shape. In that case, atoms could be both corrupted and generated. Now in fact atomists do generally endorse the further claim that atoms are not just indivisible, but fully indestructible, ingenerable, and indeed even inalterable in any way (§28.3).[9] But it is good to remember that these are further claims, not specifically entailed by the core doctrine of atomism. In general, as §5.4 will discuss, atomism is a much more narrow, even peripheral doctrine than is generally supposed.

Second, the endurance of integral parts does not entail atomism, because one could think that bodies are indefinitely divisible and still think they cannot be destroyed (or generated). This is Descartes's view. He rejects atomism in favor of the view that bodies can be divided without limit (§5.4). But still he endorses the conservation and substratum theses, not of course because he postulates some sort of metaphysical prime matter beneath ordinary bodies, but because he thinks ordinary bodies, although divisible, nevertheless endure through all change:

Absolutely all substances, or things that must be created by God in order to exist, are by their nature incorruptible and cannot ever cease to exist unless they are reduced to nothingness by God's denying his concurrence to them. Further, body, taken in general (*in genere sumptum*), is a substance, so that it too never perishes. (*Meditations* synopsis, VII:14)

It is odd to suppose that all substances must be created by God, and can go out of existence only by divine fiat. In §28.3 I will argue that Descartes does not intend nearly so strong a claim. What he clearly does mean, however, is that there is some level at which body is the enduring substratum for all physical change. Because Descartes rejects atomism, he can offer no definite story about where that level is, but this is no barrier to his supposing that, at some level, bodies do endure.

---

[9] For the complete inalterability of atoms, see, e.g., Hill, *Philosophia* n. 116: "Prima corpuscula sunt vere solida, impenetrabilis, inalterabilia, multiformis, divinae actioni in natura terminos ponentia."

The temptation to conflate atomism with permanence is evident in Walter Charleton's deduction of the atoms. He begins with a claim quoted in the previous chapter, that all agree on the need for a material substratum. From here, quite properly, he infers the incorruptibility of that substratum. Next, however, he makes two very dubious assumptions. First, he assumes that a material substratum must be extended; second, he assumes an incorruptible extended material substratum must consist of atoms. Here is the whole argument, with the inessential parts abridged and the premises numbered:

[1] That there must be some one catholic material principle . . . is unanimously confessed by all. And consequently, [2] that this matter is incorruptible . . . has been indubitated by none. . . . Insomuch therefore, as [3] the essential reason or formality of *corporiety* does solely consist in *extensibility*, . . . and insomuch as [4] nothing can be the root or beginning of material or physical extension but something indissoluble, . . . therefore, from manifest necessity, may we determine, that [5] no principle can justly challenge [≈ lay claim to] all the proprieties or attributes of the first universal matter, but Σώματα ἀδιαίρετα, indivisible bodies, or atoms. (*Physiologia* II.1.1.3)

The argument is not a success. Although (3) is true by definition (§16.1), what Charleton really needs is not (3) but rather the claim that the prime matter of (1) and (2) is extended, something that many scholastic authors denied (see Ch. 4). And even if we grant that prime matter must be a body—which comes close to presupposing the corpuscularian framework—the ultimate introduction of atoms in (5) is still neither necessary nor sufficient for enduring corpuscular prime matter. Not necessary, as we have seen, because (4) might be challenged by a Cartesian who insists on indefinite divisibility. Not sufficient either, as we have seen, because mere indivisibility does not yield incorruptibility. Once again, then, we see that corpuscular prime matter need not be atomistic, and atoms need not be prime matter.

Another unsettled issue concerning corpuscular prime matter is whether those enduring corpuscles possess any fixed, permanent nature, beyond simply their materiality. For the Aristotelian, the answer was clearly no. Aristotle had offered his account of prime matter as an alternative to a view like that of Empedocles, according to which there are a small number of elemental kinds—Earth, Air, Fire, Water—that serve as fixed points, enduring through all change. Aristotle and his followers embrace those four elements (§21.2), but do not regard them as truly primary. Beneath the level of the so-called elements there is the even more elemental level of prime matter, which is the only stuff that endures through all change. This is to say that the four elements are not permanent: a particle of pure Earth can change into Air, and so on, and indeed transmutations of this sort provide the most fundamental explanation of all natural change.[10]

Post-scholastic authors generally take Empedocles's side in this old dispute, and ascribe to their basic corpuscles a fixed, enduring nature. The material realm, on this sort of picture, was created with a certain number of different kinds of particles, the ranks of which are fixed for all time (pending further divine intervention). For some

[10] Aristotle sets out the case for a level of enduring matter beneath the elements at *Gen. et cor.* II.1 329a25–b2, where he claims that if Empedocles were right that the elements could not change, then no alteration would be possible at all. The theory of elemental change is a stock topic in any scholastic commentary on the *Gen. et cor.*—the most impressive being those of Buridan and Oresme.

early corpuscularians—such as David Gorlaeus, Isaac Beeckman, and Sebastian Basso—these kinds are some variation on the four familiar elements, but now understood in geometric terms, so that fire corpuscles are such because they have a certain shape and size, and so on. To be sure, once one turns from qualitative to geometric explanations, there is little reason to retain the traditional list of four, and indeed the example of the ancient atomists encouraged the idea that atoms might come in a virtually infinite variety of shapes and sizes. Still, it was commonly supposed that, however many different kinds of basic corpuscles there are, each corpuscle was essentially and permanently a thing of that kind.[11] As an example of this sort of view, we might consider Jean Chrysostome Magnen, whose *Democritus reviviscens* (1646) was published just before the first of Gassendi's publications in this area (although Gassendi began work on his Epicurean project in the 1630s). Magnen describes himself as the first in modern times to try to rehabilitate atomism (p. vii), which is at best an exaggeration, but he does stand out among post-scholastic authors in taking the central point at issue between Aristotelians and their critics to be the status of prime matter.[12] As noted in §2.1, Magnen treats the existence of some sort of enduring prime matter as uncontroversial. He proposes, however, that our "ignorance about true prime matter" is "the origin of all the difficulties" that plague natural philosophy (p. 51). In defense of this hypothesis he makes the reasonable remark that one's conception of matter will determine what one thinks about both substantial and accidental forms, since they inhere in matter, and that hence one's conception of matter will determine the overall contours of one's philosophy. Thus the work's first *disputatio* (which occupies nearly a quarter of the volume) answers in the negative the question "whether one should postulate a prime matter that is distinct from the elements."

Magnen's work makes more explicit than any other I have seen the case for treating prime matter in corpuscular fashion. His argument rests on identifying four hallmarks of prime matter:

---

[11] David Gorlaeus recognizes only two elemental kinds, water and earth (*Idea physicae* 7.1), neither of which can be converted into the other (7.9). Isaac Beeckman accepts the standard list of four, but insists they be explained in terms of differences in shape (*Journal* I:152–3, II:118–19, III:138). Sebastian Basso regards the traditional list of four as a live option, but possibly not the final story: "Materia rerum ex minutissimis particulis diversae naturae comparata est; quae quidem naturae sive sint quatuor elementa ignis, aer, aqua, terra; sive quid aliud prius ex quo haec elementa componantur, speciei diversissimae sunt.... Haec principia post primam creationem ortus interitusque sunt experta" (*Phil. nat.*, De materia et mixto II.5.4, p. 125). Walter Charleton, in contrast, is willing to recognize the traditional four elements only as "elementa secundaria"— "the four vulgar elements cannot justly be honored with the attributes of the first matter" (*Physiologia* II.3.1.3). For further details on Beeckman's and Basso's chemical theories see §19.6 and §21.4, as well as Kubbinga, "Premières théories."

Claude Berigard argues for infinitely many different kinds of atoms—as well as an infinite number of atoms within each kind: "facio infinitas atomorum species tota substantia inter se distinctas, et rursus in unaquaque specie atomos infinitas" (*Circulus Pisanus*, De ortu VIII, p. 419). See §22.4 for brief discussion.

[12] Magnen's claim to be the first to recover ancient atomism comes in the preface to *Democritus reviviscens*: "id opus a nullo hactenus fuerit pertractatum" (n. p. [= vii]). In claiming priority, Magnen fails even to mention Gassendi, which he could hardly have done if his work on Epicurus was generally known at that time. He does mention Sennert, and dismisses him with the remark that he proved the existence of "minima physica" rather than atoms (see §26.3 for the distinction). In another context he mentions Sebastian Basso (p. 45), but apparently does not think of him as an atomist.

On prime matter as the core problem of natural philosophy, see ibid.. p. 51: "Sed *tertium* mihi potius omnium difficultatum origo videtur, ignoratio verae materiae primae. Ratio meae conjecturae haec est: forma praesupponit materiam, ut ab aliis etiam accidentibus praesupponatur subjectum, ergo ut erit materia, ita et continuitas: forma enim, et accidentia, quae educuntur, debent sequi naturam materiae, cum quidquid recipitur per modum recipientis recipiatur...."

There are four distinctive features (*proprietates*) of prime matter, inseparable from it: (1) that it is the first subject of every body; (2) that the same elements are found to inhere in all natural bodies; (3) that it is ingenerable and incorruptible; (4) that all bodies, through their final dissolution, are broken down into it. (Proposition 1, p. 58)

From here, Magnen tries to establish that his basic corpuscular elements, his atoms, satisfy all four criteria. He takes it to be unproblematic that his elements satisfy (2), inasmuch as every natural body contains each kind of element. (Since this was part of the standard Aristotelian theory of elements [§21.2], he seems within his rights to treat it as non-controversial, but we will see below that it has an important and surprising implication.) Feature (1) is essentially equivalent to the substratum thesis. If Magnen could establish this, he realizes that he could infer that (3) and (4) hold of his atoms, but he does not seem to think any direct proof of (1) is possible. Still, "although to prove this [(1)] is most difficult, neither has it yet been proved sufficiently by the Peripatetics that their pure potentiality, their empty prime matter, is to be posited" (p. 61). In the face of this standoff, Magnen instead takes up a different strategy, and attempts to prove that (3) holds of his atoms. From (3), he claims, (1) follows. This is not obviously true, but he offers this rationale: "if another subject were postulated, the generation and corruption of the elements would be postulated" (p. 61). That is, the negation of (1) entails the negation of (3). Magnen leaves it at this, but on reflection his remark seems correct. It would make no sense to posit some more basic substratum, beyond the atoms, unless that further substratum were the substratum for the atoms themselves. (Otherwise, in what sense would it be *more basic*?) But to say that it is the substratum for the atoms is to say that it serves as the substratum over which the atoms go into and out of existence. Hence the negation of (1) entails the negation of (3). Hence (3) entails (1). So whereas the Aristotelian contends that the four elements are mutable, and that hence some further prime matter is required, Magnen aims to show that his basic atomic elements are permanent, and that hence they can serve as prime matter.

Of the four arguments Magnen offers for (3), the most promising is the second: "If the elements were corruptible and generable, then the world could be destroyed through natural causes, applied through their own proper force" (p. 62). The consequence of the whole world's destruction is absurd, Magnen claims, and so (3) must be maintained. This is an argument with a history. Epicurus had used an argument of this form to argue for the conservation of matter, and so had his Latin spokesman, Lucretius. Something like it appears in Aristotle, too, who raised the query that, if what exists passes away into nothing, "why has not the universe been used up long ago and vanished away?" (*Gen. et cor.* 318a17–18). The Jesuit Pererius offered it among his list of arguments for prime matter: "If matter is not necessary, then either generation would have ceased long ago, given that all physical forms are corruptible, or matter could be fashioned and refashioned *ex nihilo*, which has many seriously implausible consequences" (*De communibus principiis* V.4, p. 282).[13]

---

[13] For the threat of the world's disappearing, if there is no perpetually enduring stuff, see the Epicurean texts in Long and Sedley, *Hellenistic Philosophers* 4A and 4C. Magnen states the impossibility of the whole world's natural destruction as an initial axiom: "II. Mundus destrui non potest per causas naturales, vi propria et naturaliter applicatus" (*Democ. reviv.* p. 55).

Given that this argument gets used by both Aristotelians and atomists, we might immediately wonder whether it can be used to yield the specific result Magnen is after, rather than the more general conservation thesis of the previous chapter. Moreover, as an argument for conservation, it does not look very effective, since it seems to ignore the possibility (familiar from the previous chapter) that the corrupted thing will give rise to something new, without any part of it enduring through the change. If it is a law that corrupted things give rise to something new, at the same time that they themselves go out of existence (§2.3), then the end of the world need not loom. But Magnen seems to have in mind a special version of the argument that both has some plausibility and yields (3) in particular. What he must assume, to make the argument run, is the thesis discussed above: that each of the basic corpuscles essentially and permanently belongs to a certain kind. Magnen contends there are three such kinds—earth, fire, water—and that elements of each kind must be present in every body. Now suppose, contrary to (3), that the atoms can be corrupted—that, for instance, a fire atom can become an earth atom. Then it is possible for *all* the fire atoms to go out of existence. But in that case the physical world as a whole would go out of existence. Since that is not in fact possible, atoms must be incorruptible.

The argument is surprisingly powerful (at least for incorruptibility; it does not yield ingenerability). If Magnen's key empirical claim is correct—if there is one or more kind of corpuscle that must exist, for the physical world to exist—then those corpuscles must be indestructible, or else we must admit the possibility of the physical world's ceasing to exist. Now one might suppose that we should reply by simply allowing this as a possibility—a very remote possibility, on a par with the often-cited possibility that all the air in the room might congregate into one corner, but even more unlikely than that. Yet I think most people, on reflection, will have the intuition that there is a genuine impossibility here—that the world cannot, at least through natural processes, simply cease to exist entirely, so that where there was something, there now is nothing at all. If it did, where would all that matter go? (This is the converse of the highly plausible weak *ex nihilo* principle of the previous chapter.) In effect, Magnen's argument boils down to the claim that, given the conservation of matter, any necessary ingredient of matter must be incorruptible.

The heart of the disagreement over prime matter concerns just what features can be said to be necessary to it. For the atomist, matter is essentially composed of indivisible particles. If those particles are further thought to be immutable, and to come in kinds, then such kinds will themselves be a fixed, necessary feature of prime matter. A view like Magnen's that endorses this whole package of claims provides a highly clear and concrete notion of what prime matter is, and inevitably such clarity looked attractive in comparison to the obscurities of scholastic prime matter. Still, just as corpuscularians could endorse prime matter without endorsing atomism, they could likewise endorse a conception of prime matter free of immutable kinds. One finds this sort of approach in Descartes, and later in Robert Boyle, both of whom refuse to endorse atomism and further allow that matter is capable of unlimited transmutations from one kind into another. For Descartes, this is a consequence of his view that the essence of matter is simply to be *res extensa*. Although this extended stuff takes on various modes in virtue of the motion of its parts, the matter itself does not admit of differences in kind. Boyle was critical of Descartes in many respects, but this feature of the theory is one he accepted, because it fit with his own view, developed through his chemical research, that anything can be changed into anything else.

Considered as a thesis about ultimate kinds in chemistry, Boyle's theory looks like a dead end: a minority view even in its own time, it would eventually be rejected altogether, as incompatible with Lavoisier's theory of the elements.[14] Considered as a metaphysical thesis, however, it raises intriguing questions about the contrast between metaphysical and corpuscular prime matter. Earlier I described how various scholastic views, by actualizing matter, threatened to make it corpuscular. Here we can see the opposite phenomenon. Because Descartes and Boyle sharply limit the features they recognize as essential to matter, they run the risk that their view might collapse into a version of Aristotelianism. For consider what Descartes has as his enduring substratum of change: he has purely *res extensa*, matter without any features whatsoever beyond extension, but with unlimited potentiality for taking on various modes. To be sure, Descartes's version of prime matter is extended, but as we will see in the next chapter this hardly serves to distinguish it from many scholastic accounts. Bare extension is not enough to save Descartes from the paradoxes of Aristotelian prime matter, because for Descartes shape and motion are modes. *Res extensa*—the stuff that endures through change to its modes—would seem to be, in its own right, the kind of shapeless, indeterminate substratum that the scholastics postulate. Subsequent chapters (esp. §8.2 and §13.7) will return to this issue.

3.3. The Arguments: A First Rehearsal

The arguments for and against the various notions of prime matter encapsulate the broader range of arguments for and against the scholastic hylomorphic framework. This is as it should be if, as Magnen argues, prime matter is "the origin of all the difficulties" in natural philosophy (as above). Given that this is so, however, there is little point in attempting to discuss these arguments in any great detail here. Entwined as they are with debates over extension, substance, accident, mode, unity, and individuation, the arguments can scarcely be adjudicated, or even fully understood, until those other issues have been brought on board. Still, a sketch of the terrain may prove useful.

Very often, as we will see in the chapters to come, critics of scholasticism do not attempt a direct refutation of the various elements of the hylomorphic scheme. Instead,

---

[14] On the inconvertibility of the elements, see Kahn, "Entre atomisme" p. 258; Wilson, *Epicureanism* pp. 80–1; and Kuhn, "Robert Boyle" pp. 22–3, who contends that Boyle is almost alone in the seventeenth century in insisting on the mutability of the elements from one kind to another. Boyle puts the claim as follows: "So that though I would not say that any thing can immediately be made of every thing, as a gold ring of a *wedge* of gold, or oil or fire of water; yet since bodies, having but one common Matter, can be differenced but by accidents, which seem all of them to be the effects and consequents of local motion, I see not why it should be absurd to think that (at least among inanimate bodies) by the intervention of some very small addition or subtraction of matter, (which yet in most cases will scarce be needed) and of an orderly series of alterations, disposing by degrees the matter to be transmuted, almost of any thing, may at length be made any thing" (*Origin* V:332; Stewart pp. 49–50). For the standard scholastic view, see e.g. Jandun, *In Phys.* I.24 ad 4: "omnia materialia sunt adinvicem transmutabilia, vel immediate...vel mediate et per plures transmutationes...." Another early seventeenth-century denial of the transmutability of the elements can be found in Jungius, *Disp. Hamb.* XXII thes. 4, who cites various figures in support, including Sennert, as well as de Clave's 1624 broadsheet. Lasswitz (*Geschichte der Atomistik* I:332–59) surveys various early seventeenth-century claims of immutability, remarking that this "ist ein wichtiger Schritt zur Korpuskulartheorie und damit zur Fundamentierung der modernen Naturwissenschaft" (I:332).

they content themselves with showing that such metaphysical parts are not needed, leaving considerations of parsimony to do the rest. In the context of prime matter, Magnen again exemplifies this strategy. What he seeks to show, as we saw in the previous section, is that there are ingenerable and incorruptible atoms. This, however, does not *prove* that metaphysical prime matter does not exist; it simply makes any such further substratum unnecessary. For all we know, there might be something still more basic, a kind of metaphysical sub-basement beneath the atoms. Magnen sees this clearly. For immediately after concluding that his elements satisfy the four conditions of prime matter, he adds further not that Aristotelian prime matter does not exist, but that it is "altogether useless" (prop. 4, p. 79). He then reasons that since there is nothing pointless in nature, we should not posit any such further prime matter. From Peter John Olivi forward (see, e.g., §14.1), this is how the proponents of ontological austerity very often argue, on a wide range of fronts.[15]

Simply appealing to considerations of parsimony would itself be quite a parsimonious argumentative strategy, and post-scholastic authors usually cannot resist going at least a bit further. The most common further complaint is that the various elements of the hylomorphic scheme are unintelligible. This is what we have seen both Gassendi and Magnen suggest regarding prime matter: as Gassendi puts it, the Aristotelian theory does not yield "any way to describe" the matter it postulates; Magnen similarly protests against "the Peripatetics [and] their empty prime matter," where emptiness is intended to reflect not just that the stuff is purely potential, but that it lacks any intelligible content. Descartes, too, cannot accept "the prime matter of the philosophers, which they have stripped so thoroughly of all its forms and qualities that nothing remains in it that can be clearly understood" (*The World*, XI:33). Such charges of unintelligibility are extremely significant for debates throughout this period. As we will see in the chapters to come, advocates of the mechanistic–corpuscularian framework pride themselves on the top-to-bottom intelligibility of their approach: on the way their accounts genuinely *explain* the natural world. Scholastic authors are in no position to gainsay the desirability of intelligibility. The object of Aristotelian inquiry is *scientia*, an ideal systematic understanding of a given domain, and such understanding requires a grasp of the reasons why a certain phenomenon is the case.[16] Unintelligibility, then, is the enemy of *scientia*. Still, it is not obvious that the true theories are always the most clear and intelligible. Even if we aim at intelligibility, there is no guarantee that the world will cooperate. The scholastic doctrine of prime matter is certainly paradoxical, and perhaps

---

[15] Magnen argues for the uselessness of Aristotelian prime matter as follows: "Materia prima, quam Aristoteles proponit ex Aegyptiorum mente [?!], omnino inutilis est, tum physico, tum medico. Probatur primo, quia ea omissa facilius explicantur omnia, ut patebit inferius; *deinde*, quia elementa ad omnimodam mixtionem sufficiunt; *tertio*, quia medicus elementa tantum in corporibus contemplatur, physicus autem nullam materiae primae Aristotelicae necessitatem ostendere potest, quare cum nihil in natura frustra sit, eam materiam non dari concludendum" (*Democritus reviviscens* disp. 1, prop. 4, p. 79).

It is commonplace, albeit not very illuminating, to reject scholastic prime matter simply on the grounds that there is no room for it in an author's preferred ontology. See, e.g., Gassendi, *Syntagma*, II.6.1 (I:372ab): "cum ipsae ergo atomi tota sint materia substantiave corporea quae in ipsis corporibus est, constat si quid aliud in ipsis corporibus concipimus esseve animadvertimus id non esse substantiam, sed solum substantiae modum aliquem—hoc est certam quandam materiae materialiumve principiorum contexturam, concretionem, compositionem...." And Charleton, *Physiologia* IV.1.1.2: "every mutation requires a subject to be altered, and that subject must be something compound, complete, and already constituted in some determinate genus of beings."

[16] On Aristotelian *scientia* as requiring a grasp of the reasons why a thing is so, see Pasnau, "Science and Certainty."

in certain ways unintelligible (§7.2), but that does not make it false. Sometimes, from our vantage point, the world itself just is paradoxical.

Just beyond the charge of unintelligibility lies the more serious charge of incoherence. Here is Joseph Glanvill, in his *Scepsis scientifica* (1665):

That the Aristotelian philosophy is an huddle of words and terms insignificant has been the censure of the wisest; and that both its basis and superstructure are chimerical cannot be unobserved by them that know it and are free to judge it. To detect the verbal emptiness of 3 this philosophy, I'll begin at the foundation of the hypothesis. . . . Therefore the *materia prima* of this philosophy shall be that of my reflections. In the consideration of which I shall need no more than the notion wherein Aristotle himself has dressed it, for evidence of what I aim at; 6 for *Nec quid, nec quale, nec quantum* is as apposite[17] a definition of *Nothing* as can be. So that if we would conceive this imaginary matter, we must deny all things of it that we can conceive; and what remains is the thing we look for. (ch. 18, pp. 127–8)

The Latin tag is a paraphrase of Aristotle (*Meta.* VII.3, 1029a20; see *Gen. et cor.* I.3, 318a15), and though it is not clear whether Aristotle himself meant to endorse this conception of matter, scholastic authors do routinely cite the passage in favor of the view that prime matter has "neither kind, nor character, nor size." This tracks the three primary Aristotelian categories of Substance, Quality, and Quantity (§12.1). Technically speaking, prime matter cannot be in any of these categories, because it is the subject of all these categories and so in some sense prior to them.[18] But Glanvill is of course not concerned with the technicalities; he simply wants to push the claim that what has no such features cannot exist at all. Again, as in Descartes, there is a suggestion (lines 7–9) that the case against prime matter rests simply on its unintelligibility. But the overall course of the argument makes it clear that Glanvill is pushing the stronger line that prime matter is not just unintelligible to us, but positively incoherent, inasmuch as what is of no kind, character, or size must be nothing at all.

The charge of incoherence is one to which a would-be defender of the scholastics must reply. In this case, it will surely not do to insist that a thing can exist without having any character. A completely bare substratum seems not just incoherent but also unable to carry out the function for which it is intended—to be a substratum. We saw in §3.1, however, a reply from Peter Auriol that is more satisfactory: the idea that the character of prime matter precisely is its determinability. This idea is more familiar than it might initially seem. It would not be odd, for instance, to think that reflective material objects all share the property of being colored. Color, however, is a determinable property, open to any of various determinate shades. Auriol himself compares prime matter to the genus *animal*, and suggests that if there are determinable genera, then there can be prime matter. This precise analogy is perhaps a doubtful one for a scholastic audience, since they did not tend to think that higher genera correspond to any separate property or form in objects (§4.3, §12.2 and §25.1). One might insist in general that there are no such determinable properties, only the most specific,

---

[17] 'Apposite' corrects 'opposite'—following the parallel text at *Vanity of Dogmatizing* p. 153.

[18] Prime matter has no place at all in the ontological scheme of the *Categories*. This did not trouble scholastic authors, not because they thought of it as an early work, prior to Aristotle's hylomorphic insights, but because they thought of it as a more elementary treatise that passed over many of the subtleties raised in the *Physics*, *Gen. et Cor.*, and the *Metaphysics* (§12.1).

determinate species-kinds and quality-kinds, such as this particular species of animal, and this particular shade of color. Certainly, there are reasons for taking that route, but doing so would be quite a blow to the ordinary way we think and talk about properties, and so it can hardly be assumed that there are no such purely determinable features of the world. Hence there seems some room for Auriol's approach, and the charge of incoherence is not immediately decisive.[19]

Of course, if there is such a property as *color*, it is not radically indeterminate in the way that prime matter is, open to being determined in any sort of way. Only certain determinate qualities (specific shades of red, orange, etc.) count as determinations of *color*. But although prime matter is radically determinable, it too is not *wholly* determinable. If it were, then the charge of Glanvill might really stick: prime matter would seem to be just nothing. Even if authors like Auriol sometimes come close to suggesting that the whole of prime matter's nature is its indeterminateness, that cannot really be right. After all, we saw earlier pseudo-Marsilius's list of the features of prime matter, which included *perpetual, basic, uniform,* and *hidden*. Set aside *hidden*, which follows from its indeterminacy (§7.2), and that still leaves us three quite determinate ways to characterize prime matter. Indeed, these are precisely the features that explain its status as a substratum. So in the face of the paradox of a bare substratum, it seems we can reply that its bareness is a function of its indeterminacy, and that yet it is a substratum, because it is not completely indeterminate, having various characteristics that qualify it to endure through all change.

Superfluity, unintelligibility, incoherence—these are the three stock charges we will confront over and over against scholastic metaphysics. Such charges will have to be considered as we go, but in many cases a given set of views must stand or fall as a whole. The tenability of a given theory of prime matter cannot be judged apart from the account of form that accompanies it, and in light of the consequences the whole story has for questions of unity, individuation, and the like.

It is at the level of consequences that scholastic authors make their stand against attempts at a more reductive, parsimonious ontology. Here the principal concern of scholastic authors is to preserve the ontology of common sense. This will perhaps seem an unlikely claim, since scholastic metaphysics in its details often run well beyond the wildest dreams of common sense at its most fanciful. Yet as wild as its hypotheses often are, they are usually put at the service of preserving our ordinary ontology of dogs and cats and stones. The topic of prime matter illustrates this point particularly well.

---

[19] Auriol's defense of the reality of prime matter by appealing to other sorts of determinables, such as genera, is difficult to follow: "nulla est contradictio ponere materiam esse ens positivum, et tamen hoc, quod non habeat propriam et distinctam actualitatem, imo ponere oppositum esset facere fallaciam consequentis. Hanc conclusionem probo, quia non est contradictio intelligere divisum aliquod sub una differentia et quod non intelligatur sub alia, sicut non est contradictio quod reperiatur animal cum rationali, et quod, ut sic, non intelligatur sub irrationali; sed ens dividitur in esse distinctum, et ens esse in potentia; ergo non est contradictio intelligere ens aliquod positivum, quod tamen non sit in actu distinctum, sed tantum in potentia" (*Sent.* II.12.1.1; II:154bBC). The argument itself is not very clear, and moreover the generally unreliable Rome edition seems particularly muddled at this point, inasmuch as it seems to give us a long and involved objection to that argument without Auriol's reply, and then moves onto the *tertio ratio principalis* (II:155aD) without having given us the second principal argument.

Another interesting analogy Auriol offers in support of prime matter as purely potential and yet existent appeals to the parts of a continuum, which Aristotle had claimed to exist merely potentially (thus allowing for the continuum's infinite divisibility without an actual infinity of parts—see *Gen. et cor.* I.2): "Non sequitur: Existit, ergo in actu. Patet de partibus continui..." (*Sent.* II.12.2.2, II:179bD; cf. *Sent.* II.12.1.1, II:154aD). See §26.3 for the notion of potential parts.

The most commonly adumbrated consequence of abandoning metaphysical prime matter is that this would undermine our picture of the world as composed of things—substances—with a special sort of unity, enduring through time for a while and then going out of existence, to be replaced by other things. More specifically, the charge against those who let actual corpuscles be their enduring substratum is that they could not account for substantial unity, and could not account for the ordinary generation and corruption of substances. John of Jandun, for instance, contends that as soon as one actualizes prime matter, one eliminates the substantial differences between individuals: "beings would be substantially the same—indeed, there would be nothing other than that [one] actualized subject, and so all things would differ only accidentally" (*In De subst. orbis* q. 3, f. 52vb). Others make the opposite complaint: that without Aristotelian prime matter, the world dissolves into indefinitely many substances. The two lines of objection amount to the same thing: that without purely potential prime matter, we can no longer account for the privileged status that common sense accords to the familiar substances around us. Looking back to the ancient atomists, Auriol complains that "the ancients did not recognize that there is something halfway between pure being and pure non-being... This was the reason why the ancient natural philosophers denied generation" (*Sent.* II.12.1.1, II:152b–153a).[20] And when Nicholas of Autrecourt actually did deny generation and corruption in his radical *Tractatus* (1330), he dismissed metaphysical prime matter in just the way his contemporaries would have predicted, as something wholly unnecessary once the pretense of commonsense ontology is abandoned.[21]

When prime matter is understood most austerely, as the pure potentiality of the Thomists, then there is a clear distinction between the alteration of an enduring substance and the generation of a new substance. In the first case, there is an enduring actual substratum of change, the composite substance; in the second case, all that endures is indeterminate, unactualized matter. Our four centuries witness a steady retreat from that sort of view, with fully corpuscular prime matter marking merely the most extreme version of a picture on which determinate, actualized stuff endures through all change. As we will see, Scotus takes one step down this road when he insists against Aquinas that matter has its own existence and substantial parts (§4.2). Ockham goes farther still when he insists that prime matter has extension (§4.4). The

---

[20] On metaphysical prime matter as essential to the theory of generation and corruption, Auriol is paraphrasing Averroes (*In Phys.* I.78), who is paraphrasing Aristotle (*Phys.* I.8, 191b31–34): "It was this reason that also caused some of the earlier thinkers to turn so far aside from the road which leads to generation and corruption and change generally. If they had come in sight of this nature, all their ignorance would have been dispelled." This form of argument is very common in scholastic texts. See, e.g., Jandun, *In De subst. orbis* Q3 (f. 52bG): "Alia fuit opinio quorundam antiquorum quod materia prima est actu ens, sicut corpus ignis vel aeris, ut patet primo *Physicorum*. Sed haec opinio non tenet, quia si esset vera cum in utroque termino transmutationis subiectum maneat, scilicet materia, quicquid adveniret illi subiecto esset accidens, quia adveniret enti in actu.... Et haec opinio non stat, immo sequeretur quod entia essent eadem substantialiter: immo non essent nisi illud subiectum in actu, ideo omnia non different nisi accidentaliter. Sed hoc est falsum, ideo materia prima non est ens in actu."

[21] Autrecourt rejects prime matter as follows: "si res transirent de non esse ad esse, sequeretur quod esset necessarium aliquid esse quod subiceretur, quod esset materia, et aliquid quod esset forma in esse; sic enim ponit Aristoteles generationem. Nunc vero non est necessarium esse materiam..." (p. 192). See also p. 204: "Non enim habent locum nec sunt vera quae dicta sunt ab eo de materia prima, quia fundamentum in illa inquisitione est quod res transeunt de esse ad non esse et e converso." On Autrecourt's denial of generation and corruption, see §28.2. On his skeptical doubts regarding substance in general, see §7.3.

doctrines that accidents inhere directly in prime matter (§4.3, §6.3) and that substances can have multiple substantial forms (§25.1) are yet further manifestations of this same tendency. Each of these moves has powerful motivations behind it, but each threatens to undermine what is ultimately the chief motivation of Aristotelian metaphysics: to explain why ordinary composite substances—dogs and cats and stones—are the prima-ry constituents of the material world. To safeguard this commonsense ontology, one needs an account of what gives these ordinary substances a special sort of unity and endurance through time. Rival theories of prime matter should be judged, in large part, in terms of their consequences for those subsequent issues.[22]

For proponents of one or another corpuscular theory of prime matter, it becomes tempting to conclude that ordinary substances are in fact not substances at all, and that what really exists, in the material realm, is simply prime matter. Such a conclusion is by no means inevitable: no matter what one's preferred ontology, one can always insist that dogs, cats, and stones are fundamental because these are the fundamental essences or kinds in the natural realm. But when this bare claim derives no support from one's basic ontology, a great deal of weight falls on one's theory of natural kinds, and post-scholastic authors would increasingly come to have doubts about the sustainability of those distinctions (see Ch. 27). Hence the denial of generation and corruption—once regarded as an immediate *reductio* of corpuscularianism—came to be seen as a live possibility. Author after author in the seventeenth century—including Hobbes, Des-cartes, and Locke—would find it difficult to escape this conclusion, and in some cases they did not even try. By the time we confront this issue squarely (Chs. 27–9), we will have collected quite a list of ways in which the seventeenth century rejected scholastic philosophy. Yet it will be worth keeping in mind, at that point, that the root difficulty faced by the corpuscularians goes back to the disagreement over prime matter.

---

[22] Paul of Venice contends that any sort of extended prime matter would preclude generation and corruption: "Impossibile est quantitatem esse substantiam quantam. Probatur . . . Secundo, sequitur quod generatio simpliciter dicta est augmentatio . . ." (*Summa phil. nat.* VI.12, f. 101ra). Scotus argues that his somewhat actualized prime matter allows for substantial change at *Lectura* II.12 nn. 39, 43 (XIX:83, 85). See too Gabriel Biel's defense against the charge, at *Sent.* II.12.1.3: "quomodo salvatur generatio ut distinguitur ab alteratione, si materia est entitas positiva et per consequens ens in actu."

For the argument from substantial unity against actualized prime matter, see, e.g., De Soto, *In Phys.* I.7 n. 6 (pp. 52–3); Scotus, *Lectura* II.12 n. 41 (Vatican XIX:84), who raises it as a potential criticism of his own view. Suárez refers to "illa communis ratio, quod forma adveniens enti iam in actu constituto non facit unum per se, sed per accidens" (*Disp. meta.* 13.3.11).

4

Matter and Extension

One might suppose that the essential difference between corpuscular and metaphysical prime matter is that only the first is extended. Consider Robert Boyle, who begins his introduction to the corpuscularian philosophy by remarking that "I agree with the generality of philosophers, so far as to allow that there is one catholic or universal matter common to all bodies, by which [matter] I mean a substance extended, divisible, and impenetrable" (*Origin of Forms* V:305; Stewart p. 18). With this one might think Boyle first reaches out a hand to the scholastics, in postulating prime matter, only to take it away by describing that matter as extended. In fact, however, scholastics quarreled among themselves over matter's relationship to all three of the characteristics Boyle lists: extension, divisibility, and impenetrability. Indeed, although the topic has hardly been considered among recent scholars, these questions were perhaps the most hotly disputed aspects of the scholastic debate over prime matter.

In view of the complexity of the terrain, a roadmap may prove useful. The most basic scholastic disagreement concerns whether or not the enduring substratum of change is extended. Those who say no divide into those who treat prime matter as intrinsically simple (that is, lacking in parts) and those who ascribe parts to it, intrinsically, but deny that those parts are spread out. Those who argue instead for an extended substratum divide on whether it is intrinsically or accidentally extended. These distinctions yield four different views, which can be labeled as follows, with their chief proponent in parentheses:

Extensionless Theories
Simple View (Aquinas)
Extensionless Parts View (Scotus)

Extended Theories
Accidentally Quantified View (Averroes)
Intrinsically Extended View (Ockham)

This chapter will sketch these different views.

4.1. The Simple View

The case for extensionless prime matter is predictable enough, given the general tenor of the scholastic theories described in the previous chapter: prime matter cannot be extended because it is unformed and purely potential, whereas extension requires form and actuality. The argument should certainly be appealing to anyone who accepts that prime matter is pure potentiality, and it was often accepted. There was also a widespread suspicion, however, that the notion of extensionless prime matter is ultimately incoherent. To begin to see why this was so, consider what exactly it means for a thing to have or to lack extension. There seems to have been general agreement, throughout our four centuries, over what extension is: it is to have *partem extra partem*—or, in English, spatially distinct parts.[1] In view of this definition, we can see that there are a number of ways in which prime matter might fail to be extended. One way would be to lack parts. Another would be to be wholly located at an extensionless point, and so fail the requirement of spatial distinctness. A third way would be to lack location entirely. This last possibility, so far as I can find, was not regarded as a serious contender. Even if philosophers today are often tempted to treat one or another entity as locationless, our period treated it as axiomatic that everything that exists exists somewhere (§16.3). This principle was applied even to God, angels, and human souls, and so was hardly likely to admit of exception in the case of matter. This leaves two possibilities: that prime matter might exist without parts, or that it might have parts and yet fail to be spread out.[2]

---

[1] On the nature of extension, see, e.g., De Soto, *In Praed.* 6.1, p. 173C: "Prima et per se ratio quantitatis est esse rationem extensionis: nempe ratione cuius substantia habet partem extra partem, et huic proximum est, quod ratione quantitatis substantia et accidenta corporalia sunt divisibilia in partes secundum extensionem." Aristotle had connected quantity with divisible parts, and so with extension, at *Meta.* V.13, 1020a7–8: "We call a quantity that which is divisible into two or more constituent parts of which each is by nature a one and a this (ἔν τι καὶ τόδε τι)." The connection endures into the seventeenth century, in Digby, *Two Treatises* I.2.8, p. 15: "So that looking over all the several species of quantity, it is evident our definition of it is a true one, and expresses fully the essence of it, when we say it is *divisibility*, or a capacity to be divided into parts, and that no other notion whatsoever, besides this, reaches the natures of it." See also Gassendi: "Seu enim talis species procedit ex corpore, illa haud dubie corporea est, habetque partes extra partes, atque adeo extensa est" (Fifth Objections, VII:337); Descartes: "ita illud solum quod est imaginabile, ut habens partes extra partes, quae sint determinatae magnitudinis et figurae, dico esse extensum, quamvis alia per analogiam, etiam extensa dicantur" (to More, V:270); Locke: "For to say, as is usually done, that extension is to have *partes extra partes* is to say only that *extension is extension*" (*Essay* II.xiii.15); Chauvin: "...extensionem physicam, quae nihil aliud est quam plures materiae partes extra se invicem positae" (*Lexicon*, 'quantitas' p. 549a).

[2] The question of whether anything can exist without a location is complicated by scholastic terminology, according to which many things exist without being in a place (*locus*). Since a thing's *locus* is the two-dimensional surface of the surrounding body (§17.1), there are various ways of having a location (in the English sense of the term) without having a *locus*. In particular, something that exists at an extensionless point has no *locus*. For further discussion, see §14.4. The closest I have seen anyone come to countenancing prime matter without location is this passage from Scotus: "Dices, ubi erit illa materia in potentia ad omnem formam? Qualiter etiam habebit materia partem extra partem sine quantitate? Ad primam dico, quaerendo ab opposito, ubi erit angelus, vel potest eum Deus creare sine *ubi*? Et non erit maior ratio quare non posset creare materiam. Vel si dicas quod non posset, assignes mihi *ubi* quod est necessarium angelo, et assignabo ego *ubi* necessarium materiae" (*Rep.* II.12.2 n. 7; XI:322a). But exactly what possibility does Scotus have in mind here? Does "sine ubi" mean locationless? Compare the parallel passage printed in old editions of the *Opus Oxoniense*: "Et si quaeras ubi esset illa materia sine forma, dico quod sicut angelus qui non est quantus est in loco aliquo definitive, non circumscriptive, supposito quod sit in universo, si tamen fieret extra universum, ubi locus non est, non esset in loco definitive, sic materia, si fieret in universo sine forma, esset definitive alicubi; si autem fieret extra universum, nusquam esset localiter, vel definitive, tamen esset natura quaedam absoluta" (II.12.2, VI.2:683). According to the editors of the Scotus critical edition, this is not part of the *Ordinatio*; it is presumably an alternate redaction of the Parisian *Reportatio*. Here locationlessness is not at issue at all: prime matter will either exist within the physical universe "*definitive*"—that is, holenmerically (§16.5)—or will exist *extra universum*, beyond the outermost sphere of the heavens, in which case it will

Let us begin with the Simple View—the view that prime matter lacks parts. John Capreolus, the important Thomistic philosopher from the early fifteenth century, takes this line. On his view, prime matter is "actually indivisible and one, but potentially divisible, multiple, and plural." Or, to avoid the impression that prime matter is *actually* anything, he goes on to say that it is "actually indivisible—that is, not actually divisible" (*Defensiones* II.13.1.3, IV:37a). A Thomistic treatise from the late thirteenth century, probably by Robert Orford, reaches the same conclusion: "for matter to have distinct parts in its own right (*secundum se*) is impossible, because distinctness of parts properly belongs to the composite that is constituted out of distinct parts" (*De natura materiae* ch. 5, n. 390). The doctrine seems to be in Aquinas himself, inasmuch as he holds that "prime matter is said to be numerically one in all things" (*De principiis naturae* ch. 2). This is the 'is said' of the Commentator—that is, Aquinas means that Averroes said it, and indeed Averroes defended this view at some length.[3] Averroes's position was in turn spelled out by his leading Latin spokesman, John of Jandun. Jandun, lecturing at Paris and then Navarre during the second decade of the fourteenth century, devotes an entire disputed question to answering in the affirmative this question: Is prime matter numerically one in all generable and corruptible things? (*In Phys.* I.24) An anonymous question published with some of Jandun's work makes the same claim: "In everything that has matter, the matter is numerically one, inasmuch as it has nothing by which it differs" (Anon. B, f. 63raB). In §4.3 below we will see how the Averroists part ways with the Thomists on the question of what endures through substantial change. With respect to the intrinsic nature of prime matter, however, the two camps are in basic accord.

These last claims are striking because they ascribe unity and indivisibility to prime matter even within ordinary form–matter composites (within, for short, *bodies*). Does this mean that prime matter, as it is ordinarily found in bodies, is not spread out within those bodies? Surely it does not mean that, because at the same time these authors are saying that prime matter is "in" such bodies, and there is no suggestion that this means anything other than what it would naturally seem to mean, that it is spread out throughout the whole body. But how can prime matter be spread out in bodies, and yet be indivisible? Most authors are not very clear about this. So far as I can find, however, the only possibility considered is its having a mode of existence more commonly ascribed to spiritual beings: existing wholly in each place that it exists. Following Henry More's coinage (§16.4), I will refer to this as holenmerism.

---

have no surrounding body and so will lack a *locus*. The possibility of existing nowhere at all does not arise. Although this second passage is a clear statement of the idea that prime matter exists holenmerically, I consign it to the footnotes because it would seem to clash with Scotus's commitment elsewhere to the idea that prime matter has parts (§4.2). If it has parts, then one would not expect it to exist holenmerically. I am not sure what Scotus's settled view is, if he has one.

[3] For Averroes on matter as *una numero*, see *In Meta.* XII.14. Jandun remarks that this text "considerandum est diligenter" (*In Phys.* I.24, f. 22vaE).

Jandun gives a clear statement of the predictable case against extended prime matter: "omnis diversitas et pluralitas est per aliquem actum. Actus est enim qui distinguit et separat, ut communiter accipitur ex octavo Metaphysicorum. But ipsa prima materia nullam formam habet de se: ergo de se non est distincta in diversis entibus naturalibus" (*In Phys.* I.24, f. 22raD; cf. f. 22rbD). See also the argument of an anonymous *quaestio* printed at the end of Jandun's *In De subst. orbis* (f. 63aB): "Pro solutione est notandum quod materia de se est solum pura potentia, nec habet aliquem actum de se; et ideo, quod materia sit multa vel pauca, hoc non habet a se, sed a quantitate." (This is the second of two questions, the first of which [I will call it Anonymous A] takes a broadly Thomistic line, and the second of which [I will call it Anonymous B] takes a line much like Jandun's.)

Although, as we will see in some detail in later chapters, it was commonplace to discuss holenmeric existence in the context of God, the angels, and the human soul, few were keen to advertise their commitment to this doctrine in the case of prime matter. Indeed, the doctrine is most readily seen in its opponents, who understandably reject it as quite absurd.[4] An unusually express defense of the theory can be found in the Jesuit Gabriel Vasquez, writing toward the end of the sixteenth century. Vasquez contends that indivisibility is the natural intrinsic state of all substances, material and immaterial. Material substances are extended in virtue of taking on the accidental form of quantity, but "neither prime matter nor any corporeal substance of itself has parts without quantity" (*In summam theol.* III.187.2 n. 10). To lack parts, though, entails "the distinctive mode of existing in a place indivisibly: either at a point, or so as to be whole in the whole place and whole in each part" (ibid. 190.3 n. 27). Conceived in the latter way, prime matter can both lack parts and exist within bodies. For if a thing exists wholly in every place it exists, then it need have no spatial parts, and it is in some sense indivisible. Accordingly, given the standard scholastic definition of extension as having *partem extra partem*, prime matter is not extended.[5]

As usual with prime matter, it is easy to see how one might arrive at such a counterintuitive result. For if one is committed to a seriously austere conception of prime matter, then it will lack even those features that would serve to distinguish it into distinct parts. One might try to squirm out of this result by holding that prime matter is so austerely bare that it neither has parts nor lacks them. Jandun describes someone who tried to take this line, maintaining that prime matter would be neither many nor one, but indeterminate even with regard to number. Although the previous chapter considered the appeal of treating prime matter as indeterminate, Jandun seems right that this would push the paradox of prime matter too far. In his words, one and many "sufficiently divide being"—that is, there is nothing that is neither one nor many. So if prime matter exists, we cannot escape having to decide whether it is a single, indivisible thing, or else divisible. Jandun therefore concludes that "prime matter is numerically one in all generable and corruptible things."[6]

---

[4] Many are explicit in rejecting the idea that prime matter could be numerically one in all things. Burley, for instance, rejects the literal reading of "illud commune dictum" as "impossibile" (*De formis* pp. 8–9). See also Dabillon, *Physique* I.3.2 thesis 6, p. 111. Ockham in effect argues that the Simple View leads to holenmerism when he argues that every extended material substance must have real parts spatially distinct from each other, or otherwise it would exist as the soul does, "tota in toto corpore et tota in qualibet parte." For this to be true of a material substance "est absurdum" (*Tract. de corp. Christi* ch. 12; *Opera theol.* X:114). David Gorlaeus (*Exercitationes* 6, p. 98) sees two ways in which matter might exist without quantity: as an extensionless point, or as spread out but without *partem extra partem*. He regards both as patently absurd, and so insists that bodies have parts intrinsically. He treats their shape and size, however, as modes (§13.4).

[5] I have not found Aquinas commit himself to prime matter's existing holenmerically, but he expressly leaves room for this when he considers the objection that God cannot be everywhere because "quod est totum alicubi, nihil eius est extra locum illum." He responds by distinguishing between metaphysical and integral parts (the former expressly includes matter and form; his terminology is *pars essentiae* and *pars quantitatis*), and then explains that whereas "quod est totum in aliquo loco totalitate quantitatis non potest esse extra locum illum . . . , non oportet quod illud quod est totum totalitate essentiae in aliquo nullo modo sit extra illud" (*Summa theol.* 1a 8.2 obj. 3 & ad 3).
John Major expressly recognizes the possibility that a body without quantity would exist holenmerically, and as far as I can tell this is the view he favors (*Sent.* IV.12.1, f. 55rb).

[6] On the excluded middle between one and many, Jandun writes: "Et de ista quidem prima et remota materia dixerunt aliqui quod ipsa de se nec est una nec plures: quod probaverunt ex hoc, quod ipsa de se nec habet quantitatem indivisam, quae est principium unitatis numeralis secundum eos, nec multas quantitates distinctas, a quibus est pluralitas numeralis, cum ipsa sit ens pure in potentia. Sed istud non sufficit: quia unum et multa sufficienter dividens ens secundum Arist. in decimo Metaphys" (*In Phys.* I.24, f. 22rbB).

4.2. The Extensionless Parts View

One might reasonably complain that the Simple View does not yield a truly extensionless conception of prime matter. For although prime matter so conceived does not have parts, and so *a fortiori* cannot be described as having *partem extra partem*, still the view allows that such matter can be spread out in a certain way, holenmerically, existing (wholly) in more than one place at once. Whether or not such existence should properly be regarded as a way of being extended is an issue that will be considered in more detail later, in discussing the soul's similar mode of location in the body (§16.4). Here, rather than worry about how best to apply the term 'extension,' let us simply move on to discuss a second way in which prime matter might fail to satisfy the scholastic definition: by having parts that fail to be spread out. On this sort of view, matter is not intrinsically extended, which is to say that it might exist without extension. Ordinarily, of course, matter is spread out, and so extended, but it is so only in virtue of the accidental form of quantity. The Coimbrans take this view:

Matter of itself, apart from quantity, has substantial parts from which it is intrinsically composed. It does not have them extended and arranged in order, however, one outside another, without the aid of quantity. It is the role of quantity to take those parts, which would otherwise be mixed up and entangled, and spread them out and unfold them. (*In Phys.* I.2.2.3, p. 96)

This is picturesque, but not very illuminating, and the Coimbrans have nothing more to say here about what substantial parts are, or what it is for them to be "entangled" or "spread out." They identify Scotus as the source of this doctrine, and Scotus does indeed speak of prime matter, apart from quantity, as having substantial parts.[7] But the clearest discussion I have found is in Paul of Venice, from around the start of the fifteenth century. Paul gives a deflationary reading of Averroes's claim that matter is "numerically one" in all bodies. It does not mean that matter exists simply (partlessly) and holenmerically; rather, Averroes's formula should be read merely as a statement of the substratum thesis: that there is numerically one stuff enduring through any given material change (§2.2). To the objection that prime matter cannot be a basic principle because it has parts, Paul grants that it does have parts, and then contends that having homogeneous parts is no obstacle to being a basic principle. So what are these parts? He explains this, somewhat, in a discussion of what prime matter would be like apart from quantity:

Matter stripped of quantity is quantitatively divisible not actually but aptitudinally or potentially. This is clear, because such matter does not actually have *partem extra partem*, but is apt by nature to have *partem extra partem* through the addition of a quantity that extends it.[3] This is the reason why non-quantified matter can be made quantified, whereas a point or an

---

[7] Scotus appeals very briefly to substantial parts at *Opus Ox.* II.12.2 n. 5 (VI.2:683 [not in *Ordinatio*]): "Si quaeras etiam an habeat partes, dico quod partes substantiales habet: illas enim non habet per quantitatem"; see also *Rep.* II.12.2 n. 7 (XI:322b). Gabriel Biel describes the view without endorsing it (*Sent.* II.12.1.3, II:306–7). Suárez discusses it in detail at *Disp. meta.* 40.4, and refers to many other discussions. For critical discussion, see also Vasquez, *In Summam theol.* III.186.4 nn. 24–5 (VII:266); III.190.3 nn. 32–3 (VII:304). For references to further defenders of the view, see §14.1, although the focus there is on whether the matter–form composite is extended, which entangles the role of prime matter with the role of substantial form.

intellective soul cannot. For non-quantified matter has integral parts, each one of which can be outside (*extra*) another. A point or an intellective soul, in contrast, is entirely indivisible in virtue of lacking parts. (*Summa philosophiae naturalis* VI.13, f. 102ra)   6

This nicely situates Paul's view, relative to the opposition. Unlike the Simple View, he takes prime matter to have parts, even describing them as "integral parts" (line 5). This is a large step toward a corpuscular theory of prime matter: Paul evidently conceives of matter as a stuff composed of parts in the straightforward way in which ordinary bodies are ordinarily composed of integral parts. This is to give prime matter what I will call *corpuscular structure*.[8]

On this Extensionless Parts View, prime matter has its corpuscular structure intrinsically, and so necessarily, but it does not necessarily have any particular size. Not only can the same matter become larger and smaller, as it is informed by different quantities, but it can cease to have any size at all, if stripped of quantity entirely. This last possibility is what unites the Simple View and the Extensionless Parts View. The two theories agree that since prime matter is not intrinsically extended, it can exist without being spread out. This is to say that the extension of material substances (bodies, for short) is not a product of prime matter, but of something else, of accidents in the category of Quantity. But if prime matter is not what accounts for the extension of bodies, then what does it account for? Here the two theories disagree. On the Extensionless Parts View, prime matter explains the corpuscular structure of bodies: that is, the way larger bodies are composed of smaller bodies, perhaps infinitely far down. (On the complex question of how many such integral parts a body has, see Ch. 26.) The Simple View does not allow prime matter to do even that much: as pure potentiality, it cannot account for anything on the side of actuality, which is where corpuscular structure would seem to fall. So what does it do? Its role, on the Simple View, is simply to serve as the barest of substrata for all material change— an entity whose existence is mandated by the substratum and conservation theses (Ch. 2), but whose nature is both unknowable (§7.2) and fraught with paradoxical indeterminacy (§3.1).

As abstruse as the topics of prime matter and accidental quantity may seem to be, the questions they raise about corpuscular structure go to the very heart of post-scholastic seventeenth-century thought. One of the defining features of corpuscularianism is that it takes corpuscular structure to be a basic feature of the material realm, not subject to any deeper explanatory account. I will return to these issues in Chapter 14, from the perspective of accidental forms in the category of Quantity. (There corpuscular structure will come to include not just having integral parts, but having those parts spread out spatially.) For now, however, I want to consider briefly a third sort of extensionless view regarding prime matter, which might seem to be more attractive

---

[8] Paul of Venice readily grants that both prime matter and substantial form are composed of parts: "Item, cum dicitur quod materia et forma fiunt ex aliis tanquam ex suis partibus, concedo: non tamen ex aliis diversarum rationum" (*Summa phil. nat.* I.4, f. 3ra). On the important debate over whether substantial forms have parts, see §26.6.
With respect to the Averroistic dictum that prime matter is numerically one, Paul of Venice responds as follows: "Ad tertium dicitur quod propositio Commentatoris est sic intelligenda: eadem materia numero erit successive sub cuiuslibet generabilis et corruptibilis specie, et hoc est verum" (ibid.). Ockham had already offered much the same reading of the Averroist tag: "materia est una numero in generato et corrupto, quamvis sint in diversis generatis simul exsistentibus diversae materiae . . ." (*Summula* I.9, *Opera phil.* VI:180).

than either of the two just discussed. This third view combines elements of the first two: it describes prime matter as intrinsically simple, apart from quantity, as on the Simple View, and then supposes that, when informed by quantity, prime matter acquires parts, as on the Extensionless Parts View. This hybrid account might seem to capture the best elements of the other two views. Like the Simple View, it preserves the pure potentiality of prime matter, but it does so without having to embrace the weird notion that prime matter exists holenmerically throughout bodies. For within bodies, when informed by quantity, prime matter on this third view takes on a familiar corpuscular structure.

Despite the apparent attractions, I have not found any scholastic author defending this hybrid approach. What I have found are authors who attack it, construing theories of extensionless prime matter as committed to this sort of account rather than to either of the first two approaches. It is no surprise the view attracts criticism. For if one does think of the doctrine of extensionless prime matter in this third, hybrid way, then it seems vulnerable to devastating criticism, because it requires matter to go from existing as something simple to existing as something constituted of distinct parts. The problem with this is that it seems doubtful whether anything could change so radically, and yet retain its identity. But retaining its identity is of course the *raison d'être* of prime matter. Peter Auriol makes this kind of objection. Beginning with the stock complaint of unintelligibility—that "prime matter cannot be imagined or understood without dimension"—he goes on to offer this very specific objection:

> Matter cannot be understood in terms of something indivisible, in the manner of a point. For it is impossible for what is divisible (*partibile*) to be conceptually separated and grasped as indivisible (*impartibile*). For in that case multiple and distinct things would pass into what is really identical and undivided (*indivisam*), which is impossible. (*Sent.* II.12.1.4, II:164bD; cf. II:163bB)

Consider prime matter as present in all material objects. Now conceive of it as unextended. This requires conceiving of something as first "multiple and distinct" and then "really identical and undivided" (line 4), in the manner of a mathematical point. Nothing can "pass" from the one state to the other. But if prime matter is not intrinsically extended, then it will have to make just such a passage, whenever it functions as the bare substratum of change.

Auriol's objection would be effective against the hybrid view, which treats prime matter as going back and forth between a simple, indivisible state and a divisible, structured state. Perhaps there were authors who defended such a view. But on the two most prominent versions of the theory, extensionless prime matter is either *never* divisible, because it never has parts, or else it is *always* divisible, because it always has parts. In either case, prime matter serves as the substratum underlying all bodies, no matter how they change, but it does so without going through the sort of fundamental phase change that Auriol finds objectionable.

Is there anything that could go back and forth from being divisible to indivisible? Interestingly, Auriol considers a familiar potential counterexample to his claim. It might well seem that human beings go from being divisible to being indivisible, and then back to being divisible, as they go from being wayfarers in this life to being disembodied souls to being reunited with their resurrected bodies in heaven or hell. Auriol considers

this, and denies it, on the grounds that human beings are essentially extended things—
that is, they essentially have bodies. This might seem quite a bold claim to make, but it
in fact is a perfectly orthodox scholastic view that the separated soul is not a human
being, and that therefore human beings go out of existence when they die, and come
back into existence only at the resurrection. This has a theological payoff, for if a
human being is essentially corporeal and cannot exist as a mere soul, then the
resurrection of bodies is shown to be necessary for human salvation, as Christian
doctrine teaches.[9]

4.3. Accidentally Quantified Matter: Averroism

It is not easy to get one's mind around the idea of extensionless prime matter. Jacob
Zabarella finds the view flatly inconceivable, and so takes it to be virtually self-evident
that prime matter by nature is an extended stuff:

> This is so completely certain that, for me, it is as if the thing speaks for itself. For if our mind
> contemplates matter apart from forms, we can conceive of nothing other than a certain vast and
> indistinct body, and a certain empty mass, as Plotinus said. When, on the other hand, we
> consider form without matter, we conceive of something incorporeal and indivisible, which is
> subsequently extended in quantified matter. If others have been granted such mental acuity
> as to imagine incorporeal matter, I myself (let me confess my simplicity) cannot in the slightest
> do so. (*De rebus naturalibus*, De prima rerum materia II.17, cols. 217–18)

This is a nice example of the relatively colorful, personal style of sixteenth-century
Italian scholasticism. Anyone who comes to the great Paduan scholastics after being
immersed in earlier work from Oxford and Paris can hardly help but feel like a witness
to the beginnings of a transition from the dry, technical work of the thirteenth- and
fourteenth-century schoolmen to the comparatively airy, accessible prose of Galileo,
Descartes, or Hobbes. In content, too, there is something unscholastic about this
passage. The point Zabarella wants to make is much the same as the point we saw
Descartes and others make in §3.3: that prime matter, if stripped of everything,
including extension, becomes utterly unintelligible. What makes this alien to scholastic
thought is that the scholastics positively embraced the unintelligibility of prime matter
(§7.2). Although it would be a commonplace of seventeenth-century thought that the
natural philosopher should postulate only what is intelligible, this was not an idea that

---

[9] Auriol confronts the potential human counterexample as follows: "Sed hic oritur duplex dubium. Primum est quod
ratio concludit de omni partibili; non ergo est propter hoc proprium materiae, immo concludit de omnibus corporalibus
formis....Ad primum concedo consequens. Impossibile est enim intelligi hominem sine quantitate" (*Sent.* II.12.1.4,
II:165aA).

The best-known expression of the view that human beings are essentially corporeal is Aquinas's. See, e.g., *In I Cor.*
15.2: "constat quod homo naturaliter desiderat salutem sui ipsius; anima autem cum sit pars corporis hominis, non est
totus homo, et anima mea non est ego; unde licet anima consequatur salutem in alia vita, non tamen ego vel quilibet
homo." For discussion, see Pasnau, *Thomas Aquinas* pp. 385–93. There is room for doubt, however, over just how to
interpret such passages; see Stump, *Aquinas* pp. 51–4.

Suárez makes an argument much like Auriol's against extensionless prime matter. He rests his case on the interesting
claim that a thing's principle of individuation must be intrinsic to it: "in universum censeo impossibile rem aliquam, quae
veram ac propriam realitatem habet, distingui ab alia simili per aliam entitatem a se distinctam" (*Disp. meta.* 40.4.8).
Given this principle, Suárez judges it impossible for matter to be simple and then to be divided into parts by quantity.

had much currency among the scholastics. They did not tend to take for granted that we can understand the natural world.[10]

What exactly is obscure about extensionless prime matter? At the top of the list, to be sure, is the way that the Simple View denies corpuscular structure to matter, and so apparently requires it to exist holenmerically throughout bodies. This is weird, and perhaps even inconceivable, but it seems to be a consequence of taking the pure potentiality doctrine with complete seriousness. Setting that consequence aside, both versions of the extensionless view are committed to something further: that prime matter is not necessarily spread out, but might instead lack extension altogether, inasmuch as it might be located at an extensionless point. At a minimum, this is supposed to be a logical possibility. Even those who deny that God could make matter apart from all form (§3.1) ought to grant that God could make matter without the form of quantity.[11] Is anything at stake beyond this sort of bare logical possibility? Certainly no one thinks that there is a naturally occurring moment at which prime matter is reduced to a point. Many hold the view that substantial change goes "down to prime matter," in the sense that in such change there is a complete stripping away of all forms, and the introduction of brand new forms (§25.1).[12] But even so there is no period of time over which the bare prime matter endures. As Capreolus puts it, "the fire that is a body is generated from matter that, at the instant of generation, totally loses its prior dimensions and all preceding substantial and accidental forms, and at the same instant acquires a substantial form and new dimensions" (*Defensiones* II.18.1.3, IV:156b). Yet even if there is no time during which prime matter is reduced to a point, still there is a sense in which unquantified prime matter plays a fundamental role in the natural order. To see this, consider the one role that everyone agrees in ascribing to prime matter: its serving as a substratum for substantial change. On the views in question, what endures through substantial change is extensionless stuff. So although prime matter is never naturally reduced to a point, still the causal role it plays (as the prime material cause of change) gets played without quantity, and so without extension. In this sense one might

---

[10] Zabarella's appeal to Plotinus seems disingenuous, since no one is more insistent than Plotinus in holding that prime matter is extensionless (see *Enneads* II.4). As far as I can make out, Plotinus's strategy is to deny the excluded middle between one and many that Jandun insists on. The doctrine of extensionless prime matter also occurs in Plato, *Timaeus* 51ab: "if the thing that is to receive repeatedly throughout its whole self the likenesses of the intelligible objects, the things that always are—if it is to do so successfully, then it ought to be devoid of any inherent characteristics of its own.... But if we speak of it as an indivisible and characterless sort of thing, one that receives all things and shares in a most perplexing way in what is intelligible, a thing extremely difficult to comprehend, we shall not be misled."

[11] Suárez (*Disp. meta.* 40.4.5) reports that Paulus Soncinas held a quite unusual combination of views: that matter and quantity are distinct, but that it is contradictory for matter to exist without quantity (Suárez immediately goes on to add that "Et haec sententia est valde vulgaris inter Thomistas," but the context makes it clear that he is referring not to Soncinas's odd view, but rather to the thesis of indivisible prime matter. Regarding matter without quantity, Suárez a little later remarks that "nemo ... rationabiliter negare potest id fieri posse a Deo" [*Disp. meta.* 40.4.11]).

[12] For endorsements of the claim that substantial change goes down to prime matter (*resolutio usque ad materiam primam*), see, e.g., Nicole Oresme, *In Gen. et cor.* I.7; Cremonini, *De formis elementorum* II.6, pp. 71–4. This doctrine is always understood to be qualified by the remark that there is not any moment of time at which bare prime matter exists by itself. See, e.g., Oresme (ibid., p. 60): "nihil est illud instans medium, quia instans non est mensura aliqua, et adhuc posito quod esset, tunc forma sequens haberet esse in illo instanti"; Anonymous A (f. 62rbB): "materia nunquam denudatur a dimensionibus indeterminatis, quia nunquam est sine dimensione, licet sit sine hac vel illa: sicut etiam materia nunquam denudatur a formis substantialibus, licet denudetur ab hac vel illa." See too Albert the Great, *In De gen. et cor.* I.1.21.

say that it is almost as if the material substratum of change actually did occupy an extensionless point.[13]

This feature of the extensionless view gave rise to a family of arguments in favor of extended prime matter. These arguments are all variations on the general problem of where extension comes from, if not from prime matter. All parties to the debate agree that it does not come from substantial forms, which are not intrinsically extended. Instead, as stressed already, extension is generally supposed to come from quantity. Quantity, however, is an accidental form, and as such it would normally be expected to inhere in the composite substance. Hence, if prime matter is extensionless, extension would turn out to be an accident of composite material substances and so in some sense posterior to those substances. To many, however, it seemed implausible that material substances could in any sense be prior to quantity. In order to avoid this result, quantity was often posited as inhering immediately in prime matter itself.

Various arguments of this general form were advanced, but the one most commonly discussed was that of Averroes, in his treatise *De substantia orbis*.[14] Perhaps because this work is largely concerned with the heavens, it has not received much attention from modern scholars. It was, however, one of the most important philosophical influences on fourteenth-century conceptions of matter. Many commentaries were written on it, and the overview of Aristotelian physics found in its first chapter did much to shape how later scholastics thought about these issues. Averroes had argued that if the

---

[13] On the idea that prime matter apart from form would exist at a point, see Pomponazzi, *In De subst. orbis* q. 3 (p. 275): "materia prima non denudatur a quantitatibus, quia sic esset sicut punctum." (Pomponazzi is appealing to Averroes, *In Gen. et cor.* I.27, who remarks that "punctum esse materiam et vacuum manifestum est quod impossibile est.") See also Robert Orford, *De natura materiae* ch. 5 (n. 392): "Si enim possibile esset ipsam totam spoliari et denudari ab omni forma quam modo habet, certum est quod nihil diversitatis in ea reperiretur in aliqua partium distantia, cum quantitas sine forma substantiali in materia esse non possit, ut dictum est." Vasquez denies that matter without quantity would collapse to a point, because he thinks that without quantity it could not move (*In Summam theol.* III.190.3 n. 30, VII:303a). Surprisingly, even though he thinks quantity is what makes matter have parts, he nevertheless thinks that matter stripped of quantity would retain whatever parts it already has (ibid., 190.5 n. 52, VII:309b). (Magnen reports Vasquez's view, but gets this particular detail wrong: "Materia spoliata quantitate est tota in toto et tota in qualibet parte, et totius mundi materia in punctum mathematicum conflueret, si quantitate spoliaretur; ita Vasquez et alii" [*Democritus reviviscens* p. 51].)

The idea that matter without quantity would exist at an extensionless point is challenged by Peter John Olivi, who contends that the notion of such a point has meaning only in the context of quantity: "... cum punctus sit aliquid de genere quantitatis nec dicat aliquid extrinsecum ultra partes quantitatis situatum" (*Summa* II.58, II:441). Hence he argues that matter without quantity would have to be incorporeal in the way spiritual entities are, which he dismisses as absurd. (In §14.4, we will see Ockham saying something similar about the natural possibility of existence at an extensionless point.)

Anonymous A takes prime matter, conceived of as the subject of generation, to lack *locus*: "Philosophus quinto Physicorum probat per talem rationem quod generatio non sit motus: quod movetur est in loco; quod generatur non est in loco. Sed subjectum generationis est materia prima. Ergo materia prima non est in loco. Ergo materia prima ut est subiectum generationis non est quanta" (f. 61vbE). This might suggest that prime matter lacks location entirely, but the passage is more plausibly understood as describing existence merely at a point (see note 2 above). The passage is also noteworthy for focusing on prime matter "as it is the subject of generation," which seems to be the maneuver suggested in the main text of focusing on prime matter as the stuff that endures, by itself, through substantial change. Another instance of that maneuver comes in Cajetan, *In De ente* q. 17 (n. 139, tr. p. 305): "corpus enim fit ex materia quae non est corpus et indivisibilis in actu licet sit corpus et divisibilis in potentia."

[14] I translate from the Latin *De substantia orbis*, as printed in Aristotle, *Opera*. The Hebrew text is available along with a good English translation by Hyman. Printed Latin commentaries include those of Alvaro de Toledo, Jandun, Theodoricus de Magdeburg, Pietro Pomponazzi, Tiberio Baccilieri, and Agostino Nifo. Jandun's commentary was seemingly the most influential, judging from its having been reprinted eight times, all in Venice. See also Zimmermann, "Kommentare." Edward Mahoney has questioned whether Jandun is indeed the author of the commentary printed under his name, but the views described there seem to fit with what Jandun says elsewhere, and I provisionally retain the attribution.

enduring subject of change "did not have dimensions, it would not receive at the same time forms that are distinct either in number or kind; instead, there would be found at one time only one form" (*Opera* IX:3va). In effect, Averroes asks us to consider a variation of the old question, *Why is there something rather than nothing?* Averroes's variation asks: *Why are there many things rather than just one thing?* and his answer is that there are many things because there is extended matter to compose the many. This answer would fuel much speculation about whether quantitative dimensions might be the much sought after principle of individuation for material substances. But here we need concern ourselves only with a more modest claim: that, as far as material things are concerned, the extension of matter is a necessary precondition for any sort of variety among forms. The argument can be applied, and was applied, to forms of all kinds. Why is there a white surface of such shape and size? Not because of the form *whiteness*, but because the subject of that form is extended. Why does a human being have a complex organic body with different parts organized in various different ways? The soul gives rise to this complex structure, but it can do so only because there is an extended body that serves as the canvas, as it were, for these various parts. Why are there many human beings, as well as many substances of other kinds? The individual substantial forms give rise to the individual substances (Ch. 24), but can do so only if there is matter enough to provide a sufficiently extended subject for this variety.

Many scholastics would advance this same argument, in various permutations.[15] It seems to compel us to ascribe extension to prime matter prior to generation. To say that a substantial form cannot inform extensionless matter is to say that generation cannot take place when the enduring subject is extensionless. Hence we get the very specific result that what endures through substantial change is not austerely bare, but extended. If prime matter did not, prior to substantial form, already have extension— having both parts and having those parts be spread out—then there could be but one, simple material being. If the notion of a simple material being seems contradictory, then you are seeing precisely Averroes's point.

It cannot be said that this argument settled anything. Its evaluation crucially depends on the notion of priority: matter is said to be prior to the substantial form, which in turn is prior to accidental form. For a scholastic author, hardly anything was so likely to precipitate a lengthy *disputatio* as talk of priority, in its various kinds. In the present case, the priority of matter can be understood in the straightforward temporal sense, given matter's endurance through change. The priority of substantial over accidental form has to be understood in some subtler way, however, since there is no point in time at which the composite substance exists prior to all accidents, like some sort of featherless hatchling. Hence Averroes's argument gave rise to all sorts of subtle discussions— which I will not try even to summarize—over how quantity might supply the necessary extension while still being posterior, in the appropriate sense, to substantial form.

---

[15] For versions of Averroes's argument see Jandun (*In De subst. orbis* q. 6, f. 54aC), Auriol (*Sent.* II.12.1.4, II:163bF), Pererius (*De communibus principiis* V.18, p. 323), Zabarella (*De rebus nat.*, De prima rerum materia II.8, col. 194), and Burgersdijk (*Collegium Physicum* II.16, p. 23). Anonymous B (f. 63raD) remarks that "tota necessitas ponendi dimensiones interminatas praecedere formam est ut det ei esse partibile et transmutabile." Perhaps the most sophisticated attempt to refute Averroes is that of Cajetan, *In De ente* q. 17.

Those who reject extensionless theories in favor of an extended substratum of change face a choice over whether to treat matter as extended, intrinsically, by its very nature, or else as extended in virtue of some superadded form. The first view was Ockham's (§4.4), and although it is by far the most straightforward of the different theories of prime matter, it was a minority view until the seventeenth century. Much more common among scholastic authors was Averroes's solution: that prime matter exists "coeternally" with an accidental form that gives it "indeterminate dimensions." Even Aquinas himself took this view in his earliest work, and his later change of mind on this score—in favor of the view that all accidents inhere in the composite substance (§6.3), and that bare prime matter is all that endures through substantial change (§25.1)—is perhaps his most dramatic change of mind in any area.[16] Authors who follow Averroes, as do John of Jandun and Peter Auriol, agree with the Thomists on the nature of prime matter itself. This is why, earlier, I could quote Jandun in support of the Simple View. Jandun believes that prime matter, in its own right, is numerically one in all things (§4.1 above). But Jandun thinks there is another sort of matter, "propinquitous matter," which is always informed by quantity, and so is always extended (*In Phys.* I.24). So if we think of prime matter more broadly, as whatever it is that endures through all change (the broad usage of Chs. 2–3), then the Averroistic view in effect supplants extensionless prime matter with an enduring stuff that is extended. (Yet another view, associated with Avicenna, holds that prime matter is extended in virtue of a *substantial* form that endures through all substantial change. This view is interesting in the context of debates over whether there can be a plurality of substantial forms in a single substance [Ch. 25], but can be set aside for the purposes of this study, because it received essentially no support from scholastic authors.)[17]

The Averroistic theory holds that an accidental form inheres directly in prime matter. This in itself was a controversial claim; as we will see in §6.3 there was considerable debate over whether accidents should ever be conceived of as inhering in prime matter, rather than in the matter–form composite. But the Averroistic theory must hold something more: that the quantity of prime matter is an accident it never loses, even in the process of substantial change. Matter is created by God under the form of quantity, and retains that form for as long as it exists. Here again we can see the purity of the Simple View being relaxed in the direction of a corpuscular conception of matter. The enduring substratum of change, for the Averroist, is something rather like Cartesian *res extensa*. But the similarities go only so far, because Averroists always insisted that the quantity of prime matter is indeterminate, and that in generation the

---

[16] Aquinas expressly endorses Averroism at *Sent.* II.3.1.4c, *Sent.* IV.12.1.2.4c, *Sent.* IV.44.1.1.1 ad 3, *De veritate* 5.9 ad 6, but implicitly rejects it in later works, such as *Summa theol.* 1a 76.6 ad 2. Important later advocates include Jandun (*In De subst. orbis* q. 6), Auriol (*Sent.* II.12.1), Gregory of Rimini (*Sent.* II.12.2.1), and Pomponazzi (*In De subst. orbis* q. 3). Pomponazzi contrasts Averroism with the *communis modus dicendi*, of Aquinas, Giles of Rome, and Scotus—although in fact Giles at least sometimes defended an idiosyncratic version of Averroism (see note 23 below).

[17] The idea that it might be an enduring substantial form that gives prime matter its quantity is ascribed to Avicenna by Averroes (*De subst. orbis* ch. 1 [*Opera* IX:3vab]) and also by subsequent Latin authors (see, e.g., Robert Orford, *De natura materiae* ch. 4 [n. 379]; Zabarella, *De rebus nat.*, De prima rerum materia II.12, col. 206; Suárez, *Disp. meta.* 13.3.5). Hyman, "Aristotle's 'First Matter'," tends to bear out this understanding of Avicenna (and is also helpful on Averroes's view, and on the background prior to Avicenna). A hybrid version of Avicennism and Averroism is defended by Theodoricus de Magdeburg, *In De subst. orbis* qq. 7–8. Both Scotus and Henry of Ghent appeal to a *forma corporeitatis* that can endure through substantial change (see Ch. 25), but this is not the same view because they do not regard this *forma corporeitatis* as enduring incorruptibly through all material change.

matter takes on a determinate quantity in virtue of some further form.[18] This way of developing the theory allowed Averroists to account for a substance's changing its quantity, which is something that nearly every scholastic wanted to allow (§4.5). But it raised various troubling issues. One sort of issue concerns the theory's apparent profligacy: it seems on its face to postulate both multiple accidental quantities and multiple matters within the same substance. Jandun, for one, denies that he is committed to the first, but seems committed to the second, since he postulates both simple prime matter and quantified "propinquitous" matter. Another problem for the theory is its notion of indeterminate dimensions. Jandun contrasts the indeterminate, potential quantity of prime matter with "dimensions as they are in complete actuality and under their proper limits" (*In De subst. orbis* q. 6, f. 54bH). Hence prime matter—that is, the enduring substratum of change—is allegedly extended in such a way as to lack any boundary. This might make good sense if prime matter were infinite in extension. But of course that itself would be just the sort of actuality and determination that Averroism seeks to avoid. Hence their strategy again flaunts the central paradox of prime matter (§3.1): that it is a real stuff, now really extended in virtue of having inseparable quantity, but without being a stuff of any determinate kind, and now without being of any determinate size.

One might think that extending the paradox to the case of extension adds no further liability to the theory. If the concept of indeterminate prime matter is coherent in general, then why not add extension to the mix? Jandun in effect tries to motivate the theory along these lines, by repeatedly treating indeterminate quantity as exactly analogous to the indeterminacy of prime matter. Critics of Averroism thought that it faced a special problem, however, in virtue of treating indeterminate extension as arising from the side of *form* (namely, from an accident in the category of Quantity). Perhaps matter, by its very nature, has the paradoxical character of indeterminacy. But form, by its very nature, is determinate, and so it makes no sense to suppose that prime matter's indeterminacy springs in part from its having a certain form. This is a line of argument that Nicole Oresme advanced, in the middle of the fourteenth century. Insisting that no forms endure through substantial change, he argues against Averroism that "every material quantity is corruptible" (*In Gen. et cor.* I.7, p. 59) inasmuch as anything can be made to change its shape and size. In saying that, he is presupposing that all quantities are determinate quantities. No quantities can be determinable, he believes, because in general no forms can be determinable. Just as a piece of wax can have only one shape at a time, so matter can have only one form of a given kind. "If one understands what 'form' signifies, it seems to imply a contradiction for the form of fire to inhere in something without that thing's being fire" (ibid.). Similarly, Oresme wants to claim, there cannot be a quantity that inheres in a subject without making that subject be a certain quantity. Suárez, several centuries later, makes this same point more explicitly. "There can be no form that gives generic being solely, without also giving something specific being within that genus" (*Disp. meta.* 13.3.17). He argues for

---

[18] Averroism usually is spelled out in terms of a single form of quantity, indeterminate when conceived apart from substantial form, and then made determinate in the composite. See, e.g., Jandun, *In De subst. orbis* q. 6 (f. 54aFG); Auriol, *Sent.* II.12.1.3 (II:162bF); Pomponazzi, *In De subst. orbis* q. 3 (pp. 291–8). On scholastic conceptions of indeterminate dimensions, see Donati, "The Notion of '*Dimensiones indeterminatae*'."

this by induction, working his way through different sorts of forms, and claiming, for instance, that there is no form of *color* but only forms for specific colors, and no form that makes an angel be *spiritual*, but only forms that give an angel its specific nature, and so on.[19]

In §3.3, following Auriol's lead, I tried to defend the notion of indeterminate prime matter by appealing, in effect, to indeterminate forms like *color* and *spiritual*. If there is nothing incoherent in determinable properties like this, the thought was, there should be nothing incoherent in determinable prime matter. Oresme and Suárez would find the comparison unhelpful because they think indeterminate forms are much worse than indeterminate matter. Indeterminacy just is part of the character of matter (and to that extent, Suárez remarks [ibid., n. 18], it actually has a specific character). Forms, in contrast, by their very nature, are always determinate: they make a thing be such and such, and so cannot bring about the sort of partial being that stands in need of completion by some further form. Admittedly, however, this amounts to little more than the bare assertion that there are no determinable forms. Someone who fails to see the plausibility in that should not be moved by these considerations to give up Averroism.

4.4. Intrinsic Extension: Ockham, Zabarella, Pererius

The taxing subtlety of the discussion up until now has sprung from the scholastic desire to give a metaphysical analysis of why material objects are extended. If this project seems quite alien to our modern sensibilities, we perhaps have the seventeenth century to thank for that. But the idea that extension might just be a brute feature of matter goes back much earlier, all the way to the ancient atomists, and would receive an extremely powerful and systematic defense in the scholastic period, in the hands of William Ockham. As we will see in §14.3, Ockham regards Quantity as an entirely superfluous ontological category. His ultimate foundation for that controversial stand is the conviction that matter is intrinsically extended. His account of this view starts out by rejecting the Simple View's indivisible matter, numerically the same in all bodies.

Matter successively receives distinct forms. . . . This matter is numerically one in the thing generated and the thing corrupted, but in distinct generated things existing at the same time there is distinct matter. Such matter is of entirely the same nature and can make numerically one matter—in the way in which two pools of water that are separate from one another can be united and make numerically one water. (*Summula* I.9, *Opera phil.* VI:180)

If matter is not indivisible, then of course it must be divisible:

It is impossible for matter to exist without extension, because it is not possible for matter to exist unless it has part distant from part. Hence although the parts of matter can be united in the way in which the parts of water and air can be united, still the parts of matter can never exist in the same place. (*Summula* I.13, VI:191)

---

[19] For further discussion of Suárez's argument against indeterminate dimensions, see Des Chene, *Physiologia* pp. 89–90.

Against the Simple View, matter always has parts, even if those parts can be combined into something, like a pool of water, that we regard as one thing. Against the Extensionless Parts View, the parts of matter must (naturally speaking) be spread out in space. Moreover, prime matter is intrinsically extended, which is to say that its extension obtains not in virtue of any further form, accidental or substantial, inhering in matter, but as a feature of matter itself. Ockham's constant attention to questions of ontological parsimony leads him to stress that "just as the distance of one part of matter from another part is not an absolute thing distinct from those parts, so neither are extension nor quantity nor dimensions distinct things" (VI:192). To be extended just is to have parts spread out in space, and this is a naturally necessary, intrinsic feature of matter.

Ockham's conception of matter is the foundation of his entire natural philosophy. His reductive arguments against various kinds of real accidents—which later four-teenth-century authors developed to the verge of corpuscularianism (see Ch. 19)—are all grounded on a conception of matter as consisting of parts spread out in space. This broader ontological program can succeed only if Ockham can make good on his claim of parsimony at the ground level, but the issues extend too widely to be pursued in detail here, and so will have to wait until more of the theory comes into view (see esp. §14.3, §17.4, and §19.2).[20]

Subsequent scholastic authors were not generally moved by Ockham's position. Although one finds it in some later nominalists, such as Albert of Saxony, it struck most scholastics as too great a departure from an Aristotelian conception of matter as standing in potentiality to the actuality of form. The view does, however, begin to come into prominence in the sixteenth century, even among scholastic authors. Zabarella, for instance, defnds the view that "prime matter, according to its own proper nature, apart from every form, is a body in the category of substance" (*De rebus naturalibus*, De prima rerum materia II.17, cols. 214–15).[21] It is somewhat surprising to find this view in Zabarella, because he takes a much more austere line than does Ockham on the pure potentiality of matter. Sounding very much like a proponent of

---

[20] Ockham, at *Summula* I.12 (VI:188–91) runs through a series of arguments and counter-arguments against prime matter's numerical unity in distinct bodies. See also *In Phys.* I.18.7 (*Opera phil.* IV:207). Where the *Summula* argues that matter is necessarily extended, he must have in mind natural necessity, because elsewhere he allows that God could deprive matter of its extension, by making all its parts exist at the same point (see note 23 below). For a very good discussion of Ockham's overall view, see Adams, *William Ockham* II:671–95.

Others who take a view like Ockham's are John Dumbleton, *Summa* II.11; Oresme, *In Phys.* I.14; Albert of Saxony, *In De gen. et cor.* I.5; Dabillon, *Physique* I.3.3 p. 122.

[21] Zabarella, oddly enough, seems unaware of Ockham's view in this regard: "Ego puto primam materiam secundum propriam naturam, et seclusa omni forma esse corpus de categoria substantiae: quam sententiam, quanquam a nullo recentiorum receptam, nitar et ratione et antiquorum philosophorum testimonio comprobare" (*De rebus nat.*, De prima rerum materia II.17, cols. 214–15). This description fits Ockham's view even down to the willingness to characterize prime matter as a body; see Ockham, *In Phys.* I.15.9 (IV:165) and IV.9.1 (V:106), where he describes matter as a *corpus* only in a broad sense, reserving the narrow sense for something extended that can exist *per se*. Zabarella was certainly well aware of Ockham's general nominalist agenda, and Ockham's *Summula* was published in two Italian editions around the start of the sixteenth century. Even so, Ockham's position on matter seems not to have been taken up by subsequent scholastic disputes in the way so many of his other views were. The ancient sources Zabarella has in mind are Plotinus and the Greek commentators. The closest ancient counterpart is perhaps the view of Philoponus, whom Zabarella says "aliorum omnium proxime ad veritatem Ioannes accessit" (II.18, col. 219). But Zabarella thinks Philoponus made the mistake of treating matter as *identical* with three dimensions, rather than as *having* three dimensions. For recent discussions of Philoponus's views here, see Grant, *Much Ado* pp. 19–21; Sorabji, *Matter, Space, and Motion* pp. 23–30. Philoponus's alleged mistake will come up again in §8.4, in the context of Descartes.

the Simple View, Zabarella insists that matter has no actuality whatsoever, not even the actuality of existence. (Its existence comes through form.)[22] Still, it must have extension, he argues, reciting many of the standard arguments for Averroism. But just when it seems that Zabarella will defend some version of the Accidentally Quantified View, he announces that matter is a body in its own right—or, in other words, that matter, prior to form, is extended. (Given that Zabarella identifies prime matter as a body, we could now switch terminology and speak of *body* rather than *matter*, thereby making a transition to the dominant vocabulary of the seventeenth century. For the sake of continuity, though, I will continue to speak throughout of matter, even in discussing post-scholastic authors.) Zabarella probably has no precedent in supposing that matter can be both pure potentiality and extended, but given that he goes down this road, it is no surprise that he treats matter's extension as indeterminate:

Body in the category of substance is taken in two ways. . . . The first is taken for a perfect body having the actuality of existence per se, which is not only a body, but such a body, assigned to some certain nature, and this of necessity is a composite consisting of matter and form. . . . Body can be taken in a second way for an indeterminate body, assigned to no certain nature, which is only a body, but not such a body, and this signifies prime matter. (*De rebus naturalibus*, De prima rerum materia II.19, col. 225)

Because Zabarella locates this indeterminacy immediately in matter, he can avoid the objections to indeterminate form. Yet whereas Zabarella thinks it incomprehensible that prime matter should have no extension (as quoted earlier), he evidently finds it perfectly intelligible for prime matter to have extension without any definite shape or size.

Ockham is less enthusiastic about the doctrine of pure potentiality, endorsing it in name but insisting that matter nevertheless has some degree of actuality. Unsurprisingly, he likewise hedges on the indeterminacy of matter's extension. Like anyone who could be considered an Aristotelian, he takes the determinate extension of a particular body to come from the side of form. So extension of matter is indeterminate insofar as "matter is not of itself necessarily of any certain quantity—for example, this extended matter is not of itself necessarily of one-foot in quantity or two-feet, but has a greater or lesser quantity in virtue of differences in form" (*Summula* I.13, VI:192). He goes on to consider the objection that if matter gets its determinate extension through form, then it is not extended in its own right—implicitly suggesting that indeterminate extension is not extension at all. To this he replies that "although it does not have it of itself to be of a certain, determinate quantity, still it has it of itself to be of such or such a quantity" (VI:193), meaning that matter is intrinsically the sort of stuff that can have an extension of one foot, two feet, etc. Still, he pushes the objection, wondering what extension

---

[22] Zabarella opts for a pure potentiality account of matter as follows: "Si entitas pro existentia sumatur, materia non habet entitatem proprium . . ." (*De rebus nat.*, De prima rerum materia II.4, col. 186B); "Materia prima in sua essentia nullum continet actum, sed solam potentiam" (ibid., col. 186F). In his concluding remarks on prime matter, he connects the pure potentiality doctrine with the indeterminacy of extension: "in ipsa materiae natura nullus actus inest, sed est substantia quaedam indeterminata, potestatem habens recipiendi quemlibet actum. Ab hac materiae natura duae proprietates emanant, quae ab ipsa nunquam separantur: una est quantitas nullum secundum se terminum habens; prima enim radix et fons a quo in rebus naturalibus quantitas, ac dimensio derivatur, est ipsa natura materiae: altera vero est potestas illa universalis recipiendi omnes formas indistincte" (II.21, col. 231AB). For Ockham's take on the pure potentiality doctrine, see Ch. 3 note 3.

matter would have apart from form. To this he first responds that the hypothetical assumption is impossible—matter cannot exist apart from form—and that one should not worry about the absurdities that follow from an impossible assumption. Unable to leave things at that, though, he hazards an answer to the question he had just cautioned against answering: "If matter were separated from all form, substantial and accidental, it would be of a certain quantity that suits it either by its nature or by the action of what acts on it" (ibid., VI:193).

With this last remark, Ockham abandons the indeterminacy of extension, in the sense that he allows that matter, all by itself, would have a perfectly determinate quantity. It is easy to see how he might have arrived at this conclusion, given that on the one hand there are compelling reasons for thinking that matter has quantity, and on the other hand there is something very strange about a quantity that is perfectly indeterminate. Still, in the context of scholastic discussions, this is an absolutely startling outcome. It is almost as if someone defending the reality of *color* as a determinable property were finally persuaded, after much cajoling, to admit that the property *color*, if it occurred by itself, would have to make a thing be some determinate shade—even if we will never know which one, since we will never encounter the determinable property *color* on its own. To find someone else taking a position of this kind, ascribing determinate quantity to matter, we again have to jump ahead several centuries to Zabarella's era, but this time to Benedictus Pererius. Pererius accepts a form of Averroism, but in one crucial respect he is closer to Ockham than is Zabarella, because Pererius thinks that accidental quantity gives prime matter not an indeterminate extension, in the usual sense of that phrase, but a determinate extension that is fixed for the duration of the matter's existence:

It seems to us extremely likely to be true that the quantity out of which God created matter inheres in matter, precedes substantial forms, and is indeterminate of its own nature while being determined by natural agents for the variety of substantial forms that are imposed on the   3 matter. Of itself (*per se*) it is never generated or corrupted, but only by accident—that is, with respect to its determination and shape. Take a ball of wax, for instance, and give it various shapes. Let it be either round, long, or a cube. The wax's quantity is not changed, whereas   6 its boundaries and shape vary. In this way a natural agent, by the addition and subtraction of natural forms, changes the boundaries and shapes of a quantity. The form itself of the quantity, however, which the matter possesses by its power, we understand to be fixed, stable, and   9 immutable. (*De communibus principiis* V.18, p. 322)

Pererius abides by the tradition of treating prime matter as having indeterminate quantity (line 2), but he gives this a special sense: the quantity of prime matter is indeterminate in the sense that it has no precise boundaries (lines 5–8). Still, the quantity of the quantity, as it were, is fixed, as the example of the wax ball makes clear. The idea, then, is that God creates a certain amount of matter, which is fixed for all time (barring some subsequent act of creation or annihilation). Natural events subsequently shape that matter in various ways, but the overall size of the material universe cannot naturally change.

Because Pererius denies the indeterminacy of quantity, in its usual sense, he can handle with ease some of the stock objections to extended prime matter. So to this natural objection,

There is no indeterminate quantity, even if it is considered in its own right apart from substantial forms. For the universal mass (*moles*) of matter taken on its own is not infinite but finite, inasmuch as the whole is contained beneath the orbit of the moon. (V.19, p. 328)

he can make this straightforward answer:

Although the universal mass of quantity is limited —that is, the bounded whole that is contained by the ends of the heavens—nevertheless it is called indeterminate on account of the innumerable limits and shapes which it does not have in itself, but which it can take from natural agents in virtue of the variety of substantial forms that are imposed on the matter. (V.20, p. 331)

These ideas mark a fundamental shift. Although Pererius shares with Ockham the desire to ascribe a determinate quantity to matter, he goes one step farther to assert that this quantity is invariable. This was not Ockham's view. Ockham, when pressed, thinks that matter on its own might have a determinate quantity—it might occupy so much space—but he thinks that in the natural course of things it is form that determines just how much quantity matter has. Thus, as quoted earlier, what determines whether matter occupies one foot or two feet of space is the matter's form. Readers unfamiliar with scholastic natural philosophy might wrongly suppose that form can stretch matter in this way only by introducing gaps into the matter. (Since scholastic authors were in general agreement that there are not literally gaps in the sense of empty space anywhere, such gaps would have to consist in some foreign material being pulled in as a body is spread out.) But, as we will see in §15.2, scholastics before Pererius thought a certain body could come to have greater or lesser extension without gaps being introduced or eliminated. To make this clear, I will use the term 'absolute volume' to refer to the sum total of an object's extension, excluding any internal gaps, and speak of absolute growth and absolute shrinkage to refer to a change in absolute volume, as opposed to a mere reconfiguration into a more or less diffuse, gappy structure. Ockham, along with all his contemporaries, believed that a body could undergo absolute growth or shrinkage without adding or subtracting more matter. Although matter was taken to be permanent in its existence, naturally capable neither of coming into nor going out of existence (§2.5), it was not taken to possess a fixed absolute volume.

To the modern reader, this conception of rarefaction and condensation—to use the scholastic terms—may look as if it involves a kind of miracle. To scholastic authors, it was usually taken for granted. We saw Oresme, in the previous section, claim that "every material quantity is corruptible." What he means by this is precisely the idea that any given body can undergo absolute growth or shrinkage, in any part of that body. The consequences of this for prime matter are set out starkly by pseudo-Marsilius of Inghen:

The whole of matter, as far as itself is concerned, does not determine itself to have any quantity, shape, place, rarity, or density. Instead, as far as itself is concerned, the whole mass (*massa*) of prime matter—and even a part of it—could occupy the place occupied by the whole body of the heavens. There is no conflict in its existing under any imaginable rarity or density; indeed there is no conflict in the whole of it being a point. (*In Phys.* I.20, f. 19vb)

When Ockham remarked earlier that matter's being one foot or two feet in extent depended on form, one might have wondered just how far he was prepared to extend that claim. Just how big or small could a given bit of matter be? Pseudo-Marsilius's answer to that question is uncompromising. Even a bit of our terrestrial matter could actually grow to occupy as much space as the whole of the heavens. Conversely, the whole of matter could shrink to a dimensionless point. Although Ockham claims that matter is necessarily extended, naturally speaking, he too allows that it is logically possible for matter to be contracted to a point. In denying these claims, Pererius is pointing ahead toward one of the central ideas of post-scholastic thought.[23]

4.5. The Conservation of Quantity

It is unclear which of these very different scholastic conceptions of prime matter deserves to be considered dominant. The Paduan scholastic John Paul Pernumia, in the mid-sixteenth century, ascribes indeterminate dimensions to prime matter, with

---

[23] Pererius expressly considers an objection to his view from condensation and rarefaction: "Decimaquinta. Cum ex minori quantitate fit maior, id quod accidit in rarefactione non manet eadem quantitas, alioquin idem esset maius et minus; ergo acquiritur de novo aliqua pars quantitatis. Sed in quantitate eadem est ratio unius partis et totius. Si igitur una pars eius de novo est generabilis, similiter etiam tota erit generabilis" (De comm. princ. V.19, p. 328). He replies by rejecting the standard conception of rarefaction and condensation: "Ad decimamquintam. In rarefactione eadem est ratio quantitatis et materiae, nam sicut ibi plus existit quantitatis, ita quoque plus materiae: quemadmodum enim per rarefactionem partes quantitatis multiplicantur, sic etiam partes materiae: quare si nolunt in rarefactione ullam materiae particulam de novo acquiri, idem quoque sentire debent de quantitate" (ibid., V.20, p. 331). This is precisely the move Descartes would later make (Principles II.6–7). I know of no recent discussions of Pererius's view in this area.

Oresme argues at length against the conservation of quantity at In Phys. I.21. There he defends one special case of conservation: that since the whole of the sublunar material realm has as its absolute limit its boundary with the heavens, and since that boundary cannot naturally be moved, the whole of prime matter must conserve its quantity. "Tota massa materiae primae de mundo determinat sibi certam et praecisam mensuram ita quod non potest esse maior vel minor" (f. 16ra). Hence the rarefaction of any part must be accompanied by the equal condensation of another part. And if God were to create more matter, he would have to make corresponding condensations elsewhere (or else move the boundary of the heavens).

Pseudo-Marsilius's remarks against conservation are offered in support of an extensionless theory of matter. Marsilius of Inghen himself, in contrast, defends either an Averroistic or Ockhamistic view, depending on whether one holds that quantity is a real accident or simply the matter itself: "Secunda conclusio. In generato manet eadem quantitas quae fuit in corrupto. Probatur, quia vel quantitas ponitur ipsa res quanta, et sic cum maneat eadem materia habetur propositum; vel ponitur res distincta, et si sic tunc est accidens materiae et per consequens manet in ipsa materia in generato sicut in corrupto" (In Gen. et cor. I.7). Marsilius himself is a quantity realist along Buridan's lines; see his In Gen. et cor. I.15 and Ch. 15 note 6.

Since Ockham understands rarefaction and condensation reductively, in terms of locomotion (§15.1), the case of condensation to a mathematical point is just a special case of the ordinary natural process, albeit a case that is only supernaturally possible. See Sent. IV.6 (Opera theol. VII:79): "cuicumque non repugnat esse sub maiori extensione et minori, non repugnat sibi esse sine omni extensione"; Tract. de corp. Christi 40 (Opera theol. X:220): "Et eodem modo posset omnipotentia Dei conservare quamcumque substantiam et quamcumque qualitatem quantumcumque quaelibet talis esset false: 'haec substantia est quanta', 'haec qualitas est quanta'." For discussion, see Weisheipl, "Place of John Dumbleton" pp. 443–4; Adams, William Ockham II:685.

One very interesting attempt to put limits on how much rarefaction or condensation a given amount of body could undergo is that of Giles of Rome, who distinguishes between two quantities, one that belongs unchangeably to prime matter and so is akin to Averroes's indeterminate dimensions, and another that comes from form and makes a body have a certain extension in space. What makes this view distinctive is that Giles takes the first kind of quantity to determine the amount of variation possible in the second kind of quantity. "Naturaliter enim fieri potest quod materia occupans parvum locum postea occupet maiorem locum, quia naturaliter ex aqua fit aer et ex aere ignis; sed nulla virtus naturalis agentis potest immutare quantitatem illam per quam materia est tanta et tanta: non enim naturaliter fieri potest quod parum de materia fiat multum, quia tunc ex grano milii posset fieri mons unus et turris una et posset aliquid augeri eo non rarefacto et nullo addito.... Non est ergo eadem quantitas per quam materia est tanta et per quam occupat tantum locum ..." (Theoremata de corpore Christi, prop. 44, f. 31vbBC; cf. Quaest. meta. VIII.5, f. 41rF). Giles's view represents an early attempt to characterize an object's mass in distinction from its volume. For detailed studies (to which this paragraph is largely indebted) see Maier, Vorläufer Galileis ch. 2 and Donati, "La dottrina."

"the best Peripatetics," but against "almost all the Latin schools" (*Philosophia naturalis* I.7, f. 18rv). By this he probably means that he is following the non-Latin Averroes, and going against the schools of Albertism, Thomism, and Scotism. That might imply that his was the minority view, at least in Italy. Seventeenth-century scholastic textbook authors, in contrast, often assume without hesitation that prime matter is extended.[24] Given this uncertainty, it is unsurprising that post-scholastic authors have quite different understandings of the scholastic doctrine. Charleton takes prime matter to be "absolutely devoid of all quantity" (*Physiologia* II.1.1.9), whereas, according to Hobbes, 'prime matter' "signifies body considered without the consideration of any form or accident except only magnitude or extension, and aptness to receive form and accidents" (*De corpore* 8.24). Locke comes down somewhere in between: "matter is but a partial and more confused conception, it seeming to me to be used for the substance and solidity of body, without taking in its extension and figure" (*Essay* III.10.15). This looks hardly coherent, but then that is precisely Locke's point.

It is in general hard to be too critical of the great seventeenth-century authors for their sometimes tenuous knowledge of scholasticism, since even so they tend to know this material better than anyone does today. In the present case, if their various discussions of prime matter do not seem even to be taking up the same topic, they can hardly be blamed, because there simply was no one scholastic view on even the most fundamental questions concerning prime matter.

Pererius's version of the conservation thesis, according to which matter has a fixed absolute volume, is extremely unusual for the scholastic era. Post-scholastic authors, in contrast, widely embraced this doctrine, which we can call the conservation of quantity (C^Q). Thus, as already quoted in §2.5, Hobbes makes the very opposite of the claim we saw earlier from Oresme, holding that "that magnitude on account of which we name something a body is neither generated nor destroyed" (*De corpore* 8.20). Descartes realizes that the scholastic conception of condensation and rarefaction is the leading objection to his own theory of matter as essentially extended, and argues in response that "it is clearly contradictory for something to be augmented by a new quantity or a new extension without a new extended substance—that is, a new body—being added to it at the same time" (*Principles* II.8). Although Descartes's own famous use of wax as an example (*Med.* II, VII:30–1) is strikingly like Pererius's in the previous section, one need not see any direct debt. The use of wax as an example of a changeable material substance was commonplace, and C^Q itself is a natural outgrowth of the conservation thesis described in §2.5. Whereas that earlier thesis had insisted merely on the conservation of prime matter, C^Q insists that prime matter necessarily has a fixed absolute volume. Hence both matter and quantity are conserved.[25]

---

[24] See Eustachius, *Summa* III.1.1.2.4 (II:122): "Nonnullae sunt materiae proprietates sigillatim hic explicandae, quarum prima est quod sit quanta. Adeo enim materiae propria est quantitas, ut ipsi primo et per se competat"; Burgersdijk, *Collegium Physicum* II.16 (p. 22): "Tandem quemadmodum materia actu est substantia quaedam, quae sit potentia corpus, ita etiam quantitatem quandam ex se actu habet...."

[25] Before Hobbes and Descartes, one finds C^Q in Sebastian Basso, as a premise in his argument for interstitial vacua. He argues that since bodies appear to condense and rarify, and since the absolute quantity of a body is fixed, one must postulate empty space within bodies, growing and shrinking as bodies appear to grow and shrink (*Phil. nat.* De natura II.2). See also Dabillon, *Physique* III.4.6, who in effect embraces C^Q when he denies the possibility of change in absolute volume. For rival explanations of condensation and rarefaction, see §15.1.

Whereas the conservation thesis is obviously a purely metaphysical doctrine, C^Q may seem empirically testable. After all, we can at least in principle *measure* absolute volume. Understood as an empirical claim, the doctrine has to be judged an unfortunate one, inasmuch as it is very difficult to make out a case for the conservation of absolute volume. Before the seventeenth century was out, volume would be replaced by mass (Newton),[26] and ultimately mass would be identified with energy (Einstein). If forced to choose between C^Q and its scholastic rejection, we would be better off following the scholastics. Still, in keeping with the strategy of previous chapters, it is probably better to treat C^Q as a metaphysical rather than an empirical doctrine. When, for instance, Descartes claims that cases of absolute growth require the addition of new matter, this can be viewed as a metaphysical claim, inasmuch as it is a question for philosophy to decide whether what is being added is in fact matter, as opposed to, say, energy. In general, it is ultimately for metaphysics to decide whether we want to say that what gets conserved is matter, quantity, mass, energy, or perhaps even form. The truth of any conservation principle rests on a philosophical story about the stuff that is allegedly conserved.

Given the embrace of C^Q by seventeenth-century authors, it is interesting to ask whether its adoption marks the shift from metaphysical to corpuscular prime matter. More generally, given the spectrum of positions considered in this chapter, we might reconsider the whole question of when matter goes from being a metaphysical part to being an integral, corpuscular part. It is natural to think that matter becomes corpuscular when it becomes extended, but we have seen that there are many ways in which matter can have extension. Can a precise line be drawn? Thomism is of course in absolutely no danger of apostasy, since it postulates matter that is not in any sense extended. Nor do I think there is any danger for views on which matter is indeterminately extended. We can say that Averroism and Zabarella take a step toward corpuscular matter, if we like, but their conception of prime matter as extended without definite limit still seems entirely alien to the corpuscularian project. The same holds for views like Scotus's and Paul of Venice's, on which prime matter is intrinsically divisible, but actually extended only in virtue of some added form. That leaves Ockham and Pererius, both of whom take prime matter, considered in its own right, to have a determinate extension. It is easy to see that neither is thoroughly corpuscularian in his conception of matter. Ockham is not, because he thinks that, in all naturally occurring cases, the extension of matter is determined extrinsically, by form. Pererius is not, because although he accepts C^Q, he is committed to a version of Averroism, according to which matter has its determinate extension extrinsically, in virtue of an accidental, quantitative form.

Still, if we set aside these plain differences, and focus solely on that which is the enduring subject of change, there is a case to be made for the notion that Ockham and Pererius are fundamentally committed to corpuscular matter. After all, what endures

---

[26] What we call mass was in fact, by Newton, called the "quantitas materiae," and defined as a function of density and magnitude (*Principia* def. 1). The idea that it is not mere volume that gets conserved seems to have been advanced by some of the Oxford Calculators in the fourteenth century, who anticipate Newton in attempting to define quantity as a function of volume and rarity/denseness. See the discussion in Weisheipl, "Ockham and the Mertonians" pp. 631–3 and, in more detail, "Concept of Matter" pp. 165–9.

for each of them is extended stuff, shaped in various ways to form different kinds of substances, but itself intrinsically just bare extension. To make the comparison concrete, we might take Descartes as our exemplar of a corpuscularian philosopher.

The nature of matter, or body viewed as a whole, consists not in its being something which is hard, heavy, or colored, or which in any other way affects the senses, but only in its being a thing extended (*res extensa*) in length, breadth, and depth. (*Principles* II.4)

This famous doctrine is surprisingly hard to evaluate. An initial obstacle is that it can easily seem no different from what everyone thought, since it was a truism of scholastic philosophy with roots in both Aristotle and Augustine that a body is a substance extended in three dimensions (§16.1). In saying this, however, these authors were defining the logical genus *body*. Descartes is doing something very different, something very much in line with the concerns of the present chapter: he is defining the material stuff that endures through change. To say that the nature of this stuff is to be *res extensa* has many implications. First, it implies that matter cannot exist without extension. As we have seen, this is something many scholastics believed. It further implies that matter has that extension intrinsically. This is what both Ockham and Zabarella thought. Still further, it implies that a given part of matter necessarily has a fixed absolute volume or quantity. (Since Descartes takes matter as a whole to be extended without limit [e.g., *Principles* II.21], one has to speak here of a given part of the whole having a determinate quantity.) So when Descartes says that matter is essentially extended, he means that its extension or quantity is determinate. This is of course C^Q, the doctrine we have found in Pererius. There is probably no one scholastic author who endorses all three of these aspects of Descartes's account of matter. Even so, we could create a kind of composite sketch of a scholastic view that would contain something approaching corpuscular matter.

   Yet there is still more to Descartes's doctrine of *res extensa*. Like most post-scholastic authors, Descartes retains from scholasticism a substantive notion of *nature* or *essence* according to which the nature of a thing is what explains the various non-essential intrinsic features of that thing (§27.6). So in saying that "the nature of matter . . . consists . . . in its being a thing extended"—or, alternatively, that its "essence" is extension— Descartes is making an explanatory claim: that we can understand the various properties of bodies in terms of the varying modes of extension.[27] Just what ontological weight these modes should have is a difficult question that will have to await Chapter 13. But quite apart from the fact that Descartes appeals merely to modes, whereas almost all the scholastics appeal to forms, the mere fact that he chooses to regard extension as the essence of matter marks a crucial difference from scholasticism. The import of his defining matter in this way is best understood in light of what other choices he might have made. For subsequent corpuscularian critics, Descartes's account was

---

[27] Descartes speaks of the "essence" of matter as extension at, e.g., *The World* ch. 6 (XI:36): "Mais ils ne doivent pas aussi trouver etrange, . . . si je conçois son étendue, ou la propriété qu'elle a d'occuper de l'espace, non point comme un accident, mais comme sa vraie forme et son esssence"; *Principles* I.53: "sed una tamen est cuiusque substantiae praecipua proprietas, quae ipsius naturam essentiamque constituit, et ad quam aliae omnes referuntur." The last part of this sentence picks up on the point made in the main text, that essence for Descartes implies that from which a thing's other properties flow. Hence I.53 continues: "Nam omne aliud quod corpori tribui potest, extensionem praesupponit, estque tantum modus quidam rei extensae."

controversial primarily because it ignored solidity (§15.5), and foreclosed the possibility of space as something distinct from matter. But from Descartes's point of view the chief rival on which he was turning his back was a metaphysical account of prime matter. For scholastic authors, almost invariably, the essence of prime matter was its indeterminate potentiality for the substantial form that gives the composite substance its nature. This was the verdict not just of the classical traditions founded by Aquinas, Scotus, etc., but also of the Averroists, and of heterodox figures like Auriol, Ockham, Zabarella, and Pererius, among many others.[28] So although both Ockham and Zabarella regard matter as intrinsically, necessarily extended, both explicitly deny that extension is the essence of matter.[29] When Descartes insists that this is precisely what matter's essence is, he is issuing a direct challenge to the scholastic tradition of defining matter in terms of its relationship to form. Regardless how far a scholastic author might go down the road of making extension intrinsic to matter and subject to stringent conservation laws, there remains that fundamental divide between their prime matter and that of the corpuscularians.

What marks the rise of the corpuscularian movement, therefore, is not just the rejection of form, but the rejection of matter as dependent on form.[30] In its place lies a conception of prime matter not only as extended and actualized, but as capable of explaining all the phenomena of nature. Whereas the scholastics had postulated only the conservation of indeterminate prime matter, seventeenth-century authors would come to agree that it is body itself—the corpuscles that compose all material

---

[28] On the essence of matter as incomplete potentiality, see Averroes, *De subst. orbis* ch. 1 (*Opera* IX:3rb): "Unde natura huius subiecti recipientis substantiales formas, videlicet primae materiae, necesse est ut sit natura potentiae—scilicet quod potentia sit eius differentia substantialis. Et ideo nullam habet formam propriam et naturam existentem in actu, sed eius substantia est in posse, et ex hoc materia recipit omnes formas"; Aquinas, *Quod.* III.1.1: "esse autem actum repugnant rationi materiae, quae secundum propriam rationem est ens in potentia"; Auriol, *Sent.* II.12.1.7 (II:173bC): "materia habet quidditatem suo modo: est enim formabile purum et possibile"; Ockham, *Summula* I.9 (VI:179): "materia est quaedam res actualiter existens in rerum natura, quae est in potentia ad omnes formas substantiales, nullam habens necessario et semper sibi inexsistentem"; Zabarella, *De rebus nat.*, De prima rerum materia II.21 (col. 231): "dicemus enim, primam materiam suapte natura esse corpus de categoria substantiae indeterminatum, nulli certae naturae alligatum, et aptum omnia fieri, quod significat corpus generalissimum in categoria substantiae, et ipsum univocum esse facit; ideo in ipsa materiae natura nullus actus inest, sed est substantia quaedam indeterminata, potestatem habens recipiendi quemlibet actum"; Pererius, *De comm. princ.* V.21 (p. 333): "There are two kinds of potentiality, one that belongs to matter of its own force and nature. . . ."

[29] Both Ockham and Zabarella expressly say that 'matter is extended' is necessary *per se*, but *secundo modo* rather than *primo modo*, which is to say that it is true not in virtue of extension's being part of the essence of matter, but in virtue of matter's being part of the essence of extension. See Ockham, *Summula* I.13 (VI:191); Zabarella, *De rebus nat.* II.11 (col. 204B). It used to be commonly held that Ockham's theory of matter is essentially the same as Descartes's. De Wulf, for instance, wrongly claimed a century ago that Ockham treats extension as "l'essence des corps comme pour Descartes" (*Histoire* II:171n.). Weisheipl, however, seems to have put an end to this sort of talk; see, e.g., "Place of John Dumbleton" pp. 443–5.

[30] Others have articulated the idea that what ultimately distinguishes scholastic prime matter is its indeterminate potential for form. See, e.g., McMullin, "The shift here is a crucial one, because it means that (1) matter is no longer either a Receptacle or a co-principle with form, incomplete in itself and mysterious in its ontological indeterminacy; and (2) it is that which physical science may claim to describe and explain" ("Introduction" p. 18) and Des Chene: "The Aristotelians, however much they differed on the essence of matter, agreed that its essence includes being in potentia to form. As long as that remains—as long as substantial change is thought to be the actualization of matter's indifferent potentia to form—the attribution to matter of quantity, or even the characterization of it as 'indeterminate quantity' that we find in Zabarella, does not take one beyond the bounds of Aristotelian physics" ("Descartes and the Coimbra Commentaries" p. 37). Although I think these remarks insightfully capture a core area of disagreement, I have come to think that they will not do as a characterization of what is distinctive in Descartes. As I will argue in Chapters 8 and 13, his conception of substance and mode is precisely that of an indeterminate, "mysterious" subject, standing "in potentia" to its modes.

substances—that is conserved through all change. Descartes is the first well-developed and most influential proponent of this sort of view. As we will see, his own conception of substance as the subject of modes is surprisingly prone to relapse into something not so different from scholastic prime matter (§13.7). But the trend of post-scholastic thought is toward the doctrine of a permanent, fully actualized substratum. This both grounds the attack on scholastic hylomorphism, and at the same time leads to severe difficulties in attempting to save our commonsense ontology of ordinary material substances persisting through time. These and still further consequences will have to wait until later to be developed. What we have done so far is consider the most basic foundation for the overthrow of scholastic thought: the way that, in the seventeenth century, matter becomes body, and body becomes the object of natural science.

5

Philosophiae Perennes

5.1. A Modest Historiographic Proposal

It is sometimes said that the history of philosophy consists in a series of choices between Plato and Aristotle. This is too simple, but only slightly so. In truth, the history of philosophy consists in a series of choices between three primordial rivals: Plato, Aristotle, and Democritus. When the old saying is thus enlarged, it serves very nicely.

I am serious. Although one might suppose it the disreputable province of textbooks to produce this sort of simplified gloss on the history of philosophy, it seems to me quite plausible that some such schema can fruitfully be applied. There being little or no change over the centuries in either the fundamental character of our world, or the character of our minds, or the tools with which we do philosophy, we should expect philosophers to circle over and over above the same kind of views, to be tempted in the same directions, and to clash at the same places. So, in place of a perennial philosophy, I propose these three *philosophiae perennes*.

It is easy enough to see, in reflecting on our four centuries, why the familiar Plato–Aristotle schema is too simple. What it predicts is that critics of Aristotelianism would turn toward Platonism. This is not, however, how it went. To be sure, authors from the latter part of our period had every opportunity to make the Platonic turn, inasmuch as from the mid-fifteenth century forward, for the first time, the whole Platonic corpus was available in Marsilio Ficino's Latin translation. (Before the fifteenth century, only the first half of the *Timaeus* had circulated widely in Latin.) And, of course, there are a few instances of Platonism assuming a central role, especially in fifteenth-century Italy. Yet Platonism never really caught on, not in anything like the way Aristotelianism had. This is particularly clear when one comes to the seventeenth century: none of the principal philosophers from that century can plausibly be regarded as Platonists. There are, of course, places where one might see Platonic influences. Most famously, there is Cartesian dualism, which recalls the dualism of the *Phaedo*. And perhaps the nativism of the rationalists bears an affinity to Platonic epistemology. But these look like accidental resemblances rather than marks of some deep influence. Quite generally, Plato seems to have made little impact on the early modern era— indeed, even less so than his impact on the scholastic era, where it is easy to see the influence of the Neoplatonic tradition as transmitted through figures like Augustine, Proclus, and pseudo-Dionysius.[1]

Lines of development over our four centuries become much more intelligible once one envisages the range of philosophical possibilities as stretched out on a continuum where one extreme is occupied by Platonic idealism and the other by reductive corpuscularianism. Aristotelianism, on this picture, represents not the contrary of Platonism, but a middle ground between two opposing extremes, an attempt to resist the idealism of his teacher without falling into an austerely reductive corpuscularian approach. To be sure, this seems to suit how Aristotle thinks of himself, as mediating between Plato's Forms and Democritus's atoms. This also illuminates the later history of Aristotelianism, when critics of scholasticism consider their alternatives. The choice they face, broadly speaking, is between the idealism of Plato and the corpuscularianism of the atomists. And with this schematic picture in mind, what we can say is that all the leading figures of the seventeenth century chose corpuscularianism.

Of course, these claims require qualification as soon as they are submitted to close scrutiny. Some authors illustrate my thesis better than others, and in general different authors end up at all different points on the continuum. As we will see over and over in the chapters to come, it is hard to find anyone committed to a strictly corpuscularian view—that is, one that recognizes no metaphysical entities at all (§1.3). Moreover, some authors, such as the Cambridge Platonists, move at once both toward corpuscularianism and toward an explicitly Platonic idealism, seeing these as both necessary to a complete account of nature. (The title of one of Henry More's early philosophical poems is *Democritus Platonissans*.) And while one might make a case for Leibniz as situated at various places on my continuum, it seems most plausible to read him as trying to hold onto the center of the continuum, not by embracing Aristotelianism but, ultimately, by installing there his own philosophical system.[2] To be sure, judgments about where to locate an author on this continuum depend crucially on what part of their theory one is considering. Hardly anyone in the seventeenth century was willing

---

[1] On Plato in the Renaissance curriculum, see, e.g., Schmitt, "L'introduction"; Celenza, "Revival." For a recent attempt to give a larger role to Platonism in seventeenth-century thought, see Hedley and Hutton, *Platonism at the Origins of Modernity*. Despite the editors' ambition to make a case for "the vitality of the Platonic tradition" (p. 1), the cumulative impact of the essays is to highlight the peripheral influence of Platonism during the period. One of the most telling remarks from the volume is Rogers' offhand remark that one can find just a single Platonist active at Oxford in the first half of the seventeenth century ("Locke and Platonism" p. 195).

The question of "Platonism" can be fruitfully debated only in the context of a reasonably precise account of what Platonism is. In some broad sense, one might see Platonism everywhere, inasmuch as Plato's fecund and wide-ranging genius touched on virtually the whole spectrum of philosophical inquiry. This is what Whitehead had in mind with his famous remark about the history of philosophy as a series of footnotes to Plato. To determine whether a philosopher is Platonic in some more substantial way requires defining what is distinctive of Platonism, as opposed to Aristotelianism, Democriteanism, etc. This might or might not incorporate later Platonism, as well as (or as opposed to) the dialogues of the master himself, and would require going doctrine by doctrine. This, in effect, is what the present study attempts to do with scholastic Aristotelianism and its legacy in the seventeenth century.

Oderberg, "Introduction," offers a modern version of the notion that Aristotle is a *via media* between Platonism and reductive materialism.

[2] On the Cambridge Platonists, and their attitude toward corpuscularianism, see Gabbey, "Henry More and the Limits of Mechanism"; Gregory, "Ralph Cudworth"; Hutton, "Aristotle and the Cambridge Platonists"; Jesseph, "Mechanism, Skepticism, and Witchcraft."

Leibniz is the most prominent seventeenth-century philosopher to acknowledge a significant debt to Plato in his thought. For a helpful attempt to evaluate this, see Mercer, *Leibniz's Metaphysics* chs. 5–6 and, more recently, "Platonism at the Core of Leibniz's Philosophy."

to embrace the corpuscular approach all the way up to the human mind. In that domain one might find more Platonic elements, fused together with corpuscular theories of the material realm. Ethics is still another matter. Although my historiography applies most naturally to the realm of natural philosophy and metaphysics, it has applications in the moral domain as well. Reductionism in metaphysics goes naturally with hedonism in ethics, as the example of the Epicureans shows. Accordingly, the moral theory of Hobbes or Hume can be regarded as another instance of an author's moving away from Aristotelianism, but toward a more reductive rather than idealistic account.[3]

My proposal is, in the first instance, a thesis about the contours of philosophical positions, but it is also, perhaps less frivolously, a claim about actual lines of historical influence. One finds hardly any examples, throughout the history of philosophy, of an author's rejecting an entrenched philosophical theory without relying on the support of some other, pre-existent theory. That is, philosophers almost never strike out on wholly new ground, without the historical inspiration of some figure or another. Descartes is the most striking example of a philosopher who had the ambition to begin completely anew, casting away everything that had come before (§20.4). Whatever one thinks of such aspirations to methodological solipsism, the seventeenth century provides a particularly clear case-study of how in general philosophers do not work that way, even in tumultuous times. What one finds over and over, throughout that century, is that those who sought to abandon scholasticism were searching for some alternative source of inspiration. It was, however, not clear where else to look, especially if one did not want to move in the direction of Platonism. Sebastian Basso puts on the title page of his bold *Philosophia naturalis adversus Aristotelem* (1621) the well-worn saying *Amicus Plato, amicus Socrates, sed magis amica Veritas*. (Calvin had already invoked this motto, and both Walter Charleton and Newton would later do the same.) Yet Basso does not suppose that it is easy simply to set the history of philosophy aside, and start anew. On the contrary, he worried about where his contemporaries might draw inspiration:

Where should they turn? To whom should they go, once Aristotle has been abandoned? The ancient texts have been lost, with a few of their fragments dispersed over other books, mainly Aristotle's. When interpreted, they resemble feverish dreams. With what fidelity do you suppose that Aristotle recorded them? Is it still any wonder that philosophers adhere so stubbornly to Aristotle? Whom else would they follow? (ad lectorem, f. ¶6r)

Basso himself vows to follow the arguments wherever they lead, without prejudice to their source. But in practice this means abandoning Aristotle in favor of what he regarded as the grand consensus of ancient philosophy in favor of corpuscularianism,

---

[3] The influence of Epicurean moral theory on post-scholastic thought was well recognized at the time. Thomas Creech, for instance, in his preface to his English translation of Lucretius's *De rerum natura* (1682), remarks that "the admirers of Mr. Hobbes may easily discern that his politics are but Lucretius enlarged..." (f. b3v). This was not intended as a recommendation. Creech begins his preface with the remark that "the best method to overthrow the Epicurean Hypothesis (I mean as it stands opposite to Religion) is to expose a full system of it to public view" (f. b2r). The whole issue of influence in the ethical domain is quite complex, given the extensive sixteenth- and seventeenth-century literature. See, e.g., Valla, *De voluptate*; Erasmus, *Epicureus* (tr. Thompson); Sarasin, *Discours de morale sur Épicure*; Charleton, *Epicurus' Morals*. Recent studies include Jones, *The Epicurean Tradition*; Sarasohn, *Gassendi's Ethics*; Wilson, *Epicureanism*.

an approach he finds in Plato's *Timaeus* and in aspects of Stoicism, and of course also among the ancient atomists.[4]

Basso puts on display the two rival tendencies of early seventeenth-century thought: either to reject all authority, and insist on the autonomy of one's own reason, or to look for some authority sufficient to countervail Aristotle's. Although Descartes championed the first route, the second was more common. This meant not only finding an alternative to Aristotle, but also somehow pushing Aristotle out of the way, which was often accomplished by treating him as a marginal figure. Thus Daniel Sennert describes the corpuscularian doctrine as that "of virtually all the ancients before Aristotle . . . and even many after Aristotle" and he contrasts this with the view of Aristotle, "for he alone divorced himself in this regard from the ancients and rejected their view" (*Hypomnemata physica* III.2; tr. *Thirteen Books*, p. 456). When the history of philosophy is so understood, Aristotelianism can be rejected as an historical aberration, leading away from the main path toward the truth.[5]

5.2. The Revival of Atomism

Seventeenth-century authors might have gone in other directions. They had the resources to embrace Platonism, Stoicism, skepticism, or of course to advocate a revised Aristotelianism. Overwhelmingly, however, they took as their paradigm the tradition of reductive corpuscularianism that had been founded by Democritus.[6]

---

[4] For Basso, see especially Lüthy, "Thoughts and Circumstances," and also Gregory, "Sébastien Basson"; Nielsen, "Seventeenth-Century Physician"; Ariew, "Descartes, Basso." On the various manifestations of the saying *Amicus Plato* (the ultimate source of which is unclear), see Guerlac, "Amicus Plato." For another instance of the worry about where to turn, if not Aristotle, see John Webster, *Academiarum examen* ch. 10, p. 104: "Secondly, it will be urged, that if the peripatetic philosophy which the schools maintain should be taken away, where would any such perfect, complete, and methodical piece be found to supply the place thereof." Webster replies that Aristotelianism is not at all perfect, that there are better options, and that if there are not then the "academies" should be ashamed that, after so many centuries, they have not themselves put forward anything better. See §5.4 below for more of Webster's prescription.

[5] Basso's musings on reason and authority in the preface to his *Philosophia naturalis* represent a common theme in philosophical writings from the early seventeenth century. For other instances, see the introduction to Sennert's *Hypomnemata physica* (translated as *Thirteen Books*, bks. IX–XIII) and the whole of Francis Bacon's *Instauratio magna*, which is the leading example of the genre.

Another, quite remarkable strategy for coping with the influence of Aristotle was to give his works a developmental reading. Jungius (*Disp. Hamb.* XXVI.11) takes this approach, contending that although in the *Physics* and *De gen. et cor.* "communem plerisque veterum . . . minus probare videatur, in posterioribus tamen scriptis syndiacrisin manifeste profitetur"—referring to *Meteor.* IV.9–10. Pomponazzi, while not going that far, had exclaimed that here "Aristoteles Democrizat" (*In quartum Meteor.* dub. 92, 102). On this issue in general, seeLüthy, "Aristotelian Watchdog."

[6] Although I treat Democritus as the figurehead of reductive corpuscularianism, the historical sources are complex. In addition to the later Epicureans, there are extensive critical discussions of the theory not just in Aristotle but also in Cicero, Galen, and Maimonides, all of which were influential. Hero of Alexandria provided another ancient model for this kind of view, although his corpuscles were not indivisible.

An older and somewhat crude statement of the case for Democritus's influence on seventeenth-century thought can be found in Löwenheim, *Die Wissenschaft Demokrits*. For a more sophisticated treatment, see Lüthy, "The Fourfold Democritus." Regarding Democritus's limited influence before the end of the sixteenth century, Lüthy remarks: "concrete traces of his influence on the development of sixteenth-century scientific thought are sporadic" (ibid., p. 450). As late as the 1650s, it could still seem to the young Boyle that its development was a very recent event: "The atomical philosophy invented or brought into request [≈ vogue] by Democritus, Leucippus, Epicurus, and their contemporaries, though since the inundation of barbarians and barbarism expelled out of the Roman world all but the casually escaping Peripatetic Philosophy, it have been either wholly ignored in the European schools or mentioned there but as an exploded system of absurdities, yet in our less partial and more inquisitive times it is so luckily revived and so skillfully celebrated in diverse parts of Europe by the learned pens of Gassendus, Magnenus, Des Cartes, and his disciples

Although many of the core claims of the atomist tradition admitted of no more empirical confirmation than did Aristotelianism (§5.4), it appeared to have a certain status that the disreputable scholastic tradition lacked. The substantive reasons for this preference are complex, and are indeed the subject of this study as a whole. But there were also various incidental reasons why ancient atomism loomed large among competing positions. For one thing, as the previous section suggested, it was taken to have a certain ancient authority to it, with roots even older than Aristotle's or Plato's. Moreover, atomism was thought to have primacy not just in philosophy but also in ancient science and medicine. Emblematic of this was a widely credited legend—based on a series of letters falsely ascribed to the Greek physician Hippocrates—which held that Democritus had been Hippocrates's teacher. This association, which was widely accepted throughout the seventeenth century, seemed to position atomism at the foundations of scientific medicine.[7] Hence Walter Charleton refers to the members of the London College of Physicians as the "genuine sons of Democritus" (*Immortality* p. 34). Charleton is the best-known English-language example of a long-running seventeenth-century effort to rehabilitate ancient atomism, an effort that includes works mentioned already in previous chapters, such as Nicholas Hill's *Philosophia Epicurea, Democritiana, Theophrastica* (1601) and Jean Chrysostome Magnen's *Democritus reviviscens* (1646). The most prominent such example of all, however, was Pierre Gassendi. In his early *Exercitationes* (1624), Gassendi describes Democritus as the "most learned of all the ancients" (II.6.6, p. 495), and speculates that Plato's notable silence about Democritus reflects the fact that he alone, among the Presocratics, was above attack. Eventually, Gassendi decided to take Epicurus as his champion around which to build a rival philosophy to the Aristotelians. To read his long and difficult magnum opus, the *Syntagma philosophicum* (1658), is to see the teachings of Epicurus and Lucretius brought to life again, doctrine after doctrine, with the same sort of dogged fidelity with which the scholastics followed Aristotle.[8]

---

our deservedly famous countryman Sir Kenelm Digby and many other writers, especially those that handle magnetical and electrical operations, that it is now grown too considerable to be any longer laughed at, and considerable enough to deserve a serious enquiry" (*Of the Atomical Philosophy* [*Works* XIII:227]).

[7] See Lüthy, "The Fourfold Democritus" pp. 461–70.

[8] For the motivations behind Gassendi's study of Epicurus, see Joy, *Gassendi* pp. 38–9. Nielsen, "Seventeenth-Century Physician," stresses that Sebastian Basso's atomism takes Plato's *Timaeus* as its inspiration, much more than Democritus, and plausibly suggests that this is so because Democritus was still a controversial figure in the early seventeenth century (p. 343). There was, moreover, reason to be cautious about invoking Democritus, given a dispute that had raged in the first decade of the seventeenth century over a work of Joseph Duchesne (also known as Quercetanus), the *De priscorum philosophorum verae medicinae materia* (1603), which had credited Democritus as the father of chemistry. Gassendi's later remark about Plato's not daring to criticize Democritus had already appeared in Duchesne: "Legimus insuper principem Graecum Democritum, quem Plato ne reprehendere quidem est ausus" (p. 4). This work was immediately condemned by the Paris medical faculty, whose Aristotelian-Galenic orientation made any appeal to the atomic tradition completely unacceptable. Subsequently, however, Duchesne's ideas were forcefully supported by the German physician Andreas Libavius, whose advocacy of Democritus seems likely to have been influential on later philosophical thought. (My information on this dispute comes from Nielsen, "Seventeenth-Century Physician" pp. 339–41, and Lüthy, "The Fourfold Democritus" pp. 474–9, who shows that the Democritus at issue in this dispute was neither the atomist with whom we are familiar nor the alleged founder of modern medicine, but yet another legendary Democritus, the founder of alchemy.) For further information on Libavius's version of atomism see Newman, "Experimental Corpuscular Theory" pp. 306–17, who highlights the distance between Libavius's views and Democritus's.

Although Gassendi is the most vivid instance of this approach, the tendency to appeal to ancient atomism can be found throughout the seventeenth century. Francis Bacon, for instance, complains that the river of time has transmitted to us only those works that are "lighter and full of wind" (he means both Plato and Aristotle!) "while letting the heavier and solid stuff sink" (*Novum organum* pt. I, n. 71). That weightier stuff is the work of the Presocratics, especially the atomists, whose school of philosophy "saw the deepest into nature" (n. 51). Robert Boyle too refers to "that great and ancient sect of philosophers, the atomists" (*Free Enquiry* sec. 6 [*Works* X:511; Davis and Hunter p. 91]). And Joseph Glanvill writes that "the atomical hypothesis was the first and most ancient which there is in any memory in physiology" (*Scire tuum nihil est* p. 89). It may in fact have been Glanvill who wrote the Ballad of Gresham College, in honor of that early meeting-place for the Royal Society:

> Thy Colledg, Gresham, shall hereafter
> Be the whole world's Universitie,
> Oxford and Cambridge are our laughter;
> Their learning is but Pedantry.
> These new Collegiates doe assure us
> Aristotle's an Asse to Epicurus.
> (Stimson, "Ballad" p. 109)

Looking back from 1669, Leibniz praises Galileo, Bacon, Gassendi, Descartes, Hobbes, and Digby as "revivers of Democritus and Epicurus" (*Confessio naturae* pt. 1). In a 1697 letter, Leibniz describes himself as having been drawn into this debate from an early age: "I was not yet fifteen when I walked for whole days in the woods to choose sides between Aristotle and Democritus" (*Phil. Schriften* III:205). Even critics of these developments recognized them for what they were. In his 1631 attack on atomism, Libert Froidmont, a professor at Louvain, criticized those "who have deserted Aristotle, Plato, Zeno, that is, those great men of illustrious fame and erudition of the schools, and have fled to Epicurus . . ." (*Labyrinthus*, ad lectorem). Edward Stillingfleet, later Locke's most prominent detractor, was railing already in 1662 against "that which makes most noise in the world, which is the atomical or Epicurean hypothesis" (*Origines sacrae* III.2, p. 447). Berkeley's youthful notebooks from 1707–8 record this quick impression of world history: "Fall of Adam, rise of Idolatry, rise of Epicurism and Hobbism" (n. 17, *Works* I:10). Judging from its company on the list, the revival of Epicurus did not strike Berkeley as a good thing—a later entry characterizes Epicurus, along with Hobbes and Spinoza, as "a declared enemy of religion" (n. 824, I:98)—but at least it struck Berkeley as important.[9]

---

[9] The question of Epicurus's influence is even more complicated than in the case of Democritus, because Epicureanism was associated with a wider range of doctrines: not just reductive corpuscularianism, but also, most prominently, materialism, hedonism, and the denial of divine providence. When Calvin, in the mid-sixteenth century, described the growing number of Epicureans as the "argumentum certissimum" that the end of the world was near (see Jones, *Epicurean Tradition* p. 163), he surely had in mind a moral standpoint rather than a thesis in natural philosophy. Perhaps this is what Berkeley later had in mind, too, though by then, and given his philosophical orientation, this is less clear.

For a recent attempt to trace the influence of Epicureanism across its varied spheres of influence, see Wilson, *Epicureanism*. She reaches the quite bold conclusion that the downfall of Aristotelian theories of matter is the result of the revival of the ideas of the ancient atomists: "Aristotelian matter theory was repudiated and the dethronement of its author is best explained by the rediscovery and reconsideration of the arguments of the ancient atomists, especially the

It did not take the seventeenth century's scholarly rehabilitation of ancient atomism to see that these were the philosophical choices available. A 1403 letter from William Euvrie, a young arts master at Paris, to John Gerson, the University's powerful chancellor, describes the choices:[10]

I ask of you, good father, which path of doctrine will we follow? Which way do you offer to the young? . . . Do not reply to me that it is up to you to choose and judge for yourself as you wish. For it is not permitted (*licet*) that I choose, especially where the determination among such a variety of views would be daunting. And even if it were permitted to me, still right reason would seek paternal counsel. For there have been three sects that by the fame of their celebrated names have come down to us in present times. The first they call the sect of the formalizers, which they hold to be derived from Plato, through Augustine. Another, that of the nominalists, shifts the differences among nearly all things to human concepts. The first author of this sect is unknown, I gather, because there has been such an intermission of time, but they ascribe to Epicurus both its origin and its development. The third sect mediates between the above two. Begun by Aristotle, it has been propounded with careful and continual labor up to our age by Alexander, Philoponus, al-Farabi, Themistius, Avicenna, Averroes, Boethius, Albert, St. Thomas, and other Peripatetics. How then should a young man choose among such a variety of doctrines? (Kaluza, *Les Querelles* p. 17)

Euvrie's three sects correspond perfectly, on their face, with my own historiography, but strictly speaking the views he describes all belong to the middle Aristotelian ground. The "formalizers" (lines 6–7) are Scotists, and so this hardly counts as a Platonic view at all by modern standards; it is simply a form of Aristotelianism that tilts somewhat more toward realism. The "nominalists" (lines 7–10) are Ockham and Buridan, among others, and although nominalism deploys the sort of reductive approach favored by Epicurus, the view remains solidly Aristotelian, inasmuch as it retains its commitment to prime matter, substantial form, and real qualities. As Euvrie's letter indicates, students at the University of Paris at the start of the fifteenth century could choose among only a relatively narrow range of options, and felt moreover that ultimately "it is not permitted [to] choose" (line 3) (see Ch. 20). Even so, from among these limited options, Euvrie's letter reveals just the possibilities we should expect: a middle ground, "begun by Aristotle" (line 11), with reductive Epicureanism on one side and idealistic Platonism on the other.

5.3. 'Nominalism'

One of the most remarkable features of modern scholarship on our four centuries is how badly it has performed at identifying the crucial organizing concepts. Indeed, perhaps the main obstacle to writing a narrative of this period—aside from the

---

arguments to be found in Lucretius, and by the conformity the moderns perceived between their aims and the atomic philosophy" (p. 50). I would say on the contrary that the revival of the ancient atomists—at the hands of authors like Magnen, Gassendi, Charleton, etc.—is an effect rather than the cause of the rejection of Aristotelianism, and that authors embraced the corpuscularian program only because (a) they were dissatisfied with Aristotelianism, and (b) they finally, after centuries of enforced conformity, were free to pursue other options. For the last claim, see Chapter 20.

[10] The context of Euvrie's letter is analyzed in careful detail by Kaluza, *Les querelles* ch. 1, who identifies many of the specific contemporaries to whom Euvrie is reacting.

sheer quantity of texts—is that one must break free from the usual classifying schemas, which obscure as much as they illuminate. I have already set aside the most obvious of these—the distinction between medieval, Renaissance, and modern (§1.1)—and have now offered further grounds for treating the fabled phenomenon of Renaissance Platonism as peripheral. As one moves closer to the ground—closer, that is, to the issues themselves—the lines of demarcation remain tangled. For researchers focused on the later scholastic era, perhaps the principal organizing concept has been that of *nominalism*. For scholars of the seventeenth century, two central concepts have been *atomism* and *skepticism*. Yet any attempt to understand our period in terms of these concepts is bound to fail, because skepticism is a view that no one held, atomism a view that barely mattered, and nominalism not a view at all. To be sure, there are interesting issues in the neighborhood. For instance, although there are no true skeptics during our period, there are many interesting discussions of certainty and doubt, often occasioned by reflection on skepticism. Atomism and nominalism too, although flawed as organizing concepts for the period, come very close to the issues that matter most, and so they have served to get scholars into the right territory, even while obscuring the overall narrative. Here I will focus first on nominalism and then on atomism, saving a discussion of skepticism for another time.[11]

Although the fourteenth century is regarded as the heyday of nominalism, the term itself did not come into usage until the beginning of the following century. Indeed, not only did fourteenth-century authors not use this term, but in fact they recognized no common philosophical movement of this sort at all. As for the term 'nominalist,' although it had been applied to various logicians back in the twelfth century, its distinct usage in the scholastic context is first found at the start of the fifteenth century, as witnessed by the above-quoted letter from William Euvrie. When Jerome of Prague visited the University of Heidelberg in 1406, he described the nominalists as those who deny the reality of universals outside the human mind, and realists as those who affirm that reality—a usage that was guaranteed to be memorable because of his shocking attack on such nominalism as heresy. (Jerome was ultimately found guilt of heresy himself and burned at the stake in 1416. Among the subsequent charges made against him was that by making such rash charges he had posed a threat to academic unity.) The growing sense of a systematic divide between two schools of thought becomes explicit in a 1425 document from the University of Cologne, where a distinction is drawn between "the *via* of saint Thomas, Albert the Great and such ancients," and the *via* of "the modern masters [John] Buridan and Marsilius [of Inghen]." This notion of two distinct ways, a *via antiqua* and a *via moderna*, became widespread in the later fifteenth century, and was associated with realism and nominalism. At some universities one or the other school was banned; at others, there were separate chairs

---

[11] My original plan for this book called for a series of chapters on knowledge and skepticism, which would have fleshed out the claim that "no one defended skepticism." I have published some of this material in "Science and Certainty," and hope to publish more elsewhere. The central idea is the need for a distinction between ordinary knowledge, our possession of which was never seriously doubted during our period, and *scientia*, which authors were very frequently skeptical of our possessing, in one or another domain.

For recent state-of-the-art discussions of skepticism's influence in the scholastic era, see Perler, "Skepticism" and Schüssler, "John Gerson."

for realists and nominalists; in Heidelberg, it was eventually forbidden to criticize the different *viae*; ultimately, in the sixteenth century, the dispute simply dried up.[12]

Sometimes Buridan was described as the founder of the *via moderna*; other times the doctrine was traced back to Ockham. Often it was the opponents of nominalism who stressed its association with Ockham. His views were under a cloud of suspicion throughout the scholastic era, as is attested by a 1339 prohibition among the arts faculty in Paris against "listening to . . . , lecturing on . . . , disputing . . . , or referring to" Ockham's work. The 1339 statute mentioned no specific doctrines, however, and seems to have been lifted around 1360. Subsequently, Ockham's views were discussed quite extensively, and sometimes defended, but there was never a proper school of Ockhamists, in the way that there were Thomists, Scotists, and even Albertists. Was there even a school of nominalists? In 1474, Louis XI issued an edict commanding that realism alone be taught at the University of Paris, and that the books of various "renovating doctors" be confiscated. These offending scholars are listed as Ockham, John of Mirecourt, Gregory of Rimini, Buridan, Peter of Ailly, Marsilius, Adam Wodeham, John Dorp, and Albert of Saxony, as contrasted with the realists: Averroes, Albert, Aquinas, Giles of Rome, Alexander of Hales, John Duns Scotus, and Bonaventure. As for the "nominalists," this term is used of certain students at Paris who "are not afraid to imitate" the renovators. These students, or perhaps their teachers, subsequently made a reply to the French king, in which they conceived of nominalism as a movement going back to Ockham, which had been persecuted repeatedly, but which in fact represents the truer philosophy, inasmuch as "for each error found in the doctrine of the nominalists—if any are found—four or five appear in the doctrine of the realists." Ultimately, the king's edict seems to have had little influence, even in Paris. Indeed, Desiderius Erasmus remarked of Paris in 1525 that "the faction of the realists, as they are called, had once flourished, but now that of the nominalists largely rules" (Gabriel, "Via antiqua" pp. 455–6).

More or less the same names are listed over and over, with the list of realists taken from the late, great champions of the thirteenth century—thus justifying the sobriquet *via antiqua*—and the list of nominalists from the more recent, and hence in most eyes more suspect, fourteenth century. (On aversion to novelty, see §20.2.) But what were the doctrines of these separate camps? The question is best not even asked, inasmuch as these two schools of thought are simply the creations of a later time. This is most obviously the case for the so-called realists, since the differences between the authors who show up on that list are both significant and well known. It is also the case, however, for the nominalists. None of the canonical authors described as nominalists explicitly patterns his work on any of the others, or even conceives of himself as part of a movement. Although one might speak of a family resemblance among the views of

---

[12] For general information on the fifteenth-century dispute between *via antiqua* and *via moderna*, see Gilbert, "Ockham, Wyclif"; Gabriel, "Via antiqua"; Hoenen, "Fifteenth Century"; Kaluza, *Les querelles*. For the Cologne document of 1425, I follow the discussion in Hoenen, "Fifteenth Century" pp. 14–15. On the status of Ockhamism, see Courtenay, "Was there an Ockhamist School?", which summarizes earlier research by him and others on Ockham's standing in Paris in 1339–40. For the edict of 1474, and the nominalists' reply, see the English translation in Thorndike, *University Records* n. 158, and the discussions in Gilbert, "Ockham, Wyclif"; Kaluza, "La Crise." On Scotism, see Honnefelder, "Scotus und der Scotismus"; on Albertism, see Kaluza, "Les débuts de l'albertisme."

Ockham, Buridan, Marsilius, and others, there are also striking differences, as will emerge in subsequent chapters.[13]

Even if one could focus on a single issue as definitive, it would be very hard to justify the notion of a distinctive nominalist camp. Today, nominalism is most closely associated with the problem of universals. The canonical nominalists did believe that everything that exists is particular. But Aquinas and many other thirteenth-century authors believed this too, which makes it hard to see how that can serve to define the nominalist movement. Moreover, the status of universals was just one and not the most important of the issues that came to be seen as distinctive of nominalism. The 1474 Parisian defense of nominalism begins with this remark:

Those doctors are called nominalists who do not multiply the things principally signified by terms in accord with the multiplication of terms. Realists, on the other hand, are those who contend that things are multiplied in accord with the multiplication of terms. For example, nominalists say that deity and wisdom are entirely one and the same thing, because everything that is in God is God. Realists, however, say that divine wisdom is divided from deity. (Ehrle, *Der Sentenzenkommentar* p. 322)

This characterization of the disagreement focuses on whether the surface structure of language corresponds to the structure of reality, in such a way that distinct terms match up with distinct things in reality. This, however, has little to do with the problem of universals; it refers mainly to a dispute over the categories (see Ch. 12): does every predicate across Aristotle's categorial scheme—e.g., *warm, six-feet tall, next to, sitting*—have corresponding to it a real accidental form? It was disingenuous for the nominalists to have taken as their example (lines 3–5) the one case, God, where such realism seems most clearly precluded, in view of God's simplicity. The heart of the debate in fact concerned material substances, and it is here, if anywhere, that one can speak most aptly of nominalists and realists. Ockham's view that only predicates in the category of Quality correspond to a real accident—with its attendant rejection of realism regarding both Quantity and Relation—had always been the most controversial aspect of his philosophy. It seems to have been the principal cause behind the conflicts in Paris in the 1330s, for instance, and remained the focus of extended discussion among sixteenth-century scholastics. Inasmuch as this dispute spills over into both metaphysics and semantics, it has the potential to constitute a movement. But here too the lines of demarcation are obscure. It is not clear that Albert the Great and Aquinas accept real accidents at all (§10.2), nor do they seem committed to a realistic interpretation of the category scheme (§12.3). And although Ockham is the scholastic paradigm of anti-realism with respect to the categories, his views met with resistance from Buridan and later Marsilius, both of whom were realists about the category that Ockham had fought the hardest to reject, Quantity (see Chs. 14–15).[14]

---

[13] The *Sentences* commentary of Peter of Candia (1378–80) is perhaps an important step toward the rise of nominalism as a distinct school of thought, for although it does not, so far as I know, use the term *nominales*, it does refer to Ockham quite extensively, by name, something that is quite unusual in earlier texts (see Ehrle, *Der Sentenzenkommentar* pp. 56–73; Moody, "Ockham, Buridan" p. 159).

[14] The view that Ockham was most controversial for his take on the categories has been championed by Courtenay over a series of works—see, in particular, "Reception at Paris" and "Reception in England" p. 93. An interesting contemporary source is the anonymous "Commendation of a Clerk," probably from the 1340s, which criticizes clerks for being "deficiens in statu scolastico" if they take up the views of "frater Wilhelmus de Octhan anglicus atque sui

There is, in short, nothing like a coherent body of thought that one might refer to as nominalism—at least not in the fourteenth century. Ockham was known as the *venerable inceptor* primarily because of his perceived role as the founder of nominalism (rather than, as is often said, because he failed to serve as a master of theology),[15] but if there ever was a nominalist movement, it came well after the figures who were conventionally supposed to constitute it. To be sure, even well into the seventeenth century, nominalism appeared to critics of scholasticism as a bright spot amidst the darkness of Aristotelianism. The young Leibniz speaks of "the nominalist sect, the most profound of all among the scholastics, and the most consistent with the character of our present-day, reformed philosophy" ("Preface to Nizolius," *Phil. Schriften* IV:157; tr. Loemker p. 127). But no wonder Leibniz is enthusiastic, for he characterizes nominalism as tantamount to what I am calling corpuscularianism: as the belief "that all things beyond individual substances are mere names." As we will see in later chapters, none of the canonical nominalists—not even Ockham—came even close to holding so extreme a view.

These cautionary remarks are largely familiar to specialists, on whose work the preceding paragraphs draw heavily. But the implications of this research have not yet quite dawned on the broader community of scholars, who continue to think of nominalism as a central organizing concept for later scholasticism. Inasmuch as a recurring theme of this volume will be the way in which Ockham's ideas often foreshadow the eventual rejection of scholasticism in the seventeenth century, it would be quite convenient if later scholastic thought could be conceived along the lines of this conventional historiography, as a dispute between Ockham and his followers, and their realist opponents. But this is an historical fiction, an early attempt to construct a narrative for scholastic thought that is not without some basis in reality,

sequaces"—views that are subsequently characterized entirely in terms of Ockham's parsimonious treatment of the accidental categories (Thorndike, *University Records* pp. 203, 409). This is not to say that the link between nominalism and universals is entirely a modern construction. As quoted in the main text, this is how Jerome of Prague understands nominalism. Scheibler too, in the early seventeenth century, takes it for granted that the "nominales" take their name from their view that universals are mere names (*Metaphys.* I.7.7.2, p. 102).

For the semantics behind nominalism, see Klima, "Nominalist Semantics," which summarizes much earlier research. For a nuanced discussion of what it means to be a nominalist, see Biard, "Nominalism," who begins by characterizing the term 'nominalism' as "uncertain and equivocal" (p. 661) and in the end settles for characterizing it as "a common approach, a way of doing philosophy" (p. 671).

[15] There is some truth in the widespread notion that Ockham was called the *venerable inceptor* because he failed to incept as a regent master at Oxford. What is true is that the term 'inceptor,' as opposed to 'doctor,' was sometimes (rather counterintuitively) used as an honorific for those who failed to incept (e.g., the term was applied to Robert Cowton and William of Ware, neither of whom became regent master [see Ehrle, *Ehrentitel* p. 55]). Also, Ockham was sometimes referred to as the *inceptor singularis* (ibid.), presumably both because of his nominalistic focus on particulars and his originality. Still, although *inceptor* was sometimes used in this sense, other manuscripts describe Ockham as the *doctor singularis* (ibid., pp. 37, 41, 43, 47). The reason why the title *inceptor* caught on, surely, is that it contained a *double entendre* pertaining to Ockham's status as the founder of nominalism. This sense is well attested in scholastic texts. De Soto refers to "Occham, . . . quem inceptorem huius viae Nominales venerantur" (*In Isag.* prol. q. 1, p. 30I). A Franciscan sermon from 1502, speaking of Ockham's immense influence, remarks that "tota Parisinsa facultas patrem novique dogmatis venerabilem inceptorem adamavit" (Doncoeur, "La théorie" p. 22). Fonseca reports: "Guillelmus Ockham . . . qui apud recentiores nominales tantum authoritatis obtinuit, ut quasi novam philosophandi viam primus invenerit, venerabilis inceptoris nomen assequutus sit" (*In Meta.* V.28.2.1, II:952). This last passage expressly asserts that the title was assigned *because* Ockham was regarded as the founder of nominalism. Whether or not this gets the origin of the title right (how would Fonseca know that?), it at least attests to how the title was understood in the later sixteenth century.

but that has to be approached with the same sort of caution as the seventeenth-century distinction between rationalists and empiricists.

5.4. 'Atomism'

Atomism, I remarked at the start of the previous section, is a view that barely mattered. This is true when atomism is understood as it is usually understood today, as the view that the divisibility of bodies extends down only so far, and that the smallest bodies in nature are indivisible.[16] If atomism is just this—a belief in indivisible atoms—then it should be treated as a thoroughly peripheral issue, inasmuch as very little turns on whether one thinks the material realm is or is not infinitely divisible. Although Aristotle happened to opt for infinite divisibility, there is little in his broader views that rests on this. And although most scholastics were divisibilists, not all were. Nicholas of Autrecourt was an atomist, and so were John Wyclif and Nicholas of Cusa.[17] To be sure, these are three quite heterodox thinkers, but the fact that each is so different from the others suggests just how little the doctrine of atomism matters to one's broader views. Atomism becomes increasingly prevalent in the late sixteenth and the seventeenth centuries, among authors such as Giordano Bruno, Bernardino Telesio, Tommaso Campanella, David Gorlaeus, Nicholas Hill, Walter Warner, Isaac Beeckman, Sebastian Basso, Antoine de Villon and Etienne de Clave, Galileo, Claude Berigard, Daniel Sennert, Magnen, Joachim Jungius, Gassendi, Charleton, and Newton.[18] But of course not every critic of scholasticism was an atomist, and indeed many of the major figures were not. Descartes found the view positively incoherent, as did Hobbes and Leibniz, while Francis Bacon and Robert Boyle treated it as a speculative, unverifiable hypothesis, and one that was indeed quite irrelevant to their broader anti-

---

[16] It is important to distinguish atomism as a thesis about bodies from atomism as a mathematical thesis about the structure of the continuum. This form of atomism was also a minority position among scholastics, but also had its defenders. See, e.g., Maier, *Die Vorläufer Galileis* ch. 7; Murdoch, "Atomism and Motion" and "Naissance"; Wood, "Introduction."

To show that an author is an atomist, in the sense at issue here, one must show that he endorses *indivisible* atoms. The mere postulation of "atoms" is not enough, because that word is often used for any fundamental corpuscle, divisible or not. See, e.g., Digby, *Two Treatises* I.5.8: "By which word *Atome*, nobody will imagine we intend to express a perfect indivisible, but only the least sort of natural bodies." This is in effect to use 'atoms' in the sense of the Aristotelian notion of *minima*—that is, the smallest bodies that still count as instances of the kind in question. So, a *minimum* of gold is the smallest particle of gold that still counts as gold. For this commonplace scholastic notion, see §26.3. The tendency to use 'atom' in this broad sense suggests the need for some wariness in how we take talk of "atomists." For in at least some contexts it may be possible to count as an atomist without postulating indivisible corpuscles—that is, as we would put it, to be an "atomist" without believing in atoms.

[17] Autrecourt's commitment to atomism is clear in the *Tractatus*—e.g., ch. 1, p. 201: "corpora atomalia...ipsa indivisibilia." See Grellard, "Atomistic Physics" and *Croire et savoir* ch. 7, and Pabst, *Atomtheorien* pp. 285–306. For Wyclif, see Michael, "John Wyclif's Atomism" and Pabst, *Atomtheorien* pp. 306–16. For Cusa, see *De mente idiotae* III.9: "Secundum mentis considerationem, continuum dividitur in semper divisibile, et multitudo crescit in infinitum, sed actu dividendo, ad partem actu indivisibilem devenitur, quam atomum appello. Est enim atomus quantitas, ob sui parvitatem, actu indivisibilis."

[18] The still-unmatched history of atomism in the late sixteenth and the seventeenth centuries is Lasswitz, *Geschichte der Atomistik*, which discusses all the figures mentioned here. See also Hall, "Establishment," and, more recently, Pabst, *Atomtheorien*; Clericuzio, *Elements, Principles, and Corpuscles*; Lüthy et al., *Late Medieval and Early Modern Corpuscular Matter Theories*; Pyle, *Atomism and Its Critics*; Grellard and Robert, *Atomism*. On the atomism of Villon and de Clave, see Kahn, "Entre atomisme," who stresses that their 1624 broadsheet (§19.6) was controversial not for its atomism, but for its rejection of Aristotelian form and matter. For Hill and Warner, see Clucas, "Infinite Variety."

Aristotelian agendas.[19] Why can an author's attitude toward atomism serve as a rough and fallible symptom of his attitude toward Aristotelianism? Precisely because this is a question for which there was absolutely no good evidence available one way or the other, which meant that for the main run of authors it simply fell out as a consequence of their broader philosophical sympathies, pro- or anti-Aristotelian. For many in the seventeenth century, this rough and ready principle sufficed: if Aristotle is wrong, then atomism is true.

The case of Descartes, who resisted this blind inference from reverse authority, is instructive just for this reason. Descartes thought he had an argument against atomism, on the grounds that it is possible to divide anything that is extended, just in virtue of the concept of what it is to be extended (*Principles* II.20). The argument seems willfully oblivious to the fact that atomists almost always assert only the natural impossibility of splitting an atom, which means that they could grant Descartes's bare conceptual possibility.[20] Still, Descartes's rejection of atoms is unequivocal. Hence it is interesting that he is quite concerned about the charge of being a latter-day atomist, insisting that "my method of philosophizing has no more affinity with the Democritean method than with any of the other particular sects" (*Principles* IV.202). Descartes had reason to be concerned. Libert Froidmont, for instance, had pressed this very charge upon him. In Froidmont's eyes, Descartes is simply another atomist: "not rarely does he unknowingly, I think, fall into the physics of Epicurus, crude and overblown" (Descartes, *Oeuvres* I:402). Descartes predictably protests that his view is not at all like the ancient atomists, inasmuch as he postulates neither atoms nor void space (I:413), but this reading of Descartes stuck. Henry More, in his first letter to Descartes, is tactless enough to appeal to the views of Epicurus, Democritus, and Lucretius, to which Descartes makes the rather prickly reply that he does not accept their authority.[21] Still, the association endured beyond Descartes's death. John Webster's *Academiarum examen* (1654) advocates throwing Aristotle's natural philosophy out of the university and replacing it with, among other things, Ficino's version of Plato, Gassendi's version of Epicurus, and Descartes's version of Democritus.[22] Boyle, although well aware of the

---

[19] For Francis Bacon's view of atomism, see *Novum organum* II.8: "Neque propterea res deducetur ad atomum, qui praesupponit vacuum et materiam non fluxam (quorum utrumque falsum est), sed ad particulas veras, quales inveniuntur." See also ibid., I.66 at end. For Boyle, see *Origin of Forms and Qualities* (*Works* V:292; Stewart p. 7): "I have forborne to employ arguments that are either grounded on, or suppose, indivisible corpuscles called *atoms*"; *History of Fluidity and Firmness* (*Works* II:165): "I am willing to decline clashing with them [the atomists] . . . , especially since the dim and bounded intellect of man seldom prosperously adventures to be dogmatical about things that approach to infinite, whether in vastness or littleness." (See too Anstey, *Philosophy of Robert Boyle* pp. 43–4.) For some general remarks on the unverifiable character of the atomistic hypothesis, see Meinel, "Early Seventeenth-Century Atomism." For Hobbes, see *De corpore* 27.1. For Leibniz, see e.g. his letter to Remond from July 1714 (*Phil. Schriften* III:620; tr. Loemker p. 657).

[20] On the merely natural indivisibility of atoms, see also Beeckman, *Journal* II:245: "Ego vero, cum statuo atomos, non tales imaginor ut nequeam eas mente dividere, sed tales quae, cum poris careant, reipsa nequeant dividi."

[21] More, criticizing Descartes's denial of the possibility of empty space: "Idem non sensit literata antiquitas, Epicurus, Democritus, Lucretius, aliique" (Descartes, *Oeuvres* V:241). Descartes replies: "Nec dubitavi a magnis viris, Epicuro, Democrito, Lucretio, hac in re dissentire; vidi enim illos non firmam aliquam rationem esse secutos, sed falsum praeiudicium, quo omnes ab ineunte aetate fuimus imbuti. . . . Quod praeiudicium cum ab Epicuro, Democrito, Lucretio non fuerit umquam reiectum, illorum authoritatem sequi non debeo" (V:271).

[22] John Webster's prescription for a post-Aristotelian philosophy runs as follows: "That the Philosophy of Plato, revived and methodized by Franciscus Patritius, Marsilius Ficinus, and others, that of Democritus cleared and in some measure demonstrated by Renatus des Cartes, Regius, Phocylides Holwarda, and some others; that of Epicurus illustrated by Petrus Gassendus; that of Philolaus, Empedocles, and Parmenides, resuscitated by Telesius, Campanella,

disagreements between atomists and Cartesians, stresses instead their areas of agreement, in rejecting substantial forms and real qualities in favor of "deducing all the phenomena of nature from matter and local motion." So he concludes that the two camps "might be thought to agree in the main, and their hypotheses might by a person of a reconciling disposition be looked on as, upon the matter, one Philosophy" (*Certain Physiological Essays* [*Works* II:87]). In adopting the term 'corpuscularian' to describe the mainstream of post-scholastic thought, I am following Boyle's "reconciling" strategy.[23]

Another instance of the tendency to construe atomism broadly is its association with nominalism. This is surprising on its face, since none of the canonical nominalists believed in indivisible atoms, nor did they even embrace full-blown corpuscularianism. Still, the connection was persistently drawn. We saw William Euvrie propose Epicurus as the ultimate founder of the nominalist movement—a connection he seems to have picked up from a contemporary arts master at Paris, Johannes de Nova Domo. Pedro Fonseca still sees a link between nominalism and Epicureanism in the later sixteenth century. Joachim Jungius, in 1625, finds it illuminating to describe Democritus as an Ockhamist.[24] This makes little sense when atomism is understood narrowly, as the belief in indivisible atoms. But that narrow construal is not the usual one. Throughout our four centuries, it is common to associate the atomists with corpuscularianism in general. Thus Ralph Cudworth, in making the usual claim that Aristotle was outside the mainstream of ancient thought, characterizes the atomists in terms that do not even mention atoms:

Wherefore, I think, it cannot be reasonably doubted but that the generality of the old physiologers before Aristotle and Democritus did pursue the atomical way, which is to resolve the corporeal phenomena not into forms, qualities, and species, but into figures, motions, and fancies. (*True Intellectual System* I.1.16)

It is this construal of "the atomical way" (line 2) that made its association with Descartes so irresistible, and made it natural to think that nominalism was a kind of proto-

---

and some besides; and that excellent magnetical philosophy found out by Doctor Gilbert; that of Hermes, revived by the Paracelsian School, may be brought into examination and practice, that whatsoever in any of them, or others of what sort so ever, may be found agreeable to truth and demonstration, may be embraced and received; for there are none of them but have excellent and profitable things, and few of them but may justly be equalized with Aristotle and the Scholastic learning, nay, I am confident upon due and serious perusal and trial, would be found far to excel them" (*Academiarum examen* ch. 10, p. 106).

Other examples of Descartes's being placed in the tradition of ancient atomism include Honoré Fabri, who repeatedly characterizes him as a "Democritean" (Des Chene, "Wine and Water" pp. 363–4) and Creech, whose preface to his translation of Lucretius suggests that "on these leaves you find the pearls of Cartesianism" (f. b3v).

[23] On Descartes and atomism, see Roux, "Descartes atomiste?" Garber, "Descartes and the Revolution," contains an illuminating discussion of the exchange with Froidmont, although it strikes me as too simple to remark that "Descartes was right, of course . . . he was also quite clear in rejecting both atoms and the void, the *sine qua non* of atomism" (p. 476). Accordingly, I think it wrong to remark, of Descartes's departures from atomism, that "Froidmont seems to have seen none of this. What he saw was the shade of Epicurus *redivivus*; he immediately assimilated Descartes to a familiar category" (ibid.). My view, on the contrary, is that Descartes did belong to that familiar category, and that he departed from it in only incidental ways. For a subsequent rejection of indivisible atoms much like Descartes's, see Margaret Cavendish, *Observations upon Experimental Philosophy* pp. 125, 263. For earlier versions of the objection that what is extended cannot be indivisible, see Suárez, *Disp. meta.* 13.2.2 and, even earlier, Giles of Rome, *In De gen. et cor.* I, f. 217v.

[24] For Johannes de Nova Domo as the source of the link between nominalism and Epicureanism, see Kaluza, *Les querelles* pp. 19–20. For Fonseca, see *In Meta.* V.28.2.1 (II:951), where the focus is the theory of universals, but still the link to Epicureanism is present. I owe the remark from Jungius to Lasswitz, *Geschichte* II:248–9.

atomism or, as we saw Leibniz remark earlier, the scholastic theory "most consistent" with modern ideas.

Here are seven theses associated with the doctrine of atomism:

1. There are indivisible corpuscles (= atoms).
2. There is void space.
3. Corpuscles are ingenerable and incorruptible (= corpuscular prime matter; see §3.2).
4. All bodies are composed solely of corpuscles and their aggregates (= corpuscularianism; see §1.3).
5. Causation among bodies is limited to collisions among corpuscles and their aggregates (= mechanism; see §1.3).
6. The only kinds of bodily qualities are those kinds that can be found at the microcorpuscular level; sensible qualities are in fact sensations (Chs. 22–3).
7. The only genuine entities are the corpuscles: (a) they themselves are simple (§26.4), and (b) what they compose are mere aggregates (Chs. 28–9).

Taken together, these seven theses amount to an extremely radical conception of the material world, according to which neither you nor I exist, nor is anything in the world the way it superficially seems to be. Democritus himself may have endorsed all of these theses,[25] but it is hard to find any subsequent atomist who went so far. Still, the reason the atomist tradition has been an object of such enduring interest—ever since the seventeenth century—is that it has implicitly been understood as a broader thesis than the label 'atomism' would suggest, as including not just (1), or (1) and (2), but often (3), (4), and (5) as well, and perhaps even (6) and (7), at least in some attenuated form. The canonical nominalists accept not one of these theses, and so their association with atomism is misleading. But it is more reasonable to think of Descartes as a part of the atomist movement, at least for a person of Boyle's "reconciling disposition," for even if Descartes denied (1) and (2), he accepted much of the broader agenda. (Just how much of it he accepted is a question for future chapters.)

It seems hopeless to try to disassociate 'atomism' from (1) on the above list—the verbal connections are just too strong. But it is quite wrong to suppose that (1) bears any close connection to the subsequent theses. Admittedly, there is some connection between (1) and (2), inasmuch as the standard rationale for the indivisibility of the atoms was the thought that only they are entirely free of void space, and therefore (?) are unbreakable. But even that connection was not inviolable, inasmuch as there were advocates of (1) who rejected (2), and advocates of (2) who rejected (1).[26] And once one goes farther down the list, the connection to (1) disappears entirely. Hence Descartes's rejection of atoms is irrelevant to his defense of (3)–(5), and Sennert's embrace of atoms is perfectly consistent with his rejection of (3)–(7) and indeed with his thoroughly conservative views regarding forms, qualities, and other core Aristotelian doctrines. It is

---

[25] The character of Democritus's own broader ontology is difficult to determine. For discussion, and an argument for a radical reading, see Pasnau, "Democritus."

[26] It was a central thesis of the paradigmatic seventeenth-century atomists that the atoms are unbreakable because they lack void space. See, e.g., Gassendi, *Syntagma* II.1.3.5; Charleton, *Physiologia* II.1.1.4. On atomists holding (1) but not (2), see Meinel, "Early Seventeenth-Century Atomism" p. 89, and Lüthy, "The Fourfold Democritus" p. 453: "we find that almost all early modern atomists—from Giordano Bruno, Sebastien Basson, and David Gorlaeus up to Pierre Gassendi and Isaac Newton—replaced Democritus's empty space with some ether."

not too much to say that for every substantive metaphysical question at issue in the seventeenth century, one can find an advocate of atoms on either side of the question.

The conclusion that should be drawn is not merely that atomism can be understood in multiple senses, as a more or less bold and comprehensive thesis. My claim is stronger: that the prominent place modern scholars have given to atomism has dramatically distorted the philosophical landscape, by implying that divisibility is a central issue when in fact it matters hardly at all, and was not generally even supposed to be fundamental. The core of ancient atomism, for authors during our four centuries, lies in its reductive corpuscularianism. Accordingly, an author's views about the divisibility of bodies are of far less consequence than dozens of other questions in metaphysics and natural philosophy, such as questions concerning prime matter, substantial form, substance, quality, quantity, place, and successive entities. These are the issues around which the study of post-scholastic thought needs to be organized. In what follows, then, the doctrine of atomism will generally stay on the sidelines.[27]

5.5. How Descartes Saved Philosophy

The phrase *philosophia perennis* suggests that philosophical questions reoccur, century after century, and that to those questions there will be the same good answers. This is a view I endorse, once it is given a sufficiently pluralistic formulation. But the doctrine of a perennial philosophy assumes something more that is quite dubious: that there will always be a tradition of asking philosophical questions. Indeed, I think that our four centuries provide an ideal illustration of the fragility of philosophical thought. For as scholasticism collapsed in seventeenth-century Europe, one thing that might easily

---

[27] Sennert provides a nice illustration of how the focus on atomism tends to distort our perspective. Throughout his career, he takes an extremely conservative position in natural philosophy. Even in his late *Hypomnemata physica* (1636) he is still insisting on the central tenets of scholastic Aristotelianism: that "omnium actionum causa prima formae sunt" (I.5 p. 32; tr. *Thirteen Books* p. 426), that "formae per qualitates agunt" (ibid., pp. 34–5; tr. p. 427), and that "dari in rerum natura quatuor elementa, atque ea per suas qualitates, primas dictas seu manifestas et sensui obvias, efficacia esse, extra dubium est" (II.1 p. 43; tr. p. 430). Yet because Sennert's later works are sympathetic to atomism—in the narrow sense of there being a natural limit to the possibility of division (see e.g. *Hypo. phys.* III.1–2)—he commonly gets included in the camp of the "moderns," or at least as a transitional figure. For useful summaries of Sennert's views, see Newman, "Experimental Corpuscular Theory" and Michael, "Daniel Sennert" and "Sennert's Sea Change."

My critical remarks about how to understand 'atomism' in the seventeenth century are by no means unprecedented among sophisticated discussions of the topic. For instance, Pyle, *Atomism and Its Critics* p. xi, treats atomism as resting on four "pillars," roughly equivalent to my (1), (2), (4), and (5). Yet this way of proceeding still puts (1) at the heart of the story, as a necessary condition for making it into the discussion, and so tilts the focus away from the core issues. Marie Boas Hall, more than 40 years ago, questioned whether the atomist tradition is important at all for seventeenth-century developments: "Democritus, Epicurus and Lucretius were much read, . . . but they had relatively little to offer seventeenth-century natural philosophers" ("Matter" p. 77). To this it seems to me that Weisheipl made just the right response, that atomism *is* important for its corpuscular and mechanistic commitments, but not for its commitment to atoms and the void. "In the last analysis it is really irrelevant to seventeenth-century thought whether the particles of matter are absolutely indivisible, as Beeckman, Gassendi and Democritus would have it, or not. It is even irrelevant whether the vacuum exists in nature, or whether space is really empty, or whether the universe is a plenum" ("Comment" p. 101). More recently, and on the basis of a great deal of important new research, Lüthy et al., "Introduction," insist on "corpuscular matter theories," rather than atomism, precisely because "in almost all cases, the choice to use corpuscles instead of atoms did not influence the type of mechanical, micro-anatomical, or chemical explanations that were given" (p. 18). Their verdict, grounded in the history of science, should be extended to philosophy as well.

have happened is that philosophy simply died. That this did not happen is due in large part to René Descartes.

In speaking of the death of philosophy, I am imagining the end of any flourishing public inquiry into abstract questions about nature, values, and the like, approached largely in terms of *a priori* conceptual connections, developed in terms of carefully articulated theses, and supported by arguments in light of potential objections. One might suppose that such modes of thought could never die. Kant remarks in the First Critique that "in all men, as soon as their reason has become ripe for speculation, there has always existed and will always continue to exist some kind of metaphysics" (B21). Perhaps this is so, in our hearts. But whatever private metaphysical musings we might be inclined to undertake, it is surely the case that the survival of institutions that foster the teaching and publication of philosophy cannot be taken for granted. Such institutions have not emerged in all cultures, and they have faded in some, such as early medieval Europe and the modern Islamic world, after thriving there for centuries.

The early seventeenth century was a particularly vulnerable time. When ambitious thinkers considered how best to surmount the stifling legacy of scholastic philosophy, it was an open question just how much of scholasticism to throw out. To be sure, much of Aristotle would go, along with the syllogistic form and the technical vocabulary. But if one looks over the various ways in which authors attempted to go beyond scholasticism, one finds very often that they gave up much more than this—that they gave up the very practice of doing philosophy. Consider, for instance, so-called Renaissance humanism. It is perhaps too much to say that there is *no* philosophy in authors like Giovanni Pico della Mirandola and Marsilio Ficino, but one can at least say that if this sort of work had become the model for post-scholastic thought, then philosophy would have become something very different. The same might be said, a century later, for authors ranging from Giordano Bruno to Michel de Montaigne. Montaigne's "Apology for Raymond Sebond" is a famous landmark of post-scholastic skeptical thought. It is not, however, a work of philosophy. Montaigne, in his free-wheeling way, does from time to time cross onto recognizably philosophical ground, but his way of proceeding is utterly unphilosophical, free of any argumentation or conceptual analysis.

Consider, too, Gassendi's *Exercitationes paradoxicae adversus Aristoteleos* (1624). This was his first published work, and he would later do much better. But reading these *Exercitationes* is a painful exercise for someone with the slightest philosophical sensitivity, because Gassendi's attack is based not just or even primarily on certain specific Aristotelian doctrines, but on the very fact that the Aristotelians were doing philosophy. Gassendi criticizes Aristotle's followers, for instance, for focusing on the most obscure parts of his oeuvre, such as the *Metaphysics* and the *Organon*, rather than concentrating on those parts that are clearest, such as the *Economics*, the *Politics*, and the *De animalibus* (I.1.5). A little later he complains that the Aristotelians have neglected topics like plants, minerals, and elements, in favor of more obscure and metaphysical questions (I.1.7)—and he gives as an example their interest in obscure questions of possibility, such as whether God could make matter without form. Criticisms such as this amount simply to attacking the Aristotelians for asking philosophical questions. What this illustrates is the difficulty, for an early seventeenth-century intellectual, in articulating just what was wrong with scholastic philosophy, and what ought to replace it.[28]

Now consider the case of Galileo. His vision was of course utterly different from those earlier Italian humanists, but he is plainly no philosopher, in our sense of the term. Galileo's remarks on secondary qualities from *The Assayer* are philosophically important (§22.5), but they are peripheral to the monumental intellectual achievement of his later works in cosmology and mechanics. It was in these later dialogues that Galileo set out his own conception of how philosophy should proceed, and though we rightly celebrate that conception today, we no longer think of it as philosophy. Galileo himself of course knew that he was doing something very different. He was trained as a philosopher, and we still have notes from some of his Aristotelian lectures. In his mature work, however, he quite intentionally spurns this traditional, philosophical approach in favor of his own mathematical procedure. In a telling passage from the Second Day of his *Dialogo dei massimi sistemi* (1632), he has the Aristotelian Simplicio make a lofty speech in favor of Aristotle's focus on universals—what motion in general is, for instance, "leaving to mechanics and other low artisans the investigation of the ratios of such accelerations and other more detailed features." To this, Sagredo mildly asks of Salviati whether "you, descending sometimes from the throne of His Peripatetic Majesty, have ever toyed with the investigation of these ratios of acceleration in the motion of falling bodies?" (ed. Flora pp. 524–5; tr. Drake, p. 190). The reference, of course, is to one of Galileo's most famous scientific achievements. And though we of course cheer Galileo on, it is worth keeping in mind that he is in effect asking us to set aside philosophy in favor of doing something else.

Robert Boyle provides another case where scholasticism gets replaced by something very different. Although Boyle thought of himself as a philosopher, he only rarely works in a manner that we would recognize as such. Most of his work is concerned not with abstract analysis but with careful laboratory observation. When confronted with a properly philosophical thesis like the doctrine of substantial forms, Boyle characteristically remarks that "to engage very far in such a metaphysical and nice speculation were unfit for me" (*History of Fluidity and Firmness* [*Works* II:163]). Such remarks all by themselves do not show that Boyle is not a philosopher. We could just as easily imagine words of this sort coming out of the mouth of modern masters such as Gilbert Ryle or John Rawls. The point is that, in reacting against the scholastic era, Boyle chose to replace their arch metaphysics with something that is much closer to science than to philosophy. Of course, it is a commonplace that science grew out of philosophy in the

---

[28] Sennert, although generally conservative in his views, is hostile to metaphysics, and he provides another vivid example of an author's proposing in effect to do away with philosophy. In the prologue of his *Hypomnemata physica* he complains about the discussions ad *nauseam* of questions from Aristotle's physical works that are more metaphysical than physical, such as the status of prime matter, form, privation, and motion: "Physicae enim non satis excultae causam praecipuam esse existimo, quod superioribus seculis, qui maxime subtiles esse sibi visi sunt, maximam aetatis partem in generalissimis illis quaestionibus de materia prima, forma, privatione, motu, et similibus consumserunt, et disputationibus illis toties ad nauseam repetitis tempus triverunt; specialia vero, e quorum tamen observatione principia constituenda sunt, et ea quae Medicinae et aliarum disciplinarum fundamenta constituere debuerunt nunquam aut veluti canes e Nilo bibentes, summo ore vix delibarunt. Hinc adeo factum, ut tot plaustra fere commentariorum in libros Aristotelis physicae generalis nata sint, maximam partem quaestionibus, non physicis sed potius metaphysicis, et saepe inanibus speculationibus referta. Qui vero Aristotelis libros Meteorologicos, De historia animalium, De partibus animalium, De generatione animalium, De plantis legeret, vel in eos commentaretur, pauci reperti sunt, et vix totidem, quot *Thebarum portae, vel divitis ostia Nili*" (ff. †† 6v–7r; tr. *Thirteen Books* p. 415).

early modern era, and that for a time 'philosophy' referred to both disciplines. What I am further suggesting is that science might well have *replaced* philosophy in the seventeenth century, in such a way that our two-thousand-year history of philosophy might have come to an end, replaced by science on the one hand, and by the *belles lettres* of Montaigne, on the other. If this scenario seems absurd, that is only because today we take for granted the discipline of philosophy as a mainstay of higher education, an obligatory offering for any university. There is, however, nothing inevitable in that state of affairs. Consider the cautionary case of theology. Although one can still find theology departments in some modern universities, there is hardly anyone today who does theology in the way that the scholastics did. Philosophy survived, in a way that theology did not. In place of theology, in most universities, we now have religious studies.[29]

Why did philosophy not die a similar death? To the extent that it is credible to focus on the role of any single individual, it seems to me that we have Descartes to thank. Although it is fashionable to stress Descartes's activities as a scientist and mathematician, progress in these areas might have gone on quite unimpeded without Descartes, and indeed might have gone better, inasmuch as most of what Descartes touched in those areas he got wrong. But without the example set by Descartes in his philosophical writings, it is unclear what philosophy today would look like. Descartes was of course every bit as opposed to scholasticism as the other figures I have been mentioning. But unlike Galileo, Boyle, and the young Gassendi, Descartes refused to throw out the philosophy along with the scholastic method. For all that has been written about the *Meditations*, it has not been sufficiently appreciated how remarkable it is that this brilliant man, perhaps the leading mind of his generation, would insist on still doing philosophy—indeed, doing what the *Meditations* calls "first philosophy"—in a way continuous with the ancient and medieval tradition. For all of Descartes's ambitions as an original thinker, he continued to believe that the methods and problems of philosophy were real problems, best solved through the old-fashioned methods of conceptual analysis and *a priori* argument. In the wake of Descartes came Spinoza, Malebranche, Locke, Leibniz—and philosophy was back in business. But if not for the example set by Descartes, the collapse of scholasticism might have meant the end of philosophy.[30]

---

[29] For various educational reformers who are hostile to philosophy, see Jones, *Ancients and Moderns* ch. 5. These proposals for progressive reform met with conservative responses championing the traditional Aristotelian curriculum, a standoff that in effect gets resolved by authors like Descartes and, in England, Locke, who show how it is possible to continue doing philosophy in the post-scholastic context.

[30] I have found that Gibbon long ago voiced something very much like my remarks in this final section. In his *Essai sur l'étude de la littérature* (1761), Gibbon argues that Descartes is the decisive figure in the seventeenth-century's move away from *belles lettres*, toward a mode of discourse focused on physics, mathematics, and (I would stress) philosophy: "Sans doute elle poussa trop loin l'admiration pour ces savans. Souvent leur deffenseur, jamais leur zélateur, j'avouerai sans peine que leurs moeurs étoient grossières, leurs travaux quelquefois minutieux; que leur esprit noyé dans une érudition pédantesque commentoit ce qu'il falloit sentir, et compiloit au-lieu de raisonner. On étoit assés éclairé pour sentir l'utilité de leurs recherches; mais l'on n'étoit ni assés raisonable ni assés poli pour connoitre qu'elles auroient pû être guidées par le flambeau de la Philosophie. La lumiere alloit paroître. Descartes non fut pas Littérateur, mais les Belles-Lettres lui sont bien redevables" (pp. 8–9). I owe the reference to Joy, *Gassendi the Atomist* pp. 204–5.

PART II

SUBSTANCE

6

Subjects and Substances

Prime matter, together with a substantial form, yields a composite substance. The addition of substantial form brings us into the familiar territory of dogs and cats and stones. The territory is not quite as familiar as one might suppose, however, because prime matter plus substantial form yields the substance apart from its familiar sensible qualities. Hence although the composite substance just is, say, Sophie the dog, its character is nearly as obscure as the character of prime matter itself. That obscurity will be the topic of the next chapter. Here I will consider the composite substance as the subject of accidents, and show how the standard view of substance throughout our period is not nearly as straightforward as one might naturally suppose. (Substantial forms themselves will have to wait until Chapter 24.)

6.1. Substance, Thick and Thin

It may look like a mistake from the start—philosophical and exegetical—to distinguish the substance from its sensible qualities, as if it makes sense for there to be a human being of no particular size or color. Whether this does make sense, philosophically, is a question we will come to. There is no doubt, however, that this was the consensus view. Ockham puts this point in his customarily stark way, when introducing prime matter and substantial form:

[Matter] receives nothing other than form. For it should not be imagined that form causes anything else in matter, as if the matter receives from the form something in between matter and form. Rather, matter receives that form and the existence that in reality is the form, and receives nothing else. And these two partial existences, or two partial entities, constitute or make one whole thing or (more properly speaking) are the two parts of one being or total existence that is the whole composed from them. (*Summula* I.9, *Opera phil.* VI:180)

Not everyone would insist quite so strongly that the composite substance is just prime matter and substantial form. Thomists claim that existence (*esse*) is a really distinct component of composite substances, something that Ockham here expressly denies when he identifies existence with form (line 3). Others, such as Scotus, suppose that the individuation of substances requires another, formally distinct ingredient—his famous haecceity. Still others, as we saw in §4.3, think that substantial form inheres in matter that is already informed by indeterminate dimensions. Setting such subtleties aside, however, there was a shared scholastic consensus on this basic formula: that a material substance just is a composite of prime matter and substantial form.[1]

Two features of this formula deserve special attention. First, everyone agreed that this sort of metaphysical analysis, in hylomorphic terms, yields the whole substance. Form and matter are not parts that get added onto the body's integral parts, coexisting at the same level of analysis. If one wants to count integral parts, then form and matter do not enter into the picture. To the question, how many organs does a dog have, one counts all the organs and then stops. To the question, how many corpuscles, one counts corpuscles, then stops. If, on the other hand, one wants to count metaphysical parts, then one does only that, adding substantial form to prime matter and then stopping (again, setting aside certain controversial subtleties). This is especially important to keep in mind in the post-scholastic context, because those authors often proceed as if form and prime matter would have to be some further ingredient *within* a corpuscularian account, without which that account would be incomplete. When the scholastic theory is so understood, it can then be attacked as superfluous, on the grounds that a corpuscular–mechanistic story is sufficient to explain all the phenomena. One of the most important questions to ask about our period is whether this is the right way to understand scholastic thought, and in general whether it is the right way to develop an Aristotelian metaphysics. Often, as we will see in various contexts in the chapters that follow, scholastic authors do offer metaphysical entities as principles of explanation on a concretely physical level, as efficient causes in competition with a corpuscular–mechanistic account of the natural world. The hylomorphic theory admits of an alternative formulation, however, as an explanatory schema at a different level of

---

[1] Walter Burley—Ockham's realist archrival—provides another example of an author's excluding accidents from substances. From his unedited *Topics* commentary: "aggregatum ex Sorte et albedine est ens per accidens, et nullum ens per accidens est Sortes" (Conti, "Ontology in Walter Burley" p. 132n). And from his discussion of relations in his late *ars vetus* commentary: "Illud quod est aggregatum ex rebus diversorum generum non est per se in aliquo genere uno. Sed illud quod significatur per terminum concretum accidentale est aggregatum ex rebus diversorum generum. Ergo non est aliquod tale in aliquo praedicamento vel genere per se. Et ideo illud quod significatur per huiusmodi nomina 'pater' et 'filius' non est per se in genere. Major patet, quia quod est per se in genere debet esse per se ens et per se unum . . . , sed aggregatum ex rebus diversorum generum non est per se ens nec per se unum" (f. e6va).

It is uncontroversial among scholastic authors that the substance, strictly speaking, excludes accidents. It is a more controversial question whether the substance just is, as Ockham says, prime matter plus substantial form. Auriol thinks that it is, but indicates that not everyone agrees: "Secundo, quod huiusmodi entificatio non importat aliquod derelictum ex forma, sicut imaginantur quidam. Primo quia tunc in composito essent tres realitates, scilicet materia, forma, et ille modus a forma in materia derelictus, et si sic tunc materia et forma non perfecte diffinirent compositum, cuius contrarium dicit Commentator" (*Sent.* II.12.2.1, II:175bC). Auriol's interest here is in whether a form's inhering in a subject requires some further entity—which here, anticipating Suárez's later view, he calls a "mode"—in virtue of which it actualizes that subject. This issue will be discussed in §11.4. Also controversial are various further metaphysical components such as Aquinas's distinction between *esse* and *essentia* (see Wippel, *Metaphysical Thought of Thomas* ch. 5) and Scotus's haecceity (see Noone, "Universals and Individuation" pp. 118–21). Finally, there is the question of whether the composite whole just is its parts, or is something over and above its parts. For the view that the whole just is the parts, see Buridan, *In Phys.* I.19 (f. 23vb), where he considers whether it is matter, form, or the composite that is generated. He explains the fact that we customarily speak of the composite as what is generated on the grounds that the composite is what we are familiar with. Strictly speaking, though, the generation of a composite is just the generation of a form in some enduring matter. The composite is nothing more than this. See also Pererius, *De comm. princ.* V.4 (p. 282): " . . . immo non est proprie alia materia nisi prima, nam quae sunt praeter materiam primam sunt formae . . . " and V.18 (p. 323): " . . . in toto composito, hoc est in materia et forma (ponatur enim nunc quod posterius ostendetur, totum compositum nihil esse aliud quam partes eius simul iunctas). . . . " For the broader debate over whether the whole is something over and above its parts, see §28.5.

analysis, not competing with a corpuscular–mechanistic theory, but accounting for abstract, structural features of the world—in particular, the unity and endurance of substances. This is the sort of work that prime matter was put to in Part I of this study, in accounting for the substratum and conservation theses, and in Part VI we will see similar possibilities for substantial form. One diagnosis of the decline of scholastic thought—not that any one diagnosis can really be plausible, on its own—is that the scholastics lost their grip on hylomorphism as a metaphysical theory, conceiving of it instead as a concrete, physical hypothesis about the causal forces at work in the natural realm. Once form and matter were enlisted as explanatory principles of this kind, and so made subject to empirical research into phenomena ranging from embryonic development to the nature of heat, their days were inevitably numbered.

The distinction between metaphysical and integral parts points toward a second feature of the formula, one that lies at the heart of this chapter's concerns. Given that we are counting metaphysical parts when we describe substance as prime matter plus substantial form, we are entitled to infer that the substance contains no other metaphysical parts. This means, in particular, that a substance does not include its accidental forms. That result may seem strange if one thinks of material composites as the ordinary primary substances described in Aristotle's *Categories*, such as "the individual man or the individual horse" (2a15). But the *Categories'* distinction between substance and the nine genera of accidents would standardly be treated as not just an exhaustive but also a mutually exclusive division of being, so that substances are one kind of thing, accidents another, with neither remainder nor overlap. Thus, again according to Ockham, "human being and whiteness are two things (*res*) outside the soul, totally distinct, so that nothing that is one of these or part of one of these is the other or an essential part of the other" (*In Praed.* 7.1, *Opera phil.* II:158). Hence "it is clear both to Christian authors and to the philosophers that an accident is not part of a substance. For it is known to all that a substance is composed of substances, not of accidents. Therefore, no accident can be part of any substance" (*Tract. de corpore Christi* ch. 14, *Opera theol.* X:117–18). Similarly, according to Francis of Marchia, writing not long after Ockham, "it is impossible for an accident to be part of a substance" (*In Meta.* V.5, in Amerini, "Utrum inhaerentia," p. 137 n. 93). Accordingly, it is standard in scholastic discussions to treat the substantial unity of matter and form as different in kind from the merely accidental unity of substance and accident. Here is Scotus:

[F]rom these—namely, from matter and form—comes one thing *per se*. This is not so for subject and accident. For since both matter and form are intrinsic causes of a composite being, they make one thing *per se*. Whiteness and a human being, in contrast, are not intrinsic causes, because a human being can exist in its ultimate actuality without whiteness, and so *per se* it has no potentiality toward whiteness. Thus they make one thing only *per accidens*. (*Sent.* II.12.1.14 [Wadding VI:673; not in *Ordinatio*])

Set aside (until §25.5) Scotus's rationale for distinguishing between these two kinds of unity, and consider just the metaphysical structures described here. Form and matter make one thing, a human being, and that human being is in turn the subject of a further, accidental form, whiteness. Although each level of composition yields unity, the unities are of different kinds, and so apparently we have two rather different kinds of substances: the thin but more strongly unified form–matter composite, and the thick but more loosely unified composite-plus-accidents.[2]

Scotus suggests no names for these two kinds of composites. For that, we might go nearly to the end of our period, to Franco Burgersdijk's *Institutiones metaphysicae* (1640), which distinguishes the (thin) "corporeal substance" from the (thick) "concrete being":

> We speak of a potential composition when two things are united in such a way that one is in potentiality to the other, and the other is the act and form of the first. What is potentially the other is always some sort of substance, and is actualized by either information or inherence. 3
> *Through information*, when a potentiality that is incomplete in its genus takes on the actuality of its genus—that is, takes on substantial actuality—and with it constitutes a body, or a corporeal substance.... *Through inherence*, when a potentiality that is complete in its genus takes on 6 the actuality of another genus—accidental actuality—and with it constitutes a concrete being, such as a white thing, a black thing, etc. (*Institutiones* I.14.4; see also I.22.8, I.24.10)

We might well call the thick substance a "concrete being" (line 7). After all, only at this point have we arrived at a whole, ordinary individual of the sort we can observe. In contrast, the thin "corporeal substance" is something non-concrete, something abstract and metaphysical. Following Burgersdijk's lead, then, I will speak of a *thin metaphysical substance*, versus a *thick concrete substance*. Some such special terminology is needed, because scholastic texts are rife with different senses of '*substantia*,' using the term to refer, among other things, both to thick concrete entities and to thin metaphysical ones. In reading both scholastic and post-scholastic texts, it is crucial to recognize that talk of substances can have either of these senses. Even if authors from our period managed not to confuse themselves in this regard, there is every danger of their confusing us.[3]

6.2. Substance Criteria

This dual usage, thick and thin, can be seen as a consequence of the very concept of *substance*, as it was understood throughout our four centuries. The standard scholastic definitions make this clear. On one standard definition, a substance is an independent entity, capable of existing on its own. On another standard definition, a substance is the

---

[2] On the substance–accident distinction as "totally and perfectly" dividing all beings, corporeal and incorporeal, see Dabillon, *Physique* I.2.1, p. 54. On the thin rather than the thick substance as what has *per se* unity, see Toletus, *In Phys.* I.9.19 concl. 2; Coimbrans, *Physics* I.9.10.1; Eustachius a Sancto Paulo, *Summa* III.1.1.2.5 (II:123–4).

[3] On Aristotle's changing views about substance, from *Cat.* to *Meta.*, see the very comprehensive discussion in Wedin, *Aristotle's Theory of Substance*, ch. IV. On the thick concrete substance as *ens per accidens*, see, e.g., *Meta.* V.7, 1017a8–12, and the discussion in §25.5. Despite Aristotle's frequently distinguishing between the substance and the substance together with its accidents, the standard scholastic view is today controversial. For an extended reading of Aristotle in this way, see Frank Lewis, *Substance and Predication* chs. 3–5. Lewis shares precisely the scholastic view that "accidental compounds are not identical with individual substances, and they are not identical with accidents. Instead, they are *per accidens* beings, constructed out of individual substances and accidents, each of them beings *per se* . . . " (p. 85).

There are hardly any discussions of the thin metaphysical substance in the secondary literature on scholasticism. One exception is some brief remarks in Conti, "Ontology in Walter Burley," who suggests the label 'macro-object' for "an aggregate made up by a primary substance and a host of substantial and accidental forms existing in it and by it" (p. 174). That is effectively the same notion as my talk of a thick concrete substance, though I would demur from his remark that the macro-object is "the basic component of the world" (ibid.). Although this is a natural way to view the situation, I think it fails to respect the implications of the claim that such thick/macro composites are mere *per accidens* unities.

subject of inheritance for properties. Eustachius a Sancto Paulo sets both of these out clearly:

So that you may understand more plainly why particular substances are most properly called substances, note that a substance is so-called both from substanding and from subsisting: for it is proper to substance both to stretch out or exist beneath (*substerni seu subesse*) accidents, which is to substand, and to exist *per se* or not in another, which is to subsist. (*Summa* I.1.3b.1.2, I:51)

If technical terms are wanted for these two identifying characteristics of substance, Eustachius provides them: substances *substand*, which is to say they serve as the subject of accidents, and they *subsist*, which to say they exist *per se*, on their own. These twin features of substance have roots in the *Categories*,[4] and were readily accepted by post-scholastic authors as well. Both criteria appear in Descartes, for instance, in different places,[5] and in Robert Boyle they appear together: "substance is commonly defined to be a thing that subsists of itself and is the subject of accidents—or, more plainly, a real entity or thing that needs not any (*created*) being, that it may exist" (*Origin of Forms and Qualities* V:308; Stewart p. 21).

Spinoza famously deployed the subsistence criterion to show that God is the only substance, a consequence that this criterion might seem obviously to invite.[6] (Boyle, as just quoted, feels he has to guard against this outcome by parenthetically requiring that a substance not be dependent on any "*created*" being.) Certainly, Spinoza was not the first to propose this. John Wyclif reports having heard it argued that all creatures are accidents of God, the one substance. Wyclif himself seems to think that this is a perfectly coherent position, but that it is better to avoid controversy and adhere to the ordinary meaning of 'substance' and 'accident.' (Ironically, he would posthumously be condemned by the Church for, among other things, adhering to just this sort of monism.)[7] When one does adhere to the standard scholastic senses of the terms, the

---

[4] *Categories* ch. 5 points toward these twin criteria for substance in holding that substances are not in a substance (3a7), that substance terms "signify a certain 'this'" ($\tau\acute{o}\delta\epsilon$ $\tau\iota$ $\sigma\eta\mu\alpha\acute{\iota}\nu\epsilon\iota\nu$) (3b10), and that they "receive contraries" (4a10–11).

[5] Descartes offers the substanding criterion in the Second Replies (VII:161): "Omnis res cui inest immediate, ut in subiecto, sive per quam existit aliquid quod percipimus, hoc est aliqua proprietas, sive qualitas, sive attributum, cuius realis idea in nobis est, vocatur *Substantia*. Neque enim ipsius substantiae praecise sumptae aliam habemus ideam, quam quod sit res in qua formaliter vel eminenter existit illud aliquid quod percipimus. . . ." He offers the subsistence criterion at *Principles* I.51 (VIIIA:25): "Per *substantiam* nihil aliud intelligere possumus, quam rem quae ita existit, ut nulla alia re indigeat ad existendum. Et quidem substantia quae nulla plane re indigeat, unica tantum potest intelligi, nempe Deus. Alias vero omnes, non nisi ope concursus Dei existere posse percipimus." For careful discussion of Descartes's various definitions of 'substance,' see, e.g., Markie, "Concepts of Substance" and Stuart, "Descartes's Extended Substance."

[6] Spinoza's monism culminates at *Ethics* I P14: "Except God, no substance can be or be conceived." This has its roots in his definition of 'substance' in I D3: "By 'substance' I understand what is in itself and is conceived through itself, that is, that whose concept does not require the concept of another thing from which it must be formed."

[7] Here is Wyclif's reaction to a proto-Spinozistic monism: "Aliam opinionem audivi, quae est conformior virtuti sermonis, dicentem quod claudit contradictionem aliquam creaturam esse, nisi sit accidens cuius substantia, omnem creaturam induens et substentans, est deus. . . . Ideo pepigi fedus cum me ipso, quod amplius non acciperem occasionem infructuose contendere in talibus, sed supponam famosam significationem terminorum ac distinctionem entium conformiter ad antiquos philosophos et scripturam, quod tota universitas creata, licet sit accidens deo, tamen ipsa dividitur in substantiam et accidens. Substantia est res primae categoriae, quod, licet non possit esse nisi a deo, tamen inter genera entium creata est prius substantia aliis" (*De materia et forma* ch. 1, pp. 168–9). In *De ente praedicamentali* ch. 5, Wyclif himself offers an interesting and lengthy criticism of the stock definitions of substance as *esse per se* and *substare accidentibus*. The leading argument against the first (p. 34) is not that it would make God the *only* substance, but merely that it would make God *a* substance. Like most scholastics, Wyclif thinks this is a bad result, because he thinks that God lies outside the genera described by the categorial scheme. Nevertheless, the Council of Constance (1414–18)

Spinozistic result can scarcely arise. God is plausibly said to be the only substance when 'exists *per se*' is understood as *existing on its own, independently of everything else*. Scholastic authors, however, understand 'exists *per se*' as *not existing in another*—that is, not inhering in a subject. The idea has roots in Aristotle—"it is common to every substance not to be in a subject" (*Cat.* 3a7)—and in Avicenna's often cited discussion of this definition in his *Metaphysics*. Among Latin scholastics, this meaning becomes commonplace.[8] Thus Aquinas: "*Per se* seems to import only a negation, for a being is said to be *per se* as a result of its not being in another, which is a pure negation. . . . Therefore the character of substance must be understood in this way: that a substance is a thing suited to exist not in a subject" (*Summa contra gent.* I.25.236). This view endures until the end of the scholastic era. Eustachius makes this clear when, in the above quoted passage, he glosses 'to exist *per se*' as meaning "not in another" (line 4). A page earlier he had remarked that "to subsist, or to exist by itself, is nothing other than not to exist in another thing as in a subject of inherence" (*Summa* I.1.3b.1.1, I:50). And Burgersdijk: "to subsist *per se* is nothing other than not to be in another as in a subject. Therefore, for a substance to be said to subsist *per se* it is not necessary that it not depend on something else. All that is required is that it not depend on another as on a subject" (*Inst. logicae* I.4, p. 15).[9] Even at the end of the seventeenth century, Pierre Bayle objects against Spinoza that, on the standard view of the philosophers, "to subsist by itself signifies only not being dependent on any subject of inhesion" (*Dictionnaire*, "Spinoza" [XIII:463a; tr. p. 331]). To insist that substancehood requires absolute independence is thus, from the scholastic perspective, an absurdly strong requirement, and amounts to a kind of undergraduate mistake about what *per se* existence involves. Here, as we will see repeatedly in the chapters to come, philosophy displays the sort of pattern that Harold Bloom has argued for in poetics (§1.4): that innovation, very often, is a byproduct of misinterpretation.[10]

condemned, among a long list of views ascribed to Wyclif, the doctrine that "every being is everywhere, since every being is God" (see Michael, "John Wyclif's Atomism" p. 187).

[8] For the Latin Avicenna's discussion of how to define 'substance,' see *Meta.* II.1 (I:65); VIII.4 (II:403–4). For scholastic accounts, see Henry of Ghent, *Summa* 32.5 (*Opera* XXVII:76ff.); Thomas of Sutton: "Quod autem subsistit et substat, illud per se exsistit, et non est in alio et etiam aliis suponitur. Neque materia per se exsistit, neque forma, sed compositum ex utroque; et ideo compositum ex materia et forma proprissime dicitur substantia, quia ipsi convenit per se exsistere et aliis substare. Principaliter autem et maxime convenit hoc substantiis individuis, quia illae non solum subiciunt accidentibus, sed etiam substantiis universalibus, quae de ipsis praedicantur" (*In Praed.*, in Conti, "Thomas Sutton's Commentary" p. 197); Alexander of Alexandria, *In Meta.* I.3; and Francis of Marchia, as quoted in Ch. 7 note 12. Broackes, "Substance" pp. 135–6, is very good on the proper meaning of subsistence in scholastic authors.

In effect, to characterize substances as beings that do not inhere in a subject is to define them as entities that are not accidents. This is Ockham's approach. "[S]ubstantia multipliciter accipitur. Uno modo substantia dicitur quaecumque res distincta ab aliis. . . . Aliter dicitur substantia magis stricte omnis res quae non est accidens realiter inhaerens alteri. Et sic substantia dicitur tam de materia quam de forma quam etiam de composito ex utrisque. Aliter dicitur substantia strictissime de illo quod nec est accidens alteri inhaerens nec est pars alicuius essentialis, quamvis possit componere cum aliquo accidente" (*Summa logicae* I.42, I:118).

[9] For later definitions of 'substance,' see also Scheibler, *Metaphys.* II.1.3.2 (p. 432) and *Philosophia compendiosa* II.2.1.3–4: "Substantia est ens per se subsistens, ut *Homo*. Per se subsistere est non subsistere in alio inhaesive, tanquam in subjecto"; Crakanthorpe, *Intro. in meta.* ch. 5 p. 43: substance is "ens finitum per se subsistens, id est, nulli inhaerens." Suárez: "ex quo colligitur differentia inter substantiam et accidens, quod substantia etiam creata non requirit in universum materialem causam, ut supra ostensum est, accidens vero omne illam requirit" (*Disp. meta.* 14.1.3). To require independence only from a material cause is, in effect, to require only that a substance not inhere in something.

[10] Thomas Manlevelt (*circa* 1330) nicely identifies the ambiguity in the subsistence criterion that leads to monism: "Secunda distinctio est ista, quod per se existere accipitur multipliciter. Uno modo scilicet pro illo quod non est pars alicuius per se unius, et a nullo dependet vel sustinetur. Et isto modo solus deus per se subsistit. Alio modo accipitur pro

The subsistence criterion appears to rule out accidents, but is otherwise, taken by itself, highly latitudinous. The thick concrete substance counts, since even if some of its parts (the accidents) inhere in some of its other parts (the thin substance), still the thick substance as a whole does not inhere in anything. But of course the subsistence criterion does not uniquely pick out thick substances. The thin metaphysical substance qualifies, as does any given integral part of such a substance, as does any collection of substances, up to and including the whole universe. Even prime matter qualifies, despite its dependence on form, because it is independent in the relevant sense, since it does not inhere in anything else. Thus Suárez proves that prime matter counts as a substance by reasoning that "prime matter is a being that is not in a subject, for nothing could be more incompatible with that which is the first subject" (*Disp. meta.* 13.4.4). Corpuscularian critics of scholasticism, who themselves tended to think that only substances exist, could not see how the scholastics could keep from treating *all* of their various metaphysical parts as substances, including even accidents. Setting aside that question until §10.1, let us observe only that the subsistence criterion by itself hardly does much to narrow down the field of substance candidates, and certainly does not get us to the thin metaphysical substance.

The substanding criterion gets us farther, and in particular it seems to rule out thick concrete substances. To say, with Eustachius, that a substance is what "stretches out beneath accidents" suggests that the substance is something apart from those accidents, and thus we arrive at the thin metaphysical substance. To be sure, the two criteria together still do not *uniquely* pick out thin substances. The integral parts of a substance, such as a hand, certainly satisfy the two criteria, and if aggregates like a pint of strawberries can be the subject of accidents, then they too would satisfy the criteria.[11] This is, however, no objection to the theory. The twin criteria we are considering are intended only to carve off substances from other items in the categorial scheme—that is, from other beings. A pint of strawberries is not a substance not because it fails the twin criteria, but because it fails to be a being at all, except *per accidens*. The same is true, as we saw in the previous section, for the thick substance, which we can call "a substance" as a matter of courtesy, but which strictly speaking is not *a* thing at all. In the case of integral parts, the story is rather different. A hand is a substance, and if we are talking about a thin metaphysical hand, then it is a *per se* unity, and so counts as a substance in the strongest sense. That is, hands and other integral parts do have a place

---

illo quod non est pars alicuius per se unius, nec est in aliquo tamquam in subiecto. Et isto modo substantiae separatae et substantiae compositae perfectae per se subsistent" (*In Praed.* q. 16 nn. 18–19 [Andrews, "Thomas Maulevelt" p. 361]).

   Although Descartes was probably not the first, he is surely the most influential proponent of the notion that *per se* existence should be understood as "needing no other thing to exist." (For this conception of the subsistence criterion, see also his August 1641 letter to Hyperaspistes [III:429].) It is difficult to know whether Descartes means to defend the standard criterion, but expresses himself in a way that would subsequently be liable to mislead, or whether he in fact means to be doing something new. Modern scholars, without being aware of this interpretive choice, tend to read Descartes as requiring absolute causal independence, which leads them to suspect Descartes of various further unorthodox views regarding causality and the nature of material substance. I will have a great deal more to say about Descartes's conception of material substance in Part VI, but the argument will not turn on the dubious doctrine of substances as causally independent.

   [11] Even some thick substances satisfy both the subsisting and the substanding criteria, on some accounts. Thomists, for instance, think that qualities and other accidents inhere not directly in the thin substance, but in the thin substance as informed by quantity. This means that, on this view, there is a substance halfway between thick and thin, the quantified thin substance, which satisfies both criteria. Even this halfway substance, however, will be a mere *per accidens* unity.

on the categorial scheme, and they are substances rather than accidents. It would indeed be a problem if these substance criteria *did not* extend to integral parts, because they would then have no place at all among the genera of beings. Of course, once such parts are counted as substance, a host of further questions arise, and some of these will be the subject of future chapters: What makes some collections of parts count as genuine substances, whereas others are mere accidental unities? (Ch. 24) Is there any principled basis for distinguishing between what counts as a whole substance and what counts as a mere part? (Ch. 25) Does each and every integral part of a substance count as an actual substance? (Ch. 26) Since the theory of substance at issue here is not intended to resolve such questions, we should set them aside for now and focus on what that theory does yield: the substance–accident distinction.

The substanding criterion seems to make the substance–accident distinction inevitable. To say that a property inheres in some subject just is to conceive of the subject apart from that property. (Obviously, the usual spatial metaphors only make the implication stronger.) To say that a set of properties inheres in some one subject is, by the same token, to conceive of that subject apart from any of those properties. Thus the subject of inherence for all the properties of a certain substance will itself be free of all those properties. And once we get a thin metaphysical substance, we immediately get accidental forms, as the complementary metaphysical ingredients of the analysis. With that we have arrived at the venerated and scorned Aristotelian distinction between substance and accident.

It is natural to fear that our discussion has just made a disastrous wrong turn, blithely jumping from the unremarkable observation that substances have properties of one sort or another to the conclusion that there must be a metaphysical part of those substances, the thin substance, in which those properties inhere, and another kind of metaphysical part, the accidental form, that does the inhering. To be sure, we have made an unwarranted jump. Whereas earlier chapters worked hard to reach the very tentative conclusion that there might be reasons to postulate metaphysical prime matter, here we have simply helped ourselves to the substance–accident distinction, as if it fell off the back of a truck. The truck, here, was the standard, two-part definition of substance. So rather than scoop up for free this scholastic ontology, we might reject that definition, and hold that the scholastics have the wrong concept of *substance*. Better yet, we might hold that definition in abeyance until we decide on a fundamental ontology. The two-part definition is not supposed to settle such fundamental issues; rather, the definition presupposes that we have already embraced some sort of substance–accident distinction, and then tells that if we want to find the substances, we should go looking for the things that (1) are not accidents and (2) are the subjects of accidents. What we are seeing, then, is that these much-discussed definitions of substance actually do not do very much work: perhaps they describe what a substance essentially is (§7.3), but they do not motivate the substance–accident distinction, no more than they settle any of the hard questions about what is and is not a substance.

If the substance–accident ontology does not fall out of the definition of what a substance is, then how does it arise? No doubt, part of its appeal comes from an uncritical reliance on the surface structure of language. Since language attaches predicates to subjects, it is easy to suppose that the world's structure corresponds. This sort of simple-minded thought should have carried little weight with scholastic authors, however. They had at their disposal a variety of semantic theories that explained predication without any commitment to a substance–accident ontology, such as Ockham's version of supposition theory, which he formulated in the interests of his own austere ontological program.[12] Still, Ockham and almost every other scholastic author accepted a substance–accident ontology. They did so because, working from the ground up, they found themselves committed to the various pieces of the ontology; first, as we have seen, to prime matter, then to accidental forms, and finally to substantial form, as what gives unity to the whole composite. The real heart of the substance–accident framework, then, lies in its arguments, one by one, for the various metaphysical ingredients of the hylomorphic story. Subsequent chapters will work through various pieces of this theory.

From the post-scholastic, corpuscular perspective, this scholastic ontology certainly looked like a disaster. As late as 1739, one finds Hume still complaining of "those philosophers who found so much of their reasonings on the distinction of substance and accident" (*Treatise* I.1.6). What exactly is so bad about that? One sort of problem, with which Hume was much concerned, centers on whether such a distinction leaves room for any knowledge of substances themselves. This will be the topic of the next chapter. A second sort of problem would arise if the thin metaphysical substance that serves as the subject for accidents were nothing more than a bare substratum. This, however, is far from being the case. On the contrary, a form–matter composite is quite rich in character, having not just whatever characteristics arise from the side of prime matter, but also those characteristics that arise from the side of substantial form. Most importantly, the thin substance contains the essence of the substance. Indeed, in a very real sense, the thin substance just is the dog or cat or stone. Such things, inasmuch as they are genuine, truly unified substances, are thin substances. The thick concrete substance, in contrast, as stressed already, is not a genuine unity at all, and so not properly a thing. As Francis of Marchia puts it, "an accident is not the same as its subject, nor does any third thing result from them, since that third thing would be formally neither a substance nor an accident" (*In Meta.* V.4, in Amerini, "Utrum inhaerentia" p. 127 n. 76). In saying this, Marchia relies on the substance–accident schema's being both exclusive and exhaustive. The result is that the thick substance, though naturally viewed as an ordinary concrete object, is in fact not a being at all. Instead, the thin metaphysical substance, far from being a bare substratum, is the ordinary substance.

A third, related problem would arise if the thin substance, though not completely bare, did not have the accidental properties that inhere in it. In one sense that is just what the theory claims: that the thin substance is free of the accidents that inhere in it. In another sense, though, that is plainly absurd. Elizabeth Anscombe complains in this connection of the idea "so idiotic as to be almost incredible, namely that the substance is the entity that has the properties, and so it itself has not properties" ("Substance"

---

[12] For an overview of scholastic theories of predication, and their ontological commitments, see Klima, "Nominalist Semantics" and Ebbesen, "Concrete Accidental Terms." Ebbesen remarks that, on Ockham's semantics (and also Buridan's), "the substance/accident distinction becomes superfluous" (p. 157). This is perhaps true if one thinks only of semantic considerations; Ockham certainly takes there to be metaphysical considerations behind the substance–accident distinction. For a broader survey of medieval semantics, see Spade, *Thoughts, Words and Things*. For Ockham's semantics in particular, see the various relevant chapters in Spade, *Cambridge Companion to Ockham*.

p. 71). The situation can of course be put more perspicuously. What is beyond dispute is that various accidental predicates can be truly affirmed of a given substantial subject. Does this mean that the substance *has* the corresponding accidents? Yes, on the theory in question, in the sense that those accidents inhere in the thin substance. Also yes, on the theory, in the sense that the accidents are a constitutive (albeit metaphysical) part of the thick concrete substance. But no, in the sense that those accidents are not a part of the thin substance, but are somehow attached to it, or resting on it.

Again, there is no disaster, but perhaps now we can see just where trouble does lie, inasmuch as it has become clear what the theory must maintain. First, obviously, it must maintain an ontology of thin substances and accidents, understood as the metaphysical parts that constitute the thick concrete substance. This is bad enough from the corpuscular perspective, though of course there may be a story to be told about just why we need to postulate such metaphysical entities. Second, the theory understands thin substances and accidents to constitute thick substances in a special way: not simply by overlapping, but through the seemingly obscure relationship of inherence. The subject stretches itself out, as Eustachius puts it, leaving the accidents to lay down on top, and perhaps even penetrate. Unless some sort of good sense can be made of these obscene metaphors, we would have good reason to reject the whole theory. To get clear about this inherence relationship, we need to understand each of the relata: what the subject of inherence is, and what the accidents are that inhere. Both of these issues were highly controversial among scholastic authors. In the remainder of this chapter I take up the first, and defer the second until Chapter 10, before turning in Chapter 11 to the question of the inherence relation itself.

6.3. Subject Candidates

If substances necessarily substand—serve as subjects for accidents—then it becomes especially important to work out just what sorts of things accidents do inhere in. Accidents do not inhere in God, which is one reason why scholastic authors do not generally regard God as a substance. Accidents do, however, inhere in the rational soul, inasmuch as our various intellectual and volitional states are thought to be forms inhering in the powers of intellect and will. If this were not the case, then the rational soul could not count as a substance. One notorious foray down that road was made by Blasius of Parma, the *Doctor diabolicus*, who argued in lectures on the soul given in Padua in 1385 that prime matter is the subject of all our intellectual and moral states. This implies that such states cannot exist apart from the body, which seems to imply further that the soul itself cannot exist apart from the body. Stopping just shy of that conclusion, Blasius urged that the intellect's separability be accepted solely on faith, since on philosophical grounds we have reason to deny it.[13] (Reprimanded by the ecclesiastical authorities for such claims, Blasius adopts a much more blandly orthodox

---

[13] Blasius reaches this key conclusion: "Tertia conclusio: omnium habitum intellectualium et moralium est materia rerum subiectum immediatum" (*In De an.* I.8, p. 65). See also II.13, p. 120: "Quarto conclusio: cuiuslibet formae, tam substantialis quam accidentalis, materia est subiectum.... Et tunc sequuntur corollaria. Primum: nulla scientia est in anima.... Secundum corollarium: nullus conceptus est in anima, nec species lapidis est in anima, dum anima intelligit lapidem."

position in another set of lectures some eleven years later—just one of innumerable instances where religious pressure circumscribed the permissible boundaries of philosophical speculation [Ch. 20].)

Blasius may be the only instance of a scholastic author's denying that our intellectual and volitional states inhere in the soul. It is not at all unusual in general, however, to suppose that the accidents of material substances inhere in prime matter. Although I have been assuming, so far, that accidents would inhere in the form–matter composite, there was in fact considerable controversy over this issue. The two great masters of the classical period of scholasticism—Aquinas and Scotus—treat the material composite as the subject of accidents, as did Ockham. But as it became more common to ascribe indeterminate dimensions to prime matter (§4.3), it also became common to think that other accidental forms inhere in prime matter. This was Blasius's view, but in this he was simply following a well-established tradition. That tradition goes back at least to Peter Auriol, but was given its most influential statement by Gregory of Rimini, who in 1343 produced the last in the line of great scholastic *Sentences* commentaries.[14]

Rimini distinguishes three views: that accidents inhere in the composite, that they inhere in the accident of quantity (a view associated with Thomism), and that they inhere in prime matter. He argues for the last of these on the grounds that a form inheres in what has potentiality for it, and that it is matter that has the appropriate potentiality. On its face, this does not seem very persuasive. Why not say instead that the composite (the human being, say) is what is potentially hot or cold, pale or dark? Moreover, the view seems to face an obvious and devastating difficulty: that we ascribe such accidents to the composite, inasmuch as the composite is what is said to be hot or cold, pale or dark. Surely such facts about predication correspond to facts about inherence. Yet, despite appearances, and despite contradicting the grand old men of scholasticism, Rimini's view would become enormously influential. It would soon be championed by John Buridan, Marsilius of Inghen, and Paul of Venice, and by the end of the sixteenth century the cautious Jesuit commentators, always eager to defend the *opinio communis*, found themselves forced to choose between two equally established theories—what Franciscus Toletus called *duae celeberrimae opiniones* (*In Gen. et cor.* I.7 f. 262vb). Perhaps the best testimony to the influence of Rimini's view is that all the most important Jesuit authors— Toletus, Pererius, Suárez, and the Coimbrans—took his side. (The third possibility, that accidents inhere in quantity, is best set aside in this context, partly because it is intimately connected to the theory of the Eucharist, and partly because it simply leads to the question of where quantity inheres.)[15]

---

[14] Auriol, *Sent.* II.12.1.6 (II:169bB): "Quantum ad primum pono conclusionem unam, scilicet quod materia est subiectum immediatum respectu omnium accidentium quae sunt in composito...." Gregory of Rimini, *Sent.* II.12.2.2: "Per illud sui tantum compositum est subiectum formae sive substantialis sive accidentalis, per quod tantum ipsum, antequam ipsam haberet, erat in potentia receptiva ad illam. Hoc patet, quia cuius est potentia, eius est actus. Sed per solam materiam compositum erat in potentia receptiva ad formam quamlibet corporalem quam habet. Ergo etc."

[15] In favor of accidents inhering in prime matter: John Dumbleton, *Summa* II.19; Buridan, *In Gen. et cor.* II.7; Marsilius, *In Gen. et cor.* I.7; Paul of Venice, *Summa phil. nat.* III.14, f. 43rv; John Major, *Sent.* II.16, f. 33v; Jean Paul Pernumia, *Phil. nat.* I.7, f. 21r; Toletus, *In Gen. et cor.* I.7; Pererius, *De communibus principiis* V.20, pp. 328–9; VI.4, pp. 355–6; Suárez, *Disp. meta.* 14.3; Coimbra, *In Gen. et cor.* I.4.4.1; Zabarella, *De rebus nat.*, De generatione chs. 7–10, cols. 414–22; Dabillon, *Physique* II.3.8, p. 120.

Against accidents inhering in prime matter: Anonymous A [see above, §4.1], f. 62raA; Oresme, *In Gen. et cor.* I.8, *In De an.* II.1, pp. 127–8, *In Phys.* I.17, f. 12va; Capreolus, *Defensiones* II.13.1.1, IV:19–20; De Soto, *In Phys.* I.7.12, pp. 55–6;

What was the attraction of letting accidents inhere in prime matter? It was not Rimini's explicit argument from potentiality, but a different argument, which he made elsewhere, and which others would take up over and over. That argument depends on the generally accepted principle that accidents are naturally bound to their subject of inherence, and so cannot jump from one subject to another. This principle has important implications for our present question, for if accidents inhere in prime matter then they can endure through substantial change, whereas if they endure in the composite, they cannot. This gives us a way to grapple with the question of where accidents inhere (and still more reason to care about the issue), because we can now return to the question raised in §4.3 of whether anything beyond prime matter endures through substantial change. The main arguments in favor of letting accidents inhere in prime matter were variations on arguments showing that accidents must survive substantial change. Marsilius of Inghen offers a particularly clear version:

If the qualities that dispose the matter of the thing that is corrupted to generate a new form were corrupted when the thing's form is corrupted, then what brings about the form that is generated? It is unacceptable to say that [i] nothing does. It also cannot be said that [ii] an outside agent does, because this can bring about such a form only through qualities introduced into matter. Nor can it be said that [iii] the qualities themselves do, because according to the view in question those qualities are corrupted along with the corrupted form. This corruption precedes, in order of generation, the generation of the substantial form. Therefore since, when the substantial form is brought about, these qualities do not then exist, they will not bring it about, nor did they bring it about earlier, since none of that substantial form had ever existed, in the case in question. And by the same means it is proved that [ii] no outside agent does it through qualities introduced into the matter. (*In Gen. et cor.* I.7, f. 72vb)

An example will be helpful, and Auriol offers a very clear one in a similar context. Consider water's changing into ice. For a while, the water undergoes accidental change, becoming progressively colder, but eventually the water undergoes what we can suppose for the sake of the example is a substantial change, and becomes ice. The natural assumption would be that the cold of the ice is numerically the same as the cold of the water. Those who argue that accidents inhere in the composite, like Aquinas, are prepared to deny this. If we deny it, however, then Auriol and Marsilius thinks we have no explanation for the ice's generation. For consider that instant when the ice is generated. What explains why that happens? Not the cold of the water, because it has been corrupted. But what else could produce ice? As everyone knows, one makes ice by making water cold. For that to be so, the cold must endure through the change, and so the cold must inhere in the prime matter, since that is the only subject that endures through substantial change.[16]

This argument may look familiar, because it has the same structure as an argument we met in Chapter 2. There the strong *ex nihilo* principle was defended on the grounds that at least some of the ingredients of change must endure through change. The most impressive of such arguments was Scotus's causal simultaneity argument (§2.4), which

---

[16] For Auriol's ice example, see *Sent.* II.12.1.6 (II:169bEF): "... sicut patet de alteratione quae fit circa frigiditatem aquae. Abiicit enim finaliter formam aquae, sicut quando ex aqua fit cristallus, motus[?]. Cum non abiiciatur subiectum, non potest talis alteratio esse in alio quam in materia, et per consequens [non potest] terminus eius, cum motus et terminus aspiciant idem pro subiecto primo." Rimini runs his own argument from ingredients at *Sent.* II.12.2.1, pp. 272–3. Since Rimini knows Auriol's work well, and since their arguments are similar, it seems plausible that Auriol was Rimini's source.

claims that, for the prior ingredients in some new substance to play a causal role in generation, those ingredients have to exist when the new substance begins to exist, and so outlast the corrupted substance. Scotus uses this argument to show that prime matter endures, but the argument proves something more. For in saying that the prior ingredients must endure, we require more than just indeterminate stuff. Ingredients of a certain kind must endure. In the example just considered, we need more than just prime matter to make ice; we need, at a minimum, *cold* prime matter. Hence what endures is not just bare matter, but matter of a certain kind, the right kind to make whatever new thing is to be generated. (The question of exactly how new substantial forms arise was immensely contentious [§28.1], but here I suppose we have a story about that.) Marsilius's argument is therefore extremely powerful. For inasmuch as we do think that the ingredients consumed in making something new play a role in the generation of that new thing, we have reason to accept that what endures through substantial change is something more than bare, indeterminate prime matter.

Such arguments from ingredients make some controversial assumptions, as we saw in §§2.3–4, and so they do not decisively establish that prime matter is the subject of accidents. Still, anyone who accepts this kind of argument for prime matter should think that more than just bare prime matter endures through substantial change. For the Jesuits listed earlier, this was the decisive consideration in favor of prime matter as the subject of accidents. Still, accepting this sort of argument does not straightaway entail that accidents inhere in prime matter. What it entails is that something more than bare prime matter endures through substantial change. For Scotus and Ockham—as we will see in detail in Chapter 25—this something more is a form–matter composite, with multiple substantial forms, one of which can be lost in substantial change while another endures. Hence, at least in the case of living things, which is where their theory applies, they can maintain that accidents endure through substantial change in virtue of inhering in an enduring composite rather than in prime matter. Marsilius, in contrast, and the Jesuits listed earlier, all deny that substances have multiple substantial forms, and so these ingredients arguments force them to locate accidents in prime matter.

6.4. Inherence versus Predication

The previous section briefly sketched a powerful argument against the inherence of accidents in prime matter: that we say the composite is hot, cold, and so on, not that prime matter is. Auriol's example requires our speaking of "cold prime matter," but there seems something absurd about this, inasmuch as it is surely the water that is cold, not the prime matter. Neither Auriol nor Rimini seem to confront this issue explicitly, but Rimini implicitly gestures toward a way out, by claiming that although accidents inhere primarily (*primo*) in prime matter, they inhere *per se* in the composite. He does not spell out what this means, but the idea seems to be that the immediate subject of an accident is prime matter, and yet in some other sense it is proper to treat the composite as the subject. Just a few years after Rimini's lectures, Nicole Oresme describes a much clearer distinction along these same lines, between the subject of reception or inherence and the subject of denomination. This idea would be extensively employed by later authors. Albert of Saxony, lecturing in the 1350s, also in Paris, sets out the distinction clearly:

Being the subject of an accident is said in two ways: either as the subject of inherence or as the subject of denomination. So according to this view [in favor of enduring accidents] it should be said that, for every accident of a material composite, prime matter is its subject with respect to inherence, even if the composite is its subject with respect to denomination. Hence because the composite is better known to us than the matter, it is the composite that we denominate on the basis of the accident, even though the accident is in the matter. Hence we say that the human being is hot, not that his matter is. (*In Gen. et cor.* I.6, f. 136ra)

As Albert understands the distinction, it seems to amount to an error theory. That is, he thinks our language predicates *hot* of *human being* because the metaphysical truth of the situation is too obscure to be reflected in natural languages. The implication of error comes from his ascribing our linguistic practices to our unfamiliarity with matter (lines 4–6)—as if we would do things differently if we were better informed metaphysically. Since language gets the metaphysics wrong here, the metaphysician should simply disregard the linguistic data.

Albert does not himself endorse the view that prime matter is the subject of accidents; he regards both sides of the dispute as defensible. Oresme positively rejects the inherence–denomination distinction, and with it the inherence of forms in prime matter. He argues that facts about predication track facts about inherence, on the ground that a thing is made to be white, say, just in virtue of whiteness's inhering in it. Seemingly, Oresme and Albert agree on this fundamental principle: that an accident makes a thing be such (white, cold) by inhering in that thing. The view Albert recites takes this premise, combined with the premise that accidents inhere in prime matter, to show that we wrongly predicate accidents of composite substances. Oresme, in contrast, cannot believe that language goes so wrong. Prime matter is not truly white, except *per accidens*, he says, just as the soul is white only *per accidens*. The composite is what is truly white; hence, white and other accidents must inhere in the composite.[17]

Although Oresme's discussion of the inherence–denomination distinction is very brief, he is clearly aware of its dramatic implications. One who accepts the distinction either must deny that facts about inherence are the truth-makers for predication, or else must charge ordinary language with massive and systematic error. The first of these alternatives—severing the link between inherence and true predication—resembles a strategy that Ockham and others customarily employed in other contexts, as a consequence of their nominalist semantics. Ockham was after the result that '*S* is *a*' could be true even if there is no accident picked out by *a*. Here, though, we are contemplating a

---

[17] Oresme introduces the inherence–denomination distinction with this remark: "Et si diceretur quod materia prima esset calida, quia accidens denominat suum subiectum tale, dico quod quoddam est subiectum receptionis, et aliud est subiectum denominationis. Modo ad propositum materia prima est subiectum receptionis, recipiens accidentia et sustenans, et totum aggregatum denominatur illo accidente" (*In Gen. et cor.* I.8, pp. 64–5). He rejects it at ibid., p. 69: "Tunc ultimo concludo quod videtur mihi quod secunda via sit probabilior propter hoc: et suppono primo quod illud est subiectum accidentis quod dicitur tale secundum illud accidens, quia accidentis esse est inesse; ideo albedo non est accidens alicui nisi illi cui accidit esse album; secundo, suppono quod materia prima non dicitur esse alba nisi per accidens, sicut etiam anima vel forma non dicitur alba, sed totum compositum." See also *In Phys.* I.17, f. 12va: "non dicimus quod materia est alba aut calida sed homo est albus et ignis est calidus etc, unde materia non est alba nec forma sed totum compositum. Ex isto sequitur quod materia non est subjectum immediatum vel proprium talium accidentium, patet quia solum illud est subjectum quod denominator tale et materia non est huius <modi>."

situation where 'a' does pick out an accident, but the accident inheres in something other than S. Oresme's complaint is that, in such a case, the thing that is a, most properly speaking, is the thing in which a inheres. It would be true to say that 'S is a' only derivatively, in the way that a whole can have some character in virtue of one of its parts. Oresme believes both that locating accidents in prime matter would render ordinary language false, and that that is an unacceptable outcome. Others, however, were prepared to accept that outcome. Albert gestures toward it, and his remarks were restated more vigorously a few years later, in a very similar passage from Marsilius of Inghen. He remarks that the reason we do not ascribe accidents to prime matter is that "ordinary folk are unaware of matter" (In Gen. et cor. I.7, f. 72va). Where Albert had hesitated, Marsilius positively endorses this sort of error theory regarding ordinary predication.[18]

The ultimate source of the inherence–denomination distinction is perhaps John Buridan, who exercised a strong influence on Oresme, Albert, and Marsilius.[19] In his *Physics* commentary, Buridan wonders why, in cases of accidental change, we say that the underlying substance (the composite) is what is changed, in virtue of its receiving something, whereas in cases of substantial change we say that what is changed is not the thing that endures and receives a new form (the prime matter), but the thing that comes into existence (the composite substance). Buridan's diagnosis of this asymmetry is very similar to Albert's and Marsilius's earlier-quoted remarks: "substances actually subsisting on their own are known to us and to ordinary folk.... Prime matter, however, is not known to ordinary folk and so we attribute changes and mutations not to prime matter but to the composite substance subsisting on its own."[20] Hence although consistency would seem to require that we predicate substantial change of prime matter, ordinary language attaches to the things we know. Does that mean that ordinary language is false here? Interestingly, for Buridan it does not. He immediately adds that "these things are not said wrongly, because names signify conventionally" (In Phys. I.19, f. 23vb). The implication is that although natural language may not be metaphysically ideal, it can still be true if used in accord with the way we decide to use it. Hence even if cold inheres not in the water but in the water's prime matter, it can still be perfectly true to say that the water is cold, and false to say that the prime matter is cold. Buridan therefore embraces the other horn of Oresme's dilemma, and contends that facts about inherence need not be the truth-makers for predication.

Nothing could be more discouraging to the project of philosophical analysis than Buridan's claim that language works simply by convention, irrespective of the

---

[18] Marsilius of Inghen, In Gen. et cor. I.7, f. 72va: "Secunda conclusio: aliquae qualitates donominant totum compositum et non materiam primam, quia materia non dicitur calida aut frigida, sed aqua vel ignis. Et causa huius est quia vulgares materiam ignorant, et ideo sibi denominationem non attribuunt." Most of the authors cited earlier in favor of accidents inhering in prime matter appeal to this inherence–denomination distinction.

[19] On the relationship between Buridan, Oresme, Albert, and Marsilius, see Thijssen, "The Buridan School," who cautions against the idea that these figures constituted a "school" in any meaningful way.

[20] Buridan expressly invokes the inherence–denomination distinction with respect to accidents at In Gen. et cor. II.7: "Nota pro solutione rationum quod aliud est subiectum cui tales primae qualitates attribuuntur, et aliud est subiectum de cuius potentia educuntur et quod est per se ex natura sua receptivum earum. Nam subiectum de cuius potentia egreditur caliditas vel frigiditas passive et receptive est prima materia.... Sed subiecta quibus tales qualitates attribuuntur sunt substantiae compositae ex materia et forma propter maiorem notitiam earum. Vulgus enim non percipit primam materiam. Igitur illas qualitates sibi non attribuit, sed attribuit eas composito sensato."

metaphysical realities. To some, indeed, this sort of picture of predication seemed flatly incoherent. According to John Wyclif, for instance, "it is contradictory for an accident to inhere in its subject and for one not to say that its subject is thusly characterized (*sic accidentatum*)" (*De materia et forma* ch. 1, p. 167). Yet it is not clear exactly what the contradiction would be here, unless one thinks of prime matter on the model of an integral part. To be sure, it is hard to imagine a form's inhering in an integral part, P, of some whole S, without qualifying P immediately and qualifying S mediately if at all. But metaphysical parts may be different. Earlier we saw how intellectual and volitional states were standardly thought to inhere in the rational soul. Even so, Aristotle had remarked that it is not the soul that thinks, but the human being (*De an.* I.4, 408b13). Perhaps, in a similar way, some forms might inhere in prime matter and yet get ascribed to the whole composite. It is, in any case, hazardous to draw inferences about metaphysical parts on the basis of what is true for integral parts.

7

The Veiled Subject

7.1. Casting Off Naive Empiricism

It is natural to think that we know the world around us by perceiving it, and that what we do not know of material reality is unknown only because it is too small, too far away, or buried too deep under other things. For things near enough and big enough, we perceive them, and by perceiving, know them. Call this naive empiricism. Over the centuries, it has been practically definitive of the philosopher's job to subject naive empiricism to a withering critique. Indeed, stages in the development of philosophy can be measured in terms of how far they depart, and in which direction, from our natural but naive pre-theoretical orientation toward empiricism.

Embracing metaphysical parts is one way to withdraw from naive empiricism, but it is not as straightforward a withdrawal as one might suppose, because scholastic authors regard a kind of metaphysical part—accidental forms in the category of Quality—as the things that are, in themselves, perceived (Chs. 21–2). Hence, for the scholastics, we do not perceive bodies, or their integral parts, except accidentally, inasmuch as we perceive accidental qualities. These metaphysical parts are what our senses directly inform us about. Still, even if not all metaphysical parts are intrinsically obscure, most are. Our perceptual grasp of a certain range of accidental qualities gives us direct acquaintance with only a fragment of what there is, leaving us quite in the dark about the underlying subjects of those accidents, in all their metaphysical complexity.

The move toward corpuscularianism was in some cases a move toward empiricism. To the extent that post-scholastic authors cast off metaphysical parts, they have that much less baggage in need of non-empirical handling. The result was not naive empiricism, of course, given the seventeenth century's famous doubts about whether sensible qualities are in the world (Ch. 22). Moreover, corpuscularian authors retain a surprising degree of commitment to the scholastic idea that beneath the sensible qualities of things lies something more, a subject of those qualities, imperceptible even in principle. In this and the following two chapters, I argue that the retention of this veiled-subject doctrine represents one of the most significant enduring legacies of scholasticism on seventeenth-century thought.

An early corpuscularian restatement of this scholastic idea can be found in Nicholas Hill in 1601: "substance is a subsistent being, independent, ancestor to generation and forebear to matter, not only existing outside of the intellect, but transcending the faculty of understanding, a grasp of which we have only by analogy" (*Philosophia* n. 119). Versions of this same idea would turn up throughout the seventeenth century, in the most thoroughly unscholastic of places. It can be found in Descartes and Locke, as the next two chapters will argue, and also in Gassendi:

> Nothing beyond qualities is perceived by the senses. For a quality is whatever is open to sight, touch, and the other senses. And although the eye is said to see not only color but also a colored body, and also the hand to touch not only hardness but also a hard thing, still this very being 3 colored, or being hard, is a quality. That at the same time we refer to the substance in which the quality inheres, we do this through induction, by which we reason that some subject lies under the quality. . . . The main point is this: although it is granted that a common subject or substance 6 exists, it nevertheless always remains veiled, nor can we either understand or say what sort of thing it is, except through what affects it and what lies open to the senses, its qualities. (*Syntagma* II.1.6.1, I:372a)

This is a remarkable claim for an author engaged in rehabilitating ancient atomism. One might have thought that the substance–accident distinction would have been one of the first pieces of scholastic baggage to be jettisoned by corpuscularian philosophers, and with it the doctrine that beneath the sensible qualities of a thing lies some sort of veiled subject. But although Gassendi does not describe his qualities as accidents or forms—instead, they are modes (§13.4)—he does accept the core idea of a distinction between the quality and what has the quality. And since he thinks that it is the qualities we perceive, he finds it natural to think that the thing that has the qualities—the "common subject or substance" (line 6)—is by nature hidden, and revealed only by some kind of inference that he does not here spell out. (His talk of "induction" [line 5] should not be understood in the modern sense.)[1]

The doctrine of a veiled subject did have its critics. Thomas Hobbes, for instance, flatly denies that there is any such composition of form and matter, or substance and accident:

> His Lordship expounds simplicity, by not being compounded of matter and form, or of substance and accidents, unlearnedly. For nothing can be so compounded. The matter of a chair is wood; the form is the figure it has, apt for the intended use. Does his Lordship think the chair compounded of the wood and the figure? (to Bramhall, IV:302)

Part of the reason Hobbes treats it as self-evident that a chair is not composed of wood and figure is that he refuses to countenance any sort of composition other than integral

---

[1] Gassendi similarly invokes the veiled-subject doctrine in his objections to Descartes's *Meditations* (VII:271). For further discussion of his views in this domain, see §8.4 and §27.2.

A remarkable fifteenth-century instance of the veiled-subject doctrine is that of Lorenzo Valla, who claims that it is not possible to give even an example of a substance, because they lie unknown beneath qualities and actions. Apparent examples of substances are in fact substance–accident composites: "Nam si dicam 'homo,' non est haec substantia, sed res constans ex substantia, qualitate et actione; 'lapis' ex substantia saltem et qualitate, et ita in ceteris" (*Repastinatio* I.1.2; see also I.10.2–3, I.12). For discussion, see Nauta, *In Defense of Common Sense* pp. 20–1.

Broackes, "Substance," collects many seventeenth- and eighteenth-century texts endorsing an underlying subject, finding the doctrine even in Thomas Reid: "all the information that our senses give us about this subject is, that it is that to which such qualities belong. From this, it is evident that our notion of body or matter, as distinguished from its qualities, is a relative notion, and I am afraid it must always be obscure, until men have other faculties" (*Intellectual Powers* II.19; see Broackes p. 156). Broackes's own understanding of these issues is quite different from my own, however, in that he attempts to downplay the significance of appealing to an underlying subject of qualities.

composition. So if there is a substance–accident distinction to be drawn, it will have to be drawn in terms of one body's inhering in another, which is obviously absurd as a theory of accidents. Elsewhere he writes:

An accident's being said to be in a body is not to be taken as if something were contained in that body—as if, for example, redness were in blood in the way that blood is in a bloody cloth, that is, as a part in the whole; for if so then an accident would be a body too. Instead, just as size, rest, or motion is in that which has the size, or is at rest, or moves (everyone understands how this is to be understood), so too every other accident's being in its subject ought to be understood. (*De corpore* 8.3)

So what exactly is an accident for Hobbes, if not one body's inhering in another? He defines it as "the mode of conceiving a body" (*De corpore* 8.2). With this, Hobbes is not just making the commonplace switch from talk of accidents to talk of modes (§13.4), but further giving the notion of mode a subjective character, so that what counts as a mode depends entirely on how we conceive of a thing. In a phrase, this definition undermines both the substance–accident distinction and the veiled-subject doctrine. The first is ruled out because accidents are no longer something in bodies distinct from the substance. The second is ruled out because to grasp a body's accidents just is to grasp something about the body itself. There is no room here for the concept, introduced in §6.1, of a thin metaphysical substance, shorn of its accidents. For Hobbes, everything that exists is a body—"being and body are the same" (*De mundo* 27.1; see §16.2)—and so there is no room for metaphysical entities like the thin substance and its inhering accidents. The only non-reductive conception of accident that could make sense for Hobbes would be an absurd one—if accidents were bodies as blood inheres in a cloth. Hence the scholastic account can never get off the ground on Hobbes's theory. Everything in the world is a body, and so when we perceive the world, we perceive the bodies in it. Those bodies have sizes, shapes, and so on, but the only parts such bodies have are their integral parts—that is, further, smaller bodies. It is only when accidents are conceived of as parts of a different kind—as *metaphysical* parts—that we then get substances of a different kind, as the veiled, metaphysical subject of those accidents.[2]

Hobbes's reductive account seems so clear and straightforward that it is surprising, at first glance, not to find it everywhere in the seventeenth century. Yet, as we will see in the following two chapters, prominent post-scholastic authors like Descartes and Locke decline to take this approach. As a measure of just how influential the

---

[2] For Hobbes's rejection of the substance–accident distinction, see also *Seven Philosophical Problems*, VII.28: "I see by this that those things which the learned call the accidents of bodies are indeed nothing else but diversity of fancy, and are inherent in the sentient and not in the objects, except motion and quantity"; *Answer to Bramhall*, IV:308: "So also in speaking, the thing understood or named is called hypostasis, in respect of the name; so also a body coloured is the hypostasis, substance and subject of the colour; and in like manner of all its other accidents. Essence and all other abstract names, are words artificial belonging to the art of logic, and signify only the manner how we consider the substance itself." See too *De mundo* 27.1: "moveri, quiescere, albescere, et similia accidentia corporum vocamus, et inesse corporibus putamus, quia sunt diversi modi quibus corpora concipimus." And see some English notes on a draft of the *De corpore*: "An accident is not a part of natural things. It is the manner (modus) of conceiving a body or according to which a body is conceived. Or it is the faculty of a body by which it imprints the conception thereof upon us. Or that power or faculty by which a body is conceived. . . . When we say *accidentia in corpore inesse*, it must not be understood as if something were contained in the body: for example, as if redness were in blood as blood is in a bloody cloth i.e. ut pars in toto, for so an accident were also a body" (in Hobbes, *Critique du De mundo* appendix II, pp. 452–3). For further discussion of his rejection of qualities, see §10.2. For his ontology of bodies alone, see §16.2. For his anti-realism regarding sensible qualities, see §22.5. For his nominal view of powers, see §23.1.

substance–accident distinction is, we might consider the lengths to which Newton goes to avoid it. In a fascinating discussion from his *De gravitatione* (*c.*1671)—one of the most impressive philosophical works of the seventeenth century, but published only in modern times and still not sufficiently appreciated—Newton describes a theory of body that does away with the veiled subject. The discussion begins by conceding that it is not possible to prove one or another theory of the structure of bodies. From the observable phenomena, various metaphysical accounts are, for all we know, possible. That is, God could have made bodies in various ways, and we have no way of decisively settling how in fact he did it. Here is one possibility: Take some region of space (Newton had just finished setting out his theory of absolute space), and suppose God makes it impenetrable. Let that region have a certain size and shape; let it reflect light in a certain way, and in general let anything that impinges on it be affected in familiar ways. Suppose that this region *moves*, not in the sense that there is some enduring stuff that changes position in absolute space, but in the sense that God first makes one region of space impenetrable in this way, and then makes another, overlapping region of the same size to be impenetrable in the same way. For all we could tell, this just would be a body:

If God should exercise this power, and cause some region of space above the earth, like a mountain or any other body, to be impervious to bodies and thus stop or reflect light and all impinging things, it seems impossible that, by means of our senses (our sole judges in this matter), we should not consider this space to be truly a body. For it would be tangible on account of its impenetrability, and visible (opaque and colored) on account of the reflection of light, and it would resonate when struck because the adjacent air would be moved by the blow. (pp. 105–6; Janiak pp. 27–8)

An impenetrable region of this sort would be indistinguishable from body. Indeed, it is possible that *all* bodies could be like this. Moreover, although there is no decisive evidence one way or another, Newton suggests some powerful reasons for thinking that in actual fact this *is* what bodies are. The very first is that it avoids postulating a veiled subject:

For the existence of these beings there is no need to imagine some unintelligible substance serving as the subject in which a substantial form inheres. Extension and an act of the divine will suffice. Extension takes the place of the substantial subject, in which the form of the body is   3 conserved by the divine will. That effect of the divine will is the form or formal nature of body, which designates that every dimension of space in which it is produced is a body. (pp. 106–7; Janiak p. 29)

So in place of prime matter, Newton offers extended space. In place of substantial form, he offers the "effect of the divine will" (line 4), which directly makes it the case that a certain region of space will behave *as* a body—or, rather, if Newton's speculative proposal is right, makes it *be* a body. There is no more direct evidence for one theory than for the other, but Newton's account at least avoids the need to postulate a subject that is entirely "unintelligible" (line 1).[3]

---

[3]   Newton specifically argues that his prime-matter analogue, extended space, is preferable because of its reality and intelligibility: "Differunt autem quod extensio—cum sit et quid, et quale, et quantum—habet plus realitatis quam materia prima, atque etiam quod intelligi potest, quemadmodum et forma quam corporibus assignavi" (p. 107; Janiak

In many respects, nothing could be farther from the scholastic approach. Although Newton offers analogues to form and matter, there are no enduring things that constitute the substance. Space as a whole endures, to be sure, but what counts as an enduring body on this view will change its 'matter' whenever it moves. Perhaps one can speak of an enduring divine volition, but that can hardly be a constituent of the body, and moreover the content of that volition changes as the body moves, inasmuch as the volition targets first one region of space and then another. Here, then, Newton's theory of absolute space allows him to reject not just the veiled-subject doctrine, but also the substratum thesis—even the weak doctrine of a substratum that endures through accidental change (§2.2). Still, as radical as this proposal is, it takes for granted that there is something right about the veiled-subject doctrine. Even if that doctrine is wrong in postulating an enduring subject beneath the veils, it is right at least about the veils themselves. That is, Newton accepts that there is no path from the qualities of a thing—its impenetrability, its reflecting light, etc.—to the thing itself. So even in rejecting an underlying subject, in favor of the idea that bodies are simply space so-and-so disposed, Newton displays the enduring attraction of the veiled-subject doctrine. And although the speculative account of the *De gravitatione* does not appear in his later works, the veiled-subject doctrine does. Thus, according to the General Scholium of the *Principia* (2nd ed., 1713), "we grasp nothing (*minime*) of what the substance of any thing is. We see only the shapes and colors of bodies, we hear only their sounds, we touch only their external surfaces, we smell only their smells and taste their flavors. We grasp their inner substances through no sense or reflective act."

7.2. Unknowable Form, Unintelligible Matter

Why should the doctrine of a veiled subject have retained such influence over the whole of our period? One reason, as I have suggested already, is that the substance–accident distinction, combined with the thought that it is accidents we are directly acquainted with, leads almost directly to the idea that the subject of those accidents is something more obscure, either entirely unknowable or else knowable only by inference. This, at any rate, helps to explain the doctrine's prevalence among the scholastics. Even William Ockham, unorthodox in so many respects, accepts that sensible qualities

---

p. 29). He goes on to concede that he has not explained *how* God imposes his will on space in this way—a gap in the intelligibility of his own proposal—but remarks that we are stuck with this puzzle anyway, since it is the same as the puzzle of how *we* will to move our own bodies. Later, he returns to the "vulgar"—that is, scholastic—idea of body as containing a veiled subject: "Quod si vulgarem corporis ideam (aut potius non ideam) amplectimur, scilicet quod in corporibus latet aliqua non intelligibilis realitas quam dicunt substantiam esse in qua qualitates eorum inhaerent..." (p. 109; Janiak pp. 31–2). See Ch. 8 note 22 for Newton's view in the context of Descartes's theory.

Bennett offers Newton's account as a helpful starting point for Spinoza's conception of space as the one extended substance (*Spinoza's Ethics* pp. 88–92). For reasons I do not understand, however, Bennett thinks that Newton makes his proposal as a "joke" (p. 90). It seems to me clear, on the contrary, that Newton is quite serious about his proposal as both physically and epistemically possible. Whether he thinks it likely I do not know. In the much later Query 31 of the *Optics* (1718), Newton takes for granted a more orthodox corpuscularian theory, which embraces the usual substratum thesis.

For the dating of the *De gravitatione* to *c.*1671 see Feingold, *Newtonian Moment* p. 26. The editors of *De grav.* suggest that it dates from the mid-1660s, when Newton was in his early twenties. A comparison with his philosophical notebooks from 1664–5 (ed. McGuire and Tamny) makes this seem unlikely, however, inasmuch as the notebooks are clearly philosophical juvenalia whereas the *De grav.* is a work of considerable philosophical brilliance. (Admittedly, Newton was doing important mathematical work in 1665.)

are really distinct from their subjects (§19.2). He reasons that since it is these qualities that we grasp of external objects, the underlying subjects cannot in themselves be known: "we can naturally cognize no external corporeal substance in itself" (*Ordinatio* I.3.2 [*Opera theol.* II:412]). Although Ockham leaves room here for us to have a grasp of our own intrinsic nature, through introspection, he denies any knowledge of external "corporeal" substances in themselves. To say we cannot know or cognize a substance in itself is to say we cannot grasp its intrinsic, distinctive character. To this extent, substance is unintelligible. Scholastic authors were in general agreement that substance itself is either completely unknowable, or knowable only obliquely, with great difficulty.

Such pessimism—what I am calling the veiled-subject doctrine—is motivated by more than the substance–accident distinction. For inasmuch as scholastic authors conceive of the substance as simply prime matter plus substantial form (§6.1), they can hardly regard it as knowable unless at least one of its parts is knowable. Thus Scotus argues for the unknowability of substance by considering its constituent metaphysical parts: "If matter does not impress upon intellect any actuality with regard to itself, and neither does substantial form, then what simple concept will intellect have of matter or form?" (*Ordinatio* I.3.1.3 n. 146). The consensus answer to this question, going back to the classical authors of the thirteenth century, was that we could have no concept of either matter or form. Aquinas, for instance, holds that "substantial forms, which are unknown to us in their own right, become known through their accidents" (*Summa theol.* 1a 77.1 ad 7). As this passage reflects, Aquinas takes a more optimistic position than some, regarding substantial forms as veiled but not unknowable. He is less optimistic, though, about prime matter: "matter in its own right neither has existence nor is cognizable" (ibid., 15.3 ad 3). Ockham agrees, despite his very difficult conception of what prime matter is: "however much matter is a thing actually existing and necessarily distinct from form, still it is not intelligible of itself (*per se*)—that is, it is not intelligible by a cognition that is simple and proper to it" (*Summula* I.14 [*Opera phil.* VI:194]). Ockham goes on to allow that we can say true things about prime matter. We do so, however, by cobbling together various other concepts, not proper to prime matter, such as *being deprived of a thing* and *being under a thing* and *being a thing*. In this way, we can frame a description that uniquely picks it out, but without having any concept of prime matter in its own right. Ockham takes this to be true not just for prime matter, though, but also for substantial form: "substantial form can be grasped by us through no other way; instead, just as matter is cognized by analogy to form, so substantial form is cognized by analogy to matter" (ibid., VI:195). We break into this apparently closed loop by grasping accidental forms, which lead to an underlying subject, and eventually to its two metaphysical parts.[4]

---

[4] For the veiled-subject doctrine in Ockham, see also *Ord.* I.3.2 (*Opera theol.* II:416–17) and *Quod.* III.6 (*Opera theol.* IX:227): "de substantiis non habeamus experientiam nisi per accidentia, et illa non probant sufficienter quod sit distinctio specifica vel unitas." For the case of substantial forms, see also Henry of Ghent, *Quod.* IV.13 (ed. 1518, I:104vI): "formae enim proprium est agere; unde etiam forma dicitur actus ab agendo, et formas nobis occultas cognoscere non possumus nisi ex actibus earum nobis manifestis." For a later scholastic statement, see Scipion Dupleix: "nous ne voyons pas ni ne touchons les corps, comme le vulgaire pense, ains seulement voyons leurs couleurs, et touchons leur surface extérieure" (*Physique* VIII.20.17).

For Aquinas on knowing essences, see also *De ente* 5.76–81, *Quaest. de spir. creat.* 11 ad 3, *In Post. an.* II.13.119–21 [§533], and *In De an.* I.1.254–5 [§15]. See the discussions in Brown, *Accidental Being* pp. 80–3; Reynolds, "Properties"; Pasnau,

The knowability of substantial form is closely connected to the knowability of essences. A thing's substantial form either is its essence or is the principal part of a thing's essence, together with its common matter. Either way, the thin substance just is, in effect, the stripped-down essence of a thing, conceived of apart from the accidental properties of the thick substance. Hence doubts about our grasp of essences go hand in hand with doubts about our ability to grasp a thing's substantial form. These issues will be discussed in some detail in Chapter 27, once we have a more complete picture of what substantial forms are.[5]

The case of prime matter can be considered in somewhat more detail here. There was no dispute, among scholastic authors, over the basic claim that prime matter is unintelligible. Aristotle had famously spoken of grasping matter by analogy (*Phys.* I.7, 191a8), but given that the nature of prime matter was thought to be so different from the nature of other things, the analogy could at most point in the general direction of an enduring, indeterminate stuff, without showing anything about what that stuff is.[6] Descartes quite rightly highlights the comparative advantage of the corpuscularian account:

No one who uses his reason will, I think, deny the advantage of using what the senses perceive to happen in large bodies as a model (*exemplum*) to judge what happens in tiny bodies that elude our senses merely because of their small size. This is much better than explaining matters by thinking 3 up I know not what new things that have no resemblance to the things that are sensed, such as prime matter, substantial forms, and the whole range of qualities that people habitually introduce. These are all harder to understand than the things they are supposed to explain. (*Principles* IV.201) 6

As Descartes acknowledges (lines 1–3), the corpuscularian must also make an inference from visible bodies to a substratum of invisible corpuscles. Still, at least the corpuscularian analogy runs between things that have a "resemblance" to each other (line 4), differing only in size. The scholastics, in contrast, make an inference from enduring subjects like *bronze* to a subject of an entirely different kind.

As we have seen (Chs. 3–4), it is essential to the metaphysical prime matter of the scholastics that it lacks the completeness and actuality of corpuscularian prime matter. Such incompleteness accounts for its obscurity, inasmuch as it lacks the actuality to make itself known. (The actuality of substantial form, in contrast, makes it at least a possible object of knowledge.) Thus Albert of Saxony, in a characteristic treatment of whether matter is cognizable in itself, reaches the conclusion that we cannot have a "proper concept" of prime matter, on the grounds that it is in no respect active, and so cannot give rise to any understanding of itself.[7] This much was fairly uncontroversial among scholastic authors. Some went even further, however, and described prime matter as unintelligible even in principle. When Aquinas, as quoted above, describes

---

Thomas Aquinas pp. 164–70. On the unknowability of prime matter in particular, see Wippel, *Metaphysical Thought of Thomas* pp. 325–7.

[5] On whether essences are something more than just substantial form, see, e.g., Buridan, *In Meta.* VII.12; Coimbra, *In Phys.* I.9.5. The impetus for thinking that essence might just be form is Averroes, *In Meta.* VII.34.

[6] On how to interpret Aristotle's call to understand form κατ' ἀναλογίαν, see Ockham, *In Phys.* I.16.6; Albert of Saxony, *In Phys.* I.16, pp. 223–4; Zabarella, *De rebus nat.*, De prima rerum materia I.4.

[7] Albert of Saxony describes the inconceivability of matter as follows: "Tertio conclusio: materia non est per se cognoscibilis conceptu proprio. Probatur, quia materia non potest cognosci sine discursu, propter hoc quod non potest agere speciem suam in intellectum mediante sensu: patet, quia non est sensibilis. Secundo, nam, si sic, ipsa esset activa: ageret enim in intellectum; sed hoc falsum, quia, secundum quod dictum est in primo articulo, materia nullius est activitatis" (*In Phys* I.16, p. 223).

prime matter as neither having existence nor being cognizable (*Summa theol.* 1a 15.3 ad 3), he seems to mean this in the strongest possible sense: that is to say, that not even God can understand prime matter. In *De veritate* 3.5c, Aquinas remarks that God has an idea of neither prime matter nor material substantial forms, in themselves, because neither can exist apart from the other. This suggests the intriguing prospect that not even an omniscient mind—the mind that *created* matter—can understand its true nature.

Scholastic authors were aware of Aquinas's bold claims, but almost always denied that prime matter is absolutely unintelligible—that is, unintelligible even to God. Scotus argues that prime matter is intelligible to both God and angels, and Ockham insists that God has an idea of all the parts of created substances, integral and metaphysical. Suárez, looking back with the perspective of three centuries, remarks that "although theologians dispute whether God has a proper idea of matter, and some seem to deny it..., still in truth it *cannot* be denied, except perhaps in a manner of speaking" (*Disp. meta.* XIII.6.1). Even the Thomists, who at least attempt to accept Aquinas's austerely bare conception of prime matter, try to soften the doctrine: thus Cajetan, while insisting that strictly speaking there is no divine idea of prime matter, allows that God has the theoretical concept (*ratio speculativa*) insofar as God has the general idea of body *qua* body. Some sort of softening really does seem inescapable. If the doctrine of omniscience means anything, it means that God knows everything that is knowable. For prime matter to be unknowable, there would have to be something contradictory in the claim that God understands its nature. The only contradiction that seems possible would be if prime matter has no nature at all. Aquinas's temptation to go that far is of a piece with his temptation to think that prime matter does not exist at all (§3.1), but neither of these conclusions were taken seriously by later scholastic authors.[8]

Prime matter's knowability for us is another question. Although there was agreement that we can truly characterize prime matter, there was disagreement over whether those characterizations amount to a grasp of matter's proper nature, or simply a description of various accidental features that serve to pick it out uniquely. Ockham, as we saw above, takes the latter view, as do Scotus, Albert of Saxony (also quoted above), and the Coimbrans. Others, however, while conceding that we have no immediate grasp of prime matter, held that inferential reasoning can lead us to at least a partial grasp of its proper nature. This seems to be the view of John of Jandun and of pseudo-Marsilius of Inghen. The latter's detailed characterization of prime matter (*In Phys.* I.20), considered in §3.1, is offered by way of an affirmative answer

---

[8]   Against Aquinas's claim of absolute unknowability, see Scotus, *Lectura* II.12 n. 79 (Vatican XIX:101); *Opus Ox.* II.12.2 (Wadding VI.2:697 [not in *Ordinatio*]); *Opus Ox.* II.12.1 (Wadding VI.2:676 [not in *Ordinatio*]): "Dico igitur quod materia secundum se in sua essentia est cognoscibilis, sed non a nobis. Primum patet, quia omnis entitas absoluta in se est cognoscibilis; materia est huiusmodi; ergo." And see Ockham, *Ordinatio* I.35.5 (*Opera theol.* IV:493): "Alia conclusio sequitur quod materiae et formae et universaliter partium essentialium et integralium omnium sunt distinctae ideae."

Cajetan attempts to sort out Aquinas's view as follows: "idea ut ratio, respondens materiae primae, est idea corporis, quod est genus in praedicamento Substantiae " (*In Summam theol.* I.15.3, IV:205). Cajetan thinks it clear that *Summa theol.* takes a deliberately harder line than the earlier *De veritate*. Vasquez criticizes Cajetan for trying to have it both ways, and argues that either prime matter has no being, and so no idea in God, or it has being, and so has a divine idea. Vasquez—no Thomist even in the midst of a commentary on the *Summa theol.*—takes the second view (*In Summam theol.* I.74.3, I:392b).

to the question of whether prime matter is cognizable. Although pseudo-Marsilius does not expressly say that he is showing us matter's true nature, the tenor of the discussion makes it fairly clear that this is his ambition. Suárez characteristically makes these disputes explicit, and attempts, also characteristically, to reach a moderate conclusion. We do have a proper concept of prime matter, he argues, but one that is in part negative and in part confused (as opposed to picking out prime matter uniquely). So, for instance, in describing prime matter as the *first subject*, we do describe a concept that is proper to prime matter alone. But 'subject' applies confusedly, inasmuch as it applies to many things other than prime matter. The addition of 'first' gives the description its specificity, but does so negatively, by denying that there is any prior subject. This is in the end not very different from Ockham's superficially more negative verdict. He and Suárez agree that we can uniquely describe prime matter, but that we do so in largely negative terms, without having any distinctive positive idea of what it is. No proponent of metaphysical prime matter seems to have contended otherwise.[9]

Which is explanatorily prior, the metaphysical indeterminacy of prime matter, or its epistemic obscurity? Francis Bacon argues that scholastic authors go from the latter to the former, fallaciously deriving the unactualized potentiality of prime matter from the mere fact that it is hidden:

> The ancients maintained that prime matter (of the sort that can be the principle of things) is formed and endowed, not abstract, potential, and unformed. To be sure, that stripped and passive matter seems nothing more than an invention of the human mind, one that arose from $\quad$ 3 its seeming to the human intellect that what exists above all is what it imbibes most strongly and by which it is most affected. Thus it is that forms (as they call them) seem to exist more than does matter or action, the first of which is hidden and makes a less strong impression, whereas $\quad$ 6 the second is in flux and inheres less constantly. Those images, on the other hand, are judged to be both manifest and constant, with the result that prime, common matter seems to be a kind of accessory and to stand as a substratum, whereas any kind of action seems to be a mere $\quad$ 9 emanation from form. So it is that forms are given all the leading parts. (*De principiis* [*Phil. Studies* p. 206])

Although Bacon leaves open whether there are in fact unbreakable atoms (§5.4), he approves of the Democritean method of treating enduring matter as something corporeal, "formed and endowed" (line 2). The mistake of both Plato and Aristotle, as Bacon characterizes it, was to take the obscurity of the material substrate as a guide to its true nature, so that its epistemological status is made to have metaphysical import. Forms, in contrast, because they are the most prominent features of the natural world, are "given all the leading parts" (line 10).

This is a clever piece of rhetoric, but not very plausible as an accusation. Part I of this study considered in some detail the motivations that scholastic authors had for thinking

---

[9] Jandun is among those who argue we can grasp at least part of the proper nature of prime matter, albeit through form (*In De subst. orbis* Q5). The Coimbrans argue we cannot (*In Phys.* I.9.2.2). Suárez's attempt at a compromise runs as follows: "Quoad secundum autem dicendum est pervenire quidem nos in aliquem proprium conceptum materiae primae, non tamen omnino distinctum et prout in se est, sed negativum partim, partim confusum. Tota haec assertio constat ex definitione materiae tradita ab Aristotele, scilicet, esse primum subiectum, etc.; nam per illam descriptionem aliquem conceptum obiectivum explicamus; ille autem est proprius materiae, sicut et ipsa definitio. In ea vero definitione *subiectum* quid confusum est et commune; additur vero quod sit *primum*, ut ad materiam limitetur: *primum* autem negationem importat prioris subiecti" (*Disp. meta.* 13.6.1).

that prime matter must be indeterminate and dependent on form. It is on metaphysical grounds such as these that prime matter is judged to be unknowable in some deep, in-principle way. This is to say that, contrary to Bacon's charge, the metaphysics drives the epistemology. When the hylomorphic metaphysical framework gets abandoned in the seventeenth century, it becomes natural to treat prime matter in corpuscularian fashion, which means that it is veiled only because of its size. On this sort of view, as we saw Descartes suggest earlier in this section, the stuff that endures through all material change is no different from the macro-sized stuff we see all around us, except in being smaller. If such prime matter is unknowable, it is so only for lack of sufficiently developed technology. The scholastic view suggests something different: that prime matter is not body at all, but a thing of an entirely different kind, metaphysical rather than physical, unknowable to us even in principle, because it lacks the sort of actuality that we are capable of grasping.

7.3. Substance Shrouded: Scotus and Marchia

Just how far off the mark is the naively empirical idea that we perceive things in themselves? A characteristic thought of the seventeenth century was that the external world is veiled by our ideas, and known at best indirectly through them. A characteristic scholastic thought, the one we have been considering, was that the things in themselves are veiled by their accidental qualities, and known only through them. The veil of ideas was as familiar to scholastic audiences as the veil of qualities was in the later seventeenth century, and so one might consider superimposing the two veils, thereby introducing two degrees of separation between us and the world: first we grasp our own impressions, which lead us to the sensible qualities of things, from which we derive some information about the underlying subject of those ideas. Might we lie twice removed from material substances?[10]

Perhaps this was Locke's picture of the world (§9.1, §23.4). It was more common, however, to choose one or the other veil, inasmuch as each tends to undermine the other. If one thinks that we perceive our own ideas, then it is natural to shift the manifest characteristics of sensible qualities into our own mind. To that extent, though, there is less reason to insist on a distinction between a substance and its qualities. It becomes tempting to say that there are only substances in the world (aggregates of corpuscles), and that the ideas we perceive are merely one step removed from that reality. On the other hand, a commitment to the substance–accident distinction makes the veil of ideas less tempting, because it allows for a middle ground between seeing our own ideas and seeing corpuscles in motion. The character of that middle ground— that is, the character of sensible qualities—is a topic for later discussion (Chs. 21–3). Here the crucial point is that the veiled-subject doctrine has as its natural counterpart the idea that what we are directly acquainted with are the sensible qualities of material substances. This is the idea that Bacon alludes to at the end of the previous section when he describes forms as having been "given all the leading parts" (line 10). To some

---

[10] For one scholastic version of the veil of ideas, in Peter John Olivi, see my *Theories of Cognition* pp. 236–47. For the notion of twin veils, see also Stuart, "Descartes's Extended Substances" p. 85, as a possible reading of Descartes.

extent this remark applies to substantial form, but what Bacon is mainly thinking of are accidental forms in the category of Quality, whose alleged causal role was the principal obstacle to corpuscularianism (Ch. 19). Just as Bacon charges that the metaphysical incompleteness of prime matter is illicitly deduced from its epistemological obscurity, so he charges that the causal prominence of form is illicitly deduced from its being "manifest and constant" (line 8). One way to sever that connection is to put manifest qualities into the mind, and so outside the causal nexus of material objects. Bacon himself, however, takes a different route, leaving sensible qualities in the world but denying that they are either manifest or constant. Investigation shows that heat, for instance, quite contrary to its manifest appearance, is just the motion of corpuscles (§21.4).

For the remainder of this chapter, let us follow the scholastic route, and locate sensible qualities in the world, as the immediate objects of perception. What then becomes of our knowledge of substance? Some authors were, in effect, skeptics. Consider Scotus's account of why prime matter can be grasped only indirectly:

[Prime matter] cannot be cognized by us, except by analogy to form, because of the defectiveness of our intellect. Neither can [substantial] form be cognized by us, except by analogy, because from the sensible [qualities] we cognize we are led to a grasp of form, through sensible operations. Matter, however, is the principle of no sensible operation, and so from subsequent forms, which are principles of other operations, we reach the further conclusion that matter stands to them analogously to how what receives stands to the thing received. (*Lectura* II.12 n. 79)

Suppose we are sitting in front of a fire. On Scotus's account, we start with *sensibilia*, by which he means accidental qualities. (As he says elsewhere, "accidents are principles of acting and principles of cognizing substance, ... and the *per se* objects of the senses" [*Ordinatio* IV.12.1; Wadding n. 16; see §10.5 for the larger context of this claim].) The fire's heat and light are the product of the "operations" that produce these sensible qualities, and from those operations we infer an underlying principle, the substantial form, that accounts for those operations. (See §24.4 on the relationship between substantial form and its sensible qualities.) This route does not get us to prime matter, however, because we cannot make an inference of that sort from observables to prime matter. To grasp prime matter, we have to wait until the form of fire is replaced by some other form, perhaps the form of ash. Matter can then be understood as the enduring subject of first one substantial form and then another (§2.2).

Scotus takes the standard scholastic theory of perception—that what we perceive are the sensible qualities, and that these are distinct from their underlying subject—to create an insuperable difficulty for our grasp of substance itself. In arguing, in the passage just quoted, that we can achieve only an indirect, inferential grasp of substantial form and prime matter, he is implicitly saying that this is the best we can do in understanding the thin metaphysical substance, which just is the composite of prime matter and substantial form. Elsewhere he sets out this conclusion starkly, remarking that "no substance is understood in its own right, except in the most universal of concepts, namely *being*" (*In Meta.* II.2–3 [*Opera phil.* III n. 116]). As for the fact that we do seem to offer definitions of various substances, Scotus dismissively replies that "with respect to substances we have a vocal disposition, just as someone blind is naturally able to syllogize about colors" (ibid., n. 119). That is to say that we have words that we use, but we do not know what we are talking about. Making explicit the veil that sensible qualities draw across substance, he remarks:

If substance does not immediately impress our intellect with some understanding of itself, but only sensible accidents do, then it follows that we could have no quidditative concept of substance except what could be abstracted from the concept of accident. But the only quidditative concept that can be abstracted from the concept of an accident is the concept of *being*. (*Ordinatio* I.3.1.3 n. 139)

For Scotus, there is a barrier in principle to our understanding substances. All we have immediate access to are accidents, but from the concept of an accident we cannot get to the concept of a substance, except for that one concept, *being*, that both substances and accidents share. Hence the most we can do is describe substances in terms of the accidents they manifest. With respect to the (thin) substance that lies beneath those accidents, we can say only that it is a being. (We can say this much, indeed, Scotus thinks, only if we insist on something that most early scholastic authors denied: that 'being' is univocal between substance and accidents [§10.5].)[11]

Scotus's remarks about substance were widely endorsed, and were understood to hold up and down the Porphyrian tree, at different levels of generality. At the top of the tree, they imply that we cannot define the true nature of substance in general. They also imply, branching out as we move downward, that we cannot define any of the more specific genera, all the way down to the species of a given kind of substance, such as *homo*. Finally, at the very bottom of the tree, they imply that we cannot specify the nature of an individual substance, such as you or me. With respect to this lowest level, there could hardly have been any disagreement. Most agreed that individual substances of the same species differ in more than their accidents—that is, that their natures are intrinsically different, although not different enough to locate them in different species. But no one supposed that human beings, at least in this life, could ever come to grasp those subtle intra-specific differences. With respect to the highest level, the definition of substance in general, §6.2 considered the two stock scholastic definitions: subsisting *per se*, and serving as a subject in which accidents inhere. Do either of these pick out the real nature of substance? According to Francis of Marchia, lecturing in Paris around 1320, they do not. Presumably influenced in this regard by Scotus, Marchia describes the subsistence definition as proper to substance but purely negative, inasmuch as it simply rules out inhering in something else. The inherence definition, in contrast, is positive, but extrinsic and accidental, inasmuch as it rests on facts about something other than the substance itself. Hence neither definition tells us what substance itself is. What about the real natures of species? Marchia again takes Scotus's pessimistic line:

One who has a proper essential concept of a prior object can distinguish it through that concept from anything that is not it, once any posterior concept has been removed that is not a part of its

---

[11]   For other statements of Scotus's pessimism with regard to our grasp of substances, see *In De an.* q. 21; *Lec.* I.3.1.1–2 (Vat. XVI nn. 110–12); *Ord.* I.3.1.1–2 (Vat. III nn. 139–46); *Lectura* I.22 (Vat. XVII nn. 2–3); *Ord.* I.22 (Vat. V nn. 5–7). For very helpful discussions of Scotus's views in this area, see Pini, "Scotus on Knowing and Naming" and "Scotus on Doing Metaphysics." Pini points to Richard of Middleton (*Sent.* II.24.2) as an earlier instance of similar sorts of doubts.

On the argument for univocity between substantial and accidental being, as essential to our knowledge of substance, see the discussions in Fonseca, *In Meta.* IV.2.1.2 and Suárez, *Disp. meta.* 32.2.2.

nature. . . . But our intellect, in this life, following the natural order, with all the accidents   3
removed from substances, has nothing within itself with which to distinguish between those
substances. For let all the accidents and dispositions for accidents be removed intellectually from
a lion and a horse. Nothing remains within the intellect with which it can distinguish them.   6
Anyone can experience this within himself, because the intellect distinguishes a lion from a
horse only by analogy to the accidents that are proper to each. Therefore the intellect does not
have any proper essential concept of either one. (*Sent.* I.3.1, pp. 508–9)   9

This argument from indiscernibility puts in terms of a concrete example Scotus's
conclusion that our only concepts about substance kinds are concepts drawn from
accidents. Marchia is claiming that if we try to articulate the difference between a bare
(accident-free) lion and horse, we come up empty: we have no distinct idea at all of the
one versus the other (lines 5–9).[12]

In view of the general scholastic consensus over the difficulty, if not the impossibility,
of making the jump from accidents to substance, it is ironic how often seventeenth-
century critics attack scholasticism for being, in Locke's terms, "pretenders to a
knowledge that they had not" (*Essay* III.8.2). Locke contrasts scholastic philosophers
with uneducated craftsmen:

And yet those ignorant men, who pretend not any insight into the real essences, nor trouble
themselves about substantial forms, but are content with knowing things one from another by
their sensible qualities, are often better acquainted with their differences, can more nicely
distinguish them from their uses, and better know what they expect from each, than those
learned quick-sighted men, who look so deep into them, and talk so confidently of something
more hidden and essential. (ibid., III.6.24)

No doubt philosophers have never, in any era, known as much as ordinary folk. But
Locke gets the scholastic position quite wrong by suggesting that it gave an important
role to speculation about the essential character of things. Indeed, if anything, matters
are exactly the opposite. Scholastic authors tend to think it impossible to say anything
very substantive that goes beyond the sensible qualities of a thing, and so they typically
do not even try, contenting themselves instead with empty placeholders like *bovinitas*
and *humanitas*. It is the corpuscularian philosophers who attempt to offer speculative
hypotheses about such things—often at great, tedious length—which we shield modern
readers from by leaving those sections untranslated and unanthologized. The English
Descartes is sanitized of his vortices and his subtle matter, and we are spared Gassendi
almost entirely (§19.7).

---

[12] Francis of Marchia characterizes our grasp of substance as follows: "Secundo, dico quod intellectus habet
naturaliter conceptum negativum substantiae. Patet, quia non esse in aliquo sicut in subiecto est proprium substantiae;
hoc autem intellectus attribuit substantiae, non accidenti; igitur habet aliquem conceptum proprium negativum
substantiae. Tertio, dico quod habet aliquem conceptum proprium positivum accidentalem extra rationem substantiae.
Patet, quia substare omnibus accidentibus est proprium substantiae; hoc autem intellectus attribuit substantiae, non
accidentibus; igitur habet de substantia proprium conceptum negativum et proprium conceptum positivum extrinsecum
et accidentalem" (*Sent.* I.3.1, p. 508).
  Marchia's skeptical tendencies seem to have influenced Gregory of Rimini, *Sent.* I.3.2: "Tertium dubium est de
substantia, quomodo cognoscatur, an scilicet in se immediate vel in sua specie vel tantum in conceptu formato per
intellectum" (p. 382). "Ad tertium dubium pro nunc potest dici, sicut dicit unus doctor, quod substantia cognoscitur in
aliquo conceptu proprio negativo, qualis est 'ens naturaliter per se existens'" (p. 385).

Of course, some post-scholastic authors, such as Locke himself, were embarrassed by the speculative nature of the corpuscularian movement.[13] And insofar as one might want to defend such speculations, they can be thought of as early expressions of modern science. Such scientific musings—if that is what they are—are famously absent from scholastic thought. The reasons for that are of course complex, but one very important reason is the veiled-subject doctrine. Scholastic authors did not generally attempt to go beyond appearances to explain the nature of fire or water, let alone the nature of lion or horse, not because they lacked any interest in doing so, or because they thought they lacked the technology. Instead, very commonly, they took it to be metaphysically impossible to reach any substantive conclusions about the nature of substance from information about sensible accidents. This is the point of Scotus's insistence that we can arrive only at the shared concept of *being*. Marchia reaches a very similar conclusion:

Substance, in this life, does not of itself move our intellect immediately, but only mediated by accidents. For it moves intellect only mediated by the senses, which are not receptive of substance. An accident, however, cannot cause a concept that is more perfect than its own proper concept, and a proper essential concept of substance is more perfect than the proper concept of an accident. Hence neither an accident nor the intellect, by virtue of an accident, can have the proper essential concept of a substance. (*Sent.* I.3.1, p. 509)

Whereas Marchia's earlier argument from indiscernibility appeals simply to what listeners take themselves to know about substance, here Marchia argues for the theoretical impossibility of passing from accidents to substance. The key premises of the argument—that substance concepts are more perfect than accident concepts, and that less perfect concepts cannot lead to more perfect concepts—are perhaps too abstract to seem very persuasive on their own. These are, however, simply a way of insisting on the metaphysical understanding of substance that is the shared foundation of scholastic thought. When the thin substance is understood as a composite of prime matter and substantial form, and when this matter and form are understood as metaphysical parts of substances, they are positioned out of reach of ordinary empirical inquiry. Call their concepts "more perfect" or more abstract or simply more obscure, but in any case the scholastic framework does raise an in-principle barrier to the move from accidents to substance.

Setting aside for later (§27.2) our knowledge of essences, we can consider here the more fundamental question of whether we can have any grasp of substance at all. Given the substance–accident distinction, our inability to go beyond accidents implies that we have none. This is to say not just that we lack a precise account of what distinguishes lions from cheetahs, say, but moreover that we lack any substantive information about lions themselves, as opposed to the accidental qualities they might, singly, share with many other animals. We grasp part of the thick concrete substance, inasmuch as we grasp certain accidental forms, but we grasp the thin metaphysical substance not at all. Given that the thin substance just is the thing itself—the lion or the cheetah—our grasp of the material world turns out to be radically impoverished. In

---

[13] On Locke's commitment to the corpuscularian–mechanical philosophy, see Ch. 9 note 13.

view of this outcome, it is unsurprising that the most skeptical of scholastic authors, like William Crathorn and Nicholas of Autrecourt, take seriously the prospect that there simply are no substances at all. In the second of his notorious letters to Bernard of Arezzo (1335–6), Autrecourt proposes that "Aristotle never had evident knowledge of any substance other than his own soul" (n. 22), inasmuch as such knowledge would have to be based on an invalid inference from sensory experience. Autrecourt would subsequently be condemned for having held that "it cannot evidently be shown, in pointing to some bread, that there is some thing (res) there that is not an accident" (*Correspondence* Appendix A 2.2)—this being just one of many cases where fertile avenues of philosophical inquiry were shut down in the fourteenth century by ecclesiastical opposition (Chs. 19–20). The character of Autrecourt's preferred ontology will concern us later (§19.4, §28.2). Here we need note only that one of the great attractions of corpuscularianism (at least when developed along Hobbes's lines) is that it promises to put our acquaintance with substances on a solid foundation. To grasp a sensible quality of a material substance just is to grasp something about that substance. Because qualities—as they are in the world—are simply ways in which matter is structured, and because matter variously structured is just what substances are, there is no gap between qualities and substance, and hence no danger that qualities might veil the substances.[14]

[14] Autrecourt's second letter makes his doubts about our knowledge of substance quite evident: "Et quod de aliqua substantia coniuncta materiae alia ab anima nostra non habeamus certitudinem apparet, quia demonstrato ligno vel lapide, quod substantia sit ibi clarissime deducetur ex uno credito coaccepto. Sed hoc non potest inferri evidenter ex uno credito coaccepto, nam cum omnibus apparentibus ante huiusmodi discursum potest esse per aliquam potentiam, utputa divinam, quod ibi substantia non sit. Igitur in lumine naturali non infertur evidenter ex istis apparentibus quod substantia sit ibi" (n. 25).

Crathorn's doubts about substance run like this: "Prima [conclusio] est quod nulla res corruptibilis possit proprie dici substantia—ut natura ligni vel lapidis vel aliquid consimile. Et hoc patet sic: istud nomen 'substantia' derivatur ab isto verbo 'substo, substas'; unde illud proprie vocatur substantia quod stat sub alio vel aliis. Sed nihil est in isto ligno de quo proprie possit dici quod stet sub aliquo alio quod est in ligno. Licet enim in ista re sint multae naturae coextensae, tamen una illarum non est magis sub alia quam econverso. Igitur nulla illarum potest proprie dici substantia" (*Sent.* I.13, pp. 391–2).

Yet another example of a scholastic author tempted to deny the reality of material substances—contemporary with both Autrecourt and Crathorn—is Thomas Manlevelt, *Quaest. super vet. art.*, De praed. q. 16: "Prima conclusio est ista, quod probabiliter posset susteniri physice loquendo, nullam penitus substantiam esse in istis inferioribus, accipiendo substantiam pro composito ex materia et forma, vel pro aliqua parte talis compositi." To say this thesis can be sustained "probabiliter" is a weak claim: not that it is in fact *probable* in the modern sense, but merely that there are plausible arguments to be made in its favor. (Accordingly, he goes on to argue that it can also be held *probabiliter* that substances do exist.) Manlevelt makes clear just how weak a claim this is by going on to contend that something should be held *probabiliter* if its opposite cannot be evidently proved. He then argues that in fact it cannot be evidently proved that there are material substances: "omnes apparentiae possunt evidenter salvari, non posita aliqua tali substantia . . . quia posita tantummodo accidentibus sibi invicem subsistentibus et adhaerentibus, salvatur generatio et corruptio, aug-mentatio et diminutio, alteratio et loci mutatio, sicut patet in hostia consecrata" (n. 21). An obvious problem for this sort of bundle theory is that it might violate the substratum thesis (§2.2). Manlevelt considers this. He contends that there will usually be accidents enduring through all cases of change (n. 29), but allows as "satis probabiliter" the possibility that in some cases there might be no enduring substratum at all, but just a *generans* giving rise to a *generandum* (n. 31). Will that violate the *ex nihilo* principle? Manlevelt considers this, and argues that that principle places a restriction on natural change only when understood weakly, as requiring only a *terminus a quo* (n. 32)—what in §2.2 I call "the ingredients." For a detailed discussion of Manlevelt's arguments, with an edition of the whole question, see Andrews, "Thomas Maulevelt." In §8.2 I will consider how Descartes argues against this sort of bundle theory of substance.

7.4. Lifting the Veil I: Oresme

Is it possible to escape the veiled-subject doctrine from within scholastic Aristotelianism? Not everyone took the extreme position of Scotus and Marchia. Perhaps more common was the incrementalism of Aquinas, who thought that the substances of things are hidden, but can become gradually known to us through the study of their accidental qualities.[15] This sort of view had already received a classic formulation in Robert Grosseteste's highly influential commentary on the *Posterior Analytics* (1220s):

And so when, over time, the senses act through their many encounters with sensible things, reason, which is mixed up with the senses and in the senses as if it were carried toward sensible things in a ship, is awakened. Once awakened, reason begins to draw distinctions and to consider separately things that had been confused in the senses. Sight, for instance, confuses color, size, shape, and body, and in its judgment all these things are taken as a single thing. Awakened reason, however, distinguishes color from size and shape from body and then shape and size from the substance of body, and so by drawing distinctions and abstracting, it arrives at a grasp of the substance of body, which supports size, shape, and color. (*In Post. an.* I.14, p. 214)

Grosseteste seems to describe here only the initial grasp of what it is to be a body in general, a genus far removed from a grasp of the essence of some particular kind of body. Still, this provides a model for the larger project, and I suspect the majority of scholastics thought that, somehow, the project could be worked out, over time, at least in principle.

It is hard to assess the merits of this sort of model, in part because it is so difficult in general to know where perception proper ends and where inference begins. Opinions on this topic have ranged so widely that there is not even agreement on whether non-inferential perception can take us outside the mind at all. There was a pervasive worry, however, that if our initial data are limited to information about accidents, then we will never bridge the gap and arrive at information about substance. This suggested to some that we have to build some kind of grasp of substance into what is empirically given. Nicole Oresme, for instance, lecturing in the middle of the fourteenth century, mocked the veiled-subject doctrine:

According to the vulgar opinion of the philosophers (or rather of the philosophizers), the substance is somehow covered up and buried by accidents, so that the intellect first understands accidents and then discursively, by conjecture, judges that the substance exists. The substance is not sensed, but rather only the accidents under which it lies hidden. Indeed, according to them it is no more sensed than is the mover of the heavens, which is also conjectured on the basis of accidents. (*In De an.* I.4, p. 119)

Oresme sees something absurd in the common doctrine of a veiled subject—that material substances could be all around us, and yet that their existence would be a kind of refined philosophical hypothesis, requiring subtle metaphysical reasoning.

---

[15] For Aquinas's method of working from the sensible qualities inward, see Jenkins, "Aquinas on the Veracity"; Pasnau, *Thomas Aquinas*, pp. 164–70; Reynolds, "Properties." Kretzmann, "Infallibility," reads Aquinas as treating our grasp of essences as something that comes in stages, from an initially impoverished general grasp of what a thing is, up to, at least in principle, something much more determinate. The most sophisticated incremental treatment I have found is Buridan's, particularly in *In De an.* I.6. For discussion, see Zupko, *John Buridan* pp. 103–13, 214–18.

Rather than shore up the inference from accidents to substance, Oresme wants to show that our grasp of substance is non-inferential: that in seeing the color of the horse, we see the horse itself. His strategy is similar to that of a strict corpuscularian like Hobbes, in its intent to undermine the substance–accident distinction. On Oresme's account, accidents do not have their own proper existence or nature, and so they depend on substance in such a way that "in cognizing an accident one cognizes the substance." To grasp just a single accident is to have a confused and accidental concept of substance, but as one begins to put together various accidental features of the substance, one can have a progressively more clear understanding of what a substance is, all the way to an ultimate grasp of its essence.[16]

Whether this strategy has a chance of success depends on how we understand accidents—a topic that still lies before us. Oresme is here following a thirteenth-century tradition of denying that accidents (ordinarily) have any proper existence of their own (§10.2). Siger of Brabant, one of the leading advocates of that conception of accidents, had made very much the same suggestion as Oresme, contending that to apprehend an accident just is to apprehend something about its subject. As we will see, such ways of conceiving of accidents—what I will call deflationary accounts—fall out of favor in the fourteenth century, in favor of the doctrine of real accidents, a view advanced most prominently by Scotus (Chs. 10–11). It is a curious fact that both parties to this dispute maintain that their approach is the key to preserving our knowledge of substance. For Scotus, it is only when accidents are treated as beings just like substances (beings in a univocal sense) that one can make an inference from accident to substance. In contrast, the deflationary camp holds that it is precisely because accidents are not beings in the way that substances are that one can know substances by knowing accidents. Thus John Wyclif, the most prominent critic of the growing later-scholastic consensus in favor of real accidents (§11.1), argues that when accidents are given their own, separable being, there is no way of going from knowledge of accidents to knowledge of the underlying substance: indeed, "no sense or intellect establishes that there is any sort of material substance, since it appears compossible and consistent with every sensory awareness or experience that the whole created universe is a cluster (*globus*) of accidents" (*De*

---

[16] The details of Oresme's story of how we get from accidents to substance go as follows: "Et ideo ista via [vulgaris] est longe ab opinione Aristotelis, quae fuit quod accidens non est separabile a substantia non solum secundum existentiam, ut glossant, sed etiam secundum quidditatem, quia non habet esse proprie: unde imaginabatur quod, sicut impossibile est esse figuram sine figurato, ita de quolibet alio accidente, et hoc est verum nisi per miraculum. Et tunc secundum ipsum esset conclusio prima quod ad cuiuslibet accidentis cognitionem necessario concomitatur cognitio substantiae. . . . Et ideo vult Aristoteles quod conceptus accidentis non est absolutus, nec in concreto nec in abstracto, sed includit conceptum substantiae in abstracto: unde sequitur: *albedo est, igitur alicuius albedo est*; et sic cognoscendo accidens cognoscitur substantia, conceptu tamen confuso et accidentali. . . . Tunc secunda conclusio est quod ex aliquibus accidentibus communibus cognoscitur substantia determinate et etiam quidditative . . ." (*In De an.* I.4, p. 119). See also Oresme, *In Phys.* I.9: "[substantia] cognoscitur per hunc modum quia videmus accidentia et scimus per inductionem quod omne accidens est in subiecto, ex quo substantiatur hoc complexum *subiectum est*, quod [subiectum] vocatur substantia."

For a conclusion similar to Oresme's, see Peter of Ailly, *Tract. de an.* 12.5, p. 80: "Haec autem opinio non videtur omnino dicere verum, scilicet quantum ad hoc, quod dicit sensum et phantasiam non apprehendere substantiam, cum ipsemet Aristoteles dicat substantiam sensibilem per accidens, immo videtur quod sensus percipit substantiam cum accidente confuse potius quam accidens per se et distincte, ut supra dictum est. Unde potest concludi quod, cum sensus apprehendat confuse simul substantiam et accidens, intellectus potest abstrahere ex illa confusione conceptum proprium substantiae et alium proprium et distinctum accidentis, et per hunc modum notitia accidentium facit ad notitiam substantiarum." Ailly here agrees with Oresme that the senses perceive substance. But it is not clear how Ailly can get this result, since he does not take Oresme's dramatic step of questioning the substance–accident distinction.

eucharistia ch. 3, p. 78). Wyclif's views, however, were condemned. Also condemned were views, like those of Autrecourt and John of Mirecourt, that denied the reality of accidents altogether (§§19.3–4). Hence the mainstream of later scholastic thought maintained a sharp divide between two kinds of entities, substances and accidents. On such a picture it is very natural, if not inevitable, to treat the substance itself as an obscure metaphysical postulate.[17]

Although the reality of accidents could not be denied for the majority of our period, the substance–accident distinction could be blurred. The principal strategy in this regard, among later scholastics, was the doctrine of modes, which postulated a kind of entity midway between substance and accident. This is how both Oresme and Wyclif understand accidents (§13.2), and the idea of course becomes central to seventeenth-century thought, once real accidents are dispensed with entirely (§13.4). It is not clear, however, whether the theory of modes offers a route to the knowledge of substance. Gassendi, as quoted at the start of this chapter, maintains that what we conceive of or notice in bodies is not the substance itself, but the modes (or qualities) of that substance, leaving our knowledge of the substance itself obscure. Descartes too, as we will see in the following chapter, fully accepts the view that substance is veiled by modes. These are issues that can only be touched on here, however, pending a fuller evaluation of what accidents and modes are.

7.5. Lifting the Veil II: Cremonini

Aside from reconceiving the nature of accidents, is there any way around the veiled-subject doctrine? As one final attempt at this, we might look at Cesare Cremonini, the last of the great Paduan scholastics. Doomed to be remembered for his legendary refusal to look through his friend Galileo's telescope, Cremonini was nevertheless a philosopher of some interest.[18] In his treatise on the elemental forms (1605), he describes the common view—the one "everyone agrees on"—regarding the nature of the four basic elements (Earth, Air, Fire, Water). On this view, the sensible qualities associated with these elements (Hot, Cold, Wet, Dry) are merely accidents, and the substantial forms of the elements are something prior, unknown, and even un-named. This is just a special case of the veiled-subject doctrine, at the elemental level, and Cremonini is quite right to treat it as the consensus view.[19] He is persuaded,

---

[17] Wyclif's discussion of these issues is quite remarkable and deserving of further attention. He argues, among other things, that postulating real accidents as the objects of perception would make untenable the cognition of brute animals. For they, he thinks, surely do grasp substances themselves, in virtue of perceiving sensible qualities, and yet surely do not do so by making some kind of inference from the qualities to the underlying substance (*De actibus animae* II.4, p. 127).

Siger of Brabant also makes explicit how a proper understanding of what accidents are yields a path to the substance itself: "Qui intelligit aliquid in habitudine ad aliud, de necessitate intelligit terminum habitudinis.... Sed qui intelligit accidens, et praecipue per modum accidentis, ut convenit in nomine denominativo, intelligit aliquid cuius intellectus et ratio non est nisi in habitudine ad substantiam. Ergo intelligens accidens, et praecipue per modum accidentis, de necessitate intelligit subiectum istud" (*In Meta.* [Cambr.] V.23; ed. Maurer, p. 238).

On the implications of varying theories of accidents for our knowledge of substance, see also Amerini, "Utrum inhaerentia" pp. 128–9.

[18] For information on Cremonini, see Schmitt, "Cesare Cremonini"; Kuhn, *Venetischer Aristotelismus*; Riondato and Poppi, *Cesare Cremonini*.

[19] On the usual distinction between the elemental qualities and the substantial forms of the elements, see e.g., Albert the Great, *In De gen. et cor.* II.2.7; Aquinas, *In De gen. et cor.* I.8 n. 62; Giles of Rome, *In De gen. et cor.* II, f. 250va; Coimbra,

however, that this view is a mistake, and he devotes this 175-page treatise to showing that various aspects of the scholastic theory of elements can be maintained, and put on a less obscure, more parsimonious footing, if we identify the natures of the elements with their four manifest qualities, and deny that those qualities are accidents. This is, to be sure, still very far from anything that might count as corpuscularianism, because Cremonini is still crucially appealing to accidental forms in the category of Quality. Still, it is a giant step toward rendering the scholastic theory of the elements more intelligible, by rejecting, at least in this fundamental case, the veil of qualities.

Cremonini's proposal might seem too narrow and technical to be of general interest. In fact, however, the account has potentially radical implications for scholastic theory in general. The elements are the building blocks of all material substances, such that every sublunary body is composed from a mixture of these four elements (§21.2). So long as the nature of these elements is out of reach, it is hard to see how we stand any chance of grasping the natures of more complex, mixed bodies. If it turns out, however, as Cremonini argues, that the nature of the four elements lies right in front of us—if there is nothing more to their substantial forms than Hot, Cold, Wet, and Dry—then it suddenly becomes at least thinkable that we might be able to account for the nature of mixed bodies in terms of mixtures of these basic qualities. Indeed, this is what the first generation of post-scholastic thought often looked like. Authors such as Gerard and Arnold Boate, Jean Chrysostome Magnen, and Joachim Jungius introduced a corpuscularian theory that had not yet shed the elemental qualities, and so attempted to account for natural phenomena in terms of various mixtures of corpuscles endowed with various qualities (§19.6, §21.4). Cremonini does not go this far: he rejects neither substantial form nor metaphysical prime matter, and he does not explicitly extend his conclusions about elemental forms to the case of mixed bodies. There are hints, however, as to the wider repercussions his views might have. He considers, for instance, the objection that on his account material substances become sensible *per se*, inasmuch as what we sense *per se*—qualities such as hot and cold—are in fact the nature of the elements. In replying, Cremonini hedges somewhat, pointing out that we do not perceive these qualities *as* elemental natures, but simply as qualities. Still, in the end, Cremonini concedes that the doctrine of the veiled subject is simply false: we do perceive material substances, directly and *per se*.[20] Elsewhere, he considers the objection that we never come to grasp the ultimate *differentiae* that locate substances within their proper species. He replies that "there is no reasonable doubt that these ultimate

---

In Gen. et cor. II.3.1. For an overview of scholastic theories of the elements, see Maier, *An der Grenze*, pp. 3–22 (tr. Sargent pp. 124–42), and Wood and Weisberg, "Interpreting Aristotle on Mixture." With regard to the agreement among Latin authors, Cremonini writes: "Conveniunt igitur omnes quod hae qualitates sint accidentia; formas substantiales dicunt antecedere has qualitates, et esse innominatas" (*De formis elementorum* I.6, p. 41).

In addition to the question of whether the elemental qualities are the essence of the elements, there were questions regarding our grasp of the elemental qualities themselves. It was a commonplace, for instance, that the familiar terms 'Hot,' 'Cold,' etc. should not lead us to suppose that we understand exactly what these qualities are, since the pure elemental qualities are not the same as the mixed qualities we encounter in nature. See, e.g., Averroes, *Comm. medium de gen. et cor.* pp. 71–2, and the extensive discussion of such issues in Zabarella, *De rebus nat.*, De qual. element. I.

[20] The objection Cremonini considers is this: "substantia non est per se sensibilis; istae qualitates sunt per se sensibiles; ergo non sunt substantiae" (*De formis elementorum* III.12, p. 160). To this he tries the reply: "...non sentitur illa caliditas quatenus substantia, sed sentitur solum ut qualitas" (ibid., p. 162). Eventually, though, he hugs the monster, concluding the chapter with the remark that "substantia materialis debet esse per se sensibilis" (ibid., p. 166).

differentiae are sometimes unknown and unnamed. But this is not perpetually the case, and with respect to the elements it is in no way the case" (*De formis elementorum* II.8, p. 83). So Cremonini flatly denies that essences are shrouded at the elemental level. And he goes one step further and denies in general that there is some sort of "perpetual"— that is to say *in principle*—obstacle to grasping the natures of material substances. These are not moves away from scholasticism in the usual sense, but they are moves away from one of the most restrictive features of the scholastic framework. Cremonini is thus an early landmark in the seventeenth-century's drive toward putting philosophy on a more intelligible footing.

8

Cartesian Substances

8.1. Descartes's Thin Substance

It has become something of a cliché to say that Descartes looks, depending on one's perspective, like either the first modern philosopher or the last scholastic philosopher. To be sure, it is easier for us to see him as the first of the moderns. To read Descartes as a scholastic requires taking him seriously in places where we are inclined to think that he cannot mean what he says, places where his premises look so alien as to make his line of argument seem utterly untenable. (The most notorious examples are the causal principles that the Third Meditation uses to prove God's existence.) We have to imagine, though, that to a seventeenth-century audience it would be precisely these claims that would slide right by, so familiar as to be unnoticed, and so not in need of any special argument. It is as if Descartes is affecting a modern accent, but sometimes slips into his native medieval brogue. For us, the slips are what get noticed, more than the accent, whereas for his contemporaries, the accent got all the attention. Nothing better illustrates this phenomenon than Descartes's treatment of substance, where the metaphysical framework of scholastic Aristotelianism endures in ways that have not generally been recognized.[1]

The most obvious way in which Descartes retains the scholastic conception of substance is by embracing the two standard scholastic criteria for substance (§6.2): substances as independent entities, subsisting *per se*, and substances as the subjects of accidents. My interest here, however, is not in these criteria themselves, but in the way in which Descartes accepts the picture of substances as the subject of the things revealed by sense. Substances, in other words, for Descartes, are to be understood in the thin metaphysical terms of the last two chapters. Here, for instance, is one of his official definitions of the term, from his geometric reformulation of the *Meditations*:

'Substance' refers to [a] every thing in which the items we perceive exist immediately, as in a subject, or [b] every thing through which those items we perceive exist—the items we perceive being any property, quality, or attribute whose real idea is in us. (Second Replies, VII:161)

[1] For Descartes as the last scholastic, see, e.g., Muralt, *L'enjeu* p. xi: "On ne peut plus aujourd'hui par exemple voir en Descartes le 'père de la philosophie moderne', car sa pensée apparaît manifestement, si on la compare à ses origines médiévales, comme l'un des produits les plus composites de la pensée scolastique tardive."

The (a) clause refers to finite substances—minds and bodies—which Descartes goes on to characterize as the immediate subjects, respectively, of thought and extension. The (b) clause alludes to the traditional role of substances as the cause of their qualities (§24.4), and by mentioning it Descartes is able to allow for immaterial substances—God and angels—which lack the properties, qualities, etc. that we perceive, but "through which" such items exist (line 2).[2] The clause after the hyphen (lines 2–3) clarifies what it is that exists within material substances, or rather makes it clear that Descartes is not here attempting to speak with precision about what those properties are. Elsewhere, as we will see, Descartes speaks of *accidents* existing within substances. His willingness to use that terminology, together with this definition of substance as something accidents exist within, serves as an initial suggestion that Descartes is yet another proponent of the substance–accident distinction studied in the previous two chapters. As we progress, it will be quite important that Descartes's theory of accidents is really a theory of modes, but for present purposes let us simply note that he distinguishes between substances and their properties, call them what you will.

(In the above translation, 'item' = *aliquid*, and 'thing' = *res*. The Latin '*res*' is often reserved for substances, or for substances and real accidents [Ch. 12], and in keeping with this usage Descartes refrains from referring to properties as *res*. For them, he uses the noncommittal term '*aliquid*.' In the chapters to come, I will often leave '*res*' untranslated, allowing 'thing' to be used in a loose, broad sense.)

Many other passages attest to Descartes's commitment to the substance–accident distinction, and also to the further idea that substances are known only indirectly, via accidents:

We cannot initially become aware of a substance merely through its being an existing thing, since this alone does not of itself have any effect on us. We can, however, easily be made aware of a substance by any of its attributes, in virtue of the common notion that nothingness possesses no attributes, that is to say, no properties or qualities. For based on perceiving the presence of some attribute, we conclude there must also be present an existing thing or substance to which it can be attributed. (*Principles* I.52)

This just is the veiled-subject doctrine of the previous chapter. Through an attribute, such as a sensible quality, we are "easily made aware of" (*facile agnoscimus*) the underlying substance, but here Descartes commits himself to nothing more than our recognizing there must be *something* underlying such qualities. Whether we can know anything about the character of that underlying substance is at this point unclear. A very similar passage had appeared already in the Third Replies:

---

[2] Descartes's willingness to count God as a substance appears on its face to put some distance between him and his scholastic forebears, who generally do not want to treat God as a substance, and who use God's failure to satisfy the (a) clause as a reason to exclude him from that genus (§6.3). The situation is rather complex, however, because *Principles* I.51, where Descartes sets out his independence criterion for substancehood, insists that 'substance' does not apply univocally to God and creatures. The Second Replies definition quoted in the main text, as I read it, bears out this judgment of non-univocity, inasmuch as it requires two clauses to capture the cases of God and creatures. And if Descartes is going to treat 'substance' as meaning something different for God than for creatures, then he is not really in disagreement with the common scholastic view that God is not a substance.

It is certain that a thought cannot exist without a thing that is thinking; and in general no act or accident can exist without a substance for it to belong to. But we do not come to know a substance immediately, through being aware of the substance itself; we come to know it only through its being the subject of certain acts. (VII:175–6)

These texts, and others we will consider below, make a compelling case that Descartes endorses both the substance–accident distinction, and the veiled-subject doctrine. Moreover, so far as I can see, there are no texts in Descartes that speak against these doctrines.

The last of these passages was provoked by some remarks made by Hobbes. He writes in the Third Objections that "all the philosophers distinguish the subject from its faculties and acts—that is, from its properties and essences. For a being is one thing, its essence is another" (VII:172–3). A little later he remarks that "even the old Peripatetics taught clearly enough that substance is not perceived by the senses but is inferred by reasoning" (VII:178). Descartes readily endorses these remarks, but it is odd to find Hobbes of all people pushing them. For, as we saw in §7.1, Hobbes articulates a strictly corpuscularian conception of material substance according to which what we perceive of a body is simply the body itself, not some further item that inheres in the body, through which we must infer the body's existence. (And since Hobbes is an avowed materialist [§16.2], the case of material substances is the only case.) Now we know that Hobbes did not begin writing the *De corpore* until the mid-1640s, whereas the Objections and Replies date from 1641. So it may be that he changed his mind on this topic. What seems more likely, though, is that Hobbes is making an *ad hominem* argument here, appealing in each of the quoted passages to what others have standardly thought, and then using these as premises against Descartes.

Imagine Hobbes in a more constructive mood. Instead of offering Descartes these poisoned premises, he might have made a friendly corpuscularian suggestion: that Descartes not distinguish between a substance and its properties, but instead treat those properties as simply ways of conceiving the substance, so that in knowing about properties we immediately know about the substance itself. Since on this view the substance itself—the body—is all there is, there is no substance–accident distinction and no way even to formulate the veiled-subject doctrine. It is interesting to contemplate how Descartes might have responded to such a suggestion, which would have drawn him toward a purely corpuscularian account. As things actually played out, however, Hobbes was not in a constructive mood: he encouraged Descartes to draw a clear distinction between the substance and its properties, and Descartes took the bait. Moreover, as we have seen and will continue to see, this is not the only place where Descartes commits himself to these scholastic ideas. Hence despite his concern to reject the central tenets of scholastic metaphysics, Descartes retains a commitment to perhaps the most fundamental feature of that theory: the idea that concrete, particular entities can be distinguished into two kinds of metaphysical parts: the immediately observable properties, and the underlying substance. This is not to say, however, that Descartes failed to pursue his ideas to their logical end, and that we should instead look to Hobbes for a more developed post-scholastic ontology. On the contrary, as we will see,

Hobbes's radical views come at a price, a price that Descartes is unwilling to pay, and that he avoids paying by retaining the substance–accident distinction.[3]

8.2. The Wax Passage

Why did Descartes retain the scholastic substance–accident distinction, rather than embrace a fully corpuscularian account? As I stressed in the previous chapter, this is a puzzle that arises not just for Descartes, but for many post-scholastic authors. Their reasons for continuing to endorse the substance–accident distinction are complex and varied, as later chapters will show. In Descartes's case, however, there is one argument that seems especially important. Although he never sets this argument out explicitly, it lies particularly close to the surface in the wax passage from the Second Meditation. The main thrust of that passage is to establish that we apprehend substances through the mind rather than through the senses. Along the way to that conclusion, Descartes needs to distinguish between the substance itself and its sensible qualities. That passage begins with an invitation to "consider the things that ordinary folk think they understand most distinctly of all—the bodies that we touch and see." Descartes focuses on a piece of wax, and describes its various and changeable appearances. Then, after stressing that the wax remains through those sensible changes, he returns to that original invitation:

So what was it in the wax that was understood so distinctly? Certainly none of the items that I arrived at by means of the senses; for whatever came under taste, smell, sight, touch or hearing has now altered—yet the wax remains. Perhaps what it *was* is what I am *now* thinking about: for surely the wax itself was not the sweetness of the honey, or the fragrance of the flowers, or that whiteness, shape, or sound, but rather the body that appeared to me a little while ago to manifest itself in certain ways, and now in different ways. But what precisely is it that I so imagine? Let us concentrate and, after taking away what does not belong to the wax, let us see what is left: surely, it is nothing other than a thing that is extended, flexible, and changeable. (VII:30–1)

Descartes goes on to stress that this conclusion about what the wax is must be understood not through sensory imagination, but rather through "purely mental scrutiny" (VII:31). Only in this way can we properly grasp the wax's capacity for change in shape and size. In effect, Descartes is making an argument against the sort of naive empiricism described in §7.1: against the idea that sensory perception informs us directly about objects in the world around us. He does not deny that perception takes us to the qualities of those objects, but he insists on a distinction between the

---

[3] Loeb, *From Descartes to Hume* pp. 78–93, offers a sustained reading of Descartes as committed to the substance–accident distinction, and remarks that "perhaps the clearest example" in the case of body is the wax passage (p. 91). It is, however, much more common to deny that Descartes has a theory of substance as something beyond a thing's properties. Thus Broackes, "Substance," thinks the sorts of passages on which I rely cause the issues to be "muddied" (p. 158), whereas in fact "Descartes's basic view is that, to learn the true nature of a substance, he needs to find one set of properties (the fundamental ones) and set aside another set (the superficial and changeable ones)—rather than, so to speak, looking for an underlying substance that stood entirely opposed to its properties. In learning of the superficial qualities, he was already learning (superficially) of the substance" (p. 159). See also Clarke, *Descartes's Theory of Mind* ch. 8, and Schmitter, "The Wax and I," esp. p. 189.

qualities and the objects, and contends that only the mind can get all the way to the things themselves.

Descartes's argument for a distinction between the wax and its properties, as I understand it, is grounded in the indiscernibility of identicals: that if two things are in fact the same thing, they must have the same properties. This is an old method of argumentation, which we will encounter over and over in the chapters to come. Scotus in fact had claimed that appeals to discernibility are the *only* way to establish the distinctness of two things. In the context of a different debate over identity, Scotus remarks: "What is it [that establishes their distinctness]? It is, to be sure, that which is *universally* the reason for distinguishing one thing from another: namely, a contradiction. . . . If this is, and that is not, then they are not the same entity in being" (*Ordinatio* IV.11.3 [Wadding VIII n. 54]).[4] In the wax passage, Descartes appeals to successive cases of discernibility to show that the wax itself is distinct from its properties. The passage begins by describing what the senses perceive: the changeable properties of the wax: its hardness, odor, heat, etc. As for the wax itself, here things get tricky, because it is unclear how to characterize the substance side of the distinction. To employ the method of discernibility, we must of course know something about the substance. But the only things we seem to know about it, at first glance, are the very things we want to exclude: its sensible qualities. Descartes accordingly moves very carefully toward a characterization of the substance itself. First, the wax endures through change; it "remains" (line 3). Hence the wax is not its qualities, because any and all of those qualities can cease to exist while the wax endures. Next, the wax is not just something that endures, but something enduring that is "extended, flexible, and changeable" (line 8). This adds further grounds for discernibility, because none of the sensible qualities is so changeable: round is not potentially square, and so on. The final stage of the argument fills in the character of the wax substance still further, explaining that each of the three characteristics just listed has to be given a meaning that extends beyond simply all the *imaginable* states of the wax. Thus Descartes adds: "I understand that the wax is capable of countless changes of this kind, yet I cannot run through this immeasurable number of changes in my imagination" (VII:31). With this, Descartes appeals to the full modal force of his characterization of the wax. The wax is not to be identified with its current sensible qualities, nor with all of its observed sensible qualities, nor even with any finite list of potential qualities. The wax has a potential for variation that goes beyond any such characterization.

This much is given by the text itself. To see the real force of Descartes's argument, more needs to be said, and I will try to develop the argument more fully at the end of this section. Before going that far, however, it may be helpful to consider an alternative reading of the wax passage. Very often, it is supposed that this passage has as its goal nothing more than to show that the essence of the wax is distinct from its sensible qualities, and so distinct from anything we perceive through the senses. But

---

[4] Scotus's remark about discernibility as the key to establishing distinctness shows up later in Ockham, when he remarks that if the same thing can have contradictory properties, "ita perit omnis via probandi distinctionem vel non-identitatem realem inter quaecumque" (*Ordinatio* I.2.1, *Opera theol.* II:16). The idea goes back to Aristotle, *Topics* VII.1, 152a33–37: "any accident belonging to the one must belong also to the other. . . . If in any of these respects there is a discrepancy, clearly they are not the same."

although the essence–accident distinction is certainly something that Descartes needs to establish at this point in the *Meditations*, that cannot be the principal aim of the passage. If the wax passage concerned only our grasp of the wax's essence, and not the wax itself, then the intended conclusion could have been reached without nearly so much fuss, since no one would suppose that we get at the wax's essence through the senses alone. The passage's principal aim is not to show that the senses do not grasp the essence of the wax, but to show that they do not grasp the wax at all. Thus in the final paragraph of the Second Meditation he offers this summary:

I now know that bodies themselves are perceived not by the senses or the faculty of imagination, properly speaking, but by the intellect alone, and that this perception derives not from their being touched or seen but from their being understood; and in view of this I know plainly that nothing can be more easily or evidently perceived by me than my own mind. (VII:34)

This great triumph for rationalism—against naive empiricism—requires not just that the senses do not perceive the *essence* of bodies, but that they do not perceive bodies at all. With that we have the second of the principal theses announced as the title of the Second Meditation: "On the nature of the human mind: that the mind is better known than the body." Although existence proofs like the *cogito* always require some discussion of what the thing is whose existence is asserted—and hence Descartes's discussion must make its way through some thorny questions about the nature or essence of the mind—the result he is really after in the latter part of the Second Meditation is a comparison between our knowledge of minds and our knowledge of bodies.[5]

The wax passage itself is not perfectly clear at every stage about its target. The long passage quoted at the start of this section concludes by saying that the accidents do not "belong to the wax" (line 7) and that the wax is "nothing other than a thing that is extended" etc. (line 8)—phrases that point toward the view I am describing. But that passage had begun by asking "what was it *in the wax* that was understood so distinctly?" (line 1)—as if the discussion were focused on the essence within the thick concrete substance. Then a page later, in drawing conclusions from the argument we have been considering, he asks:

What is this wax that is perceived by the mind alone? It is of course the same wax that I see, touch, and imagine, the same in short that I took it to be from the start. And yet what should be

---

[5] The wax passage is standardly read as concerning our grasp of essences exclusively, rather than also our grasp of the substances themselves, so that Descartes's remarks about our grasp of the wax through mind alone are replaced with claims about our grasp of the *nature* of the wax. For prominent examples, see Margaret Wilson, *Descartes* pp. 76–99, and Hatfield, *Descartes and the Meditations* pp. 125–37. To be sure, the Second Meditation is concerned with the nature of mind and body. And Descartes does elsewhere confine himself to showing that a substance's changeable qualities are not part of the nature of that substance (e.g., *Principles* II.4 and II.11, where he considers the nature of a stone). But the wax passage is both explicit about its stronger claim, and also *needs* that stronger claim, for the larger purposes of the Second Meditation. For a reading of the passage more like my own, see Secada, *Cartesian Metaphysics* pp. 133–9.

The usual reading of the wax passage is so distorting that even the title of the Second Meditation is commonly misread, so that "De natura mentis humanae: quod ipsa sit notior quam corpus" is understood to announce the intention of showing that the *nature* of the mind is better known than the *nature* of the body. Although *ipsa* could refer back to *natura*, its paring with *corpus* suggests *mentis* as its antecedent. Moreover, the French translation renders *ipsa* as *il*, which can refer only to *esprit*, not to *nature* (IXA:18). Finally, and decisively, we have the correspondence in which Descartes asks Mersenne to insert the phrase after the colon, and that letter makes it clear that *ipsa* refers to *mens* (III:297). The ambiguity in the final version in fact seems to result from Descartes's forgetting how he had worded the original title, and Mersenne's not making the necessary adjustment to avoid the ambiguity.

noted is that its perception is not vision, touch, or imagination—nor has it ever been, although it seemed that way before—but of purely mental scrutiny. (VII:31)

It is hard, at first glance, to know what to make of this passage, given that it seems to contradict itself from line to line: first claiming that only the mind perceives the wax, then that the senses do, then again that only the mind does. Descartes goes on almost immediately, however, to correct what he had just said:

Yet here I marvel at how weak and prone to error my mind is. For although I am thinking about these matters within myself, silently and without speaking, nonetheless the actual words bring me up short, and I am almost tricked by ordinary ways of talking. For we *say* that we *see* the wax itself, if it is present, not that we *judge* it to be there from its color or shape. From this I might immediately have concluded that the wax is grasped (*cognosci*) by the eye's seeing it, and not solely by the mind's inspection. I might have, at least, if I had not then happened to see through the window men crossing the square. Ordinarily, I say that I see the men, no less than the wax. But what do I *see*, other than hats and coats, which could conceal automatons? I *judge* that they are men. And so something that I thought I was seeing with my eyes is in fact comprehended solely by the faculty of judgment which is in my mind. (VII:31–2)

Stylistically, nothing like this deservedly famous passage is to be found in scholasticism. Descartes puts things one way, then stops himself short, then explains just what it was, passing by on the street below, that actually stopped him short, then puts his point just the way he wants it. We can envision the man himself in his study, as if in a Vermeer painting.

The passage makes it quite clear that we do not see the wax. Sensible qualities stand to the wax as hat and coats stand to the men, and so we do not perceive the wax in virtue of perceiving the wax's sensible qualities.[6] Of course there is a sense in which it is absurd to deny that one sees the wax, just as it is absurd to deny that one sees people walking by on the street. Descartes is well aware of that, which is presumably why he lets the original, contradictory passage stand, and then carefully corrects it. In a broad sense, we can speak of seeing many things that are, strictly speaking, only inferred on the basis of something else. If we are to speak strictly, however, all we see are the sensible qualities of things. These are no part of the things themselves, and so to grasp the substance one needs to, as he puts it in the next paragraph, "distinguish the wax from its external forms—take the clothes off, as it were, and consider it naked" (VII:32). There could be no starker statement of the substance–accident distinction.[7]

---

[6] The comparison of a substance's accidental qualities to clothing is repeated in a passage added to the French translation of the Third Meditation: "Pour ce qui est des autres qualitez dont les idées des choses corporelles sont composées, à sçavoir l'étendue, la figure, la situation, et le mouvement de lieu, ... ce sont seulement de certains modes de la substance, *et comme les vestemens sous lesquels la substance corporelle nous paroist* ..." (IXA:35).

[7] Williams, *Descartes* pp. 220–1, considers a reading of the wax passage much like I offer here, but rejects it as too metaphysical in its understanding of Descartes's aims. Williams thus cannot take at face value Descartes's claim at VII:31–2 that we do not see the wax. See too Carriero, *Between Two Worlds* p. 440 n. 32, who thinks it "not false" but merely "misleading" to say that we see the wax itself. Carriero evidently thinks it would be equally misleading to speak of seeing *anything* under a specific description, on the grounds that descriptions require intellectual judgment. Similarly, Carriero cannot believe Descartes really means it when he says that shape etc. "does not belong to the wax," and so he proposes we understand the passage as a claim about the wax "simply insofar as it is a body, cutting away from everything else that belongs to it" (*Between Two Worlds* p. 110). This, it seems to me, introduces a crippling subjectivity into the foundation of Descartes's thought. Descartes needs objective facts about enduring substances and their natures, if he is ever to distinguish mind from body.

As explicit as the Second Meditation seems in reaching this conclusion, it has not often been read this way. Perhaps that is partly because readers have been unfamiliar with the scholastic tradition of identifying the underlying subject of the accidents as the substance itself (§6.1), and so have simply been unable to see the text for what it is. Partly, too, it is not obvious what role such an identification might play within the Second Meditation. In fact, it plays a crucial role, extending the epistemological results of earlier discussions in a new direction. Whereas the main focus of the discussion up until this point had been to stress the *certainty* with which we grasp the mind, the wax passage shows that the mind is grasped more *distinctly* than is the body. (The passage [VII:29–34] uses cognates of 'distinctly' a dozen times.) Thus when Descartes turns to consider the passage's implications for the mind, the first conclusion he reaches is this: "Do I not grasp myself not only much more truly and certainly, but also much more distinctly and evidently?" (VII:33). That the mind is grasped more truly and certainly was established by cogito-style arguments, juxtaposed with the skeptical scenarios of the First Meditation. Now, however, a further conclusion has been reached: that our grasp of the mind is more distinct. Here 'distinctly' is a technical term, so that to apprehend a thing distinctly is to grasp it in isolation from other things, as opposed to having a confused apprehension of multiple things at once.[8] This helps clarify the exact sense in which the senses do and do not perceive the wax. In a sense they do, because they perceive other things (sensible qualities) that are a sign of the wax's presence, and so reliably give rise to a grasp of the wax. (This is what the scholastics referred to as sensation *per accidens*.)[9] In the strict sense the senses do not perceive the wax, however, because they do not grasp the wax distinctly, but grasp it at most as part of grasping some larger, thicker cluster of things. To say that the senses can be *reliable* detectors of the wax is of course to ignore the skeptical worries of the First Meditation. Those worries have not yet been discharged, and part of the Second Meditation's case for the mind's being better known rests on the potential fallibility of the senses. The wax passage broadens the case, however, by showing that quite apart from challenges to the reliability of sense perception, the senses even in the best case never get at the wax itself, distinctly. Hence even once the skeptical worries are discharged in the Sixth Meditation, and the certainty of sensory perception has been vindicated, it remains the case that bodies are grasped no more directly and readily than is the mind. (Although Descartes does not stress the point, what is true here for the sense's grasp of body is true likewise for introspection's grasp of the mind: because introspection reveals individual instances of thought rather than the mind itself, the mind can be grasped distinctly only through further reasoning [§8.4]. Hence the wax passage by itself shows only that bodies are not *more* readily perceived than is the wax— and this is how he carefully puts the case in the concluding paragraph of the Second Meditation: "nothing can be more easily or evidently perceived by me than my own mind" [VII:34]. Only when the wax passage is supplemented by the earlier reflections

---

[8] On Descartes's use of 'distinct,' see *Principles* I.45 (VIIIA:22): "Distinctam autem [voco] illam [perceptionem], quæ, cum clara sit, ab omnibus aliis ita sejuncta est et præcisa, ut nihil plane aliud, quam quod clarum est, in se contineat."

[9] On the scholastic theory of sensation *per accidens*, see my *Thomas Aquinas on Human Nature* pp. 270–8. Descartes himself offers an account of very much this form, though without the scholastic jargon, in the Sixth Replies (VII:437–8). See also Carriero, *Between Two Worlds* p. 123.

on the certainty of introspective knowledge do we get the conclusion that the mind is *better* known.)

Having now tried to motivate Descartes's insistence on the substance–accident distinction, let me return to the argument of the wax passage itself. What that argument shows, through an appeal to the indiscernibility of identicals, is that accidents are not substances. That all by itself is not a very interesting result, however, because no one could propose simply identifying substance and accident. Any credible account would have to tell a sophisticated story about how substances are constructed from accidents, or accidents constructed from substances. Begin with the first. The simplest such story would treat a substance as just a cluster of sensible qualities, an idea that was at least occasionally broached by scholastic authors (§§7.3–4). Here Descartes can appeal to discernibility in quite a straightforward way, showing that such a cluster endures only for as long as its elements do, whereas the wax endures through all such change. That the wax does indeed endure is axiomatic for purposes of the argument: as he puts it right at the start of the discussion, "Does the same wax remain? It must be admitted that it does; no one denies it, no one thinks otherwise" (VII:30). Given this axiom, and given the changeability of the wax, the wax cannot be any one particular cluster of sensible qualities.

One might wonder whether, in developing the argument in this way, I am going too far beyond what Descartes's texts actually give us. In fact, however, the synopsis to the *Meditations* expressly considers bodies that are in effect bundles of accidents. In that discussion, Descartes makes the surprising claim that all substances are incorruptible—a puzzling remark that will have to await discussion until §28.3. For now, we can consider only how that claim gets applied to human beings:

> The human body, insofar as it differs from other bodies, is nothing other than the assemblage of a certain configuration of limbs, together with other such accidents. The human mind, in contrast, is not made up of any accidents in this way, but is a pure substance. For even if all its accidents change, so that it understands, wills, and senses different things, and so on, it does not on that account become a different mind. The human body, in contrast, becomes a different body merely as a result of a change in the shape of some of its parts. (VII:14; see also VII:153–4)

The human mind, as a pure substance, "is not made up of any accidents" (lines 2–3), and so is able to persist through change. The human body, in contrast, fails to be an enduring substance precisely because it is a mere "assemblage" of accidents. If this were what the wax were, it would not endure either, but since the wax does endure, it cannot be a mere assemblage. Instead, the wax must be a pure substance, just as the mind is. Hence Descartes remarks, as quoted above, that we should strip the wax of its sensible qualities and "consider it naked" (VII:32). (How the wax can be a better substance candidate than the human body—if indeed it really is—is a question that interacts with the puzzling doctrine that all substances are incorruptible, and also with the puzzling status of the Cartesian mind–body composite; it will have to wait until §25.6 and §28.5.)

Now consider a more complex theory, according to which a substance is a changing cluster of accidents. At t_1 the wax is a cluster of accidents including cold and hard; at t_2 it is a cluster including hot and soft, and so on. Here again discernibility applies: Descartes can appeal to his conception of the wax as not determinately one quality or another, but as indeterminately extended and changeable. Invoking a varying series of constituent accidents over time is not enough, because Descartes describes the wax as having a wide-open potentiality for qualities beyond those that have been or will be actual, as not just a body having a sequence of determinate shapes, but as "extended, flexible, and changeable" (VII:31) in an open-ended way, "capable of countless changes of this kind." By appealing to such *modal* properties, which go beyond any actual observable properties, Descartes can reject any theory of the wax that treats it as a simple sequence of successive, concrete wax instantiations. A sequence of that sort would seem to lack the resources to explain why the wax has an almost unlimited capacity for transformation. It would remain open to Descartes's opponent to deny that the wax does endure, in favor of an ontology according to which one thing is replaced by another, moment after moment. This, however, would not only violate the primary axiom of the case—that the wax endures—but also leave no room for the idea that this very piece of wax could become hotter or cooler, harder or softer. That fundamental feature of substances—their capacity to take on a wide range of new qualities—gets built into the level of the underlying substance, and helps to distinguish it from the superficial sensory level of reality. (The indeterminacy of the Cartesian substances is an important but startling feature of his view; for further discussion, see §13.7.)

So much for reducing substance to some sort of collection of accidents. What about the converse move, reducing accidents to substance? This is the line we saw Hobbes take in §7.1, according to which an accident is simply "the mode of conceiving a body" (*De corpore* 8.2). On Hobbes's ontology, there is no substance–accident distinction, but only substances, and substances are simply bodies, composed of nothing other than their integral parts. One of the attractive features of this sort of approach is that it holds out the possibility of avoiding the veiled-subject doctrine: one can instead say that to see the shape or color of a body just is to see the body itself. The wax passage explains why Descartes rejects this line of thought, because again the indiscernibility of identicals can be brought to bear. If the accidents are nothing other than the substance, then no change to the accidents is possible without a change to the substance. Since Descartes takes it as axiomatic that the wax endures through change, he has to draw a distinction between substance and accident, allowing accidents to change while the substance endures.[10]

It may seem implausible to suppose that Descartes would need to hold onto so much scholastic metaphysical baggage simply to retain something as mundane as enduring substances. Yet quite apart from what the texts we have considered seem on their face to say, the context in which they were written bears out this line of thought, both retrospectively and prospectively. First, the way Descartes defends the substance–accident distinction coincides closely with the standard scholastic story in this domain: that to reject an ontology of substances and accidents leaves one unable to account for the endurance of substances through change. Second, looking ahead, those who do

---

[10]   On accidental forms as required to explain the endurance of substance through change, see Scheibler's interesting remarks in *Metaphysica* I.22.20.1 (p. 311): "Sceptici aiebant nihil esse nisi quod videretur. . . . Iuxta hanc sententiam nulla forma erit. Nam nulla forma videri potest. . . . Quod formae dentur, inprimis inde primo manifestum est, quia secus nulla daretur corruptio. Nam corruptio non est, nisi per separationem vel secussum formae a materia quam informavit." His claim is not that there could be no endurance without form, but that there could be no change. For a similar claim, see Burgersdijk, *Inst. meta.* II.17.12.

reject the substance–accident distinction during our period seem to recognize the radical consequences of so doing. When Hobbes, for instance, reduces accidents to substances, he accordingly insists that our talk of things going in and out of existence is merely a manner of speaking, and that in actual fact the things that exist have their existence permanently, unless God intervenes (§28.4). In this respect, as in others, a wholly reductive corpuscularianism comes at the cost of commonsense ontology. It is certainly possible to read Descartes as offering his own sort of radical ontology, and in fact he is often read in that way (§28.3, §28.5). But if we take at face value his professed commitment to ordinary substances like living organisms and even artifacts, then we should be on the alert for the features of his system that allow him to retain something like a commonsense ontology. Foremost among these, I believe, is the substance–accident distinction.

8.3. Substance and Principal Attribute

To take Descartes's substance–accident distinction seriously requires confronting the question of what substances are. One would expect Descartes to have something fairly clear to say about such a fundamental question, but in fact he does not. Broadly speaking, there are two possibilities. One is that the substance underlying the modes is just the principal attribute: that the substance of bodies is *extension*, and that the substance of minds is *thought*. The other possibility is that substances are something beneath the principal attribute—a still deeper underlying subject. Each view has texts in its favor, and each view presents serious difficulties. On balance, though, the first suggestion seems closer to being right: that extension just is what a body is, and that thought just is what a mind is. Such claims are, however, deeply obscure, and this obscurity in the end undermines Descartes's pretensions to transparency and intelligibility.[11]

Descartes formally introduces the notion of a principal attribute in *Principles* I.53:

[E]ach substance has one principal property that constitutes its nature and essence, and to which all its other properties are referred. Thus extension in length, breadth, and depth constitutes the nature of corporeal substance; and thought constitutes the nature of thinking substance.

There is no dispute that the principal attribute counts as the essence (or, equivalently, nature) of a substance. Given this much, one would expect the principal attribute to be at least *part* of the substance. Yet it is easy to find passages that suggest a very different picture: that the substance is something beneath all the properties of a thing, completely veiled from our comprehension. According to the Fourth Replies,

We do not grasp substances immediately, as I have noted elsewhere, but only as a result of perceiving certain forms or attributes, which must inhere in some thing (*res*) in order to exist. That thing in which they inhere is what we call *substance*. If we subsequently wanted to strip that same substance of those attributes by which we grasp it, we would be destroying our entire

---

[11] The starkest text in favor of a distinction between substance and principal attribute comes in the *Conversation with Burman* (V:156), but I think that second-hand report is not reliable enough to be worth even quoting in this context, especially since, a page earlier, Descartes is reported as identifying a substance with all its attributes (V:155). It is amazing how many scholars have quoted one of these passages but not the other, depending on which favors their own view.

knowledge of it. We could pronounce some words about it, but we would not clearly and distinctly perceive their meaning. (VII:222)

'Attribute' is used here generally for any accident, and would seem to include what the *Principles* later calls the principal attribute. Only when the passage is so read would stripping the substance of all attributes leave us with no knowledge of it. The passage thus seems to say quite clearly that substance is something distinct from all its attributes. In remarking that this point had been noted earlier (line 1), Descartes might be thinking back to a remark quoted earlier from the Third Replies (VII:176), or perhaps to his definition of 'substance' as the subject of attributes (also quoted earlier, from the Second Replies). Immediately after offering that definition, he had continued as follows:

For nor do we have any idea of substance taken by itself (*praecise*), other than that it is the thing (*res*) in which the items we perceive ... exist formally or eminently. For we know by the natural light that no real attribute can belong to nothing. (VII:161)

To consider substance *praecise* is to consider it apart from everything else.[12] If substances just were their principal attributes—if Descartes really means that a mind, say, just is its principal attribute—then the idea of a substance *praecise* just would be the idea of a principal attribute. Yet what Descartes says here is that our idea of substance by itself is the bare idea of a subject for accidents. And in case any doubt remains about where the principal attribute fits into this scheme, he immediately turns to the separate cases of mind and body, defining mind as "the substance in which thought immediately inheres," and body as "the substance that is the immediate subject of local extension and of the accidents that presuppose extension" (VII:161).

The more technical discussion in the *Principles* offers a much more fine-grained understanding of these matters. At first, Descartes's use of 'attribute' seems to coincide with the view just described, so that an attribute is something that the substance "has" (I.53), and something that is "in a subject" (I.56). Something new begins to happen, however, in I.62 and I.63, where Descartes claims that substance and principal attribute are distinct only through a distinction of reason (distinct conceptually, as I will sometimes say). The starkest passage here occurs at the start of I.63, which holds that the principal attributes "should be considered as nothing other than thinking substance itself and extended substance itself—that is, as mind and body." This is not quite as decisive as it might seem, however, because what he goes on to say might imply that we identify substance and attribute more for strategic reasons than because they are in fact identical: "In this way, they are understood most clearly and distinctly. Indeed, it is easier for us to understand extended substance or thinking substance than substance on its own, leaving out the fact that it thinks or is extended." These remarks do not unambiguously assert that substance and principal attribute are identical—only that this is a distinction best left undrawn.

---

[12] *Substantiae praecise sumptae* (VII:161) looks exactly equivalent to *substantiam solam* (VIIIA:31), and in exactly the same context. For its scholastic sense, see, e.g., Aquinas, *In Sent.* I.21.1.1.2 sc 1: "de quocumque praedicatur commune praecise, praedicatur cum praecisione et proprium." The term also appears in Descartes's definition of a distinct perception (*Principles* I.45, VIIIA:22), where it is paired with 'separate' (*sejuncta*). Carriero, based on a close reading of the *Meditations*, comes to a similar conclusion about how to understand '*praecise*' (*Between Two Worlds* pp. 94–7).

What these passages do unambiguously assert is that substance and principal attribute are distinct only by reason. It is not obvious, however, what this amounts to. In his official account of this distinction, he characterizes a substance and an attribute as distinct by reason alone when the substance is unintelligible apart from the attribute (I.62). No mention there is made of such a distinction's requiring real identity. Moreover, in a letter commenting on this very passage from the *Principles*, Descartes writes that he does not speak of a distinction of reason in cases where there is "no foundation in reality" (IV:349). This might well suggest that, for Descartes, a distinction of reason obtains only between things that are, in reality, distinct (albeit mutually dependent and so not *really* distinct in the technical, independence-requiring sense [esp. §13.6]). And indeed there seems no reason why one could not have two distinct things that are mutually dependent—no reason, in other words, why mutual dependence entails identity.

Yet even if mutual dependence without identity seems possible, and even if all Descartes expressly commits himself to (in analyzing the conceptual distinction) is mutual dependence, and even if we have a letter stressing that a conceptual dependence requires a foundation in reality, still—viewed in the proper historical context—it is hard to believe that Descartes could regard *two* things as merely conceptually distinct. Although there was controversy among scholastic authors over the subtleties of the conceptual distinction, it was a bedrock principle that where there is only a conceptual distinction between x and y, then $x = y$. The very point of speaking of a conceptual distinction—a distinction of reason—is to stress that the only true distinctness occurs on the side of our concepts. For Descartes to deviate from this usage would amount to a gross and embarrassing misuse of one of the basic philosophical concepts of his era. The letter quoted from above, moreover, shows Descartes to have a good grasp even of the subtleties here. For when he insists that even a conceptual distinction has a foundation in reality, he is appealing to a standard distinction between a conceptual distinction motivated by some feature of reality, and one where reason does all the work, without any encouragement from reality. An example of the first kind would be the distinction between God's goodness and wisdom, which has a foundation in the created world inasmuch as some things reflect God's goodness, and others reflect God's wisdom. An example of the second would be to think of a thing as identical to itself. Descartes says he recognizes only the first sort of conceptual distinction; even such cases, however, involve no distinctness within the thing itself. Thus a conceptual distinction within God can be grounded in reality, but cannot be grounded in God, who is perfectly simple. Although Descartes does not explain things to this extent, he uses the right sorts of examples. He speaks, for instance, of God's justice and mercy as conceptually distinct. He then goes on to describe essence and existence as conceptually distinct, but says that the things themselves are "in no way distinguished" (IV:350). Although he does not make this same claim expressly in the case of substance and principal attribute, an addition to the French translation of *Principles* I.63 seems to strain to get this idea across: "they [the principal attributes] differ from substance by this alone, that we sometimes consider thought or extension without reflecting on the thing itself that thinks or that is extended" (IXB:54). This passage replaces the Latin text's remark that substance and principal attribute are "only conceptually distinct." Even in this later French addition to the text, there is room to see Descartes distinguishing the attribute (thought or extension) from "the thing itself." The point Descartes seems to want to make, however, even as language works against him, is that such a distinction is purely conceptual, in the sense that the two differ *only* in our thoughts.[13]

Admittedly, Descartes's treatment of the conceptual distinction is not clear enough to bear a great deal of weight. In fact, perhaps the most decisive considerations spring not from any specific text, but from the larger consequences for his view if substance is something beyond its principal attribute. To take such a stance would commit Descartes to a particularly extreme version of the doctrine of a veiled subject. Descartes's version would be more extreme than the standard scholastic version, and less attractive, because the scholastics at least had the general outlines of what a substance is: a composite of substantial form and prime matter. All Descartes has in that vicinity is his principal attribute. If substance is not that, even partially, then it is a complete and utter mystery what substance would be. Some Descartes scholars have been surprisingly willing to tolerate this conclusion, at least implicitly. Yet it seems a complete disaster for Descartes's larger project. First, as Malebranche and others would later

---

[13]   On the identity of substance and principal attribute, see McCracken, "Knowledge of the Soul" pp. 803–4: "Hence, in clearly conceiving the principal attribute of a thing, we are really conceiving the thing—the substance—itself." Nolan, "Reductionism," makes an extended argument for this identification. Indeed, Nolan takes *Principles* I.62 at its word in identifying a substance with *all* of its inseparable attributes, including not only its principal attribute but also necessary attributes like duration and existence. Kaufman, "Divine Simplicity," accepts that the principal attribute is identical with the substance, but denies that all attributes are identical with their substance, even though they are conceptually distinct. For a similar conclusion, see Rozemond, *Descartes's Dualism* pp. 221–2, note 19. My remarks in the main text commit me to siding with Nolan, inasmuch as Descartes is clear that duration, for example, is merely conceptually distinct from substance. Hence I oversimplify in speaking only of the *principal* attribute as identical with the substance. It is not clear to me—and so I set aside—the issue of whether it makes Descartes's view more or less tenable to identify the substance with all of its inseparable attributes.

Other appeals to a conceptual distinction confirm the impression that it entails identity. E.g., space and corporeal substance "non in re differunt . . . sed tantum in modo quo a nobis concipi solent" (*Principles* II.10); number, relative to the thing that is numbered "in re non differt, sed tantum ex parte nostri conceptus" (*Principles* II.8), where the case of number is introduced as analogous to the relationship between quantity and extended substance.

For scholastic instances of the sort of technical terminology for distinctions to which Descartes appeals, see Fonseca, *In Meta.* V.6.6–7 (II:395–410); Suárez, *Disp. meta.* VII.1.4; Eustachius a Sancto Paulo, *Summa* IV.3.3.5–8 (III:45–7); Scheibler, *Metaphys.* I.8. Suárez is particularly clear on the sort of foundation at issue in a conceptual distinction: "Unde fundamentum quod dicitur esse in re ad hanc distinctionem non est vera et actualis distinctio inter eas res quae sic distingui dicuntur; alias non fundamentum distinctionis sed distinctio ipsa antecederet; sed esse debet vel eminentia ipsius rei quam sic mens distinguit . . . vel certe habitudo aliqua ad res alias vere et in re ipsa distinctas, penes quas talis distinctio excogitatur seu concipitur" (*Disp. meta.* I:251a). De Soto offers *Peter's being a friend to himself* as a distinction of reason, but does not distinguish between different species of such a distinction (*In Isag. De universalibus* q. 3 [p. 41B]). The distinction between two sorts of conceptual distinctions can be found even in Aquinas, speaking of the divine attributes: "Et quia unumquodque eorum est in Deo secundum sui verissimam rationem, et ratio sapientiae non est ratio bonitatis, inquantum huiusmodi, relinquitur quod sunt diversa ratione, non tantum ex parte ipsius ratiocinantis, sed ex proprietate ipsius rei" (*Sent.* I.2.1.2c). Although Aquinas himself may well be following an earlier tradition, this at least counts as an early precedent for the often-mentioned distinction between a *distinctio rationis ratiocinantis* and a *distinctio rationis ratiocinatae*.

The Latin of *Principles* I.62–3 is clear that it is the substance and attribute themselves that are distinct. Cottingham's translation, however, mistakenly suggests that our *concepts* are conceptually distinct, rendering "Nonnulla enim est difficultas in abstrahenda notione substantiae a notionibus cogitationis vel extensionis, **quae** scilicet ab **ipsa** ratione tantum diversae sunt" as "For we have some difficulty in abstracting the notion of substance from the notions of thought and extension, since the distinction between these *notions* and the *notion* of substance itself is merely a conceptual distinction" (I:215, emphasis added). The Latin pronouns in bold are most naturally read as referring back to *substantiae* and *cogitationis vel extensionis*, rather than to their corresponding *notions*. Moreover, the translation makes no sense philosophically, inasmuch as these *notions* are distinct modally, not conceptually. The French translation makes the intended sense clear, and then goes on to make this addition (translated in the main text): "car **elles** ne different **de la substance** que par cela seul que nous considerons quelquefois la pensée ou l'étendue, sans faire reflexion sur la chose même qui pense ou qui est étendue" (IXB:54).

note, this sort of picture invites an infinite regress of substances, since if we could ever identify the nature of that underlying, mystery substance, we would have reason to distinguish again the substance from that nature, taking us down one level deeper, *ad infinitum*.[14] Second, this approach violates one of Descartes's most fundamental desiderata: a thoroughly intelligible philosophical system. His early, unpublished treatise, *The World*, highlights this idea, optimistically describing a new world containing nothing unintelligible: no scholastic prime matter; no real qualities; no quantity over and above substance. In short, "a world in which there is nothing that the dullest minds are incapable of conceiving" (XI:36). This is the same world that the *Principles* more boldly identifies as our world. How could this scheme contain a conception of substance so deeply unintelligible? How could Descartes so bitterly criticize the scholastics for their obscure metaphysical doctrines if he himself was committed to something even more unintelligible, and not just in some dark corner of his system but right at its heart, as the very substances themselves that are minds and bodies?[15]

These are results we should resist. Although I will argue in the following section that Descartes cannot escape a certain amount of unintelligibility in his conception of substance, he makes it clear enough in various passages that he does not want to treat the principal attribute as something that inheres in some further, unknowable subject. Perhaps the most clear-cut of these passages occurs in his critical commentary

---

[14] Malebranche, *Search after Truth* III.2.8 amounts to a commentary on Descartes's claim that the non-necessary attributes of a substance lead to a grasp of the substance's essence. Against the (implicitly scholastic) notion that extension might inhere in some further substance, Malebranche invokes the threat of a regress: "Et ce qu'on dit que c'est le subjet et le principe de l'étendue se dit *gratis*, et sans que l'on conçoive distinctement ce qu'on dit, c'est-à-dire sans qu'on en ait d'autre idée qu'une générale et de logique, comme de sujet et de principe. De sorte que l'on pourrait encore imaginer un nouveau sujet et un nouveau principe de ce sujet de l'étendue, et ainsi à l'infini, parce que l'esprit se représente des idées générales de sujet et de principe comme il lui plaît" (p. 477; tr. p. 245). Kant is characteristically either deep or obscure on this subject, depending on one's taste and mood: "Man hat schon längst angemerkt, daß uns an allen Substanzen das eigentliche Subject, nämlich das, was übrig bleibt, nachdem alle Accidenzen (als Prädicate) abgesondert worden, mithin das Substantiale selbst unbekannt sei, und über diese Schranken unsrer Einsicht vielfältig Klagen geführt. Es ist aber hiebei wohl zu merken, daß der menschliche Verstand darüber nicht in Anspruch zu nehmen sei, daß er das Substantiale der Dinge nicht kennt, d.i. für sich allein bestimmen kann, sondern vielmehr darüber, daß er es als eine bloße Idee gleich einem gegebenen Gegenstande bestimmt zu erkennen verlangt" (*Prolegomena* sec. 46).

[15] Concern over the status of Descartes's fundamental substances has been a perennial subject of discussion among French and German scholars, and has its origins in the post-Kantian tradition that runs through Heidegger. According to Alquié, "Expérience ontologique" p. 25: "le moi n'est pas constitué par la pensée . . . ; il est le substrat ontologique de la pensée"; p. 33: "la chose est étendue, elle n'est pas l'étendue." These remarks are sharply attacked by Gueroult, in comments printed in that same volume (pp. 32–57), who remarks that on Alquié's account, "Descartes ne sera plus Descartes" (p. 36). One might deny that Descartes's theory is symmetrical with respect to mind and body. Marion, *Metaphysical Prism* pp. 150–69, suggests an asymmetrical account on which the mind is identified with thought, and "substance is extended to other beings only after the fact, and perhaps illegitimately" (p. 168). English-language scholars broach the topic less often. Blackwell, "Descartes' Concept of Matter," argues that body must have a further subject beneath extension. Loeb, in contrast, thinks that Descartes identifies body with extension, but thinks of mind as a subject underlying thought (*From Descartes to Hume* pp. 91–3). According to Des Chene, *Physiologia* p. 69: "Descartes, with misgivings, treats extension as an attribute of substance rather than as substance itself."

The worry that Descartes was (or should have been) committed to a mind beneath consciously available experiences goes back to seventeenth-century Cartesianism. Bayle, for instance, remarks that "Souvenons-nous que les plus subtils cartésiens soutiennent que nous n'avons point d'idée de la substance spirituelle. Nous savons soulement par expérience qu'elle pense, mais nous ne savons pas quelle est la nature de l'être dont les modifications sont des pensées; nous ne connaissons point quel est le sujet, et quel est le fond auquel les pensées sont inhérentes" ("Simonides" XIII:297a; Popkin p. 282). Presumably, he chiefly has in mind Malebranche, who rejected the identification of mind with thought even though he insisted on the identification of body with extension. For Malebranche's criticisms of Descartes on this score, see e.g. Jolley, *Light of the Soul* pp. 114–31; Schmaltz, *Malebranche's Theory*. For a very helpful survey of seventeenth-century views on this general theme, see McCracken, "Knowledge of the Soul."

on a broadsheet published in 1647 by his one-time disciple, Henricus Regius. Regius, implicitly invoking Descartes's authority, had characterized extension and thought as "attributes that inhere in particular substances, as in subjects" (VIIIB:342). Descartes rejects this way of talking, remarking that "I did not say that these attributes inhere in substances as in subjects distinct from them" (VIIIB:348). Surely Descartes is objecting not just to the idea of inherence (*inesse*) in a subject, but more generally to the idea that the substance is something beyond the principal attribute. A few lines later, Descartes further characterizes *extension* as "the subject" of modes, and *thought* as "the internal principle" in which modes "reside" (VIIIB:348–9). This effectively identifies the principal attribute as the substance, given that elsewhere (as we have seen repeatedly) Descartes is so clear in defining *substance* as the subject of modes.

Further pieces of evidence in favor of identifying substance and principal attribute come from special considerations peculiar either to body or to mind. With respect to body, since its principal attribute is extension, we can bring to bear Descartes's various remarks on the status of extension. In this context—motivated by his keenness to reject the scholastic theory of quantity (Ch. 14)—he is quite clear in denying that extension is anything other than substance. Those who do accept that common scholastic distinction simply fail to have a clear conception of what they mean:

When they distinguish the substance from its extension or quantity, they either understand nothing by the term 'substance,' or they have only a confused idea of incorporeal substance, which they falsely attribute to corporeal substance, relegating the true idea of this corporeal substance to extension, which instead they call an accident. (*Principles* II.9)

This looks like very strong evidence for identifying the principal attribute of body with the substance of body itself—assuming Descartes is talking about the principal attribute. And it is hard to see what else he could be talking about.[16]

With respect to mind, Descartes famously insists on its transparency: for instance, that "nothing can be in me of which I am entirely unaware" (First Replies, VII:107). (Elsewhere he glosses the "in me" of this remark as *in my mind* [III:273].) This hardly seems to leave room for the idea of a veiled subject beneath the principal attribute of thought. Admittedly, there is a way to escape that conclusion: one could read "in my mind" as limiting the scope of transparency to the modes and attributes of the substance—the things that are "in" the mind—thereby leaving the mind itself as a veiled, unknown substratum. By the end of the following section, this reading may come to look attractive. On its face, however, we should not want to empty the doctrine of transparency of so much of its force.[17]

These passages, together with the untenable consequences of distinguishing between the substance and its principal attribute, suggest that we should reconsider the passages offered earlier as evidence for such a distinction. A first step toward such a reconsideration is to consider that perhaps they are meant to be read not as descriptions of a

---

[16] On extension (quantity) as identical with substance, see also *The World* ch. 6 (XI:35–6). But compare *Principles* II.18, where once again there is the implication of their distinctness.

[17] Regarding transparency, McDowell, "Singular Thought," describes a "fully Cartesian picture" according to which "there are no facts about the inner realm besides what is infallibly accessible to the newly recognized capacity to acquire knowledge" (pp. 150–1). Descartes's own view is perhaps not quite so fully Cartesian, but it would be surprising to find it so far off from this picture.

mysterious unknowable substratum, but rather as cautionary remarks about the disaster that looms if we try to distinguish the substance from all of its properties. So when Descartes speaks, in the Fourth Replies, as if we might "strip that same substance of those attributes by which we grasp it" (VII:222), he means to be describing a kind of absurd mistake that we might make. Now, to be sure, on my reading of Descartes, it is not a mistake to distinguish between the substance and its properties, and to that extent we are entitled to strip away those properties, to get down to the substance itself and to "consider it naked" as he says of the wax (VII:32). In doing so, we are obviously not "destroying our entire knowledge of it," as the Fourth Replies would seem to say (VII:222), since in the case of the wax such a stripping down is precisely Descartes's strategy for coming to an understanding of what the wax is: "a thing that is extended, flexible, and changeable" (VII:31). A second thought, then, building on the first, is that the Fourth Replies and other such passages have in mind a situation where we would try to conceive of a substance without working our way to it through its properties. The main point of that passage, after all, was to show that "we do not grasp substances immediately" (VII:222). This is not incompatible with the lesson of the wax passage, which is that if we begin by thinking about the properties of the wax, and, crucially, thinking about its possible properties, then we can arrive through "purely mental scrutiny" (VII:31) at the wax itself. Those properties—those modes, to use Descartes's later, technical terminology—are not part of the substance, but they point toward the substance, precisely because they are *modes of the substance*, rather than fully distinct real accidents. Accordingly, the nature of the wax itself, extension, is something delivered by reflection on the modes, and the wax is not an unknowable substratum, at least not entirely.[18]

How Descartes's conception of properties as modes rather than real accidents helps with the knowability of substance is a subject that has to await a discussion of what real accidents and modes are, in Chapters 10 and 13. For now, however, there is still more to say about what exactly a principal attribute might be. Reflection on this issue will lead us to see that, no matter how tightly modes and substances are linked, Descartes is not going to be able to escape a certain amount of unintelligibility at the core of his metaphysics.

8.4. Where Transparency Ends

The evidence on balance seems to suggest identifying a substance with its principal attribute. A mind just is thought; a body just is extension. Yet once we put things so baldly, we can see why Descartes might have been hesitant about reaching this conclusion. For it is very hard to see what such claims of identity actually amount to. If, instead, a substance were just an assemblage of modes or, to go to the other extreme,

---

[18] The idea that there is a difference between two ways of stripping off accidents is brought out fairly clearly in a response to Gassendi's *Disquisitio*, printed with the French edition of the *Meditations*, which insists on the distinction between *distinguishing* and *abstracting*: "en distinguant une substance de ses accidens, on doit considerer l'un et l'autre, ce qui fert beaucoup à la connoître; au lieu que, si on separe seulement par abstraction cette substance de ses accidens, c'est à dire, si on la considere toute seule sans penser à eux, cela empêche qu'on ne la puisse si bien connoître, à cause que c'est par les accidens que la nature de la substance est manifestée" (IXA:216). The first corresponds to the strategy of the wax passage, the second to the misguided sort of stripping away described in the Fourth Replies and elsewhere.

some sort of veiled subject beneath the principal attribute, then the principal attribute would not seem so important. Since on either view the substance itself would lie elsewhere, the principal attribute could be set aside as some sort of ontologically lightweight construct. It might, for instance, be regarded as a higher-order determinable property, as some scholars have supposed.[19] If, however, the substance—the mind itself, or the wax itself—is the principal attribute, then we face hard questions about what a principal attribute could possibly be. Descartes regularly speaks of *thought* and *extension* without elaboration, almost glibly, as if everyone knows what he means. But when such talk is juxtaposed against his apparent desire to identify principal attribute and substance, it comes under more theoretical pressure than it can bear. To the most elementary questions—*What is the extension of the wax itself? Is it different from the extension of the candlestick? How exactly?*—Descartes has no apparent answers. Of course, many possible answers suggest themselves; indeed, the idea that the basic material stuff of the universe might just be extension is an old one. Zabarella had found it in Philoponus, and rejected it on the grounds that matter must be what *has* extension, rather than extension itself (Ch. 4 note 21). That certainly sounds right. If it is not right, Descartes owes us an account of why.

Admittedly, the case of corporeal substance in Descartes is particularly vexed, because it is notoriously difficult to get clear on the most basic of questions here, like *Is the wax really a substance at all?* Since I will not be considering such questions until Part VI—where I will eventually despair of finding a developed theory of material substance in Descartes (§25.6, §28.5)—it will be better for now to focus on mental substances, where at least we know what result Descartes is after: he wants my mind to be one substance, yours to be another, and so on. Things here, however, are in some respects just as bad as in the case of bodies, because the question still remains of what it could even mean to say that I am identical to thought. In a letter from 1648, Anteine Arnauld asks how thought can be the essence of mind. It does not seem that a *particular* thought or a series of thoughts can be the essence of mind, Arnauld reasons, since then the essence would be constantly changing, and would seemingly be the product of the mind. Yet neither does it seem that something *universal* could be an essence, since that universal would be an intellectual abstraction (V:213–14). In reply, Descartes rejects both options:

Just as extension, which constitutes the nature of body, differs greatly from the various shapes or modes of extension that it assumes, so thought, or a thinking nature, which I take to constitute the essence of the human mind, is very different from any particular act of thinking. It depends   3
on the mind itself whether it produces these acts of thinking or other ones, but not that it is a thinking thing, just as it depends on a flame itself, as an efficient cause, whether it extends in one direction or another, but not that it is an extended thing. So by 'thought' I do not mean some   6

---

[19]   For attributes as determinable properties, see Ayers's reading of Descartes: "every accident is ultimately or in itself a determinate mode of a determinable property or essence, as roundness is a mode of extension. Any other conception leaves us with an unintelligible notion of 'real accidents' existing 'in' their substances in an unintelligible way" (*Locke*, II:28). Also Beck, *Metaphysics*, à propos the wax passage: "All in fact he is saying is that the essential and fundamental property which persists throughout its modifications, and which is alone grasped by the intellect, is the determinable character of being extended" (p. 102). My own view, as will become more clear in §13.7, is that such indeterminacy is a feature of the substance, but of the substance itself rather than of some harmless determinable property distinct from the substance.

universal that covers all modes of thinking, but a particular nature that receives all those modes, just as extension is a nature that receives all shapes. (V:221)

In denying that the principal attribute is a "universal" (line 7), Descartes seems pretty clearly to rule out the idea that the principal attribute is just some sort of higher-order determinable property. Instead, it is a "particular nature" that "receives" various modes (line 7). Descartes twice switches from the abstract noun 'thought' to the comparatively concrete phrases "thinking nature" (line 2) and "particular nature" (line 7). This suggests a number of things. First, it suggests that we should not conceive of a substance's principal attribute as literally *thought* or *extension*, whatever that might mean. Those terms should instead be bent into their adjectival form, yielding the notion of the mind as something that has a thinking nature—the mind as *res cogitans*. Second, it suggests that particular substances will have their own principal attribute: my mind will have its own nature, distinct from the nature of your mind. Third, Descartes does not quite say here that the principal attribute *is* the substance. Rather, he says that it is the essence or nature (lines 3, 7, 8) of the substance. This leaves room for the idea that even if, as the previous section insisted, the principal attribute is not *distinct* from the substance, it is also not the *whole* of the substance. Does that make sense? At the risk of explaining the obscure through the more obscure, consider how Christian theologians have traditionally wanted to ascribe to God properties such as goodness, but without wanting to say either that goodness exhausts the nature of God, or that God's goodness is distinct from God. In insisting on a mere distinction of reason between substances and their attributes, Descartes is similarly insisting on the metaphysical simplicity of finite substances, when conceived thinly (apart from their modes). But that does not require supposing that it exhausts the nature of my mind to characterize it simply in terms of *thought*. After all, if it did, then my mind would not be intrinsically distinct from your mind.

This last remark takes us decidedly beyond the scope of what Descartes has to say on these subjects. He offers absolutely no theory of how minds are individuated, and only the barest gestures toward a theory in the case of body (§28.5). This might reasonably suggest to some readers that a mistake has been made at some point in the line of reasoning that has led me to this juncture. My own view, however, is that Descartes is well aware of the many puzzling issues that arise regarding the underlying metaphysics of his view, and that he has made the strategic decision to embrace quietism regarding these issues—not because they are not real problems, but because he did not *need* to address them to get the results he was after. Consider the start of the Fifth Meditation:

There are many matters that remain to be investigated concerning the attributes of God and the nature of myself, or my mind, and perhaps I shall take these up at another time. But now that I have seen what to do and what to avoid in order to reach the truth, the most pressing task seems to be to try to escape from the doubts into which I fell a few days ago, and see whether any certainty can be achieved regarding material objects. (VII:63)

I take this caveat to remain in force throughout the *Meditations*. Descartes does not suppose that he has resolved all—or even very many—of the great metaphysical puzzles regarding the nature of substances and their individuation. His goal is the (relatively) more modest one of reaching complete certainty regarding a few very important matters: in particular, the existence of God and the distinction between soul and body (the two topics mentioned on the title page of the second Latin edition of 1642). His later work occasionally attempts to go a bit deeper, but in general remains more or less on the metaphysical surface of things, perhaps because Descartes did not think it possible to go any deeper. As he would remark to Princess Elizabeth in 1643, "there are two facts about the human soul on which depend all the knowledge we can have of its nature. The first is that it thinks, the second is that, being united to the body, it can act and be acted upon along with it. About the second I have said virtually nothing; only the first have I tried to make well understood" (III.664–5). Descartes does not claim that the mind's thinking and interacting with the body tells us everything about its nature, only that it is the key to "all the knowledge we can have."

One reader who did not see this was Gassendi. In the Fifth Set of Objections, and then in exhaustive detail in his *Disquisitio metaphysica* (1644), he rebukes Descartes for supposing that one could account for the essence of mind or body simply by appealing to thought or extension. Here is a characteristic complaint:

> When you go on to say that you are a *thinking* thing, we know what you are saying; but we knew it already, and it was not what we were asking you to tell us. For who doubts that you are thinking? What we are unclear about, what we are looking for, is that inner substance of yours whose distinctive property is thought. (Fifth Objections, VII:276)

Descartes does not deny the basic assumption of Gassendi's argument, that what is wanted is an account of the substance underlying the thing's observable properties. As we have seen, Descartes is as fully committed to the substance–accident doctrine as Gassendi is, and the *Meditations* is certainly aimed at grasping the substance. But whereas Gassendi is also committed to a strong version of the veiled-subject doctrine, according to which a grasp of the mind's nature requires a difficult "quasi-chemical" (VII:277) analysis (§7.1, §27.2), Descartes appears to think the methods of the *Meditations* get us to the very essence of mind and body. To Gassendi, indeed, Descartes seems infuriatingly glib about this process, as when he remarks: "I have never thought that anything more is required to reveal a substance than its various attributes; thus the more attributes of a given substance we know, the more perfectly we understand its nature" (Fifth Replies, VII:360). Here 'attribute' is being used in a non-technical sense for properties of all kinds, and so the picture once again, as in the previous section, would seem to be that we work through those properties or modes to a grasp of the substance itself. Gassendi's reply to this sort of strategy seems reasonable enough: "an attribute or property is one thing, and the substance or nature to which it belongs or from which it flows another. So to grasp the attribute or property, as well as the aggregate of properties, is not thereby to grasp the substance or nature" (*Disq. meta.* II.8.2). Given the reading of Descartes I am advancing, it is easy to be sympathetic to Gassendi's charge. Descartes seems to propose simply a crude piling up of data. This might be good enough if we were to suppose that *thought* is a determinable property that can be grasped by cataloguing the determinate instances that fall underneath it.

But once we recognize that talk of *thought* is shorthand for a "particular nature" (line 7 to Arnauld above), it looks as if Gassendi's criticisms are right on target.[20]

Descartes is incredibly dismissive of Gassendi's complaints, barely deigning to make a reply. This makes it natural to suppose that Gassendi has stupidly misunderstood the Cartesian system—that Gassendi's questions are in effect meaningless within the scheme of the *Meditations*. As I understand their exchange, however, the problem is not that Gassendi is asking meaningless questions, but that he is asking questions Descartes does not wish to consider, and that Descartes does not think he needs to consider to get the results he is after. Hence, as Descartes puts it in a further response to Gassendi published with the French edition of the *Meditations* (1647),

Our author was in the wrong when, under the pretext of objecting to my views, he put to me a great many questions of a kind that do not need to be answered in order to prove what I asserted in my writings, and that the most ignorant people could raise more of, in a quarter of an hour, than all the wisest people could deal with in their whole lifetimes. This is why I have not bothered to answer any of them. (IXA:213)

Descartes specifically has in mind Gassendi's queries about mind–body interaction, but I take his point to extend to Gassendi's queries about the "inner substance" beneath thought and extension. Part of what justifies reading the passage into this domain is Descartes's above-quoted remark from the start of the Fifth Meditation, where he makes it clear that he does not take himself to have settled the question of what the mind's nature is. Perhaps more decisively, though, I think we have to understand the exchange with Gassendi in this way, if we are to make any sense of Descartes's position. If we were to suppose that thought and extension yield a full account of what mind and body are, then Gassendi's criticisms of Descartes would look to be just obviously, painfully on target, with Descartes's replies amounting to a crude evasion of the real issues. Once we understand the debate over the nature of mind and body in the light of this passage, however, Descartes's position becomes clear. It is not quite that Gassendi's complaints are illegitimate—they are, in a certain sense, excellent questions—but they are bad questions to ask in the context of the *Meditations*, because they raise the sorts of issues that would throw the whole project hopelessly off track, bogging it down in the sort of scholastic metaphysical terrain that does not dry up in Descartes's system, but that he simply wishes to circumnavigate, in the interest of focusing on what can be established with certainty. Gassendi is not the naive kid in the front row who misunderstands everything; he is the smart but annoying kid in the back whose questions always come at the wrong time.[21]

---

[20] Similar criticisms from Gassendi regarding the inner substance of things can be found at VII:271–2 (with an even terser reply from Descartes at VII:359) and at VII:338. Gassendi airs these objections at greater length in his *Disquisitio metaphysica*, esp. II.6.3, II.7.2, II.8.2–3, VI.4.2–3, though these later discussions do not add much to his original set of objections (perhaps, in fairness, because Descartes's replies did not give Gassendi much to work with). For a helpful summary of Gassendi's position, see McCracken, "Knowledge of the Soul" pp. 821–3. For another statement of Descartes's claim that piling up non-necessary attributes leads to a grasp of the substance, see *Principles*. I.11: "et quo plures [affectiones sive qualitates] in eadem re sive substantia deprehendimus, tanto clarius nos illam cognoscere."

[21] The question of how completely Descartes grasps the nature of mind and body gets discussed in some detail in the Fourth Replies, where Descartes contends he does not need a "plane adaequatam" grasp of mind and body, one that would contain "omnes omnino proprietates quae sunt in re cognita" (VII:220). All he needs for the sake of the real-distinction argument, he contends, is that the mind and body be conceived "ut res completa" (VII:223).

We should be charitable enough to Descartes to read the Fifth Replies as pursuing a strategy of quietism, rather than as purporting to solve Gassendi's objections. It would be too charitable, however, to leave things where Descartes would like us to. First, from within the framework of the *Meditations*, Gassendi's objections raise a serious worry regarding whether Descartes will be able to reach the culminating result of the whole treatise, the real distinction between mind and body. The argument for that conclusion depends crucially on Descartes's having a distinct grasp of what mind and body are: in particular, that "nothing else belongs to my nature or essence except that I am a *res cogitans*" and that "I have a distinct idea of body, insofar as it is simply a *res extensa, non cogitans*" (VII:78). Descartes surely does not need to resolve *every* metaphysical question regarding mind and body to run the real-distinction argument, but he needs enough of a grip on their nature to underwrite these premises. These issues, unfortunately, lie outside the scope of this book.[22]

Second, even if Descartes does not need to go any deeper than he does to run the arguments of the *Meditations*, we can still think that Gassendi's questions are worth asking, especially in the context of evaluating the fate of scholastic metaphysics. As we have seen in the previous section and elsewhere, a crucial alleged advantage of the post-scholastic corpuscularian scheme is its intelligibility. No one highlights this claim more than Descartes. The claim can hardly be defended, however, if Descartes purchases intelligibility at the price of superficiality. Hence we have the right to ask: how deep does this vaunted intelligibility go?

There is no reason to think that the answer to this question will be the same in the case of mind and body, and as before I will continue here to focus on the question of what the mind is. I have argued that it is only the beginning of an answer to appeal to the principal attribute of thought. This tells us that the mind is a *res cogitans*, and that thinking is essential to the mind, but it leaves quite unanswered the sorts of further questions that one would expect to have answered. Although Descartes does not give the reader a great deal to go on here, he does occasionally shed light on the mind's status as a faculty or power. There is a hint of this in Descartes's commentary on Regius's broadsheet, when he remarks that "so far as I know, no one before me has stated that the rational soul consists in thought alone—that is, in the faculty or

---

[22] Gassendi's worry about whether the mind–body distinction can be sustained without a clearer grasp of the nature of mind and body is also expressed by Newton, who presents his theory of bodies as space so-and-so disposed (§7.1) as an alternative both to the Cartesian identification of body with extension, and to the "idea vulgaris" of a veiled subject. Naturally, given Newton's theory of absolute space, he thinks it untenable to identify body with extension. This, Newton then argues, forces the Cartesian into the veiled-subject doctrine, which then undermines the mind–body distinction: if we do not know what mind and body are, we cannot be confident of their distinction.

Wilson, *Descartes*, raises a worry at roughly the same juncture about Descartes's entitlement to grasp the nature of mind. She thinks Descartes can appeal to the mind's transparency as a first step to avoiding trouble, but then suggests that the appeal to transparency clashes with his non-mechanistic account of mind: "It seems likely that Descartes's conception of mind as outside the appropriate realm of scientific explanation includes both the view that the operations of the mind are mysteriously non-mechanical, and the view that mind is somehow transparent to itself. Unfortunately, it also appears that these two views are in tension with each other" (p. 99). My own view is somewhat different. I think the trouble begins with a failure of transparency: that when we see the kind of thing the mind's essence, thought, can and cannot be, we see that transparency fails at that level. For a similar line of thought, though in ignorance of the scholastic background, see Jolley, *Leibniz and Locke* pp. 76–81.

Criticisms closer to my own play an important role in Heidegger's *Sein und Zeit*. See, e.g., p. 24: "Mit dem '*cogito sum*' beansprucht Descartes, der Philosophie einen neuen und sicheren Boden beizustellen. Was er aber bei diesem 'radikalen' Anfang unbestimmt lässt, ist die Seinsart der *res cogitans*, genauer den Seinssinn des '*sum*.'"

internal principle of thinking" (VIIIB:347). Those last words, "faculty or internal principle," belong to Regius. But that does not diminish their authority, because Descartes is
exceptionally careful in his language throughout this work, scrupulously rejecting every
phrase in Regius's broadsheet that he finds objectionable. Later in the broadsheet,
moreover, he describes thought, by which he here means "an attribute that constitutes
the nature of a substance," as "the internal principle from which these modes spring and
in which they reside" (VIIIB:349). Given such claims, the mind itself can of course not
simply be *thought*, understood as a generic, determinable property. The mind is instead a
power; it is that which gives rise to the various modes of thought that we are directly
acquainted with. This sort of language can be found in one of Descartes's last letters
(to Henry More in February 1649), where he describes incorporeal substances as "powers
or forces" (V:270). It is already in play back in the *Meditations*, which distinguish a faculty
(*facultas*) of knowing and a faculty of choosing (*Med.* 4, VII:56). The most telling remark
there, however, comes in the Sixth Meditation, where the case for the distinction
between mind and body is developed on the basis of the mind's simplicity:

There is a great difference between the mind and the body, inasmuch as the body is by its very
nature always divisible, whereas the mind is utterly indivisible. For when I consider the mind, or
myself insofar as I am solely a thinking thing, I am unable to distinguish any parts within myself;
I understand myself to be something quite single and complete. . . . As for the faculties of willing,
sensing, understanding, and so on, these cannot be termed parts of the mind, since it is one and
the same mind that wills, senses, and understands. (VII:85–6)

This reinforces the picture of the mind, conceived thinly, as metaphysically simple. One
can speak of it as having various faculties, just as one can speak of its essence as thought,
but such ascriptions are not to be understood as introducing any sort of composition. If
the goal is to understand the mind by dint of teasing apart its different aspects, then
Descartes hardly offers much encouragement. We can draw conceptual distinctions
aplenty, but the mind itself resists analysis, inasmuch as mind = substance = thought =
power of thinking.

To deny any distinction between the mind itself and its powers is not to deny that the
mind is a power. Indeed, Descartes's position here falls neatly into one prominent
scholastic camp regarding the relationship of the soul and its powers, in a debate where
the open positions ran the full spectrum from a real distinction, to a formal distinction,
all the way to a mere distinction of reason. What all parties to this debate agreed on,
however, was that one could quite properly speak of the soul's powers. Indeed, to claim
that the mind or soul has a power is just about the most trivial claim one could make in
this domain. For inasmuch as it is practically definitive of the mind or rational soul to be
that which gives rise to acts of thought, the ascription of a power to the soul is simply
another way to state the obvious.[23] Taken all by itself, it is tantamount to ascribing a

---

[23] Nolan and Whipple, "Self-Knowledge," note that Malebranche shows signs of conceiving of the Cartesian mind as
a faculty. They dismiss the idea out of hand, however, remarking that "Philosophers often speak loosely of 'capacities'
but, strictly speaking, there is no place for such items within Descartes's austere, substance–mode ontology" (p. 73n).
This is right if they mean that there is no room for powers that are something distinct from the substance itself. But it
surely is right—in the strictest sense—to say that the mind itself, for Descartes, *is* a power. On powers in general, see Ch. 23.

The thesis that the soul is identical with its powers was standard in the twelfth century, particularly among Cistercian
authors (see McGinn, *Three Treatises*), and in the early thirteenth century (see Lottin, *Psychologie et morale* I:483–90), and
would be taken up again by Ockham (*Sent.* II.20) and the later nominalist tradition. Aquinas, in contrast, championed a

virtus dormativa to opium. Such dubious explanatory strategies are of course familiar enough in the context of the scholastics, but the moral I wish to draw from the present discussion is that the same charge could be made against Descartes's conception of substance. Despite all of his claims of intelligibility and transparency, what he ultimately is able to tell us about the nature of mind is in fact quite limited and disappointing. To assert that the mind is simple is, to be sure, a substantive and controversial thesis, but it is a thesis that, perhaps necessarily, closes the door to any further theses about the mind's character.

Yet if Descartes sacrifices transparency and intelligibility, he does so for a reason. One should not suppose that he has absorbed this scholastic framework unwittingly, as if he did not notice its influence and so was unable to shake himself free of it. On the contrary, as we have seen, Descartes expressly argues for metaphysical substances as something distinct from their accidents or modes. He takes himself to need that framework, to account for facts such as the difference between one substance and another, and the endurance of substances through change. The subsequent history of seventeenth-century thought displays a huge variety of attempts to deal with these very issues. In Descartes, such issues are not worked out in any kind of detail; in this respect Descartes stands, just as the cliché has it, halfway between two traditions, aiming at the clarity and intelligibility promised by the eschewal of scholasticism, but needing the explanatory power of the substance–accident distinction. Hence even while he sought transparency, he failed to escape the obscurity that metaphysics brings.

real distinction between the soul and its powers (*Summa theol.* 1a q. 77), and Scotus argued for a formal distinction (*Reportatio* II.16; Wadding XI.1). For further discussion, see King, "Inner Cathedral"; Pasnau, "The Mind–Soul Problem"; Pasnau, *Thomas Aquinas on Human Nature* ch. 5; Shields, "Unity of Soul."

Lockean Substances

9.1. Substratum as Ordinary Substance

John Locke's theory of substance is as reviled as any part of his philosophy. It has, however, been spectacularly misunderstood, subject to interpretations that neither he nor his contemporaries could ever have imagined. As Locke is read today, it is baffling both what he means by substance and what ever could have led him to such a theory. Read in the proper historical perspective, it becomes perfectly obvious both what Locke thinks substance is, and what motivates the theory. For better or worse, however, once his theory of substance is properly understood, it becomes quite unoriginal, even banal.

The proper historical perspective is that described in the last three chapters, of a distinction between the properties of a substance and the substance itself, where the substance just is the individual thing (the gold, the wax) apart from its properties. This substance–accident distinction is a commonplace of scholastic discussions, and gets absorbed without much resistance in authors like Gassendi and Descartes, two very prominent sources for Locke's own philosophical thinking. A close reading of Locke's remarks on substance makes it clear that he takes this distinction for granted. We might begin by looking closely at the initial paragraphs of *Essay* II.23, where he offers his canonical statement on substance.

The first section of II.23 gives a preliminary statement of the whole account. In §2, Locke takes up the idea of "substance in general"; then in §§3–5 he turns to our ideas of "particular sorts of substances," first corporeal substances (§4) and then spiritual substances (§5). Finally, §6 offers a summary of the preceding pages. (At least, this would count as "finally" in most other authors; in Locke, it leads into 31 more sections of diffuse discussion on more or less the same themes, which I will not attempt to put into any logical order, but on which it will occasionally be useful to draw.) Here is §1 in full:

The mind being, as I have declared, furnished with a great number of the simple ideas, conveyed in by the senses, as they are found in exterior things, or by reflection on its own operations, takes notice also, that a certain number of these simple ideas go constantly together; which being presumed to belong to one thing, and words being suited to common apprehensions, and made use of for quick dispatch, are called, so united in one subject, by one name; which, by inadvertency, we are apt afterward to talk of and consider as one simple idea, which indeed is a complication of many ideas together; because, as I have said, not imagining how these simple

3

6

ideas can subsist by themselves, we accustom ourselves to suppose some *substratum* wherein they do subsist, and from which they do result, which therefore we call *substance*.

Our idea of substance is complex in two different respects. First, from the many simple ideas obtained through sensation and reflection, we notice in certain cases that "a certain number of these simple ideas go constantly together" (line 3). These are "presumed to belong to one thing" (line 4) and hence are given "one name" (line 5). This leads us to the mistake of supposing ourselves to have "one simple idea" when in fact what we have is "a complication of many ideas together" (lines 6–7). At this first stage of the argument, the idea of a substance is just the complex idea of various simple qualities. If Locke had left matters here, his theory of substance would be no more memorable than, say, his theory of relations. But Locke thinks our idea of substance contains something more, "some *substratum* wherein they do subsist, and from which they do result, which therefore we call *substance*" (lines 8–9). This is the second respect in which our idea of substance is a complex idea. In addition to a complex idea of qualities that go constantly together, we have the idea of a substratum in which those qualities subsist. (I assume that Locke here—as is sometimes his custom—uses 'simple ideas' on lines 7–8 to refer to the qualities that give rise to the simple ideas in our mind.)[1] So when we think about a given substance, we do not just have the idea of a collection of simple qualities. Besides that, we also have the idea of a substratum that is the subject of those qualities.

Of all Locke's efforts to craft an English philosophical vocabulary that is not simply an Anglicized scholasticism (§21.1), perhaps most unfortunate was this choice of the word 'substratum.' The word is used only seven times in the whole *Essay* (in contrast with the 243 occurrences of 'substance'), and always it is used in an attempt to get at the real meaning of the frozen scholastic term 'substance' (*substantia*). Hence Locke introduces 'substratum' at line 8 as his own gloss on our ordinary usage—what "we call *substance*." Unfortunately, the seductive vividness of the notion of a *substratum* has contributed to the impression that Locke is discussing some sort of ineffable sub-substance, lying beneath the substance and insusceptible of further inquiry. Quite to the contrary, Locke's various skeptical, sarcastic discussions are focused not on this sort of mysterious entity, but on our grasp of the thing itself—the gold or the horse—as distinct from its qualities. That is, the substratum *just is* the ordinary substance. Everything in §1 points toward this conclusion. To say that the substratum, and not the qualities, subsists of itself (lines 7–8) is to ascribe to the substratum the most familiar characteristic of ordinary substances (§6.2). To say that the qualities subsist in the substratum, and result from it (lines 8–9), is to ascribe to the substratum the principal functions ascribed to ordinary substances (§6.2, §24.4). In short, Locke means to identify

---

[1] Locke is notoriously frank about his customary conflation of 'idea' and 'quality': "Which ideas, if I speak of sometimes as in the things themselves, I would be understood to mean those qualities in the objects which produce them in us" (II.8.8). This usage is not as perverse as it is usually made out to be, however, because it was a perfectly common contemporary usage for 'idea' to stand for a quality of objects, rather than for something in the mind (see *OED*, "idea" II; Goclenius, *Lexicon*, "Idea" 1; Descartes, *Meditation* preface [VII:8]). Hence Locke's usage of 'idea' is not a careless misuse of language, but merely ambiguous in a way that was both common at the time and easily discerned, and that he repeatedly alerts the reader to.

the substratum with the substance, and thereby to situate it within a perfectly familiar metaphysics of substance and properties.[2]

Having made this opening statement of his view, Locke proceeds to distinguish between our idea of substance in general and our idea of particular substance kinds. This way of dividing up the territory corresponds exactly with how we saw skeptical scholastic authors attack our understanding of substance: first, there is the question of whether we can formulate a positive definition of substance in general; second, there is the question of whether we can positively characterize any given kind of substance (§7.3). Here is §2 in full:

So that if anyone will examine himself concerning his notion of *pure substance in general*, he will find he has no other idea of it at all, but only a supposition of he knows not what support of such qualities, which are capable of producing simple ideas in us; which qualities are commonly 3
called accidents. If any one should be asked, what is the subject wherein colour or weight inheres, he would have nothing to say, but the solid extended parts. And if he were demanded, what is it that solidity and extension adhere in, he would not be in a much better case than the 6
Indian before-mentioned [II.13.19], who, saying that the world was supported by a great elephant, was asked what the elephant rested on; to which his answer was, a great tortoise. But being again pressed to know what gave support to the broad-backed tortoise, replied, 9
something he knew not what. And thus here, as in all other cases where we use words without having clear and distinct ideas, we talk like children; who being questioned what such a thing is, which they know not, readily give this satisfactory answer, that it is *something*. Which in truth 12
signifies no more, when so used either by children or men, but that they know not what; and that the thing they pretend to know and talk of, is what they have no distinct idea of at all, and so are perfectly ignorant of it, and in the dark. The idea then we have, to which we give the 15
general name Substance, being nothing but the supposed, but unknown support of those qualities we find existing, which we imagine cannot subsist, *sine re substante*, without something to support them, we call that support *substantia*; which, according to the true import of the 18
word, is in plain English, *standing under* or *upholding*.

An inquiry into "substance in general" (line 1) is an inquiry into the genus *substance*, traditionally conceived of as appearing at the top of a Porphyrian tree, way above the specific level where one finds kinds like *horse* and *water*. The question in its classical form is how to define 'substance.' Locke does not quite put it that way here; instead, his question is what that thing is that lies under the qualities or accidents, where an answer in general would not appeal to idiosyncratic features of a kind of substance, but would apply equally to all kinds of substances. The words "anyone" (line 1) and "supposition" (line 2) highlight one of the main points of §1, that he is not offering a theory of his own,

---

[2] Scholars sometimes treat 'substratum' as a received technical term that Locke is subjecting to criticism. On the contrary, it is Locke who is quite consciously introducing the term into the discussion as a synonym for the traditional 'substance' (*substantia*). Thus, e.g., Goclenius's *Lexicon* (1613) has a lengthy entry for *substantia*, but nothing for *substratum*. Aquinas uses 'substratum' in its various forms fourteen times, but never in the general sense of that which underlies accidents. Suárez's long discussion of substance (*Disp. meta.* 32–8) uses 'substratum' only once, and again not in the relevant sense. The word appears just once in all of Descartes's corpus, and again not in the relevant sense, and appears not at all in Hobbes, or in Bacon's principal works. (In the passage from *De principiis* quoted in §7.2, 'substratum' translates Bacon's *suffulcimentum*, itself seemingly a neologism from *suffulcio*.) Although 'substratum' is sometimes said to correspond to Aristotle's ὑποκείμενον, scholastic translations rendered that word as *subiectum*. See, e.g., *Meta.* VII.3, 1028b36, and Aquinas's commentary (VII.2.1273), which confidently offers the gloss "subiectum, idest substantia particularis."

or even a critique of a philosophical theory, but an investigation of a supposition we all make. By stipulating that we are talking about *"pure substance"* (line 1)—Descartes's phrase as well in the synopsis to the *Meditations* (VII:14)—Locke stresses that we are talking about the substance apart from its qualities. His appeal to scholastic vocabulary, "commonly called accidents" (lines 3–4) further highlights the intended sense of substance as the thing itself apart from its non-essential features. (The *Essay* almost never uses 'accident' except as contrasted with 'substance,' in passages where Locke intends to challenge our very grasp of the distinction.)[3]

The problem of §2, then, is simply the familiar metaphysical problem of how to define *"substance"*—the problem of what it is to be a "substance in general." Locke's first attempt at an answer appeals to integral parts: that a substance, at least in corporeal cases, is the "solid extended parts" (line 5). This answer goes nowhere, however, because it offers us not pure substances but impure, thick substances, substances with the accidents of "solidity and extension" (line 6). But when we try to characterize the substance apart from these qualities, we hit a brick wall, and the remainder of the paragraph consists in various rhetorical devices intended to stress our complete ignorance on this score. The closest he comes to any sort of characterization of substance in general is that it is a *res substans*, which he translates as "something to support" qualities (lines 7–18). All by itself, this is not much, but Locke elaborates a bit more in a passage from the Stillingfleet correspondence:

[I] should be very glad to be convinced by your lordship, or any body else, that I have spoken too meanly of it [substance]. He that would show me a more clear and distinct idea of substance would do me a kindness I should thank him for. But this is the best I can hitherto find, either in   3 my own thoughts or in the books of logicians; for their account or idea of it is that it is *ens* or *res per se subsistens et substans accidentibus*; which in effect is no more but that substance is a being or thing; or in short, something they know not what, or of which they have no clearer idea than   6 that it is something which supports accidents or other simple ideas or modes, and is not supported itself as a mode or an accident. (*Works* IV:8)

Clearly Locke is thinking here of substance in general, and means to be expanding on his remarks in §2. The fuller Latin tag offered here alludes to the two standard definitions of substance considered in previous chapters, even down to the terminology of "subsisting" and "substanding" (§6.2). These are of course definitions not of some mysterious sub-substance beneath ordinary substances, but of what it is in general to be a substance. In this familiar theoretical context, it would be nothing short of bizarre for Locke to have anything else in mind. Moreover, he immediately goes on, after the quoted passage, to invoke Burgersdijk in support of this conception of substance. As we have seen (§6.1), Burgersdijk expressly articulates a thin conception of substance as the thing itself, apart from its accidents.[4]

---

[3] The *Essay* uses 'accident' nine times in the relevant sense. All but two of those occurrences occur in critical discussions of our idea of substance—twice in II.23 and five times in II.13, where the context is the traditional scholastic question whether space is a substance or an accident. In that context, what is crucial is that substance and accident allegedly divide being exhaustively (§6.1). Hence it would make no sense for Locke's famously sarcastic remarks about an "Indian Philosopher" and an "Intelligent American" to target anything other than the ordinary scholastic sense of substance apart from its accidents.

[4] Burgersdijk offers the standard definition of substance at *Inst. logicae* I.4, p. 15: "Substantia est ens per se subsistens, et substans accidentibus." Locke also appeals to Sanderson, who offers the standard definition at *Compendium* I.9, p. 29.

In §3, Locke moves from substance in general to substance kinds. The transition tends to perplex modern commentators, to whom it looks as if Locke is moving from a mysterious substratum to ordinary substances, but the transition would have seemed perfectly natural to contemporaries, since it involves going from a discussion of how to define the genus *substance* to how to define distinct species of substance under that genus. Here is §3 in full:

An obscure and relative idea of substance in general being thus made we come to have the ideas of *particular sorts of substances*, by collecting such combinations of simple ideas, as are by experience and observation of men's senses taken notice of to exist together, and are 3
therefore supposed to flow from the particular internal constitution, or unknown essence of that substance. Thus we come to have the ideas of a man, horse, gold, water, etc., of which substances, whether any one has any other clear idea, farther than of certain simple ideas 6
coexisting together, I appeal to every one's own experience. It is the ordinary qualities, observable in iron, or a diamond, put together, that make the true complex idea of those substances, which a smith or a jeweler commonly knows better than a philosopher; who, 9
whatever substantial forms he may talk of, has no other idea of those substances, than what is framed by a collection of those simple ideas which are to be found in them; only we must take notice, that our complex ideas of substances, besides all these simple ideas they are made up 12
of, have always the confused idea of *something* to which they belong, and in which they subsist. And therefore, when we speak of any sort of substance, we say it is a *thing* having such or such qualities, as body is a *thing* that is extended, figured, and capable of motion; a spirit a *thing* capable 15
of thinking; and so hardness, friability, and power to draw iron, we say, are qualities to be found in a loadstone. These, and the like fashions of speaking, intimate that the substance is supposed always *something* besides the extension, figure, solidity, motion, thinking, or other observable 18
ideas, though we know not what it is.

The first two lines assume that our ideas of particular substance kinds presuppose the idea of substance in general. I discuss this below, in the final section of the chapter. In lines 3–5, Locke goes from the by now familiar "combination of simple ideas" to something new: that these ideas that "exist together" (that is, the qualities existing together in the substance) "flow from" the "internal constitution" or "unknown essence of that substance." Why do real essences get introduced here? Because "thus" we arrive at our ideas of substance kinds: "ideas of man, horse, gold, water, etc." (line 5) Locke had already remarked at the end of §1 (line 9) that the qualities of substances both "subsist" within substance and "result" from it. The "result" clause is often viewed as an aberration, but §3 confirms that Locke means it. We arrive at the idea of substance kinds by thinking of the substance both as the thing in which a cluster of sensible qualities inhere, *and* as the thing that gives rise to those qualities. Why think the latter? There is a quick inference here, marked by 'therefore' (line 4), that goes from the

Sanderson's textbooks on logic and physics are far too elementary, however, to shed light on any substantive philosophical issues. (Neither author, it should be said, uses the term 'substratum' in this context.) Compare Boyle, *Origin of Forms* (*Works* V:308; Stewart p. 21): "substance is commonly defined to be a thing that subsists of itself and is the subject of accidents." Once again, there is no sign of the word 'substratum,' and no sign that Boyle is thinking about anything other than ordinary substances.

Anyone still tempted to suppose that the "substance in general" is some sort of sub-substance beneath the ordinary substance should consider Locke's remark to Stillingfleet that "by general substance here, I suppose your lordship means the general idea of substance.... And if your lordship should mean otherwise, I must take the liberty to deny there is any such thing in *rerum natura* as a general substance that exists itself, or makes any thing" (*Works* IV:27).

qualities' existing together to their flowing from the real essence. The inference can be quick because Locke is taking for granted a standard scholastic thought: that the essence of a substance explains the accidental features of that substance (§24.4, §27.6). There is no reason to think that essence is *identical* with the substance, as some Locke scholars have suggested, but it is *of course* a part of the substance. As the previous chapter stressed in the case of Descartes, it would be strange to the point of nonsensical to think of the essence of a substance as outside of the substance. Moreover, the logic of §3 requires such a reading, because the inference at line 5 goes from the idea of the substance's essence to the idea of the substance itself. If essence did not at least partly constitute substance, this would be a complete *non sequitur*. In that case, real essences would be just one more item inhering in the mysterious sub-substance, and there would be no particular reason to invoke essences here.[5]

Although Locke will later have much more to say about real essences (see *Essay* III.6), it is crucial to his purposes here to mark those essences as "unknown" (line 4). If the essences were known, then the substance would be (at least partly) known, and Locke could no longer conclude that "we know not what it is" (line 19). In *Essay* II.31.6–7, an important later passage that should be read in conjunction with §3, Locke defends his appeal to real essences as another supposition that is so common (at least among learned Europeans) that it can and should be taken for granted (for discussion see §27.6–7). Our ideas of substance are "imperfect and inadequate" because we fail to grasp these real essences: "since they who so use the names know not [these essences], their ideas of substances must be all inadequate in that respect, as not containing in them that real essence which the mind intends they should" (II.31.7). By contrast, if we could grasp these real essences, we would then have at least something approaching an adequate idea of substance. As things are, we have no idea of a substance kind that goes beyond "the ordinary qualities" (line 7) grasped through the senses. A smith's grasp of iron, or a jeweler's grasp of a diamond, goes no farther. Nor does a philosopher's. Locke needs to say something about substantial forms here (line 10), because this is how the "philosopher"—even at the end of the seventeenth century, the philosophers are still Aristotelians—accounts for what a substance kind is. Of course, Locke contends this is just talk, with no idea behind it. This point too is developed more fully in II.31.6: "But when I am told that some thing besides the figure, size, and posture of the solid parts of that body is its essence, some thing called *substantial form*, of that, I confess, I have no idea at all, but only of the sound *Form*, which is far enough from an idea of its real essence, or constitution."

After stressing that our complex idea of substance consists of a "collection" of simple ideas grounded in perception (lines 5–9), Locke adds the complication that makes his account so interesting: that beyond this collection of simple ideas representing the

---

[5] Sympathetic discussions of the thesis that the substratum is the real essence include Mandelbaum, "Locke's Realism"; Bolton, "Substances"; Jolley, *Leibniz and Locke* pp. 81–91; Loeb, *From Descartes to Hume* p. 87. For decisive criticisms, see Bennett, "Substratum" and McCann, "Locke's Philosophy of Body."

One ground for identifying substance and real essence would be the thought that Locke might be using 'substance' as synonymous with 'essence,' a usage that is well established in Latin. We know from the Stillingfleet correspondence, however, that this is not Locke's meaning. Instead, he appeals there to standard scholastic usage—"the authority of the schools" (IV:24)—according to which 'substance' refers to the subject of accidents. This appeal to authority again suggests that we should read Locke as talking about the thin metaphysical substance of previous chapters.

sensible qualities of the substance, we "have always the confused idea of something to which they belong" (line 13). It is this further step that gives rise to the misconception that Lockean substances are somehow distinct from and underneath ordinary particulars. To be sure, the substance lies underneath the sensible qualities. But it is the horse itself, and the gold itself, that so underlies the qualities. Lines 14–17 are clear on this score, moving from our speaking of "any sort of substance" as a "thing" to our speaking of "body" or "spirit" as a "thing," and finally to "a loadstone" as an instance of a substance thing. With this in mind, we can appreciate what is going on in §4 (quoted in full):

Hence when we talk or think of any particular sort of corporeal substances, as *horse, stone,* etc., though the idea we have of either of them be but the complication or collection of those several simple ideas of sensible qualities, which we use [≈ are accustomed] to find united in the thing   3 called *horse* or *stone,* yet because we cannot conceive how they should subsist alone, nor one in another, we suppose them existing in and supported by some common subject; which support we denote by the name *substance,* though it be certain we have no clear or distinct idea of that   6 *thing* we suppose a support.

As line 1 makes clear, the topic remains particular substance kinds (cf. §3 lines 1–2), now focusing exclusively on the corporeal case. As before, the only idea we have of *horse* and *stone* is a collective idea of sensible qualities, but because we "cannot conceive" of these qualities "subsist[ing] alone, nor one in another" (lines 4–5), we arrive at the further idea of a "common subject" (line 5). That common subject just is what we call the substance. The standard modern reading of Locke must take him to be switching in mid-sentence from one sort of substance (horses and stones) to another (a substratum beneath horses and stones). This reading is virtually forced on us if we suppose that horses and stones include their sensible qualities, since if so we certainly could not be said to have "no clear or distinct idea" (lines 6–7) of the substance. (We would know its qualities.) But just as, in the previous chapter, we saw Descartes distinguish the wax and its qualities, and then proceed to argue that we do not perceive the wax with the senses, so Locke is distinguishing horses and stones from their qualities, and arguing that horses and stones themselves are obscure to us.

This understanding of Locke allows us to avoid having to read him as switching back and forth, in a bewildering manner, between ordinary substances and some sort of mysterious sub-substance. It also makes much better sense of his correspondence with Stillingfleet. Locke's first letter begins by addressing Stillingfleet's complaint that he has "almost discarded substance out of the reasonable part of the world" (IV:5). Locke flatly denies that he doubts the reality of substance, remarking that he certainly believes in "man, horse, sun, water, iron, diamond, etc." (IV:7). Modern commentators have largely had to treat this as a cheap trick, evading the real issue of Locke's attitude toward the substratum beneath ordinary substances. Once we see Locke's true view, however, we can see why he would have been genuinely baffled by Stillingfleet's complaint. How could anyone suppose him even to have questioned the reality of substance? His response is entirely appropriate, not just because the things on this list count as substances, but because things like those are the only substances there are. We can now see, too, why Locke would go on to consider another reading of Stillingfleet's complaint: that he might have "destroyed and almost discarded the true idea" of substance (IV:7–8). This is a charitable and constructive gloss on Stillingfleet's imprecise remark, and moves us into the heart of things. Locke invites Stillingfleet to show him what he is missing, even while insisting that, so far as he can see, we simply lack a clear and distinct idea of substance. (The key passage at IV:8 was quoted above.) Again, he is not changing the topic; we are still talking about man, horse, and sun. Locke believes in these *things*, but denies we have a clear and distinct idea of them, either at the species level, or at the genus level. (It goes without saying, as it usually does for scholastic authors too, that we lack any idea of substances as individuals [§7.3]. Locke takes up this issue in III.6.4–6.)[6]

I have suggested that Locke's treatment of corporeal substance is closely analogous to Descartes's treatment of the wax. Just as Locke has scholastic theories of substance constantly in mind, so too he surely had Descartes in mind. Hence extension gets prominently mentioned in both §2 and §3, as a possible account of corporeal substance, only to be dismissed on the grounds that there is "always *something* besides" (§3 line 17) this and other sensible qualities. The discussion of spiritual substance even more clearly has Descartes in the background. Here is the first half of §5:

The same thing happens concerning the operations of the mind, viz. thinking, reasoning, fearing, etc., which we concluding not to subsist of themselves, nor apprehending how they can belong to body, or be produced by it, we are apt to think these the actions of some other   3
substance, which we call *spirit*; whereby yet it is evident, that having no other idea or notion of matter, but *something* wherein those many sensible qualities which affect our senses do subsist, by supposing a substance wherein thinking, knowing, doubting, and a power of moving, etc. do   6
subsist, we have as clear a notion of the substance of spirit as we have of body: the one being supposed to be (without knowing what it is) the substratum to those simple ideas we have from without; and the other supposed (with a like ignorance of what it is) to be the substratum to   9
those operations we experiment in our selves within.

Again we are talking about ordinary corporeal substances ("body" [line 3]) and ordinary spiritual substances ("spirit" [line 4]). Up to a point, Locke is following quite closely in Descartes's footsteps. He makes a quick nod toward inconceivability arguments against materialism (lines 2–3), and then makes just the maneuver of the Second Meditation, undermining our grasp of body (lines 5–6) in order to show that "we have as clear a notion of the substance of spirit as we have of body" (line 7). The difference is that Descartes at times suggests we have a completely transparent grasp of mind, in virtue of apprehending its modes. The previous chapter considered the difficulties Descartes faces in making good on this claim. Here Locke enters into none of the complexities, but simply takes for granted that our grasp of "the operations of the mind" (line 1) leaves us entirely in the dark with respect to knowing "what it is" (line 9).[7]

---

[6] On Locke's commitment to the existence of substance, see also *Works* IV:448, where he tells Stillingfleet that "those passages were not intended to ridicule the notion of substance, or those who asserted it, whatever that 'it' signifies: but to show that though substance did support accidents, yet philosophers who had found such a support necessary had no more a clear idea of what that support was, than the Indian had of that which supported his tortoise, though sure he was it was something."

[7] The similarities to the Second Meditation are even starker in §15, a passage that reiterates §5 but appeals more clearly to cogito-style considerations as establishing "some spiritual being within me, that sees and hears." Here 'me' evidently refers to the mind–body composite, but the thing that "sees and hears" is not the composite but the veiled, spiritual subject, the mind. In §§24–7, Locke takes up the question of extension at greater length, and makes the interesting argument that we understand extension no more than we understand thought, inasmuch as we do not

It would be easy to go on and on in this way, through both the *Essay* and the Stillingfleet correspondence, showing how the standard scholastic notion of a substance apart from its accidents is also Locke's notion of substance. The evidence presented so far, however, seems so thoroughly decisive that it would be merely tedious to prolong the discussion.[8] My hope is that enough has been said to make it seem puzzling why anyone has ever taken seriously the idea of a bare substratum, the unknowable sub-substance beneath the substance. What we have here is another example of Bloomian Interpretation (§1.4, §6.2)—this time, not because seventeenth-century authors have misinterpreted the scholastics, but because modern historians have misinterpreted the seventeenth century, and so arrived at a theory of substance that philosophers never would have dreamed of putting forth as their own idea.[9]

---

understand how the parts of bodies cohere, which is requisite for extension. Locke never mentions Descartes by name in his discussions of substance, but later, in the context of debates over the vacuum, he specifically invokes Descartes in connection with his doctrine that body just is extension (IV.7.12–13). *Essay* II.1.9–10 argues (in keeping with §5 here) that thought is an operation of the soul, rather than its essence. Descartes is clearly the target there, although again he goes unnamed.

[8] The texts of the *Essay* that I rely on are so familiar that, I fear, they may carry little weight with scholars who have long been accustomed to their own preferred readings of this material. It may be helpful, then, to present some unfamiliar passages from Locke's correspondence where the substance is clearly the hidden substratum of II.23, and yet it is also surely the ordinary material thing itself. Consider, then, this remark from a letter of 1698: "Pour moi qui ne connois pas ce que c'est que la substance de la matière, je connois encore moins ce que c'est que la substance de Dieu; mais je sçai pourtant que cette substance est quelque chose, et qu'elle doit exclurre d'où elle est toutes les autres substances de la même espéce" (*Correspondence* VI:324). Surely, the unknown material substance here is just the body that excludes other bodies from the same space. And clearly the substance of God just is God. Consider also this letter to Anthony Collins from 1704: "Extension and solidity we have the ideas of and see that cogitation has no necessary connection with them nor has any consequential result from them, and therefore is not a proper affection of extension and solidity nor does naturally belong to them. But how does it follow from hence that it may not be made an affection of or be annexed to that substance which is vested with solidity and extension? Of this substance we have no idea that excludes cogitation any more than solidity" (*Correspondence* VIII:255). Here Locke distinguishes between extension and solidity and the substance "vested" with them, which is surely just the body itself. Those who want to show that a body cannot think need to show that thought is incompatible with that substance. We cannot do this because, in keeping with II.23, "we have no idea" of the substance itself that would allow such an argument to proceed.

[9] To my knowledge, no recent Locke scholars have argued for identifying substance with the thing itself, stripped of its accidents. My ideas in the chapter are much indebted, however, to Daniel Z. Korman, beginning with a Boulder graduate seminar on Locke, and continuing through many conversations and exchanges of papers. In a forthcoming work that antedates this chapter, Korman argues that Locke's substratum just is the ordinary gold and horse. Korman's claim becomes indisputable, as I see it, once Locke's work is situated in the proper historical context, that of the thin metaphysical substance of the Aristotelian tradition.

Since at least the 1960s, readers have generally agreed on distinguishing two senses of 'substance' in Locke: one by which he means ordinary substances, and the other by which he means a hidden substratum, which readers usually associate with Locke's talk of "pure substance in general" (II.23.2). It would be interesting to discover how this strange and historically blinkered notion of a sub-substance got started. There is no sign of it in older scholarship like Aaron, *John Locke* pp. 172–9; Gibson, *Locke's Theory of Knowledge* pp. 91–104; or Pringle-Pattison's notes on the *Essay*, pp. 233n.–234n.

Ayers's account of Locke on substance sometimes comes rather close to my own, although he never sees that Locke's substances just are the ordinary things themselves (apart from their accidents). He does, however, seem to see that in some sense the real essence must be a part of the substance, without being identified with it. Thus his *Routledge Encyclopedia* entry on Locke remarks that "Locke sometimes distinguishes both the notion and knowledge of real essence from the notion and knowledge of substance. That is not, however, because the 'substance' is an irremediably unknown subject underlying even essence, but because it is the common stuff of a variety of species of things …" (§5). This gets things right up until the last clause, which unfortunately suggests that the substance is just the particles that endure through change (Locke's corpuscular prime matter). Closer still are a few brief remarks from Wiggins, inspired by Ayers, who contrasts a "sympathetic" reading that is something like my own with the "traditional" substratum reading, and discusses how Locke's way of putting things has led readers to the latter ("Substance" pp. 225–6). More recently, Jacovides, "Locke on Propria," seems to have sympathy with a view like my own, although the focus of his discussion is quite different.

9.2. Locke's Tenuous Metaphysical Commitments

Locke's ideas about substance go back to the earliest surviving draft of the *Essay*, the so-called Draft A from 1671. Many of Locke's most famous themes are not yet present there, including the primary–secondary quality distinction, ideas defined as the immediate objects of perception, identity over time, and real versus nominal essences. The very first topic of Draft A, however, is the theory of substance, presented in much the same terms as would ultimately appear as *Essay* II.23. As Locke is usually read today, it must seem odd to find that the obscure doctrine of a sub-substance goes back to his earliest known work on the *Essay*. Once we see that Locke is just talking about ordinary substances, however, those thoughts begin to look rather banal. Indeed, compare them with these remarks from Samuel Parker's *Free and Impartial Censure of the Platonick Philosophy* (1666):

> [W]e are so far from attaining any certain and real knowledge of *incorporeal beings* . . . that we are not able to know anything of *corporeal substances* as abstract from their accidents. There's nothing can more perplex my faculties, than the simple idea of naked matter. And certainly it   3
> was never intended that mere essences should be the objects of our faculties. And therefore the truly wise and discerning philosophers do not endeavor after the dry and sapless knowledge of abstracted natures, but only search after the properties, qualities, virtues, and operations of   6
> natural beings, the knowledge whereof may be acquired by observations and experiments, but there are no certain means or rational methods (that I could ever yet meet with) to investigate the mysterious ideas of bare and abstracted essences. (pp. 63–4)

Parker distinguishes substance from accidents (line 2), and then takes for granted that an account of substance would be either an account of "naked matter" or else "mere essences" (lines 3–4), precisely mirroring the scholastic analysis of substance into prime matter and substantial form. Parker does not claim any originality for the notion that we cannot arrive at any knowledge of substance. This is a conclusion that "wise and discerning philosophers" have already accepted. Presumably, he is not thinking of Scotus, say, or other scholastic skeptics regarding our grasp of substance, since he goes on to inveigh against "the School Doctors, who pretend too by their definitions to unfold the most hidden and abstracted essences of things" (p. 65). (Compare the passage from Locke criticized in §7.3: " . . . the doctrine of substantial forms, and the confidence of mistaken pretenders to a knowledge that they had not" [*Essay* III.viii.2].) Instead, Parker means to praise his contemporaries—the proponents of "the mechanical and experimental philosophy" (p. 45)—who have turned away from scholastic thought and toward corpuscularian theories of the natural world.

Viewed as a critical, negative claim, Locke's treatment of substance contains nothing new. The idea that we have no distinctive positive idea of substances, apart from their accidents, is found both in prominent scholastic texts, and also among earlier seventeenth-century critics of scholasticism. The more difficult and interesting issue regarding Locke's discussion is whether he commits himself to any positive metaphysical theses regarding substance. It is easy to conclude that he does not, given how often he appeals not to his own convictions regarding substance, but to something "we accustom ourselves to suppose" (II.23.1, as above, line 8). Many scholars have been attracted to the thought that Locke is not offering his own theory, but simply reporting on a widely held set of ideas.[10] And, to be sure, it is good to keep in mind that Locke's principal ambition in the *Essay* is not to construct a metaphysics but to describe our ideas (Book II) and language (Book III). Hence to my claim that there is nothing very original in Locke's thinking about substance, it would be fair to respond that Locke never intended to say anything original about such metaphysical questions. Still, even if Locke is usually very careful to hedge his remarks with provisos to the effect that this is the view of "every one who understands the language" (II.23.6), it seems possible to discern various positive commitments on Locke's part, some of which go well beyond the sort of platitudes that literally everyone believes. One near platitude is the existence of substance. When Locke's theory is properly understood, it becomes obvious why he would find the existence of such things uncontroversial. Even so, once substances are understood in this way, as the thing itself beneath its sensible qualities, their existence becomes something less than platitudinous, and indeed Locke himself provides as good a foundation for doubt in that regard as one could want. Perhaps this is how we should understand Stillingfleet's complaint that Locke "almost discarded substance out of the reasonable part of the world" (IV:5)—not that this is what Locke *says*, but that it is an attitude his views *encourage*. And if proof is needed of just how vulnerable Locke made substance, we have Berkeley's famous attack, based on Lockean principles, on the very reality of material substance:

As to what philosophers say of subject and mode, that seems very groundless and unintelligible. For instance, in this proposition, *a die is hard, extended, and square*, they will have it that the word *die* denotes a subject or substance, distinct from the hardness, extension, and figure which are predicated of it, and in which they exist. This I cannot comprehend: to me a die seems to be nothing distinct from those things which are termed its modes or accidents. And to say a die is hard, extended, and square is not to attribute those qualities to a subject distinct from and supporting them, but only an explication of the meaning of the word *die*. (*Principles* n. 49)

No sub-substances here; Berkeley is attacking the reality of the thing itself, the die that is hard and square. Locke was the inspiration for this line of argument,[11] although, as we

---

[10] Locke's treatment of substance as a shared supposition has been widely noted. See, e.g., Mackie, *Problems from Locke* pp. 74–5: "It is plain from these passages themselves that Locke is primarily describing what he takes to be our ordinary way of thinking, and is not necessarily endorsing it himself. He is certainly not constructing here anything that we could call his own theory of substance. . . ." Another way of doubting whether Locke is offering a theory of substance is proposed by McCann, "Attack!", who ascribes to Locke a no-theory theory of substance, by which he means that it is an account that does none of the work for which theories of substance are standardly put forward. My own view, on the contrary, is that Locke thinks we can be certain there are substances because we take them to do *all* the work that substances were standardly said to do, as the enduring subjects of accidents, accounting for the enduring continuity of the thick concrete substance with its properties.

[11] It is explicit in Berkeley's notebooks that Locke is the inspiration for his remarks on our inability to have any idea of substance (see, e.g., nn. 89, 517, 601). Throughout his work, Berkeley takes for granted that the substratum in question just is the material substance itself. To reject such a substratum just is to reject the existence of material entities such as horses, gold, etc. Sometimes Berkeley associates the postulation of such a substance with the postulation of matter (e.g., *Principles* 16 and *Notebooks* n. 517, where "nec quid nec quantum nec quale" alludes to Aristotle's discussion of matter at *Meta.* VII.3, 1029a20). Other times the substratum is associated with speculation over "unknown natures and philosoph-ical quiddities" (Third Dialogue [*Works* II:238]). Of course matter and nature (substantial form) are the two components of ordinary material substances. Berkeley never considers that Locke might be discussing some further substratum beneath these.

Although Leibniz is often associated with the doctrine of the mysterious sub-substance, in fact the *Nouveaux essais* suggests no such thing. Most tellingly, Leibniz has Locke's spokesman remark that "les mots de substance et d'accident sont à mon avis de peu d'usage en philosophie." This is offered as a summary of II.13.20 where, if anywhere in the *Essay*, Locke would be talking about sub-substances. If Leibniz understood Locke to be describing any such thing, then one

have seen (§7.4), it is a thought one finds in various scholastic authors too. Locke himself reassures Stillingfleet, however, not just that he believes in substance, but that we have good reason for that belief: "I held we might be certain of the truth of this proposition, that there was substance in the world, though we have but an obscure and confused idea of substance" (IV:236).

Here, then, is a metaphysical commitment, to the by now familiar doctrine of a distinction between substance and accidents. Even if Locke has nothing further to say about what substances are, he thinks we can be certain of their existence. On what does this certainty rest? Evidently, it rests on an assumption about what substances do. For although Locke disavows any idea of what substances are, he takes himself to grasp something of their function, remarking that "of substance, we have no idea of what it is, but only a confused obscure one of what it does" (II.13.19). By far the most prominent function he ascribes to substance is to serve as the subject or support for qualities. (For instances, see II.23.2, lines 2, 4, 15–19 above, and II.23.4, lines 4–6 above.) This, he tells Stillingfleet, is the "true reason" on which our supposition of a substance "is grounded" (*Works* IV:19). It is a reason, however, that commits Locke to still more metaphysical baggage, because it commits him to the existence of qualities that depend on substance. We postulate substance because we are not capable of "imagining how these simple ideas [viz., qualities] can subsist by themselves" (II.23.1, lines 7–8 above). It can seem a mere platitude to say that color requires a colored object and shape an object to have the shape—or that jumping requires a jumper, as Hobbes mischievously put it to Descartes (§8.1, §16.2). But the history of scholastic philosophy is full of attempts to deny that the surface structure of perception and language should be cashed out in terms of a substance–accident distinction (§6.2), and we have seen that Hobbes himself proposes the thoroughgoing elimination of accidents in favor of an ontology of substances alone, conceived in various ways (§7.1). In contrast, and very much like Descartes before him, Locke gives ontological status to both substance and accidents. Indeed, Locke's strategy for inferring substance from quality is reminiscent of Descartes's own strategy: "nor do we have any idea of substance taken by itself, other than that it is the thing in which the items we perceive . . . exist formally or eminently. For we know by the natural light that no real attribute can belong to nothing" (Second Replies, VII:161). Whether either Descartes or Locke had good reasons for treating properties as dependent entities, over and above substance, is a question to which I will return (§13.5, §23.4).[12]

---

would expect him to agree that they are of little use. Instead, Leibniz positively endorses substance in the sense at issue in II.13.20, remarking that "J'avoue, que je suis d'un autre sentiment, et je crois que la considération de la substance est un point des plus importans et des plus féconds de la philosophie" (p. 150). Yet, obviously, Leibniz does not wish to endorse the doctrine of a sub-substance.

[12] Locke repeatedly stresses to Stillingfleet that the primary ground for a belief in substance is the need for qualities to inhere in something: "as long as there is any simple idea or sensible quality left, according to my way of arguing, substance cannot be discarded; because all simple ideas, all sensible qualities, carry with them a supposition of a substratum to exist in, and of a substance wherein they inhere" (IV:7); "by 'carrying with them a supposition,' I mean, according to the ordinary import of the phrase, that sensible qualities imply a substratum to exist in" (IV:447).

The suggestion that Locke's theory of substance is partly driven by his realism regarding qualities is made as well by Lowe, who speaks of Locke's "mistaken reification . . . of qualities as ontologically independent entities in their own right" (*Locke* p. 90). For Locke, though, one might better speak of qualities as ontologically *dependent* entities, especially since it is their dependence that leads to the postulation of an underlying substance.

The second way in which Locke repeatedly characterizes our idea of substance is as that which unifies the various sensible qualities we conceive of as constituting the substance:

Whatever therefore be the secret, abstract nature of substance in general, all the ideas we have of particular distinct sorts of substances are nothing but several combinations of simple ideas, co-existing in such, though unknown, cause of their union as makes the whole subsist of itself (II.23.6).

[O]ur specific ideas of substances are nothing else but a collection of a certain number of simple ideas, considered as united in one thing (II.23.14).

[T]he greatest part of the ideas that make our complex idea of gold are yellowness, great weight, ductility, fusibility, and solubility in aqua regia, etc., all united together in an unknown substratum (II.23.37).

[I]n substances, besides the several distinct simple ideas that make them up, the confused one of Substance, or of an unknown support and cause of their union, is always a part (III.6.21).

It is significant that Locke regularly says not just that ideas (that is, the qualities that give rise to them) are united in a substance, but that the substance *causes* their union. The phenomenon he has in mind, I take it, is not just the momentary co-presence of various qualities, but their stably enduring over time. The reason we think of certain things as substances, after all, is that we associate them with stable, predictable clusters of sensible qualities. Thus, in the case of a swan, we notice its "white colour, long neck, red beak, black legs, and whole feet, and all these of a certain size, with a power of swimming in the water, and making a certain kind of noise" (II.23.14). From such facts about the world, which can after all scarcely be denied, Locke takes us to infer the existence of substances as the cause of such enduring property clusters. Viewed in this light, the hackneyed example of a pincushion to illustrate the concept of a substratum gets things completely backwards. Locke is postulating not just some thing to which various random properties can be attached, but some thing that explains the stable concurrence of these properties rather than others, because it is the *cause* of its various properties. Instead of pincushions, think of porcupines.

This sort of argument for the existence of substance is very much a traditional scholastic argument (§24.4). For now we need note only that, just as scholastic authors advanced this claim in the context of arguing for substantial form, so Locke advances it in the context of his real essences. This is clear, for instance, in a passage from II.23.3 quoted above (lines 2–5): "... such combinations of simple ideas, as are by experience and observation of men's senses taken notice of to exist together, and are therefore supposed to flow from the particular internal constitution, or unknown essence of that substance." To say these ideas—viz., qualities—exist together just is to advert to their union. Locke appeals here to the thing's real essence because that is the aspect of the substance that accounts for the thing's observable properties. Here, then, we seem to have a further substantive metaphysical thesis: not just that we should distinguish between substance and accidents, but that we should postulate a causal relationship between the two, so that what explains why a certain thing has certain properties is the substance of the thing, and that the particular explanatory feature of the substance is its real essence, which is what gives rise to these properties and hence explains their unity both at a time and over time.

Real essences are a kind of organizational principle: "I do not take them [real essences] to flow from the substance in any created being, but to be in every thing that internal constitution, or frame, or modification of the substance..." (IV:82). This characterization suggests that the substance itself is a kind of composite: an organizational principle, together with a stuff that gets organized. Once again, then, Locke's commitments seem surprisingly close to scholastic views, according to which the stuff that gets organized is prime matter. Locke is as dismissive of prime matter as he is of substantial form, describing scholastic discussions of it as "obscure and unintelligible" (III.10.15). Yet, as we have seen in the case of other authors (§2.1, §3.2), what Locke really objects to is a certain understanding of prime matter, "as if there were some such thing really in nature, distinct from body" (III.10.15). The core idea of a stuff that endures through all natural change is one that Locke seems to accept. Thus he remarks that a human being "can do nothing towards the making the least particle of new matter, or destroying one atom of what is already in being" (II.2.2). And he contrasts supernatural creation—"when a new particle of matter does begin to exist, *in rerum natura*, which had before no being"—with ordinary generation:

When a thing is made up of particles, which did all of them before exist, but that very thing, so constituted of pre-existing particles, which considered altogether make up such a collection of simple ideas [that is, qualities], had not any existence before: as this man, this egg, rose, or cherry, etc. (II.26.2)

In general material substances are entirely alike on the stuff side: "as a tree and a pebble being in the same sense body, and agreeing in the common nature of body, differ only in a bare modification of that common matter" (II.13.18). The reference to the "modification" of matter is a reference to the substance's internal constitution, its real essence. Hence an egg or a cherry just is a collection of particles, organized in a certain way, such as to give rise to its various distinctive sensible features.

There is ample evidence, therefore, for ascribing to Locke a robust metaphysics of substance. For all his assertions of ignorance, he has in fact quite a lot to say about what substance is. Yet it would be quite out of keeping with the spirit of his thought, I think, to treat him as committed to any very specific hypothesis. Although he describes various suppositions that the educated folk are committed to, such as the existence of substances, each with its own real essence, Locke seems perfectly ready to give up these hypotheses for others. Even the overarching corpuscularian framework that he inherits from Gassendi, Boyle, and others is, for Locke, merely the best available hypothesis at the time. Hence there is no good reason to ascribe to Locke any definite metaphysical scheme. Perhaps the real essence of a thing is more than simply a spatial arrangement of its parts; perhaps the very idea of a real essence is a mistake. Once one sees that the theses advanced by Locke are the most commonplace of seventeenth-century views, there becomes little reason to read Locke as dogmatically committed to any particular metaphysical story. As suggested earlier, Locke is always a reluctant metaphysician, pursuing the strategy of quietism as far as possible. His true agenda is simply to put on a rational footing the ideas and language we in fact use to talk about the world.

9.3. How Metaphysics Matters

We should not quite conclude, however, that Locke has no interesting positive metaphysical theory of substance. For even if Locke is committed to no specific theory, and perhaps even thinks it impossible to arrive at any specific theory, he does nevertheless maintain the very interesting position that a complete grasp of substances would include a grasp of their metaphysical structure. This comes out most clearly in his discussions of what it is to be a substance in general. As we have seen, Locke has nothing at all to say of a positive nature about what it is to be a substance (see II.23.2 and the parallel discussion in Stillingfleet [IV:8], as quoted above). This familiar claim takes on a new meaning in Locke, however, because he takes it to have consequences for our grasp of individual substance kinds. For Locke, the idea of substance in general is a constituent in our ideas of particular substance kinds. Thus "an obscure and relative idea of substance in general being thus made, we come to have the ideas of particular sorts of substances" (II.23.3, lines 1–2 above). Indeed, the "supposed or confused idea of substance, such as it is, is always the first and chief" idea in the complex of ideas that "represent distinct particular things subsisting by themselves" (II.12.6). Moreover, Locke makes it clear that our failure to grasp a given kind of substance arises not just from our failure to grasp real essences, but also from our ignorance about substance in general:

For since the powers or qualities that are observable by us are not the real essence of that substance, but depend on it and flow from it, any collection whatsoever of these qualities cannot be the real essence of that thing. Whereby it is plain that our ideas of substances are not adequate; are not what the mind intends them to be. Besides, a man has no idea of substance in general, nor knows what substance is in itself. (II.31.13)

The second sentence, as following from the first, asserts that the failure to grasp real essences makes our ideas of substance inadequate. (This follows, of course, only if real essences are a part of the substance.) The third, final sentence adds the qualification that a grasp of the real essence is not sufficient to understand a particular kind of thing, because even if one knew that, one would still lack a grasp of substance in general. (That final clause also refers, obscurely, to "substance in itself." Perhaps this reflects the idea that the real essence would not tell the whole story about the intrinsic structure of a given substance, since it would leave out, minimally, the stuff that gets structured by the essence.)

Scholastic authors do not generally suppose that one must grasp the nature of substance in general in order to grasp a particular kind of substance. Indeed, the idea is rather surprising: why should an understanding of gold or horse require a metaphysical account of what it is to be a substance? We now suppose, for instance, that we do understand gold, in virtue of understanding its chemical structure. This seems to be just the sort of understanding that Locke had in mind as knowledge of a thing's real essence. But Locke thinks we do not fully understand gold until we have a metaphysics of substance. In other words, a scientific understanding of any kind of thing is incomplete unless married to a philosophical account of what it is to be a thing, a substance. Although Locke does not make it clear why he thinks this, the claim is on reflection a plausible one. The judgment that modern chemistry understands what gold is has to be made gingerly, based on certain background assumptions that lead us to treat this sort of information (chemical structure) as fully revealing what stuff of that kind is. These background assumptions are largely philosophical assumptions, about what counts as a full understanding of something like gold. So even if there is a sense in which we think we understand gold through chemistry alone, the very conclusion that chemistry alone suffices must itself be supported by a background philosophical theory about the metaphysical status of things like gold—that is, of substances in general.

Although Locke is provisionally willing to accept a broadly corpuscularian theory of the material world, he is unwilling to treat this as the whole truth about material substances. Indeed, the most striking feature of his whole discussion is not the commonplace attacks on scholastic metaphysics, or even his professions of ignorance regarding the true nature of substance, but rather the way he refuses to exempt contemporary corpuscularian thought from the scope of his attack.[13] As we have seen, he rejects the Cartesian strategy of identifying substance with thought or extension. He equally dismisses the common but glib corpuscularian strategy of identifying material substances with the basic corpuscles. Treating substance as the "solid extended parts" (II.23.2, line 5 above) gets us nowhere, as remarked earlier. Whereas a strict corpuscularian like Hobbes rejects the very notion of an accident as something over and above the substance itself, and accordingly rejects the inquiry into some sort of veiled subject (§7.1), Locke accepts that there is metaphysical work to be done here. It is not enough simply to say that big bodies are composed of small bodies, arranged in a certain way. That gets us not at all to the things themselves.

Locke therefore stands curiously poised between scholastic theories of substance, which he rejects, and corpuscularian theories of substance, which he also rejects. Here perhaps the best comparison is with Leibniz. Just as Leibniz endorses corpuscularian explanations at a certain level, but thinks there is a further metaphysical story to be told, so too Locke is a corpuscularian who thinks that we would understand ordinary substances—horse, gold, etc.—only if we understood their metaphysical structure. This means not just that we would need a positive idea of what it is in general to be a substance, but also that we would need an account of the metaphysical structure of individual substances: of what exactly a real essence is, and what the other constituents of a substance are. This is required, Locke believes, not just in order to have a complete metaphysics, but even in order to understand what gold is, or what a cherry is. But whereas Leibniz is willing to construct a positive theory, Locke remains steadfastly unwilling to do so. Indeed, he seems to regard the project as impossible in principle, going so far as to remark that

---

[13] Locke's doubts about our ability to grasp the underlying natures of things emerge in his discussions of substance, of course, but also of cohesion (*Essay* II.23.23–27), impulse (II.23.28), the relationship between primary qualities and secondary qualities (IV.3.28), and the laws of nature (IV.3.29). In general, he bemoans "what a darkness we are involved in, how little it is of being, and the things that are, that we are capable to know" (IV.3.29). The most he will say of the "corpuscularian hypothesis" is that it goes "farthest in an intelligible explication of the qualities of bodies" (IV.3.16). For nuanced discussions of Locke's views in these areas, see McCann, "Lockean Mechanism," and Rozemond and Yaffe, "Peach Trees." For the extent of Locke's commitment to mechanism in the early drafts of the *Essay*, see Walmsley, "Locke's Natural Philosophy."

the simple ideas we receive from sensation and reflection are the boundaries of our thoughts; beyond which the mind, whatever efforts it would make, is not able to advance one jot; nor can it make any discoveries, when it would pry into the nature and hidden causes of those ideas. (II.23.29)

Perhaps what ultimately makes Locke's account of substance so provocative is that he at once both rules out a metaphysics of substance, and insists on it as essential to a full understanding of the familiar things around us. This is an important development for the history of philosophy, because—as suggested already (§5.5)—one of the consequences of scholasticism's demise might have been a wholesale rejection of metaphysics. By positioning metaphysical inquiry as obligatory for a complete grasp of reality, Locke provoked successive generations to attempt the discoveries and advances that he had ruled out.

PART III

ACCIDENTS

10

Real Accidents

10.1. The Holy Grail

Any list of the really big ideas from the history of philosophy, no matter how short and selective, would have to include the idea that the fundamental objects of philosophical analysis are *forms*. The idea was of course initially Plato's, offered as a way of dealing with various kinds of reductionism, and then became domesticated at the hands of Aristotle, who paired form with matter, as the two chief principles of his metaphysics and natural philosophy. So far, this study has concentrated first on matter, and then on the substance constituted by matter, underlying the sensible qualities. Although forms have inevitably come into the picture at various junctures, I have tried to enter as little as possible into the many complexities surrounding the topic. It was, however, controversies over form, above all else, that constituted the subject matter both of scholastic disputes in the fourteenth through sixteenth centuries, and of the seventeenth-century rejection of scholasticism. Accordingly, the heart of this book, beginning now, concerns the theory of forms.

For those who aspire to a modern revival of Aristotelianism, the concept of *form* can easily take on the aspect of a kind of Holy Grail, such that if only we could get these ideas clearly in focus, we could then see our way forward on any number of philosophical fronts, such as the union of mind and body, the coherence and endurance of substances, the nature of causality, and so on. The historical record, however, suggests that this hope is a snare and delusion. There has never been any such thing as *the* theory of form; instead, form is just a conveniently pliable catchword that takes on substantive meaning only when developed in one controversial direction or another. So although scholastic philosophers of all kinds used this terminology incessantly, it had no more of a fixed meaning than does our ubiquitous modern philosophical talk of "properties." Correspondingly, there can be no simple answer to the question of how far post-scholastic authors retain the conception of form. The concept is so polymorphous as to make generalizations almost meaningless. Among post-scholastic authors, the elusiveness of the concept is sometimes framed as an objection. Joseph Glanvill, for instance, the English propagandist for the Royal Society, remarks in his *Scepsis scientifica* (1665) that form "is a mere word," something that even "votaries of that philosophy themselves can scarce tell what to make of" (ch. 18, pp. 125, 130). These remarks might give the misleading impression that scholastic authors have nothing to say about what forms are. On the contrary, they have an enormous amount to say, as we will see. What Glanvill is perhaps registering, though, is the lack of consensus. The only points of agreement regarding form were the merest of platitudes, such as that form is actuality, or that it (ordinarily!) inheres in a subject. All of the hard questions were contentious ones. We will see this confirmed over and over as we proceed, but the point comes out especially clearly in considering those forms that were traditionally characterized as accidental.[1]

One of the most remarkable features of the debate over accidental form is the way conceptions of form travel full circle, from the thirteenth to the seventeenth century. The first scholastic efforts to make sense of Aristotle's metaphysics, in the thirteenth century, tend toward an understanding of accidental form that is deflationary, in the sense that such forms are regarded as lacking any proper being of their own. From the start of the fourteenth century, under the influence of John Duns Scotus, this deflationary reading is generally rejected, in favor of a conception of accidents as real entities in their own right. When seventeenth-century authors in turn reject the doctrine of "real accidents," they are in many cases returning to the sort of view that was first in favor among scholastic authors. Remarkably, then, the lines of demarcation on this fundamental issue are not simply a matter of dividing medieval against modern, Aristotelian against mechanistic. Rather, early scholastic authors line up on the same side as the "modern" seventeenth-century approach, against the dominant realism of the later scholastic era. Accordingly, when seventeenth-century authors attack the doctrine of real accidents, they are not attacking an essential feature of scholastic Aristotelianism, but merely a peculiarity in how the scholastic theory developed from the fourteenth century onward.

According to this later scholastic realism, accidental forms are beings in their own right, capable of existing independently of their subjects. For most of the period with which this study is concerned, this was the dominant view, enforced by ecclesiastical authority (Chs. 19–20). Hence seventeenth-century authors were well within their rights to complain, as does Robert Boyle, that the scholastic theory of accidental form is "manifestly contradictious"—treating such forms as both accidents and substances. This complaint was not only legitimate, but was in fact a standard objection throughout the scholastic era.[2] Moreover, although we will see that scholastic authors had ready replies to this sort of criticism, there is a sense in which the later scholastic

---

[1] For platitudes regarding form, see e.g. Buridan, *In Praed.* q. 16 (pp. 164–5): "forma dicitur communiter de omni actu perficiente materiam vel subiectum aliquod, cui inhaeret"; Wyclif, *De materia et forma* p. 163: "forma . . . significat rem per quam vel secundum quam aliquid est formaliter quid, vel alicuius modi." In the case of each author, the platitude conceals some rather remarkable and unorthodox views, as discussed in §11.1.

For a useful overview of the continuing talk of form and matter among seventeenth-century authors, see Lüthy and Newman, "Preface." See also the many interesting examples collected in Emerton, *Scientific Reinterpretation of Form*, and also the remarks in §24.5.

[2] The contradiction Boyle discerns runs as follows: "For, speaking in a physical sense, if they will not allow these accidents to be modes of matter, but entities really distinct from it and in some cases separable from all matter, they make them indeed accidents in name, but represent them under such a notion as belongs only to substances" (*Origin of Forms* V:308–9; Stewart p. 22). Similar complaints can be found in countless places, among both scholastic and post-scholastic authors. It appears as early as Alexander of Hales (before 1236): "si ergo ens in alio fit ens non in alio, videtur quod accidens fiat substantia" (*Quaest. disputatae* 51.4.3, p. 939), and was widespread enough to have been condemned in 1277 (see prop. 139, quoted in note 15 below). For the seventeenth century, see, e.g., Digby, *Two Treatises* I.6 (p. 39), I concl. (p. 345); Descartes, Fourth Replies (VII:253–4). Menn, "Greatest Stumbling Block" is useful on the scholastic context to Descartes's objections.

tradition precisely does want to construe accidents on the model of substances, inasmuch as accidents are said to be beings in just the way that substances are. These scholastic authors *sought* the result that, at the deepest level, substances and accidents are things of the same metaphysical kind.

10.2. Deflationary Accounts

I use the term 'deflationary' to cover a broad range of views on which forms are somehow less than full-fledged beings in their own right, which is to say that they do not exist in the same sense that substances exist. The most extreme sort of deflationist account, which we might call *eliminativism*, is the view that there simply are no such things as accidental forms. This strategy has its explicit defenders in the seventeenth century. We have already seen Hobbes, for instance, endorse this sort of view, with his remark that an accident is just "the mode of conceiving a body" (§7.1). To prove his point, Hobbes initially focuses on motion, rest, and shape, those cases where it is easiest to suppose that the accident is just the body itself, variously situated. He then adds:

It could seem to some that not all accidents are in their bodies in the same way that extension, motion, rest, or shape are in them—for example, that color, heat, odor, virtue, vice, and the like are in bodies in a different way and, as they say, *inhere* in them. I would ask them to suspend   3
their judgment on this matter for now, and wait a little, until it be investigated by reason whether even these accidents are not also certain motions, either of the mind that imagines them or of the very bodies that are sensed. For such an inquiry is a large part of natural   6
philosophy. (*De corpore* 8.3)

Hobbes is quite right to think of natural philosophy as being concerned in "large part" (line 6) with the status of accidental forms. On his own eliminative view, however, accidents are either nothing more than bodies variously situated and moved, or else sensory experiences that we mistakenly project onto bodies (§22.5). Thus, "whatsoever accidents or qualities our senses make us think there be in the world, they are not there, but are seemings and apparitions only. The things that really are in the world without us are those motions by which these seemings are caused" (*Elements of Law* I.2.10). All change, according to Hobbes, is simply the motion of bodies, and so there is no need to postulate the succession of accidental (or substantial) forms. As he firmly puts it, "I have denied, as he knew, that there is any reality in accidents" (*Answer to Bramhall* [*Works* IV:305]).[3]

---

[3] For further passages from Hobbes, see §7.1. For Hobbes's account of change as corporeal motion, see *De corpore* 9.9 and 25.2 and also *De mundo* 5.1 and 7.1. Regarding his hostility toward substantial form, see *Lev.* IV.46: "to be a body, to be speaking, to live, to see and the like infinitives, also corporeity, walking, speaking, life, sight and the like, that signify just the same, are the names of nothing." See Leijenhorst, *Mechanisation* pp. 163–5.

Leijenhorst thinks that Hobbes has two conceptions of accidents. In the strict sense, an accident "is not an objective 'mode of a body,' but our subjective 'mode of *conceiving* body'" (*Mechanisation* p. 156). This corresponds with my eliminativist reading. But Leijenhorst thinks that Hobbes is also committed to a realistic conception of accidents, at least with respect to size and motion: "the *phenomenalist* accidents are the fruits of *realist* accidents" (p. 157). I do not believe this is correct, even for size and motion. Malherbe distinguishes between the subjective accident in the perceiver and the external reality that causes the perception ("Hobbes et l'accident" pp. 50–1). But this much is consistent with my reading of Hobbes, since of course I can accept that it is an external reality that produces our subjective mode of conceiving. Malherbe goes on to remark: "L'accident n'est pas un être, ni une partie d'un être; sa réalité n'est que phénoménale . . ." (p. 55). Hobbes does talk of accidents in bodies as powers; see §23.1 for my reductive reading of such remarks.

It is not as easy as one might suppose to find other clear instances of authors eliminating forms from their ontology. Throughout the later scholastic era, to be sure, the doctrine is effectively incontrovertible. Nicholas of Autrecourt does reject forms of all kinds in the mid-fourteenth century, but he would be condemned for so doing (§19.4), and subsequent thinkers, however heterodox, toed the party line in this regard. Even Nicholas of Cusa, no Aristotelian, allows that Aristotle got it right when he divided the world into substances and accidents.[4] Giordano Bruno foreshadows what was to come in 1584, when he describes the view that "forms are nothing other than certain accidental dispositions of matter" and associates it with a long list of philosophers from Democritus onward. But although he says that he himself held this view for a long time, he adds that he has since come to believe in forms (*De la causa* dial. 3, p. 63; tr. p. 55). It is only in the seventeenth century that one begins to find sustained opposition. Isaac Beeckman seems to be one early proponent of eliminativism (§19.6). Looking around for encouraging precedents, he quotes in his journal the above passage from Bruno (III:360). Francis Bacon is perhaps another early example, judging from a remark in the *Novum organum* (1620) that "nothing truly exists in nature beyond individual bodies." Yet at the same time he urges that "the task and aim of human science" is to discover the forms of those bodies (II.1–2). Bacon's appeal to forms has been interpreted in many ways. If we take him at his word here, however, and hold that only individual bodies exist, variously situated, then form must be reducible to facts about how those bodies are situated. This, I take it, amounts to eliminating form altogether, and we will see this strategy at work later (§21.4), in Bacon's doctrine that the form of heat is not any "positive nature" (ibid., II.18), but simply a kind of motion.[5] Nicholas Hill, in 1601, provides an even earlier example of this same general approach: "form is the state and condition of a thing, a result of the connection among its material principles; it is a constituting principle, not an operative one" (*Philosophia* n. 35). Hill's remark about form, undeveloped as it is, offers a useful suggestion about what it might mean to deny the reality of form. Although we will see that commitment to form comes in many kinds and degrees, one of the most important questions about form is whether it plays any causal role. This is precisely what Hill seems to deny when he describes form as "constituting," not "operative." That is, the concept of form is useful in explaining how a body is constituted: the body has such and such a shape, with its parts so and so arranged. What we should not suppose, according to Hill, is that the form acts as some further agent within a body, playing its own causal role. This, however, as we will see, is precisely what most scholastic authors were prepared to affirm about forms, both accidental and substantial.[6]

---

[4] Cusa treats substance and accident as exhaustively dividing being: "recte divisit Aristoteles omnia quae in mundo sunt in substantiam et accidens" (*De docta ignorantia* I.18.53). On his attitude to Aristotle, see Moran, "Nicholas of Cusa."

[5] There is an extensive literature on Bacon's use of form, and much disagreement. For a Platonizing reading, see e.g. Rossi, *Francis Bacon*. The case for Aristotle's influence is made in Larsen, "Aristotelianism" and Zagorin, *Francis Bacon*. See also Malherbe, "Bacon's Method" and the essays in Malherbe and Pousser, *Francis Bacon*. For a reductive interpretation, *Novum organum* I.51 is particularly notable: "formae enim commenta [≈ fictions] animi humani sunt, nisi libeat leges illas actus formas appellare." This suggests that forms are nothing more than the laws according to which bodies move.

[6] By the second half of the seventeenth century, statements of eliminativism are easier to find. The young Leibniz, for instance, embraces a strict corpuscularianism, declaring to Thomasius in 1669 that "formam supponamus nihil aliud esse quam figuram" and that "has omnes [mutationes] putant recentiores per motum localem solum explicari posse" (*Phil.*

Further discussion of seventeenth-century views will have to wait until later (Chs. 13, 19, 21–3). Here I will concentrate on the state of the scholastic dispute. From the earliest scholastic studies of Aristotle's hylomorphism, in the mid-1200s, up until the end of that century, the dominant tendency was deflationary. Although no one proposed eliminativism, it was commonly supposed that the existence of accidents should not be understood in the same sense as the existence of substances: that 'existence' is equivocal in the two claims, and that talk of an accident's existing is best understood as shorthand for a substance's existing in a certain way. This was how Averroes had read Aristotle's talk of τὰ πάθη καὶ αἱ κινήσεις (*Meta.* 1071a2), remarking that "accidents are in truth states and changes (*passiones et motus*) of substances;...they are nothing other than dispositions of a substance" (*In Meta.* XII.25). This would become the common thirteenth-century reading as well. Richard Rufus of Cornwall, for instance, in his *Scriptum in Metaphysicam* (*c.*1237), describes an accident as having no existence in its own right, inasmuch as it is "nothing other than the being of the substance." Hence, "the nature of an accident is not distinct from the nature of a substance, but is merely the being of that substance" (VII.1.4). Albert the Great takes essentially the same position in his commentary on the *Metaphysics* (1260s), concluding that "an accident is truly only the mode of a substance" (VII.1.1) inasmuch as it has no existence of its own: "an accident is not by its nature an essence taken in its own right that gives rise to some existence (*esse*), but instead is some sort of existence of the substance, constituted by the substance" (VII.1.4). Running through the various qualities and quantities that are the paradigm accidents, Albert concludes in every case that the accident is not something over and above the substance, but simply a mode of the substance, such that "if the substance were taken away, nothing at all would remain of the nature of the accident, neither in reality nor in the intellect" (VII.1.1). (Although Albert repeatedly describes accidents as modes, I will for now refrain from using this heavily freighted term, pending a fuller discussion of the topic in Ch. 13.)

It is not clear that the view Albert describes here is his own. He elsewhere warns that his commentaries present only Aristotle's views, and indeed in his earlier *Sentences* commentary he had offered a less deflationary account of accidents.[7] Still, as we will see, the question of what Aristotle thought was a significant aspect of the scholastic debate. Moreover, readings of Aristotle of course influenced authors' own views. Consider this remarkable discussion of form from the start of Aquinas's *Quaestiones de virtutibus in communi* (1271):

Schriften IV:165–6; tr. Loemker pp. 95–6). Of course Leibniz later came to be much more sympathetic to form. For a detailed discussion of his early views, and this letter in particular, see Mercer, *Leibniz's Metaphysics* ch. 3.

[7] For Albert the Great's deflationism, see also *In Meta.* VII.1.7: "...accidens ordinabile in genere et specie non absolvitur ab esse substantiae, quia ipsum est quaedam substantia sub tali esse, et ideo non est nisi modus substantiae"; ibid., VII.1.8: "...accidens non habet differentiam entis, qua ordinetur in praedicamento, nisi accipiatur sic, quod dicat substantiam sub esse tali vel tali." And see *In Praed.* I.2: "ens dicitur aequivoce de omnibus entibus per se et in alio existentibus, eo quod per se ens solum naturae est ens, alii autem quaedam modi sunt illius entis, et non entia vera et principalia." For a caution against assuming that such remarks from his commentaries represent Albert's own thoughts, see the epilogue to his *Politics* commentary: "Nec ego dixi aliquid in isto libro, nisi exponendo quae dicta sunt, et rationes et causas adhibendo. Sicut enim in omnibus libris physicis, nunquam de meo dixi aliquid, sed opiniones Peripateticorum quanto fidelius potui exposui." On how to read Albert's commentaries, see Wieland, *Untersuchungen* pp. 6–15. For a less deflationary stance on accidents, see *Sent.* IV.12.16, which distinguishes two sorts of accidental *esse*: "esse quod habet accidens in subiecto est quasi esse entis compositi; sed esse quo essentia est id quod est intelligitur in accidente secundum se" (ed. Jammy XVI:185b).

Many err regarding form because they judge it as if they were judging substance. This seems to happen because forms are signified as substances are, in the abstract, as *whiteness* or *virtue*, and so on. As a result, some follow this mode of speech and judge accidents as if they were substances. . . . For they hold that forms are suited to be made just as substances are, and so when they do not find what it is that generates forms, they claim that they are either created or preexist within matter. What they do not notice is that just as existing belongs not to form, but to the subject through the form, so too being made (which culminates in existing) belongs not to form, but to the subject. For just as a form is said to be a being not because *it* exists—if we are to speak properly—but because something exists by it, so too a form is said to be made not because *it* is made, but because something is made by it, when a subject is brought from potentiality to actuality. (q. 11c)

Throughout his work, Aquinas invokes the principle that what exists, strictly speaking, is substance. All other putative entities, even if we talk about them as if they exist, are not truly existent, but are merely aspects of substance. In the case of form—Aquinas means to include here both accidental forms and substantial forms other than the rational soul—they are the explanatory principles for why a substance has certain features. Aquinas never claims that accidents do not exist, or that only substances exist. The idea, instead, inspired by Aristotle's remarks on the homonymy (equivocity) of *being*, is that although we can truly say that accidents exist, that claim can come out true only if we give 'exists' a different—albeit connected, and so analogous—sense from what it has in the case of substance. This idea of treating 'exists' equivocally sounds on its face desperately obscure, given that it is hard enough to understand what existence amounts to in the paradigm case of substantial existence. But Aquinas does not mean to ascribe to accidents any sort of twilight, halfway mode of existence. Instead, he understands the claim that an accident exists as meaning that a substance exists in a certain way (as white, or tall, etc.). Thus "whiteness is said to exist not because it subsists in itself, but because by it something has existence-as-white" (*Quodlibet* IX.2.2). Admittedly, this leads directly to the question of what existence-as-white (*esse album*) amounts to, and one might reasonably worry that Aquinas has just shifted the difficulty from one place to another. But at least he has expressly warned us away from one sort of potential confusion, the confusion of thinking that there are things such as accidents that have their own existence. Instead, only substance "properly and truly has existence or exists" (ibid.). As we will see in §§26.3–5, Aquinas extends such deflationism even to a substance's integral parts. Reflection on his position in that context will require reconsidering how his view fits in between eliminativism and full-blooded realism.[8]

---

[8] For Aquinas, see also *Summa theol.* 1a 45.4c: "Illi enim proprie convenit esse, quod habet esse; et hoc est subsistens in suo esse. Formae autem et accidentia, et alia huiusmodi, non dicuntur entia quasi ipsa sint, sed quia eis aliquid est; ut albedo ea ratione dicitur ens, quia ea subiectum est album. Unde, secundum Philosophum, accidens magis proprie dicitur entis quam ens. Sicut igitur accidentia et formae et huiusmodi quae non subsistunt magis sunt coexistentia quam entia, ita magis debent dici concreata quam creata." See also *Summa theol.* 1a2ae 55.4 ad 1 and 110.2 ad 3. *In Meta.* XI.3.2197; *In Meta.* XII.1.2419; *De occultis* (ed. Leo. 43:184); *Sent.* III.6.2.2c. *De ente* puts a similar kind of thought into somewhat different terms, remarking that "ens absolute et primo dicitur de substantiis et per posterius et secundum quid de accidentibus" (ch. 1, ed. Leo. 43:370). For discussion, see Brown, *Accidental Being* passim, esp. pp. 142–4; Reynolds, "*Per se* Accidents" pp. 211–30; Wéber, "L'Incidence" pp. 196–8; Wippel, *Metaphysical Thought of Thomas* pp. 253–65; Klima, "Thomistic 'Monism'." On the rational soul as a special case, in virtue of its subsistence, see *Summa theol.* 1a 90.2c.

On the homonymy of being in Aristotle, see *Phys.* I.3, 186a22–187a12; *Meta.* IV.2, 1003a33–b11; *Meta.* V.7, 1017a7–b9; *Meta.* VI.2, 1026a33–b3; *Meta.* VII.4, 1030a19–b13; and Shields, *Order in Multiplicity* ch. 9. For Aquinas on the homonymy of being, see his commentaries on these texts, as well as *Quod.* IX.2.2 and *De substantiis separatis* ch. 8 (ed. Leo. 40:D54):

Thirteenth-century arts masters, in their lectures on Aristotle, likewise take for granted this standard deflationary account of accidents. Siger of Brabant is typical, remarking *circa* 1273 that "an accident is not a thing that exists nor does it have the characteristic of existing except in relation to substance."[9] A contemporary English *Physics* commentary puts this idea vividly:

> The essence of an accident consists in its relationship (*dispositione*) to a substance. For we should not imagine that an accident is a thing in its own right to which gets attached a relationship or link (*respectus*) to the substance in which that accident exists. For if so then an accident would   3
> be something absolute in its own right, dependent on substance only as something extrinsic, and on this view an accident could be cognized apart from the substance. These outcomes are impossible, however. Hence what an accident is is to be something *of* the substance: either   6
> a measure (as a quantity is), or a state (as a quality is), and so on. Thus the Philosopher says that an accident is a being only because it belongs to a being. (Oriel ms. 33, in Donati, "*Utrum accidens*" p. 600)

The reference to Aristotle (lines 7–8) alludes to a passage from the start of *Metaphysics* Zeta that was quoted constantly in this context: "all other [non-substantial] things are called beings because they belong to what is such a being—such as quantities, qualities, affections, and so on" (1028a18–20). This was taken as a summary statement of the idea that accidents can be said to exist only in an equivocal sense, inasmuch as they inhere in a substance that exists.

10.3. The Problem of the Eucharist

Classical thirteenth-century discussions can ordinarily be expected to furnish the foundations on which later scholastic thought builds. In the present case, however, these foundations are shaky in the extreme. For even while theologians offered up a deflationary account of accidental form, they defended transubstantiation as the standard, even obligatory, account of the sacrament of the Eucharist. What transubstantiation maintains, however, is that the accidents of the bread and wine endure after consecration without inhering in any substance. (According to transubstantiation, the bread and wine are no longer there, having given way to the substance of Christ. Since it seemed out of the question for Christ to serve as the subject of those flavors, smells, etc., and since no other substance candidate seemed available, the accidents were held

---

"Cum enim ens non univoce de omnibus praedicetur, non est requirendus idem modus essendi in omnibus quae esse dicuntur; sed quaedam perfectius quaedam imperfectius esse participant: accidentia enim entia dicuntur non quia in se ipsis esse habeat, sed quia esse eorum est in hoc quod insunt substantiae." On the kind of equivocity in question as analogy, see, e.g., *Sent.* I.19.5.2 ad 1, *Sent.* II.42.1.3c.

[9] For Siger of Brabant's deflationism, see *In Meta.* (Paris) VII.5 (ed. Maurer, p. 454): ". . . accidens non sit id quod est nec habeat rationem essendi nisi in habitudine ad substantiam." See also an anonymous *In Phys.* I.12 (ed. Zimmermann, pp. 21–2): "Quia quaedam sunt entia secundum rationem essendi absolute dictam, sicut substantia, quaedam ratione essendi ad aliud attributa, ut accidens est ens ratione essendi ad substantiam dicta." This work has also been attributed to Siger, which is easy to believe if one compares its language with the following passage from Siger, *In Meta.* (Cambr.) V.23 (ed. Maurer, p. 237): "Accidens non habet essentiam absolutam, sed dictam in habitudine ad aliud. . . . Nec solum intelligo quod accidens, secundum quod accidens vel secundum quod qualitas vel quantitas, habeat rationem ad aliud dictam, sed etiam rationem essendi tantum habet in habitudine ad substantiam. Unde dicitur ens quia entis." For further references, drawing on unpublished manuscripts, see Donati, "*Utrum accidens*."

to exist without inhering in a subject.) Remarkably, the need to make room for transubstantiation did not generally drive thirteenth-century theologians away from their deflationary conception of accidents. Even so, it seemed to many that there simply was no room for accidents to exist apart from their subject. The passage quoted at the end of the previous section from an anonymous *Physics* commentary is part of a larger argument attempting to show that accidents are inseparable from their subject (as indeed was the earlier quotation from Averroes). This is a conclusion one finds over and over in the works of arts masters from this period. Their main argument was the same that one finds in the seventeenth century: that to allow accidents to exist apart from a substance is to countenance a thing's being at the same time a substance and an accident. This, everyone agreed, was impossible. Yet the doctrine of transubstantiation required that it be possible, at least logically (that is, possible for God), for accidents to exist apart from any substance. (Many authors, it should be noted, require only the *quantity* of the bread and wine to subsist on its own, and treat the remaining accidents as inhering in the quantity. Since quantity itself is an accident [Ch. 14], this in no way evades the core question of how to reconcile a deflationary account with transubstantiation, and so in what follows I set this detail aside.)[10]

In the face of this conundrum, one relatively straightforward solution emerged: that an accident be defined not as something that inheres in something else, but as something that naturally *tends* to do so. This is an idea that seems to stem from Bonaventure's *Sentences* commentary (*circa* 1252):

An accident's *aptitudinal* relationship to a subject is essential, and this is never taken away from accidents..., for it is true to say that they are *suited* to be in a subject. Its *actual* relationship to a subject, however, even though by nature it is always actually present, is nevertheless subsequent to its essence. Hence there is nothing absurd about its being able to be separated from its subject, by a supernatural power. (IV.12.1.1.1c)

This is a perfectly reasonable suggestion about how to distinguish accidents from substances. Just as a physicist might make definitions that presuppose certain laws of nature, without worrying about what might happen if those laws were abridged, so

---

[10]   Transubstantiation is defended by all the leading thirteenth-century theologians, including Albert (*Sent.* IV.12.16), Bonaventure (*Sent.* IV.12.1.1.1), and Aquinas (*Sent.* IV.12.1.1.1). By the time of the Coimbran commentaries, its implication for the theory of accidents was entirely beyond dispute: "Sit vero conclusio de qua Christiano Philosopho dubitare non licet: posse Deum conservare accidentia extra subiectum" (Coimbrans, *In Gen. et cor.* I.4.6.2). On transubstantiation's historical development, see Goering, "Invention," McCue, "Doctrine of Transubstantiation," and Macy, "Dogma of Transubstantiation." It should be noted, however, that there was a constant undercurrent of sympathy for consubstantiation, motivated in large part by the desire to avoid separable accidents (see, e.g., Ockham, *Reportatio* IV.8 [*Opera theol.* VII:137–40], Peter of Ailly, *Sent.* IV.6 art. 2 [f. D4rb–va], the latter of which was cited explicitly by Luther [see Pluta, "Ailly"]). For wide-ranging discussions of the theological and philosophical issues surrounding the Eucharist, see Adams, "Sacrament of the Altar" and Sylla, "Autonomous and Handmaiden Science." On the metaphysics of separability for accidents, see Des Chene, *Physiologia* pp. 129–33.

For qualities as inhering in the quantity of the host, rather than having no subject at all, see Albert, *Sent.* IV.12.16, Aquinas, *Summa theol.* 3a 77.2, Giles of Rome, *Theoremata de corpore Christi* props. 36, 39. It is not always clear whether, for these authors, a quality (or other non-quantitative accident) could in principle exist by itself, apart from quantity. The principal difficulty here concerns what would individuate a non-quantitative accident. (Quantity was widely thought to be self-individuating.) Godfrey of Fontaines (*Quod.* IV.22) takes the view that qualities seemingly cannot exist without quantity, as does Thomas of Sutton (*Quod.* II.6). James of Viterbo (*Quod.* II.1) argues to the contrary that absolute accidents (including qualities and motion) can exist without any subject, and Suárez would later describe the separability of quality as "longe probabilius" (*Disp. meta.* 37.2.4). For a retrospective discussion, see Coimbrans, *In Gen. et cor.* I.4.6.2, p. 76. Imbach, "Metaphysik," also surveys various positions on this issue.

Bonaventure suggests that we define accidents in terms of how they behave under natural circumstances, setting aside the anomalous supernatural case. Not surprisingly, this idea was widely embraced by other theologians. The suggestion, however, goes only so far. Although it nicely handles the objection that accidents would become substances, it leaves untouched the real core of the problem: to explain how it is even logically possible for a dependent entity to take on independent existence. Accidents, as they were generally conceived in the thirteenth century, just do not seem to be the kind of thing that *could* be made to exist in this way.[11]

To see exactly where the difficulty lies, we might consider Aquinas's third set of *Quodlibetal Questions* (Easter 1270). He begins the series by considering whether God can make prime matter exist without form. The only argument in favor depends on an analogy to accidental form: just as God can make an accident exist without a subject, so God can make matter exist without form. The comparison is in fact quite apt, because both prime matter and accidental form, as Aquinas conceives of them, lack existence in their own right. In each case, then, we might wonder how something that lacks such existence could possibly be made to have it. For prime matter, Aquinas goes on to argue that this is utterly impossible, on the grounds that for matter to have actual existence just is for it to have a form. Hence it is an immediate contradiction for *prime matter* (matter without form) to have *actual* existence (§3.1). But since accidents of course *are* forms, and so are actual, no such consideration applies. Instead,

An accident depends on a subject for its existence as a cause that sustains it. Since God can produce all the effects of secondary causes without those secondary causes, God can conserve an accident in existence without a subject. (ad 1)

Aquinas here takes for granted a view that has already arisen in various other connections, and that we will consider in some detail later (§24.4): that accidental properties are caused by their subject. (The whiteness of snow, for instance, is a result of the nature of snow.) His point, then, is that we can do without a subject for accidents if we think of God as playing the necessary causal role. Yet although this takes us somewhere, by showing that there is no immediate contradiction in the notion of an independently existing accident, it leaves unanswered the hard question of *how* something like whiteness can possibly exist on its own. Even if we think of God as taking over the causal role of sustaining accidents, we still have no explanation of what it would be for an accident to exist without a subject, and so the suspicion may still remain that some sort of impossibility lurks here. Indeed, the grounds for such a suspicion lie close at hand. For on the deflationary account that Aquinas and his contemporaries accept, an accident's existence just is the existence in a certain respect of a substance. God certainly cannot play *this* role for substance, both because then God would be the subject of

---

[11] For Bonaventure as seemingly the first to appeal to an accident's natural tendency to inhere, see Bakker, *La raison* I:314. Bakker is especially helpful in showing how little is new in Aquinas's much discussed treatment of the Eucharist: "En somme, la doctrine de Thomas, loin d'être une innovation, entre parfaitement dans le consensus des théologiens à partir d'Alexandre de Hales" (I:316). Given this, one should be cautious in accepting Pini's conclusion that "it is nevertheless his [Aquinas's] way of dealing with the issue that set the agenda for the debates on the status of accidents in Paris in the last two decades of the thirteenth century" ("Substance, Accident" p. 283). For an interesting later criticism of the view that even the aptitude to inhere is essential to an accident, see Paul of Venice, *In Meta.* VII.1.1.2 (in Amerini, "Alessandro di Alessandria" pp. 233–5). For a still later defense of the thesis that it is, see Fonseca, *In Meta.* VII.1.1 (II:199–201).

accidents (this was out of the question), and because we would then no longer have what we were after, accidents without a subject. Hence the problem remains: how can it be even logically possible for an accident to exist on its own?[12]

Thirteenth-century authors come closest to answering this question when they appeal to a change in an accident's *modus essendi*. The idea is to draw a distinction between what is essential to a thing and what is merely its accidental mode of existence. This sounds modest enough, but its application in this context is nothing short of audacious, inasmuch as it requires claiming that an accident's inhering in a subject is just one mode of existence that it can have, and that it might instead have the sort of existence characteristic of a substance. The miracle of the Eucharist, then, requires that God change an accident's *modus essendi*, so that what was a dependent being now takes on an independent mode of existence. This is an especially bold claim to make within the context of the deflationary approach, because the claim must be not just that accidents go from inhering to not inhering, but that they change their ontological status radically: accidents go from being mere ways in which a substance exists to being subsistent entities in their own right. To gauge the audacity of this move, we might think in terms of more familiar modern ontological kinds. Imagine, for instance, an event's existing as an object, or an abstract object's taking on a concrete mode of existence. How can we make any sense, for instance, of the number nine's existing concretely? In effect, this is the sort of radical transformation being countenanced in the case of accidents.[13]

Still, audacious as this strategy may be, its defenders need to establish only its bare, logical possibility. Until their opponents can produce an express contradiction in the notion of a freestanding accident—of the sort Aquinas produces in the case of

---

[12] The heart of Aquinas's reasoning on the inseparability of matter from form goes as follows: "Videtur quod Deus possit facere quod materia sit sine forma. Sicut enim materia secundum suum esse dependet a forma, ita accidens a subiecto.... Responsio.... [I]dem est dictu, materiam esse in actu et materiam habere formam. Dicere ergo quod materia sit in actu sine forma est dicere contradictoria esse simul; unde a Deo fieri non potest" (*Quod.* III.1.1). On the causal story that Aquinas requires to allow the separability of accidents, see Côté, "Siger of Brabant and Thomas Aquinas."

[13] Bakker, *La raison* I:307–10, traces the *modus essendi* doctrine back to the Franciscan William of Middleton, *circa* 1250: "Praeterea, inesse non definit proprie loquendo essentiam accidentis, sed prout concernit modum essendi. Unde cum dicitur 'accidentis esse est inesse,' hoc verum est secundum quod 'esse' dicit modum essendi. Unde, quia modus essendi est extra rem, non de esse rei simpliciter, ex separatione huius esse non destruitur esse simpliciter" (*De sacramentis* IV.6.26, as quoted in Bakker, *La raison* I:308 n. 34). The idea later appears in Aquinas, e.g., *Sent* IV.12.1.1.1 ad 1 and *De substantiis separatis* ch. 8 (as quoted in note 8 above). See also Simon of Faversham, *In Praed.* q. 1, p. 73: "Quodlibet praedicamentum constituitur ex duobus, scilicet ex re et ex modo essendi sibi superaddito." It plays a very prominent role in Giles of Rome, e.g., *Theoremata de corpore Christi* prop. 27, f. 16vb: "Non tamen est inconveniens, rem unius praedicamenti habere modum alterius praedicamenti, et universaliter unam rem habere modum alterius, quia licet reale esse competat rei per suam essentiam et naturam, modus tamen potest rei competere ex eo quod alteri coniungitur, vel secundum quod ad aliud comparatur"; ibid., prop. 40, f. 27vb: "Non naturaliter ergo, sed miraculose in sacramento altaris est quantitas per se existens; non tamen propter hoc quantitas illa erit substantia, sed habebit quemdam modum substantiae: per se enim esse dicit quemdam modum essendi substantiae, sicut inesse dicit modum essendi accidentis. Et sicut dicebatur superius, potest substantia non per se esse, et tamen non erit accidens, sed habebit quemdam modum accidentis, quia forma substantialis substantia quaedam est, nec tamen per se est, sed non ideo est accidens; habet tamen quemdam modum accidentalem et quemdam modum qualem. A simili ergo, si ponitur accidens per se esse, non erit illud accidens substantia, sed habebit quemdam modum substantiae." See also Giles, *Sent.* (Rep. Monacensis) IV.9 (p. 465), and for a study of Giles's use of this concept, in various contexts, see Trapp, "De doctrina modorum." Giles himself seems to adhere to a deflationary account of accidents: "Accidentia autem existunt, non quod habeant per se esse, nec quod habeant proprium existere, sed quia sunt in existente et existunt per existere subiecti" (*Quod.* II.2 [Easter 1287], as quoted in Wippel, *Metaphysical Thought of Godfrey* p. 211 n. 6). In §12.3, *modi essendi* will reappear in another context, as a strategy for distinguishing between the accidental categories. So far as I can see, these two usages are not directly related.

freestanding prime matter—it is open to suppose that God can make accidents exist on their own. Hence the appeal to a change in a thing's *modus essendi* is an extremely powerful device for reconciling transubstantiation with a deflationary account of accidental form. Contrary to what one might naturally suppose, it is by no means clear that an orthodox theory of the Eucharist requires forms to be independent entities. Until the *modus essendi* strategy is proved incoherent, it is open to combine transubstantiation with even the most deflationary theory of accidents—perhaps even a theory of accidents as modes—just so long as accidents are not eliminated altogether.[14]

Yet even if incoherence was not *proved*, it was nevertheless widely suspected. Aristotle, after all, had categorically ruled it "impossible" to separate accidents from their subjects (*Phys.* I.4, 188a10; cf. *Meta.* XII.5, 1071a1–2). Manuscripts survive from a great many arts faculty lectures in the latter thirteenth century contending that, at least on philosophical grounds, accidents are inseparable from their subjects. The standard argument for this conclusion was that actual inherence, rather than mere aptitudinal inherence, is essential to being an accident. Why one should define an accident in that way was never made very clear (§11.2), but nevertheless such claims were prominent enough to be condemned four times over by the condemnations of 1277 in Paris. This did not seem to have had any decisive effect on the course of the debate, however. Certainly it did not outside of Paris, which is the only place those condemnations were formally in effect. Thus Dietrich of Freiberg composed an extended treatise *De accidentibus* (*circa* 1280) in support of a deflationary account on which separated accidents are impossible. Even in Paris, the condemnations seem to have had the effect only of making arts masters more careful in stating their conclusions. Radulphus Brito, for instance, writing around the turn of the fourteenth century, acknowledges that "it is true according to our faith that an accident can exist without a subject." Still, "I say according to the intention of the Philosopher that the essence of an accident is to exist or inhere within a subject" (*In Isag.* q. 33; ed. Ebbesen, "Termini" p. 85). This is to say that an accident, as Aristotle conceives of it, is not the kind of thing that can have independent existence. Although incompatible with Church teachings, this is the soundest interpretation of Aristotle, Brito holds, and so is what an arts master ought to teach. Brito does not say that both views are true, nor does he say which view he himself believes. He claims only that different sets of premises lead to different conceptions of what an accident is. (This stance sidesteps the condemnations of 1277, by framing the debate not in terms of what is true according to the faith, but instead in terms of "the intention of the Philosopher." In §19.3 we will see how the condemnations of 1347 go farther by condemning not just the teaching of certain views as true, but even the teaching of them as philosophically defensible.)[15]

---

[14] If accidents can take on the *modus essendi* of a substance, then can substance take on the *modus essendi* of an accident, and inhere in a subject? Some, like Gabriel Biel, thought consistency required an affirmative answer (*Canon* lec. 44 H, II:166), whereas others, like Pedro Fonseca, denied it (*In Meta.* VII.1.1, II:200b–201a). Such considerations are relevant to the question of how to define substance, and would strictly speaking require qualifying the discussion in §6.2, so that what is essential to the substance is merely the *natural tendency* to subsist. Aquinas, for one, makes this explicit in *Quod.* IX.3 ad 2.

[15] Dietrich of Freiberg describes his deflationary account as follows: "accidens dicitur ens per attributionem ad vere ens, quod est substantia, quia ipsum non est nisi quaedam dispositio veri entis, quod est substantia: et hoc est essentia eius" (*De accidentibus* 10.2 [*Opera* III:66]; "Igitur nulla virtute vel naturali vel supernaturali potest hoc fieri, ut tale accidens sit actu sine subiecto" (ibid. 21.4, p. 83). For discussion, see Imbach, "Pourquoi." For Brito, see also *In Phys.*, as

Hence, as I remarked earlier, the situation at the close of the thirteenth century was extremely unstable. The initial and most influential Latin reading of Aristotle on accidental form had been deflationary, but there was persistent doubt over whether this could be reconciled with the Church's most important sacrament. Within the arts faculty, the result was an unhealthy distinction between the teachings of the faith and the teachings of philosophy. Among theologians, the result was often an unsatisfying appeal to the brute mystery of God's infinite power. Thus, according to Giles of Rome, writing *circa* 1275, "just as we know *that* God exists, but cannot know *what* God's nature is, so we can know *that* God can conserve an accident in existence apart from a subject..., but we cannot intellectually grasp...*how* God conserves an accident in existence." Indeed, he adds, given that accidents are by nature the sort of thing that exist within a subject, we cannot even understand a separated accident at all, without understanding how they are conserved in existence by God (*Theoremata de corpore Christi* prop. 41, f. 28va). In light of this situation, it is easy to see how a very different understanding of accidental form could have come to seem so persuasive, and could have led later scholastic thought to develop a radically different conception of what an accidental form is.

10.4. Toward Real Accidents

I have been speaking in somewhat vague terms of the consensus thirteenth-century view as "deflationary" so as to generalize over a spectrum of views. Setting aside for a moment the subtleties of their debates, what I take these deflationary views to have in common is the denial that accidents have the same sort of being that substances have. Aristotle's claim that 'being' is equivocal between substances and accidents was

---

quoted in Donati, *"Utrum accidens"* p. 596). For a very similar discussion from an anonymous *Metaphysics* commentary, perhaps also by Brito, see Ebbesen, "Radulphus Brito" pp. 483–4. See also the similar post-1277 treatment in Giles of Orleans, *In Gen. et cor.* I.14 (pp. 54–7).

Thirteenth-century arts masters who deny that accidents can be separated from their subject include Boethius of Dacia, *In Top.* III.1 (p. 167) and III.6 (pp. 176–8) and anonymous, *In Phys.* I.13 (ed. Zimmermann, pp. 23–7). Amerini, *"Utrum inhaerentia"* p. 114, concludes that "apart from rare exceptions, the most common trend" within the arts faculty was to deny that accidents can be separated from their subject, citing additional manuscript sources. It is, however, difficult to generalize, because authors take a range of views, from concluding that *Aristotle* denied the separability of accidents, to concluding that philosophical principles entail the inseparability of accidents, to concluding simply that accidents are inseparable. For further references and discussion, see Bakker, *La raison* ch. 4; Donati, *"Utrum accidens"*; Imbach, "Le traité de l'eucharistie"; and Pini, "Substance, Accident." Although this topic has been extensively discussed in recent years, these studies have failed to recognize just how closely the arts masters are following the standard theological account of accidental forms. Thus Imbach takes Siger's account of accidents to be so contrary to that of the theologians as to make the Eucharistic separability of accident from substance a logical impossibility: "il [Siger] ne critique *nulle part* explicitement la thèse de la *séparabilité*. Cette critique serait une conséquence *logique* de sa conception de l'accident, mais il faut avouer qu'il ne la formule pas *expressis verbis* ("Le traité de l'eucharistie" p. 190). This would come as a surprise to Aquinas, however, whose conception of accidents is very much Siger's conception, and who of course regards it as consistent with separability. In part, scholars have missed just how widespread the deflationary consensus was; in part, they have missed the force of the appeal to a change in *modus essendi*. On the condemnations of 1277, see Piché nn. 138–41 and the discussion in Hissette, *Enquête* pp. 287–91: "Quod accidens esse sine subiecto habet rationem impossibilis implicantis contradictionem. Quod Deus non potest facere accidens esse sine subiecto nec plures dimensiones simul esse. Quod accidens esse sine subiecto non est accidens, nisi aequivoce; et quod impossibile est quantitatem sive dimensionem esse per se; hoc enim esset ipsam esse substantiam. Quod, cum Deus non comparetur ad entia in ratione causae materialis vel formalis, non facit accidens esse sine subiecto, de cuius ratione est actu inesse subiecto." See too Giles of Rome (?), *Errores philosophorum* I.10 and XII.8, which ascribes the error of treating accidents as inseparable both to Aristotle and to Maimonides (cf. *Guide* III.15–16).

understood as implying a fundamental ontological divide, such that accidents could be considered beings only in some sort of special sense, distinct from the proper sort of being that belongs to substances. It is this idea that Scotus attacks at the end of the thirteenth century. Although he does not wish to eliminate the fundamental Aristotelian distinction between substance and accidents, he denies that it marks a distinction between things that truly exist and things that only derivatively exist. On the contrary, entities in all ten categories are genuine beings, all existing in the same, univocal sense of 'exist.' What marks off accidents from substances are various kinds of priority, such that substances give rise to accidents, and accidents (ordinarily) inhere in substances. Yet even if accidents are posterior to substance in various ways, they do not on that account exist any less, or have any less claim to be counted as beings.

Only when accidents are so conceived can we justly speak of "real accidents" in the sense that term was used—most often opprobriously—in the seventeenth century. Although the critics of real accidents did not take much care to define their target precisely, it is possible in retrospect to say with some precision what was at issue. For an accident to count as *real*, it is neither necessary nor sufficient that it be separable from its subject. This should not be regarded as necessary, both because not everyone regarded real qualities as separable from quantity, and because later Protestant scholastics would defend real accidents and yet reject the separability claims of the "Papists."[16] Separability is not sufficient either, given that even highly deflationary theories claimed to allow the separability of accidents (in virtue of a change in *modus essendi*, as we have seen). What does define a real accident is its being a genuine, irreducible entity, existing in its own right even while inhering in a subject. I do not know whether Scotus was the first to have conceived of accidents in this way, but in virtue of his prominence he was surely the principal force behind the new consensus. As I have already indicated, however, the climate was ripe for this sort of sea change, inasmuch as the prevailing conception of accidents left transubstantiation at best an utter mystery, and arguably an outright contradiction. When accidents are reconceived along realistic lines, transubstantiation becomes hardly mysterious at all. Although it remains a natural law that accidents inhere in a subject (and so the Eucharist remains a miracle), that fact of their inherence becomes, in a sense, more of a puzzle than their ability to exist separately. As Fabrizio Amerini has put it in an important recent study of Scotus, the Eucharist becomes "a case that *reveals* what the real metaphysical order of the actual world is rather than a case that *violates* this order" ("*Utrum inhaerentia*" p. 139). Yet although the case for accidents as real entities is made in a theological context, the arguments rest largely on philosophical considerations, and consequently they inspire a thoroughgoing philosophical reevaluation of accidental form.

Scotus's arguments for the reality of accidents can be understood only in light of a more fine-grained taxonomy of the various deflationary positions. The most radical such position defended in the thirteenth century held that accidents have no nature

---

[16] Burgersdijk is an example of a Protestant scholastic committed to real accidents—viz., "entia quae a substantia different reipsa" (*Inst. meta.* II.17.3). Still, "Pontificii putant accidens ideo accidens esse non quod revera inhaereat substantiae, sed quod possit inhaerere. . . . Nos contra contendimus, *essentiam accidens esse non solum posse inhaerere, sed actu inhaerere substantiae*, ideoque absolute simpliciterque impossibile esse ut accidens aliquod per se sine substantia existat" (ibid., II.17.15, original emphasis). See also Crakanthorpe, *Intro. in meta.* ch. 4, pp. 28–30; Keckermann, *Systema phys.* II.1 (*Opera* p. 2037); Carpenter, *Phil. libera* II.1.

or essence of their own. Both Richard Rufus and Albert the Great seem to say this in their *Metaphysics* commentaries (§10.2), both wanting only the substance to have a nature. This comes perilously close to eliminativism, because if we agree that there *are* accidents it then becomes hard to see how we can refrain from ascribing to them some sort of nature. There must, after all, be some fact of the matter about *what* a certain accident is, and that would just seem to be its nature or essence. Accordingly, most thirteenth-century discussions presuppose that accidents have a nature. Still, to say they have a nature is not to say they have existence. Here, too, there were various positions. The most deflationary claim one could make here would be to deny that there is any such thing as accidental being. On this view, only substances exist, and so the claim that there are accidents has to be cashed out in terms of the substance's existing in a certain way. Giles of Rome takes this view, and we will see Scotus single it out for attack below. A somewhat less deflationary stance allows accidental being, but treats it as belonging to the substance rather than to the accident. This is the view Aquinas seems to take, as when he characterizes the accidents of ordinary (pre-sacramental) bread and wine as follows: "Such accidents, so long as the substance of the bread and wine remained, did not themselves have existence (*esse*), and neither do other accidents. Instead, their substance had such existence because of them—snow, for instance, is white because of whiteness" (*Summa theol.* 3a 77.1 ad 4).[17]

None of these views count as embracing real accidents. On my taxonomy, at any rate, accidents are real only if they have their own proper existence, in the way that substances do. There is, however, a common thirteenth-century stance that goes part way toward real accidents, inasmuch as it gives them a kind of diminished existence. This is how Peter of Auvergne talks in the 1270s: "an accident is said to have the character of a being—not a being *simpliciter*, but a diminished being." The most prominent version of this sort of view, and the version that most closely approaches the doctrine of real accidents, is that of Henry of Ghent. In his tenth quodlibetal question (1287), Ghent explicitly argues for the view that accidents have an existence distinct from the existence of their subject. His opponent is someone who treats accidents as mere "modes" of substantial existence, without any existence of their own. Ghent, however, urges a different understanding of Aristotle's doctrine that accidents are beings only because they belong to a being (*non dicuntur entia nisi quia entis* [*Meta.* VII.1, 1028a18]): the claim is true "not because they do not have their own

---

[17] The question of whether an accident has a nature or essence admits of various further complexities. One view, defended at length by Dietrich of Freiberg and more briefly by Siger of Brabant (*In Meta.* [Cambr.] V.23, ed. Maurer, pp. 237–8), treats accidents as having an essence, but only derivatively so, in virtue of their subject. For Dietrich, this is the root difference between substances and accidents (see esp. *De accidentibus* 9 [*Opera* III:64–6]). It is hard even to state this view, however, without in the end claiming that having this sort of derivative essence just is the nature of an accident. In general, it seems to have been widely accepted that accidents must have some sort of nature. See, e.g., Radulphus Brito, *In Isag.* q. 33 (ed. Ebbesen, "Termini" p. 87): "quantumcumque accidens inhaeret subiecto essentialiter, tamen accidens per suam essentiam est essentia distincta a subiecto."

Interacting with the question of whether accidents have an essence is the question of whether an accident's essence is identical with its *esse*. Godfrey of Fontaines, for instance, affirms this identity, whereas Giles of Rome denies it (see Wippel, *Metaphysical Thought of Godfrey* ch. 5). Klima, "Substance, Accident and Modes," suggests that the success of the *modus essendi* strategy hangs on whether there is such a real distinction between essence and existence. If there is, then, according to Klima, the *modus essendi* of an accident need not be part of its essence.

For Giles's denial that there is any accidental *esse* over and above the accident and its subject, see *Theoremata de esse et essentia*, th. XV, and the discussion in Wippel, *Metaphysical Thought of Godfrey* pp. 210–12.

existence and their own essence, but because they do not have their existence and essence separately, but within the substance and along with that substance's existence and essence, and also causally from that substance" (*Quod.* X.8 [*Opera* XIV:215]). Accordingly, Ghent treats accidents—or, more precisely, certain kinds of accidents (§12.3)—as *res*, things in their own right. Terms for substances, qualities, and quantities "agree in this, that they signify a *res* that is a nature and essence to which existence belongs" (*Quod.* V.6 [ed. 1518, I:161vO]). But Ghent does not go all the way to univocity: he holds onto the standard view that substances and accidents exist in a different sense, just as God and creatures do. Accordingly, substance has a "truer reality" and a "truer existence" than do accidents, which are beings only "in a qualified and diminished sense (*secundum quid et diminute*), because they are not called beings, nor are they beings, except because they are dispositions of an unqualified being, a substance" (*Quod.* XV.5 [ed. 1518, II:577vG]).[18]

Ghent's views are interestingly poised between the prevalent deflationism of his time and the realism that would later sweep scholastic thought. Since Ghent denies that accidents exist in the same sense that substances do, he does not count as a proponent of real accidents, as I use that label. But his insistence that accidents have their own proper existence, over and above the existence of the substance in which they inhere, makes it scarcely appropriate to describe his view as deflationary. He is a transitional case. It is hard to evaluate the merits of this position, or even assess just how realistic or deflationary it is, because of the obscurity in the idea of a being that is diminished and less than fully true. It may be that, for Ghent, accidents have diminished existence simply because their existence (ordinarily) depends on a substance, but it is not clear why a dependent entity should be regarded as any less of an entity. One can of course stipulate that entities exist more truly to the extent that their existence is less dependent on other things, and perhaps this is how Ghent should be understood, but that manner

---

[18] The view Ghent describes and subsequently criticizes holds that "substantia existit quia ei formaliter competit existere, quantitas existit quia est mensura existentis, qualitas existit quia est modus quidam existentis secundum se, relatio existit quia est modus existentis in ordine ad aliud" (*Quod.* X.8; *Opera* XIV:199). This gets defended on the grounds that "per hoc, ut dictum est supra, dicunt salvari analogiam in ente super decem praedicamenta, et aliter non" (ibid.). Giles of Rome would seem to be Henry's target (see the references (at ibid.), XIV:199n.–200n.).

Ghent argues for the equivocity of 'being' at *Summa* 21.2, focusing on the case of God and creatures, but explicitly applying it to the case of substance and accident as well (ed. 1520, I:124rF). On this topic, see also Paulus, *Henri de Gand* pp. 52–6.

Amerini, speaking of the thirteenth century, claims that "the majority of masters in the Arts Faculty tend to say that accidents are something on their own other than substances' modes of being" ("*Utrum inhaerentia*" p. 107; cf. p. 106 n. 25). It is unclear to me whether this is in fact the *majority* view among any thirteenth-century group—and we are a long way from a comprehensive grasp of the surviving manuscripts—but there certainly are a significant number of authors who take a view like Ghent's, holding that accidents have some sort of *esse* on their own. For Peter of Auvergne, as quoted in the main text, see *In Meta.* VII.2 (as quoted in Pini, "Substance, Accident" p. 285n). Compare James of Viterbo, *Quod.* II.1, p. 6: "Accidens enim est ens imperfectum et debile." For an earlier statement, see Alexander of Hales: "Respondeo, accidens habet quoddam esse secundum suam essentiam quod non dependent a subiecto, et quoddam a suo subiecto" (*Quaest. disputatae* 51.4.3, p. 940). See also Geoffrey of Aspall: "omne accidens est aliquid in se praeter hoc quod est esse substantiae . . . " (*In Meta.* VII.4, as quoted in Amerini, "*Utrum inhaerentia*" p. 105 n. 22). Godfrey of Fontaines might seem to be denying accidents their own *esse* at *Quod.* I.20 (Christmas 1285), p. 43: "Respondeo dicendum quod, cum ens primo et per se dividatur in ens secundum rationem essendi absolutam dictum ut substantia, et in ens secundum rationem essendi ad aliud attributum ut accidens, quod est non ens, nisi quia entis quod est substantia disposita [ed. *dispositio*]." A year later, however, he expresses himself rather differently: "Ad tertium similiter patet, quia accidentia non dicuntur esse nisi quia sunt entis propter hoc quod suum proprium esse non possunt habere nisi ut innixum ipsi esse simpliciter quod est esse substantiale" (*Quod.* III.4 [brevis], p. 311).

of speaking seems unhelpfully to confuse two different things: ontological status and causal dependence. To some extent, this complaint of obscurity might be lodged against any of the deflationary accounts we have considered, inasmuch as they all try to articulate an account that falls in between outright eliminativism and full-fledged univocal realism. Since most of these discussions lie in the background of the period officially under study, it seems best not to investigate this thorny problem here. These same issues will arise again, however, in several different contexts: first in Chapter 13, where I will attempt to say something more satisfactory about the sense in which modes have a kind of diminished existence, and then in Chapter 26, where I will consider views on which parts in general—integral and metaphysical—have some sort of lesser existence.

10.5. Scotus's Univocal Account

Scotus's most extensive discussions of the ontological status of accidents come in his discussions of the question "Whether accidents exist in the Eucharist without a subject" (*Ordinatio* IV.12.1). He begins his response to the question by sketching a deflationary account:

Here it is said that since for a single composite entity there is just a single existence, that existence belongs consequently and accidentally to any accident belonging to the whole. Consequently, if an accident is separated from its subject, God gives it a new existence, because it cannot now have the existence of the whole that it once was the accident of. (Wadding VIII n. 3)

The view described here is one of the more extreme deflationary theories described above, associated most closely with Giles of Rome, according to which the only existence is substantial existence, leaving no room for any distinct accidental existence at all. On its face, this might seem quite a natural view to take. For it might seem that either one should endorse accidental forms as metaphysical parts that exist in their own right, as substances do, or else treat them as merely an aspect (a mode?) of the substance. In the latter case, however, it would seem odd to say, as Aquinas seems to, that a substance has multiple existences, substantial and accidental. On a strictly deflationary view, it would seem better to say that only the substance exists.[19]

Taking off from strict deflationism, Scotus mounts his own theory of accidents in two stages, first arguing that accidents must have their own existence, then arguing that such existence is not in any way derivative or analogical, but must be of the same kind as substantial existence. The arguments Scotus makes for the first stage are difficult to evaluate. Some of them are strictly theological, grounded in Eucharistic considerations; others are philosophical, but trade on obscure questions such as whether an accident can have a nature without having its own existence, or whether it is better to postulate

---

[19] The Wadding edition of 1639 attributes to Aquinas the view under attack by Scotus here in *Ord.* IV.12.1, that accidents lack any *esse*. It has sometimes been suggested that Aquinas does reject any accidental *esse* over and above substantial *esse*, but the consensus view—and certainly the weight of the textual evidence—indicates that he accepts both. (For discussion and further references see Wippel, *Metaphysical Thought of Thomas* pp. 253–65.) Giles of Rome is a much more plausible source for the view.

a single composite existence or multiple existences for the whole and for its parts. (It is a measure of Henry of Ghent's influence that his arguments get deployed extensively by Scotus at this stage, before Scotus turns in the second stage to attacking Ghent's view.)[20] I will eventually try to say something about how to understand such debates over existence, in §§26.5–6. Here, however, it will be more illuminating to focus on the second stage of Scotus's argument, where the line of argument is clearer and had greater influence.

Suppose we accept the conclusion of the first stage: that accidents have their own existence. This precludes one sort of deflationary account, but leaves the heart of deflationism untouched. For although an accident can be said to exist on this view, it does so only equivocally, in virtue of its subject's having a certain existence. The first of four doubts that Scotus raises against his account invokes this sort of ambiguity, and in particular Aristotle's comparison between 'being' as said of substances and accidents, and 'healthy,' as said of an animal and its urine (*Meta.* IV.2, 1003a33–b10). Just as the sense in which urine is healthy is completely different from (although derivative on) the sense in which an animal is healthy, so the sense in which an accident exists is completely different from the sense in which a substance exists. Scotus, however, adamantly rejects this reading of Aristotle:

'Healthy' is purely equivocal when it is used to denote *having health* formally and *having health* as a sign. On the other hand, 'being' is not purely equivocal, as was said elsewhere [*Ord.* I.3.1.1–3]. There is something absolute on the part of both substance and accident, on which account each is formally called a *being*, even though there is an ordering from one of those absolutes to the other. (*Ordinatio* IV.12.1 [Wadding VIII n. 17])

Urine is healthy in a completely derivative way, inasmuch as it serves as a sign for something that is healthy in the proper sense. A direct application of this metaphor to the present case would suggest precisely the sort of deflationary account accepted by earlier authors, according to which an accident exists only insofar as, in virtue of it, a substance exists in the proper sense. Scotus, however, contends that the analogy "does not run on four feet" (ibid., n. 16). Although the existence of accidents does differ from the existence of substances, inasmuch as accidents by nature depend on substances for their existence (this is the "ordering" of line 4 above), this does not mean that accidents do not properly exist: "Neither the substance's causal role with respect to the whole accident, nor the greater perfection of its being (*entitatis*), nor the essential ordering of being shows that an accident is not formally a being (*ens*)" (*In Meta.* VII.1 n. 30). In effect, Scotus is urging that questions of ontological status be separated from questions of causal dependence.

Scotus uses 'formally' (*formaliter*) here where another writer might use 'strictly' or 'properly.' An animal is formally healthy whereas urine is not, but both substances and accidents have being formally.[21] Of course, it is not a simple matter to define what it is

---

[20] For Ghent's version of the arguments against the Giles-like view, see *Quod.* X.8 (*Opera* XIV:209–10). Godfrey of Fontaines also argues against a Giles-like view, and seemingly a year earlier, in 1286 (*Quod.* III.4). A reason for thinking that Scotus gets the argument from Ghent is that, after considering this argument, Scotus immediately turns to attacking Ghent's own account of how accidents can exist apart from their substance (*Ord.* IV.12.1 [Wadding VIII n. 4]).

[21] For 'formaliter,' see Wuellner, *Dictionary*, "formally": "1. according to the definition of a thing; in the precise or proper meaning that describes its specific nature" (p. 110). Scotus is very clear that he is offering not just his own view regarding accidents, but also a reading of Aristotle. See, e.g., *In Meta.* VII.4 n. 17: "non sit intentio Philosophi negare omnem entitatem formaliter ab accidentibus praeter entitatem substantiae actu." As for Aristotle's express denial that

to be a being, or to exist. But whatever we mean when we say that a dog or a cat exists, that is what we mean when we say that the animal's color or size exists. So whereas Aquinas warned against talking about accidental forms in the abstract, as if 'whiteness' picks out a thing (§10.2), Scotus thinks that such abstract terms work in just that way. Indeed, "it seems that an accident as conceived in the abstract is a *more* true being than an accident conceived in the concrete" (*In Meta.* VII.1 n. 31). How so? Scotus thinks '*albedo*' (whiteness) picks out a thing, a form, that exists in the truest sense. In contrast, according to the standard scholastic analysis of a sentence like *Albus currit* (the white thing runs) or *Hic equus est albus* (this horse is white), '*albus*' picks out not an accidental form, but rather the thing that is white. As we saw in earlier chapters, however, the white horse is not a true thing at all, but a *per accidens* unity, and so counts as less of a true being than does whiteness. In this way we arrive at the standard scholastic metaphysical scheme for material substances, as it was generally understood from the fourteenth century forward, and as it was eventually attacked by corpuscularian philosophers. The thick concrete substance that is, say, a white horse, is a mere aggregate, a composite of two kinds of more fundamental entities, a thin metaphysical substance and its various real accidents. That thin substance is a fundamental entity, an *ens per se* (§25.5), but is nevertheless further composed out of prime matter and substantial form. These disparate ingredients—real accidents, prime matter, and substantial form—are the chief metaphysical parts of scholastic philosophy, each of which would be subject to a withering assault in the seventeenth century.

With this we have a good picture of how Scotus wants us to understand accidents, but we have not yet seen Scotus's reasons for his view. In part, those reasons rest on a broader metaphysical issue—Scotus's commitment across the board to the univocity of being, not just between substances and accidents, but also between God and creatures.[22] Elsewhere he defends this doctrine for reasons that focus on the nature of God's existence. Here in *Ordinatio* IV.12, though, he offers an argument that focuses on the existence of accidents:

Accidents are principles of acting and principles of cognizing substance (according to *De anima* I [402b21–25]), and are the *per se* objects of the senses. But it is ridiculous to say that something is a principle of acting (through either a real action on matter or an intentional action on sense or intellect) and yet does not have any formal being (*entitatem*). For so we might say that a chimera acts or is sensed. It is also ridiculous for something to be *per se* a state (*passionem*) of a being, unless it has some being *per se*, or to be the endpoint of some change or mutation, unless it has some being. But all substances, if they have any states, [these states] are accidents. And any change involving growth, alteration, and location is a change toward an accident, as its endpoint. (*Ordinatio* IV.12.1 [Wadding VIII n. 16])

Scotus in effect presents us with a laundry list of the principal roles played by accidental form in scholastic thought:

---

accidents can exist apart from a subject, Scotus takes this to follow not from the essential nature of what an accident is, but from Aristotle's refusal to allow God to violate the usual causal orders by sustaining an accident supernaturally (see *Ord.* IV.12.1 [Wadding VIII n. 10]). For a later instance of the sort of reading of the urine analogy that Scotus wants to reject, see Eckhart, *In Exodum* n. 54 (*Werke* II:58–9).

[22] For a good overview of Scotus's views on the univocity of being, see Dumont, "Univocity." As remarked in §7.4, debates over the univocity of 'being' for substance and accidents are tied up with debates over the knowability of substance, with each camp contending that their view saves us from complete skepticism in this domain. Scotus's views here are nicely summarized in *In De an.* q. 21.

- as principles of acting (e.g., heat makes water hot) [line 1];
- as objects of sense and intellect (e.g., color acts on sight) [lines 1–2];
- as states (or, we might say, properties) of substances (e.g., a certain extension makes an object square) [lines 5–6];
- as the endpoints of change (e.g., a person grows to be six feet tall) [line 6].

It is, Scotus argues, ridiculous (*truffa*) to give these roles to accidental form, and at the same time to insist that such forms do not really (properly, formally) exist. We might just as well assign these roles to any other non-existent entity, like a chimera (line 4).[23]

In a way, this is the most important argument we will encounter over the course of this whole study, because it encapsulates the later scholastic case for the doctrine of real accidents. Although an assessment of scholastic thought might range over any number of a vast range of different questions, the central issue is the status of the standard Aristotelian metaphysical parts. Even if the diversity of scholastic views bears constant emphasis, there is something right in Descartes's 1640 remark to Mersenne that

I do not regard the diversity of their views as making the philosophy of the schools at all difficult to refute. For one can easily overturn all the foundations on which they agree with each other. Once that has been done, all their particular disputes will seem foolish. (III:231–2)

The foundations Descartes has in mind are the various metaphysical parts of material substances. Among these foundations, first and foremost, is the doctrine of real accidents. As subsequent chapters will make clear, these serve as the fundamental explanatory principles of natural philosophy and psychology.

Part of what makes Scotus's argument important is that not only does it attempt to end one line of thought (deflationary theories of accidental form), but it also sets another line of thought in motion. For as soon as one accepts the argument's conclusion, that the various roles played by accidental form require them to have serious ontological weight as entities in their own right, one is forced to consider very carefully just what sorts of ontological commitments one wants to make in that regard. Does the fact that a person grows to be six feet tall commit us to an ontology of *heights*? Does the fact that colors are the object of sight commit us to the reality of *color*? As subsequent chapters will consider in some detail, many of the most prominent philosophical disputes of later scholasticism concern the status of these various kinds of accidents. By treating accidents as real things, Scotus forced subsequent generations to reexamine just where accidents were needed, and where they could be dispensed with. Earlier scholastic authors, with their deflationary attitude toward accidents, worried about this problem almost not at all.[24]

Scotus's argument can therefore be regarded as yielding a template to be applied to specific cases:

If a certain accidental form plays a fundamental explanatory role, then we must regard it as a real, genuinely existing thing.

---

[23] For a rather different reading of Scotus's argument here, see Cross, *Physics of Duns Scotus* pp. 95–7.

[24] For another instance of Scotus's arguing for real accidents on the basis of causal considerations, see *In De an.* q. 7 n. 13, where the focus is actions: "Item, impossibile est aliquod creatum fieri de non-agente agens nisi mutetur ad aliquam formam in eo exsistentem."

Applying the inference requires going case by case through the various kinds of accidents, a project that occupied the scholastics from Ockham all the way through Suárez and beyond. Parts IV and V of this study will look in some detail at various specific applications, where the inference itself is taken for granted, and where the central question is whether the antecedent holds: do the accidents in question play a fundamental explanatory role? As remarked in §10.2 above, it would not be until the seventeenth century that a sustained case was made for the eliminativist answer: that there are no accidents that play any such role.

What about the inference itself? Could it be challenged? From Scotus's perspective, with deflationary accounts foremost in mind, this is the real issue. He assumes that his opponent will grant the antecedent—that accidental forms play the various roles he describes—but yet will resist the conclusion that such forms genuinely (univocally, formally) exist. As an example of this stance, consider again Aquinas's remark that "whiteness is said to exist not because it subsists in itself, but because *by it* something has existence-as-white" (*Quod.* IX.2.2). Accidents do not have existence in their own right, then, but rather make a substance have accidental *esse*. Yet Aquinas cannot even state his deflationary account without making the form itself do some work: the form *makes* the substance be white, inasmuch as "by it" the substance has such *esse*. Aquinas puts his position in just this way repeatedly, and it does not look as if he can avoid it. He wants the accident to be real, in some sense, but wants to distinguish it from the *esse* that can belong only to the substance. The accident has to be related to that *esse*, however; indeed, the presence of the accident must be the proximate explanation of why the substance is white. But here Scotus's argument seems to apply directly: how can the accident *do* that, without itself genuinely existing? Aquinas seemingly wants to have it both ways, so that accidents play a robust explanatory role, but yet without serious ontological standing. It is here, even more than in dealing with the Eucharist, that thirteenth-century deflationary accounts are most unstable.[25]

One way to save a deflationary account, without falling into eliminativism, is to treat forms abstractly, so that they are explanatory principles of a kind, but not causal principles (in our modern sense of 'cause'). So, we might say that the peg will not go into the round hole because it is square—and that this is a kind of basic explanation—but not suppose that *squareness* plays a causal role over and above the corpuscular facts about the peg. And we might say that one reason he was attracted to her is that she was tall, but deny that her *height* played a causal role over and above the facts at the corpuscular level. There is a tension here, mentioned already (§6.1), and which we will encounter repeatedly in the chapters to come (esp. §24.3), between two ways of developing an Aristotelian metaphysics of form. On one line of development, forms play a concrete, causal role in the physical make-up of reality, so that even the most fundamental, reductive analysis of the natural world would be incomplete—the equations, as it were, would not come out right—without accounting for the causal role of forms. Developed in a different way, forms are abstract principles of analysis, essential

---

[25] For Aquinas's commitment to accidental forms as acting on their subject see also *Quaest. de virt. comm.* 11c (translated in the main text earlier): "Sicut enim forma ens dicitur, non quia ipsa sit, si proprie loquamur, sed quia aliquid ea est; ita et forma fieri dicitur, non quia ipsa fiat, sed quia ea aliquid fit"; *Summa theol.* 1a2ae 55.4 ad 1: " . . . accidentia et formae non subsistentes dicuntur entia non quia ipsa habeant esse, sed quia eis aliquid est. . . . "

to a complete understanding of the world, but not acting within the world at a fundamental level. Both of these tendencies can be found in Aristotle, but the scholastic tendency was to favor the concrete, physical understanding of form. Scotus's argument consists in reminding his audience that this is what forms are supposed to do, and then urging the absurdity of such a stance, when combined with a deflationary ontology.

The following chapter will consider the altered conception of accidental form that arrives in the wake of Scotus's arguments.[26]

---

[26] I am not the first to suggest that a new conception of accidents takes hold after Aquinas. Calvin Normore has been arguing for some years now, in a series of works in progress, that the later scholastic rejection of the equivocity of accidental being is crucial for understanding accidental forms and modes. I am indebted to this work and to many conversations with him about these issues. De Rijk, "Buridan's View," begins with the remark that "one of the most striking characteristics of late medieval metaphysics is the upgrading of 'accidental being.' The strict opposition between 'esse per se' and 'esse per accidens,' which had been of paramount importance ever since Aristotle, has lost its relevance in the ontological discussions of the fourteenth century" (p. 41). Other authors have focused on Scotus as the crucial figure. Muralt highlights Scotus's acceptance of univocity, especially as it concerns accidents: "L'apparition de cette nouvelle forme de pensée entraîne des conséquences immenses" (L'Enjeu p. xiii). Wald regards Scotus as the crucial influence in the rise of the scholastic conception of real accidents that is later attacked by Hobbes and others ("Accidens"). Pini remarks that "Scotus's mature doctrine of substance and accident is a daring new conception of how things are in the world" ("Substance, Accident" p. 273). Amerini also recognizes that Scotus plays a role, but Amerini contends that the shift to real accidents happens earlier: "while the first Aristotelian interpreters regard accidents principally as inhering modes of being of substances . . . , the majority of theologians and philosophers in the second half of the thirteenth century regard accidents as absolute beings" ("Utrum inhaerentia" p. 139). Far from showing that this is the majority view, however, Amerini offers not a single instance of this view prior to Scotus. He seems on firmer ground, however, in saying that by 1320—after Scotus—it was "set in stone" that accidents have their own being and essence (p. 122).

11

Inherence

11.1. The Realistic Consensus

The previous chapter described a transformation in scholastic thinking about accidents around the end of the thirteenth century. Whereas the dominant tendency had been to think of accidents as aspects of substance, rather than as full-fledged beings in their own right, scholastic thought after Scotus largely accepts that accidents are real entities in a univocal sense. The change is apparent in Walter Burley, who in his early *Categories* commentary (before 1310) had endorsed the equivocity of 'being' over the ten categories, but in his later work comes to accept univocity.[1] It becomes especially apparent in William Ockham, whose attempt to eliminate most kinds of accidents (Chs. 12, 14, 19) is driven by the conviction that if an accident exists it must *really* exist, as a "true thing, distinct from substance." The subsequent dispute over the status of the various accidental categories presupposes that accidents be understood in the full-bodied, non-deflationary sense that Scotus had set out at the turn of the century.[2]

---

[1] See Conti, "Ontology in Walter Burley" pp. 151–2, quoting from his unedited *In Praed.*, and then citing *In Phys.* I.2.1, ff. 12vb–13ra. The latter acknowledges univocity only *communiter*, but that is the sense at issue here, according to which things are denoted by a single term in virtue of a single concept. Henry of Harclay, *circa* 1313, also accepts the univocity of substance and accident (*Quaest. ord.* 12 nn. 69–100).

[2] Alexander of Alexandria, *circa* 1305, affirms that "accidentia de se habeant aliquam entitatem" (*In Meta.* VII.1.1), but denies that "accidentia sint entia simpliciter" (ibid., VII.4.6). His arguments for the first conclusion closely follow Scotus's argument from causal role discussed in §10.5. Still, Alexander continues to treat accidents as having an "entitas diminuta." More than a century later, Paul of Venice is still using Scotus's arguments—perhaps following Alexander—for the conclusion that accidents are "ens formaliter" (*In Meta.* VII.1.1, part 1 concl. 2). Paul goes on (ibid., part 2 concl. 4) to defend the univocity of 'ens' over all the categories. (Thanks to Fabrizio Amerini for making available his forthcoming texts of both of these works.) Bakker has uncovered other cases where fourteenth-century theologians simply copy Scotus's conclusions verbatim. See, esp., Michel Aiguani de Bologne (1363) and Nicolas Biceps (1386), as quoted in Bakker, *La raison* II:186–93, II:259–61.

Ockham accepts the univocity of substance and accident at *Summa logicae* I.38, *Ord.* I.2.9 (*Opera theol.* II:317–18), and *In Isag.* 2.10. His remarks have to be interpreted with some care, however, for although he insists that any *res*, substantial or accidental, can be described univocally (see, e.g., *In Isag.* 2.10 [II:44]: "de omnibus rebus potest aliquid univoce praedicari"), he nevertheless argues that 'ens' is equivocal over the ten categories, inasmuch as terms in the categories function in such different ways. For Ockham on the reality of accidents in general, see *Rep.* IV.8 (*Opera theol.* VII:141): "...cum accidens sit res distincta a substantia et vera res, habet vere causam efficientem." See also *Rep.* IV.9 (*Opera theol.* VII:154): "accidens dependet a subiecto sicut a causa extrinseca," and *In Praed.* 14.12 (*Opera phil.* II:287): "...aliquando illa res propter quam aliquid dicitur quale est realiter differens ab illo quod est quale, et informans ipsum; sicut homo dicitur albus et qualis propter albedinem quae realiter distinguitur ab homine et quae est in homine subiective. Aliquando autem hoc non contingit, sed nulla est talis res in eo quod est quale, sed propter hoc quod ipsa se habet

The case of John Buridan, around the middle of the fourteenth century, nicely illustrates this new consensus. Buridan reads Aristotle as holding that only substance is a being (*ens*) or thing (*aliquid*). Although it is tempting to treat accidental terms like 'whiteness' on a par with substantial terms like 'horse,' so that they pick out entities of a certain kind, in fact accidental terms have a much less straightforward meaning: they refer to a substance's being a certain way. For Aristotle, there are no such things as accidents for accidental terms to refer to.[3] This sort of account would have fit quite comfortably among the thirteenth-century discussions described in §10.2, but Buridan neither appeals to this recent history nor feels himself able to defend the approach. So, after setting out the view in careful detail, he rejects it, without argument: "if we hold that whiteness subsists by itself, without inhering in any subject, then clearly this whiteness is genuinely a being and a thing" (*In Meta.* VI.4, f. 17rb). The thirteenth-century appeal to a change in *modus essendi*, designed to circumvent such an inference (§10.3), is not mentioned as a possibility. Nor is any mention made here of Scotus's (or any other) philosophical arguments for real accidents. Instead, the case is grounded entirely on faith. This shows that, although Scotus's view had become ascendant, his arguments were not themselves always influential. For whereas Scotus seemed to think that the best arguments for real accidents are philosophical rather than theological, Buridan holds that the theological considerations are decisive, but that there are no philosophical grounds for departing from a deflationary account. (On how to read such professions of faith, in the face of the philosophical evidence, see §20.5.)[4]

By Buridan's time, the doctrine of real accidents had become the *opinio communis*. This is by no means to say that everyone after Scotus defends it. Nicole Oresme defends a view on which only substances have true existence, leaving accidents to exist equivocally as modes (§13.2, §19.3). Marsilius of Inghen, too, argues against the univocity of 'being' as applied to substance and accident, inasmuch as accidents "according to their nature, barring a miracle, in no way have existence of their own."

---

aliter quantum ad aliquid extrinsecum et quantum ad partes suas intrinsecas, non quia ipsis tale aliquid extrinsecum adveniat absolutum quod formaliter inhaereat, sed propter hoc quod aliquid extrinsecum advenit. . . . "

Another interesting fourteenth-century case is Durand of St. Pourçain, who in effect follows Scotus's lead with respect to absolute accidents, but holds onto a deflationary account for relative accidents. See, e.g., *Sent.* IV.12.1 n. 5, f. 322ra: "accidens absolutum est quaedam natura in se cui competit aliquis modus essendi. Accidens autem respectivum solum est modus essendi alterius partis." Durand takes it to follow that absolute accidents can exist without their subjects, whereas relative accidents cannot (ibid., n. 6). For further information on Durand's view, see Ch. 13 note 2.

[3] Buridan characterizes Aristotle's position as follows: "Homo enim simpliciter loquendo est aliquid et asinus est aliquid sed albedo vel nigredo non est aliquid, ut dicebatur, ita quod hoc nomen 'ens' vel 'aliquid' non dicitur de albedine vel nigredine secundum rationem simplicem, immo secundum rationem connotativam. Et de terminis diversorum praedicamentorum dicitur secundum diversas additiones et connotationes: albedo enim est aliquid esse aliquale; magnitudo autem non sic sed aliquid esse aliquantum. Ideo patet quod accidentia non dicuntur simpliciter entia, immo entia secundum quid, scilicet cum additione et cum attributione ad substantiam, quia conceptus accidentis explicatur per conceptum substantiae, cum additione" (*In Meta.* VI.4, f. 17ra).

[4] Buridan invokes the faith in these terms: "Nunc videndum est quomodo respondendum est ad quaestionem motam ponendo ea quae posuimus ex fide. Dico ergo quod nos tenemus ex fide quod per potentiam dei accidentia possunt separari a substantiis et separatim conservari sine substantia sibi subiecta; unde dicimus quod sic sine subiecto subsistant in sacramento altaris. Si igitur ponamus quod albedo sic per se subsistat absque hoc quod alicui subiecto inhaereat, tunc manifestum est quod illa albedo manifeste est ens et vere est aliquid et etiam ex hoc manifestum est quod conceptus a quo sumitur hoc nomen 'albedo' est ita simplex sine aliqua connotatione sicut 'deus' vel aliquis terminus [ed. *terminis*] substantialis" (ibid., f. 17rab). For further discussion, see Bakker, "Aristotelian Metaphysics"; de Rijk, "On Buridan's View." Buridan argues in greater detail against this sort of reductive conception of accidents at *In De an.* III.11, as discussed in Ch. 19.

Even so, both Marsilius and Oresme acknowledge the univocity doctrine as "the common view." Peter of Ailly wants at least to consider the view that accidents are not things distinct from substances. The view should not be regarded as heretical, he says, but he himself declines to affirm it, on the grounds that to do so "would fall outside the common philosophy, which posits that accidents are things (*res*) distinct from their subjects, as whiteness is distinct from the thing that is white" (*Sent.* IV.6 art. 3, f. D5rb).[5]

The most prominent opponent of real accidents is John Wyclif. Although Wyclif is generally a realist in metaphysics, and insists in particular on the irreducible reality of accidents in each of the nine accidental categories (Ch. 12 note 22), he combines that view with a staunchly deflationary conception of what accidents are. The claim that accidents exist in substances is true only in an analogical sense, he holds, and he blames "modern" confusions over accidents on an equivocation in what it means for substances and accidents to exist. Whereas the essence of a substance is to exist *per se*, "accidents do not have existence unless they inhere, since all accidents are modes of substances" (*De ente praedicamentali* ch. 5, p. 38). Indeed, "every accident is a substance's accidentally so standing (*se habere*)" (ibid., p. 42). But whereas thirteenth-century deflationists had combined such claims with one or another strategy for allowing the separability of accidents from their subjects (§10.3), Wyclif chose to defy Church authority and insist that not even God could separate accidents, so conceived, from their subject. Given that an accident is "nothing other than a substance's accidentally existing in some mode" (*De eucharistia* ch. 3, p. 63), they are simply not the sorts of things that can exist on their own. For accidents to exist apart from a substance, as required by the doctrine of transubstantiation, one would need to postulate that inhering in substances there are some further absolute entities—real accidents—over and above the substance's so-and-so standing. Wyclif regards this both as absurdly redundant and as undermining our knowledge of the substance itself (§7.4).[6]

---

[5] Oresme notes the common view regarding quality at *In Phys.* I.13: "uno modo accipitur 'ens' pro aliqua re demonstrata vere existente, sicut est homo, animal et albedo secundum communem viam." Marsilius of Inghen rejects this approach at *In Meta.* IV.5: "Quibus premissis, sit secunda conclusio haec: quod nullus est conceptus univocus et absolutus substantiae et accidentis.... Correlarium responsale ad quaesitum est: iste terminus 'ens' non significat univoce substantiam et accidentia." (See Bakker, "Aristotelian Metaphysics," for discussion and for lengthy excerpts from this unedited text.) In characterizing univocity as the *opinio communis*, Marsilius cites "multi theologi" and adds "et est bonae memoriae magistri Iohannis Biridani." Then he adds, quite remarkably, "quamvis non credam quod in fine vitae fuerit illius opinionis"—implying that Buridan eventually took a deflationary view more like the one he ascribed to Aristotle, and indeed more like Marsilius's own (see Bakker, "Aristotelian Metaphysics" p. 258 n. 25). Another interesting defense of equivocity from this period is that of pseudo-Marsilius of Inghen, *In Phys.* I.7. Among later scholastics, the doctrine of equivocity can most readily be found among Thomists—e.g., De Soto, *In Praed.* IV.1, p. 131AB: "Tertia conclusio, ens non univoce, sed analogice, significat substantiam et accidentia.... Confirmatur ex modo concipiendi: quia re vera solas substantias apud homines censentur esse entia, nec duo lapides existimantur plura quam duo entia, licet multa sint illic accidentia."

[6] Wyclif rejects the univocity of existence between accidents and substances as follows: "Et patet quod contentio de quidditate formarum accidentalium stat pro magna parte in equivocationibus terminorum. Unde quando homines inceperunt philosophari, aliqui negarunt accidentia...; aliqui dubitaverunt si accidentia sunt entia...Sed post, subtilius philosophantes, invenerunt quod ens dicitur analogice de substantia et accidente.... Unde opiniones modernas pro magna parte reor stare in equivocationibus terminorum. Unde unus dicit quod nullum accidens est ens, quia statuit sibi saltem verbaliter quod ens significat solum illud quod potest per se esse" (*De materia et forma* ch. 1, pp. 167–8). For good discussions of his view, see Kenny, *Wyclif* ch. 7 and Conti, "Wyclif's Logic and Metaphysics" pp. 103–13. As Conti discusses, a full treatment of Wyclif's theory of accidents needs to distinguish between inherent accidents, which is my subject here, and accidents considered absolutely, where Wyclif's realism applies. For the broader context of Wyclif's theological thought, see Levy, *John Wyclif*, and Penn, "Wyclif and the Sacraments."

Predictably, Wyclif's views were declared heretical, and his association with a deflationary theory of accidents must have discredited even further the sort of deflationism championed by classical thirteenth-century authors. From the fourteenth century forward, debate continued over the merits of Scotus's univocal theory of being, but even so there was never any doubt that accidents are genuine entities in a very strong sense. Thomists continued to insist that the being of accidents is not the same as the being of substances, making the two uses of 'existence' analogical, but their views are never deflationary in anything like the pervasive thirteenth-century sense. In general, for later scholastic authors, deflationism was as far out of bounds as was the denial of accidents altogether (§19.5). This state of affairs would endure until the Reformation made it possible, at least in some parts of Europe, to challenge Church authority with impunity (§20.4).[7]

The doctrine of real accidents immediately gives rise to the question of what it is for an accident to inhere in a subject. What makes it the case, for instance, that a certain color is the color of this dog, rather than of another dog, or indeed of nothing at all? Locke would memorably express his doubts regarding the meaningfulness of talk about inherence:

> But were the Latin words *Inhaerentia* and *Substantia* put into the plain English ones that answer them, and were called *Sticking on* and *Under-propping*, they would better discover to us the very great clearness there is in the doctrine of *Substance* and *Accidents*, and show of what use they are in deciding of questions in philosophy. (*Essay* II.13.20)

Although the *Essay* is concerned more with substance than with accidents, Locke here takes aim at the latter as well, and treats the notion of *inherence* as part of the problem. Locke does not in fact do away with accidents (§23.4), no more than he does away with substance (§9.1), but one manifestation of his skepticism concerning our grasp of substance and accident is his skepticism over whether we know what it means for an accident to inhere in a substance. It is perhaps natural to react to this passage by complaining that Locke simply does not understand Aristotelian philosophy, and that if he did he would see just what inherence amounts to. This inclination has to be resisted. The quest for the one genuine Aristotelian theory of inherence is just as illusory as the quest for the one genuine Aristotelian theory of form (§10.1). Instead of one canonical theory there are many, wildly divergent theories. In fact, as an historical matter,

---

[7] Capreolus's version of a Thomistic theory of accidents is particularly instructive for the way it tries to secure the realist credentials of such a theory, while retaining the theory's distinctive core, which is that accidents by nature are the kind of thing that give *esse* to a subject, rather than have *esse* of their own. To do this, he makes heavy use of the distinction between *esse* and essence, so that the claims that [accidens] "habet entitatem realiter distinctam ab aliis entitatibus" and "accidens . . . est realitas vel entitas terminata" come out true in virtue of accidents having their own essence, but not their own *esse*. Echoing the terminology we will see Auriol use in §11.4, Capreolus holds that "sic ergo [accidens] est entitas terminata termino propriae essentiae, licet non termino propriae exsistentiae" (*Defensiones* II.18.1.3, IV:150b).

For other late scholastic accounts of being as analogous between substance and accident see Fonseca, *In Meta.* IV.2.1; Suárez, *Disp. meta.* 32.2; Scheibler, *Metaphys.* II.1.2.3 (pp. 427–31). For all three authors it is clear that accidents have their own proper being, just as much as substances do. (Similarly, creatures have their own proper being, just as much as God does, even if 'being' should be understood analogically between God and creatures.) Fonseca cites Giles of Rome as a proponent of the stronger deflationary view that denies accidents any proper being, and remarks "absurdam illam sententiam, Accidentia non habere propriam existentiam, sed per solam existentiam substantiae existere" (*In Meta.* IV.2.1.7, I:706B).

Locke's remark is completely apt. Scholastic talk of forms inhering in a subject just is a way of saying that forms *stick on* or *belong to* or *are associated with* their subject. The impressively Latinate 'inherence' is just another word for talking about the completely familiar but metaphysically opaque relationship that a thing stands in to its properties, and the scholastics no more shared a theory of how that happens than do philosophers today.

Advocates of a deflationary account may not need a theory of inherence at all. If accidents have no existence in their own right, but exist as aspects (or modes, or dispositions) of their subject, then there are not really two things there at all, and so talk of inherence would hardly seem appropriate. Of course, such a view may raise puzzles of its own, such as what an aspect (mode, disposition) is, and how a thing's aspects stand relative to the thing itself. But such questions do not seem to be questions about inherence. Accordingly, scholastics from the fourteenth century on, with their anti-deflationary commitments, worry about inherence in a way that earlier generations do not. Nicholas of Autrecourt, for instance, complains that we do not know what it means when we say that an accident inheres in a subject, and Autrecourt himself is almost unique among scholastic authors in arguing for the elimination of accidents entirely (§19.4). Wyclif argues in some detail against the coherence of the idea that one independent thing could inhere in another, in support of his own deflationary account.[8] Autrecourt and Wyclif, however, are outliers. Most later scholastic authors are committed to embracing some sort of theory of inherence. In what follows I consider first a general question regarding inherence, and then two different kinds of approaches: Scotus's attempt to connect subject and accident by introducing a third, intermediary thing, and Peter Auriol's attempt to explain inherence without recourse to any such intermediary.

11.2. Must Accidents Inhere?

Thirteenth-century arts masters who argued against the separability of accidents almost always did so on the grounds that inhering in a subject is essential to an accident. The question of whether this is so should be distinguished from the debate between realist and deflationary theories. Although it is natural to associate deflationism with the claim that inherence is essential, we saw in the previous chapter that many theologians were prepared to defend the first but not the second. Moreover, one might be a realist about accidents—in the sense of treating accidents as genuine entities in their own right—and yet think that such entities essentially inhere in something else. We will in fact see that Peter Auriol defends this kind of view. Accordingly, as stressed in §10.4, a *real accident* should be defined not in terms of separability, but in terms of real existence.

---

[8] For Wyclif, see *De actibus animae* II.4, p. 122 and *De eucharistia* ch. 3, p. 64: "...et per consequens oportet dare informationem quae sit vinculum quo substantia et tale accidens colligantur...."

Autrecourt's doubts about inherence are evident in these remarks: "non est apparens quid intelligendum sit per hunc sermonem: accidens inhaeret subiecto" (*Tractatus* first prol., p. 194); "nec apparet modus inhaerentiae quia non sicut pellis inhaeret ossibus poterat poni, et circa hoc contingebant multae difficultates ut an inhaerentia sit de substantia accidentis" (ch. 1, p. 204).

Nathanael Carpenter can be seen as a transitional figure in discussions of inherence, for although he accepts real qualities (*Phil. libera* I.1), he denies that they should be said to "inhere" in their subject, and instead offers a causal analysis of the relationship between substances and qualities (*Phil. libera* III.8).

The thirteenth-century debate over whether inherence is essential to accidents is not for the most part an argument-rich terrain. On one side one finds, unsupported by argument, the Bonaventurean claim that actual inherence is not essential, and that only the tendency to inhere is essential (§10.3). On the other side one finds the equally unsupported claim that actual inherence is essential.[9] How one is supposed to distinguish between what belongs to a thing's essence, and what belongs merely to its accidental *modus essendi*, is unclear. To some extent, this impasse reflects the divide between the arts masters, who were not responsible for explaining transubstantiation, even if they had to accept it, and the theologians, who were expected not just to accept transubstantiation but also to explain it. Almost all the theologians (except, as we will see, for Auriol) agree that transubstantiation requires that inherence not be essential to accidents. This conclusion is not very satisfying intellectually, however, if the best philosophical arguments favor the conclusion that accidents essentially inhere.

Once again Scotus is particularly interesting, inasmuch as he has philosophical arguments for the separability of accidents. His best argument for this conclusion (one that seems likely to have been inspired by Henry of Ghent)[10] is extremely difficult but well worth the trouble of unpacking. (Readers already feeling overwhelmed by the scholastic subtleties might proceed directly to Chapter 12 at this point.)

[1] There is no absolutely necessary dependence of an absolute accident on something else that [a] does not belong to its essence but is only an extrinsic cause—unless [b] on the absolutely first extrinsic cause, God. But [2a] a subject does not belong to the essence of an accident, because if it did then a white man would not be a being *per accidens*, which is contrary to the Philosopher. . . . For by adding to a thing something belonging to its essence, the result is not a being *per accidens*. . . . [2b] Nor is a subject the absolutely first extrinsic cause; rather, God alone is a cause of this sort, and God is not the subject of an accident. [3] Therefore the dependence of an absolute accident on a subject is not absolutely (*simpliciter*) necessary—where what is "absolutely necessary" is that whose opposite involves a contradiction. (*Ord.* IV.12.1; Wadding VIII n. 9)

The argument's focus is an "absolute accident" (line 1), by which Scotus means a non-relational accident. For such an accident, the conclusion holds, there is no "absolutely necessary" dependence on a subject (line 8), by which he means there is no logical necessity, even if there is natural necessity. The structure of the argument is simpler than it initially appears. Premise (1) contends that an absolute accident will be absolutely necessarily dependent on some subject only if either (a) that subject is part of its essence or (b) that subject is God. Premise (2) shows that neither (a) nor (b) is the case: first that the subject of accidents is not part of the essence of the accident, and then that the subject is of course not God. From these premises, the intended conclusion (3) clearly follows.

The (b) case obviously need not detain us. We might wonder, though, why that leaves (a) as the only remaining option. This is to wonder what supports premise (1).

---

[9] John of Jandun offers a notably strong fourteenth-century statement of the view that accidents are essentially inherent, at least "secundum mentem Aristotelis et Commentatoris" (*In Meta.* VII.1; ff. 87v–88v). So far as I have found, however, Jandun does not contest the full-fledged being of accidents.

[10] See Ghent, *Quod.* X.8 (*Opera* XIV:205), which makes this argument for the conclusion that accidents have their own proper existence: "Et similiter in composito per accidens ex substantia et accidente, quotquot sunt in eo essentiae diversae substantiae et accidentis, tot sunt in eo esse utroque modo. Si enim accidens non haberet esse proprium in subiecto, sed solum esse subiecti, nullo modo compositum esset unum ens per accidens."

Scotus immediately goes on to argue for (1) as follows: "The major is proved, because the first cause can completely supply the causality of any extrinsic cause, with respect to any effect whatsoever. This is because it has in itself all such causality more eminently than does a secondary cause" (ibid.). In effect, Scotus reasons as follows. In cases where an absolute (non-relational) accident is dependent on a cause that is *extrinsic* to that accident, that dependence will be absolute only if the cause in question is God, because God can always take the place of any other extrinsic cause, and so allow the accident to exist apart from that cause. If, to take the most obvious case, one supposes that the accident is dependent on its subject—whiteness on the man—then God can play the causal role of the subject. (We saw in §10.3 how this was a standard move among earlier authors.) If, on the other hand, an absolute accident is dependent upon something *intrinsic* to that accident, then that cause must be part of the accident's essence, or otherwise the dependency would of course not be essential, and so inherence would not be absolutely necessary. Hence, as (1) asserts, the only relevant cases are (a) and (b). Now although the (b) case is obviously a non-starter, the (a) case is indeed a very natural way to think about accidents. Consider a color. Philosophers today tend to think of colors as either physical states, mental states, or dispositions. In any of those cases, however, a definition of what a color is—which is to say, an account of its *essence*—would ineliminably refer to the kind of thing that is the subject of the state or disposition: to a surface, say, or perhaps to a perceiver's mind. This is to say, more generally, that states and dispositions—as well as functions, aspects, and attributes—are all most naturally conceived of in such a way that a description of their essence makes reference to a subject. The idea that there is something incoherent about an accident (or property, etc.) without a subject arises not because the subject is required as a *cause* of the accident, but because *having a subject* is part of what it is to be an accident. This is the view Scotus must refute.

We can now see, then, that the crux of the argument is the (a) case. To rule it out (lines 3–6), Scotus makes a very interesting appeal to a doctrine introduced in §6.1: that the conjunction of substance and accidents does not yield an *ens per se*, but only a thing that exists *per accidens*. This was a standard part of the scholastic case in favor of the substance–accident distinction in general, the idea being that the whole, thick aggregate of a thing together with its accidents is not a unity in the full sense. Rather, what is truly one thing is the substance that lies beneath the accidents, the thin metaphysical substance constituted out of form and matter. Scotus here argues that if we take that line of thought seriously, we are forced to conceive of accidents as separable from their subjects. It is by no means perfectly obvious why this is so, but consider the standard Aristotelian example that Scotus adduces, a white man. Whiteness of course does not belong to the essence of the man (call him Socrates), but on the account in question the subject, Socrates, would belong to the essence of whiteness. One might suppose that we have a merely *per accidens* unity here because Socrates can endure with or without the whiteness, but Scotus insists that this is not enough. Thus at lines 5–6 he invokes the plausible premise that when two things are joined, if one is part of the essence of the other, then their union is not *per accidens*. This is the crucial premise of the argument.

Ultimately, the argument turns on two ways of understanding the sense in which the thick concrete substance is an *ens per accidens*. On a weak reading of that doctrine, the thick substance is an *ens per se* because the thin substance can endure without the accidents: that is, because the accidents fluctuate, whereas the thin substance itself endures. This is a dubious claim, however, because it would seem that even the thin substance can fluctuate, inasmuch as it can gain and lose integral parts. This is an issue that will become extremely important in Chapter 29. We can set it aside for now, though, because Scotus offers a different reason for rejecting the weak reading. His claim, in effect, is that we should treat the thick substance as an *ens per accidens* in a stronger sense: not just because it is a thing that may change its parts over time, but because it is a thing that, at each instant, given the accidents it has, lacks essential unity. His opponents' account requires the accidents that a subject has at an instant to be essentially united to that subject. What Scotus insists, with the crucial premise of lines 5–6, is that this kind of union would make the whole thick composite into an *ens per se*. Effectively, then, the claim that accidents necessarily inhere in a subject undermines a core principle of Aristotelian metaphysics.

Once the argument comes clearly into focus, however, a weakness stands out. The crucial premise holds that "by adding to a thing something belonging to its essence, the result is not a being *per accidens*" (lines 5–6 above). Here there looks to be a dangerous slide from the claim that an accident essentially has *some* subject (whiteness must inhere in *a* surface) to the claim that an accident essentially has *this* subject (whiteness must inhere in *Socrates*). Scotus seems to need the second of these for his argument to go through, whereas his opponent seems to need only the first. Yet although Scotus does not consider this objection, he perhaps has a reply available. Inasmuch as Scotus's opponents wish to block the possibility only of an accident's floating free from any subject, they need think of accidents as essentially inhering only in *some* subject. But this is not all his opponents wish to deny. They also wish to block the possibility of an accident's migrating from subject to subject. To make their case here, they need more than essential inherence in some subject or another; they need the claim that *this* accident inheres essentially in *this* subject. Otherwise, Scotus can run the very same argument as above, appealing again to divine power, to show that nothing prevents whiteness from inhering in something other than Socrates. So it would seem plausible, after all, that to block migration one really must turn the composite of Socrates and whiteness into an *ens per se*, not an *ens per accidens*. Whether Scotus's argument would work against an opponent who concedes the possibility of migration and denies merely the possibility of free-floating accidents is less clear. But I know of no one during our four centuries who took such a stance, which is to say that Scotus's argument may have been effective enough against his actual opponents.[11]

---

[11] Although I will not enter into the details, it is worth comparing Scotus's *Ord.* IV.12.1 (Wadding VIII n. 9) with the similar argument at *Rep.* IV.12.1 (Wadding XI.1 n. 3). For a different reading of the *Ordinatio* argument, see Cross, *Physics of Duns Scotus* pp. 100–3. Cross also holds (ibid. p. 101) that, for Scotus, accidents can migrate from subject to subject by divine power, relying on *Ord.* IV.12.6 (Wadding VIII n. 12). Here Scotus seems to allow that, after the sacrament, a numerically different but qualitatively similar bread and wine will return as the subject of the same accidents that have endured through transubstantiation. What matters for the argument presented in the main text, however, is the natural impossibility of migration, which Scotus clearly asserts at *Ord.* II.3.1.4 n. 118 (Vat. VII n. 118).

The *Ordinatio* goes on to extend the argument to an objection often considered by earlier writers in similar contexts: that although God can replace any efficient cause, God cannot take the place of the material cause sustaining the accident. Scotus, however, can wield against this the same argument as in the main text, that to treat an accident's subject as its material cause is to make the substance–accident composite an *ens per se*. Here he seems on even firmer ground than in the argument considered in the main text, inasmuch as treating *homo albus* as an *ens per accidens* surely entails that accidents are not related to their subjects as form to matter. That form of composition, after all, is precisely what gives rise to an *ens per se*.

The present argument complements and extends Scotus's argument from the end of the previous chapter, inasmuch as we now have the conclusion that accidents both really (univocally, formally) exist, and that they are separable from their subjects. The arguments also share several important similarities. First, they have force only against an opponent already committed to certain Aristotelian presuppositions. The crucial assumption of that earlier argument concerned the explanatory role played by forms. Here, the crucial assumption is the substance–accident distinction, and in particular the doctrine that the thick concrete substance exists only *per accidens*. No doubt this claim would have been widely accepted at the time, and in Chapter 29 we will see how the thick–thin distinction plays an important role in some scholastic accounts of identity over time. Even so, one might worry that Scotus simply begs the question by insisting that the thick substance be merely an *ens per accidens* in just the way he specifies.

A second similarity is that this argument, like the earlier one, can be viewed both retrospectively and prospectively. Retrospectively, it shows that thirteenth-century authors were committed to a metaphysical distinction between substance and accident that presupposes accidents have a certain independence. Prospectively, it points toward a line of argument regarding accidents (and other putative entities) that would be employed continuously among scholastic authors from the fourteenth century onward: the argument that two (created) things are really distinct if and only if they are separable. This is not a line of thought that one commonly finds among authors prior to Scotus. By and large, however, it would come to be taken for granted that the crucial test for being a genuine thing—a *res*—is separability. As we will see repeatedly in the chapters to follow, this Scotistic strategy would be crucial in shaping the scholastic dispute over the status of various kinds of accidental forms. Yet, as we will also see (esp. §13.6, §14.3), it is extremely difficult to determine just what sort of separability ultimately matters.

11.3. Glue-and-Paste Theories

When accidents are thought of in Scotus's terms, as real things distinct from substances, ordinarily but not necessarily inhering in those substances, it becomes obvious that one needs an account of what makes one thing inhere in another. The most obvious sort of account—at least from the perspective of scholastic authors already up to their necks in metaphysical parts—was to appeal to yet further metaphysical parts to explain inherence. Kenelm Digby's *Two Treatises* (1644) mocks scholastic authors for making accidents into substances and then having "to look for the glue and paste to join these entities unto the substance they accompany: which they find with the same facility, by imagining a new entity whose nature it is to do that which they have need of" (treat. I concl., p. 345). This looks on its face as if it must surely be a caricature, but in fact Digby describes quite precisely the most common scholastic approach to the problem.

Yet again, it is useful to focus on Scotus. In a brief but interesting passage from his early *Lectura* (*circa* 1298), he shows himself to be keenly aware of the problem of inherence, but uncertain of how to solve it.

I believe that 'unity' is one of the more difficult words in philosophy. For there are in things many hidden (*occultae*) unities that are obscure to us. There was a period when I often considered how man–white makes one thing more truly than if they were separate. For whiteness's inherence in a man does not produce any added reality, and yet when whiteness is in a man, then the man–white is one, and not when they are separate. (*Lec.* I.17.2.4; Vato XVII n. 239)

Instead of "white man" (*homo albus*), Scotus speaks here of "man–white" (*homo album*), so that not even grammatical agreement is allowed to smooth over the deeply problematic question of what unites subject and accident. He offers no account here of how to explain that union, only ruling out an account on which inherence would "produce" (*facit*) some further *realitas* (line 4). One can see why Scotus might have wanted to resist that sort of glue-and-paste theory (to adopt Digby's phrase), but he eventually decided that some such account is the only viable solution. His reason for thinking this draws on the conclusion of the previous section: that it is not necessary for an accident to inhere in a subject. Just as it is possible (by divine power) for an accident to exist after its subject has gone out of existence, so it is possible for an accident and its subject to continue existing, but separately, without inherence. This shows that inherence must be something more than just the bare existence of the subject and an accident.[12]

What more *could* inherence be? From a strict mechanistic–corpuscularian point of view, the only obvious way to relate two beings is to appeal to their spatiotemporal relationships. (Any account of unity, endurance, causality, belonging-to, etc. would seemingly have to be cashed out in this way, which is why seventeenth-century philosophers find it so difficult to remain within the bounds of this sort of thoroughgoingly reductive account.) Scotus does not even bother to consider whether inherence might be explained in terms of some sort of spatial relationship—namely, in terms of being next to or, better, overlapping each other. Perhaps one reason this seems not worth discussing is that it does nothing to explain why accidents have a natural tendency to inhere in a particular subject. If inherence were merely a matter of spatial location, then it would seem that giving a substance a good enough shake might knock off its accidents, so that a color, say, might fall from one substance and float onto another. (Shaking off an accident would be quite different, of course, from the ordinary case where a piece [an integral part] of a thing is broken off.) In general, the "sticking on" of metaphysical parts—as we saw Locke put it earlier—can scarcely be explained with corpuscularian tools.

Scotus's solution is to introduce further metaphysical parts: specifically, he argues that inherence is a kind of relational accident. Inherence must be relational rather than something absolute, he argues, because it is not independent in the way that absolute accidents are. As we saw in the previous section, Scotus's absolute accidents do not essentially inhere, or essentially depend on anything other than God. Inherence, in contrast, like all relations, essentially depends on other things: in this case, an absolute accident to do the inhering, and a subject for that absolute accident to inhere in. But although this shows that inherence is not an absolute accident, inasmuch as it is not separable in the proper way, Scotus nevertheless takes inherence to be a genuine entity,

---

[12] For other expressions of Scotus's puzzlement over the difference between two things as united and as separated, see *In Meta.* VII.1 (*Opera phil.* IV n. 22) and *In Meta.* VIII.4 nn. 2–3, 16, 54, 56, and the related discussion in §25.5.

really distinct from both accident and subject, inasmuch as there is a kind of separability here. For although inherence requires an absolute accident, that absolute accident can, as we have seen, exist without inherence. And where one thing can exist without another, a real distinction between those two things must obtain (see §13.6 for various complicating details). The general scheme in place here, therefore, which will be considered more closely in the next two chapters, is that absolute accidents are separable from their subject in both directions (the accident can exist without the subject, and vice versa), whereas relational accidents are separable in only one direction (inasmuch as the subject can exist without them, but not vice versa). Scotus's specific conclusion regarding inherence is that it falls into the category of either Action or Passion, depending on whether one focuses on the form's acting on the subject or the subject's being acted on by the form. (Just as each of two white things has the relational property of being *like* the other, so Scotus seems to think there is an inherence relationship in both subject and accident, as a passion and an action, respectively.)[13]

This way of handling inherence may seem so abstrusely metaphysical as to be entirely unsatisfactory. One way to respond to this sort of complaint is to stress the cogency of Scotus's argument at every step of the way. *If* you accept that accidental forms are genuine explanatory principles, and *if* you accept the substance–accident distinction, *then* you need a theory of inherence, and it is hard to see how that will be framed if not in terms of still further metaphysical parts. In other words, as soon as one begins to make use of metaphysical parts at all, one has to follow that road where it leads, even if in the end one must postulate many more metaphysical parts than one originally wanted. A sense of dissatisfaction, however, may arise less from worries over the cogency of Scotus's arguments, and more from a sense that nothing of any explanatory value has been achieved by all this philosophizing. Of course, that is the timeless complaint made of all philosophy, and perhaps the most that can be said here is that the charge is no more apt in the present case than in others. To be sure, to say that whiteness inheres in snow in virtue of the snow's standing in a being-acted-on relation to the whiteness does not offer the sort of explanation that we expect today from

---

[13] For Scotus's argument from separability to inherence as a third thing, see *In Meta.* VII.1 nn. 18–20, *Lec.* II.1.4–5 (Vat. XVIII n. 191), *Ord.* IV.12.1 (Wadding VIII n. 6): "Et si quaeras, ad quod genus pertinet illud quod per se significat hoc quod est accidens vel inhaerens? Respondeo, ad genus aliquod respectus extrinsecus advenientis. Patet enim quod dicit respectum: quia non potest intelligi ratio eius ad se. Non autem dicit respectum intrinsecus advenientem, quia non necessario consequentem positionem extremorum, quia sicut patebit in ultima conclusione fundamentum eius et terminus possunt manere sine isto respectu. Si quaeras ad *quod* genus, vide si forte ad genus passionis, ut sic passio dicat non tantum respectum passi ad agens, sed ad formam; vel si forte ad genus actionis, ut sic actio dicat non tantum respectum agentis ad patiens, sed formae informantis ad illud quod informatur. Sed utroque modo erit respectus extrinsecus adveniens." See also ibid., n. 21, and *Rep.* IV.12.1 (Wadding XI.2 n. 7). For other discussions of Scotus on inherence, see Amerini, "*Utrum Inhaerentia*," Pini, "Substance, Accident," Menn, "Suárez and Modes" pp. 232–5, though I would dissent from Menn's charge that "Scotus is trapped" in a contradiction in his strategy for dealing with the regress argument (p. 234). His criticism there loses sight of the fact, which Menn himself stresses elsewhere (e.g., p. 233), that a real distinction for Scotus requires only one-way separability. The main text suppresses a complication made explicit in the passage just quoted: that inherence is an extrinsic rather than an intrinsic relation. Intrinsic relations fall into the category of Relation, whereas extrinsic relations cover the remaining six categories. For the difference between them, see e.g. *Rep.* IV.12.1 (Wadding XI.2 n. 7): ". . . posito solo fundamenta non sequitur respectus intrinsecus adveniens necesse, sed ipso et termino positis, oritur ex natura extremorum; respectus autem extrinsecus adveniens tantum contingenter consequitur extrema posita in esse." For further discussion of Scotus's theory of relations, see the following two chapters, as well as Adams. *William Ockham* I:215–76. Cross, *Physics* pp. 107–15. Henninger, *Relations* ch. 5.

physics. But Scotus was not trying to offer that kind of explanation. If he were, then his answer would have been quite different: he would have said that snow is white because it has a certain mixture of the primary qualities (Ch. 21). The scholastics were convinced, however, that side by side with such physical answers there are metaphysical answers couched in hylomorphic terms. It is useful to know, Scotus thinks, not just that whiteness arises from a certain mix of Hot, Cold, Wet, and Dry, but also that whiteness is an accidental form, and so a real being, and that its inherence in another real being can be given an analysis along the same lines that we give when we speak of one thing's acting and another thing's being acted on. By appealing to accidents in the categories of Action and Passion, Scotus is in effect suggesting that a metaphysics of inherence will take the same general form as an analysis of action. If that metaphysical project can be explanatory, then Scotus's may be as well.

Scotus's discussion of inherence takes on further interest, moreover, because of the way it can be generalized as an approach to problems concerning unity. Since Scotus regards accidents as real beings, he regards the inherence of accidental forms in their subjects as just a special case of the general problem of how to explain the unity of distinct things. Indeed, he stresses in his discussion of inherence that his approach here applies generally: "every union of one absolute thing to another is an extrinsic relation" (*Ord.* IV.12.1; Wadding VIII n. 21). This is to say that the problems of unifying substantial form with prime matter, or soul with body, or integral parts with one another as a complete substance, will all require this same sort of solution: appealing to a further relational entity to account for the fact that *these* things altogether make one thing—a single substance—whereas *these* things together with *that* make one thing only in some lesser sense. Hence the fact that a white dog is one thing *per accidens* follows from the character of the action/passion that is inherence, whereas the fact that a soul and its body is one thing *per se* follows from the sort of relationship that obtains in that case. As we will see when we consider these matters further (§25.5), Scotus is ultimately skeptical about whether we can give very deep explanations here, but insofar as any explanation is possible, it must advance along these lines.

One risk that this kind of analysis runs is that we will end up not just up to our necks in metaphysical parts, but positively drowning—that once we begin to postulate such entities, we will be forced to postulate infinitely many more. That risk has perhaps been obvious for some time with respect to glue-and-paste theories. If one thing inheres in a second in virtue of some third thing, we would seem to need some further account of that third thing's inherence, and that fourth thing will in turn require a fifth, *ad infinitum*. This objection is almost omnipresent in discussions of inherence, beginning with the commentaries of thirteenth-century arts masters.[14] These texts most often appeal to the threat of a regress as a way of arguing that an accident's inherence cannot

---

[14] For a brief contemporary version of the regress argument, see Anonymous Matritensis, *In Praed.* quest. 34 (pp. 164–5): "Ad hoc dicendum quod dependentia qua dependet accidens ad subiectum idem est in esse cum accidente; quia si accidens dependet ad subiectum, non per suam essentiam sed per aliquid aliud accidens sibi additum, tunc quaeritur de illo ulterio accidente per quid dependeret ad subiectum. Si diceres quod per suam essentiam, eadem ratione fuit standum in primo. Et si diceres quod per aliquid additum, tunc quaerendum est de illo, et sic in infinitum. Ex hiis dico quod dependere accidentis sit qualitas, et illa dependentia erit qualitas. Sed dependentia accidentis quae est relatio non est ad subiectum, sed ad terminum." For other versions, see Olivi, *Summa* II.54 (II:261); Scotus, *In Meta.* VII.7 nn. 6, 36; *Ord.* IV.12.1 (Wadding VIII n. 12); Francis of Marchia, *In Meta.* V.4 (in Amerini, "*Utrum inhaerentia*" p. 127 n. 77); Auriol, *Sent.* IV.12.1.1 (III:109bDE, 110aAB); Jandun, *In Meta.* VII.1 (f. 88rvHI); Fonseca, *In Meta.* VII.1.1 (III:198aA).

be something added to it, and so must be essential to an accident. Here, for instance, is Radulphus Brito, around the turn of the fourteenth century:

Inhering in a subject either belongs to an accident's essence or it is a [further] accident added on. If it belongs to the accident's essence then I have my conclusion. If it is something added to the accident's essence, then it is certainly an *accident* of the accident, because what is added is   3
something additional, and so is either a substance or an accident. What is added is not a substance, because nothing inheres formally through a substance, but the accident does inhere through it. Therefore what is added is an accident, and therefore it inheres, because every   6
accident inheres. Therefore the inherence of what is added either belongs to its essence or is instead something added on. If it belongs to its essence, then for the same reason we should have stopped with the first, namely that inherence belongs to an accident's essence. If it does not   9
belong to its essence, then it is something added. Therefore what is added is either a substance or an accident. It is not a substance, as before; therefore it is an accident, and if it is an accident, then it inheres, because inherence, even given that it does not belong to an accident's essence,   12
still cannot be separated from it. Therefore it inheres either through its essence or is instead something added on. And in this way the same problem always returns. Therefore either there will have to be an infinite regress or it will have to be granted that inhering belongs to an   15
accident's essence. (*In Isag.* q. 33 [ed. Ebbesen, "Termini" p. 86])

Brito spells things out so carefully that the argument needs no further elaboration. The regress he identifies seems thoroughly vicious, in the sense that an infinity of such metaphysical entities is entirely unacceptable. There are, moreover, only a few places where one can potentially escape Brito's line of argument. First, of course, one can reject glue-and-paste theories altogether, and so not treat inherence as something "added on" (line 1). We will consider theories of this sort shortly. If inherence *is* something new added on, then one might deny that it is an accident (lines 2–4). To be sure, it does not seem plausible to treat inherence as a *substance*, since this would make it the sort of thing that could naturally exist on its own. Brito assumes that if inherence is not a substance, then it is an accident, but here is another place one might try to escape. Suárez, three hundred years later, would treat modes as entities falling in between substances and real accidents, and offer inherence as a particular clear example of why modes must be postulated (§13.3). Since modes *are* the sort of thing that inhere of their own nature, the regress stops at this second level. Brito, however, does not consider the possibility that accidents might come in two types.

If inherence is a further accident, then it does seem, as Brito twice claims (lines 6, 11–13), that it must itself inhere. As remarked earlier, 'inherence' is just a technical term for a form's attaching to its subject, however that happens. Hence there is no point in trying to argue that inherence is the kind of form that does not itself inhere in anything. This leaves just one final way out: that we stop at this second level down, and hold that inherence here *does* belong to the accident's essence. This is how Scotus handles the threat of regress. He claims that, at the second level down, the inherence$_2$ of inherence$_1$ is not really distinct from inherence$_1$ (using subscripts to mark the different levels). Why stop the regress here, and not (as Brito says at line 9) at the first level? Recall that Scotus's reason for distinguishing inherence$_1$ from the accident was that the accident and the subject can exist without inherence$_1$. Hence, he reasoned, inherence must be a third thing. In the present case, however, Scotus thinks it an outright contradiction to have inherence$_1$ without inherence$_2$. As he puts it, "it is a contradiction for the inherence$_{[1]}$ of whiteness in a surface to exist actually, and for that inherence$_{[1]}$ not to inhere actually, or not to have inherence$_{[2]}$" (*Ord.* IV.12.1; Wadding VIII n. 17). This seems right, inasmuch as inherence$_1$ presupposes that form and subject are actually attached to one another, all the way down. If some lower-level inherence were missing, inherence$_1$ would be missing too. But then, Scotus argues, making his characteristic appeal to separability, if it is absolutely impossible both for *a* to exist without *b*, and for *b* to exist without *a*, then it must be the case that *a* and *b* are not really distinct. Since that is the case here, inherence$_2$ must be the same as inherence$_1$, and the regress stops.[15]

11.4. Inherence without the Glue: Auriol

Treating inherence as a thing in its own right, above and beyond the accident and the subject, has not been shown to be incoherent. Still, it requires a proliferation of entities that, other things being equal, might best be avoided. Deflationary accounts can readily avoid this route, inasmuch as an accident's existence, on that view, at least presupposes (if it is not equivalent to) the subject's being in a certain state. Hence it is easy for the late-thirteenth-century arts master Martin of Dacia to dismiss the idea that inherence is a relation between accident and subject. Instead, "this dependence is not any thing (*res*) and so will be in no category. For whatever is in a category will be a thing. Instead, it is merely a mode of understanding, and so merely a thing of reason (*res rationis*)" (*In Praed.* q. 47, p. 209). Because Dacia is not thinking of accidents in realistic terms, he can be dismissive of inherence. But can a realist about accidents leave out the glue in this way?

Perhaps the most striking effort along these lines is that of Peter Auriol.[16] Writing *circa* 1316 on the same distinction from Lombard's *Sentences* as Scotus, Auriol stresses repeatedly that he is committed to the reality of accidents, in the sense that accidents are genuine beings. Hence, he describes an accident as a "true *res*," in opposition to "the ancients who say that an accident is not a reality outside the soul" (*Sent.* IV.12.1.1, III:109aC). (Both the atomists and the Eleatic monists are often mentioned in this connection.) Again, an accident is "a thing that is not the substance itself" and "has a reality that is not its substance" (ibid.). For that conclusion he offers this brief argument, appealing to the reality of change in the same sort of way that Scotus had (§10.5):

So I say, then, that an accident is distinct from its substance. For change above all else makes one know the distinctness of realities. But a substance is changed from accident to accident. Therefore, etc. (Ibid., III:111bE)

---

[15] Marchia takes a generally Scotistic line with respect both to Scotus's realism and to his account of inherence, but with some interesting modifications (see Amerini, "*Utrum inhaerentia*" and Bakker, *La raison* I:400–4). Another interesting example of a glue-and-paste theory is that of Buridan, who calls it a *dispositio*. Although he never goes into the details of what this *dispositio* is, he does try to avoid the regress argument along lines very much like Scotus's (*In Meta.* V.8 ad 2, f. 33ra). Most interesting, perhaps, is that Buridan expressly rejects the idea that inherence might be merely a matter of spatial proximity. Relying on theological examples, Buridan claims that an accident can exist where a substance is, without informing that substance—e.g., as the accidents of the host do not inform the body of Christ (f. 32vb).

[16] There is no modern secondary literature on Auriol's theory of inherence. My translation of *Sent.* IV.12.1.1, based on a corrected version of the nearly unintelligible 1605 edition, is available at www.peterauriol.net. An electronic version of the entire 1596–1605 edition is available on my Provisionalia website.

In contrast to the commonplace thirteenth-century appeal to the equivocity of 'exists,' Auriol acknowledges that "being is predicated of an accident *in recto* and *per se*" (ibid., III:111bF). He even criticizes those "moderns" who characterize accidents as having "being that is weak and in need of support" (ibid., III:109bA). On Auriol's view, accidents have full and unqualified existence.[17]

Yet Auriol thinks it possible to endorse fully the separate reality of accidents without treating inherence as anything above and beyond subject plus accident. Thus, after expressing his commitment to realism, he adds:

Nevertheless, it is not a bounded and complete thing without its substance. Thus it has a reality that is not its substance, and yet it is not a thing that is divided (*divisa*) from its substance. Consequently, it is a thing that is absolutely undivided in its own right, but not divided relationally from the substance that is its subject. (Ibid., III:109aC)

Auriol wants to distinguish the question of whether an accident has real existence of its own from the question of whether it is—as he variously puts it—"bounded," "complete," and "divided" (from other things). An accident is "absolutely undivided in its own right," which is to say that it has the sort of unity that is a prerequisite for being a genuine entity, but at the same time it is an incomplete and attached entity, in the sense that its existence presupposes (at least by nature) a subject to inhere in. Auriol devotes a long and dense article to establishing this conclusion. To reach it, he needs to show that although substances and accidents are distinct things, they are not distinct complete things of the sort that must be joined by some further relation. So, "from the whiteness and the surface there comes about one thing: not through their being linked together in the way one complete thing is linked together with another complete thing" (III:109aE). So how are a subject and an accident attached? In answering this question, Auriol appeals to the strategy we have seen so often used in the thirteenth century, that of treating an accident as simply a mode or state of its subject. Thus, "color is nothing other than the coloration itself and a state (*affectio*) that belongs intrinsically to another" (*Sent.* IV.12.1.2, III:112aC). Likewise, when talking about shapes it is more appropriate to use 'figuration' (*figuratio*) than 'figure' (*figura*), because 'figure' implies a thing with its own independent existence, whereas 'figuration' implies a thing bounded by another (*Sent.* IV.12.1.2, III:112aEF). Auriol expressly rejects the view on which quantity is nothing beyond substance, expressly insisting that "when I speak of a [body's] part I am speaking of two things—namely, the substance itself with its matter, and its divisibility—and these are not one and the same." Even so, "quantity just is the divisibility of a thing's parts." Hence this divisibility (literally, partibility) is not a complete distinct thing, but an incomplete, unbounded thing. Accordingly, "this divisibility is not added to that wood through a mediating relation" (*Sent.* IV.12.1.1, III:111aBC). (On the relationship between quantity, divisibility, and having parts, in the context of the debate over the reality of quantity, see Ch. 14.)

---

[17]   Like so many thirteenth-century authors, Auriol invokes the Aristotelian slogan (*Meta.* 1028a18) that the accident is not *ens* but *entis*: "Intentio Philosophi est quod accidens, eo quod non est ens, sed entis, non sit res terminata, sed res in adiacentia, immo ipsa adiacentia ad alterum. Unde proprius figura exprimitur per hoc nomen figuratio quam per hoc nomen figura, quia figura rem suam importat per modum cuiusdam terminati, figuratio vero per modum adiacentis" (*Sent.* IV.12.1.2, III:112aEF).

Auriol repeatedly tries to explain his view by analogy to how a line stands to its endpoint. If we were to imagine the two as detached, distinct things, "then each would be bounded (*terminata*) without the other.... The point would not be the boundary of that line, but would be something impressing that boundary" (*Sent.* IV.12.1.1, III:110aB). In fact, however, the endpoint's relation to the line is much more intimate than that—the two are in a certain sense bound together. The analogy has a certain appeal, inasmuch as it suggests the sort of mutual dependence that Auriol sees in the case of subject and accident. Of course, the analogy also has its limits—in particular, because it suggests treating inherence on the unhelpful model of a spatial relationship.

Perhaps more helpful than any analogy is to consider Auriol in the context of the evolving scholastic debate. What Auriol is really after is a way of combining realism about accidents—that they *really* exist—with the standard thirteenth-century view that an accident just is a state (mode, disposition) of its subject. In the wake of Scotus, Auriol could no longer ignore the tendency of deflationary theories to slide toward anti-realism. What gives his account such interest, then, is the way it tries to maintain an expressly realist position while still treating accidents as, in effect, modes. Suárez, looking back at Auriol's view, seems to see that this was the project, but he finds it unintelligible, because he takes modes by their very nature to be the sorts of things that are not really distinct from their subject. Thus he writes, "it is hardly intelligible what this means, unless perhaps he [Auriol] thought that no accident is a thing distinct in reality from the being of the substance, but only a mode" (*Disp. meta.* 16.1.2). What Auriol was after, however, is a theory on which accidents are both mode-like entities and genuine things, really distinct from substances. Setting aside (until Ch. 13) the question of whether 'mode' is the appropriate term to use for this conception of accident (and it is not Auriol's own term), still the project is clearly an important one.

Auriol offers five complex arguments in favor of the conclusion that accidents are incomplete, unbounded entities. Each turns on the advantage of letting accidents be immediately united to their subjects, so that inherence is not a third, intervening thing. The simplest of the five, the second, revisits Scotus's appeal to the nature of substance–accident unity (§11.2), but reaches a very different conclusion:

When several things make one thing with a unity that is a positive relation, rather than with a unity that is the negation of a relational division, then it is necessary that their unity be the unity of a heap. (The proof is that this is how the Philosopher argues in *Metaphysics* VIII [ch. 6].) But an accident and a subject are not one in the way that a heap is. Therefore their union is not a relation, but a relational indivisibility, or the negation of division. (*Sent.* IV.12.1.1, III:110aD)

Whereas Scotus had contrasted the unity of substance and accident with the *per se* unity of form and matter, Auriol contrasts the unity of substance and accident with the *per accidens* unity of a heap. Scotus had warned that to bind accidents too tightly to their substance is to do away with the distinction between the thin metaphysical substance and its peripheral accidents. Auriol argues that if substance and accident are not immediately joined, their union will become too weak, like that of a pile of stones. Of course, there are a great many differences between a pile of stones and a thick concrete substance like a white dog, and so there would be considerable room here for Scotistic subtlety in replying to Auriol. But, setting the details aside, the basic disagreement here is illuminating. Given Scotus's full-blown realism, there is a sense in which a thick substance, a substance–accident composite, is a heap-like entity. To be sure, accidents are not substances, and so a thick substance will not be a heap in quite the way that a pile of stones is. But inasmuch as Scotus makes accidents into things that are very much like substances, he cannot escape the result that a thick substance comes to look more like a heap than like a tightly unified *ens per se*. Indeed, Scotus *wants* that result, inasmuch as he insists on distinguishing the thin substance from the thick substance that is, like the heap, an *ens per accidens*. Auriol, in contrast, in his relatively brief discussion of this argument, does not even acknowledge the familiar thought that a substance–accident composite is one thing only *per accidens*. On the contrary, he accepts (and does not think it necessary to argue for) the minor premise that a thick substance and a heap are not one thing in the same way (lines 3–4). Ultimately, he even asserts that a substance–accident composite is a *per se* unity, something Scotus would of course stoutly deny. The reason behind this disagreement is that Auriol wants to treat all cases of hylomorphic composition alike. Hence he takes Aristotle's often quoted comments from the end of *Metaphysics* Eta—What is the cause of unity? The difficulty disappears if we say one is matter, the other is form (§25.5)—to apply both to the composition of substantial form with prime matter and to the composition of an accident with its subject. Elsewhere, in fact, Auriol offers an extended analysis of substantial form that is exactly parallel to the account he offers here of accidental form. In each case, then, we have a *per se* unity. Obviously, the disagreement between Scotus and Auriol on this point runs very deep.[18]

The showpiece of Auriol's whole discussion is the long, first argument (the first of the five) for the conclusion that accidents are incomplete, unbounded entities. It begins like this:

Form and formal effect are the same reality (*formalitas*). But the formal effect of an accident is not a thing divided from its subject; instead, the subject and the formal effect are one through their being internally indivisible. Therefore the form or accident and its subject are not divided things, but are one through their being indivisible in every way. (Ibid., III:109bAB)

The crucial concept in this desperately difficult argument is that of a *formal effect*. The idea is that a form is a kind of cause, a formal cause, so that for any form there is an associated effect that it has on its subject. The concept of a formal effect is roughly the same as the concept of inherence, inasmuch as to ask whether a form inheres in a subject just is to ask whether its formal effect is at work on the subject. In Aquinas's terms (§10.2), the formal effect would be the accidental *esse* of the subject that the accidental form brings about; in Scotus's terms, the formal effect would be the action or passion that is the form's inhering in its subject (§11.3). Auriol, in contrast, denies that the formal effect is anything other than the form itself (premise 1). But since the formal

---

[18] Auriol's views on substantial form are intriguing and, so far as I know, also unstudied. Whereas his broadly deflationary conception of accidental form has many precedents, a deflationary conception of substantial form is quite unusual. The key text is *Sent.* II.12.2.1, which asks "Utrum forma substantialis sit aliqua determinata entitas in actu in materia, vel sit tantummodo actu actio ipsius materiae, et communicatio sive communicabilia, pro quanto ipsa cum forma integrant rationem unius simplicis naturae" (II:174a). His view is the second.

effect is incomplete and indivisible from its subject (premise 2), the form is likewise incomplete (conclusion).

Each of Auriol's premises is supported by a version of a regress argument, of just the sort we looked at earlier (§11.3). Since we have already seen how Scotus can reply to that sort of move, it seems better to focus on a different kind of argument that Auriol offers for the crucial first premise:

> The formal effect of a form and act is to form and actuate matter. Then I ask: Is the form the actualization itself, or is the actualization something deposited (*derelictum*) by the form in the subject? The second cannot be maintained, since what is deposited would be either [a] something absolute or [b] something relational. If [a] it were something absolute (as one doctor imagines), then quantity would deposit some sort of extension and redness would deposit reddening (*rubicundatio*). If so, then it follows that something can be actualized without the act, and formed without the form, because, as a result of its being absolute, God can through his power separate the thing deposited [from the form that deposited it]. Further, the form is then not a formal cause, but an efficient cause, for the form would in this way impress its effect in matter just as would an efficient cause. Nor [b] can that which is deposited be something relational, for if it were a relation then to be actualized and formed will be to be related. (Ibid., III:109bBD)

This is a powerful line of thought. If form and its formal effect are distinct, then the role of a form will be to "deposit" some further thing in the subject (line 2). If so, then we would have to say that the accidental form of quantity would deposit extension, or some such thing, and the form of redness would deposit reddening. Auriol plainly intends for this to look unattractive on its face, but he thinks that when we consider the possibilities for what might be deposited, we will realize that the account is entirely implausible. The deposit will be either something relational or something absolute (line 4). If it is relational, then we would be committed to the view that every case of a thing's being made actual or informed consists in its being related somehow (line 11). This does not seem plausible. If, on the other hand, the deposit is something absolute, then Auriol sees two other implausible consequences. First, for every acci-dental form it would be possible to distinguish two absolute things: the form itself and its deposit. But where there are two absolute things, it is logically possible for one to exist without the other. Hence it is possible, at least by the power of God, for a thing to undergo reddening without the form of redness, and so on in other cases (lines 6–8). This seems absurd—how could a thing become red without taking on the form of red? Second, if an accidental form acts as a cause by impressing something on the effect, then it is hard to see what distinguishes formal causality from efficient causality. The distinction seems to collapse (lines 8–10). Auriol similarly goes on to criticize Scotus's view that inherence falls into the category of Action or Passion, remarking that "then the causality of form will not be distinct from the causality of an agent" (ibid., III:109bD).

Scotus would have to grant some of these consequences. First, it just is his view that all cases of an absolute accident's informing a subject are relational. Given that, for Scotus, there are two absolute things there, it must follow for him that they are united in virtue of some kind of further relational entity. As we have seen already, forms understood along Scotus's lines involve more metaphysical entities than one might have supposed. Although one can sympathize with Auriol's desire to avoid this, it is not clear that he has thereby shown Scotus's account to be flatly unacceptable. Second, Scotus would have to acknowledge that an accidental form is a kind of agent. After all, if inherence is an action (or a passion), then it is hard to escape the conclusion that an accidental form acts on its subject. Hence formal causality is more like efficient causality than one might have supposed. Yet Scotus need not embrace this to the extent Auriol imagines, because Scotus is not committed to an accidental form's depositing "something absolute" in the subject. His view is rather that for a subject to have an accident is just for that accident to stand in a certain relationship to its subject. So we can speak of an accidental form's acting on a subject, and this action is itself a third thing in addition to the subject and the accident, but there is no fourth thing that gets "deposited" by the accident. Hence Scotus is not committed to the most absurd consequence of all here, that there could be a reddening without the form of redness (lines 6–8).

Unsurprisingly, then, Auriol's arguments do not prove decisive against a sophisticated opponent like Scotus. To be sure, Auriol does hold a dramatic advantage with regard to parsimony. Against that, however, is the worry that Auriol's theory cannot account for one of the chief desiderata of any theory of accidents during this era: separability. Given that Auriol does not share Scotus's concern with treating the thick substance as an *ens per accidens*, he would not have been impressed by the philosophical argument considered earlier in favor of treating accidents as separable from their subjects. Yet on theological grounds—to account for transubstantiation—there was no escaping the absolute requirement that accidents be separable. Auriol's later readers tend to reject his account on that basis. John Capreolus, a Thomist writing a century after Auriol, labels the view "false and pernicious with respect to the faith" (*Defensiones* II.18.1.3, IV:152b). Suárez, after charging that Auriol wants to turn accidents into modes, continues that such a view is "repugnant and incompatible in many ways with the truths of the faith" (*Disp. meta.* 16.1.2). Just as there can be no sitting without a sitter, so in general modes cannot exist without a subject (ibid., n. 21).[19]

---

[19] Suárez makes it clear that he does not have Auriol's text, but is relying on Capreolus's lengthy verbatim report. He goes on to consider whether Auriol might be denying not that accidents have being, but rather this: "Fortasse tamen non fuit hic sensus illius auctoris, sed quod accidens, sive sit res distincta a subiecto sive non, in re non distinguatur ab actione seu inhaerentia in subiecto" (*Disp. meta.* 16.1.2). This clearly is part of Auriol's view. Even this much, for Suárez, amounts to treating accidents as modes, inasmuch as Suárez takes precisely this to be a distinctive feature of modes: "haec accidentia, cum non sint res distinctae, sed modi tantum, non afficiunt subiecta mediante aliquo modo unionis ab ipsis distincto ex natura rei, per quem eis uniantur, sed seipsis immediate coniunguntur.... Unde fit, in his formis modalibus causam ipsam formalem non distingui a sua causalitate actuali, quia causalitas formae, ut saepe dixi, non est aliud ab unione actuali formae ad subiectum" (16.1.22).

Suárez's own line on inherence is similar to Scotus's, but still more complex. According to him, inherence is a mode of an accident essentially including a relation of the accident to the subject. This means that inherence is both absolute and relational, and it gives Suárez the results that (a) the accident can endure without inherence; (b) inherence cannot endure without the accident; (c) inherence entails the subject's being informed by the accident. Unlike Scotus, the relation is "transcendental" in the sense that it is not in any category. See *Disp. meta.* 16.1.9, and the further discussion of Suárez in §13.3.

What about Ockham? Since he accepts that there are some real, Scotus-style accidents, one might expect him to embrace inherence as a kind of relation. On the other hand, given Ockham's rejection of relational accidents, one might expect him to take an account more like Auriol's. Officially, he does neither, and as a result his view seems unhappily conflicted. He clearly does not treat real qualities as mode-like (§19.2), and so Auriol's strategy is not open to him. On the other hand, there are texts where he seems to commit himself to inherence. According to Adams, who lays out the evidence, Ockham treats inherence as "a thing really distinct from Socrates and his whiteness," while yet at the same time, "Ockham does not acknowledge this consequence" (*William Ockham* I:275). On Adams's view, it is not that Ockham is inconsistent, but that he hides behind the qualification that inherence is an extra-categorial relation. This

To be sure, Auriol digs himself a deep hole in this regard. Repeatedly, he characterizes subject and accident as "indivisible," remarking for instance, in the conclusion to an argument quoted earlier, that "the form or accident and its subject are not divided things, but are one through their being indivisible in every way" (*Sent.* IV.12.1.1, III:109bB). Noting later that "many make a great difficulty here over whether inherence is the essence of an accident," he declares that "inherence is the accident itself" (ibid., III:110bBC). But if the color of the bread, as it inheres, *just is* that inherence, then how can it continue to exist without inhering? The standard thirteenth-century deflationary move, at this juncture, was an appeal to a miraculous change in the accident's *modus essendi* (§10.3). But Auriol rebuffs this strategy, insisting that the miracle of the Eucharist does not involve God's making accidents into independent, bounded things. Quite plausibly, he holds that this would be to turn accidents into substances, and so would not be a way of preserving the accidents of the host at all. Accidents are essentially unbounded and incomplete, in their own right, and so cannot fail to be such (*Sent.* IV.12.2.1, III:113aBC). What room does this then leave Auriol? Ultimately, he must appeal to the mystery of God's infinite power. God can cause accidents to exist on their own despite their incompleteness. Auriol concedes that we cannot conceive of how this is possible. Accidents are so dependent on their subject that, to us, it *seems* impossible for them to exist on their own. But Auriol denies that our intuitions are any guide to possibility: "God through his power can do more than our intellect can reveal or intuit" (ibid., III:113bC). To the objection that, on this account, "God could make straightness without a line, and roughness and lightness in weight without parts," Auriol just hugs the monster: "Show me the reason why God can do whatever does not imply a contradiction, yet cannot do these things" (*Sent.* IV.12.2.2, III:115bC).

With this remark, Auriol usefully reminds the reader of something we saw in the previous chapter: that when it comes to divine omnipotence, the burden of proof lies with those who would circumscribe it. Unless an explicit contradiction can be found in Auriol's account, the assumption should be that God can separate accidents from their subjects, even when accidents are so conceived. Rational intuition or conceivability may count as positive evidence for what is possible, but inconceivability is no guide to impossibility, inasmuch as God can do things that are inconceivable to us. (Aquinas had made just this claim at a similar juncture.)[20] So whereas Scotus's account makes the Eucharist hardly mysterious at all—at least with respect to the endurance of accidents without a subject—Auriol, for better or worse, restores the doctrine to its full obscurity. Yet whereas in the previous chapter I was optimistic that appeal to a change in *modus essendi* leaves open a window of possibility in this domain, in the present case I am not so sure. After all, even if we accept that the showing of a contradiction is required to

---

seems an unhappy result, however, because it saves the parsimony of Ockham's categorial scheme only by introducing unexplained entities outside that scheme. To get a happier outcome, one would need to contend that Ockham is not committed to the reality of inherence, a view he takes, for instance, in *Summa logicae* I.51. This, however, would leave him with no story at all about what inherence is. For other perspectives, see Henninger, *Relations* p. 142 and Menn, "Suárez and Modes" pp. 235–8.

[20] For the idea that inconceivability does not entail impossibility, see, e.g., Aquinas, *Summa contra gentiles* IV.65.4018: "manifestum est autem quod plus potest Deus in operando quam intellectus in apprehendo"; Giles of Rome, *Theoremata de corpore Christi* prop. 41 (f. 29ra): ". . . multa sunt deo possibilia, quae intelligere non possumus; facit enim deus accidens sine subiecto esse, quod intelligere non possumus, non intellecto subiecto."

establish metaphysical impossibility, Auriol might seem to furnish us with the material to show just that. Consider the whiteness that inheres in the bread. Auriol holds that this accident is identical with its inherence in the bread—the inherence is not some further thing. But now let it cease to inhere. How can the accident continue to exist? The logic of identity is perhaps obscure enough that, even here, more work would be needed to show an express contradiction. But the consensus among later scholastics was that a view such as Auriol's could not be made to work, and that—on theological if not on philosophical grounds—a fully realistic theory of accidents had to be maintained, at least for some kinds of accidents.

The differences in kind among accidents is our next subject.

12

Categories

12.1. The Significance of the Categories

Reflection on language is enough all by itself to suggest the distinction between substance and accident. Does language suggest further basic distinctions among kinds of accidents? Perhaps comparison of *Socrates is ugly* to *Socrates is married* suggests the distinction between monadic and polyadic predicates, and hence a distinction between properties and relations. Setting aside relations, however, can one go any further in drawing fundamental distinctions between kinds of monadic properties? It has been the recurrent dream of philosophers that some such further categorization could be made. The Stoics proposed a rather modest distinction between Substrate, Quality, Disposition, and Relation. Decidedly un-modest attempts to develop an ideal language—such as al-Farabi's tenth-century *Book of Letters* or John Wilkins's *Essay Towards a Real Character and a Philosophical Language* (1668)—began by putting things in the world into their proper categories, and then structuring language accordingly. Immanuel Kant offered his own categorial scheme, and similar efforts continue to this day.[1]

The most influential theory of the categories was of course Aristotle's, whose treatise by that name counts as one of the few philosophical works to have been studied almost continuously in Christian Europe through antiquity into the Middle Ages. Once Latin authors had access to the full Aristotelian corpus, in the thirteenth century, it became important to understand just where the *Categories* fits into Aristotle's larger system. Since hardly anyone proposed a developmental reading, there was little discussion of Aristotle's having outgrown the doctrines of the *Categories*. Still, there was the thought that it is a work for beginners, and so not the place to find answers to the deepest metaphysical questions. Thus Godfrey of Fontaines speaks of it as "the Philosopher's first book, read by boys just starting out" (*Quod.* I.20, p. 44). Tellingly, Thomas Aquinas wrote commentaries on twelve of Aristotle's works, covering all the most significant

---

[1] For the Stoic categories, see Long and Sedley, *Hellenistic Philosophers* I:162–79. For doubts over whether this should be regarded as a category theory at all, see Barnes, "Les cátegories" pp. 24–6. For al-Farabi, see Khalidi, *Medieval Islamic Writings*. For Wilkins, see *Real Character* pt. II, and the remarks of Rutherford, "Universal Language" sec. 2. For Kant, see *Critique of Pure Reason* A64/B89–A83/B116. For modern versions, see e.g. Chisholm, *Realistic Theory*, Westerhoff, *Ontological Categories*, and Thomasson, "Categories."

philosophical treatises—all except the *Categories*.[2] Beginning in the early fourteenth century, however, and throughout the late scholastic era, questions about the status of the ten categories become central topics of metaphysical inquiry. This new tendency is vividly on display throughout Ockham's work, which is full of lengthy discussions that traverse the various categories *seriatim*. It remains a constant feature of late scholastic thought all the way through Suárez's philosophical masterpiece, his *Disputationes metaphysicae*, roughly a quarter of which is devoted to working one by one through all ten categories. It is scarcely possible to understand any area of philosophy during our four centuries without coming to grips with the status of the Aristotelian categories. The task is not easy, however, because as usual there is no one dominant theory—on the contrary, the scholastics hold a bewildering variety of views regarding how to understand the categorial scheme.[3]

The previous two chapters have suggested an explanation for why the theory of categories became so important to later scholastic authors. When accidents are conceived of in deflationary terms, as entities whose existence is identified with a substance's existing in a certain way, then the project of categorizing accidents will not seem like a fundamental issue. To know what exists, one counts substances, not accidents. In contrast, once the doctrine of real accidents becomes the *opinio communis* in the fourteenth century, the list of ten categories—Substance, Quantity, Quality, Relation, Where, When, Action, Passion (= Being Acted On), Position, and Having—begins to look like an inventory of the kinds of things there are. That is, the *Categories* now comes to look like Aristotle's fundamental metaphysical text.

The importance of the *Categories* for later scholastic thought was not lost on seventeenth-century critics. Consider this florid passage from Pierre Gassendi:

There is no one unaware of how celebrated this distribution of categories, predicaments, or highest genera has always been among Aristotelians. It is the whole apparatus from which the Lyceum was built, or rather, it is the treasure house in which the Peripatetics have piled up all their riches. Hence it is that they fight so constantly for these ten categories that if someone were to take one away, they would think their palladium to have been carried off. Indeed, these are as it were the ten ramparts and towers on which the well-being of Philosophy depends, so much so that they must be fought over no less zealously than hearth and home. One should not be surprised, then, if they use hardly any other word as often as 'category.' (*Exercitationes* II.3.1, p. 311)

---

[2] Scholastic authors have varying suggestions about the place of the *Categories* within Aristotle's corpus. Buridan describes it as tending to follow received views, rather than as offering Aristotle's own considered account (*Summulae* III.3.2). Zabarella describes it as a kind of metaphysical prolegomenon to the logical works, offering logicians a rough guide to the kinds of things in the world that need to be handled by a logical theory. Still, according to Zabarella, it is not properly a metaphysical work, because it does not offer a detailed, contemplative scientific treatment of *res*, but merely one *gratia operandi*—hence its superficial character (*De natura logicae* II.2, II.5–6). For an unusual developmental reading, drawing on Simplicius, according to which Aristotle wrote the *Categories* when he was young, see the anonymous text quoted by Ebbesen, "Catégories au Moyen Âge" p. 248.

[3] Scheibler's *Metaphysica* is another illustration of the importance of the categorial scheme for late scholastic metaphysics. Its entire second half, some 400 pages, is structured around the ten categories, beginning with substance in most detail, and then devoting gradually less attention to each of the subsequent genera.

The importance of the *Categories* for later scholastic thought is widely appreciated among recent scholars. See, e.g., Kaluza, "Les catégories" p. 123: "Elle [la question des catégories] a été posée parce que, au XIVe siècle, la réponse qu'elle peut obtenir montre immédiatement le caractère globale de la philosophie qui soutienne et la porte." Among the many recent studies, see these collections: Biard and Rosier-Catach, *La tradition médiévale*; Bruun and Corti, *Les Catégories*; Gorman and Sanford, *Categories*; Newton, *Medieval Commentaries*.

When scholastic authors speak of categories, according to Gassendi, they refer to "certain classes and receptacles, as it were, to which absolutely all things are referred distinctly and in order" (ibid.). This then leads Gassendi to question whether there really are exactly ten such classes of things, no more and no less, and he has an easy time finding fault with Aristotle's list, both for being non-exhaustive and for being redundant. When the Aristotelian project is so conceived, it becomes an easy target of ridicule. But did the scholastics actually conceive of the ten categories as ten classes of things? As we will see, along the wide spectrum of scholastic views, some authors come close to satisfying Gassendi's description whereas others are as skeptical of the categorial scheme as Gassendi himself is.[4]

One generally accepted reason for rejecting Gassendi's characterization of the debate is that not all beings are included in the ten categories. This was thought to be true above all for God, who was typically said to lie outside the genera of the categories. Indeed, the thesis that God belongs to some genus of being was condemned at Oxford in 1277.[5] Other entities were sometimes said to fall outside the categories as well. Prime matter, for instance, was often judged to be a substance, but in some kind of extra-categorial sense.[6] The thick substance-accident composite likewise does not fall into any category. John Wyclif lists among non-categorial entities not just accidental aggregates but also privations, hypothetical truths, and truths concerning past, future, and possible states of affairs. It is not clear how much of a realist Wyclif wants to be about such *entia*. He seems to indicate that they are mind-dependent, inasmuch as he says that they are accidents having merely *esse intelligibile*. Still, according to Wyclif, these count as beings, even if not ones that belong to any category. Wyclif's remarks here do not seem to have been particularly eccentric. Walter Burley, earlier in the fourteenth century, similarly restricts his claim of all-inclusiveness: "Every non-complex term signifying a created thing outside the soul that is one *per se* signifies either substance or quality, etc." (*In art.*

---

[4] For other seventeenth-century critiques of scholastic category theory, see, e.g., Digby, *Two Treatises* tr. 1 concl., p. 344: "Upon this occasion, I think it not amiss to touch how the latter sectators or rather pretenders of Aristotle (for truly they have not his way) have introduced a model of doctrine (or rather of ignorance) out of his words which he never so much as dreamed of; howbeit they allege texts out of him to confirm what they say, as heretics do out of scripture to prove their assertions: for whereas he called certain collections or positions of things by certain common names (as the art of logic requires), terming some of them *qualities*, others *actions*, others *places*, or *habits*, or *relatives*, or the like, these his latter followers have conceited that these names did not design a concurrence of sundry things, or a diverse disposition of the parts of any thing, out of which some effect resulted, which the understanding considering all together has expressed the notion of it by one name; but have imagined that every one of these names had correspondent unto it some real positive entity or thing, separated (in its own nature) from the main thing or substance in which it was." Also Arnauld and Nicole, *La logique* p. 51: "Voilà les dix catégories d'Aristote, dont on fait tant de mystères, quoique à dire le vrai, ce soit une chose de soi très-peu utile, et qui non-seulement ne sert guère à former le jugement, ce qui est le but de la vraie logique, mais qui souvent y nuit beaucoup...." As usual, Leibniz is more sympathetic: "... ich auch in der bisherigen Logick viel gutes und nützliches finde.... Die gröste lust empfand ich an den so genantem *praedicamenten*, so mir vorsam als eine Muster-Rolle aller Dinge der Welt" (to Wagner [1696], *Phil. Schriften* VII:516; tr. Loemker pp. 463–4).

[5] On God as not falling into the category of substance, see, e.g., Albert the Great, *In Praed.* I.7, I:103b and Ch. 6 note 7. More generally see Tabarroni, "*Utrum Deus*," who shows that although this was the thirteenth-century consensus, shared by fourteenth-century authors as heterodox as Auriol and Ockham, some amount of dissent develops, most prominently in Gregory of Rimini, *Sent.* I.8, and also among arts masters in Paris and Italy. Still, God's exclusion from the categories remained the *opinio communis* throughout the scholastic era, a point that Descartes reflects when he remarks that "atque ideo nomen substantiae non convenit Deo et illis univoce, ut dici solet in Scholis" (*Principles* I.51).

[6] For prime matter as a substance outside the category of Substance, see Alexander of Alexandria, *In Meta.* VII.3.4, Paul of Venice, *In Meta.* VII.1.2. For further discussion of the sense in which prime matter and substantial form count as substances, see §26.1 and Ch. 26 note 15.

vet. [*In Praed.*] f. d1ra). The claim must be limited to simple linguistic expressions, because a complex expression—a sentence—might be said to signify a proposition or state of affairs, which would not be in any category. The claim must also be limited to creatures, to exclude God, and to *per se* unities, to exclude thick concrete substances, heaps, and the like. Finally, Burley limits the claim to things outside the soul, presumably so as to exclude the sort of beings of reason (*entia rationis*) that Wyclif lists. (Burley surely does not mean to exclude all mental items, given that knowledge and virtue are paradigmatic qualities [cf. *Cat.* 8].) Of course, the more beings that get counted as extra-categorial, the more cause one has to wonder just what the point of the categorial scheme is. Burley attempts to delimit precisely the range of Aristotle's category theory, but his various qualifications hardly induce confidence in the soundness of the project. Still, in what follows I will set aside worries of this sort. For present purposes, we might begin by thinking of the ten categories as a classification of the basic (non-composite) physical (extra-mental) entities. This, at least roughly, is what the category realist thinks.[7]

12.2. Category Nominalism: Ockham and Buridan

Not all scholastic authors were category realists. According to one prominent line of thought, the categories do not divide things at all, but instead divide language or concepts. Despite the perils of 'nominalism' as a classificatory label (§5.3), there is a tight enough connection here that it is appropriate to label views on which the categorial scheme is purely linguistic or conceptual as *category nominalism*. For purposes of this chapter, then, 'nominalism' means category nominalism. The most prominent nominalist was the venerable inceptor himself, Ockham:

These categories are not things outside the soul, really distinct among themselves. To be sure, human being and whiteness are two things (*res*) outside the soul, totally distinct, so that nothing that is one of these or part of one of these is the other or an essential part of the other. But it should not be imagined that it is this way for Substance, Quantity, Relation, and so on—namely, that a substance and a relation are two really distinct things, so that nothing that is a substance or part of a substance is a quantity or a part of a quantity or relation, and that conversely   6

3

---

[7] On Burley's commitment to propositions see Cesalli, "Le réalisme propositionnel" and Conti, "Ontology in Walter Burley" pp. 126–36. Wyclif's remarks on entities that transcend the categories run as follows: "Istis suppositis patet quod restringendo ens praedicamentale ad illud quod per se est in aliquo decem praedicamentorum, sunt quotlibet entia quorum nullum est formaliter ens praedicamentale, ut patet de Deo, unitate et puncto.... Secundo patet idem de quotlibet privationibus.... Tertio patet idem de aggregatis per accidens, de multitudinibus et multis similibus, quae oportet omnem loquentem ponere, ut patet tam de artificialibus quam naturalibus. Quarto patet idem de praeteritionibus, futuritionibus, potentiis et negationibus, quae, quamvis dicerentur accidentia vel posteriora ipsis subiectis secundum esse intelligibile, tamen non possunt dici accidere alicui substantiae secundum esse existere" (*De ente praedicamentali* ch. 1, p. 5). See also Robert Alyngton's similar remarks, at *In Praed.* p. 249: "Per hoc ergo quod [Aristoteles] dicit quod 'secundum nullam complexionem dicuntur' [1b25] excludit aggregata per accidens, et veritates negativas, ac veritates de possibili, de praeterito et futuro—quae veritates nec sunt substantiae nec accidentia, sed entia rationis." Much the same exceptions are made by Eustachius a Sancto Paulo, *Summa* I.1.3b.1.3 (I:48), even though just a few pages earlier he had remarked that "nihil enim est in tota hac rerum universitate, sive substantiale sive accidentale, quod ad unum horum [categoriarum] non pertineat" (I:45). Here Eustachius, in place of 'praedicamenta,' adopts the Hellenic 'categoriae,' a term that goes back to the influential pseudo-Augustinian *Categoriae decem*, but which rarely appears in scholastic authors, even as late as Suárez. This is a typical instance of the influence of Renaissance humanism on late scholastic philosophical vocabulary. For some typical remarks in this vein, see Valla, *Retractatio* I.1.2.

quantity is a single thing really and totally distinct from substance, relation, and quality, and that substance, quantity, relation, action and so on are so many things really and totally distinct from one another. Instead, what should be imagined is that these are distinct words and distinct intentions or concepts in the soul, signifying external things. And it should not be said that as these intentions are distinct from one another (no one of which is another), so too the corresponding things are distinct. For distinctions among signifying words or intentions in the soul do not always line up with distinctions among the things that are signified. (*In Praed.* 7.1, *Opera phil.* II:158)

This passage is worthy of attention in various respects. First, it provides a clear statement of Ockham's commitment to real accidents in the sense described by the previous two chapters. In cases where accidents exist—always in the category of Quality, according to Ockham—accident and substance are two *res*, "totally distinct" (lines 1–3). (As in earlier chapters, I leave '*res*' untranslated when it serves as a technical term for entities that have independent existence in a very strong sense—the requisite strength varying from author to author.) Second, it makes explicit Ockham's commitment to the substance–accident distinction, according to which the substance, strictly speaking, is the thin metaphysical substance, shorn of its accidents (§6.1). For cases where we have a real accident, "totally distinct" from its substance, the accident is not the substance or even a "part" of the substance (lines 2–3, 5–6). The substance–accident distinction is exclusive and non-overlapping.

The third noteworthy feature of the passage is of course its insistence that the categories carve up language and concepts, not external reality. The passage can in fact be read as making a kind of argument for that conclusion, as follows:

1. If accidents exist, they *really* exist, as things "totally distinct" from their subjects.
2. No accidents outside the category of Quality really exist.
∴ 3. The categories are not a guide to what exists (but merely to our ways of talking and thinking about what exists).

The difficulty with this sort of argument is that it depends on a long and contentious discussion of the various accidental categories, by way of establishing premise (2). Rather than depend on the results of that discussion, Ockham offers various more direct arguments for the conclusion stated in (3). (With that conclusion in hand, he can then take up the various accidental categories without having constantly to fend off the objection that such accidents *must* exist, because they are found on Aristotle's list.) Most of these arguments turn on textual details from the *Categories*, and so focus on Aristotle's intentions rather than on the philosophical issue. Ockham does, however, offer one sort of general philosophical argument for his conclusion. This argument rests on an issue that has arisen several times already in earlier chapters, regarding the status of determinable properties (§3.3, §§4.3–4). Ockham notes that each category seems to contain accidents at different levels of generality. Category realism would therefore seem to entail a hierarchy of increasingly general accidents, so that, for instance, "belonging to the essence of this whiteness are, at a minimum, whiteness in general, color in general, and quality, which is the most common genus" (ibid., II:159). It is, however, "impossible" to be a realist about such determinable qualities, because there is no good account of what would hold such a hierarchy together. It is not the case, for instance, that they are linked by one's inhering in another, as if they were related as matter to form. But if they are not somehow linked together, then the absurdity threatens that a thing could go from having this whiteness to having this blackness and yet still have the determinable accident of whiteness in general. No doubt one might reply to this argument by constructing some new machinery for linking together determinate and determinable accidental forms, something that goes beyond the familiar Aristotelian appeal to inherence. Alternatively, one might simply deny that category realism requires embracing the whole hierarchy of determinate and determinable forms. But Ockham's argument at least shows just how problematic a naive embrace of category realism would be. A manageable theory requires saying that *some* of the items described in Aristotle's *Categories* are really just manners of speaking.

For Ockham, manners of speaking (or conceiving) are the *only* items cataloged by the categorial scheme. As it happens, those manners of speaking do have ontological import in the categories of Substance and Quality. In every other case, however, the linguistic–conceptual items that fall into the categories pick out not a distinctive kind of thing, but merely substance and quality in some oblique way. Thus 'sitting,' from the category of Position, picks out not a distinct form but simply a substance with its parts suitably organized. (I capitalize when referring to the categories themselves; and use lowercase when referring to the entities contained in the categories.) Ockham runs through the various categories carefully, showing how in each case there is no need for anything beyond an ontology of substances and qualities.[8] Later we will look closely at his arguments for the most controversial of cases, that of Quantity (§14.3), and also at why Ockham continues to accept that there are real accidents in the category of Quality (§19.2). For now, though, consider a general difficulty that a view of Ockham's sort faces in maintaining the categorial scheme. Whereas a realist can of course pin categorial differences on differences in reality, the nominalist must somehow find those differences within language. And it is hard to see how language by itself can be made to give rise to this sort of ten-fold division. (Or how concepts could do so. Given the symmetry that scholastic authors generally accept between words and concepts, I will not distinguish sharply between these two positions.) One crude criticism of nominalism was that, on such a view, there can be only one category, since spoken words are sensible qualities. (See, e.g., Burley, *In art. vet.* [*In Praed.*] f. c6vb. One might just as well argue that all such linguistic items should all go into the category of Quantity [cf. *Cat.* 6, 4b24–35].) This simply begs the question against the nominalist, by assuming precisely what the nominalist denies: that it is things that get categorized. But the objection serves to highlight the difficulty of finding seams in language that will match up with those that Aristotle describes.

Ockham's solution is to divide the categories according to the different interrogatives that can be applied to a thing. Thus, when one asks of a thing *What is it?*, the answers to such a question—'human being,' 'animal,' 'stone,' etc.—fall into the category of Substance. When one asks *How much?* (*Quantum?*), the answers fall into the category

---

[8] Ockham's austere ontology comes with a significant qualification. For although he thinks that there are no philosophical arguments for entities outside the categories of Substance and Quality, he concedes that relations are necessary to account for the Trinity and Incarnation. (As Ch. 11 note 19 discusses, he may also have to allow inherence as a real relation.) Still, he is able to insist that there are no entities corresponding to the category of Relation, because all such relations are extracategorial. For excellent discussions of this issue, see Adams, *William Ockham* I:267–76 and Henninger, *Relations* pp. 140–5. Hereafter, I will ignore this complication.

of Quantity. Thus it is linguistic considerations that divide up the categories, and linguistic (or conceptual) entities that get categorized. This is, however, not an easy view to defend. Ockham has to concede that Latin does not have distinct interrogatives for each of the ten categories (no more than does Greek or English). In place of a distinct interrogative for Position, for instance, one has to ask a question like *Is he sitting or lying down?* In the face of this difficulty, Ockham calmly remarks that "sometimes we lack interrogative terms that ought to exist, because they have not been introduced" (*In Praed.* 16.2, *Opera phil.* II:303). Hence the categories arise not from the interrogatives actually present in language, but from the interrogatives that "ought" to be present. Yet this should lead one to wonder about the basis for concluding that there ought to be exactly ten different interrogatives in any language. The most obvious basis would be the shape of reality itself: that, in view of that reality, there are ten different basic kinds of questions to be asked of things. But then we are back to the view that the categories reflect a divide at the level of external reality.[9]

John Buridan, writing a generation later, attempts to refine Ockham's general approach. The categories are not distinguished by external things, he says, inasmuch as there certainly are not ten different kinds of things corresponding to the ten categories. But neither are the categories distinguished simply by language, "because different languages do not require a change in the number of categories, which philosophers generally agree on. Also, words are given whatever signification we like. Hence the categories would be multiplied whenever we like, which is absurd" (*In Praed.* q. 3, pp. 17–18). Buridan's solution is to appeal to our distinctive predicative intentions, the idea being that behind the variety of natural languages lies a common conceptual framework. Although there are infinitely many possible patterns of predication, these can all be reduced to ten basic kinds, as determined not by any structural feature of language, but by the way we conceptualize reality. Buridan seems well aware that the gerrymandered character of Aristotle's categories makes this view look just as implausible as does category realism. He softens the blow, however, in two ways. First, he argues that there is no systematic method for deriving the categories, as if the number ten could be made to fall out a priori from some more basic division. "Many have labored in vain" who sought to construct such a scheme, he argues (ibid., p. 19). The only possible method for establishing the number of categories, he argues, is the empirical method of finding language being used in a way that cannot be reduced to any other predicative form. Second, Buridan leaves open the possibility that such inquiry could yield a number larger than ten. Aristotle never said that there are no more than ten categories, he simply offered these ten, leaving it open that others might find more. "So if we were to find some common predicates possessing other modes of predication beyond the ten mentioned, it seems entirely clear to me that it should not

---

[9] Ockham derives the categories from interrogatives at *In Praed.* 16.2 (*Opera phil.* II:301–3); *Summa logicae* I.41 (*Opera phil.* I:116–17); *Quod.* V.22 (*Opera theol.* IX:567–9). His argument against determinable accidents is more complex than the main text indicates. After ruling out that determinate accident might stand to determinable accident as form to matter, he proceeds to consider this case: "Similiter, si sint distincta realiter ista albedo et albedo communis, et ista albedo est primo in subiecto particulari, ergo albedo communis erit primo in subiecto communi" (*In Praed.* 7.1, *Opera phil.* II:160). This amounts to the idea that determinate whiteness will inhere in the primary substance, while determinable whiteness inheres in the secondary substance. Ockham of course does not accept the reality of secondary substances, but he has to take this view seriously because the category realist is likely to embrace the reality of secondary substances as well (see Conti, "Realism" pp. 648–50).

be denied that there are more than ten categories" (ibid.). For Buridan, then, the categories cannot be read straight off of language; rather, natural language points toward an underlying conceptual scheme, and this is what the ten categories track.[10]

As Buridan's comments suggest, there were many proposals for how to derive the ten categories systematically. Those derivations are not our topic here—indeed, it is important to distinguish sharply the derivation problem from the question of ontological commitments, because an author might appeal to linguistic considerations to derive the categories, and yet think those linguistic considerations reflect distinctions in reality. It should be said, however, that Buridan's skepticism regarding the possibility of a systematic derivation was widely shared, even by realists. Scotus, for instance, although he thinks that the reality of each of the ten categories can be proved one by one (§12.5), criticizes systematic attempts to divide reality in such a way that the ten-fold distinction falls out as a consequence. Suárez too, much later, would similarly remark that "it cannot be demonstrated *a priori*, by a special argument, that there are so many highest genera [of being], no more and no less. Hence neither does Aristotle anywhere try to demonstrate this, but instead always treats it as certain" (*Disp. meta.* 39.2.18). It is, therefore, not essential to the scholastic project—even among realists—to defend the ten categories as exhaustive.[11]

What distinguishes realists from nominalists over the categories—most basically—is whether they take the categories to correspond to some non-conceptual, non-linguistic distinction among things—in short, whether they regard the categories as *metaphysically*

---

[10] Buridan's positive account of how the categories are distinguished runs as follows: "[Praedicamenta] sumuntur ex diversis intentionibus, secundum quas termini sunt diversimode connotativi vel etiam non connotativi. Et quibus diversis connotationibus proveniunt diversi modi praedicandi terminorum de primis substantiis; et ita directe et immediate distinguuntur penes diversos modos praedicandi de primis substantiis. . . . Et sciendum quod haec distinctio praedicamentorum non est per divisiones sufficientes alicuius rationis communis in rationes speciales, sicut esset divisio generis in suas species, ut animalis in ratione et irrationale, quoniam Aristoteles supponit quod huiusmodi diversis intentionibus seu rationibus, secundum quas proveniunt tales diversi modi praedicandi, non est aliqua communis ratio vel intentio. . . . Credo ergo quod non possit aliter assignari vel probari sufficientia numeri praedicamentorum, nisi quia tot modos praedicandi diversos invenimus non reducibiles in aliquem modum praedicandi communiorem acceptum secundum aliquam unam communem rationem, ideo oportet tot esse" (*In Praed.* q. 3, pp. 18–19). See also, more briefly, *Summulae* III.1.8.

Regarding Buridan's relationship to Ockham, see Klima, "Nominalist Semantics" pp. 171–2: "it was Buridan's careful attention to theoretical detail, coupled with prudent practical judgment and pedagogical skill, that in his hands could turn Ockham's innovations into relatively uncontroversial, viable textbook material, capable of laying the foundations of a new, paradigmatically different conception of the relationships between language, thought and reality."

Another interesting nominalist treatment of the categories is Albert of Saxony's *Quaest. in artem vet.* His "Quaestio de sufficientia praedicamentorum" follows Ockham in arguing that the ten categories derive from the different kinds of questions that we customarily ask, and denies that the categories are ontologically committing. To the question of why Aristotle distinguishes *Actio* and *Passio* but not *Habere* and *Haberi*, Albert responds that this would not correspond to the linguistic–conceptual framework we in fact use (par. 398). Of course we *could* embrace a different framework, and if we did then *Haberi* would be a further category (par. 399).

[11] On attempts to derive the categories, the so-called *sufficientia praedicamentorum* arguments, see Bos and van der Helm, "Division of Being"; Ebbesen, "*Catégories au Moyen Âge*" pp. 251–3; McMahon, "Reflections"; Pini, "Scotus on Deducing." For Scotus's skeptical remarks, see the *additio* at *In Meta.* V.5–6 nn. 73–80. Suárez offers a useful summary of various competing strategies (*Disp. meta.* 39.2.18). He attributes his own conclusion to Avicenna, who, in a discussion often cited by scholastic authors, had remarked: "Nos enim non cogimur observare hanc regulam famosam qua dicitur quod decem sunt genera quorum uniuscuiusque est certissima generalitas, et quod nihil est extra ipsa" (*Sufficientia* II.2, f. 25va). Even so, Suárez does eventually try to show why ten *might* be the right number of categories (*Disp. meta.* 39.2.33). For another skeptical discussion of the possibility of a derivation, see Godfrey of Fontaines, *Quod.* VII.7 (pp. 349–50). Even Burley, an arch-realist, remarks: "Intelligendum est quod quamvis numerus praedicamentorum non possit demonstrari [ed. demonstrant], tamen aliqui acceperunt sufficientiam praedicamentorum sic . . ." (*In art. vet.* [*In Praed.*] f. d1ra).

committing. To say this is not to say that the *Categories* is a work of metaphysics. On the contrary, because the *Categories* was standardly grouped among Aristotle's logical works, it was customary to assert that the official topic of the work is language. Yet one might say this and still go on to hold that those linguistic–conceptual divisions have a foundation in reality, thereby endorsing category realism. Not surprisingly, these claims sometimes get confused. Thus Boethius—author of the most influential commentary among scholastics—is quoted by nominalists in support of the doctrine that the *Categories* concerns words, and by realists in support of the doctrine that the *Categories* is metaphysically committing. What Boethius seems to have thought—and what was by far the most common scholastic view—was that the *Categories* is about language, but that it is a study of language that reveals the metaphysical structure of the world. The nominalist view, in contrast, was that metaphysics cannot be read off of language in this way. As Ockham put it above (lines 12–13), "distinctions among signifying words or intentions in the soul do not always line up with distinctions among the things that are signified." Accordingly, for the nominalist, the fact that there are ten categories shows nothing whatsoever about the structure of reality.[12]

12.3. Structures: Aquinas and Ghent

Later scholastics do not usually follow Ockham in treating the categories as purely linguistic. To be sure, one finds authors taking that view, from Nicholas of Autrecourt in the fourteenth century to Franco Burgersdijk in the early seventeenth. Still, the usual view was that the categories divide things. One finds this view defended by the full range of late scholastic authors, from Zabarella to De Soto to Suárez.[13] Yet even when later scholastic authors commit themselves to treating the categories metaphysically,

---

[12] For the standard view that the *Categories* is a logical work, and so properly concerned with language rather than metaphysics, see Pini, *Categories and Logic* ch. 1. For a clear example of this claim combined with category realism, see Simon of Faversham, *In Isag.* q. 1, p. 17: "Logica considerat intentiones quas intellectus fundat in rebus et ⟨quae⟩ sunt extraneae rei"; ibid., q. 2, p. 19: "Cum autem intellectus causat tales intentiones, et movetur ab apparentibus in re, et propter hoc intellectus diversas intentiones logicales attribuit diversis rebus propter diversas proprietates. Unde logicus non diceret hanc esse veram, *Homo est genus*, sed hanc, *Homo est species*. Ideo tota logica accipitur a proprietatibus rerum, quia aliter logica esset figmentum intellectus, quod non dicimus." For discussion see Pickavé, "Simon of Faversham." For an overview of the scholastic dispute over the subject of the *Categories*, see Ebbesen, "Catégories au Moyen Âge" pp. 257–67.

The passage from Boethius favored by nominalists runs as follows: "Adeo non de rebus sed de vocibus tractaturus est, ut diceret 'Dicuntur.' Res enim proprie non dicuntur, sed voces. Et quod addidit, 'singulum aut substantiam significat,' late patet eum de vocibus disputare; non enim res, sed voces significant, significantur autem res" (*In Praed.* I, col. 180C). Yet compare that with ibid., col. 161A: "Dicendum est in hoc libro de primis vocibus prima rerum genera significantibus" and col. 162D: "Quoniam rerum prima decem genera sunt, necesse fuit decem quoque esse simplices voces, quae de subiectis rebus dicerentur." Ockham quotes the first passage (*In Praed.* 7.1, II:158), Scotus the second (*In Meta.* V.5–6 n. 38).

[13] Strictly speaking, Autrecourt prefers to think of the categories as conceptual rather than linguistic. Speaking even more strictly, Autrecourt leaves room for the view that the categories might contain *res*: "... et istos decem conceptus primos vel res sic conceptas appellat decem praedicamenta" (*Tractatus* ch. 5, p. 226). Still, Autrecourt clearly prefers the conceptual view. What he is most concerned with rejecting, however, is the sort of view that finds *res* for every category: "Et si per decem praedicamenta vis aliud intelligere puta decem res ex natura rei distinctas negarem simpliciter" (ibid.).

Burgersdijk's commitment to category nominalism comes out as follows: "Sed si decem istae classes entia non continent, dicat aliquis, cur ergo dicuntur summa genera? Respondeo. Dicuntur summa genera τῶν κατηγορουμένων, non τῶν ὄντων" (*Inst. meta.* II.17.11, p. 362).

For various late scholastic versions of category realism, see Zabarella, *De natura logicae* II.2–5; De Soto, *In Praed.* prol. p. 109C; Suárez, *Disp. meta.* 39 prol. par. 1: "... non quia nomina in praedicamentis ponantur, sed quia dialecticus magis consideret res in praedicamentis collocandas quoad quid nominis quam quoad quid rei...."

they do so in various different ways, most of which fall well short of Gassendi's caricature in §12.1. It is, indeed, not clear that anyone defended the reality of the ten categories in quite the way that Gassendi suggests. To clarify the situation, we can first consider various weaker examples of category realism, and then some more robust varieties.

The weakest sort of view that I am counting as realist endorses the idea that each of the categories marks off a distinct kind of being, but without supposing that there is a one-to-one mapping from categories to basic entities. This would seem to be Aquinas's view, judging from his few scattered discussions of the topic. He accepts the common-place claim that the proximate cause of the distinction among categories is linguistic, in terms of different modes of predication. (This idea was hard to resist among scholastics, inasmuch as the Latin word for categories is *praedicamenta*, which just means *things that are predicated*.) But this is not to say that the categories divide linguistic items. Rather, "something is put into a category only if it is a thing (*res*) existing outside the soul" (*Quaest. de potentia* 7.9c). Not surprisingly, then, the different modes of predication that give rise to the categories are ultimately grounded on distinctions within reality: "Being is delimited into different genera in accord with different modes of predicating, which depend on different modes of being (*modum essendi*)" (*In Meta.* V.9.890). Still, this basic realist commitment is tempered by the concession that a single thing can be classified into either of several categories. The same change (*motus*), for instance, can be put into the category of either Action or Passion, depending on whether that change is linked to the patient or the agent. If one says,

This table was built by Mary

then a *passio* is ascribed to the table. If one says,

Mary built this table

then an *actio* is ascribed to Mary. In one sense there obviously is a difference in reality between actions and passions—to build and to be built are not the same thing. This, according to Aquinas, is what the categorial difference is capturing. In another sense, however, it would be odd to suppose that these two sentences involve different metaphysical commitments, as if the shift from the passive to the active voice involves appealing to different entities in the world. Aquinas does not believe this: he is perfectly happy to allow that the two sentences come out true in virtue of the same metaphysical constituents: the agent, the patient, and the change (*motus*). (I do not mean to suggest that *change* is itself basic for Aquinas; that raises still further questions that must be set aside until Chapter 18. One might also suppose, as other authors do, that relations will come into play in this analysis. Aquinas, however, does not say so.) So the difference between *actio* and *passio* is real, but that is not to say that each category contains a kind of irreducible entity. At least in the case of *actio* and *passio*, Aquinas believes that one could give a reductive analysis in terms of more basic entities. (Lying in the background here are Aristotle's remarks at *Phys.* III.3 regarding there being just one actuality for any agent–patient pair—e.g., in the case of mover and moved, there is just one motion. But although "the road from Thebes to Athens and the road from Athens to Thebes are the same," there is still a difference between "being here at a distance from there and being there at a distance from here" [202b14–19].)[14]

There is perhaps some temptation to suppose that, if Aquinas is willing to embrace such reductionism, then (a) he is at least implicitly rejecting Aristotle's categories scheme, and (b) he is venturing rather close to category nominalism. The basis for supposing the latter would be not that he thinks the categories are purely linguistic, but that even a nominalist such as Ockham ought to be willing to grant that these linguistic differences have *some* basis in external reality. After all, surely even Ockham would be prepared to recognize the difference between *building* and *being built*. No doubt, but still there is a critical difference between Aquinas and Ockham here, inasmuch as Ockham denies that the categories should be read as showing us anything about how the world is. Although different categorial claims naturally come out true in virtue of different features of the world, the ten-fold division cannot be put to any metaphysical work, and was not intended to do so. Aquinas, in contrast, sees the ten categories as significant for the nature of reality.

Although this is not the place to go into detail regarding Aquinas's views, it will be helpful to have at least a sketch, because it will serve as a useful foil for the realism of subsequent generations. In a sense, for Aquinas, the only basic entities are substances. Given his deflationary theory of accidents (§10.2), accidental forms do not properly exist at all, but exist only in the derivative sense that their subjects exist in a certain way. Accordingly, Aquinas is not very concerned with the ontology of the categories. Although the categorial scheme has metaphysical implications, they cannot, for Aquinas, map reality at its most fundamental level. But what then do the categories demarcate? Although Aquinas's talk of *modi essendi* is not very clear, I think we can get a sense of his view by introducing the idea of a *structure*. A structure, as I will use that term, is ontologically innocent: it is an attempt to account for how the world is organized, but without postulating any further items in the world. The term 'structure' is not intended to correspond to any particular scholastic term, but it does I think capture how Aquinas thinks about at least some of the categories. The categories of

---

[14] Aquinas sets out his views on Action and Passion as follows: "Sed si actio et passio sunt idem secundum substantiam, videtur quod non sint diversa praedicamenta. Sed sciendum quod praedicamenta diversificantur secundum diversos modos praedicandi. Unde idem, secundum quod diversimode de diversis praedicatur, ad diversa praedicamenta pertinet. Locus enim, secundum quod praedicatur de locante, pertinet ad genus quantitatis. Secundum autem quod praedicatur denominative de locato, constituit praedicamentum ubi. Similiter motus, secundum quod praedicatur de subiecto in quo est, constituit praedicamentum passionis. Secundum autem quod praedicatur de eo a quo est, constituit praedicamentum actionis" (*In Meta.* XI.9.2313); "Sic igitur patet quod licet motus sit unus, tamen praedicamenta quae sumuntur secundum motum sunt duo, secundum quod a diversis rebus exterioribus fiunt praedicamentales denominationes. Nam alia res est agens, a qua sicut ab exteriori sumitur per modum denominationis praedicamentum passionis; et alia res est patiens a quo denominatur agens" (*In Phys.* III.5.323).

I am unsure whether Aquinas's reductionism might extend to other lesser categories, but one might consider the following text: "Alia vero genera magis consequuntur relationem quam possint relationem causare. Nam Quando consistit in aliquali relatione ad tempus, Ubi vero ad locum. Positio autem ordinem partium importat, Habitus autem relationem habentis ad habitum" (*In Meta.* V.17.1005). This is too compressed to be regarded as decisive, but it certainly points toward the idea that these last four categories might be reduced to the category of Relation. Even the irreducibility of relations might be questioned, as the discussion in Henninger makes clear (*Relations* ch. 2), although Henninger himself—notably without textual support—concludes that, for Aquinas, relations are "really distinct" from their foundations (pp. 29–31). One might look to *Quaest. de potentia* 7.9c as evidence for the reality of relations: "Sic ergo oportet quod res habentes ordinem ad aliquid realiter referantur ad ipsum, et quod in eis aliqua res sit relatio." Such a claim leaves room for a reductive account, however, and indeed that same article might be read as suggesting that the *res* that is a relation is either a quantity, or else some active or passive power.

Actio and *Passio*, for instance, do not contain distinct, irreducible things, but they describe distinct fundamental structures. To say that there are ten categories of being is to say that there are ten fundamentally different ways in which the world may be arranged.[15]

This notion of an arrangement of being—an ontologically innocent structure—takes on a more prominent place in Henry of Ghent. As we saw in §10.4, Ghent's views mark a transitional stage on the path toward real accidents. Although 'being' is equivocal for Ghent, accidents nevertheless have their own existence and count, along with substance, as *res*—in the ontologically robust sense of that term. Yet Ghent does not extend his realism to all ten categories; instead, only accidents in the categories of Quantity and Quality count as *res*, leaving the other categories to be mere modes or aspects of those basic entities:

In the whole universe of creatures there are only three *res* belonging to the three first categories—Substance, Quantity, and Quality. All the others are aspects (*rationes*) and intellectual concepts (*intentiones intellectus*) with respect to those three *res*, with no proper reality unless insofar as they are grounded on the *res* of those [three] categories. (*Quodlibet* VII.1–2 [*Opera* XI:34–5]; cf. *Quod.* V.6 [ed. 1518, I:161O])

It is hard to say whether passages of this sort disqualify Ghent from category realism. He does here treat the lesser seven categories as concepts. Strictly speaking, however, he regards all ten categories as conceptual. This is simply a reflection of the standard view described already, according to which the categories are a conceptual/logical construct. The question, then, is what sort of foundation this construct has. And although Ghent is clear that there are only three fundamental *res* within the categorial scheme, still the other categories correspond to something that he calls either a mode of being (*modus essendi*) or a categorial aspect (*ratio praedicamenti*). The ten distinct categories arise from the various modes or aspects of these three fundamental *res*: "these two—namely, the categorial *res* and the aspect of its being which is its categorial aspect—constitute a category and distinguish one category from another" (*Summa* 32.5, *Opera* XXVII:79).[16]

---

[15] Aquinas is often credited with a much more thoroughly realistic theory of the categories than he in fact holds. See, e.g., Kenny, *Aquinas on Being* p. 3: "when a predicate in a particular category is actually true of something, according to Aquinas, there exists in the world an entity corresponding to the predicate"; Gracia and Newton, "Categories, Medieval" sec. 4.1: "Fundamental to Aquinas' derivation of the categories is an isomorphism between language and reality. Only because language parallels reality in some way can Aquinas derive the ten categories of extramental things from the ten different kinds of predication he accepts; we know that there are ten different kinds of things based on the different ways something is 'said of' or 'predicated of' a subject." Suárez in contrast cites Aquinas in support of the view that the categories do not always mark a real ontological distinction (*Disp. meta.* 39.2.22–23).

Wippel characteristically sees the subtleties here, and reports on a secondary literature devoted to the question (*Metaphysical Thought of Thomas* pp. 208–28). Wippel's own conclusion, however, is that "in every case Thomas regards the mode of being which justifies a distinct predicamental name as a distinct and irreducible mode of being" (p. 225). My response to this is the argument of the main text: that this is right in the sense that Aquinas thinks each category captures a distinct structure of reality, but strictly speaking it is wrong inasmuch as Aquinas does not think each category is ontologically irreducible.

[16] Ghent's view that Substance, Quantity, and Quality are foundational for the other categories is widespread, even among authors that are less inclined toward a reductive view. Indeed, we will see in §12.5 that even the most robustly realist theories of the categories accept the primacy of those three categories. For another example, see Dietrich of Freiberg, *De accidentibus* 7.4 (*Opera* III:63): "... quantitate et qualitate, quae sunt quasi radices et fundamenta aliorum septem generum."

The terms 'modus' and 'ratio' may well be the two most slippery words in Latin. As we have seen, the phrase 'modus essendi' is Aquinas's. As for 'ratio,' that might here be translated as *aspect* or *character*. There is really no hope in understanding what either of these expressions mean, except by looking at how they are used in context. Sometimes Ghent seems to suggest that they should not be given any sort of realistic interpretation, as when he remarks above (line 3) that the lesser categories have "no proper reality" and, earlier in the same text, that "there is beyond a doubt nothing real in the category of Relation, except for what is a *res* from another category" (*Quod.* VII.1–2, *Opera* XI:24). Yet to say that there is no *realitas* and nothing *realis* may just be another way of saying that there is no *res* in these relational categories, leaving room for some other sort of lesser ontological status. Moreover, Ghent seems to disassociate himself from the view that the lesser categories are merely conceptual when he approves of the Boethian dictum that "the ten categories are the ten first genera of *res*," cautioning only against inferring from this that the categories describe ten distinct kinds of *res*. As for what sort of reality the lesser categories have, Ghent's talk of *modus essendi* often abbreviates to the claim that items in these categories are modes. It is only in a very broad and improper sense that modes can count as *res*, inasmuch as "a mode is grounded on a true *res*" (*Summa* 55.6, ed. 1520, II:111vQ). Still, it is plausible to think that modes are not purely an intellectual construct. On the other hand, there seems to be nothing in Ghent to suggest the more realistic conception of modes to be described in the following chapter, according to which modes are irreducible entities with their own causal powers. Instead, I suggest that it is again the notion of a structure that best captures Ghent's view. Although a few of the categories pick out distinct kinds of *res*, in general the categorial scheme makes far more modest ontological commitments. What the lesser seven categories describe are seven different ways in which *res* are organized in the world.[17]

Ghent is sometimes described as reducing the categorial scheme to three, as in Paulus, *Henri de Gand* pp. 158–9. Recent scholarship, however, has inclined to the view that although there are only three kinds of *res*, still there are ten fundamental categories. See, e.g., Pickavé, "Simon of Faversham" p. 206: "It is therefore wrong and exaggerated to conclude Henry is cutting down the list of categories to just three . . ."; Pini, "Scotus's Realist Conception" p. 72: "Since each category is the result of a combination of a thing and a mode and since there are no fewer than ten modes, the categories are ten. . . . This mode is a real feature, so even non-absolute categories must be regarded as mind-independent constituents of the world. But they should not be considered as things on their own."

For all ten categories as conceptual on Ghent's view (literally, as *intentiones secundae*) see *Quod.* V.6 (ed. 1518 I:161vO): "hoc nomen accidens sit nomen intentionis secundae impositum a modo essendi, scilicet in alio, et non a re cui convenit esse secundum illum modum a qua imponuntur illa nomina quantitas et qualitas. Unde et nomen substantiae inquantum distinguitur contra nomen accidentis et imponitur a modo essendi per se sicut accidens a modo essendi in alio est nomen secundae intentionis, sicut est nomen accidentis"; *Quod.* V.2 (ed. 1518 I:154vF): "Ex quo est hic advertendum quod sicut nomen accidentis, quia imponitur a ratione praedicamenti quae est modus essendi inhaerendo alteri, ideo est nomen intentionis non rei, sic nomen substantiae, inquantum imponitur a ratione praedicamenti quae est modus essendi subsistendo, [ideo] est nomen intentionis non rei."

A full discussion of Ghent's categorial theory would need to consider the role in his thought of an intentional distinction, which distinguishes, for instance, a relation from its foundation. For discussion and references, see Henninger, *Relations* pp. 46–7, 168–9.

[17] For the Boethian dictum, and Ghent's gloss, see *Quod.* VII.1–2 (*Opera* XI:34): "Et quod assumitur secundum Boethium [*In Praed.* I, 64:161A], quod 'decem praedicamenta sunt decem prima genera rerum,' bene verum est, sed non decem res, nec dixit Boethius aut aliquis philosophorum quod sunt decem res decem primorum generum." On the thought that modes are *res*: "Sed tunc non est disputatio nisi de nomine, appellando extenso nomine rem quod alii appellant modum rei. Attamen si sic respectus possint dici res, hoc non est nisi quia ex natura rei fundantur in vera re" (*Summa* 55.6, ed. 1520 II:111vQ).

It may seem odd to find this notion of *structure* playing a role in the present context, in the heart of the scholastic era. In the seventeenth century, to be sure, one might expect to find extensive appeals to structure, and indeed the next chapter will make clear just how much turns, for post-scholastic authors, on the question of whether their so-called modes are simply structures. But what—one might wonder—are structures doing in the thirteenth century, in solidly Aristotelian figures like Aquinas and Ghent? Of course, I have not argued that either of these figures seeks to employ the notion of structure wholesale, across their whole categorial scheme. For both Aquinas and Ghent, the concept plays a role only at the margins of their categorial scheme, as a way to defend the scheme's reality all the way down the list. At the critical points— Substance, Quantity, Quality—the metaphysical commitments of the theory are not in doubt, and are solidly Aristotelian (albeit in rather different ways, given Aquinas's more deflationary stance). Still, there may seem something peculiar in structures, so conceived, having a place in any solidly Aristotelian theory. After all, isn't a structure just precisely what a form is, for Aristotle? How does *ba* differ from *ab*, if not in structure, and is this not just how Aristotle wants us to think about form? (See *Meta.* VII.17, 1041b11–33.) A scholastic author's attempting to avoid the ontological commitments involved in form by appealing to structure may therefore look like a rather gross conceptual confusion. Or like a dog chasing its own tail.

Of course, the term 'structure' is my own, and amounts to a considerable extrapolation from what these texts actually say. Yet even if I am wrong in ascribing this sort of view to Aquinas and Ghent, the view itself is worth having in mind, because it describes an important region of conceptual space that is not necessarily closed off to a scholastic Aristotelian. As I stressed in §10.5, the scholastic conception of form is concrete and causal rather than abstract. Qualities, for instance, are real features of the world because they play an irreducible causal role. Scotus relied on these points to argue against deflationary theories of accidents. Such arguments would apply all the more, however, to any view that would turn accidents into ontologically innocent structures. If structures are not things in any sense, if they are nothing over and above the things that are structured, then they will hardly seem suited to play the sort of causal role that

McMahon, "Some Non-Standard Views" p. 58, suggests that Ghent's talk of modes has "far-reaching consequences for the history of metaphysics," inasmuch as it gives rise to later theories of modes. (For a similar suggestion, see Klima, "Buridan's Logic" p. 481n.) This seems overstated, inasmuch as Ghent's use of modes falls well short of the use to be described in the following chapter, and inasmuch as there are many other thirteenth-century precedents. Still, Ghent does seem to have been an important source for the subsequent idea that the categories can be distinguished in terms of *modi essendi*, which surely played an oblique role in the decision by later authors to use 'mode' for a kind of less than fully real accident. The phrase *modus essendi* appears in a similar role in Aquinas, as quoted earlier in the main text, and at *Quaest. de veritate* 1.1c. Ghent, however, appeals to the phrase much more prominently, and subsequent authors use the notion quite extensively, e.g. Simon of Faversham: " . . . praedicamenta distinguuntur penes modos essendi et non penes quoscumque modos essendi, sed penes tales modos essendi qui in nullo communicant" (*In Praed.* q. 12, p. 85); "Praedicamentum autem nihil aliud est quam coordinatio praedicabilium—secundum, sub, et supra—habentium rem distinctam ab aliis rebus vel modum essendi distinctum, a quo accipitur diversus modus praedicandi. Et ideo illa quae significant res distinctas vel habent modos essendi distinctos qui in nullo alio conveniunt habent modos praedicandi distinctos et constituunt diversa praedicamenta" (*In Phys.* III.10, in Pini, "Scotus's Realist Conception" p. 73n.). See also Radulphus Brito, *In Praed.* q. 8 ad 3, p. 94: "Quando non est relatio, sed est modus essendi. . . . Etiam Habitus non est relatio, sed est modus essendi. . . . Etiam Positio est quidam modus essendi. . . . " See also an anonymous Madrid text: "Modi autem praedicandi oriuntur ex modis essendi. . . . Modi autem essendi sunt decem, quorum unus non est alius. Et ideo sunt tantum decem modi praedicandi distincti" (*In Praed.* q. 7, in Andrews, "Anonymous" p. 129). The doctrine subsequently comes in for criticism from authors who argue that something else should individuate the categories—e.g., Olivi, *Summa* II.28, I:485–6; Paul of Venice, *In Meta.* VII.1.1.

scholastic authors almost universally wanted to ascribe to accidental forms. Hence, for the scholastics, forms are not structures. This leaves room, however, for ontologically innocent structures to play a role at the margins of scholastic theories, not as a substitute for form, but as a conceptual tool that supplements form. When we come to the seventeenth century, the question will be whether such structures replace form entirely. But before we get there, we should not be surprised to see scholastic authors making a more limited use of this same tool.

12.4. Modest Category Realism: Olivi

Both Ghent's assimilation of quality and quantity to substance, insofar as all three count as *res*, as well as his reluctance to ascribe any reality to the remaining categories, are precisely the outcomes one would expect from the shift toward a more realistic theory of accidents. The greater reality accidents are thought to have, the more like substances they become, but also the harder it becomes to postulate them all the way down the categorial scheme. In the decades to come, Ghent's commitment to *res* in the category of Quality would be accepted by almost every subsequent scholastic author (Ch. 19). His commitment to *res* in the category of Quantity would likewise become the standard view, despite the criticisms of Ockham and others (Chs. 14–15). In the case of the remaining seven accidental categories, however, Ghent's approach only fueled a scholastic controversy that would never be settled. Among the very most controversial of authors in this respect was Ghent's contemporary, Peter John Olivi. Olivi's various discussions of the *Categories* are particularly striking for their hostility toward the whole Aristotelian project. Whereas even an iconoclast like Ockham is an enthusiastic supporter of Aristotle—once suitably interpreted—Olivi makes no effort either to be charitable or to bend Aristotle to his own purposes:

Some followers of Aristotle believe that he wanted the ten categories to be ten genera of things essentially distinct from one another. They accept that this is so as if it were a first principle, even though Aristotle is not found to have said much that implies that their essences are always   3 necessarily distinct—and much less is he found anywhere to have furnished any argument, necessary or probable, proving the distinction and number of the categories. For in the *Categories* he does nothing on this score but set out the various genera, as if whatever he   6 might say would count as known *per se*. Nor in the *Metaphysics* does he prove anything in this regard, but rather presupposes it as known. (*Summa* II.28, I:483–4)

Olivi is partly criticizing Aristotle for presupposing without argument his list of ten, and partly criticizing Aristotle's readers for treating the categories as ten kinds of "essentially distinct" things (lines 1–2). To say that the ten categories are essentially distinct is to say that the categories distinguish ten kinds of irreducible, basic entities. Olivi argues at some length that this is wrong, for every category other than Quality. Again we might focus on *Actio* and *Passio*, which Olivi understands in much the same way that Aquinas had, in terms of a change associated with either a patient or an agent. Those who criticize the essential-distinction view "marvel at how, given that the same effect is an action and a passion, distinct [only] in relation, he can take there to be two essentially distinct categories" (*Summa* II.28, I:489).

That Olivi puts this last criticism into the third-person singular illustrates how, instead of blaming this view on his contemporaries, and proposing his own reading of the *Categories*, Olivi focuses the blame squarely on Aristotle. Along with many other ancient philosophers, Aristotle "was deceived in arguing for essential diversity on the basis of a plurality of real *rationes*" (*Summa* II.14, I:264). This last remark points toward the most distinctive feature of Olivi's positive view, a feature that puts some distance between him and the nominalists. For whereas Ockham would eschew any alleged ontological commitments arising from the categorial scheme, in favor of a linguistic interpretation, Olivi contends that categories beyond Substance and Quality are metaphysically committing in a certain way. Although they do not categorize essentially distinct *res*, they do capture distinct *rationes reales*—appealing to that same slippery term 'ratio' that one finds in Ghent. So, instead of treating the categories as marking out distinctions among *res*, Olivi treats them as distinguishing *aspects* of reality: "They say that the number and differences among the categories are not in all cases derived from a real difference, but sometimes from merely a difference of real aspect, and so they say that the same thing according to different aspects can be in such categories at the same time" (*Summa* II.25, I:444). Such aspects are real inasmuch as they are mind-independent features of the world. For instance, in the case of relations,

It does not seem that a relation adds anything real to that on which it is founded, but only makes for (*dicit*) another real aspect belonging to the same thing. This aspect is *real* inasmuch as such an aspect of the relation exists *in re*, not solely in the intellect. But it is not really *another* in the sense of being another *res* or essence. . . . (*Summa* II.54, II:260)

To take a specific example, the similarity of one white thing to another is not a *res* added onto the thing's whiteness, but just an aspect of it. Quite generally, Olivi thinks we should understand the project of categorization in these terms. (The views I am ascribing to Olivi are in fact ones he always articulates in the third person plural, but at great length and with obvious enthusiasm. This is his general approach for setting out controversial theses, even in cases where the views he describes are quite obviously novel. When his views, including his theory of the categories, later came under censure [see below], Olivi is able to reply that "I have said nothing assertively about this, that I know of, although I did recite something to this effect, among many other opinions" [Laberge, "Tria scripta" n. 15, p. 130]. Without taking a stand on whether this sort of response is disingenuous, we can fairly speak of these ideas as Olivi's, thereby giving him the credit for first formulating them.)[18]

---

[18] Olivi is not perfectly explicit, so far as I have found, that he accepts quality and only quality as a real accident. Others, indeed, have read him differently. Courtenay describes Olivi as having accepted the reality of three categories: Substance, Quality, and Action ("Categories" p. 244). This characterization, however, is based solely on an accusation that Olivi categorically rejects, remarking: "Nec assertorie nec recitatorie omnino tale quid dixi" (*Epistola ad R.* n. 15, p. 57). It is, moreover, quite clear that this cannot be Olivi's view about Action, inasmuch as (a) actions and passions are understood reductively in terms of a relation between an agent, a patient, and a *motus* (*Summa* II.28, I:489); (b) relations are themselves understood reductively (see *Quod.* III.2 and *Summa* II.54, II:260–3); and (c) a *motus* is nothing more than the presence of one quality after another, or one location after another (where location is not a distinct category). For Olivi on location, see §17.5; for his views on motion, see Ch. 18 note 10. For Olivi on relations, see also the material from *Summa* Bk. I edited in Schmaus, *Liber Propugnatorius*, pt. II.1.

According to Pini, Olivi denies the reality of all nine accidental categories: "From the remark that categories are not always distinct things and essences, Olivi drew the conclusion that there is never an essential distinction among categories. Accordingly, the categories are to be seen not as a classification of the world into mind-independent kinds

Olivi's distinction between *rationes* and *res* leaves us with the same sort of interpretive puzzle that we face in the case of Ghent's contemporary work. One way to understand these aspects is as mere structures, so that, for instance, the difference between *actio* and *passio* amounts to nothing at all in the world beyond a difference in the structures we choose to pick out. Relations of similarity might be like that, too. Socrates may be really similar to Plato, in virtue of their both being pale, but there is nothing further in Socrates, beyond his skin color, in virtue of which he is similar to Plato. What there is is a structure, an isomorphism between the two, and we might well think of such structures as distinct in kind from the sorts of structures that characterize actions, which would in turn be distinct in kind from the structures that characterize passions. I have ascribed this sort of view to Aquinas, with regard at least to *Actio* and *Passio*, and to Ghent, with regard to all seven of the lesser categories. Possibly, this is Olivi's view too, but in his case there is strong evidence for thinking that he is committed to something beyond mere structures. In the passage just quoted, for instance, the sense in which aspects are not something in addition to whiteness is that they are not a further *res* (line 4). His desire to make these *rationes* into something real, but still not *res*, suggests that he is attempting to formulate a theory of the categories in terms of entities that fall in between mere structures and full-blown *res*. Indeed, as we will see in §13.2, Olivi is quite explicit in conceiving of these in-between entities as modes, which he understands as something that is not a real accident but yet is "added" to the substance. Understood in this way, Olivi's theory of *rationes* should be understood not as a reductive theory, and not as a version of the sort of minimal realism advocated by Ghent for the lesser seven categories, but as an attempt to describe a kind of entity that is neither substance nor real accident, but yet does really exist.

Even if Olivi treats some categories as containing entities of a diminished, modal sort, he does not take this approach all the way through the categorial scheme. Instead, in the case of some alleged categories, Olivi doubts whether there is even a distinct *ratio* to be found. This is true of Position (e.g., sitting, lying), which strikes Olivi as reducible to Where. Hence "they marvel at how it can be a category distinct from Where—I mean not only as distinct things (*secundum rem*), but even as distinct aspects (*secundum rationem*)" (*Summa* II.27, I:490). He makes the same criticism for *Actio* and *Passio*—not that they should be thought of as a single category, but that the sort of *ratio* involved here is the same as the *ratio* that characterizes the category of Relation (*Summa* II.25, I:444). These sorts of criticisms of Aristotle's categories distinguish him from Ghent's

but as a classification of our modes of describing the world according to distinct aspects (*rationes*) of the extramental things. So, Olivi applied to all categories what Henry of Ghent and Simon of Faversham said about the last seven non-absolute categories" ("Scotus's Realist Conception" p. 75). There is, however, no reason to think that Olivi wants to treat qualities reductively, and significant positive evidence that he accepts real accidents in the category of Quality. See, in particular, *Summa* II.28, I:487: "si enim quantitas est accidens, tunc oportet quod dicat quandam formam accidentalem absolutam; omnis autem forma talis videtur esse qualitas, quia per suam informationem reddit materiam talem vel talem"; *Tractatus de quantitate* ad 3, f. 51v: "Potest igitur dici quod si ratio quantitatis diceret unam solam essentiam essentialiter distinctam ab omnibus aliis, sicut videmus in substantia et qualitate...." Pini also seems wrong in treating Olivi as an anti-realist along the lines of Ghent with respect to all the lesser categories. This will become clearer in §13.2, in the context of Olivi's theory of modes.

For thoughts on Olivi's careful practice not to defend controversial views as his own, see Burr, "Olivi and the Limits of Freedom."

more realistic outlook. Whereas Ghent is prepared to defend the reality of all ten categories, at least in the minimal sense that each of the categories captures some metaphysical feature of reality, Olivi thinks that Aristotle's list of ten gets the metaphysics wrong. In this respect Olivi's views are even less realistic than the nominalists, inasmuch as they at least wish to preserve the ten categories, whereas Olivi thinks the list needs to be wholly rewritten in certain areas, and that Aristotle's authority should count for nothing.[19]

Olivi's views epitomize the many options that scholastic authors have in evaluating the Aristotelian categories. So far, we have seen five different sorts of views regarding how a given category should be understood:

1. As a distinct kind of *res* (a substance or a real accident);
2. As a distinct kind of *mode* (a real item in the world, but somehow not a *res*);
3. As a distinct kind of *structure* (a feature of reality, but not an item [*res* or *mode*] over and above the items in other categories);
4. As a distinct linguistic or conceptual kind;
5. As not a distinct kind at all, but wholly eliminable.

With these distinctions in mind, we can summarize the previous discussion as follows. Aquinas counts only substances as *res*. Some accidental categories—he is explicit about *Actio* and *Passio*, but one might wonder whether the point extends more widely—describe mere structures, whereas the remainder—including at least Quality and Quantity—fall roughly into the category of modes (§13.1). Ghent treats Substance, Quality, and Quantity as kinds of *res*—this is what puts him on the road to the doctrine of real accidents—and treats the remainder as kinds of structures. Olivi holds that Substance and Quality categorize *res*, and seems to treat Quantity, Relation, Where and When as kinds of modes (§13.2). Action, Passion, Position, and Having all seem to be treated eliminatively, as part of Aristotle's categorial scheme but no part of God's. The nominalist, finally, preserves the entirety of the categorial scheme, but does so by treating every category as merely linguistic or conceptual. Still, the nominalist may think that, as it happens, some of those categories correspond to real ontological divisions. Ockham, for instance, thinks that substances and qualities (the things, not the categories) are distinct *res*, although he generally shows no interest in metaphysical correlates for the other categories. (There is controversy over whether Ockham's ontology needs, in certain cases, to go beyond substance and quality; see §17.4 as well as Ch. 11 note 19 and note 8 above.)

---

[19] On Olivi's treatment of the categories as marking off *rationes reales*, see *Summa* II.14 (I:264–5), II.25 (I:444), II.28 (I:483–98), II.54 (II:260–3), II.58 (II:446), *Quod.* III.2, *Epistola ad R.* n. 15, pp. 57–8. For discussions of Olivi's category theory, see Boureau, "Concept de relation"; Burr, "Persecution" pp. 54–61 and "Quantity and Eucharistic Presence"; Pini, "Scotus's Realist Conception" pp. 74–7. On the condemnation of Olivi in 1283, with respect to the categories, see Bakker, *La raison* I:355–60. More generally, see Piron, *Parcours d'un intellectuel franciscain* pp. 35–56.

Olivi might seem to embrace nominalism at *Summa* II.13 (I:253), where he remarks that "Aristoteles in praedicamentalis sicut et in omnibus logicalibus multa tradit modo logicali et intentionali seu secundum modum intelligendi et loquendi plus quam modo reali et metaphysicali." He then uses this remark to downplay the ontological import of the doctrine of secondary substances. But this sort of comment on the *Categories*—treating it as a logical work—is standard among scholastic authors (see Pini, *Categories and Logic* passim). Moreover, Olivi does not here disavow all metaphysical commitments in the *Categories*, and clearly does not do so when actually discussing the categorial scheme.

12.5. Robust Category Realism: Scotus

There is still one development left to be explored in this overview of scholastic category theory, and that is the rise of robustly realistic interpretations of the categorial scheme. The theories so far canvassed all fall short of robust realism, inasmuch as they all deny that the categorial scheme describes ten irreducible kinds of basic entities. Minimally, then, a robustly realistic theory of the categories would have to accept the irreducibility of the ten categories, in the precise sense that each category contains a distinct kind of basic entity. (If one did not insist on this further precision, then both Aquinas and Ghent might be said, misleadingly, to embrace the irreducibility of all ten categories, inasmuch as each takes the categories to describe ten basic structures of reality.) Yet here right away we face the question of just what will count as robust realism. In light of the five-fold distinction of the previous section, we can distinguish between two ways of satisfying the above minimal requirement: either weakly, by treating all ten categories as describing either *res* or modes, or strongly, by treating the categories all the way through as a division among *res*. At first glance, there seem to be many examples of this last, maximally strong sort of view, but on closer inspection it becomes difficult to distinguish among views in this domain. Although it is not hard to find authors defending the doctrine that each category picks out a distinct kind of *res*, it is not always clear what exactly they mean by a *res*, and whether it is ultimately distinct from a mode. Pending a clearer account of the *res*–mode distinction—something I will attempt in the following chapter—the discussion here will have to be somewhat provisional.

The existence of a robustly realistic stance on the categories is well attested in scholastic texts. Peter of Candia, for instance, lecturing on Lombard's *Sentences* in Paris in 1379, contrasts the view of Ockham and "many modern doctors," who say that the only accidents are qualities, with the view of "the Subtle Doctor and many ancient doctors," that "to every accidental category there naturally corresponds some positive *res* really distinct from a *res* in any other category." (Characteristically, Candia declines to take a stand, wryly recommending the realist view to those who wish to be liberal, and the nominalist view to those who are inclined to be harsh.) So Candia takes the realist camp as holding that each of the ten categories contains *res* distinct from *res* in every other category.[20] Suárez, as usual, offers a more fine-grained set of choices, distinguishing between three forms of realism: one that posits a real distinction between items in each of the ten categories; another that allows a mere modal distinction between some categories; and a third that allows some of the categories to be distinct merely rationally (that is, conceptually), so long as there is a foundation in reality. Suárez characterizes the second view as *valde communis*, highly popular, but does not associate it with any particular philosopher. He himself defends the third view (§13.3), and ascribes

---

[20] Peter of Candia describes robust category realism as follows: "Secunda opinio...ponit quod cuilibet praedicamento sub ambitu accidentis correspondet ex natura rei res aliqua positiva a re alterius praedicamenti realiter condistincta....Et istius opinionis videtur fuisse Doctor Subtilis et multi antiqui doctores" (*Sent.* II.1.2, in Bakker, *La raison* I:424 n. 316). "Sic igitur apparet imaginatio antiquorum doctorum. Si vultis esse liberales, ista opinio vobis porrigit multitudinem copiosam; si vero amari, praecedens opinio vobis profert pauca et minus scrupulosa; utraque opinio est multorum venerabilium doctorum" (ibid., I:425 n. 320).

it to, among many others, Aquinas and Ghent (quite rightly, as I have argued). The first view is the one I am describing as maximally robust category realism.[21]

Scotus is undoubtedly the principal authority for views of this last sort. One might well think there are earlier precedents. In a 1283 condemnation of Olivi, for instance, a group of seven Franciscan theologians conclude that "to say that the categories are not really distinct is contrary to the Philosopher, and is especially dangerous in the cases of Quantity and Relation" (Fussenegger, "Littera" n. 16). Olivi himself seems to acknowledge this as the orthodox view: his discussions of the categories repeatedly distinguish between the sort of view he favors and a view on which the ten categories are "essentially distinct," by which he might seem to mean a view on which the ten categories mark off ten distinct kinds of res. It is not clear, however, who the proponents of this sort of view are supposed to be in the earlier part of the thirteenth century, given the deflationary character of most earlier views. As I have suggested already, the debate over the categories comes into focus only once one articulates a theory of real accidents, which is a development that takes place only with Scotus. Inasmuch as earlier authors want to insist on the reality of all ten categories, and a real distinction among them, I suspect they mean to insist only that each category has a distinct foundation in reality, whether that foundation be res, mode, or structure.

It is only with Scotus, then, that one finds the conceptual framework that makes it possible to formulate the doctrine of robust category realism. According to Scotus, the ten categories are not merely distinct according to distinct modes of predicating, but "distinct essentially" and "distinct formally" (In Meta. V.5–6 nn. 56, 81). This is the same sort of language that Olivi had already attacked, but now it comes attached to a worked-out theory of what an accident is. Hereafter, the view begins to attract other distinguished proponents. Walter Burley defends it in his 1337 commentary on the ars vetus, arguing against "certain moderns" (that is, Ockham) who distinguish only Substance and Quality, in favor of the view that the ten categories are "really distinct" (In Praed. f. d1ra), and that the categorial scheme divides res rather than words (f. c6vb). Paul of Venice, another notable late medieval realist, writing in 1408, likewise speaks in this context of a real distinction: relations are really distinct from their foundations

---

[21] Suárez distinguishes between the three versions of category realism as follows: "Dicunt ergo aliqui, ad distinguenda genera accidentium, necessariam esse mutuam realem distinctionem rerum sub illis generibus contentarum" (Disp. meta. 39.2.19); "Secunda sententia, et valde communis, esse videtur saltem esse necessariam distinctionem modalem inter diversa genera accidentium" (ibid., par. 20); "Est ergo tertia opinio, quae ad praedicamentorum distinctionem sufficere censet distinctionem ex modo concipiendi nostro fundato in re, quae a quibusdam vocatur distinctio rationis ratiocinatae, ab aliis appellatur distinctio formalis" (ibid., par. 22). Suárez does not mention Scotus at all in this connection, perhaps because he feels unsure whether Scotus belongs in the first or second category. The only reference to a defender of the first view is a marginal reference to Paul of Venice, Summa phil. nat. VI.31 (misprinted in the 1866 edition as ch. 21). I take it that Suárez himself is responsible for the marginalia in the 1596 edition. Generally, however, the 1866 edition mangles those marginal annotations quite badly, either printing them as footnotes or else positioning them in italics at the start of a paragraph, and in the process often so misplacing them as to render them quite unintelligible. Sadly, modern translations have generally followed the later edition. Serious work on Suárez should at least consult the earlier edition.

For a similarly unsympathetic reference to robust categorial realism, see De Soto, In Praed. 6.2, p. 181: "Haud nos latet quam sit persuasu⟨m⟩ difficile, omnia decem praedicamenta sic esse realiter distincta, ut ex realibus multi videntur contendere: nempe quod distinguantur omnia sicut albedo distinguitur a substantia, quam in sacramento altaris sine substantia certo credimus existere. Quinetiam mihi nunquam persuasum erit relationem et sex ultima praedicamenta hoc modo a substantia esse realiter distincta."

(*Summa philosophiae naturalis* VI.24, f. 111rab); *actio* is really distinct from *passio* (VI.31, f. 116vb); and so on.[22]

With this we would seem to have the tradition that Candia and Suárez both invoke, the maximally realist view according to which each of the ten categories describe independent, really distinct *res*. Here, however, is where the puzzles really begin. For although it is easy to find later scholastic authors asserting a real distinctness between accidents in all ten categories, such authors do not endorse the sort of independence for accidents that one might suppose would follow. As the following chapter will discuss, standard theories of distinctions (as found, e.g., in Suárez and later in Descartes) hold that a real distinction is said to obtain between two things that can each exist without the other. For Scotus, however (as §11.3 already noted in passing), a real distinction requires only that one of the pair be able to exist without the other. A relation is distinct from its foundation, for instance, because the foundation (say, whiteness) can continue to exist while its subject is first similar to another thing and then dissimilar (as that other thing goes from being white to black) (*In Meta.* V.5–6 n. 91). Yet, although the quality whiteness can exist without the similarity relation, Scotus explicitly holds that the similarity relation cannot exist without some foundation.[23] Burley's position is in this regard just the same. A relation is really distinct from its foundation because the latter can exist without the former. But this does not mean that relations can exist apart from their foundations. On the contrary, relations of equality or inequality require quantities, and likeness and unlikeness requires quality. In general, "a relation inheres in a substance only mediated by some more perfect accident" (*In art. vet.* [*In Praed.*] f. e6vb). Hence for both Scotus and Burley, some categorial items are not really distinct in the sense of being capable of existence apart from their subjects. Indeed, despite how category realism is commonly described by both its advocates and its critics, there seems to be no scholastic author who supposes that accidents in every category are capable of independent existence.

---

[22] For another statement of Scotus's realism, see *In Praed.* 11.26: "Dicendum quod tantum sunt decem generalissima rerum, quorum distinctio non sumitur penes aliquid logicum tantum, sed penes ipsas essentias."

Another clear case of robust category realism in Scotus's tradition is that of Petrus Thomae (*circa* 1320), e.g., "omnia praedicamenta distinguuntur sicut res et res" (ed. Bos, "Petrus Thomae" p. 307). Wyclif is another category realist, though of an attenuated sort, since none of his inherent accidents are *res*, but instead mere modes (§11.1): "quantitas, qualitas, relatio et cetera genera convenientia in eodem subiecto singulari sunt omnia idem subiecto singulari, licet in suis naturis different in genere" (*Tract. de univ.* 4, p. 91). See Conti, "Wyclif's Logic and Metaphysics" p. 86: "Wyclif's (metaphysical) world consists of molecular objects, that is, singular items classified into ten different types or categories."

On later scholastic category realism in general, see the groundbreaking work of Conti, who has studied in detail how the realist tradition of Burley gets taken up by what he calls the Oxford Realists, especially Wyclif, Robert Alyngton, and Paul of Venice (who studied at Oxford). See, for instance, most recently, "A Realist Interpretation." For an extended discussion of Scotus's importance for realist theories of the categories, see Pini, "Scotus's Realist Conception." On Burley's significance, see again Conti, "Ontology in Walter Burley" and "Walter Burley." Pini and Conti both characterize Scotus and Burley as defending an earlier tradition of category realism, but without making it very clear what constitutes that tradition. For Pini, the 1283 condemnation of Olivi "should probably be considered as the first self-conscious statement of a realist interpretation of the categories in the thirteenth century" (p. 76). I myself also cannot find anything earlier, but still Pini's claim would be surprising, given that Olivi himself repeatedly acknowledges this sort of realism. Conti speaks of the "Boethian tradition, according to which the ten categories correspond to ten distinct kinds of things," and lists Albert the Great, Thomas of Sutton, Simon of Faversham, and Scotus as adherents prior to Burley ("Ontology in Walter Burley" p. 146). I have not found clear evidence, however, that any of these authors (other than Scotus) adhere to any form of what I am calling robust realism. (Indeed, in a more recent work, Conti includes Faversham among reductionists like Ghent ["A Realist Interpretation" p. 318].)

[23] See *Ord.* IV.12.1 (Wadding VIII nn. 5, 8); *Ord.* II.1.4–5 (Vat. VII n. 269); *Lec.* II.1.4–5 (Vat. XVIII n. 253); *Quod.* III.3 nn. 46–7; *In De an.* q. 7.

The puzzle, in short, concerns why Scotus, Burley, and others insist on a real distinction between all ten categories, when in effect they seem to be treating the lesser categories as mere modes. Suárez, as we have seen, tells us that these are two different kinds of views, but he does not offer much help on who the proponents of these two views are, and on close inspection it is hard to find anyone who wants to maintain the maximally realistic view. This is so even for Scotus, the supposed champion of robust category realism. In his *Quodlibetal Questions* (1306/7), he distinguishes three different senses of 'res' (III.1.7–14). In one sense, most broadly, a *res* is anything that is not nothing, by which he means anything that does not include a contradiction. (This would include the sorts of *possibilia* and other beings of reason that earlier we saw to be excluded from the categorial scheme.) In another sense, most strictly, a *res* is a substance. In between these two extremes is a meaning of *res* that he ascribes to Boethius, and that can best be appreciated in light of what Boethius himself had said in his *De trinitate*:

> Is it not now clear what the difference is between items in the categories? Some serve to refer to a thing (*res*), whereas others serve to refer to the circumstances of a thing. The first are predicated so as to show that a thing is something, the others not that it is something, but instead they attach something extrinsic in a certain way. (ch. 4 [*Theol. Tractates* pp. 22–4])

According to Boethius, those categorial items that refer to a thing are substances, qualities, and quantities, whereas the remaining categories concern merely "the circumstances" of a thing. Scotus reads this passage as marking the distinction between *res* and mode. Only entities in the categories of Substance, Quantity, or Quality count as *res*, whereas items in the remaining categories are mere modes. On the strength of this distinction, Scotus goes on to argue that relations are *res* in the first and weakest sense, and yet not *res* at all in the second and third senses, but merely modes. Paul of Venice cites the same passage, as a potential counter-argument to his claim that relations should count as *res*. In reply he makes the same move as Scotus:

> If one uses *res* strictly, as it is applied only to absolute beings, then the seven relative categories are not *res* but only modes or circumstances of things. . . . But if one uses *res* as equivalent with 'being' taken transcendentally, in a broad manner of speaking, then all the categories are *res*. (*Summa phil. nat.* VI.25, f. 112rb)

This is the same view that had appeared in Scotus and Burley: that only items in the first three categories are *res* in the strictest sense, things capable of independent existence apart from their subjects.

What then is this Boethian-inspired view? To be sure, it is a much stronger form of realism than Henry of Ghent's, even if like Ghent it insists that only items in the first three categories are *res* properly speaking. This is easy to see, because as it happens Ghent too discusses the above-quoted passage from Boethius. Whereas Scotus and Paul of Venice take it as a license to distinguish two senses in which accidents are things, Ghent takes it as support for his view that the lesser seven categories are not entities at all. Thus he glosses the passage from Boethius as showing that these categories "do not imply anything's inhering in creatures" (*Summa* 32.5, *Opera* XXVII:93). What distinguishes the later tradition of category realism made prominent by Scotus and Burley is their conviction that items in all ten categories are things of some kind, irreducible to other things, and inhering in substances.

Hence these authors are defending some form of robust realism, as defined at the start of this section. But the view is not as robust as it initially seems. For even these most robust of realists want to distinguish between *entia absoluta* (absolute beings, in the categories of Substance, Quantity, and Quality) and *entia respectiva* (relative beings in the remaining categories), whose existence is dependent on items in the first three categories. Hence this view lends itself to the sort of caricature offered by Ockham, who describes the "moderns" as adhering to the view that for each of the categories there are corresponding *parvae res*, "little things" (*Quod.* V.22, *Opera theol.* IX:564–5). This is derisive, to be sure, but it is also a fair statement of how category realism took shape in the fourteenth century. No one was so bold as to say that items in every category are fully separable *res*, but yet Scotus and others still want to insist that they are things in some sense.[24]

In light of the increasing importance that modes take on in the later scholastic tradition, and in the seventeenth century, what we want to know is whether these *parvae res* count as modes or as real accidents, or perhaps as entities of still another sort, in between the two. Given that there was no well-established theory of modes in the thirteenth century, it is no surprise that Scotus and others do not provide a clear answer to this question. It is now time, though, to attempt an answer ourselves, by directly addressing the difficult but extremely important question of what authors at the end of our period are talking about when they talk about modes. To summarize what is to come: the idea of a class of accidents with diminished reality runs through the whole scholastic period, appearing in one form in Aquinas and other thirteenth-century deflationists, and eventually in another form in Suárez and Descartes. Scotus's labeling of the lesser accidents as modes was perhaps influential on these developments, but Scotus cannot really be considered a part of that movement. His so-called modes are in fact real accidents, and so Scotus's form of robust realism is indeed a theory on which accidents in all ten categories are *res*, really distinct from one another.

---

[24] For Scotus on non-absolute accidents as modes, see *Quod.* III.1.12. "Secundo modo, accipit Boethius distinguendo rem contra modum rei, sicut loquitur libro *De trinitate*. . . .Vult ergo distinguere rem contra circumstantiam, et sic, secundum eum, sola tria genera, substantia, qualitas et quantitas, rem monstrant, alia vero rei circumstantias. Hoc ergo nomen 'res,' in secundo membro acceptum, dicit aliquod ens absolutum, distinctum contra circumstantiam sive modum, qui dicit habitudinem unius ad alterum." I have oversimplified Scotus's remarks about *res* in the broadest sense, which he further distinguishes into (a) anything at all that is intelligible and (b) anything that is intelligible as existing outside the soul. The crucial question about the category of Relation—which is the topic at issue in *Quod.* III—is whether it is a *res* in sense (b). For other passages where Scotus accepts the characterization of non-absolute accidents as modes, see *Ord.* II.1.4–5 (Vat. VII nn. 215, 228); *Lec.* II.1.4–5 (Vat. XVIII nn. 188–9, 198, 210); *Quod.* III.2 n. 31.

On the *absoluta–respectiva* distinction, see Scotus, e.g., *Ord.* IV.12.1 (Wadding VIII n. 5); Burley, *In art. vet.* (*In Praed.*) f. f1rb: "fundamentum relationis est res absoluta quae per se potest instituere intellectum. Sed relatio est res respectiva quae non potest intelligi nisi in habitudine ad aliud." The distinction is commonplace before Scotus. For an early statement, see Albert the Great, *In Praed* I.7 (Jammy I:104ab). It also appears, e.g., in James of Viterbo, *Quod.* II.1, pp. 8–9, where quantities and qualities are the only absolute accidents, and so the only ones that can exist without a subject. See also Richard of Middleton: "Dicendum ergo quod, extendendo nomen 'accidentis' ad omne illud quod nec est substantia nec pars substantiae, quaedam sunt accidentia quae non sunt nisi respectus, et quaedam de quorum ratione est res absoluta et respectus (sicut simitas), et quaedam de quorum essentia nihil est nisi absolutum" (*Sent.* IV.12.1.1, IV:150a). This leads to his main conclusion, which is that absolute accidents—quantities and qualities—are separable, by the power of God, from their subjects. Middleton's discussion is particularly interesting, in the present context, because it begins with an objection that treats accidents as modes: "Impossibile est habitudinem seu modum separari a re cuius est; sed accidentia sunt quidam modi seu habitudines substantiae; ergo impossibile est accidentia a substantia separari" (ibid., IV:149a). Middleton simply denies the minor premise: "Ad primum in oppositum dicendum quod minor est falsa, nisi accipiatur 'modus' secundum quod comprehendit sub se non tantum modum se habendi ad alium, sed etiam dispositionem substantiae secundum seipsam" (ibid., IV:150a). This suggests that 'modus' is appropriately used only of relative accidents. It is unclear to me, however, whether Middleton takes the sort of robustly realist position on these relative categories that Scotus and others would later take.

13

Modes

13.1. Overview

If we set to one side the many mind-numbing intricacies of the metaphysical debates that run through our four centuries, and ask ourselves where the Aristotelians and their critics most crucially agree and disagree, the answer is plain. By far the most significant point of agreement is that what primarily exist are substances, enduring through time as the subjects of the changeable properties we perceive through the senses. By far the most significant point of disagreement concerns the status of these changeable properties: are they real accidents, or are they mere modes of substance? Although there were of course many other quite fundamental metaphysical disagreements during the period, this and the next ten chapters will make clear just how much depends on the status of accidents.

It would be convenient if all the scholastics believed that all accidents are real, and if their opponents all believed instead that all accidents are mere modes. Alas, the situation is far more complex. On one side, it is easy to find scholastic authors from the very start of our period treating at least some accidents, if not all, as modes. On the other side, although post-scholastic authors quite uniformly describe accidents as modes, it is far from clear what exactly they mean. For some, such talk seems to be wholly reductive: just a way of signaling that all there really are in the world are substances, variously modified. For others, modes seem to be a distinct category in their ontology. The focus of this chapter will be on the modal realists, setting aside those authors who speak of modes reductively. To use again the terminology of the previous chapter, I am distinguishing between *modes*, understood as things in some sense, and *structures*, understood as ontologically innocent ways in which things are.

There are so many different and overlapping sources for the doctrine of modes that it seems hopeless to give a precise account of its origins, and probably would have seemed hopeless to anyone at the time. Talk of modes plays a role in speculative grammar, for instance, and in the analysis of syncategorematic terms, as well as in discussions from natural philosophy of how qualitative forms can be more or less intense.[1] Probably the central strand of development, however, is that described over

---

[1] For speculative grammar, with its connection between *modi significandi* and *modi essendi*, see, e.g., Pinborg, "Speculative Grammar," esp. pp. 262–3. On syncategorematic terms, see Peter of Spain's claim that they signify not

the last three chapters. As we have seen, Albert the Great describes accidents as modes in the 1260s, and Aquinas, soon after, proposes distinguishing the ten categories in terms of ten distinct modes of being (*modi essendi*). After Henry of Ghent, the phrase *modi essendi* becomes associated especially with the seven lesser categories, leaving items in the categories of Substance, Quality, and Quantity to be identified as *res*. Once Scotus's theory of real accidents becomes ascendant, the debate over the status of the categories can be understood as a debate over whether all nine accidental categories describe *res*—fully real and distinct things—or whether some of them describe mere modes of *res*.[2]

Generalizing, we might say that from the earliest Latin attempts to understand Aristotelian hylomorphism there was a concern with describing a halfway sort of existence associated with certain accidents. On the earliest, deflationary accounts, such halfway existence was associated with all the accidents, whereas after 1274 only items in the lesser, "relative" categories were characterized in this way. When accidents are so understood, the question inevitably arises of what it could possibly mean to speak of a thing as having diminished existence. Insofar as we understand existence at

---

things but instead *modi essendi* (see Klima, "Peter of Spain" p. 530). For the suggestion of a link between the theory of modes and the intension and remission of forms, see Normore, "Accidents and Modes" p. 683, who would seem to have Scotus in mind (see note 11 below).

[2] For other early scholastic examples of the *res*–mode distinction, see Nicholas of Strasbourg, *Summa phil.*: "Dicendum est enim quod res dupliciter potest accipi. . . . Uno enim modo dicitur res omne illud quod non est nihil. . . . Alio modo dicitur res proprie, secundum quod distinguitur contra modum rei . . ." (in Imbach, "Metaphysik" p. 363 n. 22); Alexander of Alexandria, *Quod.* q. 6: "de accidentibus enim respectivis, quae sunt sex, puta quae magis dicunt modum rei quam rem, satis videtur manifestum quod non possunt fieri sine subiecto, alias fierent sine suo essentiali. . . . Sua enim essentialitas est quod sint . . . modificationes rerum" (in Amerini, "Alessandro" p. 207 n. 66); James of Viterbo, distinguishing absolute and respective absolutes, remarks that the latter cannot exist without a subject, not even by divine power, because "haec enim accidentia non dicunt rem, sed modum rei" (*Quod.* II.1, p. 8)—in contrast, for James, color and other such qualities are *res* rather than *modi essendi* (ibid., p. 18); Dietrich of Freiberg, *De accidentibus* 17.9 (*Opera* III:77): "Concluditur ergo ex inductis quod accidens non est nisi quidam modus seu dispositio substantiae, et hoc est essentia eius in eo, quod ipsum est ens, nec habet aliquam essentiam absolutae quidditatis secundum se ipsum"; Auriol (*Sent.* IV.12.1.1, III:110aA) criticizes the strategy of accounting for inherence in terms of a mode rather than a relational accident; Franciscus de Prato (1330s), *Logica* I.5.1, p. 381: "Hic tamen nota quod 'res' potest accipi dupliciter. Uno modo proprie et stricte, scilicet pro ipsa essentia reali. Et isto modo accipiendo 'rem,' illa dicuntur distingui realiter quae dicunt plures essentias intrinse distinctas realiter. Et isto modo non distinguuntur realiter omnia praedicamenta, sed solum tria praedicamenta isto modo distinguuntur realiter, scilicet substantia, quantitas, et qualitas. Alio modo accipitur 'res' communiter et large non solum pro ipsa essentia, sed pro modo essendi sive pro modo reali ipsius essentiae. Potest enim una res habere diversos modos reales secundum quod res potest diversimode exigere et connotare aliam rem. Et isto modo accipiendo 'rem,' non oportet quod illa quae distinguuntur realiter habeant diversas essentias vel quod differant realiter intrinsice, Et isto modo distinguuntur septem ultima praedicamenta . . . ." None of these authors say enough to make it clear whether their talk of modes should be understood realistically or reductively.

A particularly interesting early case is Durand of St. Pourçain, who distinguishes between absolute and relative (*respectivum*) accidents, in such a way that only the former count as *res* "per prius et simpliciter" (see also Ch. 11 note 2). On the other hand, "res dicitur . . . per posterius autem et secundum quid de respectu, qui non est res nisi quia est realis modus essendi; unde habet minimum de entitate, quia est solum modus entitatis" (*Sent.* I.30.2 n. 15, I:84vb). In a subsequent discussion, however, this talk of modes gets developed not along the realist lines that are the focus of this chapter, but in the sort of deflationary way considered in §10.2, such that modes exist only in the sense that their subject exists: "respectus autem et universaliter omnes modi essendi sunt entia quia entis, non solum concomitative sed quidditative et formaliter, quia nullam entitatem habent nisi hanc quae est esse huius." In contrast, absolute accidents have their own existence: "verbi gratia albedo quae est esse huius ut subiecti, puta cygni, est aliquid esssentialiter praeter esse huius, quia esse huius non est eius essentia, sed modus essendi. . . . Sed essentia vel quidditas seu entitas horum modorum tota consistit in hoc quod est esse huius" (*Sent.* I.33.1 n. 15, I:89rv).

all, it hardly seems to be the sort of thing that admits of degrees. What exists, wholly exists, and what does not exist, does not exist at all. So one might suppose, at any rate, if not for this pervasive tradition of locating certain accidents in this dubious region of gray.

There seem to be two basic scholastic strategies for explaining the diminished existence of certain accidents. One strategy, formulated quite explicitly by Aquinas (§10.2), treats accidents as entities of a lesser sort inasmuch as they lack any existence of their own. This strategy of treating a thing as distinct from its existence, which Aquinas similarly applies to prime matter (§3.1), has interesting implications for substantial unity and the relationship of a whole to its parts, as we will see in §26.5. On its face, however, the doctrine looks quite obscure, inasmuch as it seems to separate the question of what things there are (substances, forms, prime matter, etc.) from the question of what things exist (substances). The second basic strategy understands accidents to exist in a lesser way inasmuch as their existence depends on something else. That is, such lesser accidents exist in their own right, but cannot exist apart from their subject. One great advantage of this way of proceeding is that it is less obscure, inasmuch as we have some sense of what it means for one thing to be separable from another. A disadvantage, however, is that it is unclear what this sort of dependence has to do with having a diminished ontological status.

Although there are no easy generalizations that can be drawn here, the overall trajectory of the debate runs from a long unsettled period during which there was no fixed technical sense of mode, toward an increasing consensus that modes are to be understood as real and distinct entities in the second of the above ways: as depending on their subjects in a way that makes them somehow less real and less distinct. This is how the notion of *mode* tends in general to develop, but unfortunately there is no point during our four centuries where a given usage becomes canonical. Since '*modus*' is simple the ordinary Latin word for *way*, it is often difficult to tell whether an author is simply speaking casually about the way something is, or whether "the way" is to be taken with full metaphysical rigor, as a thing in its own right. As our period develops, '*modus*' becomes more entrenched as a technical term, but even then talk of modes remains equivocal between various more or less realistic senses. In contrast to a term like 'substance,' whose meaning remains roughly constant throughout our period (see Part II of this study), one cannot take for granted, at any point, that 'mode' is being used in any particular way. All one can do is go case by case, looking carefully at how individual authors employ the concept.

Here, then, I will begin by looking at several isolated cases where modes are being treated with ontological seriousness. These treatments, as we will see, anticipate the decisive contribution of Suárez, who explicitly formulates a realistic conception of modes and gives them a central role in his metaphysics. Suárez's treatment in turn shapes the main seventeenth-century line of thought regarding modes, most prominently Descartes's. After working through all this material, I will attempt to address the most difficult questions of all: what is a mode, and what does it mean for a mode to exist but in a lesser way than substances or real accidents exist?

13.2. Modal Realism: Olivi and Oresme

Talk of modes does not take on the technical precision of a theory until the late sixteenth century. Throughout the first of our four centuries, however, one can find authors here and there who use 'mode' in the sort of ontologically committing way that would eventually become so important. I have already discussed the case of Peter Auriol (§11.4), who without using the term 'mode' offers what is nevertheless a theory of this sort, in order to account for how accidents inhere in their subject. Another case considered briefly above is John Wyclif (§11.1), whose opposition to real accidents manifests itself as a theory of modes—a term he uses repeatedly to capture the sort of deflationary account he seeks to revive.[3] Here, I will focus on two other figures, Peter John Olivi and Nicole Oresme.

Olivi is the first scholastic author I have found to set out a theory of modes as an ontological category distinct from both substances and accidents. That this is his view is not at all clear from most of his discussions of the categories, where—as we saw in the previous chapter—he tends not to use the term 'mode,' preferring instead to distinguish between the view that the categories distinguish between things that are essentially distinct, and the weaker view that he himself defends, that they mark merely distinct real aspects of things (*rationes reales*). Taken on its own, it is not clear whether such aspects are ontologically innocent structures, or whether they are modes in an ontologically committing sense. In other places, however, Olivi makes clear his commitment to an ontology of modes. In his *Tractatus de quantitate* (1282), for instance, he writes that "quantity is not a kind of absolute form or essence, but only a kind of actual mode of being, since it cannot in any way without contradiction be or be brought about without some absolute essence to which it belongs and in which it is grounded" (f. 52vb). Expanding on that passage in an analytical table of contents that accompanies this treatise, he considers whether this conception of mode violates a dictum that Olivi himself elsewhere accepts, that every accident can exist apart from its subject, at least by the power of God. He responds that "I would want to be understood to have made use of such claims only against those who do not distinguish between accidents that are absolute forms and essences, and accidents that are only actual modes of being" (f. 63vc). These passages are remarkable because they clearly distinguish between accidents, which are separable from their subjects, and modes, which are a kind of accident but yet, in virtue of their inseparability, are not real accidents. Olivi goes on in this same passage to give two other examples of modes: spatial location and the arrangement of a thing's integral parts.[4] Elsewhere, as we will see in §17.5, he also treats temporal location as a mode.

---

[3] For Wyclif, in addition to the passages quoted in §11.1, see *De actibus animae* II.4, p. 123: "illa non habendat in superfluis, cum ponit omnem rem esse substantiam, et accidentia esse modos substantiarum"; ibid., p. 127: "accidentia, quae sunt modi subiectorum . . . "; *De eucharistia* ch. 3, p. 63: "omne accidens formaliter inhaerens substantiae non est nisi veritas quae est substantiam esse accidentaliter alicuius modi, ut hic supponitur, sed nulla talis veritas potest esse sine substantia."

[4] It is not perfectly clear how to read this particular passage. Here is how it is printed in the 1509 edition: "huiusmodi accidentia quae tantum dicunt actuales modos essendi quale est: ubi: vel esse: hoc vel ibi vel contactus seu contiguitas duorum se tangentium aut unio continuitatis partium et consimilia non possunt fieri absque hiis quorum sunt" (*Tractatus de quantitate*, tabula f. 63vc). This could be read as describing as many as five different modes, but I think Olivi in fact means to describe only two: the location of a thing and the arrangement of its parts.

There can be no doubt that for Olivi these modes are something beyond the substance itself, because he argues that they are "something added" to the substance. Consider this passage, which takes up two objections to his account of angels as having spatial location in virtue of having a certain *modus essendi*:

You might object to this argument by saying that being in a corporeal location (*loco*) does not add anything to the *res* that is located, or to its being in itself, because if it were added, then [1] it seems [a] that what is added could miraculously be made by God without that *res*, and also [b] that the *res* could be made by God without any such accident and so without any such location; and [2] it seems that what is added would be a quality, from which it would follow that local motion (motion to somewhere) would be the motion of alteration. To this it should be said that where (or being here or there) does add something to the *res* that is here or there, but not something that should be called a quality or a form that is absolute (or absolutely applying to its subject). Instead, it is a thoroughly relational mode of being, which is called location or situation. (*Summa* II.32, I:586)

Olivi is imagining an objector (such as Ghent or, later, Ockham) who would favor a reductive account of the category of Where. Both of the objections take for granted that what is added will be a real accident, separable from its subject. Objection 1, at lines 2–4, points to the absurdity of (a) a where without a subject, and (b) a subject without a where. (On the absurdity of the latter, see §16.3.) Objection 2, at lines 5–6, further takes for granted something that Olivi himself believes, that the only real accidents are qualities (§12.4). But if locomotion involves the gain and loss of a quality, then we lose the standard Aristotelian distinction between locomotion and alteration. Olivi's reply is to deny that what is added, when a thing acquires a new spatial location, is a real accident. Instead, it is a mode. (It is less clear whether Olivi's real accidents, in the category of Quality, are real in the precise sense described in §10.4. Plainly, though, his distinction between modes and accidents requires treating accidents far more realistically than is standard in the thirteenth century. We will encounter evidence of Olivi's realism regarding accidents again in §14.1.)

Olivi goes on, following the passage just quoted, to offer his most detailed extant account of modes, by way of explaining exactly why a mode does not face the absurdities described above in objection 1:

As for what is said against this—that God could miraculously [a] make a where without a *res* that is located, and [b] make that *res* without any where—it should be said (as has been shown elsewhere more fully [loc. unknown]) that [ad a] these accidents are actual and correlative modes of being in such a way that they necessarily include in their meaning or character the actual existence of their subject. Such accidents cannot, without contradiction, be made without a subject. And [ad b] although the subject does not depend on its accident, as if it were conserved

---

For Olivi on quantity as a mode, see also *Summa* IV.11 (in Maier, "Das Problem der Quantität" p. 168): "accidentia alia non possunt esse sine quantitate eadem ratione qua nec substantia corporalis potest sine illa esse, cuius altera duarum causarum dare oportet: aut quia scilicet quaelibet essentia corporalis habet propriam extensionem nil aliud dicentem nisi partes illius essentiae prout sunt in situ diverso continuare, aut quia ipsa quantitas dicit quendam modum existendi, a cuius totali genere non potest aliquid corporale abstrahi, quamvis posset abstrahi a quocumque particulari ipsius." It is unclear whether relations can be modes. In *Quod.* III.2, he gives a negative answer to the question "An relatio addat aliquid realiter differens ab illo in quo immediate fundatur." As the wording of the question suggests, however, and as the text itself confirms, Olivi means to deny only that a relation is a *res* really distinct from its foundation. Unfortunately, he does not there offer any positive account of what relations are.

by it, still a subject is limited by its species to certain modes of being and standing disposed (*se habendi*). This is so inasmuch as such subjects cannot, without contradiction, be put into existence without some such accident, although they could without this or that one. (Ibid., I:586–7)

Predictably, in response to (a), he insists on the feature of modes we saw him stress earlier, that they are dependent on their subjects. Here, however, in response to objection (b), Olivi adds a further feature of modes, that they are properties of a subject such that the subject must have some one instance of their kind, although not any determinate one. In this case, a *res* must be somewhere, although not anywhere in particular. For short, I will say that modes *depend* on their subjects, inasmuch as they cannot exist without their subject, and also that they *determine* their subjects, inasmuch as the subject of a mode must possess one or another mode from certain determinable classes. Among later authors, as we will see, both determinacy and dependency are defining characteristics of modes.[5]

Another interesting example of modal realism can be found in the early work of Nicole Oresme. His *Physics* commentary (*circa* 1346) makes the remarkable proposal that accidents in all nine categories should be understood as modes rather than "true forms."[6] In one respect, this is a more radical proposal than Olivi's, because it denies to quality the status of a real accident (§19.3). In another respect, however, the proposal is less radical, or at any rate less austere, because it leads Oresme to countenance a much wider ontology than Olivi would tolerate, including not just items in all ten categories, but also *res successiva*, entities that wholly exist only over time, rather than wholly at any one time (Ch. 18). For now, however, let us focus simply on Oresme's account of what a mode is.

Oresme prefaces his discussion by stressing how useful it is to consider opposing viewpoints. In that spirit—"not asserting that the following opinion is true, but open to the correction of others"—he offers his unorthodox view. First, he offers the standard account of what a substance is, and then this striking account of three ways of understanding accidents:

It should secondly be noted that an accident can be conceived of in three ways:
In one way, an accident can be conceived of as a true form inhering in a substance, like a substantial form (although not intrinsically in such a way that it is a demonstrated true essence), divisible and extended with the extension of its subject and properly signifiable by a substantial term, as is conceived to be so in the case of whiteness.

3

---

[5] The great Anneliese Maier has documented Olivi's commitment to modes in a series of works to which I am much indebted. See "Das Problem der Quantität" pp. 159–75; "An der Schwelle" pp. 355–62; "Die naturphilosophische Bedeutung" I:358–61 [tr. Sargent, pp. 82–5]; "Bewegung ohne Ursache" pp. 290–325. Maier remarks that, although Olivi comes back "immer wieder" to the question of modes, he does so "ohne jemals eine präzise ontologische Definition oder Analyse dieser *modi* zu geben" ("Das Problem der Quantität" p. 170). This is perhaps fair, inasmuch as Olivi's discussions are scattered and unsystematic, but at the same time I think that he does manage to identify quite precisely the distinctive features of modes.

[6] I am indebted to Stefan Kirschner and his collaborators for a copy of their forthcoming edition of Oresme's *Physics* commentary. There is already a considerable literature on Oresme's use of modes in this text, in particular a series of works by Stefano Caroti. A good place to begin is Caroti's "Nicole Oresme et les *modi rerum*," along with the other papers found in that same volume, and the collection of papers in Caroti and Celeyrette, *Quia inter doctores*. On the dating of the commentary to before 1347, and its relationship to the condemnation of that year, see Caroti, "Les *modi rerum* . . . Encore une fois." For Oresme's use of modes to account for motion and time, see §18.2.

In a second way, it can be conceived that in no way is an accident outside the soul any *res*   6
other than the substance that is the subject. All there is is that substance, standing in such a way
as various predicates are said of it. In this way, the accident would be nothing other than the
substance (nothing except a predicate), and this is how some speak of every accident except   9
quality.

In a third, distinct way, one can conceive of an accident not as a proper extended or inherent
form as in the first way, nor merely as the substance (or the predicate or linguistic item), as in   12
the second way, but as something's being such or so much. For example, whiteness would be
nothing other than *being white*, which would be properly signified by the concrete term ['white']   15
together with the infinitive 'being,' and by the adjectival term. (*In Phys.* I.5)

The standard later scholastic view treats at least whiteness and other such qualities as
accidents in the first way—as real accidents (Ch. 10). Ockham and his followers (the
"some" referred to at line 9) think that qualities are the only real accidents, and that all
other so-called accidents can either be reduced to substance and quality, or can be
treated as mere linguistic entities. But after setting out this familiar contrast between
realists and nominalists, Oresme introduces a third kind of view (lines 11–18), on which
accidents have some sort of positive ontological status, but not as true forms inhering in
a subject. Rather, an accident would be understood as a subject's being a certain way—
for instance, being white or being round.

Very cautiously, Oresme proceeds to argue for this third view, across all nine of the
accidental categories. His first conclusion is that 'being' is equivocal between substance
and accident. Second, he concludes—again only as a position that is "plausible and open
to correction"—that no accident is a form in the first of the above senses. (The principal
argument for this conclusion is that, if there were real accidents, then—contrary to his
first conclusion—'being' would be univocal between substance and accident. Such
univocity, recall, is precisely the result that proponents of real accidents after Scotus
are seeking [§10.5].) Third, Oresme argues against the second account of 'accident,'
arguing that no accident, in any of the categories, is simply a substance. (The argument
here is simply that, with respect to many authoritative passages, this reductive approach
"destroys the text.") Finally, Oresme concludes that every accident should be understood in the third of the above senses, on the grounds that the other options have been
eliminated.[7]

To be sure, there is no *argument* here that would cause concern to Oresme's
opponents on either side. The passage is significant simply because it clearly sets out
a third way, that of modes. Although Oresme does not use the term 'mode' here, he
uses it in many other places in connection with this theory. The following passage is
particularly striking:

---

[7] Oresme offers another general classification of forms at *In Phys.* III.6: "Tertio distinctio est quod quaedam formae
sunt per se existentes, aliae sunt formae accidentales inhaerentes, ut imaginaretur consequenter de aliqua albedine, aliae
sunt quae dicuntur conditiones, vel modi rerum, vel taliter se habere, sicut quaedam relationes et huiusmodi." Here
Oresme goes on to argue that motion is a mode. See also *In Phys.* I.13: "suppono distinctionem quod haec nomina 'res,'
'ens,' 'unum' sunt equivoca. . . . Et ideo uno modo accipitur 'ens' pro aliqua re demonstrata vere existente, sicut est
homo, animal et albedo secundum communem viam. Secundo modo accipitur equivoce et large pro modo rei sive
conditione que proprie esset significabilis per orationem vel complexe; verbi gratia aetas non est aliquid demonstratum
sed est rem tantum durasse et fuisse a longo tempore, et sic de multis aliis rebus." Another, similar division of senses of
'ens' appears at *In Phys.* I.15.

We should also take note of what the best division of being is. 'Being,' 'res,' and 'something' can be taken in one way for that which truly is, and in this way it is sometimes the case that to be something is [rightly] said to be nothing. Thus we say that he who heats a thing does nothing, but instead he makes that which was earlier cold to be hot. In this way, unless a body or a substance is produced, it is not said that something is made. In another way, broadly, those terms are taken for an accident, condition, disposition, or mode of a thing, or for that which is a thing's being situated thus. (*In Phys.* II.6)   3

   6

Oresme distinguishes two senses of 'being.' In a strict sense, all that counts is "a body or a substance" (lines 5), and when we casually speak of a body as *being hot*, we should say strictly speaking that there is no further being there—no heat—but just the body that becomes hot. If we want to count such accidents as beings, then we need to speak "broadly" and include the "condition, disposition, or mode of a thing" (lines 5–6). This way of dividing the territory reflects Oresme's commitment to the equivocity of 'being,' and to the idea that accidents—even qualities like heat—are beings only in some weaker sense. Here, and throughout Oresme's *Physics* commentary, 'mode' is simply one among various terms that might equally well be used to talk about accidents. But whatever the terminology, his discussion is significant because it attempts to make space for a kind of ontological item falling in between a genuine entity and nothing at all. It is hard to tell exactly what Oresme thinks a mode is, but the general tenor of his remarks points back toward thirteenth-century deflationary views, and the idea that for a mode to exist just is for its subject to exist in a certain way.

   Modal realism remained an isolated phenomenon in the fourteenth century. Considered as a challenge to the orthodox doctrine of real accidents, the theory of modes looked suspicious and perhaps even heretical. Indeed, Olivi and Wyclif were both censured for their theories of accidents, among other things, and Auriol's views were perennially under a cloud of suspicion. Oresme was not so disreputable a figure, but only because he was more cautious. When it became clear after the condemnation of 1347 that his theory of accidents as modes was untenable (§19.5), Oresme backed off, and his later work abandons his early modal realism.[8] It is, indeed, only very recently that scholars discovered the existence of a manuscript containing Oresme's *Physics* commentary; perhaps the work was too controversial to have widely circulated. Inasmuch, then, as none of the writings considered in this section were widely known, the theory of modes lacked a visible champion until Suárez, in the late sixteenth century. Suárez, as we will see, found a way to introduce modes without controversy, by postulating them not in place of but over and above real accidents. This is an

---

[8] In a work that seems to be slightly earlier than the *Physics* commentary, Oresme describes Aristotle as holding "quod accidens non est separabile a substantia non solum secundum existentiam...sed etiam secundum quidditatem, quia non habet esse proprie: unde imaginabatur quod, sicut impossibile est esse figuram sine figurato, ita de quolibet alio accidente, et hoc est verum nisi per miraculum" (*In De an.* I.4, p. 119). Oresme shows every sign of endorsing this view, which makes particularly clear the close connection between his view and deflationary thirteenth-century accounts (and with Buridan's reading of Aristotle on accidents [see §11.1]). Interestingly, however, a very similar reworking of this question (ibid., p. 500.74–81) takes a much more conventional view, declining to treat accidents as without any *esse proprie*. It seems likely these revisions reflect the influence of the 1347 condemnations.

   For another seemingly pre-1347 text, see *In De gen. et cor.* I.2, pp. 11–12: "si dicatur quod albedo incipit esse per alterationem, hoc non valet, quia albedo nihil est nisi hoc esse album."

instance of a phenomenon we will become increasingly familiar with as this study unfolds (esp. Chs. 19–20): the way in which ecclesiastical authority suppressed philosophical innovation throughout the scholastic era, closing off fertile avenues of inquiry that would come open only in the seventeenth century. The most significant consequence of censorship in the present context was to preclude a debate over the different ways in which a theory of accidents might be formulated. The doctrine of real accidents became scholastic dogma, and to the extent that it was no more than dogma it became that much more difficult to defend in the seventeenth century. A further, more subtle consequence is that it remained unclear throughout the scholastic era exactly what modes are. Because these early champions of modal realism had so little influence, the terminology never became firmly entrenched, and it is at least as common, in the fourteenth century, to find 'mode' being used reductively. Thus, as we will see in §19.3, when John of Mirecourt suggests that only substances exist, and that accidents are nothing at all, he uses the term 'mode' to make this point (§19.3). And when John Buridan and others attack this sort of reductive view, they attack it as a theory of modes (§19.5). Buridan is aware of views that lie in between real accidents and full-blown reductivism (indeed, as we saw in §11.1, he ascribes such a view to Aristotle), but he does not describe these as theories of modes. Not long after Buridan, Albert of Saxony shows himself aware of the ambiguities here. Noting that an accidental form can be either "a *res* inhering in a subject" or else a mode, he asks: "Is this mode of standing (*modus se habendi*) the thing that so stands, or is it not that thing?" and responds that either answer is possible: "it can be said that it is, and it can be said that it is not" (*In Phys.* I.19, p. 251). With respect to his own ontology, however, Albert leaves no room for anything but substances and real accidents: "I hold that everything that exists is either a substance or an accident, and that nothing—whether it is called a *modus rei* or a *complexe significabile*—exists in reality unless it is a substance or an accident" (ibid., I.18, p. 239).[9]

In general, throughout the fourteenth century, realistic and reductive uses of 'mode' exist side by side. And although future research will doubtless uncover much more information about how 'mode' was used in the fifteenth and sixteenth centuries, I can see no sign of its playing a central role in scholastic metaphysics until the end of the sixteenth century, when Suárez gives modes a crucial place in his metaphysics.

---

[9]   Buridan's hostility toward modes, understood reductively, is particularly clear in this passage: "Ideo propter tales rationes, aliqui antiquissimi posuerunt accidentia non esse entia distincta a substantiis suis, sed deberet dici 'modos substantiarum': quod idem non solum nunc est calidum et post frigidum, aliter et aliter se habens, immo etiam ipsum nunc est caliditas et post frigiditas, aliter et aliter se habens, sicut est idem nunc sphaericum et post cubicum. Et hanc opinionem tenuerunt et tenent, ut puto, non quia credant eam esse veram, sed quia est difficile eos redarguere demonstrative" (*In De an.* III.11). For Marsilius's similar remarks, see *In De an.* III.7: "accidentia essent solum quidam modi se habendi substantiarum, qui non sunt distincti a substantia" (in Caroti, "*Modi rerum* and Materialism" p. 223 n. 39).

Albert of Saxony unfortunately says nothing more about his views on modes. He remarks that the place to take this issue up is not in the *Physics*, but in his lectures on the *Metaphysics*, which have not survived. His reference to the *complexe significabile* is to an abstract, proposition-like entity postulated by Gregory of Rimini and others. There was a close link between fourteenth-century debates over modes, as ways in which substances exist, and states of affairs, as ways in which the world exists. For *complexe significabile* in general, see Nuchelmans, *Theories of the Proposition* and de Libera, *Référence vide*. For the connection between propositions and modes, see Adams, "Things versus 'Hows'"; Biard, "Les controverses"; and Caroti, "La position" pp. 335–42.

13.3. The Suarezian Model

Suárez's importance for late scholastic thought tends to be absurdly exaggerated by students of the period, with one going so far as to remark, in a prominent reference work, that: "Francisco Suárez was the main channel through which medieval philosophy flowed into the modern world." This makes as little sense as describing David Lewis as the main channel through which analytic philosophy flowed into the twenty-first century. Arguably, Suárez was the best metaphysician of the sixteenth century, but his philosophical influence was felt mainly in that area, and even there he was just one voice among many. In view of the vast number of scholastic texts available in the seventeenth century, and the vast number of important authors holding widely divergent views, it is absurd, even if convenient, to single out any one figure as the dominant influence. Seventeenth-century authors often do cite Suárez, and rely on his views implicitly, but not markedly more than they rely on Fonseca, Toletus, Zabarella, the Coimbrans, Pererius, and Scaliger—to say nothing of towering classical figures like Aquinas and Scotus. Moreover, focusing on the big names of the era does not even capture the principal avenues through which scholastic ideas passed, which were textbooks and the tradition of studying and commenting directly on Aristotle, which for many students remained their principal point of access to scholastic thought.[10]

Even so, Suárez does seem to have been extremely important on the subject of modes, given his very clear and careful account of what they are, and the extraordinary importance they have in his metaphysics. He introduces the terminology of 'mode' and 'modal distinction' in such a way as to make clear that he takes himself to be doing something new:

We ought to posit among created things an actual distinction in the nature of things (*ex natura rei*), prior to the operation of intellect, which is not such as there is between two *res* or entities that are entirely distinct. This distinction could be called *real* in the general sense of the term, **3** because it does truly occur on the side of reality, and not through an extrinsic denomination made by intellect. Still, to distinguish this from the other, greater real distinction, we can call it either a distinction in the nature of things,...or it can more properly be called a modal **6** distinction because, as I will explain, it always occurs between some *res* and its mode. (*Disp. meta.* 7.1.16)

The whole course of Disputation Seven—Suárez's well-known discussion of distinctions—leads up to this point. Suárez has already explained how he understands a real distinction, and a distinction of reason—topics that he regards as relatively straightforward. The hard question, he thinks, is whether any distinction falls between the two. In

---

[10] For an even stronger statement of the view that Suárez's influence is overstated, see Clemenson, *Descartes' Theory of Ideas* pp. 11–12. Clemenson doubts Suárez's influence even with regard to the theory of modes, and even with respect to Descartes. This seems to me to go too far. For the contrasting credulous view regarding Suárez's influence, see Doyle, "Suárez, Francisco."

On the role of scholastic textbooks, see, e.g., Reif, "Textbook Tradition" and Schmitt, "Galilei and the Text-Book Tradition." The practice of teaching directly from Aristotle's texts was common in the early part of the scholastic era, and was reinvigorated by the textual concerns of the humanists. Late in our period, the practice seems to have been particularly common in Protestant universities (see Methuen, "Teaching of Aristotle"). For one seventeenth-century reading list, apparently from a tutor at St. John's College, Cambridge, see Curtis, *Oxford and Cambridge in Transition* pp. 108–13. Among the many works listed, Suárez is not included, not even in metaphysics, where instead Fonseca's works are recommended.

one sense he thinks there clearly is not, since there can be no middle ground between being dependent on mind and independent of mind, and no middle ground between being the same and being different (ibid., par. 10). Even so, among things that are different independently of mind, and so really distinct "in the general sense of the term" (line 3), Suárez here announces that there is a distinction to be drawn between two kinds of distinctions, real and modal, where the first distinguishes between *res* and *res*, and the second distinguishes between *res* and mode (lines 2, 7). (Later [ibid., par. 26], he allows that two modes within the same subject can also be counted as modally distinct from one another.)

The sense that Suárez is breaking new ground is borne out by a comparison with previous discussions. Although we have seen many precedents in earlier scholastic thought for the term 'mode,' the notion of a modal distinction is uncommon before Suárez. De Soto, for instance, remarks in 1543 that "among all the philosophers before Scotus, there were only two distinctions: a distinction of reason, and a real distinction" (*In Isag.* "De universalibus," q. 3, p. 41ab). Moreover, the only further sort of distinction that De Soto recognizes (only to reject it) is Scotus's formal distinction, which is generally understood as a distinction within a thing that is numerically one, and so would seem to be quite different from the modal distinction. Now to be sure it would be possible to interpret the formal distinction in a way that brings it close to the idea of a modal distinction. But this is not Suárez's path, nor is it a path that Scotus encourages. Scotus himself does, occasionally, speak of distinguishing between *realitas* and *modus*, but the contexts in which he does so are not closely related to the modal distinction as we know it.[11] A more important precedent is Pedro Fonseca's discussion of the modal distinction in his *Metaphysics* commentary (1577), which Suárez explicitly draws on. Fonseca treats the notion of a modal distinction as if it were commonplace, which suggests there are earlier precedents I am unaware of. But Fonseca too has an entirely different understanding of what a modal distinction is, and he does not uses 'mode' to talk about a kind of lesser accident.[12]

---

[11] See *Ord.* I.8.1.3 (Vat. IV nn. 138–40), where Scotus appeals to a distinction between *realitas* and *modus* to distinguish between whiteness and its degree of intensity. It seems doubtful to me that this plays any important role in the later theory of modes. Although Scotus does, as we saw in §12.5, treat the lesser categories as describing modes rather than *res*, and although *this* is surely an important step toward the later theory of modes, he explicitly postulates a real distinction between these modes and their subjects, and has nothing to say in this context about a lesser, modal distinction. Interestingly, Fernández García's Scotistic *Lexicon* contains a lengthy discussion of the various kinds of distinctions (pp. 225–32), but does not even mention the modal distinction.

[12] Fonseca (*In Meta.* V.6.6.2, II:400) recognizes three senses of *modi essendi*, all of which have figured in earlier chapters: (1) real accidents like shape, white, and sweet (§10.5); (2) the *modi essendi* that serve to distinguish the categories (§12.3); (3) the *modus essendi* that changes when an accident goes from inhering in a subject to subsisting on its own in the Eucharistic host (§10.3). Modes in the first sense are really distinct from their subject. Modes in the second sense are distinct merely by reason. Only modes in the third sense count as modally distinct from their subject.

On the modal distinctions as predating Fonseca, see his *In Meta.* V.15.2.5 (II:816E): "Opinio eorum qui sentiunt relationem a fundamento distingui modali distinctione…recentiorum quorundam est propria." Unfortunately, he mentions no names. Responding to this discussion, Suárez (*Disp. meta.* 47.2.7) ascribes this view to Scotus (with some justification, as we saw in §12.5), and to the Thomist Chrysostomus Javelli, but Fonseca cites the same passage from Javelli as supporting a formal distinction (II:818B). I have not been able to consult Javelli's work. Báñez too describes Scotus as distinguishing shape and quantity "non realiter tanquam res a re, sed distinguunter formaliter ex natura rei, vel realiter formaliter, ut alii dicunt, vel distinguuntur sicut res et modus rei" (*In Summam theol.* I.3.4; I:147b).

Part of what makes it difficult to pin down the history of the modal distinction is that a distinction between mode and *res* can appear in so many contexts. Here my interest is in modes as items in the accidental categories, but the origins of the modal distinction may well lie elsewhere, as the case of Fonseca illustrates. For a detailed discussion of how the

Suárez, then, seems to be doing something new, and the tone of the discussion suggests he is well aware of this. He begins his case for the existence of a modal distinction by describing what a mode is:

So as to prove and clarify the assertion [of the previous passage], I claim that among created things, beyond the *entities* that are there—the substance and root of things, so to speak—there are found certain real *modes*, which are both something positive, and which in their own right (*per seipsos*) act on those entities, giving them something that is outside their whole essence as individuals existing in reality. (*Disp. meta.* 7.1.17)

Modes are here contrasted with entities (*entitates*), a term that for Suárez is at least roughly synonymous with 'res.' Suárez does not initially mention the two distinguishing features of modes described in §13.2: their dependence on a subject, and their determination of a subject. For now, Suárez's concern is only to establish the credentials of modes as a mind-independent feature of reality: thus they are "real," "positive," and causal agents "in their own right." Elsewhere he further makes it clear that modes "have some proper existence" and are "something existing *in rebus*" (*Disp. meta.* 47.2.8). (This is said explicitly in contrast to Fonseca, whose modes lack existence entirely, and so cannot be categorial items at all. Also, unlike Oresme and Wyclif, Suárez makes no appeal to the equivocity of 'being' to explain the diminished status of modes.) The attraction of this way of proceeding should be immediately clear. If Suárez can show that modes are genuine features of the world, and then go on to show that they are in a certain way lesser entities than *res*, we would then have very strong reason for recognizing two sorts of mind-independent distinctions, a greater one and a lesser one.[13]

Of course, simply describing what a mode is leaves open the question of whether any such things exist. This is the task Suárez immediately takes up, remarking that he will establish "by induction" that modes exist, which is to say that he will establish it by listing various examples of modes. At this point, especially to a reader working backwards to Suárez from the seventeenth century, the discussion may seem to take a strange turn. For rather than appeal to what might seem to be paradigmatic modes like shape or motion, Suárez appeals instead to the inherence of quantity in a subject as his leading example of what a mode is:

This [the claim of the previous passage] is clear by induction: for in the case of a quantity that is in a substance, for example, two things can be considered: first, the entity of the quantity itself;

modal distinction appears in late scholastic discussions of essence and existence, for instance, see Wells, "Suarez, Historian."

Suárez cites Fonseca as a precedent for his use of 'mode,' but acknowledges that Fonseca "aliqua ponat exempla quae incerta nobis sunt" (*Disp. meta.* 7.1.19). Fonseca is quite clear that modes lack their own existence: ". . . si relatio sola modali distinctione distinguatur a fundamento siquidem illud *ad* non significabit entitatem ullam, cui peculiaris existentia conveniat, sed purum quendam modum essendi ipsius fundamenti" (*In Meta.* V.15.2.5, II:817BC). Suárez, in addition to criticizing Fonseca in this regard, also criticizes him for including shape among real accidents: "et in hoc ordine ponit figuram, sed immerito, quia in tertio constituitur, quia respectu quantitatis illam afficit tanquam modus, non tanquam res omnino ab illa distincta" (*Disp. meta.* 7.1.19; cf. Fonseca, *In Meta.* V.6.6.2, II:400).

[13] For further discussion of the causality exercised by modes, and their immediate union with their subjects, see *Disp. meta.* 16.1.21–22. This passage describes the relationship between subject and mode in terms very close to those that Auriol had used to describe the relationship between subject and accident (§11.4). For another useful discussion of the real and modal distinctions, see *Disp. meta.* 47.2.7–9, where it is especially clear how different Suárez's modal distinction is from Fonseca's.

second, the union or actual inherence of that quantity with its substance. The first we call simply the *res* of the quantity, including whatever belongs to the essence of that individual quantity occurring in reality, which remains and is conserved even if the quantity is separated from its subject.... The second (that is, the inherence) we call the mode of the quantity.... (*Disp. meta.* 7.1.17)

After running through a list of things he does not mean by 'mode' in this context, he concludes:

The inherence of quantity is called its mode because it is something affecting that quantity, which serves to ultimately determine the state and character of its existence, but does not add to it any new proper entity, but only modifies the preexisting entity. (Ibid.)

The discussion, which had been proceeding in a clear enough fashion, may at this point seem to have run off the rails. (My earliest notes on Disputation Seven make just one remark at this point: "This is really obscure!") Viewed in the proper perspective, however—the perspective of the last three chapters—it is easy to see what Suárez is up to. Although both shape and motion are modes, for Suárez, he takes these to be hard and controversial cases, wrapped up in disputes over the categories of Quantity, Quality, and Where. He picks inherence as his leading example because he takes it to be a clearer case. Indeed, as we have seen (Ch. 11), there was close to a consensus among scholastic authors that *something* is needed to explain the unity of accidents with their subjects. When quantity, for instance, is understood as a real accident (Ch. 14), it becomes the sort of absolute entity, or *res*, that may or may not be joined to a subject. But if an accident is not by its nature the sort of thing that necessarily inheres in a subject, then some further explanation—beyond simply appealing to the thing's nature—is required for why it ordinarily does inhere. Moreover, and crucially, since that something will itself need to be joined to its subject, it cannot be a *res*, as Suárez goes on to argue in the following paragraph, because in that case we would be embarked on the sort of vicious regress we encountered earlier (§11.3). Hence we need modes—things that are immediately united with their subject—to account for inherence. As obscure as the example looks through modern eyes, to a scholastic it would have looked like the paradigm case of the usefulness of modes: here, and in other domains, they are the ideal regress-blockers, explaining inherence without requiring any further explanation.[14]

Suárez goes on to fill out the induction by appealing to various other contexts in which modes are required:

- a quality's inhering in a subject (quality being the only other kind of real accident, beyond quantity, that Suárez recognizes);
- the union of substantial form with matter;

---

[14] Although Suárez's choice of inherence as his leading example of a mode doubtless reflects his sense that this is a relatively clear case, his choice also reflects his desire to adhere to as much of a tradition as possible. The case of inherence brings him into connection with Fonseca's third sense of mode (above), and so in turn with the earlier *modus essendi* tradition that Fonseca is following, which was made especially prominent by Giles of Rome (Ch. 10 note 13). The fact that Suárez, in his discussion of precedents for his view, is unable to cite any clearer precedents (he also mentions Giles, Durand of St. Pourçain [note 2 above], and Didacus de Astudillo), is evidence of how slight a foothold the theory of modes has even at the end of the sixteenth century, and so of how important Suárez is in bringing this theory into prominence. Toletus, interestingly, regards the division into real distinctions and distinctions of reason as exhaustive—he does not even mention the modal distinction (*Comm. in univ. logicam*, De praed. in comm. q. 3 [*Opera* II:193]).

- the divine persons with respect to the divine nature;
- presence and local motion (§17.5);
- an action or a dependence on something else.

Suárez goes into detail regarding only the last of these, taking as his example light's dependence on the sun, but he issues a promissory note that announces one of the main themes of the many disputations that lie ahead: "this is not the place to talk about all of these cases, although as this work progresses the occasion will arise" (ibid.). Indeed it does. If we confine our attention only to the implications of Suárez's theory of modes for his categorial theory—setting aside its place in causation, motion, and substantial unity, to say nothing of its various theological applications—then we find the distinction applied to the accidental categories in general at Disputation 39.2, and then in detail over the subsequent fourteen disputations, covering nearly 500 pages of dense Latin text. To foreshorten the discussion radically, he distinguishes between

(1) real accidents;
(2) modes; and
(3) improper and extrinsic accidents (*Disp. meta.* 16.1),

and classifies items in the nine accidental categories as follows:

(1) quantity, some qualities;
(2) action, where, some relations;
(3) passion, when, having, position.

Subsequent chapters will consider some of the details of this framework, as we turn to accidents in the individual categories.

Returning to the main line of argument in Disputation Seven, Suárez goes on to supplement his "inductive" argument—that is, enumerating cases—with what he calls an *a priori* argument for modes:

Creatures are imperfect, and so either dependent, composite, limited, or changeable with respect to various states of presence, union, or determination. As a result, they need such modes, by which they are made complete with respect to all these [states]. This is so because, necessarily, this making complete does not always occur through entirely distinct entities— indeed this cannot even be reasonably conceived as being the case—and so as a result real modes are required. (*Disp. meta.* 7.1.19)

This does not seem particularly effective as an *argument* against a more parsimonious ontology. A strict corpuscularian, for instance, will simply deny that things are intrinsically incomplete. A material substance, as such, has a certain shape, size, and spatial location, and this in turn determines its interactions with other things. Of course, whether such an austere picture can be made to work has to be assessed on a case by case basis, but for now the point is just that Suárez has hardly presented us with a compelling *a priori* argument for modes in general. Still, although not effective as an argument, this passage seems quite effective as a statement of the deeper metaphysical picture that lies behind Suárez's account. Substances on this view are not simply free agents to which accidents may or may not be added, but are radically incomplete entities that cannot exist at all until determined in various ways by things of another kind, modes. I will return to this in §13.7.

Suárez's picture of substances as indeterminate suits perfectly the conception of modes we have seen others developing, because it accounts for determinacy as a feature of the *res*–mode relationship: *res* do not depend on any particular mode, but must be determined by some one mode within a determinable class. This is one half of the mutual dependence identified earlier between *res* and mode. The second half—the dependency of mode on *res*—is implicit above, inasmuch as modes are regarded not as complete things in their own right, but as completers for their subjects, suggesting that they are united in a particularly intimate way. Suárez goes on to make this explicit at the end of this same paragraph:

[A] mode is not properly a *res* or an entity, unless one is using the term 'being' (*ens*) broadly and in the most general sense, for whatever is is not nothing. In contrast, if we take 'entity' for that *res* that of itself and in itself is something, in such a way as not at all to require its being   3 intrinsically and essentially affixed to another, but instead either is not capable of union with another, or else can be united only by means of a mode that is distinct in the nature of things from itself, then a mode is not properly a *res* or an entity. Here is where its imperfection shows   6 best: it must always be affixed to another, to which it is immediately united *per se*, not by means of another mode. . . . (Ibid.)

Modes are beings, inasmuch as they are "not nothing" (line 2), but they are beings of a lesser sort, inasmuch as they are dependent on their subjects in a special way (lines 6–8). Substances, in contrast, even if they need modes, do not need to be "affixed" to any particular mode. From here it is a simple matter, to which he immediately turns (*Disp. meta.* 7.1.20), to establish his intended conclusion: that there is a lesser distinction on the side of things, a modal distinction. Suárez reaches this result, it should be noted, without resting anything on the familiar idea that really distinct things are separable in two directions, whereas modally distinct things are separable in only one direction. In the following section of Disputation Seven, Suárez introduces these as the principal marks (*signa*) of the two kinds of distinctions, and I will return to this issue in §13.6. For now the important point is just that such facts are a *consequence* of there being distinct kinds of things in the world, existing in different ways. Hence the true basis for the modal distinction is the existence of an intermediary kind of thing in the world, a thing that is neither fully distinct nor fully identical with its subject.[15]

13.4. The Seventeenth Century

After Suárez, modes become an established part of the metaphysician's toolkit. But this is not to say that there was, at least at first, any clear consensus on what modes are. Among scholastics, one finds some, such as Franco Burgersdijk, who closely follow

---

[15]   There are few good discussions of the scholastic theory of modes. The best I know of is that of Menn, "Suárez and Modes." Still, I take issue with Menn at various places. He holds, for instance, that "the theory of modes is characteristic of Jesuit philosophy" ("Suárez and Modes" p. 226), but it is not clear what his basis for this conclusion is, since the only Jesuit authors he discusses are Suárez and Fonseca, and he himself establishes quite clearly that Fonseca's theory of modes is very different from Suárez's. Also, Menn overstates the place of modes in Suárez's category theory: "Suárez maintains that figures (in the category of quality), and all beings in the categories of action, passion, where, when, and position, are modes rather than *res*" (p. 242). This gets the various categories only about half right, as I discuss in the main text.

For a good discussion of modes from the side of semantic considerations, see Klima, "Buridan's Logic," esp. pp. 490–1.

Suárez's usage. Although Burgersdijk acknowledges that the nature of modes is "so abstruse as to make it difficult to define them justly or appropriately," he goes on to stress that a mode is "something positive" that has an effect on its subject by limiting or circumscribing it in a certain way (*Inst. meta.* I.7.1)—very much the terms that Suárez had used.[16] Christoph Scheibler's *Metaphysica* (1617) is also deeply influenced by Suárez's theory of modes, embracing the idea that they complete substances that are otherwise imperfect (I.8.5.2 n. 68). But Scheibler resists the Suarezian view that modes are beings in their own right: "They do not add to the preexisting entity a new entity—as does heat, for instance, when it comes to be in water—but only modify the pre-existing entity" (n. 69). Moreover, although Scheibler accepts that the distinction between mode and substance is more than merely conceptual, he rejects Suárez's modal distinction, insisting that all distinctions are either real or conceptual, with nothing in between.

Various critics of scholasticism found it useful to appeal to modes in their attacks on real accidents. David Gorlaeus, for instance, retains a short list of real qualities, including most importantly heat (§21.4), but dismisses other accidental forms—including shape and size, as well as the substantial union of soul and body—as mere modes. The great question, in cases such as this, is whether these modes are to be understood realistically, as in Suárez, or in the wholly reductive way that Buridan and others had supposed. In Gorlaeus's case, the answer lies somewhere in between, since like Scheibler he wants to say that modes are not real entities, but yet that they are not mere beings of reason:

A mode in itself, as it is distinguished from a real being, does not have any real being. Rather, all this comes to it through that being of which it is a mode. For to be a real mode is to have real existence—not, to be sure, its own proper existence, but another's, and not through itself, but through another, through whose existence it too exists. It is in this way that the shape and the size of the wax are modes of it. They are distinct from it, since they can be separated, as when the wax is made round, but yet as distinct they do not have any proper existence of their own. (*Exercitationes* 2.1, pp. 27–8)

---

[16] Burgersdijk's full account of modes runs as follows: "Horum natura ita abstrusa est ut difficile sit eam justa convenientive definitione explicare, faciliusque sit, docere quid modus non sit quem quid sit. Ne tamen nihil dicamus, videtur *modus esse positiva quaedam, interna, et absoluta appendicula, qua res modificata, vel quoad esse vel quoad fieri, ut ita dicam, limitatur*" (*Inst. meta.* I.7.1, original emphasis). See also ibid., I.7.4: "Effectum modorum est res modificatas limitare, seu determinare, ac circumscribere"; ibid., I.7.9: "Modi additi rebus modificatis efficiunt aliqualem haud dubie compositionem...." And see ibid., II.17.12, where secondary qualities grounded on the four Aristotelian primary qualities are real accidents, whereas accidents based on shape and location are mere modes.

Another scholastic case is Eustachius a Sancto Paulo, who characterizes the four principal categories as *res* and the lesser six as mere modes. Eustachius gives no indication that modes are anything over and above the thing they modify, and in general his discussion betrays no sign of Suárez's influence. See *Summa* I.1.3b.1.2 (I:46–7): "Ex iis etiam sequitur, quatuor duntaxat esse praecipuas categorias; nempe Substantiae, Quantitatis, Qualitatis, et Relationis.... Sunt enim ista quatuor entium genera proprie loquendo formaliter seu essentialiter inter se et ab aliis distincta. At vero reliqua sex summa genera non proprie dicuntur formaliter seu essentialiter inter se aut ab aliis differre, neque enim si praecise spectentur, essentiae sunt ab aliis distinctae, sed modi tantum reliquorum entium. Ex. gr., actio et passio sunt modi rei quae producitur, quatenus ab agente fit et in patiens recipitur: neque enim *calefactio* sive active sive passive accipitur aliter a *calore* distinguitur, neque locus aliud quam quantitas essentialiter, sicut nec tempus aut situs; denique habitus essentialiter est ipsa res quae haberi dicitur." For the characterization of the four principal categories as containing *res*, see Eustachius's accompanying table (ibid., I:47). Eustachius's discussion of the modal distinction likewise fails to encourage even slightly the idea that modes have any positive ontological status (*Summa* IV.3.3.2.7, III:46). Indeed, that discussion, dependent as it is on Fonseca's discussion of the modal distinction (note 12 above), does not even mention modes in our sense as candidates for a modal distinction.

In effect Gorlaeus returns to the deflationary conception of accidents standard in the thirteenth century, retaining a robustly realistic account only in the case of a few central qualities.[17]

Other texts from the early seventeenth century, although they appeal to modes, do not explain what they mean. Nathanael Carpenter might seem to be a modal realist in his *Philosophia libera* (1621), when he remarks that "every mode of a being adds something to that being" (I.1, p. 11), but his remarks are too compressed to engender any confidence. The case of Joachim Jungius is even less clear. Sounding like so many earlier figures throughout our period, he remarks that "there are not as many entities in the natural world as there are attributes; an attribute does not always add to its subject some *res* distinct from that subject, but often only a mode as it were of being (*modum quasi entis*)" (*Praelectiones physicae* I.4). So far as I have found, Jungius offers no theory of modes.

As always when discussing modes, one can only go case by case. The tendency, however, as the seventeenth century progresses, is toward an increasingly realistic conception of modes. Pierre Gassendi, for instance, takes it to be just obvious in his polemics with Descartes that "modes are not nothing but something more than mere nothing; they are therefore *res* of some kind, not substantial of course, but at least modal" (*Disquisitio* II.3.4, p. 117). Gassendi flies in the face of time-honored usage when he insists that modes count as *res*, but his point is clear enough: modes are either something or nothing, and they cannot be nothing. Given the particular weight he puts on the idea that our knowledge of substance is veiled by its properties (§7.1), and given that he conceives of those properties as modes, he can hardly fail to be a modal realist.[18] Leibniz takes for granted a similar realism, again in response to Descartes: "To deny a real distinction between modes is an unnecessary change in the accepted use of words. For until now modes have been considered as *res* and have been viewed as differing in reality—as in a piece of wax, for instance, a spherical shape differs from a square one" (*Animadversiones in Principia Cartesiana* ad art. I.60–1 [*Phil. Schriften* IV:365; tr. Loemker p. 390]). Malebranche too does not hesitate to treat modes as features of reality: "it is absolutely necessary that everything in the world be either a being or a mode (*manière*) of a being" (*Search after Truth* III.2.8.ii [tr. p. 244]).[19]

---

[17] For Gorlaeus on modes in place of accidents see *Exercitationes* 1.3, p. 13: "Nam peripateticorum accidentia non omnia nobis sunt entia, sed entium modi: et quae entia sunt, scilicet lumen, calor, frigus etc. non accidentis sed physicae naturae sunt species." His *Idea physicae* ch. 12 gives a quick overview of where he thinks one should invoke modes.

[18] For Gassendi, see also *Syntagma* II.1.6.1, where modes are "something further" within substances: "Cum ipsae ergo atomi tota sint materia, substantiave corporea quae in ipsis corporibus est, constat, si quid aliud in ipsis corporibus concipimus, esseve animadvertimus id non esse substantiam sed solum substantiae modum aliquem—hoc est, certam quandam materiae materialiumve principiorum contexturam, concretionem, compositionem, aut consequentem ex ea raritatem vel densitatem, mollitiem vel duritiem, magnitudinem sive molem, delineationem seu figuram, colorem ac speciem, mobilitatem vel torporem, et quae id genus talia sunt, ex quibus ipsum corpus cui insunt tale potius sit ac denominetur quam aliud.... Hinc potest quidem Qualitas universe definiri Modus sese habendi substantiae, seu status et conditio qua materialia principia inter se commista se habent" (I:372ab).

[19] The long entry for '*modus*' in Goclenius's *Lexicon* (1613) does not come anywhere close to the idea of a mode as an alternative to a real accident. But the idea appears in Micraelius's *Lexicon* from a half-century later, and is perfectly familiar a half-century after that, in Chauvin's *Lexicon*. His entry for 'form' remarks: "est ergo forma corporis naturalis, iuxta Recentiorum placita, nihil aliud quam, ipsius materiae cui inest, modus" (*Lexicon* p. 260b).

Spinoza's is of course the most prominent seventeenth-century use of 'mode,' at least after Descartes. Given that, for Spinoza, all creatures are modes (see, e.g., *Ethics* I P14 cor. 2), the realist–reductivist question obviously takes on special salience here, but would require a separate study. Another noteworthy case is the *Port-Royal Logic* (I.2, p. 47): "J'appelle

As an exception to this pattern, one might think of Hobbes. Although I have argued for Hobbes as the clearest case of an austerely reductive theory of accidents (§7.1, §10.2), he nevertheless defines accidents in terms of modes: an accident, he says, is "the mode of conceiving a body" (*De corpore* 8.2). But an accident here is not the mode of a *body*, but the mode of *conceiving* a body—that is, accidents have been made into subjective features of our conceptual framework. (Admittedly, since for Hobbes everything is a body [§16.2], he is strictly speaking not entitled even to the existence of modes of conceiving. But we cannot expect him to get to the rock bottom of everything all at once.) When Hobbes is at his rigorous best, he makes it clear that bodies have neither accidents nor modes. Thus what he tells Bramhall is not that accidents are mere modes, but that "I have denied that there is *any* reality in accidents" (*Works* IV:305).[20]

Pierre Bayle's *Dictionary* (1697) offers a remarkable retrospective account of how talk of accidents and modes developed over recent centuries. To a considerable degree, his account corresponds with my own.

The general doctrine of the philosophers is that the idea of being contains, immediately under it, two species, substance and accident.... With regard to accidents, they all agreed, before the wretched disputes that divided Christendom, that they depend so essentially on their subjects of   3
inhesion that they cannot exist without them. This was their specific character, which differentiated them from substances. The doctrine of transubstantiation overthrew this whole idea and forced philosophers to say that an accident can subsist without its subject.... They   6
therefore admitted a real distinction between a substance and its accidents.... But some of them continued to say that there were accidents whose distinction from their subject was not real, and which could not subsist outside of it. They called these accidents "modes." Descartes,   9
Gassendi, and in general all of those who have abandoned scholastic philosophy have denied that an accident is separable from its subject in such a way that it could subsist after its separation, and have ascribed to all accidents the nature of those that are called "modes"....   12
("Spinoza" DD, XIII:463 [tr. pp. 331–2])

As we saw in §10.2, Bayle is quite right to think accidents were initially conceived of as dependent on their subject (lines 2–4). To be sure, the role he ascribes to the Eucharist is oversimplified. Transubstantiation was already orthodoxy by the mid-thirteenth century, at a time when deflationary theories of accidents were still prevalent. As we have seen, deflationism could allow for subsisting accidents by appealing to a change in *modus essendi* (§10.3). So although transubstantiation no doubt contributed to the move toward real accidents, it did not decide the case, and in part the case was decided on philosophical grounds (§10.5). Even so, Bayle is again on target when he describes the theory of modes as a return to that earlier deflationary view (lines 7–9). Talk of modes is not a way of rejecting the substance–accident distinction—on the contrary, that

---

manière de choses, ou mode, ou attribut, ou qualité, ce qui étant conçu, dans la chose, et comme ne pouvant subsister sans elle, la determine à être d'une certaine façon, et la fait nommer telle." See also Wilkins, *Essay towards a Real Character* II.1, p. 26, distinguishing substance and accidents: "...such things as subsist by themselves, or which (according to the old logical definition) require a subject of inhesion, though they are indeed nothing but the modes of substance." Neither of these latter texts makes clear the extent of its metaphysical commitments.

[20] Hobbes does occasionally use the term '*modus*' in connection with accidents, remarking for instance that being white and the like "nihil aliud esse praeter corporis modum (possem apertius dicere actionem), quo varie agens in sentientes nunc uno modo nunc alio modo apparet" (*De mundo* 28.4). What the parenthetical remark tells us is that modes for Hobbes are not to be construed realistically, but are a description of the actions that a body undertakes in virtue of which it causes a certain experience in a perceiver.

distinction is part of "the general doctrine of the philosophers" (line 1), and it never was overthrown. But, as Bayle suggests, the term 'accident' had to go, debased as it was by the disreputable scholastic doctrine of real accidents. Hence authors like Descartes and Gassendi switched terminology entirely (lines 9–12), referring to accidents of their preferred sort as *modes*. As we have seen, the way had been prepared for that terminological shift by a long line of scholastic authors.

13.5. Cartesian Modes

The previous section looked briefly at a wide range of figures. To reach any firm conclusions, however, we need to slow down. Let us look more carefully, then, at the most influential seventeenth-century proponent of modes, Descartes, to see whether his usage fits the realistic conception of modes that I have traced through the scholastic era.

I have already argued for Descartes's commitment to the substance–accident distinction from the side of substance (Ch. 8). That conclusion, all by itself, entails that Descartes is committed to some sort of accident-like entities. If this commitment is genuine, however, then we would expect to find evidence of it in what he says about modes. Given the background just surveyed, it will obviously not be enough to cite the bare fact that Descartes speaks of modes and the modal distinction. Without knowing how he is using those terms no conclusions can be drawn. What we have to ask, then, is whether Descartes's modes satisfy the various characteristics of modes construed realistically. Those characteristics can be summarized as follows:

- dependency: modes cannot exist apart from a substance;
- determinacy: although a substance can exist apart from any given determinate mode, it must possess some mode from within each determinable kind;
- reality: modes exist, independently of the mind, although they are lesser entities than *res*;
- causality: modes exercise causal influence on their subjects.

It is uncontroversial that Descartes's modes satisfy the first two of these characteristics. When the *Principles of Philosophy* (1644) begins to use 'mode' in a systematic way to talk about the accidental properties of a thing, it does so by invoking the terminology of real and modal distinctions. There is not a real distinction between them, because for two things to be really distinct it must be the case that each could exist apart from the other (I.60). Any two substances meet this test, but modes do not, because a mode cannot exist apart from its substance. (There can, for instance, be no thoughts apart from a mind, and no shapes apart from a body.) Still, Descartes holds that not all distinctions are real distinctions, and that there is a modal distinction between modes and their substances (I.61). This distinction then gets applied specifically to the modes of thought and extension:

Thought and extension can also be taken as modes of a substance, in so far as one and the same mind can have many different thoughts, and one and the same body, with its quantity unchanged, can have many different modes of extension. . . . In this way, thought and extension are modally distinct from substance, and can be understood no less clearly and distinctly than substance can, provided they are regarded not as substances or *res* separate from other *res*, but simply as modes of *res*. (*Principles* I.64)

Descartes's modes thus satisfy the dependency test, inasmuch as they cannot exist without substance. They also satisfy the determinacy test, inasmuch as a mind must always be thinking something, and a body must be extended somehow.[21]

Like Suárez, Descartes treats one-way and mutual separability as marks of the modal and real distinctions, respectively. As in Suárez, however, these are merely marks, ways in which we "recognize" the distinctness of things (*Principles* I.60–2). What *defines* the different distinctions are the fundamental ontological categories that Descartes and Suárez both endorse. A real distinction occurs between two or more substances (*Principles* I.60); a modal distinction occurs between substance and mode, or between two modes of the same substance (even if two distinct modes will often be mutually separable). This way of proceeding is significant because it means we should not look to Descartes's various distinctions as a way of understanding his ontological scheme. Rather, the different distinctions are a consequence of the scheme: it is because Descartes has an ontology of substance and mode that he can appeal to two sorts of distinctions.[22]

This remark brings us back to the question of just what sort of ontological weight modes have for Descartes. Although they satisfy the dependency and determinacy test, there will be no reason to interpret them realistically unless they also satisfy at least the reality test, if not also the causality test. Evidence for the first of these is not hard to find. In the Third Meditation, Descartes remarks that "the ideas that represent substances to me are something greater and, so to speak, contain within themselves more of objective reality than the ideas that merely represent modes or accidents" (VII:40). This is to say that there is more reality in what is represented by those two kinds of ideas, which is just to say that substances are more real than modes. (The French translation, after the phrase "more objective reality," adds this: "that is to say, [these ideas] participate through representation in a higher degree of being or perfection" [IX:32].) This certainly suggests that modes have some degree of reality. If that is not what Descartes meant, he had an opportunity to explain himself, because Hobbes would press him on just this point:

---

[21] Given what Descartes thinks the modes of body are—e.g., size, shape, motion—it is obvious that they satisfy determinacy, at least with respect to any finite body. The situation is much less obvious for the modes of thought, but Descartes notoriously insists on the point even here—e.g., to Burman: "Et mens nunquam sine cogitatione esse potest; potest quidem esse sine cogitatione hac aut illa, sed tamen non sine omni, eodem modo ut corpus ne quidem per ullum momentum sine extensione esse potest" (V:150).

[22] Kaufman, "Divine Simplicity," contains a careful presentation of Descartes's various distinctions. Regarding dual separability and the real distinction, see *Med.* VI (VII:78) and the Sixth Replies (VII:434): "quidquid est reale potest separatim ob omni alio subiecto existere; quicquid autem ita separatim potest existere est substantia, non accidens." Regarding one-way modal separability, see *Med.* VI (VII:78), *Broadsheet* (VIIIB:350), and a letter from around 1645: "Ita figura et motus sunt modi proprie dicti substantiae corporeae, quia idem corpus potest existere nunc cum hac figura, nunc cum alia, nunc cum motu, nunc sine motu, quamvis, ex adverso, neque haec figura neque hic motus possint esse sine hoc corpore" (IV:349). Rozemond, *Descartes's Dualism* pp. 5–6, is very good on the point that separability is merely a sign of a real distinction, and that both the real and modal distinctions—in both Suárez and Descartes—are defined in terms of the sorts of things being distinguished.

Moreover, D. C. should reconsider what he wants to say by "more of reality." Does reality admit of more and less? Or, if he thinks that one *res* is more of a *res* than another, he should consider how this can be explained to us with that degree of clarity that every demonstration calls for, and that he himself has employed elsewhere. (Third Objections, VII:185)

This is just the line we should expect from Hobbes, who flatly insists that only substances exist and that accidents are nothing beyond ways of conceiving substance (§7.1, §10.2). Descartes might have seized on Hobbes's query as an opportunity to make clear that—at least among creatures—substances are all equally real, and what is not a substance is nothing at all. Remarkably, however, Descartes restates his original claim even more forcefully:

I have explained well enough how reality admits of more and less: it does so, of course, inasmuch as a substance is more of a *res* than a mode; and if there are real qualities or incomplete substances, they are more of a *res* than are modes, but less than are complete substances; and, finally, if there is an infinite and independent substance, it is more of a *res* than a finite and dependent substance. All this is completely self-evident. (Third Replies, VII:185)

This kind of hierarchy of being could scarcely be more scholastic, and seems utterly incompatible with a reductive conception of modes.[23]

The *Principles* puts this same ontological scheme on a more systematic foundation. That account begins at I.48: "All the objects of our perception we regard as either *res*, or affections of *res*, or else as eternal truths, which have no existence outside our thought." The next twenty paragraphs set out this ontology in detail. According to this initial division, only eternal truths are excluded from having existence outside our thought. This certainly suggests that "affections" (he will soon shift to talking of modes) do have mind-independent reality. This suggestion gets amplified considerably in the later French edition, where Descartes introduces a series of changes that allow his technical terminology to be introduced in a less haphazard way. Here, I.48 reads: "I distinguish all the objects of our perception into two kinds: the first contains all the things (*choses*) that have some existence, and the other, all the truths that are nothing outside our thought" (IXB:45). Included on the side of "things that have some existence" are both substances and their associated properties (*proprietez*). The term 'properties' includes modes, but the terminology of 'mode' is held back until it can be explained in I.56. Accordingly, where I.51 had begun "In the case of those items that we regard as *res* or modes of *res*..." (VIIIA:24), the French version begins "In the case of those items that we regard *as having some existence*..." (IXB:46–7), a phrase that looks ahead to both substances and modes. So what the Latin version suggests, the French version makes explicit: that both substances and modes are things that exist.

There thus seems to be quite solid textual support for the conclusion that Descartes's modes satisfy the reality test. So far as I can find, moreover, there is no textual evidence against that conclusion. If Descartes had wanted an ontology of substance alone, he ought to have said so, as both Bacon and Hobbes do (§10.2). He never does. If modes

---

[23] The *Meditations'* account of degrees of reality is set forth yet another time in the geometric restatement at the end of the Second Replies, axiom 6 (VII:165): "Sunt diversi gradus realitatis, sive entitatis; nam substantia plus habet realitatis, quam accidens vel modus; et substantia infinita, quam finita." See also to More, Aug. 1649 (V:403): "Translatio illa quam motum voco non est res minoris entitatis quam sit figura: nempe est modus in corpore."

were meant to be understood reductively, as mere structures (in the sense of §12.3), one would expect him to have said so or, instead, to have refrained from using the terminology of 'mode' at all. So although there is certainly historical precedent for an ontologically innocent understanding of 'mode,' that interpretation gains no support from anything that Descartes actually says.

What of the final feature of modes conceived realistically, *causality*? Here matters are less clear. To be sure, it is easy enough to find Descartes appealing to modes in causal contexts, as either causes or effects. Motion, after all, is a mode (see, e.g., *Principles* I.65), and so if there is creaturely causation at all in Descartes, modes must surely play a central role. The problem, however, is that someone who wants to read Descartes's modes reductively can also read these claims reductively, so that to speak of a mode's causing or being caused is simply shorthand for the claim that a substance-so-structured either causes or is caused. Given this sort of reductive strategy for explaining away apparent appeals to the causal role of modes, it might seem that an interpretive standoff will be inevitable here. There is, however, a special context that *requires* Descartes to isolate the distinct causal role played by modes—the Eucharist. At the end of the Fourth Replies, in an unusual foray into theological territory, Descartes proposes an account of how the appearances remain unchanged in the host, despite the bread's and wine's going out of existence. What gives rise to the appearances, he argues, is not the bread and wine, but the surface that surrounds the bread and wine, which can endure through transubstantiation. Crucially, for our purposes, this line of thought requires two claims:

1. "I am convinced that there is nothing else whatsoever that affects our senses beyond that surface alone that is the boundary of the dimensions of the body that is sensed" (VII:249).
2. "The surface of the bread or wine or any other body should not here be understood as a part of the substance or even of the quantity of that same body, nor should it be understood as a part of the surrounding bodies. It should be understood as simply the boundary that is conceived to lie in between the individual particles and the bodies that surround them; and this boundary has no reality whatsoever except a modal one" (VII:250–1).

According to (1), it is the surface of a body that acts on our senses. According to (2), that surface is a mode. There is no other way to read these claims, because transubstantiation requires Descartes to find something other than a substance to account for the ongoing continuity of appearances. (It cannot be a substance, because according to transubstantiation the substance of the bread and wine ceases to exist.) Of course, one might well complain that this is yet one more case of the pernicious influence of transubstantiation on philosophy during this era. We know, indeed, that two of Descartes's most sympathetic readers, Mesland and Clerselier, felt uneasy about this account. Although we do not have their letters, we have Descartes's replies, where he tries to explain how a surface, conceived as a mode, can endure through the replacement of both the underlying substance (the bread and wine) and the surrounding air. The more Descartes says about this, the stranger the view seems, but what matters for our purposes is that these letters continue to rely on the two claims quoted above. Indeed, just about the least controversial claim made in this correspondence is that a mode can be a cause. I conclude, then, that Descartes's theory of modes is fully realistic, in very much the same sense as Suárez's. This becomes the prevailing usage in the later part of the century.[24]

13.6. Separability

Even if we now have some rough taxonomy of the different theories of modes, and who their proponents are, we are still a long way from understanding what a mode is. This is one of the most perplexing questions that will arise over the course of this study, and to make any headway it is crucial to set aside an issue with which it can easily be entangled: the question of the separability of modes and accidents from their subject. As noted earlier, when Suárez and Descartes describe real and modal distinctions in terms of two-way versus one-way separability, they mean to be offering a rough and ready mark of how to tell these two kinds of distinctions apart. They do not suppose that such facts about separability are what *define* the real and modal distinctions. Hence Suárez readily admits various counterexamples, such as that of creatures being inseparable from God and yet being really distinct from God (*Disp. meta.* 7.2.25). Descartes, too, in the Fourth Replies, admits that God might be able to separate modes from their substance, even if this is inconceivable to us (VII:249). What defines these different distinctions, for both Suárez and Descartes, are the different ontological statuses of the entities in question. A real distinction just is a distinction between two *res*, whereas a modal distinction just is a distinction that involves entities of a lesser sort, modes. It is important to avoid the mistake, then, of supposing that modes can be understood through an understanding of the modal distinction, and that the modal distinction in turn can be understood in terms of a certain kind of separability. That gets the order of analysis precisely backwards. Rather, to understand why Suárez and Descartes

---

[24] For Descartes's ongoing correspondence regarding the role of modes in the Eucharist, see the Feb. 1645 letter to Mesland (IV:163–4): "...par ce mot de superficie, je n'entens point quelque substance, ou nature réelle, qui puisse être detruite par la toute puissance de Dieu, mais seulement un mode, ou une façon d'être...."; see also the recently discovered spring 1646 letter to Clerselier, where, by analogy, the surface in between the candle and the air endures through changes to each, "et ayant les mêmes dispositions et mouvements excite ensuite les mêmes sentiments" (IV:743). Then, discussing the Eucharistic case directly: "la grandeur, la situation, la figure, cette superficie moyenne, etc., comme ce n'étaient que des modes ou des façons d'être du pain et non point quelque chose de réel different du pain, il est aisé de concevoir que n'y arrivant aucun changement en ces modes a cause que le Corps de N. S. J. C. prend precisement la place du pain, ils doivent encore paraître les mêmes *et produire les mêmes effets, c'est a dire exciter en nous les mêmes sentiments*" (ibid., emphasis added). For surfaces both as modes and as the objects of sensation, see also the Sixth Replies (VII:434): "cum omnis sensus tactu fiat, nihil praeter superficiem corporum potest sentiri,...quae nihil aliud est quam modus." See as well a 1641 letter to Mersenne (III:387 n. 7).

For a careful and nuanced discussion of the historical context of Descartes's discussion of the Eucharist, see Ariew, "Descartes and the Jesuits." On Descartes's appeal to the surface as a mode, see Laymon, "Transubstantiation." For some reflections on why Descartes had to get into this theological territory, given his rejection of real qualities, see §20.3.

It is unclear to me how controversial it is among modern scholars to identify Descartes as a modal realist; there is surprisingly little discussion of the issue in the recent literature. For one particularly forthright example of the sort of reductive reading I mean to reject, see Nelson, "Introduction": "The inventory of substances is the complete inventory of Descartes's ontology..." (p. 103); "It should not be thought, however, that modes have a kind of existence apart from the modified substance" (p. 104); "Modes are not a separate item in the inventory of the universe. Instead, they provide ways of conceiving substances as limited" (p.104). In contrast, Normore has argued for the reality of Descartes's modes in an unpublished paper, "Cartesian Modes," putting particular emphasis on Descartes's need to give motion some reality. See also Chappell, "Descartes on Substance" pp. 252–3.

postulate a modal distinction, one needs to understand what modes are. Once one understands modes, both the modal distinction and inseparability will follow.[25]

Still, rather than set aside questions of separability entirely at this point, it will be useful to understand something of how scholastic views in this area evolved over the centuries. For although Descartes's way of setting out this territory comes from Suárez, Suárez's usage is idiosyncratic, and so liable to mislead. The more usual scholastic practice, as noted already (§13.3), is to recognize only two sorts of distinctions, real and conceptual. Since things that are merely conceptually distinct are really identical, the question of a distinction on the side of reality is for most scholastic authors quite straightforward: things are either the same or they are different. No further nuances are required, or even possible. This was the *opinio communis* across the spectrum of scholastic authors, from Ockham to Scotus to the Thomists. (As noted earlier, Scotus's famous formal distinction holds between things that are really identical, and so is not relevant here.)[26]

Supposing one accepts just a single distinction on the side of reality, the question then arises of whether that sort of real distinction requires two-way or merely one-way separability. The situation here is confusing. One thing that is reasonably clear is that if *a* can exist without *b*, then *a* is not the same as *b*. That is, one-way separability is sufficient to establish non-identity. This is a point that Scotus relies on in arguing for the reality of items in all ten categories. With respect to relations, for instance, he argues as follows:

Nothing is really the same as something without which it can really exist without contradiction. But there are many relations without which their foundations can exist without contradiction. Therefore there are many relations that are not really the same as their foundation. (*Ord.* II.1.4–5, Vat. VII n. 200)

The argument might at first seem to be airtight. As an example to support the minor premise, Scotus offers the way a white thing can first be dissimilar to another thing, then similar if that other thing becomes white (ibid., n. 205). As for the major premise, it seems incontrovertible, because everyone accepts that a thing cannot be separable from itself. So where there is any sort of separability, even in one direction, there is not full and real identity. Scotus shows, indeed, that the major premise follows directly from the first principle that the same thing cannot at the same time be F and not-F. For suppose that *a* can exist without *b*. Then it can be the case that *a* exists and *b* does not exist. But then, if *a* = *b*, it follows that the same thing at the same time exists and does not exist, a violation of our first principle. Hence one-way separability entails non-identity (ibid., n. 201). To deny the premise is, moreover, a philosophical disaster, inasmuch as monism would then inescapably follow: "if that major is denied, there does

[25] Scheibler has an excellent discussion of the real distinction and how two-way separability serves as a defeasible test (*Metaphys.* I.8.3). Regarding the modal distinction he writes: "Ego primo dico non esse prosus necessarium ad distinctionem realem et rationis addere tertiam, quomodocunque dicatur, modalis an aliter" (ibid. I.8.5.1 n. 55). He thinks this even though he admits modes into his ontology (§13.4).

[26] For Ockham against an intermediary distinction, see e.g. *Ord.* I.2.9 (*Op. theol.* II:317): "... omnia quae sunt extra animam, saltem in creaturis, si sint aliquo modo distincta, sunt res realiter distinctae." For further references and discussion, see Adams, *William Ockham* I:46–52. Suárez remarks that "multi negant posse excogitari aut intelligi mediam aliquam distinctionem" (*Disp. meta.* 7.1.9), and goes on to cite a long list of Thomists. See also the discussion in Fonseca, *In Meta.* V.6.7 (II:404–10).

not seem to remain any basis from which the distinction of beings can be proved" (ibid., n. 202).[27]

It is, however, not so easy to prove the reality of items in the various accidental categories. If Scotus's argument were successful in establishing that relations are really distinct from their subjects, then it could be used to yield the reality of any accidental property you like—whiteness, musicality, fatherhood, sitting, being a U.S. citizen, living in Colorado. Inasmuch as each can be separated from its subject, each would be a real property. What gives Scotus's argument its superficial appearance of success is the gap between being "not really the same" (line 3 above) and being *really distinct*. There is a gap here not because there is some sort of distinction that falls short of a real distinction, but because the failure of identity between *a* and *b* entails the distinct reality of *a* and *b* only if we presuppose that *a* and *b* are both things. If *a* and *b* fail to be identical because *a* is real and *b* is nothing, then we do not have a real distinction, or at any rate not the sort of real distinction that establishes the reality of relations. Hence the category anti-realist has nothing to fear from the above argument. (For another way to block this sort of simple appeal to separability, see §14.3.)

Suppose, however, that we establish the existence of substances and the existence of modes, and that we then appeal to their separability in one direction to establish their distinctness. (This is Suárez's strategy, quite explicitly, in Disputation Seven, and this is how in effect I take Descartes to be arguing in the wax passage [§8.2, §13.7].) The question then arises of what we are to make of the alleged fact that modes are separable in only one direction—that is, that they are dependent on their subjects. For Suárez and Descartes, this is a sign (albeit defeasible) that they are entities of a lesser sort. But this was by no means the standard verdict. Scotus, as we saw in §12.5, takes a position much like Suárez's in distinguishing between those categories that contain *res*, separable in both directions from their subjects, and the lesser, relational categories that contain mere modes, and that are dependent on their subjects. But Scotus does not conclude from this that the relational categories are entities of a lesser sort, or that they are any less distinct from their subjects. They are, he argues, fully and really distinct. Ockham, in contrast, contends that for any two things that contingently exist, each can, at least by divine power, exist without the other—that is, he insists that separability always runs in both directions. (Hume would later say something similar.) Ockham wields this principle against Scotus's realistic ontology, arguing that if a thing exists then it can exist

---

[27] For discussion of separability and the real distinction in Scotus, see King, "Scotus on Metaphysics" pp. 21–2; Henninger, *Relations* pp. 79–97; Pini, "Scotus's Realist Conception" p. 95. It is unfortunately common among recent scholars to suppose that a real distinction requires two-way separability—see, e.g., Des Chene, *Physiologia* p. 124: "Substantial form and prime matter are really distinct only if each is capable, at least by the absolute power of God, of existing without the other."

Ockham makes a long and careful reply to Scotus on relations (*Ord.* I.30.1, *Op. theol.* IV:281–319), in which he accepts Scotus's major premise (IV:310). See the discussions in Adams, *William Ockham* ch. 7 and Henninger, *Relations* chs. 5, 7. Adams agrees with Ockham on Scotus's major premise, calling it "uncontestable" (I:218). In the very similar discussion of *Lectura* II.1.4–5, Scotus remarks that "maior est ita manifesta quod est primum principium" (n. 185). Menn identifies Suárez as "the 'shameless' person of Scotus's fears, who denies that 'things one of which can remain without the other are really distinct'" ("Suárez and Modes" p. 241). This is misleading, however, because Scotus is talking about someone so shameless as to deny all real distinctions, even between Socrates and Plato, or Socrates and a stone (*Ord.* II.1.4–5; Vat. VII nn. 202–3). His argument is then that if we deny this, in an effort to avoid real relations, we have no way of responding to the shameless monist. In fact Suárez himself offers an argument much like Scotus's for the sufficiency of one-way separability as a refutation of identity (*Disp. meta.* 7.2.3).

all by itself, something that seems absurd for many of Scotus's *parvae res*—relations? actions? where? when?—up and down the list of categories (§12.5). Generations of scholastics would subsequently line up in favor or against Ockham's principle: realists against it in order to safeguard the reality of the relational categories, and Thomists also against it in order to save the notion of purely potential prime matter as really distinct but inseparable from form. Suárez, in his characteristic way, is proposing a compromise: let Ockham's strict criterion hold for genuine *res*, but let there be another class of lesser entities that satisfy only the weaker criterion.[28]

The history of these ideas reveals just how precarious a position Suárez (and Descartes) have staked out. There is nothing at all inevitable about the idea that all genuine *res* should be mutually independent. There is nothing particularly natural in the idea that less independent things are thereby less real. These are the terms of the Suarezian compromise, but their truth is far from intuitively obvious, and both principles were widely rejected. The way forward, however, is to set aside these debates over dependence and separability, since these issues are posterior to the question of what modes and *res* are. As I have urged in earlier chapters (esp. §10.4), the notion of a real accident cannot be fleshed out in terms of its independence from a subject. Similarly, here, although modes are necessarily dependent on their subject, that dependence is a consequence of their nature and indeed merely a defeasible mark of it. So with the issue of separability now set to one side, let us finally take up the question of what modes are supposed to be.

13.7. What Are Modes?

I have stressed from the start of this chapter that there are various approaches to modal realism. One approach treats modes as real but without having their own proper existence. What exists, on this sort of view, is the substance. For a mode to exist just is for the substance to exist in a certain way. We have seen this understanding of mode in Oresme, Wyclif, Scheibler, and Gorlaeus, and it is in this sense that Aquinas (and many of his contemporaries) can rightly be said to treat accidents as modes (§10.2). One great advantage of this approach is that it points toward a non-skeptical account of our knowledge of substance. If modes are ways of being of substances, then it seems

---

[28] For Ockham's insistence on two-way separability, see e.g. *Quod.* VI.6 (*Op. theol.* IX:605): "omnis res absoluta, distincta loco et subiecto ab alia re absoluta, potest per divinam potentiam existere, alia re absoluta destructa." See also *Sent.* prol. q. 1 (*Op. theol.* I:38) and the discussions in §14.3 and §19.2. The formulation in the main text is worded so as to exclude the case of God and creatures. Since God cannot not exist, creatures cannot be separated from God, even though they are really distinct from God. For a brief but very helpful discussion of these issues, see Adams, *William Ockham* I:16–19. Adams alludes to a further complication here regarding wholes and parts, when she exempts from two-way separability two distinct things that stand to each other as whole to part. This is a tricky issue, given that Ockham denies that wholes are really distinct from their parts taken together (§28.5). Still, inasmuch as a whole is distinct from any one of its parts (§26.2), and yet cannot exist without it (§29.2), something like her further restriction does seem necessary. Because of the complexity of the issues, the formulation in the main text, and in subsequent chapters, regretfully ignores these complications.

Against the requirement of two-way separability, see Burley, *In Phys.* I, f. 14vb: "illud principium est falsissimum et contradictionem includens, scilicet quod deus possit omnem rem absolutam distinctam ab alia re absoluta facere sine ea." The same point is constantly urged by Thomists—see, e.g., Durand of St. Pourçain, *Quod.* II.4, p. 189; Capreolus, *Defensiones* II.18.1.3 (IV:150b); Cajetan, *In De ente* q. 9 (tr. p. 191); Báñez, *In Summam theol.* I.3.4, q. 2.

For Hume's version of the separability principle, see *Treatise* I.4.5, p. 233, and appendix, p. 634.

plausible to say that, in grasping a mode, one just is grasping something about the substance itself. This does not necessarily make the nature of a substance entirely transparent, but at least it allows us to know some things about them. We saw Oresme make this sort of argument in §7.4. Despite this significant advantage, I will not try to say more about this here. The view strikes me as seriously obscure, inasmuch as it requires distinguishing between the reality of a thing and its existence. Moreover, this is not the version of modal realism that would prove most influential in the seventeenth century. (I will return to the distinction between a thing and its existence in §18.5 and again in §26.5.)

A second approach toward modal realism would hold that although modes are real, they supervene on non-modal features of the substance itself. This is, to be sure, a theory that will seem much more natural to modern sensibilities, and for a while I thought it could be found in one or another author from our period. Since I no longer think that, I will again describe this option only briefly, but it is worth at least mentioning, because it sheds light on the spectrum of possibilities open to a modal realist. To treat modes as supervening on substances requires distinguishing between two sets of facts, and then supposing that facts of the first kind undergo change only in virtue of facts of the second kind. So let our first kind of facts be shape, size, and motion. Let our second kind of facts be the location of the substance's parts. Then facts of the first kind—call them modes—supervene on facts of the second kind, inasmuch as the shape, size, and motion of a thing all depend on facts about how the parts of that thing are located.

Why would anyone want to import this anachronistic notion of supervenience to explain the theory of modes? One reason is that this provides a neat explanation for why modes are associated with both dependency and determinacy. Dependency obtains, of course, because such modes depend on their subvening base—since there is no shape, say, without the location of the thing's parts, the mode would depend on the substance, but the substance would not depend on the mode. At the same time, determinacy follows as well, because the subvening facts about location always give rise to one or another supervening mode. No matter how the parts are located, there must for instance be *some* further fact about the thing's shape. A second advantage is that this approach suggests an explanation for why modes are said to have their puzzling halfway sort of existence, real but not as real as substances. We can understand such claims as meaning simply that modes supervene on their subjects. Of course, there is the risk that such claims of supervenience will fuel a demand for reduction. In effect, this is Ockham's view. As we will see shortly (§14.3), he thinks that facts about shape, size, and motion can be wholly accounted for in terms of facts about the location of a thing's parts. The present line of thought, in contrast, contends that the supervenience relationship—at least in certain cases—describes a distinction that falls in between strict identity and real distinctness. A final advantage of this approach is that it fits the way these authors sometimes talk. Consider this passage from Descartes:

By the word 'surface' I understand not any substance or real nature, which could be destroyed by God's omnipotence, but only a mode or manner of being, which cannot be changed without a change in that in which or through which it exists—just as it involves a contradiction for the square shape of a piece of wax to be taken away from it without any of the parts of the wax changing their place. (To Mesland [1645], IV:163–4)

What comes before the dash constitutes a clear statement of supervenience, and what comes after the dash looks to be just the right sort of example: the shape of the wax supervenes on the location of its parts, and so counts as a mode of the wax.

All the same, I think this cannot be the right way to understand modes during our period. Certainly, it cannot be right for the scholastic modal realists we have been considering, because they are very explicit in treating temporal location itself as a mode (§17.5). If location is a mode, then there would seem to be no non-modal base for modal properties like size, shape, and motion to supervene on, and the theory falls apart. What about Descartes? Here there may be more room for supervenience, because the standard examples of modes of extension are size, shape, and motion. One could therefore try to read Descartes as building facts about location into the substance-level of his ontology, and then treating the various canonical modes of extension as supervening on such facts. This might have the further appeal of minimizing the impact of Descartes's modal realism, for although we could still take seriously his commitment to modes as real, we would not have to regard them as fundamental in a way that threatens his overriding commitment to corpuscularianism. The facts about position, we might say, are the deep facts that explain the way the material realm is, and the modal facts simply ride on top of these. A grasp of such modes might not constitute a grasp of the underlying substance, but inasmuch as the modes supervene on facts at the substance level, the door would be open to working our way from the modal level to the substance. Still, even if the appeal is clear enough, the texts do not bear it out. For Descartes regularly does mention location as a mode of extension—most notably in his official introduction of the modes of extension in *Principles* I.48:

Perception, volition, and all the modes both of perceiving and of willing are referred to thinking substances. To extended substance belong size (that is, extension itself in length, breadth, and depth), shape, motion, position (*situs*) of its parts, their divisibility, and the like.

In listing the "position of its parts" on the side of the modes, Descartes does not seem to retain any facts at the substance level on which the modal facts could supervene.[29] And if this is true for body, it seems even more clearly true for mind, where it is hard to see how the supervenience interpretation could possibly go. What sorts of facts at the substance level could particular thoughts and volitions possibly supervene on?

This leaves, so far as I can see, just one other way to understand what modes are. This third approach is, in a sense, the polar opposite of the previous one. Whereas supervenience treats the substance as determining its modes, this final approach treats the substance as radically indeterminate, and necessarily in need of modes in order to

---

[29] Descartes also mentions location as a mode of extension at *Principles* I.65: "figuras omnes, et situs partium, et ipsarum motus." This passage suggests that the Latin of *Principles* I.48 is probably mispunctuated: rather than the somewhat peculiar phrase '…situs, partium ipsarum divisibilitas, et talia…' it should likely read '…situs partium, ipsarum divisibilitas, et talia.' The main text translates accordingly. The French translation also corrects the mistake, with the phrase "situation des parties." See also the third paragraph of Meditation V (VII:63), which likewise lists '*situs*' among the modes, although without using the term '*modus*.'

exist at all. One great advantage of this approach is that it fits very closely with how Suárez describes his theory. As we saw in §13.3, part of Suárez's case for modes is an "a priori" argument, according to which "creatures are imperfect, and . . . as a result they need such modes, by which they are made complete with respect to all these states" (*Disp. meta.* 7.1.19). We are now in a position to say a bit more about the sort of picture Suárez is invoking, and what this shows about the nature of modes. If one takes modal realism seriously, and furthermore places on the modal side *all* the facts about location, arrangement, and the motion of particles, the result is to leave the substance itself "imperfect" or incomplete, in the sense that it will have no location, no shape, no size. Those are facts on the modal side, not the substance side, and so to take seriously the reality of modes as something distinct from the substance just is to strip the substance itself of such geometric–kinetic properties. Now there is something admittedly odd in this way of putting things—in saying that the substance will have no location, shape, or size. For in a sense *of course* the substance has a location etc.—it has one precisely in virtue of its modes. In part we are revisiting the familiar puzzle that confronts anyone who would distinguish between a thing and its properties, and yet want to say that the substance has the properties (§6.2). What is new in this connection is that we are dealing with properties that a substance cannot lack. On Suárez's picture, the substance is radically incomplete when considered all by itself, and cannot coherently exist without the addition of entities of another sort, modal entities. This is in contrast to the case of real accidents, which have a very different relationship to their subject. Although real accidents inhere in substances, and thereby license the ascription of a property to a substance, the substance does not need any such real accident in order to exist. Real accidents like heat and color are ones that a substance can exist without (Chs. 19, 21)—they add something to the substance, but they do not complete the substance in the way that modes do. Accordingly, determinacy applies to modes, but not to real accidents. Dependency too applies only to modes. Modes are dependent on their substance, because what they are, essentially, are completers of incomplete substances. Real accidents, in contrast, have no such character. There is nothing about the nature of a material substance that demands color, for instance, given that bodies can be transparent. Hence substance and real accident do not lock together in the way that substance and mode do.

I believe this is the picture that both Suárez and Descartes have in mind when they claim that modes are entities of a lesser kind. The obscure idea of a halfway sort of existence should be understood in terms of the very special relationship that modes have to their subjects. What does the work here is not simply the fact of one-way separability. That fact all by itself has no particular ontological implications: creatures, for instance, do not exist any less than God simply because they are causally dependent on God. What matters instead is that both modes and substances are radically incomplete in the way just described, so that neither is conceivable without the other. Suárez captures this mutual interdependence by speaking of a *modal distinction*. Or, and this is perhaps the more illuminating way to put it, he describes mode and subject as *in a certain way identical*. Modes, he says, are neither fully identical with their subjects nor fully distinct, but partly identical and partly distinct. Thus, between a mode and its subject there is "a certain kind of identity" (*Disp. meta.* 7.1.20), and a mode "has some identity with the thing on which it acts" (ibid., par. 26). Such ways of talking look hopeless on their face, but can be made sense of if understood to refer to the sort of dependence at issue between mode and substance—not merely a contingent causal dependence as obtains between two *res*, but a necessary metaphysical dependence, such that substances cannot exist without modes, and a mode cannot exist without its substance.[30]

An interesting feature of the Suarezian model is that it crucially depends not just on facts about modes, but on facts about substance. One cannot understand his picture simply by thinking hard about what a mode is supposed to be—one also needs to think about what substances are. It is because *substances* have a certain incompleteness that we must postulate entities of a certain special kind, partly distinct from their subjects and partly the same. Yet if this is a strength of the theory, it might also seem to be a weakness, because it requires embracing a conception of substance that seems deeply obscure. The official grand narrative of this study (§1.3, §4.5) runs from the development of a scholastic ontology of metaphysical parts, toward the corpuscularian rejection of such parts in favor of an ontology of substance alone. Viewed from that perspective, the finding that Descartes, say, is a modal realist might look like a minor wrinkle in the overarching narrative. Yes, Descartes endorses modes, but modes are things that barely exist at all, leaving substances to be the stars of the corpuscularian show. This narrative could be sustained on the supervenience approach to modes. But the Suarezian model will not bear this construal, because Suárez builds up a theory of modes by tearing down the notion of substance. Whereas we would naturally suppose that substances exemplify the concrete and particular, Suárez's substances are indeterminate and to that extent metaphysical. They are, indeed, the counterparts at a higher level of composition to scholastic prime matter. The Suarezian substance is not quite as indeterminate as prime matter—it is characterized by a certain specific nature (dog, cat, stone) and endures only for as long as that nature is preserved. Still, Suárez's dogs and cats and stones not only lack heat and color, but also lack shape, size, and location. Of course, in another sense they most definitely *have* all of these features, but they do so only in virtue of being joined with further metaphysical parts. This is a familiar picture in the case of the real accidents, and one would expect Descartes to have nothing to do with it. But what we are now seeing is that the Suarezian model extends this story to the geometric–kinetic properties. Inasmuch as Descartes needs properties of that kind, and does not reduce them to the level of substance, he too embraces this Suarezian picture. To return to Francis Bacon's memorable image (§7.2), substance gets shunted

---

[30] The obscurity of the notion of partial identity makes it tempting to treat the modal distinction as entailing either that mode and *res* are not in any respect identical, or that they are wholly identical. Menn, for instance, writes that the Jesuits "think that all accidents in the last seven categories are really identical with some substance or quantity or quality, and distinguished at most formally or modally" ("Suárez and Modes" p. 231). This is true, however, only if "really identical" is understood in a rather special sense, not as meaning *wholly identical*, as one would expect, but as meaning *not really distinct*. Suárez's own practice, however, is to think of identity as coming in degrees (see, e.g., *Disp. meta.* 7.3.5). For other examples of his appealing to a "kind of identity" see *Disp. meta.* 7.2.9, where two modes of the same substance are merely modally distinct, "quia licet non ratione sui, formaliter loquendo, saltem ratione rei quam modificant habent inter se quamdam realem identitatem"; ibid., par. 10: "quae huiusmodi sunt non habent ex proprio conceptu sufficientem entitatem in qua conserventur, sed solum ex quadam identitate ad ea quibus insunt."

off into a minor role, as the indeterminate substratum, leaving modes to be given all the leading parts.

The theory of modes is of course supposed to reduce one's ontological commitments, by avoiding the sorts of obscurities that arise from treating accidents as real. Cartesian accidents are *mere* modes, and so supposedly unobjectionable. But if modes too are real, even if less real, then it is not clear that the theory can avoid its own sort of metaphysical obscurities. These consequences may indeed seem bad enough to prompt a reevaluation of the evidence in favor of modal realism, or at least to make one wonder whether the Suarezian model is the right one for Descartes. In defense of these conclusions, I would again point to the wax passage from the Second Meditation. I discussed this text at some length in §8.2, while arguing for this same substance–mode distinction from the side of substance. Here I will confine myself to indicating briefly how Descartes's argument applies in the present context, setting aside the details that were discussed more fully already. The aim of the wax passage is to show that we perceive modes of substance, not the substance itself. That requires some kind of substance–mode distinction that goes beyond a mere distinction of reason. (If the distinction were merely of reason, then the most Descartes could conclude is that we perceive substance but without realizing it, because we do not realize the identity between mode and substance. But he clearly thinks that even a philosophically enlightened observer does not perceive the substance.) To get a distinction on the side of reality, Descartes invokes the changeability of substance:

[S]urely the wax itself was not the sweetness of the honey, or the fragrance of the flowers, or that whiteness, shape, or sound, but rather the body that appeared to me a little while ago to manifest itself in certain ways (*modis*), and now in different ways. But what precisely is it that I so imagine? Let us concentrate and, after taking away what does not belong to the wax, let us see what is left: surely, it is nothing other than a thing that is extended, flexible, and changeable. (VII:30–1)[31]

The passage appeals, in a way that is by now familiar, to the indiscernibility of identicals. The substance (body) had certain modes, and now it has other modes. The substance endures whereas the modes do not. Therefore the substance is something distinct from the modes. The crucial assumption here is that the substance endures through change. Those who would deny this—a line of thought that stretches from Ockham and Buridan all the way to Hobbes and then Locke (chs. 29–30)—do not face the same sort of pressure to separate the thing from its properties. But since Descartes wants to retain at least this much of our commonsense ontology of enduring particulars, he feels the need to distinguish between that which endures and that which

---

[31] It seems to me Gassendi has in mind the indeterminacy of substance apart from its modes in the Fifth Objections when he wonders how Descartes can strip the forms off and still claim to grasp what the wax is. "miror qui dicas te, peracta illa detractione formarum quasi vestium, perfectius atque evidentius percipere quid cera sit. Nam percipis quidem ceram ejusve substantiam debere esse aliquid præter ejusmodi formas; at quid illud sit, non percipis, nisi nos fallis. . . . Si dicas te absque ulla extensione, figura, coloreque concipere, dic, bona fide: qualenam ergo?" (VII: 271–2). Gassendi, I take it, accepts the indeterminacy of substance, but wants Descartes to acknowledge the epistemic consequences.

A conception of Descartes's indeterminate substance much like my own can be found in Secada, *Cartesian Metaphysics*, e.g., pp. 14, 190, 249, though Secada does not seem to feel the obscurity of this doctrine.

changes. Since he cannot tolerate real accidents, he embraces Suárez's conception of modes, which is still a realistic theory of properties but not quite so realistic. This diminished ontological commitment comes with a price, however—the indeterminacy of substance. The logic of the wax passage requires removing all the changeable properties from the substance, and leaving it only with that which is essential to it. When we do this to the substance—when we "distinguish the wax from its external forms—take the clothes off, as it were, and consider it naked" (VII:32)—we make it into something wholly metaphysical, something that could not possibly exist on its own, and something we can seemingly have no idea of, other than as the determinable subject of various determinate modes, existing in potentiality for those modes. To a startling extent, we recreate the scholastic doctrine of prime matter.

PART IV

EXTENSION

14

Quantity and Extension

We tend to take corpuscular structure for granted. We assume, that is, that physical reality, by its very nature, is composed of extended integral parts, that those parts, however far down they go, yield the basic structure of reality, and that we have reached a fundamental understanding of things when we can explain them in terms of that structure. Of course, simply to suppose that bodies are composed of parts is not on its face a controversial view. What is controversial, however, or at least ought to be controversial, is that this corporeal structure is a basic feature of reality, requiring no further explanation.

This perspective is so familiar that it may be hard to imagine what it would be like to deny it. Indeed, if one wanted to make a case for the modernity of seventeenth-century thought, in the sense of its having introduced a conceptual framework that has shaped our understanding of reality today, one could hardly do better than to focus on this idea. For most scholastic authors, however, the corpuscular structure of reality is not its fundamental nature, but something accidental and posterior, something that it might—at least by divine power—lose. Hence an inquiry into the most fundamental nature of the material world, an inquiry into the thin substance (apart from its accidents) or, even more fundamentally, an inquiry into prime matter, would transcend the extended reality with which we are familiar, and get at the basic stuff from which *res extensa* is constituted. As we will see, looking at material substance in this way raises deep questions not just about extension but also about universals and the problem of individuation.

For our four centuries, the debate over corpuscular structure is the debate over Quantity. Of the various kinds of being described by the categorial scheme, none was more controversial and none was more central to the corpuscularian revolution, inasmuch as it is here, in the category of Quantity, that the various geometric–kinetic properties lie. This is not, however, one of those debates that serves to define the boundaries of scholastic Aristotelianism. For although most scholastic authors were quantity realists, some were not, insisting instead that corpuscular structure is a basic feature of matter. By the seventeenth century, talk of quantity largely gives way to talk of extension, but the issues remain much the same. Indeed, for seventeenth-century authors these issues become all the more pressing, because it is crucial to the reductive corpuscularian project that this structure be taken as metaphysically basic, so that material substances can be built up from there. Indeed, the basicality of corpuscular structure becomes so prevalent an assumption among post-scholastic authors that they tend to take it for granted. When this idea is put forth by earlier authors, in contrast, it is as a thesis they have to argue for strenuously, and always against the common consensus. Precisely for this reason, it will be illuminating to focus on them in preference to their seventeenth-century heirs.

14.1. Against Quantity: Olivi

A large part of the reason there were such long-running disputes over quantity is that there was little agreement about precisely what it is. Nicholas of Autrecourt remarked on how most of the doctors he had heard lecture at Paris in the 1320s did not think it even worth arguing in favor of quantity realism, regarding its truth as self-evident (*Tractatus* prol. 2, p. 197). Well attuned to the gap between what is said to be self-evident and what truly is self-evident, Autrecourt goes on to make the confidence of these realists look quite absurd. But how one judges this dispute depends entirely on what one takes quantity to be, a question that came into focus only once the reality of the category came into question at the start of our period. Scholastic authors were strongly disposed to defend quantity realism—that is, to treat accidents in the category of Quantity as real accidents in the sense defined in §10.4. They did so, however, in many different ways. One line of argument, which we will consider in the following chapter, connects quantity with impenetrability. The most common scholastic view, however, and the focus of this chapter, treats quantity as a real accident that serves to make a material substance extended.

Yet even if a link between quantity and extension was taken for granted for much of our period, it was quite unclear just what it is that quantity adds to a substance or—to put the same point differently—just what would be missing if quantity were removed from a substance. On one version of quantity realism, which I will call the *A theory*, quantity is what makes a body have parts. On another version, the *B theory*, quantity makes the body's parts be spread out in a continuous and unified way. This disagreement should look familiar, inasmuch as we considered an analogous debate in Chapter 4, over prime matter and extension. According to the Simple View (§4.1), prime matter is intrinsically without parts, and has parts only in virtue of being informed by quantity. This was the standard Thomistic view, endorsed by Averroists in a certain way as well, and it accords with the A theory of quantity. According to the Extensionless Parts View (§4.2), in contrast, prime matter of itself, intrinsically, has parts, but those parts are not spread out—extended—until prime matter is actualized by quantity. This view was suggested by Scotus,[1] and defended by Paul of Venice and others; it corresponds with the B theory of quantity. The debate as it arose in Chapter 4 was, in the first instance, a disagreement over the nature of prime matter. But it was, equivalently, a disagreement over the role of quantity, inasmuch as quantity is what was standardly conceived of as explaining extension. In this chapter, we are considering the debate from a higher level of composition: not as a disagreement over prime matter and extension, but as a

---

[1] For Scotus's defense of quantity, see *In Meta.* V.5–6 nn. 82–9 and V.9, as well as *Ord.* IV.12.2 (Vat. VIII n. 15).

disagreement over material substance and extension. Once the issues are set out from this perspective, as concerning not just the abstruse topic of prime matter, but what is essential or accidental to material substances in general, they take on a new light. For we are now in a position to see how this is a dispute over the very nature of corpuscular structure: the way in which bodies are composed of smaller bodies, spread out in space to form a larger whole.

Peter John Olivi seems to have been the first scholastic author to treat corpuscular structure as basic. Writing in 1279, Olivi describes his contemporaries as adhering to the position that "quantity adds something really distinct to the thing to which it belongs first and *per se*, and not just the position or continuity of the parts of that thing, in virtue of which they are located outside of one another" (*Summa* IV.10, in Maier, "Problem der Quantität" p. 169). What exactly that added thing might be is not clear, and indeed Olivi argues against quantity realism by insisting that there is nothing more for quantity to add—nothing more to be explained—that is not already accounted for by matter's and form's having parts arranged in a certain way. Thus, "'quantity' refers to nothing other than the parts of the thing quantified, together with their location or position, being extrinsically coordinated with each other" (*Tractatus de quantitate* f. 49vb). More precisely, "quantity or extension adds absolutely nothing really distinct to the quantified matter or to the extended and quantified form, except perhaps the union and location and position of those parts" (*Summa* II.58, II:440). This is more precise because it adds the essential further requirement that, for a thing to count as having quantity, it must have parts that have some sort of *unified* location. Otherwise, instead of a single, continuous quantity, we would have simply a discrete collection of multiple things. Olivi's wording in this last passage is interesting for several reasons. First, he casually identifies quantity with extension. As we will see, this is a common assumption in discussions of continuous quantity (as distinct from what Aristotle called discrete quantity [*Cat.* ch. 6], which will not concern us here). It is a particularly natural assumption for Olivi in this context, inasmuch as he expressly understands quantity in the way authors universally understand extension—as a thing's having *partem extra partem*, or spatially distinct (albeit unified) parts (§4.1).[2] Second, the passage is a bit coy about whether quantity adds anything to substance, remarking that "quantity adds nothing really distinct except perhaps..." Now it is quite clear, in texts we have already looked at (§12.4), that Olivi means to reject quantity as something really distinct from substance or quality (the only real accident he allows). But we have also seen signs that Olivi accepts quantity as a mode (§13.2), and so we can understand this passage as leaving room for that option.

Setting aside for now the issue of Olivi's exact ontological commitments (§17.5), let us concentrate on Olivi's arguments against treating quantity as a real accident. Immediately after offering what I labeled above a "more precise" statement of his view, he offers a series of six impressive arguments for it, the first two of which I will

---

[2] On the definition of extension as a thing's having *partem extra partem*, see §4.1. Dutton observes that, when extension is defined in these terms, the idea of an extended simple becomes impossible ("Nicholas of Autrecourt" p. 81). Scholastic authors would not have regarded this as an objection to their view, but as a welcomed consequence. As we will see in Ch. 16, immaterial entities were not regarded as extended, even if they exist in more than one place at once. That leaves the question of whether all bodies, no matter how small, have integral parts. For this complex issue, see §26.2.

consider here. Here is the first, which as usual (§12.4) he puts safely into the third-person plural:

They prove this from the fact that every extended matter and form has parts that are constitu-tive of its essence, are infinitely divisible, have distinct locations or positions, and are united and made continuous with one another. All these things, they say, are completely self-evident. We   3
see this, for instance, in whiteness, one part of which is in one part of matter, and another in another part, and so on in short for all other cases. But 'extension' or 'quantity' does not seem to refer to anything other than that multitude of parts having distinct locations in this way, and so   6
being united to each other. For if we suppose that 'quantity' refers to a form that is really distinct from these parts, it will still be necessary to postulate, within that [distinct form], parts other than these parts, standing to one another with respect to the aforesaid conditions in just the way   9
that these parts stand to one another. (ibid.)

The argument begins (lines 1–3) with the "completely self-evident" assertion that when either matter or form is extended, it has parts that are (a) essential to it; (b) infinitely divisible; (c) distinctly located; and (d) continuous. Notably, the claim holds not just for a composite substance, but for the metaphysical parts of that substance (prime matter + substantial form), and also for any inhering accidental forms. Hence Olivi takes as his example whiteness (lines 3–5), which is the sort of quality he is a realist about. So far, this is just a restatement of Olivi's view: that things have extension (= *partem extra partem*) intrinsically, and that extension (when continuously unified) just is quantity. The clever part of the argument comes at the end (lines 7–10), where he considers what would happen if we postulated quantity as some further form, to account for extension. That form, too, Olivi argues, would have to have parts, and they too would be extended. But—the reader has to supply the punchline—we would then need a further explanation to explain the extension of that new form, and off we go on a regress, or else we allow that no further explanation is needed, in which case we did not need to introduce any further form in the first place. This seems plausible. For if one considers the color on a surface, it does seem right to think that it has parts, and that those parts have a continuous location, and that the color's having continuously located parts is *essential* to it. How could a color lack those features? (Infinite divisibility [line 2] is another matter, especially for color, but we can set that aside until §26.2.)

The plausibility of this first argument is brought out by his second argument:

They also prove this from the fact that, if every accident and every other quantified real nature (*essentia quanta*) were taken away, [A] the constitutive and essential parts of those forms and that matter would not on that account be taken away, nor would [B] their essential union, in virtue   3
of which they constitute and make up their whole. Now although the union of the parts of that matter does refer to something formal and so to something really distinct from its parts, that union of parts without which they cannot exist necessarily points toward a substantial form,   6
not an accidental one, since accidental forms do not give substantial being or existence to matter or to its parts. If, however, [C] division applied *per se* only to quantity, then having divisible parts would apply *per se* to it alone, and so if it alone were removed then all the parts would be   9
removed, since wherever parts remain, divisibility and union also remain, given that everything having parts is divisible into those parts. But however matter and corporeal form are claimed to be united with respect to their parts, by that very fact some extension and continuity is always   12
claimed as well. Therefore regardless what quantity is removed from them, they will always have quantity, by the very fact that they have their parts united in this way. (ibid., II:440–1)

This dense passage is worth considering closely. Its overarching assumption is that if quantity is an accident, then it should be possible for the substance to exist without any quantity. (In setting out the debate in this way, Olivi shows himself to be a forerunner of the doctrine of real accidents that would become ascendant from Scotus forward [§10.5 and §11.1].) The question, then, is what difference it would make to a material substance, if the quantity were removed. If we could pinpoint what would be lost when the quantity is lost, we would know what quantity does, and why it must be postulated. The passage runs through three possible stories about what quantity, as a real accident, does for the substance:

A. Quantity is what makes a thing have parts.
B. Quantity is what makes a thing's parts be spread out in a continuous and unified way.
C. Quantity is what makes a thing be divisible.

With respect to A, Olivi argues that if quantity could be removed, the remaining substance would still have continuously united parts (lines 1–3). Their having parts, the previous argument had held (lines 1–2 earlier), is just constitutive of what they are, and requires no further explanation. As for B, Olivi agrees that the unity of these parts does require some further explanation (lines 4–8). But that explanation, he contends, will depend on a substantial rather than an accidental form (Chs. 24–5). So what is left for quantity to do? The argument considers one more possibility, C, that quantity might explain divisibility, as opposed to unity (lines 7–9). But again the substance alone, with its parts, is sufficient to explain divisibility, since as long as those parts remain, both union and divisibility remain (lines 9–11). The absurd result of removing quantity from a substance, then, is that it makes no difference: the substance remains quantified (lines 13–14). The conclusion we are left to draw for ourselves is that quantity, conceived of as something over and above a thing's parts so-and-so organized, is completely otiose, and so should not be posited.

Olivi could scarcely have been very clear about exactly what role his opponent would want to ascribe to quantity, because it is hard to find a sustained statement of quantity realism before our period begins. Here, as we will see in other domains, a proper defense of the standard scholastic framework had to wait until after it came under attack. At this early juncture in the debate, Olivi has to guess at exactly what work the realist might invoke quantities to do. His guesses, however, would prove to be right on target, inasmuch as he singles out what would become the two leading versions of quantity realism—what I call the A theory and the B theory. As for C, one often does find later authors talking of quantity as what explains divisibility, doubtless under Aristotle's influence (e.g., *Meta.* V.13, 1020a7–8). Olivi's diagnosis, though, would seem to be widely accepted: that divisibility follows directly from the having of parts. Hence talk of quantity as explaining divisibility can generally be understood as another way of framing the A theory.[3]

---

[3] Olivi devotes two extended discussions to quantity, first in *Summa* II.58 (*circa* 1278), and then in the *Tractatus de quantitate* (1282). For the fourth of Olivi's six arguments in *Summa* II.58, based on the incoherence of an extensionless point outside of the context of some quantity, see Ch. 4 note 13. Another important statement can be found in the *Tabula* printed at the end of the 1509 edition of the *Quodlibet*: "quantitas continua non addat ad formas vel materias per ipsam extensas nisi solum duo, scilicet exteriorationem seu exteriorem situm seu positionem partium materiae vel formarum, et continuitatem earum seu unionem continuitatis, qua una pars est alteri unita et continuata" (f. 63vb). Olivi's views

It would not take long for the terms of the debate to sharpen. Olivi wrote his lengthy *Tractatus de quantitate* (1282) because he was already being criticized, as he himself puts it, for holding "ridiculous and pernicious opinions" (49vb). The next year he was censured by his Franciscan order, in general for denying that the ten categories are really distinct (§12.4), but more specifically for holding the "dangerous" doctrine that neither Quantity nor Relation are really distinct categories. Branding a doctrine as *dangerous* bears a precise ecclesiastical meaning: that although the content of the proposition itself does not contradict Church dogma (in which case it would be heretical or erroneous), still it has consequences that threaten Church dogma. In the case of Relation, the main threat is to the Trinity. In the case of Quantity, the main threat is to the Eucharist, because standard theories of transubstantiation maintained that quantity is what subsists apart from the host, and that the other real accidents inhere in it. To this there is a straightforward reply: that the qualities of the host subsist on their own, and are intrinsically extended, and so do not need to inhere in quantity. Olivi, however, characteristically, responds by stressing that he had not defended any of these views *in propria persona*, but only "recited" them.[4]

On the heels of this controversy came an effort by others to explain why quantity is not reducible in the way Olivi had proposed. One way in which the debate might have gone, at this juncture, is for Olivi's adversaries to have identified some further work for quantity to do, beyond ABC above. This would eventually happen, as we will see in the next chapter, but not for several generations. Olivi's contemporaries wanted to defend the reality of quantity in just the way Olivi had supposed they would, by claiming that a real accident is necessary to account for a body's being extended. Indeed, this understanding of quantity remains dominant throughout the scholastic era. Thus Gabriel Vasquez, at the end of the sixteenth century, would assert that "extension is the proper nature of quantity, as it has been hitherto defined by all the philosophers" (*In summam theol.* III.190.5 n. 52; cf. ibid., I.196.3 n. 10). This is not true, as the next chapter will make clear, but it is close.[5]

Even when authors agreed that quantity is that which makes a thing be extended, in one of the ways listed above, there was still disagreement about exactly which of these

regarding quantity, as well as the later reaction to those views, are discussed in detail by Maier, "Problem der Quantität" pp. 159–75; Burr, "Quantity and Eucharistic Presence"; and Bakker, *La raison* I:342–66.

[4] For Olivi's censure in 1283, see Fussenegger, "Littera septem sigillorum" n. 16, p. 52: "Item dicere quod praedicamenta non distinguuntur realiter est contra Philosophum et maxime de relatione et quantitate est periculosum"; Laberge, "Tria scripta" n. 15, p. 129: "De hoc nihil assertive quod sciam dixi, licet inter multas opiniones aliquid de hoc recitaverim; et quia de huiusmodi philosophicis non multum curo, paratus sum (ed. *sunt*) revocare, quamvis communem opinionem in scholis semper tenuerim." For detailed information, see Piron, *Parcours d'un intellectuel franciscain* pp. 35–56.

[5] For other later scholastic accounts of quantity in terms of extension, see Fonseca, *In Meta.* V.13.1.3, II:639: "crediderim igitur, rationem formalem quantitatis esse ens per se extensum"; ibid., V.13.23, II:652: "cum quantitas sit ipsa extensio..."; Eustachius a Sancto Paulo, *Summa* I.1.3b.2.1 (I:56): "Quare in ratione formali extensionis consistit ipsius quantitatis ratio et natura"; Nathanael Carpenter, *Phil. libera* I.1, p. 3: "ubicumque enim est partium extensio, ibi est quantitas." Compare Ficino, *Platonic Theology* I.2.1: "quantitas autem nihil est aliud quam extensio ipsius materiae, aut si quid aliud est, est tamen res quaedam talis, ut et divisioni subiecta sit semper..."; Biel, *Sent.* IV.10.1: "omnes loquentes de quantitate continua seu extensiva in hoc concordant, quod quantitas est illud per quod res aliqua divisibilis est extensa, id est habet partem extra partem localiter seu descriptive, ita quod una pars determinat sibi aliquem praecisum locum et adaequatum et alia alium, ita quod duae partes extensivae non sint simul in eodem loco adaequato."

Although, as I will be indicating, the scholastic debate over quantity has received some amount of attention in the secondary literature, work on this topic remains in its infancy, with even the most basic conceptual distinctions, such as between what I call the A and B theories, having gone unnoticed.

roles quantity plays. The most prominent early defender of quantity realism, Richard of Middleton, is quite ambiguous. Middleton, another Franciscan and a member of the committee that censured Olivi's work, attacks those views in a quodlibetal question composed three years after the censure. Taking up Olivi's query about what would happen when this supposedly real quantity is removed from a substance, Middleton responds that it would leave behind a substance that is extendible, but not extended. In contrast, he says, a spiritual substance is neither extended nor extendible. What exactly does it mean, though, to be extendible? Middleton might be thinking in terms of the B theory: that the substance has integral parts which fail to be spread out, but are instead, as it were, all folded into one another. Or he might have in mind a version of the A theory: that a material substance without quantity lacks integral parts but *potentially* has them, in a way that a spiritual substance, by its nature, never could. Presumably, Middleton has one or the other of these views in mind, but he does not make it clear which.[6] Other discussions from this era, however, are more explicit. Roger Marston, also a Franciscan, allows that matter has parts intrinsically. He, then, is explicitly a B theorist: he defends quantity as that which spreads those parts out in a continuous fashion. Thomas of Sutton, in contrast, as one might expect from a Dominican follower of Aquinas, is expressly an A theorist: he ascribes to quantity the role of giving parts to matter. The arts master Simon of Faversham, similarly, devotes an entire question to "Whether substance apart from quantity has parts," and answers in the negative (*In Praed.* 34).[7]

Through the subsequent centuries, quantity realists continue to argue between themselves over these two theories. John Capreolus, for instance, takes a substance without quantity to lack parts entirely, as does Eustachius a Sancto Paulo, two centuries

---

[6] For Richard of Middleton's response to Olivi, see *Quod.* II.14, p. 52a: "Substantia enim quae est corpus per intellectum abstracta a quantitate non intelligitur ut quid extensum, sed ut quid extensibile. Unde non intelligitur ut spiritus, quia spiritus non est aliquid extensum, nec extensibile." Middleton takes up Olivi's view again, more briefly, at *Sent.* IV.12.1.1. Compare Giles of Rome, *Theoremata de esse et essentia* th. 15, p. 93: "Quantitas extendit materiam et dat ei esse extensum. Ipsa ergo extensio materiae est quoddam esse eius quod recipit a quantitate. Debemus enim imaginari quod materia de se non dicit quid actu extensum, sed dicit aliquid quod est in potentia ut extendatur. Sed materia actu coniuncta quantitati vere actu extenditur et habet esse extensum." Moody, "Ockham and Aegidius of Rome," argues that Giles rather than Aquinas is the target of Ockham's later attack on quantity realism. Although Moody is quite right that Aquinas has nothing to do with this dispute, it is hard to say whether Giles is a principal source.

[7] For Roger Marston, see *Quod.* II.29, p. 292: "Unde, omni quantitate a mundo subtracta per divinam potentiam, remaneret materia cum suis partibus ordine essentiali distinctis. . . . Forma vero materialis adveniens materiae perficit eam, et per consequens distinguit a ceteris, faciens quantitatem distinctam; et quia perficiendo materiam facit partem extra partem, efficit quantit atem continuam." Marston goes on to associate this conception of quantity with the indeterminate dimensions of Averroes's *De substantia orbis* (§4.3).

For Thomas of Sutton, see *Quod.* III.17: "licet materia partes habeat substantiales eiusdem rationis sicut et quantitas, tamen materia de se partes non habet, sed per quantitatem. Et similiter forma tam substantialis quam accidentalis non habet partes eiusdem rationis de se, sed per quantitatem. Quantitas vero habet partes eiusdem rationis de se formaliter. Hoc enim est de ratione quantitatis." Sutton's discussion is particularly interesting because it attempts to grapple with Olivi's point that, if quantity explains extension, we then need a further story about why quantity itself is extended. Sutton's reply is to grant that quantity is extended, and that this is a separate extension from the extension of the substance, and one that quantity has intrinsically, in such a way that no further story is required. Peter Auriol would later take a different route, holding that quantity makes a substance have parts but without itself having parts (*Sent.* II.12.1.5). Auriol is sometimes included among quantity anti-realists (see, e.g., Suárez, *Disp. meta.* 40.2.2), and no wonder, given that he says things like this: "quantitas sit ipsamet partibilitas partium" (*Sent.* IV.12.1.1, III:111aB). But this is of a piece with his broadly deflationary conception of accidents (§11.4), which is not the same as a reductive conception of accidents. Thus, he goes on to insist that "cum dico partem, duo dico, scilicet ipsam substantiam et materiam eius, secundo partibilitatem eius, et haec non sunt unum et idem" (ibid.). Indeed, Auriol here treats it as a distinct argument for his view that it avoids anti-realist attacks on quantity.

later. Distinguishing between a thing's external extension, in virtue of which it has parts spread out in space, and its internal extension, in virtue of which it simply has distinct parts, Eustachius appeals to quantity to explain both. (Hence Eustachius in effect defends both the A theory and the B theory. This is often what the A theorist seems to think.) Walter Burley, in contrast, holds that without quantity a body ceases to have *partem extra partem*, but yet "a substance without its accidents has all the same parts that it had before—both its essential parts (matter and form) and its integral parts" (*De formis*, pars post., p. 58). This same view would be defended, later, by Paul of Venice and, much later, by the Coimbrans.[8]

14.2. The Seventeenth Century

By the middle of the seventeenth century, a reductive theory of quantity along Olivi's lines is taken for granted by all but the most conservative remnants of scholasticism. If it seems hard to imagine that events could have developed any other way, then consider the case of Kenelm Digby, whose *Two Treatises* (1644) combines a thoroughly post-scholastic rejection of real qualities with the retention of quantity. For Digby, Aristotle's four elemental qualities, and all subsequent qualities, can be reduced to bodies arranged in certain ways. Moreover, "all operations among bodies are either local motion, or such as follow out of local motion" (I.5.5). These claims sound as if they entail a thoroughgoing corpuscularianism, but Digby thinks that his reductive story requires more than just substance—it requires substance and quantity:

If all physical things and natural changes do proceed out of the constitution of rare and dense bodies in this manner, as we do put them (as the work we have in hand intends to show), then, so manifold effects will so convince the truth of this doctrine which we have declared, that there can remain no doubt of it, neither can there be any of the divisibility of quantity from substance, without which this doctrine cannot consist. (I.3.9, p. 25)

What quantity adds to the story is "divisibility, or a capacity to be divided into parts" (I.2.8, p. 15). This just is to say that quantity gives the material realm its corporeal structure. With that structure in place, a familiar sort of corpuscularian story can be told. Without quantity, in contrast, material substance would be indivisible, without parts. (On the status of parts in Digby's theory, see §26.4.)[9]

---

[8] For Capreolus, see *Defensiones* II.18.1.3, IV:148ab: "si Deus separaret substantiam ab omni quantitate, illa substantia non haberet partes distantes, nec propinquas; immo, nullam haberet in actu." For Eustachius, see *Summa* I.1.3b.2.1 (I:56): "Verum cum duplex esse possit extensio rei quantae: altera velut externa et sensibus perspecta, nempe extensio partium in ordine ad locum; altera vero interna, a sensibus plane remota, nempe extensio earundem partium in ordine ad se."

Although something like Eustachius's distinction appears in Fonseca, who is frequently a source for Eustachius, Fonseca goes on (*In Meta.* V.13.2.3, II:649–51) to take a view like that of his fellow Coimbran Jesuits. The Coimbran view had been suggested by Scotus (Ch. 4 note 7), and is also developed by Paul of Venice (§4.2). See also Burley, *De formis*, pars post. p. 64, and *Super artem veterem*, Praed. f. e3va: "concedo quod partes substantiae praesupponuntur a partibus quantitatis in essendo, sed non in essendo quantae.... Et cum dicitur quod Deus potest facere substantiam panis vel hominis sine aliqua quantitate, dicendum quod hoc concesso substantia hominis vel panis haberet partem vel partes sed non partem extra partem."

[9] For Digby on material substance without quantity, see *Two Treatises* I.3.8, p. 22: "if besides quantity there be a substance or thing which is divisible, that thing, if it be condistinguished from its quantity or divisibility, must of itself be indivisible, or (to speak more properly) it must be not divisible. Put then such substance to be capable of the quantity of the whole world or universe and, consequently, you put it of itself indifferent to all, and to any part of quantity: for in it,

Today, Digby's view seems almost unintelligible. Lacking the proper historical context, modern readers scarcely know what to make of his work. Why abandon qualities, and yet hold onto quantity? From the scholastic perspective, however, this is a perfectly natural halfway house on the road toward pure corpuscularianism. For one might well think that a mechanistic story about corpuscles could explain all the qualitative phenomena in nature, and yet still think that the corpuscular structure of nature itself needs explanation. This seventeenth-century strand of quantity realism appears in other places, such as Thomas White,[10] but it was quickly overwhelmed by accounts on which corpuscular structure is basic. Most influential of all was Descartes. When he characterizes the essence of matter as extension, he means—among many other things (§4.5)—that there is no deeper account to give of what the stuff is. To be extended means to have *partem extra partem*, for Descartes, but this scholastic formula does not explain anything, and cannot be explained any further. *Extension* is one of those "primitive notions" that serve as the basis for our subsequent ideas, just as *thought* is a primitive notion (to Elisabeth [1643]; III:665). One begins with the idea that matter is extended, and from that fact (together with certain laws of nature [§15.5, §16.4]), one explains the rest of what we know about bodies.[11] Very much the same idea can be found in Walter Charleton, in describing the way each atom has its own magnitude, from which arises the extension of the whole. He then adds:

This duly perpended, no man need hereafter fear the drilling of his ears by those clamorous and confused litigations in the Schools, about the formal reason for Quantity; for nothing can be more evident than this, that the extension or quantity of a thing is merely *modus materiae*, or (rather) the *matter* itself composing that thing; insomuch as it consists not in a point, but has parts posited without parts, in respect whereof it is diffuse: and purely consequent from thence, that every body has so much of extension as it has of matter, extension being the proper and inseparable affection of matter or substance. (*Physiologia* III.10.1.4)

Again, the idea, so familiar as to be nearly invisible, is that the only explanation one need give of a thing's corpuscular structure is that it is a body. To have "parts posited without parts" (line 5), Charleton's translation of *partes extra partes*, is just what it is to be a body. Charleton flirts with the thought that one might appeal to modes to explain corpuscular structure (line 3) but then immediately corrects himself: extension is not explained by something added to matter, but just is "the matter itself" (line 4). Oddly, however, Charleton soon goes on to spoil the force of this passage by allowing that God could separate extension from a body [ibid., III.10.1.7], which makes nonsense of the passage just quoted, and, if taken seriously, would force him to enter into the "clamorous and confused litigations in the Schools" (lines 1–2) over what this quantity–extension is, above and beyond the body.

---

[10] See *Peripateticall Institutions* IV.1.3: "Substance as it is condistinct from Quantity is indivisible, since Quantity is divisibility." White's discussion closely follows Digby's views, and indeed the work's sub-title is *In the way of that eminent person and excellent philosopher Sir Kenelm Digby.*

[11] On extension in Descartes as meaning to have *partem extra partem*, see *Med.* VI, VII:337–8: "seu enim talis species procedit ex corpore, illa haud dubie corporea est, habetque partes extra partes, atque adeo extensa est"; to More, Feb. 1649 (V:270) "ita illud solum quod est imaginabile, ut habens partes extra partes, quae sint determinatae magnitudinis et figurae, dico esse extensum." For a general overview of the relationship between Descartes and scholastic theories of quantity, see Biard, "La conception Cartésienne." See also Des Chene, *Physiologia* pp. 97–109.

To be sure, the idea of body as intrinsically corpuscular in its structure is not novel to the seventeenth century. Leucippus and Democritus had this same idea in the fifth century BCE, as did, following them, Epicurus. The idea is present in various Islamic philosophers,[12] and then appears again, as we have seen, among the scholastics. Thus, as we saw in the previous section, Olivi takes as his fundamental premise against quantity realism the claim that "every extended matter and form has parts that are constitutive of its essence." Olivi immediately goes on to describe this structure as "infinitely divisible," thus distinguishing his view from that of the ancient atomists, but—as suggested already (§5.4)—the much-discussed debate over atomism is merely a footnote to the more basic question of whether physical reality is fundamentally corpuscular in structure.

According to Olivi, as just quoted, having parts is essential not just to matter but also to extended forms—that is, to anything that informs matter (as opposed to, for instance, an idea in the mind of a human being or an angel, which would count as a non-extended form). This makes it clear that one can treat corpuscular structure as fundamental without being a corpuscularian in my sense of the term (§1.3)—that is, one can think of corpuscular structure as applying not just to bodies, but also to properties, forms, forces, fields, or whatever entities one's metaphysics contains. Indeed, as we have seen, Olivi offers color—conceived of as a form—as an exemplary case from which to argue for the thesis that extended reality essentially has parts. Now, to be sure, the thesis that corpuscular structure is intrinsic is a crucial first step toward corpuscularianism, inasmuch as it puts in place the framework on which authors like Ockham, Autrecourt, Galileo, Descartes, and Hobbes would mount their reductionist projects. But having the machinery with which to stage this sort of attack does not commit one to carrying the attack through all the way to a thoroughly corpuscularian conclusion. Moreover, to go all the way to the corpuscularian extreme—as Hobbes, most notably, does—should in no way be regarded as a characteristically *modern* idea, but rather as a short-lived regression to the vulgar reductivism of ancient atomism, an experiment that would be discredited before the seventeenth century had even come to a close (§19.7).

14.3. Corpuscular Structure as Basic: Ockham

Although pride of place in any discussion of quantity should go to Peter John Olivi, a thorough treatment of the debate must ultimately turn to William Ockham, who takes very much the same view as Olivi, and for similar reasons, but offers a much more thorough defense—more thorough, indeed, than any seventeenth-century author would provide. Although Ockham, like Olivi, was a Franciscan, it seems unlikely that he knew Olivi's work at first hand, since it was suppressed by the Franciscan authorities. But we can be certain that Ockham knew of the view, since he quotes verbatim and responds to Richard of Middleton's criticisms of it. Just like Olivi, Ockham was attacked by Church authorities for his reduction of quantity. But whereas Olivi's name was

---

[12] On Islamic atomism, see Dhanani, *Physical Theory of Kalām*, and Pines, *Studies in Islamic Atomism*. On the attitudes of the ancient atomists to sensible qualities, see Pasnau, "Democritus and Secondary Qualities."

subsequently lost to history—until his works were rediscovered in the late nineteenth century—Ockham became positively notorious.[13]

Ockham discusses quantity in many different places, the most sustained of these being his *Tractatus de corpore Christi* (*circa* 1323), which is almost entirely devoted to a discussion of quantity, in and out of the Eucharist.[14] The case he makes there for the reducibility of quantity proceeds in what we now think of as Cartesian style—that is, from the ground up, from strictly philosophical premises, "so that the claims being made should be seen to be supported by a solid and unshakable foundation" (ch. 12, *Opera theol.* X:112). His first premise is the assertion that bodies have corpuscular structure:

1. "Every extended material substance is composed of substantial parts distant from one another in place or location" (ibid.).

This is a claim that he says "no rational person should doubt" (ibid.). One can see why, since to be extended just is to have *partem extra partem*. As we will see below, more turns on this first premise than Ockham admits, but let us grant it for now. By itself, it falls well short of showing that corpuscular structure is intrinsic or essential to a material substance, because that structure might be a consequence of some accidental feature of body, in virtue of which it is extended. In other words, Ockham has not yet ruled out quantity as something over and above substance. To get that conclusion, he needs three more premises, which he defends in the three subsequent chapters:

2. "The infinite and incomprehensible power of God can naturally make and conserve any prior absolute *res* without an absolute *res* that is really distinct in itself as a whole and that is naturally posterior" (ch. 13, *Opera theol.* X:115).
3. God "can produce and conserve any substance without any absolute accident formally inhering in it" (ch. 14, X:116).
4. God can "destroy an absolute accident inhering in a substance and conserve that substance, without a local change to the substance" (ch. 15, X:119).

We have already discussed the issues surrounding (2), in §13.6, and so it should be no surprise to see Ockham appealing to separability here. By confining his attention to

---

[13] For Ockham's discussion of Middleton, see *Tract. de quantitate* q. 3 (*Opera theol.* X:65–78). Ockham himself was attacked in terms even stronger than those used against Olivi: "Dicimus quod ponere quantitatem non esse rem distinctam a substantia est contra communem sententiam sanctorum, doctorum et philosophorum, quam reputamus veram. Quo supposito dicimus esse erroneum et periculosum et contra determinationem Ecclesiae, quae ponit in sacramento altaris solam substantiam converti, quantitate et ceteris accidentibus remanentibus" (2nd ser., art. 21, in Koch, "Neue Aktenstücke" p. 178).

[14] The discussion in the *Tract. de corp. Christi* often closely parallels, verbatim, the discussion in *Quod.* IV.19–34. Although the *Quodlibeta* seems to have been debated before the *Tractatus* was written, it seems to have been written out in its surviving form later. (For a summary of what we know about the chronology of Ockham's work, see Spade, "Introduction.") A close comparison of the two works indeed suggests that the *Quodlibeta* clarifies and in some cases expands upon the version offered in the *Tractatus*. Ockham mounts another extensive discussion of quantity in his *Tract. de quantitate*. For briefer, and for that reason somewhat more accessible discussions, see *In Praed.* 10.4, *Summa logicae* I.44, *Rep.* IV.6 (*Opera theol.* VII:71–8), *Summula* III.12. For modern discussions, see Maier, "Problem der Quantität" pp. 176–98; Burr, "Quantity and Eucharistic Presence"; Adams, *William Ockham* ch. 6.

In the fifteenth century and beyond, quantity anti-realism would be regarded as one of the characteristic doctrines of the "nominalists." The situation is not so simple, however, given that Buridan, the most prominent of the so-called nominalists after Ockham, defends a B theory of quantity, albeit for original reasons (§15.1). For straightforward versions of quantity anti-realism along Ockham's lines, see John Dumbleton, *Summa logicae et philosophiae naturalis* II.12–13; Albert of Saxony, *In Phys.* I.6; Peter of Ailly, *Sent.* IV.6.3; Marsilius of Inghen, *Sent.* IV.9.2; Gabriel Biel, *Sent.* IV.10.1, *Sent.* IV.12.1.1, and *Canon lec.* 43–4.

cases where *a* is prior to *b*, Ockham insures that (2) is entirely uncontroversial, but it should not be inferred that this is the strongest principle he accepts, since elsewhere he asserts that for any two contingently existing things, either can exist without the other. Here, though, all Ockham needs is (2), because from it, (3) follows immediately, given the realistic understanding of accidents that Ockham accepts (§11.1). What everything turns on, then, is whether (3) can be leveraged into the stronger (4). If Ockham is allowed (4), then quantity anti-realism follows straightaway, at least when quantity is understood to be that which accounts for extension. For (4), together with (1), entails that a material substance could exist without any accidents and still be spread out, *partem extra partem*. But since that just is to have extension, and to have extension just is to have quantity—as Ockham like others takes for granted—a substance has quantity intrinsically. At this point Ockham's razor takes over, because *frustra fit per plura quod potest fieri per pauciora*—"it is pointless to do through more things something that can be done through fewer" (ibid., ch. 29, X:157). Since a material substance is intrinsically extended, there is no need for any further accident in the category of Quantity, and if there is no need for it, it should not be posited.

Quantity realists of the sort under discussion in this chapter—those who associate quantity with extension—will need to deny (4). But if we can get to (4) from (3), then Ockham has a powerful argument, inasmuch as (3) is relatively uncontroversial among the parties to this dispute. As it happens, however, Ockham's arguments for (4) are notably feeble. Here is his leading argument:

Who among the faithful will dare to say that God, if he wills to separate or destroy an absolute accident inhering in a subject without destroying its substance, that God is compelled to move that substance or a part of it from one place to another? For if natural causes force out and draw in to the same subject many absolute accidents, without that subject's changing locally, then cannot God...? (ibid., ch. 15, X:119–20)

Ockham takes for granted that qualitative change naturally occurs without any local motion, which is a crucial part of his case for why qualities, alone among accidents, should be retained (§19.2). But if this can happen naturally in the case of quality, he here reasons, then surely God can make it happen in the case of quantity, if quantities are real accidents. Yet this clearly begs the question. For if quantity has the function of explaining a thing's locational properties, then there might well seem to be a special incoherence involved in removing quantity without a change in location, and we would have the only sort of good reason one can have for limiting God's power, a logical contradiction.

This is precisely the reply that gets made in an anti-Ockhamist *Logica* (*circa* 1325), a work of unknown authorship formerly attributed to Richard of Campsall. After quoting Ockham at some length, pseudo-Campsall flatly denies (4), remarking that it is as much a contradiction for God to remove the quantity from a body without a change to its location as it would be for God to remove the whiteness from a body without a change to its being white. Insisting from the start that quantity both makes a thing have parts and spreads those parts out, pseudo-Campsall deploys against Ockham the principle that has come to be known as the anti-Razor:

Whenever an affirmative proposition is truly stated of things, if one thing does not suffice to account for that proposition's truth, then one must posit two things, and if two do not suffice, then three, and so on to infinity. (*Logica* 41.19)

The anti-razor does not conflict with Ockham's more famous principle of parsimony; indeed, Ockham himself articulates the anti-razor on more than one occasion. To invoke it is simply a way to stress something that is fairly obvious in any case: that parsimony is a theoretical virtue only in cases where the theory in question truly is adequate. In the present case, Ockham's opponents are convinced quantity is required to account for corpuscular structure. Against such an opponent, Ockham can make no headway by presupposing that quantity plays no part in accounting for spatial location.[15]

Even if Ockham's appeal to (4) in this context is doomed to failure, it is understandable that he appeals to it. Indeed, his strategy here of considering questions of separability while holding fixed certain features of the enduring subject sheds a great deal of light on how separability functions as an argument. As we have seen already, appeals to separability run throughout our period, and seem to have been brought into particular prominence by Scotus (§11.2). The strategy is much more difficult to employ than it appears at first glance, however, because there is a sense in which separability is all too easy to come by. As noted in §13.6, an incautious use of this strategy could yield real accidents corresponding to any predicate you like, from lying down to living in Colorado. One way to avoid this result, as we saw, is to insist that there be an entity of some sort corresponding to the predicate. Then the fact of separability decisively shows that this entity is distinct from its subject. In most cases, however, this is not a helpful approach, because whether or not the predicate corresponds to any entity is precisely what is in question. Ockham is here using another approach, which I will refer to as an appeal to *fixed separability*: he asks whether an accident is separable from its subject while holding fixed certain features of the subject. When we do this, and find that separability is still possible, we have not absolutely proved that accident and subject are distinct, but at least we have proved that the accident cannot be reduced to that which we are holding fixed. So, suppose you are something of an Ockhamist regarding *lying down*—that is, suppose you think that the property of lying down is nothing over and above the body's limbs being positioned in a certain way. Now you confront an opponent who wishes to invoke separability against you, and so points out that you can remain in existence while the property of lying down comes and goes. The appropriate response, in line with Ockham's strategy here, is to demand that your opponent show that *lying down* is separable while holding fixed those features of the substance that you think it reduces to. Separability would show something, you should insist, only if that property can come and go while holding fixed the facts about the

---

[15] For pseudo-Campsall's rejection of (4), see *Logica* 41.49: "quia sicut dictum est in principio istius capituli [41.3–6], quantitas est illud per quod tanquam per principium formale aliquid habet partem extra partem et per quod aliquid in loco existit. Sicut, ergo, est contradictio quod Deus possit conservare Sortem, si Sortem sit albus, destruendo esse posterius natura, absque hoc quod Sortes mutetur secundum esse album, ita est contradictio quod Deus conservet omnem natura priorem quantitate, destruendo quantitatem absque mutatione locali istius prioris." Burley makes a very similar reply at *In Phys.* I tr. 2 c. 1, f. 15rb. See also the extensive reply in Paul of Venice, *Summa phil. nat.* VI.12–13.

Walter Chatton, another of Ockham's opponents, formulates the anti-razor at *Rep.* I.30.1 n. 57. Ockham himself deploys the principle at *Quod.* VII.3 obj. 2 and *Quod.* I.5 (*Opera theol.* IX:30–1). See also Maurer, "Ockham's Razor."

position of your limbs. (In fact it *might* still be separable even when the bodily facts are fixed, if you think that lying down requires your lying down on something, and that floating in a recumbent position is not lying down. Such examples illustrate why the notion of fixed separability is a useful analytic tool.)

The bare, non-fixed appeal to separability is perhaps the most common argument for quantity realism. Over and over again, authors from Middleton to Digby urge the reality of quantity on the grounds that a body can gain and lose a certain quantity, through rarefaction and condensation (§15.2). Hence the quantity must be something distinct from the body. Ockham accepts that quantity is not conserved, but rejects the general form of the argument, on the grounds that it would prove far too much. His response is to insist on fixed separability. Specifically, since he thinks items in the various non-real accidental categories can be explained in terms of motion within the subject and its integral parts, he offers the formulation of (4) above. Shapes are therefore not real, because although a subject can be separated from its shape, it does not admit of fixed separation. Elemental and sensible qualities, in contrast, pass the test of fixed separation, and so they are real (§19.2). No doubt Ockham thought that quantity is the very clearest of cases where his test should be insisted on. But in this context, where his opponents are claiming that quantity is what accounts for corpuscular structure, it simply begs the question to hold those facts fixed. (It is worth considering whether Ockham's strategy similarly begs the question in the case of other accidental categories.)[16]

Although the argument just discussed is Ockham's most famous, he gives quite a few others. One holds that just as substances do not depend on accidents, so neither do the integral parts of those substances. Hence although a substance's parts might be modified by an accident, they could not have been brought into existence by an accident.[17] Another argument reasons that an accident presupposes a subject to inhere in. Hence any accident, like quantity, that is somehow going to modify the parts of a substance must inhere in those parts, which is to say that those parts must precede the accident. If, instead, the subject of that quantity has no parts, then quantity itself can have no parts, but will be a simple accident informing a simple subject. In that case, however, how can extension ever arise? Both of these arguments are aimed at the A theory of quantity. Proponents of the B theory need not be troubled by them, and might even wield these arguments themselves, as Burley does, in support of the B theory of quantity.[18]

---

[16] For examples of simple, non-fixed appeals to separability, see e.g. Middleton, *Quod.* II.14 (p. 51a); Digby, *Two Treatises* I.3.9 (pp. 24, 26); Auriol, *Sent.* IV.12.1.1 (III:111ab): "aliqui putaverunt quod quantitas esset idem realiter cum substantia, quod faciliter improbatur...quia substantia manente invariata transmutatur nunc in unam quantitatem, nunc in aliam." Ockham considers this line of argument in detail at *Quaest. Phys.* 93 (*Opera phil.* VI:647–52). For other instances of Ockham's insisting on fixed separability, see *Ord.* I.30.4 (*Opera theol.* IV:369) and *Rep.* II.1 (*Opera theol.* V:14–15), where Ockham holds fixed not only the motion of the thing's parts, but also the passage of time and the addition or subtraction of any parts.

[17] See *Tract. de corp. Christi* ch. 29 (*Opera theol.* X:160): "Nec valet dicere quod substantia non habet partes nisi per quantitatem quae est res distincta a substantia, nam substantia non dependet ab aliquo suo accidente, nec per consequens partes substantiae dependent a partibus accidentiae." Suárez gives a very forceful endorsement of this argument at *Disp. meta.* 40.4.8–9. Suárez himself, however, is a quantity realist of a different kind, as §15.3 will discuss.

[18] For Ockham's argument that accidents presuppose a subject already divided into parts, see *Tract. de corp. Christi* ch. 12 (*Opera theol.* X:113–14), ch. 28 (X:155–7), and *Summula* I.13 (*Opera phil.* VI:192–3). Burley summarizes the argument as follows: "Sed si dicatur quod circumscripta omni alia re quantitatis substantia non haberet partem extra partem—

These last two arguments are really just two aspects of the same argument, an argument that depends on treating the integral parts of a substance as having the same ontological status as the complete substance. If one accepts this view, then it will seem quite compelling to treat corpuscular structure as basic, inasmuch as one will treat both substances and their integral parts as part of the basic furniture of the universe, and then it will seem quite natural to build everything else up on that basis. Some of the force of Ockham's long discussion in this *Tractatus de corpore Christi* comes from his building this picture in at the start, in arguing for (1) above. Although (1) is supposed to be an indubitable foundation for what follows (and can indeed be read that way), Ockham at times treats (1)—with its talk of "substantial parts"—as having established the much more controversial conclusion that a substance's integral parts are full-fledged substances in their own right. The status of the integral parts of a substance is a topic we will consider in more detail in Chapter 26. For now, it is enough just to note that the quantity realist need not accept that integral parts are substances on a par with the complete substance they compose, but can instead treat these parts as an accidental feature of body, and so ontologically derivative.

Perhaps the most effective of all Ockham's arguments against quantity is not one of the ones just mentioned, but an argument that might better be described as a challenge: if quantity explains corpuscular structure, and is a real accident, then what could possibly happen to a material substance if that quantity were removed? Would it no longer be a body? Discussion of this issue raises many complex questions, and will occupy the remainder of this chapter.

14.4. Body without Extension

If corpuscular structure is not intrinsic to material substances, but instead some kind of superadded accident, then it ought to be possible for material substances to exist without corpuscular structure. It ought to be possible, in short, to have bodies that lack extension. The alleged incoherence of this lies at the heart of Ockham's case against quantity realism.

What options do Ockham's opponents have? They obviously cannot allow that the body remains where it is, structure unchanged. But what other options are there? Quantity realists do not usually have anything very illuminating to say about this, and indeed none of the options seems very promising. The situation here is analogous to that for extensionless prime matter (Ch. 4) but worse, because now we are talking about *bodies*, which by definition are things extended in three dimensions (§16.1). No wonder Franco Burgersdijk would later complain that he cannot see how quantity realism can be defended "without the most obvious contradiction." For inasmuch as

---

contra: secundum ponentes quantitatem rem aliam a substantia, quantitas est accidens et per consequens praesupponit substantiam tanquam subiectum suum. Ergo eodem modo partes quantitatis praesupponunt partes substantiae. Ergo substantia ex se habet partes et non per quantitatem" (*Super artem veterem* [*Praed.*] f. e2va). He goes on to grant it at f. e3va. Crathorn endorses it at *Sent.* I.14 concl. 7. Burgersdijk offers it as his main argument in support of quantity anti-realism (*Collegium Physicum* 5.3). An argument of this same sort appears as late as Chauvin's *Lexicon* (2nd ed. 1713), pp. 548–9. Vasquez, a proponent of the A theory, explicitly confronts this sort of argument and rejects it, arguing that a substance's integral parts are not essential to it, and so can arise from an accident (*In summam theol.* III.190.5 nn. 51–3).

the view requires the possibility of a material substance's existing apart from quantity, "it is as if they proclaim that a corporeal substance exists and does not exist" (*Collegium physicum* 5.4). Now there is a quick reply that can be made to this complaint, to the effect that a material substance is only accidentally corporeal, when 'corporeal' means *a thing with corpuscular structure* (see §16.6 for further discussion). But in the present context that only makes more pressing the question of what such a quantityless substance is, if not corporeal.

The B theorist, for whom the body intrinsically has parts, and requires quantity only for those parts to be spread out, has only two options: a quantityless substance must either exist at a point, or lack location entirely. Gassendi, in his youthful anti-Aristotelian polemic, mocked the first idea at great length. How could a mountain come to exist at a point, he wondered, and still have all its integral parts intact? In what sense could one speak of corporeal parts, in a thing that has been compressed in this way?[19] Ockham had already criticized this same idea in a much more subtle way. First, he argues, points are not what we imagine them to be. By this, he seems to mean two things: first, that points are not tiny regions into which a body might be contracted, but are instead perfectly extensionless; second, that points are not things of any sort at all, but merely geometric constructs, or shorthand for talk about the limits to a line. Neither observation seems a decisive objection to locating a material substance at a point. For even if points lack extension, and indeed are not things at all, still talk of points is, if nothing else, a way of talking about locations, which is all the quantity realist needs. Ockham has two further objections, however, which are more effective: first, that there would be no internal explanation for why the substance's parts collapse in that way; second, that there could be no answer to the question of *which* point a material substance would collapse into, or why each part would go to that same point rather than to some other. Still struggling to supply an answer to such questions some 250 years later, Pedro Fonseca proposes that since it is God who removes the quantity from the substance, God can simply pick any point he likes for the substance to collapse into. This, however, misses the force of Ockham's argument. To say that a body's spreading out *partem extra partem* requires some explanation—a real accident in the category of Quantity—implies that, without quantity, material substances have some other propensity. If that propensity is to exist at a point, then the quantity realist should frankly acknowledge either that there is something intrinsic to material substances in virtue of which they have this propensity, or that there is some extrinsic natural force that compacts quantityless material substances in this way. These options are analogous to the choices available for explaining why a body falls to earth when its support is removed. And, as in that case, the best Ockham's opponent can do here is simply to insist that a fully developed physics would answer the question of exactly how a material substance would behave if not stretched apart by quantity, just as it explains exactly how a body behaves in free fall.[20]

---

[19] See *Exercitationes* II.3.10, p. 339. The explicit target of his discussion is a view, like Eustachius's, that distinguishes between "internal" and "external" quantity, and supposes that the former, which is to have ordered parts, is compatible with lacking the second, which is to be spread out in three dimensions.

[20] Ockham's arguments against existence at a point appear at *Quod.* IV.22 (*Opera theol.* IX:405) and *Tract. de corp. Christi* ch. 15 (*Opera theol.* X:120–1). On the ontology of points and lines, see Ockham, *Summa logicae* I.44, *Tract. de*

The remaining option for the B theorist is that a material substance without quantity would cease to have any location at all. Suárez describes this as the Thomistic option (*Disp. meta.* 40.4.19), and indeed Cajetan seems to take this view.[21] It is not easy, however, to find other explicit defenses of it. Burley is perhaps an example, when he remarks that "no part of a substance existing without quantity would have position or location (*situm aut locum*)" (*Super art. vet.* [*Praed.*] f. e3va). This is less clear cut than it seems, however, because a thing might fail to have *situs* and *locus* just in virtue of lacking extension. (Strictly, a thing's *locus* is the outermost edge of the body that surrounds it, and a thing's *situs*, if understood as falling within the category of Position, consists in its spatial arrangement.) Hence Burley's remark is consistent with his treating quantityless material substances as point-like. Buridan, who also ascribes to the B theory (though for distinctive reasons, as we will see in §15.1), says something very similar:

If magnitude were removed from matter by divine power, that matter would still have parts distinct from one another, but its parts would not be positioned either outside one another or inside one another, because the position (*situs*) that characterizes magnitude would be removed. Nor would its parts be located or positioned close to or far from other parts, or above or below, and so on. (*In Phys.* I.8, f. 11va)

A quantityless material substance would have parts, but not *partem extra partem*, nor *partem intra partem*. The idea may be that the body would lack any sort of location whatsoever, but again Buridan does not expressly commit himself to that. If one reads carefully, with an eye to the exact meaning of the technical Latin expressions, one sees that all he actually denies is that the parts of a quantityless body would be spread out. In general, although authors often talk about the possibility of locationless bodies, they hardly ever affirm that this is in fact a possibility. Ockham typifies this tendency when he dismisses the possibility of non-location out of hand, remarking that even an angel has some location. Subsequent authors tend to agree, all the way up to Fonseca and Suárez. (See Chs. 16–17 for further discussion.)[22]

---

quantitate q. 2, and the discussion in Adams, *William Ockham* I:201–12. Burley takes a particular interest in this topic, and replies at length against the anti-realist *moderni* (*Super art. vet.* ff. e2vb–e3va; *In Phys.* I tr. 2 c. 1, ff. 13rb–14vb).

For Fonseca on existence at a point, see *In Meta.* V.13.2.3, II:653D: "Itaque si Deus auferat quantitatem a ligno eiusque substantiam conservet, ne continuo esse desinat, uno e duobus modis manere poterit substantia ligni. Altero, in aliquo puncto eiusdem spatii aut alterius, in eo videlicet quem Deus elegerit, ut enim solus Deus nudam ligni substantiam conservaturus est, ita solus ipse designabit punctum in quo illam conservet." Vasquez rejects this possibility at *In Summam theol.* I.196.3 n. 12 and III.190.3 n. 30. For further references relevant to the question of bodies compressing to a point, see Grant, "Principle of Impenetrability."

[21] Cajetan seems to insist unequivocally that bodies without quantity would lack location: "Ad exemplum quod adducitur de hac aqua existente in vase, remota per intellectum quantitate, etc., dicitur quod imaginatio in hoc decipitur. Quoniam, seclusa quantitate, aqua illa nusquam remaneret, quoniam nullam habitudinem haberet ad locum; sed restaret cum negatione distantiae ab illo loco et quocumque alio" (*In Summam theol.* I.52.1.X).

[22] Burley also flirts with the non-location solution at *De formis*, pars post., p. 64: "Dicendum quod separatis omnibus accidentibus ab homine substantia capitis manet et substantia pedis similiter sine omni figura nec est una pars extra aliam nec sunt partes simul secundum locum nec separatae secundum locum, quia non sunt in loco." This is ambiguous in the usual way, however, between genuinely lacking location and simply not satisfying the Aristotelian conception of *locus*. For clear rejections of non-location, see Ockham, *Ord.* I.37 (IV:568–9); Fonseca, *In Meta.* V.13.2.3 (II:654AB); Suárez, *Disp. meta.* 40.4.19. Suárez goes on to allow that a quantityless body might exist at a point (par. 20), or holenmerically (par. 21). His own preferred solution, however, is that a quantityless body would simply cease to resist penetration by other bodies (§15.3).

For the A theorist there is still one more option, holenmerism. On this sort of view (§16.5), a quantityless material substance would not cease to be spread out, but would be spread out in an unstructured, partless way, so that the whole substance occupies not just the whole of its place, but also each and every part of that place. This is how immaterial entities (the human soul, angels, God) were standardly thought to exist during our period, and it was commonly agreed that such things are not extended, inasmuch as they lack *partem extra partem*. This seems to be how pseudo-Campsall imagines quantityless material substances, and Fonseca identifies this as a second way in which a material substance could exist without location. The most extensive defense of this sort of view I have found is that of Gabriel Vasquez, the sixteenth-century Jesuit whose views in this connection were mentioned earlier (§4.1). Vasquez takes a firm and unambiguous stand in favor of the view that quantity is what makes a thing have parts: "It should be said therefore that a material substance (or matter), of itself and without quantity, does not have integral parts but is entirely indivisible. It is through quantity alone that it actually has such parts" (*In Summam theol.* III.190.3 n. 33). This of course leads to the question of what that quantityless condition would look like, and here too Vasquez is quite clear. He expressly rejects the possibility that a quantityless body might collapse into a point, for reasons much like Ockham's. This leaves the conclusion that a body would be spread out, but in such a way as to exist wholly everywhere it exists. Thus "the proper mode of existence for a corporeal substance"—that is, its mode of existence apart from all accidents—"is such that it is whole in the whole and whole in each part, which is [also] proper to an indivisible and spiritual thing" (*In Summam theol.* III.187.2 n. 10).[23]

The fairly staggering implication of this view is that corporeal and incorporeal entities are not fundamentally distinct, with respect to extension. It is an accident, in the technical sense, that certain entities happen to be spread out *partem extra partem*, and although it may be that in the natural world this is how bodies *always* are, still from a metaphysical point of view that is not their intrinsic nature. Ockham had anticipated this sort of move, and had understandably judged it to be completely unacceptable:

Unless wood and in general every extended material substance were to have real and substantial parts, distinct in position, such a substance would be no more really extended than would the intellective soul. For just as the intellective soul is whole in the whole body and whole in each part, so every material substance would be whole under its whole quantity and whole under each part. That is absurd. (*Tract. de corp. Christi* ch. 12, *Opera theol.* X:114)

---

[23] For pseudo-Campsall's suggestion that a quantityless body would exist wholly in each place, see *Logica* 41.49. Also Fonseca, *In Meta.* V.13.2.3, II:653D, continuing the passage in note 20: "Altero, in toto eodem spatio, aut in alio diverso, si maluerit: ita tamen ut iam substantia non sit tota in toto spatio et partes singulae in singulis partibus spatii (isto enim modo adhuc esset extensa formaliter, quod sine quantitate fieri nequit) sed ita ut tota sit in toto, et tota in qualibet parte." John Major is very explicit about the holenmeric possibility for bodies without quantity, though it is not entirely clear whether he means to endorse this as his own view (*Sent.* IV.12.1, f. 55rb). The term 'holenmeric' is adapted from More; see §16.5.

Suárez expressly rejects the idea that material substances might naturally, apart from quantity, exist holenmerically: "non est connaturale materiali substantiae vel partibus eius ut habere possit realem praesentiam in diversis locis, etiam partialibus.... ipsamet substantia materialis ex se habet hanc limitationem. In quo magna est differentia inter illam, etiam nude sumptum, et substantiam spiritualem, nam haec natura sua est apta ad illum modum existendi..."(*Disp. meta.* 40.4.22). He can easily say this, because he denies that quantity accounts for extension.

This is one of Ockham's arguments for (1) above, and so understood it is unquestionable: inasmuch as a body is *extended*, it must have *partem extra partem*. But the absurdity Ockham sees here applies to a view like Vasquez's, inasmuch as Vasquez's understanding of quantityless body just does make it into a thing with the same organizational structure as an immaterial soul. To many—including some scholastic authors (§16.6)—it seemed incredible that the soul has this sort of whole-in-each-part structure. But if this seems bad in the case of an immaterial soul, then it must seem unspeakably worse to ascribe this sort of structure to material substances as well, as their intrinsic nature.

Can we even make sense of this view? Begin with something homogeneous in the strictest sense: a thing such that each part of that thing, however small, is qualitatively the same as any other part. (One might wonder whether there are any such things, but this is a theoretically useful place to start, and anyway scholastic authors accept strictly homogeneous entities.) In such a case, holenmerism is not so far away, for we would simply have to imagine, in place of a thing with qualitatively the same parts, a thing with *quantitatively* the same parts. Consider again the example that Olivi had initially used, that of whiteness (an accidental form in the category of Quality). Olivi thinks it clear that whiteness has its parts intrinsically, such that, within the whole entire whiteness of a table, we can distinguish the part that inheres in the left half of that table, and so on. On the opposing view we are now considering, whiteness has that corpuscular structure, but has it only in virtue of another accident, quantity. (Usually the whiteness is said to inhere in the quantity, rather than vice versa, but we can set this detail aside.) Without quantity, the whiteness of the table would be holenmeric in structure, which is to say that numerically the same form would exist throughout the table, informing the whole and informing each part. (Since Ockham treats corpuscular structure as intrinsic both to accidents and to substances, it is not surprising that he denies this is possible; instead, at least with respect to material substances, "no accident is indivisible, existing whole in the whole and whole in each part" [*Summula* I.20, *Opera phil.* VI:209].)[24]

The analysis of holenmeric whiteness can be extended to other homogeneous entities, including substances. If gold is strictly homogeneous, then it is easy to imagine it as holenmeric, by once again replacing qualitative sameness with numerical sameness. This is easy to *imagine*, to be sure, because to sensory imagination the two kinds of sameness are indistinguishable anyway. But there seems nothing troubling here even on a fuller conceptual scrutiny, so long as one is willing to endorse not just universal forms (properties), but also universal substances.

Indeed, far from being unintelligible, we have arrived at quite a familiar view: a theory of forms (or properties) as universals. That we should have suddenly arrived here makes perfect sense, given that quantity was a leading scholastic contender for the

---

[24] Ockham raises the question of individuation in the context of the holenmeric hypothesis, as applied to prime matter: "Et si quaeratur per quid distinguitur una materia prima ab alia cum omnis distinctio sit per formam, dicendum est quod illae materiae primae se ipsis distinguuntur sicut duae formae aeris se ipsis distinguuntur" (*In Phys.* I.18.7, *Opera phil.* IV:207). For an excellent overview of scholastic theories of individuation, see King, "Problem of Individuation." For more detail, see Gracia, *Individuation in Scholasticism*.

Whereas Ockham treats individuation as basic, Digby explicitly treats unity as basic, precisely as one would expect given his retention of quantity to explain corpuscular structure: "to ask absolutely why a body sticks together were prejudicial to the nature of quantity, whose essence is to have parts sticking together, or rather, to have such unity, as without it, all divisibility must be excluded" (*Two Treatises* I.5.4).

principle of individuation. Take away quantity, then, and what would one expect, if not universals in place of individuals? Conversely, Ockham treats individuation as basic, and this too is precisely what one would expect. Individuality, for him, is given at the start, along with the whole corpuscular structure. That chasing quantityless body down this rabbit hole has led us to universals makes good sense for another reason, too: because this is, of course, the other great topic of dispute between nominalists and realists. Nominalists like Ockham never get to universals, because—at least with respect to material substance—they build extension and individuation into the foundation of their theory. For the sort of realist currently under discussion, in contrast, quantity comes later, and so individuation comes later. If there is any validity at all to the picture of realists and nominalists locked in battle (§5.3), it is these two issues around which they circled, their views in one domain putting oblique pressure on their views in the other. To be sure, not every "realist" holds the conjunction of views that leads to holenmerism. But for those that do, the startling implication—implicit in the theory, even if never explicit, so far as I have found—is that it is the universal, rather than the particular, that is basic within the physical world. This is not to say that the physical world *is* universal in some deep sense. Quantity makes the world particular, just as quality makes the world colored. But individuation comes later, conceptually speaking; it is not basic. This is to say that material substances in themselves, and forms in themselves (at least those outside of Quantity), are universal and not particular. If, miraculously, the world were stripped of all quantity, that universal structure would be manifest.

This is deep, but I confess to being unsure it is coherent. If one sticks to the strictly homogeneous, the view is perhaps defensible, but things become quite obscure as soon as one considers anything heterogeneous. What would it be for a tree, for instance, to exist holenmerically? How, that is, could the whole tree exist in each part of the tree? For a complex object, this seems to make no sense. Here is where Ockham's objection to turning corporeal entities into holenmers seems quite compelling. Probably the only way around it is to distinguish between kinds of entities. Paul of Venice, for instance, a leading champion of realism, distinguishes between divisible forms and two kinds of indivisible forms. A divisible form, like whiteness, is in its subject in such a way that the whole is in the whole, and part in the part. They do not exist holenmerically—that is to say, as universals—but they could if quantity were miraculously removed. Immaterial forms like the human soul, in contrast, are indivisible but still may be spread out through their subject, in which case they would exist holenmerically, as the human soul in fact does. Finally, some forms are indivisible in such a way that they exist only in the whole, not in the part. Shape is like this; it makes no sense to imagine each part of a circle having the form of circularity. Something similar seems true of heterogeneous substances, for whereas each particle of gold might be gold, it is not the case that each part of a tree is, or could be, a tree. In these cases, holenmerism does not seem possible for the whole. It might, however, even in this case, still be possible at the level of the parts, inasmuch as something indivisible in this third way might be composed out of parts that are divisible. One might even contemplate a view on which complex indivisible forms are reduced to simple divisible forms, allowing everything to bottom out in holenmeric structure. In §26.6, indeed, we will see how some late scholastic authors thought that complex substantial forms are nothing more than an aggregate of simple partial substantial forms—the form of the liver, the form of the kidney, and so on.[25]

This is barely a beginning to understanding these issues, but at least we can see the direction in which this form of quantity realism points. If extension is not part of the essence of material substances, then such substances can (at least by the power of God) exist without being extended. So far as I can find, these aspects of scholastic thought have never been discussed by modern scholars, but there is no doubt that authors of the time were aware of the implications and, indeed, sometimes prepared to hug this monster. Pseudo-Campsall, for instance, is untroubled by the idea that "God can make Socrates exist without his being quantified" (*Logica* 41.19), and Burley likewise says that although a human being deprived of all accidents would not be *homo physicus*, it would be *homo metaphysicus* (*De formis*, pars post., p. 64). Admittedly, this consequence seems less absurd in the human case, because we are tempted to understand it in the manner of Cartesian dualism. But for an Aristotelian, or for a Christian committed to the necessity of the resurrection of the body for immortality, the human case is just as bad as any other. Vasquez positively embraces the apparent absurdity, remarking that "without quantity, there cannot be an organic body, or flesh and bones" (*In Summam theol.* III.187.2 n. 10). As an A theorist, he has no way around this outcome, because without quantity a body does not have any parts at all. But how is this at all tolerable? How can a tree continue to function without roots and branches? How can an animal continue to function without organs? Yet if living things do not function, surely they are not alive. And surely being alive is essential to living things.

Although Vasquez is unusual in tackling these problems head-on, they are the direct consequences of what seems to be the most widely accepted scholastic conception of quantity: that quantity makes a thing have parts, and that it inheres as an accident in the composite substance. To be sure, there are other ways of being a quantity realist. One can embrace the B theory, and let material substances have their parts intrinsically. Or one can let quantity inhere in prime matter, as the Averroists did (§4.3). But these views too, as we have seen, are obscure in their own ways. What is perhaps most remarkable in all this is that the nominalist strategy of treating corpuscular structure as basic— which to us seems so natural as to be almost inevitable—was during this time the position of a distinct minority, and indeed at times a persecuted minority. If we begin reading only in the seventeenth century, we blind ourselves to that fact.

---

[25] Paul of Venice sets out his distinction between kinds of forms in *Summa phil. nat.* VI.16 (f. 104rb): "Intelligendum quod forma est in subiecto tripliciter: primo modo partibiliter, et sic forma extensa est in subiecto quia totum est in toto et pars in parte; secundo impartibiliter per multiplicationem, et sic forma extensa est in subiecto et eadem in aliqua parte sui; tertio impartibiliter et absque multitudine, et sic forma figurae est in subiecto, ac unitas praedicamentalis, et numerus mathematicus. Talis namque forma est in subiecto et non in aliqua parte sui secundum se vel secundum aliquid sui; quaqumque enim additione vel subtractione facta corrumpitur prima forma secundum se et quodlibet sui, et altera generatur, sicut patet octo metaphysicae."

15

Extension and Impenetrability

It is a sign that you are dealing with an ideologue when, over and over, you decisively refute his theory, only to find him refashioning that same theory so as to escape your objections. Perhaps we are all ideologues, in one domain or another. Perhaps, too, this is not such a bad thing. At least my imagined ideologue is responsive to your arguments. Perhaps, eventually, if you keep after him, he will arrive at the truth.

Certainly, the scholastics were ideologues, and their ideology was Aristotelianism as sanctioned by the Church. In the face of challenges to the cogency of Aristotle's category scheme, for instance, almost none of them simply abandoned the scheme. Instead, they reinterpreted it, either by producing new and more powerful arguments for a realistic interpretation, or by moving to some sort of less ontologically committing position. Even the nominalists do not abandon the category scheme; they just understand it differently, in linguistic terms.

The case of quantity provides a rich case-study of these developments, because here one finds not only the usual spread of opinion from realist to nominalist, but also an interesting range of realistic options. The dominant view of quantity, throughout our period, associated it with extension. Hence those who argued that extension is an intrinsic feature of material substances—a line of thought that Chapter 14 traced from Olivi to Descartes—generally took themselves to have eliminated the need for any real accidents in the category of Quantity. But it is characteristic of the scholastic ideology not to be so easily discouraged. For even while most authors assumed that quantity accounts for extension, there was a persistent minority effort at saving a realistic interpretation of quantity by finding some other work for members of that category to do. The most important such tasks were to account for a variety of phenomena that I will group under the heading of impenetrability.

It is easy to ridicule the scholastics for their zealous efforts at saving the Aristotelian program, one way or another, revising the theory as necessary to defend their master's views. Olivi, perhaps an ideologue in his own right but no Aristotelian, mockingly remarked that "without reason he is believed, as the god of this age" (*Summa* II.58 ad 14, II:482). But there comes a point when one's ideology becomes so flexible that the term becomes a misnomer, and one's fidelity to a certain system becomes little more than a matter of terminological convenience. No one has ever invented their philosophical vocabulary from scratch, disdaining all previous attempts to conceptualize the world.

So if the scholastics chose to rally around one particular vocabulary, Aristotle's, we should not think less of them for that. We are all so far from an adequate grasp of the core questions of philosophy that it scarcely matters whose terminology we use—one starting point is as good as any other.

I have stressed already the way in which central Aristotelian terms like 'form' admit of so many distinct meanings among the scholastics as to be bare placeholders for a dizzying variety of theories (esp. §10.1). The category of Quantity is another such case. There might seem something absurd about the way various authors scurry to find some other use for quantity once they come to have doubts about whether it explains extension. It is as if they know Aristotle had to be right, and just cannot quite decide *how* he was right. But the apparent absurdity comes from *our* putting their exegetical cart before their philosophical horse. The authors we will be considering in this chapter have philosophical reasons for thinking that the impenetrability of bodies is something more than just an intrinsic feature of material substances. Those arguments stand on their own, but of course they need a word to talk about that which makes bodies be impenetrable. Since they conceive of it as an accident, they naturally want a word that bears those sorts of associations. And if accidents in the category of Quantity are not going to do the work of explaining extension, then why not use that term 'quantity' for this new purpose? Since extension and impenetrability are intimately related, the usage seems quite natural. The resulting theory is Aristotelian in vocabulary; whether it is Aristotelian in some stronger sense is not really important, and was not very important to the authors we will be considering.

This chapter begins by considering two kinds of phenomena that led some scholastic authors to insist on the reality of accidents in the category of Quantity: condensation and rarefaction, and co-location. We will then look at how Suárez's work points toward a systematic, proto-scientific theory of impenetrability, and how a third phenomenon associated with impenetrability, solidity, remained outside the theory. Finally, we will consider how Descartes attempted to get impenetrability for free from within his system—as a consequence not of extension, but of the laws of nature.

15.1. Condensation and Rarefaction: Buridan

A body is said to condense when it becomes less extended without losing any material, and to rarify when it becomes more extended without gaining new material. Although the previous chapter mentioned this phenomenon only in passing, debates over quantity throughout the entirety of our period take condensation and rarefaction as a central issue. As early as Richard of Middleton, it appears as a central objection to Olivi's anti-realism. It is still a central issue in Descartes, who treats it as one of two main obstacles to accepting extension as intrinsic to body (the other is the confused idea of empty space), complaining that "there are some so subtle that they distinguish the substance of a body from its quantity, and even distinguish that quantity from extension" (*Principles* II.5). The reason the phenomenon was thought to be problematic for a view like Olivi's or Descartes's is that it seems to involve a body's changing its extension, which suggests that extension is an accident inhering in the body. One way to deny this is to hold that extension is invariable—the conservation of quantity principle earlier dubbed C^Q (§4.5). Beginning at least with Benedictus Pererius, this came to be the dominant view, so much so that by the middle of the seventeenth century its denial seemed worthy only of mockery. Thus Charleton speaks of "the extreme absurdity of those high-flying wits who imagine that a body, when rarified, though it has no more of matter, has yet more of quantity or extension than when condensed" (*Physiologia* III.10.1.4). Charleton, like Descartes and Pererius, argues instead that a given amount of matter will always have the same quantity or extension, and that apparent changes in size (rarefaction or condensation) must be the result of an increase or decrease in the amount of extraneous stuff (air, etc.) mixed in among the matter. Although Descartes and Charleton disagree about whether empty interstitial space could be among the causes of condensation and rarefaction, with Descartes of course denying it, they agree that matter conserves its quantity. Condensation and rarefaction must therefore always arise from a body's becoming more or less gappy in its structure.

Scholastic authors almost universally deny this claim, not even allowing that sort of gappy change to count as true rarefaction or condensation. They hold instead that a given amount of matter can change its absolute volume, growing or shrinking without taking on or losing stuff, or becoming more or less gappy. The same stuff, on this view, simply occupies more or less space. Hereafter I will follow this usage, assuming that 'condensation' and 'rarefaction' refer to true, non-gappy change in absolute volume. I suggested in §4.5 that this is a perfectly reasonable view, and that if scientific developments have undermined anything in this area, it is C^Q itself that seems most vulnerable. With respect to quantity, however, the implications of denying C^Q are uncertain. To say that rarefaction and condensation occur in virtue of a change in quantity is to offer the most paradigmatic of scholastic explanations: change as change in form. But not all cases of change occur in this way, as any scholastic author will admit, and so one can scarcely defend quantity realism simply by pointing to the alleged phenomenon of rarefaction and condensation. (This is another way of making the same point made in §14.3: that bare non-rigid separation, a thing's continuing to exist apart from something else, goes nowhere toward establishing the ontological credentials of what is removed.) Even so, many and perhaps most authors assume that condensation and rarefaction are to be explained by a change to an accident in the category of Quantity. This seems to have been the standard view before Ockham, who referred to it as the *opinio vulgi*. But he raised so many difficulties for this view that it subsequently becomes very common—even among quantity realists—to deny that condensation and rarefaction are the result of a change in quantity.[1]

---

[1] On condensation and rarefaction as a standard argument for quantity realism, see Middleton, *Quod.* II.14, p. 51a; Descartes, *Principles* II.5, VIIIA:42: "Duae vero adhuc causae supersunt, ob quas potest dubitari an vera natura corporis in sola extensione consistat. Una est, quod multi existiment pleraque corpora sic posse rarefieri ac condensari ut rarefacta plus habeant extensionis quam condensata." As usual, Leibniz is less narrow-minded than his peers: "tous les Peripateticiens ordinaires et plusieurs autres croyent qu'une même matière pourroit remplir plus ou moins d'espace, ce qu'ils appellent rarefaction ou condensation, non pas en apparence seulement (comme lorsqu'en comprimant une éponge, on en fait sortir l'eau), mais à la rigueur comme l'Ecole le conçoit à l'égard de l'air. Je ne suis point de ce sentiment, mais je ne trouve pas qu'on doive supposer d'abord le sentiment opposé..." (*Nouveaux essais* II.4.1).

On the *opinio vulgi* that quantity explains condensation and rarefaction, see Ockham, *Quaest. Phys.* 97 (*Opera phil.* VI:657): "Praeterea, secunda est opinio vulgi, quod rarefactio est per hoc quod quantitas corporis densi eadem numero omnino exsistens primo est minor et postea maior, et hoc quia partes illius quantitatis remotius iacent sive magis distant localiter nunc quam prius." For Ockham's complex objections to this sort of view, see, e.g., *Quod.* IV.25 ad 2, *Tract. de*

There are two main ways of explaining condensation and rarefaction without appealing to quantity. The most obvious, although not the most palatable, is to maintain that a body condenses when its parts overlap—that is, come to be partly co-located. This is the view of William Crathorn, whose *Sentences* commentary (1330–2) is full of these sorts of eccentric ideas. On Crathorn's theory, bodies are in a constant state of overlap, except in the unusual case when they are maximally rarified. Only then will there be no overlap of particles. This really is an eccentric idea, because it was taken for granted by most authors throughout our period that bodies, by their nature, cannot ever be co-located. Hence Carthorn's hypothesis of overlapping, telescoping bodies was almost never taken seriously.[2]

The second strategy available to those who would explain condensation and rarefaction without appealing to quantity is a surprisingly straightforward reductive appeal to local motion: the parts of the body simply move closer together or farther part, all the way down. This was the view that quantity anti-realists—including both Olivi and Ockham—almost always took. Ockham puts it like this:

[M]atter is made to have a greater or lesser quantity not through its receiving any absolute accident, but through condensation and rarefaction alone. This is nothing other than for the parts of matter to come more or less close to each other, which can happen through local motion alone with respect to those parts—that is, through the parts of matter being dilated and contracted. (*Summula* I.13, *Opera phil.* VI:194)[3]

Ockham is talking about true condensation and rarefaction. He does not have in mind the compression of void space, since he accepts the usual Aristotelian plenum theory. Nor does he have in mind the Cartesian picture, on which a body rarifies or condenses in virtue of taking in or squeezing out foreign material. On either of these pictures, as he remarks, "it is only the gaps that would be rare or dense, whereas what lies between the gaps would be no differently disposed than before" (*Quaest. Phys.* 97, *Opera phil.* VI:657). Of course, this is just what the proponent of C^Q is after, but since Ockham thinks a body can change its absolute volume, he wants an account on which it is the body that rarifies and condenses, not the gaps. So, consider a perfectly homogeneous, solid body, and consider how it might be condensed. Descartes would take this to be impossible: since such a body has no gaps, it cannot be condensed any farther. Ockham, in contrast, sees no difficulty: all that is required is for the parts of the body to move closer together. A modern reader, at this point, may have the strong intuition that Descartes is right, and that the parts of a perfectly solid body cannot move closer

---

quantitate q. 3 (*Opera phil.* X:63–4, 71–5), and the very useful discussion in Adams, *William Ockham* I:178–84. Des Chene (*Physiologia* pp. 107–9) gives a nice overview of the scholastic debate.

[2] Crathorn offers his unorthodox theory of condensation and rarefaction in *Sent.* I.14 concl. 15, p. 420: "Decima quinta conclusio est quod impossibile est fieri naturaliter vel per agens naturale, quin multa corpora eiusdem species sint simul, et hoc patet sic: impossibile est aliquod corpus esse rarius quam prius fuit, vel esse rarius quam modo sit, nisi habeat multas partes loco et situ indistinctas." Given this, it is unsurprising that he goes on to allow that a body can be compressed to an extensionless point, with all its parts precisely overlapping (ibid., concl. 20). For a critical discussion of this sort of view, see pseudo-Marsilius, *In Phys.* IV.14, f. 56ra (tr. Grant, *Source Book* p. 351a). For a recent discussion, see Robert, "William Crathorn's Atomism" pp. 156–8. Galileo recognizes overlap as one way to explain condensation, but treats it as so clearly unacceptable that it is better to embrace his theory of infinite indivisibles (*Two New Sciences* first day [ed. Favaro VIII:93; tr. Drake p. 54]).

[3] For Olivi, see *Summa* II.58 (II:443–5).

together, except by overlapping. This is what Crathorn too had thought. But although Ockham accepts that overlap is at least supernaturally possible—he thinks God could contract a body until it exists at an extensionless point (Ch. 4 note 23)—he sees no need for overlap here. Since he denies C^Q, he simply holds that the parts are able to move closer together because they *get smaller*. And if one wonders *how* they get smaller, Ockham's straightforward answer is that they get smaller by their parts' moving closer together. And so it goes, infinitely far down. For Ockham, this is no more strange than it is strange for us to imagine a chemical reaction occurring at once within each and every molecule of a substance. Indeed, so far as I can see, there is nothing incoherent about this reductive conception of condensation and rarefaction. If we persist in seeing this as puzzling, it is only because of an abiding commitment to C^Q at some level or another.

Ockham's version of quantity anti-realism persuaded some to abandon realism altogether with regard to the category of Quantity. Others, however, even if they found his arguments compelling, nevertheless attempted to find some other basis for defending the category. The most prominent example of this second sort of reaction is that of John Buridan. Although Buridan would later be regarded as a leading nominalist, he defends a traditional B theory of quantity, much like that of the arch realist Walter Burley. (On the A and B theories of quantity, see §14.1.) Like Burley, Buridan takes material substances to have their parts intrinsically, and holds that although a quantity-less material substance would continue to have parts, it would cease to have *partem extra partem*. The parts, in other words, would cease to be spread out, and would apparently be compressed into an extensionless point. (As discussed in §14.4, it is not entirely clear how we are supposed to think about the not-naturally-possible case of a body stripped of all quantity.) What gives Buridan's defense of this thesis its distinctive character is that he regards the traditional arguments for this traditional view as generally bad, "sophistical or facile" (*In Phys.* I.8, f. 10va). Accordingly, he offers his own argument, based on the phenomenon of condensation and rarefaction.

Sensitive as ever to Ockham's views, Buridan recognizes that the anti-realist has a coherent story available to explain the mere fact of condensation and rarefaction. The only way to establish the reality of quantity, then, is to introduce some further phenomenon for which the anti-realist has no explanation. To this end, Buridan introduces an example of condensation and rarefaction complex enough to be called an experiment, even if it presumably took place only in thought. He describes how the air trapped within a bellows that has been plugged at the opening can be significantly rarified and condensed by heating and cooling. Yet that same air cannot be significantly compressed or expanded by attempting to push the handles together or apart. This gives us an interesting discrepancy to account for. A given body—the air within the bellows—retains its extension when acted on in one way, but changes that extension when acted on in another. To explain this, Buridan argues, we must appeal to something beyond facts about the location of a thing's parts. We need quantity.

To make his case, Buridan attempts to rule out all other potential explanations for the phenomenon in question:

It seems to me that the others cannot plausibly give an explanation of the case just described. For they say that condensation and rarefaction occur not through the generation or corruption

of magnitude [≈ quantity], but solely through the local motion of parts, through which those   3
parts come closer or go farther from each other. Now I can move bodies by pushing or pulling
them. What then stops me from being able to compress the parts of air all at once, condensing
them into a smaller place? The matter does not stand in the way, since there could be more   6
matter in a much smaller place. Nor does the air's substantial form stand in the way, since that
whole form is made to be in a smaller place when the air is condensed by cooling it, as has been
said. Nor does heat stand in the way, in and of itself, since there could be much more heat in   9
a much smaller place—for there is much more heat in a small, red-hot piece of iron. (*In Phys.* I.8,
f. 11rb–va)

Buridan's target is plainly Ockham, and so he reasonably enough confines himself to
considering only the limited resources that Ockham's parsimonious ontology accepts.
The passage eliminates these options one by one. First, if condensation and rarefaction
are explained simply by the local motion of the thing's parts, then we ought to be able
to bring this about in the case of the closed bellows, since we can easily enough move
bodies "by pushing or pulling them" (lines 4–5). So why is this not possible in the
bellows case? (lines 5–6) Something else must be at work. Buridan proceeds to consider
all the remaining options: the explanation will be either matter (lines 6–7), substantial
form (lines 7–8), or a quality (lines 9–10). (These are the options from within Ockham's
ontology.) Matter gets ruled out because Buridan and his opponent agree that matter,
of itself, could be compressed much farther than what he is attempting here (lines 6–7).
To rule out substantial form, Buridan counts on the bellows experiment, which shows
that the air could be condensed by cooling it. If, however, it were the nature of air to
resist condensation beyond a certain point, then neither cooling nor mechanical
pressure ought to produce an effect. The fact that the air can be condensed in one
way, then, rules out the substantial form as a cause of its resistance to mechanical force.
Finally, as for quality, the obvious candidate is heat. For since heat is what causes
rarefaction, it is really the only quality that seems to offer a potential explanation for
why the air resists condensation. But it too gets ruled out because a much smaller body
could be much hotter (lines 9–10). Hence there is nothing about heat in itself that
precludes the air from occupying less space. The only option left, then, is to postulate
something further, which we might aptly call *quantity*.

As vivid as Buridan's thought experiment is, it is not at all easy to see what the
resulting picture of quantity is supposed to be. One thing that is clear is that Buridan is
not providing a new understanding of how condensation and rarefaction work. With
regard to the kinetic story about what happens—that is, a description of the motion of
the parts and their impact on one another—the only two options are those described by
Crathorn and Ockham, and Buridan evidently favors Ockham's approach. Rather than
offering an alternative to Ockham at this level, Buridan is arguing that we must
supplement that account with something else. Local motion is the whole of the story
in one regard, with respect to the actual kinetic change that occurs, but it does
not explain why air has the extension it does, and water its own extension, let alone
why certain kinds of causes can change that extension whereas others cannot (cooling
versus squeezing, for instance). In effect, this is simply to defend what Ockham called
the *opinio vulgi*: that condensation and rarefaction occur in virtue of a change in
quantity.

Yet even once we see roughly where Buridan's view lies, it takes some work to see precisely what quantity is adding to the story. Clearly it is not supposed to determine the *location* of a body and its parts, as if each and every body were given its absolute location in the world in virtue of having a certain quantity. In general, no one supposed that quantity plays this role, because one would then have to suppose that a thing changes its quantity whenever it moves, a view that no one held. Still, although quantity does not account for location, exactly, it must do something in this neighborhood. After all, condensation and rarefaction ultimately just do concern the location of a body's parts. Buridan's idea is that quantity explains why the parts of a body are stretched apart from one another to one degree or another. More quantity stretches a thing out farther, whereas when quantity is removed the parts draw back inward. It is an important part of Buridan's view that quantity is the kind of form that admits of stacking, so that a body becomes progressively more rarified in virtue of taking on more and more of the appropriate accident:

Dimension [≈ quantity] yields something extended just as heat yields something hot, or light something luminous. So it seems reasonable that if more heat or light yields a subject that is more hot or luminous, and less heat or light yields one that is less hot or luminous, so too more dimension yields something more extended and less yields less. So just as more quality yields a more intensely qualified thing, so more dimension yields a more extended thing. (*In Phys.* IV.11, f. 78rb; cf. ibid., I.8, f. 11rb)

This picture of adding one accident on top of another was a standard scholastic way of thinking about qualities like heat or color. Buridan wants to apply this picture to quantity, so that when the air in the bellows is heated, it does not lose one quantity and gain another, but simply takes on further degrees of quantity, and in virtue of gaining one or more additional forms, it becomes that much more extended. Conversely, as a body sheds quantitative forms, its parts draw closer together, until that point when it loses quantity altogether and so ceases to be extended. (Much of what motivates this way of conceiving quantity is an effort to escape Ockham's attack on earlier theories of quantitative change, but I am setting this aspect of the debate aside.)[4]

Many subsequent authors were persuaded by Buridan's argument. Yet one might wonder whether they ought to have been. The whole point of the elaborate bellows experiment, and the disparity it establishes between the effects of heating and cooling versus mechanical pressure, is to yield the result that the air's extension cannot be attributed to its substantial form. Yet this conclusion is easily evaded: it could simply be part of air's nature, for instance, and so a fact about its substantial form, that it is more

---

[4] Quotations from Buridan, *In Phys.* I.8 rely on the often significant emendations in Maier, "Problem der Quantität" pp. 211–15. For another substantial statement of Buridan's view see his newly edited *In Gen. et cor.* I.11, which is especially clear on the way quantitative forms will be layered: "additio magnitudinis ad magnitudinem in eodem subiecto non est impossibilis ubi subiectum plus distaret per illas duas magnitudines quam per unam. Et sic est in proposito. Unde sicut caliditas addita caliditati in eodem subiecto reddit subiectum calidius, sic extensio sive magnitudo addita extensioni in eodem subiecto reddit subiectum extensius. Et aliter impossibile esset et contra rationem extensionis quod extensio extensioni adderetur." This text also redescribes the bellows experiment, referring back to the discussions at *In Phys.* I.8 and IV.11, and makes it clear that quantity is not the *tendency* to maintain a certain extension, but that which "formally" accounts for the actual distance between a thing's parts: "Prima [conclusio] est haec, quod in rarefactione magnitudo generatur, hoc est dictum quod res aliqua sive dispositio aliqualis faciens formaliter distare generatur sive acquiritur, ita quod non sufficit solus motus localis partium." For Buridan's account of qualities as successively acquired, see *In Phys.* III.4–5.

easily compressed by cold than by mechanical force. (Buridan's junior colleague on the arts faculty at Paris, Albert of Saxony, one of the most influential quantity anti-realists, in effect seems to respond in this way.)[5] But even if other scholastic authors have various ways around Buridan's result, it is not clear that the strict corpuscularian does. For by resting his argument for quantity not just on change in rarefaction and condensation, but on a body's variable resistance and susceptibility to compression and expansion, Buridan takes the scholastic debate over quantity into a new domain, one that asks not just about the extension of a body, but about why it tends to retain that extension, even under pressure. As we will see in this chapter's final section, seventeenth-century authors ran into very serious difficulties in just this domain. Indeed, this is one of the areas where corpuscularianism ultimately foundered.[6]

Yet even if Buridan's account points in this direction, it is instructive to see that he is not offering quantity as an account of why bodies resist compression and expansion. Buridan does discuss the inclination of a body to maintain a certain extension:

Such condensation or rarefaction is in effect (*quasi*) violent with respect to the bodies that are rarefied or condensed. For given the air's most suitable disposition with respect to rarity and density, if it is further rarefied or condensed without any alteration to its primary qualities [that is, without heating or cooling]—either by being compressed extrinsically or else by being pulled extrinsically so that it fills in to avoid a vacuum—this is outside its proper inclination. Hence it tends and is inclined naturally to revert to the prior state that is most suitable to it, and it does revert naturally once the compression is removed. (*In Phys.* IV.11, f. 78ra)

Thus the air in the bellows, at a certain temperature, is inclined to extend the bellows to a certain degree, and it resists being squeezed or stretched. This is not, however, what Buridan takes quantity to do. On his view, quantity is simply that which makes a thing be extended: when the bellows is pulled apart, against its natural inclination, it gains quantity. What this means is that Buridan has no account of why air compressed under mechanical pressure springs back when relieved of that pressure. This risks looking absurd: why is it not enough to say that a body with such an inclination to maintain its

---

[5] For Albert of Saxony see the highly compressed response at *In Phys.* I.6 ad 6: "Ad sextam de vesica dico quod nec materia aeris resistit, nec forma abstracte, sed forma existens in tanta massa materiae. Unde bene verum est quod forma aeris posset bene esse sub minore quantitate quando non esset in tanta massa materiae; cum tamen est in tanta massa materiae, cum non possit stare in materia quantumcumque densa, ipsa est illud quod resistit comprimenti." It is far from obvious that Albert means to appeal to substantial form here, but I cannot see what other "forma" he could have in mind.

[6] Oresme, like Buridan, insists that quantity can explain condensation and rarefaction, although so far as I have found he discusses the matter only in passing (e.g., *In Gen. et cor.* I.7, pp. 58–9; *In Phys.* I.21). Also quite clearly following Buridan is Marsilius of Inghen (*In Gen. et cor.* I.15). For examples of quantity realists who disassociate quantity from rarefaction and condensation, see Coimbra, *In Gen. et cor.* I.5.17.3 and Paul of Venice, *Summa phil. nat.* VI.12 ad 3: "Ad tertium dicitur quod quando aer condensatur manet tota quantitas praecedens, et praecise illa quae prius fuit, et quod eadem quantitas est nunc minor quam prius fuit, per hoc quod partes quantitatis propinquus iacent; sed non ponitur quantitas propter istam causam solum...."

Buridan's bellows experiment is subsequently endorsed by Marsilius of Inghen, *Abbrev. in Phys.* I, f. 3vb; *In Gen. et cor.* I.15; pseudo-Marsilius, *In Phys.* I.8. For some of these discussions, as well as Albert of Saxony's, see Maier, "Problem der Quantität" pp. 217–23. (Maier's lengthy quotation from a *Quaest. de Gen. et cor.* that she ascribes to Oresme [pp. 218–19] is in fact from an alternate version of Buridan's commentary [see Michael, *Johannes Buridan* II:631–48].) Maier also discusses Albert of Saxony's view, and criticizes him for failing to grapple with the real force of Buridan's arguments, which seems fair enough, although it may be that behind the highly compressed remarks that have been left to us lies a more developed criticism. On Buridan, see also the interesting discussions in Adams, *William Ockham* I:185–6, and Normore, "Buridan's Ontology."

extension is acted on externally with such force as to result in the body's being moved in such a way? Why do we *also* need a story about that in virtue of which a body has a certain extension?

Buridan has his reasons for preferring to associate quantity with actual extension rather than with the tendency to preserve extension. For one thing, this allows him to avoid treating real accidents as tendencies or dispositions. Like scholastic authors in general, Buridan thinks of accidents as actual, categorical properties, rather than mere dispositions (§23.5). Also, the association of quantity with actual extension puts Buridan in a better position, as we will see in §17.4, with respect to explaining location. Although reductivists from Ockham to Descartes take for granted that they can have for free the facts about where a thing and its parts are located, it is by no means obvious that this is so. Buridan's theory of quantity is not a theory of location, as noted already, but we will see that it gives him at least part of the tools necessary to explain location. In any case, although Buridan appeals to the phenomena of impenetrability to motivate his theory, he does not appeal to quantity to explain impenetrability.

15.2. The Co-Location Argument: Francis of Marchia

Buridan's argument for quantity gives a prominent place to phenomena associated with impenetrability, but does so in an essentially conservative way, inasmuch as it preserves the standard link between impenetrability and extension. The next sort of view to be considered, that of Francis of Marchia, severs that link, associating quantity with impenetrability while granting that bodies are intrinsically extended. It was not easy for Marchia to see the possibility of making this move, because the conceptual ties between quantity, extension, and impenetrability had traditionally been so tight as to be wholly taken for granted. Thus, when Olivi took aim at quantity realism, he took for granted as his target the view that quantity accounts for a body's having extended parts (*partem extra partem*). He made no separate mention of impenetrability, presumably because he assumed that a body extended in this way just would be impenetrable, in virtue of being spread out. This, at any rate, was how thirteenth-century realists— drawing on Averroes—had tended to conceive of the situation. According to Giles of Rome,

The reason why body resists body and why it does not allow another body to co-exist with itself is taken from the very fact of its occupation of a place. Therefore that through which a body has its occupying a place is that through which it has its resisting another body and its not allowing another body to co-exist with itself. It has this not through quality, but through quantity. (*Phys.* IV.15.76, f. 83ra)

Giles offers no explanation for why a thing's occupying a place—in effect, its being spread out in three dimensions—is sufficient to explain its resisting other bodies. Since immaterial things can also be located over an extended region (Ch. 16), the point cannot be a general conceptual one about what it is to be spread out, but rather is a special feature of how bodies occupy a place. Since a body's special way of occupying a place is what it has in virtue of quantity, Giles concludes that quantity explains both extension and impenetrability. This was the consensus view through

Ockham, who similarly takes for granted that an account of extension will yield an account of impenetrability.[7]

Although it is of course to the advantage of both Olivi and Ockham to get impenetrability for free, along with extension, this causes them trouble in a certain way, and it is this that motivates Marchia's rethinking of the connection between quantity and impenetrability. The trouble begins in this way: quantity anti-realists hold not only that material *substances* have quantity intrinsically, but also that material *qualities* do. This is a view we encountered in the previous chapter in several contexts. First, from a theological point of view, the quantity anti-realist needs qualities to be intrinsically extended so that they retain their extension when apart from the substance, in the Eucharist. Second, from a purely philosophical point of view it also makes good sense to suppose that real qualities are extended. Colors, for instance, seem to be extended just as much as bodies do themselves, and in fact we saw in §14.1 that Olivi treats whiteness as an exemplary case from which to argue that things are intrinsically extended. But now here is the trouble. If material qualities are extended, and material substances are extended, and if extension is what explains impenetrability, then it seems as if accidents should not be able to co-locate with substances. This, however, is an intolerable result. A quality is not to be understood as a body that is contiguous with the substance, like a layer of paint on top of a wooden bed. Colors and other qualities are not bodies but forms that inhere in their subject. And although the nature of inherence is obscure, as we saw in Chapter 11, at least one clear necessary condition on it is co-location.

I call this *the co-location argument*. It is one of the earliest and most commonly made objections against quantity anti-realism, going all the way back to Richard of Middleton's arguments against Olivi. It is, moreover, an argument that both goes deep and extends widely, inasmuch as it has ramifications across all four of our centuries, and across the spectrum of philosophical positions. The argument takes its force from the fact that co-location is such an important issue during this time. For Aristotelians, that is obvious, because their various metaphysical parts must be understood as spatially overlapping. Where the strict corpuscularian might postulate only a single thing at a given place, the Aristotelian will see prime matter (Chs. 2–4) and substantial form (Ch. 24), the substance that is a composite of these (Ch. 6), and also whatever accidental forms inhere in that substance (Chs. 10–12). More extravagant theories might postulate modes (Ch. 13), *entia successiva* (Ch. 18), dispositions (Ch. 23), multiple substantial forms (Ch. 25), and integral parts distinct from their whole (Ch. 26). All of this, moreover, covers just the material realm. Any author from our period, scholastic or not, will also suppose that immaterial entities standardly overlap bodies: the rational soul occupying the whole of the human body, angels from time to time occupying one or another corner of the material realm, and God constantly overlapping with everything (Ch. 16). So for the Aristotelian in particular, but to some extent for everyone during our period, co-location is a familiar fact of life. The fact that bodies *cannot*

---

[7] For Giles of Rome and other thirteenth-century treatments of impenetrability as a consequence of extension, see Maier, "Problem der Quantität" pp. 146–58. See also Adams, *William Ockham* I:171, who translates a different part of the same passage from Giles of Rome. For Averroes, see *In Phys.* IV.76 (commenting on 216b6–8). Maier goes on to show that the doctrine is present in Albert the Great, Thomas Aquinas, Richard of Middleton, and William of Ware.

interpenetrate is, from this perspective, a puzzling anomaly that demands some special account.[8]

The co-location argument has force against anyone who would explain impenetrability simply in terms of extension, but then at the same time allow that extended entities overlap. Early statements of the argument are not always so powerfully presented, but by the time of De Soto the argument had taken on its canonical status as the "best of all" arguments in favor of quantity realism. Noting that quantity anti-realists simply grant the conclusion that quantified things overlap, he tries to saddle them with this consequence:

If there were multiple quantities interpenetrating one another in the same subject, it would follow that no natural explanation could be assigned for why two distinct bodies cannot naturally interpenetrate in the same place. (In Praed., De quantitate q. 2, p. 186aH)

Although De Soto thinks that both realism and anti-realism are plausible views, neither of which can be decisively proved, he ultimately opts for realism on the basis of this argument. Suárez too, later in the sixteenth century, thought that although there are various plausible arguments in favor of quantity realism, only the co-location argument is decisive.

For an anti-realist in the mold of Olivi or Ockham, there is no easy escape from this argument. For if one is committed to

(a) the reality of interpenetrating entities of any kind;
(b) extension's being an intrinsic feature of those entities; and
(c) extension's entailing impenetrability,

then the disastrous outcome follows: qualities cannot overlap with substance, and so cannot inhere in substance. To escape, one needs to reject, or at least weaken, one of these three principles. Quantity realists of the sort we have hitherto considered deny (b), and so leave room for a substance and its properties to overlap. It is the composite material substance as a whole—the thick substance—that is extended, in virtue of an accident in the category of Quantity, and this explains why it is extended material *substances*—bodies—that cannot overlap. The strict corpuscularian, in contrast, denies (a). Substances can be intrinsically extended and so impenetrable, on this view, without running into difficulties about co-location with accidents or other properties, because there are no properties. A third way out would be to restrict (b) so that only material substances are intrinsically extended. This is how I read Descartes. Descartes does not reject (a), inasmuch as his ontology embraces both modes (§13.5) and immaterial entities (§16.4). But these entities are not truly extended, and hence can be co-located with material substances. If modes or minds were *res extensa*, then they would be material substances, bodies, since all and only bodies are extended and impenetrable.

---

[8] The co-location argument appears early on in the debate, in Richard of Middleton, *Quod.* II.14, p. 50b, and subsequently gets mentioned in virtually every scholastic discussion of the topic, all the way through to the end of the sixteenth century, where it is still being discussed at great length (see, e.g., Fonseca, *In Meta.* V.13.2.3 [II:647]; Vasquez, *In summam theol.* III.194.3 nn. 27–9). Ockham responds to Middleton's original formulation at *Tract. de quantitate* q. 3 (*Opera theol.* X:77–8). Burley, *De formis* pars post., pp. 52–7, contains a particularly detailed discussion of this argument. For Suárez, see *Disp. meta.* 40.2.17: "Quae argumenta sunt probabilia, illud vero solum est efficax quod ex impenetrabilitate dimensionum sumitur, et in priori discursu [nn. 11–13] explicatum est."

(The relation between mind and extension in Descartes is complex and controversial; I take this up in detail in §16.4–5 and §17.3.)[9] Part of the co-location argument's force, then, comes from its wide appeal. The quantity realist likes it, because it can be used to make a case for real quantities on the basis of real qualities. The corpuscularian likes it too, because it can instead be used to claim that there are neither qualities nor quantities. The only faction that is in trouble is the one that wants to hold onto overlapping entities (particularly real accidents in the category of Quality) while treating those qualities and also substance as intrinsically extended.

What about (c) above? Here is where Francis of Marchia enters the story. Lecturing on Lombard's *Sentences* at Paris in 1319–20, Marchia was a contemporary of Ockham's and a decade senior to Buridan. His great insight was to see that one could hold onto (a) and (b) but deny (c), by distinguishing between extension and impenetrability. After setting out the anti-realist position on quantity in terms that are unmistakably Ockham's, Marchia offers a quick version of the co-location argument. He then considers a reply on Ockham's behalf that we have not yet considered: that one might distinguish substantial extension from accidental extension, and hold that while two things having substantial extension cannot overlap, accidental extension does not preclude overlap. Marchia immediately rejects this way out: "given that the extension of substance and of quality has the same account (*ratio*), if the one accounts for the impossibility of two things being together at the same place and time, then so does the other" (in Maier, "Problem der Quantität" p. 205). This is exactly right: if to have extension just is have *partem extra partem*, and if *this* is what explains impenetrability, then either impenetrability will characterize both substance and quality, or else it will characterize neither. Indeed, to distinguish two kinds of quantities would make it quite mysterious just what quantity is, and so undermine the whole point of Olivi's and Ockham's project, which is to explain quantity in clear, reductive terms. Not surprisingly, neither Olivi nor Ockham seems to have proposed this sort of obscurant distinction between kinds of extension.

With that first attempt at a solution to the co-location argument rejected, Marchia offers his own solution, which amounts again to distinguishing two kinds of extension, but in a much more illuminating way. To have what Marchia calls *negative extension* is simply to have parts that are located at a distance from one another. This is intrinsic both to material substances and to qualities. There is, however, something else which he calls *positive extension*: having parts that are not just spread out but that resist co-location. As he explains:

A thing's parts can be spatially distant in two ways: in one way merely negatively (*privative*); in another way positively. The parts of a whole are distant from each other *negatively* when one part is distant from another in such a way that one is not where the other is, but yet does not resist it. Instead, it is in its own right naturally suited (*nata*) to exist with it at the same time and location or place. That this in fact does not occur results from some external obstacle. A whole is said to have parts at a distance from one another *positively*, on the other hand, when one of its parts is spatially distant from another and outside it in such a way that it is not naturally suited to

---

[9] Descartes's complaint against those who distinguish quantity and extension appears in almost identical terms at *Rules* 14 (X:447); see also *World* ch. 6, XI:35–6.

exist with it at the same time and place. Instead, when one enters into the place of another, it expels it from that place. (ibid., p. 207)

This distinction allows Marchia to accept (b), that substance and quality are intrinsically extended, understanding 'extension' in the first, negative sense. But because only the substance as a whole, the body, has positive extension, there is no obstacle to qualities inhering in substance. With respect to negative extension, then, Marchia agrees with Ockham that it comes for free, intrinsic to the nature of both material substances and material qualities. But since impenetrability is not entailed by that first sort of extension, we need some account of what explains it. He appropriates 'quantity' as a label for that which explains the resistance between bodies.

Ultimately, Marchia is a quantity realist, but of a new and quite distinct kind. By overthrowing the common assumption that quantity is that which makes a thing be extended, he gives the debate a complexity that blurs any straightforward contrast between realists and anti-realists. For although Marchia does postulate real accidents in the category of Quantity, and so officially counts as a quantity realist, at the same time he accepts the fundamental metaphysical thesis of Ockham's reductive project: that extended corpuscular structure is a basic feature of material entities. It is this step that is crucial to the corpuscularian reductive agenda, from Ockham to Hobbes. Even so, Marchia's theory poses a fundamental challenge to that agenda, by insisting that impenetrability is irreducible to corpuscular structure. The details of his proposal are, moreover, ideally situated to respond to Ockham. In particular, against the famous argument that God could remove a thing's quantity without moving its parts, yielding the absurd result that a thing without quantity would still have quantity (§14.3), Marchia can grant that a body without quantity could be extended in the negative sense. But it does not follow that—if God were to do that—nothing would be changed, and hence the body would still have quantity. For what would be lost once the quantity was removed is the power of those parts to resist overlap. They might stay where they are, spread out in the normal non-overlapping way, but there would no longer be anything keeping them from drifting inward on top of each other.[10]

15.3. Toward a Unified Scientific Account: Suárez

John Buridan's arguments for quantity were much discussed, but his theory did not change the character of the debate. Francis of Marchia's views were much bolder, but did not circulate widely and were quickly forgotten, until their rediscovery by modern scholars. Not even Buridan, working at the same university just a few years later, shows any sign of familiarity with them. Still, Marchia's idea was such a good one that someone was bound to reinvent it. Indeed, one finds it worked out in considerable detail almost three centuries later, in Suárez. Suárez firmly denies that quantity should be invoked to explain either a thing's having parts, or those parts being spread out. To think of quantity in this way is to fall into the trap of those he calls the nominalists, because they were clearly right to deny that any real accident is required to explain

---

[10] Marchia's discussion of quantity, in *Sent.* IV.13.1.1, is not yet edited, but large parts have been transcribed by Maier, "Problem der Quantität" pp. 200–9 and Bakker, *La raison* I:404–8.

corpuscular structure. Yet Suárez regards as "quite absurd" the supposition that this is all that quantity is (*Disp. meta.* 40.2.17). Instead, quantity accounts for a body's "locational aptitude" (40.4.15), the natural tendency of its parts to spread out:

This [conception of quantity] displays itself between two matters or two bodies. For that the matter of this body is substantially and really distinct from the matter of that one results not from quantity but from its proper being, as the above arguments prove. But that those two 3 matters are so affected that they necessarily need (*necessario debeant*) to be extended or separated in place, this comes formally from quantity. Therefore what we see in distinct whole bodies or matters we should understand to be the case also in the parts of the same body or matter, united 6 to one another. (40.4.15)

Without quantity, then, a body might still have parts; Suárez agrees with Ockham (and Marchia and Buridan) that a thing has its parts intrinsically. But in a body without quantity, those parts would not "necessarily" (line 4) be spread out. That is, there would be nothing to resist condensation or rarefaction as far as one likes, and indeed nothing to resist one body's floating into the same place as another's. It is quantity that explains why such things do not happen:

To the argument, I grant that a [material] substance [without quantity] would have distinction, composition, and union of its parts. I also grant that the parts of that substance could be conserved by God in distinct locations, as the argument made there proves. But all these things 3 do not suffice for a substance to be a quantity, unless it has the corporeal bulk (*molem*) on account of which it resists other bodies in the same location, and also its parts naturally repel each other from the same space. This is what that substance, deprived of quantity, would not 6 have. For it could be penetrated by other bodies in the same location, just as much as an angelic substance could, and its parts could exist indifferently either in the same place (*ubi*) or in different places. (40.2.21)

Suárez knows nothing of Marchia's long-forgotten work. So far as I can see, however, the two men hold essentially the same view. Marchia describes quantity as that which makes one part of a body "not naturally suited (*nata*) to exist with another at the same time and place" (as above); Suárez instead speaks of a resistance to penetration that is an "inclination." Both think that this natural tendency is the work of accidents in the category of Quantity. On the strength of this argument, quantity takes its place in Suárez's scheme as the only kind of real accident other than qualities. Every other accidental category either describes a mode or else fails to describe any sort of genuine entity (§13.3).[11]

Although Suárez's idea is not wholly new, he deploys it in a more systematic way, so as to cover not just resistance to co-location, as in Marchia's theory, but also the tendency of bodies to retain the same volume, along the lines suggested by Buridan's

---

[11] Suárez's line on quantity would be defended in the seventeenth century by Scheibler, *Metaphys.* II.7.4.1. For a critical discussion of Suárez's theory, see Vasquez, *In Summam theol.* III.190.3 n. 20: "Aliqui recentiores paucis ante annis docere caeperunt essentiam propriam quantitatis non esse quamcumque extensionem aut divisibilitatem, sed talem quae virtute propria postulet dispositionem partium in loco ita ut occupet illum. Occupare autem locum dicunt idem esse quod cum alia quantitate in eodem loco esse non posse—id quod alio nomine impenetrabilitatem appellant."

Marchia does not discuss condensation and rarefaction at all in his remarks on quantity. Suárez says that he does not want to enter into the elaborate details of the debate on this subject (see *Disp. meta.* 40.4.29), but his broader description of the phenomena in question seems pretty clearly to cover not only co-location but also condensation and rarefaction.

theory. By associating quantity with these various aspects of impenetrability, Suárez puts himself on the brink of a unified, scientific account of the physical phenomena associated with extension. Quantity can be understood in terms of the internal mutual resistance and attraction among a body's parts, balanced in such a way that those parts maintain a determinate, stable extension. Outside pressure on that body can then be balanced against these internal inclinations, in such a way that the overall sum of forces could in principle be measured, by calculating how much external force it takes to alter the body's extension. The only aspect of this that is actually foreign to Suárez is the idea that we might put these results into quantitative form. Famously, this played almost no role in scholastic thought. That it did not do so is surely a result, in part, of a failure to see just how fruitful that sort of project could be. Today we can only smile at Cesare Cremonini's cautioning his students that "those who are too practiced in mathematics are deficient in physics" (Meinel, *In physicis* p. 25n.). Really, though, how could poor Cremonini have foreseen what was to come? Indeed, even if he had been more sympathetic with the efforts of his friend Galileo, he would have been unable even to conceive of the possibilities that lay ahead, because scholastic theories were not couched in terms that facilitated the right sort of quantified treatment. Suárez's theory of quantity provides an instance of how a reconceptualized metaphysics—even one as highly dependent on the scholastic tradition as Suárez's—might naturally lead toward a recognizably modern scientific inquiry.

The developing scholastic debate over quantity provides another illustration of what is perhaps the most important characteristic of late scholasticism: the trend toward understanding Aristotle's increasingly suspect ontology in physical rather than metaphysical terms. To think of quantity metaphysically is, for instance, to think of it as what gives a body its corpuscular structure. As we have seen, early scholastic discussions revolve around highly abstract philosophical arguments, such as the idea that for quantity to yield corpuscular structure is for it to serve as the principle of individuation, without which bodies and forms would be universals (§14.4). The situation begins to look different when we consider the work of Marchia and Buridan. At the hands of these authors, quantity begins to take on a concrete aspect. Two bodies cannot overlap, according to Marchia, because they have quantity. Air when heated and cooled behaves differently from how it behaves under mechanical pressure, according to Buridan, because of its quantity. These are recognizably scientific claims, and even if one might complain that the hypothesis of quantity is not very well defined, still we can see it as an early attempt to label something that modern science has described with a great deal of precision. In Suárez these lines of thought are developed in considerably more detail, and stand just on the verge of what we think of as modern science. (I return to these issues in §23.5, where we will see that Suárez's talk of inclinations should be construed in categorical rather than dispositional terms.)

15.4. Solidity

A fully unified account of the phenomena surrounding corpuscular structure would also embrace hardness, or *solidity*. Whereas all bodies, even air, resist being compressed, dilated, or co-located with other bodies, not all bodies are solid: water is not very, and air is not at all. A solid body is a highly cohesive body; in general, a thing is solid insofar as it is cohesive. One might think for a moment that the bellows experiment is getting at the case of cohesion, too, when it focuses on the case of rarefaction. But these are different phenomena: air resists rarefaction, as Buridan showed, but even so it is not even slightly cohesive. Hence we might distinguish three physical phenomena under the broad heading of impenetrability:

1. Resistance to co-location;
2. Resistance to change in absolute volume;
3. Solidity.

All three phenomena concern the attraction and resistance of particles; it would be natural to attempt to give them a unified explanation. This, however, never happened. As we have seen, Marchia focused on the first, Buridan on the second. The third is not discussed in the context of quantity.

Certainly, solidity might have found a place in these discussions. When Olivi characterized quantity as explaining both the extension and unity of a body (§14.1), he was presupposing that an adequate account would explain not just why the parts of a body are spread out, but also why they are together. This aspect of quantity was never much developed, however, in part because it was unclear what was at issue. To say that the parts of a body are *together* might be understood in the sense of their being merely contiguous, or in the stronger sense of their cohering. Inasmuch as one wants the subject of quantity to be a unified substance, mere contiguity is surely not enough. But although scholastic authors have a great deal to say about substantial unity, they thought of this as a quite distinct issue from the present issues surrounding quantity. So although Olivi, for example, does think to mention unity in the context of quantity, he quickly dismisses it as the product of a body's substantial form (as quoted in §14.1). In their discussions of quantity, they tend to take for granted, as we have seen Buridan do, that a merely contiguous body (such as the air inside the bellows) counts as having quantity. Hence the question that is central to solidity—the question of cohesiveness—remains outside the debate. Even the most extensive and systematic treatment of the phenomenon of impenetrability, that of Suárez, fails to embrace the question of solidity.

Here is a place, then, where the Aristotelian ideology distorts the issues. No matter how much flexibility the scholastics show in their thinking about what quantity might be, they cannot abandon the rigid distinction between accidental and substantial forms. Since the phenomenon of cohesiveness gets associated with substantial unity, it falls under the heading of a different category, Substance rather than Quantity. Hence it must be explained in different terms, by a substantial rather than an accidental form. So although there is a perspective from which all three of the above phenomena are tightly linked, they could not be so linked within the normal scholastic framework. Here we see one of the frustrations of the history of philosophy: that we are bound, for better or worse, to the conceptual framework of our period. I remarked at the start of this chapter that one starting point is as good as any other in philosophy. Perhaps that was over-optimistic. Here, at any rate, is a place where a certain starting point leads to a framework that keeps apart issues that might have been fruitfully considered together. Even so, the historian's perspective has its advantages, for while we bridle under the conceptual constraints of our period, we can also learn from them. Although we are now inclined to treat coherence as a physical phenomenon, to be explained within the same theory that explains the mutual resistance of bodies, it may also be that there is a metaphysical story to be told about coherence—not as part of a theory of atomic forces, but as a metaphysics of substance. Nothing like a satisfactory theory of atomic attraction and repulsion can be found during our four centuries, but the period has what is perhaps the compensating advantage of a highly developed metaphysics of substantial unity and persistence. That will have to wait, however, until the final part of this study.[12]

15.5. Impenetrability as a Natural Law: Descartes

When scholastic authors postulate quantity to explain impenetrability, this is just one more item added to their rather long list of ontological commitments. In addition to the thin metaphysical substance and its parts, integral and metaphysical, these authors almost always endorse a further ontology of real accidents including the four elemental qualities, various sensible qualities (color, flavor, etc.), and occult qualities (magnetism, etc.) (Chs. 21–2). Given that the corpuscularian dream of a thoroughgoing reductivism is off-limits for scholastic authors (Ch. 19), there is relatively little cost in adding impenetrability to their list.

Conversely, the scholastic debate over quantity provides a clearer picture of what a reductive, corpuscularian account of extension would have to accomplish. It would have to account not just for corpuscular structure—a body's having integral parts, spread out *partem extra partem*—but also for a body's tendency to remain spread out, resisting rarefaction, condensation, and co-location. When one turns to the seventeenth century with these topics in mind, one finds that much is taken for granted. Because

---

[12] The idea of an atomic force to explain the coherence of bodies was famously proposed by Newton, in the General Scholium to the *Principia* and in Query 31 to the *Optics*. Compare his youthful talk of particles being wedged together, in his philosophical notebooks of 1664–5 (pp. 349–50). Naturally, the idea of invoking forces goes back farther, showing up for instance in Walter Warner's unpublished notes from the early seventeenth century (see Clucas, "Corpuscular Matter Theory" pp. 183–96). Even earlier, Nicholas of Autrecourt presciently compared magnetic forces to that which holds together the atoms of a solid body: "Et forsan sicut adamas ferrum, ita est ibi unum quod connectit et retinet in tali colligatione ipsa indivisibilia, et secundum hoc quod est maioris vigoris magis durat illlud suppositum in ratione suppositi; et illud, si sic esset, diceretur quasi principium formale rei" (*Tractatus* ch. 1, p. 201). The last clause, suggesting that this atomic attractive force might just be what others call the substantial form of a thing, brings out Autrecourt's anti-Aristotelian reductivism (§19.4, §28.2), but also brings out the way authors of the period assimilate cohesion to substantial unity, and hence to the metaphysics of substance.

One very common seventeenth-century attitude toward solidity is despair. Glanvill criticizes Descartes for explaining coherence in terms of nothing more than the parts of a body being at rest relative to one another, and regards the puzzles here as emblematic of our impoverished cognitive situation: "I think the emergent difficulties, which are its attendants, unanswerable: proof enough of the weakness of our now reasons, which are driven to such straights and puzzles even in things which are most obvious and have so much the advantage of our faculties" (*Scepsis scientifica* p. 46). Locke thinks the character of extension is as mysterious as the character of thought, because understanding the first requires understanding "wherein consists the union and cohesion of its parts, which seems to me as incomprehensible, as the manner of thinking, and how it is performed" (*Essay* II.23.24).

Henry More, characteristically, treats the problem of coherence as a reason to abandon the strict Cartesian program and allow immaterial forces (*Ench. meta.* 9.12).

Perhaps the most developed discussion of these matters from within our period is Boyle's "History of Firmness" (*Works* II:150–203). For a survey of seventeenth-century views, see Millington, "Theories of Cohesion" and Hill, "Locke's Account of Cohesion."

post-scholastic authors almost always take corpuscular prime matter as basic (§3.2), they see no need to account for corpuscular structure in the way that many scholastics had, in terms of quantity. As for those parts being spread out, if this means their location, absolute or relative, this too often gets taken for granted as something that requires only a story about the extrinsic efficient cause that gave those parts their location (Ch. 17). With respect to condensation and rarefaction, that gets largely ruled out from the start, as we have seen, on the grounds that quantity is always conserved (§4.5, §15.1). Given all of these assumptions, there is a strong temptation among many seventeenth-century authors to suppose that all one needs to have a complete meta-physics of body is corpuscular prime matter. And so it is easy to suppose that Democritus was ultimately right, at least with respect to the physical world: that all there are are atoms and the void, and maybe not even the void.

Even so, worries about impenetrability plague the seventeenth century. Despite Descartes's insistence that impenetrability comes for free with extension, others would have serious doubts. Atomists like Magnen and Gassendi insist that impenetrability has to be built-in at the foundations, as an essential feature of atoms in virtue of which all bodies are impenetrable.[13] Henry More, in his first letter to Descartes (December 1648), urges that body be conceived not just as extended—something that might be said even of spiritual entities—but also as impenetrable.[14] Controversy over this issue would continue through-out the seventeenth century. Locke, as early as the A Draft of the *Essay* (1671), criticizes Descartes for treating it as a self-evident principle that body just is extension, contrasting this with the equally plausible principle that body is extension plus impenetrability. By the time of the published *Essay* (1689), he is ready to insist that extension alone could not adequately capture the essence of body: "therefore the essence of body is not bare extension, but an extended solid thing" (III.6.21).[15] Ralph Cudworth, in his *True Intellectual System of the Universe* (1678), denies "the general heads of all entity to be *Extension* and *Cogitation*," arguing instead that "the first heads of being ought rather to be expressed thus: *Resisting* or *Antitypous Extension*, and *Life*" (III.16). Finally, and perhaps most notably, Leibniz eventually rejects extension altogether as part of the essence of body, and replaces it with resistance. But even

[13] On impenetrability as located at the atomic level, see Magnen, *Democritus reviviscens* p. 190: "Atomus itaque substantialis est entitas corporea, substantialis simplex, et purissime homogenea, indivisibilis ex natura sua, per se primo exigitiva quantitatis, cuius beneficio sit impenetrabilis, et ad continuum physicum componendum ordinata." For Gassendi, see *Syntagma* II.1.6.3 (I:381b): "adnoto…primariam causam quare penetratio corporum non detur, seu unum corpus excludatur ab eodem loco in quo est aliud, non tam videri extensionem sive quantitatem, praecise spectatam, ut vulgaris opinio est, quam soliditatem sive corpulentiam." On solidity as a basic feature of Gassendi's atoms, see ibid., II.1.3.5 (I:256b): "ita solida et, ut ita dicam, dura compactaque sit, ut divisioni, sectionive, et plagae nullum locum faciat."

[14] More remarks to Descartes (V:240): "Quod et aliam innuit materiae sive corporis conditionem, quam appellare poteris impenetrabilitatem; nempe quod nec penetrare alia corpora, nec ab illis penetrari possit."

[15] Locke is particularly interested in the issue of impenetrability for what it allegedly shows about the possibility of a vacuum. See Draft A §27, p. 46: "But yet though both of these propositions (as you see) may be equally demonstrated—viz., that there may be a vacuum and that there cannot be a vacuum—by these two certain principles—viz., what is is and the same thing cannot be and not be—yet neither of these principles or ways of demonstrations prove to us or can prove that body does exist or what it is as it exists. But for that we are left only to our senses to discover to us as far as they can." Judging from this passage— which appears in essentially the same form at *Essay* IV.7.12–14—Locke may not at this time have made up his mind about the adequacy of extension to account for impenetrability. Such an attitude suggests that of Boyle, who insists on impenetrability as a feature of body (as nearly everyone does, including Descartes), but seems agnostic on whether it can be accounted for by extension alone. See *Possibility of the Resurrection* (*Works* VIII:308; Stewart pp. 202–3): "the true notion of body consists either alone in its extension, or in that and impenetrability together."

in his earliest works, before arriving at that view, he doubts that extension alone could account for impenetrability, holding instead that "the nature of body is constituted by extension and antitypy. . . . Nothing should be posited in bodies that does not flow from the definition of extension and antitypy" (to Thomasius, April 1669, *Phil. Schriften* IV:173–4 [tr Loemker pp. 101–2]). ('Antitypy' is simply the Hellenized form of the Latinate 'impenetrability.')[16]

There is at least some truth to Locke's complaint that Descartes simply assumes, as a self-evident principle, that body is simply extension. At least as far as impenetrability is concerned, Descartes often tends to take for granted that corporeal extension entails it. Sometimes he makes this explicit, as in the Sixth Replies: "the true extension of a body is such as to exclude any interpenetration of parts" (Sixth Replies, VII:442). Often, though, he takes the connection entirely for granted, as in his most systematic treatment of natural philosophy, the *Principles*, where impenetrability is not even mentioned. Still, in making this presupposition, Descartes is simply adhering to the standard scholastic view. For despite this chapter's focus on a few unusual cases, the most common scholastic view (that of, for instance, Giles of Rome, as quoted at the start of §15.2) was that impenetrability is a consequence of extension. Descartes, we might say, is simply taking advantage, as he so often does, of what the scholastics are prepared to grant him. This is the situation, at least, up until the very end of his life, when More pushed him on these issues.

In the face of More's suggestion that body has to be defined not just by extension, but by impenetrability as well, Descartes offers the following argument to show that extension entails impenetrability:

One cannot understand one part of an extended thing to penetrate another part that is equal to it without thereby understanding the overlapping part of its extension to have been taken away or annihilated. What is annihilated, however, does not penetrate anything else. And so, in my view, it is demonstrated that impenetrability belongs to the essence of extension and not to the essence of any other thing. (To More, April 1649, V:342)

Consider two solid balls, each one cubic meter in volume. Let them exactly overlap. Whereas we once had two cubic meters of extended stuff, we now have only one cubic meter. But to say that we now have only one cubic meter of extension is to say that half of the matter of those two balls must have been annihilated. But "what is annihilated does not penetrate anything else" (line 3). Hence it is in fact impossible for one extended thing to penetrate another.

There is no argument in this book that I have gone back and forth on so many times. My own indecision reflects the diverging assessments of recent experts. Daniel Garber is enthusiastic, describing the argument as "simple and ingenuous" (*Descartes' Metaphysical Physics* p. 147). According to Jonathan Bennett, however, it is circular, and "should

---

[16] Leibniz offers a particularly detailed negative assessment of the prospects for explaining impenetrability in terms of extension in his 1692 *Animadversiones* on Descartes's *Principles* (*Phil. Schriften* IV:364; tr. Loemker p. 390), and in his 1712 *Conversation of Philarète and Ariste* (*Phil. Schriften* VI:579–94; tr. Loemker pp. 618–28; tr. Ariew and Garber pp. 257–68). He surely has Descartes in mind in his early *Confessio naturae* when, lumping together under the heading of *consistentia* a body's *resistentia, cohaerentia*, and *reflexio*, he writes: "quarum rationem qui ex materiae figura, magnitudine et motu mihi reddiderit, eum ego magnum philosophum libens fatebor" (*Phil. Schriften* IV:108; tr. Loemker p. 112). His mature views on extension are complex and changing. For discussion, see Nason, "Leibniz's Attack"; Sleigh, *Leibniz and Arnauld* chs. 5–6; Robert Adams, *Leibniz* pt. 3; Garber, "Leibniz on Form and Matter" pp. 339–40.

not convert anybody" (*Learning from Six Philosophers* I:31). The reason the argument is so hard to evaluate, I have come to believe, is that it can be construed in two different ways: either as making a purely conceptual point about extension, or as making a claim about how extended bodies must behave in the natural world. When the argument is understood in the first way (as it almost always is by scholars today), impenetrability is made to follow from the very nature of what it is to be extended. So understood, the argument is a failure, because it begs the question when it assumes that the volume of our two overlapping balls will be one meter. What the proponent of overlap will contend, instead, is that the total volume is two meters, compressed into a one meter region. That is just what overlap is. In effect, this is Bennett's objection to the argument.

Admittedly, the charge of begging the question here is somewhat obscure. It is perhaps easier to see that the argument cannot succeed, when so construed, by considering how it would fall prey to the co-location argument of §15.2. If extension, by its very nature, entails impenetrability, then it ought to be impossible for *any* two extended things to overlap. Hence Descartes's argument would rule out, for instance, the possibility of space as a distinct thing that bodies exist in, since it would show that a body's existing in space entails the annihilation of either the body or the space. Although Descartes would of course be content with that outcome, it is ridiculous to think his argument could yield such a powerful result. Moreover, the argument when so construed also seems to rule out cases of overlap that Descartes does embrace. It suggests, for instance, that the mind could not overlap with any part of the body, but instead either one or the other would have to be annihilated. Similarly, it seems that God could not be everywhere, without everything else's being annihilated. Admittedly, for Descartes, neither the mind nor God is extended strictly speaking (§16.4), and so neither is strictly relevant. But the problem is that, when the argument is construed in its most general, conceptual form, it seems to apply to any sort of co-location. It seems to rule out, for instance, that God could be immense at the same time that the created world is immense, because their immensities would have to overlap. If there is something special about corporeal extension that makes it by nature impenetrable, then that ought to figure in the premises of his argument.

For Descartes's argument to have a chance at success, it needs to be construed in the second way, so as to follow from facts about bodies as they are in the natural world. For Descartes, one of the most fundamental such facts—and the one that is decisive here—is the conservation of quantity (C^Q). Suppose we accept that the quantity or extension of bodies is always conserved. This would be a natural law, violable only by divine power. Hence an exception to C^Q would require divine intervention. One form such divine intervention might take would be for God to make more or less matter, by creating or annihilating it. This violates not just C^Q but also the even more widely accepted conservation of matter thesis (§2.5): that matter never comes into or goes out of existence. Descartes's argument supposes that the alleged case of overlap would in fact not be overlap at all, but instead a violation of the conservation of matter—God would break a natural law and "annihilate" (part of) a body. In focusing on this possibility, the argument might seem to suggest that not even God could make two bodies genuinely overlap in a way that would conserve quantity. This, however, strikes me as an implausible reading of the passage, given Descartes's generous understanding of divine power. On my reading, the point is merely to stress that *some* sort of miracle would have to occur, in cases where two bodies come together. This is to say that Descartes would allow the possibility of a second sort of miracle's occurring in the imagined case: that God would allow the overlap to happen, preserving the conservation of matter thesis but still violating C^Q. This is to say that it is logically possible for bodies to overlap, and that the fact they do not is a result of the laws of nature rather than any conceptual point about extension.[17]

The clearest advantage of this construal of the argument is that it excludes the unwanted cases of space and immaterial entities, on the grounds that C^Q does not apply to them. Still, the argument may seem to beg the question, in just the way described above, since one might contend that no violation of C^Q has been proved to occur. For two bodies to overlap, as above, is for them to *maintain* their extension, but now in one and the same region. Once the argument is construed as I have suggested, however, Descartes is in a better position to respond. For now the issue is whether this is how C^Q ought to be understood, and whether when so understood it is defensible. As far as exegesis goes, it seems quite clear that Descartes and others understand C^Q to require the conservation of *non-overlapping* quantity. Surely, when Descartes insists that "it is impossible to remove the least bit from this quantity or extension without also taking just as much from the substance" (*Principles* II.8), he did not mean to leave open the possibility of bodies coming to occupy less space by overlapping. This would be the sort of telescoping universe envisaged by William Crathorn as an explanation of condensation (§15.1), and clearly Descartes takes C^Q to rule that out, just as much as it rules out condensation and rarefaction of the usual sort. Hence, just as C^Q blocks true condensation and rarefaction, it likewise blocks the co-location of bodies.

---

[17] With respect to impenetrability, Descartes tells Hyperaspistes in 1641 that "quomodo mens corpori extenso coextendatur, etsi non habeat ullam veram extensionem, hoc est ullam per quam locum occupet, atque aliud quid ab eo excludat" (III:434). And to Elizabeth, June 1643: "l'extension de cette matière est d'autre nature que l'extension de cette pensée, en ce que la première est determinée à certain lieu, duquel elle exclut toute autre extension de corps, ce que ne fait pas la deuxième" (III:694). The second passage in particular suggests that impenetrability follows from C^Q, inasmuch as being "determined to a certain place" does not mean being immobile, but rather having a determinate extension. These two notions are also closely connected in *The World* ch. 6 (XI:33): "... chacune de ses parties occupe toujours une partie de cet espace, tellement proportionée à sa grandeur qu'elle n'en sauroit remplir une plus grande, ni se resserrer en une moindre, ni souffrir que, pendant qu'elle y demeure, quelqu'autre y trouve place."

Gassendi is quite explicit in treating C^Q as a law of nature: "... ex lege naturae unumquodque corpus suum occupat locum, et tantum quidem quantum ipsum est, adeo ut, sive quiescat sive moveatur, intelligamus semper vel eundem vel aequalem locum, in quo sit extensum" (*Syntagma* II.1.6.3, I:381a). As quoted above in note 13, however, Gassendi appeals neither to this law nor to the nature of extension to account for impenetrability, but rather to *solidity*, a basic feature of atoms.

Descartes scholars seem generally to take for granted that impenetrability is supposed to follow purely from the nature of extension. See, e.g., Woolhouse, *Descartes, Spinoza, Leibniz* p. 81: "His idea, it seems, is that simply in being extended, body is consequently impenetrable; being impenetrable is part of what it is to be extended"; Williams, *Descartes* p. 229: "for Descartes, any extended thing that completely occupies a given space excludes any other extended thing from occupying that space—matter keeps out other matter. This he regards, consistently with his general position, as a pure conceptual necessity"; Gabbey, "Force and Inertia" p. 234: "impenetrability, which for Descartes is a logical consequence of the idea of body as extension..." Perhaps Garber's enthusiasm for Descartes's argument against More results from his understanding the argument in the way I propose. For although Garber does not say that the argument should be read in terms of natural rather than conceptual necessity, he does emphasize the conservation of quantity in connection with the argument, which is the crucial idea (*Descartes' Metaphysical Physics* p. 147).

On laws of nature in seventeenth-century philosophy, see Ott, *Causation and Laws of Nature*; Henry, "Metaphysics and Origins"; Milton, "Laws of Nature"; Daston and Stolleis, *Natural Law and Laws of Nature*. For Descartes in particular, see also Schmaltz, *Descartes on Causation* pp. 105–24. For Boyle's interesting views, see Anstey, *Philosophy of Robert Boyle* ch. 7. On the scholastic background see Ruby, "The Origins of Scientific Law." On occasionalism before the seventeenth century, see Perler and Rudolph, *Occasionalismus* and Schmaltz, *Descartes on Causation* pp. 9–48.

So, at least, Descartes contends. The question remains, however, of whether this non-overlapping version of C^Q is defensible. As I understand Descartes's response to More, the argument is only as strong as C^Q is; since I have criticized that principle already (§4.5), my enthusiasm here can go only so far. Still, when we read the argument as resting on C^Q, it no longer looks like a facile and question-begging bit of sophistry invoked to save his theory. Instead, the argument reveals itself as a special application of a general principle that lies at the heart of his account of corporeal substance. Even if C^Q is not true, it was very widely accepted by seventeenth-century authors, in precisely the strong non-overlapping form that yields the natural impossibility of co-location. This puts Descartes in a much stronger position on this topic, at least historically speaking, than is commonly recognized. For supposing one wants neither to follow the scholastics in rejecting C^Q, nor to weaken C^Q by allowing overlap, one then ought to concede to Descartes that impenetrability follows from this fundamental principle. From this vantage point, one no more needs a special account of why bodies do not interpenetrate than one needs a special account of why they are not susceptible to rarefaction or condensation.

Quite right, a stubborn scholastic will reply: one very much does need an account of all these things. Hence a corpuscularian treatment is inadequate unless supplemented by accidents in the category of Quantity. Descartes's later critics say something quite similar: even if they accept C^Q, they in effect want an account of *why* C^Q is true. They differ from scholastic quantity realists in expecting to find that account in the nature of corporeal substance rather than in some sort of real accident, but they are in other respects aligned with their scholastic forebears. Indeed, once we get past our modern allergy to scholastic talk of *forms*, keeping firmly in mind instead that such talk is as open-ended and flexible as is our talk of *properties* (§10.1), we can see that it makes no fundamental difference whether one speaks of a body's being impenetrable in virtue of a form in the category of Quantity, or whether one speaks of it as a force, as Locke among others would (*Essay* II.4.1). (For more on the status of dispositions and forces, see Ch. 23.)

Descartes is doing something very different. Instead of offering any sort of intrinsic explanation of impenetrability, Descartes appeals to a law of nature:

I have noticed certain laws that God has so established in nature, and of which he has implanted such notions in our souls, that after adequate reflection on them we cannot doubt that they are exactly observed in everything that exists or occurs in the world. (*Discourse* pt. 5, VI:41)

If C^Q is one of these laws for Descartes, as I am claiming, then neither it nor its consequences are entailed by the nature of bodies. On the contrary, God might have created and then set in motion a material world that did not adhere to C^Q. In such a world, bodies might rarify, condense, and overlap. Such bodies would not satisfy Descartes's standard for having "true extension" (Sixth Replies, VII:442), but 'true' there is keyed not to any *a priori* feature of extension, but to *res extensa* as it behaves under the laws that govern it. In the hands of some later figures—Newton most clearly—the appeal to a law might serve in place of a full explanation, as a way of describing the phenomena without having to frame hypotheses about the causal mechanisms at work. This is not Descartes's attitude; he shows no sign of thinking that his account is in any sense incomplete. Instead, the appeal to God's laws is the whole story in this domain, and there is nothing further about material substances that explains why they are naturally unable to overlap. In effect, this is a kind of localized occasionalism, governed by the laws of nature. Bodies resist co-location not because of any intrinsic feature they possess, which causally prevents penetration from occurring, but because God's laws prevent it. Descartes is hardly clear on how we are to understand the causal role of such laws, but we can take a clue from how he understands the annihilation of bodies: as "God's denying his concurrence to them" (*Meditations* synopsis, VII:14). This is the traditional view that the conservation of matter is a consequence of God's constantly acting on the created realm, conserving it, leaving annihilation to be simply the cessation of such activity. It seems plausible to suppose that the conservation of quantity should be understood in a similar way, as God's constantly conserving the same non-overlapping volume of matter. In the context of his argument to More, then, Descartes is imagining that God might cease to conserve one of the two bodies, creating merely the illusion of overlap. Another possibility, I take it, is that God might continue to conserve the two spheres in existence, but might cease to conserve their non-overlapping volume. This would be genuine, albeit miraculous, overlap. It would require not God's taking action, but his ceasing to act.

In this way, impenetrability rests on a kind of law-governed occasionalism. This is a framework that scholastic authors were familiar with from its prominence among Islamic authors, but that hardly anyone found attractive until late in the seventeenth century. Hence, the focus of discussions for most of the century continued to rest where they did in previous centuries, on discovering the intrinsic basis of impenetrability. The familiar criticism of the scholastics was of course that their forms failed to explain anything. But, as Locke realized, this sort of complaint might be made about many post-scholastic discussions as well:

If anyone asks me *What this solidity is*, I send him to his senses to inform him: let him put a flint or a football between his hands and then endeavor to join them, and he will know. If he thinks this not a sufficient explication of solidity, what it is and wherein it consists, I promise to tell him what it is and wherein it consists when he tells me what thinking is or wherein it consists, or explain to me what extension or motion is, which perhaps seems much easier. (*Essay* II.4.6)

This marks the beginning of a new attitude toward our subject. Among scholastics, no one doubted that the goal of the discussion was to identify the role, if any, played by forms in the category of Quantity. One reached a conclusion on what such forms do, and moved on to the next *quaestio*. Many seventeenth-century discussions are not fundamentally different, even if they shift to talk of forces and powers. In Locke one finds a new kind of worry: that even once those sorts of fights have been successfully fought, one still has not explained anything. This is not entirely fair. Scholastic theories of forms, and their post-scholastic counterparts, can be metaphysically explanatory, and/or they can be forerunners of a more complete, quantified, physical account. In appealing to the laws of nature, Descartes is doing something quite different, but his own approach would only fuel the questions about just how much either metaphysics or physics explains about the natural world. With the rise of worries such as these—in Malebranche, Leibniz, Berkeley, Hume, etc.—there stretches before us a new episode in the history of philosophy, one that extends into the eighteenth century and beyond.

16

Mind and Extension

16.1. The Material–Immaterial Divide

From the start, this study's focus has been on material substances. Indeed, many of the topics of discussion so far do not even apply to immaterial things. Such things lack both matter and quantity, at least as they were standardly construed during our period, and so do not raise the sorts of issues with which we have largely been preoccupied. Here I consider how these issues apply or fail to apply to the case of immaterial substances.

One might say that *of course* immaterial substances lack matter and quantity, but the issues are not quite so simple. There was, first, a lively debate among the earliest scholastics over the doctrine of universal hylomorphism: the thesis that all substances contain matter of some kind. Since this doctrine was largely abandoned by the time our period begins, we can set it aside here.[1] As for the second claim, that intellectual substances lack quantity, this was never in much doubt among scholastic authors, who almost always associate quantity with extension, and deny that an intellectual substance could have either. Yet this assumption comes into question in the seventeenth century, in the work of Thomas Hobbes and Henry More, both of whom claim, in rather different ways, that all things—even minds—are extended. Hobbes and More can be regarded as two corners of a triangle, with Descartes the third. Reflection on this Philosophers' Triangle is especially interesting, as we will see, for the light it sheds on how best to distinguish the material from the immaterial.

The material–immaterial divide is problematic for us moderns in a way it never was for scholastic authors. Although we still readily speak of materialists and dualists, it has become very hard to know what that distinction amounts to. For the scholastics, the situation is relatively straightforward: material entities can be marked off as those that either contain or are by nature dependent on prime matter. Belonging to the first group are composite substances and their integral parts, and aggregates of composite substances. In the second group are material forms, substantial or accidental. Immaterial entities either exist independently of matter (God and angels) or at least are naturally able to do so (human souls). It is this way of viewing the divide that makes the terminology of 'material' and 'immaterial' particularly apt. The clarity of this

---

[1] For universal hylomorphism, see, e.g., Kleineidam, *Das Problem der Hylomorphen*; Lottin, *Psychologie et morale* I:427–60; Dales, *Problem of the Rational Soul*; Long, "Of Angels and Pinheads."

distinction depends on two things: a firm distinction between form and matter, and a clear understanding of where prime matter is found. (Hence the significance of rejecting universal hylomorphism.) When seventeenth-century authors call into doubt the form–matter distinction, in favor of a view on which only substances (and perhaps modes) exist, they take the first step toward undermining that standard distinction between the material and the immaterial. For now instead of a world divided into form, matter, and composites of the two, we have a world only of substances. How are we to know which of those substances count as material and which do not?[2]

For the most part, seventeenth-century authors do not take themselves to have a problem here. Indeed, they are more likely to congratulate themselves on escaping from a problem. Thus Malebranche remarks in 1674 that "it can be said with some assurance that the difference between the mind and the body has been known with sufficient clarity for only a few years" (*Search after Truth* preface, p. 115 [tr. p. xl]). The remark pays homage to Descartes, and his account of mind as essentially thought, body as essentially extension. To be sure, there *is* something new about this, inasmuch as Aristotelian prime matter has dropped out, replaced by an account in terms of these two principal attributes of mind and body. As quickly as this, the terms 'material' and 'immaterial' begin to lose their aptness. Even so, both of Descartes's principal attributes are grounded in earlier traditions. The identification of *thought* as the essence of mind goes back to Augustine, although the idea goes undeveloped among scholastics, who tend to conceive of thought as conceptually removed from soul twice over (as an activity of the intellect, which is in turn a power of the soul).[3] Treating *extension* as the essence of body is a thoroughly commonplace idea, found in both Aristotle and Augustine, and subsequently throughout scholastic texts as well. Aquinas, for instance, had taken it for granted that bodies are those substances "in which one finds three dimensions" (*Summa theol.* 1a 18.2c), and subsequent scholastics agree.[4]

Authors during our four centuries tend to agree that all and only thinking things are immaterial, which makes this a convenient criterion for immateriality. Even so, this half of Descartes's account contributes little to understanding what it is to be immaterial, and so does not help very much to clarify the nature of the material–immaterial divide. More promising is the idea that extension defines materiality. Although on its face the extension criterion simply repeats a scholastic commonplace, in fact the situation here

---

[2] For the idea that the spiritual (i.e., God, angels, and rational souls) can be defined as what lacks matter, see for instance Scheibler, *Metaphys.* II.2.5.2.2 (p. 457): "ergo substantia immaterialis sive incorporea sive spiritus *est substantia quae intrinsece ex materia non componitur*, sive, *quae est expers materiae*...."

[3] For Augustine, see, e.g., *De trinitate* X.10.16, and the discussion in Pasnau, "Mind and Extension." The Cartesian idea that the mind, as essentially a thinking thing, must always be thinking, was widely regarded as eccentric. See, e.g., this remark from the *Journal* of François Babin, a traditionalist attempting to stem the tide of Cartesianism: "On n'apprenoit plus aux jeunes gens qu'à se défaire des préjugés de l'enfance, et à douter de toutes choses, même s'ils étoient au monde. On leur enseignoit que l'âme est une substance dont l'essence est de penser toujours quelque chose; que les enfants pensent dès le ventre de leur mère..." (p. 2; see Ariew, "Modernity" p. 121).

[4] On body defined as what has three dimensions, see Aristotle, *De caelo* I.1, 268a20–23; Augustine, *De trinitate* X.vii.9. The definition is entirely commonplace among scholastic authors, e.g. Aquinas, *Summa theol.* 1a 18.2c: "hoc nomen corpus impositum est ad significandum quoddam genus substantiarum, ex eo quod in eis inveniuntur tres dimensiones." This meaning remains standard into the seventeenth century, e.g. in Goclenius's *Lexicon*: "corpus quod est substantia est subiectum triplicis dimensionis" (s.v. 'corpus,' p. 481a), and Hobbes, *Lev.* 34.2: "The word *body*, in the most general acceptation, signifies that which fills or occupies some certain room or imagined place, and depends not on the imagination, but is a real part of that we call the *universe*."

is quite complex. Extension for Descartes is no longer a formal constituent of a composite body (in the way it is for most scholastics, under the label 'quantity'), but is instead in some sense (§8.3) the body itself. This is not quite to say that Descartes no longer has prime matter. As I have argued (Chs. 2–3), Descartes and his post-scholastic contemporaries still have prime matter in the sense that they still have an enduring subject of physical change. These bodies or *corpora*, composed of *corpuscula*, now play the functional role of prime matter, and so define what it is to be material. For this reason, we might now more properly distinguish between the *corporeal* and the *incorporeal*. Yet, of course, to say that the corporeal is that which is composed of *corpora* does not get us very far, without some further analysis of what bodies are. Hence the importance of Descartes's account of bodies in terms of extension. For most scholastic authors, in contrast, extension lacks any such significance. Since they tend to be quantity realists (Ch. 14), they are generally committed to the possibility of extension-less material substances (material substances that are, strictly speaking, not bodies [§16.6]). Indeed, many scholastics, whether in the Averroistic or Thomistic tradition, treat prime matter as itself unextended (§4.1). Hence, for most scholastic authors, questions about extension and quantity come apart from questions about materiality, and the materiality of a substance depends on the presence of prime matter. So even if Descartes's account of body as essentially extended is verbally no different from what the scholastics said, and even if it yields the same verdict in central cases, still it gives extension a more central role—literally, a more essential role—than it plays in scholastic discussions. With this comes an increased interest in just exactly what it means for a thing to be extended, and whether extension can be applied in any sense to immaterial entities. The main focus of this chapter will be on how these debates played out in the seventeenth century.

16.2. All Things Are Extended: Hobbes

Given how common it is to treat bodies as essentially extended, it should be no surprise to find Descartes's contemporaries agreeing with him here. A case in point is Hobbes. Although the Third Set of Objections and Replies to the *Meditations* depicts two authors talking past each other at almost every step, they do in fact agree that body is essentially extended. What makes Hobbes an interesting case is that he further asserts that *all* things are extended, with the result that all things are bodies. Here is how that point comes out in his exchange with Descartes, from near the beginning of Hobbes's Objections:

How do we know the proposition 'I am thinking'? It can come only from our inability to conceive any act without its subject—such as jumping without a jumper, knowing without a knower, or thinking without a thinker. It seems to follow from this that a thinking thing is something corporeal. For it seems that the subject of any act can be understood only under a corporeal aspect or under the aspect of matter. (VII:173)

In reply, Descartes agrees with the first point, that we cannot conceive of an act without its subject (lines 1–3). But he expresses complete bewilderment at what follows, remarking that the inference to the mind as corporeal is made "without any argument and contrary to all usage and all logic" (VII:175). Quite right, it seems. What could possibly lie behind Hobbes's utterly unsupported inference from an act's needing a subject to that subject's being corporeal?

In the objections to Descartes, these issues remain obscure, but in Hobbes's own work a somewhat clearer picture emerges. In part, his materialism arises from his brand of empiricism. In the *Elements of Law*, written just a year before his exchange with Descartes, he remarks that "we who are Christians acknowledge that there be angels good and evil, and that they are spirits, and that the soul of man is a spirit, and that these spirits are immortal." Then he adds the crucial qualification:

But to know it, that is to say, to have natural evidence of the same: it is impossible. For all evidence is conception, as it is said, and all conception is imagination and proceeds from sense. And spirits we suppose to be those substances which work not upon the sense, and therefore not conceptible. (I.11.5)

Consequently, we have no conception of anything spiritual if that means something imperceptible. To the extent we do conceive of something spiritual such as the mind, the angels, or God, we conceive of something extended, which "fills up the place which the image of a visible body might fill up.... To conceive a spirit is to conceive something that has dimension" (ibid., I.11.4). But, since what has dimension is a body, it follows that spirits must be bodies. So Hobbes concludes this discussion in *Elements of Law* by saying that angels and spirits are corporeal substances. Later, in the *Leviathan* (1651), he puts the point still more plainly, remarking:

[E]very part of the universe is body, and that which is not body is no part of the universe. And because the universe is all, that which is no part of it is nothing (and consequently, nowhere). Nor does it follow from hence that spirits are nothing. For they have dimensions, and are, therefore, really bodies. (*Lev.* 46.15)

When we say that God is a spirit, this is simply "a signification of our reverence" (*Elements* I.11.4), showing "our desire to honor him with such names as we conceive most honorable among ourselves" (*Lev.* 34.4). In the Latin Appendix to the *Leviathan*, he writes that he "affirms, of course, that God is a body" (3.6).

All of this points toward one way to understand the above enthymeme from the Third Objections: that the subject of an act must be corporeal, because we can conceive only of what is corporeal. It is, however, not very satisfying to understand Hobbes's materialism as arising purely from his empiricist scruples—as if from the fact that we cannot perceive and therefore imagine and therefore conceive of something incorporeal, it follows that there is nothing incorporeal. To be sure, he wants that stronger conclusion. He claims not just that we have no concept of the immaterial, but that such a concept would be positively incoherent. Thus, the words 'substance without dimension' "do flatly contradict one another" (*Elements of Law* I.11.4). And, "*substance incorporeal* are words which, when they are joined together, destroy one another, as if a man should say *an incorporeal body*" (*Lev.* 34.2). The words destroy one another, because they are contradictory in their signification, and hence the phrase fails to signify (*Lev.* 4.21; 34.24). Still, if the only basis for Hobbes's materialism were the limits of what we can conceive, he would hardly have grounds for asserting this sort of contradiction.[5]

Another reason for seeking a better account of Hobbes's view is that it would be good to understand why he puts things as he does in the Third Objection—that is, why from an act's needing a subject "it seems to follow that a thinking thing is something corporeal" (as above). So far as I can see, there is nothing about subjects of acts, as such, that lends itself to this conclusion. What Hobbes *is* entitled to here is the inference from actions to entities. Indeed, given that his austere ontology recognizes only substances (§7.1, §10.2), actions for him must be nothing at all. Hence there can be no question of whether actions are corporeal or incorporeal; the question must concern the thing that acts. Unfortunately, the above passage accomplishes nothing more than to make this shift from thinking to the thing that is thinking; it is as if Hobbes has forgotten that he still needs to show that all things are bodies. Elsewhere, though, he tries to do that, by appealing to these two premises:

1. Whatever exists has a spatial location;
2. Spatial location entails extension.

With these added premises, along with

3. What is extended is a body,

we get the conclusion

4. Everything that exists is a body.

Whether or not this is exactly what Hobbes had in mind in the Third Objections, it is certainly the way he reasons elsewhere. Regarding (2) and (3), he remarks in the *Elements of Law* that "locality is dimension, and whatsoever has dimension is body, be it never so subtle" (I.11.5). With respect to (1), Hobbes remarks that there could be no such thing as incorporeal ghosts, because they would be "ghosts that are in *no place*; that is to say, that are *nowhere*; that is to say, that seeming to be *somewhat*, are *nothing*" (*Lev.* 34.15). The whole argument comes together in a passage attacking the immateriality of the rational soul: "For seeing they will have these forms to be real, they are obliged to assign them some place [= 1]. But because they hold them incorporeal, without all dimension of quantity, and all men know that place is dimension [= 2], and not to be filled but by that which is corporeal [= 3], they are driven to . . . absurdities" (*Lev.* 46.19). (See §16.5 for the elided part of the passage.)

---

[5] The idea that Hobbes's materialism falls directly out of his empiricism is common, and seems to be how Descartes himself reads Hobbes, judging from this remark to More: "Quod vero nonnulli substantiae notionem cum rei extensae notione confundant, hoc fit ex falso praeiudicio, quia nihil putant existere vel esse intelligibile nisi sit etiam imaginabile; ac revera nihil sub imaginationem cadit quod non sit aliquo modo extensum" (Feb. 1649, V:270).

On another reading, Hobbes simply has no argument; see Mintz, *Hunting of Leviathan* p. 67: "But his assumption that there can be no other substance but matter is gratuitous and unproved. Hobbes was most impressive when he worked out the logical consequences of his assumptions; he showed no inclination for proving those assumptions to be true beyond a firm belief that they were self-evident and attainable by all reasonable men who exercise their minds with due and proper care."

Curley, "Hobbes versus Descartes," suggests yet another way, too complex to be summarized here, to understand the quoted argument from the Third Objections. On God's materiality more generally in Hobbes, see Leijenhorst, "Hobbes, Heresy." See also Hobbes's criticisms of the incorporeal in *De mundo* 5.3 and 27.1, and his blanket statement in some English notes on a draft of the *De corpore*: "There is nothing that truly exists in the world but single individual bodies producing single and individual acts or effects from law, rule or form and in order or succession" (in Hobbes, *Critique du De mundo* appendix II, p. 449).

Descartes of course accepts (3), but the first two premises look very dubious. Why should existence require spatial location? And, even if we accept that, why should location entail extension, as opposed to merely an extensionless point? This is territory we have visited before, in the context of trying to understand what it would be for prime matter or a material substance to lack quantity (§§4.1–3, §14.4). We can now set aside those rather arcane questions pertaining to supernatural, merely logical possibilities, and focus on what were almost universally supposed to be actual cases: the extensionless, incorporeal existence of the human soul, angels, and God. Hobbes's contrarian view is that it is incoherent to treat any such entities as extensionless, and hence incoherent to treat them as incorporeal. Although Hobbes offers no more support for these claims beyond what we have seen, that does not mean his arguments lack force. For even if philosophers today very often take for granted that immaterial entities have no location, this is in fact quite an extraordinary view, historically speaking. The next section takes up this issue, putting Hobbes's argument in the proper historical context.

16.3. What Exists Must Exist Somewhere

For almost the whole history of philosophy, going all the way back to ancient times and forward to Hobbes's own contemporaries, it was commonly supposed that whatever exists exists somewhere. This idea was promoted by Plato, who seems to endorse both (1) and (2) when he remarks that "everything that exists must of necessity be somewhere, in some place and occupying some space, and what does not exist either on earth or somewhere in heaven does not exist at all" (*Timaeus* 52b; cf. *Parm.* 151a4–5). Indeed, according to Aristotle, "everyone supposes that what exists is somewhere, for what does not exist is nowhere. Where is the goat-stag or the sphinx?" (*Phys.* IV.1, 208a29–30). The obvious *non sequitur* in the first sentence marks this as an *endoxa*, rather than a claim Aristotle himself necessarily endorses, and indeed his ultimate view is more nuanced. (The soul, for instance, has a location only accidentally, in virtue of its informing a body.) Still, the idea that nothing exists nowhere endures. Augustine takes it to be so obvious that "what exists must exist somewhere" that he says "nothing compels my consent as that does" (*Soliloquia* I.15.29).[6]

Scholastic authors were in substantial agreement that immaterial entities have locations. They did not always go so far as to say that what exists *must* have a location, because they often thought it at least possible that immaterial entities might lack

---

[6] Immediately after Augustine rules out a thing's existing nowhere, he adds that "esse in loco" applies only to bodies, and that accordingly truth "non est in loco" (*Soliloquies* I.15.29). Similarly, Boethius treats it as a "communis animi conceptio" that "quae incorporalia sunt, in loco non esse" (*De hebdomadibus* [*Theol. Tractates* p. 40]). The idea that there is something about *locus* in its technical sense that excludes immaterial entities has its roots in Aristotle. See *Phys.* IV.5, 212b27–29: "not everything that exists is in place, but only movable body." For a typical treatment of such claims, see Aquinas, *Summa theol.* 1a 52.1, where *esse in loco* is said to be equivocal, allowing that in one sense angels can exist in a place. For a more detailed discussion, similarly insisting that angels are in some sense located, see Scotus, *Ord.* II.2.2.1–2. Anselm, *Monologium* chs. 20–3, contains a brilliant discussion of God's omnipresence that is another important source for the distinction between being in place (which applies only to bodies, and implies containment) and being somewhere (which applies to God, everywhere). For Anselm, as for Aquinas and the later tradition, immaterial entities are not in a *locus*, strictly speaking, because there is no surrounding body that *contains* them. When I speak of location I use the term not in this technical sense, but in the ordinary sense that means simply being somewhere.

location. God, for instance, might not be thought to exist anywhere before there was a physical world to inhabit (§17.3). Still, as things are, it was generally supposed that everything exists somewhere. This is particularly clear in those authors who treat location as a mode, such as Peter John Olivi. Olivi argues that everything created has some determinate mode of location:

> Every created thing is limited to a partial or particular existence, and to an existence that is related and connected (or connectable) to everything that can be added to it on the inside or outside. As a result, it is impossible for it to have an existence that is absolutely free of every local relation, or to have an existence that is immense, absolutely and immensely attaining every actual and even possible place. For this reason, it cannot be posited as either outside every place or in every place possible to God, and accordingly it must always be in some place that is proportionate to its limited size. (*Summa* II.32, I:587; see §13.2 and §17.5 for further details)

This is not so much an argument as a statement of a view: all creatures must have a location because they are made that way, not intrinsically having one location, but also not capable of existing apart from every location. A creature without location would therefore be incoherent, very much as Hobbes would later insist. Olivi's account is remarkably similar to the way Suárez, three centuries later, would argue in general for the existence of modes, based on the incompleteness of finite substances (§13.3). Suárez would likewise agree that location counts as a mode of creatures (§17.5), and so agree that any substance must have some determinate location. So, for instance, even if God had created angels before creating the physical world, Suárez insists that still those angels would have some kind of location. In general, "no *res* can be understood that does not exhibit its real presence somewhere" (*Disp. meta.* 40.4.19).[7]

The issue of how immaterial entities are located comes up for discussion most often in considering the nature of God's omnipresence. There seems to have been complete agreement, throughout our period, on the principle that God is everywhere in the strongest and most literal sense. The most influential text here is from Lombard's *Sentences* (1157), which asks: "Who would dare to say that the divine essence is nowhere?" (I.37.4.3) So far as I can find, no one would. Scotus, discussing this passage, remarks that "nor can it be said that God is nowhere, since that seems proper to nothing" (*Reportatio A* I.37.1–2 n. 27). Ockham, in this same context but generalizing, holds that "there is no thing that really exists that is nowhere, remote from everything" (*Ordinatio* I.37, *Op. theol.* IV:568–9). And, according to Gabriel Biel, "no existing thing

---

[7] One of the few places where the possibility of locationless entities is expressly considered is in the Condemnation of 1277, which condemns the thesis "Quod intelligentia, vel angelus, vel anima separata nusquam est" (n. 218). Hissette, *Enquête* pp. 104–10, claims to find this view in various contemporary arts masters, but what he actually finds is the familiar claim that such entities "non sunt in loco." A possible exception to the consensus over location is the anonymous but influential twelfth-century *Liber sex principiorum* n. 49: "[Ubi] videtur autem non omni adesse; anima etenim nusquam est, nullum etenim locum occupat neque implet." But this again can be read as denying only being *in loco*.

A remarkable letter from Walter of Mortagne to Peter Abaelard (1140) attempts to get Abaelard to sign onto the doctrine that God, angels, and souls lack location entirely, contending that this is a view Abaelard used to hold: "Praeterea notificate mihi, si adhuc creditis, quod Deus essentialiter non sit in mundo vel alibi, et quod angeli et animae nusquam sint. Quod, si bene memini, audivi vos fateri, quando novissime invicem contulimus de quibusdam sententiis. Praeterea apud nos ventilatum est vestram affirmare sapientiam, quod Christus praedicando, laborando, ad extremum moriendo nihil meruerit, et quod nemo propter opera sua bona vel mala nisi pro sola voluntate remunerari debeat vel puniri" (Gousset, *Actes* II:286). Clearly, Walter is hoping to get Abaelard into trouble; so far as I know, Abaelard never took the bait.

can be postulated that exists nowhere" (*Sentences* I.37, I:678). If God is not nowhere, then the other options are that he is somewhere in particular, or everywhere. Although Aristotle had located the first mover in the outermost region of the heavens, and although Averroes had called it "puerile" to say that God is in everything,[8] there seems to have been no disagreement among Christians that literal omnipresence is a tenet of the faith. As Suárez would later put it, "God is intimately present to this corporeal universe, not just by presence (that is, cognitively) and by power or action, but also by his essence or substance, just as all the theologians teach, as certain to the faith, on account of divine immensity" (*Disp. meta.* 51.2.8).[9]

This consensus holds up through the seventeenth century. Franco Burgersdijk, summarizing scholastic views, remarks that what lacks location does not exist (*Inst. meta.* I.21.1). Nathanael Carpenter, though critical of many scholastic doctrines, accepts that "whatever exists exists either at a point or in space" (*Phil. libera* III.1, p. 226). According to Pierre Gassendi, "there is no substance or accident to which it does not belong to be somewhere or in some place" (*Syntagma* II.1.2.1, I:182a), a sentiment that Walter Charleton later echoes (*Physiologia* I.6.1.9). Gassendi takes God to exist everywhere, in all space; indeed "the divine substance is quasi-extended, since it exists not in one place alone, but in many, indeed in all" (*Syntagma* II.1.2.2, I:191a). Moreover, since according to Gassendi there has been space from all eternity, God has *always* existed everywhere. Newton would famously go one step beyond that, apparently treating space as a divine attribute.[10] Minimally, at any rate, Newton is committed to the idea that everything that exists is in space: "space is an affection of being *qua* being. No being exists or can exist that is not related to space in some way: God is everywhere, created minds are somewhere, body is in the space that it fills, and whatever is neither everywhere nor anywhere does not exist" (*De gravitatione* p. 103; Janiak p. 25). Newton goes on to apply this to the Cartesian soul:

If we say with Descartes that extension is body, then . . . the distinction between mind and body in his philosophy becomes unintelligible, unless at the same time we say that the mind is in no

---

[8] Aristotle puts the first mover in the outermost heaven at *Phys.* VIII.10, 267b6–8 and *De caelo* I.3, 270b5–8, where he describes this as the universal view: "For all men have some conception of the nature of the gods, and all who believe in the existence of gods at all, whether barbarian or Greek, agree in allotting the highest place to the deity...." For Averroes, see *Destructio* 14, p. 375: "Et sermo similis sermoni dicentis ex antiquis quod Deus est in omni re, et sunt pueri." Both of these texts are cited by Suárez, *Disp. meta.* 30.7.2, but it is noteworthy that in this detailed discussion of God's location, Suárez does not even *consider* the possibility of denying that God has location. Similarly, the prospect of God's being out of the world entirely does not even occur to Aquinas—in any of his various discussions—as a potential objection to the doctrine of omnipresence (see *Sent.* I.37, *Summa contra gent.* III.68, *Summa theol.* 1a 8).

[9] Modern scholars have often thought that one or another scholastic author denies literal omnipresence. Funkenstein, for instance, reads Aquinas as giving God a location only analogically, and contrasts this with Scotus, for whom it is taken univocally, and so literally (*Theology and the Scientific Imagination* pp. 50–7). Hudson also thinks Aquinas denies literal omnipresence ("Omnipresence" pp. 201–2). Rozemond, in contrast, thinks that it is Scotus who denies God's genuine omnipresence ("Descartes and Holenmerism" pp. 346, 358), as does Jasper Reid ("Spatial Presence" pp. 95–6). The reason one might misread both authors in this way will become clear in the following chapter. Wierenga, "Omnipresence" §2, rightly remarks that the standard medieval view "has the consequence that, strictly speaking, God is present everywhere that some physical thing is located."

[10] The relationship for Newton between God and space is a controversial matter. For a particularly nuanced discussion, see McGuire, "Existence." His insistence that whatever exists has location gets reiterated in a manuscript from *circa* 1692-3: "Tempus et locus sunt omnium rerum affectiones communes sine quibus nihil omnino potest existere. In tempore sunt omnia quoad durationem existentiae et in loco quoad amplitudinem praesentiae. Et quod nunquam nusquam est, id in rerum natura non est" (as quoted in McGuire, ibid., p. 465).

way extended, and so is not substantially present to any extension, that is, exists nowhere. This seems the same as if we were to say that it does not exist, or renders its union with body minimally intelligible—not to say impossible. (Ibid., p. 109; Janiak p. 31)

Locke too, by way of trying to get clear on what spiritual substances are, insists on their being capable of location, and so being mobile (*Essay* II.23.19–21). The most striking case of all is More, who devotes several chapters of his *Immortality of the Soul* (1659) to collecting Hobbes's most important arguments for materialism and replying to each. After quoting and responding to various passages, he turns finally to *Leviathan* 46.19, as quoted above, which he calls "more considerable than any of the former, or all of them put together," and which he casts in this general form: "Whatsoever is real, must have some place: But spirits can have no place." In reply he denies not the first premise but the second, holding instead that "spirits are as truly in place as bodies" (I.x.8). Given the context in which Hobbes and More were writing, it makes perfect sense that Hobbes would take for granted that what exists has location, and that More would seek to attack the argument not by denying that, but by finding a sort of extension that immaterial entities could have.

Most of the passages just quoted bear on the first of Hobbes's two vulnerable premises, rather than the second. But if we understand 'extension' broadly, as simply occupying a three-dimensional spatial area, then the second premise too begins to look plausible. Indeed, premise (2) is a tautology if we understand 'location' in the Aristotelian sense of *locus*, as the surface of the body that contains the thing. (The *locus* of the egg whites, roughly speaking, is the shell [§17.1].)[11] Any object with location in this sense must be spread out in three dimensions, in order for there to be a surrounding body. Of course, if this is how we understand 'location,' then all the work of the argument rests on premise (1), which would now be asserting that all things have not just some spatial position, but three-dimensional location. But this further jump to existence as necessarily three-dimensional—whether read into the first premise or the second—was widely regarded as uncontroversial. Indeed, we have already seen resistance to the alternative: to the possibility that anything—corporeal or incorporeal—could be said to exist at a mathematical point (§14.4). The worry arises not just in discussions of quantity, but also in discussions of the soul. Aquinas, for instance, had called it "ridiculous" to imagine that "the soul's simplicity is like that of a point—as if it were something indivisible that has an indivisible location" (*Sent.* I.8.5.3c). Gassendi, considering the various ways in which Descartes's soul might exist in the body, remarks that it would be "surely incredible" for it to exist at a point—especially an extensionless mathematical point, which Gassendi labels "purely imaginary" (Fifth Objections, VII:340). (Descartes's response does not dispute this.) In general, according to More, "to take away all extension is to reduce a thing only to a mathematical point, which is nothing else but pure negation or nonentity" (*Immortality* pref. §3). Hence, "if a thing be at all, it must be extended" (ibid.).[12]

---

[11] Hobbes dissents from the scholastic Aristotelian conception of place (*locus*) as the two-dimensional exterior limit to a body. Instead, for Hobbes, place is extended in three dimensions over the whole area occupied by a body (see Leijenhorst, *Mechanisation* pp. 102–23). Still, on either view, only something extended occupies place.

[12] Gassendi extends his attack on Descartes's lack of clarity over the location of mind in *Disquisitio metaphysica* VI.4.4. Descartes, in the Fifth Replies, strangely ignores Gassendi's original queries on this subject. Perhaps his later response to

None of this shows that Hobbes's first two premises are true, only that they were widely accepted, provided that we understand 'extension' broadly enough. Indeed, in this broad sense, as we will see, even Descartes is willing to allow that both God and embodied minds are extended. But it is possible to say more than just that these claims were widely endorsed; it is possible to see why they were endorsed. For suppose we accept that an immaterial entity acts on the physical world. Suppose, to pick a specific case, the human mind is immaterial, and that it acts on the brain. In that case, we would have extremely strong evidence that the human mind is located in the brain. For we would then be forced to choose between that conclusion and the conclusion that agents need not be located where they act—that is, that action at a distance is possible (where things that have *no* location are counted as being at a distance from things that have location). Perhaps there are circumstances in which we might be tempted to allow action at a distance. But surely—in the absence of other evidence—we should take the default position that things are located where they act. I say that this line of thought provides extremely strong evidence, because it is the same line of thought that we employ for locating *anything* in the world, material or not. We think the Lincoln Memorial is in Washington because that is where it makes its causal impact on the sensorium of the tourist. We don't think it is located in Colorado, because it does not *do* anything there. Now perhaps action at a distance is possible; if so, then perhaps the Lincoln Memorial is in Colorado. Yet if we cannot quite *prove* that this is not so, I think we can say that we have at least very good evidence against that possibility. Our evidence for locating the mind in the brain seems just as strong, if we accept that the mind acts on the brain. Since it was the nearly universal consensus of our period that spiritual entities of all kinds do act on the material world, these authors had extremely strong evidence for treating those entities as existing in that world. (The following chapter discusses the relationship between action and location in more detail.)

Philosophers today tend to assume, without argument, that immaterial entities lack location. In part this is another instance of Bloomian Interpretation (§1.4). The famous Cartesian doctrine that only bodies are extended, ripped from its historical context and subsequently misunderstood, has made credible an idea that if not so frequently repeated would seem quite incredible: that minds have no location. But of course there are reasons why a particular misinterpretation gains currency. What drives this one, I suspect, is the absence of any other story about what makes immaterial entities be things of a fundamentally different, non-material kind. For if one thinks of the soul or mind as literally existing in the brain, or thinks of God as literally existing everywhere

Gassendi's *Disquisitio*, with its reference to the "quantité de telles questions" (IXA:213) that are easy to ask but best not to answer, should be read as extending to this issue, the point being that this is one of those questions that are not bad ones in their own right, but that it is best not to take up when searching for clarity, because we have no clear answers (see my discussion of this passage at §8.4).

More also takes up the impossibility of existence at an extensionless point in attacking a group he calls the *Nullibists* (§17.3), who treats immaterial entities as lacking location. The denial of point-like existence is one of their three axioms, along with the claims that all and only thinking things are immaterial, and that whatever is extended is material (*Ench. meta.* 27.2). More accepts the first two of these axioms, but rejects the third.

Reid, "Spatial Presence," collects many interesting passages from later Cartesians regarding God's omnipresence, some of which come close to rejecting literal omnipresence. But, as Reid's careful discussion shows, in the end all these authors agree that "God was substantially present in the spatial world" (p. 101), a finding Reid goes on to extend to Descartes himself, based on the correspondence with More (p. 105).

on earth, the question then looms of why the mind is not just a part of the brain, or why God is not just part of the natural world. That is, one needs to say something more about what makes such things immaterial. Authors throughout our period do not have to resort to the peculiar notion that immaterial things exist nowhere, because they have other ways of demarcating the material–immaterial divide. The most straightforward of these is to invoke prime matter. But this was only one strategy for trying to mark that divide, and it was of course not Descartes's strategy. In the remainder of this chapter I turn to consider another strategy, which can be found throughout our period, in both scholastic and post-scholastic authors. This strategy appeals to a concept we have encountered repeatedly in earlier chapters, the concept of holenmerism: existing as a whole in more than one place at once.

16.4. True Extension: Descartes and More

It is time to get clear on the sense in which, for Descartes, only bodies are extended. To that end, let us draw the Philosophers' Triangle mentioned earlier. One line of the triangle is the claim that whatever exists must be extended. This is the line that connects Hobbes and More, and which each used in a different way to criticize Cartesian dualism: Hobbes from the side of materialism; More, as we will see, in support of a different conception of immaterial entities. A second line of the triangle is the claim that extension demarcates the material. This joins Hobbes and Descartes, against More, in the view that immaterial entities would have to be in some sense extensionless. The final line, connecting Descartes and More, is dualism: the thesis that there are both material and immaterial entities. Where two of the lines meet at a point we can identify a thesis distinctive of one of our three philosophers: Descartes's thesis that there are unextended substances; Hobbes's materialism; and More's defense of extended immaterial substances. The relationship, then, is shown in Figure 16.1.

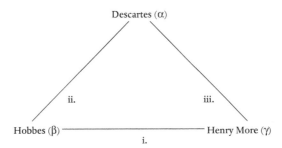

i. All things are extended
ii. Extension demarcates the material
iii. A dualism of material and immaterial entities

α. There are unextended substances
β. Materialism
γ. There are extended immaterial substances

Figure 16.1. A philospher's Triangle

Having discussed Hobbes's relationship to Descartes already, we can turn now to the relationship between Descartes and More.

By the end of his career, More's dualism was in fact much more thoroughgoing than Descartes's, in that More postulated spirit throughout all of nature. He accordingly came to think that Descartes's mechanistic approach was indefensible, remarking that "there is no purely mechanical phenomenon in the whole universe" (*Divine Dialogues*, I:A6v). For our purposes, however, we can set aside this dispute about the success of mechanistic explanation, and focus on the different ways in which More and Descartes defend their version of dualism against the other sides of the triangle. The principal texts bearing on this issue are a fascinating series of letters between the two men.

The discussion begins with More's letter of December 1648, in which he argues that Descartes's extension criterion for body is unacceptably broad, because both God and angels are extended. To show this, he appeals to God's causal connections with the material world. More reasons that God impresses motion on every part of the world, which requires some sort of "quasi" touching of each part, which requires him to exist everywhere in the world (V:238–9).[13] In reply, Descartes readily accepts the doctrine of God's omnipresence, and grants that God is in a certain way extended, as are angels and the human soul:

> It is not my custom to argue about words, and so if someone wants to say that God is in a way extended, since he is everywhere, I have no objection. But I deny that true extension, as it is commonly conceived by everyone, is to be found in God or in angels or in our mind or in any   3 substance that is not a body. By 'extended being' everyone standardly means something imaginable. . . . In this being they can imaginatively distinguish various parts of determinate size and shape, each in no way the same as the others. Each can be imagined as transferred to   6 the place of others, but no two can be imagined simultaneously in one and the same place. (V:269–70)

This is one of Descartes's most developed statements of an idea that is crucial to his understanding of the distinction between mind and body: the idea that what distinguishes body is not just being spread out in space in any fashion—what I will call *bare extension*—but a certain way of being spread out. The previous chapter's discussion of impenetrability made a start toward understanding this distinction, and §17.3 will complete the picture with an account of how only bodies, for Descartes, are essentially extended. As for the passage before us, it suggests three criteria for "true extension" (line 2):

a. It must be imaginable (lines 4–5);
b. It must have distinct parts of determinate size and shape (lines 5–6);
c. Such parts must not be able to coexist simultaneously at one and the same place (line 7).

---

[13] More's talk of God's quasi-touching bodies is presumably informed by the sophisticated scholastic tradition regarding how precisely to define contact. The denial of action at a distance, understood as a requirement that proximate efficient causation requires contact, required a clear sense of just what it means for two bodies to be in contact. The action of form on matter, as well as the action of a spiritual entity (God or angel) on a body, were standardly said to involve contact only in an improper sense. This is not to say that forms are not located where their subjects are, or that spiritual entities are not located where they are acting, only that the strict conditions for contact are not satisfied. See, e.g., Nichole Oresme, *In Gen. et cor.* I.17; Marsilius of Inghen, *In Gen. et cor.* I.16; Paul of Venice, *Summa phil. nat.* III.22.

Criterion (c) is clearly ruling out penetrability in the sense of co-location, and so need not be discussed further here. With respect to (a), it is clear as the correspondence develops that Descartes does not intend it to play a part in defining true extension. For in this and the following letter he shows quite effectively that More cannot define body as *perceptible substance*, because it would then be defined by a contingent relationship to the human senses. Surely the same is true of imaginability. This leaves us to focus on (b).

In insisting that having parts is a fundamental feature of body, Descartes is in effect appealing to the idea of corpuscular structure: that bodies will have parts spread out, *partem extra partem* (§14.1). He insists on this as far back as *The World* (*circa* 1630): "Let us add that this matter may be divided into as many parts having as many shapes as we can imagine" (XI:34), and again, alongside impenetrability, in his last letter to More: "each part of this space or body is distinct from all other parts and is impenetrable" (V:403). Descartes of course does not think that accidents in the category of Quantity need to be invoked here. Like Ockham (§14.3), he takes corpuscular structure to be an intrinsic feature of body, and indeed, also like Ockham, he takes that structure of distinct parts to be actual all the way, infinitely far down (§§26.1–2). Thus, indivisible atoms are said to be impossible because atoms are bodies, hence extended, and hence divisible (*Principles* II.2; see §5.4). To say that all bodies are composed of integral parts is to say that all bodies are divisible, a fact that Descartes regularly appeals to in demarcating bodies from minds. He appeals to divisibility to establish that God is not a body: "since bodily nature includes divisibility along with local extension, and since being divisible is an imperfection, it is certain that God is not a body" (*Principles* I.23). He also uses divisibility to distinguish the human body from the human mind: "there is a great difference between the mind and the body, inasmuch as the body is by its very nature always divisible, while the mind is utterly indivisible" (*Med.* VI, VII:86).

Descartes and More agree to a surprising extent about all of this. Responding to the above passage regarding true extension, More agrees that impenetrable, tangible extension is not found in immaterial entities (V:301), but that bare extension is.[14] Replying in turn, Descartes remarks that "at last we agree about the facts (*de re*); what is left is a question of terms (*de nomine*): whether this second sort of [bare]

---

[14] More's letters to Descartes have almost nothing to say about divisibility or corpuscular structure. His embrace of divisibility as a mark of corporeality, and his rejection of holenmerism, become clear only later. But More does, from the very first letter, insist on impenetrability: "Quod et aliam innuit materiae sive corporis conditionem, quam appellare poteris impenetrabilitatem; nempe quod nec penetrare alia corporea, nec ab illis penetrari possit. Unde manifestissimum est discrimen inter naturam divinam ac corpoream, cum illa hanc, haec vero seipsam penetrare non possit" (V:240). In reply, Descartes accepts that all and only bodies are characterized by impenetrability, but insists that the essence of body is captured by extension rather than impenetrability. This is what he means when he says that impenetrability is a *proprium quarto modo* (V:269). The fourth kind of *proprium*, according to Porphyry's *Isagoge*, is one that characterizes all and only the members of a certain species, all of the time, but which as a mere *proprium*, does not get at the essence of the thing.

Descartes immediately goes on to suggest that impenetrability is associated with having parts: "...tangibilitas et impenetrabilitas habeant relationem ad partes, et praesupponant conceptum divisionis vel terminationis; possumus autem concipere corpus continuum indeterminatae magnitudinis, sive indefinitum, in quo nihil praeter extensionem consideretur" (V:269). Although I cannot see why either tangibility or impenetrability implies having parts, the passage is notable for seeming to allow the possibility of a body that has bare extension, without parts or limits. This again points to the way that both impenetrability and corpuscular structure are consequences not of the bare concept of extension, but of extension supplemented by certain contingent features of the world as it was created—namely, so as to be in motion in various complex ways, but with quantity always conserved.

extension should be described as equally true" (V:342). There is no reason to treat this remark as ironic. The two really do seem to be in agreement, at this point, regarding how to discriminate the corporeal from the incorporeal.[15] If this has not always been obvious to readers, that is because they have not recognized that Descartes accepts the conventional view that spiritual entities exist where bodies exist, and are spread out in three dimensions. God, for instance, not only acts on everything, but also exists everywhere: "it is certain that God's essence must be present everywhere so that his power can exert itself there" (to More, August 1649, V:403). With respect to the human mind, he writes: "we need to recognize that the soul is really joined to the whole body, and that we cannot properly say that it exists in any one part of the body to the exclusion of the others" (*Passions* I.30). Although subsequent passages go on to clarify that the mind acts directly only on the pineal gland (ibid., I.31–2), Descartes never retreats from the claim that the mind exists throughout the whole body. Indeed, he even encourages Princess Elizabeth to conceive of the soul as extended, provided that this be understood as "extension of a different nature" (III:694)—that is, bare extension, lacking impenetrability and corpuscular structure.

The idea that bodies can be defined in terms of a certain sort of structure, part outside of part, has a rich history. Descartes was deeply influenced, in this respect as in so many others, by Book X of Augustine's *De trinitate*, where body is defined as that "of which a part is less than the whole in spatial extension" (vii.9). Augustine goes on to say, in this same passage, that if some insist on using 'body' (*corpus*) so broadly as to encompass even the mind, "we should not argue with them over a question of terminology" (see also *De genesi* VII.21.27). Augustine, in turn, may well have been hearing echoes of Plotinus:

We say that there are things primarily apt to partition, by their very nature prone to scatter. They are things in which no part is the same as either another part or the whole, things of which a part is necessarily less than the total and whole. These are sensible magnitudes and masses, each of which has its own place and cannot itself be in several places at the same time. (*Enneads* IV.2.1)

Descartes embraces just this conception of the corporeal. Reiterating the above quoted account of true extension, he tells More that "I call extended only what is imaginable as having *partes extra partes*, of determinate size and shape—although other things are also called extended by analogy" (V:270). Locke would later mock this way of talking, remarking that he need not explain the nature of space, since his opponents cannot explain the nature of extension: "For to say, as is usually done, that extension is to have *partes extra partes* is to say only that *extension is extension*" (*Essay* II.13.15). Locke knows perfectly well, however—as his journals attest—that the appeal to distinct parts is doing

---

[15] The last word in the correspondence belongs to More, who wrote a *post mortem* reply to Descartes's last letter (a letter that Descartes never completed nor sent, and that consequently More saw only five years later). In that letter, from 1655, More writes: "De Dei etiam, quam vocant omnipraesentia nullum superest inter nos dissidium, cum ubique eum esse agnoscat, vimque suam in subiectam materiam exerere, extensionem porro aliqualem ei competere, sed longe diversam ab ea quae divisibili ac impenetrabili corpori competit" (*Collection*, I:106). On the circumstances of this final letter, and on the relationship between More and Descartes in general, see Gabbey "Philosophia Cartesiana Triumphata." On the development of More's antipathy to holenmerism, see Reid, "Evolution." There is still no published English translation of More's letters to Descartes, although there is a French translation by Rodis-Lewis.

a certain sort of work here, distinguishing between bare extension and extension that has corpuscular structure.[16]

How could a thing be extended without corpuscular structure? As we have seen several times already (§4.1, §14.4), something can be extended in this way if it exists *holenmerically*: wholly at each place where it exists. Such a being may not be perfectly simple, inasmuch as it might admit of structure in terms of, for instance, dispositions or powers. (Some say that the human soul, for instance, is complex in virtue of its various powers for thought and volition, and in virtue of its various moral and cognitive dispositions.)[17] But if a thing exists holenmerically then it does not have proper integral parts: the 'part' of it that exists at any sub-region would be the whole of it. Hence holenmers do not satisfy Descartes's account of true extension.

Holenmerism is the standard view regarding immaterial entities—God, angels, and rational souls—from Plotinus, Augustine, and Anselm all the way through the scholastic era. Nearly all the leading scholastic authors embrace this position, including Bonaventure, Aquinas, Scotus, Ockham, and Buridan.[18] (The standard scholastic terminology is of existing in a place *circumscriptively*, as bodies do, versus existing in a place *definitively*, as the human soul or an angel does. This is inconvenient terminology for our purposes, however, because the scholastics do not always use these terms in quite the same way, and because these are two ways of existing in a limited place, and hence do not cover the case of God. Thus I prefer More's neologism 'holenmeric,' meaning *whole in part*.)[19] Later scholastic authors persist in this view. Here, for instance, is Jacob

---

[16] Locke's *Journals* make it clear that he fully understands the implications of insisting on having parts as something over and above bare extension: "Extension or their *partes extra partes* seems to be proper only to body because body alone has parts and is divisible—i.e., whose parts are separable one from another" (June 20, 1676, p. 77). He goes on to discuss whether bare extension by itself might satisfy this criterion for being a body.

Dabillon offers a contemporary treatment of the material–immaterial divide that stresses divisibility and having parts in much the way that Descartes's does—not because Dabillon is influenced by Descartes, but because both share Ockham's conception of matter as intrinsically corpuscular in structure. So, e.g., "l'être corporel est un être divisible. Or l'être divisible, c'est avoir des parties et être tel de sa nature que l'on ne puisse être dans un espace indivisible" (*Physique* I.2.1 p. 50). Dabillon goes on to reject both having prime matter and impenetrability as definitions of corporeality. Later, he distinguishes between the true claim that immaterial entities are co-located with bodies, and the false claim that they are extended (III.1.1, p. 197).

[17] The soul's powers are often thought of as parts of a certain kind. See, e.g., Aquinas, *In De an.* I.14.58–75. For the debate over whether there is in fact any distinction between the soul and its powers, see Ch. 8 note 23.

[18] On the holenmeric existence of immaterial entities, see, e.g., Plotinus, *Enneads* IV.2.1; Augustine, *De trinitate* VI.6.8; John of Damascus, *De fide orthodoxa* 13.3; Anselm, *Monologium* chs. 20–3, *Proslogium* ch. 13; Bonaventure, *Sent.* I.8.2.3; Aquinas, *Summa theol.* 1a 8.2 ad 3, 1a 76.8; Scotus, *Ord.* II.2.2.1–2 (Vat. VII n. 245); Ockham, *Quod.* I.12, *Tract. de corp. Christi* ch. 7; Buridan, *In De an.* II.7, III.4, III.17; Oresme, *In De an.* II.4, III.4; Suárez, *Disp. meta.* 51.4.2, *In De an.* 2.8, *In Summam theol.* pt. I, tract. 3 (De anima), 1.13.13, 1.14.9–10 (*Opera* III:566b, 570–1).

As crucial as the distinction between holenmeric and corpuscular structure is throughout our four centuries, there is almost no secondary literature on it. For what there is, see Grant, *Much Ado* pp. 223–8, 350 n. 127, and Rozemond, "Descartes and Holenmerism," whom I follow in taking 'holenmeric' as a technical term.

[19] On existing in a place definitively versus circumscriptively, see, e.g., Ockham, *Quod.* I.4, *Opera phil.* IX:25: "Circa secundum articulum, dico quod esse in loco dupliciter accipitur: circumscriptive et definitive. Circumscriptive est aliquid in loco cuius pars est in parte loci, et totum in toto loco. Definitive autem est quando totum est in toto loco et non extra, et totum est in qualibet parte illius loci, quo modo corpus Christi est in loco definitive in Eucharistia, quia totum eius corpus coexistit toti loco speciei consecratae, et totum coexistit cuilibet parti illius loci." See also *Quod.* IV.21, IV.31; *Rep.* IV.6 (*Op. theol.* VII:78–105). The inspiration for this distinction is Lombard, *Sent.* I.37.6. Other early instances are Hales, *Summa theol.* I.1.1.2.3.2 (I:64) and Aquinas, *Sent.* I.37.3.1, *Summa theol.* 3a 76.5 ad 1, 1a 52.2c: "Nam corpus est in loco circumscriptive, quia commensuratur loco. Angelus autem non circumscriptive, cum non commensuretur loco, sed definitive, quia ita est in uno loco, quod non in alio. Deus autem neque circumscriptive neque definitive, quia est ubique." Not every author defines this distinction in terms of holenmerism, or even in terms that clearly entail holenmerism, as this last passage from Aquinas shows. Moreover, sometimes existing in a place definitively is treated

Schegk, who served as professor of philosophy at Tübingen for nearly half of the sixteenth century:

Quantity is an inseparable accident from corporeal things, because the incorporeal differs from the corporeal in no other way than that every body, on account of its quantity, has *partem extra partem*, rather than the whole's being everywhere where it is. Every incorporeal thing, in contrast, never exists divided on account of its parts, nor is part *extra partem*; rather, each part is *intra partem*, so to speak, and so the part is nothing other than the whole itself. I will give as an example the case of soul and body. It is clear to everyone how the body is divided into parts. But the parts of the soul, as the powers from which it is said to be a whole (which in the human soul are the nutritive, sensory, motive, and intellectual) are so related that wherever one is, there they all are. For this reason, the soul is also said to be whole in the whole body, and whole in each part. God too, because he is incorporeal, is said to be whole everywhere, however far as the corporeal universe is divided into parts. (*In Organon* [*Praed.*], p. 34)

The idea by no means disappears among post-scholastic authors. Gassendi embraces it, in the case of God.[20] Newton too, although he insists that all things occupy space, cautions against imagining that God is like a body, "extended and made of divisible parts." As we might now predict, what Newton denies is not extension, but having divisible parts, and he offers this lovely analogy:

The moment of duration is the same in Rome and London, on earth and on the stars and heavens everywhere. And just as we understand any moment of duration to be diffused in its own way throughout all spaces, without any concept of its parts, so it is no more contradictory that mind too, in its own way, can be diffused through space without any concept of parts. (*De gravitatione* p. 104; Janiak p. 26)[21]

In light of all this, it should be no surprise to find Descartes insisting on holenmerism for the human mind, remarking that "this is exactly the way in which I now understand the mind to be coextensive with the body—the whole mind in the whole body and the whole mind in any one of its parts" (Sixth Replies, VII:442).[22]

---

[20] Gassendi invokes holenmerism as God's manner of "quasi-extension" at *Syntagma* II.1.2.2 (I:191a) "Dico autem quasi extensionem, ne imaginemur divinam substantiam ritu corporum per locum extensam: quippe cum sit summe individua, ac semel et ubique tota, sed nimirum ut corporea substantia dicitur extensa, quod non in uno solum puncto sed per plureis loci parteis fusa sit."

[21] Grant, *Much Ado* pp. 253–4, argues that Newton rejects holenmerism with regard to divine extension. Grant's only argument, however, aside from his own view that holenmerism is "unintelligible" (p. 416 n. 420), is the alleged absence of textual evidence in support of holenmerism, a point entirely vitiated by Newton's explicit remarks in *De gravitatione* (as quoted in the main text). McGuire, "Existence" pp. 504–6, correctly discerns Newton's commitment to the doctrine.

Grant, *Much Ado* p. 416 n. 419, rightly points out that Leibniz denies holenmerism (and extension in general) for the human soul, on the grounds that "to say that it is, the whole of it, in every part of the body, is to make it divided from itself" (to Clarke, third paper, n. 12, in Alexander, *Leibniz–Clarke* pp. 28–9). But God's case is different, since God is present everywhere "by essence" (ibid.). Clarke accepts both of these points (ibid., pp. 33–4). Neither author expressly indicates in this discussion whether they are thinking of God as holenmeric. But when Leibniz denies here that God is present "par situation," he likely has in mind the scholastic category of *situs* or Position, which implies the sort of spatial arrangement typified in the canonical example of *sitting*. Presumably, God is not extended in this way because God lacks corpuscular structure.

[22] Descartes asserts the soul's presence throughout the body at *Med.* VI (VII:86): ". . . quamvis toti corpori tota mens unita esse videatur . . ."; *Principles* IV.189: "Sciendum itaque humanam animam, etsi totum corpus informet, praecipuam tamen sedem suam habere in cerebro." One might read a passage from the Fifth Replies as a clear text to the contrary: "Etsi enim mens sit unita toti corpori, non inde sequitur ipsam esse extensam per corpus, quia non est de ratione ipsius ut sit extensa, sed tantum ut cogitet" (VII:388–9). But given what he says elsewhere, I read this as denying only that the mind has true extension—that is, in such a way as to have parts and be impenetrable.

Scholars have often wondered why Descartes would embrace holenmerism, a doctrine that might seem to epitomize scholastic obscurity. We are now in a position to see exactly why he does. For given that he thinks minds exist spread out in the material world—a doctrine that, as we have seen, virtually everyone accepts, for both God and creatures—he needs some way to distinguish this bare extension from the true extension that is definitive of bodies. True, he still has impenetrability, and might have relied on that alone to distinguish spiritual from corporeal extension. But this is a weak reed on which to rest this distinction, especially given that impenetrability is a consequence not of *res extensa* in itself, but of how the laws of nature happen to have been written out (§15.5). Moreover, distinguishing these two kinds of extension is critical to Descartes in a way it is not for most scholastic authors, since for him extension is no mere accidental feature of material substances, but is the very essence of what it is to be material. Hence if minds were extended in the way material things are extended, minds would simply be material things. To prevent this devastating result, Descartes needs holenmerism.

16.5. Prospects for Holenmerism

Holenmerism had its critics, even among the scholastics. It was rejected by Albert the Great, and treated with suspicion by various heterodox fourteenth-century authors, such as William Crathorn, although by then the view seems to have become too entrenched to be rejected outright.[23] By the late sixteenth century, while more conservative authors continue to defend holenmerism, mainstream scholastics like Jacob Zabarella feel able to reject the doctrine. Zabarella argues that holenmerism takes its plausibility from a confusion between two claims. What is true is that the whole

---

Jasper Reid has made a detailed argument against supposing that Descartes locates the mind in the body, claiming that "the balance of probabilities" goes against this view ("Spatial Presence" p. 107). Crucially, he takes the passages I rely on to be consistent with the claim that the mind has mere "operation presence" in the body, by which he seems to mean merely that it produces an effect there. On its face, this is a surprising thing to say about those passages where Descartes describes the soul as holenmeric. Part of the point of holenmerism, as it applies to the human soul, is to distinguish between the way in which the soul itself is present to the body, wholly in each part, and the way its power is present, partly in each part. For an Aristotelian, it would be obvious nonsense to suppose that the operations of the soul are wholly present in each part, unless one supposes that one can see with one's feet. Yet one might be able to defend Reid's position, even here, since it may be that the Cartesian soul, unlike the Aristotelian soul, does exercise its power uniformly over the whole body. Still, it is hard to see what would motivate taking what Descartes plainly says about the mind, and giving it this very peculiar construal. Reid agrees, after all, that Descartes's God is genuinely located in the world (see note 13 above). So why not allow that the human mind is, too? And what are we to make of Descartes's remark that he and More are in agreement *de re* (V:342)? On Reid's view, this would have to be read as disingenuous. I agree, though, that the texts are tricky, and I return to these issues in §17.3.

[23] For Albert the Great against holenmerism, see *In De an.* II.1.7 (VII.1:75a): "et tunc dicendum quod anima est in corde, et inde influit potestates suas in totum corpus, et sic non est in toto tota, ita quod in qualibet parte sit tota, sed quod in qualibet parte est secundum aliquam suarum potentiarum." On the thirteenth-century debate, see Pegis, *St. Thomas and the Problem of the Soul* pp. 141–7. Zabarella, *De rebus nat.*, De part. animae, cols. 727–64, also gives a thorough account of earlier scholastic views. Crathorn, *Sent.* I.15 raises many worries about both God and the soul's being spread out in three dimensions, but also argues in favor of each view, and in the end declines to settle the matter. Later authors commonly refrain from criticizing the view, except to label it "mirabile et super naturam" (Buridan, *In De an.* II.9, ed. Sobol p. 138). See, similarly, Suárez, *In De an.* 2.4 ad 1 (ed. Castellote p. 282).

In considering the prospects for holenmerism, and its relationship to immateriality, it is important to keep in mind that different authors embrace the holenmeric to different degrees. Aquinas, for instance, holds that all substantial forms are holenmeric (*Summa theol.* 1a 76.8c), whereas Ockham holds that only the rational soul is (*Quod.* I.10). There seems to have been no consensus among later authors.

essence of the soul is in each part of the body, just as the whole essence of whiteness is in each part of a wall. (Each part of the wall is really white; each part of a person is really alive.) But it is not true that the whole quantity of the soul is in each part of the body, no more than the whole quantity of whiteness is in each part of the wall. This is an important distinction to draw (something like it can be found as far back as Aquinas), and Zabarella seems right to stress that holenmerism requires the second claim as well as the first. Indeed, shortly we will see how More appeals to this very feature of holenmerism in attacking the doctrine. Zabarella, however, is concerned less with refuting holenmerism than with replacing it with something else. So, in place of treating the soul as quantitatively or numerically the same in each part of the body, he takes the soul to be extended so as to have corpuscular structure: "every form informing matter and constituting a composite is extended with the extension of matter, so that with respect to its extension the whole is in the whole but the whole is not in the part; instead, part is in part" (*De rebus nat.*, De part. animae ch. 11, col. 755A).[24]

To deny holenmerism by ascribing extended parts to the soul runs the obvious risk of making the soul into a body. Although, as we will see, this is not Zabarella's aim, it is precisely Hobbes's ambition. No wonder, then, that Hobbes is one of the most outspoken seventeenth-century critics of holenmerism. As Hobbes is well aware, to show that minds are bodies he must do more than show that they have bare extension. He must also show that they have corpuscular rather than holenmeric structure. To meet this further burden of proof, then, Hobbes, in his most complete argument against immaterial entities, combines an argument against extensionless entities with an argument against holenmeric entities. The focus is the rational soul:

For seeing they will have these forms to be real, they are obliged to assign them some place. But because they hold them incorporeal, without all dimension of quantity, and all men know that place is dimension, and not to be filled but with that which is corporeal, they are driven to   3 uphold their credit with a distinction: that they are not, indeed, anywhere *circumscriptive*, but *definitive*—which terms, being mere words, and in this occasion insignificant, pass only in Latin, that the vanity of them may be concealed. For the circumscription of a thing is nothing else but   6

[24] For Zabarella against holenmerism, see *De rebus nat.*, De part. animae ch. 11 (col. 755CD): "et quisquis illa omnia bene consideret, quae a Latinis dicuntur ad probandum animam esse in qualibet parte totam, manifestam in eorum dictis ambiguitatem animadverteret. De ipsa namque animae substantia verum est id quod dicunt: sicut enim tota et integra est albedinis essentia in parte parietis, nec minus quam in toto pariete, ita in singula viventis parte inest essentia animae integra; non tamen tota secundum quantitatem, quam per accidens adepta est ex coniunctione cum corpore." Aquinas is very clear about the difference between a form's being essentially and quantitatively whole at *Summa theol.* 1a 76.8c, and at 1a 8.2 ad 3: "albedo enim est tota in qualibet parte superficiei, si accipiatur totalitas essentiae, quia secundum perfectam rationem suae speciei invenitur in qualibet parte superficiei, si autem accipiatur totalitas secundum quantitatem, quam habet per accidens, sic non est tota in qualibet parte superficiei. In substantiis autem incorporeis non est totalitas, nec per se nec per accidens, nisi secundum perfectam rationem essentiae. Et ideo, sicut anima est tota in qualibet parte corporis, ita Deus totus est in omnibus et singulis."

Encouraged, most likely, by Zabarella, Burgersdijk finds it easy to dismiss holenmerism out of hand, remarking that the phrase "tota in qualibet parte" is a "locutio impropria" (*Collegium Physicum* 21.11). For Burgersdijk's own view of immaterial extension, see §17.3. Another early seventeenth-century attack on holenmerism can be found in Gorlaeus, *Idea physicae* X.2.

the determination or defining of its place; and so both the terms of the distinction are the same. And in particular, of the essence of a man, which (they say) is his soul, they affirm it to be all of it in his little finger, and all of it in every other part (how small soever) of his body, and yet no more soul in the whole body than in any one of those parts. Can any man think that God is served with such absurdities? And yet all this is necessary to believe, to those that will believe the existence of an incorporeal soul, separated from the body. (*Lev.* 46.19)

The first part of the passage (lines 1–3, discussed in §16.2) sets out Hobbes's case for why anything that is real must be extended. Hobbes rightly sees that his opponent will accept this, and will insist that immaterial entities are extended in a special way, definitively rather than circumscriptively (lines 3–5). From here, Hobbes makes two arguments against holenmerism: first, he criticizes the scholastic terminology for being meaningless (lines 5–7); second, he mocks the implications of holenmerism (lines 8–10). This part of the passage, it must be said, shows Hobbes at his philosophical worst. First, the two lines of thought work against each other, since the mockery is effective only if we do indeed understand the meaning of the distinction. And of course Hobbes does understand the distinction perfectly well—well enough to see that it stands in the way of his materialism. As for the mockery, the consequences he describes are ones that proponents of holenmerism insist on, and that they take to be distinctive of immaterial entities. To be sure, these look superficially like weird results, but it is their very weirdness that justifies a dualism between two fundamentally different kinds of entities, material and immaterial. Since this is precisely how Hobbes's opponents understand immaterial entities—as he is clearly aware—his whole defense of materialism collapses unless he can show there to be some incoherence in holenmerism, or some consequence that is plainly unacceptable. But Hobbes goes no farther.[25]

Holenmerism's most trenchant critic is Henry More, who coined the term to facilitate his attack. More's early correspondence with Descartes had embraced the concept, at least for the case of God, who is "whole everywhere, and his complete essence is present at all points or spaces and points of space. It therefore does not follow [from his being extended] that he has *partes extra partes*" (V:305). But in *Immortality of the Soul* (1659), More expressly takes Hobbes's side on this question, rejecting the "scholastic riddle" of *tota in toto et tota in qualibet parte*, and criticizing Hobbes only for being "so frightened" by this "mad jingle" that "he never since could endure to come near the notion of a spirit again" (I.10.8). Here More goes no farther than Hobbes toward showing what is wrong with holenmerism, remarking only that it "seems to verge too near to profound nonsense." In his *Enchiridion metaphysicum* (1671), however, he offers a series of interesting arguments:

a. "they make one and the same thing many thousands of times greater or less than itself at the same time, which is absolutely impossible" (27.12),

---

[25] Hobbes attacks holenmerism even more briefly at *Elements of Law* I.11.5: "And it is a plain contradiction in natural discourse, to say of the soul of man, that it is *tota in toto*, and *tota in qualibet parte corporis*, grounded neither upon reason nor revelation." At *Lev.* 34.23 he implicitly recognizes that his account of how angels are extended needs to rule out holenmerism: "there is no text in that part of the Old Testament which the Church of England holds for canonical from which we can conclude, there is or has been created any permanent thing (understood by the name of *spirit* or *angel*) that has not quantity *and that may not be by the understanding divided, that is to say, considered by parts, so as one part may be in one place and the next part in the next place to it*, and, in sum, which is not (taking body for that which is somewhat or somewhere) corporeal" (emphasis added).

   b. "it is the same as if someone were to say that there is nothing of the soul that is not included within [bodily part] A, and yet that, at the same moment of time, . . . the whole soul is in [some distinct bodily part] B, as if the whole soul were outside its whole self. This is clearly impossible in any singular and individual thing. As for universals, they are not things, but rather notions we apply in contemplating things" (ibid.);

   c. "if the whole of a spirit exists in individual physical points, then it is clear that the essential amplitude of the spirit . . . is not greater than that physical point in which it exists. . . . This cannot but appear wholly ridiculous when applied to any created spirit. But when applied to the majesty and amplitude of the divine numen, it is flatly intolerable, if not enormously insulting and blasphemous" (ibid.).

This makes for a fairly robust attempt to identify the incoherence that authors like Zabarella and Hobbes felt to lurk within holenmerism. But has More actually shown the doctrine to be contradictory, or just that it is weird and counterintuitive (something its proponents readily grant)? Surely the result described in (a) is a contradiction. But does holenmeric structure entail it? Prima facie, it seems to. For when we keep in mind Zabarella's distinction between whole essence and whole quantity, and that holenmerism entails the second as well as the first, then the view does seem to lead to the contradictory result that an immaterial substance, at the same time, has many different sizes. For we surely cannot say that a spirit wholly existing in some tiny space A has just that size, if it also exists at other places. At the same time, we also cannot say that its size corresponds to the sum of all the non-overlapping places where it exists, because to say that would seem to make nonsense of the claim that it exists *wholly* at A. At first glance, then, this looks like a strong argument.

   Turning to (b), modern readers will likely not be troubled here. As More acknowledges, it insists on the absurdity of the mode of existence associated with universals—whose existence we are now taught to regard as perfectly intelligible. More might have granted that being wholly at A and wholly at B is possible for universals, but just not possible for individuals. This, however, would simply invite the response that, strictly speaking, immaterial entities turn out to count as a kind of universal. What More instead seems to think is that being wholly located at more than one place at the same time is incoherent for anything, and that accordingly universals are not things at all. The closest one can come to universals are concepts that merely *represent* more than one thing, rather than being literally *in* more than one thing. In taking this view of universals, he was reflecting the overwhelming consensus of our period (§5.3, §27.4). But has he shown anything contradictory about having multiple locations at once? I think not. Although it is weird to allow "the whole soul" to be "outside its whole self," it does not seem to be a contradiction, given the view that the whole soul is in multiple places.

   Objection (c) is particularly interesting because it makes explicit that these criticisms apply specifically to the case of God, and so definitely shows that he has abandoned his early support of divine holenmerism (as in his second letter to Descartes, quoted above). The objection does not attempt to establish a contradiction, but might still be effective, if it points to a result that the holenmerians cannot accept. The alleged result is that a soul, an angel, or God is of such slight "amplitude" as to fit comfortably within a single physical point. To be sure, this is a consequence of the view, but it is a consequence that More's opponents embraced. Descartes, for instance, allowed that the mind could be reduced to a point.[26] Moreover, as we will see in the next chapter, it was commonly granted that God had no location at all when there was no physical world for him to inhabit. Hence (c) is effective only if one accepts More's view that all entities, even immaterial ones, have some sort of fixed, intrinsic extension. When that assumption is in place, it will seem absurd that a whole spirit—especially God—could fit within the smallest of physical spaces. As noted already, however (and as the following chapter will discuss in detail), Descartes denied that minds are intrinsically extended, and treated this as a further feature that distinguishes them from true *res extensae*.

Even (a), on further reflection, can be seen to depend on More's view that immaterial substances are intrinsically extended. For what More assumes, in generating that contradiction, is that there is an intrinsic fact about the size of an immaterial substance. As soon as we admit that, we face contradiction along the lines set out in (a). The solution is to deny that holenmers have any intrinsic size at all. This allows us to say that the soul wholly exists at A, without having to accept the implication that being so located captures the whole of its size or extension. Instead, we can restrict the range of 'wholly' to intrinsic properties of a thing. The soul, in the eye, is wholly there, but this does not mean that its whole size is there, no more than the whole of its causal actions are there. (It does not, for instance, act on the foot there.) Causal relations are extrinsic in the way that size is. It does not follow from this that immaterial substances lack a size, which would suggest that they lack extension entirely. They have a size just as surely as they have causal connections with bodies, and we can measure that size by adding together all the places where the soul exists, just as we can measure the cumulative causal connections between a holenmer and bodies. (Thus God's size is that of the universe, and a soul has the size of its body, and God acts everywhere all the time, and the soul acts everywhere that its body is.) But since size is extrinsic, it is a confusion to suppose that a holenmer's size is wholly present at each place it exists. When holenmerism is so understood, it escapes More's criticisms.

More's attack on holenmerism, however, is not based solely on its incoherence. In part, he simply thinks the view is unnecessary. As More explicitly recognizes, holenmerism is motivated by the need to distinguish between the extension of minds and the extension of bodies, lest minds just turn out to be bodies. Yet we can do this, he claims, without invoking holenmerism—and, indeed, while accepting the Cartesian view that what distinguishes bodies is impenetrability and having distinct parts. What holenmerism adds to the Cartesian story is an explanation of how something could be extended without distinct parts. But More thinks there is another way to go: that an immaterial thing could be extended, not holenmerically, and yet without parts, provided that it is indivisible. His idea comes in two steps. First, a thing can be extended and yet indivisible:

We acknowledge some extension (namely, material) to be endowed with such strong and invincible antitypy that it necessarily . . . repels and excludes every other matter . . . , even though

---

[26] Descartes, in the Sixth Replies (VII:442), after describing how gravity could be contracted to a mathematical point on his old way of looking at things, goes on to explain that this is precisely how he now thinks of the mind. This is not to say that the mind ever will exist this way. I take it that Descartes's mind, apart from the body, simply lacks location, and that this is part of the reason More refers to him as a *Nullibist* (§17.3).

this wonderful power is not at all contained in the simple idea of extension. . . . Why can we not   3
equally easily conceive that another extension (namely, immaterial), although extension in
itself includes no such power, is so constituted that it cannot be divided into parts by any
other thing, either material or immaterial, but is so united and so coheres with itself   6
everywhere by an indissoluble, necessary and plainly essential link that, although it can
penetrate everything and be in turn penetrated by everything, nothing can so insinuate itself
into it as to dislodge or perforate any of its essence anywhere, or to dig or scratch a hole in it?   9
(Enchiridion metaphysicum 28.9)

Here the idea is that immaterial things are characterized by a cohesiveness so strong
that nothing, material or immaterial, can divide it into parts (lines 5–6). The second step
is then to claim that what is indivisible in this way lacks parts:

The Nullibists [§17.3] offer nothing when they say that every extended thing implies parts, and
all parts division. For the first of these is false, since the idea of a being that is one in its own right
(unum per se), although extended, contains no parts. Instead, it is conceived according to its
proper essence as a thing that can be made perfectly simple, and so composed of no parts. . . .
(ibid. §10)

Immaterial entities, then, are unum per se in a very strong sense, so as to be "perfectly
simple" and accordingly "composed of no parts" (line 4). These claims yield the result
that immaterial entities fail to be truly extended because they fail to have corpuscular
structure: not because they are holenmerically structured, but because they are perfectly simple albeit extended entities.

One might want to object to the first step, on the grounds that anything that is
extended is at least divisible, even if not actually divided. This, as noted earlier, was
Descartes's argument against atomism. It is not clear to me how More would reply to
this obvious objection. Sometimes he allows that we can conceive of dividing anything
extended, even spirits, and that this therefore implies the logical possibility of division.
But he can hardly think that what distinguishes immaterial entities is merely the
physical impossibility of division, because More is also an atomist, holding that "matter
consists of indiscerpible particles" (Immortality pref. §3). This is to say, seemingly, that
atoms are physically indivisible. Perhaps More is after some sort of indivisibility that lies
in between physical and logical possibility, but at this point we get no guidance from
More himself.

For the second step of the argument to be plausible—the move from indivisibility to
lacking parts—one would presumably have to take 'indivisible' in a very strong sense. If
all More wanted from spirits was physical indivisibility, then it would be hard to see
why they should fail to have integral parts—e.g., a left half and a right half. Moreover, if
one's concept of integral part did require physical divisibility (Ch. 26), it would then be
hard to see why lacking integral parts would mark a fundamental ontological divide
between the material and the immaterial. For one could certainly imagine a physically
indivisible body, atomic-sized or even larger. Hence I think More must have in mind
something more than the mere physical indivisibility of spirits. The following passage,
indeed, suggests as much: "[a spirit] cannot be created or in any way produced except
under this condition, that all its parts are inseparably and indiscerpibly one—just as a
right triangle can be produced only under this law, that the squares of the cathetus and
the base equal the square of the hypotenuse" (Ench. meta. 28.13). Sadly, however, More

cannot even figure out how to state his view without contradicting himself, by making reference to the "parts" of spiritual substances. And although he subsequently apologizes for putting the claim in these terms, his treatment of these issues does not do much to encourage careful scrutiny.[27]

16.6. Holenmerism and Immateriality

We have now encountered four different ways to divide material from immaterial things:

1. All and only material things naturally depend on prime matter.
2. All and only material things have bare extension—that is, are spread out in three dimensions.
3. All and only material things have integral parts.
4. All and only material things have corpuscular, non-holenmeric structure.

For seventeenth-century authors, (1) is a non-starter and so let us continue to set it aside. The only author we have found defend (2) is Hobbes, but he uses (2) as a premise to argue that everything is material, and his contemporaries universally rejected his conclusion on the basis of rejecting this premise. We have just seen More give a prominent place to (3), and indeed (3) would be widely accepted throughout our period as a mark of the material. (Since the notion of an integral part was initially defined in terms of *body* [§1.3], it might be regarded as tautologous to say that everything with integral parts is a body.) Even so, (3) by itself does not seem to *explain* the material–immaterial divide, because one still needs an account of how immaterial entities can fail to have integral parts. One way to do so would be to lack even bare extension, but since no one wanted to take this route, some further story is required. The most promising strategy we have seen is (4), which entails that what makes immaterial entities special is their holenmeric structure.

Supposing holenmerism is coherent, we can now consider its prospects as the mark of immateriality. It should be said from the start, however, that proponents of holenmerism do not themselves always embrace this application of the concept. Perhaps Descartes does, inasmuch as he treats its contrary, corpuscular structure, as a necessary condition on true extension, and so materiality. Hobbes, too, as quoted near the start of §16.5, claims that holenmerism would be "necessary" for the soul's immateriality. The scholastics, however, do not generally see an entailment in either direction. As we saw in §14.4, A theorists sometimes suggest that the fundamental structure of the material

---

[27] For More, although a spiritual substance is extended, "tamen sit in partes physicas ac reales prorsus indivisibilis sive indiscerpibilis" (*Ench. meta.* 28.3). On the difference between discerpibility and the logical possibility of divisibility, see *Ench. meta.* 28.10: "nihil causae nostrae nociturum esse si concederemus extensionem hanc spirituum metaphysicam esse etiam divisibilem, sed *logice* duntaxat, non *physice*—hoc est, non esse *discerpibilem.*" Elsewhere he suggests that "being divisible only conceptually" is definitive of any extension, "it being of the very essence of whatsoever is, to have parts or extension in some measure or another" (*Immortality* pref. §3). At *Immortality* I.2.10, discerpibility is characterized as the "gross tearing or cutting one part from another."

More might distinguish between his atoms and spirits on the grounds that, even if both are indiscerpible, atoms are also impenetrable. But this isn't the end of his difficulties, for not only does he define the spiritual realm in terms of indiscerpibility, but he also defines body as "a substance impenetrable and discerpible" (*Immortality* I.3.1). So are atoms not bodies? Amazingly, More fails to recognize the problem.

realm might itself be holenmeric, and might take on corpuscular structure only through quantity. Indeed, as we saw back in §4.1, some even supposed that prime matter itself is intrinsically holenmeric, and takes on corpuscular structure only when informed. In general, the scholastics more commonly appeal to (1) in marking the divide, and treat (4) as quite a different issue.

An apparent exception to this pattern is Jacob Schegk, as quoted in §16.4, who treats corpuscular structure as definitive of bodies, inasmuch as "the incorporeal differs from the corporeal in no other way" (lines 1–2). But Schegk cannot really suppose that this is what distinguishes these two genera of substance, because corpuscular structure, as he clearly explains, arises from quantity, which is an accident, and no accident can be the ultimate explanation of distinctions at the level of genus or differentia. Schegk must therefore be thinking of the corporeal–incorporeal distinction as accidental to substances. Whatever is corporeal must have quantity as its "inseparable accident" (line 1), but still a substance may cease to be corporeal, if it miraculously loses that quantity. In effect, we have already encountered this view in Gabriel Vasquez (§14.4), who explicitly treats corpuscular structure as accidental, and indeed holds that material substances are intrinsically holenmeric, and so would exhibit that structure if not informed by quantity. This understanding of corporeality is explicit in Walter Burley, who distinguishes two senses of the term: one sense meaning actual corpuscular structure, which is accidental, and another sense meaning the "aptitude" for such structure, which is what appears on the Porphyrian tree as the differentia of the genus *body*. Hence there seems little enthusiasm for treating actual corpuscular structure as necessary to bodies.[28]

It likewise seems doubtful that immaterial entities must have holenmeric structure. Zabarella of course denies it. On his account, when the rational soul informs the body, it has corpuscular structure and so is a corporeal form in just the sense in which whiteness is a corporeal form. Still, the rational soul is immaterial inasmuch as it is naturally possible (and indeed inevitable) for it to lose that structure, upon separation from the body, at which point it would no longer be corporeal at all. How it would then exist is a further question, but in any event what makes the rational soul immaterial is not its having one sort of structure or another, but its natural separability from prime matter. Even advocates of holenmerism are unlikely to suppose that immaterial entities must be so structured. To suppose this, one would have to think that such entities are always extended—that God was and will be extended, even when there is no material world, and that the rational soul is extended, even apart from the body. Some authors do take this view, as we will see in the next chapter, but proponents of holenmerism generally assume that immaterial entities can exist even without bare extension, and so *a fortiori* without holenmeric extension.

---

[28] Burley explains the way in which 'corporeal' can be accidental to material substances as follows: "Ad aliud, dico quod 'corporea' accipitur dupliciter: uno modo pro illo in quo sunt actu tres dimensiones, et sic 'corporea' non est differentia substantiae. Alio modo accipitur 'corporea' pro eo in quo est aptitudo ut in eo ponantur tres dimensiones, sive actu habeat dimensiones sive non, et sic 'corporea' est differentia substantiae" (*De formis* pars post., p. 59). Burley needs this distinction to explain how quantity can both be an accident and account for the extension of a body's integral parts (see above, §14.1). For a similar account of how extension can be accidental to a human being, see Blasius of Parma, *Quaest. logicales* III.5, pp. 269–70.

Contrary to the general tendency of scholastic thought, however, there is something to be said for the idea that holenmeric structure is at least sufficient for immateriality. For it seems fundamentally alien to materiality for there to be things that exist wholly in one place, and at the same time wholly in another. If More's complaints about this mode of existence have not already made this point obvious, then consider that such a thing would have the following peculiar property: its destruction in any region of space—that is, its being made not to exist in a place where it formerly did exist—would not entail the destruction of any part of it. So long as it continues to exist elsewhere, the *whole* of it continues to exist elsewhere. Descartes highlights this feature of holenmers:

The soul is of such a nature that it has no relation to extension, or to the dimensions or other properties of the matter of which the body is composed; it is related solely to the whole assemblage of the body's organs. This is obvious from our inability to conceive of a half or a third of a soul, or of the extension that a soul occupies. Nor does the soul become any smaller if we cut off some part of the body.... (*Passions of the Soul* I.30; cf. *Med.* VI, VII:86)

Read in isolation, the start of this passage would suggest that Descartes's soul lacks any sort of extension, and indeed perhaps lacks location entirely. But since Descartes had just finished saying "that the soul is really joined to the whole body, and that we cannot properly say that it exists in any one part of the body to the exclusion of the others" (as quoted earlier), we know that he must here be speaking of true, corporeal extension. The soul lacks that kind of extension, as "is obvious" (line 3) if we try to map the parts of the soul onto the parts of the body. We find ourselves unable to do that, since the soul lacks parts that would allow us to conceive of any fraction of it. Moreover, and most startlingly, although we can make the soul cease to exist in any one place, this does not make the soul "any smaller" (line 4), because it still wholly exists elsewhere. According to More, the very idea of such existence is absurd, but the conclusion Descartes draws is that whatever so exists deserves to be treated as a separate class of entities.

This is fairly compelling, but would have been rejected by many scholastic authors, on the grounds that corpuscular structure is accidental. This is shown most vividly by the insistence of some (including both Scotus and Ockham) that God could make a body exist in more than one place at the same time—which seems to allow that it might exist holenmerically. Indeed, many authors hold that something like this supernatural possibility is routinely actualized in the sacrament of the altar, when the body of Christ is made to exist holenmerically where the bread and wine once was. This is miraculous, of course, but it is a miraculous way in which Christ's *body* exists, and so would count as a counterexample to the principle that holenmeric structure is sufficient for immateriality. For a less forbiddingly theological case, we might recall §14.4's discussion of how, for some scholastic authors, forms or substances apart from quantity would exist holenmerically, which is to say in effect that they would be universals. Such existence would also be miraculous, since even if a body can be naturally rarefied and condensed, it cannot be naturally made to lose its quantity altogether. Still, the logical possibility of such separation points toward the idea that material entities are not intrinsically corpuscular in their structure. But this, of course, is not to say that these entities are intrinsically immaterial, inasmuch as prime matter is what accounts for materiality. Even a universal form, wholly instantiated in more than one particular, would not count as an immaterial entity so long as it is a form that naturally depends on prime matter.[29]

One way in which focusing on prime matter rather than holenmeric structure seems advantageous is that it has the potential to explain why immateriality should be associated with the mental. As I noted at the start of the chapter, and then quickly set aside, Descartes appeals to *thought* as the principal attribute of immaterial entities. Scholastic authors tend to agree that all and only immaterial entities think. A good example of this is Richard Crakanthorpe's 1619 metaphysics textbook, which offers twelve *proprietates* of spirits (*Intro. in Metaphys.* 8). His list includes holenmeric structure (nn. 6–9) and also penetrability (n. 10), but begins (nn. 1–5) with various psychological capacities: understanding, volition, free action, moral action, and language. (Characteristics 11–12 concern the way in which spirits move.) By 'spirits' Crakanthorpe means angels, and so this is not exactly an account of how to draw the material–immaterial divide. But the idea that immaterial entities are necessarily thinking entities is pervasive among scholastic authors. They have, moreover, a principled reason for thinking that only immaterial entities can think, inasmuch as they take prime matter to be incompatible with intellectual (that is, abstract, universal, conceptual) thought. It is of course quite a separate matter to evaluate these much-discussed arguments for the immateriality of intellect, but at least the general strategy is clear enough: all and only material beings are made out of a certain kind of stuff, prime matter, and this stuff is incompatible with abstract thought. Once prime matter is taken out of the equation, and the material–immaterial divide is made to rest on the presence or absence of a certain kind of extension, it is hard to see why thinking should belong only to immaterial things. Descartes must hold that thinking is impossible for *res extensa* because of the presence of one or more of the features of true extension, but it is very hard to see how such an argument might go. What, for instance, does penetrability have to do with thought? What does holenmerism? Some authors during our period do try to make a case for holenmeric structure as what enables the unity of consciousness, but this is not an idea that Descartes develops.[30]

In general, then, the trend toward defining materiality in terms of corpuscular structure creates as many difficulties as it solves. Although it is undoubtedly attractive to leave behind the obscure scholastic notion of prime matter, the resulting picture is

[29] The weight of thirteenth-century opinion had gone against the possibility of a body's existing in multiple places—see, e.g., Aquinas, *Quod.* III.1.2; Henry of Ghent, *Quod.* IX.32; Godfrey of Fontaines, *Quod.* IV.5. In defense of such a possibility, see Scotus, *Ord.* IV.10.2; Ockham, *Rep.* IV.6 (*Op. theol.* VII:93–105); Biel, *Canon* 43B: "Deus per suam absolutam potentiam potest facere unam aliquam substantiam secundum se totam coexistere pluribus corporibus"; Dabillon, *Physique* III.4.5, thesis 2. Ockham's position was singled out for censure as "false and impossible" (Koch, "Neue Aktenstücke" p. 193), but opinion would remain divided on the question. For instance, Michael de Massa, a strident critic of Ockham's in most respects, likewise takes this to be possible for God (Courtenay, "Categories" p. 259). Locke would later take the impossibility of multi-location as a fundamental principle in our ideas of identity and diversity (*Essay* II.27.1). On various late scholastic endorsements of the possibility of multi-location, see Ariew, "Descartes and the Jesuits" p. 146.

For holenmerism as applied to Christ's mode of presence in the Eucharist, see, e.g., Ockham, *Rep.* IV.6; Buridan, *In De an.* III.4; Biel, *Canon* 43; and the discussion in Adams, *William Ockham* I:186–201.

[30] For the possible role of holenmerism in accounting for thought, see More (*Ench. meta.* 27.11), who identifies the unity of consciousness (or something like it) as the second principal argument in favor of holenmerism. He of course attacks this claim (27.14). I do not know which contemporary authors More had in mind as his target, but arguments of this general sort go as far back as Proclus's argument that nothing with distinct parts could be self-aware (see my *Thomas Aquinas on Human Nature* p. 194).

problematic in its own ways. Without some sort of ineffable stuff to mark off the material realm, it becomes hard to know what exactly does define bodies, and what even could be special about the 'immaterial' realm. Moreover, just as these developments raise puzzles over what makes immateriality special, so they leave open the question of why thinking should require immateriality. A consequence of this new conception of matter, then, is that it becomes possible to wonder, along with Locke (*Essay* IV.3.6), whether there might in fact be thinking matter.[31]

---

[31] On the extensive debate in the wake of Locke over the possibility that something material might think, see Yolton, *Thinking Matter.*

17

Location

17.1. Space and Place

Every reductionist project from our period, Aristotelian or post-scholastic, relies crucially on facts about location. Olivi's and Ockham's anti-realism regarding quantity depends on a story about the parts of bodies and the location of those parts. Seventeenth-century corpuscularians count on facts about shape and motion to take the place of all real accidents, and ultimately understand shape and motion in terms of location, spatial and temporal. (On motion, see the following chapter.) If these accounts are to be successful in reducing accidental forms to substance, then location itself had better not introduce any ontological commitments over and above substances. In view of how much work location does for such authors, it is rather surprising that the topic is not more discussed. Here I attempt to set out the main lines of debate regarding spatial location.

Let our question be this: How do objects get their location? One sort of answer would advert to facts about who or what put the object there. This, however, is not our question. What I am interested in, in scholastic jargon, is not the efficient cause of location but the formal cause: What is it to be located somewhere? It may be that this is a bad question to ask. Perhaps facts about location are simply brute facts, there being nothing more possible to say beyond the fact that a thing is so located. Or it may be that this is a topic where the quietism of a Descartes or Locke is to be preferred to the metaphysical ambitions of the scholastics—that whether or not facts about location lie at rock bottom, they at any rate go too deep for us. It is, however, not obvious that our question is a bad one. We certainly regard it as fair game to investigate other properties in this way, and in some cases we take ourselves to have discovered the answer, as when we learned that heat is a kind of molecular motion (§21.4). Is it not reasonable to suppose that we might similarly come to understand what it is for an object to have a certain location?

One might suppose that the central issue here is the nature of space. On one view, objects are located in a space that is a three-dimensional, motionless, indivisible, perhaps limitless, perhaps eternal entity with which bodies overlap. To have a location, on this view, is to occupy a certain region of space. The great objection to this view, historically, was the obscurity of such an alleged entity, and so to avoid postulating any such thing, Aristotle and his followers denied that there is anything that bodies occupy. As an alternative to talking about space (*spatium*), orthodox Aristotelians describe the place (*locus*) of a given body as the surface of whatever surrounds that body (see *Phys.* IV.1–5). The *locus* of a floating balloon, then, is the air that is in immediate contact with the surface of that balloon. On this view, to have a location just is, as the English term suggests, to have a certain *locus*.

This much-discussed dispute over the nature of space impinges on many other important questions, in philosophy and science, and the growing diversity of views on this question in the later sixteenth century is something of a harbinger of the end of scholasticism. It is not the concern of this chapter, however, because regardless of whether one wants to speak of bodies as being in a place or in space, one still needs an account of what it is in virtue of which they are located there. Simply to postulate space (or else to insist there is only place, and no space at all) is by itself no answer at all to that question, because it leaves unexplained what must be true of objects for them to count as being *in* space (or place). It is of course also no answer to say just that objects are *located* there, since that is precisely what we seek an account of. Our present topic, therefore, is not the famous debate over the nature of space, but the comparatively neglected debate over what accounts for a thing's location in space.[1]

17.2. The Causal Argument for Location

For our purposes, there are two broad kinds of things for which one needs a theory of location, and two broad strategies for explaining their location. The kinds are material things and immaterial things—that is, bodies and minds. The strategies are intrinsic and extrinsic. Intrinsic strategies explain a thing's location in terms of a feature of the thing itself, whereas extrinsic strategies relate the thing to something else that has location. The easy test for telling these strategies apart is that a theory counts as extrinsic if and only if it entails that a thing, conceived of apart from other things, could not have any location. If a theory is not extrinsic, it is intrinsic. The strongest sort of intrinsic theory would treat location as a product of a thing's essence. It is in this sense of the term that Ockham, for instance, insists that corpuscular extension is intrinsic to bodies (§14.3).

---

[1] Given how little attention the primary texts give to the topic of location, it is unsurprising that there is essentially no secondary literature.

There is, of course, a massive secondary literature on the history of debates over space. See, e.g., Koyré, *From the Closed World*; Sorabji, *Matter, Space, and Motion*; Grant, *Much Ado*; Sylla, "Space and Spirit." The concept of space goes back to the Presocratics and is defended in one form or another by many subsequent authors, but subsequently falls entirely out of favor among Aristotelian scholastics. Ockham writes of such a view, "quamvis non habeat multos sapientes defendentes, apparet tamen vulgo" (*Summula* IV.18, *Opera phil.* VI:392), showing both that the theory had little support from philosophers, but that yet it had an intuitive appeal even during the heyday of scholastic Aristotelianism. The attractions of the theory are recognized by Oresme, who seems to reject it only because it is un-Aristotelian: "Alia est imaginatio multum rationalis, si esset usitata, quod motus localis est locus non continentis sed spatium interceptum inter latera continentis. ... Et secundum hoc, ponendo tale spatium, non oporteret concedere aliqua absurda, quae conceduntur secundum alias vias. Sed tamen, quia hoc est expresse contra Aristotelem, qui improbat illam opinionem, ideo conformiter ad praecedentem quaestionem" (*In Phys.* III.5, ed. Caroti, "La position" p. 368). The view begins again to receive the unqualified support of philosophers in the sixteenth century, thanks in large part to the influence of Gianfrancesco Pico (*Examen Vanitatis* VI.4–5), who draws heavily on the Philoponus, and in turn influences other Italians, such as Bernardino Telesio, Francesco Patrizi, Giordano Bruno, and Tommaso Campanella (see Schmitt, *Gianfrancesco Pico* pp. 138–44). Subsequently, the theory begins to appeal even to authors who are otherwise quite traditional, such as Daniel Sennert (*Epitome* I.7), Burgersdijk (*Collegium Phys.* 6.12–13; *Inst. meta.* I.21.2–3), and Isaac Barrow (*Lectiones* 10). Of course, these authors often disagree among themselves in significant ways.

Clearly, however, no body could have its *location* intrinsically in this way, since bodies are able to change their location. Indeed, only God is intrinsically located in this strong sense, since, according to everyone during our four centuries, God is by nature omnipresent. More important for our purposes, then, will be a weaker version of an intrinsic theory, according to which a thing takes on some absolute, non-relational location in virtue of possessing some sort of accidental property. Suárez, as we will see in §17.5, takes this sort of view when he sets out his modal theory of location.

Since the previous chapter was concerned with minds, let us begin with them, and with the principal extrinsic strategy for explaining their location. From Aquinas and other classical scholastic authors of the thirteenth century all the way through Descartes and beyond, the usual way of locating minds was to appeal to their causal influence on bodies. This is a clear instance of the extrinsic strategy, because it takes for granted that bodies are located, and then attempts to derive the location of minds by appealing to their relationship to bodies. This causal argument, as I will call it, runs as follows:

1. Immaterial entities act on bodies.
2. Action at a distance is impossible.
3. Immaterial entities are located where bodies are.

Applying this template to specific cases, we get the result that God is everywhere, that angels are located among us (and so move among us), and that the human soul exists throughout the body.[2]

The causal argument was endorsed widely, but not universally. Since it was uncontroversial that immaterial entities act on bodies, the case against the causal argument rests entirely on (2). Although almost everyone was prepared to agree that action at a distance is physically impossible (Ockham was one of the few who denied that), many doubted whether this impossibility extends to the immaterial realm.[3] The divine case seemed especially ripe for challenge. Scotus, whose criticisms were far and away the most influential on the later debate, makes this interesting argument:

That which is omnipotent causes with its will whatever it wills. But for the will to will something to be, it need not necessarily be present to that thing, just as neither is our will present in this way to the thing that we will. Therefore that which acts through its will need not be present to that which it acts on. Therefore even if God were not present to an effect through his essence, but were in a determinate place—as old ladies imagine that he is seated on a throne in heaven—still he *could* cau2se the effect through his will that in fact he *does* cause. (*Reportatio A* I.37.1–2 n. 19)

---

[2] Aquinas applies the causal argument to both God (*Summa theol.* 1a 8.1) and angels (ibid., 52.1). The case of the human soul is rather different, since its direct application there would require the sort of mover–moved theory of soul and body that he is determined to reject (see ibid., 76 passim). But a version of this same argument, tied to actuality, applies to the soul: "Anima vero est forma substantialis: unde oportet quod sit forma et actus non solum totius, sed cuiuslibet partis.... Actus autem est in eo cuius est actus. Unde oportet animam esse in toto corpore, et in qualibet eius parte" (ibid., 76.8c). In view of Descartes's criteria for true extension (§16.4), it is notable that, immediately after establishing God's omnipresence, Aquinas stresses that this mode of existence involves neither impenetrability (*Summa theol.* 1a 8.2c) nor having parts (ibid., 8.4c).

[3] Ockham embraces action at a distance among bodies at *Rep.* III.2. See Goddu, "Ockham's Arguments." For subsequent discussions, see Oresme, *In Gen. et cor.* I.17 and Marsilius of Inghen, *In Gen. et cor.* I.16, Biel, *Sent.* I.37 (I:679), Suárez, *Disp. meta.* 30.7.4–10. For the broader scholastic debate, see Kovach, "Enduring Question."

The key premise is that God's omnipotence works simply by his willing something (line 1). He wills it, and it happens. But (minor premise), it is easy to will something at a distance (lines 1–3)—even we do that, when we will, say, for there to be peace in the Middle East. One might quibble over that minor premise, holding that we cannot *really* will something at a distance, because one can truly will only what one takes to be within one's power. The most we can do with distant or future events is intend or plan for a certain outcome, which is not the same as willing it. This is just a quibble, however, because if the major premise is true, then God—unlike us—can do anything (that is logically possible) just by willing it, and so he might quite reasonably sit on his throne and will things to happen at the other end of the universe (lines 4–6). Not that Scotus agrees with the old ladies (line 5), or with Aristotle, for that matter, who held the same view, minus the throne (§16.3). The point is that God *could* act on the world in this way, if one were to deny the doctrine of omnipresence. Like everyone else I have found from our period, Scotus takes omnipresence to be a non-negotiable tenet of the faith. What he denies is that it is demonstrable: "it does not seem to me that it can be demonstratively proved that God is everywhere through his essence; this is merely believed by me" (ibid., n. 24). The qualifying phrase 'through his essence' means *really existing there*, as opposed to being there merely cognitively (*per praesentiam*) or merely causally (*per potentiam*). (This is the language used in Lombard's *Sentences* I.37, and so became standard throughout our period.)[4]

Scholastic authors from this point forward debate the causal argument in considerable detail, with Thomists and Scotists at the head of the respective camps. To see what is at stake in these debates, one needs to notice an important ambiguity in the argument: should it be read as simply licensing an inference, or should it be read as offering an explanation for *why* minds are located at a given place? That is, does the causal argument tell us merely that we can be confident minds have locations, on the grounds that we know they act on bodies? Or does it in fact offer an answer to the question raised at the start of the chapter, of how it is that minds get their locations? In scholastic terms, we could label these the *a posteriori* and *a priori* readings of the argument, but since that terminology was co-opted for other purposes in the eighteenth century, it will be better to label these, respectively, the *evidential* and the *explanatory* reading. In §16.3, I offered in effect the evidential version of the argument: that the human mind should be taken to be located in the brain, on the grounds that it acts there. Scotus's argument above attacks this evidential argument as it applies to God: we cannot be sure that God is located just from the fact that he acts on bodies, according to Scotus, because God could act on a body without being located there.[5]

---

[4] Lombard's account of the various ways in which God is present to creatures is constantly discussed (see, e.g., Bonaventure, *Sent.* I.37.1.3.2; Aquinas, *Summa theol.* 1a 8.3; Scotus, *Rep. A* I.37.1–2). Lombard is himself drawing on Gregory the Great, who also mentions God's being in things by presence and grace: "Licet Deus communi modo omnibus rebus insit praesentia, potentia, substantia, tamen familiariori modo per gratiam dicitur esse in illis...." Reid, "Spatial Presence" pp. 96–105, shows how this language remained important among Cartesians, who continued to accept literal omnipresence.

[5] For Scotus's criticisms of the causal argument, see also *Lec.* I.37, *Ord.* I.37, *Lec.* II.2.2.1, *Ord.* II.2.2.1. Scotus is very clear about the distinction between what I call the evidential and explanatory version of the argument, but thinks Aquinas is confused about which version he wants. For Scotus's argument from creation, see *Rep. A* I.37.1–2 n. 20.

It is perhaps not entirely clear which reading of the causal argument Aquinas means to endorse, but it seems at least likely he intends the explanatory reading. See, e.g., *Summa theol.* 1a 52.1c: "Per applicationem igitur virtutis angelicae ad

It is sometimes difficult to tell whether a given author means to endorse only the evidential reading, or also the explanatory reading. Each reading faces its own difficulties. According to the evidential reading, a mind must first be located somewhere, so that it can then act there. (Here, and throughout this discussion, words like 'first' and 'then' need not be given temporal force; they describe the explanatory/causal order.) An angel, for instance, on this view, needs to position itself properly in the world if it is to have any causal impact on the world—just as, of course, you and I need to position our bodies properly in the world, if our bodies are to have the right sort of impact. The parallel to physical cases highlights the intuitive character of this way of thinking about the location of minds, but even so this way of going is problematic in two ways. First, it leaves us no closer to an understanding of the central problem of the chapter: what it is for a thing to have a location. For even if we now have an argument *that* minds must have a location in the world, given that they act there, we have no conception whatsoever of *how* minds have a location. Second, the merely evidential reading seems to render the world's creation incoherent, at least on its usual construal through our four centuries. The usual view about creation is that, before God created the world, there was only God, which is to say that there was no space (or place) and no facts about location. When God created the world, he created facts about location. But that is to say that the creation comes first, which is to say that the causality comes first, which is to say that it is incoherent to suppose God must always *be* somewhere, before he can *act* there. Since there was no *there* before there was a world, God's causal activity must be prior, at least in this case. The same would be true even now, if God were to create something new outside the universe. God's being there, then, must be posterior to his action. These arguments too are due to Scotus, as one might have guessed.

Later Thomists are not swayed by these considerations, because they insist that the causal argument must be understood in its stronger explanatory form: that minds are located somewhere *because* they act there, and not vice versa. Thus Capreolus insists:

God need not be present to a creature before he acts on it. Indeed, this implies a contradiction, because before God acts externally, there is nothing external, and if there is nothing external to God, then there is nothing for God to aid. Therefore God produces and conserves creatures *before* God is present to them. (*Defensiones* II.2.1.3.1.1, III:130b)

This is not to reject the causal argument, but merely to reject it on its weaker, merely evidential reading. But the explanatory reading faces difficulties of its own—indeed, Scotus contends that the argument becomes straightforwardly incoherent when understood in this way. The heart of the causal argument, of course, is the idea that action at a distance is impossible, and that a mind must therefore be present to a body *so that* it can act on that body. Yet if the argument is given explanatory force, we must suppose that a mind acts on a body and *as a result* is located there. It does not seem as if the argument can have it both ways: location may be a pre-condition for causality, or it may

---

aliquem locum qualitercumque, dicitur angelus esse in loco corporeo." See also, for similar language, *Sent.* I.37.3.1c and *Quod.* I.3.1. This last discussion, too, seems to anticipate the worry that location ought to be prior to causality, in the form of this argument: "Prius est esse quam operari, ergo prius est esse in loco quam operari in loco; sed posterius non est causa prioris; ergo operari in loco non est causa quare angelus sit in loco" (obj. 1). To this Aquinas replies, "nihil prohibet aliquid esse prius simpliciter quod non est prius quantum ad hoc. . . . Et similiter prius simpliciter est corpus quam tactus, tamen est in loco per contactum dimensivae quantitatis. Et similiter angelus per contactum virtutis" (ad 1).

be a consequence of causality, yet surely it is not both. Capreolus, and other Thomists, insist that the mind's causation comes first, and that God's having location is a consequence. But how can this be squared with the overall argument? If we take Capreolus's view of the situation then it looks like a complete mystery why we should want to defend premise 2 and insist that a mind must be where it acts. In God's case, if God must first create some body, before it can even make sense for God to be there, then why must God subsequently be there too? Is it an unwritten rule that God must show up to admire that which he has made? That angels cannot resist descending to earth to observe their handiwork? It is not obvious how to avoid such absurdities.

Although I have not found any authors who make it clear how to pursue the issues beyond this impasse, the explanatory version of the causal argument might be defended by treating premise 2 as a conceptual claim about what it is for a thing to be located. This is to say that the prohibition against action at a distance, in this context, has nothing to do with whether action at a distance is physically possible. If that were the point then, after all, premise 2 would surely not apply to God. As Scotus puts it, "that which is of unlimited power seems able to act at any sort of distance" (*Ordinatio* II.2.2.1, Vat. VII n. 205). Thomists can bypass this objection, however, as well as the apparent incoherence described above, by reading premise 2 as making a conceptual point: that a thing cannot act except where it is located, because, at least for immaterial entities, acting on a place is what accounts for the phenomenon of location. To be located, for a mind, just is to act there.

To explain the location of immaterial entities in these terms is not to deny that minds are literally located. The claim is not that minds have a location figuratively speaking, in virtue of having effects in the world, but that they are literally located in the world, just because they act there. Hence the explanatory reading of the argument offers what the evidential reading does not: a theory of how minds are located. The theory is, as promised, extrinsic, inasmuch as it accounts for location in terms of a certain sort of relation to other things, a causal relation. Admittedly, this may seem like a very peculiar view. How can a mind's acting somewhere be what it is for a mind to be somewhere? Such action might be a *symptom* of location (as the evidential reading would have it), but how can it just *be* the fact of location, in the way that heat might be molecular motion? To want something more here is, in effect, to want an intrinsic account of location—to think that a mind's being located somewhere is a fact about it, rather than a fact about how it is related to the world. Most scholastic authors did not think any such intrinsic story made sense. For them, facts about location are always relational facts, so that one coherently cannot speak of a thing's having some sort of absolute location, intrinsically, apart from everything else. As we will see in §17.4, this is a view they tended to take even in the case of bodies. But before leaving the case of minds behind, we should look again at the debate between Descartes and Henry More, which sheds some light on the question of how to locate minds.[6]

---

[6] The causal argument goes back to John of Damascus, e.g. *De fide orthodoxa* 13.4: "Angelus autem corporaliter quidem in loco non continetur, ut typum accipiat et formetur. Verumtamen dicitur esse in loco, qui adest intelligibiliter et operatur secundum suam naturam; et non est alibi, sed illic intelligibiliter circumscribitur ubi et operatur." The causal argument would be controversial as early as the Condemnation of 1277 (ed. Piché nn. 77, 204). Hissette, *Enquête* pp. 101–10 collects many thirteenth-century examples of the argument. For later defenses, see, e.g., Capreolus, *Defensiones* II.2.13.1; Cajetan, *In summam theol.* I.52.1; Franciscus de Sylvestris, *In Summam contra gent.* III.68. Even Leibniz attempts to put it to some work (see Robert Adams, *Leibniz* pp. 353–60). Prominent critics after Scotus include

17.3. Intrinsically Extended Minds: Descartes versus More

In §16.4, we saw how Descartes and More come to the point in their correspondence where Descartes can exclaim that "at last we agree about the facts" (V:342). What they agree on is that immaterial substances can be located and even spread out over multiple locations. Where Descartes withholds agreement is in his insistence that this does not count as true extension. True extension, on his view, requires

(1) impenetrability, in the sense of no co-location with other truly extended things (§15.5), and
(2) corpuscular structure (§16.4).

This is, however, not quite the full story regarding true extension, because Descartes also insists that true extension requires

(3) the essentiality of extension.

True extension, of course, applies to all and only bodies. The third condition means that bodies by nature, necessarily, are extended in the three spatial dimensions. Immaterial entities, in contrast, may or may not be extended in this way.

This last feature of true extension begins to emerge immediately after Descartes makes his optimistic remark about his being in agreement with More:

For my part, in God and angels and in our mind I understand there to be no extension of substance, but only extension of power, so that an angel can exercise its power now on a greater and now on a lesser part of corporeal substance. For if there were no body, I would understand there to be also no space with which an angel or God would be coextensive. But when someone attributes to a substance an extension which is only the extension of power, this is, I take it, the effect of a prejudice that regards every substance, including God himself, as imaginable. (V:342)

It is easy to misread this passage, especially if one looks at it through the lens of scholastic terminology. What Descartes might seem to be saying here, in terms of Lombard's canonical vocabulary, is that minds are not really extended, not extended

Biel, *Sent.* I.37.3 and Suárez, *Disp. meta.* 51.4.11–20. This is one of those questions where one can immediately find out what a given scholastic theologian thinks by turning to the relevant distinction of his *Sentences* commentary—in this case, Book I, distinction 37. Also relevant is Book II dist. 2, which typically takes up the location of angels.

Durand of St. Pourçain is an interesting case, because he found all the options regarding the location of angels to be so problematic that he decided to deny that angels have location, a stance that would subsequently be much criticized. See, *Sent.* I.37.2.1 n. 7 "circa hoc sunt quatuor opiniones, una quae ponit quod angelus isto modo iam dicto determinat sibi locum, in quo est definitive, et ratio essendi sic in loco determinato est sua essentia . . ."; n. 18: "Secunda opinio est quod angelus non est in loco sic quod sua essentia sit ei ratio essendi in loco, sed operatio eius circa locum . . ."; n. 22: "Ideo est tertia opinio quod Angeleus neque per essentiam neque per operationem neque per quodcumque aliud est in loco, . . . sed solum dicitur esse in loco inquantum est in corpore locato non secundum se sed secundum suum effectum . . ."; n. 26: "Quarta opinio est quod essentia angeli nusquam est, . . . [sed] est praesens cuilibet corpori quod potest movere praesentia ordinis, non situs, sive moveat corpus sive non."

In the seventeenth century, Locke endorses the causal argument: "For having no other idea of motion, but change of distance with other beings that are considered as at rest, and finding that spirits, as well as bodies, cannot operate but where they are, and that spirits do operate at several times in several places, I cannot but attribute change of place to all finite spirits" (*Essay* II.23.19). So does Newton: "Omnipraesens est non per virtutem solam, sed etiam per substantiam: nam virtus sine substantia subsistere non potest" (*Principia*, general scholium). See Grant, *Much Ado* pp. 253–4 and §16.3.

in terms of their essence or substance (lines 1–2), but only virtually extended, in a metaphorical sense, in virtue of having more or less wide-ranging effects on the world (lines 2–3). That this cannot actually be his view, however, is clear from passages elsewhere, particularly when he insists that the soul is located throughout the body, and—in his last letter to More—that "God's essence must be present everywhere so that his power can exert itself there" (V:403). In this last passage he clearly is drawing the scholastic distinction between essence and power, and insisting on both. The earlier passage is making a different claim: that whereas bodies are extended essentially— bodies just are *res extensa*—immaterial entities are extended only in virtue of acting on things that are intrinsically extended. This is not a difference in the reality of their extension, but only a difference in what explains it. Putting things slightly more perspicuously a page later, he writes: "I hold that God is everywhere in virtue of his power, but in virtue of his essence he has no relation to place at all" (V:343). Similarly, speaking of the human case, he had written a few years earlier that "the soul is of such a nature that it has no relation to extension" (*Passions* I.30).

Descartes invokes the familiar causal argument in this context because it gives him a further way to distinguish between minds and bodies. Bodies do not have to *do* anything to be extended; extension is their nature. Minds may or may not be extended, but are not essentially so. This third constraint on true extension, when combined with the first two, yields a rich and coherent account of what distinguishes material from immaterial entities. Although these three characteristics do not seem to be mutually entailing, they are closely related, as is most clearly seen by considering the situation where they are absent. Suppose that, in place of (2), a thing has holenmeric structure, existing as a whole, everywhere it exists. Then (3) must fail to obtain as well. This is so because, as More's attacks on holenmerism make clear (§16.5), holenmerism is a coherent view only if the extension of a holenmeric entity is extrinsic. Now suppose, in place of (3), a thing has extension relationally, as a consequence of acting on bodies. This requires that (1) fail. For if immaterial substances exist wherever they act, then their extension *depends* on their overlapping with bodies, as the things upon which they stretch themselves.

Descartes has a theory of extension, but he does not have a theory of location. To say that a body has its extension essentially does not show anything about why it is located at one place or another. He does, as noted in §13.7, treat the "position of parts" as a mode of extension (e.g, *Principles* I.48), but he does not develop a modal theory of location to anything like the degree that others before him had (§17.5). With respect to minds, Descartes does endorse the causal argument, but it is not at all clear how he reads it. The paragraph before the last one contains one text that suggests the strong explanatory reading (V:343) and another that suggests the weak evidential reading (V:403). It is also unclear whether the location of minds would be a mode. Presumably, it is not a mode of thought. It also does not quite seem to fit the model of an attribute like duration, since this is said to "remain unmodified" (*Principles* I.56). There seems little point in speculating further. The plain truth is that these issues go deeper than Descartes is willing to go—which is of course part of his philosophical appeal.

As in the previous chapter, Descartes's views can be interestingly contrasted with those of More. On my reading of the correspondence, More made considerable strides in illuminating the way in which Descartes must tolerate the extension of minds—all the way to the point where Descartes announces their essential agreement. But when Descartes goes on to introduce essentiality as a distinguishing feature of the true extension that characterizes bodies, he inserts into the discussion a very fundamental point of disagreement. This is not immediately obvious in subsequent letters, but by the time of More's later writings, long after Descartes's death, it emerges as the crucial point of disagreement. Consider, first, the case of God. More agrees with Descartes that the causal argument can be used, on its evidential reading, to establish God's immensity. But he thinks that God's acting on bodies does not *explain* his omnipresence. On the contrary, God would be just as immense even if there were no bodies, and moreover God was immense—infinitely extended in all directions—even before there were bodies. Just as Cartesian bodies are essentially extended, so is More's God.[7] This is an idea that gets developed at length in chapter 8 of More's *Enchiridion metaphysicum* (1671), where he describes divine extension as infinite, immobile, simple, dependent on nothing, and, in short, equivalent to God. This claim of equivalence, which he hesitates over in his earlier writings, is eventually embraced in a scholium added to the 1679 edition of his metaphysics:

[S]ince I make this immobile extension something real, and adorned with so many divine attributes, it will be impossible for me not to conclude that it itself is God, represented in a rough and general way. Nor can it be otherwise, since there cannot be any God or any absolutely perfect being if something besides him existed of itself in the way that I here describe this immobile extension: as eternal and necessary, infinite and immense. (*Ench. meta.*, scholium to VIII.13, p. 173 [tr. p. 69])

This conception of space as God plays a part, of course, in the long-running dispute over the nature of space, and More's idea would prove influential on later discussions, most famously on Newton. For More, however, as much as a solution to the problem of space, this represents a natural consequence of his thinking about immaterial entities. For once one rejects an extrinsic account of their extension, and takes God's extension to be a feature of God himself, it becomes quite natural to conceive of God as timelessly, unchangeably existing everywhere, infinitely in every direction. Perhaps such extension could lie on top of space, as it were. This would mean that in the world around us there would be at least three levels of overlapping things everywhere, space co-located with bodies, and bodies co-located with God. In

---

[7] More offers the causal argument for God's omnipresence in his first letter to Descartes (V:238–9), and later at *Ench. meta.* 27.5: "Nam et ipsi Nullibistae agnoscunt et asserunt operationes quibus anima agit in corpus esse in corpore, et potentiam illam sive vim divinam qua agit Deus in materiam eamque movet praesentem esse singulis materiae partibus. Unde facile est colligere operationem animae Deique vim motricem esse alicubi, in corpore nempe et in materia. . . . Ergo si operatio animae est alicubi, anima est alicubi, ibi nempe ubi est operatio. Si potentia Dei est alicubi, Deus est alicubi, ibi scilicet ubi divina potentia: hic in singulis materiae partibus, anima in humano corporo."

Although More's correspondence does not explicitly address the essentiality condition on true extension, one might regard it as implicit even in his first letter to Descartes, when he objects to *Principles* II.18 for its claim that not even God could keep the two sides of a vessel apart while removing all the intervening matter. More replies that even without matter, the space would be filled by "divine extension" (V:241). This shows, at any rate, that although More thinks the causal argument has evidential force, he does not regard it as explaining extension, inasmuch as God can occupy an area where there are no bodies. For More's evolving views on the relationship between God and space, see Reid, "Evolution."

preference to that picture, however, it is easy to see the appeal of simply identifying space and God.[8]

Just as God is intrinsically extended, existing everywhere by virtue of his nature, so too the human soul might have its own extension. This idea is quite alien to most scholastic authors, but begins to take hold in the latter part of our period. Franco Burgersdijk, in his generally conservative physics textbook (1632), takes the surprising view that "the rational soul exists and is coextended with the whole body, not by the body's quantity, but by its own proper quantity, which accords with its nature" (*Collegium physicum* 21.11). This is More's view as well:

That we may now have a more clear and determinate apprehension of the nature and condition of the soul out of the body, let us first consider her a while, what she is in her own essence, without any reference to any body at all, and we shall find her a substance extended and indiscerpible, as may be easily gathered out of what we have above written. (*Immortality* III.2.1)

We have run into the indiscerpible extension of More's spirits already (§16.5); here our concern is with the soul's being extended "in her own essence." More thinks that finite minds—human souls and angels—can change their location and their shape. What is essential is that they possess a certain fixed quantity of extension: "the soul is numerically the same from infancy to extreme old age and is neither greater nor less through that entire period of time, but is more spissated or contracted in infancy, and more expanded in adulthood" (*Ench. meta.*, scholium to 28.7). So even while the body changes throughout life, the soul remains the same, numerically and quantitatively. When More says that it expands or contracts without becoming "greater or less," he does not have in mind the usual scholastic theory of rarefaction and condensation (§15.1); his idea, instead, is that in becoming more contracted or "spissated" the soul will fold in upon itself: "I mean nothing else by spissitude, but the redoubling or contracting of substance into less space than it does sometimes occupy" (*Immortality* I.2.11). Since immaterial substances are penetrable, More finds it natural to suppose that souls and angels contract by collapsing in upon themselves.[9]

Whereas the doctrine of intrinsic divine extension leads More to identify God with space, the essential extension of finite minds leads More to place finite minds in their own fourth dimension:

Although all material substances considered in themselves are contained in only three dimensions, a fourth should be admitted into the natural world, which can, I think, be aptly enough called *essential spissitude*. This, although it applies most properly to those spirits that can contract their extension into a smaller place, can however by an easy analogy be referred further to spirits' penetrating both matter and each other, so that wherever either many essences or more

---

[8] Burtt, *Metaphysical Foundations* pp. 135–48, provides a useful overview of More's views on the relationship between spirits and extension, with a particularly detailed discussion of how More in various works comes more or less close to identifying God with space. For an earlier version of More's thinking on this last subject, see *Antidote*, appendix ch. 7.

An earlier precedent for thinking of God as having extension seems to be the sixteenth-century German Protestant Nicholas Taurellus. See the remarks in Lüthy, "Gorlaeus's Atomism" pp. 279, 284.

Grant is particularly strong on the subject of space as extending infinitely far beyond the corporeal realm. For the general (but not universal) scholastic rejection of that possibility, see *Much Ado* chs. 6–7, and for its subsequent embrace among various post-scholastic authors, see Ch. 8.

[9] More spends some time speculating on the shape that a soul might have apart from matter: "whether there be any peculiar figure natural to her, answerable to animal shape, or whether she be of herself a round or oval figure ... [or] change her shape according as occasion requires" (*Immortality* III.2.2). In the end he does not hazard a guess with respect to the soul in heaven, confining himself to the claim that its shape there will be like the shape of the angels, whatever that may be.

essence is contained in one place than the size of that place permits, we there recognize this fourth dimension, which I call its essential spissitude. (*Ench. meta.* 28.7)

As above, 'spissitude' refers to a spirit's contracting into a smaller area, but here the term is applied more generally to any case where two extended substances interpenetrate. If those substances are perfectly dense in three dimensions, then their overlap requires a fourth dimension. Since More accepts Descartes's prohibition on material overlap, this fourth dimension is accessible only to immaterial substances. In offering this account, More makes it explicit that he is trying to address the argument against overlap that Descartes had made in his second letter to More (V:342): that any apparent case of overlap would in fact be a case of one body's being annihilated. As discussed in §15.5, that argument risks proving too much, by ruling out not just body overlapping body, but also spirits overlapping body, something that Descartes wishes to allow for just as much as More does. Descartes, as I understand him, has to insist that the argument applies only to bodies. More can say something different: that spirit and body do not destroy one another when they interpenetrate because the spirit occupies a fourth dimension.[10]

More's conception of spirits as essentially extended leads him to refashion a quip of William Chillingworth's into its now famous form:

She [the soul] has as ample, if not more ample, dimensions of her own than are visible in the body she has left. Which I think worth taking notice of, that it may stop the mouths of them that, not without reason, laugh at those unconceivable and ridiculous fancies of the schools, that first rashly take away all extension from spirits, whether souls or angels, and then dispute how many of them booted and spurred may dance on a needle's point at once. (*Immortality* III.2.1)

This has endured through the centuries as a familiar jibe against scholastic abstruseness.[11] It is a fairly staggering irony, however, that More thinks the way out of such "ridiculous fancies" is to insist that souls and angels have dimensions of their own, in hyperspace, that are too "ample" to admit of joining together in dance on a needle's point. Indeed, if anything, More's talk of essentially extended but possibly spissated angels would seem to encourage such fancies, because it raises the question of just how small a spirit might get, and whether they might overlap in ever-higher dimensions of space.

---

[10] It is quite clear that More offers his fourth dimension as a response to Descartes's argument against the overlap of extended entities. See *Ench. meta.* 28.6 and *Immortality* I.2.11: "For what some allege, that it implies a contradiction that extended substance should run one part into another, for so part of the extension, and consequently of the substance, would be lost, this I say (if nearly looked into) is of no force. For the substance is no more lost in this case than when a string is doubled and redoubled, or a piece of wax reduced from a long figure to a round."

[11] On angels and pinheads, Chillingworth's 1637 *Religion of Protestants* pref. §19, defending "the Divines of England" against the charge that they lack "deep knowledge of philosophy, especially of metaphysics" responds: "As if forsooth, because they dispute not eternally, *Utrum chimera bombinans in vacuo possit comedere secundas intentiones? Whether a million of angels may not sit upon a needle's point?* Because they fill not their brains with notions that signify nothing, to the utter extermination of all reason and common sense, and spend not an age in weaving and unweaving subtle cobwebs, fitter to catch flies than souls, therefore they have no deep knowledge in the acroamatical parts of learning." Mayo describes this work as "one of the most influential books of seventeenth-century England" (*Epicurus in England* p. 24). More's talk of angels dancing reappears a mere two years later in Glanvill, *Vanity of Dogmatizing* ch. 11, p. 100. Thomas Reid would later remember this as Chillingworth's example (see the editors' note to *Essays on Intellectual Powers* p. 474n.). For an instance of the sort of scholastic disputation that Chillingworth had in mind, see Aquinas, *Summa theol.* 1a 52.3: "Utrum plures angeli possint simul esse in eodem loco," which answers in the negative, and the commentary in Vasquez, *In Summam theol.* I.193, which answers in the affirmative.

To have extension essentially does not entail having some determinate location essentially. In general, as I have stressed already, a theory of extension is not a theory of location. Only in the special case of God, given his omnipresence, do facts about where God is located follow from facts about how God is extended. So far as I can see, More offers no account of what makes a mind be located. He cannot allow that the familiar causal argument explains the location of spirits, because that would make their location (and hence extension) contingent on there being bodies for them to act on. More must resist that outcome, since he thinks it a necessary truth that whatever exists must be located somewhere: "if a thing be at all, it must be extended" (*Immortality* pref. §3; see §16.3). Indeed, his main argument against the causal account of location proposed by Descartes (and earlier Thomists) is that it has the consequence that immaterial entities at least potentially exist nowhere. If God, for instance, has location only in virtue of acting on bodies, then God would be nowhere before the world was created. This is a consequence that scholastic authors were generally willing to embrace,[12] but for More this is unacceptable. His most extensive attack on these views comes under the banner of an attack on the *Nullibistae* or "nowhere men," a group at whose head he puts Descartes. On its face this is a surprising way for More of all people to characterize Descartes's views, since it is in his letters to More in particular that Descartes makes clear his willingness to give location to immaterial substances. It may be that More does not see this because he misunderstands the passage quoted at the start of this section, where Descartes distinguishes between extension of substance and extension of power.[13] Or it may be that although More knows perfectly well that Cartesian minds are usually located, he objects nevertheless to the implication that they *can* exist without location. This, to be sure, is a possibility that Descartes accepts, as when he remarks to More that the extension of power goes away once "the extended thing corresponding to it is taken away" (V:343). Indeed, this is no idle possibility, since it obtained in God's case before the physical world existed, and will presumably be the case for human minds when separated from their bodies.

It is interesting to see how something we now take for granted—that immaterial entities may (or even must) exist without location—could have seemed so absurd to More. He was not alone in this. Hobbes, of course, was among his allies (§16.2), but so too, perhaps, was Pietro Pomponazzi, back around the turn of the sixteenth century.

---

[12] There seems to have been general agreement among the scholastics that God cannot have existed anywhere before there was a physical world to exist in. See, e.g., Aquinas, *Summa contra gent.* III.68.2430: "Unde nec determinatur ad locum, vel magnum vel parvum, ex necessitate suae essentiae, quasi oporteat eum esse in aliquo loco: cum ipse fuerit ab aeterno ante omnem locum." And see Scotus, *Rep.* I.37.1–2 (Bychkov n. 20): "ante creationem universi, non magis fuit Deus hic ubi modo est universum quam extra universum imaginatum, ubi nihil est." In general, since scholastic authors do not postulate any sort of space beyond the physical world itself, they have no way of making sense of the idea of things being located prior to the creation of the world.

Among Scotus's various attacks on the causal account of location for minds is his contention that this would leave angels frequently without location, inasmuch as they are often not exercising any causal influence on bodies (e.g., *Ord.* II.2.2.1–2, Vat. VII n. 207). This is a result that the Condemnation of 1277 (nn. 77, 218, 219, 204) seems to have targeted. Aquinas, however, had embraced that result without qualms (e.g., *Sent.* I.37.3.1 ad 4) and later Thomists follow his lead in insisting on it (see, e.g., Cajetan, *In Summam theol.* I.52.1.XXVIII).

[13] As evidence that More misunderstands Descartes's distinction between *extensio substantiae* and *extensio potentiae* see his third letter, where he complains: "putarem implicare contradictionem, quod potentia mentis sit extensa, cum mens ipsa non sit extensa ullo modo" (V:379). Evidently, he understands Descartes's text as if it were following the standard scholastic terminology stemming from Lombard. For a reading of Descartes's view here in line with my own, see Schmaltz, *Descartes on Causation* p. 171n.

Pomponazzi considers the following objection against the soul's being able to exist apart from the body:

If the rational soul gives existence to the body, etc., and yet becomes separated (since it is a unified being existing on its own), then in what place will it be? Where will it be? What will it do? Oh, it will be in purgatory! This is laughable. (*Corsi inediti* II:9)

The point seems to be that any imaginable story about where the soul might be located is laughable. Not even worth considering, evidently, is the possibility that the soul might simply have no location at all. Pomponazzi goes on to argue in favor of immortality, but with the remark that in such a difficult matter he wishes he were a student rather than a teacher (ibid.). Tellingly, our record of this disputation contains no response to the above argument.[14]

17.4. Reductive Bodily Location: Ockham and Buridan

In virtue of what does a body have a certain location? One very common scholastic view is, again, extrinsic. A body's location is to be explained not in terms of anything intrinsic to the body itself, but in terms of its relation to something else—specifically, to its place. This is to say that a body has location in virtue of being contiguous with whatever surrounds it. Aquinas, like many others, sets out this sort of view as the natural counterpart to the causal theory of how immaterial minds are located:

Everything that is in a place, or in anything at all, in some way touches that thing. For a corporeal thing is in something as a place in virtue of the contact of its dimensional quantity, and an incorporeal thing is said to be in something in virtue of the contact of its power, since it lacks dimensional quantity. (*Summa contra gent.* III.68.2424)

An immaterial entity, then, is located somewhere in virtue of one kind of contact—by acting on something that is there. A body has location in virtue of another kind of contact: the contact of "dimensional quantity." What this means is that a body's location is fixed in terms of the body that surrounds it. As before, it is important to distinguish between an evidential and an explanatory reading of this claim. Thinking in merely evidential terms, one might well say that we know the cup is in front of us because light is reflecting off of it there, into our eyes, and because we can reach out and touch it there. But scholastic authors often want to read the claim in a stronger way, so that the contact explains what it is for the cup to be located there. It is located in a place because it is touching that place.

This sort of approach faces as many difficulties as does the analogous causal approach in the case of minds. One difficulty arises when one considers what to say about the

---

[14] Another seventeenth-century voice in favor of the possibility of minds without location is Digby, who argues, perhaps with Hobbes in mind, that "out of a thing's being in no place, it cannot be inferred that it is not, or that it is no substance" (*Two Treatises* II.10.2). In part, Digby makes his case here in terms of the Aristotelian theory of place, which makes it easy to find counterexamples. (In particular, since there is no surrounding body for the universe as a whole, it is standardly acknowledged not to be in a place.) But he goes on to make it clear that, with respect to the separated soul, he is after the stronger claim that it has no location at all: "that she is nowhere and yet (upon the matter) that she is everywhere; that she is bound to no place and yet remote from none; that she is able to work upon all without shifting from one to another, or coming near any; and that she is free from all, without removing or parting from anyone" (ibid.).

location of the located body—the body in virtue of which the first body has its location. In discussing the location of minds, we simply helped ourselves to the fact that bodies would have location. This gave the theory a stable ground to rest on. Here, in contrast, we are locating one body in relation to another, and of course the location of that located body must itself be analyzed in this same extrinsic way, and this will go on and on, without any stable ground to land on. Hence the whole story will float together, in a circular or web-like way, unable to attach itself to something with absolute, intrinsic location. One scholastic strategy for coping with this issue is to privilege certain fixed points, like the center of the earth and the poles of the heavens. But if one presses the issue by asking about the location of the universe as a whole, and how that is determined, the usual scholastic answer is that there can be no answer, because the question does not make sense. Location, that is to say, is always relative to other locations, and so one cannot intelligibly talk about the location of everything, as if the whole universe might be shifted over a few feet. Although this sort of answer did not satisfy everyone—its unpalatability led John Buridan to realism regarding motion (§18.2) and led Newton to space—still most scholastic authors were content to give up on absolute location. (Another notable exception is Suárez; see §17.5.)[15]

Suppose we grant, as the extrinsic approach demands, that location is ultimately relative rather than absolute. Even if we agree on this, there is still room to wonder whether this sort of extrinsic approach genuinely explains location at all. It was clear enough that the causal strategy for locating minds might be explanatory, inasmuch as it accounts for location in terms of something quite different, causation. Here, in contrast, location is explained in terms of contact or touching. This is not supposed to be a causal relationship; part of the point of the analysis is that a body can have a certain location without exercising any causal influence on its environment at all. Yet if touching a body is not acting on that body, then what is it, other than a certain fact about location? This of course suggests that we still do not have an explanation of location.

It is to Ockham's credit that he sees this worry clearly, and attempts to deal with it by working out the details of this sort of extrinsic theory of bodily location. His account is quite intricate, but worth taking the time to consider:

> It is not the Philosopher's intention to say that in the located body there is some *res* related to its [surrounding] place (*locus*), distinct from both [the located body and the surrounding place]. Rather, a body's being in a place is nothing other than a body's not being distant from a place—that is, that there is not anything in between the body and the place. And so 'being next to' (*propinquitas*) implies only that between this and that there is no body. And so when one posits that this body exists and that body exists and they are not overlapping (*simul*), and that there is no body in between them all, then one is truly next to the other, setting aside any other *res* [that one might postulate]. (*In Praed.* 16.2, *Opera phil.* II:300)

[15] For an overview of scholastic theories of place, including the appeal to fixed locations, see Trifogli, "Change, Time, and Place." For a typical instance of the scholastic willingness to give up absolute location, see Aquinas, *Summa contra gent.* II.35.1116: "Particularia enim corporea, sicut in tempore determinato, ita et in loco determinato producuntur; et quia habent extra se tempus et locum a quibus continentur, oportet esse rationem quare magis in hoc loco et in hoc tempore producuntur quam in alio. In toto autem caelo, extra quod non est locus, et cum quo universalis locus omnium producitur, non est ratio consideranda quare hic et non ibi constitutum est." For another statement of Aquinas's view that location is a matter of being surrounded by another body, see *Quod.* III.1.2c: "aliquod corpus esse localiter in aliquo loco nihil est aliud quam secundum commensurationem propriarum dimensionum."

Ockham begins (lines 1–2) by insisting that Aristotle does not want to explain location in terms of some further location-explaining thing (*res*) within the body. Instead, location is to be explained more parsimoniously, in terms of being in a place, a notion that he proceeds to analyze in detail. First, he introduces this account of 'being in a place':

1. Body a is in place b = a is not distant from b (line 3).

Then he further analyzes the right hand side:

2. a is not distant from b = there is nothing in between a and b (line 4).

Then he backs up and reformulates. Since to be in a place is simply to be touching, adjacent, or next to some surrounding body, Ockham shifts the focus of the analysis to the 'next to' relationship:

3. a is next to b = there is nothing in between a and b (lines 4–5).

Although put in slightly different terms, (3) is supposed to follow from (1) and (2). But then, introducing complexities gradually, he recognizes that (3) is not quite rigorous enough, and so he arrives at this:

4. a is next to b = a exists, b exists, a and b do not overlap, and there is nothing in between a and b (lines 5–8).

This gives us a full analysis of 'being in a place.'

(Ockham's analysis, it should be noted, presupposes a plenum theory of matter. If there could be empty space between bodies, then the right hand side of (4) might be satisfied and yet it might not be the case that the two bodies are next to each other. Since scholastic authors almost all embrace a plenum theory, it is understandable that Ockham feels able to make this assumption.)

An analysis along the lines of (4) is a start to a general theory of location, but it cannot be the whole story: a general theory, even of the relational variety, must account not just for the special case of contiguity, but for the relative locations of each and every body, including those at a distance from each other. One way to do this would be to construct a theory on which the facts about location are constructed out of a myriad of spatial relationships between distinct bodies, such that a given body is close to a second, farther from a third, even farther from a fourth, and so on. Ockham, ridiculing this sort of view, points out that, since bodies are infinitely divisible, there would have to be an infinite number of such relationships—indeed, that any one body would stand in infinitely many such locational relationships: "as many parts as there are from which a thing is distant, so many relations will there be; and since those parts are infinite, there will be infinitely many relations in each" (ibid.). Ockham, seeking in general to avoid an ontology of relations, is especially keen to avoid this sort of infinite proliferation. So he immediately extends the account of (4) one step farther, to a general theory of spatial relationships between all bodies. He does this by using the analysis of 'being next to' to generate an analysis of its contrary, 'being distant from.'

In the same way, 'distance' implies only this body and that body, and this one's not overlapping that one, and that there is some body in between them. And inasmuch as the intervening body is larger or smaller, the distance is greater or less, and not because of some further *res* formally existing in them. (ibid.)

First he builds on (4) to analyze 'distant from':

> 5. *a* is distant from *b* = *a* exists, *b* exists, *a* and *b* do not overlap, and there is some further body *c* in between *a* and *b*.

This in turn points the way to an account of how to measure degrees of distance:

> 6. The degree of distance between *a* and *b* is given by the size of *c*.

With that, we have a complete account of the locational relationships between bodies.[16]

What drives the theory is Ockham's reductive agenda. One could maintain an extrinsic theory of bodily location, analyzed as being next to some other surrounding body, and yet think that this "next to" relationship requires some sort of relational property. This was, indeed, what robust category realists like Scotus generally maintained (§12.5). The intrinsic–extrinsic distinction is therefore orthogonal to the reductivist–realistic distinction. But it is because Ockham wants to nail down the possibility of a reductive line that he takes such pains to understand what being in a place involves. Still, although this is Ockham's program, it should not be supposed that his account manages to reduce all the locational facts into some other kind of fact. We saw in the previous section an instance of this sort of complete reduction, when causal relationships were invoked to account for the location of immaterial entities. But that strategy had a chance of working because it could take for granted the location of bodies. In the present context, where there is nothing further on which to ground location, it seems hopeless to think the locational facts can be analyzed away entirely. All Ockham can do, then, is to offer an analysis in terms of a smaller number of such facts. Hence, in place of *next to* and *distant from*, he appeals to the fact that *a* and *b* are not co-located, and the fact of there (not) being something between them. What Ockham takes as basic, then, are facts about spatial order in any given direction. That is, he needs to know whether, for any two objects, those objects are co-ordered (overlapping) and, if not, whether any other object is ordered in between them. (Think of how one might do this with any two numbers, or the hues of any two colors.) Given this limited information, he can construct a general theory of spatial relationships.

A sticking point, however, is step (6), which attempts to go from the binary *next to/distant from* pair to a generalized analysis of how to measure distance. This is absolutely essential to the project, since what matters about distance is not the mere fact of it, but the extent of it. The analysis in (6) depends entirely on the size of intervening body *c*. But how do we get that? The most obvious thought is that size can be determined simply by the repeated application of the analyses in (4) and (5). One takes the two endpoints of *c*, and asks whether they are next to or distant from each other. If they are

---

[16] Ockham appeals to his analysis of location more briefly at *Summula* III.10. The strategy is picked up later by Autrecourt, in his account of motion (*Exigit ordo*, pp. 214, 225).

One seventeenth-century attempt to explain bodily location in extrinsic terms is that of Digby, who argues at some length for the view that "the locality of motion is but an extrinsical denomination, and no reality in the thing moved" (*Two Treatises* I.5.5).

distant, in virtue of some intervening c', then we perform the same analysis again, on c', and we keep going until we arrive at two points that are next to each other. The size of c is determined by how many times we have to repeat that process. Unfortunately, this method will not work, given that bodies are infinitely divisible. For as we go from c to c' to c'' and so on, we must be considering progressively smaller bodies. But how much of the body are we meant to take off at each step? If Ockham had atomic units, we might have a definite answer, and might conceive of a body's size in terms of the numbers of its atoms. But since Ockham recognizes no smallest unit of a body, the above method can work only if we stipulate that what is to be taken off at each step is a piece of a certain size. Yet that, of course, presupposes the notion of *size* that we are trying to analyze. What this objection suggests is that Ockham's approach, if it is to yield a fully adequate theory of location, needs more than facts about co-location and lying in between. It also needs at least some facts about distance.

Ockham has nothing more to say about how to solve this problem. One way forward would be that suggested by Euclidian geometry, which takes as primitive the notion of coincidence or equidistance. For if we allow ourselves facts about whether distance ab coincides with distance cd, we can then measure other distances as a proportion of any given distance. (For instance, the length of ef will be twice the length of ab just in case there is a point g between e and f such that both eg and gf coincide with ab.)[17]

Another way forward would be to accept John Buridan's theory of quantity. As we saw in §15.1, Buridan dissents from Ockham's minimalist ontology with respect to the category of Quantity, postulating accidents there as the explanation for why the parts of a body are extended to a certain distance. When Ockham's theory of location, as just described, is supplemented by Buridan's theory of quantity, the result is a general theory of spatial relationships. Buridan's quantities add an account of (6): the size of body c can be explained in terms of its quantity. To be sure, Buridan's account does not yield a complete theory of location all by itself. Since only individual substances have quantity, such quantitative facts cannot explain the spatial relationships between distinct objects. Two objects might swap positions, for instance, without any change in quantity. So quantity could not track location unless one were to introduce quantity to account for the distance between all bodies. This is something that neither Buridan nor Ockham would want, however, since it would in effect generate an infinity of distance relationships of just the sort Ockham had railed against. Still, we could use Buridan's theory of quantity, as it stands, to supplement Ockham's account, by giving him a way to explain the size of a given body. Ockham would presumably not approve of this strategy, since this involves invoking real accidents in the category of Quantity, but the theory is undeniably useful in this context.

The interest of Ockham's account lies in making explicit the ontological commitments involved in locating bodies. I have stressed that he does not succeed in reducing away locational facts entirely, since he still must take as basic certain facts about spatial ordering, as well perhaps as further facts about coincidence (Euclid) or size (Buridan). But to say that Ockham must take certain *facts* as basic is not necessarily to say that he

---

[17] Euclid invokes coincidence as Common Notion 4: "Things that coincide with one another are equal to one another." This was put at the center of a rigorous nominalistic reconstruction of Euclidean geometry by Hilbert; see Heath's commentary on the *Elements* I:228–32, and Field, *Science without Numbers* ch. 3.

has therefore incurred a corresponding number of *ontological* commitments. If the reductivist agenda is to be fairly evaluated, it is crucial not to assume from the start that for every fundamental fact of the world, there is a corresponding entity. That issue has to be explored with care. Buridan, for instance, thinks that facts about the extension of a substance (its size) do depend on accidents in the category of Quantity. He agrees with Ockham, however, that facts about location do not require some further ontology in the category of Where (*Ubi*). Speaking of both Where and When, Buridan writes:

> It is not to be believed that *when* is a *res* distinct from both time and the temporal thing, which time deposits into the temporal thing, or that *where* is a *res* distinct from both place and the thing in that place, passing from the place to the thing in that place.... Such claims appear to me strong enough to kill dogs, and those ensnared in them can no more get out than can fish from nets. (*In Praed.* 18, p. 145)

It is the robust category realists whom Buridan is imagining as poisoned and netted by the category scheme. Like Ockham, Buridan contends that we can account for locational facts without introducing further ontological commitments. Unfortunately, Buridan has little to say about just how such commitments can be avoided.[18]

Ockham too does not have a great deal more to say, beyond what we have seen, but one point he insists on is that a substance is itself, immediately, present to a place. This is to say that the spatial ordering described above is not a product of any sort of accidental form, relational or otherwise, but is an immediate feature of substances.[19] Ockham's theory is still an extrinsic theory, in my terminology, because to have a location is still a matter of being in a place, understood as one body's being next to another, which is itself understood in terms of (4) above. What Ockham wants to insist on, however, is that all these relational facts can be accounted for without invoking any further ontology beyond substances. Facts about spatial ordering are, in other words, ontologically innocent.

The legitimacy of this approach has been widely questioned. Ockham's Parisian critic Michael de Massa, for instance, writing in the mid-1330s, argues that where an agent really acts on an object, it produces some real effect in it, and that this is so when one body moves another. Since such an effect cannot be the thing that is moved or the thing's place (neither body *a* nor body *b*, in Ockham's terms above) it must be some kind of accident in the category of Where. So Michael concludes that "this *where* is some positive reality beyond the thing moved and beyond its place."[20]

---

[18] Buridan, in the passage quoted, is specifically attacking the *Liber sex principiorum* n. 48: "Ubi vero est circumscriptio corporis a loci circumscriptione procedens." Suárez later focuses on this anonymous twelfth-century text as the leading statement of a realist theory of *Ubi*, associating it also with De Soto and Scotus (*Disp. meta.* 51.1.5). For a more extended realist defense of both *Ubi* and *Quando*, see pseudo-Campsall, *Logica* 46–7. Buridan also urges an anti-realist line regarding *Ubi* at *Summulae* 3.7.3, but without offering any metaphysical details.

[19] Ockham argues that bodies are immediately present to a place at *Quod.* IV.20: "substantia materialis ex hoc ipso quod est immediate praesens quantitati sic quod tota est praesens toti et pars parti est immediate praesens loco illius quantitatis per partes suas intrinsecas." I discuss the key argument for this thesis at the start of the next section. See also *Tract. de corp. Christi* ch. 16.

[20] Michael de Massa argues for realism regarding location as follows: "Praeterea, agens reale applicatum applicatione reali circa passum dispositum reale causat aliquem [*ed.* aliquando] effectum realem in ipso; sed movens mobile motu locali, puta movens caelum, est huiusmodi; ergo causat in ipso aliquem effectum et hoc positivum realem. Sed talis effectus nec est ipsum mobile nec locus, sed est ipsum ubi; ergo ubi est aliqua realitas positiva praeter mobile et praeter locum..." (in Courtenay, "Categories" p. 258).

Paul Vincent Spade has recently generalized this form of argument, applying it not just to causal relationships but to any sort of locational ordering, and indeed to anything in virtue of which statements come out as true or false:

Does it not sound paradoxical, even absurd, to say truth and falsehood are determined in part by the arrangements of things along various orderings and then to *deny* the reality of those same orderings? If truth is based in reality, not merely in subjective fancy, then any factor that really affects the truth values of propositions must be given *some* reality in one's ontology. ("Ockham's Nominalist Metaphysics" p. 108)

Spade frames this as an interpretation: that Ockham must believe in some reality corresponding to such facts, because it would be absurd to do otherwise. But since there is no positive textual evidence to support this reading, as Spade himself admits, it seems best to set aside these exegetical pretenses as merely a concession to modern scholarly convention. (One *criticizes* one's contemporaries, and *charitably interprets* historical figures.) Let us therefore treat Spade's remarks as an argument against Ockham's view. There is certainly no doubt about what we might call the major premise: that Ockham relies on locational orderings to account for the truth-values of sentences. More doubtful is the minor premise: that what determines the truth-values of sentences must have some reality. In some sense, Ockham can agree. After all, there is no suggestion that he is an eliminativist about locations. Objects really have locations—it is just that those locational facts are a primitive feature of substances, rather than the result of some positive reality beyond the subject itself (borrowing Michael de Massa's useful formulation). So for the minor premise to cut against Ockham, it must be read in a certain way: that distinct determiners of truth value must be distinct realities.

Now Spade's principle is beginning to sound like quite a strong and implausible version of the correspondence theory of truth, where not only does truth depend on reality (a plausible claim), but moreover the distinct elements of any truth depend on distinct elements of reality. Part of the reason this is implausible is that it seems just hopeless to know how to draw these distinctions, on the side of either language or reality. For instance, as Spade stresses, Ockham's reductionist program depends on locational facts of both the spatial and temporal kind. Each, as he puts it, "affects the truth values of propositions" (line 4 above). Does this mean that we need distinct truth-makers in reality for the spatial and the temporal facts? Could there not instead be one spatiotemporal truth-maker for both, as modern physics would have it? Presumably, some amount of multi-tasking is allowed. But then why not go all the way to Ockham's view, which is that just one truth-maker, the substance, can account for both spatial and temporal location? Indeed, this is a perfectly familiar move of his in other contexts. In the face of the great scholastic conflict over how to account for the individuation of substances, for instance, Ockham urges that there is no principle of individuation, other than the substance itself. Substances just are individuals, he argues, and so it is a mistake to go looking for something else that individuates them. Spade's minor premise, if it is to have any teeth at all, would rule out this sort of move regarding individuation, just as it would in the case of location.

Of course, these two cases are not entirely analogous. A thing's principle of individuation is wholly intrinsic and unchanging, whereas location changes, and seems to be relational. To capture these aspects of his view, we might think of how Ockham understands qualitative similarity. For two objects to be the same in color, according to Ockham, it must be the case that each has its own distinct, qualitative property (an accidental form). But there is, in addition to this, no further relation of sameness or similarity—it just is the case that those two qualities are similar. So this is another example where we have a "factor that really affects the truth values of propositions" (Spade), but no distinct corresponding ontological reality, beyond two colored objects. And here we have quite a close analogue to locational facts, because as noted earlier what Ockham is after in those cases is an ordering in any direction between any two objects, just as one might order any two objects as more or less similar in color. Here too there is a disanalogy, for whereas the qualitative similarity between two bodies results from a distinct accident in the category of Quality, there is of course no distinct accident in the category of Where or Quantity to ground spatial proximity. As with the principle of individuation, it is the substance itself that has the location.[21]

17.5. Location as a Mode: Olivi and Suárez

Ockham's theory is extrinsic and reductive, but these two aspects of his view might easily be pulled apart. Indeed, the sort of view Ockham is worried about most is a view that would retain the extrinsic strategy of locating bodies in terms of their proximity to some surrounding place, but invoke some sort of accidental property to explain this relation. Ockham has an ingenious argument against this sort of view, in favor of his view that "an extended material substance is immediately present to a place through its intrinsic parts":

Everything that is present to a place is present there either through itself or through something else to which it is present. . . . If a material substance is present to a place through its intrinsic parts, then I have my conclusion. If through something else (such as quantity), then I argue as follows. When any two things are present [to one another] without local distance, then whatever is immediately present to one of them is, for the same [reason], immediately present to the other. But a quantity and its place are present [to one another] without local distance, and the material substance that exists under the quantity is immediately present to the quantity through its own intrinsic parts. Therefore, it is immediately present to the place of that quantity through those same parts. (*Quod.* IV.20 [first proof], *Op. theol.* IX:398–9; see *Tract. de corp. Christi* ch. 16, *Op. theol.* X:122–3)

Suppose a body's location were explained by some further property (line 3). In this case, Ockham contends that the property would be immediately present to the place (line 6),

---

[21] For a good overview of Ockham's theory of individuation, see King, "Problem of Individuation." For his theory of resemblance, see Adams, *William Ockham* ch. 4. For his reductive account of temporal location, see e.g. *Summa logicae* I.59. A fuller defense of Ockham's reductive views in these areas would need to discuss his extremely extensive and interesting arguments against the line of thought that where a substance undergoes change there must be some entity that it gains or loses. See *Summula* III.10 and *Tract. de quantitate* q. 3 (*Opera theol.* X:72–5).

Spade's reading/criticism of Ockham develops over a series of papers, beginning with "Critical Notice," and then in "Three Versions," but is given its most developed statement to date in "Ockham's Nominalist Metaphysics," as quoted here in part.

and the body would be immediately present to the property (lines 7–8). But now, applying the transitivity of location (lines 4–6), he concludes that the body itself would be immediately present to the place (lines 8–9), which is the conclusion he seeks.

To see how clever an argument this is, consider the analogous situation for other properties, like colors. A body is colored in virtue of having an accident in the category of Quality. It is the accident that is immediately colored, and the body is colored when that accident inheres in it. Ockham sees no incoherence in this, and indeed he accepts the reality of qualities (§19.2). But the analogous story for location is not coherent. For suppose there is an accident in the category of Quantity or Where that explains location. In that case, the body that is located in virtue of that accident will acquire its location when that accident inheres in it. But inherence—however we are to think about it—minimally requires co-location. This means, absurdly, that a body must already have its location before it can be given that location by an accident. The accident is therefore superfluous.

We have seen in other cases (Ch. 11) how the inherence relationship lends itself to paradoxes of this sort. And we have seen that various scholastic authors have a very effective strategy for coping with such problems: they invoke modes to do the work that real accidents cannot do. One finds this strategy as early as Peter John Olivi, *circa* 1278. In a passage quoted in full earlier (§13.2), Olivi considers and rejects the doctrine that being in a place is nothing over and above the thing that is located. To be sure, there is no real accident involved here, but there is *something*, a mode: "where (or being here or there) does add something to the *res* that is here or there, but not something that should be called a quality or a form that is absolute.... Instead, it is a thoroughly relational mode of being, which is called location or situation" (*Summa* II.32, I:586). Although Olivi's view has to be gleaned from scattered passages, and although he sometimes offers several possible accounts, without choosing among them, it seems that his preferred view distinguishes modes corresponding to Quantity, in virtue of which a body's parts are spread out to a certain extent, and modes corresponding to Where, in virtue of which bodies are given their relative ordering, as situated next to one another. This sort of view does not require postulating two located entities, the accidental locator and the located substance. Modes are not things that have locations, but are that by which substances have location. Ockham's paradox is therefore evaded.

Olivi's theory is non-reductive and extrinsic. It is non-reductive, of course, because it invokes modes. It is extrinsic because it uses those modes to articulate a theory along the same lines that Ockham and Buridan would later develop, explaining location as being relative to other bodies, and invoking modes in the category of Quantity to account for the size of those bodies. Olivi goes on to say that every creature—material and immaterial—"must always be in some place" (*Summa* II.32, I:587; see §16.3 for the full passage). This fits with what I earlier called the *determinacy* of modes—the way a given subject must always have some one or another mode from a determinable class. It suggests that Olivi's theory might in fact be intrinsic—that modes serve to give their subject an absolute place, independent of everything else. I think that what Olivi means, though, is that given a world in which there are other things with their own places, any further thing must fit somewhere into that ordering. Locational facts remain, therefore, ultimately relational.[22]

For an explicitly intrinsic theory of location in terms of modes, we can look ahead some three hundred years to Suárez. He begins his discussion of the category of Where by distinguishing three theories of location: (1) the extrinsic Aristotelian theory of place; (2) a realistic theory of the sort Buridan had criticized above; (3) a theory of space as that which bodies fill. Rejecting all of these, he instead contends that the category of Where contains "a real and intrinsic mode of the *res* that is said to be somewhere, from which mode that *res* has its being here or there" (*Disp. meta.* 51.1.13). The discussion subsequently focuses in turn on the claims that it is a mode, that it is real, and that it is intrinsic. As for the first, Suárez predictably appeals to one-way separability (Ch. 13): that a thing can exist without any particular location, but a location is unintelligible without a thing (ibid.). But how do we know there is a real thing at all here? Suárez argues as follows:

This is proved, because (a) when a body is said to be here or there, these words signify something real applying to such a body; (b) this is true on the side of reality, without any invention of the mind; (c) being here or there can be gained or lost through real change, since local motion is a real change and being here or there is the only thing that is lost or gained; (d) being here or there is a necessary condition on really acting or being acted on, and is supposed to be the foundation of real relations. (51.1.14)

Location must be something real within bodies, because we truly ascribe locational facts to bodies (a–b), and need facts about location to make sense of various real changes, actions, and relations (c–d). This is a version of the charge we have seen made against Ockham's attempt to handle locational facts reductively (§17.4), and is reminiscent of the strategy we saw Scotus apply more generally in defense of real accidents (§10.5)—that realism is best defended by showing that certain entities are necessary for our best theories about the way the world works. As stressed already, moreover, this is a particularly vulnerable place to lodge such charges, because no reductivism along Ockham's lines can afford to deny the explanatory role played by location. Ockham and others may be willing to rip out large chunks of the categorial framework, but when they do so they end up putting all the more weight on facts about location.

After arguing for the reality of these locational modes, Suárez turns to their intrinsicalness. He argues at length against the coherence of absolute space, and then against the standard scholastic theory of location as relative to a surrounding place. Against the second sort of view, he argues that a body can maintain its location even if the surrounding bodies change, and can change its location without any change to what surrounds it. Examples to illustrate both of these claims are easy enough to come by: a

---

[22] Olivi's most important passages on location as a mode have been quoted already in §13.2. Regarding items in the category of Where, as something over and above Quantity, see also *Summa* II.58, II:447–8: "Ubi non sint aliud quam praesentialis applicatio locati et partium eius ad locum suum." He makes it clear there that there is no need to postulate anything corresponding to Position. Regarding temporal location, he writes: "Ergo instans nil aliud est quam praesentia mobilis, et ideo nil aliud ponit in re nisi mobile praesens esse vel non esse, sicut omnia accidentia, quae nihil aliud dicunt nisi substantiam sic esse, eo quod non dicunt nisi modos essendi substantiae vel eorum quae sunt in substantia" (Maier, "Problem der Quantität" p. 170n.).

tree in a river maintains its location, for instance, even while the water around it moves; a man on a boat moving down a river changes his location, even while his place—the boat—remains the same. Such cases had been much discussed by earlier authors. Suárez's position is remarkable, because he insists on a purely intrinsic account, according to which a thing, in virtue of the mode that locates it, has an absolute location apart from everything else that exists: "as long as a thing conserves in itself this mode of presence, it always remains in the same *where* as it was before, even if other things are changed around it" (*Disp. meta.* 51.1.17). Seemingly, such independence extends not just to a thing's immediate surroundings, but to *anything* that might serve to fix a body's relative location, since Suárez contends that "if it were anything extrinsic [that explained its location], it would above all be the body surrounding it" (51.1.15). Hence, since that account fails, Suárez concludes that "if a body is now here and later there, it is changed intrinsically and really; therefore what varies within it is not just some extrinsic denomination, but something intrinsically existing within it" (ibid.)

With this we have arrived at the sort of absolute conception of location that Newton and Clarke would famously defend against Leibniz. One might have supposed that this sort of view would be attractive for an extremely austere ontology like Ockham's or Hobbes's. After all, when facts about location are made to bear so much explanatory weight, it is natural to want those facts to be intrinsic facts, for fear that otherwise there may be no intrinsic facts whatsoever. There is indeed a real possibility here that, for the strict corpuscularian, there will be no intrinsic facts in the material realm. According to the strict corpuscularian, after all, the various qualities, powers, and states of bodies can all be reduced to a body's geometric/kinetic features (§1.3). Such features, however, at least for the corpuscularian, consist simply in facts about location. If, therefore, the facts about location are all extrinsic, then there would seem to be absolutely no intrinsic feature of bodies. To be sure, there is something odd about this, but of course there is also something quite odd about the notion of absolute spatial location, and for Ockham and other proponents of a reductive, extrinsic account, such oddities are apparently worse.

Suárez recognizes the oddity of the idea of absolute location, remarking that "such a mode ... is something absolute, although we can explain this only by grounding it in relations of distance or nearness, which is why in a manner of speech it is said to be relative" (*Disp. meta.* 51.1.13). In other words, although Suárez thinks the arguments in favor of absolute location are decisive, he sees the utter obscurity in the very idea of such a thing. For this reason, we cannot help but speak of location in relational terms, locating one thing relative to another. Still, he thinks, such relational facts cannot be the whole story about location.

Although Suárez's use of modes to explain spatial location is more radical than Olivi's, inasmuch as it grounds a theory of absolute location, in another domain it is Olivi who gives a more robust role to modes. On Olivi's view, temporal location is a mode just like spatial location is. Suárez, in contrast, sharply distinguishes the two, insisting that whereas spatial location is the product of a distinct mode, temporal location can be analyzed entirely in terms of the existence of substances and accidents. There is, he claims, just a distinction of reason between a thing's existing and its duration over time (*Disp. meta.* 50.1.5–9). In insisting that the category of When is ontologically innocent in this way, Suárez acknowledges that he is effectively taking the reductive Ockhamist line with regard to temporal properties. There is, to be sure, something attractive about the idea that the temporal location of a thing is nothing over and above its existence. But if Suárez is going to go Ockhamist on this score, then why not do the same with spatial location? An illuminating exercise is to return to Suárez's arguments above (a–d) in favor of the reality of spatial modes, and try substituting 'now or then' for every occurrence of 'here or there.' Are the arguments any more compelling? It seems to me that deep questions lurk here regarding the nature of time, and the reality of past and future events. But all these brief remarks can accomplish is to reinforce the thought that the subject of temporal location requires its own separate treatment. The following chapter will have some bearing on this matter, but the fundamental issues will have to wait for another occasion.[23]

---

[23] Another example of an author treating location as a mode is Burgersdijk, *Inst. meta.* I.7.7: "Ubi sive potius praesentia localis modus est locatae rei." Scheibler also describes location as a mode (*Metaphys.* I.17.2.2 n. 19), but the real interest of Scheibler's discussion is his very clear insistence on an intrinsic theory of location: "Esse alicubi non consistit formaliter et solum in denominatione extrinseca. Extrinsecae denominationes illae dicuntur quae sumuntur ab actu alienae alicuius rei, vel per coexistentiam alterius rei—quomodo paries dicitur visus, non per aliquid sibi intrinsecum, sed sumpta denominatione ab extrinseco actu videntis. Patetque, quia esse alicubi est proprietas cuiusque entis actualis. Proprietates autem non sumuntur ab extrinseco. Deinde, quia remoto omni extrinseco, adhuc res relinquitur esse alicubi. Id enim extrinsecum, unde sumeretur haec denominatio, inprimis esset res alia circumdans vel circumscribens. At omni circumdante remoto, veluti remoto aere ex conclavi per divinam potentiam, atque ita conclavi evacuato, nihilominus res eo immissa esset alicubi et non nuspiam" (I.17.2.1 n. 7). Scheibler goes on, as one would expect, to argue against a causal account of location.

Suárez's insistence on distinguishing the spatial and temporal cases might be seen as having made its mark on Descartes, who likewise distinguishes between the spatial and the temporal case, allowing that spatial location is a mode of bodies, but that duration is an attribute rather than a mode. Why is it not a mode? Descartes's brief remarks suggest that it is not because, unlike spatial location, temporal location remains unmodified (*Principles* I.56). Time flows, that is, but flows smoothly, without variation.

18

Entia Successiva

18.1. What Are Successive Entities?

So far we have been presupposing that what fundamentally exist are substances, enduring through time. This is a reasonable enough assumption to make, because there was a quite general consensus throughout our four centuries that enduring substances lie at the foundation of what there is. The final chapters of this study will consider how this consensus begins to unravel in the hands of what I will refer to as nominalist approaches to diachronic identity. But before we get that far we ought to explore how authors during our period had the conceptual resources to contemplate a radically different sort of existence, one on which things exist not wholly at a time, but part by part over time, as *entia successiva*.

The previous two chapters point us naturally toward this new topic, because to consider how things are located in space and time leads to the question of how things move through space and time. To say that substances are in motion, and endure through time, suggests the existence of entities, motion; and time. It is not, to be sure, *obvious* that a theory of motion needs to postulate the reality of some thing, a motion, over and above the facts about bodily location. On one school of thought, associated above all with Ockham, a theory of location can be parlayed into a theory of motion by simply considering whether or not the located object is changing its location, which change in turn is nothing more than for an object to have one location and then another. Others, however, argued for realism in this domain, insisting that an adequate theory of change requires an ontology of motions and perhaps time. Reflection on the character of these alleged entities suggests, in turn, that they possess a manner of existence quite unlike that of substances. Hence was born a fundamental distinction between two kinds of entities, permanent and successive.

The topic of successive entities, once widely discussed among scholastic authors, is today quite obscure. This may be in part because post-scholastic authors largely ignore the topic or, when they do discuss it, do so in much the same terms as before. Gassendi, for instance, embraces successive entities, whereas Leibniz offers the usual scholastic arguments against them. Although modern metaphysicians are aware of the scholastic terminology, thanks to Roderick Chisholm, it has received virtually no attention from scholars with the competencies necessary for investigating its origins. Yet, as soon as one begins to look, one finds the permanent–successive distinction everywhere. It has roots in Aristotle, Augustine, Avicenna, and Averroes, and is already taken for granted, as well established, before our period begins. (It is invoked regularly by Thomas Aquinas, for instance.) The fourteenth century features an extensive debate between those, such as Ockham, who think that there are no successive entities, and others who contend that there are. One would like to say that the lack of attention devoted to this topic is surprising, but in truth it is simply a typical instance of how little we yet understand about the scholastic era.[1]

In considering this topic, it is even more important than usual to define the subject clearly. This is, however, difficult, and is so for the same reason that it is important: because different authors define the phrase in quite different ways, and often seem to mean different things even when they use the same formulas. There seems, however, to be one formulation of the distinction that is universally accepted: that a permanent entity exists all at once, whereas a successive entity does not. This is, for instance, Walter Burley's formulation:

This is the difference between permanent and successive things: that a permanent thing exists all at once (*tota simul*), or at least can exist all at once, whereas it is incompatible with a successive thing to exist all at once. (*In Phys.* III text 11, f. 65rb)

To say that a permanent thing exists all at once is to say that, when it exists, it wholly exists, which is to say that all of its parts then exist. As Burley himself says, "a permanent thing has all of its parts at once" (ibid.). As in earlier chapters, it is best at least for now to understand 'part' in a very broad sense, as any aspect of a whole. So the core idea of the permanent–successive distinction, on this way of framing it, is that successive entities exist partly at one time and partly at another, and never wholly at any one time, whereas the whole of a permanent entity—every part of it—exists at the same time.[2]

---

[1] For Gassendi's embrace of *entia successiva*, see *Syntagma* II.1.2.7, I:223ab, where he considers the usual paradoxes regarding successive entities (§18.3), and dismisses them on the grounds that this is just what successive entities are: "at nihil est revera nisi permanens? Fatendum nihil esse revera permanenter, nisi permanens; et esse revera quoque suo modo, hoc est successive, quod est successivum." Locke also seems willing to admit successive entities, at *Essay* II.27.2 (§30.2). For Leibniz's contrary view, see his fifth paper to Clarke, n. 49: "Whatever exists of time and of duration, being successive, perishes continually, and how can a thing exist eternally which (to speak exactly) does not exist at all? For how can a thing exist of which no part does ever exist? Nothing of time does ever exist but instants, and an instant is not even itself a part of time. Whoever considers these observations will easily apprehend that time can only be an ideal thing."

For Chisholm, see *Person and Object*. For the doctrine's roots in Aristotle, see *Phys.* III.6, 206a20–30, where being is spoken of in many ways, as when "we say it is day or it is the games, because one thing after another is always coming into existence." See also *Cat.* 6, 5a15–37, where the parts of time and language are said not to be *permanens*, and hence to lack position *ad se invicem* (in Boethius's standard translation). As Kretzmann points out ("Incipit/Desinit" p. 135 n. 32), the permanent–successive distinction is not developed in Boethius's commentary on this passage, but can be found in Abaelard's *Glossae in Categorias* (pp. 62–3): "...ipsae substantiae dicuntur continuae succedenter aut permanenter, succedenter ut tempus, permanenter ut linea." For various thirteenth-century occurrences, see de Libera, "Le traité" pp. 262–3 note p.

[2] On *entia permanentia* as *tota simul*, see William of Sherwood, *Syncategoremata* p. 76 (tr. 16.3): "Et sunt permanentia quorum partes simul sunt; cuiusmodi est album. Successiva quorum partes non sunt simul, cuiusmodi est currere"; Peter of Spain, *Syncategoremata* VI.3: "Prima differentia est quod res permanentes dicuntur quarum esse est totum simul.... Secunda autem differentia est quoniam partes permanentium simul sunt omnes...et non est una post alteram. Successivarum vero partes non sunt simul omnes sed una est post alteram successive." Aquinas, *Sent.* I.8.2.1 ad 4: "in successivis est duplex imperfectio: una ratione divisionis, alia ratione successionis, quia una pars non est cum alia parte: unde non habent esse nisi secundum aliquid sui"; Aquinas, *In De caelo* I.29.278: "tempus non est totum simul, sed est successivum"; pseudo-Aquinas, *De tempore* ch. 1: "omnia successiva, quae secundum se tota non extant, sed secundum

When the distinction is so understood, it is not at all clear how to divide things up as either permanent or successive. If we interpret the criterion for permanence strictly, it is hard to see how anything other than God could count. A tree, for instance, gains and loses leaves, and never has all of those leaves at once. Something similar seems true of finite minds: their thoughts come and go in such a way that the mind never possesses all of its thoughts at once. Moreover, even if we were to conceive of a completely unchanging substance, that substance would still endure through time. This suggests that the entirety of its existence could not be captured at any one instant, inasmuch as its existence extends through time, having one part now and other parts at other times. If 'part' is understood broadly enough, such an entity does not have all its parts at once. When matters are so described, only God counts as permanent.[3]

This conception of the created world, as impermanent and partial in contrast to God, has an impressive pedigree. On Boethius' famous definition of divine eternity, it is "the all-at-once and complete possession of unending life" (*Consolation of Philosophy* V.6), where "all-at-once" translates *tota simul*, the very phrase that is later used to mark the permanent–successive distinction. Hence God would seem to be the only thing that can be said in the strictest sense to be whole (that is, have all its parts) at any given time.

---

aliquid indivisibile sui"; Chatton, *Rep.* II.2.1, p. 89: "…aliqua non essent nata esse simul in rerum natura nec per consequens esse permanentia per causas naturales…"; Rimini, *Sent.* II.1.4, p. 125: "Habet quoque haec entitas [i.e., motus] partes intrinsecas sibi invicem succedentes secundum prius et posterius, quarum nulla simul in aliquo tempore vel instanti existit vel aliqua virtute existere potest cum alia. Et ex hoc dicitur entitas successiva"; John Major, *Sent.* II.2.2: "res successiva…quod non potest habere plures partes simul"; Scheibler, *Philosophia compendiosa* II.1.9.9: "Permanens est, quod suum esse habet simul. Successivum est, quod partes sui esse habet in fluxu quodam, ut motus, tempus, sub quo sunt hora, dies, annus, etc."

Seventeenth-century authors continue to use the standard phrase *tota simul*. See, e.g., Descartes, *Rules* 11 (X:407): "ad mentis intuitum duo requirimus: nempe ut propositio clare et distincte, deinde etiam ut tota simul et non successive intelligatur"; Arnauld to Descartes in 1648: "Sed quaeri potest, de quo tempore hic agatur. Si enim de ipsius mentis duratione, quam tempus appellas, negant vulgo Philosophi ac Theologi, rei permanentis et maxime spiritalis, qualis mens est, durationem esse successivam, sed permanentem, et totam simul (quod quidem de Dei duratione certissimum est), ac proinde non esse in ea partes quaerendas, quarum priores a posterioribus non dependeant" (Descartes, *Oeuvres* V:188); Leibniz, *Phil. Schriften* IV:394 (tr. Ariew and Garber p. 251): "Continua autem duorum sunt generum: alia successiva, ut tempus et motus; alia simultanea seu ex coexistentibus partibus constantia, ut spatium et corpus."

[3] Arnauld, as just quoted, represents a rare case of someone suggesting that timeless, Boethian eternality be applied to something other than God. Descartes rejects this idea, insisting that created minds go through time just as bodies do (V:193). For a detailed retrospective discussion of the scholastic debate, see Suárez, *Disp. meta.* 50.3–5. Most in our period accept that Boethian eternality does apply to God; for exceptions, see Hobbes, *Of Liberty* §24: "As soon as I can conceive eternity to be an indivisible point, or anything but an everlasting succession, I will renounce all that I have written on this subject"; Charleton, *Physiologia* I.7.3.4: "What wit is so acute and sublime as to conceive that a thing can have duration, and that duration can be as a point without fusion and continuation from one moment to another, by intervenient or mediate moments? Easy enough, we confess, it is to conceive that the *res durans* is altogether at once, or does retain the sameness of its nature, without mutation, diminution, or amission [≈ loss] of any perfection: but that, in this perseveration, there is not many nows, or many instants, of which, compared among themselves, some are antecedent and others consequent, is to us absolutely incomprehensible."

For the possibility that God might be the only permanent entity, see Albert of Saxony, *In Phys.* III.3, p. 483: "possumus imaginari aliquid esse permanens simpliciter, scilicet tam secundum eius substantiam totaliter quam etiam secundum eius dispositionem: isto modo forte nihil est permanens, nisi prima causa." See also Oresme, *De configurationibus* II.13: "Rerum quaedam sunt ita successivae quod non possunt aliquo modo permanere, sicut tempus et motus. Aliae sunt ita permanentes quod licet habeant esse vel durare temporaliter, divisibiliter, et successive, tamen earum essentia toto illo tempore eadem permanet nec potest esse aliqualiter successiva, sicut substantiae indivisibiles et immateriales. Sed prima illarum, quae Deus est, nec habet essentiam successivam nec esse sive durare quoquomodo successivum. Immo indivisibiliter et infinite permanet per seipsam aeternitate sua indivisibili et interminabili, quae est idem quod ipsemet Deus."

Everything else exists partly at one time and partly at another. Augustine's *Confessions* contains a sparkling depiction of this idea:

Why, my soul, do you perversely follow your flesh? It would follow you, if you turned away. Whatever you sense through it is partial. You are unaware of the whole of which these are the parts, and yet these parts delight you. But if the sense of your flesh were 3 suited to comprehend the whole, and were not, in punishment, justly confined to a part of the universe, you would wish to pass over whatever exists in the present, so that the whole would provide you with more pleasure. For so it is that you hear, with the same sense of 6 the flesh, the words we speak, and you certainly do not want to stop at the syllables, but to pass on so that other syllables may come and you may hear the whole. So it always is when all of what makes up some one thing does not all exist at once (*omnia simul*): if it could all 9 be sensed, it would be more enjoyable than it would individually. But far better than these is he who made all things, our God. He does not pass away, because nothing succeeds him. (IV.11.17)

As things are, we are confined to perceiving the present. (Augustine seems to treat this as a consequence of original sin [line 4].) But this is just part of the whole past and future course of affairs, and if we could break out of our time-bound perspective and perceive that whole, we would care much less about the present, and our current fleshly preoccupations. This would make us happier. But "far better" (line 10) would be to perceive God, author of all those parts. Augustine does not expressly formulate Boethius's later conception of eternality, as complete existence all at once, but it is implicit here, in the contrast between the sequential character of the created world, constructed out of temporal parts, and the successionless nature of God.

This strict conception of permanence is a perfectly congenial result for scholastic authors, who generally agree that God is permanent in a way that nothing else could be. Thus Albert of Saxony, responding in the 1350s to the question of whether there are both permanent and successive things, takes the main objection to permanent entities to be the argument that only God is permanent, and in reply allows that God may be the only thing that is permanent *simpliciter*. In general, it went without saying that God exists all at once in a way that material substances do not. Yet in the present context this scholastic commonplace is potentially problematic, because it makes it hard to see how to arrive at the permanent–successive distinction as scholastic authors saw it. For although God is certainly the preeminent example of a permanent entity, human beings are supposed to count as well, as are trees, as is matter and at least most forms, both substantial and accidental. (Souls count as permanent, and so do colors.) To see how we might arrive at the distinction as it is intended, we need to consider more closely what exactly it means to exist all at once, *tota simul*.

A closer look at the texts reveals two quite different ways of applying this concept to the permanent–successive distinction. On what I will call the *synchronic* approach, the distinction is drawn in terms of whether an entity *could* wholly exist at an instant. This is what Burley seems to have in mind. What he says, in the passage quoted above, is that a permanent thing either "exists all at once, or at least *can* exist all at once" (lines 1–2). Correspondingly, a successive entity not only in fact does not exist all at once, but actually cannot do so—such existence is "incompatible" with being successive. Although the simple assertoric formula is very common—it appears in the thirteenth century, for instance, in the logicians William of Sherwood and Peter of Spain—Burley seems at first to offer it and then to retreat to the modal formulation. Perhaps he does so because he recognizes that the first formulation is too strict. Unfortunately, it is not entirely clear how we are to understand the possibility of such all-at-once existence. What I think Burley must have in mind, however, is the possibility of an entity's existing for just a durationless instant. So consider an instantaneous tree. Whatever parts it has, at that instant, would be all its parts, and so it would be *tota simul*. In general, on this synchronic approach, that which is permanent *could* exist at an instant, whereas that which is successive could not. It is an oddity of this way of understanding the distinction that an *instantaneous* entity counts as a *permanent* entity, but this does seem to be the way many of our sources conceive of the distinction. Burley, for instance, explicitly discusses the case of instantaneous entities, and rules both that they are possible, and that they count as permanent rather than successive.[4]

Just like that, we have gone from a very strict conception of permanence to a very loose conception—apparently loose enough to include any sort of substance, material or immaterial, as well as properties like color, size, and shape. Indeed, one might well wonder at this point what would *not* count as a permanent entity—what would be such as to be incompatible with existing all at once, even for an instant. As I suggested at the start of the chapter, the standard scholastic examples of *entia successiva* are time and motion. On this synchronic understanding of the permanent–successive distinction, it is easy to see why these should count as successive. In the case of time, Aristotle had stated the case succinctly:

Time has parts, some of which have been, others of which are going to be, but no part of it is. The now is not a part, because a part is a measure of the whole, which must be composed of parts. Time, however, does not seem to be composed of nows. (*Phys.* IV.10, 218a5–8; cf. 220a19)

What is true for time seems likewise true for motion, inasmuch as there can be no motion in an instant. Motion requires time—again citing Aristotle, "every motion is in time" (*Phys.* VI.2, 232b20). Hence motion and time, if they exist, seem to exist in a fundamentally different way from how substances and other permanent entities exist. Like permanent things, they exist through time, but in a strange way they seem unable to exist at any given moment of time.

The other principal understanding of the permanent–successive distinction shifts the focus away from the synchronic question of whether a thing can be whole at an instant, toward the *diachronic* question of whether a thing endures for more than an instant. Nicole Oresme, *circa* 1346, describes the distinction explicitly in these terms. After

---

[4] Burley defends the possibility of instantaneous permanent entities in *De primo et ultimo instanti* II.2: "Distinctio ulterius est de re permanente, qua quaedam est res permanens quae [*ed.* qua] solum durat per unum instans, sicut mutatum esse, et instans in tempore, et ubi in medio motus. Unde lapis, si non haberet nisi unum instans, adhuc esset res permanens, quia habet omnes suas partes simul. Alia est res permanens quae durat per tempore, sicut homo et asinus et simile...." This work defines the distinction in terms almost identical to those used in his *Physics* commentary: "Circa primam est sciendum quod differentia est inter res permanentem et successivam, quoniam res permanens, communiter loquendo de re permanente, est illa cui non repugnat ex natura rei habere omnes partes simul. Et res successiva est illa cui repugnat ex natura rei habere omnes suas partes simul; immo est de natura sui quod habeat unam per temporem, et aliam posteriorem, et quando pars prior est, pars posterior non est" etc. (ibid., II.1).

setting aside two improper senses of 'successive,'[5] Oresme explains the term's proper sense:

Third, ['successive' is used] for that which at no time is such that what existed in its first part exists in its second part. Instead, for any time you take, some of that successive entity exists in one of its parts, and a totally different such exists in another part. This is how we conceive of time, because the first part does not exist when the second exists, and so such a thing is said to be not permanent but in continuous flux and transition. To illustrate: something is said to flow with respect to place that is not in one and the same place of its own through time; likewise, something is said to flow with respect to existence that does not have the same existence over the whole of some time. This is why past time is spoken of in terms of flowing water. 'Permanent' is used in the opposite way, when for some time, over some instants, the same thing exists all at once (*totum simul*), from one instant to another. (*In Phys.* III.6, dist. 1)

Oresme too takes off from the commonly accepted view that permanent entities exist *totum simul* (line 10), whereas successive entities exist partly at one time and partly at another. But whereas the synchronic approach marks a distinction in how things exist at an instant, making no claims about sameness over time, Oresme focuses on such diachronic identity. Permanent entities are those that are literally enduring (*permanens*), numerically the same, from one instant to another (lines 9–10), whereas successive entities go through time in flux, meaning that "some" of it exists at one time and "a totally different such exists" at a different time (lines 2–3). The successive entity is the whole made up of these distinct "parts."

Insisting on diachronic identity is one way to try capturing the idea of all-at-once existence. For if permanent entities are numerically the same over time, then the past and future careers of such entities are in some sense not distinct: the thing, as it exists earlier or later, is the *same* as the thing as it exists now, and so not a proper part of the thing. Hence a permanent entity seems to be *tota simul*, whole at any given time. It is not clear to me whether this is how the permanent–successive distinction is usually understood by scholastic authors, since what one usually finds are the same stock phrases, without further elucidation. It does seem clear that the diachronic approach is employed by Gregory of Rimini, John Buridan, Albert of Saxony, and John Wyclif, who compares the way permanent entities occupy time to the way holenmers occupy space, wholly at each point (§§16.4–6). On the other hand, many discussions of the distinction make no mention of diachronic identity at all, and many agree with Burley in appealing to the *possibility* of all-at-once existence, a qualification that seems unnecessary on the diachronic approach. As late as Christoph Scheibler's *Metaphysica* (1617), one finds the synchronic approach defended very explicitly, so that an entity that exists for just an instant, and then is subsequently replaced by a new entity of the same kind (his example is new light's being constantly generated by the sun), counts as a permanent entity, inasmuch as "at any moment it has its essence all at once, and even if it exists for no more than that one moment, still the light is light, which is incompatible with a successive entity" (I.16.8.2 n. 99). What makes things even less clear is that it would

---

[5] According to Oresme (*In Phys.* III.6, dist. 1), 'successive' is used least properly to refer to a permanent entity that undergoes change. It is used less improperly for a thing that comes to obtain successively, in degrees, in the way that heat is successively acquired by an object. He makes no mention of the synchronic version of the distinction.

be possible to combine the two approaches, requiring permanent entities to pass both the synchronic and the diachronic tests, and also (or instead) requiring successive entities to fail both tests. Still, although these waters are muddy, the difference in approaches is important to bear in mind, because they sometimes yield quite different results, as we will see.[6]

18.2. Are There Any Successive Entities?

Although the notion of a successive entity has many prominent antecedents, it is not until Avicenna that one finds an extended argument for treating the notion with full ontological seriousness—that is, for the view that successive entities are things over and above permanent entities. But since Avicenna's view was sharply critiqued by Averroes, the first Latin authors who attempted to address the issue were left with no clear authoritative guidance on how to proceed. Of course, this is just the normal state of philosophy, and so the normal outcome followed: disagreement and debate. The first round of scholastic commentaries, in the middle of the thirteenth century, took a realistic stand, endorsing the reality of motion and time as successive entities. At the same time, the two most distinguished Parisian theologians, Aquinas and Bonaventure, were anti-realists. Bonaventure, for instance, accepts the claim that "everything successive reduces to something permanent" (*Sent.* II.2.1.1.3 ad 5). Subsequently, one's impression of the debate seems a matter of local perspective. According to Hervaeus Natalis, writing in Paris at the start of the fourteenth century, "it is generally held that the form acquired through motion is really the same as the motion itself" (*Sent.* I.17.4),

---

[6] For Albert of Saxony's embrace of the diachronic approach, see §18.4. For other clear statements of that approach, see Suárez, *Disp. meta.* 50.5.1; Rimini, *Sent.* II.1.4 (IV:175): "Permanens vero describitur quod secundum se totum primo potest durare per tempus et in diversis instantibus esse. Et ex hoc sequitur quod si aliquod eiusmodi habet partes, partes suas possunt simul esse"; Buridan, *In Phys.* III.7 concl. 6: "motus ultimae spherae est res pure successiva cuius scilicet est pars prior et pars posterior non manentes simul"; Wyclif, *De ente praedicamentali* ch. 20, pp. 195–6: "Ex istis patet quod sicut nullum multiplicatum per locum est extensive per locum, sic nullum permanens per tempus est extensive per illud tempus; quia sicut multiplicatum per locum est secundum se totum ad omne punctum dati loci, sic permanens est ad omne instans dati sui temporis secundum se totum, quod est impossibile de successivo. In hoc enim differt permanens a successivo, quod permanens est illud quod manet successive in extensum, cuiusmodi est omne illud quod sufficit manere per tempus sine innovatione vel deperditione partis. Successivum vero omne quod per tempus extenditur; quamlibet autem partem divisibilem taliter extensi oportet habere tempus sibi appropriatum, in quo non sit aliquid sui totius praeter ipsum vel partem eius, sicut est de localiter extenso." Wyclif's parallel treatment of the temporal and spatial cases can be found much earlier in Anselm, *Monologium* chs. 20–3.

For the synchronic approach, see also Cajetan of Thiene, *In Phys.* III.1 f. 24va: "rei successivae repugnat omnes partes simul habere, qualiter non est de re permanente." Scheibler sets out the synchronic approach in considerable detail at *Metaphys.* I.19.1. The very case of light that he describes as permanent had been treated by Buridan as successive, and indeed as analogous to the case of motion; see Maier, *Zwischen* pp. 179–80, quoting from the unedited earlier redaction of *In Phys.*: "dico de motu sicut de lumine. . . . "

I have not found any scholastic author who recognizes the existence of a synchronic–diachronic disagreement over how to characterize the permanent–successive distinction. Modern scholars are similarly unaware. Solère seems to understand the distinction synchronically ("Postérité d'Ockham" p. 296), as does Trifogli: "The body has extension and physical parts, and these parts are such that they can all exist at the same time. Medieval authors call a thing with this property a permanent thing. . . . The body's becoming hot also has parts (that is, phases), but these parts are such that they cannot exist simultaneously but only one after the other" ("Change, Time, and Place" p. 269). Brower-Toland sees the potential for an "ambiguity" in 'permanent' very much along the lines I am describing ("Instantaneous Change" p. 40). She describes what I am calling the synchronic sense of 'permanent' as "its technical usage," and finds it in Henry of Ghent. As for what I am calling the diachronic sense, she dismisses this as the "ordinary" non-philosophical sense of the term—unaware that it would later be put forward as the proper philosophical interpretation.

thereby marking anti-realism as the *opinio communis*. Just fifteen or so years later, however, in England, Ockham reports it as "the general view of everyone that motion adds something distinct in reality beyond the thing moved and its end-point" (*Reportatio* II.7, *Opera theol.* V:100). Yet although Ockham proceeds to argue at great length for a reductive account of motion and other successive entities, his arguments would not carry the day. Indeed, his views on motion and time appear in John Lutterell's list of suspect propositions. And although the papal commission formed in Avignon to review the list did not pursue this particular accusation against Ockham, anti-realism had clearly become a dubious position. Gregory of Rimini does defend it at great length in 1343, and a few years later John of Mirecourt offers the thesis that "every *res* is permanent" as "a supposition accepted by many, whether true or false" (*Sent.* I.2.3, p. 327). Yet this claim would subsequently figure in Mirecourt's condemnation (§19.3), and the vanguard of later fourteenth-century thought—John Buridan, Nicole Oresme, Albert of Saxony, and Marsilius of Inghen—would all defend the reality of motion as a successive entity. By the time Cajetan of Thiene was writing in Padua in 1439, the thesis that motion is a successive entity would be something "everyone holds" (*In Phys.* III.1, f. 25ra).[7]

Let us at this point distinguish three questions, and take each of them up in turn:

1. Do we have good reasons for postulating successive entities?
2. Is the very idea of a successive entity coherent?
3. Might there be more successive entities than is usually supposed?

The first question amounts to asking why we should postulate time and motion as entities over and above permanent things. This issue must be addressed, because otherwise the permanent–successive distinction goes unmotivated. Here, however, I will address it only very briefly, because these issues are so vast that they threaten to eclipse this chapter's intended focus, which is the general nature of successive entities.

One prominent scholastic motivation for rejecting a wholly reductive theory of motion was to account for a projectile's ongoing motion apart from its initial mover. (Why does a ball continue to move, even once it leaves the hand?) Many scholastic authors, such as Francis of Marchia, John Buridan, and Nicole Oresme, proposed attributing to bodies in motion an *impetus* that accounts for why they continue to move on their own. Of course, this is a place where the seventeenth century really has overturned scholastic thought: we now recognize it as a mistake to look for an explanation of constant motion, regarding constancy as the default situation. (This

---

[7] For the history of the debate over successive entities from Avicenna forward, see Maier, *Zwischen* pp. 1–186. For Averroes in particular, and his later influence, see Trifogli, *Oxford Physics* pp. 37–66. Regarding the status in ancient times of the question whether there is a successive entity involved in change, beyond permanent entities, Trifogli ("Change, Time, and Place" pp. 268–9) remarks: "Medieval commentators were much concerned with this question. Indeed, it is distinctively medieval, inasmuch as Aristotle does not even explicitly consider it; nor do Greek commentators on the *Physics*." Trifogli (ibid.) documents the extent to which the earliest Latin commentaries, in England, take a realistic view.

For Lutterell's list of suspect propositions drawn from Ockham, see Koch, "Neue Aktenstücke" n. 40, p. 377. For the condemnation of Mirecourt, see Stegmüller, "Zwei Apologien" n. 45, p. 67. As in Ockham's case, this charge against Mirecourt was dropped before the final list of condemned propositions was drawn up. Two other fourteenth-century anti-realist accounts of motion are Autrecourt, *Tractatus* ch. 5, p. 224 (see Dutton, "Nicholas of Autrecourt") and pseudo-Marsilius, *In Phys.* III.7, who responds to Buridan's and Oresme's arguments in detail. For Marsilius's realist stance, see *Abbrev. Phys.* III, not. 2 dub. 1, f. 10rv.

principle of inertia became enshrined as Newton's First Law of Motion, but developed out of the earlier work of figures like Isaac Beeckman, Galileo, Descartes, and Christiaan Huygens.) Yet this whole issue is in fact irrelevant for present purposes anyway, because the *impetus* possessed by a moving body was not generally conceived of as a successive entity. Rather than being the motion itself, the *impetus* was thought of as a permanent, intrinsic quality that is the *cause* of motion. In general, regardless of what causal story one tells about how bodies are put into motion and retain their motion, it is a separate question to determine the ontological status of the motion itself. This is our present concern.[8]

The principal reason to give motion itself some sort of irreducible ontological status is to account for absolute motion. On the standard anti-realist approach, as set out in most detail by Ockham, motion is (very roughly) just an object's having one location now and another location later, where location is understood according to the relational account described in the previous chapter. This has the consequence that there will be various scenarios that we intuitively want to count as cases of motion, but that the theory cannot account for. The Condemnation of 1277 offers one very simple such case—God's moving the whole of the heavens "in a straight line" in one direction or another (ed. Piché n. 49)—something that would be impossible if motion were understood in terms of location relative to other bodies, but that the authors of the condemnation insisted was a real possibility for God. This proposition was often cited in the context of debates over the status of motion. Buridan, for instance, describes the case where the whole universe is moved in a circle, a scenario that is impossible on a relationalist account, but to him seemed clearly possible. Oresme describes a series of similar scenarios. Suppose that the whole universe contains just one thing, and that this thing moves for an hour, then rests for an hour, then moves for an hour, and so on. Or, more cleverly, suppose that there are two bodies, *a* and *b*, and that for one hour *a* moves circularly, while *b* stays at rest, then for the next hour *b* moves circularly while *a* rests, and so on, back and forth. No relational facts among the bodies can account for the hourly variation. For a listener who finds none of these scenarios, not even the last, compelling as evidence of absolute motion, Oresme has this retort: the two-body scenario is similar to the actual state of the universe, where we can say either that the heavens revolve diurnally around the earth, or that the earth rotates diurnally and not the heavens. No observations can distinguish between the two cases, since "it cannot be experienced whether it is the earth that moves circularly or the heavens" [*In Phys.* III.7].) On a relational account, there is no way to distinguish the cases even in principle. But neither Buridan nor Oresme find it plausible to suppose there is no absolute fact of the matter. For Oresme, what these cases show is rather that the *epistemic* status of motion is doubtful: we can never be completely certain that one thing

---

[8]   There is a large literature on scholastic *impetus* theory. See, e.g., Maier, *Zwischen* chs. 6–7; Maier, "Die naturphilosophische Bedeutung" (tr. Sargent ch. 4); Maier, "Galilei" (tr. Sargent ch. 5); Moody, "Galileo and his Precursors"; Schabel, "Francis of Marchia's *Virtus derelicta.*" Although Francis of Marchia attempted to locate *impetus* in between permanent and successive entities, Buridan insisted that it must be one or the other, and that it could not be successive: "tertia conclusio est quod ille impetus est res naturae permanentis, distincta a motu locali, quo illud proiectum movetur" (*In Phys.* VIII.12, f. 121ra). On this issue, see Maier, *Zwischen* pp. 350–7.

For early statements of the principle of inertia, see Beeckman, *Journal* I.24–5 (1613–14); Descartes, *The World* ch. 7 (XI:38–9). For Galileo's complex role, see Dijksterhuis, *Mechanization* pp. 347–59. For Huygens, see Barbour, *Discovery of Dynamics* pp. 462–86.

rather than another is moving. All we can do is treat one hypothesis as more likely than another. Thus, if *a* is the whole earth, and *b* is my walking across it, "it is not truth-like (*verisimile*) that the earth moves on account of a person's walking, and indeed that is unbelievable. Instead, it is truth-like that the earth is at rest" (*In De an.* II.15, p. 239).[9]

The proponent of a relational theory of motion will simply have to deny that these scenarios are possible. It makes no sense to speak of the whole universe's moving, and in cases where the relational facts are entirely symmetrical, there can be no fact of the matter about whether it is *a* or *b* that is in motion. Of course, this is a large topic, and there are many options other than postulating motion as an irreducible entity. Newton, who had even more sophisticated arguments of the same kind as Buridan's and Oresme's, postulated absolute space. Olivi reduces local motion to a series of intrinsic modes of location (§17.5).[10] Both of these approaches might be used to yield facts about absolute motion without having to treat motion as something over and above an object's being located first here and then there.

So far, I have been focusing only on the case of local motion. Analogous arguments were crafted for time. To the claim that time is simply a measure of motion, William Crathorn responded that there could be time even if nothing is in motion. For suppose God annihilates everything, and then creates something new. The vacant interval could last a shorter or longer time, Crathorn contends, and hence there are facts about time independent of facts about motion.[11] There are also cases of 'motion' in the scholastic

---

[9] For Ockham's anti-realist theory of motion, see *Quod.* I.5, VII.6, *Summula* III, *In Phys.* III.2, *Quaest. Phys.* 8–36, and the discussions in Shapiro, *Motion, Time, and Place* pp. 24–91 and Adams, *William Ockham* II:799–827. For an overview of Buridan's view, see Biard, "Le statut du mouvement." For Oresme, see Caroti, "La position" and Kirschner, *Nicolaus Oresmes Kommentar.* For Albert of Saxony's similar views, see *In Phys.* III.6–7 and Sarnowsky, *Die Aristotelisch-Scholastische Theorie.*

[10] For Olivi on motion, see *Summa* II.27 (I:467): "motus enim per quem forma educitur non est aliud quam successiva et continua formae acquisitio et eductio; unde non est aliud quam continuum fieri ipsius formae; fieri autem formae et primum esse partium eius idem sunt secundum rem.... Tale autem fieri nihil reale addit ad ipsam formam et ad eius esse quod sit essentialiter diversum ab essentia ipsius formae aut ab eius esse." Later he acknowledges that he is, in effect, identifying successive with permanent things: "totus iste modus de identitate motus et formae et de identitate successivi et permanentis multis videtur esse impossibilis et ridiculosus" (I:481) and he characteristically offers to such readers the opposing view of motion as a successive entity, although he himself now regards the anti-realist view as "magis probabilem" (I:466). See also *Summa* II.32 (I:586–7), as well as the text edited in Maier, *Zwischen* pp. 299–319. It seems to me that Maier goes badly astray in her reading of Olivi here, regarding his view as much closer to Buridan's than to Ockham's, so that "liegen Olivis und Buridans Auffassung des motus localis durchaus auf der gleichen Linie" (ibid., p. 329). On the contrary, Olivi accepts nothing of what Buridan does in this domain: he rejects both an ontology of successive entities and any permanent entity along the lines of Buridan's *impetus* theory. Although Olivi's locational modes go beyond Ockham's even more minimalist ontology, as we saw in the previous chapter, this is in no way a step toward Buridan's position. Indeed, were Buridan to recognize Olivi's locational modes, he would no longer need to treat local motion itself as an entity, but could handle it reductively, as he does qualitative change (see *In Phys.* III.2).

[11] Regarding time, Crathorn argues: "Deus posset adnihilare omne positivum creatum et post diu, quando placet sibi, aliquid creare. Igitur inter adnihilationem omnis positivi creati iam et productionem vel creationem sequentem vel possibilem sequi posset esse duratio maior et minor, igitur tempus. Sed pro tunc nulla res moveretur; igitur non est de ratione temporis quod sit motus" (*Sent.* I.16, concl. 2). From this Crathorn concludes that time is independent of motion, but he does not further conclude that time is something real. It is instead "quid imaginativum" (ibid., concl. 6).

Similar attempts to treat time as something distinct from motion can be found in the sixteenth-century Italian naturalists. Bernardino Telesio, for instance, holds that "nihil enim a motu cum pendeat tempus, sed per se (ut dictum est) existat; quas habet conditiones, a se ipso habet omnes, a motu nullam prorsus" (*De rerum natura* I.29, p. 44).

For an extended defense of realism regarding time, see Buridan, *In Phys.* IV.12–16, although on Buridan's view time just is a certain motion—namely, the motion of the outermost heaven (see Dekker, "Buridan's Concept of Time"). Oresme treats time as "primum omnium successivorum," and, predictably, as a mode (*De configurationibus* II.2). On scholastic views more generally, see Maier, "Das Zeitproblem"; Porro, *Medieval Concept of Time*; Jeck, *Aristoteles contra Augustinum*; Imbach and Putallaz, "Olivi et le temps"; Trifogli, *Oxford Physics* ch. 4, who pays particular attention to time's status as an *ens successivum*.

sense that go beyond mere local motion. Under the heading *motus* are changes of all kinds, including growth and shrinkage, qualitative alteration, and substantial generation and corruption. (These can be thought of as changes in the categories of Quantity, Quality, and Substance, respectively.) Not everyone endorsed successive entities for all kinds of motion. Buridan, for instance, does so only in the case of local motion. Oresme, in contrast, accepts the doctrine in its full generality, as covering any sort of qualitative or quantitative change. Indeed, Oresme thinks that in cases of qualitative change— when water becomes hotter, or a surface whiter—what persists is a successive quality, inasmuch as the substance possesses over time a series of qualities, each lasting for only an instant, which is then replaced by a distinct, more or less intense quality of the same kind. (Buridan's account of accidental change in terms of forms piled on top of forms was offered precisely so as to avoid this sort of result. On Buridan's view, as discussed in §15.1, a substance becomes larger not by losing one accidental form and gaining another, but by having a new form piled on top of the existent ones, as it were, which makes the substance one degree larger or hotter or whiter. Forms remain permanent, on Buridan's account, even when undergoing change.)[12]

Once one sees the full generality of what is at issue, it becomes clear that the scholastic proponent of successive entities is making quite a broad metaphysical claim: that in addition to enduring substances and their properties, there are entities of a fundamentally different kind, which in English we would speak of as *events*. I have said nowhere near enough to make plausible the case for widening our ontology to include such things, and have said nothing at all about how they would fit into the usual scholastic frameworks. Authors disagreed about which category they should go into, or in what sense successive entities are beings at all. Oresme, for instance, counted them as modes, whereas Albert of Saxony excused himself from locating them on Aristotle's category scheme by insisting that although successive things exist, they are not entities, and so neither substances nor accidents in any category. All of this of course might be discussed at much more length, but so much will have to suffice for motivating the permanent–successive distinction.

18.3. Is the Idea of a Successive Entity Coherent?

When the status of successive entities became controversial in the fourteenth century, it was clear right away what the main argument against them would be, because it was an argument that Aristotle had made very clearly, against the reality of time:

---

[12] Buridan denies any need for a successive entity to account for qualitative change at *In Phys.* III.2. For Oresme's contrary view, see *De configurationibus* II.13. Maier, *Zwischen* pp. 177–85, contains a very helpful discussion of their disagreement, focusing in particular on Oresme's conception of accidental change in terms of a series of instantaneous forms.

Albert of Saxony denies that motion is an *ens* at *In Phys.* III.3, pp. 482–3: "non de omni termino significative accepto de quo est verificabile esse, est verificabile ens. . . . Et ita secundum ponentes motum non esse aliud a rebus permanentibus, sed esse ipsas res permanentes taliter vel taliter se habere ad invicem, non concederetur motus esse ens, quamvis bene concederetur esse, et per consequens bene concederetur esse de numero eorum quae sunt, sed non de numero entium."

A rare later example of someone who follows Ockham in rejecting *entia successiva* entirely is John Major, *Sent.* II.2.2 and *In Phys.* III.4.

Part of it has been and is not, and part of it is going to be and is not yet. Now time . . . is composed of these parts. But it might seem impossible for a whole to have any share in being, if it is composed of parts that are not. (*Phys.* IV.10, 217b33–218a3)

Aristotle goes on, in a passage partially quoted already, to insist that the now is not a part of time. Hence we get the paradoxical result that time, if it exists, would be a thing none of whose parts exist. Aristotle presents this as an initial puzzle about time, but it is a puzzle that his subsequent discussion does nothing to dispel, inasmuch as he ultimately makes time dependent on the mind (*Phys.* IV.14). Subsequent scholastic discussions of time naturally deal with this argument at great length, but it was obvious that the same argument might be thought to apply to motion as well, and indeed to anything that satisfied the synchronic conception of a successive entity. Hence Ockham argues:

If motion is a thing distinct from permanent things, it is either divisible or indivisible. It is not indivisible, according to those [who defend its reality]; therefore it is a divisible thing; therefore it is composed out of parts. Therefore it is composed either out of parts existing together at once   3 (*simul*)—and then motion will truly be wide, high, and deep, which they do not grant—or out of parts not existing together at once, which is what they grant. This cannot be said, however, because that which does not exist cannot be part of any being; for no being is composed out of   6 non-beings. Therefore motion cannot be said to be a being distinct from permanent beings on the basis of such non-beings. (*Summula* III.5)

Most of the intricacies in this argument can quickly be set aside. No one supposes that motion is indivisible (lines 1–3); no one supposes that its parts are *simul* (lines 3–4). Hence it seems one must grant that at least most of its parts, if not all of them, do not presently exist. But how can a thing exist if its parts do not? This same argument can be found in almost every scholastic discussion of this material, but there was very little agreement on how it ought to be handled.[13]

One kind of reply is purely linguistic, in that it attempts to explain how we can truly speak in the present tense of events as occurring when, strictly speaking, no event unfolds *now*.[14] But since this line of thought does not grapple with the metaphysical question of how a successive entity could exist, I set it aside to focus on replies to the metaphysical question. Three different strategies of this kind stand out. One simply grants that motion is composed of parts that do not exist, and insists that such a thing can nevertheless exist. So Burley argues in response to Ockham:

---

[13] Ockham reiterates the standard argument against successive entities at *In Phys.* III.2.6 (*Opera phil.* IV:431). Other particularly detailed versions occur in Rimini, *Sent.* II.1.4, pp. 134–5; Autrecourt, *Tractatus* ch. 5, p. 224; Suárez, *Disp. meta.* 50.9.19.

A remarkable, if brief, post-scholastic discussion of *entia successiva* can be found in Arnold Geulincx (d. 1669), whose posthumously published *Metaphysica vera* endorses the standard objection to the existence of such entities, and then goes on to suggest that this impugns the reality of everything other than God, who is the only truly permanent entity: "Plato olim collegit, motum, tempus, eaque omnia quae haec involvunt, ut mundus partesque eius, itemque nos, quatenus homines, non proprie exsistere. Nihil enim proprie exsistit, nisi quod partes suas simul habet (nam quod succcessive partes suas habet, id partim non est). Haec igitur talia quae motum successionemque involvunt, ita sunt, seu exsistunt, sicut pica alba est (nam partim alba est et partim non est alba); haec vero non est propria alba. Unde Deus seu res aeternae proprie solum simpliciterque sunt" (II.13; tr. Wilson p. 82).

[14] For a detailed and impressive instance of the linguistic reply, see Oresme, *In De an.* II.15, pp. 243–5.

This is the difference between permanent and successive things: that a permanent thing exists all at once, or at least can exist all at once, whereas it is incompatible with a successive thing to exist all at once. And so I grant that a successive being is composed out of non-beings, as is clear of a day, week, month, and year, which are composed out of non-entities. And it is certain that some part of this day is past and some part future, and yet this day is, and so it is for this year and its parts. (*In Phys.* III text 11, f. 65rb)

The first sentence of the passage was quoted earlier, as Burley's account of what a successive entity is. Now we can see that that definition is embedded in a response to the main argument against successive entities. Burley's straightforward reply is just to accept that this is what it is to be a successive entity. A generation later, Albert of Saxony takes the same approach. To the argument that "nothing exists whose parts do not exist; but the parts of a successive entity do not exist; therefore etc." Albert boldly denies the major premise:

To the second argument—"that does not exist whose parts do not exist"—it can be replied by granting that something exists whose parts do not exist. This is clear in the case of God and the [angelic] intelligences; hence there is something no part of which exists. But another reply has to   3 be given for what has parts. What should be said is that, for existence to hold of permanent entities, it is required that their parts exist. For existence to hold of completely successive entities, however, it is not required that their parts exist, but that one part succeed another, as a   6 future part succeeds a past part. (*In Phys.* III.3 ad 2)

Albert begins with a quibble (lines 1–3): that which lacks parts, like God and the angels, does not need to have its parts exist. (It is to deal with such quibblers that Ockham's above formulation carefully stresses that what are at issue are divisible entities [lines 1–3].) As for the case that matters, Albert just denies that its parts must exist. Again, the implication is that this is just what it is to be a successive entity. Of course, Ockham and other opponents of successive entities will happily accept this characterization—that is precisely why they think such things cannot exist. Does this leave us in a standoff between opposed intuitions? I think instead that, so far, it is a rout. Rimini, quite rightly, mocks Burley's response, on the grounds that once we start constructing entities out of non-entities, we might as well allow that while neither chimeras nor goat-stags exist, there is nevertheless an entity composed of them.[15] The problem is that neither Burley nor Albert has provided any way of dealing with the eminently plausible principle that if a thing exists, then at least some of its parts must exist. The best Burley can do is offer some examples where it is supposed to be obvious that successive entities—days, months, years—exist. But although Burley's listeners would have immediately recognized the allusion to Aristotle's discussion of how a day exists (*Phys.* III.6, 206a19–34), the example nonetheless does not get him very far, because although we are just as inclined to affirm facts about the calendar as we are facts about motion, it hardly follows that either set of facts requires an ontology of motions or days or years.

---

[15]   Gregory of Rimini mocks Burley as follows: "Tum quia non est intelligibile quod aliqua non-entia, nec possibilia esse entia, continuentur alicui enti aut insimul entitatem aliquam constituant. Unde posset aequaliter dici quod, licet chimaera nihil sit neque tragelaphus, continuantur tamen ad invicem mediante aliquo ente, et quod simul sumpta vel praecise ipsa aut etiam cum aliquo ente sunt una entitas constituta ex chimaera et tragelapho et entitate una. Quod nullus sapiens diceret" (*Sent.* II.1.4, p. 135).

Both Burley and Albert are willing to grant that no part of a successive entity exists. The implausibility of that stance naturally makes one wonder what else might be said. The most obvious alternative is to hold that, even if not every part of a successive entity exists, still some part of it does. This is how Walter Chatton, in his commentary on the *Sentences* (1321–3), responds to Ockham. To the standard objection that nothing exists whose parts do not exist, etc., Chatton responds by denying not the major but the minor premise:

> To the other argument I reply that, on the contrary, some part of motion does exist, because, assuming the motion is not interrupted, no instant or time can be assigned in which there is no true *passiva motio*, and this is part of that motion (*motus*). (*Reportatio* II.2.1 n. 37; see also II.2.2 n. 27)

Chatton's idea is that motion can be understood as composed out of instantaneous parts. This is, he realizes, a claim fraught with paradox, because it was widely regarded as impossible for a continuum to be composed out of dimensionless entities. (This is part of the reason that Aristotle, and those following him, denied that the now is a part of time.) Although this is an issue that he takes up at some length in a subsequent question (*Reportatio* II.2.3), I must here set aside all such paradoxes concerning the continuum. Suppose, for the sake of argument, that we can make sense of a temporal continuum composed of durationless parts. The next question, it would seem, is how there can be motion at an instant. In fact, however, Chatton is not committed to affirming this. What exists at an instant is what he calls a *passiva motio*, and although this is a part of a motion (*motus*), it does not follow that the *passiva motio* itself is a motion. Even in Latin, this looks tendentious, since *motio* and *motus* often serve as mere stylistic variants, but there is nothing incoherent in Chatton's distinction, since it is common for the parts of an F not themselves to be instances of F. (My arm is not a human being.)

I have left *passiva motio* (line 3) in Latin because there is no good English translation, but even so the concept itself is a familiar one. Chatton has in mind the state a body is in, at an instant, in virtue of which it is true that that body is undergoing change. This is something we seem to be able to account for. For if we compare at an instant two objects, one in motion and one at rest, but otherwise identical, there would seem to be something intrinsically different about them, just insofar as one is in motion and the other is not. In modern physics, this issue arises in discussions of instantaneous velocity, where we want to make some sense of the claim that, at an instant, an object has a certain velocity. Chatton's account has the potential of explaining this, whereas Ockham's view cannot, and neither can the line taken by Burley and Albert of Saxony, since on either kind of account there is nothing to ground facts about motion at an instant.

Since just one instantaneous *motio* cannot, by itself, be a motion, Chatton's theory of motion satisfies the synchronic test for being a successive entity. It is less clear that it satisfies the diachronic test, because it might seem an object in constant motion would retain the same *passiva motio* over time, which would explain its constant speed and trajectory. On such an account, the entity in question would seem to be a permanent quality rather than some sort of successive thing. This is not, however, Chatton's view: his *passiva motio* is in constant flux, inasmuch as a different *motio* is responsible for every change in position that an object undergoes.[16] Yet once we see this, it becomes clear that Chatton's account is still vulnerable to a version of the main objection to successive entities: for even if it is not the case that no part of a motion exists, still it remains the case that most of the parts of a motion do not. Indeed, as Ockham points out, on a theory of this sort there would appear to be infinitely many such instantaneous *motiones* whenever a thing undergoes motion, only one of which would exist at any moment (*Summula* III.2). How bad is this? The worry about infinity is another of the paradoxes that plague any discussion of continuous entities, and so I will again set it aside, and focus just on the complaint that motion would be a thing some of whose parts do not exist. Chatton himself formulates this objection in a very strong form, as the complaint that motion would be "composed from being and non-being" (*Reportatio* II.2.2 n. 11). This gets at the heart of what is worrisome about Chatton's conception of motion, for if we think of motion as a thing, and treat its parts as what compose it, then the inescapable result seems to be that we are imagining an entity made up partly of non-existent things, which seems flatly absurd. Chatton's response to this objection grants the absurdity: it would be contradictory for a thing to be composed of beings and non-beings. But to suppose this of motion is to treat motion as a permanent entity, having all its parts at once. Motion is composed of its parts in a different way: "There is one *motio* now, another one was and is not, and a third also is not but will be. That which we now have is, and at once will not be. In no other way is motion (*motus*) composed of beings and non-beings" (*Rep.* II.2.2 n. 31).

This reply comes close to being an instance of the strategy we saw earlier: to respond to an alleged absurdity by insisting that this is just how successive entities are. But Chatton is in a somewhat stronger position than this suggests. He is not simply embracing the absurdity, but distinguishing two ways of being composed of parts, one of which allows that some of a thing's parts do not exist. His opponent must take the very strong view that when a thing exists, all of its parts exist. Ockham in fact says this explicitly, but as we will see below, and at more length in Chapter 29, this leads to some trouble, because it is not clear how even paradigmatic permanent entities can satisfy so strong a condition. At this stage, then, I judge the discussion between Chatton and Ockham a standoff.[17]

One more approach to defending successive entities deserves mention. Although every author I have discussed so far takes for granted that what is in the past or future does not exist, one might question that assumption. To do so is of course to undermine entirely the standard Aristotelian argument we have been considering, for if past and

[16] Chatton is quite explicit that there is a distinct *motio passiva* at each instant; see *Reportatio* II.2.2 n. 68: "Si intelligas de motione passiva, illa non est eadem modo et prius." Instead of speaking of an instantaneous *motio*, scholastic authors more often distinguish between a *motus* and an instantaneous *mutatio*. See, e.g., Wlliam of Alnwick: "motio et mutatio distinguantur essentialiter et specifice.... Una via est continua et successiva, alia autem est subita et simul tota" (Maier, *Zwischen* p. 91). Crathorn is notable in following Chatton in treating this *subita mutatio* as a part of motion (*Rep.* II.16, n. 11). On instantaneous velocity, see Lange, "How Can?"

[17] Part of Chatton's case for an instantaneous *motio*—too complicated to be discussed in detail here—is the role such a state plays in explaining causation via impact. On Ockham's view, such causation looks like nothing more than constant conjunction. Chatton argues that this cannot distinguish between a true case of causation and a case where God is in fact the causal agent (*Rep.* II.2.1 n. 16), and invokes his *passiva motio* to account for that difference. Ockham replies at length (*Quod.* I.5), and in subsequent discussions adds to his analysis a counterfactual element: if the cause had not been present then, all else being equal, the effect would not have occurred (see *Quod.* VII.3).

future states exist, then the proponent of successive entities can happily maintain that every part of such entities exists. This is the line that John Wyclif takes, *circa* 1369. Turning Aristotle's argument inside-out, he reasons as follows:

It is clear from the way in which one must speak about time and other successive entities that talk about "the present" must be enlarged. For otherwise it would have to be denied that any such successive entity could exist, which is impossible according to the foregoing. The inference   3
is clear, for if we posit that hour-long motion *a* exists, it is clear that it must be a divisible successive thing, and have all its parts successively, not at the same instant. Therefore it must be that many things exist outside the present instant. For if something is successive, it is   6
successive with respect to its individual parts, which cannot exist at the same instant. Therefore it follows that many of its parts are lodged outside that instant. (*De ente praed.* 20, p. 189)   9

This neatly inverts the standard argument against successive entities, turning it into an argument for the existence of past and future entities, as follows:

1. Successive entities exist (line 4);
2. If a thing exists then all its parts exist (tacit);
3. The parts of a successive entity exist successively, "not at the same instant" (lines 4–7);
∴ 4. "Many things exist outside the present instant" (line 5).

Against Ockham and Rimini, Wyclif thinks that (1) is undeniable. Against Burley and others, Wyclif thinks (2) is unquestionable. Since (3) is just what it means for an entity to be successive, we should therefore embrace the reality of past and future objects.

Although the passage just quoted looks quite clear, one might hesitate to believe that Wyclif really means what he seems to say. The assumption that only the present exists seems so engrained in pre-modern thought that it is hard to believe anyone would question it. To be sure, among fashionable metaphysicians today, it is virtually *de rigueur* to hold that all events in time are equally real. But modern metaphysicians can appeal to Einstein's theory of general relativity, according to which facts about simultaneity are relative to spatiotemporal frames of reference. Hence it is now plausible to suppose what would otherwise seem simply fantastic: that there is no absolute now in which all things exist. Yet we can be sure that Wyclif really did think this, because he argues for the claim persistently, using just the sorts of arguments we would expect. So, he offers his own version of a frame-of-reference argument, contending that the only way to make sense of divine omniscience is to understand past and future entities to be as real as present ones. Quoting Augustine—"To God there is neither past nor future, but all things are present" (*De diversis quaest.* 17)—Wyclif remarks that "there is no doubt but that if something *is* with God, then it *truly is*" (*De ente praed.* 20, p. 192). To be sure, proponents of divine eternality did not traditionally think that the doctrine entails the reality of the past and future. But, at least on its face, Wyclif's point seems a reasonable one. For as long as we think of our temporal frame of reference and God's eternal frame of reference as at least equally valid, it is hard to see what basis there could be for giving a privileged metaphysical status to what is, for us, the present.[18]

---

[18] Wyclif returns to divine eternality at the end of *De ente praed.*, arguing that Thomas Bradwardine is likewise committed to the reality of past and future. The treatise ends on this note: "patet ergo quod si partes temporis sunt apud Deum, tunc vere sunt" (ch. 22, p. 219).

Wyclif also argues for the reality of past and future on the basis of causation, contending that "the way in which we must talk about causes, time, and many similar things necessitates our positing something to exist outside the present instant" (ibid., 19, p. 184). He goes on to offer various examples of causal relationships where cause and effect cannot be simultaneous, but yet both cause and effect must exist. The general template is this: "It is clear that if *a* causes or is the principle for *b*, then each of those exists; but it is plainly contradictory for both to be in the same instant at once" (ibid.). In general, as we saw in §2.4, scholastic authors embrace the simultaneity of a cause and its proximate effect, and so Wyclif has to make the case that at least sometimes this is not the case. He offers various examples of non-simultaneous efficient and final causes, but his leading example is one we encountered in §2.4, in discussing the endurance of prime matter. There we saw Scotus contend that, since (i) cause and effect must be simultaneous, but (ii) the generation of something new must build on the corrupted thing that furnishes the ingredients of the new thing, therefore (iii) there must be some stuff— prime matter—that endures through the process of corruption and generation, providing the raw material of the new entity. Wyclif, appealing to Aristotle's talk of the privation as a cause (*Phys.* I.7), contends that a causal story about generation must appeal not only to the newly generated form and the enduring matter, but also to the condition of the corrupted thing—that is, the fact that the matter was in such-and-such state, before becoming something new (e.g., the man was non-musical, before becoming musical [*Phys.* 190a1]). Since generation must build on that prior state, the prior state figures as a cause. But then, Wyclif reasons, if it is a cause in generation, it must exist, even if it is in the past. Hence past things exist.[19]

So far as I can find, Wyclif's important views on this subject have never before been noticed.

18.4. Might Everything Be Successive?

There was never much interest, during our period, in extending the scope of what counts as a successive entity. Discussion focused on whether there were *any* successive entities, and tended to take for granted that the principal if not only candidates were time and motion. In retrospect, however, it is natural to wonder just how broadly this class of entities might extend, once let in the door at all. As noted already, 'motion' extends to changes of all kinds, and so readily extends to cover what we now call events. From a scholastic perspective, this class of entities, even on its broadest construal, seemed clearly distinct from substances, qualities, and other accidental forms. With the rise of corpuscularianism, however, that distinction becomes less clear, because so much of what scholastics took for granted as permanent entities comes to be analyzed in terms of corpuscles in motion. If that sort of analysis bottoms out in motion, so that heat, say, becomes a kind of corpuscular motion (§21.4), then we would seem to have added a sensible quality to our list of successive entities. This

---

[19] Regarding causal relationships, Wyclif later remarks: "Omnis modus habendi, etiam alienissimus, quo vir habet uxorem, requirit habitum esse cum habente actuali; ergo causantia requirit actualem existentiam causantis, etsi ampliet quo ad causatum" (*De ente praed.* ch. 20, p. 191).

assumes we accept the reality of successive entities, but one can see how the corpuscularian project—despite its general orientation toward parsimony—might find it quite convenient, if not indispensable, to do just that. Hence Descartes does not treat motion along Ockham's lines, as simply one location after another, but treats it in the way Oresme does, as a mode (§13.5). And although Gassendi, in defense of the minimalist ontology of the ancient atomists, has no qualms in throwing out almost all of scholastic metaphysics, he holds onto successive entities (§18.1). This is not really surprising, given the centrality of motion to post-scholastic thought.

We can see a glimmer of this trend among scholastic authors, inasmuch as they often treat sound as a successive entity. If one can say this about sound in the fourteenth century, the point can easily be extended to heat in the seventeenth, and perhaps even to color today, inasmuch as we now know that an object's "reflection" of light is really a complex process of absorbing and then reemitting energy. Once one starts down this road, it is not easy to see where to stop. Descartes argues that we should regard not only motion as a "quality," but also rest (*The World* ch. 7, XI:40). This goes one step beyond scholastic authors, who postulated successive entities to account for *change*, but assumed that where there is no change, there is nothing successive.[20] The road goes farther. For once motion and rest come to rule all phenomena in natural philosophy, it is tempting to conclude that there are no phenomena independent of motion and rest, which might inspire the thought that there are no entities that are not successive.[21] This is, however, not what happened. As usual, the story of seventeenth-century philosophy is not that of a rush to the extreme reductive opposite of scholastic views. Rather, what is both interesting and typical of the era is the attempt to resist an indiscriminately reductive impulse, without simply falling back into a scholastic metaphysics.

What keeps post-scholastic thought from losing hold of permanent entities entirely is the doctrine of substance. Part VI of this study will consider some of the various disputes that arose over the unity and persistence of substances. Yet, as for the very fact of there being unified and persistent substances, here there was no dispute. This is a result that has been in place from as far back as Chapter 2, in virtue of the doctrine of prime matter. Prime matter is, most fundamentally, a manifestation of the substratum thesis (§2.2): that there is some sort of enduring stuff beneath all change. To endorse that thesis, as virtually everyone during our period does, just is to accept an ontology grounded in enduring substances. How to conceive of those substances—how they are individuated, whether they are thick or thin in terms of their properties, how they relate to the ordinary substances of common sense—these are further, highly contentious questions. But inasmuch as everyone during our period endorses some kind of

---

[20] Contrary to Descartes's later claim that both motion and rest are qualities (or modes), Oresme, *De configurationibus* II.12, p. 300, insists quite explicitly that where there is no change, there is no successive entity.

[21] Scheibler argues that time and motion are the only genera of successive entities (*Metaphysica* I.19.4.1 n. 26). Sound is included as a successive entity by both Oresme (*In Phys.* III.6; *In De an.* II.19, p. 287) and Albert of Saxony (*In Phys.* III.3 concl. 6). Suárez argues for sound as a successive entity at *In De an.* 7.6.2. This need not be a counterexample to the claim that time and motion are the only kinds of successive entities, because one might say that sound just is a kind of motion. But Neither Oresme nor Albert takes that approach; instead, each speaks of sound as a quality that "consequitur motum." For more information on sound, see §21.3. For the general issue of whether sensible qualities reduce to primary qualities or anything else, see Ch. 22. On scholastic theories of sound more generally, see Pasnau, "Sensible Qualities." On color as event-like, see Pasnau, "The Event of Color."

substratum enduring through change, no one can suppose that all entities are successive. Prime matter is the ultimate, uncontroversial *ens permanens*.

Even so, and before engaging in some of the famous and not so famous controversies over the nature of substance, it is interesting to consider in a general way the possibility that all entities might be successive. The most straightforward road to this conclusion would be to show that there is something incoherent in the notion of a permanent entity. As a first try at this result, consider the permanent--successive distinction in synchronic terms, so that a permanent entity is one capable of existing at an instant. There are no sounds at an instant, just as there are no motions, and hence, so the argument goes, sounds are successive entities. Might there, along the same lines, be no living things at an instant? If to be alive is to carry out the distinctive operations of life—nutritive, locomotive, sensory, and intellectual—then one might argue that no living thing exists at an instant either, since all of these operations at least arguably require time. This is not an argument I have actually found, presumably because, for an Aristotelian, there is a clear reply. Instead of defining living things in terms of occurrent operations, a definition needs to be couched in terms of the powers to perform those operations, thus making the characteristically Aristotelian shift from second actuality to first (see, e.g., *De an.* II.5). A human being, then, need not actually be doing anything, but needs to have the power to do various things. This is a familiar Aristotelian strategy, but it is also a move one finds in the seventeenth century, most famously in Boyle and Locke, when they describe various sorts of qualities as powers within objects. If such powers are something over and above the familiar kinetic–geometric story about particles in motion, then this gives us a way to flesh out our picture of what permanent entities are. Now, in fact, I do not think that this is the Boyle–Locke picture; I will be arguing in Chapter 23 for a reductive understanding of their talk of powers. But if powers have no more reality, for the strict corpuscularian, than they suppose substantial and accidental forms do, then the threat looms that prime matter, whatever that be, will be the only permanent entity to survive the great post-scholastic purge, and that ordinary substances—dogs and cats and stones—will be no more than a mélange of *entia successiva*, running through time on the back of some obscure underlying substratum.

When permanent entities are understood diachronically, as things that endure from instant to instant, different sorts of issues arise. Most basically, the question arises of whether anything actually does endure in this way, and how we might come to know it. Suppose, as the synchronic view would have it, that it is possible for there to be a substance that exists for just an instant and then goes out of existence. If this is possible, then it would also seem possible to construct a successive substance, composed out a series of instantaneous substances. Indeed, if the series were made congruent enough, so that each successive item closely resembled the previous one, then such an entity might be indistinguishable from a permanent substance. Given that possibility, the question naturally arises of how we know that ordinary substances are permanent, rather than successive. One might suppose that this is a natural question only for a modern reader, but in fact these issues are quite at home in the scholastic context, and were explicitly discussed. Albert of Saxony, for instance, in setting out his diachronic account of what it is to be a successive entity, finds it simplest to illustrate by describing a substance that would be like that:

> The second distinction is that something can be conceived of as successive *simpliciter*, both with respect to its substance and with respect to its state. An example of this would be if Socrates were continually made and made again by the First Cause, corresponding to the way in which the Seine continuously flows and flows, so that nothing of the preexisting [river] remains. (*In Phys.* III.3, pp. 483–4)

If God had chosen to create Socrates over and over again, moment after moment, rather than to create him once and then conserve him until his death, then Socrates would be a successive entity—just like time and motion are in fact thought to be. Both Albert and Nicole Oresme (whose discussion is most likely the inspiration for Albert's) explicitly hold that this scenario is possible. Here is Oresme:

> Fourth conclusion: it does not imply a contradiction nor is it strictly impossible for there to be a substance that is successive *simpliciter*. For instance, if *a*, which is twice *b*, is successively diminished, there is no contradiction in God's creating one substance—even a human   3
> being—that will endure for just as long as *a* will be twice *b*, that is for a single instant, and so too when *a* will be one-and-a-half times *b*, and so on for every other proportion. Therefore such an aggregate from all these would be a human being, a successive substance, of which nothing   6
> that existed in a given part of time existed in a subsequent part. (*In Phys.* III.6)

The passage is illuminating in various ways. First, Oresme makes it clear that such a successive entity would be an "aggregate" of instantaneous substances (line 6). Second, he explicitly says that the instant-substance would indeed be a substance, and even a human being (lines 3–4). (On the synchronic view, this would disqualify the aggregate from being a successive entity, but that of course is not how Oresme understands the distinction.) Third, he also explicitly says that the resulting successive entity would also be a substance, a human being (line 6). Since he uses the grammatical singular to make this point, he evidently does not think that it would be a series of different human beings, as one might suppose. Instead, it would be a single human being. Fourth, the main thrust of the passage is to show that such a successive substance is possible.

   To be sure, Oresme shows no signs of being even tempted to suppose that human beings are like this. As we saw in §18.2, Oresme does think that when an accident undergoes gradual change, it become a successive rather than a permanent entity, inasmuch as the persistent accident is a series of instantaneous forms. But stable accidents are permanent, on his view, and so are substances. Albert of Saxony is perhaps more willing to take seriously at least the possibility of a fully successive ontology, even at the level of substance:

> Let this be the first conclusion: it does not imply a contradiction for there to be a substance that is successive *simpliciter*. ... This is clear, because it does not imply a contradiction—indeed, perhaps it is the case—that we continuously exist and are produced by the First Cause in just the   3
> way that light is produced by a luminous body, so that just as light or a visible species of color is continuously one and then another [at a given place] ..., so Socrates is continuously one and then another human being, in such a way that, on this conclusion, just as a human being   6
> depends on the First Cause for its conservation [at every moment], so too [at every moment] for its being made. Nonetheless I hold, as it is the general custom to hold, that although every being

that is not the First Cause is conserved by it, nevertheless it is not continuously made by it, but   9
rather, after it has once been made, it is thereafter conserved in its existence. (*In Phys.* III.3,
p. 484)

Albert begins with Oresme's conclusion, that a successive substance, even a successive human being, is possible. But he then goes on, seemingly, to recognize that, for all we know, we are successive substances (lines 2–3). That is, he seems to go from the metaphysical possibility to the epistemic possibility. This is quite a startling notion, because if one were to hold that substances are successive entities, then—since all the other categories of being depend for their existence on the substance they inhere in—it would follow that everything (other than God) is a successive entity. Now Albert does immediately go on to argue as his second conclusion, in a subsequent passage (ibid.), that no substance is successive in this way. But the argument there is obviously feeble,[22] and so it is tempting to think that his actual grounds for rejecting successive substances are what he says in the passage just quoted, that he wishes to adhere to "general custom" (line 8). This is, at any rate, as close as I have found anyone in our period come to taking seriously the idea that there are no permanent entities.[23]

Albert's discussion makes clear just why it is natural for authors during our period to contemplate the possibility of an entirely successive created world: that the doctrine of divine conservation makes this possibility readily conceivable. According to that doctrine, God not only creates all things but also conserves all things, at every instant of their existence, in such a way that if God's conserving activity were to stop, then everything would cease to exist. Hence, as was commonly agreed, God's conservation amounts to more than just his choosing not to annihilate; rather, annihilation is in a sense the default option, and for that not to happen God must act, which of course he does. It is a common saying, during our four centuries, that conservation is simply continuous creation. What exactly this amounts to is a difficult question, which goes beyond the scope of this chapter, but one thing at least that is clear is that the doctrine of conservation is supposed to be consistent with the numerical identity of substances through time. God creates at every instant, but somehow recreates the very same thing over and over. The great question, of course,

---

[22] It runs as follows: "Sit secunda conclusio quod nulla substantia est simpliciter successiva. Probatur, nam omnis substantia vel est perpetua vel aliquando incepit esse. Si dicatur primum, tunc non est simpliciter successiva. Si dicatur secundum, tunc ipsa incepit esse per generationem, et per consequens fuit terminus generationis, et per consequens, si esset simpliciter successiva post illam generationem qua incepit, adhuc continue fieret et generaretur, et sic postquam fuit generatum, adhuc generaretur, et sic non fuisset terminus generationis completus; quod est falsum" (*In Phys.* III.3, pp. 484–5).

[23] Cross reaches the remarkable conclusion that Bonaventure's theory of divine conservation commits him to treating substances in general as successive entities. Putting the discussion into modern terms, Cross remarks that "Bonaventure's four-dimensionalism is probably unique in the middle ages" ("Four-Dimensionalism" p. 414). Cross's inspiration is a critical discussion in Henry of Ghent, which does seem to be aimed at Bonaventure, and which expressly does attack the view that all created substances are a series of instantaneous substances, created for an instant by God and then succeeded by a newly created substance (*Quod.* V.11). But although Bonaventure brings this sort of criticism on himself, by comparing God's conservation of the angels to water from a fountain or rays from a sun (*Sent.* II.2.1.1.3c), he goes on to make it clear that an angel retains its existence through time: "etsi esse totum habeat, tamen continuationem esse non habeat totam simul, et ideo est ibi successio *sine aliqua innovatione circa esse vel proprietatem absolutam.*" Indeed, Ghent signals his awareness that this is the intended view of the "aliqui" he criticizes, remarking "aliquorum intentio" is founded on the view "quod res in sua essentia et in esse suo substantiali et essentiali manet una et eadem" (ed. 1518, I:169rG). But still Ghent presses his attack, because he thinks Bonaventure's view entails the result, intended or not, that no creatures are permanent.

is whether even God could preserve numerical identity by this method. It can be tempting to suppose that one or another account of conservation during our period amounts to treating ordinary substances as successive entities. I can see no good basis for thinking that anyone during our period intends this result. But what we see in both Oresme and Albert is that reflection on the doctrine of conservation raises the specter that God *could* create distinct but congruous instantaneous substances. The doctrine of successive entities might then be invoked to explain the sense in which this series of discrete substances is also a single substance.[24]

It is only on the diachronic account, however, that such a series counts as a successive entity. Scheibler considers as an objection to the permanent–successive distinction the argument that "every *res* is conserved by God; but conservation is nothing other than continuous generation" and therefore there are no permanent entities in creation. He responds by invoking his synchronic account: that even when conservation is so understood, still at each moment what is created is a complete human being, and so a permanent entity.[25] This illustrates the divergent sorts of results that one gets from these two different accounts of the permanent–successive distinction.

18.5. Permanence and Eternity

Suppose we set aside the difficulties of the previous section, and agree that substances endure through time, numerically the same. Do we then have permanent entities? This satisfies the diachronic approach, as I have described it. But one might yet have qualms. After all, identity through time was invoked to account for permanent entities because that looks like a way to get the result that such things exist all at once, *tota simul.* But does mere diachronic identity really get that result? There was agreement that the notion of a permanent entity applies preeminently to God, who exists *tota simul* in the

---

[24] For a comprehensive look at scholastic theories of conservation, see Suárez, *Disp. meta.* 21. For recent discussions of Descartes's views in this domain, see Gorham, "Cartesian Causation" and Schmaltz, *Descartes on Causation* pp. 71–84.

The striking remarks of Meditation III might encourage the thought that Descartes treats even human beings as successive entities: "omne tempus vitae in partes innumeras dividi potest, quarum singulae a relinquis nullo modo dependent, ex eo quod paulo ante fuerim, non sequitur me nunc debere esse, nisi aliqua causa me quasi rursus creet ad hoc momentum, hoc est me conservet" (VII:48–9). Descartes is quite clear here both that a thing's life (*tempus vitae*) is composed of distinct parts, and that divine conservation causes the very same I to exist over time. Could that I be an *ens successivum*? Gorham has indeed recently made such a claim ("Descartes on Persistence"). This result does seem to follow if we suppose that the distinct parts of a thing's life are what constitute the thing. If, instead, we could ascribe to Descartes a distinction between essence and existence, then we could say that what has temporal parts is the event that is a life or an existence. This is a successive entity. The thing itself—the substance that is I—is a permanent entity that wholly exists at each moment it exists. (See the following section for more on the essence–existence distinction.) It seems on its face unlikely that this will work since, as Gorham stresses, Descartes explicitly insists that the essence–existence distinction is merely one of reason: "quia substantia quaevis, si cesset durare, cessat etiam esse, ratione tantum a duratione sua distinguitur" (*Principles* I.62; see also *Oeuvres* IV:350 and V:164). Schmaltz, however, has recently suggested that Descartes does have a distinction here: that although duration as an attribute of substance is distinct only by reason from the substance, there are also modes of duration, modally distinct from the substance, and that these are the innumerably divisible parts of life described at VII:48–9 (*Descartes on Causation* pp. 80–1).

[25] See *Metaphysica* I.16.8.2 nn. 98–9: "Sic igitur et homo, quia in quovis momento est homo, et in nullo momento quicquam ei deest quod pertineat ad essentialem eius integritatem, hinc ergo is—non obstante conservatione divina a Deo per continuatam generationem dependentia—absolute est ens permanens et non successivum."

fullest sense. What this amounts to is that God is not only unchanging but even unaffected by time, inasmuch as God wholly exists at every instant that he exists. In other words, God lacks temporal parts. Creatures, however, are evidently not like that: the very point of the Boethian doctrine of eternality is to draw a distinction between God's permanence and our successiveness. This, as noted at the start of the chapter, would seem to pose a quandary for scholastic authors. For it would seem they either have to admit that only God is a permanent entity, and that all creatures, strictly speaking, are successive, or they have to find a way of saying that creatures themselves, somehow, share something of divine eternality, and hence count as permanent in their own right.

Scholastic authors want to say neither of these things, and their way out is quite interesting. They insist that finite substances are genuinely permanent by distinguishing between different aspects of a thing, some of which are permanent whereas others are successive. Oresme begins to make this point by distinguishing two senses in which a thing counts as successive:

'Successive' is used in two ways: in one way non-absolutely (*secundum quid*) and categorema- tically, when a thing does not endure as a whole, but yet something of it always endures (*permanens*). For instance, that to which continuous addition is made in each instant is, as a   3 whole, one thing and then another. In a second way, 'successive' is used absolutely (*simpliciter*) and syncategorematically, for what neither with respect to itself nor with respect to some of it endures through any time. This is how we conceive of motion and time. (*In Phys.* III.6,   6 dist. 2)

Understood *simpliciter*, a successive entity does not in any respect endure. This is what, earlier, we saw him claim to be *possible* for substances. In the weaker, *secundum quid* sense, however, substances usually *are* successive entities, inasmuch as they are con- stantly gaining and losing substantial parts. Albert of Saxony takes up just this same distinction, and notes that living things are always successive in the *secundum quid* sense. As for an entity that would be permanent in the strongest sense, excluding even partial change, Albert remarks (as noted earlier) that "perhaps nothing is permanent, except the First Cause" (*In Phys.* III.3, p. 483).

These distinctions point toward a solution to the above quandary. For even if created substances are not wholly permanent, in the way that God is, it will be the case that at least "something of it always endures" (line 2). The idea is that any permanent entity, even if it undergoes considerable change, will always have an enduring core that satisfies the diachronic requirement. What is this core? It is the substance's essence. As Oresme says elsewhere, "some things are so successive that they cannot endure in any way, like time and motion; other things are permanent in such a way that although they have existence or endurance temporally, divisibly, and successively, nevertheless *their essence* remains the same for that whole time" (*De configurationibus* II.13, p. 298). Here again, then, as in earlier chapters (esp. §8.2, §13.7), the substance–accident distinction plays a crucial role in accounting for the endurance of substances through time, allowing us to say that the thing itself, essentially, exists as a whole at every moment that it exists. If substances were simply bundles of ever-changing properties, they would be wholly successive entities.

To make sense of material substances as genuinely permanent entities requires more, however, than just the substance–accident distinction. For beyond change at the level of accidents, material substances change their integral parts. The tree gains and loses leaves, the cat grows and expels waste, and even the stone suffers erosion. The substance–accident distinction helps not at all with change of this sort, because the integral parts of a body fall not onto the accident side of that exhaustive distinction, but onto the substance side (§26.1). This means that, on the most straightforward account of substances and their parts, material substances are not genuinely permanent entities with all of their parts *tota simul*. They may last for more than an instant, but are unlikely to last the day. This is a result that many authors in the nominalist tradition were prepared to tolerate, as we will see in Chapter 29. There was, however, a very extensive later scholastic discussion over whether something else might be said. If the parts of things are in some sense not actual (§26.3), then this so-called change of parts may not have such dire implications for permanence. Similarly, if the whole is something over and above the aggregate of its parts (§28.5), then the whole may remain *tota simul* even while its parts change. These are issues that will have wait until Part VI.

There is, however, still more. To make sense of the idea that created substances are genuinely permanent, it is not enough to seclude their accidents and integral parts. That might seem to be enough to get us to the sort of unchanging, essential core that Oresme describes above, but it is not quite. What Oresme says is that "although they have *existence or endurance* temporally, divisibly, and successively, nevertheless *their essence* remains the same for that whole time" (as above). This contrast is not between essence and accidents, but between essence and existence. What Oresme is invoking, in other words, is the hoary distinction—found in Boethius and Avicenna, and later, most famously, in Aquinas—between being and essence. On this sort of picture, a substance itself may be permanent, even while the event that is its existence unfolds progressively through time in the way that all successive things do. This is, indeed, the heart of the difference between the permanence of creatures and the eternality of God: although both exist as a whole through time, it is only in God's case that essence and being can be identified, with the result that even God's mode of existing is *tota simul*, all at once, without temporal succession. Such existence is what Boethius called *eternality*.

The fascinating consequence of this idea is that creatures, with respect to their essential natures, are permanent entities in the fullest sense. They are of course not eternal—they lack the illimitability of God—but with respect to their essences they have precisely the sort of all-at-once, *tota simul* nature that God has, existing wholly at every instant they exist, rather than being stretched out in temporal parts across time. Reflection on the nature of permanent entities thus reveals that the very most obscure of the traditional divine attributes, eternality, is in fact just the most perfect example of an entirely familiar phenomenon.

Perhaps even more interesting is the way in which the famous Thomistic distinction between being and essence might be deployed to block the idea that all beings are successive entities. By embracing this distinction, one can account for the intuition that in some sense (with respect to its essence) a created substance does wholly exist at each moment of time, whereas in another sense (with respect to its existence) it persists only through part-like segments. I will have more to say about the essence–existence distinction in §26.5. For now, though, we will have to content ourselves with this faint glimmer of the glories that might await the committed neo-Thomist.[26]

---

[26] For a general overview of the essence–existence distinction, see Wippel, "Essence and Existence." I discuss the relationship between permanence and eternity in more detail in "On Existing All at Once." That paper also considers in more detail the textual basis for a distinction between being and essence as crucial to understanding the sense in which creatures do and do not persist through time.

Boethius's famous invocation of divine eternity in *Consolation of Philosophy* V prose 6 implicitly distinguishes between the thing and its existence or "life," remarking that "nihilque est in tempore constitutum quod totum vitae suae spatium pariter possit amplecti." Boethius more explicitly distinguishes between being and essence in the axioms of his *De hebdomadibus* (*Theol. Tractates* pp. 40–2).

PART V

QUALITY

19

Real Qualities

19.1. The Significance of Qualities

The most important issue dividing the scholastics from their seventeenth-century critics is the status of qualities. No question so thoroughly shaped the changing character of philosophical thought. Although other topics—like prime matter and substantial form—were in a sense more fundamental, the debate over qualities was the door through which seventeenth-century thought passed from its criticisms of scholastic natural philosophy into wholly novel terrain in epistemology and the philosophy of mind. Indeed, it is the conviction that the scholastics were wrong about quality, more than anything else, that fueled the wholesale rejection of Aristotelianism. For it seemed clear to many that, if qualities had to go, the whole scholastic framework must be flawed. This is how central the topic was to our four centuries.

Belief or disbelief in real qualities can practically serve to define the scholastic–post-scholastic divide, inasmuch as virtually every scholastic author endorsed the doctrine, and all of the canonical seventeenth-century figures rejected it. Subsequent chapters will consider the various kinds of qualities, and their interrelationships. Here I will describe the overall trajectory of the debate, beginning with the standard scholastic rationale in favor of qualities, then a brief fourteenth-century rebellion against the doctrine, and finally the emergence of a sustained opposition, which would happen only in the seventeenth century. The final section of the chapter will attempt to identify the root philosophical disagreement, which I believe lies in disagreements over the conceivability of various kinds of reductive explanations.

Building on the conclusions of earlier chapters, we can quickly and precisely define what it means to believe in real qualities: it means to think that there are real accidents (Ch. 10) in the category of Quality (Ch. 12). Unpacking this a bit, to believe in real qualities is to believe that there are fundamental qualitative features of reality, qualitative in the sense that they are neither relational nor quantitative (or, to use a later term, geometrical), nor are they understood in terms of either motions or events of any kind (they are permanent, not successive entities [Ch. 18]), or spatial or temporal location (Ch. 17). This thinly veiled survey of the main Aristotelian categories amounts to little more than the claim that qualities are those entities that are not in any other category, which is of course less than ideally helpful. It is not clear, however, that there is any more adequate characterization available. Among quality skeptics, this difficulty was naturally seen as a liability. Robert Boyle, for instance, ridicules Aristotle for the claim that "quality is that by which a thing is said to be *qualis*" (*Origin of Forms and Qualities* [*Works* V:315; Stewart p. 29]), quoting the first sentence of *Cat.* 8). Likewise, Kenelm Digby remarks of recent scholastic discussions of quality, "I confess ingenuously, I understand not what they mean by them, and I am confident that neither do they" (*Two Treatises* I.6.1). But since almost everyone during our four centuries wants to talk about qualities in some sense or another, this is a difficulty that everyone must confront. Indeed, as we will see (§19.7, §23.6), various seventeenth-century departures from a strict corpuscularian framework, such as Newtonian forces, were met with the charge of being simply real qualities under a different name. Because it is unclear what counts as a quality, this charge is difficult to evaluate.

The issues become clearer if we shift from the general to the specific, inasmuch as qualities come in many, often familiar kinds. The most basic division is between the elemental (Hot, Cold, Wet, Dry), the sensible (heat, color, sound, taste, odor), and the occult (magnetism, medicinal properties). Since this list includes both the primary causal agents in the natural world (Ch. 21), and the immediate objects of sensation (Ch. 22), their status is of paramount importance to both natural philosophy and epistemology. And inasmuch as one common post-scholastic approach to the sensible qualities is to locate them within the perceiver, their status becomes central to the philosophy of mind as well. These ramifications are so wide and profound, indeed, that it would scarcely be possible to make sense of scholastic philosophy without its commitment to qualities, and scarcely possible to imagine a post-scholastic philosophy that retained qualities in the scholastic sense.[1]

19.2. Quality Realism: Ockham

The profligate ontology of the scholastics had no greater critic than William Ockham. Yet Ockham, though he rejects accidents in every other category, retains qualities. Who better, then, to serve as spokesman for quality realism?

If Ockham feels any temptation to subject qualities to the razor, it never shows; on the contrary, he mounts a vigorous defense of their reality, and holds out their unimpeachable ontological credentials as a standard that alleged entities in the other accidental categories inevitably fail to meet. His principal argument on behalf of quality realism is just what one would expect, in light of what we have seen of his views in previous chapters. He argues that the predicates in a language are ontologically committing if and only if their truth value cannot be explained in terms of the spatial position of a substance and its integral parts. Here is a typical version of that argument:

---

[1] For a detailed discussion of how to define 'quality,' see Scheibler, *Metaphys.* II.8.2 (pp. 738–41).

For the idea that the primary–secondary distinction is what gives rise to the mind–body problem in the seventeenth century, see King, "Why Isn't the Mind–Body Problem Medieval?" p. 204.

There is shockingly little literature on the status of qualities in scholastic thought—much less, for instance, than there is on the relatively peripheral topic of relations. The most useful general discussion I know of remains Maier, "Die Mechanisierung," originally published in 1938 (!), which shares my view that the rejection of qualities lies at the heart of the seventeenth-century rejection of scholasticism.

In order to know when a quality should and should not be viewed as a thing distinct from a substance, it is appropriate to use the following test. When several predicates (*praedicabilia*) that cannot be truly ascribed to the same thing at once can be truly ascribed to the same thing in   3 turn, on account of local motion alone, then it need not be the case that those predicates signify distinct *res*. Now predicates such as 'curved' and 'straight' can be truly ascribed of the same thing, in turn, on account of local motion alone. For when something is straight, if later,   6 without any other *res* being introduced, its parts are brought closer together through local motion, so that they are less distant than before, then it is said to be curved. For this reason, curvature and straightness do not imply *res* other than the *res* that are straight and curved. The   9 same is true for shape, since through the local motion alone of some of the parts something can be made to have distinct shapes. And so it is for rare and dense and the like.

But this is not so for whiteness and blackness, heat and cold, and the like. For something is   12 not made hot or cold through this alone that the thing or its parts are moved locally. Hence all such qualities imply *res* distinct from the substance. (*Summa logicae* I.55, *Opera phil.* I:180–1)   14

The strategy Ockham deploys here is the same that he deployed against quantity realism (§14.3). There, he had argued that alleged entities in the category of Quantity can be explained in terms of corpuscular location. Quantitative change would therefore be explained in terms of local motion. Here (lines 5–11) he argues against the reality of straightness, curvature, and shape on the same grounds. (These examples arise in the context of Quality because Aristotle had treated shape as the fourth species of Quality [*Cat.* 10a11–15]. Since Ockham thinks that the categories in general divide up language rather than reality [§12.2], he is perfectly content with the result that some of the terms gathered under Quality fail to refer to anything beyond substances so-and-so arranged. Even many category realists were inclined to think that, from a strict ontological point of view, this fourth species of Quality in fact describes quantities.) Yet even if some terms from the category of Quality refer only to substances arranged in one way or another, there are other terms that refer to real and irreducible entities of another kind, *qualities*. Ockham's examples are whiteness, blackness, heat, and cold (line 12). In these cases the local motion of a thing's parts cannot account for a substance's having these qualities. Hence such qualities are *res*—that is, real accidents—distinct from and irreducible to substance (lines 13–14).[2]

Ockham's test, as it stands, is not very rigorously formulated. There are many cases where we can truly ascribe a predicate and then truly ascribe a contradictory predicate, without the subject's undergoing any local motion or change to a real accident. Here is an example: *now* I am 39 years old, and *now* I am 40. In fact Ockham himself sometimes blocks this particular sort of counterexample, by adding the further qualification that the passage of time not explain the change in truth value. But even once we make an exception for change in both spatial and temporal location, there are still obvious counterexamples of other kinds. Here is one: *now* I am not an uncle; *now* I am. Time is passing in this case, but what explains the change in truth value is not the passing of time, but the birth of my niece. Later in the fourteenth century, John Buridan recognized Ockham's vulnerability to this and other sorts of counterexamples. Buridan

---

[2] For other versions of Ockham's test for ontological commitment, see *Quod.* VII.2 (*Opera theol.* IX:707); *Rep.* III.7 (*Opera theol.* VI:197–8); *In Phys.* I.15.8 (*Opera phil.* IV:160–1); *Ord.* I.30.4 (*Opera theol.* IV:369): "Unde pro omnibus istis est una ratio solum quae est ista: impossibile est contradictoria successive verificari de eodem nisi propter motum localem alicuius, vel propter transitionem temporis, vel propter productionem vel destructionem alicuius."

accepts that something like Ockham's test is correct, but he sees that there will be a whole class of counterexamples unless it is modified. So, in addition to changes to a subject that consist purely in local motion, and changes to a subject that involve the addition or subtraction of a real accident, Buridan describes changes that do not involve any real change to the subject itself, but that are wholly extrinsic to that subject. As examples of predicates that work in this way, Buridan offers *being a father, being wealthy, being nearby,* and *being on the left.* According to Buridan, we can be confident that some change to a subject involves change to a real accident within that subject only once we rule out both local motion and these sorts of extrinsic changes.[3]

Buridan's friendly amendment to Ockham's test is obvious enough. Presumably, Ockham himself does not mention it because he took the discussion to be implicitly restricted to cases of intrinsic change. Hence Ockham regards even the mention of time as not strictly necessary for his purposes, and in one passage where he does mention it he describes it as a response to a "quibble that could be made" (*In Phys.* I.15.8, *Opera phil.* IV:161). The passage of time, like becoming an uncle and other so-called extrinsic denominations, implies nothing at all in the thing itself, but only a change in other things. Thus Ockham, impatient to get to the heart of the matter and set aside technical quibbles, focuses on the case that matters: local motion. As we have seen (§17.4), location for Ockham is an intrinsic feature of substances and their integral parts, and local motion is nothing other than a thing's having one location and then another. But although location, and so local motion, are very much real features of things, they are not features that are ontologically committing. This is what makes possible his austere nominalist project, where the critical question is always whether a certain putative entity can be understood reductively in terms of a substance and its parts, positioned in a certain way. Motion, time, and quantity can be so understood, as can shapes. Sensible qualities such as color, however, and elemental qualities such as heat cannot be so reduced. In these cases, no corpuscular treatment is possible.

Both Ockham and Buridan are persuaded that a wide range of such qualities cannot be understood in corpuscularian terms. Buridan, for instance, after presenting his more careful version of Ockham's test, accepts that heating and cooling are changes that require something intrinsic's being added or lost: "this is how it is when water is first hot and later cold" (*In De an.* III.11). In effect, these are claims of the sort that we saw

---

[3] Buridan offers his much more rigorous formulation of Ockham's test at *In De an.* III.11: "Nam res *uno modo* potest aliter et aliter se habere prius et posterius ad aliquod extrinsecum, sine aliqua sui mutatione, per mutationem illius extrinseci. Sic enim columna prius mihi dextra sit posterius mihi sinistra. *Secundo modo* aliqua res dicitur aliter et aliter se habere per hoc quod partes eius quantitativae mutant situm ad invicem per motum localem earum, sic enim eadem magnitudo fit aliter et aliter figurata. Et hoc est aliter et aliter se habere ex alietate partium ad invicem, et ex motu earum partum per quem fiunt aliter figuratae, qui est etiam alius ab illis partibus et a totali magnitudine. Sed si res *tertio modo* dicatur aliter et aliter se habere prius et posterius (scilicet circumscriptis exterioribus et quod eius partes non mutent situm ad invicem), tunc alietas designata per 'aliter et aliter se habere' non potest salvari, nisi per generationem vel corruptionem alicuius dispositionis sibi inharentis et distinctae ab ea. Sic enim est de aqua, si prius est calida et post frigida; et de materia, si prius est sub forma aquae et post sub forma ignis; et de intellectu, si prius fuit sic opinans et post contrarie: nam homine dormiente, et omni repraesentatione sibi per sensum circumscripta, adhuc aliter haberet se posterius quam haberet se prius, quod non potest salvari nisi per alietatem illarum opinionum ab invicem et ab intellectu." See the similar passage at *In Phys.* II.3 (f. 31rab).

Ockham's test for ontological commitment, often in its more precise Buridanian form, can be found again and again in later authors associated with nominalism, such as Albert of Saxony (e.g., *Quaest. in artem vet.* par. 635) and André Dabillon (e.g. *Physique* I.1.3, pp. 31–2).

Scotus urge in defense of real accidents: that various accidental entities are real, because those entities have an impact on the world that cannot be explained in any other terms (§10.5). Today it is scarcely necessary to observe just how dubious a thesis this is in the case of qualities such as heat and color. We are so used to the idea that heat is just molecular motion, for instance, that it can be hard to understand how anyone could think otherwise. Moreover, there are plenty of perfectly obvious cases where local motion at least leads to qualitative change. Motion can make a thing warmer, for instance, or accentuate its smell, or change its color. (Such facts were surely clear enough well before Locke's example of the pounded almond that ceases to be clear white [*Essay* II.8.20]; indeed, Lucretius had already offered very similar examples of this phenomenon [*De rerum natura* II.749–833].) Even so, both Ockham and Buridan, along with almost all of their contemporaries, seem so convinced of their anti-reductionist claim that neither thinks it necessary to provide any sort of argument.

Instead of arguments, we get bare assertions. Ockham, for instance, insists that God could conserve an extended material substance without its parts undergoing local motion, while destroying every real accident within it, including color, heat, smell, flavor, weight, and a wide range of other dispositions and capacities (*Quod.* IV.22). So, an apple might remain just as it is, with respect to each of its material parts, down to the very finest corpuscular details of its microstructure, and yet might suddenly change its color or lose its color entirely. (Evidently, this would involve its becoming transparent. How could the apple lose its temperature entirely? Presumably, the idea is that it would be neither hot nor cold, but lukewarm. Cold, for the scholastics, is a quality in its own right, not a mere privation, which implies that there can in principle be a neutral state, analogous to transparency, that is neither hot nor cold.) Such loss of qualities would, to be sure, be an unnatural and hence miraculous event. But Ockham thinks it would not be impossible, because color and other qualities are not the product of the thing's corpuscular structure. In contrast, Ockham insists that God could not leave that apple just as it is, in terms of its corpuscular structure, and change the *shape* of the apple. The impossibility of that is what shows there is no real distinction between a substance and its quantity.

The almost universal embrace of quality realism, in Ockham and others, combined with the lack of strong arguments in its favor, even in Ockham, is a striking fact that calls for some explanation. One possibility is that the scholastics were forced to hold onto qualities for theological reasons—largely, in order to save the doctrine of transubstantiation. On this way of explaining the sacrament of the Eucharist, the look and taste of the bread and wine endure without the bread and wine itself, as accidents without a substance to inhere in (§10.3). It was a matter for debate whether this story requires real accidents in the category of Quantity, but it certainly seemed to require real accidents in the category of Quality—it requires, that is, that the sensible qualities of the bread and wine be really distinct from the bread and wine. Hence this may look to be one of those cases where even the most freethinking of scholastic philosophers, such as Ockham, are forced by their religion to take philosophical positions contrary to their better philosophical judgment. The following chapter will consider the difficult question of whether it is ever legitimate to read between the lines of scholastic texts in this way. In the present case, though, I believe we do not need to engage these issues, because Ockham in fact believes that there are solid *philosophical* grounds for insisting on quality realism.

This conclusion—that Ockham's quality realism is based on more than just theological convenience—has been championed in recent years by Marilyn Adams, but has struck others as hard to believe.[4] To understand the issues aright, it is crucial to distinguish, as in earlier chapters (esp. §10.4, §11.2), between two sorts of views: *quality realism*, which is the view that the category of Quality contains genuine entities irreducible to entities in any other category, and *separability*, which is the view that accidents might exist apart from their subject. It is not implausible to think that the separability thesis is a deliverance of the faith. Buridan, for instance, with respect to his account of how accidents inhere contingently in subjects, remarks that "I in no way would have conceded this if not for that separability that I hold on faith" (*In Meta.* V.8, f. 33ra). Indeed, according to Pedro Fonseca in the sixteenth century, "everyone, before this mystery was divinely revealed, supposed . . . that it implied a contradiction for an accident to be able to be separated in this way from its underlying substance" (*In Meta.* VII.1.1.2). The separable existence of accidents, however, is neither necessary nor sufficient for quality realism. The distinction between these two issues becomes quite clear by the early seventeenth century, when we find scholastic Protestants, such as Franco Burgersdijk, insisting that qualities are accidents really distinct from substances, while yet, at the same time, holding against the *Pontificii* that "it is absolutely and unconditionally impossible for an accident to exist on its own without a substance" (*Inst. meta.* II.17 ths. 3, 15).[5]

Given that the thesis of separability is so easily entwined with the notion of a real distinction, it will perhaps be helpful to recall how these issues can come apart. One place they come apart is in deflationary theories of accidents (§10.2), according to which only substances properly exist, and talk of an accident's existing is shorthand for a way in which its substance exists. Authors who take this sort of view do not endorse real accidents and so count as quality realists only in a lesser sense, but even so they may or may not regard accidents as separable from their subjects (Aquinas does [§10.3]; Wyclif does not [§11.2]). A second place quality realism and separability come apart is in the idea that merely one-way separability is sufficient for a real distinction. This is an idea we have encountered in Scotus, among others, and that he uses to defend his across-the-board category realism (§10.5 and §13.6). For this approach to make any sense, however, separability has to be understood in carefully circumscribed ways: it has to be

---

[4] Adams offers a forceful, though I think incomplete, case for the view that Ockham's quality realism is motivated by independent philosophical considerations. Her best argument is this: "Where Ockham thinks that faith and natural reason lead to different conclusions . . . he does not hesitate to distinguish what must be said 'by those who follow unaided natural reason' . . . and what must be held according to 'Truth' and 'the Faith'" (*William Ockham* I:279). Clearly, as Adams stresses, Ockham never draws such a distinction in defending quality realism. Adams's view goes against the general judgment of earlier scholars, such as Weisheipl, "The Concept of Matter" pp. 157–8: "Were it not for the Eucharist, Ockham would have denied absolute reality to every accident." More recent scholars continue to be doubtful of whether Adams can really be right—see, e.g., Ebbesen, "Les *Catégories* au Moyen Age" p. 250: "Il fait selon moi peu de doutes que la doctrine de l'eucharistie constitue la principale raison de la particularité de cette ontologie. . . ."

[5] Pierre Bayle, as quoted in §13.4, agrees with Fonseca's judgment that the separability of accidents from their subjects was motivated by the doctrine of transubstantiation.

A case where separability was not motivated by the Eucharist can be found in Islamic philosophy: Maimonides disapprovingly reports that some of the Mu'tazilites held that accidents can, by the power of God, exist without a subject. But this looks to be the proverbial exception that proves the rule, inasmuch as Maimonides goes on to say that they "have arrived at this conclusion not by philosophical research alone, but mainly by the desire to defend certain religious principles" (*Guide* III.15). For further information on this case, see Imbach, "Metaphysik" p. 373 n. 81.

For references to other Protestant scholastics who endorse inseparable real accidents, see Ch. 10 note 16.

understood, in short, as fixed separability (§14.3). This is to say that a substance's ability to exist without a given accident is grounds for the reality of that accident only if the change is possible while holding fixed various features of the substance. Which features? Those that one's anti-realist opponent might regard as plausible candidates for a reductive analysis. If separation in one direction is sufficient for a real distinction, then qualities could be really distinct from their subjects and yet not be able to exist apart from them, just as later Protestant scholastics would urge.

How does all this apply to Ockham? Ockham does not hold a deflationary theory of accidents; he holds that if they exist, they really exist, in just the sense that substances exist (§11.1). But his argument for quality realism, as quoted above, is not couched as an argument for separability in both directions. On the contrary, it is an appeal to one-way fixed separability. He is urging that a substance can have and then lose a quality such as heat while holding fixed certain crucial features of the substance. Which features? Those he regards as the only plausible candidates for a reductive analysis of quality: facts concerning that body's corpuscular structure. If a quality can come and go without any change to the location of the body and its integral parts, then the quality must be something over and above those parts—it must be real. The issue of whether it can exist apart from the substance need not even arise. Now, in fact, it is an interesting and idiosyncratic feature of Ockham's position that he thinks the only distinction between things is a real distinction, and that a real distinction entails two-way separability. This is so, on his view, because of his conviction that for any two things that contingently exist, each can, at least by divine power, exist without the other (§13.6). This was, to be sure, a controversial view. But, since Ockham holds it, he need not draw the distinction I am urging, between the reality of qualities and their separability. If qualities are real, on his view, then they can exist apart from their subject. This means that Ockham has a thoroughly philosophical basis both for the doctrine of real qualities and for the doctrine of separability. He need not appeal to the Eucharist to justify his views.[6]

Still, a puzzle remains. The standard scholastic argument for quality realism, as we have seen it in Ockham, does not look at all persuasive. Indeed, part of what makes it tempting to see the invisible hand of faith here is that Ockham offers nothing in support of his conviction that sensible qualities cannot be explained in corpuscularian terms. If we suppose, as I do, that he and at least some of his contemporaries sincerely find this argument persuasive, then we need an account of why this is so. The best way to understand their position, it seems to me, is as an argument from conceivability. For the first three centuries of our period, authors are in almost universal agreement that it is flatly inconceivable to suppose that something like color, or heat, could be a product of corpuscular motion. Yet if this is right, it is a remarkable fact, not just because such an intuition is likely to strike us as so alien, but because it is an intuition that seems to collapse completely in the seventeenth century as well. How could a certain kind of explanation seem simply impossible, for generations, and then suddenly seem not just conceivable but true? I will return to this question in §19.7, but first we need to collect more data.

---

[6] Ockham's insistence that substance and quality, as distinct existences, can each exist apart from the other finds a later champion in Hume: "Every quality being a distinct thing from another, may be conceived to exist apart, and may exist apart, not only from every other quality, but from that unintelligible chimera of a substance" (*Treatise* I.4.3, p. 222). For Hume, however, this is a way of making trouble for quality realism.

19.3. *Anno* 1347: Mirecourt and Oresme

The year 1347 deserves to be remembered as one of the great milestones in the history of philosophy. It was then that the route to modern philosophy was blocked by Church authorities, and effectively put on hold for almost 300 years. In that year, the University of Paris condemned the following view:

That it is plausible, by natural light, that there are no accidents distinct from substance, but that every *res* is a substance, and that if not for the faith this view should be held as plausible or could be held as plausible. (Stegmüller, "Zwei Apologien" n. 43, p. 65; cf. Denifle, *Chartularium* II.1147 n. 29)

The target of this and forty other condemned propositions was John of Mirecourt, a Cistercian monk and theology master at the University of Paris. We met Mirecourt briefly in §18.2, in the context of his suggestion that successive entities might not exist. All by itself, this claim would not have attracted much attention, and Mirecourt would no longer be remembered. But this was just one of various controversial theses that he aired. Over the course of his *Sentences* commentary (1344–5), Mirecourt questioned not only the reality of event-like entities, but also, most notably, the reality of states or properties—that is, the reality of qualities.

Although Mirecourt's view is well-known, in virtue of its being condemned, it is not easily reconstructed on the basis of his text, and it is worth taking a little time to see exactly what he thought. A first glimmer of his position emerges in a passing remark from earlier on in his commentary:

There could be another opinion, and perhaps—if it were permissible—I would hold it to be quite plausible. This opinion would be to claim that action is nothing, and neither is motion or thought, but these are modes of how things stand (*modi se habendi rerum*). (*Sent.* I.2, p. 329)

Actions and motions are paradigmatic successive entities, and so it is no surprise to see them mentioned here, given his anti-realism in that domain. It is somewhat surprising, however, to see thought (*intellectio*) included on the list, because mental states are ordinarily understood as permanent entities, and indeed as qualities. This is a thesis for which he would later be condemned:

It can plausibly be maintained that thought or volition is not distinct from the soul, but rather that it is the soul itself. And someone maintaining this would not be forced to deny any self-evident proposition, or any authoritative proposition that must be admitted. (Stegmüller, "Zwei Apologien" n. 42, p. 64; cf. Denifle, *Chartularium* II.1147 n. 28)

In issuing this condemnation, the censors perhaps thought that they were safeguarding the existence of qualities in the soul. But this is not how Mirecourt conceived of the situation. He makes it explicit that he takes both thoughts and volitions to be actions rather than states. Hence his rejection of these as independent entities is tantamount to rejecting not qualities, but successive entities.[7]

---

[7] On thoughts and volitions as actions, see Mirecourt, *Sent.* I.2, p. 327: "Quarta propositio est ista, quod quaelibet intellectio creata est quaedam actio potentiae intellectivae et motus eius, et quaelibet creata volitio est quaedam motio potentiae motivae et quaedam actio eius; ista patet per tertiam conclusionem huius quaestionis primi articuli." That earlier conclusion (pp. 322–3) makes these claims in even stronger terms, remarking: "quaelibet cognitio est actio."

It is only in a later question from his *Sentences* commentary that Mirecourt takes on the category of Quality. First, he restates his earlier conclusion: "it can be said that a given cognition of the soul is the soul itself, and likewise for volition" (*Sent.* I.19 n. 67.1). Then he considers the objection that his view proves too much, proving that there would be not only no successive entities, but no real accidents as well. Remarkably, he grants the possibility:

If you say further that, by the same reason, all the world's accidents would be denied, I grant the conclusion. Indeed, I believe that, if not for the faith, many might well have said that every *res* is a substance. (ibid., n. 73.2)

As always, '*res*' has the connotation of a real entity, really distinct from other entities. What Mirecourt thus judges to be quite possible, and perhaps even probable if not for the faith, is in effect corpuscularianism, the doctrine that the only material entities are bodies and their integral parts. (Mirecourt's formulation of course leaves room for immaterial substances as well, just as do most seventeenth-century corpuscularians.) Clearly it was this passage—as scribbled down by the censor who read through Mirecourt's work—that gave rise to the condemned proposition quoted at the start of this section.

Mirecourt is in effect offering his own view about how quality realism would fare if stripped of all theological support. Whereas I urged in the previous section that there were philosophical reasons behind quality realism, Mirecourt thinks that "many" would instead embrace corpuscularianism, if not for the faith. (Of course both claims might be true.) In the next passage, Mirecourt attempts to sort out the respective evidential weights of faith and reason:

If it were said that the faith holds the opposite; therefore it is not plausible [that there are no accidents]—I say that this inference is not good. For although this does follow: *faith holds the opposite of this; therefore this is not true*, still it does not follow that the opposite [of the faith] is not plausible. On the contrary, the opposites of some articles [of faith] are more plausible to us than are the articles themselves. (*Sent.* I.19 n. 73.3)

This is couched provocatively, but in substance Mirecourt's claims are not really so bold. He does not say that corpuscularianism is true, and does not even say it is the best-supported philosophical thesis. He regards it only as one of several equally plausible views, and moreover he acknowledges that it is contrary to the faith and so must be rejected. Still, this was not enough for the Paris censors, who—as quoted above—condemned not just the affirmation of the thesis in question, or even its bare plausibility, but even the notion that it is a view that would be plausible if not for the faith. That is to assert, in effect, that there are decisive philosophical reasons for maintaining the reality of at least some accidents.

We have two sets of responses that Mirecourt made to the charges that were brought against him. Regarding the thesis that the soul's actions can plausibly be identified with the soul, Mirecourt offers a rather creative interpretation of what it means for a thesis to be "plausible" (*probabilis*). For him, 'a plausible claim' is not understood in the Aristotelian sense, as a claim for which there are strong but non-demonstrative arguments. Instead, he takes any thesis to be plausible so long as it has the status of being an open question, in the sense that neither it nor its opposite is demonstratively known to be the case or is entailed by Church teachings. He then goes on to insist that he does not *know*, strictly speaking, whether the soul is identical with its actions, and so continues to regard the proposition in question as plausible, in his sense of the term.[8] Even so, he allows that the arguments for a distinction between the soul and its acts are better than those for the opposite, and so he asserts it as his opinion that there *is* a distinction. Then he turns to the proposition concerning accidents, and says this:

I reply to this just as I did to the preceding proposition, with this addition, that I adhere more firmly and certainly to the distinctness of substance and accident than to the distinctness between thought and soul, both on account of the faith, and also because the arguments for this are stronger, and many think that they have demonstrations for this, at least *a posteriori*. Still, I do not know whether the arguments that we have for this can be called demonstrations. (Stegmüller, "Zwei Apologien" pp. 65–6)

Now, under pressure, Mirecourt allows that—in addition to the faith—there are strong philosophical arguments for the reality of accidents. But he cannot resist adding that these arguments are *a posteriori* (line 4), in the Aristotelian sense that they begin with effects rather than causes. This just is the method of argument that Scotus had set out for real accidents, and that Ockham and Buridan were following: to show that accidents are needed to explain natural phenomena. Strictly speaking, however, *a posteriori* arguments are not demonstrations, and accordingly Mirecourt hesitates in counting the existence of real accidents as demonstratively *known*.

Mirecourt does not say enough about these issues to justify further discussion of his views. Indeed, although he is bold enough to raise interesting philosophical questions, his very limited remarks regarding these questions are wholly unsatisfactory. In particular, it is not at all clear why he is prepared to accept that if successive entities are in trouble then so are real accidents. Certainly, he recognizes that these are quite different issues, and in his response to the process against him he carefully distinguishes between the view that the soul's operations are actions (and so successive entities), and the view that they are accidents in the genus of Quality.[9] The only apparent link between these claims is that, just as there are no decisive arguments in favor of successive entities, so there are no decisive arguments in favor of real accidents. Moreover, Mirecourt fails to acknowledge that anti-realism in these two domains, far from being mutually supporting, is actually in tension. When authors offer reductive accounts of successive entities, they generally do so by claiming that the apparent event

---

[8] My characterization of Mirecourt's reply to the charges against him extrapolates somewhat from what he actually says, focusing on the first response. (The second response is much briefer, and more concessive.) What he says is that he regards a thesis as *probabilis* if it is neither known nor established by authority. He must mean that neither it nor its opposite has this status. Although he goes on to remark that "sic communiter vocari solet" (Stegmüller, "Zwei Apologien" p. 65), surely the standard sense of 'probabilis' requires a thesis to have the support of arguments that have some force.

[9] Mirecourt clearly signals the difference between treating *intellectio* and *volitio* as actions and treating them as qualities when he responds to the charge of questioning the reality of successive entities (Stegmüller, "Zwei Apologien" pp. 67–8): "de entitate intellectionis et cuiuslibet talis actionis animae,...possunt esse tres opiniones. Una est quod sensatio est quaedam qualitas in potentia sensitiva et intellectio quaedam qualitas in anima intellectiva de genere Qualitatis, et non est actio....Alia opinio poneret quod etsi intellectio et sensatio et huiusmodi sint quaedam qualitates, sunt etiam actiones animae....Alia est via quae poneret intellectionem esse qualitatem absolutam, et poneret cum hoc quod quandocumque anima intelligit, est in anima quaedam actio de genere Actionis, tamen illa actio non est illa qualitas nec est anima nec est aliqua res...."

is nothing more than a substance's being in one state, then another, and then another. But this works only if one has an account of what it is for a substance to be in the relevant state, and this was ordinarily supposed to require *accidents*. Thus Buridan, for instance, can give a reductive account of those successive entities that are alterations, because he can appeal to real qualities. But Buridan thinks local motion must be a thing in its own right, because there are no further states to reduce it to. Olivi, in contrast, is able to give a reductive account of local motion, because he has temporal modes (§18.2). And even Ockham, though refusing to acknowledge any entities corresponding to location, at least acknowledges primitive locational facts, in virtue of which he can construct a reductive theory of local motion (§17.4). It is clear, then, how Mirecourt might hold that the soul's actions are nothing more than its going through a series of successive qualitative states. But if he then also wants to pursue anti-realism with regard to qualities, it is not clear what resources he has available for offering any sort of account of thought or volition. And although of course matters are especially perplexing with regard to the rational soul, given its immateriality, the point applies more generally to any theory that eliminates both qualities and events. Without, in short, *some* kind of distinction between a substance and its changing states, it is hard to see how a theory can account for change at all. This is why, as I suggested in the previous chapter, neither of the great corpuscularian theorists of the seventeenth century, Gassendi and Descartes, are willing to embrace a reductive account of motion.[10]

Even if Mirecourt's work goes only so far, he is symptomatic of a broader trend of thought in Paris at this time. As a more sophisticated instance of this trend, we might remember Nicole Oresme, whose own case against real accidents is contemporary with Mirecourt's. Oresme explicitly describes and then tentatively rejects the view that an accident is a "true form inhering in a substance" (§13.2). Instead, for Oresme, forms are modes. This positions him, along with Mirecourt, as a quality anti-realist. And although it is only in his *Physics* commentary that Oresme discusses these issues in enough detail to set out a positive view, his early work persistently casts a skeptical eye on the reality of qualities. In his questions on the *De generatione et corruptione*, for instance, Oresme contrasts generation and qualitative alteration by saying that "when something is altered, it does not begin to be but begins to be such" (I.2, p. 11). So much is uncontroversial, but then Oresme goes on: "If it is said that whiteness begins to be through alteration, this does not hold, because whiteness is nothing other than this-being-white." This is an unambiguous rejection of the doctrine of real qualities. The first book of Oresme's *De anima* commentary takes a similarly deflationary approach, rejecting the vulgar view that accidents are independent entities that surround and therefore conceal substances (§7.4), in favor of an account that hearkens back to the deflationism of Albert the Great and Thomas Aquinas. This amounts to a clear rejection

---

[10] The tension in general between anti-realism regarding permanent accidents and anti-realism regarding successive entities applies for Mirecourt as well to his reductive account of species in cognition. Like Ockham, Mirecourt denies the existence of *species in medio*, as well as sensible and intelligible species, postulating instead merely acts of cognition (*Sent.* I.4; for Mirecourt, see Maier, "Problem der Species" pp. 445–6; for the larger debate, see Pasnau, *Theories of Cognition*). But if an act of cognition is not a successive entity, what is it? It seemingly cannot be a permanent quality either, because that is just what an intelligible species is. The interaction between the debate over successive entities and the debate over the reality of species deserves further attention.

of the doctrine of real qualities, as that view was commonly defended from the time of Scotus onward.[11]

Scholars have compared Oresme's view with Mirecourt's, because Mirecourt too, in a passage quoted above, speaks of accidents as modes.[12] But here is a very clear case where 'mode' is being used in two quite distinct senses. Oresme, as we have seen, expressly distinguishes his theory of modes from the view that accidents do not exist at all. Modes, on his view, are entities of a kind, even if they somehow have a lesser existence than do substances. Mirecourt, in contrast, uses the term 'mode' to make a reductive claim: that the only things that exist are substances. That this is so is perhaps not perfectly obvious, because when he suggests, for instance, that the only *res* that exist are substances (as quoted above), this might be read as leaving room for some lesser sort of non-*res*-like entities. Still, the passage quoted above in which he invokes modes is itself telling, since what he says is that "action is nothing, and neither is motion or thought, but these are modes of how things stand" (*Sent.* I.2). Oresme, in contrast, certainly did not think that modes are nothing. Mirecourt's view becomes even more clear in subsequent discussion from his *Sentences* commentary, discussing the sense in which God might be said to have accidents:

To the first, I say that 'accident' is taken in many ways. In one way, it is taken for a really inhering form, and in this sense no accident is in God, neither eternally nor in time. In another way, 'accident' is or can be taken for a mode of accidentally standing (*modo se habendi*), as when we say that nakedness or poverty pertains (*accidit*) to someone—not that in this case any entity pertains to him, but because he so stands. And according to this way of speaking, doctors grant that many things pertain to God in time, because sometimes he is the creator and sometimes not, without any change on his part. (*Sent.* I.25 n. 31; see also *Sent.* I.26 n. 36)

Here God is said to have modes. But given the general consensus of the time that God is perfectly simple and changeless, it must be that Mirecourt's modes have no ontological status, and are instead simply a reductive way of talking about how a thing is constituted.

19.4. Nicholas of Autrecourt

Both Mirecourt and Oresme look positively moderate in their views when compared to Nicholas of Autrecourt, whose radical ideas had made their way around Paris during the previous decade. Autrecourt is best known for a series of letters in which he attempts to undermine all certainty regarding the tenets of Aristotelian philosophy.

---

[11]   Other passages in Oresme's *In Gen. et cor.* hint at a reductive conception of form in general, such as I.6, p. 50: "forma non est aliud nisi materiam esse per hoc in tali vel tali supposito et quod sit tale suppositum"; I.9, p. 73: "cum forma non sit aliud quam formatio materiae, impossibile est quod formatio istius materiae eadem numero fuerit formatio alterius materiae." But both of these passages admit of less radical construals. There is no room for ambiguity in *In De an.* I.4, p. 119: "Et ideo ista via [vulgaris—see §7.4] est longe ab opinione Aristotelis, quae fuit quod accidens non est separabile a substantia non solum secundum existentiam, ut glossant, sed etiam secundum quidditatem, quia non habet esse proprie; unde imaginabatur quod, sicut impossibile est esse figuram sine figurato, ita de quolibet alio accidente, et hoc est verum nisi per miraculum."

[12]   Mirecourt's views on quality are considered in careful detail by Caroti, "Les *modi rerum*." Although I am persuaded by his claim that the 1347 condemnation served to moderate Oresme's subsequent views (§19.5), I think Caroti is wrong to see Mirecourt as a basis for Oresme's theory of modes.

His most impressive philosophical achievement, however, is his *Tractatus* (1330)—also known by its opening words as the *Exigit ordo*—a systematic treatise of natural philosophy that is nothing short of a full-blown attempt to revive ancient atomism.[13] The foundations of this treatise are a long series of arguments for the thesis that nothing comes into or goes out of existence. This conclusion—which §28.2 will consider in detail—entails not only that the material world is fundamentally composed out of atoms, but also that atoms are the only material things that exist. In accord with this strictly corpuscularian account, Autrecourt contends that all natural change can be accounted for in terms of the motion of these particles:

So then in the case of natural things there is only local motion. When from such motion there follows an aggregation of natural bodies that are gathered to one another and acquire the nature of a single subject, this is called *generation*. When those bodies separate, it is called *corruption*. And when through local motion a subject has joined to it atomic bodies that are such that their arrival seems to bring about neither the motion of the subject nor what is called its natural operation, then this is called *alteration*. (*Tractatus* ch. 1, pp. 200–1)

This amounts to the utter rejection of Aristotelian natural philosophy, as thoroughgoing as anything in the seventeenth century. To say that there is only local motion (line 1) is to say that there is no other kind of change. What Aristotelians think of as distinct sorts of change—in particular, generation, corruption, alteration—are merely distinct sorts of local motion.

When change is so understood, there is no need to postulate any further entity—a form—that comes into or goes out of existence. Accordingly, Autrecourt rejects both substantial and accidental forms. The latter result he makes quite explicit: "according to the aforesaid, it would be said that such accidents are nothing other than various atomic bodies, existing in their subject as parts in a whole" (p. 204). In a sense, accidents exist in their subjects, just as the Aristotelians would have it. But they are there not in virtue of some mysterious relationship of inherence (§11.1), but as parts—that is, integral parts— are in a whole. As in most defenses of corpuscularianism, the case rests largely on the absence of arguments for a wider ontology. After stating his positive case in favor of the thesis that nothing in the natural world goes in or out of existence, he issues the following, remarkable challenge:

Even if these arguments are not found to be entirely conclusive, still the position is plausible— more plausible than the arguments for the opposite conclusion. For if those who hold the opposite conclusion have arguments, let them state them, and let the lovers of truth compare   3 them with these. I believe that, to anyone not biased one way or the other, it will be apparent that these arguments have the greater degree of plausibility. I speak this way because in the books of others I have seen few arguments for occult conclusions to which I have not known   6 how to give plausible responses. And if they say that I deny self-evident principles, it is amazing how openly they state falsehoods, which they cannot do without lying. . . . It is also amazing how they judge to be self-evident principles whose opposite virtually all of Aristotle's prede-   9 cessors agree on, or at least the more serious among them. . . . Philosophers should not allow

---

[13] The sole surviving manuscript of Autrecourt's *Tractatus* describes it as the *Tractatus utilis ad videndum an sermones peripateticorum fuerint demonstrativi*. Although generally known in English as the *Universal Treatise*, that title depends on what is probably a misreading of the second word of the Latin title. For 'utilis' as more plausible than 'universalis,' see Kaluza, *Nicolas d'Autrécourt* pp. 153–5.

these men, who do not know how to resist the truth, to shield themselves behind such verbosities. (ibid., p. 203)

Even if Autrecourt's general metaphysical arguments are not conclusive, still he insists they are at least plausible (line 1). If there are strong, countervailing arguments in favor of real qualities, the proponents of that view have certainly not succeeded in articulating them (lines 2–7). This leaves the possibility that the doctrine of qualities (and allied tenets of Aristotelianism) might be self-evident (*per se notum*), a possibility Autrecourt treats most scornfully of all, given that such claims can hardly have the status of first principles. Anticipating a familiar theme of later anti-scholastic rhetoric (§5.2), Autrecourt wonders how Aristotle's metaphysics could be self-evident, if "virtually all of Aristotle's (more serious) predecessors" rejected it (lines 8–10).

A decade before Mirecourt, then, and even in stronger terms, Autrecourt reflects the view that there are no good philosophical reasons for quality realism, and that indeed consensus on this score is the product of intellectual bullying rather than reasoned arguments. The corpuscularian alternative strikes him as, if not clearly true, then at least clearly deserving of a hearing. But although that view would eventually get its hearing, it would take 300 years for this to happen. In the short run, Autrecourt faced the same fate as Mirecourt. A process begun by Pope Benedict XII in 1340 led to the condemnation of sixty-six propositions as (variously) false, dangerous, presumptuous, suspect, erroneous, and/or heretical. Autrecourt was made to bring this list to Paris, and in November 1347 he publicly recanted and then burned it, along with a copy of his books. Among the condemned propositions were the theses that all permanent entities—substances and accidents—are eternal, and that in the natural world there is only local motion. Both theses were condemned as not only false and erroneous, but also heretical—the strongest possible charge, punishable by death if not recanted. Strictly speaking, Autrecourt did not recant his corpuscularianism in Paris, because he denied ever maintaining these theses. And indeed, he does periodically insert remarks into the *Tractatus* to the effect that these conclusions hold only "according to natural appearances," that he knows that "the truth and the Catholic faith hold otherwise," and that he does not mean to contradict the faith—although he is vastly less cautious in this regard than either Oresme or Mirecourt would be. Still, these qualifications notwithstanding, Autrecourt was required to declare that all the condemned propositions are false, etc., and that they should never be taught again. This was enough to keep him from the flames, but it did not save his books or his ideas, which went into eclipse for centuries.[14]

---

[14] For a reconstruction of the process against Autrecourt, see Kaluza, *Nicolas d'Autrécourt* pp. 100–28 and Thijssen, *Censure and Heresy* pp. 74–82. Strictly speaking, Autrecourt's condemnation should be dated to 1346, which was when the censure was determined in Avignon. But its pronouncement in Paris, which is where it would have had the most direct impact on philosophy, occurred the following year. For the text, with a partial translation, see the appendices to de Rijk's edition of the correspondence with Bernard—appendix A, 13.3: "Quod res absolutae permanentes, de quibus dicitur communiter quod generantur et corrumpuntur, sunt aeternae, sive sint substantiae sive accidentia.—Falsum, erroneum, et hereticum"; ibid., 13.4: "Quod in rebus naturalibus non est nisi motus localis, ita quod quando ad talem motum sequitur congregatio corporum atomalium naturalium quae colliguntur adinvicem et sortiuntur naturam unius suppositi, dicitur generatio; quando segregantur atomalia, dicitur corruptio; et quando per motum localem atomalia fuserunt cum aliquo supposito, quae sunt talia quod aut adventus illorum facere videtur ad mutationem suppositi vel ad id quod dicitur operatio naturalis eius, tunc dicitur alteratio.—Falsum, erroneum, et hereticum"; ibid., 13.12: "Quod isti conclusioni quod res permanentes sunt aeternae, magis est assentiendum quam oppositae [*ed.* opponendum]. Et si

19.5. After 1347

It would be difficult to exaggerate the significance of these two condemnations—of Mirecourt and Autrecourt—for the history of philosophy. If the debate over quality had been allowed to take its course in the 1340s, subsequent events would look utterly different. Inasmuch as the theory of qualities lay at the heart of scholastic Aristotelianism, a challenge to the standard view would have blown the doors off the narrow confines of later scholastic thought, potentially giving rise, centuries earlier, to the whole range of new questions that emerge in the seventeenth century. But whereas in other domains the late fourteenth and early fifteenth centuries were a time of dazzling innovation (Chaucer and Boccaccio in literature, for instance, and van Eyck in painting), philosophy was—at least comparatively speaking—frozen in place at mid-century, and would remain there until the pressure to change finally reached the point of explosion, three centuries later. I do not mean to suggest that nothing interesting happens in scholastic philosophy after 1347. Obviously, we have already seen many examples to the contrary. But I do think that, from this point forward, scholastic thought locks itself into a relatively narrow conceptual framework, within which there is a great variety of views, but which nevertheless in retrospect takes on the aspect of a black-and-white picture, waiting for the seventeenth century to arrive in Technicolor.

Obviously, these are bold and speculative claims. I will pursue them further in the following chapter, but for now they rest on two theses. First is the view that quality realism lies at the heart of scholastic thought and its subsequent rejection. This is a contention that is difficult to document, but that I hope will look increasingly plausible over subsequent chapters. Second is the claim that the condemnations of Autrecourt and Mirecourt are critical for subsequent events. This can, to some extent, be documented. First, as we have seen, it was possible to challenge quality realism quite openly before 1347—hence the condemnations. Second, these condemnations not only put an end to the academic careers of their targets, but also led others to take a conventionally realistic line on the subject. This is certainly what we would expect to find, at least in Paris, since the language of the condemnations leaves so little room for negotiation. Here is how the condemnation of Mirecourt begins:

We, Robert de Bardis, chancellor of Paris, doctor of sacred theology, and the other active regent masters in the faculty of theology at Paris, prohibit all bachelors of theology, both those reading the sentences in this year and those who have read or will read in any future year, either in reading or responding, to assert, dogmatize, hold, or defend publicly or privately the articles listed below, nor any one of them. For of these, in the form in which they have been proposed, we have judged some erroneous, others suspect and bad sounding to the faith and also to good morals. Whoever does the opposite will find himself deprived of all honorable standing in the faculty of theology. (Courtenay, "Mirecourt's Condemnation" p. 191)

---

aliqui dicant eum ex hoc negare principia per se nota, dicit quod hoc non possunt dicere nisi mentiendo.—Erroneum et hereticum."

For Autrecourt's occasional qualifications, see e.g. *Tractatus* ch. 1, p. 204: "Ista sunt sic dicta secundum apparentia naturalia quibus nunc participamus; scio vero quod veritas est et fides Catholica hoc tenet quod non omnes res sunt aeternae nec huic rei videor contradicere quia solum dico quod ista conclusio secundum apparentia naturalia quibus nunc particpamus est probabilior opposita."

Unsurprisingly, this had a chilling effect on teaching in the faculty of theology at Paris. But since the arts masters at Paris were expected to take their lead from the theologians in such matters, it also changed the way philosophy was taught. Thus although Oresme's earliest writings take quite adventuresome positions on the subject of quality, this abruptly stops in his later writings. Stefano Caroti, the leading authority on Oresme's work in this area, speaks of "the almost complete silence of Nicole Oresme on the doctrine of *modi rerum* after his commentary on the *Physics*," a fact Caroti uses to date the commentary to before 1347 ("Les *modi rerum*" p. 197). Oresme's other works from this period show similar signs of influence. His commentary on *De anima* I, for instance, takes a strikingly deflationary view of accidents. But when he gets to Book III and takes up the very question that Mirecourt had raised regarding the distinction of the soul and its accidents, he takes a completely bland, orthodox stance, offering a series of stock arguments and then this: "Finally, this thesis is confirmed, because to hold the opposite is condemned by a certain Parisian article; hence to say that the soul is its operation is an error" (*In De an.* III.9, p. 381). Moreover, we have an alternative version of the discussion in Book I that follows the original discussion quite closely but entirely leaves out the controversial material on the status of accidents.[15]

Buridan too cites the Mirecourt condemnation in insisting on the distinction between the soul and its operations. After very carefully setting out both sides of this dispute, he remarks that "not withstanding these [arguments on behalf of the other side], I firmly adhere to this conclusion: that when I think and know, my intellect is neither the thought nor the knowledge; rather, the thought and the knowledge are dispositions distinct from it and inhering in it" (*In De an.* III.11). His first argument for this conclusion is the authority of the Mirecourt condemnation, and the second is the potential threat to the Eucharist. It is hard to know, however, to what extent Buridan is relying on authority rather than reason. For he goes on to give two philosophical arguments against Mirecourt's identity thesis. First, he contends that the arguments in its favor naturally lead to the thesis he associates with Democritus and Melissus: that reality is nothing more than changing clusters of ingenerable and incorruptible bodies. Of course, this is precisely the view Autrecourt had defended. Buridan calls it "dangerous," which is to say that it is problematic on theological grounds, but he also calls it "utterly obscure" and concludes: "this has been sufficiently disproved by Aristotle and others, and I in no way wish to assert it" (ibid.; see §24.2 for further discussion). Second, Buridan argues that the reductionist talk of the soul's "standing thus and then thus" (*aliter et aliter se habere*), although intended as an alternative to postulating any entity that comes and goes, is in fact equivalent to the claim that the soul "stands in one way (*modo*) and then another," with the result, ultimately, that "the intellect is distinct from these modes" (ibid.). He concludes that one might as well posit qualities. This leads Buridan to a detailed discussion, along Ockham's lines (§19.1), of which sorts of changes are ontologically committing in this way and which are not. In the case of both mental

---

[15] The redacted version of Oresme's *In De an.* I.4 is edited as an appendix to that work (I.5). Although the editor attributes these redacted questions to John Buridan, there seems no good evidence for this. On the other hand, the near-verbatim relationship between these questions and Oresme's is absolutely no guarantee that the redactions are by him; disputed questions were copied in this era in the way that lecture notes get passed around within a modern university department. Still, no matter who the author, the point remains that the omission of this controversial material seems to mark the influence of 1347.

states and elemental qualities like Hot and Cold, change is ontologically committing, and so the reductive agenda of a Mirecourt or Autrecourt must be rejected. As usual, neither of those authors are mentioned by name, but the reference to the 1347 condemnation makes the target perfectly obvious. It is not clear whether Buridan regards the philosophical considerations as decisive on their own, but it seems clear that although he might have sympathy for the sort of non-reductive modal theory proposed by Oresme (and which Buridan thinks can be found in Aristotle [§11.1]), he is not at all tempted by a more strictly corpuscularian account. Because of 1347, however, there is no way of knowing where he thinks the philosophical arguments might actually lead. (I return to this case in §20.5, as an instance of the difficulty in distinguishing between what an author truly believes, and what he feels forced to say.)[16]

Strictly speaking, Mirecourt's condemnation had force only in Paris. But since the theology faculty of Paris was far and away the most influential such body in Christendom, its influence was massive. The list of condemned propositions was expanded in subsequent years (drawing on theses found in the works of other authors), and circulated under the heading of the *articuli novelli Parisius*—"the new (smaller) Paris articles"—as distinct from the long list of 1277. When the University of Bologna established a faculty of theology in 1364, the list was incorporated into their statutes. As for Autrecourt's condemnation, since it was determined in Avignon, its force was more general. As with Mirecourt's, this list of condemned articles can be found in some subsequent *Sentences* commentaries, and even some early printed texts.[17]

Of course, the real test of influence is whether subsequent authors dared to contravene these condemnations. At least with respect to qualities, they hardly ever did. Around the end of the fourteenth century, Blasius of Parma boldly proclaims that "no physical argument concludes that any accident should be posited; rather, this conclusion was plausibly established: that everything that is is a substance" (*De intensione* p. 489). Other evidence of such views is either anonymous or second hand. Peter of Candia reports having heard this view defended in Oxford *circa* 1370, and allows that the view is philosophically defensible, but cannot be squared with theological principles. Peter of Ailly, in 1377, likewise describes the view that accidents are not distinct from their subject, and urges his listeners not to brand this view as heretical, since its denial cannot be inferred from any "evident" tenet of the faith, but merely from plausible ones. This discussion amounts to a plea not to cut off discussion of the topic, and Peter offers various ways in which quality anti-realism might be squared with the Eucharist. Even so, he himself does not presume to defend anti-realism. Describing the view as "outside the common philosophy," he proceeds to maintain

---

[16] For Buridan's argument that change in thought entails at least distinct modes, see *In De an.* III.11: "Item 'aliter et aliter se habere' significat idem quod 'alio et alio modo se habere.' Si ergo intellectus noster nunc est una opinio, et cras erit opinio contraria, alio et alio modo se habens, iste modus non erit iste modus; ex quo modi ponuntur alii. Si ergo modi sunt plures et alii ab invicem, et intellectus non est nec erit alius, sed semper idem, necesse est intellectum esse alium ab illis modis et ab unoquoque illorum." For a general discussion of Buridan's response to Mirecourt, in light of the condemnation, see Maier, *Zwischen* pp. 331–9. For both Buridan and Oresme on this topic, see Zupko, *John Buridan* pp. 218–25.

[17] For the Autrecourt condemnation, see de Rijk's edition (*Correspondence* pp. 142–3). For brief remarks on the circulation of the Mirecourt articles, see Denifle, *Chartularium* II:613, and Courtenay, "Mirecourt's Condemnation." On the significance of the Autrecourt condemnation, see Weinberg: "as important an event in the intellectual history of the fourteenth century as was the condemnation of Averroism in 1277 in that of the thirteenth" (*Nicholas of Autrecourt* p. 3).

the orthodox realist line. Paul of Venice, in his lectures on the *Metaphysics* from the 1420s, reports that "many have denied that sensible substances are substantially distinct from their accidents" (citing only ancient views) and argues on that basis that the distinction cannot be self-evident (*manifestum per se*). But he too favors realism.[18]

What is most striking of all, however, is that when one looks for interesting discussions of this material in late scholastic texts, one finds very little. The great late scholastic authors—such as De Soto, Toletus, Zabarella, Suárez—all of course talk about the various accidental qualities, at length. But whereas their discussions of quantity and relation can be quite fascinating, the discussions of quality are invariably disappointing. Suárez is typical. Although he devotes an entire metaphysical disputation to the category of Quality (*Disp. meta.* 42)—as he does to each category—this particular dispute contains little of interest. Whereas elsewhere he works hard to defend the reality of substantial form (§24.4) and accidents in other categories (esp. §15.3, §17.5), he does not seem to regard quality realism as an open question. And when he does confront the view that there are no accidents, only substances and modes—a claim that, tellingly, comes up in an entirely different context—he deals with it in brief, brusque terms, labeling it "repugnant and incompatible in many ways with the truths of the faith" (*Disp. meta.* 16.1.2, referring to Auriol's theory of inherence [§11.4]). Suárez must have known about the fourteenth-century controversies over this issue. But it seems as if, by the end of the sixteenth century, the whole issue is beyond dispute, at least among scholastics.[19]

19.6. Cracking the Ice

The decline of scholasticism coincides with the decline of quality realism, in the seventeenth century. We have seen why this event did not happen in the fourteenth century, but one might have expected its time to come faster than it did. In particular, one might have expected qualities to come under suspicion in the fifteenth century, when the research of the humanists yielded a renewed acquaintance with ancient atomism. Lucretius's *De rerum natura* was discovered in 1417 (and printed 37 times from 1473 to 1620); Epicurus's letters could be read in Diogenes Laertius's *Lives of the Philosophers* once that was translated into Latin in the 1420s. So whereas earlier scholastics drew mainly on Aristotle's critical accounts of Democritus, authors from the fifteenth century forward had access to something much closer to a well-developed version of reductive corpuscularianism. Even so, they were extremely hesitant to embrace any part of it. The great publisher Aldus Manutius, in a preface to his edition of Lucretius's poem (1500), justified its publication "not because he wrote things that are true and that we should believe..., but because he put the teachings of the

---

[18] Peter of Candia is quoted in Bakker, *La raison* I:423–4. For Peter of Ailly, see *Sent.* IV.6 art. 3, f. D5rb–va. For Paul of Venice, see *In Meta.* VII.1.1, part 2 concl. 3. Maier quotes an anonymous critic of qualities, from the later fourteenth century: "Tunc sit prima conclusio incidentalis ista, quod bene possibile est, quod nec caliditas nec frigiditas sint res distinctae a suis subiectis.... Quando ignis calefacit aquam, nihil facit, sed facit aquam aliter se habere, quod nihil est, nec aliquis nec aliqua, nisi idem subiectum stare in tali dispositione sub qua prius non steterat" (*Zwischen* p. 330, from a *Physics* commentary found in Vat. lat. 3019, f. 89r).

[19] For the negative evidence from later scholastics, see, e.g. De Soto, *In Praed.*, "De quali et qualitate"; Schegk, *In Praed.*; Toletus, *In Praed.* ch. 8; Zabarella, *De rebus nat.*, De qual. elem. I–II; Coimbra,*In Gen. et cor.* II.3.2.

Epicurean sect into elegant and learned verse." To be sure, Epicureanism is suspect not just, or even mainly, because it undermines real qualities; its all-embracing materialism calls into question the immortality of the soul and even the very existence of God. (Dante had put the Epicureans in the sixth circle of Hell, along with heretics.) But those features of the view only made it harder to embrace any aspect of the corpuscularian agenda.[20]

The so-called Renaissance philosophers never seriously challenged quality realism—and this is one reason that movement seems disconnected from seventeenth-century developments. Early in his career, Marsilio Ficino had written a commentary on Lucretius's poem, but he came to regret his earlier enthusiasm, and in his *Platonic Theology* (1474) he gives quality a place among the five preeminent substances: God, angel, soul, quality, body. The young Giovanni Pico della Mirandola would likewise posit quality as one of his five primary categories, in his *900 Theses* (1486): oneness, substance, quantity, quality, relation (*Theses* 3>27). Pico did embrace the sort of deflationary account common in the thirteenth century (Ch. 10), according to which "accidents should in no way be called beings, but of beings" (2>78)—a thesis he rightly sees as departing from "the common philosophy." And Pico even took the dangerous further step, like Wyclif earlier, of suggesting that the Eucharist could be explained without positing separable qualities (4>1). As with Wyclif, this was not tolerated, and for this among other reasons Innocent VIII ordered all printed copies of the *900 Theses* to be burned within three days. (This appears to have been the first such episode in the young history of the printed book.) Still, again like Wyclif, Pico was not arguing for a reductive treatment of quality, but only arguing against the separability thesis.[21]

The aspect of the ancient atomist program that was easiest to accept was the atomic thesis itself: the claim that there is a point where bodies become too small to be naturally divided any further. This thesis was easy to defend because very little rests on it (§5.4). Once one sets atoms to the side as a distraction, and focuses attention instead on the issue that matters most—real accidents in the category of Quality—one finds that the scholastic doctrine was incredibly resilient. Throughout the fifteenth and sixteenth centuries, quality realism remains intact, defended even by figures who are otherwise quite hostile to scholasticism, including humanists such as Lorenzo Valla, scientists such as Johannes Kepler, and the Italian naturalists: Francesco Patrizi, Bernardino Telesio, and Tommaso Campanella. Well into the seventeenth century, the story remains much the same. Even among the most stridently anti-scholastic of early seventeenth-century figures, most retain qualities in their ontology, including David

---

[20] For the passage from Manutius, as well as other information in this paragraph, I am indebted to Kraye, "Moral Philosophy" pp. 376–7, 382–3. See also Garin, *La cultura filosofica* pp. 72–92 and, most recently, Wilson, *Epicureanism*, esp. pp. 15–38.

[21] For Ficino on qualities, see *Platonic Theology* I.1.3, I.2.4–9, I.3.1: "qualitas forma quaedam est." For Pico's attitude toward quality and other accidents, see Farmer's introduction to the *Theses*, pp. 97–102. Pico himself never asserts that accidents are in fact inseparable from their subject, but he clearly finds the view tempting. See also *Theses* 2>51: "Necessarium est dicere secundum Averroem quod substantia est de intrinseca quidditate accidentis, et est opinio et Aristoteli et philosophiae maxime consona." His first controversial thesis regarding the Eucharist is this: "Qui dixerit accidens existere non posse nisi inexistat Eucharistiae poterit sacramentum tenere etiam tendendo panis substantiam non remanere ut tenet communis via" (*Theses* 4>1). This amounts to the assertion that transubstantiation can be maintained without the separability of qualities. His second thesis (4>2) then argues, in effect, that the Eucharist could occur through consubstantiation (which of course would make separability entirely unnecessary). Pico's *Apologia* subsequently discusses his views on the Eucharist in great detail (*Opera* I:181–98).

Gorlaeus, Nathanael Carpenter, Daniel Sennert, William Pemble, Joachim Jungius, Gerard and Arnold Boate, and Jean Chrysostome Magnen.[22]

All the way then from 1347 into the 1600s, quality realism remained effectively unchallenged. Its first clear rejection, so far as I can find, appears in Isaac Beeckman. In a journal entry from around 1617, he remarks that "there is no doubt that the nature of cold and hot are taken from the swiftness and slowness of the motion of corpuscles" (I:132). A year or two later: "all powers emerge from motion, shape, and quantity" (I:216). In 1621, Sebastian Basso, a French student of medicine, endorsed the notion that "by solely the local motion of particles, from which all things are brought about, all the most distinct changes are brought about that things undergo" (*Philosophia naturalis* VIII pref., p. 430). At this same time, in England, Francis Bacon published his corpuscularian views, in his *Novum organum* of 1620, identifying heat with corpuscular motion (§21.4), and arguing in general that "nothing truly exists in nature beyond individual bodies" (§10.1). In 1623, in Italy, Galileo's *Assayer* challenged the reality of all the sensible qualities, arguing that they exist not in bodies but in the mind (§22.5). Aside from Bacon, however, none of these works were well known, and indeed Beeckman's ideas were never published at all. (His journal records his reaction, however, to each of the books just mentioned, as they became available to him, and in each case he records the melancholy and largely true remark that their ideas were already anticipated in his journal. As for why he never published his ideas, perhaps this charming passage is illuminating: "By nature I am timid.... I also easily believe others, and so I am used to being often deceived and to changing my mind" [ibid., III:220].)[23]

The defenders of orthodoxy fought back. In 1624, three young Parisian scholars—Jean Bitaud, Antoine de Villon, and Etienne de Clave—attempted to hold a public disputation calling into question the core doctrines of Aristotelianism: metaphysical prime matter, substantial form, and real qualities. With respect to the last, they offered up the following thesis:

The Peripatetics were dreaming when, speaking little in accord with the nature of things, they said that true and physical alterations are brought about through the introduction or loss of some new and merely accidental entity, while the subject remains unchanged with respect to its substance. For nothing can ever naturally occur without the addition or subtraction of principles, or their being variously mixed. (thesis 10, in Kahn, "Entre atomisme" p. 246)

Since "alteration" is always qualitative change, this amounts to an attack on the Aristotelian theory of qualities. Strictly speaking, the thesis does not maintain that there are no qualities, only that the gain or loss of qualities by itself could not account for alteration without some further change to the underlying substance. But in the context of the broadsheet as a whole, which goes on to attack Aristotelian theories of the elemental qualities and their mixture (theses 11–13), and ultimately defends

---

[22] Valla's ontology consists of substances, qualities, and actions (see *Retractio* I.17, *Repastinatio* I.1). Carpenter accepts only two genera of beings: substance and quality (*Phil. libera* I.1). Sennert's quality realism is unsurprising in his early works, which are rather conservative, but it extends even into his more adventuresome late writings, such as the *Hypomnemata physica*, as quoted in Ch. 5 note 27. For the other late defenders of quality mentioned in the main text, see the references in §21.4.

[23] Beeckman's journal cites Basso at II:242, Bacon at II:250ff., and Galileo's *Assayer* at III:223. For a helpful overview of Beeckman's work and influence, see Gaukroger, *Emergence of a Scientific Culture* pp. 276–82. For further details of his chemical views, along with Basso's, see Kubbinga, "Premières théories."

atomism (thesis 14), it seems clear enough that the authors were posing a fundamental challenge to the scholastic doctrine of qualities.

The debate never took place. The Theology Faculty at Paris condemned the theses, and singled out the tenth for particularly harsh judgment: "This proposition is false, rash, scandalous, and in a way threatens the holy sacrament of the Eucharist." Following the usual practice, the matter was then passed on to the secular authorities, here the Senate Council of Paris, who banished the three scholars from the city and issued the general warning that no one, on pain of death, should hold or teach any maxims contrary to the ancient authors and the theologians. Once again, the doctrine of real qualities was propped up by force.[24]

These measures made a difference for some time, at least among Catholics. Jean-Baptiste Morin, a French physician and would-be scientist, immediately published a brief work in which he characterized Villon and de Clave (evidently the principal forces behind the broadsheet) as having declared a *"guerre ouverte"* against Aristotle's philosophy (*Refutation* p. 5). Given that their theses were "full of error and heresy," he declared there to be "not the slightest doubt" that the process of condemnation was "just and necessary" (p. 17). In a similar spirit, Marin Mersenne, who would later become Descartes's chief confidant, lists all fourteen of the broadsheet's theses in a work from 1625, and then describes them as "impertinent" and "quite easy to overthrow" (*La vérité des sciences* p. 81). Yet he goes on to offer only brief and inadequate remarks about how this might be done.

In certain circles, the condemnation of 1624 remained influential for decades. Jean de Launoy, in his 1653 history of Aristotelianism at Paris, speaks triumphantly of the illustrious *fortuna* of Aristotle, to have been defended so decisively by the theology faculty in that year.[25] And indeed it could still look at mid-century as if the outcome of the battle were in doubt. But although, like all revolutions, this one appears inevitable only in hindsight, still it is clear that the conditions for change were all in place. First, the restricted lines of inquiry open within scholasticism were widely seen as intolerable, and the more so given the sudden availability of other options. As Leibniz remarked in 1678, looking back to the middle of the century, "there were many then, disgusted with

---

[24] The 1624 Parisian broadsheet is reproduced in Kahn, "Entre atomisme," and also transcribed in Launoy, *De varia fortuna*, pp. 205–11, along with the text of the condemnation. For an English translation, with extensive discussion, see Garber, "Defending Aristotle." See also Ariew and Grene, "Cartesian Destiny" pp. 87–9, who cite Jean-Cecile Frey as another contemporary critic of the 1624 broadsheet. Drawing on a work published by de Clave in 1641, they suggest that the broadsheet's rejection of form "was only partial"—a conclusion that fits with the precise way in which thesis 10 is framed, as noted in the main text. For the broader context of condemnations by the University of Paris theology faculty at that time, see Thorndike, "Censorship."

My focus on the first half of the seventeenth-century as the crucial transition point is at odds with those who focus on earlier Renaissance developments. See, e.g., Lohr, "Metaphysics and Natural Philosophy" p. 286: "Following Pletho's critique [in the early fifteenth century] the Scholastic paradigm for science broke down. The humanists brought new materials, new methods, new scientific interests and new alternatives. Aristotelianism became but one among many philosophies. Whereas for the Scholastics Aristotle had been 'the Philosopher' par excellence, from the mid-fifteenth century other philosophies—Platonism, Stoicism, Epicureanism—claimed attention." This seems to me to locate the breakdown of scholasticism 200 years too early, and to overstate wildly the influence of various Renaissance developments. It would have been little comfort to Bitaud, Villon, and de Clave, for instance, to be told that Aristotelianism was "but one among many philosophies."

[25] Launoy characterizes the events of 1624 as follows: "Haec ultima Aristotelis fortuna multo adhuc fuit illustrior, quam sexta et septima. Nam cum anno Christi MDCXXIV universa Aristotelis doctrina publicis thesibus oppugnari coepit Lutetiae, tunc Senatus, et Facultas Theologiae Parisiensis oppugnantium impetum retardarent, et sua auctoritate compescuerunt" (*De varia fortuna* ch. 17, p. 201).

the scholastic plan of studies, who sought freedom, since Bacon and others had already prepared their minds" (*Phil. Schriften* I:196; tr. Loemker p. 188). Second, by the 1640s, anti-Aristotelianism had a group of spokesmen around whom others could rally, including Gassendi, Hobbes, and above all Descartes. From mid-century on, quality realism was a thoroughly disreputable view. Descartes's mockery of "real qualities, attached to substances like little souls to their bodies" (III:648), had carried the day.

It is easy to imagine a different outcome, if scholastic thought had inoculated itself against the threat of reductionism back in 1347, and allowed the debate over corpuscularianism to run its natural course. If brilliant figures like Buridan and Oresme had been allowed free rein, the subsequent development of scholastic thought might have looked utterly different. Alternatively, if seventeenth-century Aristotelians had been able to field a philosophically worthy advocate, the scholastics might have held on. As it was, however, their only effective weapon was censorship. By 1663, Descartes's books had been placed on the Index of Prohibited Books, precisely because of his rejection of real qualities, and there was condemnation after condemnation of his views throughout the later seventeenth century. In 1662, the Theology Faculty at Louvain condemned the thesis that in bodies there is only "motion, rest, place, figure, and size," and similar decrees were issued in Paris as late as 1691.[26] The role of censorship in the story is indeed important enough to warrant a historiographic excursion, in the following chapter, on the way in which ecclesiastical censure impeded philosophical developments throughout the four centuries under study. But Church pressure is not the only factor at work here. As I have claimed already in the case of Ockham (§19.2), scholastic authors took there to be good philosophical reasons for quality realism, and it to this issue I turn in the final section of this chapter.

19.7. The Argument from Conceivability

What philosophical reasons explain the persistence of real qualities through the scholastic era, and their sudden rejection in the seventeenth century? A first step toward answering this question is to distinguish between the irreducibility thesis and the separability thesis. The first of these holds only that there are real qualitative features of bodies, irreducible to any sort of geometric–kinetic explanation. The second urges further that such real qualities can exist apart from their subjects. Here I will set this second claim aside, entangled as it is with the theology of the Eucharist and complex questions about the logical independence of distinct entities.

Once we focus our attention squarely on the essence of the debate over real qualities— on the irreducibility thesis—it becomes easier to see the nature of the philosophical disagreement: it turns on a difference in intuitions about the conceivability of certain sorts of explanations. For Ockham and nearly all of his contemporaries, it seemed simply impossible that the local motion of particles might account for qualities such as color and heat. Obviously, this sort of reductive analysis is something they had contemplated.

---

[26] On the censorship of Descartes, see Brockliss, *Moment of No Return*; McClaughin, "Censorship and Defenders of the Cartesian Faith"; Ariew, *Descartes and the Last Scholastics* chs. 8–10, and the documents translated in Ariew et al., *Background Source Materials*. For the censures in 1662 and 1691, see Des Chene, *Physiologia* p. 3.

Indeed, Ockham's principal line of argument, as considered in §19.2, turns precisely on considering such a reduction and rejecting it as impossible. What is particularly striking from our vantage point, however, is the way he takes this impossibility to be so obvious as to speak for itself, without requiring any further argument. A few, most prominently Autrecourt and Mirecourt, had been willing to embrace the geometric–kinetic reduction of qualities as at least a possibility, and no doubt their views would have had greater influence if they had not been condemned. But the general attitude of Ockham, Buridan, and other leading figures of the period is that such a line of inquiry could be ruled out from the start. In contrast, from the mid-seventeenth century forward, the reductive mechanistic–corpuscularian program came, in many circles, to be taken for granted, and again without very much by way of argument.

That the consensus among philosophers could change so dramatically is quite interesting for us today, because we face an analogous sort of dispute: Is it conceivable that explanations from the domain of neuroscience might fully explain the workings of the mind? One potential lesson to be drawn from our four centuries is that such intuitions about conceivability are far more malleable and subject to inculcation than we might like to believe. I think that there is truth to this, but the situation is complex. For one thing, one might suppose that there is more than just an analogy between the questions of reducing real qualities and mental phenomena—that, in fact, these are two aspects of the same, ongoing debate. It is, after all, heat and color that Ockham mentions in his refusal to countenance a reductive explanation of quality. This might encourage the hypothesis that it is the *perceptual* features of such qualities—what it is like to perceive them—that strikes Ockham (and his contemporaries) as irreducible. This would mean that *his* anti-reductive scruples are in fact *our* scruples—that he, too, is ultimately concerned with the irreducibility of mental states. That philosophers seemingly changed their mind about this in the seventeenth century would then admit of a neat explanation: that in fact they did not change their mind, but just became more clear on the distinction between heat and color as sensations, and heat and color as features of the external world. Once that distinction was drawn, reduction of external qualities became unproblematic.

I suspect that this is a widely held and widely taught picture of how the debate over real qualities went, but it is surely quite wrong. One mistake that it makes, as we will see in more detail in Chapter 22, is to ascribe to scholastic authors an absurdly confused account of sensible qualities, as if they could have believed that mental states exist in the external world, outside of our minds. For now, though, there is a simpler way to see what is wrong with this story: it would account for only a limited class of accidents in the category of Quality, those that are sensible. The scholastic theory of qualities is, however, a much broader and more fundamental theory. As noted in §19.1, it covers not only the familiar sensible qualities, but also qualities that are in no way perceptible, including occult qualities, and—most importantly of all—the four primary qualities, which as we will see in Chapter 21 lie at the heart of scholastic natural philosophy. So even if Ockham and others were somehow so confused as to suppose that our perceptual awareness of sensible qualities is a feature of the qualities themselves, that would not be enough to explain their thoroughgoing insistence on the irreducibility of such qualities.

Yet even if the irreducibility of quality is quite a distinct issue from the irreducibility of mental states, the analogy is worth pursuing a little farther. One of the great attractions of neuroscience as an explanatory framework for the mind is that, in contrast to dualism, it is a clear, concrete, workable proposal. We know exactly what it claims, and we have at least some sense of how we might investigate whether it is true. Something like this holds for the corpuscular–mechanical framework, as contrasted with real qualities. For whereas we have a very clear sense of what it is to be spread out in space, *partes extra partes*, in rest or in motion, the notion of a quality is utterly opaque. Descartes complains constantly that the principles of scholastic philosophy are "unintelligible" (e.g., *Principles* IV.198), and Kenelm Digby—another prominent critic of real qualities in the 1640s—mocked "that gentle and obedient philosophy of Qualities, readily obedient to what hard task so ever you assign it" (*Two Treatises* I.31.2).[27] Samuel Parker's *Free and Impartial Censure of the Platonick Philosophy* (1666) contrasts the two options in the way that is usual for the time: "The chief reason therefore why I prefer the Mechanical and Experimental Philosophy before the Aristotelian is . . . because it puts inquisitive men into a method to attain it [certainty], whereas the other serves only to obstruct their industry by amusing them with empty and insignificant notions" (p. 45). For Robert Boyle, a few years later, the Aristotelians "have better played the part of *painters* than *philosophers*," giving the illusion of solid and magnificent structures "when the whole piece is superficial, and made up of colors and art, and comprised within a frame perhaps scarce a yard long" (*Excellency of the Corpuscular or Mechanical Philosophy* [*Works* VIII:104–5; Stewart p. 140]).

What is at issue, though, is not the relative clarity of the corpuscular–mechanical framework, but its feasibility. The traditionally-minded Hermann Conring complained to Leibniz in 1678 that

Learned mathematicians have known for many centuries how to use the quantities of natural things. But that all the states of natural things are quantities, no one since the rejected deliriums of Democritus has even attempted to make this plausible. (Leibniz, *Schriften* I:191)

Conring of course knows that this is not strictly true: many had *attempted*, quite seriously, to make plausible an account of the natural world in terms of size, shape, motion, and other quantitative properties. But he means that no attempt had been credible. Leibniz's reply to Conring is fascinating. Still in his early, strictly corpuscularian phase, Leibniz insists that he recognizes nothing in bodies other than quantitative features: size, shape, position, and their changes. But rather than show that all allegedly qualitative phenomena—or even any qualitative phenomena—*can* actually be understood in these terms, he offers an indirect argument: that this is the only sort of account that *could* be genuinely explanatory. The alternative, he thinks, is to appeal to some sort of bare, primitive Aristotelian form. This, however, explains nothing at all. Leibniz then concludes:

---

[27] Digby argues at considerable length against quality realism. He denies that qualities have "a being . . . distinct from the substances in which they conceive them"; instead, they are merely "different affections or situations of the same body" (*Two Treatises* I.6.2, p. 40). See also Digby's preface and the conclusion to the First Treatise.

If these considerations can do nothing for you, I would like you to think this one thing: that if physical things cannot be explained by mechanical laws, then God himself, even if he wants to, cannot reveal and explain nature to us. (*Phil. Schriften* I:197; tr. Loemker p. 189)

That is, if a purely quantitative, corpuscularian account of the natural world cannot be given, then the world must at bottom be mysterious, inexplicable even with the help of divine illumination. This puts beautifully the inspiration behind much of seventeenth-century post-scholastic thought: that on one hand Aristotelianism cannot be right, because it explains so little, and on the other hand corpuscularianism must be right, because it explains so much.

Yet despite the confidence of philosophers working in the corpuscular tradition, their agenda cannot be said to have been vindicated. From its earliest incarnations, it was compromised by various further elements that rendered its metaphysical foundations opaque, such as the distinction between mode and substance (Chs. 8–9, 13), and the need for some sort of defining essence or structure to account for the unity and endurance of substances (Chs. 27–8). Even with regard to qualities themselves, the case against scholasticism was far from being decisive. To be sure, certain kinds of qualities readily admitted of a corpuscularian analysis. Sound, for instance, had been conceived even by the scholastics as closely connected to motion (§21.3), and heat could be readily understood on this model as well (§21.4). Other qualities, however, were much more resistant to this sort of reductive treatment, and seventeenth-century authors were driven to the most implausible and speculative hypotheses, as one sees in Descartes's various attempts to explain the nature of color.[28] Today we no longer pay much attention to these embarrassing aspects of the period, but much of the actual substance of seventeenth-century philosophy concerned topics like these, and contemporary audiences rightly saw that such details were fundamental. Thus, although Samuel Parker, in the passage quoted earlier, describes himself as a proponent of the mechanical philosophy, he stresses—in the phrase elided from the above quotation— that this "is not so much because of its so much greater certainty." Indeed, Parker quite despairs of arriving at any genuine understanding of nature along these lines:

For though I prefer the mechanical hypotheses before any other, yet me thinks their contexture is too slight and brittle to have any stress laid upon them; and I can resemble them to nothing better than your glass drops, from which, if the least portion be broken, the whole compages immediately dissolves and shatters into dust and atoms; for their parts, which rather lie than hang together, being supported only by the thin film of a brittle conjecture (not annealed by experience and observation) if that fail anywhere, the whole system of the hypothesis unavoidably shatters: And how easy a thing it is to spoil the prettiest conjecture, is obvious to the most vulgar observer. (pp. 44–5)

In retrospect, one would have to say that Parker was quite right about this. For even if one admires the general orientation of the post-scholastic era—whether that be for its anti-metaphysical quietism, its empirical tendencies, or its quantitative aspirations—one cannot say that the great philosophers of the era got very much right. Indeed, from our present vantage point, the ideal of a strictly corpuscularian–mechanistic worldview

---

[28] See *Regulae* 12 (X:413) and the *Optics* (VI:90–2), and see §22.6 for more on Descartes's views on color.

looks like a hopelessly quixotic enterprise, doomed to failure in both philosophy and science.[29]

The shining example of a seventeenth-century achievement in science is Newton, but this is hardly a case that the proponents of an austere reductionism could take much comfort in, because Newton's theories rely essentially on the notion of force. As we will see in §23.6, this was widely criticized as marking in effect a return to real qualities. According to Leibniz, "it pleases others to return to *occult qualities* or *scholastic faculties*, but since these crude philosophers and physicians see that those terms are in bad repute they change their name, calling them forces" (*Antibarbarus physicus*; *Schriften* VII:338; tr. Ariew and Garber, p. 313). Whether or not this is quite fair, it is clearly the case that an appeal to forces is tantamount to taking the scholastic side in the debate over whether purely geometric–kinetic properties could explain natural phenomena. By the end of the century, the failure of the mechanical philosophy was embarrassingly obvious. The young Newtonian John Keill begins the preface to his *Introductio ad veram physicam* (1702) with the remark that "although the mechanical philosophy is today celebrated in name, and in our era its practitioners have attained fame, nevertheless in most of the writings of the physicists one can find hardly anything mechanical beyond the name itself."

It is admittedly peculiar to ally the Newtonians with the Aristotelians, against the corpuscularians, and I will not insist on that. But even if one thinks of Newtonian forces as a friendly amendment to the corpuscularian–mechanistic program, that program remained the subject of widespread skepticism well into the eighteenth century. Consider, for instance, the article on chemistry written by the respected chemist Gabriel Venel for Diderot's *Encyclopedia* (1751–72).[30] Beginning with the opening line, "Chemistry is hardly developed among us," Venel proceeds to issue a challenge to proponents of a mechanistic approach to the distinctive qualities of bodies: "We venture to defy anyone to present us with an account of a chemical phenomenon founded on known mechanical laws that we cannot demonstrate to be false or unwarranted." Venel is reacting to Newton's speculative proposal (made in an appendix to his *Optics*) that the microphysical world might be analyzed through the same method used so successfully for planetary motion. The suggestion, in other words, is that material bodies are composed of even smaller bodies that are attracted to one another in much the way that the planets are attracted to the sun. This idea set the agenda for much of eighteenth-century chemistry, and of course would eventually be vindicated. But Venel could not see how any such account could possibly be satisfactory. In particular, he thought it inconceivable that a physical account of the internal mechanics of a substance might account for the external qualities of that substance. Consider the various qualities of gold: its color, malleability, divisibility, melting point, weight ("sixteen times more than water"), etc. We can easily imagine "a body that is similar insofar as it is formed from an assembly of the same parts that belong to gold, but which

---

[29]   On the drive for explanatory clarity, together with the speculative character of actual corpuscularian proposals, see Nadler, "Doctrines of Explanation." There is of course a very large literature on the status of the mechanical hypothesis in the seventeenth century; see, e.g., Anstey, "Robert Boyle"; Gabbey, "Mechanical Philosophy"; Jacovides, "Epistemology"; Westfall, *Construction of Modern Science*.

[30]   Venel, "Chimie," is published with only slight abridgement in Proust, *L'encyclopédisme* pp. 106–40. For information on Venel, see the entry by W. A. Smeaton in the *Dictionary of Scientific Biography*.

has none of the qualities just described." This is precisely the sort of anti-reductive approach that Ockham and other scholastic proponents of qualities had taken.

In retrospect, doubts of this sort should look quite reasonable. It would take centuries to work out in convincing detail a fully adequate account for many of the scholastic qualities. It would not be until the twentieth century, for instance, that chemists were able—in the light of quantum mechanics—to give a truly satisfying answer to some of Venel's queries, such as why gold is yellow. And if we look at modern scientific explanations, in chemistry or physics, it hardly seems to be the case that they vindicate the corpuscularian agenda. One therefore should not suppose that there was anything inevitable about the ascendance of the corpuscularian program in the seventeenth century, or about the collapse of scholastic Aristotelianism. At least with respect to the doctrine of real qualities, philosophers simply exchanged one speculative hypothesis for another.

20

Heresy and Novelty

20.1. Four Centuries of Inquisition

While generations of Dominicans and Franciscans in Paris were debating the subtleties of Aristotelian metaphysics, their confrères in southern France were harrowing the peasantry in an effort to root out the Cathar heresy. The heyday of scholastic philosophy in fact coincides precisely with the highest pitch of Christian intolerance, and moreover it was the same religious orders, the mendicant friars, who were at the forefront of each. For four centuries, the papacy's network of inquisitors into heresy—the so-called *Inquisition*—exercised enormous influence throughout large parts of Europe, with its power waxing to confront Protestantism, and then gradually waning over the course of the seventeenth century, just as the scholastic era was giving way to new philosophical approaches.

It is no coincidence that our four centuries of philosophy coincide with the Inquisition. Although the inquisitors that pursued Waldensians, Cathars, Jews, and assorted others had no authority over university scholars, it is plausible to think that the broader intellectual currents that gave rise to the one gave rise to the other. Before the turn of the thirteenth century, the Roman Church had treated heresy as merely a marginal problem. Over the course of that new century, a growing intellectual confidence appeared throughout western Europe. In Rome, it yielded an increasingly bureaucratic and theologically rigorous papacy, ready to go to war against heretics and infidels. In Paris and Oxford, it led to increasingly sophisticated systems of speculative thought. Friars like Albert the Great, Thomas Aquinas, Bonaventure, and Scotus, rather than devoting themselves to suppressing new forms of religion among the laity, were concentrating their energies on crafting beautiful new theories of their own, yielding the second great flourishing of original philosophical ideas in European history.

Yet because of the intolerant atmosphere in which these ideas were born, scholasticism never had the opportunity to develop fully. Whatever connection there may be between the rise of scholasticism and the rise of the Inquisition, it is clear that the atmosphere of intolerance that dominates these four centuries also poisons the development of philosophical thought. To be sure, the scholastic era could scarcely have been given a more powerful initiation than it received at the hands of Aquinas, and for a second act Scotus would be hard to improve upon. Beyond these first steps, however, scholastic thought was never allowed to progress. This was not for lack of trying. Peter

John Olivi attempted to move the debate in new and innovative ways (§12.4, §13.2, §14.1), but in 1283 the Franciscan authorities suppressed his writings, largely silencing whatever contribution he might have made. Ockham was able to have more influence in the early fourteenth century, and by the end of the scholastic era was recognized as the venerable inceptor of nominalism (§5.3). But Ockham too fell under the shadow of ecclesiastical censure, and spent his last two decades in exile, excommunicated. Accordingly, Ockham's career was interrupted, and he was always regarded as a dubious, suspicious figure, influential at the margins of scholastic thought but not wholly respectable. John Wyclif represents yet another missed opportunity. His innovative consuture views (§7.4, §11.1, §18.3) might have illuminated scholastic thought in many domains, but he fell afoul of Church teachings on the Eucharist, among other things, and his work would consequently be suppressed. Moreover, Olivi, Ockham, and Wyclif were all, by any reasonable measure, moderate figures. Their critiques of classical scholasticism were penetrating but hardly revolutionary; they urged reconsideration of important issues like the status of real accidents, but were hardly out to overthrow the entire Aristotelian framework. As for true revolutionaries, the only significant voice is Nicholas of Autrecourt, who really did pose a fundamental challenge to the orthodoxies of Aristotelianism (§19.4, §28.2). If Autrecourt had been allowed to state his case, the scholastic era would have been immeasurably enriched, but of course that did not happen. In 1347 he was forced to burn his books in public in Paris, and another opportunity was missed. For any given era there are only so many gifted, original figures that can be expected to emerge. The scholastic era had its chances, and squandered them. After a magnificent hundred or so years of progress, scholasticism ran up against the limits of what Church authority would tolerate, and thereafter slowly sank into intellectual sterility and irrelevance.[1]

This narrative flies in the face of the standard story of scholastic thought that dominated the discipline until recently. According to that standard story, Aquinas represents the ideal culmination of scholastic thought, while Ockham and other later figures are seen as merely skeptical, corrosive forces, dragging down the achievements of the thirteenth century.[2] Admittedly, few scholars take this story seriously anymore,

---

[1] On medieval heresy and the rise of the Inquisition, H. C. Lea's magisterial *History of the Inquisition* remains well worth reading. For up-to-date scholarship and further references, see, e.g., Lambert, *Medieval Heresy*, and Moore, *Formation of a Persecuting Society*. Regarding the rise of the Inquisition in the thirteenth century, after centuries during which heresy was not a major issue, Lea remarks that "the Church had not always been an organization which considered its highest duty to be the forcible suppression of dissidence at any cost" (I:209). For an extended argument against carelessly invoking the notion of a single, centralized Inquisition as a monolithic force, see Peters, *Inquisition*.

On the link between the rise of the Inquisition and the rise of the scholastic era, see Peters: "By the mid-thirteenth century, much of the ambiguity and hesitation that had characterized the attitudes toward heresy on the part of churchmen, councils, and popes was gone: in its place were the formal disciplines of theology and law, consisting of bodies of professional knowledge applied by professional personnel trained in the new universities..." (*Inquisition* pp. 60–1). See also Bianchi: "En effet, c'est précisément pendant ces deus siècles [XIIIe et XIVe] que l'institutionnalisation de l'enseignement dans les Universités a rendu à la fois pressante et possible la répression des divergences doctrinales; et cela alors que la professionnalisation et la bureaucratisation de l'exercice du pouvoir dans l'église provoquait une intolérance croissante à l'égard des individus dont les convictions ou les comportements s'écartaient de la norme" (*Censure et liberté* p. 12). And see Moore, who speaks of "the emergence of the bureaucratic regime, or the professionalization of the exercise of power" (*Formation of a Persecuting Society* p. 140; see also pp. 150–1, 153).

[2] Gilson is the leading spokesman for the standard twentieth-century Thomistic story about scholastic philosophy. See, e.g., *The Unity of Philosophical Experience*, pp. 90–1: "...they are all on the straight road to skepticism. Mediaeval thought entered it as soon as Ockham's philosophy took deep root in the European universities of the fourteenth century. Scholastic philosophers then began to mistrust their own principles, and mediaeval philosophy broke down; not

and in recent decades Ockham has assumed his rightful place as one of the treasures of the scholastic era. But it has not been sufficiently appreciated just how completely upside-down that old Thomistic story is. To think of Aquinas as the culmination of scholastic thought is rather like thinking of Descartes as the culmination of post-scholastic thought. Each serves as a vital cornerstone for the work that would follow, drawing the scattered ideas of their contemporaries into a brilliantly lucid system. But just as part of what makes Descartes great is the massive influence he would have on subsequent generations, so much of Aquinas's greatness lies in the movement that he, more than anyone else, began. Consider what seventeenth-century thought would look like if its innovations ran from Descartes to Malebranche, and then stopped. This is, in effect, the fate of the scholastic era, which began so promisingly only to see its natural development suppressed by the intolerance endemic to the era. Although papal inquisitors had no jurisdiction over the university system, the climate that fostered the Inquisition was very much felt there as well. We know of over fifty official judicial proceedings against academics in the thirteenth and fourteenth centuries, an oppressive climate to which even Aquinas's ideas initially fell prey in the condemnations of 1277, and which in later years ensured that no one could stray very far from the classical scholastic framework set out by the great thirteenth-century masters. Although previous chapters have stressed at every turn the rich variety among scholastic views, most of that richness falls within a fairly narrow range of options, and from the later fourteenth century on, that range becomes so narrow as to be claustrophobic. Inasmuch as those options are indeed interesting ones, later scholastic thought is not without its appeal, particularly in the hands of subtle masters like Francisco Suárez and Jacob Zabarella. But despite its glorious beginnings, these later centuries cannot be taken seriously as a great era of philosophical achievement.

My point is not that there is something wrong with Aquinas's ideas, or Bonaventure's, or Scotus's. It may indeed be, for all I have said, and for all I know, that some version of these classical systems is as close as human beings have ever come to a true metaphysics, a true ethics, or a true theory of human nature. If that is the case, then the later fate of scholasticism is all the more tragic, because those systems were never properly exposed to the light of unfettered philosophical dispute, and so were never given the chance to prove themselves in the face of criticism. John Milton's *Areopagitica* (1644), his passionate defense of freedom of the press, describes how "our faith and knowledge thrives by exercise as well as our limbs and complexion. Truth is compared in Scripture to a streaming fountain; if her waters flow not in a perpetual progression, they sicken into a muddy pool of conformity and tradition" (p. 38). There is no better example of this than scholastic metaphysics. As other chapters stress, scholastic authors were able largely to take for granted the crucial components of their hylomorphic scheme. Because no one was able to challenge the basic assumptions of prime matter, the substance–accident distinction, real qualities, or substantial forms, scholastic authors never critically reflected on the legitimacy of their approach. Perhaps every one of these elements of the scholastic system will

for want of ideas, for they still were there; or for want of men, for there never were more brilliant intelligences than at the time of that glorious sunset; mediaeval philosophy broke down when, having mistaken philosophy for reality itself, the best minds were surprised to find reason empty and began to despise it."

eventually come to take its rightful place in the ideal metaphysics to which philosophers aspire. If that is so, the case still needs to be made, because scholastic authors
themselves were never required to make it. Able to take for granted all but the subtle
details that separate one school from another, their work stagnates into the sort of
muddy pool that Milton describes.

The same institutional oppression that debilitated scholastic philosophy weighed
heavily on the seventeenth century too. That century began about as badly as it could
have, with Giordano Bruno's being burned at the stake on February 17, 1600, after
seven years of imprisonment at the hands of the Roman Inquisition. For some decades,
the Church's efforts at suppressing challenges to Aristotelianism remained quite inten-
sive. To mention just a few of the most prominent cases, Giulio Cesare Vanini was
burned in 1619. Tommaso Campanella was imprisoned for twenty-seven years.[3]
Galileo was confined for the last decade of his life. A public defense of anti-Aristotelian
principles advertised in Paris in 1624 was broken up, and its ringleaders exiled (§19.6,
§20.2). Authors in Protestant countries—such as Nicholas Hill, David Gorlaeus, Francis
Bacon, Sebastian Basso, and Daniel Sennert (§20.4)—could not be touched by the
Inquisition, but they were nevertheless far from free, nor could their ideas spread
through Europe as they might have. Descartes exercised quite a reasonable prudence in
suppressing his earliest writings, and moving to a relatively tolerant Holland before
publishing anything. Eventually, of course, scholars gained more room for innovation,
but even in France the debate between old and new raged throughout the century, with
Cartesianism becoming ascendant at the University of Paris only in the final decade of
the century.[4] In 1739, Hume could affix Tacitus as the epigram to his *Treatise of Human
Nature*: "rare happy time, when one is allowed to think what one wants, and say what
one thinks." Even for Hume, it is not clear whether Tacitus is offered in a celebratory
or an aspirational mode. For almost all of the seventeenth century, almost everywhere
in Europe, the question could not even have arisen. For those years it is instead
Descartes's motto, taken from Ovid, that is emblematic: "He has lived well who has
lived well hid."[5]

---

[3] On the place of Bruno, Campanella, and other Italian naturalists, see Copenhaver and Schmitt, *Renaissance
Philosophy* ch. 5. Schmitt elsewhere stresses that already, at the turn of the seventeenth century, there was more room
for innovation than there had been earlier: "Even taking into account the sobering examples of Patrizi, Campanella, and
Bruno, philosophers were able to move in far more directions in 1600 than they were in 1400 or even in 1500. While the
early fourteenth century produced an occasional radical thinker like Nicholas of Autrecourt, by the late sixteenth century
such figures emerged by the dozens" ("Towards a History" p. 15).

On intellectual freedom in the medieval university, see Bianchi, *Censure et liberté*; Putallaz, *Insolente liberté*; Thijssen,
Censure and Heresy; McLaughlin, *Intellectual Freedom*; Miethke, "Bildungsstand und Freiheitsforderung." Courtenay,
"Inquiry," puts the number of judicial proceedings at over fifty (p. 170).

[4] For Cartesianism's eventual conquest of the University of Paris, after protracted struggles, see Brockliss, "Moment
of No Return," which summarizes much earlier research. For Descartes at Cambridge, see the remarks of Roger North
regarding his education at Jesus College in the late 1660s: "at that time new philosophy was a sort of heresy....I found
such a stir about Des Cartes, some railing at him, and forbidding the reading of him, as if he had impugned the very
Gospel, and yet there was a general inclination, especially of the brisk part of the university, to use him, which made me
conclude, there was somewhat extraordinary in him, which I was resolved to find out, and at length did so" (Curtis,
Oxford and Cambridge in Transition pp. 257–8).

[5] For some interesting speculation regarding the subtext of Hume's epigram, see Russell, *Riddle of Hume's Treatise*
pp. 70–5. Descartes expressly links his motto with the threat posed by the Inquisition: "Vous savez sans doute que Galilée
a été repris depuis peu par les Inquisiteurs de la Foi, et que son opinion touchant le mouvement de la terre a été
condamnée comme hérétique. Or je vous dirai que toutes les choses que j'expliquais dans mon *Traité*, entre lesquelles était
aussi cette opinion du mouvement de la Terre, dépendaient tellement les unes des autres, que c'est assez de savoir qu'il y

As with the earlier scholastic period, moreover, these restraints on freedom of expression go beyond simply silencing some voices and delaying others. Here, as before, censorship serves to diminish the quality of the ideas that were eventually expressed. For when seventeenth-century authors finally were able freely to declare themselves in opposition to scholasticism, they understandably rushed to stake out views at the opposite extreme, rejecting the hylomorphic framework in its entirety in favor of austerely reductive corpuscularian accounts. Of course, as we have seen in some detail already, the post-scholastic era witnessed an immense variety of approaches ranging all over the philosophical spectrum. But the tendency among the most gifted and prominent authors—such as Descartes, Gassendi, Hobbes, Boyle, Locke—was to set their face resolutely against scholastic metaphysics in all its manifestations. Forced for so long to suffer under the tyranny of Aristotelianism, as they thought of it, the dominant seventeenth-century stance was to move as far away as possible from anything that smacked of speculative metaphysics in the scholastic style. Now, to be sure, one of the recurring themes of this study has been the difficulties such authors faced in making good on their reductive aspirations. The need to account for the familiar world of experience pushes seventeenth-century authors back toward various metaphysical commitments, even while they denounce the obscurity of such notions. Yet even if their views were not always as far from the scholastics as their rhetoric would suggest, their hostility had the unfortunate consequence that—once again—the opportunity for a serious debate between rival schools was lost. Whereas the cogency of the hylomorphic scheme was too much taken for granted to be subject to debate during most of the four centuries under study, it came to be so despised by the end of our period that, ironically, it was no longer taken seriously enough to be worthy of debate. The one prominent exception is Leibniz, who makes a sustained attempt to combine a mechanistic physics with something like a scholastic metaphysics.[6] Leibniz's views, however, were too idiosyncratic to be the savior of scholasticism, which by the close of the seventeenth century had become far too deeply unfashionable to be saved. Although one finds remnants of scholastic thought in the eighteenth, nineteenth, and even twentieth centuries, these scattered remains could have no appreciable influence. Censorship had sustained the Aristotelian program for four centuries, but once that support was lifted, these ideas fell lifeless to the ground, hopelessly discredited. It is

---

en ait une qui sait fausse, pour connaître que toutes les raisons dont je me servais n'ont point de force; et quoique je pensasse qu'elles fussent appuyées sur des démonstrations très certaines, et très évidentes, je ne voudrais toutefois pour rien du monde les soutenir contre l'autorité de l'église. Je sais bien qu'on pourrait dire que tout ce que les Inquisiteurs de Rome ont décidé, n'est pas incontinent article de foi pour cela, et qu'il faut premièrement que le Concile y ait passé. Mais je ne suis point si amoureux de mes pensées, que de me vouloir servir de telles exceptions, pour avoir moyen de les maintenir; et le désir que j'ai de vivre en repos et de continuer la vie que j'ai commencée en prenant pour ma devise: *bene vixit, bene qui latuit*, fait que je suis plus aise d'être délivré de la crainte que j'avais d'acquérir plus de connaissances que je ne désire, par le moyen de mon écrit, que je ne suis fâché d'avoir perdu le temps et la peine que j'ai employée à le composer" (to Mersenne, Feb. 1634; I:285–6).

[6] On Leibniz's distinctive position between various different currents of thought, see Brown, "Leibniz" and Mercer, *Leibniz's Metaphysics*. Mercer sees Leibniz's attempts to integrate Aristotelian and corpuscularian thought as representative of a larger tradition along these lines (see esp. ibid., pp. 100–9). She therefore rejects my depiction of the complete abandonment of Aristotelianism in favor of corpuscularianism. I readily grant her the existence of countless lesser figures aiming at one or another kind of compromise. But I persist in thinking that, if we look at the mountaintops—those figures who were and remain most influential—the picture is as I describe it.

indeed only within the last few decades that the mainstream of philosophy has taken a renewed interest in the sorts of abstract, non-reductive metaphysical questions that had once seemed to lie at the heart of philosophical inquiry.

20.2. "A Strange Presumption"

Although we should not make light of the Church's pernicious influence on philosophy over these four centuries, that influence needs to be understood in a broader context. The Church punished heresy harshly, but did so in an era in which all crimes were punished harshly, and frequently by death. Moreover, although the notion that heresy is a crime is foreign to our modern sensibilities, this attitude was taken for granted throughout the pre-modern era. It is perhaps no surprise to find Aquinas remarking that "heretics are wolves . . . and therefore ought to be eradicated" (*In Sent.* IV.13.2.3sc). But four hundred years later one can find Descartes taking a similarly hard line, at least about atheism, which he says is "the most atrocious crime, and should be tolerated in no republic, however free" (to Voetius; VIIIB:174). This attitude goes back to Plato, who had recommended five years in prison for those who deny that the gods exist or that they care about us, with death to follow if the prisoner is not reformed (*Laws* X, 909a). In general, there was little dispute during our period that heresy and apostasy are the worst of sins, and that one is not only obliged oneself to adhere to orthodoxy, but obliged to be ever vigilant regarding the orthodoxy of others. Ecclesiastical authorities counted on scholars to police themselves, relying on students to report suspicious teaching, and on expert panels, drawn from the ranks of university masters, to judge the danger. The suppression of intellectual freedom, then, was not a tyranny imposed from on high, against the will of the people, but was instead accepted widely, if not quite universally, right up until the end of the seventeenth century, in much the way that patriotism today remains an endemic passion among the masses. One finds this attitude not only in the Roman Church, but also in Protestant countries, which were often just as intolerant as Catholic ones. John Calvin's intolerance, in particular, was notorious. And even Milton agreed that freedom of the press has its limits, and should not apply to "popery" or "superstition" (*Areopagitica* p. 54). Such works, he thinks, certainly need to be suppressed.[7]

One might naively suppose that such limitations on free expression would have little bearing on metaphysics. To be sure, atheism was not a live option anywhere in Europe

---

[7] On heresy as the greatest of sins, see Lea, *History of the Inquisition* I:234–5, which also situates the brutality of the Inquisition in the context of contemporary criminal law. Peters remarks that the penalties for heresy "rivaled the most severe penalties for any offense recognized anywhere in thirteenth-century law" (*Inquisition* p. 56). He points out that the use of torture, so notoriously associated with the Inquisition, was common as well in the prosecution of civil crimes (ibid., p. 65). Aquinas had used the harshness of civil law as an argument for punishing heresy with death: "Unde si falsarii pecuniae vel alii malefactores statim per saeculares principes iuste morti traduntur, multo magis haeretici statim cum de haeresi convincuntur possent non solum excommunicari sed et iuste occidi" (*Summa theol.* 2a2ae 11.3c).

The idea of an obligation to report the heresy of others goes back to Pope Leo I: "he who does not, when he can, recall others from error shows that he himself errs" (Wakefield and Evans, *Heresies* p. 353). The Condemnation of 1277 is typical of our period in threatening to excommunicate not only anyone who promulgates any of its long list of errors, but also anyone who hears any such errors and does not report it within seven days (ed. Piché pp. 74–6). Godfrey of Fontaines says that informants of this kind were common among the "minus periti et simplices" (*Quodlibet* XII.5, p. 102).

until around the close of our period.[8] But provided one stayed within the bounds of the local orthodox Christian theology, it might seem that the possibilities in metaphysics would be wide open. Of course, as we have seen, this was far from the case. The Condemnation of 1277 is notorious for its wide-ranging intrusion into questions that might seem to be strictly philosophical (§10.3, §18.2, §29.3). Robert Kilwardby's shorter list of condemned propositions from that same year in Oxford is just as aggressive in reaching into seemingly non-theological terrain, not only proscribing the denial of hylomorphism in general—"that matter and form are not essentially distinct"—but also proscribing Aquinas's unitarian version of the theory, according to which a single material substance contains just a single substantial form (§25.1). The following century would see a retreat with respect to the censure of doctrines pertaining to Aquinas (at least after his canonization in 1323), but the general pattern of aggressive intervention on philosophical questions continued unabated. In 1312, the Council of Vienne required on pain of heresy maintaining that the soul is the form of the body. The condemnations of Autrecourt in 1346/7 and of John of Mirecourt in 1347 proscribed a long list of theses that seem on their face quite distant from theological concerns—most notably for our purposes the denial of quality as a real accident (§§19.3–5). These ecclesiastical interventions had a profound impact on theologians and philosophers. As we have seen in other chapters, scholars routinely cite them as the basis for their views. And to ensure that students and masters were familiar with the limits of orthodoxy, collections of the various condemned doctrines were assembled into a single handy *Collectio errorum*, and these circulated throughout European universities. Moreover, for every proposition that was explicitly censured, many more views were subject to less formal kinds of pressure, or were indeed never stated at all, because they so obviously fell outside the bounds of what was permissible.[9]

The censures of 1270–1347 demarcate the outer limits of debate for the duration of the scholastic era. In general, as time wore on, these limits came to be so entrenched as to be internalized in the minds of scholars, their basis in Church doctrine no longer needing to be mentioned. Consider the Council of Vienne. In 1278, Peter John Olivi thought himself free to question whether the soul is the form of the body. This was, after all, a doctrine that had been dominant in the Latin West for only a few decades. In general, remarks Olivi of Aristotle, "his authority, like that of any infidel and idolater, is nothing to me" (*Summa* II.16; I:337). Yet after Olivi's views on the soul were condemned at Vienne in 1312, it became impossible to follow his lead in this matter. Accordingly, when in subsequent years authors such as Henry of Harclay, John of

---

[8] For the origins of atheism in the latter seventeenth century, see Schröder, *Ursprünge des Atheismus* and Foucault, "Fondements." Of course, it is harder to say the extent to which people might have taken atheism seriously in the privacy of their thoughts, or outside of academic circles. Christopher Hill relates the startling example of the English Ranter William Bond, in 1656: "no God or power ruling above the planets, no Christ but the sun that shines upon us; . . . if the Scriptures were a-making again then Tom Lampire of Melksham would make as good Scriptures as the Bible. There was neither heaven nor hell except in a man's conscience . . ." (*World Turned Upside Down* p. 183; see pp. 136–45 for other cases). But this is an exceptional case, from an exceptional period. Speaking of the revolutionary period in England, Hill writes that "for a short time, ordinary people were freer from the authority of church and social superiors than they had ever been before, or were for a long time to be again" (ibid. p. 292).

[9] For Kilwardby's list of condemned propositions, see Denifle and Chatelain, *Chartularium* I:559. On the circulation of condemnations as a *Collectio errorum*, see Bianchi, *Censure et liberté* pp. 60–1 and Courtenay, "Preservation and Dissemination."

Jandun, and Peter Auriol take up the question of how the soul stands to the body, they go along with the standard hylomorphic analysis, but make it clear that they are doing so purely on the basis of faith, and stress that they do not think the doctrine can be proved. Eventually, however, the Aristotelian analysis came to be taken for granted, as beyond dispute, and in this and other domains scholastic thought took on the rigid, dogmatic aspect for which it would be so scorned in the seventeenth century. Although the fifteenth and sixteenth centuries are filled with ingenious disputes over the debatable points of scholastic metaphysics—the nature of prime matter, the role of quantity, the number of substantial forms, and on and on—the larger questions of whether we even ought to postulate prime matter, real accidents, or substantial forms were simply not open to discussion.[10]

One measure of the increasing vulnerability of the scholastic framework toward the end of our period is the reappearance of official efforts to suppress dissent. In 1513, the Fifth Lateran Council reaffirmed the Council of Vienne's earlier teaching. The newly founded Jesuit order subsequently provides the most comprehensive example of the renewed efforts at systematizing the bounds of permissible philosophical dispute. In 1562, Diego Ledesma, prefect of studies at the Jesuits' Roman College, set out a list of principles "to be taught and defended by all masters of arts and philosophy." Predictably, the list includes the principle that "the rational soul is truly the form and act of the body," but it also includes some much more sweeping language:

New opinions, especially in weighty matters, should not be introduced without the advice and express license of superiors.

    Also, it is not allowed to hold views against the most received and solemn opinions and, as it were, the axioms of nearly all the philosophers and medical scholars, such as

- natural bodies consist of matter and form, and these are the principles of natural things;
- there are four elements;
- there are four primary qualities;
- there are four kinds of causes;

and others like these, although they have nothing to do with the faith. Indeed, one should teach against any common opinion rarely, and not without great cause. (ed. Gómez Rodeles et al., *Monumenta* p. 490)

---

[10] For Olivi on the soul, see *Summa* II.51, and the discussion in Pasnau, "Olivi on the Metaphysics of Soul."

    Harclay remarks of the Averroist line on intellect that "nulla ratio probat oppositum. Unde solum propter fidem teneo quod intellectiva est forma hominis" (*Quaest. ord.* 9 n. 59). Jandun recites the stock Aristotelian line and then remarks: "omnia talia quae dicunt fideles catholici ego dico simpliciter esse vera sine omni dubitatione, sed demonstrare nescio. Gaudeant qui hoc sciunt; sed sola fide teneo et confiteor" (*In De an.* III.12, col. 291). Auriol expressly invokes the Council of Vienne: "licet demonstrari non possit animam esse formam corporis modo aliarum formarum, tamen tenendum est, secundum quod mihi videtur, quod sicut figura est forma et pura perfectio cerae, sic anima est pura actuatio et formatio corporis eo modo quo se habent caeterae formae. . . . Illam autem conclusionem teneo specialiter propter determinationem Concilii, quae ex verborum apparentia videtur ad intentionem illam" (*Sent.* II.16.1.2, II:224b).

    For the Council of Vienne, see Denzinger, *Enchiridion symbolorum* n. 902: "Porro doctrinam omnem seu positionem temere asserentem, aut vertentem in dubium, quod substantia animae rationalis seu intellectivae vere ac per se humani corporis non sit forma, velut erroneam ac veritati catholicae inimicam fidei, praedicto sacro approbante Concilio reprobamus. . . . "

    One measure of the extent to which the various condemnations from the start of our period became internalized in later discussions is that when the Paris theology faculty decided in 1520 to create a systematic register of false opinions, its first attempt at so doing omitted, remarkably, the condemnations of 1270, 1277, and 1347 (ibid. pp. 1664–5).

The remarkably specific list of principles that Ledesma put forward would be reiterated, with various additions and subtractions, in later Jesuit documents. By the time of the famous *Ratio studiorum* (1586), in which the Jesuits attempted an official statement of their pedagogical practices, these sorts of specific lists of "quasi axiomata" (lines 3–4) gave way to more general statements requiring teachers to adhere to safe and approved doctrines and texts, and above all to the opinions of Thomas Aquinas. In a letter that circulated with the *Ratio studiorum*, Claudio Aquaviva, the general of the order, allowed that in certain cases there might be other views that are "more plausible and more accepted" than Aquinas's. Still, "because of his authority and his more secure and approved teachings, which our Constitutions commend, it should be made completely sure that he is followed *ordinarily*." More generally, according to Aquaviva,

Let no one defend any opinion that the bulk of learned men would judge to go against the received axioms of the philosophers or theologians, or against the common meaning of the scholastic theologians.... In questions already dealt with by others, let no one follow new opinions or introduce new questions in matters that can pertain in any way to religion or that are of any significance, without consulting the prefect of studies or the Superior. (de Rochemonteix, *Un collège des Jesuites* IV:11n.–12n.)

Despite such strictures, many of the most interesting late scholastic authors are in fact Jesuits, including Benedictus Pererius, Franciscus Toletus, and above all Suárez. But it is obvious that in such a climate they could go only so far toward genuinely open philosophical inquiry.[11]

Today we can hardly understand the idea that philosophers ought to eschew innovation in favor of the safe and secure. To the extent we can understand this, we are likely to suppose that these strictures must have been imposed by some authority on high, and that philosophers during most of our period were accordingly living in a state of oppression, unable to express themselves freely. Perhaps this is so in some cases, and I will return to this issue in §20.5. In general, however, there is every reason to think that the various academic restrictions considered above reflect the common consensus of the intellectual class. After all, Dominicans chose to become Dominicans, thereby accepting an absolute requirement to defend the views of Aquinas. Jesuits chose to become Jesuits, and so commit themselves to the conservative educational program described above. Admittedly, for the authors we have been considering, there

---

[11] For the Fifth Lateran Council see Denzinger, *Enchiridion symbolorum* n. 1440: "hoc sacro approbante Concilio damnamus et reprobamus omnes asserentes, animam intellectivam mortalem esse, aut unicam in cunctis hominibus, et haec in dubium vertentes, cum illa non solum vere per se et essentialiter humani corporis forma exsistat... verum et immortalis, et pro corporum quibus infunditur multitudine singulariter multiplicabilis, et multiplicata, et multiplicanda sit...."

For further details regarding Jesuit restrictions on teaching, see Ariew, "Descartes and Scholasticism" and Lohr, "Jesuit Aristotelianism." For further documents in translation, see Ignatius of Loyola, *Constitutions*, esp. IV.5.4. "The doctrine that they ought to follow in each branch should be that which is safer and more approved, as also the authors who teach it" (p. 189); IV.14.1. "In general, as was stated in the treatise on the colleges, in each faculty those books will be lectured on which are found to contain more solid and safe doctrine, and those which are suspect, or whose authors are suspect, will not be taken up" (p. 219).

Although scholars tend to describe the Jesuits as a conservative philosophical force, such generalizations must be drawn with care, since they certainly do not apply across the board, as we have had occasion to see in the work of Pererius and Suárez in particular. For some valuable remarks on the more progressive trends in sixteenth-century Jesuit education, see Secada, *Cartesian Metaphysics* p. 28, who speaks of a "spirit of rational inquiry and freedom from dogmatism."

was no real choice with respect to Christianity in general, but there is also hardly any evidence that scholars wanted the sort of wide-open intellectual freedom we value so much today. Consider this 1403 letter from a young Parisian arts master to his chancellor:

I ask of you, good father, which path of doctrine will we follow? Which way do you offer to the young? . . . Do not reply to me that it is up to you to choose and judge for yourself as you wish. For it is not permitted (*licet*) that I choose. especially where the determination among such a variety of views would be daunting. And even if it were permitted to me, still right reason would seek paternal counsel. (Kaluza, *Les Querelles* p. 17; see §5.2 for further discussion)

This young scholar quite sincerely wants to be told what to think. To be sure, there were calls throughout our period for wider leeway in philosophical speculation, and these calls intensified over the course of the seventeenth century, as we will see below (§20.3). But even Locke, whose *Letter Concerning Toleration* (1689) is the most famous of all such appeals, goes only so far in his demands: freedom of inquiry is a good thing among fellow Protestants, but he allows no such freedom to Catholics, let alone atheists. Opposition to completely unfettered philosophical and theological speculation is virtually universal throughout our four centuries.

When the freedoms of many are suppressed by a powerful few, no special explanation is required beyond the usual motives of power, money, and fanaticism. Here, however, the common consensus in favor of restricting intellectual autonomy should lead us to wonder at its cause. Two factors seem particularly important. First and foremost is a line of argument that one encounters over and over in discussions of heresy: that philosophical novelty leads to theological novelty; theological novelty threatens the unity of the Church; any threat to the unity of the Church is a threat to the well-being of the Church; and the Church's well-being should be preserved above all else. The first step in this syllogism, from philosophical innovation to theological heterodoxy, has deep roots in Christian thought. Tertullian had said that "philosophers are the forefathers of heretics," and this idea would appear again and again. In the twelfth century Bernard of Clairvaux attributed Peter Abaelard's alleged theological errors to his pursuit of philosophy, blaming him for "preferring the innovations of the philosophers and their novelties to the teaching of the catholic fathers and to the faith" (*Patr. lat.* 182:355C). Around the same time, William of Conches attacked his monastic critics for their hostility toward novelty:

Ignorant themselves of the forces of nature and wanting to have company in their ignorance, they do not want people to look into anything; they want us to believe like peasants and not ask the reason behind things. . . . If they learn that anyone is so inquiring, they shout that he is a heretic, placing more reliance on their monastic robes than on their wisdom. (tr. Peters, "*Libertas Inquirendi*" p. 92)

By the time of the scholastic era, this sort of resistance to novelty was commonplace. John Gerson, chancellor of the University of Paris for over three decades (1395–1429), praised what he described as the "daily" condemnation of articles at Paris (*Oeuvres* V:430), which he justified on the grounds that "otherwise the school at Paris and from there the whole kingdom of France and indeed the greater part of Christendom would fall into numerous errors" (*Oeuvres* X:256).[12]

The notion that heresy posed a threat to the institution of the Church was commonplace. Innocent III, in 1199, compared heresy to treason, but argued that heresy was much worse, in virtue of being an offense against Christ's "eternal majesty" (*Patr. lat.* 214:539B). The Dominican Nicholas Eymerich's classic manual, the *Directorium Inquisitorum* (c.1376) describes heretics as "attacking, demolishing, and devastating the integrity of the catholic faith by subtly and damnably subverting it" (f. a3v). Even Desiderius Erasmus, though relatively liberal on the subject of heresy, accepted that "it is necessary for the preservation of the state to kill heretics who are blasphemous and seditious" (*Opera* X:1576).[13] In the early seventeenth century, this line of thought is set out with particular clarity by Jean-Baptiste Morin, in his *Refutation des theses erronées* (1624), an attack on the anti-Aristotelian broadsheet that had been posted in Paris earlier that year (§19.6). Morin's brief work begins with this memorable sentiment:

It is a maxim of which many states around the world, even today, offer a deplorable proof: that there is nothing more seditious and pernicious than a new doctrine. I am speaking not only of theology, but even of philosophy. For if... the true awareness of visible and corporeal things— that is, the true natural philosophy—elevates and delights us with an awareness and love of invisible and incorporeal things, and above all God, creator of all things,... it is indeed certain that the false philosophy or awareness of things in nature cannot bring the spirit to that same end. Instead, turning us away from there, it cannot lead anywhere other than to errors, heresies, and atheism. (pp. 3–4)

Morin goes on to work out the implied argument in detail. "All the atheists and deists" have become such by pursuing "a new philosophy and new but false principles" (p. 4). "Nearly all the heresies" are the result of "denying or perverting the philosophy of Aristotle" (ibid.). Heresies, in turn, divide the minds of the people, and so lead to the division and ruin of nations. "This is why, in every well-policed state, as soon as such a plague appears, these developments are anticipated right away and the authors are severely punished, lest it be regretted later, should this poison be tolerated even a little" (p. 5).

---

[12] On the hostility toward philosophical innovation in the centuries before our period, see Chenu, *Nature, Man, and Society* ch. 9; Peters, "*Libertas Inquirendi*," and Verbeke, "Philosophy and Heresy" (who quotes Tertullian). Stephen of Tournai was already complaining about philosophical novelty in the new universities at the turn of the thirteenth century: "Lapsa sunt apud nos in confusionis officinam sacrarum studia litterarum, dum et discipuli solis novitatibus applaudunt, et magistri gloriae potius invigilant quam doctrinae, novas recentesque summulas et commentaria firmantia super theologia passim conscribunt, quibus auditores suos demulceant, detineant, decipiant, quasi nondum sufficerint sanctorum opuscula patrum" (*Patr. lat.* 211:517). More generally, see Ginzburg, "High and Low" and Smalley, "Ecclesiastical Attitudes," who argues that the resistance to novelty ebbs and flows over the course of the Middle Ages.

[13] On heresy's seriousness arising from its threat to the unity of the faith, see Lea, *History of the Inquisition* I:211: "No matter how trivial may have been the original cause of schism, nor how pure and fervent might have been the faith of the schismatics, the fact that they had refused to bend to authority, and had thus sought to divide the seamless garment of Christ, became an offence in comparison with which all other sins dwindled into insignificance, neutralizing all the virtues and all the devotion which men could possess." For contemporary instances of this attitude, see Gregory IX's decretal *Ille humani generis* or Frederick II's *Liber Augustalis*, both from 1231, which describe in the harshest terms both the danger of heresy to the Church, and the severity of the punishments it should receive. (Excerpts from both documents are translated in Peters, *Heresy and Authority* pp. 196–8, 207–9.) See also Gregory XI's 1377 bull against Wyclif: "He has cast himself into the depravity of preaching heretical dogmas that strive to subvert and weaken the state of the whole Church as well as secular authority" (ibid., p. 271).

No doubt, Morin is a reactionary figure. But his hostility toward innovation lies very much in the mainstream of early seventeenth-century thought. In describing "a new doctrine" (line 2) as the greatest of dangers, he is echoing the conclusion reached by the Paris Theology Faculty earlier that year, in its condemnation of the anti-Aristotelian broadsheet.[14] That same sort of caution can be found in contemporary thinkers as intelligent as Marin Mersenne, whose *Quaestiones celeberrimae in Genesim* (1623) roundly condemns the opponents of Aristotle: "These men who desire to found a new philosophy, and to demonstrate it from fundamental principles, never regard the glory of God. Rather they strive with an ignorant obsessive zeal, by which—unless I am mistaken—they seek to shake up and overturn the Catholic religion, if they are able to do it" (preface). Mersenne's views would change over time; indeed, he came to be a prominent advocate for Galileo and Descartes. His early career shows vividly, however, why it was so difficult for such ideas to become established.[15] Descartes, for one, understood this quite well. In a letter from 1637 to one of his former teachers at the Jesuit college of La Flèche, he remarks: "I know that the principal reason that requires members of your order to reject most carefully all sorts of novelties in matters of philosophy is the fear they have that these novelties might also cause some changes in theology" (I:455). Descartes assures that there is nothing to worry about in that regard, and that in fact his views agree "best of all with the mysteries of religion" (I:456). We have no record of how the Jesuit priest responded.

Worrying about philosophical novelty in these ways requires taking it seriously as a powerful cultural force. This is not easy to imagine today, given how marginal the influence of philosophy is, even in the most rarified of intellectual circles. Yet philosophy during our four centuries was a much broader field, encompassing all of what we now regard as the sciences. As an analogue to the intellectual prominence and influence of philosophy, then, we might think of the modern place of science, and the controversial role it plays in religion and ethics. Yet once we take science as our point of comparison, it becomes especially striking that *novelty* was so greatly feared during

---

[14] The Faculty of Theology at the University of Paris prefaced their evaluation of the 1624 Broadsheet with this remark: "Nihil plane in Republica Christiana periculosius, nihilque communi Sanctorum Patrum iudicio cavendum diligentius, quam rerum novitas, ea praesertim, quae verae scientiae, sacraeque doctrinae manifeste dignoscitur adversari" (de Launoy, *De varia fortuna* p. 203). They go on to cite 1 Timothy 6:20: "O Timothy, keep that which is committed to thy trust, avoiding the profane novelties of words, and oppositions of knowledge falsely so called."

[15] I am indebted to Daniel Garber for most of my information on Mersenne (see Garber, "On the Frontlines"), as well as on the 1624 Paris Broadsheet and the response by Morin (see Garber, "Defending Aristotle"). Garber considers in detail the broader cultural and religious forces at work in the initial resistance to novelty, and in the eventual embrace of the new philosophy by Mersenne among many others. One of Garber's principal conclusions is that "the hold Aristotelianism had on European thought was much more than intellectual.... To oppose Aristotelianism could legitimately be read as an attack on the very institutions of the state, the government, the courts, the church, and on the learned professions that support those institutions" ("On the Frontlines" p. 157).

Even Glanvill, a leading advocate of the Royal Society, feels the need at least to recognize the worries that novelty might lead to religious unrest: "You know me too well, to think I designed anything against the appointments and purposes of our pious ancestors in those venerable nurseries of piety and learning. I too well apprehend the danger of such innovations in an age so prone to fancies and dissettlements, in which nothing, however worthy and sacred, has been able to defend itself against the rude hands of proud, because successful, violence gilded with the plundered titles of *Reformation* and *Religion*" (*Scire tuum nihil est* p. 78). But Glanvill goes on to argue that this shows only the need to teach Aristotle to "junior students" in the universities, and does not justify the practice of senior scholars "to sit down in a contented despair of any further progress into science than has been made by their idealized *sophy*; and depriving themselves and all this world of their liberty in philosophy by a sacramental adherence to an heathen authority" (ibid., pp. 78–9). Curtis, *Oxford and Cambridge in Transition* ch. 9, argues that it was in fact quite unusual, well into the seventeenth century, to suppose that the universities were a place where scholars make advances in learning, as opposed to merely passing on the learning of old.

the period in question, since of course we now take innovation to lie at the very heart of scientific inquiry. Indeed, one cannot fully appreciate why novelty was held in such bad repute during these four centuries simply by noticing its alleged connection with theological heresy. After all, our period begins shortly after one of the most abrupt and striking transformations in the history of philosophy, when Aristotelianism came to dominate the university curriculum in the mid-thirteenth century. The great figures of the classical scholastic period were at the forefront of these innovations, and spoke out strongly against those who would stifle progress. Albert the Great, for instance, memorably lashes out at those who "seek nothing in the writings [of Aristotle and others] except for what they criticize." These are, he says, "bitter and bilious men who turn everyone else to bitterness, not allowing them to seek the truth in the sweetness of society" (*In Polit.* epilogue, ed. Jammy IVb:500b). So it is not as if the scholastic era was founded on conservative principles of resistance to change. It is indeed a remarkable feature of the period that Aristotle went so quickly from being a suspect pagan to being the safest and solidest of philosophical authorities. The hostility toward innovation of the later scholastic era is quite difficult to square with the radical dislocation that Albert, Aquinas, and others championed in the mid-thirteenth century.

Accounting for this dislocation requires understanding a second aspect of our period's hostility toward philosophical innovation. Aristotle could come onto the scene as an unparalleled philosophical authority, despite the evident risks to the faith, because of the widespread conviction during our period that older authors generally have greater authority. This is one of those ideas from which the caricature of a "Middle Ages" is constructed—those supposedly fallow centuries between the fall of Rome and the rise of the Renaissance, when the highest aspiration of civilization was simply to preserve something from the crumbling edifice of classical learning. Emblematic of this picture of the era is Bernard of Chartres's famous image of dwarfs having seen farther by standing on the shoulders of giants, an image that would get reworked again and again throughout our period.[16] In general, the notion that the ideas of antiquity are to be preferred to modern innovations flourished throughout our four centuries. Aristotle's authority in philosophy, Galen's in medicine, and Ptolemy's in astronomy are all indications of the tendency to treat ancient authors as governing figures in various intellectual domains. The grip of such assumptions was slow to give way. John Aubrey remarked toward the end of the seventeenth century that "till about the year 1649, 'twas held a strange presumption for a man to attempt an innovation in learning" (*Natural History of Wiltshire*, preface p. 18). Aubrey dates this sea-change to the advent of experimental philosophy at Oxford. In other parts of Europe, that date might be put earlier, but in any case a dramatic change of attitude certainly does take place in the mid-seventeenth century. When earlier figures like Marsilio Ficino and Francesco

---

[16] For the long history of the dwarfs-on-the-shoulders-of-giants saying, see Jeauneau, "Nains et géants" and Merton, *On the Shoulders of Giants*. The ascription to Bernard of Chartres is made by John of Salisbury, *Metalogicon*: "Dicebat Bernardus Carnotensis nos esse quasi nanos gigantium humeris insidentes, ut possimus plura eis et remotiora videre, non utique proprii visus acumine aut eminentia corporis, sed quia in altum subvehimur et extollimur magnitudine gigantea" (*Metalogicon* 3.4). John himself is not so bound to ancient views: "Nec dedignatus sum modernorum proferre sententias quos antiquis, in plerisque praeferre non dubito" (*Metalogicon* prol.).

Newton invokes the dwarfs-and-giants saying with reference to his contemporaries Descartes and Hooke. According to Feingold, however, this was intended ironically (*Newtonian Moment* p. 24).

Patrizi had attempted to move away from Aristotle, it was toward the ancient wisdom (*prisca sapientia*) of Plato, Pythagoras, and Hermes Trismegistus. When early seventeenth-century authors turn instead toward corpuscularianism, they too appeal to authority, but now to the authority of ancient atomism (§5.2). The title of Jean Chrysostome Magnen's *Democritus reviviscens* (1646), for instance, displays its backward-looking character. The first sentence of the prolegomena announces its intention: "to reestablish the philosophy of atoms, first-born among all the sects of wise men." Joseph Glanvill likewise appeals to the antiquity of atomism, referring to this hypothesis as "the first and most ancient which there is in any memory in physiology," compared to which "the Aristotelian is a very novelty . . . at the best a degeneracy and corruption of the most ancient wisdom" (*Scire tuum nihil est*, p. 89). Gassendi's extensive efforts at rehabilitating Epicurus are part of this same project: rather than do something new, Gassendi seeks to uncover the lost wisdom of old. Even Francis Bacon, despite his famous insistence on forgoing authority in favor of observation, is not above appealing to the authority of antiquity: "the philosophy of Democritus seems to us worthy of being rescued from neglect, especially since it agrees in most things with the authority of the most ancient times (*prisci saeculi*)" (*De principiis* [*Phil. Studies* p. 206]).[17]

Why should the ancients be wiser than us? Perhaps there is no more hope of explaining this common assumption than of explaining why we moderns today tend to assume we are much wiser than the ancients. Still, one can find something of a theoretical underpinning behind this preference for antiquity in the common embrace of what is, in effect, the world-historical analogue to the second law of thermodynamics: the idea that the natural world constantly deteriorates over the centuries, a downward spiral that began with the Fall of Man and that will end only with the Second Coming. Although this too may look like a characteristically "medieval" view, it is one that endured well into the so-called modern era. John Donne's *First Anniversary* (1611), for instance, is an extended meditation on the world's decline:

> . . . mankind decays so soon,
> We're scarce our Fathers shadows cast at noon.
>
> . . .
>
> And as our bodies, so our minds are crampt:
> Tis shrinking, not close weaning that hath thus,
> In mind and body both be-dwarfed us.

Godfrey Goodman's *Fall of Man* (1616) discusses in painstaking detail how ours is "the old age of the world" (p. 357), decrepit and feeble. Thus "the wits of former times, certainly they did far exceed ours, their bodies were better tempered, as being nearer the first mould" (pp. 359–60). This naturally leads Goodman to an enormous pessimism regarding the prospects for any sort of intellectual progress: "For all arts whatsoever, the best authors are the most ancient, even unto this day. I could instance in every one in particular, though we, building upon their foundations, have added some ornaments,

---

[17] On humanism and the *prisca sapientia*, see Cophenhaver and Schmitt, *Renaissance Philosophy* pp. 146–8, 190–2, 336–7. For Patrizi, see Deitz, "Falsissima est ergo" p. 243: "Patrizi's discussion of Aristotle's theory of matter is informed by one of his strongest convictions—viz., that the older a philosophical tenet is, the nearer it is to original truth. . . ." For Gassendi's strategy of couching his views in the context of an ancient tradition, see Joy, *Gassendi the Atomist* pp. 10–11, 18–19.

yet such as are not necessary to perfect the art: and generally for the ancients, whatsoever you shall observe in practice amongst them, you shall find that it stood with great wisdom and providence" (p. 360).[18]

Ideas such as these shape the contours of philosophical thought over our four centuries. Although there is intrinsic power to a hylomorphic metaphysics, it would be naive to suppose that this framework dominated philosophy for so long simply because it was the best available hypothesis. Similarly, although the classical scholastic authors—particularly Aquinas and Scotus—created a powerful systematic philosophical framework for Christian theology, their ideas were not powerful enough all by themselves to remain ascendant for four centuries. That they did is the result of external factors, social and religious. Although the full story is far too complex to be handled adequately in the space I am allowing it, we have at least glanced at two important considerations: the fear of theological schism, and the valuation of antiquity over modernity. In the mid-thirteenth century it was respect for ancient thought that played the decisive role in the rapid assimilation of Aristotle, overcoming the fear of heterodoxy. Once Aristotle was accepted as The Philosopher, however, scholastic thought became locked into a fairly narrow range of options. Having identified their preeminent ancient authority—whom Vanini would mockingly call "that supreme dictator of human wisdom" (*De admirandis* dial. 2, p. 7)—scholastic thought found itself incapable of considering other options. In certain limited circles in Italy, Plato made an impact in the fifteenth century, but his influence never came close to challenging Aristotle's (§5.1). If Plato could not, who could? Aristotle's ancient pedigree, combined with the fear that philosophical novelty might lead to theological discord, rendered his authority unassailable, for four centuries. This is as good a run as any philosopher has ever had, or is ever likely to have again. In view of the social pressures at work, however, it should go into the record books with an asterisk.

20.3. Dissidents

Although the various condemnations of the scholastic era have been intensively studied, scholars have nevertheless tended to downplay their negative effects. One

---

[18] On the decline of nature, see Haydn, *Counter-Renaissance* pp. 525–44. For Goodman and subsequent debates, see Jones, *Ancients and Moderns* chs. 1–2. Remarkably, Goodman complains that even the dwarfs-and-giants metaphor gives us far too much credit, since in fact we cannot see as far as the giants of old (*Fall of Man* pp. 361–2). Goodman makes it clear, however, that his pessimistic attitude is not universally shared. For he complains "that this our age being most proud, arrogant and vainglorious, does most unjustly claim unto itself the name and title of the learned age" (p. 360).

Even Newton, it has been argued, had some sympathy for the natural-decline hypothesis, invested as he was in trying to recover the ancient wisdom of old, in religion, alchemy, and other domains (see Dobbs, "Stoic and Epicurean Doctrines" p. 231).

The trope of the world's growing older and moving toward decline is a familiar one in medieval texts (see, e.g., Wakefield and Evans, *Heresies* pp. 228–9, 290), with roots going back to Augustine (see Marrou, *L'ambivalence du temps*). It was used to justify the Church's increasingly violent response to heresy, as necessary given the increasingly evil condition of the world. Even in the scientific domain, until the very end of our period, there is little evidence of optimism regarding progress (see Molland, "Medieval Ideas" and Zilsel, "Genesis"). But see Galileo's pointed remark against Simplicio's accusing nature of a "second childhood": "E non so con che fondamento voi vogliate riprender la natura, come quella che per la molta età sia imbarbogita ed abbia dimenticato a produrre ingegni specolativi, né sappia farne più se non di quelli che, facendosi mancipii d'Aristotile, abbiano a intender col suo cervello e sentir co i suoi sensi" (*Two Chief World Systems* second day [ed. Flora p. 492; tr. Drake p. 152]).

reason why is the perception that such censorship was ineffectual. Although that is true in certain cases, such as the early thirteenth-century efforts to suppress Aristotle's natural philosophy, or the later thirteenth-century attacks on Aquinas, in many other cases censorship had a massive, crippling influence on scholastic thought. Virtually all of the ideas associated with the innovations of seventeenth-century thought—corpuscularianism, monism, occasionalism, materialism, skepticism, and on and on—were utterly familiar at the end of the thirteenth century. The sole reason why such notions failed to play a prominent role in scholastic thought is that, when they were put forward as positive theses, they were immediately censured. The indubitable evidence that such censorship was effective is the narrow range of philosophical options in play during this period. Although to Descartes it could seem as if "the majority of would-be philosophers over the last centuries have blindly followed Aristotle" (*Principles*, French preface, IXB:7), it would be more apt to say that these philosophers had been blinkered by ecclesiastic censure.[19]

A second, more plausible reason for downplaying the role of censorship would be the apparent contentment of scholastic philosophers to run along their narrowly circumscribed course. Like a man who has no desire to leave a locked room, these scholars might be thought to have had all the freedom they wanted. Yet as Luca Bianchi has shown in extensive detail, this optimistic diagnosis is untenable. Even if the rank and file of scholars thought it appropriate and even desirable to follow the lead of authority, there were always, throughout the scholastic era, a significant number of exceptions.[20] The Condemnation of 1277 itself bears witness to this phenomenon, both generally in terms of the wide range of heterodox propositions it condemns, and specifically in

---

[19] McLaughlin's formidable study, *Intellectual Freedom*, is marred by its constant insistence on the freedom of scholastic philosophers and theologians. E.g.: "By the late thirteenth century the master of arts was free to devote himself to the teaching of any and all of the parts of philosophy. He might enjoy, no less fully, it seems, than they had desired, the independence sought by his more radical colleagues in the conflicts which culminated in 1277" (p. 96); "In both theory and practice, the intellectual province of the late thirteenth-century theologian was virtually unlimited" (p. 238). From McLaughlin's Panglossian perspective, the much harassed Siger of Brabant "represents not only the fulfillment of the vocation of the thirteenth-century master of arts and the measure of his freedom, but the culmination of his struggle for the autonomy of his discipline" (p. 95). Autrecourt, likewise, is not a counterexample to her position, but rather "demonstrated very effectively how free the speculation of a master of arts might be" (p. 139). McLaughlin does not stop to ask herself why it would take nearly 300 years before anyone else would dare to say the things that Autrecourt had said. See too Peters's only slightly more judicious remarks, in reference to the various university condemnations: "these attempts at controlling teaching seem to have done little to stop a process that kept spilling beyond the tidy confines of philosophy and theology and carefully drawn schemes of the organization of knowledge" (*"Libertas Inquirendi"* p. 93). And see MacClintock, *Perversity and Error* p. 73: "... in spite of the attacks of the 1270s, the autonomous tradition of learning in the arts faculty continued actively throughout the last quarter of the 13th century, without any but the most perfunctory recognition of subordination to the ecclesiastical authorities."

A more sophisticated argument against the efficacy of scholastic censorship is offered in de Libera, *Penser au Moyen Âge*, who contends that censorship often led to more rather than less heterodoxy, and so served to promote the ideas that it sought to shut down. Although it is of course impossible to know what scholars said in the privacy of their studies, it seems clear that the written record we must content ourselves with does not bear out this optimistic picture. Instead I follow Bianchi: "les mécanismes de contrôle idéologique ... ont en général atteint leur but ou, du moins, conditionné le développement des débats, la succession des courants, l'accessibilité des textes d'une manière si remarquable que l'histoire de la pensée en a été profondément modifiée" (*Censure et liberté* p. 57).

[20] For the argument that scholastic authors had as much freedom as they wanted, see Haskins: "Even within the more carefully guarded field of theology and philosophy, it is doubtful whether many found themselves cramped. Accepting the principle of authority as their starting-point, men did not feel its limitations as we should feel them now. A fence is no obstacle to those who do not desire to go outside, and many barriers that would seem intolerable to a more sceptical age were not felt as barriers by the schoolmen. He is free who feels himself free" (*Rise of the Universities* pp. 55–6). For Bianchi's in-depth investigation of cases where scholastic authors did not feel themselves free, see *Censure et liberté*, esp. pp. 69–85.

terms of a series of articles directed at an untrammeled rationalism at the expense of authority:

37. "Nothing is to be believed unless it is self-evident or can be established from what is self-evident."
150. "One should not be satisfied to have certainty on any question through authority."
151. "To have certainty regarding any conclusion, it must be founded on self-evident principles."

These claims were objectionable because they threatened the preeminence of Church authority in theology as well as philosophy. We know of no thirteenth-century author who made claims as strident as these. Perhaps the authorities were pursuing a straw man. But it may also be the case that arts masters at the University of Paris were advancing such claims orally and not putting them in writing, or that some such radical doctrines were written down and later destroyed. We still have some manuscripts that were altered in response to the Condemnation of 1277, and no doubt others were destroyed altogether. Of the vast number of arts masters teaching at Paris—at least 120 by the 1280s, and over 500 a century later—only a very little survives, and so we effectively have no idea what sorts of things might actually have been said in the lecture halls of the average arts master, let alone in the privacy of their rooms.[21]

Although many of the voices condemned in 1277 seem, from what we can tell, to have been effectively silenced, one who was not was the Parisian arts master James of Douai. Even before the 1277 condemnations were announced, James was expressing concern over the censorious atmosphere surrounding philosophy in Paris:

As a result of this defamation it may happen that many—noble and common, those who have begun their studies and those who have not, or those who have begun and advanced, both doctors and auditors—withdraw from philosophy and from philosophical study and investiga-   3
tion or contemplation. This will be a great obstacle to grasping many truths, and especially theological truths. I say that it will be an obstacle to grasping many truths, because it is certain that philosophy pursues the grasp of truth with respect to many entities by following the path of   6
reason. That it is an obstacle to grasping theological truths is clear because, as many say, those who are informed in philosophy can achieve more on the theological faculty than can others. So if people withdraw from philosophy and from the study of philosophical contemplation, this   9
will be a great obstacle to the grasp of theological truth. (*In Ethic.* prologue [Bianchi, *Censure et liberté* p. 265n.])

James does not quite say that many *have* been abandoning philosophy because of the restrictions on intellectual freedom; he simply warns that it "may happen" (line 1), and that if it does then both philosophy and theology will suffer. In the wake of 1277, James returned to this theme, and his remarks become even more strident:

Although philosophy is a great perfection of human beings, philosophers these days are nevertheless oppressed (*oppressi*). Such oppression can have four causes: the badness (*malitia*) of people; their envy; the ignorance of some; and their stupidity. The first can be the badness of   3
people, since those people are bad who hate the good and hate those who can achieve success and attain great standing. As a result of such bad people's accusing others it can happen that

---

[21] On potential sources for the rationalist propositions from the Condemnation of 1277, see Hissette, *Enquête* pp. 20–3. On the alteration and destruction of manuscripts in the wake of 1277, see Bianchi, *Censure et liberté* pp. 37–9. For a very useful overview of the Condemnation of 1277 and of recent literature on the subject see Bianchi, "1277."

philosophers these days are oppressed. The second cause can be envy, since people who envy 6
others are more ready and inclined to accuse those whom they envy. The third cause can be the
ignorance of some, if they are ignorant of what is and is not an error. The fourth cause can be
the stupidity of some, since there are some who imagine they know philosophy, when in actual 9
fact they do not. . . . But I believe that a philosopher using reason can defend the truth, dispute
against its deniers, and even judge errors more than can someone untrained who is not a
philosopher and is not using reason. Hence the fact that philosophers are so oppressed detracts 12
greatly from the path of philosophy. (*In Meteor.* prologue [Bianchi, *Censure et liberté* pp. 263–4n.])

James's anger is palpable. Although he qualifies his accusations as mere possibilities,
there seems little doubt he thinks the Condemnation of 1277 was motivated by malice,
envy, ignorance, and stupidity. Displaying a very modern sensitivity to the impact such
restrictions have on intellectual freedom, James speaks of his fellow philosophers as
"oppressed" (lines 8, 12), and he goes on to contend—as he had in the previous
passage—that the result will be harm to both philosophy and theology. Both disciplines
are best pursued by philosophers "using reason" (line 12) rather than forced down a
narrow path set by others whose motives are dubious.

Although the strident character of James's language is perhaps unmatched by other
scholastic texts in this domain, his general sentiments are common enough. Giles of
Rome, writing in 1278 in defense of Aquinas's unitarian theory of substantial form
(Ch. 25), attacks those who have been a "pestilent disparager" of Aquinas's views,
condemning those views as "erroneous" when in fact they have "illuminated the
Church" (*De gradibus formarum* ch. 6, f. 206vb). Going beyond the usual exchange of
insults between Thomists and their critics, Giles adds that "the path toward holding
contrary views should be closed to no one where we can hold such views without
danger to the faith." To condemn philosophical views as contrary to the faith poses a
threat to the faith itself:

It ought to be plainer than plain and clearer than clear for a thesis to be counted as erroneous.
For such is the weakness of our intellect, [even] with respect to the things in nature that are
most evident, that [arguments] that on one day seem to be demonstrations appear on another 3
day to be sophistical. Anyone can follow opinions that are without danger to the faith. But what
on one day is said to be erroneous and on another day is held to be catholic—what is this other
than to assert that the faith does not have the firmest of foundations, and that it is instead the 6
feeble opinions of human beings and our various superstitions? (ibid., f. 207ra)

Giles here insists on a strict division between those theses that pose a danger to the faith
and those that do not. In cases where there is no danger, "anyone can follow" whatever
view they like (line 4). Giles does not for a moment question the importance of
imposing restrictions in cases where the faith is threatened. But the threat had better
be clear—indeed, "clearer than clear" (line 1)—because otherwise the Church exposes
itself to the inevitable flux of philosophical opinion, which would give the impression
that the foundations of the Church itself are equally uncertain.

A generation later, Durand of St. Pourçain makes a similar case for the autonomy of
reason in matters not pertaining to the faith. The preface to the third version of his
Sentences commentary (1317/27) begins by making a lavish case for the authority of
scripture in theology. Given that the Bible is the revealed word of God, its testimony
takes precedence even over human reason. But what of matters that do not touch the

faith? Here Durand declares that "we follow reason more than the authority of any doctor, however celebrated or established, and count for little any human authority when the contrary truth shines forth through reason." To do otherwise is intolerable, since "any human being who sets aside reason for the sake of human authority falls into beast-like ignorance" (f. 1vb). The implications he draws for those who would restrict the scope of reason in matters not pertaining to the faith are striking:

> From these remarks it is clear that to compel or induce someone not to teach or write things that disagree with what a given doctor teaches is to prefer such a doctor to the holy doctors, to shut down a path to the investigation of the truth, to raise an impediment to knowledge, and not merely to hide the light of reason under a bushel, but to constrain it by force. (ibid.)

Just as did Giles, Durand is insisting on the autonomy of reason in matters not pertaining to the faith.

Yet another instance of such claims can be found in Ockham's political writings. In his long discussion of heresy in the *Dialogus*, Ockham offers what amounts to an insider's history of reactions to the three most famous condemnations of the early part of our period: the Parisian condemnation of 1277; the Oxford condemnation of 1277, reiterated in 1284; and the condemnations of Peter John Olivi (*Dialogus* I.2.21–26). Without expressly taking a position of his own on these matters, Ockham recounts how he has known many who insist not only that some of the propositions condemned are not heretical, but moreover that some are actually true. Further, quite apart from the question of the truth of the various condemned propositions, Ockham reports that others criticize the authorities for straying into purely philosophical territory where the faith was not implicated: "they assert that no one should solemnly condemn or forbid purely philosophical assertions that do not pertain to theology, because in such matters everyone ought to be free to say freely whatever he likes" (ibid., ch. 24).[22]

All of these authors share a conviction that there should be a sphere of philosophical autonomy where one can say what one thinks. They agree that such autonomy has its limits, and in particular that it is limited in cases where there are implications for the faith. But therein lies the rub. Every case of ecclesiastical censure is justified as a defense of the faith. So in a sense the controversy is not over the desirability of unfettered philosophical speculation; the controversy concerns what principles do and do not threaten the Church. John of Mirecourt was condemned for denying real qualities, on the grounds that this conflicts with the sacrament of the Eucharist (§19.3), and three hundred years later Descartes's work would meet the same fate (§19.6). Given the common assumption throughout our period that tolerance should not extend to what threatens the faith, it is scarcely helpful in such a case to invoke the autonomy of philosophical speculation. Although there is some force to cautionary remarks such as those of Giles of Rome, who urged that censorship should be used only when the threat to the faith is completely clear, the only way to adjudicate these issues, ultimately, is to enter into the complex theological details. Hence as much as the philosopher might like

---

[22] Although Ockham certainly believed that heresy ought to be severely punished, it has been argued that his views in that domain are much more tolerant than many of his contemporaries, inasmuch as he is unwilling to condemn as heretical those who believe in good conscience that they are acting in accord with the faith. See Shogimen, "From Disobedience to Toleration" and Nederman, "Individual Autonomy."

to reflect on, say, the Aristotelian categorial scheme in its own right, free from theological questions, for practical purposes this could not be done. Even Descartes, averse as he was to engaging in theology, recognized that he could not eliminate real qualities from his ontology without providing his own account of the Eucharist (§13.5). Like his scholastic predecessors, then, Descartes faced a pragmatic dilemma. The safest, most direct argument for intellectual autonomy is to insist that philosophy and theology are separate domains. But the only way to *show* that they are separate domains is to engage the theological issues. In so doing, the philosopher undermines the very separation that he seeks.

Perhaps the most interesting instance of a scholastic author arguing for intellectual freedom is also the author who pushes the farthest toward heterodoxy: Nicholas of Autrecourt. The first prologue to his *Tractatus* offers a detailed rationale for the unconventional claims he is about to make. His aim, or so he tells us, is to free philosophers from their endless debates over the obscurities of Aristotle and Averroes, revolving around questions that it is not possible to have any certainty about. "What can be had with certainty will be had in a brief time if people turn their intellects immediately toward things, just as they have been turned toward the minds of men, toward Aristotle and his commentator Averroes" (p. 181). Once that work is finished, Autrecourt holds that scholars will be able to devote themselves to more important ethical matters, something, he implies, that many of these scholars might well benefit from. Then, after the formulaic profession that he "wishes to say nothing contrary to the articles of the faith, the determination of the Church, the articles condemned in Paris, etc." (p. 182), he takes up an objection to his approach based on its novelty. The objection—one that Autrecourt says "people argue for against those who try to transform widespread views and bring newly to light conclusions that lie hidden in things" (ibid.)—is that to do this one would have to have the arrogance to suppose oneself better able to reach such conclusions than are the many others who have for a long time agreed on the contrary view. This is, of course, a version of the sort of argument against novelty considered in the previous section.[23]

Rather than bothering to deny the novelty of his views, Autrecourt tries to make a principled case for what he is doing. His first step is to offer a general rule for the conditions under which it is permissible to offer a new doctrine that clashes with the majority view. The rule is that if someone grasps all the concepts pertinent to some question as well as does the majority, and also clearly grasps further concepts that permit one to see more into the truth of that question, then one can "without presumption" and "with sufficient certitude" reach conclusions contrary to the majority (ibid.). As an example he describes how the majority of young men abandon the intellectual virtues in pursuit of riches, honors, and carnal pleasures. What is one to

---

[23] When Autrecourt confronts the objection that it would be arrogant to propose novel ideas, he had in mind rebukes such as the one that Hervaeus Natalis directed against Durand of St. Pourçain. Hervaeus distinguishes between (1) those questions that have been determined by scripture or the Church, (2) those that have not been explicitly determined, but on which there is a "magis communis doctrina doctorum et sanctorum", and (3) those on which all such authorities are indifferent. Only in the third case does Hervaeus see any room for discretion. In the first case one should not even "recite" the contrary view or admit its possibility. In the second case, "licet non oporteat necessario declinare in hanc partem aut in illam, tamen magis declinare in illam a quam videntur doctrina communis et sancti magis discordare videtur mihi non esse tutum et esse presumptuosum, maxime cum nullus debeat preficere suum ingenium tot et tantis" (Koch, *Durandus de S. Porciano* p. 225).

do in the light of how the majority conduct themselves? Should one reason that the majority is likely to know best? Of course not—instead, one should follow the rule just described, and reason that one sees perfectly well what the attraction of these sensual pleasures is, and has further concepts as well, regarding "the good that lies in the contemplation of God and in the use of the moral virtues" (p. 183). This makes it permissible to ignore the masses, and follow one's own, superior judgment. Autrecourt quickly clarifies that he does not mean to apply this rule to himself: he claims no such superiority in grasping philosophical concepts. But there is a second rule that applies to his own case. If someone develops unorthodox ideas in some domain, and if that person discusses these ideas with others of good judgment, and if that person deliberates for a long time about these ideas, and they continue to seem correct, "then he can and should— especially in merely speculative matters—reveal faithfully his view and set out his claims [not] as true, but so that his view may be considered in light of these claims" (ibid.).

These two rules address the charge of intellectual arrogance. Autrecourt, however, takes the worry about novelty to have a further component: that novel, unorthodox ideas are very likely to be false, simply because they contradict what the majority think. To this he makes a remarkable reply:

> It is clear that this manner of argument is not suited to render a conclusion evident. Hence, even if God were simply to say to a blind man: "White is the most beautiful of colors," and the blind man were to know that it is God, still the claim would not be *evident* to him, because he would   3
> lack the proper concepts of the terms, even though he would assent to the proposition as true. Now in the case of speculative matters we seek only to know a thing in such a way that it becomes apparent to the soul. The case is not like that of legal conduct, where what is sought is   6
> not a cognitive grasp but rather the deed. In those cases, then, the legislator uses such arguments so as to bring people to assent, for he knows that once assent is gained, the deed will follow. But here the only thing we seek is evidentness, and so it does not seem proper to use such   9
> arguments. Instead, we seek the truth regarding the questions raised, in self-evident propositions and in experiences. (p. 184)

Even if it is true that orthodox, mainstream views are more likely to be true, Autrecourt insists that such considerations should not be invoked to block novel ideas from being considered. This might be a sound way to proceed in practical affairs, where all that ultimately matters is getting people to act in the proper way. But in "speculative matters" (line 5) we want not just to have the right answer, but for that answer to be "evident" (lines 1, 3, 9)—that is, we want to *understand* the claim. Hence when someone puts forth a novel idea in these domains, the proper way to proceed is to show *why* such claims are false.

In this reply, and throughout his discussion, Autrecourt resists appealing to the all-too-permeable distinction between philosophy and theology. Rather than plead theological irrelevance—a strategy that he would have seen fail over and over—Autrecourt attempts to draw a distinction between the speculative and the practical. This implies that the discussion of novel views should be welcomed in purely speculative matters, no matter what the domain of discourse. One who advances novel ideas should humbly expect to be proven wrong. So long, however, as the discussion has no impact on how people actually conduct their lives, new ideas will be beneficial, even if false, because they will lead to a better understanding of the truth. In retrospect, we can see just how right Autrecourt is about this. In a context where theology is so deeply rooted in philosophy, it is hopeless to try to carve out a separate domain of free philosophical discourse. What one needs to do instead is to insist on the autonomy of speculative thought, even regarding theology, on the grounds that such autonomy is crucial for the proper development of those ideas. In a climate where new ideas cannot even be considered, the established orthodoxy is doomed to wither away—not because it has been proved false, but because it ceases to command any intellectual respect.

Events would confirm Autrecourt's argument. His reductive, anti-Aristotelian views were of course condemned (§19.4) and scholastic hylomorphism carried on, sustained by authority but not understood as it might have been if permitted to face serious challenge. Autrecourt's fate was, moreover, the same as all the others we have seen protesting against censorship. James of Douai, Giles of Rome, Durand of St. Pourçain, Ockham—they were all condemned, in one way or another, with their academic careers disrupted and their ideas suppressed. Scholastic philosophy had a century or so of glorious innovation, but by the end of the fourteenth century it becomes largely hidebound, enlivened from time to time by bold controversialists like Blasius of Parma (§6.3, §19.5) and subtle conservatives like Francisco Suárez (§13.3, §15.3, etc.), but steadily slipping ever further into intellectual irrelevance.[24]

20.4. The Thaw

It would take until the seventeenth century for a new wave of philosophy to appear that would be worthy of comparison with the height of the scholastic era. Well before then, however, signs of change were everywhere. One sees it implicitly, as noted earlier, in the newly aggressive efforts of the Jesuits and others to define the essential tenets of orthodoxy. One sees it explicitly in various scientific domains. Most famous is Nicolaus Copernicus's *De revolutionibus orbium coelestium* (1543), but this is just one case among many. In that same year, the great Paduan anatomist Andreas Vesalius published his magnum opus, *De humani corporis fabrica*, which documented hundreds of errors in Galen's hitherto authoritative anatomical work. By that time Paracelsus had already caused a scandal at the University of Basel for his attacks on Galen and other authorities. After burning the works of Galen and Avicenna in the St. John's Day bonfire, Paracelsus was forced to abandon his professorship, in 1527.[25] It would of course take time for these ideas to win adherents, famously so in Copernicus's case, but just as

---

[24] Another prominent scholastic voice in favor of freedom of inquiry is Godfrey of Fontaines, *Quodlibet* VII.18 and XII.5 (see Putallaz, "Censorship"). See too De Soto, *In Praed.*, De quantitate q. 2, p. 188b: "atque hanc mihi legem, in his praesertim metaphysicis distinctionibus constitui, ut nisi prius intellexero, non credam, cum de solis fide revelatis scriptum sit, nisi credideritis, non intelligetis." As far back as the early twelfth century, Adelard of Bath was complaining about his age's hostility toward modern thought: "Habet enim haec generatio ingenitum vitium, ut nihil quod a modernis reperiatur putet esse recipiendum. Unde fit ut si quando inventum proprium publicare voluerim, personae id alienae imponens inquam: 'Quidam dixit, non ego'" (*Quaest. naturales* prol.). His near contemporary Walter Map thought that every age shared this same vice: "Omnibus saeculis sua displicuit modernitas, et quaevis aetas a prima praeteritam sibi praetulit" (*De nugis curialium* IV.5). This has turned out not to be a universal truth, though it remains to be seen whether it is our modern enthusiasm for our own age that is anomalous.

[25] For Vesalius's anatomical innovations see, e.g., Singer, *Short History of Anatomy*. For Paracelsus, see Debus, *Chemical Philosophy* pp. 48–51; Pagel, *Paracelsus* pp. 58–9.

much so in medicine and chemistry. Robert Bostocke complained in 1585 that Paracelsian views still could not get a hearing: "in the schools nothing may be received nor
allowed that savors not of Aristotle, Galen, Avicenna, and other ethnics" [≈ pagans]
(*Difference betwene the auncieent Physicke* f. Fiiv). This is the same situation that Henry
Cornelius Agrippa had complained of back in 1526:

> In many and almost all places of study, a perverse custom and damnable use is grown, in that
> they bind with an oath the scholars which they receive to teach, never to speak against Aristotle,
> Boethius, Thomas, Albert, or against any other of their scholars, being accounted as a God from
> whom, if a man differ a finger's breadth in thought, immediately they will call him heretic,
> a sinful person, an offender of godly cares, and worthy to be burned. (*Of the Vanity and
> Uncertainty of Arts and Sciences*, "To the Reader")

It would be a long time until this situation changed in the universities. As late as the
Laudian Statutes of 1636, Oxford scholars were required to follow the teachings of
Aristotle, "whose authority is paramount," and "the entire doctrine of the Peripate-
tics"—on pain of a fine of five shillings for each offense (tr. Ward, *Oxford Statutes* I:44).

Setting aside the sciences, and looking at philosophy in a narrower sense, one finds a
great deal of discontent with the status quo in the sixteenth century, but without any
clear idea of where to go next (§5.1). Gianfrancesco Pico's *Examen vanitatis* (1520)
attacks Aristotle in painstaking detail, but takes it for granted that if Aristotle is refuted,
the only alternative is philosophical skepticism.[26] Subsequent Italian authors—in particular, Bernardino Telesio, Francesco Patrizi, Giordano Bruno, and Tommaso Campanella—made a serious effort at crafting a replacement for Aristotelianism, and paid
quite a steep price for so doing. Yet despite their efforts and sacrifices, their influence
would be slight and fleeting. Of course, orthodox scholasticism marched on, but with
telling differences in tone. Benedictus Pererius's *De communibus principiis* (1562) begins
with a rousing appeal to the role of experience and reason in both theology and
philosophy:

> What is more vile and abject, what greater blindness of the mind can there be, than to grasp
> and judge nothing in its own right, and to depend for everything on another's sense and
> judgment? . . . I yield much to Plato and more to Aristotle, but to reason most of all. In setting
> out the questions, debates, and controversies of philosophy, I diligently consider what Aristotle
> thought, but much more so what reason recommends, examining myself most carefully. If
> I understand that something is consistent and fitting with the views of Aristotle, I consider it
> plausible; if I see that something is congruent with reason, however, I judge it to be true and
> certain. (preface, f. ā4r)

---

[26] For a great deal of detailed information on Aristotelianism in England from 1500 to 1650, see Schmitt, *John Case*.
Schmitt argues that Aristotle's authority ebbed and flowed during these years throughout Europe, declining in the mid-
sixteenth century and then reviving at the start of the seventeenth century. Schmitt's *Gianfrancesco Pico* remains an
excellent source for information about that author as well, and I am in particular indebted to Schmitt for noticing Pico's
tacit assumption that if Aristotle is refuted, philosophy is refuted: "In Pico's rather confined view, however, the
demonstration that Aristotelian philosophy was in error was considered to be sufficient to show that human reason
could never reach *sincera veritas*. For him, such a demonstration would be adequate to show that the reliance on 'human
philosophy' should be abandoned forever. Apparently it never occurred to him that such a destruction of the foundations
of Aristotelian science might have another consequence, that from it could develop a 'new science' to take the place of
the one which had been discredited" (p. 159).

These lines were published in the same year that Pererius's fellow Jesuit, Diego Ledesma, was first setting out his list of mandatory philosophical axioms (§20.2), and indeed Pererius's teaching seems to have been part of what motivated his effort. Six years after Pererius's book, Jacob Zabarella, in his inaugural oration as professor of natural philosophy at the University of Padua, describes his scholarly methodology as follows:

So long as I am an interpreter of Aristotle, I can neither follow nor defend any other opinion than that of Aristotle, even if in actual fact I think otherwise. Accordingly, youthful students listening to Aristotle should suppose not that what they hear and are taught should be absolutely maintained, but only that this is what human reason and the weakness of our natural light can uncover and penetrate. (Bouillon, "Un discours inédit" p. 124)

Both Pererius and Zabarella are characterizing their work on natural philosophy, and at first glance they seem radically opposed. Whereas Pererius pleas for intellectual autonomy, Zabarella seems to be committing himself to a very conservative scholarly program. Even so, it is remarkable just how much distance Zabarella wants to place between Aristotle's views and his own. Just because I am being paid to teach Aristotle, he seems to be telling his audience, you should not suppose that I am myself an Aristotelian. What Zabarella himself thinks cannot necessarily be inferred from his exegetical writings.[27]

When philosophers of the seventeenth century finally lit upon the mechanistic–corpuscular framework as an alternative to Aristotelianism, they naturally gave a prominent place to this kind of rhetoric against authority. Nicholas Hill's *Philosophia Epicurea Democritiana* (1601), although characteristically paying homage in its title to ancient tradition, begins the main treatise with these words in large, capital letters: *Philosophia nec nova nec vetus*—"Philosophy neither new nor old"—presumably meaning that he aims neither at tradition nor at novelty for its own sake, but aims simply at the truth. To the charge that he is abandoning Aristotelianism, he makes the concise reply that "I am sworn to the words of Aristotle no more than Aristotle was sworn to the words of Plato" (p. 4). A decade later, Galileo took himself to have proved, most famously with his telescope, that various aspects of Aristotelianism could not be true. His fury at those who would still not listen leaps off the pages of his third letter on sunspots (1613):

There remain in opposition to my work some stern defenders of every minute point of the Peripatetics. So far as I can see, their education consisted in being nourished from infancy on the opinion that philosophizing is and can be nothing but to make a comprehensive survey of the texts of Aristotle, that from diverse passages they may quickly collect and throw together a great number of solutions to any proposed problem. They wish never to raise their eyes from those pages—as if this great book of the universe had been written to be read by nobody but Aristotle, and his eyes had been destined to see for all posterity. (ed. Flora p. 952; tr. Drake pp. 126–7)

Francis Bacon's *Instauratio magna* (1620) puts this attitude into memorable aphorisms, such as this: "Philosophy and the intellectual sciences are, like statues, adored and celebrated, but not moved forward" (preface, p. 12). A year later Sebastian Basso puts

---

[27] On Pererius's innovations as an influence on the Jesuit drive toward a well-defined set of philosophical axioms, see Lohr, "Jesuit Aristotelianism" p. 212. For Zabarella's Aristotelian commitments, see Poppi, "Zabarella." On the broader question of Aristotle's changing place as an authority, see Kessler, "Transformation of Aristotelianism."

on the title page of his *Philosophia naturalis adversus Aristotelem* the familiar saying "Plato is a friend and Socrates is a friend, but the truth is a friend even more," a sentiment all the more apt for being traditionally ascribed to Aristotle himself (§5.1). Daniel Sennert is largely a conservative figure, but in his later writings he does warm to a few heterodox doctrines at the periphery, most notably atomism (§5.4). In the preface to his *Hypomnemata physica* (1636) he complains about the hostility his works had met with. Aristotle is "a great man, whom I admire and venerate," Sennert remarks, but his authority is not absolute. Other philosophers have a greater claim to antiquity, and moreover "even if Aristotle were the most ancient of all the philosophers, still he cannot thereby be taken as the standard of truth. For truth is the adequation of our thoughts not with the thoughts of another human being, but with things" (f. ††1v; tr. *Thirteen Books* f. B2r.).[28]

With one exception, all of the authors just mentioned are Protestant, and the exception—Galileo—tends to proves the rule. There is nothing about Protestant theology that particularly lends itself to rejecting scholasticism, and we have already encountered examples of conservative scholastic authors who are also Protestants (e.g., Franco Burgersdijk and Christoph Scheibler). Moreover, in general, many Protestant states were every bit as intolerant as Catholic ones, and sometimes more so. Still, Protestants generally had greater freedom when it came to metaphysics and natural philosophy, simply as a consequence of the historical association between mainstream academic philosophy—scholasticism—and Catholic theology. Within Catholic countries, calling scholastic Aristotelianism into question might easily be confused with calling Catholicism into question. The same associations held in Protestant lands too, and accordingly the Protestant authorities were more likely to tolerate the new philosophy, or even encourage it.[29]

[28] One of the most extended and systematic seventeenth-century defenses of innovation against the demands of authority is George Hakewill's *An Apologie of the Power and Providence of God* (1627), which responds to the arguments from natural decay advanced by Goodman and others (§20.2). For an extensive discussion, see Jones, *Ancients and Moderns* ch. 2. An earlier example is Louis Le Roy's *De la vicissitude ou varieté des choses en l'univers* (1575; English tr. 1594), whose views are discussed in Rossi, "Idea of Scientific Progress" pp. 76–7. Rossi links the increasing confidence of the sixteenth and seventeenth centuries with the discoveries made through exploration of the New World, giving rise to a whole new body of information—geographic, botanical, ethnographic, etc.—that manifestly surpassed anything known by the ancients.

The case for novelty remained enough in doubt in the later part of the century that Locke thought it necessary for the Essay to raise the issue in both the dedication ("truth, like gold, is not the less so, for being newly brought out of the mine") and the epistle to the reader ("'tis not worth while to be concerned, what he says or thinks, who says or thinks only as he is directed by another"). Compare Locke's famous remark in *The Reasonableness of Christianity*: "the greatest part cannot know and therefore they must believe" (*Works* VII:146), which suggests that Locke and the opponents of innovation agree with regard to the masses, and differ only over whether an elite few may be capable of something new. But one gets a much fuller picture of Locke's view from *Essay* IV.20.2–4, where what impedes the masses is not any innate inferiority, but their economic and political conditions. Thus, "'tis not to be expected that a man who drudges on all his life in a laborious trade should be more knowing in the variety of things done in the world than a pack-horse who is driven constantly forwards and backwards in a narrow lane and dirty road only to market should be skilled in the geography of the country" (§2), and others whose economic circumstances might permit intellectual achievement "are cooped in close by the laws of their countries and the strict guards of those whose interest it is to keep them ignorant, lest by knowing more they should believe the less in them" (§4). The A Draft adds a more pointed remark that Locke evidently thought it better to suppress in the printed version: "this is generally the case of all those who live within the reach of the inquisition, that great office of ignorance, erected very cunningly for the propagation of truth without knowledge" (§39).

[29] My remarks on the role of Protestantism in the overthrow of scholasticism might call to mind the views of Robert Merton, who influentially argued that the rise of Protestantism was an important factor in the rise of seventeenth-century science. The Merton Thesis, however, is a sociological claim about how certain values associated with Protestantism, and especially English Puritanism, fueled a certain sort of scientific practice. My own claims, in contrast,

These considerations help explain why Descartes, at the age of 32, left France for Holland, thereafter returning to his native country for only a few brief visits. As he remarked of Holland in a letter from May 1631, "in what other country could one enjoy such complete freedom?" (I:204). Ensconced in the Netherlands, Descartes proceeded to offer the most influential of all philosophical attacks on scholasticism. His first published work, the *Discourse on the Method* (1637), sets out a kind of charter for a philosophical reformation. Writing in French, rather than Latin, depicting himself as a humble man of common sense, Descartes permits himself none of the harsh rhetoric found in Galileo or Bacon. Without indeed mentioning Aristotle's name at all, the *Discourse* describes a radically new philosophical method, grounded not in a set of authoritative texts and doctrines, but in a kind of methodological solipsism, according to which Descartes seeks to "reform my own thoughts and base them upon a foundation that is all my own" (pt. 2, VI:15). One man, alone in a room without books, thinking clearly and deeply, down to the most basic foundations of knowledge. It is far from clear that this is a good way to do philosophy, but it is an approach that subsequent generations would find deeply attractive.[30]

20.5. The Disingenuity Problem

The familiar complaints of the seventeenth century against scholastic thought can be found in more or less the same form throughout our four centuries, and the alternatives to Aristotelianism also remain largely the same. What makes the seventeenth century philosophically exciting, then, is that finally philosophers got the chance to develop these ideas. Conceiving of the period in this way raises interesting questions, however, about how to interpret the claims of philosophers from earlier centuries. For once we

---

rest entirely on the boundaries of permissible speech in Catholic and Protestant countries, and rest not on any intrinsic Catholic propensity toward intolerance, which the record does not show, but on the historical accident that entwined Aristotle with the Church.

[30] The motivations behind Descartes's move to Holland are perhaps more complicated than the main text suggests. The letter to Balzac, quoted in the main text, describes a wide range of attractive features of Holland, and by no means suggests that intellectual freedom was Descartes's principal motivation (see also *Discourse* pt. 3 [VI:31]). Moreover, as Rodis-Lewis points out (*Descartes* pp. 71–2), Holland had its incidents of intolerance as well, and Descartes would later be touched by it, especially in his controversies with Voetius. Still, though Descartes may have had personal reasons for preferring Holland, he surely did, in 1628, have good reason to worry about whether his philosophical project could be safely pursued in France, given what had happened to Vanini in 1619 and to the Paris broadsheet of 1624. Further, one would hardly expect Descartes to say outright, even in his correspondence, that he had left France so as to write things that might elsewhere be judged heretical. The prudence that caused him to leave France also led him to be prudent in discussing his reasons for leaving.

By the time of the preface to the French edition of the *Principles* (1647)—quoted in the main text earlier—Descartes's rhetoric becomes more heated, and invokes Aristotle explicitly: "la plupart de ceux de ces derniers siècles qui ont voulu être philosophes, ont suivi aveuglément Aristote, en sorte qu'ils ont souvent corrompu le sens de ses écrits, en lui attribuant diverses opinions qu'il ne reconnaîtrait pas être siennes, s'il revenait en ce monde; et ceux qui ne l'ont pas suivi (du nombre desquels ont été plusieurs des meilleurs esprits) n'ont pas laissé d'avoir été imbus de ses opinions en leur jeunesse (parce que ce sont les seules qu'on enseigne dans le écoles), ce qui les a tellement préoccupé, qu'ils n'ont pu parvenir à la connaissance des vrais principes" (IXB:7).

For a general discussion of Descartes's novelty and modernity, see Cottingham, "A New Start?" Garber neatly summarizes the new attitude: "as important as these individual results, was his new attitude toward philosophizing: in a culture that esteemed authority, the authority of ancient books, the authority of the Church, the authority of the teacher, Descartes sought to advance the view that the only real authority is reason itself—and all have equal access to that" ("Voetius" p. 8).

recognize that scholastic thought operated in an atmosphere of intellectual intolerance, the question naturally arises of whether we should take at face value the claims that philosophers make. We have already seen Zabarella's remark, in 1568, than when he lectures on Aristotle it should not be supposed that he believes all the things he is saying. Does this go for John Buridan, too, back in the mid-fourteenth century, in his *Quaestiones* on the Aristotelian corpus? This would be a disastrous outcome, because these are the principal venue for Buridan's discussions of metaphysics, natural philosophy, psychology, and ethics. And if this were true of Buridan, whom else might it be true of?

There is no reason to suppose that such doubts might delegitimize all of scholastic thought. As I have stressed, philosophers and theologians of the era seem generally to have supported the processes of ecclesiastical censure. So of the hundreds of arts masters and theologians that taught in the universities at any given time, many were undoubtedly true believers, happily following the orthodox, time-honored teachings of Aquinas, Scotus, and others. But we have seen already that there were some who were not content with the enforced strictures on inquiry. Do those few who were bold enough to complain represent merely a small disgruntled minority, or do they hint at a larger reservoir of unspoken dissent? Do even the works of the very greatest of authors, such as Buridan, need to be read with the suspicion in mind that some of their claims may be disingenuous?

Suspicions such as these were certainly familiar enough at the time. An anonymous student at the University of Paris, writing in the mid-fourteenth century, lists among the requirements of any master of arts that "he shall not snarl at the catholic faith" (Thorndike, *University Records* p. 219). One might have supposed that this could go without saying, but compare the contemporary charge of a certain Friar John, who charged Oxford with being a "gymnasium haereticorum" (Courtenay, "Inquiry" p. 169). He was forced to retract that inflammatory accusation, but others were saying much the same thing. Francesco Petrarch's *De ignorantia* (1367–70) charges against scholastic philosophers that, "when there is no threat of punishment and no witnesses, they attack truth and piety and in their private dens they secretly mock Christ" (n. 87). Describing a philosopher he encountered who showed belligerent hostility toward Christianity, Petrarch remarks that "there are thousands of instances of this kind. . . . Prison and stake are alike impotent to restrain the impudence of ignorance and the audacity of heresy" (*Petrarch* p. 213). Two hundred years later one still finds these same complaints. According to Patrizi,

It has become fixed in the minds of the common people, and many of the learned as well, that most of those who do philosophy have neither good nor pious feelings about the Catholic faith or else believe incorrectly or not at all, and philosophers have become the butt of a joke common everywhere: "He's a philosopher; he doesn't believe in God." (*Nova de universis philosophia*, preface)

Such charges are familiar enough today, inasmuch as the same sort of cultural wars afflict the modern academy. This is by no means to say that the charges are baseless. Ecclesiastical decrees from throughout the scholastic era are full of references to "malignant persons" (1276), "corrupt doctrine" (1285), "unsound views" (1340), and the like. Masters were prohibited from lecturing in private, but seem to have done so anyway. Ockham assures his readers that "many people have knowingly taught secretly and publicly a number of assertions condemned at Paris" (*Dialogus* I.2.21).

Given all this, one might have expected the scholastic era to be full of heterodox, dissenting thinkers. Perhaps an atheist would be too much to hope for, but surely anti-Aristotelians ought to have been commonplace. Where were they all? The natural suspicion is that they were afraid to speak their mind in public, let alone commit it to writing. Godfrey of Fontaines complains that his colleagues are cowards when it comes to speaking their minds:

Doctors must be diligently cautioned not to be anxious where there is nothing to fear, imagining themselves to have good reason for silence when there is not. For there are few to be found who can be blamed for excess in speaking the truth, but many for their silence. (*Quodlibet* XII.6, p. 107)

Undoubtedly, there were many such cases. Peter Ceffons's scorching critique of John of Mirecourt's 1347 condemnation describes how the censors "take themselves to have labored in vain if they find nothing heretical or erroneous" (Trapp, "Peter Ceffons" p. 141). Unwilling to be persecuted by those who "turn good things into bad every day, and imagine bad where there is great virtue," Ceffons reports that he has censored himself:

I have removed much, and deleted my own words from other passages of this lecture lest it should be too distinctive of myself and too striking. So too, I have removed some of my own ideas and added some claims made by others whom I believe have not suffered persecution. (ibid., p. 151)

For anyone who has spent much time reading scholastic philosophy, it is easy to wonder just how common a practice this was.[31]

The risks of dissent should not be exaggerated. Despite the stereotype, university scholars were almost never burned at the stake. The controversies that surrounded figures like Olivi, Giles of Rome, and Durand of St. Pourçain did not prevent them from continuing their academic careers. Autrecourt's case was the most egregious, but even his fate was hardly horrific. Although stripped of his university position, he went on to become dean of the cathedral at Metz. The critical factor in all these cases is the author's willingness to recant. To count as a heretic, strictly speaking, a Christian must not only make claims that contradict the faith, but also *persist* in those claims, even after being corrected. So provided that a scholar was ready to retract his claims should they meet with official condemnation, he ran no risk of heresy, and so ran no risk of suffering the ultimate penalty. Even so, for many, the consequences were surely bad enough. Scholars were arrested, confined, and had their works confiscated. They were made to suffer the public humiliation of retraction, and the consequent opprobrium of their peers and students. Some were never able to pursue an academic career again, and those who were generally had to walk a much more straight and narrow path.[32]

---

[31] For Ceffons's protest against the condemnation of 1347, see Elderidge, "Changing Concepts of Church Authority," who provides extensive translations, and Bianchi, *Censure et liberté* pp. 66–7.

[32] The classic definition of heresy is attributed to Robert Grosseteste: "Haeresis est sententia humano sensu electa, scripturae sacrae contraria, palam edocta, pertinaciter defensa" (see Matthew Paris, *Chronica majora* V:401). On the relatively light consequences for condemned scholars, see Courtenay: "censure had little serious effect on subsequent

So the question remains: can we take these texts at face value? The problem is especially pressing, of course, in cases where an author suggests some sympathy for a view that he is prohibited from maintaining. Such cases arise throughout our period, in every domain. Here we might just consider a few examples relevant to this study.

1. In §11.1 we looked at how Scotus's robust conception of accidents as "true things" became the prevailing orthodoxy in the fourteenth century. Buridan describes quite vividly and sympathetically a more deflationary view, and ascribes it to Aristotle, but then makes it clear that he himself does not accept this view, strictly on the basis of the faith (see also §19.5). A generation later, Peter of Ailly says something very similar. Should we take these authors at their word when they say that they reject the deflationary account in favor of real accidents? Is Buridan, in offering a very detailed account of how the deflationary view can be found in Aristotle, signaling to us that he regards it as the preferable view, even if he is unable to say so? Might this have been obvious to his students? To his readers? These are immense issues for the history of metaphysics in our period, because the doctrine of real accidents, as it emerges from Scotus forward, is one of the crucial dividing lines between later scholastic thought and the seventeenth century.[33]

2. Henry of Ghent, in his first quodlibetal dispute, characterizes the unitarian theory of substantial form as a tenable if unproven doctrine (§25.1). Soon after, he was asked to meet in private with high Church officials, including Bishop Stephen Tempier and Cardinal Legate Simon de Brion. They told him that he was expected to embrace pluralism "clearly and openly," as required by the faith. Accordingly, in subsequent quodlibetal disputes Ghent did just that. But is this what he believed? Would he not have supposed himself a better judge of such matters than these Church officials? On the other hand, Henry was a member of the committee that helped formulate the Condemnation of 1277, and it is he himself who tells us of this private meeting, without any hint of resentment. Might he therefore have submitted unhesitatingly to this sort of ecclesiastical guidance?[34]

3. Such worries are not confined to the scholastic era. Descartes says that a human being is a genuine, *per se* unity of mind and body, where these two substances stand to each other as form to matter (§25.6). As a Catholic, this is what the Fifth Lateran Council required him to say. Yet, as we will see, there are plenty of reasons for wondering whether Descartes really believed this, and it is clear that

careers even for the obstreperous" ("Inquiry" p. 180). For detailed studies of the ecclesiastical process, see Courtenay, "Erfurt CA 2 127" and Thijssen, *Censure and Heresy*. Putallaz, "Censorship," offers a useful overview.

[33] Buridan, *Quaest. Phys.* IV.8 contains an interestingly frank remark regarding the restrictions he faced as an arts master. He insists on his right to discuss issues with theological implications, provided he resolve such issues in accord with the faith.

The disingenuity problem as it arises for Buridan has been discussed in some detail by Pluta, "Persecution," who makes the extraordinary claim that "Suppression of independent philosophical thought has occurred fairly frequently during the course of history. This is especially true for the Middle Ages. Consequently, medieval texts in philosophy must be studied in a special way, because their intention was often to conceal as well as to reveal. Medieval philosophers were particularly inventive in developing techniques of writing, which enabled them to shroud their true beliefs" (p. 564). I endorse the first two sentences, of course, but dissent from the Straussian project that Pluta goes on to describe.

[34] Henry of Ghent describes the meeting with Tempier and Simon de Brion, in the first redaction to *Quodlibet* X.5 (*Opera* XIV:128). For brief accounts, see Kelley, "Introduction" pp. 13–14 and Bianchi, *Censure et liberté* pp. 47–8.

he felt considerable pressure to adhere to orthodox teachings on this point. So should we believe what he says?

In each of these cases, it seems by no means implausible to question whether the author's claim should be taken at face value. But who would have the hubris to assert that an author does not mean what he expressly says? Do we understand the minds of these authors well enough to rewrite their claims so boldly? It is easy to feel torn. Moreover, worries such as these threaten to infect nearly every area of philosophy, through our four centuries. Once one gets started, it is hard to know where to stop, and even the most august and canonical texts might be suspected of disingenuity.

Yet as reasonable as such suspicions may be, I think it is generally fruitless to pursue them. First, from a philosophical point of view, the question of what an author *really believes* is not all that important. What matters to a philosophical treatment of the period are the ideas presented and the arguments for them. Whether or not the author thought an argument valid is a piece of biographical minutia that makes no difference to whether the argument is valid. This is not to deny that considerable caution and suspicion are called for. We should be aware of the external motivations that might have led Descartes, for instance, to describe human beings as a *per se* unity, especially if this claim conflicts with other things that he says. But in the end all we have to go on are the writings an author has left us, and the ideas he did put forward. The rest is gossip.

A second, more subtle reason to resist these suspicions is that the question of what someone believes is far from straightforward. Although we tend to think of belief reports as binary—yes or no—the psychological states at issue are far more complex in the best of cases, and become even more so when external pressures are at work. Whether Henry of Ghent really believed the pluralist theory of substantial form may have varied from day to day. It may be that he wanted to believe it, but was unsure himself whether he truly did believe it. As a more familiar model for this sort of situation we might consider the fate of intellectuals under modern dictatorships. In between the true believers at either end of the spectrum—dissidents and propagandists—lie the great mass of writers and artists, seeking to tell at least some vestige of the truth without destroying the lives of themselves and their families. Survival in such a context requires playing a role, and embracing certain aspects of the state-approved system. The poet Czesław Miłosz describes how, at some point, one becomes so enmeshed in such a system that "he can no longer differentiate his true self from the self he simulates" (*Captive Mind* p. 55). I suspect, similarly, that there often just is no fact of the matter about whether philosophers during our period believe the theories they are putting forward. Given the restraints they labored under, they arrived at views they could live with.[35]

This will perhaps seem a grim conclusion to reach. It ought to seem grim, because our four centuries provide the most dramatic example from the history of philosophy of the toll that the suppression of ideas takes. The would-be student of this period should recognize the situation, but ultimately there is little to be done. Our texts contain no

---

[35] Perry Link describes modern China as another case where the suppression of ideas leaves authors unclear about just what it is they really think. "How easy is it to climb out of a mental enclosure? And how easy, before one even begins the climb, is it to become conscious of all the large and small ways in which the enclosure has shaped one's perception of the world?" ("Chinese Shadows" p. 33).

coded messages, no esoteric teachings. The arguments are what they are, and one either finds them interesting or not. In my view—let me be clear—the philosophy of these four centuries is among the best ever produced. The period begins with one great philosophical leap forward, and ends with another. But that that second leap took four centuries to happen—that philosophy stood largely frozen in time, as Michelangelo, Luther, Copernicus, and Shakespeare passed on and off stage—this is a testimony to the forces of intolerance during our era.

21

Primary Qualities

21.1. Orientation

Where does the distinction between primary and secondary qualities come from? The beginner's answer is that it comes out of John Locke. A more advanced answer is that Locke gets it from Robert Boyle. The expert, black-diamond answer is that it is imported from earlier centuries. This last answer is of course the one I wish to develop here, inasmuch as the primary–secondary distinction is a core doctrine of scholastic natural philosophy, to which any student during our period would have been introduced at a tender age. For authors in the Aristotelian tradition, the four primary qualities are the bedrock of explanation in the physical realm, in that they are the foundation of their causal theories. Yet, as we will ultimately see, even if it reveals a profound ignorance of the history of philosophy to suppose that the notion of secondary qualities is an invention of the seventeenth century, still there is a kernel of truth to that supposition. Indeed, viewed in a certain light, the beginner's answer is correct: the primary–secondary distinction *was* invented by Locke, inasmuch as our modern distinction is founded not on the distinction as it was standardly understood all the way through the seventeenth century, but on various idiosyncratic features of the way Locke thinks about the distinction.

The *locus classicus* for the scholastic idea is the beginning of Book II of *On Generation and Corruption*, where Aristotle attempts to tease out the fundamental qualities of the natural bodies around us. Considering Empedocles's proposal that there are four basic elements—Earth, Water, Air, Fire—Aristotle argues that this thesis can be proved correct by establishing that there are four basic qualities:

Hot, Cold, Wet, Dry.

These qualities, in their various possible combinations, give rise to the four elements. For generations of later Aristotelians, these are the primary qualities, and the secondary qualities are those further features of things—texture, color, flavor, odor, etc.—that the primary qualities explain.

When Locke employed the terminology of primary and secondary qualities in his famous discussion in *Essay* II.8, he took for granted that it would be thoroughly familiar to any reader with even a rudimentary philosophical education. He surely could not have imagined that, in the centuries to come, familiarity with Aristotelian thought would decline to such a point that even these rudiments would cease to be familiar to most readers, and that it would be *his* essay that introduced subsequent generations to the primary–secondary distinction. Still, even if Locke is borrowing a distinction from the Aristotelians, he is not taking it over unaltered. Here, as in so many other places, the project of the *Essay* is not to reject Aristotelianism entirely, root and branch, but to bend it in a new direction, feeding on many Aristotelian concepts, but putting them both into a modified linguistic framework, English, and also into a modified conceptual framework. Just as English is not Latin, but yet is continuous in various ways with Latin, so Locke's philosophy is not Aristotelian, but is continuous with it in various ways. This is, moreover, not just a matter of unwitting, subliminal influence. There are too many places where Locke is plainly going out of his way to offer the reader a translation of old ideas into his new framework. We have seen this sort of thing already in the unfortunate case of 'substance' and 'substratum'—unfortunate because Locke's usage has come to be so misunderstood (§9.1)—and we will see it again in his use of 'essence' (§27.7). The present context is perhaps the most prominent and straightforward instance of all. In this huge English tome on the foundational topics of language, nature, mind, and knowledge—the first systematic treatise on these topics in English—Locke regularly tries to provide a bridge between the old and the new, both between Latin and English, and between Aristotelianism and the new, corpuscularian philosophy.

With respect to the observable characteristics of bodies around us, Locke could of course have eschewed the Latin *'qualitas'* entirely. But he chose not only to use the cognate word, but even to embrace the familiar primary–secondary distinction. In this he was far from alone among post-scholastic authors. The terminology is in Pierre Gassendi, for instance, and in Boyle. But these earlier precedents highlight a crucial choice regarding usage on Locke's part. When Gassendi speaks of "primary" and "secondary" qualities, he maintains the *extension* of the scholastic terms—that is, he continues to treat hot, cold, etc. as primary qualities—and so given his atomistic framework he of course must reject the primary–secondary distinction as worthless. In contrast, Boyle accepts the *intension* of the scholastic distinction, treating those qualities as primary that are explanatorily fundamental, whatever they may be. Locke of course chose this second path, with the twin results that he could embrace the distinction, and yet understand it in a radically different way, so that heat turns out to be a secondary quality, along with color, odor, etc., whereas the primary qualities turn out to be size, motion, etc.: features of bodies that, for the scholastics, were not qualities at all, but fell into some other accidental category.

Boyle's and Locke's decision was both inspired and consequential. If they had followed Gassendi's usage, readers today might be familiar with the distinction as the scholastics drew it, but would regard it as a dusty exhibit from a museum for the history of science. By reframing the distinction, Boyle and Locke were able to embrace the concept that lies behind the distinction: that there are certain features of bodies that are somehow fundamental, and other features that are somehow derivative. Thus it was that the primary–secondary distinction took on new life in the seventeenth century, and this most familiar of Aristotelian notions became a modern commonplace as well, albeit in an entirely new philosophical context.[1]

21.2. Fundamentals of the Aristotelian Theory

The distinction between primary and secondary qualities is as important for scholastic philosophy as it is for seventeenth-century philosophy. Yet whereas the latter has been the subject of massive scholarly attention, and has become obligatory reading on any undergraduate philosophy curriculum, the scholastic theory has been hardly discussed at all, even by experts in the field. It will be useful, then, to summarize the basic tenets of the scholastic theory, as it was commonly understood. The basic thesis behind the distinction is that the primary qualities, after prime matter, are the most basic principles of the natural, sublunary world (see *Gen. et Cor.* II.1, 329a32–34). The restriction to the realm beneath the moon is necessary, because the scholastics held that the heavenly bodies are made of a fifth kind of stuff, and work in fundamentally different ways. If we confine our attention to the bodies around us, however (as I will hereafter tacitly do), then we arrive at prime matter as the most basic explanatory principle, inasmuch as it lies beneath all change (§2.1). Beyond prime matter lie the four primary qualities, which are the most basic principles responsible for shaping matter. These are prior even to the four elements inasmuch as they explain those elements, according to the scheme of Figure 21.1.

This is not to say that the primary qualities define the four elements, or (equivalently) are their essence. As considered briefly in §7.5, the standard scholastic view was that these qualities are accidents of the elements, and that the elements have some further

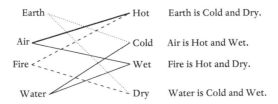

Figure 21.1 The four elements and their primary qualities

---

[1] The best extended discussion of the scholastic theory of primary qualities remains Maier, *An der Grenze* pp. 3–22 (tr. Sargent ch. 6). Scholars who work on the seventeenth century have gradually been becoming aware of the background to Locke's distinction. In 1964, Mandelbaum established the connection to Boyle ("Locke's Realism"). Wilson, in 1992, mentions Boyle as a source for the distinction and cautiously adds that "it was evidently adapted from scholastic usage. . . . I do not know whether Boyle originated the modern usage" ("History of Philosophy" p. 220n.). By 2007, Jacovides is able to begin his fine discussion of Locke's distinction by describing "a long tradition of calling the fundamental explanatory qualities or principles 'firsts'," and specifically mentioning Aristotle's primary qualities ("Locke's Distinction" p. 101). For notably good discussions of the causal role of the scholastic primary qualities, see Anstey, *Philosophy of Robert Boyle* pp. 21–2 and Miles, "Descartes' Mechanism" pp. 107–8.

Scholars sometimes fuss over the difference between the adjectives 'primary' and 'first,' and note that scholastic texts, and early English texts as well, use the Latin *prima* rather than *primaria.* The difference is, however, entirely superficial. In Latin one more naturally speaks of *'qualitates primae,'* and early English authors often mimic this locution by speaking of 'first qualities.' But it is better English to speak of 'primary qualities,' and by the time of Boyle and then Locke that becomes the standard usage. My practice, therefore, is simply to translate *'qualitas prima'* as 'primary quality.'

substantial form, unknown to us, that gives rise to these qualities (§24.4). Still, the four qualities are explanatorily basic, for it is in virtue of them that the elements function as they do. And since these elements are the building blocks of the natural world—as Aquinas puts it, they are "the cause of generation and corruption and alteration in all other bodies" (*In De gen. et cor.* prooem., n. 2)—the primary qualities get pride of place in an account of the natural world.

To say, as Aquinas does, that the elements cause "generation and corruption" and "alteration" is to make them explanatorily basic with regard to both substantial and accidental change. ('Alteration,' as we have seen in other chapters, is the technical term for qualitative accidental change, whereas 'generation and corruption' refers to sub-stantial change). Hence the primary qualities are explanatorily basic in two sorts of ways: both with respect to substances and with respect to other qualities. Eustachius a Sancto Paulo puts the first idea quite clearly in his early seventeenth-century textbook: "these qualities are called primary because from their blending (*temperie*) results the nature of a mixed body, and when this blending is dissolved, the mixed body is necessarily dissolved" (*Summa philosophiae quadripartita* III.2.2.1.1, II:208). This frame-work is complicated by various factors. First, although bodies are always the result of a mixture of the four elements and their associated primary qualities, there are other factors at play in the natural realm, such as substantial forms, spiritual qualities, occult qualities, and the heavenly bodies (see below). Second, it was controversial whether the elements, or even their qualities, continue to exist within the mixture. It was commonly claimed instead that, having been mixed together so as to constitute a body of a certain kind, the elements merge together so as to become such a body, and no longer themselves actually exist (§22.3). Third, the elements are never found in isolation. Of course we do find ordinary earth, air, fire, and water existing separately, but these are mixed bodies, each one a composite of the four elements. The elements, therefore, as Aristotle makes clear, are distinct from (albeit similar to) the ordinary bodies that we customarily refer to as 'earth' etc. (*Gen. et cor.* II.3, 330b22–25). (To mark this difference, it is useful when talking about scholastic texts to capitalize the names of the elements and their attendant qualities.) An important consequence of this last point is that both the elements and the elemental qualities, since they never appear separately, have the status of a theoretical postulate. This means that they were highly vulnerable to the charge of obscurity, and to the seventeenth century's attempt to replace these universal qualities with primary qualities of a very different sort.

The primary qualities are also explanatorily basic with respect to other qualities. As Albert the Great puts it, "the primary qualities of tangible things are the cause of all the other sensible qualities" (*In Gen. et cor.* II.1.1). And, according to Walter Burley, "secondary qualities are caused by a mixture of primary qualities" (*De formis* pars post. p. 65). Here lie the precise origins of the seventeenth-century distinction between primary and secondary qualities. This notion of two classes of qualities—one basic and the other dependent on the first—was a commonplace of scholastic discussions from the thirteenth into the seventeenth century, to be found in virtually any scholastic discussion of the elemental composition of bodies. According to the late sixteenth-century Coimbran commentary on *Generation and Corruption*, for instance, "colors, flavors, smells, and other secondary qualities arise from the various temperaments and proportions of the primary qualities" (I.10.4). Christoph Scheibler, writing in the early seventeenth century, holds that primary qualities do not depend on others, whereas "after the primary qualities follow the secondary qualities, which arise (*oriuntur*) from the primary" (*Philosophia compendiosa* III.13.1).[2]

Whereas it is a straightforward task to list the Aristotelian primary qualities, it is more difficult to say what the secondary qualities are. Roughly, we might say that the secondary qualities are the non-primary sensible qualities. But this is only roughly correct. There are many kinds of qualities, and so there are many opportunities for fine-grained distinctions, as well as many qualifications to this rough account. Scholastic authors routinely accept the following broad division among qualities:

a. the four basic, elemental, primary qualities: Hot, Cold, Wet, Dry;
b. the non-basic tactile qualities: heavy, lightweight, hard, soft, viscous, brittle, rough, smooth, coarse, and fine (cf. *Gen. et cor.* II.2, 329b20);
c. the other sensible qualities: color, sound, smell, taste;
d. occult qualities, such as magnetism;
e. the so-called spiritual or intentional qualities, such as light or color as it exists in a medium or sensory organ;
f. wholly immaterial qualities, such as thoughts and volitions.

Although one sometimes finds other usages, the most common practice is to treat only (b) and (c) as the secondary qualities. The list in (b) comes straight from Aristotle, and he is perfectly clear (329b33) that all of these can be derived from (a). (Even here, however, there is doubt regarding heavy and light. For despite their inclusion on Aristotle's canonical list, they are in other contexts treated as basic, active powers, impelling motion toward or away from the center of the earth. This is a large topic, which I will not pursue.) The sensible qualities in (c) are also standardly described as secondary qualities and, as we have already seen, are conceived of as arising from the primary qualities. (Or, at any rate, color, smell, and taste are. Sound, as we will see in the following section, is a more complex case.)[3]

The remaining qualities (d–f) are not usually described as secondary, and do not arise from the primary qualities. Those in (f) obviously do not, since they lie outside the realm of body altogether. The occult qualities (d)—sometimes referred to as tertiary qualities—are likewise famously resistant to any sort of more fundamental explanation, and I will return to them in §23.6. The qualities in (e) are yet another story. Despite their name, intentional/spiritual qualities are a part of the physical world, and interact with bodies in a straightforward way. Scholastic authors take themselves to have at least something of a

---

[2] For the doctrine that secondary qualities arise from primary, see also, e.g., Paul of Venice, *Summa phil. nat.* V.20, f. 77va: "colores, odores, et sapores, licet fiant ex omnibus qualitatibus primis, non tamen eodem modo...." Both Buridan and Nicole Oresme discuss the issue in some detail (each at *In Gen. et cor.* II.1). Oresme's discussion is followed closely, often verbatim, by Albert of Saxony (*In Gen. et cor.* II.1) and Marsilius of Inghen (*In Gen. et cor.* II.1). For essentially the same view, from a later perspective, see the Coimbrans, *In Gen. et cor.* II.3.1–2. For a compact textbook discussion see Johannes Magirus's *Physiologia peripatetica* III.6–7.

[3] For relatively detailed scholastic attempts to explain how colors arise from a mixture of primary qualities, see Auriol, *Sent.* II.13 and Suárez, *In De an.* 7.2. It is difficult to get a clear picture of the status of heavy and light as qualities. According to Maier, they are "undoubtedly active in nature," even though they are not among the basic four (*An der Grenze* pp. 9–10; tr. Sargent p. 131). Buridan, however, makes a point of arguing that heaviness can be explained in terms of cold and lightness in terms of heat, in virtue of their respective condensing and rarefying tendencies (*In Gen. et cor.* II.1 ad 1).

sense of how this process works, which is why these do not count as occult qualities. Light (*lumen*) in the air, for instance, is the product of the light (*lux*) of the sun or a flame. (Latin usefully distinguishes between a light source [*lux*] and light in a medium [*lumen*].) Colors and other sensible qualities in the air (*species in medio*) are caused by the sensible qualities on the surfaces of objects (§22.3). Still, despite being relatively well understood, these cannot be wholly explained in elemental terms. Nicole Oresme makes this clear in his account of what distinguishes "material" from "spiritual" accidents:

> Those accidents are called material that follow the conditions of matter, as are the primary qualities and those that follow them, and whose transmutation gives rise (*disponit*) in its own right to generation and corruption, and that have a contrary. The others, which do not follow the primary qualities nor have a contrary nor give rise to generation and corruption are said to have spiritual existence—for example, light (*lumen*), influences, the species of color in the air and in the organ, acts of the soul, and such things. (*In De anima* III.13, p. 412)

Here the "material" qualities are the primary and secondary ones, (a)–(c) above. Qualities outside of this group can all be classed as "spiritual," insofar as they are not a product of elemental mixture (lines 3–4), do not play a direct role in generation and corruption (line 4), and have no contrary (line 4). This is not to say that they are immaterial in anything like our modern sense, but only that they lie outside the principal explanatory framework of the elemental qualities.[4]

Although there was a general consensus that the secondary qualities "arise from" and are "caused by" the primary qualities, there was a great deal of controversy over the details. What everyone could agree on is that the secondary qualities arise from the mixture of the four elements and their attendant qualities. As for how mixture occurs, that had been a matter of tremendous controversy ever since antiquity, particularly with regard to the question of whether the elements and their qualities endure through mixture (§22.3). And when it comes to the details of how elemental combinations might yield one or another secondary quality, naturally no one had any idea. Hardly anyone even tries, for instance, to account for a particular hue of color in elemental terms.

Rather than pursue the various rather technical issues that arise regarding mixture, I want to turn to three widely accepted theses regarding primary qualities that are extremely important for our four centuries. The first is the thesis of *universality*, that the primary qualities are present in all bodies. This is to say that, in the sublunary realm, all bodies are a mixture of the four elements and their attendant qualities. The universality thesis had been articulated explicitly by Aristotle (*Gen. et cor.* II.8) and was, so far as I can find, maintained without exception by scholastic authors. To be

---

[4] An important source for the doctrine of spiritual–immaterial qualities is Averroes; see, e.g., his *Epitome* of the *Parva naturalia*, tr. Blumberg pp. 15–16. The notion that such qualities *in medio* have a special sort of status is closely tied to their ability to pass through one another in different directions, without interference. Another distinctive characteristic is that while natural qualities bring about effects of the same kind, spiritual qualities are not of the same kind as their cause: colors do not produce colors in the medium or sense organ. See, e.g., Albert the Great, *De praed.* 5.6–7; Burgersdijk, *Collegium physicum* 25.7.

There is a dispute among recent scholars regarding the materiality of spiritual/intentional qualities. My *Theories of Cognition* ch. 1 argues for their physical character. Compare the very different view in Hoffman, "Halfway State." I have come to think, however, that the whole debate is largely misguided, inasmuch as scholastic authors simply do not recognize any binary divide between the material and the immaterial (see my *Thomas Aquinas on Human Nature* pp. 70–2).

According to Zabarella, '*spiritualis*' as used of substances (like angels) and of species (sensible and *in medio*) is "entirely equivocal" (*penitus equivoce*) (*De rebus nat.*, De sensu agente ch. 3, col. 836).

sure, given the usual scholastic commitment to the separability of qualities from their subjects (§19.2), the universality thesis can obtain only as a matter of natural rather than metaphysical necessity. Yet it is far from clear why the thesis should hold of necessity even in this weaker sense. For even granted that the primary qualities are explanatorily basic, it seems clear that there could be a certain primary quality that occurs only in certain sorts of entities—a special basic quality, for instance, that is found only in living beings. This, however, was not the scholastic view. Following Aristotle, they supposed that each and every body would contain each of the primary qualities. As we will see, this is an important point of similarity with seventeenth-century thought.

A second core thesis is *supervenience*: that no change is possible to secondary qualities without a change to the primary qualities. Here, for instance, is Boethius of Dacia from around the start of our period:

In the case of these last states there can be no alteration unless there is an alteration in the primary qualities, and the primary qualities are the causes of these. For instance, this body is soft, because it is half Dry and twice Wet. If this were always to be so, then that body would not become hard. The same is evident for young and old: unless there is a change in primary qualities, a body is not changed from young to old (nor vice versa); rather, that mixed body would always remain at the same point. (*In Gen. et cor.* I.16c)

And here is Giles of Orleans, from around the same time, on the consequences of denying that there is change at the level of the primary qualities:

It would also follow that there could be no alteration in secondary qualities—that is, in colors, flavors, white and black, etc. The reason is that every alteration in secondary qualities is caused by some alteration made in the primary qualities. But there is no alteration in primary qualities, or so we are supposing. Therefore there could not be alteration in secondary qualities. (*In Gen. et cor.* I.6c)

What both passages make explicit is that no change is possible to the secondary qualities without a change to the primary qualities. This is what, in modern parlance, can be described as the supervenience of secondary on primary qualities.[5]

Supervenience, all by itself, is not a *causal* relationship; it says only that the secondary qualities co-vary, in the way just defined, with the primary qualities. Much less does supervenience entail that the secondary qualities can be *reduced* to the primary qualities—at least not in the sense that I use that term throughout this study. A reductive account of color, for instance, on my terminology, would hold that for an object to have a color is just for it to have a certain mixture of primary qualities. This is not what the scholastics think: although they believe that the colors of objects co-vary with the mixture of their primary qualities, they think that to have a color is to have a further,

---

[5] Cremonini endorses the supervenience of all qualitative change on the elemental level, since "intelligendum est nihil posse alterari nisi harum qualitatum [elementarum] mutatione. Naturaliter enim quicquid alteratur per aliquam mutationem in his qualitatibus alteratur. Unde harum mutatio est causa alterationis aliorum, ut fit dum homo canescit: mutata enim una vel altera qualitate in temperamento, fit primo alteratio secundum eam qualitatem; deinde consequitur eam alteratio in colore pilorum. Ratio igitur Philosophi est, nisi hae qualitates mutentur, non erit alteratio; quia omnis alterationis naturalis hae sunt causae" (*De formis elementorum* II.9, p. 150). See also Vasquez, *In Summam theol.* III.194.1 n. 6 (VII:338b): "hoc ipso intelligitur 'definitum', has qualitates primas, earumque temperamentum in hoc sacramento manere. Cumque naturaliter tale temperamentum consequatur non tantum colores et sapores, sed etiam alias qualitates occultas, sive illae sensibiles sint sive non, 'definitum' quoque intelligitur, caetera omnia accidentia manere."

secondary quality: a real accident from the category of Quality. Although reductive theories of color tempt some post-scholastic authors, they hold no appeal for Aristotelians, for reasons we will consider in the following two chapters. But although the supervenience thesis should not be read as licensing reduction, it is supposed to be a consequence of the causal relationships that obtain. The *reason* secondary qualities supervene on primary qualities, as both of the above passages make clear, is that the primary qualities are causally responsible for the secondary qualities. There was considerable controversy over the causal story at this point, and pursuing it would require a detailed investigation into scholastic theories of the elements. For present purposes let it suffice to say just that the primary qualities are causally fundamental to such an extent as to license the thesis of supervenience.

The causal role of the primary qualities is not limited, however, to the secondary qualities. To see as much, we can turn to the third and most significant core thesis, *causal primacy*: that the primary qualities are the primary causal agents in the physical realm. This is an aspect of how Aristotle had conceived of the elemental qualities from the start: Hot and Cold, he thought, are the two qualities in virtue of which bodies act on the world, and Wet and Dry are the two qualities in virtue of which bodies are acted on (e.g., *Meteor.* IV.5). What seems to have inspired Aristotle to give Hot and Cold this special status is that they, unlike other qualities, transfer their likeness to other bodies: a pink surface does not make other nearby surfaces pink, but a hot or a cold body does pass its temperature on to other nearby bodies. As doubtful a theoretical foundation as that is, it became unquestioned orthodoxy among scholastic authors that the elemental qualities are the primary agents in nature. Thus, according to Albert the Great, "the primary qualities are primarily active and passive, and it is in virtue of them that whatever acts acts, and whatever is acted on is acted on" (*De praed.* 5.6; ed. Jammy I:162a). Eventually, it became common to treat all four elemental qualities as active, and it is in this form that the doctrine endured all the way through the scholastic era. Here, for instance, is Benedictus Pererius in the late sixteenth century:

the four primary qualities [are] Cold, Hot, Wet, and Dry. From the alteration that occurs in these primary qualities results every alteration in the secondary qualities, which are based on the mixture of the primary qualities—namely, colors, odors, flavors, health, sickness, and others of this kind. The alteration of other things, which is properly change (*motus*), should be treated as that alone that occurs in virtue of the primary qualities alone, since it is here that there is properly acting, being acted upon, and contrariety. (*De communibus principiis* XIV.2, pp. 736–7)

Even Daniel Sennert's *Hypomnemata physica* (1636), for all its openness to atomism (§5.4), still regards the causal role of the elemental qualities as non-negotiable: "it is beyond doubt that we should posit four elements in the natural world, and that they are efficacious through their so-called primary qualities..." (II.1 p. 43; tr. p. 430).[6]

---

[6] For Wet and Dry as active, albeit less active than Hot and Cold, see Albert of Saxony, *In Gen. et cor.* II.2; Marsilius of Inghen, *In Gen. et cor.* II.2, Eustachius de Sancto Paulo, *Summa phil. quad.* III.2.2.1.1 (II:208).

For the causal primacy thesis, see Albert the Great, *In Phys.* V.1.4 (ed. Cologne IV:410b): "ad vere autem contraria quatuor exiguntur. Primum quidem est quod sint agentia in se invicem vel patientia, vel per se vel per alia, quae sunt priora ipsis: per se quidem, sicut qualitates primae; per alia ab ipsis autem, sicut qualitates secundae causatae ab ipsis quae dicuntur primae."

Toletus states the causal primacy thesis as follows: "Alteratio autem per se duplex est, altera immediata, altera mediata. Immediata est ad qualitates [ed. *quantitates*] quae contrariae sunt et per se ipsas agunt et patiuntur; huiusmodi

Since these claims were not particularly controversial among scholastic authors, they were not subject to the sort of detailed scrutiny that one finds concerning vexed topics such as the status of prime matter (chs. 2–3) or quantity (chs. 14–15), and the subject was particularly remote from the concerns of most theologians. The best place to find a discussion of these issues is in authors whose interests in natural philosophy were more practical, and hence required serious attention to causal mechanisms. Consider, for example, Paul of Taranto, the late-thirteenth-century alchemist who authored the influential *Summa perfectionis* (traditionally ascribed to "Geber," Jābir ibn Hayyān).[7] In the theoretical prologue to his *Liber tam theoricae quam practicae veritatis in arte alkimica*, Taranto provides a sketch of standard Aristotelian theory, so that readers will understand the proper method of attempting alchemical transformations. He begins with the claim that "every power in nature is a certain quality" (p. 7). This leads to the now-familiar division between primary and secondary qualities, and then the crucial claim:

The aforesaid secondary qualities are not of themselves properly active on a given nature except *per accidens*.... Taste acts on nature only through something else, namely Hot, Cold, Dry, and Wet, which are in the flavorful thing. Nor can any of the secondary qualities act within the nature and essence of anything, except through the primary qualities.... [In contrast,] Hot, Cold, Dry, and Wet are nature's hands, as it were, and principal powers, through which nature transforms and makes all generable things. (*Liber veritatis* pp. 8–9)

One could not ask for a clearer statement of the causal primacy thesis. For Taranto, the primary elemental qualities are the "hands of nature" (line 5), an idea that leads Taranto to his main conclusion about how the alchemist should proceed:

The aforesaid points to the cause of defect and error in certain unskilled, fraudulent, and false artificers, who either have not arrived at the true arrangement of things or who through sophistry compose solely for external appearance. Whoever either does not know how or cannot use such powers (other than those of the secondary qualities) will never produce, through color and superficial operations, anything other than external accidents through vain appearance, and will arrive at no truth regarding these. But he who knows these capacities of nature lying in the pure elements through Earth, Water, Air, and Fire, and recognizes how to grasp them with the power of art—and knows how to join the mineral principles to the said powers ..., will most truly be able to transform and bring about natural forms through art, ... just as nature herself brings these things about in mines. (pp. 12–13)

---

sunt solae quatuor elementares qualitates, quae primae dicuntur: hae enim secundum se agunt invicum ac immediatam habent contrarietatem. Mediata vero est secundum qualitates contrarias quidem, sed quae non secundum se agunt, sed secundum primas, ex quarum commixtione fiunt: huiusmodi sunt omnes qualitates sensibiles, quae secundae dicuntur, ut colores, sapores et odores, et aliae huiusmodi" (*In Phys.* VII.3.3, IV:198rb). This is a comment on *Phys.* VII.3, which begins with the remark that "everything that undergoes alteration is altered by sensible causes." Averroes comments on this in a passage that explicitly invokes the primary–secondary distinction: "Et est manifestum quod ista alteratio invenitur in prima contrarietate quae est in tactu, scilicet in frigiditate et caliditate, humiditate et siccitate. Et similiter videtur esse in contrariis sequentibus ista, verbi gratia duritie et mollitie. Sed tamen est primo in primo qualitatibus. In ista autem secundo mediantibus primis" (*In Phys.* VII.14; cf. ibid., VII.11). Another important Averroistic discussion of these issues is his Middle Commentary on the *De generatione*, which circulated widely in Michael Scot's translation (*c.*1230).

[7] On Paul of Taranto, see Newman, "New Light" and *Atoms and Alchemy*. For a recent general study of the role of alchemy in the emergence of post-scholastic science, see Moran, *Distilling Knowledge*.

If one wants to change the nature of things—to make true gold, for instance, and not just the appearance of gold—one must harness the primary qualities. Otherwise, one is simply scratching at the surface.

These are perfectly ordinary statements of standard scholastic thinking in this area, and yet the doctrine expressed is quite extraordinary and underappreciated. In effect, it constitutes the heart of the scholastic theory of causation. Although Aristotelians of course recognize four kinds of causes—formal, material, efficient, and final—it is form that, to again quote Francis Bacon, is "given all the leading parts" (§7.2). What the causal primacy thesis tells us is that, among sublunary bodies, the true locus of causal efficacy lies with the primary, elemental qualities. The principal and most fundamental way in which change occurs is when one body makes another hot, or cold, or wet, or dry. This not only explains the bulk of natural phenomena, but is itself explanatorily basic, in the sense that there is nothing more to be said about why a given body is hot or cold, etc. It is so because it has a high proportion of the relevant elemental qualities, which is as far down as explanation goes in this direction.

None of this is to say that the elemental qualities are the *only* causal agents in the physical realm. As we will see in detail beginning in Chapter 24, substantial forms play a very important role in accounting for why a given substance has and retains the elemental composition it has. Heavenly bodies, too, play a pervasive role, even if such explanations were sometimes mocked as "the last refuge of the weak."[8] Other qualities can also be causally efficacious: occult qualities play a role in various phenomena such as magnetism (§23.6), and spiritual/intentional qualities are critical to understanding perception (§22.3). Surprisingly unimportant, however, are the secondary qualities, which from a causal point of view are effectively epiphenomenal—involved in the propagation of spiritual qualities in the medium, but not otherwise playing a causal role in the natural world.

The reader may have noticed by now, however, that nothing has been said about the causal role of the geometric–kinetic properties, and so it is to these that I now turn.

---

[8] On the heavens as the last refuge of the weak, the most cited version is that of Oresme, *De causis mirabilium* prologue p. 136: "Nec propter hoc oportet ad caelum tanquam ad ultimum et miserorum refugium currere, nec ad demones, nec ad Deum gloriosum quod scilicet illos effectus faciat immediate plus quam alios quorum causas credimus nobis satis notas." Hansen's edition (p. 50n.) notes that this is a common saying, appearing in much the same context, for instance, in Auriol, *Sent.* IV.1.1.3 (III:16aE): "hoc est refugium miserorum in philosophia, sicut Deus est refugium miserorum in theologia."

The relationship between substantial form and elemental qualities is complex. Many hold that the operations of living things—even plants—cannot be the result purely of an elemental mixture, but must arise in part from the substantial form itself. See, e.g., Aquinas, explaining why a soul cannot simply be a description of a mixture of the "active and passive qualities," viz., the four elemental qualities: "operatio animae vegetabilis, et cognitio sensitiva, excedit virtutem qualitatum activarum et passivarum, et multo magis operatio intellectus. Complexio autem causatur ex qualitatibus activis et passivis. Non potest igitur complexio esse principium operationum animae. Unde impossibile est quod aliqua anima sit complexio" (*Summa contra gent.* II.63.1417; see also *Summa theol.* 1a 76.1c). See §24.4 for further information.

Oresme, unlike most, rejects the supervenience of the secondary qualities on the primary qualities, on the grounds that the substantial form (the "forma mixti") might produce a difference at the level of secondary qualities not explained by any difference at the elemental level: "Sed contra: qualitates secundae resultant ⟨ex primis⟩ et sequuntur earum proportionem, igitur ubi est similitudo primarum erit etiam secundarum. Respondetur negando quod qualitates secundae precise consequuntur primas, cum hoc tamen principalius consequuntur formam mixti, ideo dicunt medici quod aliquae secundae qualitas inest aliquibus a tota specie. Patet exemplo quia possibile est quod in duobus racemis sit omnino consimilis proportio qualitatum primarum et tamen unus erit albus et alter niger" (*In Phys.* I.10).

21.3. The Mechanical Affections

Viewed in a certain light, there is something thoroughly modern, or at any rate seventeenth-century, about Paul of Taranto's remarks. A forerunner to Robert Boyle, Taranto wants to reform scientific practice in accord with a clearer theoretical understanding of the foundations of nature. The alchemists he criticizes have relied, unwittingly or perhaps deceitfully, on faulty philosophical presuppositions, and their project has accordingly been doomed to failure. By taking seriously the true causal forces at work in the world, we can use nature's own tools to transmute natural kinds. Viewed in a different light, however, Taranto's ideas could not be farther from Boyle's, in that they disagree utterly on what those true causal forces are. Boyle rejects Aristotelian qualities across the board, primary and secondary, in favor of what he calls the "mechanical affections," which in Locke would be elevated to the status of the primary qualities. Taranto, in contrast, like other scholastic authors, seems entirely to ignore these sorts of geometric–kinetic properties.

It is not exactly the case, however, that scholastic authors ignore the geometric–kinetic properties. Such properties are, instead, bracketed off as cases not subject to an account in terms of primary qualities. One can see this sort of bracketing strategy at work even among the sensible qualities themselves, in the case of sound. Although one might suppose that scholastic authors would count sound as a paradigmatic secondary quality, they do not. For whereas a body's color, odor, and flavor depend on its primary qualities, this is clearly not so in the case of sound. Even if primary qualities play a role in the sound a body emits when struck, the sound itself depends on motion. It depends, first, on the motion of the body that emits the sound, which in turn is usually produced by the motion of another body, which strikes it. And since it was standardly supposed that sounds exist in the air or other medium, rather than in the body that vibrates, the sound further depends on the motion of that medium. I say "depend," because few authors went so far as to *identify* sound with motion. But it was commonplace to describe sound as arising from motion, which is to say that it does not fit the usual paradigm of a secondary quality. Buridan makes this explicit, when he qualifies his account of secondary qualities by saying that "I do not speak of sounds, which are made not through Heat, Cold, Wet, etc., but through the local motion of the air" (*In Gen. et cor.* II.1c). It was up to the terminological preferences of a given author whether or not to conclude that sound is a secondary quality, but either way its status was problematic, inasmuch as it clearly acted on the world, but not in virtue of any primary qualities.[9]

---

[9] I have discussed the case of sound in some detail in "Sensible Qualities," focusing especially on the scholastic resistance to identifying sound with motion, and the question of where sounds are located. I have since discovered that Oresme takes the view that sounds are in objects rather than the medium, and offers the argument that if sounds are in the air, then the air ought to be what we hear: "primo conclusio est quod sonus est qualitas quaedam quae est in percutiente et percusso. . . . Si sonus esset in aere, immo magis deberemus dicere quod nos [ed. *non*] audimus aerem, sicut videmus Socratem per colorem" (*Quaest. de anima* II.19, pp. 284–5). This is the only pre-twentieth-century author I have found defending this view. Apollinaris Offredus later discusses the issue in some detail, but he defends the standard view (*Quaest. de anima* II.21.2, f. 46v). Suárez also has an extended discussion, but in the end defends the "communis sententia": "mihi certum est sonum primo et principaliter esse in corpore medio, ut est aer" (*In De an.* 7.6.6, ed. Castellote p. 644).

For other cases where sound is exempted from the standard story regarding secondary qualities, see Albert the Great: "Differentiae enim sonorum non inducuntur hic: quia quamvis inferant passionem auditui, tamen ex primis qualitatibus (quae primo sunt activae et passivae, et virtute earum agit quod agit, et patitur quod patitur) non causantur" (*De praed.*

Sound is standardly assimilated to a larger set of cases. Here is Oresme, attempting to sort out the question of what counts as a secondary quality:

If all other qualities [beyond the four primary ones] are said to be secondary then a distinction must be drawn. There are some that follow from the primary qualities and their alteration—for example, whiteness and perhaps some flavors. Then there are others that, as it were, do not   3 pertain to these, because they neither are those primary qualities nor do they follow from them—light (*lumen*), for example, and also rarity or shape, which follow local motion and are not properly called *secondary*. Also in this way, as was said, sound is not properly a secondary   6 quality because it does not follow alteration but rather local motion with regard to velocity. (*In Phys.* II.5 ad 3)

On Oresme's usage, then, the true secondary qualities are only those that follow from the primary qualities. Other important qualities—light, rarity/denseness, shape, and sound—count as secondary qualities only in an improper sense. For each of these exceptions, some other account must be provided. Light—that is, *lumen*, the light propagated in a medium—is treated as a spiritual quality, along the lines discussed in the previous section. Rarity and shape, according to Oresme, "follow local motion" (line 5). Much the same might be said about size and about motion itself. Hence all of these cases have to be excluded from the ranks of the properly secondary qualities.

We might at this point distinguish three issues. First is the vexed question—considered at length in earlier chapters—of what category of being the various geometric–kinetic properties fall into. Although some, most notably Ockham, proposed a reductive explanation in terms of the location of a body and its parts, the more common view was to locate such properties in the category of Quantity (Chs. 14–15), and then to treat change in location as a successive entity (Ch. 18). The situation here was confused by Aristotle's having put shape into the category of Quality (*Cat.* 10a11), and one occasionally finds an author trying to make good on that claim. Paul of Venice, for instance, as a thoroughgoing category realist (§12.5), argues that shapes are a distinct kind of Quality, distinct from the substance and the corpuscular structure of its parts, and also distinct from the primary and secondary qualities (*Summa phil. nat.* VI.20). The usual view, however, was that none of the geometric–kinetic properties could be counted as qualities.

Second, beyond the question of what these properties are, there is the question of what explains them. No one could doubt Oresme's above conclusion that shape, size, motion, etc. cannot in general be a product of the elemental qualities. In some kinds of cases, and particularly in living things, it must be the substantial form that explains why a body has the shape and size it does (§24.4). In other sorts of cases there is clearly nothing to say other than that a body has a certain shape, size, and motion because of the impression made by some other, external body. Cases of this sort are standardly set aside as uninteresting and peripheral. When Boethius of Dacia, for instance, formulates his account of how secondary qualities supervene on primary ones, he simply excludes those properties that are "caused by an external cause, such as that a body is square" (*In Gen. et cor.* I.16c).

Third, and of most interest here, there is the question of what causal powers the geometric–kinetic properties possess. Here too, their role was marginal. We have seen this already, by implication, in discussing the causal primacy of the elemental qualities. The case of Paul of Taranto is particularly clear: to bring about real changes in nature one must wield "the hands of nature"—meaning not the size, shape, and motion of particles, but their four elemental qualities. Franciscus Toletus, to take another example, regards shape as even less of a causal agent than the secondary qualities, for whereas the secondary qualities are at least truly active, albeit indirectly, through the primary qualities, "shapes are in no way active, neither in their own right nor in virtue of anything belonging to them, because they are not composed of the primary qualities" (*In Phys.* VII.3.3, IV:198rb). It was this conviction that qualities are the primary causal agents that led the scholastics to resist identifying sound with motion: for if sound were motion then it would not be a quality, and in that case could not have the appropriate causal impact on the senses.

From a seventeenth-century perspective, all of this may seem quite incredible. Given the post-scholastic confidence in the explanatory power of the geometric–kinetic properties of bodies, how could scholastic authors not just embrace irreducible real qualities but even allow them to overshadow size, shape, and motion? Again, as at the end of Chapter 19, issues of conceivability seem to lie at the core of such questions. Although it seems obvious that motion causes motion, and can lead to further changes in geometric properties, almost no one during the scholastic era found it remotely credible that such changes could explain *all* the phenomena of the natural world. Hence there was felt to be the need for further sorts of causal agents at work, and scholastic authors simply followed the leading scientific theories of their day in appealing to the framework of the four elements and their attendant qualities.[10]

As an illustration of this mindset, we might again focus on a figure whose concerns are decidedly practical. Hieronymus Fracastorius was an early sixteenth-century Paduan physicist whose account of a germ theory of disease ought to have made him as famous today as his contemporary, Copernicus. (Compared to astronomy, however, the history of medicine gets short shrift.) In a crucial chapter from his masterpiece *De contagione*, Fracastorius attacks the dismissive view that the spread of contagious disease is simply the result of occult properties. This is nothing more than an excuse to avoid dealing with the question, Fracastorius declares, since to appeal to occult properties is

---

[10] Scotus remarks that shape and the other common sensibles (e.g., size, motion) "non inferunt passionem sensibus, sed tantummodo diversificant modum immutandi sensus a sensibili proprio, quod sensibile solum infert passionem sensui" (*In Praed.* 30–36 n. 76).

A telling sign of the scholastic focus on qualitative rather than geometric properties as the locus of change comes in how they treat a passage where Aristotle himself declares that of the various kinds of change—in size, in quality, in location—it is locomotion "that must be primary" (*Phys.* VIII 7, 260a29). Scholastic commentators always brush aside the apparent implications. Buridan, for instance, dismisses the passage as applying only to the celestial bodies (*In Gen. et cor.* II.1 ad 1). Aquinas acknowledges the passage at the start of his *De generatione* commentary by remarking that "primus autem motuum est motus localis, qui est perfectior ceteris, et communis omnibus corporibus naturalibus" (prooem. n. 1). Part of the reason it is most perfect is presumably that it is distinctive of the celestial bodies. But Aquinas also seems to reason that it is the "first" because it is even more universal in its scope than the elemental qualities, inasmuch as it is common to all bodies, celestial and sublunary.

For a useful discussion of the second-class status among the scholastics of geometric–kinetic properties, and shape in particular, see Des Chene, *Physiologia* pp. 109–21.

nothing more than to say that we do not know what the cause of contagion is. So he proposes to work through the various *possible* causes:

We must suppose that, although there are ten genera of all things, the only active principles are Substance and Quality. For it is evident that neither Quantity nor Relation nor Where nor, in short, any of the other categories produces any effect, except *per accidens*. Moreover, it is evident that substance produces nothing *per se* except for local motions up or down, rarefaction and condensation, and circular motions; for these are the motions produced by the [substantial] form of things. All other actions come from qualities. (I.6, p. 22)

Although the scant literature on Fracastorius often describes him as a corpuscularian,[11] his philosophical views here are those of a mainstream scholastic Aristotelian. Given the theoretical presuppositions he describes, there are only two possibilities for how diseases can spread: either by substance, or by quality. But all a substance itself can do is bring about locomotion, and Fracastorius goes on to dismiss this sort of causal explanation almost out of hand, remarking that "contagion is not *per se* a local motion, but rather the corruption of certain things and the generation of other things" (p. 24). Given that such mechanistic explanations strike Fracastorius as non-starters, he focuses on quality as the only viable kind of explanation. Here he draws the distinction registered earlier between ordinary material qualities and the spiritual qualities that pass through air and water.

It is clear that material qualities can bring about many things, for the so-called primary qualities generate and alter all things, whereas the so-called secondary qualities—light (*lux*), odor, flavor, and sound—bring about nothing among themselves, since they are not contraries, but still they move the senses by means of those qualities that are called spiritual. It is also clear that these spiritual qualities have many actions and are a power in nature.... (pp. 23–4)

Which of these explains contagious disease? Not the secondary qualities, obviously. The spiritual qualities might seem attractive candidates, but Fracastorius argues that they are dependent on their sources in a way that the spread of contagion is not: the light in the medium ceases, for instance, when the light source is turned off, and odors fade as distances grow greater, whereas contagions endure without their source, and can spread "even across the sea" (p. 24). This leaves the primary qualities:

If they say that contagion is brought about by some material quality, then they will appeal to nothing that is unknown unless perhaps they invent some unknown kind of quality that is neither Hot, nor Wet, nor Dry. But this certainly cannot be imagined. (p. 24)

Fracastorius thus concludes that contagion must be explained in terms of the familiar primary qualities. But since such qualities cannot naturally float free of substances, these qualities must inhere in some kind of substance, a *seminarium* or germ, which is capable of generating further such germs and thereby spreading. The distinctive mix of primary qualities found in a given kind of germ acts on the germ's host, thereby causing disease.

From our perspective, Fracastorius is indefensibly precipitate in holding that new primary qualities "cannot be imagined." But this is what it looks like, in retrospect,

---

[11] See e.g. the brief biobibliography in the *Cambridge History of Renaissance Philosophy*, which remarks that Fracastorius "favoured a Democritean corpuscular theory."

when one pins one's theory to the best fundamental science of the day. When that science collapses—as sciences are prone to do—one's theory collapses with it. Yet here it is worth insisting on a point that should by now be familiar: there is a sense in which Fracastorius—and Taranto too—are both fundamentally on the right track in their explanatory frameworks, in a way that they would not have been had they abandoned real qualities for corpuscular–mechanistic explanations. Although neither could have anticipated the complexity of the phenomena they were attempting to explain, and its resistance to human intervention, they were both correct in supposing that merely mechanical intervention in the process of nature would yield only superficial results.

To be sure, the mechanistic framework has the advantage of intelligibility (§19.7), and perhaps for the brief time it was ascendant it played an important role in stimulating the research program we now think of as modern science. Among philosophers, however, the principal consequence of rejecting qualities as causes was to engender a pervasive skepticism over whether there could be any genuine causes at the physical level. From Malebranche and Leibniz, through Berkeley and Hume, the consequences of the reductive mechanistic framework were just the opposite of what was initially intended. Far from "putting inquisitive men into a method to attain certainty," as §19.7 saw Samuel Parker hoping, the reduction of all causality to mechanical impulse led philosophers to question whether there was any such thing as physical causality at all. One path out of this impasse was Newton's appeal to force, as §23.6 will consider. In general, though, these debates lie beyond the scope of this study. They belong to the second and third generation of post-scholastic thought, inasmuch as they amount to a rejection of the first-generation approach that marks the limit of this study. Here, then, I confine my attention to why Aristotelian primary qualities were rejected, and what was initially put in their place.

21.4. The Crucial Case of Heat

Once one understands the causal primacy of the elemental qualities in scholastic natural philosophy, it is easy to see why these authors were so committed to defending real qualities. All the other accidental categories might go, but Quality had to remain. Chapter 19 discussed quality realism in general, and considered briefly its rejection in the seventeenth century. Here the focus will be on the crucial case of Heat, and its counterpart Cold. As we have seen, these are not just two sensible qualities among others, but are rather the foundation of Aristotelian natural philosophy.

The theory of the four elemental qualities was dominant into the seventeenth century. No one who could be called a scholastic philosopher challenged the theory, and even the most heterodox "Renaissance" philosophers accepted the traditional view. Consider, for instance, Francesco Patrizi's *Discussiones Peripateticae* of 1581 (not a polite "discussion" of Aristotelianism but a "violent breaking apart," the term being associated with military actions and medical treatments for tumors). Amidst Patrizi's systematic rethinking of Peripatetic doctrine, he cannot bring himself to give up the doctrine of the four elements and the primary–secondary distinction. The best he can do, then, is to distance the doctrines from Aristotle, and so he remarks that the doctrine of the four elements goes back not just to Empedocles, but even to the Egyptians, and that the primary–secondary distinction can be found in the Presocratic figure Ocellus of Lucania (II.6, p. 252). (What Patrizi in fact draws on here is the inauthentic, post-Aristotelian treatise *On the Nature of the Whole.*)

Another interesting case is Johannes Kepler. In a letter from 1599, he takes up the familiar idea that sounds are associated with motions, described in terms of mathematical ratios. He then wonders whether the point might extend farther, and remarks that "if sounds take these ratios, it is credible that colors do too" (*Werke* XIV:50). His idea is that colors might be analyzed quantitatively in terms of the angle of reflection of light, where a direct reflection would yield pure light and various oblique reflections yield the various colors. "These are suspicions," he admits, and then goes on to talk about the other sensible qualities:

The same may be said for flavors and odors. It does not seem [to hold] for the objects of touch, for they are material qualities and Heat is merely an active quality without the sort of variety that applies to the other sensible qualities. With respect to the common sensibles, what need is there to say anything, since we have said it already. For sound is a motion of the air, and it is because of that motion that it receives its ratios.... What should I say of numbers? They follow quantities.... Shapes are the cause of ratios. (XIV:51)

Kepler finds it at least plausible that the sort of reductive, mechanistic treatment standardly applied to sound could be made to work for some of the other so-called proper sensibles (color, flavor, odor), and for all of the so-called common sensibles (including motion, number, and shape). The one case to which this explanatorily reductive treatment does not apply is the case of the tangible qualities, particularly Heat.

Why not Heat? First, because (line 2) it is a "material quality"—that is, it is one of the basic, elemental qualities of the natural world, which cannot be treated reductively without destroying the core of Aristotelian natural philosophy. Also (line 2), it is "merely an active quality"—that is, its principal role is to serve as a causal agent in natural processes, which evidently seems to preclude its having this sort of purely quantitative explanation. Third (lines 2–3), it lacks "the sort of variety (*discrimine*) that holds for the other sensible qualities." It is not obvious what Kepler has in mind here, but I take the point to be that, whereas the causal activity of the other proper sensibles (that is, the Aristotelian secondary qualities) consists simply in their variegated action on the senses, Heat does not produce any such variety of tones, hues, or flavors. There are stronger and weaker sensations of heat, but this corresponds simply to proximity, not to any kind of variation on the part of the Heat itself. (Hence, unlike the other proper sensibles, one cannot tell anything about the source of Heat simply from the sensation of it, because all sensations of heat are qualitatively alike.) Accordingly, the quantitative strategy that Kepler uses to describe different tones or hues has no application in the case of Heat. It is nothing more than an active natural quality.

As long as the primary qualities held, the Aristotelian theory held. Kepler's informal speculations regarding color, flavor, and odor would have made little difference to the broader course of the debate even if they had been more influential, because these qualities were, for the scholastics, something like epiphenomena anyway. Since they played no causal role other than in sensation, it would scarcely have mattered whether they were explained in terms of the four primary qualities or else in quantitative terms, as sound was. The four primary qualities were the linchpin of the theory.

Well into the seventeenth century, that theory did hold. The innovative Italian naturalists of the late sixteenth century—not just Patrizi, but also Bernardino Telesio and Tommaso Campanella—all take Heat to be a fundamental active principle in nature. David Gorlaeus, writing c.1611, despite challenging some of the most fundamental tenets of scholastic metaphysics (§25.6, §28.4), accepts a version of the four qualities (§22.4). William Pemble's *De formarum origine* (1629) thinks that substantial forms can be rejected entirely except when it comes to human beings, but takes for granted that there are accidental qualities. Daniel Sennert, though sympathetic to atomism in his later work, endorses the doctrine of the elemental qualities up until his death in 1637. Joachim Jungius thinks that Wet and Dry can be downgraded to modes, but retains Hot and Cold as forms. Gerard and Arnold Boate attack substantial form at length in their 1641 book, but have nothing to say against the scholastic doctrine of qualities. Later in that same decade, Jean Chrysostome Magnen replaces Aristotelian prime matter with corpuscularian elements (§3.1), but allows those elements to have the familiar four primary qualities. There were a few exceptions in the early seventeenth century. Isaac Beeckman took direct aim at the elemental qualities in his journals, beginning around 1617, but these did not circulate (§19.6). Sebastian Basso eliminated any role for the primary qualities in his *Philosophia naturalis* of 1621 (§19.6), and this work did circulate widely, but Basso was an obscure figure and the radical character of his views emerges only on a very close inspection of the book. Galileo argued against the reality of qualities, and Heat in particular, in his *Assayer*, but this work too did not circulate widely (§22.5). The great champion of a mechanistic account of heat, as we will see, was Francis Bacon, but it would be some time before his arguments would prevail. For at least the first half of the seventeenth century, scholastic authors continued to assert the irreducibility of the elemental qualities with considerable confidence. Franco Burgersdijk, for instance, writes in his *Collegium physicum* (1632) that "all the primary qualities are true and positive qualities, distinct in themselves from the substance of the elements" (13.3). Although he acknowledges that doubts have been raised about Cold, Wet, and Dry, he remarks that "aside from the advocates of atoms, one finds no one who doubts this regarding Heat" (ibid.). André Dabillon, too, in his *Physique des bons esprits* (1643), recognizes doubts about Wet and Dry, and notes that some might doubt whether Cold is a positive quality. Invoking the Ockhamist principle that animates much of his work—that "one must not without reason multiply accidents distinct from substances" (II.1.1.2, p. 139)—he suggests as well that odors and flavors can be understand in mechanistic terms, as "tiny bodies" (p. 138). But he draws the line at Heat, and also color, remarking that "whatever may be the case for these others, it is certain that Heat is a distinct accident, as are colors" (p. 139).[12]

---

[12] For Patrizi, Telesio, and Campanella on the elemental qualities, see the remarks in LoLordo, "Activity of Matter" pp. 95–6, and Granada, "New Visions."

A full account of the history of heat during this period would have to take account of the views of Paracelsus and his followers. This tradition continues to have a place for the four Aristotelian elements and their associated qualities, and Hot and Cold continue to figure in their theories, but such explanations come to be overshadowed by a new explanatory

The story of how elemental Heat turns into mere mechanical heat is a fascinating one, having like all good stories an engaging beginning, middle, and end. The story begins with the Aristotelian consensus we have considered already: that Heat is a basic, active quality. We can date precisely when this consensus begins to break apart in public: in 1620, when Francis Bacon published his *Novum organum*. Amidst the many aphorisms and mandates from on high that Bacon delivers in this work—William Harvey is said to have complained that "he writes philosophy like a Lord Chancellor" (Aubrey, *Lives* II:381)—there is here one solid piece of philosophical–scientific inquiry: Bacon's treatment of heat. The discussion starts in Book II aphorism 11, where Bacon begins to collect his data: cases where heat is present; cases where it is not present; cases where it is variable. This hodge-podge of facts does not seem particularly promising as the basis for a theory, but Bacon nevertheless finds there the account of heat he is after. Setting the intellect loose, in aphorism 20, to attempt an initial "interpretation of nature in the affirmative," Bacon reaches this magnificent conclusion:

Each and every instance makes it apparent that the nature delimited by heat is motion. This is shown above all in a flame, which is perpetually moved, and in simmering or boiling liquids, which are also perpetually moved. [Bacon proceeds to run through other cases.]... What I have   3 said of motion—namely, that it stands as a genus to heat—should be understood not as that heat generates motion, or that motion generates heat (although these are both true in certain cases), but that heat itself, or the what-it-is of heat, is motion, and nothing else. (*Novum organum* II.20,   6 p. 262)

Although one might doubt whether Bacon's method and data provide adequate warrant for the result he arrives at, the conclusion itself is expressed with admirable clarity. The point is not that heat and motion stand in a causal relationship in one direction or the other (lines 4–5), but that they stand in the identity relationship: heat just is motion (line 6), or at any rate a certain kind of motion. (That is the point of describing motion as the genus of heat [line 4].) Lest Bacon's point still be misunderstood, he immediately goes on, after this passage, to warn against three potential equivocations. First, heat is not the same thing as the sensation of heat (*calidum ad sensum*); the latter is "merely an effect of heat on the animal spirits" (ibid.). Second, heat should be distinguished from the power to generate heat: some things have the latter but not

scheme in terms of Sulphur, Salt, and Mercury. For a summary, see Goodrick-Clarke's introduction to Paracelsus, *Essential Readings* pp. 27–31.

For Sennert, see *Epitome* III.1 (p. 188): "Qualitates hae vulgo primae appellantur, non quod sint absolute primae, vel primae dignitate, aut quod omnes reliquae qualitates ab iis ortum habeant, sed quod primis corporibus sublunaribus πρώτως insint." This is a weaker claim than the usual scholastic doctrine of explanatory priority, but still the doctrine is retained in some form, and Sennert maintains it even in his late *Hypomnemata physica* (1636). See Ch. 5 note 27, and Michael, "Sennert's Sea Change."

For Jungius, see *Praelectiones physicae*, assert. primae n. 55: "si nulla humiditatis aut siccitatis... univoca actio probari potest,... neque necesse est ut peculiares formae statuantur.... Sufficit enim huiusmodi corporum differentias modos entis ponere." In contrast, Hot and Cold play a central role in his physical explanations. Moreover, Jungius thinks there are many other, occult qualities at work in nature, which the usual atomistic strategies will not serve to explain: "Esse in rebus naturalibus alia praeter calorem et frigus agendi... principia, permistionis spontaneae exempla abunde evincunt.... Pororum sane et atomorum figura et situs aliquid ad hanc theoriam expediendam confert, non tamen in eo videntur sita esse omnia" (ibid., n. 66). See also *Disp. Hamb.* XXXII corr. 8, and Meinel, *In physicis* p. 31: "Jungius war kein Atomist in Sinne einer rein physikalischen Korpuskularmechanik."

For Magnen, see *Democritus reviviscens* I.2 prop. 8: "Nomine *qualitatis*... intelligo qualitates primas... calorem, frigus, humiditatem, et siccitatem." Proposition 11 argues for only three distinct elements: Earth, Water, and Fire.

the former, such as the motion of friction. Third, heat is not fire: indeed, "the notion of fire is common and worthless" inasmuch as fire is simply the combination of heat and light.[13]

There is no more important single contribution to the anti-scholastic cause than Bacon's remarks on heat. If hot and cold are simply kinds of motion, then the whole Aristotelian theory of quality falls apart, which is to say that its whole theory of causation in the natural world falls apart, which is to say that all of Aristotelian natural philosophy falls apart. Bacon does not belabor the significance of his conclusions for his broader anti-Aristotelian project, but it is certainly no accident that he alights upon the case of heat to demonstrate his method. Only once heat has been given this sort of corpuscularian analysis can Bacon reach the conclusion quoted several times already in earlier chapters, that "nothing truly exists in nature beyond individual bodies" (*Novum organum* II.2).

One might suppose that, in the reductive, anti-Aristotelian climate of the mid-seventeenth century, Bacon's idea would quickly become dominant. And indeed one does soon find other examples of this sort of pure kinetic theory—that is, a theory according to which heat is nothing more than the motion of ordinary material particles. Most prominently, it appears in Descartes, as early as in his early unpublished treatise *The World* (1629–33):

Others may, if they like, imagine the form of Fire, the quality of Heat, and the action of Burning, as completely distinct things within the wood. For my part, I am afraid of going wrong if I suppose there is anything more in the wood than what I see must necessarily be there. I content myself, then, with conceiving the motion of its parts. For you may posit 'fire' and 'heat' there, and make it 'burn' as much as you like; if you do not suppose in addition that some of its parts move about and detach themselves from their neighbors, then I cannot imagine it undergoing any alteration or change. Conversely, if you take away the Fire, take away the Heat, and keep the wood from Burning, then, provided that you grant me only some power that puts its finer parts into violent motion and separates them from the coarser parts, I find that this power alone will be able to bring about all the same changes that we observe in the wood when it Burns. (ch. 2, XI:7–8)

---

[13] The novelty of Bacon's idea is sometimes downplayed, on the grounds that this or that scholastic philosopher can be found associating heat with motion. These earlier discussions are indeed prominent, and go all the way back to antiquity, but they do not go beyond establishing a causal relationship. Grosseteste, for instance, describes how heat can be generated in one of three ways: by a hot body, by motion, or by the concentration of light rays by a mirror or lens (*De calore solis*, ed. Baur pp. 79–81). Crombie describes this as "an original theory of heat" (*Robert Grosseteste* p. 87n.), but the broad outlines are perfectly traditional. The same idea shows up, for instance, in Albert the Great, *In De caelo* II.3.1 (ed. Cologne V.1:143): "... caliditas non semper provenit ex hoc quod essentialiter est calidum, cum aliquando proveniat ex motu et aliquando ex reflexione radiorum ad locum unum, sicut apparet in speculis comburentibus...." Aristotle himself had postulated that both the heat and the light of the stars are caused by the friction produced by their motion through the sky (*De caelo* II.7, 289a20–34), and this text was very often cited. The topic of burning mirrors and lenses, though post-Aristotelian, was much studied in Hellenistic, Byzantine, and Arabic thought (see Bellosta, "Burning Instruments"). For a particularly extensive discussion of how heat arises from motion see pseudo-Avicenna, *Liber caeli et mundi* chs. 13–16, esp. pp. 266–8: "Dicam igitur quod invenimus sensibiliter, et etiam est per se notum, quod ex motu fit calor et ex quiete frigiditas." An anonymous document criticizing Galileo's views on heat refers to "that proposition proffered by Aristotle in so many places: that motion is the cause of heat" (Redondi, *Galileo Heretic* p. 333). Such remarks raise interesting questions about the supposedly limited control role of the mechanical properties, but they remain quite distinct from identifying heat with a kind of motion, as Bacon does.

Characteristically, Descartes does not positively assert that there is no such quality as Heat nor element such as Fire—he asserts only that one need not posit such things, leaving the tacit principle of parsimony to do the rest.[14]

It is easy to find the pure kinetic theory in later authors—it appears, for instance, in Thomas Hobbes, Robert Hooke, Boyle, Newton, and Locke.[15] Remarkably, however—and here we come into the middle part of our story—the pure kinetic theory would not win out, despite its impressive list of supporters, for another 200 years. It was resisted not only by the many die-hard scholastics, but even by some of the leading corpuscularian authors of the seventeenth century. Beeckman is an early symptom of what was to come: although he accepts that "the nature of cold and hot are taken from the swiftness and slowness of the motion of corpuscles" (*Journal* I:132, writing in 1617), he does not ever, for as long as his journal entries continue, abandon the doctrine of the Aristotelian four elements. For even while he accepts the sort of strict corpuscularianism that would become famous in Descartes, Hobbes, and others, holding for instance that "all powers emerge from motion, shape, and quantity" (I:216), he continues to endorse the idea of four basic elements and four associated primary qualities. Each of the four elements has corresponding to it a certain kind of atom: "the atoms seem to be of only four kinds, from one of which comes Earth, from another Water, from a third Air, and from a fourth Fire" (III:138, in 1629), and those elements are associated with their traditional primary qualities: "pure Fire, beyond Heat and Cold, impresses on us no other quality..." (II:118, in 1620). To be sure, Beeckman understands these

---

[14] For Descartes's kinetic theory, see also *The World* ch. 5 and a letter to Mersenne in 1643: "et la chaleur, les sons, ou autres telles qualitez, ne me donnent aucune difficulté: car ce ne sont que des mouvements qui se sont dans l'air" (III:649–50).

[15] Hobbes *Leviathan* I.1: "And this seeming or fancy is that which men call sense, and consists, as to the eye, in a light or colour figured; to the ear, in a sound; to the nostril, in an odor; to the tongue and palate, in a savor; and to the rest of the body, in heat, cold, hardness, softness, and such other qualities as we discern by feeling. All which qualities called sensible are in the object that causes them but so many several motions of the matter by which it presses our organs diversely. Neither in us that are pressed are they any thing else but diverse motions (for motion produces nothing but motion)."

Hooke, *Micrographia* p. 12: "Heat being nothing else but a very brisk and vehement agitation of the parts of a body"; p. 16: "Now that the parts of all bodies, though never so solid, do yet vibrate, I think we need go no further for proof, then that all bodies have some degrees of heat in them, and that there has not been yet found any thing perfectly cold: Nor can I believe indeed that there is any such thing in Nature, as a body whose particles are at rest, or lazy and unactive in the great theatre of the world, it being quite contrary to the grand economy of the universe."

Boyle, *Origin of Forms and Qualities* (*Works* V:313; Stewart p. 27): "...the productions of its heat (which itself is but the brisk and confused local motion of the minute parts of a body)"; *Introduction to the History of Particular Qualities* ch. 4 (VI:280; Stewart p. 113), where Boyle makes clear that heat is not associated with any particular kind of particle. According to Partington, however, Boyle's research in the 1670s led him back toward a material theory, on the basis of experiments that seemed to show a gain in weight through heating. See *History of Chemistry* II:530, discussing Boyle's *Essays of Effluviums*, esp. *Works* VII:317–33.

Newton, *Optics*, query 5: "Do not bodies and light act mutually upon one another: that is to say, bodies upon light in emitting, reflecting, refracting and inflecting it, and light upon bodies for heating them and putting their parts into a vibrating motion wherein heat consists?"

Locke, *Essay* IV.16.12: "Thus observing that the bare rubbing of two bodies violently one upon another produces heat, and very often fire itself, we have reason to think, that what we call heat and fire consists in a violent agitation of the imperceptible minute parts of the burning matter"; *Elements of Natural Philosophy* ch. 11: "Heat is a very brisk agitation of the insensible parts of the object, which produces in us that sensation from whence we denominate the object hot; so what in our sensation is heat, in the object is nothing but motion. This appears by the way whereby heat is produced; for we see that the rubbing of a brass nail upon a board will make it very hot; and the axletrees of carts and coaches are often hot, and sometimes to a degree that it sets them on fire, by the rubbing of the nave of the wheel upon it. On the other side, the utmost degree of cold is the cessation of that motion of the insensible particles, which to our touch is heat."

elements and qualities in geometric–kinetic terms. But although the account is rigorously mechanistic—in the sense that it explains everything in terms of bodies in motion—it is not a pure kinetic theory of heat, because it accounts for heat not in terms of motion in general, but in terms of the motion of a specific kind of body, Fire corpuscles. In place of a pure kinetic theory, then, Beeckman articulates what has become known as a *material* theory of heat.

Throughout the century, material theories of heat would be as common as pure kinetic theories, even among anti-Aristotelians. One finds this sort of view, for instance, in Galileo's *Assayer* (1623), which takes a firm corpuscularian stand against real qualities, but endorses the reality of "fire-corpuscles" (*ignicoli*): "a multitude of minimum-sized particles having certain shapes and moving with certain velocities, which upon meeting with our bodies, penetrate them by means of their extreme subtlety, and their touch as felt by us when they pass through our substance is the sensation we call 'heat'" (ed. Flora p. 315; tr. Drake p. 277). Galileo's view is made more complex and interesting by his insistence that heat (and other sensible qualities) are in the perceiver, not in external objects (§22.5). Even so, as in Beeckman, his account of heat retains at its core the Aristotelian theory of Fire as an elemental kind, transplanted into a corpuscularian context. Something similar can be found in Kenelm Digby, whose *Two Treatises* (1644), though rejecting real qualities, still retains the theory of the four Aristotelian elements, but now explained in terms of variation in quantity (§14.2).[16]

The most prominent seventeenth-century theory of this kind was Pierre Gassendi's. His Epicurean-inspired atomism does not retain the framework of the four Aristotelian elements to the extent it is found in Beeckman and Digby, but he nevertheless retains the idea that the atoms can be distinguished into different kinds, depending on their shape, and that one of those fundamental kinds will be "calorific atoms":

When I say that heat enters, penetrates, dissolves, and so on [for the various actions that heat performs in the natural world], one should not understand a certain nude and solitary quality, but rather certain atoms insofar as they are given such a size, shape, and motion.... These atoms do not have heat in their own right or (which is the same) they are not hot, but they can nevertheless be judged and called atoms of heat, or calorific atoms, insofar as they create heat, that is, have this effect of penetrating, dislodging, and dissolving. (*Syntagma* II.1.6.6, I:394b)

Again, there is nothing here that violates the strictest corpuscularian principles, but still this is not a purely kinetic theory. Calorific atoms are explained in terms of geometric properties, and they do their work through motion, with the result that a calorific atom is not itself, intrinsically, hot (line 4). But heat also requires the right sort of atom, and so we have not yet entirely given up on the idea that heat is a kind of thing. Gassendi goes on to argue that cold likewise is the product of a certain sort of atom, rather than being

---

[16] For Digby's reliance on quantity, understood as rarity or denseness, see *Two Treatises* I.6.2: "And so that which the understanding calls heat, and makes a notion of, distinct from the notion of the fire from whence it issues to burn the wood that is near it, is nothing else in the fire but the very substance of it in such a degree of rarity, or a continual stream of parts issuing out of the main stock of the same fire, that enters into the wood, and by the rarity of it makes its way through every little part and divides them." Digby's conclusion, which stresses his commitment to Aristotelianism, highlights his endorsement of "the four first qualities" (tr. I concl., p. 343); he does not mention that he reduces those qualities to differences in rarity. See also Thomas White's *Peripateticall Institutions* II.5, which explicitly takes up Digby's line on the four elements. White describes the secondary qualities as "those which most immediately follow mixtion" (ibid., II.6).

simply the absence of motion, and he echoes the Aristotelian argument that cold cannot be a mere privation, because cold is an active power (ibid., I:401b). The same doctrine appears in Gassendi's English follower, Walter Charleton.[17]

Commentators have been quite hard on Gassendi for his views in this domain, seeing it as a particularly clear manifestation of Descartes's essential superiority to Gassendi as a proponent of corpuscularianism. Such reactions are overstated. For one thing, as I have been stressing, nothing in Gassendi's theory is inconsistent with the quantitative approach. Moreover, Descartes's account, like Bacon's, is itself not purely kinetic in one fundamental respect: although they identify heat with motion, they think that only certain kinds of particle motion count as heat. Bacon, indeed, thinks that certain sorts of motion are associated with cold.[18] Still, the very fact that the kinetic theory treats heat as an event, rather than as a thing of some kind, is an important step. This is no mere change in the details of their corpuscular hypothesis, but a categorial change of perspective: the kinetic theory goes from understanding a sensible quality as a *res*—a property or substance of some kind—to understanding it as an event.[19] That in turn invites the question of what else in the familiar world around us might be an event or a process, rather than an enduring thing. Such thoughts threaten to subvert Aristotelianism even more fundamentally than does the corpuscular–mechanistic worldview, by calling into question our familiar substance-based ontology, grounded on matter as the enduring substratum of change. But inasmuch as authors throughout our four centuries almost invariably endorse this ontology, there is a sense in which even the most radically anti-Aristotelian figures of the seventeenth century retain the same basic ontological framework as their scholastic forebears.

Moreover, even in the case of heat—and here we come to the end stages of our story—it would be centuries before the kinetic approach won out. Between Descartes and the establishment of the kinetic theory of gases in the 1850s, the dominant position was one or another material theory, such as the atomism of Gassendi, the phlogiston of

---

[17] For Gassendi on heat, see Boas Hall, "Establishment" p. 430; LoLordo, *Pierre Gassendi* pp. 223–4; LoLordo, "Gassendi and the Seventeenth-Century Atomists"; Maier, "Die Mechanisierung" pp. 26–33; and Partington, *History of Chemistry* II:462–4. Boas Hall's study remains quite worthwhile as a survey of seventeenth-century views in these areas.

Charleton, speaking of the four Aristotelian "first qualities," remarks that "because the original of no one of those qualities can be so intelligibly made out from any other principles, therefore does our reason oblige us to deduce them only from the magnitude, figure, and motion of atoms" (*Physiologia* III.12.1.2). He then goes on: "we do not understand any Aristotelian, i.e. naked or immaterial quality, altogether abstract from matter, but certain particles of matter, or atoms, which being essentially endowed with such a determinate magnitude, such a certain figure, and such a particular motion..." (n. 4). Thus heat is associated with spherical atoms, and cold with tetrahedral atoms. What, then, makes water freeze? The introduction of tetrahedrical atoms into the octohedrical atoms that are the substance of water (III.13.1.8).

[18] Bacon describes the motion associated with heat as rapidly expansive in a non-uniform but generally upward direction. Cold, in contrast, is a contractive, downward-tending motion (*Novum organum* II.20). Descartes stresses that heat consists "proprement" only in the motion of ordinary terrestrial matter, and so is not to be identified with particle motion in general (to Mersenne, II:485).

[19] Westfall criticizes Gassendi's hybrid view in strong terms: "In many ways, the qualitative philosophy of Aristotle reappeared in disguise in his writings; that is, special particles with special shapes were to account for specific qualities. Descartes equated heat with the motion of the parts of bodies and took coldness to be simply the absence of heat, Gassendi, on the other hand, spoke of calorific and frigorific particles" (*Construction of Modern Science* p. 41). As I suggest in the main text, however, this is a misdiagnosis of where Gassendi goes wrong. There is nothing qualitative in Gassendi's account, even in disguise, inasmuch as his different kinds of atoms can be understood in thoroughly geometric terms. Gassendi simply does not see that what is needed is a category shift, away from the scholastic idea that heat is a thing of some kind, and toward the idea that heat is an event. The idea of the kinetic theory as a conceptual breakthrough is also stressed by Boas Hall, "Establishment" p. 521.

Georg Stahl and others in the early eighteenth century, or the caloric theory of Antoine Lavoisier and others in the later eighteenth century. These and still other views differed quite widely in their details, such as whether heat is to be identified with a certain stuff or regarded as an effect of that stuff, but they all agreed in supposing that a theory of heat and fire requires postulating some special kind of material. Although there were advocates of a pure kinetic theory in the eighteenth century—most famously Count Rumford in his 1798 paper to the Royal Society—it was not until the work of Victor Regnault and others in mid-nineteenth century that the pure kinetic approach of Bacon and Descartes was finally vindicated. Even if the kinetic theory now strikes us as obviously preferable, it would be some time before the weight of evidence favored such a view. To have arrived at the kinetic theory back in the early seventeenth century was a lucky guess.[20]

This later history has important implications for assessing the seventeenth-century reaction to scholasticism. Although Bacon's discussion of heat struck at the very heart of Aristotelian natural philosophy, the scholastic theory was not ultimately rejected because of the kinetic theory of heat. A consensus formed around that theory only in the nineteenth century—much too late to play a role in the decline of scholasticism. What happened instead, in scholastic terms, was that heat shifted from the category of Quality to the category of Substance. Such an ontological shift, however, is a product of philosophical rather than scientific debate. From a scientific point of view, accidental forms in the category of Quality would have served just as well as caloric fluid, say, as the theoretical entity postulated in a quantitative theory of heat gain and loss. To understand what happened to the scholastic theory of the primary qualities, then, one needs to look not at scientific discussions of heat, but at philosophical debates over real accidents and the category of Quality. If philosophers had not succeeded in discrediting real qualities, the eighteenth century might well have continued to formulate its increasingly quantitative and sophisticated accounts in terms of the *quality* of heat. That instead the discussion turned away from real accidents and toward various kinds of stuff is a testimony to the philosophical victory that the corpuscularians won over scholastic metaphysics.

21.5. The New Primary Qualities

Even though heat continued for centuries to be treated as a thing of some kind, it was clear by the end of the seventeenth century that heat would not be a basic, irreducible explanatory principle. The tide had decisively turned against the Aristotelian doctrine of the four elements and their associated primary qualities. When this finally happened, it happened fast. In 1643, André Dabillon could still contend that "everyone who is wise (*tous les sages*) agrees that there are four simple sublunary bodies: Earth, Air, Water, and Fire" (*Physique des bons esprits* VI.4.4.1, p. 486). A year later, however, Descartes's

---

[20] For the later history of debates over heat, I have relied heavily on Fox, *The Caloric Theory of Gases*, and the papers collected in his *Culture of Science in France*. For a discussion of seventeenth-century theories, one must, so far as I can find, go all the way back to Berthold's 1875 study, *Rumford und die Mechanische Wärmetheorie* pp. 1–39.

Principles of Philosophy would be published, followed by Gassendi's first atomistic work in 1647, Hobbes's *De corpore* in 1655, Gassendi's *Opera omnia* in 1658, Hooke's *Micrographia* in 1665, and Boyle's *Origin of Forms and Qualities* in 1666. Two years later, John Wilkins scarcely does justice to the situation when he remarks that "men do now begin to doubt whether these that are called the four elements be really the primordial rerum, First Principles, of which all mixed bodies are compounded..." (*Essay Toward a Real Character* II.3, p. 56).

By the late seventeenth century, outside of reactionary circles, the term 'primary qualities' could be used only as an object of scorn, or else in some other, non-Aristotelian sense. Already in Bacon one finds the scornful usage: the "primary elemental qualities...pertain to the empty compendia of ideas to which the mind acquiesces and is distracted from more solid things" (*Novum organum* I.66, p. 104). Descartes avoids the phrase entirely, whereas in Gassendi it continues to be used in its Aristotelian sense, albeit usually prefixed with the cautionary tag "so-called."[21] Boyle is the first author whom I have found to switch the usage around by taking the intension rather than the extension of the term, so that he can begin once again to use the terminology in a constructive way. He first employs this terminology in his *Certain Physiological Essays*, and uses essentially the same terminology in several later works. Given the prevalence of this terminology during our period, it is scarcely very surprising that Boyle would start to use the terms in this way, but the tradition he began is so important that it is worth setting out the textual data in some detail (see Table 21.1).

What can we learn from this table? First, Boyle is fairly consistent about what goes into the primary column: size (bulk), shape (figure), and motion or rest. The earliest work sometimes also mentions the arrangement (disposition or contrivance) of the body's parts. In the *Origin of Forms and Qualities* this gets replaced by the equivalent phrase "texture of the whole" (V:317), with the difference that texture is always described as something that follows from the primary affections, rather than being included among them (e.g., V:324). Second, Boyle refers to these properties as not only primary but also primitive, catholic, simple, and mechanical. Boyle himself explains his usage of mechanical: "which attributes I call the mechanical affections of matter, because to them men willingly refer the various operations of mechanical engines" (V:302). (I return to 'primitive,' 'catholic,' and 'simple' in the following section.) Third, Boyle never uses the term 'quality' to describe the items in the primary column; instead he very consistently describes them as "primary affections," only rarely using other terms like 'modes' (= 'moods') or 'accidents.' But, fourth, he always speaks of the items in the secondary column as qualities, and indeed regularly suggests that all or almost all the qualities go in this column.

Boyle's decision to continue speaking of the "secondary qualities," but to switch instead to the terminology of "primary affections" was obviously deliberate. He comments on it in the last passage excerpted in the above table:

I shall not spend time to enquire into all the several significations of the word *Quality*, which is used in such various senses as to make it ambiguous enough: since by the subsequent discourse

---

[21] See, e.g., *Syntagma* II.1.3.5, I:256b: "...vocatas illas primas qualitates, calorem, frigus, humiditatem, siccitatem, et vocatas quoque secundas, colorem, odorem, saporem, et consimileis."

Table 21.1 Bayle's references to primary and secondary properties

Text (Date)	Primary	Secondary
Certain Phys. Essays [*Works* II:21] (1661)	"the more primitive and catholic affection of matter"—ex. "bulk, shape, and motion"	"the more obvious and familiar qualities or states of bodies"—ex. "Heat, Cold, Weight, Fluidity, Hardness, Fermentation, etc."
Certain Phys. Essays II:21–2	"most primitive and simple affections"	"the familiar, though not so universal qualities of things"—ex. "cold, heat, weight, hardness, and the like."
Certain Phys. Essays II:22	"atoms or their affections"	"secondary qualities"
Certain Phys. Essays II:98	the "primary and mechanical affections (if I may so call them) of matter"—ex. "motion, figure, and disposition of parts"	"those more secondary affections of bodies"—ex. "which are wont to be called sensible qualities"
Origin of Forms and Qualities pref., V:302 [Stewart p. 17] (1666)	"the mechanical affections of matter"—ex. "Motion, Size, Figure, and Contrivance of their own Parts"	"almost all sorts of qualities"
Origin V:308 [Stewart p. 21]	"moods or primary affections of bodies"	"less simple qualities"—ex. "colours, tastes, and odours"
Origin V:317 [Stewart p. 31]	"primary accidents"—ex. "size, shape, and motion or rest of its component particles"	"sensible qualities"
Origin V:317 [Stewart p. 32]	"simpler and more primitive affections of matter"	"secondary qualities, if I may so call them"
Origin V:324 [Stewart p. 40]	"primary and catholic affections of matter"—ex. "bulk, shape, motion or rest"	"qualities"
Origin V:334 [Stewart p. 51]	"primary affections of matter"	"all these Sensible Qualities, and the rest that are to be met with in the Bodies without us"
Intro. to the History of Particular Qualities ch. 1, VI:267 [Stewart p. 97] (1670)	"primary modes of the parts of matter ... simple attributes, or primordial affections"—ex. "size, shape, motion and rest"	"all the qualities"

it will sufficiently appear in which of the more usual of those significations we employ that term. But thus much I think it not amiss to intimate in this place, that there are some things that have been looked upon as qualities, which ought rather to be looked upon as states of matter or complexions of particular qualities, as *animal, inanimal*, etc. *Health* and *Beauty*, which last attribute seems to be made up of *Shape, Symmetry*, or comely proportion, and the *Pleasantness of the Colours* of the particular parts of the face. And there are some other attributes, namely *Size, Shape, Motion*, and *Rest*, that are wont to be reckoned among qualities, which may more conveniently be esteemed the *Primary Modes* of the parts of matter; since from these simple attributes or primordial affections, all the qualities are derived. But this consideration relating to words and names, I shall not insist upon it. (*Introduction to the History of Particular Qualities* ch. 1 [*Works* VI:267; Stewart p. 97])

Boyle here acknowledges that his contemporaries use 'quality' ambiguously, in a wide variety of ways. Properly speaking, though, the term should not apply to the primary attributes of matter (lines 8–11), and it should also not apply to "complexions" of multiple qualities (lines 4–8). This suggests a three-level hierarchy of features pertaining to bodies: first, the primary features from which "all the qualities are derived" (line 11). Second, those qualities, derived from the first level. Third, "states" or "complexions" that are not immediately derived from the primary level, but can instead be derived from the secondary level—as beauty is a consequence not just of the shape but also of the color of one's face (lines 7– 8). Obviously, one might choose any terms to talk about these three levels. Boyle's choice, however, is notably in accord with scholastic tradition. As I have stressed, the "primary qualities" of Locke were not considered qualities by the scholastics at all. Conversely, inasmuch as the scholastics did of course want to take seriously the reality of qualities, they were unlikely to countenance the sorts of "complexions" that Boyle talks about here. So although the details of Boyle's account are radically different from scholastic thinking, he makes an effort to adhere to the terminological tradition.[22]

Whether or not Boyle was the very first to frame the primary–secondary distinction in this way, he was certainly influential on subsequent developments. In 1669, Leibniz cites approvingly Boyle's use of the term 'corpuscular,' which he describes as the view that "so far as can be done, everything should be derived from the nature of body and its primary qualities—size, shape, and motion" (*Confessio naturae* [*Phil. Schriften* IV:106; tr. Loemker p. 110]). Obviously, Leibniz noticed Boyle's reframing of the primary–secondary distinction, but did not share Boyle's scruples over how to use the term 'quality.' That brings us to Locke, who was Boyle's close friend and regular correspondent. Draft A of Locke's *Essay concerning Human Understanding*, written in the summer of 1671, contains no mention of the primary–secondary distinction, but in Draft B, written later that same year, the distinction appears quite clearly.[23] By the time of the first edition of the *Essay* (1689), Locke had arrived at the following, canonical list:

---

[22] On Boyle's theory in general, see Alexander, *Ideas, Qualities* and Anstey, *Philosophy of Robert Boyle*, as well as the discussion in Chapter 23 below. Alexander credits Boyle with the expression 'primary quality,' but Anstey correctly points out that Boyle never uses that phrase (p. 39). Because Boyle does not refer to his primary affections as qualities, he can still, on occasion, speak as if the primary *qualities* are those non-basic, non-geometric properties of bodies that seem most fundamental. Thus, in a passage that might have gone on my table were it not liable to confuse the issues utterly, he speaks of "the chiefest modes or qualities of matter, such as are heat, cold etc.," but then immediately contrasts these with "the above-mentioned most primitive and simple affections" (*Certain Phys. Essays* [*Works* II:21]). For a particular clear refusal to treat the primitive affections as qualities, see *Of the Systematical or Cosmical Qualities of Things*: "the qualities of particular bodies (for I speak not here of magnitude, shape, and motion, which are the primitive moods and catholic affections of matter itself) do for the most part consist in Relations" (*Works* VI:287).

[23] Locke introduces the primary qualities, and by implication the secondary qualities, in Draft B §94, pp. 209–10. "Nor after all the acquaintance and familiarity which we imagine we have with matter, and the many qualities men assure themselves they perceive and know in bodies, will it perhaps upon examination be found that they have any more or clearer primary ideas belonging to body then they have belonging to spirit; for setting aside extension and cohesion of parts, all other qualities we observe in or ideas we receive from body as distinguished from spirit (for we have some ideas common to both, as *number*) are probably but the results and modifications of these: for impenetrability or a power of receiving and communicating motion by impulse or protrusion is a necessary consequence of extension and cohering of parts; figure also is but the termination or modification of extension in the several masses of such cohering parts; and all the other sensible qualities in bodies, as heat, cold, colours, smells, tastes, and all the objects of sense and the ideas thereof produced in us are probably in the bodies wherein we imagine they reside nothing but different bulk and figure, and in us those appearances or sensations of them are nothing but the effects of various impulses made upon our organs by particles or little masses of bodies of different size, figure, and motion. . . . The two primary qualities or properties of body—viz., extension and cohesion of parts—we perfectly know and have distinct, clear ideas of. . . . We have also the knowledge of several qualities inherent in bodies and have the clear, distinct ideas of them, which qualities are but the various modifications of the extension of cohering parts and their motion."

"These I call *original* or *primary qualities* of body, which I think we may observe to produce simple ideas in us, viz. solidity, extension, figure, motion or rest, and number" (II.8.9). Like Boyle, Locke takes the intension rather than the extension of the term, which allows him to use the distinction rather than heap scorn upon it. At the same time, like the young Leibniz, Locke ignores Boyle's scruples over the proper use of 'quality.' Thus our modern usage is born.[24]

21.6. The Intension of the Distinction

Of the many issues that arise concerning the seventeenth-century usage of the primary–secondary distinction, we are now particularly well-positioned to address one of them: the vexed question of what it is that grounds the distinction—that is, why some qualities are primary and some secondary. Among scholastic authors there is a very clear and settled understanding of the distinction, as one that concerns causal or explanatory priority, so that those qualities are *primary* that are explanatorily basic and give rise to other qualities, which are in turn *secondary*. Given just how consistent that scholastic usage is, it would be perverse—without explicit indications to the contrary—to read seventeenth-century authors as meaning anything different.

The following passages are all very clear on the basis of the primary–secondary distinction:

Albert of Orlamünde (late 13th c.): "those four qualities are called primary because they do not flow from others, but all the other qualities or contraries arise from them. Thus heat neither arises from nor depends on dryness, nor vice versa, and so on for the others.... The secondary

---

The oddity of Locke's identifying only two primary qualities—extension and cohesion—is explained by the context: Locke is setting up a parallel with the case of mind, where the primary qualities we "perfectly know" are thinking and "the power of moving" (that is, desiring). Like Boyle, and like the eventual treatment in the *Essay*, Locke here adverts to "bulk," "figure," and motion, but unlike Boyle he here proposes that figure can be understood as a modification of extension and cohesion. For further discussion of this passage, see Downing, "Uses of Mechanism."

[24] I speak of Locke's canonical list of primary qualities only in the sense that this is the list he first offers. It is repeated exactly at II.8.22, but elsewhere he offers a rather confusing variety of other lists, and scholars disagree on what the true list of primary qualities ought to be. On this issue, see e.g. Alexander, *Ideas, Qualities* ch. 6, and Robert Wilson, "Locke's Primary Qualities."

The practice of using 'quality' broadly to refer to properties in general predates Locke. Gassendi, for instance, explicitly states that '*qualitas*' can serve as a synonym for '*accidens*' (*Syntagma* II.1.6.1, I:373a). The modern usage of 'quality' has morphed to such an extent that it can now seem doubtful whether the Boyle–Locke secondary qualities should count as qualities at all. See Curley, "Locke, Boyle" p. 442: "when Locke calls them *secondary* qualities what he means is that they are not qualities at all...." This takes us a long way from the natural contemporary reaction to Locke: to wonder why he refers to the mechanical affections as qualities. Locke, for his own part, shows some awareness in his Draft B (1671) that he is using the term in a broader, non-standard way: "All that I desire is to have understood what I mean by the word quality when I use it, wherein if it be used by me something differently from the common acception I hope I shall be pardoned, being led to it by the consideration of the things, and this being the nearest word in its common use to those notions I have applied it to" (§61). This last remark seems true enough, inasmuch as there is no other common word in Latin or English that will do, 'form' being unacceptably Aristotelian and 'property' having the connotation of a necessary but non-essential attribute, a *proprium*. The only real open alternative is 'mode,' a word that he puts to a different use (see *Essay* II.12.4). See also *Essay* III.4.16, which acknowledges that the "ordinary acception" of the term 'quality' excludes the primary qualities.

Rickless, "Locke on Primary and Secondary Qualities" p. 302, argues on internal textual grounds that Locke has two senses of 'quality,' one on which the primary qualities count, and another on which they do not.

qualities, in contrast, are the ones caused by these—namely, hard and soft, sweet and bitter, white and black, and the like" (*Philosophia pauperum* III.3).

John Buridan: "those qualities are called primary that are not reduced to others in the manner of their generation, but others are reduced to them" (*In Gen. et cor.* II.1c).

Christoph Scheibler: "The primary qualities are those that do not depend on others, whereas others depend on them....After the primary qualities follow the secondary qualities, which arise from the primary" (*Philosophia compendiosa* III.12.1, 13.1).

Eustachius a Sancto Paulo: "these qualities are called primary because from their blending (*temperie*) results the nature of a mixed body, and when this blending is dissolved, the mixed body is necessarily dissolved" (*Summa* III.2.2.1.1, II:208).

David Gorlaeus: "The Peripatetics distinguish qualities into the primary and the secondary. The primary are these four: Hot, Cold, Wet, Dry. The others are called secondary, because they arise from those that are primary" (*Idea physicae* 12.1).

Rudolphus Goclenius: "Those qualities are called secondary that are made from the first, and are reduced to them as to their principles" (*Lexicon philosophicum*, 'qualitas,' p. 915b).

Franco Burgersdijk: "Those qualities are called primary that do not arise from others.... The secondary are those that result from a blending (*temperie*) of others" (*Collegium physicum* 13.2).

André Dabillon: "it is standard to divide corporeal qualities into primary and secondary: the primary are those that do not arise from a mix of the others. There are four of these: Hot, Cold, Wet, and Dry. The secondary qualities are those that do arise from a mix of the others, such as color" (*Physique des bons esprits* II.1.1.2, p. 138).

Leibniz: "That the other tactile qualities—smoothness, lightness, tensity, etc.—do not constitute the nature of body is commonly recognized, from the very fact that they are called secondary and so arise from others that are constitutive" (to Thomasius, 1669 [*Phil. Schriften* IV:173; tr. Loemker p. 101]).

All these passages agree that explanatory priority is the essence of the primary–secondary distinction. I know of no texts concerning scholastic views that suggest anything else.

It is quite clear that Boyle shares this scholastic understanding of the primary–secondary distinction. Almost every one of his statements of the distinction reiterates the idea that the secondary qualities "proceed from" or "depend on" or are the "consequences of" the primary affections. Hence he refers to these as "primitive" and "simple," and even "most primitive and simple." The most telling passage, because it offers this as the reason for the label 'primary,' is this one:

There are some other attributes, namely size, shape, motion, and rest, that are wont to be reckoned among qualities, which may more conveniently be esteemed the primary modes of the parts of matter, since from these simple attributes or primordial affections all the qualities are derived. (*Introduction to the History of Particular Qualities* ch. 1 [*Works* VI:267; Stewart p. 97])

Boyle never suggests any other basis for the primary–secondary distinction. He does, however, accept two of the further claims associated with the scholastic doctrine. First, he accepts *causal primacy*: that the primary affections are the chief causal agent throughout nature. Thus he remarks that "there are simpler and more primitive affections of matter, from which these secondary qualities, if I may so call them, do depend: and that the operations of bodies upon one another spring from the same" (*Origin of Forms* [*Works* V:317; Stewart p. 32]). Second, he accepts *universality*: that the primary affections are found in all bodies. Hence he speaks of the "catholic affections of matter" or, equivalently, the "universal" affections.

What, then, about Locke? Given this unbroken consensus on how to understand the distinction, it would be extraordinary if Locke were doing something else with this terminology. Nevertheless, most scholars believe that he is, even if they disagree on what exactly he is doing. It has been variously argued that the distinction rests on the presence or lack of conceptual inseparability, physical inseparability, resemblance to our ideas, and real existence in nature.[25] To be sure, each of these lines of interpretation has solid support in Locke's text, and such passages show at a minimum that there is *more* going on in Locke than in previous statements of the distinction. Even so, I believe that his understanding of the distinction grows directly out of earlier treatments. This is, admittedly, not immediately obvious. When Locke first introduces the primary–secondary distinction, he appeals not to explanatory priority, but instead to the *inseparability* of the primary qualities from bodies.

Qualities thus considered in bodies are, first, such as are utterly inseparable from the body, in what state soever it be; such as in all the alterations and changes it suffers, all the force can be used upon it, it constantly keeps; and such as sense constantly finds in every particle of matter which has bulk enough to be perceived, and the mind finds inseparable from every particle of matter, though less than to make itself singly be perceived by our senses. (*Essay* II.8.9)[26]

This famous and much-discussed idea, although on its face rather different from explanatory priority, is in fact not incompatible with the scholastic understanding of the distinction. It is, on the contrary, equivalent to the additional tenet of the view that I am calling the universality thesis. To be sure, as noted earlier, explanatory priority does not entail universality. The entailment also does not run in the other direction, since there could be universal features of body that have no explanatory force at all. Still, the two doctrines traditionally go hand in hand, all the way back to the Presocratic supposition that the project of natural philosophy was to find the basic *and* universal ingredients of all matter. And post-scholastic authors had good reason to put particular weight on this aspect of the view, because universality is clearly a criterion that favors the corpuscularian hypothesis. For whereas it is quite dubious whether the Aristotelians are right in supposing that all bodies contain each of the four traditional elements or their elemental qualities, it seems quite plausible that all bodies have solidity, extension, figure, motion or rest, and number. The idea is endemic to corpuscularian thought,

---

[25] For the logical inseparability interpretation of Locke, see e.g. McCann, "Locke's Philosophy of Body." For physical inseparability, see Robert Wilson, "Locke's Primary Qualities." For resemblance, see Mackie, *Problems from Locke* ch. 1; Curley, "Locke, Boyle" pp. 450–1. For explanatory priority, see Alexander, *Ideas, Qualities* p. 122. For a stress on Locke's anti-realism regarding secondary qualities, see Jacovides, "Locke's Distinctions," though his ultimate view is rather like my own, in that he thinks "Locke draws more than one distinction here; he wants to convince his reader that they overlap" (p. 103). For the idea that secondary qualities are in bodies but dependent on perceivers, see Rickless, "Locke on Primary and Secondary Qualities," though Rickless would seem to state my view exactly when he remarks that "Qualities of bodies are called 'secondary' because they depend on (arise from) the primary qualities of their parts (II.viii.10, 14, 23)" (p. 300). See too Anstey, *Philosophy of Robert Boyle* pp. 39–40: "All the remaining qualities of bodies are secondary to these primaries because they are in some sense reducible to them."

[26] This passage was added in the fourth edition (1700). The same idea, however, is present from the first edition onward at IV.8.23, where it is also seemingly used to define the primary qualities. The fourth edition simply makes the point more prominent.

showing up not just in Boyle but also, for instance, in Galileo, Descartes, and the young Leibniz. Indeed, when the primary qualities are so conceived, one might suppose that the universality thesis obtains not just as a matter of natural necessity, as it does for the scholastics, but as a metaphysical truth about the nature of bodies. For Descartes and others who treat these primary qualities as modes, universality becomes part of their account of what it is to be a mode: substances depend on modes inasmuch as they cannot exist without one or another mode from within a given kind. (Compare Chapter 13, where this strong thesis of universality, grounded in metaphysical necessity, was labeled *determinacy*.)[27]

Although Locke repeatedly highlights universality as the chief characteristic of the primary qualities, he does also appeal to their priority relative to the secondary qualities, stressing over and over that the latter arise from the former, as at the end of this passage:

The first of these [sorts of qualities] . . . may be properly called real, original, or primary qualities, because they are in the things themselves, whether they are perceived or no, and upon their different modifications it is that the secondary qualities depend. (*Essay* II.8.23)[28]

Locke further endorses causal primacy: that the primary qualities are the principal causal agents throughout the natural world:

These insensible corpuscles being the active parts of matter, and the great instruments of nature, on which depend not only all their secondary qualities, but also most of their natural operations; our want of precise distinct ideas of their primary qualities keeps us in an incurable ignorance of what we desire to know about them. (IV.3.25)

Whereas scholastic authors had resisted the idea that sound might be reduced to motion, on the grounds that there would then be no good account of how it acts on the senses, Locke makes precisely the converse argument: that since "impulse" is "the only way which we can conceive bodies operate in us," it must be that "the ideas of secondary qualities are also produced . . . by the operation of insensible particles on our senses" (II.8.11). The *Essay* struggles with the status of these empirical claims, sometimes insisting on them, as here, and other times treating them as mere hypotheses on which his main line of thought does not depend. My contention is that the essence of Locke's primary–secondary distinction is an empirical claim consisting in the theses of explanatory priority, universality, and causal primacy. This explains why Locke apologizes, toward the end of the chapter in which he introduces the primary–secondary distinction, for having "been engaged in physical enquiries a little farther than, perhaps,

---

[27] On the universality doctrine among seventeenth-century authors, see Galileo, *Assayer:* "Per tanto io dico che ben sento tirarmi dalla necessità, subito che concepisco una materia o sostanza corporea, a concepire insieme ch'ella è terminata e figurata di questa o di quella figura" etc. (ed. Flora p. 311; tr. Drake p. 274, and see §22.5). For Descartes, see the remarks on his commitment to determinacy in §13.5. For Leibniz, see his 1669 letter to Thomasius (*Phil. Schriften* IV:173–4; Loemker p. 101). See also Boyle, *Origin of Forms* (*Works* V:307; Stewart p. 20), and Anstey, *Philosophy of Robert Boyle* pp. 45–7.

[28] Locke discusses the dependence of the secondary on the primary qualities in particular detail at *Essay* IV.3.11–13, where this is treated as reason for epistemic despair, inasmuch as we neither can grasp the primary qualities nor, if we could grasp them, could we grasp why certain primary qualities give rise to certain powers in objects and hence certain sensations in us.

I intended" (II.8.22). Such inquiries were necessary, he explains, "to distinguish the primary and real qualities of bodies, which are always in them, . . . from those secondary and imputed qualities, which are but the powers of several combinations of those primary ones, when they operate." The passage invokes universality and gestures at the end toward causal primacy. The implication is that Locke's discussion is fundamentally a thesis about what is explanatorily basic in the natural world.[29]

Even so, there is a sense in which all of this misses the most important part of the story. Although Locke's primary–secondary distinction is continuous with how that distinction was understood throughout our period, it contains at the same time much that is new and interesting. First, the primary–secondary distinction is made to yield a thesis about resemblance. From the fact that the secondary qualities "are in truth nothing in the objects themselves but powers to produce various sensations in us, and depend on those primary qualities," Locke concludes that "it is easy to draw this observation, that the ideas of primary qualities of bodies are resemblances of them, and their patterns do really exist in the bodies themselves; but the ideas produced in us by these secondary qualities have no resemblance of them at all..." (II.8.15). The distinction is further made to yield some sort of anti-realism regarding the secondary qualities. In a passage quoted just above, for instance, he remarks that certain qualities are primary "because they are in the things themselves, whether they are perceived or no." Evidently, the secondary qualities are not in the things themselves, or at least only there when perceived.

Neither of these are new ideas—they appear both in Descartes and in Galileo, for instance—but still they are quite unlike anything that the primary–secondary distinction was traditionally associated with, and it is remarkable that Locke thinks this traditional distinction leads directly to them.[30] They are, moreover, exceedingly interesting ideas, much more interesting today than obsolete debates over the fundamental physical qualities in matter. The primary–secondary distinction would not continue to capture our interest if it were simply another episode in the proto-scientific debate over the fundamental elements of nature. For that, we have Thales. Accordingly, our modern primary–secondary distinction is not a thesis about explanatory priority, but instead a thesis about resemblance, or response-dependence, or dispositional versus categorical properties, or sundry other matters concerning metaphysics and mind. Ours is not the scholastic distinction, and not Boyle's distinction, and in a way it is not Locke's distinction. But in another way Locke has bequeathed us the modern primary–secondary distinction, by supposing that the traditional distinction could be made to

[29] McCann ("Locke's Philosophy of Body" p. 65) objects to those who read Locke's distinction as founded in explanatory priority by pointing to a passage where Locke speaks of the secondary qualities as grounded either in the primary qualities "or if not upon them, upon something yet more remote from our comprehension" (*Essay* IV.3.11). But if that were indeed to happen (as of course it has), one would face again the question of whether to take the extension or the intension of the primary–secondary terminology. As I read the passage, Locke has simply chosen, for clarity's sake, to maintain at this point the extension of the terminology, and still speak of shape, etc. as primary. He might just as well have continued to adhere to the intension of the terms, and identified these new "more remote" qualities as the real primary qualities.

[30] McCann insightfully discusses how Locke gets resemblance failure from the primary–secondary distinction ("Locke's Philosophy of Body" pp. 63–4). Descartes raises the problem of resemblance in *Med.* III (VII:38), where it is the issue that "praecipue de iis quarendum est." See also, e.g., *Med.* VI (VII:82) and *Principles* IV.197–8. Boyle ties the failure of resemblance to his general criticism of scholastic theories of qualities in *Origin of Forms* (*Works* V:317; Stewart p. 31 and *Works* V:334; Stewart p. 51). For Galileo, see §22.5.

yield these new and interesting results. We have lost interest in the underlying tradition, but we are still fascinated with what Locke introduced. The next two chapters will consider those issues more squarely.[31]

---

[31] Ayers ("Primary and Secondary") distinguishes between a reading of Locke's distinction in terms of a "mechanistic model" and a reading in terms of a philosophical argument about perception. Whereas I put weight on the first, as a reading of Locke, he puts weight on the second, but I quite agree with his remark that if the first is all Locke is doing, then "the distinction has presumably been consigned to history by more recent science" (p. 3ts).

I myself, in earlier work, have understood the primary–secondary distinction in ways quite different from what I argue for here. In "A Theory of Secondary Qualities," I took for granted from the start that the distinction should be limited to the sensible qualities, and that it should be analyzed in terms of our concepts. I still think this is how *we* should understand the distinction. But I've come to think that that perspective is fundamentally alien to the history of the debate. More problematic is my attempt to show that Democritus does not embrace the primary–secondary distinction ("Democritus and Secondary Qualities"). My argument there likewise assumed that the distinction should be understood as a thesis about sensible qualities; I relied on the idea that Democritus offers an even-handed critique of the reality of all sensible qualities, primary and secondary. But if the primary–secondary distinction is fundamentally a distinction about the explanatory priority of certain features of nature, then surely Democritus does adhere to some kind of primary–secondary distinction, and indeed not just any kind, but precisely the kind that Boyle and Locke embrace, where what is fundamental are shape, size, and motion. What I was seeing as absent from Democritus's discussion are what I would now describe as the further theses that Locke superimposes on the distinction.

22

Secondary Qualities

22.1. Big Idea #2

If the first big idea from the history of philosophy was *form* (§10.1), the next big idea—perhaps the only other really big idea—was that the world is not the way it appears to be. In a way, this idea might seem a precondition for all philosophical speculation; if the world were as it appears, what need would there be for philosophy? But although at least implicit in the musings of the Presocratics, and a constant undercurrent in Plato, the idea lies outside the main thrust of Aristotle's thought. For him, and for his scholastic progeny, the senses are the epitome of reliability: "perception of the proper sensibles is true, or admits the least possible amount of falsity" (*De an.* III.3, 428b18). It would wait until the seventeenth century for the appearance–reality gap to become an enduring and explicit theme in philosophical speculation.[1]

Scholastic disinterest in the gap between appearances and reality is of a piece with its often-discussed disinterest in skepticism,[2] and arises from the idea that philosophy ought to treat the reliability of the senses as axiomatic. Hence, to take just one case, Thomas Aquinas's leading argument for why we should take the qualities of the bread and wine to remain in the Eucharist is simply that we perceive them there: "it appears to the senses that some quantity there is colored and affected by the other accidents;

---

[1] Democritus is the Presocratic who articulates the appearance–reality gap most explicitly: "There are two forms of judgment, genuine and bastard. To the bastard form belong all these, sight, hearing, smell, taste, touch. The form that is genuine, but separate from this one, is when the bastard form can no longer see in the direction of greater smallness nor hear or smell or taste or perceive by touch other things in the direction of greater fineness" (ed. Diels and Kranz, *Fragmente* 68 B11); "in reality we know nothing, for truth is in the depths" (ibid., B117). But he also is attested to have said things that seem to contradict this: "Democritus said straight out that truth and appearance are identical, and that there is no difference between the truth and what appears to the senses, but what appears and seems so to each individual is true, as Protagoras also said" (ibid., A113).

Hacker, *Appearance and Reality*, describes the gap as having "fascinated, obsessed and bewildered philosophers" for twenty-five centuries (p. 1). This is misleading, since although the problem is old, it has been of only intermittent interest. Rightly, though, he remarks that "since the seventeenth century these . . . questions have been brought within the ambit of a fresh field of force" (p. 2). Hume treats the appearance–reality gap as the heart of post-scholastic thought: "the fundamental principle of that philosophy is the opinion concerning colours, sounds, tastes, smells, heat and cold; which it asserts to be nothing but impressions in the mind, derived from the operation of external objects, and without any resemblance to the qualities of the objects" (*Treatise* I.4.4).

For Aristotle's doctrine of near infallibility regarding the proper sensibles, see also *De an.* III.3, 428a11–12. I discuss Aquinas's understanding of this doctrine in *Thomas Aquinas on Human Nature* pp. 187–9.

[2] See most recently Perler, *Zweifel und Gewissheit*, and "Skepticism."

nor are the senses deceived about such things" (*Summa theol.* 3a 77.2c). In context, Aquinas is making a stronger point than might be immediately evident: after all, we should not suppose the miracle of the Eucharist consists in a collective hallucination. If we can trust the senses in general, we can trust them during Mass. But the idea that we can trust the senses in general would be one of the most prominent targets of seventeenth-century criticism. In Francis Bacon's words, memorable for the whiff of paradox they contain, "it is certain that the senses deceive, but they also testify to their own errors" (*Instauratio magna*, Plan of Work p. 32). The idea that the senses are deceptive in certain domains dominates later seventeenth-century thought, and worries about just how far that domain might extend become a leading theme of the eighteenth century. As usual, it is beyond our scope to consider the iterations of idealism and skepticism that cycle through Berkeley, Hume, and Kant. The focus here will be the mixed verdict found in Galileo, Descartes, and Hobbes, which Locke would ultimately tie to the primary–secondary distinction: that with respect to kinetic–geometric properties the senses can be trusted, but that they are profoundly misleading when it comes to color, sound, smell, flavor, and heat.

Ironically, it was in just these cases—which for the sake of familiarity I will hereafter follow Boyle and Locke in calling the *secondary qualities*—that the Aristotelians were most confident of sensory reliability. These were the proper sensibles, the cases where, as Aristotle puts it above, the senses are either never wrong or at least hardly ever. A great deal of ingenuity has been put into trying to understand why Aristotle would have said this. I think it best to suppose that he said it for the perhaps banal reason that it is manifestly true: we rarely do go very far wrong with respect to the secondary qualities, whereas we are more likely to go wrong regarding shape, size, and motion, and even more likely to go wrong in identifying what sort of thing it is that we are perceiving. Such a truth is, admittedly, not very philosophically interesting, and in particular it is quite beside the point of the seventeenth-century discussions that would come to overshadow Aristotle in this domain. According to these post-scholastic authors, our perceptions of secondary qualities are problematic because they lead us to project onto the world features of our perceptual experience, so that the usual, uncritical use of the senses leaves one with a radically false view about the way the world is.

Lying in the shadow of this familiar idea is the scholastic's confidence in sensory reliability. A great deal of nonsense has been written about what the scholastics thought about appearances and reality, and some of this must be dispelled before we can go any farther. Admittedly, it is hard to know exactly what scholastic authors thought in this area, because they hardly ever talk about phenomenal experience. They talk about acts of sensation and thought, to be sure, and they talk about the representational content of those acts, but the what-it-is-like of the experience itself is not usually a subject of interest. Perhaps for this reason, two sorts of quite erroneous claims have frequently been made about scholastic thought in this domain: first, that color and the other secondary qualities are primitive, *sui generis* features of reality; second, that they are exactly like our experience of them.[3]

---

[3] For the alleged primitiveness of scholastic secondary qualities, see Nadler, "Doctrines of Explanation" p. 517; Alexander, *Ideas, Qualities* p. 41: "Questions such as 'What makes this substance yellow?' were likely to be regarded as the most fundamental kind of question about natural phenomena and as representing the point at which questioning had to

The first of these can be dispelled quite quickly, on the basis of the previous chapter. Although it is true, as we will see in §22.3, that scholastic authors were hardly ever even tempted to deny the reality of the secondary qualities, they certainly did not treat those qualities as primitive in the sense of being explanatorily basic. Instead, the Aristotelian primary qualities—Hot, Cold, Wet, and Dry—are basic, and the secondary qualities were so-called (even by the scholastics) precisely because they are causally dependent and supervenient on those elemental qualities (§21.2). (Even heat, as we perceive it, can be explained in terms of an elemental mixture in which the primary quality of Heat is particularly prominent.) Moreover, and for the same reason, the secondary qualities were as far from being *sui generis* as is possible within the Aristotelian scheme. To categorize them as qualities was to group them with the primary causal agents in the natural, sublunary world, the elemental qualities that underlie all alteration, generation, and corruption. Color and the rest were therefore given as naturalistic a treatment as one could hope for at the time, embedded squarely within the best available natural science. (Where the charge of being primitive and *sui generis* rightly applies is to the occult qualities [§23.6].)

The second misunderstanding is trickier. The notion that the secondary qualities are exactly like our experiences of them might be termed 'Projection'. Usually, Projection is treated as an error theory in the philosophy of perception—as the view that we erroneously project characteristics of our sensory experiences out onto the external world. But the scholastics are often charged with holding Projection as an affirmative thesis: that the external world really does have the various phenomenal characteristics of our sensory experiences.[4] One possible basis for Projection is the above-mentioned confidence in sensory veridicality. To say that the senses are veridical, with respect to color, for instance, is to say that when one sees a certain color, one is almost certain to have gotten it right, by correctly discerning the existence of a color in the world. This is the Aristotelian near-infallibility doctrine.

---

stop because we are at the limits of observation"; Boas, "Establishment" p. 415: "Forms and qualities were real entities attached to matter or substance. . . . They expressed the result of sense perception which was thus presumed to penetrate to the ultimate reality of matter; secondary qualities were therefore thought to be real, innate and intrinsic in bodies. . . . Whereas modern science 'explains' a property, the form or quality was accepted as a complete and satisfactory explanation of the observed phenomena, the final answer to all queries." For exact resemblance, see Robert Adams, "Flavors, Colors, and God" p. 246: "We do not think there is any quality in physical objects that resembles the peculiar qualities or qualia that make the difference between experiencing red and yellow, or between the taste of sugar and salt. . . . But the typical opinion of Aristotelian Scholastics was that phenomenal qualia are similar to, and produced by, physical qualities that we perceive in bodies by means of the qualia. There is a qualitative 'form' in the sugar that is like the quality of the taste of sugar that makes it different from the taste of salt. The quality of the appearance of red that makes it different from the appearance of yellow resembles a form or quality that is present on the surface of a typical ripe apple." John Cottingham, "Descartes on Colour" p. 238, gets both these notions into the same sentence: "What is denied is the inherence of redness *qua* redness—redness construed as a certain sort of *sui generis* quality supposed to inhere in objects in a way that exactly matches our sensory awareness of it."

[4] In part, no doubt, the ascription of Veridical Projection to scholastic authors is common now because it is common in the seventeenth century. Malebranche, e.g., writes that "lorsque les philosophes disent que le feu est chaud, l'herbe verte, le sucre doux, etc., ils entendent, comme les enfants et le commun des hommes, que le feu contient ce qu'ils sentent lorsqu'ils se chauffent. . . . Il est impossible d'en douter en lisant leurs écrits. Ils parlent des qualités sensibles comme des sentiments . . ." (*Search after Truth* VI.2.2). Locke describes Veridical Projection perfectly: "Flame is denominated hot and light; snow, white and cold; and manna, white and sweet, from the ideas they produce in us: Which qualities are commonly thought to be the same in those bodies that those ideas are in us, the one the perfect resemblance of the other, as they are in a mirror; and it would by most men be judged very extravagant, if one should say otherwise" (*Essay* II.8.16).

But this is not nearly enough for Veridical Projection, since it is something that one might accept while denying that anything like our experiences exists in the external world. Indeed, as I have already suggested, this sort of confidence in veridicality is something that everyone should accept.

A more promising place to look for Veridical Projection is in the standard scholastic thesis that all cognition requires a likeness between cognizer and cognized. (Such likeness is necessary but not sufficient for veridical cognition: some authors, such as Ockham, stress that the right sort of causal relationship is also required.) The likeness thesis was a frequent target of criticism in the seventeenth century. Descartes, for instance, remarks of vision that although there is an image in the back of the eye that resembles external objects, "we must not think that it is by means of this resemblance that the picture causes us to sense these objects—as if there were yet other eyes within our brain with which we could perceive it" (*Optics* 6; VI:130; see also VI:85, VI:112–14). Locke's objections to resemblance are also well known. Yet for the scholastic likeness thesis to yield Veridical Projection, it would have to be construed in a very strong and implausible way. When a perceiver sees color, for instance, and so has a phenomenal experience of a color, the color would have to resemble the phenomenal experience: the colors would then be exactly as the experience is. The word 'exactly' here can mean only one thing: that the qualities in the world are like our sensations all the way down to the phenomenal experience itself: that the experience itself is somehow in the external world. If less than that is meant—if the claim is merely that our experiences in some respect or another resemble the sensible qualities they represent—then the thesis is far from being implausible, and may even be true. The scholastics, however, were committed only to this weaker thesis, not to exact resemblance. We can see as much by looking more closely at the likeness thesis as they formulated it. First, it is motivated not by a theory of what the secondary qualities are, but by a general Aristotelian principle about causality: that all effects resemble their causes. That this is the motivation is clear from how authors defend the likeness thesis, and also from their willingness to apply the likeness thesis to all cognition, sensory and intellectual. Second, the very fact that the likeness thesis gets applied to intellectual cognition should make us extremely wary about understanding it in a crude and literal fashion: what would it be for the essence of horse to be exactly like our idea of horse? Third, many scholastic authors make it clear that they understand likeness in very broad terms that do not require the cognition itself to be exactly like the thing it represents. Suárez, to take just one example, while accepting that the objects of cognition are a formal likeness of the intentional species in the cognitive faculty that represents them, denies that these species have to be "of the same kind" as objects in the world. Ordinary resemblance may require sameness of kind, but "representational likeness" is special, and can obtain between very different sorts of entities (*In De an.* 5.2 concl. 2).

This sort of strategy—defining a *sui generis* category of representational likeness—is no doubt problematic if one is trying to explain mental representation in terms of some better understood concept. Even so, such claims make it clear that scholastic talk of likeness between cognizer and cognized does not require supposing that the secondary qualities are exactly as they appear to be. Admittedly, here, as always, one has to be cautious in overgeneralizing about scholastic views. Suárez is responding to Durand of St. Pourçain, who did insist that likeness requires sameness of kind. Durand was probably the inspiration for William Crathorn, a few years later in the early fourteenth century, who notoriously insisted that we can perceive colors and other sensible qualities only if the sensory faculty literally takes on the quality in question, becoming red and round, for instance. But even these authors who take likeness quite literally are not endorsing Veridical Projection. Crathorn thinks that the visual power becomes red when it sees red, but this does not mean that phenomenal experiences are projected out onto the world. On the contrary, for Crathorn, the world's sensible qualities are projected into the mind. In general, then, and even in the most extreme cases, the scholastic commitment to analyzing mental representation in terms of likeness provides no evidence for the thesis that they endorse Veridical Projection.[5]

There is, however, more than just a lack of evidence here; there is also a kind of pragmatic impossibility. We could justly ascribe the thesis of exact likeness—that is, Veridical Projection—to the scholastics only if we could find an author who sets the thesis out in reasonably explicit terms. But Veridical Projection is a thesis that, as soon as it is set out in explicit terms, shows itself to be incoherent. Anyone who gets far enough along to distinguish phenomenal experiences from things in the world, and then considers whether the latter might be exactly like the former, has to see immediately that the thesis is impossible. There could certainly be isomorphic elements between sensation and object—that is what the likeness thesis in its weak and plausible form must maintain—but it is simply incoherent to think that inanimate objects could be just like phenomenal experiences. Berkeley surely put it too strongly when he remarked that "an idea can be like nothing but an idea; a colour or figure can be like nothing but another colour or figure" (*Principles* n. 8), but the claim is manifestly true if one has in mind the sort of exact phenomenal-to-world likeness that Veridical Projection insists on. Inanimate objects cannot be characterized in terms of phenomenal experiences—that is part of what we mean by calling them *inanimate*. So not only is there no evidence that the scholastics endorsed Veridical Projection, but it is actually impossible that they could have explicitly done so. This is not to deny that many people throughout history have been *implicitly* under the spell of Projection: no doubt there are many who, failing to grasp the appearance–reality gap, have treated the appearances as if they were reality. Perhaps even some philosophers have been under the spell. But there is a pragmatic impossibility in ascribing Veridical Projection to someone as a philosophical thesis, because even to articulate the thesis requires enough sophistication to see immediately that the thesis is incoherent.

---

[5] For likeness as the key to mental representation, see my *Theories of Cognition* ch. 2, and the discussion of the role Ockham and others give to causality (pp. 113–21). The only scholastic author I have found denying a role to resemblance in mental representation is William of Auvergne (ibid., pp. 101–5)—perhaps because his *De anima* from c.1240 was written before Latin authors were fully in the grip of Aristotelianism.

Durand of St. Pourçain relies on his insistence on sameness of kind to show that angels do not have intelligible species (*Sent.* II.3.6 n. 17), and that human beings cannot perceive God through any species that serves as a likeness of God (*Sent.* IV.49.2 n. 13). For Crathorn, see *Sent.* I.1 (tr. Pasnau *Cambridge Translations* pp. 285–90; see my *Theories of Cognition* pp. 101–5). Aquinas, like Suárez, insists that the resemblance found in cognition is distinct from ordinary resemblance (see, e.g., *Quaest. de veritate* 2.3 ad 9). Brower and Brower-Toland, "Aquinas on Mental Representation," have recently argued that he treats cognitive resemblance as "primitive or *sui generis*."

22.2. Revelation

Although it is not plausible to suppose that any scholastic authors defend Projection, it can be shown that they often defend a different thesis, *Revelation*. I use this label in the same way it is used in modern discussions, as the thesis that sensory experience reveals the very nature of the sensible qualities. To have a standard visual experience of red, for instance, is to know essentially what red is. One might suppose that the only way to believe Revelation is to embrace either Projection or Anti-Realism, where the latter is the Galilean thesis to be discussed in the next section, that sensible qualities do not exist in the external world. For if sensible qualities either are nothing other than sensory experiences or else exactly resemble those experiences, then Revelation might plausibly be maintained. Can it be maintained without defending either Projection or Anti-Realism? I believe that scholastic authors commonly thought it could. The idea would be that while the senses do not reveal everything about the secondary qualities of material objects, they reveal enough to give us a clear sense of what those qualities are.[6]

We have already seen plenty of examples of what the senses do not reveal about the secondary qualities. They do not reveal that these qualities are accidents, or what the ontological status of an accident is (Ch. 10). They do not reveal that such qualities inhere in a certain kind of subject, either a quantity or a substance (Ch. 11). They do not reveal that they are accidents in the Aristotelian category of Quality (Ch. 12). All of these results are metaphysical, not empirical. The senses also do not reveal that the secondary qualities are caused by and supervene on the primary qualities (Ch. 21). Nor do they reveal the commonly endorsed Aristotelian view that the different hues of color are caused by black and white intermingling in different degrees (see *De sensu* ch. 3). These are theses of natural philosophy, not immediately revealed to sensation. One might well wonder just what content that leaves for the thesis of Revelation. What it leaves, most notably, is that the senses reveal the quality spaces of the different secondary qualities. This is to say, for instance, that although vision does not show anything about the metaphysical status or causal bases of color, it does show everything there is to be shown about the differences among the colors. Orange is similar to red; red is similar to purple; purple is more similar to blue than to green. These are important facts about color that anyone knows just by looking at the colors; indeed, it is plausible to say that they are in some sense the essence of the colors. No doubt there are other facts about color that sight reveals, but these seem the best candidates for supporting Revelation.

These last remarks regarding Revelation are speculative, because scholastic authors do not discuss the issue in enough detail to get very clear about their view. Why, then, should we think they endorsed Revelation at all? One reason is the famous distinction between manifest and occult qualities (§23.6). The phrase 'manifest quality' does not occur in Aquinas, but becomes pervasive in later scholastic thought. Stephanus Chauvin's *Lexicon philosophicum* (2nd ed. 1713) offers this definition: "A manifest quality is

---

[6] The classic statement of Revelation is in Mark Johnston, "How to Speak of the Colors." Perhaps one can see Revelation in this remark of Aquinas's: "Si qua vero sunt quae secundum se sunt nota nobis, ut calor, frigus, albedo, et huiusmodi, non ab aliis denominantur. Unde in talibus idem est quod nomen significant, et id a quo imponitur nomen ad significandum" (*Summa theol.* 1a 13.8c).

one whose cause or causes and defining character (*formalitas*) can be easily explained" (p. 546a). The paradigm cases are the secondary qualities, which are said to be readily "explained" by sensory observation. This is tantamount to embracing Revelation, because for the secondary qualities to count as manifest, on this definition of the term, it must be that the senses reveal the nature of those qualities.

Such alleged manifestness of the secondary qualities was a prime object of scorn in the seventeenth century. Just as anti-Aristotelians criticized the scholastics for yielding too much to mysterious occult qualities, so they attacked them for trusting too much in the manifest qualities. In Walter Charleton's words: "Who too boldly presuming that all those qualities of concretions, which belong to the jurisdiction of the senses, are dependent upon known causes, and deprehended by known faculties, have therefore termed them *Manifest*" (*Physiologia* III.15.1.1). For some post-scholastic authors it is hardly an exaggeration to say that the manifest and the occult trade places: it is the so-called occult qualities that admit of ready explanation, in mechanical terms, whereas the manifest qualities become occulted in the mysteries of the immaterial mind. Charleton, however, is more pessimistic across the board: he takes the obscurity of the so-called manifest qualities to show that there is nothing we understand very well: "It being a discouraging truth that even those things which are familiar and within the sphere of our sense, and such to the clear discernment whereof we are furnished with organs most exquisitely accommodate, remain yet ignote and above the moon to our understanding" (III.1.1.1). The truth, Charleton concludes, is that "all the operations of nature are mere secrets" (III.15.1.1).

All by itself, the doctrine of manifest qualities provides a fairly thin basis for reading Revelation into scholastic theories of the secondary qualities. Stronger evidence comes from discussions of the Aristotelian dictum that one who lacks some sense must lack some corresponding knowledge (*Post. an.* I.18, 81a38). Scholastic authors understand this to mean that someone who lacks vision, say, will also lack knowledge about colors. But then the question arises of whether someone would truly be barred from knowledge of a certain secondary quality without the corresponding sense? If the secondary qualities were primitive, *sui generis* properties, then the answer might seem to be clearly yes. But given that this is not the scholastic view, and that indeed we understand their underlying causes, one might think that one *could* grasp the secondary qualities without being able to perceive them. Thus John Buridan, considering the Aristotelian dictum, remarks:

The entire difficulty in this question is why through a knowledge of the [primary] tangible qualities we cannot come to a knowledge of [e.g.] flavors or odors, since these are their causes, just as in many other cases we go from knowledge of causes to knowledge of effects, and conversely. (*In Post. an.* I.28c)

Buridan goes on to allow that this is possible: even someone blind from birth can acquire knowledge (*scientia*) about color. Such knowledge will be "confused," however, in the technical sense of failing to discriminate between cases of different kinds. So Buridan's final conclusion is that "if we lack a sense from birth then it is impossible for us, with respect to the sensibles proper to that sense, to acquire naturally a knowledge of the quidditative concepts of those sensibles" (ibid.). That is, only someone who has known what it is like to see colors can know what colors essentially are. This conclusion

would seem to depend on Revelation. Although Buridan does not attempt to characterize these "quidditative concepts" of the secondary qualities that we grasp through
the senses, his point is that the senses, and only the senses, show us the secondary
qualities as they are.

The same idea is spelled out somewhat more, two centuries later, in Domingo de
Soto's treatment of this same question. De Soto's discussion, although quite different in
its details, reaches essentially the same conclusion as Buridan. The congenitally blind
can know something about colors: they can know, for instance, that one color dilates
sight whereas another contracts it, that the stuff that is known by taste as milk is white,
and that white is what dilates sight. Still, the congenitally blind cannot have a knowledge of colors "through proper and quidditative concepts":

> This is proved, because the blind do not properly understand what it is for whiteness to dilate
> sight and for blackness to contract it, but through a comparison to sound or taste. Nor do they
> understand the difference between white and black, red and green; instead, they have concepts
> of these that are just like those that I have when I discuss some sixth sense—whether, that is,
> God could make another sense by which I would perceive another sensible distinct from the five
> kinds of sensibles. (*In Post. an.* I.6, p. 388a)

De Soto mentions two shortcomings in a non-visual grasp of color. First, the knowledge that whiteness "dilates sight" (lines 1–2) is not "proper" in the way it would be if
one could actually sense whiteness. Second, a non-visual grasp of the colors does not
reveal the differences between them. Given these remarks, however, which are all De
Soto gives us, one might suppose that the blind *could* acquire a proper and distinctive
grasp of the colors. Dilation and contraction are evidently mechanical events that can
be grasped in all of their details without any visual information; why, then, couldn't
someone blind grasp the distinctive event that occurs when white acts on sight?
Similarly, given that the secondary qualities are caused by and supervene on the
primary qualities, why couldn't one arrive at a perfectly "proper" understanding of a
given color by coming to grasp just what mixture of elemental qualities gives rise to it?
What De Soto must be supposing, although he does not say so explicitly, is that even
these sorts of determinate, uniquely specifying accounts would leave out the essence of
what the colors are. One can specify just how much a given color dilates sight, but
without having the experience, one is not grasping the "quiddity" of the color itself.
Similarly, one could know what elemental mixture causes a given color, but a proper,
quidditative grasp of color requires grasping the visual differences between the colors.[7]

---

[7] De Soto takes his argument that sight reveals the essence of color to be licensed by Aristotle, *Phys.* II.1, 193a7–9: "a
man blind from birth might reason about colors. Such persons must therefore be talking about words, without any
understanding (νοεῖν)." For an argument against reading Aristotle as committed to Revelation with regard to the
secondary qualities, see Ganson, *On the Origins* pp. 192–203.

The idea that whiteness dilates whereas blackness contracts comes from Plato, *Timaeus* 67d–e. (I owe this reference to
Mark Smith.) This section of the *Timaeus* was not available in the Latin West until the fifteenth century.

It is hard to understand the traditional view that the colors result from a mixture of black and white, and the texts do
not offer much help. Dave Robb has suggested to me that the view might work if we think of white as somehow
containing all the colors, some of which are revealed while others are obscured by being mixed with varying amounts of
black. Interestingly, the view carries into post-scholastic texts. Charleton, for instance, describes how spherical and
polished bodies are white, whereas craggy ones are black, and then asserts that from these two extremes the remaining
colors can be readily explained: "The generation of the two extreme and ground colours, white and black, being attained
by this kind of inquest into the rolls of reason . . . , there can be no great difficulty remaining concerning the genealogy of

More would need to be said to make this line of thought plausible, but even in their schematic form, these passages are extremely good evidence for the doctrine of Revelation. Indeed, the texts are so suggestive that they might seem to betray a commitment to the much stronger doctrine of Projection. For why would one suppose that the essence of the secondary qualities is revealed only by perception unless one thought that the perceptual experience itself is something that the quality in the world possesses? Admittedly, it is possible that this incoherent notion is what motivates either Buridan or De Soto. But this is something that they neither say nor are committed to, inasmuch as there is room to defend Revelation without Projection. One can think that the phenomenal features of experience display the essential features of the secondary qualities—the space of similarities between them—without taking the further, incoherent step of supposing that the secondary qualities *possess* the phenomenal features of experience. Accordingly, if charity is to count for anything as a principle of interpretation, it should lead us to read these authors as committed to Revelation, not Projection.

22.3. Scholastic Realism

Anti-Realism, as I will use the term here, is the doctrine that the secondary qualities do not exist in the external world. (Realism, for purposes of this chapter, is the denial of Anti-Realism.) Galileo famously argued for Anti-Realism, and so did Hobbes, as we will see. Its prominence among seventeenth-century authors is symptomatic of the interest they took in the appearance–reality gap. Before Galileo, in contrast, Anti-Realism is virtually unheard-of. Indeed, according to the usual misunderstandings of the scholastic theory of the secondary qualities, it would have been quite inconceivable for the scholastics to have defended Anti-Realism, inasmuch as the senses show the world to be populated with explanatorily basic qualities that are exactly as they seem to be. In fact, however, Anti-Realism was a more tempting option for scholastics authors than is ordinary realized, and the reasons why they nevertheless resisted it are worth examining.

It is useful to distinguish two motivations for Anti-Realism. The first arises from the appearance–reality gap, and relocates the secondary qualities, moving them from external bodies into the mind. This is in effect a response to Projection: it amounts to supposing that we have been confusing the mental and the physical, and proposes to untangle the mess by relocating the secondary qualities. The second form of Anti-Realism is eliminativist. It takes its inspiration from a reductive account of the secondary qualities—the claim that color, say, is nothing other than a certain arrangement of primary qualities—and then decides to go one step beyond reduction and claim that in truth there are no secondary qualities in the external world at all.

Scholastic authors were aware of both of these possibilities. Peter Auriol seems to have in the mind the first when he cites "the opinion of the ancients, who say that an accident is not a reality outside the soul" (*Sent.* IV.12.1.1, III:109a). The second option was by far the more tempting, however, inasmuch as various analogous cases made

---

all other intermediate ones, since they are but the offspring of the extreme, arising from the intermission of light and shadow, in various proportions" (*Physiologia* III.4.3).

eliminativism look plausible. The four elements, for instance, along with their substantial forms, were usually thought to cease existing when mixed together. Within a mixture, according to the standard view, there is only the mixed body and its substantial form (gold, for instance, and the substantial form of gold). There are no further substantial forms for the elements, because the elements do not actually exist within the mixed body. The details here were hotly disputed, but the basic view was widely accepted. A similar sort of reduction was often proposed for the elemental qualities: that they too, being accidents of the elements, could no longer exist once the elements themselves were corrupted by mixture. Here too there was considerable disagreement, and some authors held that the elemental qualities do remain within a mixed body, but the issue was at any rate widely debated.[8]

If mixture results in the elements and their qualities ceasing to exist, then it is natural to wonder how much further this might go. No one proposed eliminating the Aristotelian primary qualities altogether, since all of scholastic natural philosophy rests on their causal role (§21.2). But might the secondary qualities be reduced, or even eliminated, so that instead of supervening on the primary qualities they would in fact be nothing more than a mixture of primary qualities? This was not a widely discussed question; the reality of the secondary qualities is almost always taken for granted.[9] But scholastic authors with strong inclinations toward parsimony were sometimes tempted. Richard Fitzralph reports in his *Sentences* commentary (*circa* 1328) that he himself had once succumbed:

Some say that every color is light (*lux*), that every flavor is a mixture of primary qualities, and that odor is flavor. Indeed I at one point did not believe that anything exists other than substance or the Equivocal Views: Descartesfive qualities—namely, the four elemental qualities and light (*lux*)—supposing there to be a small number of things. The reason was that I was focused on these few things, and I could preserve those by this stance. Hence I believed it to be true, in accord with that principle stated above Equivocal Views: Descartes[that if something can be done through few just as it can through more, then it is better that it be done through few rather than more]. And in this way those who have been well trained in logic err in recognizing too few things, whereas others who are ignorant of logic ascribe to every statement a new entity (*res*), postulating more entities than God has ever established as real. (*Sent.* II.1.2, in Maier, *An der Grenze* p. 16n.)

Anti-Realism is here depicted as a natural consequence of the sort of parsimonious ontology that would come to be associated with nominalism. And indeed, once one gets down to an ontology of substances and qualities, the natural next step is to think about whether one can make do with fewer kinds of qualities. Given that the secondary

---

[8] Excellent overviews of scholastic disputes over mixture can be found in Maier, *An der Grenze* pt. I (part. tr. Sargent, ch. 6) and, more recently, Wood and Weisberg, "Interpreting Aristotle on Mixture," and Wood, "The Influence of Arabic Aristotelianism." The Coimbran commentary on *De generatione*, at I.10, is a good place to get a sense of the range of scholastic views, as is Burgersdijk, *Collegium physicum* disp. 18. Aquinas is especially associated with the view that the elemental primary qualities cease to exist in a mixture; this follows from his insistence that all substantial change goes down to prime matter, that accidents are individuated by their subjects, and that accidents do not inhere in prime matter (see, e.g., his *De mixtione elementorum*). Oresme takes the view that the contrary elemental qualities yield a single mean quality (*In Gen. et cor.* I.5). Auriol is one of very few authors who suppose that the elements themselves remain in the mixed body (see Maier, *An der Grenze* pp. 69–74). Buridan takes the less extreme view that the elemental primary qualities remain but not the elements themselves (see *In Gen. et cor.* II.7 and Maier, *An der Grenze* p. 132).

[9] Ockham remarks: "communiter conceditur a omnibus quod color, sapor et huiusmodi qualitates sensibiles inter se realiter distinguunter et etiam a substantia" (*Tract. de quantitate* prol. [*Opera theol.* X:4]).

qualities both supervene on the primary qualities and yield to the primary qualities almost all causal activity (§21.2), it is no wonder that Fitzralph was tempted simply to eliminate them.

Ultimately, Fitzralph changed his mind about this, and I have found no one else before the seventeenth century who comes so close to Anti-Realism. Why not? The mid-seventeenth-century Ockhamist André Dabillon suggests that the issue depends on whether one thinks the primary qualities are the efficient cause of the secondary qualities or merely the material cause, in the sense that a certain mixture of primary qualities is what underlies secondary qualities of a certain kind. In the first case, the two will seem distinct, since it is not tempting to identify an efficient cause and its effect. But in the second case "it is very plausible that the secondary qualities are nothing other than the primary qualities variously mixed—although one could also say that they are entirely distinct from the primary qualities, just as mixed bodies are distinct from their elements" (*Physique des bons esprits* II.1.1, p. 139). Here the analogy to elemental mixtures is explicitly invoked, and Dabillon's point is that we are not tempted to say that mixed bodies are nothing more than their elements. The situation is clearer, however, if primary qualities are the efficient causes of secondary qualities, and this is how scholastic authors usually seem to have understood the situation. Ockham, for instance, explicitly describes primary qualities as the efficient cause of secondary qualities (*Quaest. phys.* 117), and accordingly he never subjects the secondary qualities to his Razor.

The most obvious reason why scholastic authors could not eliminate the secondary qualities from the external world is that they were understood to play a limited but important causal role. As we have seen (§21.2), the causal primacy thesis leaves the secondary qualities as nearly epiphenomenal. As Oresme describes the situation:

The second conclusion is that none of the sensible qualities is active, other than the tangible qualities. I speak of action with contrariety—that is, of corruptive action. This is clear by induction, because it does not seem that a white object is able to whiten a black object placed next to it, and so on in other cases. And if it is objected that odor and flavor seem to be active, because they infect the surrounding air, I respond that they are not. What instead does this is the heat or cold of the bodies that have the odor or flavor. (*In Gen. et cor.* II.1, pp. 186–7)

Oresme is arguing for the causal primacy of the elemental qualities. He frames his conclusion carefully, in terms of a certain sort of causation, which Oresme calls "corruptive" (line 2), and which refers to an action that causes an object to lose one state and acquire another—for instance, to go from being black to white. The secondary qualities are not active in that way, and so count as inert with respect to ordinary natural processes. There is, however, a causal role that the secondary qualities play: they give rise to intentionally existing species in the surrounding medium, which in turn gives rise to our sensations of those qualities. Here is Paul of Taranto, the late-thirteenth-century alchemist, in a passage already quoted in part (§21.2):

The aforesaid secondary qualities are not of themselves properly active on a given nature except *per accidens*, for they are properly active of themselves on sense through their species, according to the spiritual and intentional existence that these species have, and not according to their natural existence, except *per accidens*. For color moves sight according to the intentional existence that it has in the transparent medium, and not according to the natural existence it has in natural things, and taste as taste, of itself, moves the sense and not nature, for a similar reason. It is not taste, however, that nourishes, but food and drink—namely, the substance that *has* the taste. Thus taste acts on nature only through something else, namely Hot, Cold, Dry, and Wet, which are in the flavorful thing. Nor can any of the secondary qualities act within the nature and essence of anything, except through the primary qualities. (*Liber veritatis* pp. 8–9)

This is the standard scholastic view: that the secondary qualities do not act naturally on the world, but do act through spiritual/intentional qualities (§21.2). This sort of causal role in turn helps support the doctrine of Revelation: it is because the secondary qualities themselves give rise to our sensory experiences that we can expect those experiences to grasp the secondary qualities as they are.[10]

Even so limited a causal role, confined to sensation, is incompatible with Anti-Realism. As we have seen in previous chapters (esp. §10.5), the principal scholastic test for the reality of any accident is a causal test: does the supposed accident do anything in the world, such that its elimination would leave a causal void? Applying this test to the case of the secondary qualities, scholastic authors were, almost without exception, Realists. Peter John Olivi makes this particularly vivid in his discussion of the Eucharist, when he points out that if God can separate an accidental quality from its substance, then he can surely also separate that quality from all other qualities:

For it is clear that color and flavor and the four elemental qualities that are in the species of the bread and wine had a greater connection to the substance to which they belonged than they have to one another. Who then will dare to say that God could not separate them from each other, so that color stands on its own, and flavor on its own, and so too for the others. (*Sent.* IV.11, in Bakker, *La raison* I:344n.)

Naturally speaking, it would be impossible to have the secondary qualities without the Aristotelian primary qualities, since the former were held to supervene on the latter. But their separation is no more impossible than separating a quality from its subject; so if God can make accidents exist independently of substance, he can make secondary qualities exist independently of the primary qualities on which they naturally supervene. Such separation is possible, as we have seen, only given Realism regarding the secondary qualities. Hence these qualities too, just as much as the four elemental primary qualities, take their place among the real accidents that would come to be the hallmark of later scholastic thought. This is the broader causal story that provides the context for seventeenth-century theories of the secondary qualities.

---

[10] On the causal role of color, see also Toletus, *In Praed.* ch. 8 (II:158a): "colores non agere in oculos passione corruptiva, cum imprimant speciem et similitudinem, quae non corrumpit." For Zabarella, the causal story about sensation is no more mysterious than any other causal story in nature: sensible qualities are perceived simply because they produce a *species* that travels through the medium and ultimately makes an impression on the senses. Thus, "nihil aliud est sentiri per se, quam speciem suam in sensu producere" (*De rebus nat.*, De sensu agente col. 842C). Indeed, there is no more mystery in the sensory case than in the paradigmatic physical case of heat: "Quemadmodum igitur vana esset quaestio cur calor alium calorem materialem producat, cum nulla huius productionis sit alia ratio quam ipsamet caloris natura, quae apta est ad alium calorem in alio generandum; ita etiam vanum est quaerere cur sensiles qualitates in medio et in organo speciem suam producant; etenim suapte natura sunt aptae ad speciem suam multiplicandam" (col. 842A).

22.4. Post-Scholastic Realism

The Anti-Realism that we associate with the seventeenth century has little precedent in earlier philosophy. Not only is it not found among Aristotelian authors, but even the fiercest, most reductive critics of Aristotelianism, such as Nicholas of Autrecourt, still maintain some kind of mind-independent place for the secondary qualities. The only real forerunner of Anti-Realism was Democritus. And if we look at how his views were interpreted in the first half of the seventeenth century, we can see just how alien a notion Anti-Realism was. The most famous testimony to Democritean Anti-Realism is this fragment:

By convention (νόμῳ) sweet and by convention bitter, by convention hot, by convention cold, by convention color; but in reality (ἐτεῇ) atoms and void. (ed. Diels and Kranz, *Fragmente* 68 B9)

The fragment is attested in Sextus Empiricus, Diogenes Laertius, Galen, and Plutarch, none of which were available in the Latin West until the fifteenth century. Even in the mid-seventeenth century, however, the fragment was regarded as baffling. Jean Chrysostome Magnen, whose *Democritus reviviscens* (1646) aims at rehabilitating Democritus's reputation, thinks that Democritus accepts all the traditionally recognized qualities, primary and secondary. As for the famous fragment, he takes it to be making a point only about sensory variation. Understanding νόμῳ literally as *law*, he takes it that objects are sweet or bitter "by a certain law and proportion between agent and patient, one being sweet to one which is bitter to another" (III.3, p. 436). Hence the fragment does not support Anti-Realism. Pierre Gassendi, writing three years later, understands the passage somewhat differently, but is no more inclined toward Anti-Realism:

The sense is that nothing truly and of its nature (that is, eternally) endures the way (*quale*) it is, beyond atoms and the void (the atoms, I mean, along with their inseparable properties). All the rest does not exist truly and by the necessity of its nature, but depends on various accidents for   3 its existing and coming to be in one way rather than another. . . . Beyond atoms and the void, all the qualities that are seen in things (color, heat, etc.) he says to exist "by law" (*lege*)—not indeed that they depend on human convention, as translators render it, but metaphorically, appealing   6 to a kindred phrase: that just as, in the case of human actions, justice, injustice, rightness, wrongness, praise, and blame depend on the constitution of the laws, so, in the case of natural things, light, dark, sweet, bitter, hot, cold etc. depend on the various positions and orders of the   9 atoms. (*Animadversiones* pp. 230–1)

Gassendi rejects the 'by convention' translation of νόμῳ that remains standard today (line 6), pointing out reasonably enough that human convention surely has nothing to do with it. Instead, he thinks the point amounts to some kind of dependence claim: that sensible qualities depend on atomic structures just as moral evaluation depends on how the laws are set up. This "metaphorical" reading (line 6) is of course not terribly promising for anyone not inclined to make morals rest on human law. Even so, Charleton's *Physiologia* (1654) closely paraphrases this passage, endorsing Gassendi's reading of what Charleton calls a "remarkable and mysterious text" (III.1.1.2).[11]

---

[11] Charleton's gloss on Democritus's fragment, while in part amounting to a literal translation of Gassendi, elaborates in other places in a way that is worth quoting: "therefore ought all other things, and more eminently qualities, in regard

The way these critics read Democritus tells us more about their own views than it does about Democritus. Whereas readers now tend to take for granted that Democritus is anticipating the primary–secondary distinction, early readers of the passage, with no less textual evidence to go on than we have, were seriously puzzled. Their puzzlement arises because they were not even considering Anti-Realism as a live philosophical possibility. Despite being leading advocates of post-scholastic corpuscularianism, they all took for granted that the secondary qualities are in some sense in the world. They took for granted Realism.

In Gassendi's case this is not terribly surprising, because he is explicitly following the Epicurean version of atomism, which embraces Realism.[12] Accordingly, Gassendi must confront the problem of how atomism can account for secondary qualities in the world:

If it is true that the only material principles of things are atoms, and there are no other qualities in atoms other than size, shape, and weight, or motion, as was set out above, then what makes it the case that so many additional qualities are created and exist within the things themselves: color, heat, flavor, odor, and innumerable others? (*Syntagma* II.1.5.7, I:366ab)

His full answer to this query emerges slowly over the 85 dense double-column pages that he devotes to the qualities of things (ibid., II.1.6). In keeping with his reaction to Democritus, he never once stops to question whether the secondary qualities actually are in "the things themselves" (*ipsis rebus*, line 3). The general character of his Realist strategy is clear from the start:

Since these atoms, then, are the whole of the corporeal matter or substance that exists in bodies, it is clear that if we conceive or notice anything else to exist in these bodies, that is not a substance but only some kind of mode of the substance—that is, a certain contexture, concretion, or composition of this matter or material principles; or, following from that, its rarity or denseness, softness or hardness, size or bulk, outline or shape, color and image, mobility or sluggishness. (ibid., II.1.6.1, I:372ab)

These two passages together yield the view that, with respect to substance, there are only atoms and aggregates of atoms. With respect to qualities, there are the atomic qualities—size, shape, weight, motion—and then there are the qualities of the aggregate bodies. The aggregate qualities are either the texture/composition of the atoms, or else various qualities that "follow" (line 4) from that texture. This includes the macro-level counterparts of the atomic qualities (the size, shape, and motion of the aggregate body), and those qualities that are an obvious consequence of atomic texture, such as rarity or denseness, and also various further qualities that are not so obviously a result of atomic texture, such as color. As for the status of those qualities, Gassendi endorses the old Aristotelian slogan, familiar from deflationists like Albert the Great and Aquinas (§10.2), according to which "only substance properly exists," whereas an accident "is not so much a being, as it is a being of a being (*entis ens*), or a mode of standing of a

---

they arise not from, nor subsist upon any indeclinable necessity of their principles, but depend upon various transient accidents for their existence, to be reputed not as absolute and entire realities, but simple and occasional appearances, whose specification consists in a certain modification of the first matter, respective to that distinct affection they introduced into this or that particular sense, when thereby actually deprehended" (*Physiologia* III.1.1.2). Accordingly, as we will see in §23.4, Charleton holds that bodies have no color in the dark, and perhaps no color when unseen.

[12] See Furley, "Democritus and Epicurus" and Sedley, "Epicurean Anti-Reductionism."

being" (*Syntagma* II.1.6.1, I:373b). This is not to deny that there are qualities, but only to insist, as Gassendi puts it here and elsewhere, that they are modes (§13.4).[13]

Gassendi's version of Realism is what one expects to find in the seventeenth century. When one goes beyond the most famous names, however, one can find all sorts of unexpected views, views that we hardly know how to classify today. Consider, for instance, the atomism of Claude Berigard, a Frenchman teaching in Italy and writing in 1643. He describes atomism as a more plausible view than Aristotle's prime matter (at least provided that the existence of the void can be established, something that he thinks has not yet been conclusively shown). Berigard wants to modify traditional atomism, however, so that instead of postulating atoms that vary merely in shape and size, he postulates atoms of fundamentally different kinds, such that each kind of atom has its own quality: heat atoms and cold atoms and so on. There are, he contends, "infinitely many species of atoms, distinct from each other in terms of their whole substance, and further there are infinitely many atoms within each species" (*Circulus Pisanus*, De ortu VIII, p. 419). Mere difference in shape and size, according to Berigard, has too little explanatory force to ground an atomic theory. He therefore makes all of his atoms circular, remarking that "the operations of nature are revealed more brightly by a difference in species, rather than by a difference in shape" (p. 423). This is the sort of view that makes it hopeless to speak of medieval versus modern doctrines: Is Berigard's embrace of atomism modern? Or is it a throwback to ancient doctrines? Is his embrace of primitive qualities medieval? Or is it modern for rejecting an analysis into the traditional four elemental qualities? The philosopher whom Berigard most resembles, as he acknowledges, is Anaxagoras.[14]

A very different, much more austere sort of Realism can be found in David Gorlaeus, whose youthful *Excercitationes philosophicae* (c.1611; publ. 1620) defends an early form of corpuscularianism. Gorlaeus accepts the Aristotelian primary qualities—or, at any rate, he accepts some of them: "There are therefore these four entities distinct from their subjects: hot, cold, light, and darkness. We recognize no other accidents that are real entities" (7.2, p. 114). In saying that these are real entities, Gorlaeus commits himself to full-blown scholastic real accidents, fully separable from their subjects and existing in just the sense that substances exist. (He even makes the unusual claim that such accidents can migrate from subject to subject [5.2], rejecting the usual scholastic view about how accidents are individuated.) But these are the only accidents that Gorlaeus is willing to accept. Stressing over and over the nominalist slogan that entities should not be multiplied without necessity, he contends that every other aspect of the physical world must be given a reductive account in terms of bodies and these four qualities. Thus he contends that the remaining traditional elemental qualities, Wet and Dry, are

---

[13] For Gassendi's account of how atomic structures give rise to further features of body, see Boas, "Establishment" pp. 429–31; Fisher, *Pierre Gassendi's Philosophy* ch. 9; LoLordo, *Pierre Gassendi* pp. 154–8; LoLordo, "Gassendi and the Seventeenth-Century Atomists."

[14] Berigard provisionally aligns himself with Democritus rather than Aristotle at *Circulus Pisanus*, De ortu VIII, p. 419: "Si qua autem experientia sufficienti saltem vacuum comprobaretur (nam quas hactenus vidi satis efficaces non existimo) tunc Democriti atomos materiae primae Aristotelis opposuissem." Later, though, it turns out that Anaxagoras is his true master: "Infinita praeterea sunt individua specie distincta, quod accipimus ab Anaxagora potius quam a Democrito, ac propterea omnibus figuram sphaericam tribuimus; luculentius enim naturae opera declarantur specierum quam figurarum diversitate" (p. 423). For a brief but useful further discussion see Meinel, "Early Seventeenth-Century Atomism," who describes Berigard's view as "qualitative atomism" (p. 73).

not accidents at all, but inseparable features of individual atoms. (As such, they remain important to his account, even if they lack any sort of separate ontological status.) As for the secondary qualities, he regards their status as an "arduous and ambiguous question" (7.8, p. 157). They are either modes, or else a kind of motion (as is sound), or else light itself (as is color). In any event, Gorlaeus shows no interest in questioning their external reality. With respect to the secondary tangible qualities, such as hard and soft, he remarks that "one cannot deny that they should be posited, because they are sensed" (7.5, p. 139). This conviction that the sensible qualities exist, because we perceive them to exist, is the precise core of Aristotelian Realism, retained here in this more austere theoretical context.[15]

Still more austere is Kenelm Digby, whose *Two Treatises* (1644) denies that there are any real qualities. But this does not keep Digby from maintaining a steadfast Realism, albeit of a reductive variety, according to which all the qualities of things are nothing more than a mixture of rare and dense. Here, for instance, is the story about color:

Thus then you see how colour is nothing else but the disposition of a bodies superficies, as it is more or less apt to reflect light, sithence [= since] the reflection of light is made from the superficies of the same body, and the variety of its reflection begets variety of colours. But a   3
superficies is more or less apt to reflect light according to the degrees of its being more or less penetrable by the force of light striking upon it, for those rays of light that gain no entrance into a body they are darted upon must of necessity fly back again from it.... And accordingly we see   6
that if a diaphanous body...be much compressed beyond what it was, as when water is compressed into ice, it becomes more visible, that is, it reflects more light, and consequently it becomes more white.... And thus it is evident how the origin of all colours in bodies is plainly   9
deduced out of the various degrees of rarity and density, variously mixed and compounded. (*Two Treatises* I.29.4)

Digby's thoroughgoing rejection of qualities does not prevent him from affirming that there are colors in the world. Like Gassendi, he associates colors with certain non-qualitative phenomena in the world, although unlike Gassendi he appeals to irreducible quantity (§14.2) as the brute explanatory force. Although his view reduces qualities to quantity, it is not eliminativist, inasmuch as it remains true to say, on his view, that colors, flavors, etc. exist in the world. Thus he concludes his discussion of the sensible qualities with a peroration on the purpose of our senses. Their purpose, he says, is "to bring us into knowledge of the natures of the substances we converse with," something

---

[15] For Gorlaeus's views on the elements and their qualities, see *Idea physicae* chs. 7 and 12, as well as Ch. 3 note 11 above. For further discussion, see Lüthy, "David Gorlaeus' Atomism" and Gregory, "David Van Goorle."

It is possible to discern hints of Anti-Realism in Gorlaeus's *Idea physicae*, a contemporaneous summary of the *Exercitationes*. There he remarks that odor and flavor are both the result of a mixture of Hot and Cold: "Odor et sapor sunt unum et idem, sed ut diversi sentiuntur, quia organa diversa. Illud enim idem, quod sapor est in lingua, in naribus est odor" (12.8). In the more detailed discussion of the *Exercitationes*, however, it is clear that he is not interested in identifying sensible qualities with the sensation, but rather that he wants to identify odor and flavor with the same complexion of Hot and Cold, and then wants to use the senses to explain why we distinguish between the two. The *Idea physicae* also remarks of sound that "nullus datur sonus ubi nullus est qui eum ipsum audiat" (12.10). This certainly looks like Anti-Realism. Again, however, the fuller discussion of the *Exercitationes* makes it clear that the view is something different: Gorlaeus holds that sounds are a motion in the *spiritus* of the auditory nerves. This comes right up to the brink of Anti-Realism, but inasmuch as the sound is still a physical event, outside the mind, this still perhaps counts as a version of Realism. The point is debatable, however, since in note 18 below I will suggest that Galileo, the archetypical Anti-Realist, may likewise think that the sensible qualities are to be located in the body of the perceiver. Even so, Gorlaeus makes this claim only about sound.

that the senses do by bringing us "the likeness or extracts of those substances" (I.31.5). On these pages, the specter of Anti-Realism has not yet appeared.[16]

22.5. Two Anti-Realists: Galileo and Hobbes

Post-scholastic Anti-Realism begins with Galileo's *Assayer* (1623). Perhaps there are earlier texts that gesture toward removing the sensible qualities from the world, but—remarkably—one has to go all the way back to Democritus to find anyone who expresses Anti-Realism with anything like the clarity and force of Galileo's famous discussion.[17] *The Assayer* leaves no room for doubt about what it wants to maintain. Although it takes as its starting-point the commonplace claim that motion is the cause of heat (§21.4), within a few lines Galileo establishes as his target the "universal" view "that heat is a real accident, affection, or quality that really resides in the material by which we sense ourselves to be warmed." In place of this, Galileo wants to defend the position that "tastes, odors, colors, and so on are no more than mere names so far as the subject in which we place them is concerned, and that they reside only in the sensory body."[18] Here is the argument Galileo offers for this conclusion:

Now I say that whenever I conceive any material or corporeal substance, I immediately feel the need to think of it as bounded and as having this or that shape, as being either large or small in relation to other things, as being in this or that place at this or that time, as being in motion or at 3 rest, as touching or not touching another body, and as being one, few, or many. From these conditions I cannot separate such a substance by any stretch of my imagination. But that it must be white or red, bitter or sweet, noisy or silent, of sweet or foul odor, my mind does not feel 6 compelled to bring in as necessary accompaniments. Without the senses as our guides, reason

---

[16]   Digby's view is clearly not Anti-Realist, inasmuch as he clearly affirms that there are sensible qualities in bodies. I claim that the view is reductive, inasmuch as those sensible qualities just are quantitative properties, rarity and density. This is perhaps not entirely clear, however, and it would be worth considering whether Digby endorses merely explanatory dependence, rather than reduction, as this passage suggests: "the sensible qualities of bodies are made by the mixtion of rarity and density" (*Two Treatises* I.31.4). This would make his treatment of the primary–secondary distinction analogous to that of the scholastics, with rarity and density in place of the four elemental qualities.

[17]   The closest I have found to Anti-Realism between Democritus and Galileo is Nicholas Hill, in 1601: "Calor est qualitas non ignis propria per se, sed habito respectu ad sensum tactus, et secundum χρημαΤίσας (?—ed. χημαΤίσας) est partis discontinuatio sensitivae per punctiferi ignis aggregationem" (*Philosophia Epicurea* n. 60). I am not sure what this says, but here is a stab at a translation: "heat is not a proper, *per se* quality of fire, but is said in relation to, and according to its interaction with, the sense of touch. It is the discontinuity of the sensory part through an aggregation of fire particles." Hill says nothing more than this.

Doubts about color prior to the seventeenth century are not doubts about its existence in the external world, but about its true nature there. See, e.g., Sanches, *Quod nihil scitur* p. 136: "De colore multo maior dubitatio. Quando illi credendum? Quando naturae suae magis propinquus, minusque ab extraneo affectus. At quis illius naturam novit? Quis simplicem vidit? Perpetua mutatio a sole, luna, et aliis superne; inferne, terra, aqua, et mixtis." This makes sense, of course, only given that color is not primitive and *sui generis*. Hence, here, its dependence on "earth, water and mixed bodies." For color's dependence on light, and so on "change to sun and moon," see Ch. 23 notes 12–13.

Hacker, *Appearance and Reality*, credits Galileo with "the modern origins of this conception" (p. 2), which is fair enough, although he then more doubtfully goes on to remark that "Galileo's conception greatly influenced Descartes" (p. 8). One might expect to find Anti-Realism in Beeckman's journals, but it is not there. Heat is given a kinetic account (I.132–3, I.216); color too is understood mechanistically (I.327, II.76, III.105–6); sound is located in the medium (I.92–3).

[18]   Ed. Flora pp. 311–12. Drake's translation (p. 274) misleadingly renders Galileo's claim that the secondary qualities reside "nel corpo sensitivo" as the claim that they reside "in consciousness." This makes Galileo sound much more like Hobbes or Descartes, both of whose accounts are founded on the appearance–reality gap. Galileo shows no interest in that issue, but instead seems to think of the problem as a straightforward mislocation of a physical event: we put heat in the body that causes the sensation of heat, whereas instead it should go in the body that undergoes the sensation.

or imagination on its own would probably never arrive at qualities like these. Hence I think that tastes, odors, colors, and so on are no more than mere names ... (ibid.)   9

Although Galileo is not using the terminology of 'primary' and 'secondary,' the passage nevertheless offers clear guidance on how to draw such a distinction. The primary are those that a body cannot be imagined as not having: shape, size, location, motion/rest, touching/not-touching, one/many (lines 1–6). The secondary are those that (a) a body need not have; and (b) can be grasped only through the senses. These criteria rely on two ideas familiar from scholastic thought: first, the doctrine of universality, that the primary qualities are present in all bodies (§21.2); second, the status of the secondary qualities as the proper sensibles—that is, qualities of bodies that can be grasped by a specifically attuned sense and in no other way. Taking these two criteria together, we get a fairly full list of the primary and secondary qualities.

Whether these criteria are adequate to generate an exhaustive distinction between the primary and secondary qualities is a much-discussed issue. Here I will set it aside, however, in order to focus on a more pressing question: Why would Galileo have thought that this perfectly familiar way of distinguishing between qualities supports Anti-Realism? On its face, the last, concluding sentence of the passage comes out of nowhere, and on close inspection Galileo's argument seems even shakier. Consider first whether Anti-Realism might follow from universality. The conceptual impossibility of bodies without shape, size, etc. obviously shows that bodies have these qualities. But three of the items on the list appear to be disjunctive. There is no conceptual necessity in a body's being in motion, or in its being at rest; the necessity concerns the exhaustive disjunct of the two. So are we to understand this argument as maintaining that various *disjunctive* properties are among the primary qualities of bodies? Or perhaps we should think of motion–rest as a single, non-disjunctive kind, consisting in facts about location over time. If so, however, why cannot we add *colored or not-colored* to the list of primary qualities, as a single kind of property consisting in facts about behavior in light? Perhaps instead the idea is that the secondary, mind-dependent qualities are those that both fail to be universal and that can be grasped only by a single, dedicated sense. But why should we believe that this is so? Suppose that heat is, as the scholastics thought, a primitive feature of some but not all elements, perceivable only by touch. Is that impossible? Could the world not be like that? The above passage does not seem to contain anything approaching a successful argument for Anti-Realism.

The most impressive part of Galileo's discussion, however, is not his ostensible argument, but the analogy that he presents next. When we are tickled by a feather, the tickling sensation belongs to us, not to the feather, and it would obviously be a mistake to ascribe the tickle to the feather. Do we not make the same mistake when we ascribe heat to the object that produces the sensation of heat? This goes much farther toward making Galileo's case than does his opening argument. There is no denying that the tickle is in us, not in the feather, and it is not obvious why the sensation of heat should be different from a tickling sensation. Even so, this hardly shows that we should never understand sensory experiences as representing a sensible quality outside the body. A recently discovered anonymous report filed with the Vatican soon after the *Assayer*'s publication makes this telling objection:

This discourse seems to me to be at fault in taking as proved that which it must prove—i.e., that in all cases the object that we feel is in us, because the act that concerns it is in us. It is the same as saying: the sight with which I see the light of the sun is in me; therefore, the light of the sun is in me. (Redondi, *Galileo Eretico* p. 428; tr. Finocchiaro p. 203)

This gets things exactly right. Galileo needs to establish that the case of the tickle generalizes. And it is far from clear that even he would accept an across-the-board generalization: after all, he would not embrace Anti-Realism in the case of light. Why the light of the sun is a different case from the tickle of the feather is a difficult question, and it is even harder to know how to go from those paradigm cases to the usual secondary qualities (see the following section for an attempt at this). Still, even if Galileo's discussion was far from decisive, it put forward in vivid terms an idea that would grow increasingly influential in the years to come.

Although Galileo's remarks were prescient, they had limited influence. That was probably a good thing for him, for if they had become better known he would have likely run into trouble with the Inquisition even sooner than he did. The main purpose of the anonymous report quoted above is to call into question whether Galileo's view is consistent with the doctrine of transubstantiation. A similar complaint was made by Orazio Grassi, a professor of mathematics at the Collegio Romano. Grassi, writing under the pseudonym Lothario Sarsi, engaged in a long-running and bitter dispute with Galileo. Grassi was the target of *The Assayer,* and he answered in 1626 with a point-by-point response. When he comes to what he calls "the digression on heat," Grassi remarks that Galileo here "confesses himself a member of the school of Democritus and Epicurus" (*Ratio ponderum* 48 [VI:486]). (We have Galileo's handwritten marginal notes to Grassi's book, where he protests that he has never even read Epicurus [ibid., VI:476 n. 133]). Although Grassi raises some philosophical objections to Galileo's argument,[19] his main objection is that the view is incompatible with the sacrament of the Eucharist as it is understood by the Church. On its face, this looks like a very serious worry. As we have seen (§§19.3–5), the Church had been adamant since 1347 that the doctrine of real accidents is required to make sense of the Eucharist. *The Assayer* seems to challenge that doctrine in the most explicit terms.

Even so, Galileo never ran into trouble in this regard. One possible reason is that, strictly speaking, *The Assayer* does not conflict with transubstantiation, since it does not reject real accidents across the board in the way that we saw Nicholas of Autrecourt and John of Mirecourt do. Since Galileo's focus is limited to the sensible qualities, he could easily have defended himself by appealing to various other sorts of real accidents (in the category of Quantity, for instance) to endure through transubstantiation. As long as Galileo could accept some sort of accidental entity that is separable from substance, he would have been in no trouble. In effect, then, Galileo's views might have skirted controversy because they were not as wide-ranging and programmatic as that of later

---

[19] One is essentially the objection of the anonymous Vatican document: "cum hoc argumentum a particulari progrediatur, nihil omnino probat" (*Ratio ponderum* 48 [VI: 487]). Redondi, *Galileo Eretico*, identifies Grassi as the author of this anonymous document, but his suggestion has generally been rejected. Redondi also, notoriously, has argued that this discussion in *The Assayer*, and the worries it raised about the Eucharist, were the hidden cause of Galileo's eventual condemnation. The evidence for this, however, is thin to the point of being nonexistent, and this argument too has been generally dismissed by scholars.

figures such as Descartes. (It was precisely because Descartes left no room for real accidents that his works were later placed on the Vatican's Index.) And whether or not the loophole I just described was explicitly recognized, it surely mattered that Galileo's discussion occurred as a brief aside in a book concerned with other matters, and that he never developed these ideas further in his other works.

For whatever reason, Galileo's Anti-Realism was not controversial, and just as it was not controversial, so it was not influential. When Descartes and Hobbes begin to advocate their own versions of Anti-Realism in the 1630s, they show no signs of *The Assayer's* influence. Although both men refer very often to Galileo in their correspondence and published work, they never refer to that particular treatise, let alone to the discussion of Anti-Realism. Nor does *The Assayer* get discussed in Boyle's writings or, so far as I can find, in Leibniz's. It is famous today because Galileo became famous for other things, but it made little impression at the time.[20]

Descartes's own, much more equivocal version of Anti-Realism has roots in his unpublished writings of 1629–33 (published posthumously as *The World* and the *Treatise on Man*). But it is not until the *Meditations* (1641) and the *Principles of Philosophy* (1644) that Descartes published anything that squarely denies the external reality of the secondary qualities, and even then his claims are always much more equivocal than those of Galileo, as we will see in the next section. It is instead Thomas Hobbes who deserves credit as the second major advocate of Anti-Realism in the seventeenth century. Hobbes's view is stated as unequivocally as Galileo's, but is supported by a much better argument. His *Elements of Law* (completed in 1640 although not published until 1650) sets the case out in detail:

Because the image in vision consisting in colour and shape is the knowledge we have of the qualities of the object of that sense, it is no hard matter for a man to fall into this opinion, that the same colour and shape are the very qualities themselves; and for the same cause, that sound   3
and noise are the qualities of the bell, or of the air. And this opinion has been so long received that the contrary must needs appear a great paradox; and yet the introduction of species visible and intelligible (which is necessary for the maintenance of that opinion) passing to and fro from   6
the object is worse than any paradox, as being a plain impossibility. I shall therefore endeavour to make plain these four points:

(1) That the subject wherein colour and image are inherent is not the object or thing seen.   9
(2) That that is nothing without us really which we call an image or colour.
(3) That the said image or colour is but an apparition unto us of that motion, agitation, or alteration, which the object works in the brain or spirits, or some internal substance of the head.   12
(4) That as in conception by vision, so also in the conceptions that arise from other senses, the subject of their inherence is not the object, but the sentient. (I.2.4)

---

[20] Redondi, ibid., refers repeatedly to *The Assayer's* fame, and perhaps this was so within Italy, but elsewhere in Europe the only reference to the work I have found occurs once in passing in Beeckman's journal (III:223). Drake remarks that the work "is of relatively small scientific importance and has not been widely read outside Italy" ("Biographical Sketch" p. 62). Maier likewise stresses the limited influence of this work ("Die Mechanisierung" p. 34). According to Ansey, "there is no evidence that his [Galileo's] brief discussion there had any impact on Boyle or his contemporaries" (*Philosophy of Robert Boyle* p. 24). Hamilton's notes to his edition of Thomas Reid's *Works* describe the *Assayer's* discussion as "remarkable but neglected" and reports that he can find only one philosopher who has discussed it (the nineteenth-century Italian, Mamiani della Rovere) (note D, II:831). One might wonder, however, whether Descartes would have independently arrived at the example of tickling with a feather, which appears in *The World* ch. 1 (XI:6).

Quite unlike Galileo, Hobbes's argument is rooted in the appearance–reality gap. Indeed, Hobbes seems to think that Projection has become entrenched among us, so that we take "the image consisting in color and shape" (line 1) to be "the very qualities themselves" (line 3). If this is what we are doing, then (as I have stressed) there is no need to make an argument against it; it should be enough to point the mistake out, and let its incoherence speak for itself. All the same, Hobbes makes an argument. He needs to, because he wants not only to reject Projection, but also to reject the much more innocuous doctrine of Realism, as he does at the end of the passage in points 1, 2, and 4.

The above passage contains a quick parenthetical argument (line 6) contending that to make our customary Realism work one has to endorse the scholastic doctrine of spiritual/intentional species as intermediaries between object and percipient. Let us set aside this *ad hominem* attack on the scholastics, however, and focus on the much more substantial argument that immediately follows:

Every man has so much experience as to have seen the sun and other visible objects by reflection in the water and in glasses, and this alone is sufficient for this conclusion: that colour and image may be there where the thing seen is not. But because it may be said that 3 notwithstanding the image in the water be not in the object, but a thing merely phantastical, yet there may be colour really in the thing itself, I will urge further this experience: that diverse times men see directly the same object double, as two candles for one, which may happen by 6 distemper, or otherwise without distemper if a man will, the organs being either in their right temper or equally distempered. The colours and figures in two such images of the same thing cannot be inherent both therein, because the thing seen cannot be in two places: one of these 9 images therefore is not inherent in the object. But seeing the organs of sight are then in equal temper or equal distemper, the one of them is no more inherent than the other, and conse-quently neither of them both are in the object; which is the first proposition mentioned in the 12 precedent section. (I.2.5)

This is what has come to be known as the argument from illusion. Hobbes begins with the case of reflected images, as cases where there is a color but it cannot be said to inhere in the object (lines 1–3). He sees, though, that cases of this form are not enough to yield the result he is after, because they leave it open to someone to insist that in standard cases one does see the true color of the object (lines 3–5). So to get his unqualifiedly Anti-Realist conclusion, he switches to the case of double images, as when one sees two candles where there is only one (lines 5–13). The crucial thing about this case is that each eye sees a different image. That, at any rate, is the natural way to describe the situation, but as soon as one describes it that way, Hobbes wins the argument, because he then has us persuaded that we are not seeing the candle, but seeing an *image* of the candle. As soon as the image gets detached from the candle in this way, the first and second of his four points get established, and it is easy to generalize the argument to cover the other secondary qualities. Echoing Francis Bacon's memo-rable aphorism (§22.1), Hobbes concludes that "this is the great deception of sense, which also is by sense to be corrected" (I.2.10).[21]

---

[21] Hobbes reprises his case for Anti-Realism in *Leviathan* I.1 (and see I.5). His view goes back at least to 1636, in a letter to Cavendish where he remarks that "whereas I use the phrases, the light passes, or the colour passes or diffuses

Since there is a massive philosophical literature on the argument from illusion, a detailed discussion here seems unnecessary. I will content myself, then, with a remark about the scope of Hobbes's argument. He explicitly extends the argument to all of what would come to be regarded as the standard secondary qualities, including sound (I.2.9). The inclusion of sound is somewhat unusual, at this time, because of the long-standing association of sound and motion. This association makes it somewhat hazardous to be an anti-realist regarding sound, because if realism cannot be maintained here, one might well wonder whether it can be maintained for motion or the geometric properties. And indeed Hobbes seems not entirely sure about excluding those. For although he does not explicitly extend the argument from illusion beyond the standard secondary qualities, he does begin the first of the two passages quoted above by speaking of "colour and shape" (line 1), and suggesting that shape too is something we project onto bodies. Can this be squared with his corpuscularianism? Could there be phenomenal shape and corpuscular shape? These questions would get asked, of course, several generations later, but such debates lie beyond the limits of this study.

22.6. Equivocal Views: Descartes

By the second half of the seventeenth century, Anti-Realism had become a familiar view. When, for instance, Thomas Stanley's *History of Philosophy* (1655–62) comes to the famous Democritean fragment, he criticizes Magnen and Gassendi for their excessively realistic interpretations of the passage (§22.4), and glosses it as follows: "there is nothing really existent but atoms and the vacuum, all things else are only *quoad nos*, viz., in opinion" ("Democritus" XI.9.3, p. 763b). By the time Locke began writing the *Essay* in 1671, this was an utterly commonplace notion, albeit still controversial. One finds it in minor figures like Joseph Glanvill and in major figures like Newton and Leibniz.[22] François Babin, a theologian at the College of Angers, kept a journal in the 1670s in which he complained that "it is no longer fashionable to believe that fire is hot, that

---

itself, my meaning is that the motion is only in the medium, and light and colour are but the effects of that motion in the brain" (*Corresp.* I:38). See also *De corpore* 29.1, *Decameron* ch. 6, *Elements of Philosophy* IV.25.3, and *Seven Philosophical Problems* ch. 4: "those things which the learned call the accidents of bodies are indeed nothing else but diversity of fancy, and are inherent in the sentient and not in the objects—except motion and quantity." For discussion, see Leijenhorst, *Mechanisation* pp. 84–9.

[22] For Glanvill's Anti-Realism see *Scepsis scientifica* ch. 12 p. 74: "So that what we term *heat* and *cold*, and other qualities, are not properly according to philosophical rigour in the bodies, their efficients: but are rather names expressing our passions; and therefore not strictly attributable to any thing without us, but by extrinsic denominations, as vision to the wall." This leads him to say that the senses do not deceive—it is the intellect that deceives in wrongly judging on their basis (p. 77).

For Newton, see the *De gravitatione*: "Praeterea, cum corpus hic speculandum proponatur non quatenus est substantia physica sensibilibus qualitatibus praedita, sed tantum quatenus est quid extensum mobile et impenetrabile, itaque non definivi pro more philosophico, sed abstrahendo sensibiles qualitates (quas etiam Philosophi, ni fallor, abstrahere debent, et menti tanquam varios modos cogitandi a motibus corporum excitatos tribuere" (p. 91; tr. p. 13).

Leibniz explicitly credits Descartes with popularizing Anti-Realism: "Utilem Cartesius operam navavit post Veteres in eradicando hoc praejudicio, quo calores, colores aliaque phaenomena ut res quasdam spectamus extra nos, cum constet eadem manu quod valde calidum videbatur, mox tepidum sentiri. . . . [E]x quibus apparet nullam talem rem extra nos consistere, cuius phantasma imaginationi nostrae obversatur." A note added to the draft manuscript reads: "Interim recte dicimus colores et calores esse in rebus, cum horum phaenomenorum fundamenta intelligimus" (*Animadversiones in partem generalem Principiorum Cartesianorum* ad I.65–8 [*Phil. Schriften* IV:365; tr. Loemker pp. 390–1]).

marble is hard, that animate bodies sense pain. These truths are too ancient for those who love novelty" (p. 2).

It was not Galileo who made Anti-Realism famous, nor was it even Hobbes. Instead, oddly enough, it was Descartes. This is odd, because it is not clear that Descartes should be counted as an Anti-Realist at all. Modern commentators have been sharply divided on this point, with some quite confident that he puts the secondary qualities in the mind, and others equally confident that they are as real as the modes of extension. The reason for the disagreement is that Descartes can be found talking both ways. His early *Regulae* (c.1628) offers an extended corpuscularian account of color as a feature of body, remarking that "whatever you may suppose color to be, you will not deny that it is extended" (Rule 12, X:413). Similarly, *The World* (1629–33) offers a kinetic account of heat as particles in motion (§21.4). The *Discourse* and the associated essays on *Optics* and *Meteorology* continue this pattern, stressing that external things do not always resemble our sensations of them, but assuming throughout that colors etc. are features of bodies.[23] Beginning with the *Meditations*, however, Descartes often takes a more Anti-Realist line. The Sixth Replies puts the point quite starkly: "colors, smells, tastes, and so on are merely certain sensations existing in my thought, and differ no less from bodies than pain differs from the shape and motion of the weapon inflicting the pain" (VII:440). This reasserts the no-resemblance thesis that was in place from his earliest writings, but now supplemented by Anti-Realism. A letter to his friend Chanut in 1649, providing advice on reading the *Principles*, is even more explicit:

It must be remembered, while reading this book, that although I consider nothing in bodies except the size, shapes, and motions of their parts, I claim nonetheless to explain there the nature of light, heat, and all the other sensible qualities; for I presuppose that these qualities are only in our senses, like pleasure and pain, and not at all in the objects that we sense, in which there are only certain shapes and motion that cause the sensations we call light, heat, etc. This I did not explain and prove until the end of Part Four.... (V:291–2)

Yet if this seems to brook no doubt, a look at the end of the *Principles* shows Descartes to be saying something rather different. Instead of insisting that the secondary qualities "are only in our senses" (line 4), *Principles* IV.198 willingly considers "heat and other sensible qualities insofar as they are in objects" and after making the usual corpuscularian, anti-scholastic remarks, concludes that what we pick out when we talk about the secondary qualities is "nothing other than various dispositions of those objects that make them able to move our nerves in various ways" (ibid.). However we are to understand this talk of dispositions (Ch. 23), it does not look here as if Descartes is an Anti-Realist.

One natural reaction to these passages is to conclude that Descartes endorses both Realism and Anti-Realism. The claim would be not that he is inconsistent, but that the question at issue is equivocal and admits of different answers depending on how it is understood. This is how I myself view the problem, and this has been a common perspective for as long as the problem has been recognized. Gassendi, for instance,

---

[23] See, e.g., VI:44, 85–6, 92, 330–5. Descartes is still promoting his Realistic, corpuscularian account of color in a letter to Mersenne in 1638: "La différence des couleurs...[dépend] seulement de la diverse proportion qui est entre leur mouvement droit et le circulaire" (II:468).

when asked in a 1644 letter whether heat should be thought of as a motion or a perception of the motion, responded that this is ultimately just a dispute over words. Malebranche likewise regards the issue as "confused and indeterminate," but credits Descartes with helping us see the situation correctly:

Only since Descartes do we respond to these confused and indeterminate questions—whether fire is hot, grass green, sugar sweet, and so on—by distinguishing the equivocation of the sensible terms that express them. If by heat, color, flavor, you mean such and such a movement of insensible parts, then fire is hot, grass green, sugar sweet. But if by heat and the other qualities you mean what I sense near fire, what I see when I see grass, etc., then fire is not hot at all, nor grass green, etc., for the heat we sense and the colors we see are only in the soul. . . . (*Search after Truth* VI.2.2)

A distinction something like this one makes good sense of what is going on in Descartes, and in other authors like Locke (§23.4), when they seem to want both to defend Anti-Realism and yet to continue speaking of the secondary qualities as if they are in bodies.[24]

   To say only this much, however, is not very interesting. Malebranche tells us that if you are talking about the stuff in the world you are a Realist, whereas if you are talking about the sensation you are an Anti-Realist, which amounts simply to reaffirming the ambiguity. This is, moreover, not very persuasive as a diagnosis of the ambiguity, because it does not seem right that there is any pre-philosophical sense of 'color' or 'heat' on which those terms refer to the sensation.[25] The fact that Descartes and others are tempted to use the terms that way is the outcome of a philosophical analysis arising from some other ambiguity regarding the terms. The historical context we have been considering suggests just what ambiguity that is. Throughout the scholastic era and into

---

[24] Samuel Sorbiere asks Gassendi "an verum sit quod somniabam paradoxum: ferrum candens, immo ignem ipsum non esse calidum, cum inanimatum tale dici possit, et sit calor non tantum certus quidam motus particularum corporis alicuius, sed perceptio motus illius, quam perceptionem habere non potest corpus anima et sensu non praeditum" (*Opera* VI:469a). Gassendi replies: "erit quaestio de voce, si velis calorem ibi solum esse ubi est sensus, sive facultas partium divulsionem percipiens" (VI:187a).

   The *Port-Royal Logic* describes 'heat' as ambiguous between the sensation we have and a quality in the fire that is "tout-à-fait semblable à ce que nous sentons" (I.13)—a way of setting out the situation that of course admits of only one coherent disambiguation, in favor of Anti-Realism. Arnauld takes a very different approach in *Des vraies et des fausses idées* ch. 23 (pp. 313–14). There he agrees that the question of whether sensations or bodies are colored "ne sera qu'une question de nom." And while he agrees that the colors are not "réellement répandues" on the surfaces of bodies, he contends that this is a perfectly appropriate way of speaking, inasmuch as they can be said to be there as "dénominations," in the way that one can truly say that the statue of Diana was worshipped by the Ephesians.

   Among recent Descartes scholars, a good example of the compromise reading I wish to adopt is that of Perler, "Sind die Gegenstände farbig?" p. 184: "Descartes' Theorie des Sinneseigenschaften darf nicht als eine Theorie verstanden werden, die Farben vollständig auf subjektive Empfindungen reduziert . . ."; p. 194: "Widerspricht sich Descartes, wenn er Sinneseigenschaften gleichzeitig dem materiellen Gegenstand und dem Geist zuordnet? Ich glaube nicht. . . ." Claims for Descartes as a Realist can be found in Carriero, *Between Two Worlds* p. 288, Voss, "Psyche and Soma" p. 182, and Menn, "Stumbling Block," who maintains, remarkably enough, that "there is nothing anywhere in Descartes to suggest that he thinks that bodies are not really colored or hot and cold" (p. 186n.). For Descartes as an Anti-Realist, see, e.g., Wilson, *Descartes* p. 80; Broughton, *Method of Doubt* passim; and Rozemond, *Descartes's Dualism* ch. 3. Nolan and Whipple, "Dustbin Theory" (and, more recently, Nolan, "Descartes on 'What We Call Colour'") take the surprising view—seemingly against *all* the texts—that Descartes is an eliminativist about the secondary qualities, in the sense that they exist nowhere at all. Cottingham, "Descartes on Colour" appears to take a quietist approach, suggesting that the question is not a helpful one to focus on.

[25] Some evidence for this is that *The Oxford English Dictionary*'s very long entry on 'color' recognizes no meaning for the term that associates it with a sensation. The OED does recognize such a meaning for 'heat,' but offers no non-philosophical instances of the term being used in this way.

the seventeenth century we have seen two quite distinct aspects of the theory of secondary qualities, physical and phenomenological. The *physical* aspect of the theory accounts for these qualities in causal terms, by explaining both what their causal bases are, and what sorts of effects they have on other bodies, including our senses. We have seen how opinions in this domain changed dramatically over our four centuries, from the view that the secondary qualities supervene on the elemental Aristotelian qualities to the view that the secondary qualities can be explained reductively in terms of geometric–kinetic properties. The *phenomenological* aspect of the theory focuses on the experiences that arise when we perceive a secondary quality. Here too we have seen a dramatic change in views, from an uncritical acceptance of resemblance and the thesis of Revelation to a general consensus that sensation neither resembles the secondary qualities nor reveals anything about their nature.

That these are two aspects of the same theory points toward a systematic ambiguity in words like 'color' and 'heat.' These words can be understood according to either their physical designation or their phenomenal designation. When 'heat' designates physically, it refers to whatever plays the causal role we associate with heat: as that which is, depending on one's theory, either a primary elemental quality or a product of motion, and as that which is responsible for various effects in the world, such as boiling water, drying clothes, and producing a certain experience within us. When 'heat' designates phenomenally, in contrast, it refers to that which is captured by the phenomenology of my experience—that is, it refers to the stuff that has the character-istics that my perception of heat shows it to have. This way of understanding the ambiguity is importantly different from Malebranche's simplistic formulation. The point is not that 'heat' is ambiguous between an external property of bodies and a sensation, but rather that it is ambiguous between two theoretical roles that we expect heat to fill: as that which plays a certain role in our physical theories, and as that which is given in experience. When the ambiguity is formulated in this way, we can under-stand why Realism has been ascendant for most of the history of philosophy. To philosophers before the seventeenth century, who were largely committed to Revela-tion, these two roles do not come apart. That which plays the causal role, giving rise to our sensations and to various other natural phenomena, just is the stuff revealed by experience. Hence Realism comes out true on either disambiguation of the question. Once Revelation gets denied, however, then it no longer seems that 'heat'—designating phenomenally—refers to external things. The only candidate for heat, so construed, is our sensations themselves.

This way of understanding the situation is, in a sense, simply a linguistic formulation of the same point with which this chapter began: that the appearance–reality gap is a seventeenth-century development, and was not for the most part a concern of philo-sophers before that time. The linguistic formulation is useful, however, because it highlights the essential ambiguity of questions regarding the sensible qualities. The question of whether heat exists outside the mind is intrinsically ambiguous in much the way that 'The woman I love is a lucky woman' is intrinsically ambiguous between a rigid and non-rigid reading. (It depends on whether I am referring rigidly to the specific woman I in fact love or non-rigidly to whomever happens to be the object of my affection.) Because our interest in the secondary qualities is irresistibly entwined with our experiences of them, our talk about these qualities is always liable to be understood as designating phenomenally—not as referring to experiences, as Malebranche's sim-plistic formulation would have it, but as referring to that which is as experience reveals it to be. But because we are also interested in a purely physical, non-phenomenal understanding of the world around us, we use 'heat' and other such terms to refer to the stuff in the world that plays a certain causal role. Since that physical interest endures regardless of what we might decide about phenomenal experience, our secondary-quality talk continues to pull us toward the properties of bodies, even if we decide those properties are nothing like what they appear to be. When that happens, the question of where heat is cannot be given an unambiguous answer.

These remarks explain why pre-seventeenth-century philosophers were Unequivocal Realists, and why various seventeenth-century authors were Equivocal Anti-Realists. They do not explain, however, how Galileo, Hobbes, and others could have embraced Unequivocal Anti-Realism. For if the terminology is ambiguous in the way I have suggested, it would seem that a case could never be made for the unequivocal insistence that the secondary qualities exist only in the mind (at least not without going all the way to Berkeleian idealism). This too can be explained, however, and the explanation sheds further light on the case of Descartes. Although 'heat' and other secondary-quality terms are equivocal in the way described above, we feel a certain conceptual pressure not to let these two meanings drift so far apart that the terms refer to quite distinct things: to particles in motion on the one hand, and to sensations on the other. This pressure comes from what we might think of as the controlling concept behind our use of terms like 'heat' and 'color': the concept of that which is represented in experience, or that which we are sensing when we have a certain tactile or visual experience. Color, for instance, just is that familiar quality that we detect through the sense of sight. If we stop talking about that, then we stop talking about color. This controlling concept is itself ambiguous, because it leaves us wanting to use secondary-quality terms as both phenomenal and physical designators, but all the same it is the concept that governs both of these subsidiary interests. This explains how a philosopher like Hobbes could have come to be persuaded of Unqualified Anti-Realism. For what his argument from illusion purports to show is that the thing we perceive—the very image, and the very color—is not something out in the world, but something in the mind. Such a line of argument, if successful, cuts through the above-described ambigui-ty and gets directly at the controlling concept of what we take a secondary quality to be; it forces us to agree that the qualities themselves—the things we are acquainted with through experience—are not out in the world at all. We will of course still want to talk about the physical causes of those sensations, but it would now seem to be a misuse of language to refer to those causes as *colors*, *sounds*, and so on.

The trajectory of Descartes's writings on this topic points towards an increasingly unqualified Anti-Realism. Why would he think that? Although he does not offer anything quite like Hobbes's argument from illusion, Descartes suggests at times that he has come to the same sort of conclusion. For in both the *Meditations* and the *Principles* he suggests not just that secondary-quality' experiences fail to *resemble* any-thing outside the mind, but that they also fail to *represent* anything outside the mind. This idea is suggested in the Sixth Meditation, when Descartes describes various "ill-considered judgments" that he is in the habit of making: "that in a hot body there is something just like the idea of heat that is in me; that in something white or green there is the same whiteness or greenness that I sense; that in something bitter or sweet there is the same taste; and so in other cases" (VII:82). This begins with the familiar denial of exact resemblance, but after the first semi-colon switches to a much stronger claim: that the quality being sensed—the whiteness or greenness or taste—is not in the external body at all. To be sure, the passage as a whole is hardly a good example of Descartes's tendency to embrace Unequivocal Anti-Realism, given that it speaks of bodies as hot, white, green, bitter, and sweet. But even while seeming to accept a kind of Equivocal Realism, the passage makes the sort of claim that has the potential to debunk Realism entirely. For what it suggests is that the 'color' and 'taste' of external bodies are not something we sense, and so not properly sensible qualities at all.

This passing line of thought from the *Meditations* is developed at greater length in *Principles* I.66–71. Descartes first sets out the relatively modest claim that to have a clear and distinct perception of color and other secondary qualities we must regard them as merely sensations; when regarded as things outside the mind, they not only fail to be clear and distinct, but moreover "there is no way at all in which one can understand what sort of things they are" (I.68). Presumably, he means that there is no way of doing this through the senses alone; it takes reason to figure it out. So far this does not go beyond the sort of equivocal view described above: denying Revelation, Descartes wants us to see that there is a sense in which the secondary qualities just are the sensations. He goes on to explain that "if someone examines what it is that the sense of color or pain represents as existing in the colored body or in the part that is in pain, he will realize that he is wholly ignorant of it" (I.68). This is a stronger claim than one might expect. Revelation holds only that the senses show us the nature of the secondary qualities; Descartes wants to deny not only that, but further that the senses reveal *anything* about these qualities. That seems like an extraordinary claim, since one would have thought that perception shows us at least *something* about color as it is in the world (its size, shape, and location, in particular). Why would Descartes deny that? The full force of his claim emerges two sections later, when he concludes that what we are doing when we uncritically use our senses is that "we take ourselves to perceive clearly that which we do not in any way perceive" (I.70). Here we have the failure of representation that entitles Descartes to Unequivocal Anti-Realism. The claim is repeated in the following section: "what we call the sensations of tastes, smells, sounds, heat, cold, light, colors, and so on—sensations that do not represent anything located outside our thought" (I.71). It is quite clear here that Descartes is denying not only the resemblance of secondary-quality sensations to external objects, but even their representation of those objects. Accordingly, the colors we are seeing, the sounds we are hearing, and so forth, are not features of the external world. The door is open to Unequivocal Anti-Realism.[26]

---

[26] Descartes's no-representation claim also appears explicitly in the *Fourth Replies* (VII:234): "si quidem, ut dixi, verum sit illas [ideas coloris et frigoris] nihil reale exhibere." In the Sixth Meditation there is this interesting passage: "Et certe, ex eo quod valde diversos sentiam colores, sonos, odores, sapores, calorem, duritiem, et similia, recte concludo, aliquas esse in corporibus, a quibus variae istae sensuum perceptiones adveniunt, varietates iis respondentes, etiamsi forte iis non similes" (VII:81). This implies Anti-Realism, inasmuch as it treats the secondary qualities as sensations. Perhaps it also implies that these sensations do not represent, inasmuch as it speaks of having to "conclude" something about the causes of those sensations, as if this is a further inference that the mind must draw from the sensation, rather than something that the sensation itself represents. For a detailed discussion of the no-representation doctrine, see Simmons, "Are Cartesian Sensations Representational?" and Machamer and McGuize: *Changing Mind*. For another reading of how *Principles* I.66–71 bears on secondary qualities, see Downing, "Sensible Qualities."

To deny that our experiences of smells, sounds, etc. represent *anything* in the external world is every bit as extraordinary a claim as the scholastic doctrine of Revelation that Descartes means to reject. The transformation in views here is in fact emblematic of our subject as a whole. For scholastic authors, sensible qualities could be perceived only if they were genuine qualities—real accidents—that somehow resemble the sensations they cause. Sound, as we saw in §21.3, could not simply be a kind of motion, because if so then it could not be sensed. Post-scholastic Realists like Bacon and Gassendi dared to imagine that the story could be mechanistic all the way through—that geometric–kinetic properties in the world might cause sensory experiences that would represent those very properties. As always, however, rejection of the Aristotelian framework carried unforeseen consequences. In this case, what was lost was a clear account of how perception could actually work. To Galileo, and then to Hobbes and Descartes, the elimination of real qualities in favor of a corpuscular–mechanistic story paved the way to an austerely quantitative picture of the physical world. But it did more than that, because it took what had been the anchor of the Aristotelian method, perceptual experience, and rendered it thoroughly problematic.

23

Powers and Dispositions

23.1. Nominal Powers

The seventeenth century is commonly said to have bequeathed to us three ways of thinking about sensible qualities: either in reductive microphysical terms, or as internal phenomenal states, or else as powers or dispositions. Having discussed in some detail the first two kinds of theories, it is natural to turn to the third. The main thesis of this chapter, however, is that nothing like this third sort of theory can be found during our period—not among scholastic authors, nor even in the seventeenth century.

In modern terms, my claim is that authors during our period recognize only categorical properties, and never dispositional properties. Since the proper understanding of this terminology is a matter of some dispute, the distinction can be usefully employed only to the extent that it is precisely defined. What I seek to show, then, is that authors from our four centuries cannot be found postulating accidents or qualities or properties that are nothing more than *bare dispositions*, where a bare disposition is understood as having two distinctive features. First, if a bare disposition is causally efficacious at all, its efficacy is in some sense derivative or borrowed from other, more basic qualities. So, for instance, if a leaf has the bare disposition to cause in me a sensation of green, that disposition is causally efficacious, if at all, only derivatively, inasmuch as the leaf has various more fundamental qualities that act through the air on my sense organs. Second, a bare disposition is merely conditionally actual, in the precise sense that its essential nature is manifested only under certain conditions. The color of the leaf, then, if it is a bare disposition, just is the power to cause a sensation of green, a power that of course manifests itself only under certain conditions. My claim, then, is that authors during our period recognize no such things. The only accidents or qualities they recognize are categorical, which is to say they are of such a nature as to be categorically rather than conditionally actual, and have intrinsic rather than derivative causal powers.

If this is right, it is a surprising result, because we are accustomed to treating Robert Boyle, and even more so John Locke, as providing the canonical statement of a dispositional theory of color and other so-called secondary qualities. According to Locke, after all, the secondary qualities are "in truth nothing in the objects themselves but powers to produce various sensations in us by their primary qualities" (*Essay* II.8.10). The account of a bare disposition just offered is calibrated to capture the way they talk about powers and dispositions. If such claims are ontologically committing, then, I will argue, the powers they postulate can be nothing more than bare dispositions. It is, however, not plausible to suppose that they postulate any such thing. On the contrary, when Boyle and Locke talk about bodies, they use 'power' and 'disposition' in an utterly reductive sense, so that for a body to have a power or disposition is nothing more than for it to have a certain sort of corpuscularian structure, in a world with other bodies that have a certain sort of corpuscularian structure, and given certain laws of nature. This is not to make the more modest claim that these powers or dispositions supervene on the strictly corpuscularian facts, or that such facts are what "give rise" to these powers. Instead, my claim is that, for all their talk of powers and dispositions, neither Boyle nor Locke admits any such thing into his ontology, at least as far as the corporeal world is concerned.

To state my case, I will distinguish between *nominal* and *real* powers. Nominal powers, as I use that phrase, are nothing more than a corpuscularian structure embedded in a certain sort of world. I call them nominal, as will become clear, not because of any affinity with scholastic nominalism, but because of an affinity with Locke's nominal essences, which itself has its roots in Boyle (§27.4). The strictest of corpuscularians can countenance nominal powers, so understood, because they introduce no ontological commitment beyond bodies in motion. Real powers, in contrast, on my usage, are ontologically committing. In contrast to Boyle and Locke, there is no doubt that scholastic authors countenance real powers. What I will argue, however, is that their powers are almost never bare dispositions, in the above sense, but always categorically actual and intrinsically causal. Powers in this robustly actual sense are important in the seventeenth century too, as we will consider in the final section of this chapter. But before entering into the complex territory of real powers, it will be helpful to consider the more straightforward reductive position of those whose talk of powers is always nominal.

Some seventeenth-century authors expressly commit themselves to a nominal conception of powers. David Gorlaeus, for instance, whose early resistance to scholastic metaphysics is so radical in many respects (§25.6, §28.4), holds across the board that "just as we have said that quantity does not differ from the quantified body, so we further say that no powers ... are distinct from the thing's essence.... They differ solely by our reason and manner of conceiving them" (*Exercitationes* 7.1, p. 100). His argument is that entities should not be multiplied without necessity, and that the substance itself is capable of whatever operations are ascribed to the powers: "why cannot the substance exercise its actions through itself, but instead requires an accident through which it acts?" (ibid., p. 105). Thomas Hobbes's even more reductive metaphysics takes the same approach, regarding talk of powers as shorthand for a description of a substance constituted in a certain way: "the power of agent and patient taken together, which may be called the complete or full power, is the same as the complete cause, for each consists in the aggregation together of all the accidents that are required to produce an effect in both the agent and the patient" (*De corpore* 10.1). This by itself is not obviously reductive, until one remembers (§7.1, §10.2) that Hobbes's theory of accidents is itself reductive: accidents are nothing more than "the mode of conceiving a body" (*De corpore* 8.2). Hence his view of the corporeal world (which, for Hobbes, is the whole world) is rigorously corpuscular: there are bodies in motion and nothing more.

I will now argue that this nominal attitude toward powers is in Boyle and Locke as well. This is not to say, however, that powers play an insignificant role in their theories. On the contrary, after making the case for a reductive reading of Boyle and Locke in this domain, I will argue in §23.4 that their shared conception of power is quite fundamental to their philosophical thinking.[1]

23.2. Powers in Boyle

One reason to credit various seventeenth-century authors with real powers is that they commonly talk of bodies as having various sorts of *dispositions*. Thus, after setting out an account of color in terms of light, Boyle goes on to add the following:

> I did not deny but that colour might in some sense be considered as a quality residing in the body that is said to be coloured; and indeed the greatest part of the following experiments refer to colour principally under that notion, for there is in the bodies we call coloured, and chiefly in   3
> their superficial parts, a certain disposition, whereby they do so trouble [≈ agitate] the light that comes from them to our eye, as that it there makes that distinct impression, upon whose account we say, that the seen body is either white or black, or red or yellow, or of any one   6
> determinate colour. (*Experiments and Considerations Touching Colours* I.3 [*Works* IV:33])

As clearly as Boyle states the thesis that colors can be regarded as dispositions (line 4), the passage nevertheless shows nothing whatsoever about Boyle's ontological commitments. The problem is that 'disposition' and its various cognates are standardly used to refer to the corpuscular structure of a body—the spatial arrangement of its parts—without reflecting any commitment to a dispositional property over and above that structure.[2] Thus Boyle elsewhere refers to the "primary and mechanical affections" as "motion, figure, and disposition of parts" (*Certain Physiological Essays* [*Works* II:21]), where the last of these clearly refers to corpuscular structure. At a minimum, then, talk of dispositions among authors during our period can by itself decide nothing with regard to whether the author is committed to real or only nominal powers. My own

---

[1] For further evidence of Hobbes's thoroughgoing reductivism, see the passages collected in §7.1 and §10.2. For Hobbes's materialism, see §16.2. Admittedly, a determined proponent of real powers might seek to enlist Hobbes in the cause. For in the same section of the *De corpore* where he defines an accident as "concipiendi corporis modum" (8.2), he also offers this definition: "Accidens definiunt esse *modum corporis, iuxta quem concipitur*; quod est idem ac si dicerent, *accidens esse facultatem corporis qua sui conceptum nobis imprimit*." The first part of this might, on its own, be taken as equivalent to the "mode of conceiving" formula. But the second part suggests that Hobbes is thinking of accidents as in bodies, and indeed as powers or faculties. Still, I think the broader tenor of his remarks makes it clear that he does not mean to postulate powers as something above and beyond a strictly corpuscularian theory. The many passages quoted in §7.1 and §10.2 strike me as decisive. Moreover, if Hobbes did mean to analyze the accidents of bodies in terms of the powers of bodies, then his discussion of powers (*potentiae*) in *De corpore* 10 would be obviously incoherent, because that discussion, as quoted in the main text, seeks to understand powers in terms of accidents.

[2] The link between 'disposition' and the ordering of parts goes back to the Latin translation of Aristotle: "dispositio (διάθεσις) dicitur habentis partes ordo, aut secundum locum, aut secundum potentiam, aut secundum speciem" (*Meta.* V.19, 1022b1–3).

Another passage where a cognate of 'disposition' is used in such a way as to suggest a dispositional theory of the secondary qualities occurs in Descartes: "omnino concludendum est, non etiam a nobis animadverti, ea, quae in obiectis externis, luminis, coloris, odoris, saporis, soni, caloris, frigoris, et aliarum tactilium qualitatum, vel etiam formarum substantialium, nominibus indigitamus, quicquam aliud esse quam istorum obiectorum varias dispositiones, quae efficiunt ut nervos nostros variis modis movere possint" (*Principles* IV.198). For a recent discussion of the controversies over whether Descartes is committing himself here to a dispositional theory, see Nolan, "Descartes on 'What We Call Colour'."

view, however, is much stronger than that: I believe that disputes among scholars over how to understand talk of dispositions in the seventeenth century are moot, because such terminology *never* has the meaning it has acquired in modern times. One simply does not find during our period any commitment to merely dispositional, non-categorical properties.

If anyone during our period does ascribe to bare dispositions of this sort, one might expect it to be Boyle—not because he uses the term 'disposition,' but because he routinely makes appeal to seemingly bare powers at fundamental junctures of his philosophical thought. To see what such appeals amount to, we should look at his most substantial philosophical treatise, *The Origin of Forms and Qualities* (1666). Here he attacks the scholastic doctrine of real qualities on the familiar grounds (§10.1) that such qualities are treated as "real and physical entities" (*Works* V:309; Stewart p. 22). The mistake Boyle charges them with is the same that we have seen reductively minded authors accuse their opponents of throughout our four centuries: the mistake of supposing that where there are different names one may "infer a diversity of physical entities in the subject whereunto they are attributed" (ibid.). In place of this "grand mistake," Boyle offers his own account of such qualities. He begins the discussion with a famous analogy to a lock and a key that has been made to fit it, each of which can be said to have taken on a new power or quality in virtue of their "congruity":

> The lock and the key did each of them now obtain a new capacity and it became a main part of the notion and description of a lock, that it was capable of being made to lock or unlock by that other piece of iron we call a key, and it was looked upon as a peculiar faculty and power in the key, that it was fitted to open and shut the lock, and yet by these new attributes there was not added any real or physical entity, either to the lock or to the key, each of them remaining indeed nothing but the same piece of iron, just so shaped as it was before. (V:310; Stewart p. 23)

The first half of the passage makes it clear that the lock and key really have acquired a "faculty," "power," or "capacity," in the sense that one can truly say, e.g., 'the lock has a capacity that it did not have before.' But the second half of the passage is equally insistent that what allows us to say this is nothing new about the lock or the key: there is no new "real or physical entity" (line 5), and each remains "nothing but" what it was before (line 6). The same paragraph goes on to apply the analogy to sensible qualities:

> And proportionably hereunto I do not see why we may not conceive that as to those qualities (for instance) which we call sensible, though by virtue of a certain congruity or incongruity in point of figure or texture (or other mechanical attributes) to our sensories, the portions of matter they modify are enabled to produce various effects, upon whose account we make bodies to be endowed with qualities; yet they are not in the bodies that are endowed with them any real or distinct entities, or differing from the matter itself, furnished with such a determinate bigness, shape, or other mechanical modifications. (V:310; Stewart p. 24)

Boyle regards the analogy as quite close. Bodies have sensible qualities because of a "congruity" between their corpuscularian structure or "texture" (lines 2–3) and the texture of the sense organ. In virtue of this congruity, the one body can produce certain effects in the other and for this reason we are warranted in saying that these bodies are "endowed with qualities" (line 5). But again we immediately get the all-important proviso (lines 5–7): although we can make good sense of our talking this way, we should not commit the grand scholastic mistake of supposing that there are any such things as powers or qualities, beyond the matter and its various mechanical affections.[3]

As the two passages just quoted make clear, Boyle does not think that sensible qualities (and in general other powers) are to be reduced merely to the texture of the body that we speak of as having the quality. The lock "obtain[s] a new capacity" (line 1) once the key comes into existence, but since the lock itself changes not at all, this capacity cannot be identified with the texture of the lock. Bodies likewise have sensible qualities in virtue of their congruity with other, perceiving bodies, and the fact of that congruity is crucial to Boyle's analysis. These two passages are drawn from what he labels "an excursion about the relative nature of physical qualities," and in other works he reiterates the idea that qualities "for the most part consist in relations, upon whose account one body is fitted to act upon others, or disposed to be acted on by them, and receive impressions from them" (Systematical or Cosmical Qualities [Works VI:287]). This has led many commentators to suppose that Boyle is embracing an ontology of relations. But in the context of his time it is absurd to suppose Boyle is rejecting the scholastic category of Quality only to relapse into the even more obscure category of Relation, a category that even the most scholastic of authors wanted to treat reductively. In saying that such qualities are relations, Boyle means only that the reductive base for qualities and powers is the texture of the body that is said to have the power, together with the textures of the relevant surrounding bodies, and the laws of nature that govern those bodies. This, I take it, is the point behind his warning that "we must consider each body not barely as it is in itself an entire and distinct portion of matter, but as it is a part of the universe, and consequently placed among a great number and variety of other bodies, upon which it may act and by which it may be acted on in many ways" (Origin V:313; Stewart pp. 26–7).[4]

If the passages just discussed (and there are many others just like them) do not show Boyle to have rejected real powers in favor of nominal powers, then I do not know what more he would have had to say to make that point. To say, as each of the above two passages does, that bodies have powers, but that these powers are not real entities

---

[3] Boyle reiterates the reductive character of his theory of qualities over and over in Origin. The dissolvability of gold in aqua regis is "not in the gold any thing distinct from its peculiar texture" (V:310; Stewart p. 24); the poisonousness of the peas "is really nothing distinct from the glass itself" (V:311; Stewart p. 25); the heat of the sun "itself is but the brisk and confused local motion of the minute parts of a body" (V:313; Stewart p. 27); the quality of a cave by which it gives back an echo "is in it nothing else but the hollowness of its figure" (V:319; Stewart p. 34). Clearest of all, perhaps, is this: "Whence men have been induced to frame a long catalogue of such things as, for their relating to our senses, we call sensible qualities; and because we have been conversant with them, before we had the use of reason, and the mind of man is prone to conceive almost every thing (nay even privations, as blindness, death, etc.) under the notion of a true entity or substance as itself is; we have been from our infancy apt to imagine that these sensible qualities are real beings in the objects they denominate, and have the faculty or power to work such and such things; as gravity has a power to stop the motion of a bullet shot upwards, and carry that solid globe of matter toward the center of the earth, whereas indeed (according to what we have largely shown above) there is in the body to which these sensible qualities are attributed, nothing of real and physical but the size, shape, and motion or rest of its component particles, together with that texture of the whole which results from their being so contrived as they are" (V:316–17. Stewart p. 31).

[4] On the relational, situated aspect of Boyle's thought, see also Intro. to the History of Part. Quals. ch. 3 (Works VI:275): "And every distinct portion of matter, whether it be a corpuscle or a primary concretion, or a body of the first, or of any other order of mixts, is to be considered not as if it were placed in vacuo, nor as if it had relation only to the neighbouring bodies, but as being placed in the universe, constituted as it is, amongst an innumerable company of other bodies, whereof some are near it, and others very remote, and some are great and some small, some particular and some catholic agents, and all of them governed as well by the universal fabric of things, as by the laws of motion established by the author of nature in the world."

and are nothing beyond the bodies themselves with their various mechanical affections, is just what it means to defend the doctrine of merely nominal powers. This has not, however, been the majority view among commentators. Much more common has been to take Boyle's talk of powers at face value—as ontologically committing—and to suppose that Boyle's frequent cautionary remarks about powers not being "real or distinct entities" (as above) is aimed exclusively at powers in the robust, categorical sense associated with the scholastics.[5] To be sure, the scholastics are his principal target, and he particularly criticizes them for treating real qualities as separable from bodies (V:309; Stewart p. 22) and resembling our sensations of them (V:317; Stewart p. 31). Earlier chapters have cast doubt on this sort of construal of the scholastic theory of accidents, but here let us set aside such disputes and consider whether we should understand Boyle to be rejecting the reality not of powers of all kinds, but only of what he takes to be "scholastic" powers. The powers that Boyle describes would have to be not only (a) inseparable from bodies and (b) not resembling our sensations, but also (c) relational and (d) lacking in causal powers.

Read in this way, Boyle is endorsing the reality of bare dispositions, in the sense defined earlier. In virtue of (c), such powers are conditional rather than categorical, inasmuch as they exist in a body only given the appropriate surrounding circumstances. The "congruity" of lock and key, for instance, gives them each a power that they would otherwise lack, and the same is true for sensible bodies in virtue of their congruity with our senses. It is clear enough that Boyle's powers, if they are real, must satisfy (c). The case of (d) is perhaps less clear. After all, Boyle does describe them as "powers," a label that hardly encourages the thought that they are causally powerless. Moreover, Boyle tells us that "it is by their qualities that bodies act immediately upon our senses" (*Origin* V:298; Stewart p. 13). Yet even if Boyle's powers are inevitably described as *doing* things, I think the only way to defend a non-reductive reading of his conception of powers is to insist that they are not truly causes. It would be hard to see how to give *any* meaning to Boyle's repeated insistence that qualities are not "real or physical" if he does not mean, minimally, that ascribing such powers to bodies does not involve ascribing to them some further causally active entity beyond their mechanical affections. This seems, moreover, to be the point of his remark that "there are simpler and more primitive affections of matter, from which these secondary qualities, if I may so call them, do depend: and that the operations of bodies upon one another spring from the same"

---

[5] The leading proponent of a reductive interpretation of Boyle's qualities is Alexander. But he makes the mistake of neglecting the relational character of Boyle's view, and so he supposes that qualities reduce simply to the texture of the body that has them. See, e.g., *Ideas, Qualities* p. 74: "these corpuscular structures or *textures* are *identified* in the example concerning colour, with qualities in bodies producing appearances of colours to us. . . . That is, textures are identified with powers and . . . with secondary qualities." That this sort of view cannot be right has been shown in overwhelming detail by O'Toole, "Qualities and Powers" and Kaufman, "Locks, Schlocks." But both O'Toole and Kaufman wrongly slide from rejecting an oversimplified reductive view to rejecting reductivism entirely.

The classic source for ascribing irreducible bare dispositions to Boyle and Locke is Jackson, "Locke's Distinction." Along similar lines, see Curley, "Locke, Boyle." The most detailed discussion of Boyle's theory of qualities is Anstey, *Philosophy of Robert Boyle* chs. 3–4. Anstey carefully works through the relevant texts and sees the potential for a reductive interpretation, but nevertheless contends in the end that there are "two incompatible and irreconcilable aspects of his thought," one reductive and the other relational (p. 107). I find this a baffling conclusion to reach, however, since Anstey himself recognizes how historically implausible it is to suppose that Boyle is a realist about relations (p. 92), and since, as Anstey himself seems to acknowledge (p. 104), all the complicating relational aspects of the theory might be handled simply by widening the reductive base of the account.

(*Origin* V:317; Stewart p. 32). So I take it that Boyle's mechanistic hypothesis entails a very strong version of the causal primacy thesis (§21.2): that it is the primary and not the secondary qualities that are causally efficacious.

If, then, Boyle is a realist about his powers, they must be regarded as bare dispositions. Yet even if many commentators have seemed willing to assert precisely this, it seems to me utterly incredible to suppose that Boyle would advocate any such thing. One would have to suppose that when the above passages flatly abjure all "real entities" beyond matter with its mechanical affections, he means to exclude only entities of a certain kind—physical ones, evidently—and that he means to leave room for entities of another kind, a subtle sort of metaphysical entity that does not do anything and is not separable, even logically, from its subject. In our modern, metaphysically extravagant, neo-scholastic era, it does not seem so surprising to include such bare dispositions within our ontology, but this sort of attitude is quite at odds with Boyle's own anti-metaphysical approach. His *Free Enquiry into the Vulgarly Received Notion of Nature* (1686) offers this brief abstract of the more extensive earlier discussion in the *Origin of Forms and Qualities*: "the term 'faculty' may indeed be allowed of, if it be applied as a compendious form of speech, but not as denoting a real and distinct agent; since in reality the power or faculty of a thing is (at least) oftentimes but the matter of it, made operative by some of its mechanical modifications" (*Works* X:561; Davis and Hunter p. 154). He goes on to put into this category the very sorts of examples considered above, including locks and keys, and sensible qualities.

Perhaps the best text in favor of ascribing to Boyle some sort of subtle metaphysical theory of qualities is a passage in the *Origin of Forms and Qualities* where he remarks parenthetically, after one of his characteristic denials that qualities are "real and physical entities," that "we have not here to do either with logical or metaphysical ones" (*Works* V:309; Stewart p. 22). That might seem to leave the door open to just this sort of metaphysical doctrine of dispositions, but in fact what Boyle means is precisely the opposite. It is the scholastics, he takes it, who are fond of metaphysical and logical entities. This same work's "Proemial Discourse" sharply takes the scholastics to task for their discussions that are "so obscure, so perplexed, and so unsatisfactory" and then he adds that "their discourses upon these subjects do consist so much more of logical and metaphysical notions and niceties, than of physical observations and reasonings, that it is very difficult for any reader of but an ordinary capacity to understand what they mean" (V:289; Stewart p. 3). Clearly, then, Boyle is not himself going to turn away from a physical account of qualities toward a metaphysical or logical account. When he denies that qualities, understood as powers, are "real and physical entities," he means to deny that they are entities of any sort. Boyle does not have a theory of bare dispositions. His powers are merely nominal. Once we understand this about his view, we can understand much better the important role that his talk of powers plays within his theory. But before turning to this issue, it will be helpful to consider Locke's kindred theory.[6]

---

[6] For examples of Boyle's anti-metaphysical tendency, see *New Experiments* (*Works* I:198), "This reason, I say, being thus desumed seems to make the controversy about a vacuum rather a metaphysical than a physiological question, which therefore we shall here no longer debate"; *Certain Phys. Essays* (*Works* II:163): "although to engage very far in such a metaphysical and nice speculation were unfit for me"; *Origin* (*Works* V:343; Stewart pp. 57–8): "I should now examine

23.3. Powers in Locke

Locke's canonical formulation of the claim that secondary qualities are powers holds that they are "nothing in the objects themselves but powers to produce various sensations in us by their primary qualities, i.e. by the bulk, figure, texture, and motion of their insensible parts" (*Essay* II.8.10). This formulation notably lacks the Boylean proviso that these powers are not "real and physical entities" and that they are "nothing but" the matter with its mechanical affections. What Locke insists on instead, more clearly than Boyle, is that the only things doing any causal work are the primary qualities. This becomes unmistakable in later passages, where "the ideas of secondary qualities are also produced, viz. by the operation of insensible particles on our senses" (II.8.13), so that, for instance, whiteness and sweetness "are but the effects of the operations of manna by the motion, size, and figure of its particles on the eyes and palate" (II.8.18). So even if the secondary qualities are "powers," they are, in their own right, oddly powerless. If Lockean secondary qualities are to be regarded as in some sense real rather than nominal powers, they will have to be the sort of bare dispositions previously considered and rejected in Boyle's case.[7]

One reason for affirming that Locke is some sort of realist about these powers might be simply that he refers to them, over and over. But this is of course consistent with his understanding such talk in a reductive sense, as shorthand for something else. A better reason is perhaps that Locke repeatedly describes the powers of secondary qualities as "depending" on the primary qualities, rather than being *identical* to the primary qualities (II.8.14, 23, 24, 26; II.23.8). If one looks closely, however, one can find considerable evidence for a fully reductive reading. A suggestion in this direction is his repeated contrast between the "reality" of the primary qualities and the apparently less-than-real status of the secondary qualities (II.8.14, 15, 22, 23, 24; II.23.37). But these passages are not decisive, because Locke might mean only that the secondary qualities are less real insofar as they have no causal power, or insofar as they arise from the primary qualities. More generally, they might be less real simply insofar as they are secondary in the sense that was familiar from scholastic discussions. A clearer text is the following:

[T]he ideas produced in us by these secondary qualities have no resemblance of them at all. There is nothing like our ideas existing in the bodies themselves. They are in the bodies we denominate from them only a power to produce those sensations in us: and what is sweet, blue, or warm in idea, is but the certain bulk, figure, and motion of the insensible parts in the bodies themselves, which we call so. (II.8.15)

---

those arguments that are wont to be employed by the schools to evince their substantial forms, but, besides that the nature and scope of my present work enjoins me brevity, I confess that, one or two excepted, the arguments I have found mentioned as the chief are rather metaphysical or logical than grounded upon the principles and *phaenomena* of nature, and respect rather words than things, and therefore I, who have neither inclination nor leisure to wrangle about terms, shall content my self to propose and very briefly answer two or three of those that are thought the plausiblest."

[7] Locke endorses the causal primacy of the primary qualities at a particularly prominent juncture, in the last sentence of *Essay* II.21, in his summary of his whole theory of simple ideas: "Though when we go beyond the bare ideas in our minds, and would enquire into their causes, we cannot conceive any thing else to be in any sensible object, whereby it produces different ideas in us, but the different bulk, figure, number, texture, and motion of its insensible parts" (II.21.73). This passage also provides strong evidence of Locke's realism regarding primary qualities, inasmuch as they appear to play the sort of causal role that carries ontological commitment.

This familiar line of attack on resemblance in the first sentence would not seem to furnish any evidence regarding the ontological status of powers, if not for how the passage ends. Secondary qualities are only powers, the final sentence says, and then after the colon adds that all there actually are in bodies are integral parts of various sizes and shapes in motion. If Locke's understanding of powers is not reductive, then the clauses on either side of the colon contradict one another most grievously. Another, equally clear passage occurs a few sections later: "Pound an almond, and the clear white colour will be altered into a dirty one, and the sweet taste into an oily one. What real alteration can the beating of the pestle make in any body, but an alteration of the texture of it?" (II.8.20). If Locke's powers were in any sense real, then there would be an obvious answer to this rhetorical question: beyond a change to texture, pounding an almond would change the powers of a thing, adding or subtracting a bare disposition. That does not count as a real alteration, evidently, because powers are not real entities.

I admit there can be no such thing as a proof text, when one is dealing with Locke, given the notorious looseness of his prose. But these passages at least make a strong *prima facie* case against a realistic interpretation of Lockean powers. When he remarks that these are "powers barely, and nothing but powers" (II.8.24) or "nothing but bare powers" (II.23.8), it seems to me he is taking for granted that readers will understand just what he means: that talk of powers is simply shorthand for a more complex description in terms of primary qualities, inasmuch as such powers are nothing beyond those primary qualities. All of this bears the unmistakable mark of Boyle's influence. I am aware of no one else during our four centuries who takes the approach of downplaying the reality of an alleged entity by treating it as a "bare power." For scholastic authors, and for many seventeenth-century authors as well, as we will see, powers are real causal entities, and the phrase "nothing but a power" would be something like an oxymoron. The close superficial similarity between Locke and Boyle provides more *prima facie* evidence that we should interpret Lockean powers along the lines that Boyle makes so explicit, as nothing over and above bodies and their textures.

So why does Locke not state the reductive claim more explicitly, rather than repeatedly saying that powers "depend" on the primary qualities? His reason, which again underscores the similarity to Boyle, is their relational character. The chapter on powers, although not in general very illuminating with regard to their ontological status, remarks in passing that "powers are relations, not agents" (II.21.19). That they are not agents was clear enough from the earlier discussion of secondary qualities. The relational character of powers is explained in the following passage:

[M]ost of the simple ideas that make up our complex ideas of substances, when truly considered, are only powers, however we are apt to take them for positive qualities; v.g. the greatest part of the ideas that make our complex idea of gold are yellowness, great weight, ductility, fusibility   3
and solubility in aqua regia, etc., all united together in an unknown substratum. All which ideas are nothing else but so many relations to other substances, and are not really in the gold, considered barely in itself, though they depend on those real and primary qualities of its internal   6
constitution, whereby it has a fitness differently to operate and be operated on by several other substances. (II.23.37)

Here color takes its place among various other qualities that are "only powers" rather than "positive qualities" (line 2) and are "nothing else but so many relations to other substances" (line 5). Because of this the most that can be said is that these powers "depend on those real and primary qualities" (line 6). Not only can they not be identified with the primary qualities, but indeed they cannot be in the body at all "considered barely in itself" (line 6). Why not? That gets explained more clearly in this passage:

The particular bulk, number, figure, and motion of the parts of fire or snow are really in them, whether any one's senses perceive them or no: and therefore they may be called real qualities, because they really exist in those bodies. But light, heat, whiteness or coldness are no more really in them than sickness or pain is in manna. Take away the sensation of them; let not the eyes see light or colours, nor the ears hear sounds; let the palate not taste, nor the nose smell; and all colours, tastes, odours, and sounds, as they are such particular ideas, vanish and cease, and are reduced to their causes, i.e. bulk, figure, and motion of parts. (II.8.17)

This passage should be read not just in the narrow context of the secondary qualities, but in the broader context of Locke's theory of powers. Heat and color are no more in bodies than sickness or pain is in manna. This is not necessarily to say that these powers are not there, only that they not in the body "considered barely in itself," as the previous passage puts it. The powers might be said to be in bodies, but they are there as relations. As such, their existence depends on other factors, and cannot be identified with the primary qualities of any particular body.[8]

So if Locke's secondary qualities are real powers, they are bare dispositions, causally inefficacious and only conditionally actualized. A body's having color, for instance, depends on its being properly illuminated, and on perceivers of the right sort. The only categorical qualities that Locke recognizes are the primary qualities. But could Locke really believe that bodies have bare dispositions of this sort, doing nothing, and coming into and going out of existence as the environment changes? That seems very hard to believe. Anyone who does ascribe such realism to Locke had better be prepared for ontological profligacy, inasmuch as Locke is prepared to countenance a great many such powers. In addition to those with which we are familiar, "I doubt not, but there are a thousand changes, that bodies we daily handle have a power to cause in one another, which we never suspect, because they never appear in sensible effects" (II.23.9). Fortunately, we need not go down this path. Locke tells us explicitly that he is not a realist about relations: they have "no other reality but what they have in the minds of men" (II.30.4). This then fits the picture ascribed already to Boyle: what really exists, in the physical world, are bodies and their primary modes, attributes, or qualities. We can truly talk about bodies having powers—indeed, we can hardly help but do so,

---

[8] For a remarkable statement of the relational, environmental character of Locke's conception of qualities, see *Essay* IV.6.11: "For we are wont to consider the substances we meet with, each of them as an entire thing by itself, having all its qualities in itself, and independent of other things; overlooking, for the most part, the operations of those invisible fluids they are encompassed with, and upon whose motions and operations depend the greatest part of those qualities which are taken notice of in them, and are made by us the inherent marks of distinction whereby we know and denominate them. Put a piece of gold any where by itself, separate from the reach and influence of all other bodies, it will immediately lose all its colour and weight, and perhaps malleableness too; which, for aught I know, would be changed into a perfect friability. Water, in which to us fluidity is an essential quality left to itself, would cease to be fluid. . . . We are then quite out of the way, when we think that things contain within themselves the qualities that appear to us in them; and we in vain search for that constitution within the body of a fly, or an elephant, upon which depend those qualities and powers we observe in them. For which perhaps, to understand them aright, we ought to look not only beyond this our earth and atmosphere, but even beyond the sun, or remotest star our eyes have yet discovered."

inasmuch as "whatever change is observed, the mind must collect a power somewhere, able to make that change, as well as a possibility in the thing itself to receive it" (II.21.4). Yet although there is a way in which this sort of power talk can be understood as true, it should not be taken as implying the existence of any sort of thing, a bare disposition, beyond bodies and their textures. Locke's talk of powers is nominal.[9]

23.4. The Explanatory Force of Nominal Powers

To insist that Boyle's and Locke's powers should be understood nominally is not to say that their pervasive talk of powers is uninteresting. On the contrary, it is interesting and important in much the way that Locke's theory of nominal essences is interesting and important. That theory attempts to account for our ideas of natural kinds in a way that avoids postulating anything in reality that corresponds to those ideas. My claim is that Boyle and Locke want to treat our ideas of qualities in precisely the same way. We have ideas about the qualities that bodies have, and we talk as if bodies really have those qualities, but what these qualities amount to are mere nominal powers, reducible to the geometric–kinetic features of bodies and their environment.

This conception of quality is arguably Boyle's most important philosophical idea. Although it is the descendant of Hobbes's insistence that an accident is merely "the mode of conceiving a body" (*De corpore* 8.2), Boyle develops this sort of nominal approach in a way that puts it at the center of his natural philosophy. That the theory of qualities is important to Boyle cannot be doubted. The proem to *The Origin of Forms and Qualities* describes it as an attempt to write

some kind of introduction to the principles of the mechanical philosophy, by expounding . . . , as far as my thoughts and experiments would enable me to do, in few words, what, according to the corpuscularian notions, may be thought of the nature and origin of qualities and forms; the knowledge of which either makes or supposes the most fundamental and useful part of natural philosophy.

He then opens his preface with this remark:

The origin . . . and nature of the qualities of bodies is a subject that I have long looked upon as one of the most important and useful that the naturalist can pitch upon for his contemplation. For the knowledge we have of the bodies without us being for the most part fetched from the

---

[9] A realistic interpretation of Lockean powers can be found in Jackson: "by 'secondary quality' he [Locke] means, neither qualities nor ideas, but a third set of entities, which he calls 'powers of bodies to produce ideas by means of (primary) qualities'" ("Locke's Distinction" p. 55). See also, among many others, Yolton: "besides the original properties, the insensible particles have dispositional or relational properties, causal properties that Locke calls 'powers'" (*Compass of Human Understanding* p. 22). Chappell's recent essay on powers in Locke does not expressly commit itself on this ontological question, but seems implicitly committed to a realistic interpretation: he even thinks that powers can be "the cause of a change that occurs when a power is actualized" ("Power in Locke's *Essay*" p. 131).

The clearest statement I have found of a reductive reading of Lockean powers is in Jacovides, "Locke's Distinctions" pp. 126–8. Heil ("Dispositions" p. 351) also suggests this sort of reading of Locke. Ayers's treatment of Lockean powers in general tends in this same direction, although rather than view the theory as positively reductive, he treats it as an attempt to stay at the phenomenal level while remaining neutral about "the level of things as they are in themselves and as they should be conceived of in theoretical, explanatory science" ("Ideas of Power" p. 7). Perhaps in some official sense Ayers is correct to treat Locke as intending agnosticism regarding the things in themselves. But in practice all Locke's sympathies lie with a reduction to primary, mechanistic qualities.

informations the mind receives by the senses, we scarce know anything else in bodies, upon whose account they can work upon our senses, save their qualities. (*Works* V:298; Stewart p. 13)

The prominent place Boyle gives to qualities is doubtless part of what has encouraged readers to understand the theory in realistic terms. But these remarks should be understood as a reflection not of Boyle's ontological commitments, but of his pragmatic attitude toward scientific explanation. Whereas Descartes thought himself able to give a reductive explanation of all natural phenomena, Boyle recognizes that different forms of explanation need to be tolerated and even encouraged:

I consider then that, generally speaking, to render a reason of an effect or phenomenon is to deduce it from something else in nature more known than itself, and that consequently there may be diverse kinds of degrees of explication of the same thing. For although such explications   3
be the most satisfactory to the understanding wherein it is shown how the effect is produced by the more primitive and catholic affection of matter—namely, bulk, shape, and motion—yet are not these explications to be despised wherein particular effects are deduced from the more   6
obvious and familiar qualities or states of bodies, such as heat, cold, weight, fluidity, hardness, fermentation, etc., though these themselves do probably depend upon those three universal ones formerly named. (*Certain Phys. Essays* II:21)   9

This does not mean that he thinks heat and other secondary qualities (lines 6–7) are something over and above "bulk, shape, and motion" (line 5), only that it is sometimes an advance in understanding to get down to the level of the secondary qualities, pending a complete reduction all the way to "the more primitive and catholic affections" (line 5).

One of the most striking features of this nominal conception of power is its ecumenical attitude toward what counts as a power or quality. As we have seen (§23.2), Boyle regards our principal conception of the secondary qualities as perceiver-relative, with the consequence that a body's having color and other secondary qualities depends on there being suitable observers. This is simply a feature of how we talk about bodies: because our senses "may be wrought upon by the figure, shape, motion, and texture of bodies without them after several ways," the mind gives these bodies "distinct names, calling the one light or colour, the other sound, the other odour, etc." and "calling one colour green, the other blue, and one taste sweet and another bitter, etc." (*Origin* V:316; Stewart p. 31). So conceived, the sensible qualities depend on there being bodies having certain textures, in a world with perceivers that have certain corresponding textures. We might just as well, however, understand these qualities non-relationally. Thus, after raising the worry that qualities might seem to have "an absolute being irrelative to us" (V:317; Stewart p. 32), Boyle insouciantly replies that "I do not deny but that bodies may be said in a very favourable sense to have those qualities we call sensible, though there were no animals in the world" (V:318–19; Stewart p. 33). He goes on to describe a body as possessing these non-relational qualities "dispositively" rather than "actually" (V:315; Stewart p. 34). One might think that Boyle needs to make up his mind here about whether these qualities are or are not relational. But given his nominal conception of powers, he can tolerate either usage. In one sense bodies would lack colors and smells in a world without perceivers, and in another sense they would have them. Neither claim is privileged, except insofar as we wish to conceive of sensible qualities in one way or another.[10]

Such ecumenism is particularly helpful in trying to understand color. Boyle and Locke are generally understood to have treated color as a bare disposition, but they have also been read as defending each of the other two principal modern accounts of color: reductive physicalism and Galilean anti-realism.[11] In fact, their view is one that has no modern counterpart, and perhaps this is part of the reason readers have been confused. They are reductivists about color (and other sensible qualities) but, unlike modern physicalists, they do not assume that a body's having a color reduces simply to facts about that particular body. In one sense—Boyle's "dispositive" sense—a body's having a color just does reduce to facts about its own texture. But a body does not "actually" have a color, according to Boyle, unless there are creatures with color vision, and so an account of actual color must make appeal to corpuscular facts about perceivers. The theory's sensitivity to environmental factors does not preclude it from being reductive, provided that the reduction is holistic. Moreover, although I have not found Boyle saying as much, his account can readily accommodate the notorious problem of perceptual differences within or between species. If bees can detect colors on flowers that we cannot, then those flowers have one actual color in virtue of the visual capacities of bees, and they have another actual color in virtue of our visual capacities. For each and every different kind of perceptual capacity that exists, the

---

[10] In a later work, Boyle articulates within a single sentence both his "actual" relational understanding of qualities and his non-relational "dispositive" sense: "most of those powers and other attributes that we call qualities in bodies depend so much upon the structure or constitutions of other bodies that are disposed or indisposed to be acted on by them that if there were no such objects in the world, those qualities in the bodies that are said to be endowed with them would be but aptitudes to work such effects, in case convenient objects were not wanting" (*Of Men's Great Ignorance* [*Works* VI:522]).

Kaufman's "Locks, Schlocks" wonders how Boyle can recognize powers both in the usual relational sense and in this other, dispositive sense. If he is willing to endorse dispositive powers, then, Kaufman worries, they "would do all of the same work in an explanatorily adequate natural philosophy. And if that were the case, then the corpuscularian natural philosophy doesn't need actual qualities" (pp. 178–9). Kaufman's answer is that only actual, relational qualities for Boyle are real, and that the non-relational, dispositive qualities are mere "*entia rationis* with a *fundamentum in re*" (p. 190). My own view, in effect, is that all Boyle's qualities are *entia rationis*.

One of the best texts I have found for giving Boyle's powers this sort of reductive reading occurs later in *Origin of Forms*: "I doubt [≈ fear] that sometimes we mistake names for things, and because when a body by the action of proper agents obtains such a modification as fits it for such and such actions and uses, we are wont to call it by such a name, and attribute a form to it, we are prone to conclude that the faculties and qualifications it enjoys and the things it is able to perform are due to this form we have assigned it; as if this form were some distinct and operative substance that were put into the body as a boy into a pageant [≈ stage], and did really begin, and guide, and overrule the motions and actions of the *compositum*. Whereas indeed what we call the form, if it be not sometimes little more than one of those airy things that the schools call an external denomination, seems oftentimes to be rather a metaphysical conception in our mind than a physical agent that performs all things in the body it is ascribed to: as when a conveniently shaped piece of steel is by having a due temper given it turned into the spring of a watch, not only the motions of the watch, though proceeding from this spring, proceed not from the form of the iron (for a spring made of another elastical body, though it would not be so convenient, might set a watch a moving) but which is here the main observable, the springiness itself flows not immediately from the form (for steel is not less steel when it is not springy then when it is) but from the mechanical and adventitious texture that is superinduced in the metal, and may be given it by several outward agents, as the fire, the hammer, etc." (*Works* V:479) The focus here is substantial form, but I take the point to apply more widely to alleged forms of all kinds.

[11] For an anti-realist reading of Boyle—treating secondary qualities as sensations—see Keating, "Un-Locke-ing Boyle" p. 309 and Mandelbaum, "Locke's Realism" pp. 19–21. Boyle does, at least once, speak of colors etc. as sensations, but he immediately goes on to speak of the sensible qualities as being in the world (*Origins* V:334; Stewart p. 51). To my mind, then, Boyle cannot even be regarded as what §22.6 calls an Equivocal Anti-Realist.

flower has a distinct power. Provided one is willing to tolerate this sort of proliferation of colors, the theory of nominal powers can readily account for perceptual variability.

Another kind of advantage is that the theory neatly accounts for the controverted issue of whether bodies have color in the dark. Locke holds that porphyry has no color in the dark (*Essay* II.8.19), and although it is possible that he thinks this because of special features of that rock, it would not be surprising if he intended the claim to hold generally, because it was a commonplace view that goes back to the Epicureans. Inspired by that tradition, Walter Charleton, for instance, holds that "colours have no existence in the dark," and that "the substance of light, or the minute particles of which its beams consist, are necessarily to be superadded to the superficial particles of bodies, as the complement, nay the principal part of colour" (*Physiologia* III.4.1.7). He goes on to discuss a red cloth that can be made to change its appearance by being held up and exposed to light and shadow in various ways: "demand of yourself, whether any one of all those different colours can be really inherent in the cloth?" Charleton's own answer is that the cloth, intrinsically, has only a "disposition" for color, and that the actual color consists in the particles being illuminated in a certain way. What Boyle adds to Charleton, and what Locke is building on, is a worked-out theory of such dispositions. On this theory, environmental factors play a role in the individuation of sensible qualities, and so the holistic kind of reduction they propose takes into account not only the presence and absence of perceivers (and variations among them), but also the presence and absence of light (and variation in light). Because of the nominal character of the theory, we can understood both why we adhere to certain conventions in talking about color (and other sensible qualities) and also why other conventions seem equally tenable.[12]

Locke shows inclinations not only to deny that there are colors in the dark, but also to deny that there are colors outside the mind at all, as when he writes that "whiteness and coldness are no more in snow than pain is" (*Essay* II.30.2). To be sure, he does not always talk this way, but he does so enough to have persuaded some commentators that he means it. The previous chapter considered one basis for a certain indecision about what to say about this: when 'color' designates physically, it refers to something in bodies, but when it designates phenomenally, it refers to a sensation (§22.6). This ambiguity explains why an author might be tempted toward equivocal color Anti-Realism. But more is needed to explain why an author would insist on unequivocal Anti-Realism. To the extent Locke heads in that direction, I think his nominal theory of powers is the reason. If colors for him were irreducible powers, as the standard reading has it, then his Anti-Realism could be at most equivocal. But when secondary qualities are understood nominally, it becomes natural to want to stress the reductive character of the account by saying things that, strictly speaking, go beyond reduction all the way to eliminativism. Thus Locke can write that "sweetness and whiteness are not really in manna; which are but the effects of the operations of manna by the motion, size, and

---

[12] On Locke's discussion of porphyry, see Jacovides, "Locke's Distinction" pp. 121–2. For the history of the debate over whether bodies have colors in the dark, see Guerlac, "Colours in the Dark." Guerlac shows that scholastic authors disagreed on this issue. For a very sophisticated discussion of this issue see Buridan, *In De an.* II.12. Buridan insists that color, as the *per se* object of sight, must—whatever else it may be—be the external *cause* of color vision. For other highly worthwhile discussions see Oresme, *In De an.* II.16 and Suárez, *In De an.* 7.2.

figure of its particles on the eyes and palate" (II.8.18). Strictly speaking, what he ought to say is that sweetness and whiteness are powers of the manna that are nothing over and above the motion, size, and figure of its particles, in an environment where these particles are able to produce sensations of the relevant kind.[13]

In this respect, Boyle is perhaps more in control of the theory than Locke is—not surprisingly, given that it is Boyle's theory. Unlike Locke, Boyle almost never wavers from the view that secondary qualities are in the world. As we have seen, moreover, Boyle is clear on the explanatory force of accounts cast in terms of qualities, and he is clear about the way his nominal approach licenses an ecumenical tolerance for different ways of individuating powers (e.g., as relative or non-relative to perceivers). A more charitable interpretation of Locke, however, would be that he simply does not wish to develop the theory in the way Boyle suggests, because he doubts the explanatory usefulness of such powers. For whereas Boyle regards an account of qualities as "the most fundamental and useful part of natural philosophy" (as above), Locke seems much less impressed by what we learn about the world, when we describe it in terms of its qualities. He thinks that our ideas of substances consist mostly in ideas of secondary qualities, but adds that this yields very little by way of useful information: "this, how weighty and considerable a part soever of human science, is yet very narrow, and scarce any at all" (*Essay* IV.3.10). We cannot determine the connection between secondary qualities and the primary qualities on which they depend, and as a result we cannot determine any necessary connection between distinct secondary qualities. Nor can we hope to grasp the far-flung relations that a particular body may have to other bodies, potentially even to bodies beyond the "remotest star our eyes have yet discovered" (IV.6.11). The result is that "our knowledge in all these enquiries reaches very little farther than our experience" (IV.3.14).

Still, even if Locke and Boyle disagree on the explanatory usefulness of powers, it is helpful to keep in mind that Locke's conception of powers is essentially Boylean. This explains, for instance, why Locke sometimes describes all qualities, primary and secondary, as powers (II.8.8), and at other times seems to treat only the secondary

---

[13] On a realistic interpretation of colors as powers, there are delicate questions to ask about exactly how holistically to cast one's net. Beyond the issue of whether to require light there is the question of what sort of observers are required, and here there is a wide range of possible views. One might require actual observers or merely past or future observers. If actual, there is a question of how nearby they must be. Charleton, in one passage, seems to require not just actual observers but actual, occurrent observations (*Physiologia* III.1.1.2, as quoted in Ch. 22 note 11), as if a leaf that falls unseen in a forest has no color. Locke might be thought to be making a similar claim when he remarks that "let not the eyes see light or colours . . . and all colours . . . vanish and cease and are reduced to their causes" (*Essay* II.8.17). It is unclear, however, whether he refers to an occurrent act of seeing, or to the mere existence of perceivers with the appropriate capacities. For realists regarding powers, such interpretive decisions must be a matter of considerable anxiety, unless they are promiscuous realists indeed. The most impressive defense I have found of a realistic theory of powers in Locke is that of Stuart, "Locke's Colors," who argues that for Locke colors are relations to occurrent acts of seeing, and so exist only when seen. On my nominal powers account, in contrast, every way of talking is as good as the next, and the only substantive task is to track our ordinary conceptual framework.

Essay IV.2.11–13 shows Locke at his equivocal best regarding the extra-mental existence of colors. In other places he is an unequivocal Realist. In Draft B, for instance, the external existence of colors "is a certainty as great as human nature is capable of concerning the existence of any real thing but a man's self alone" (§35). The *Elements of Natural Philosophy* (late 1690s) are again equivocal: "Heat is a very brisk agitation of the insensible parts of the object, which produces in us that sensation from whence we denominate the object hot; so what in our sensation is heat, in the object is nothing but motion" (ch. 11). He reaches a clearer verdict, though, in the case of sound: "That which is conveyed into the brain by the ear is called sound; though, in truth, till it come to reach and affect the perceptive part, it be nothing but motion" (ibid.).

qualities as powers (II.8.10 etc.). On a nominal account of what powers are, one can talk either way. Likewise, the case of the porphyry that has no color in the dark yields this conclusion: "whiteness or redness are not in it at any time, but such a texture that has the power to produce such a sensation in us" (II.8.19). Read incautiously, this looks like Anti-Realism. But if we read Locke with Boyle's theory in mind, we can treat this as the claim that (a) colors are powers; (b) such powers are reducible to textures; and (c) powers can be treated either non-relationally or relationally. Understood non-relationally (Boyle's "dispositive" sense), colors are present even in the dark. Understood relationally (Boyle's "actual" sense) we get the intended result that porphyry "has no colour in the dark," since colors in this sense are grounded on the right sort of body in the right sort of conditions.

A proper understanding of Locke's conception of powers helps as well with several larger themes from the *Essay*. First, it helps explain why Locke is so drawn toward indirect realism: the doctrine that ideas rather than the qualities of bodies are "the immediate object of perception" (II.8.8). For scholastic authors, persuaded that sensible qualities are real accidents causally responsible for perception (§22.3), there is little temptation to deny that colors and other sensible qualities are the things we perceive. But when sensible qualities are identified as powers, and these powers are understood nominally, it becomes easy to doubt whether they are suitable objects of perception at all. Causally inert, the sensible qualities are an explanatorily useful construction but are hardly fundamental features of the world. These are poor candidates for objects of perception, or at least so one might well suppose.

Second, when Locke's theory of powers is understood nominally, it is easier to see what his theory of substance amounts to. I argued in Chapter 9 that substance for Locke, "the supposed, but unknown support of those qualities we find existing" (II.23.2), is simply the thing itself—the gold, the horse, the man. The standard modern interpretation of Locke, according to which he treats ordinary substances as a composite of sensible qualities and an underlying substratum, is wrong about both sides of this supposed composite entity. First, as I argued (§9.1), it misunderstands Locke's talk of a "substratum," supposing him to be positing a mysterious sub-substance when in fact he is simply talking about the ordinary thing itself. Second, it wrongly treats sensible qualities as the sort of things that require a subject to inhere in, when in fact sensible qualities are mere nominal powers, and nominal powers are nothing over and above the substance itself, as modified by certain mechanical affections. Once we see that the secondary qualities are to be understood reductively, as nothing over and above a body with its various mechanical affections, then the bare substratum interpretation loses much of its rationale. We can avoid having to suppose that Locke harbors an ontology of myriad powers, all grounded in an unknowable substratum, which all together comprises the familiar things we call horses and gold. This would go far beyond the most extravagant metaphysical systems of the scholastic era.

What about the primary qualities? Understood simply as powers, they are merely nominal, as all Lockean powers are, at least in the corporeal realm. Locke is quite clear, however, that the primary qualities are not *mere* or *bare* powers, inasmuch as they are something real and irreducible in bodies. I have made no arguments regarding how to understand Locke's primary qualities, but my view is that they are best understood along the lines of Descartes's modes of extension. As such, Locke has to face the same sorts of problems that Descartes faces in explaining the relationship between determinate modes and an indeterminate substance (§13.7), which is to say that the character of Lockean substances is by no means pellucidly clear, even if one accepts my view that Lockean substances just are ordinary substances. Thus one arrives at the picture suggested back in §7.3, that the world, for Locke, is doubly veiled from experience, inasmuch as the things themselves lie hidden beneath the primary qualities, which in turn lie hidden beneath our ideas.[14]

23.5. Scholastic Powers

Removed from their historical context, it is natural to read Boyle and Locke as committed to an ontology of bare dispositions. A Lockean theory of color is today synonymous with a dispositional theory, and Boyle is rightly credited as the inspiration for Locke's view. In the context of the seventeenth century, however, there is little precedent for this notion. Powers can be understood nominally, as they clearly were in Gorlaeus and Hobbes (§23.1), or they can be understood robustly, as categorically actual causal agents. Nothing in between was generally recognized. Of course, one might suggest that Boyle and Locke are simply doing something new. And surely their texts have been the inspiration for many modern accounts. Here again, however, we have one of those Bloomian episodes where misinterpretation is the mother of philosophical invention (§1.4). If we could confront Boyle or Locke with the idea of bare dispositions as irreducibly real, they would surely recoil from being credited with anything so thoroughly removed from the causal, physical, corpuscular mode of explanation that they favor. Indeed, although they might well have branded modern talk of dispositions as just another instance of scholastic obscurity, the fact is that the scholastics themselves reject anything like such bare dispositions. This makes it doubly implausible to ascribe any such thing to either Boyle or Locke. It is a view that not only goes against what they say and goes against the spirit of their work, but also requires anachronistically importing a metaphysical notion that is quite alien to their time.

Scholastic authors have available to them a very direct and decisive argument against bare dispositions, grounded in elementary Aristotelian principles.

1. Powers, qualities, and properties are forms.
2. Forms, by their very nature, actualize the subject they inhere in.
3. Forms, by their very nature, are causally efficacious.
4. No powers, qualities, or properties are bare dispositions.

---

[14] On the relation between substance and powers in Locke, see also *Essay* II.31.8: "The simple ideas, whereof we make our complex ones of substances, are all of them (bating only the figure and bulk of some sorts) powers, which being relations to other substances, we can never be sure that we know all the powers that are in any one body, till we have tried what changes it is fitted to give to, or receive from other substances, in their several ways of application: Which being impossible to be tried upon any one body, much less upon all, it is impossible we should have adequate ideas of any substance, made up of a collection of all its properties." This has been read, reasonably enough, as a denial that primary qualities are powers. On my own reading of Locke, which I confess to being underdetermined by the texts, it is always legitimate to attach the label 'power' to any state of affairs that acts or is acted on. Here the primary qualities are exempted from the class of powers only because they are not mere powers. For an argument against treating the primary qualities as powers, see Rickless, "Locke on Primary and Secondary Qualities."

The conclusion (4) follows immediately from the premises, given how bare dispositions were defined at the start of the chapter. Premises (2) and (3) are central to the Aristotelian program, and can scarcely be questioned. Premise (1), however, might seem to admit of counterexamples, inasmuch as scholastic ontology is full of various powers and potentialities that do crucial work, and yet do not seem to be forms. Here I will set aside prime matter: even if in some sense, according to some authors, it might count as a bare disposition, it is scarcely relevant to the sorts of qualities at issue here. When we turn, however, to any sort of complex actual entity, we immediately encounter all kinds of further properties that look something like bare dispositions. A particularly striking example is the soul, which although itself a paradigmatic form, contains various further metaphysical parts such as its faculties (will, intellect, etc.), its moral habits (virtues, vices), and its cognitive habits (memory, knowledge)—a range of examples that takes us through psychology, ethics, and epistemology. To be sure, whether one ought to be a realist about these various capacities was subject to dispute. Some, for instance, thought that the soul's faculties are nothing over and above the soul itself, whereas others insisted on a real distinction between the soul and its faculties. Everyone, however, accepted the reality of at least some of these potentialities. All of these, moreover, might seem to fit the notion of a bare disposition, inasmuch as they might be regarded as tendencies of the soul to act in various ways, actualized only under certain circumstances. Yet if one looks closely at how the scholastics understand these "tendencies," they turn out themselves to be forms. The powers of the soul, for instance, are qualities, and so a kind of accidental form, as are the habits that inhere in the soul. As forms, all of these powers and habits are conceived of as actualizing the soul in various ways, and being intrinsically efficacious. The virtue of charity, for instance, actualizes the will simply in virtue of inhering in it. When the appropriate circumstances arise, charity makes the will care for others more readily and reliably. But its performing this effect in a given situation is its "second actuality." The "first actuality" that is definitive of charity is its continual, categorical actualization of the soul. Sensible qualities, for the scholastics, are categorical in just the same way, inasmuch as they are intrinsically, non-derivatively efficacious and categorically, non-conditionally actual.[15]

The most fine-grained scholastic discussions of the various sorts of qualities occur in commentaries on *Categories* ch. 8, where Aristotle distinguishes four species of quality

---

[15] On habits as accidental forms, in the category of Quality, see Aquinas, *Summa theol.* 1a2ae 49.3 ad 1. Aquinas makes clear as well in that passage that a habit's informing a subject is itself, directly, a kind of actuality, albeit one ordered toward a further, second actuality. "Ad primum ergo dicendum quod habitus est actus quidam, inquantum est qualitas, et secundum hoc potest esse principium operationis. Sed est in potentia per respectum ad operationem. Unde habitus dicitur actus primus, et operatio actus secundus, ut patet in II *De anima.*" For Aquinas to have something like bare dispositions, in the context of this theory, he would have to postulate a distinct power associated only with the second actuality, distinct from the form that brings about the first actuality in the subject.

For the powers of the soul as qualities, see e.g. Aquinas, *Summa theol.* 1a 77.1 and 5. Scotus's argument against a real distinction between the soul and its powers makes much of the fact that such powers are not mere potentialities, but are themselves actualities: "omnes ponunt quod intellectus est quidam actus" (*Opus Ox.* II.16 [Wadding VI.2, n. 5; not in *Ordinatio*]). He then reasons that, if this is so, then there is no reason not to allow the soul itself to serve as the actuality that gives rise to the second actuality of thought and volition. On the debate over the relationship between the soul and its powers, see Ch. 8 note 23.

On the general relationship between form and actuality—premise (2) in the argument—see e.g. Aquinas, *Quod.* 1.4.1sc: "quaelibet forma, cum sit actus, facit esse in actu" and Buridan, *In Praed.* q. 16 (pp. 164–5): "forma dicitur communiter de omni actu perficiente materiam vel subiectum aliquod, cui inhaeret."

(8b26–10a27). Here is how J. L. Ackrill renders the distinction in English, together with Boethius's standard Latin translation and Aristotle's Greek:

a. States (*habitus; hexis*) and conditions (*affectio; diathesis*)
b. Natural capacities (*potentia naturalis; dunamis phusikē*) and incapacities
c. Affective qualities (*qualitates passibiles; pathētikai poiotētes*) or affections (*passio; pathē*)
d. Shape (*forma; schēma*) and external form (*figura; morphē*)

The sensible qualities, elemental and secondary, go into (c). Classed in (b) are qualities that are natural to a thing, rather than acquired: being a runner by nature, or healthy by nature, or soft by nature. Class (a) divides into stable and long-lasting "states" (knowledge, virtues) and unstable, quickly changed "conditions" (hot, cold, healthy, sick). These distinctions were the subject of a vast scholastic commentary tradition, which defies summary. So far as I have found, however, the scholastics are not at all inclined to see this as an invitation to countenance bare dispositions. Ockham's thorough discussion, although idiosyncratic in certain ways, is typical of the general trend. He is particularly struck by the oddly overlapping character of Aristotle's division. Hot and cold are paradigmatic examples of (c), but they are also listed among conditions of the body in (a). Hard and soft are examples of (b), but presumably they belong in (c) as well. Rather than attempt to reconstruct the boundaries between the classes as exclusive, Ockham simply denies that this was Aristotle's intention. Ockham argues instead that all qualities properly belong in (a), as either *habitus* or *affectiones*, depending on whether or not they are stable and long-lasting. Referring to the class as a whole as *dispositiones*, he remarks that "every quality that is in its own right one thing (*una res per se*) is contained in this first species of quality, since every such thing is either stable or unstable" (*In Praed.* 14.4 [*Opera phil.* II:273]).[16]

Given that qualities are the only accidents allowed in Ockham's ontology (§19.2), one can say that for Ockham the only things that exist are substances and dispositions. This will mislead, however, if one is thinking of bare dispositions. For although some of the items Aristotle puts into class (a)—particularly knowledge and virtue—look as if they could count as bare dispositions, Ockham recognizes no such distinction between dispositional and the categorical qualities. All of Ockham's "dispositions"—that is, all of his qualities—are not just ontologically real and irreducible but also non-relational and causally efficacious. Nothing we might want to count as a disposition gets into Ockham's ontology unless it passes his test for ontological commitment (§14.3, §19.2): a thing's gaining or losing that disposition must require more than just local motion. So although Ockham's willingness to describe qualities as dispositions bears at least superficial affinities with Boyle's and Locke's treatment of qualities as powers, the views are in fact radically different. Their qualities are bare powers, analyzed reductively. Even though Ockham is the leading representative of the reductive wing of scholasticism, he remains very far from offering a reductive treatment of powers in general. To be sure, on his view, many so-called qualities or dispositions are not truly *res* at all. Items in class (d), for instance, are nothing beyond a substance and the location

---

[16] One controversial aspect of Ockham's treatment of the four species of quality is his claim that the species are non-exclusive. See, e.g., the criticism in pseudo-Campsall's *Logica* 44.16.

of its parts (§14.3), and many putative qualities in class (b) are nothing more than an amalgam of various distinct qualities acting in concert (*In Praed.* 14.5 [*Opera phil.* II:275]). But inasmuch as Ockham thinks that certain qualities are causally efficacious in a way that is irreducible to a geometric–kinetic analysis, he must allow those "dispositions" into his ontology as robust, categorical properties. In no case does Ockham countenance bare dispositions.

Ockham's treatment of qualities is in line with the general tendency of scholastic thought to suppose that any real entity, substantial or accidental, will be causally efficacious. This is part of the broader scholastic tendency, which we have encountered numerous times already (§6.1, §10.5, etc.), to understand Aristotelianism not in abstract, metaphysical terms, but as a concrete, physical theory of the world. Given the generally friendly attitude of Aristotelianism toward metaphysical parts (§1.3), one might have expected it to be quite amenable to an ontology of bare dispositions. This is not, however, how later scholastic Aristotelianism developed. The notion of forms as functions, or as dispositions, or as anything other than individual causal agents is as alien to later scholastic thought as it is to Hobbes, Descartes, Boyle, and Locke. As a result, when seventeenth-century authors attack the ontology of scholasticism, they rightly do so from within natural philosophy, not from within metaphysics, and they offer the mechanical philosophy as an appropriate alternative. To suppose that Boyle and Locke are committed to an ontology of bare dispositions is to ascribe to them the sort of metaphysical entity that not even scholastic authors welcomed.

As always, however, it is hazardous to generalize regarding what "the scholastics" thought. On any substantive philosophical issue, there is unlikely to be agreement, unless it is the sort of enforced agreement that is the product of ecclesiastical censure (§20.1). The present case is no different. Although it is generally true that the scholastics are hostile to bare dispositions, one finds a very clear counterexample to this rule in Jacob Zabarella's discussion of the soul's powers. Zabarella works through the two main schools of thought on this issue: those, like Scotus, who deny a real distinction between the soul and its powers, and those like Aquinas who insist on a real distinction. Zabarella takes Aquinas's side in the debate, but then he offers a remarkable variation on the usual view. For although he accepts that the soul has powers—will, intellect, etc.—that are really distinct from the soul itself, he denies that those powers have any causal efficacy: "although this natural power is in a certain way an intermediary between the cause it follows from and the operation, nevertheless it is not an interme-diary *cause*. Instead, that prior cause is the immediate cause of the operation" (*De rebus nat.*, De fac. animae ch. 4, col. 692). Zabarella makes it expressly clear that he wishes to postulate the reality of the soul's powers; he sees himself as taking Aquinas's side in this debate, not Scotus's. But he does not think that such powers *do* anything. The soul needs powers because the soul needs to be in the right condition to act in certain ways, but it is the soul that acts, and not its powers. Zabarella evidently regards this as holding for powers and dispositions in general—thus he offers this example:

If someone is actually running, we do not say that the power (*potentia*) of running is the proximate cause of that running. Rather, the soul itself, or its instruments, or its condition, or whatever else it is from which that power emanates is said to be [not just] the remote cause, but rather the proximate and immediate cause. For a power is not the cause of an operation, but only the cause's aptitude for operating. (ibid.)

In the context of scholastic thought, this is an extraordinarily idiosyncratic idea. There were those who thought powers were needed, in one domain or another, and those who thought them unnecessary, but so far as I can find Zabarella is the only one to have proposed that they are needed without being causally efficacious.

Much more typical of the scholastic perspective is Suárez, who considers only to reject the idea of treating quantity as what I am calling a bare disposition. His theory of quantity, as discussed in §15.3, associates the quantity of a body—a real accident—with the natural tendency of its parts not to overlap with each other or with other bodies. But if quantity is a tendency, then it might well appear to be a bare disposition: an inclination to resist other bodies that might or might not manifest itself, depending on the environment. Suárez, however, expressly disavows this understanding of the theory. Initially, he raises the issue as an objection to his own account:

> You will say that this extension, as it has been explained, consists solely in a kind of aptitude for expelling a similar quantity from the same place. This aptitude cannot be the essential nature (*ratio*) of quantity, however, both because quantity as such is the actual form giving its formal effect in act rather than giving some aptitude, and because if it does provide some aptitude, that would be some sort of non-essential feature (*proprietas quaedam*) rather than its essential nature.... (*Disp. meta.* 40.4.16)

Quantity, according to this objection, cannot essentially consist in an aptitude. Forms have to actualize their subject, and do so not just upon certain occasions when the aptitude is manifested, but continuously, insofar as they are "the actual form" (line 3) of a body. This is to say that forms are not essentially *potentialities*, but instead that they are essentially *actualities*. In other words, forms must be categorical properties rather than bare dispositions. This is the objection. Suárez likes it well enough, however, that he grants almost all of it. Here is his reply:

> I reply, first, that we can almost never set out the essences of things, as they are in things. Instead, we work through their connection to some non-essential feature, and we seem to succeed well enough when we spell it out through that non-essential feature that is the first and   3
> closest of all to the essence of the thing. Second, we do not say that the essence of quantity consists in an aptitude for expelling another body or resisting it, so that it does not enter into the same space. For this aptitude, taken formally, is rightly counted among the non-essential   6
> properties of quantity. We instead say that to be the form that gives corporeal bulk (*molem*) or extension to things is the essential nature of quantity. As for what it is to have corporeal bulk, we can spell it out only through its connection to this effect, which is to expel a similar bulk   9
> from the same space....

Suárez endorses the objection's claim that accidents, as forms, are actualities rather than potentialities. This means, just as the objection maintains, that aptitudes are non-essential features of accidents (lines 4–7). As a result, quantity cannot essentially consist in the aptitude to resist other bodies should they come near (lines 4–6). The objection's only mistake, then, is to misunderstand Suárez's account. Quantity is not a dispositional property, but a categorical one; it is that which "gives corporeal bulk or extension to things" (lines 7–8). Why did Suárez not say that from the start? Because, alas, we do not even know what it is for a thing to have "corporeal bulk" (lines 8–9), and so our only option is to characterize quantity in terms of a non-essential aptitude that is closely associated with having bulk. We saw in §15.3 why Suárez does not want to say that having corporeal bulk is simply being spread out in space: that, he thinks, is an intrinsic feature of the body itself. What we are now seeing is that corporeal bulk also cannot be defined as an aptitude to resist other bodies, because real forms must be more than this sort of bare disposition. The form of quantity can *ground* that aptitude, and indeed pointing to the aptitude may be the best way to explain what quantity is. But, strictly, quantity is the underlying ground for that aptitude. And the quantity, rather than the aptitude, is the real accident inhering in bodies.[17]

23.6. Real and Occult Powers

Despite all the metaphysical obscurity of bare dispositions, there is a sense in which they promise transparency. By their nature, bare dispositions reveal themselves to us. If a color just is the power to cause in us a certain sensation, then our epistemic access to color is about as good as one could hope for. If, moreover, the color just is the bare power, nothing deeper, then, in effect, to see colors is to know them. Conversely, to reject bare dispositions is to abandon that sort of transparency. When Suárez insists that quantity is more than just the bare aptitude to resist other bodies, he surrenders the hope of a completely perspicuous account: although resistance is a *mark* of possessing quantity, it is not its essence. As for what that essence is, we do not know. Indeed, in general, "we can almost never set out the essences of things, as they are in things" (line 1 above). The scholastic rejection of bare dispositions, then, goes hand in hand with a willingness to appeal to the unknown essences of things.

Among seventeenth-century critics of scholasticism, this sort of appeal to the unknown was one of its most damning features. Boyle's and Locke's nominal conception of powers is one way to avoid such obscurantism—in particular, what Boyle called "that sanctuary of the ignorant, occult qualities" (*Sceptical Chymist* pt. 5 [*Works* II:328]). Treating powers nominally allows Boyle and Locke to make sense of the way we talk about the world—as having various sorts of qualities—but without postulating either unknown essences or a new ontological category of bare dispositions. Instead, their powers are nothing over and above the mechanical affections of bodies, and so, at least in principle, are not mysterious at all. In practice, of course, proponents of this sort of mechanistic–corpuscular approach were almost never successful in explaining exactly how a given quality could be reduced to such mechanical affections. Still, the explanatory payoffs were clear enough, and for authors like Descartes, Hobbes, Boyle, and Locke, the truth of their reductive strategies was an article of faith. As Descartes firmly puts it, "there are no powers in stones and plants that are so mysterious . . . that they cannot be explained in this way"—that is, "from principles that are known to all and admitted by all, namely the shape, size, position, and motion of particles of matter" (*Principles* IV.187). Inasmuch as Descartes is willing to speak of powers at all, he too understands them nominally.

---

[17] It is interesting to compare Suárez's negative attitude to bare dispositions in the context of quantity with his attempts to save middle knowledge as a theory of divine foreknowledge by postulating within free creatures a bare *habitudo* either to do a certain action in a certain circumstance, or to refrain from doing it. This *habitudo* is what God foresees, with respect to our actions. For discussion, see Robert Adams, "Middle Knowledge" pp. 81–2.

So far as I can find, Zabarella's extremely interesting view has never before been noticed.

This sort of austere metaphysics was never the only game in town, however, even among steadfastly anti-scholastic authors. Precursors of the mechanistic approach such as Johannes Kepler and William Gilbert had postulated forces to explain gravity and magnetism. Later, Walter Warner postulated an "efficient power" within bodies to account for their motion, and Charleton similarly appealed to a "motive virtue wherewith every compound body is naturally endowed" (*Physiologia* III.11.1.1). Henry More rejected the mechanical philosophy explicitly, postulating active forces within matter. Leibniz famously introduced forces as a critical ingredient in his metaphysics, and even assimilated this aspect of his views to scholastic prime matter and substantial form. Most influential of all was Newton, who postulated both a gravitational force to account for planetary motion and an atomic force to account for the hardness of bodies and their interactions. None of these powers count as bare dispositions—they are all categorically actual and intrinsically efficacious.[18]

Although this subject is too vast to be treated adequately here, something needs to be said about the general line of thought, both because it puts in relief the distinctively nominal approach of Boyle and Locke, and because real powers would prove immensely important to subsequent developments. In general, it is one of the most surprising aspects of seventeenth-century thought that, by the end of the century, the austerely mechanistic mid-century approach was on the retreat, and would never return to prominence again. Indeed, contrary to what one might suppose from the attention that philosophers give to the mechanistic movement, it was merely a brief passing fashion in the larger scheme of things. Within fifty years of Descartes's death, the Newtonians were already beginning to dominate natural philosophy, and Newton's conception of force was becoming a respectable principle of explanation.[19]

Historians of science have studied in detail how Newton's theory of gravity carried the day, and how his speculative proposal regarding atomic forces would eventually be vindicated by chemistry. For purposes of this study it will be more helpful to look at the general philosophical dispute that arose between Leibniz and Newton regarding the legitimacy of appealing to such forces. Although this dispute runs into the eighteenth century, it is important to consider it here, because Leibniz is criticizing Newton's

---

[18] For Kepler, see Dijksterhuis, *Mechanization* pp. 310–12, and Barker and Goldstein, "Theological Foundations." Henry's "Occult Qualities" discusses the role of forces in Warner, Charleton, and many other English authors before Newton. Although not all of the examples he adduces are equally compelling, that paper makes a strong case for the presence of real forces in seventeenth-century thought prior to Newton. Also on the activity of matter, see Clericuzio, "Gassendi, Charleton and Boyle." For Henry More see, e.g., *Immortality* III.13.7 and the discussion of the connection to Newton in McGuire, "Neoplatonism and Active Principles." And see Gabbey, "Henry More and the Limits of Mechanism."

For the role of forces in Leibniz, see e.g. Garber, "Foundations of Physics," and the useful summary in Garber et al., "New Doctrines of Body" pp. 594–602. For Newton there is a vast literature—see, e.g., McGuire, "Force, Active Principles"; McMullin, *Newton on Matter and Activity*; and Westfall, *Force in Newton's Physics* ch. 7, who contends that Newton's appeals to force emerged "more than anything else" from chemical rather than celestial phenomena (p. 380). For particular attention to forces at the chemical level in Newton, and to the great subsequent influence of this approach, see Thackray, *Atoms and Powers*.

It has been questioned whether even Descartes excludes forces entirely from his physics. For an extended argument that he does not, see Gabbey, "Force and Inertia." For an argument that the only force in Descartes's physics is God, see Hatfield, "Force (God)."

[19] For a compelling argument that Boyle's achievements in chemistry are quite unrelated to his mechanistic philosophy, see Chalmers, "Lack of Excellency." On Boyle's antipathy to occult qualities, see Alexander, *Ideas, Qualities* pp. 17–18 and Anstey, *Philosophy of Robert Boyle* pp. 22–4.

natural philosophy from something like the strictly mechanistic perspective of the mid-seventeenth century, and accusing him and others of returning to the obscurity of the scholastics.

> It pleases others to return to *occult qualities* or *scholastic faculties*, but since these crude philosophers and physicians see that those terms are in bad repute they change their name, calling them forces. True corporeal forces are of only one kind, namely, those that are exercised through the impression of impetus—for example, when a body is pushed forward. (*Antibarbarus physicus* [*Phil. Schriften* VII:338; tr. Ariew and Garber p. 313])

Dismayed at the return of such seemingly discredited forms of explanation, Leibniz wonders "what would Descartes or Boyle say if they returned now?" (ibid., VII:343). Given that Leibniz himself is a proponent of forces in the domain of metaphysics, he might seem an unlikely critic of Newton. But Leibniz draws a sharp distinction between the metaphysical domain, where scholastic-like entities can play an explanatory role, and the physical domain, where a purely mechanistic account holds sway. More specifically, Leibniz contends that a mechanistic account is always sufficient to explain any particular physical phenomenon, and that accounts that appeal to any other sorts of entities or causes must be either reducible to a strictly mechanistic account or else rejected. This puts him into real disagreement with Newton, who insists that a purely mechanistic account is impossible in the case of gravity, and at least doubtful as an explanation of the cohesion and complex behavior of microscopic bodies.

Leibniz's charge of occultness, which he repeatedly makes, stands in a venerable tradition of criticism. But what exactly are occult qualities, and what is wrong with them? It is important to keep in mind that, for scholastic authors, 'occult' simply means hidden, and so in general carries no exotic or pejorative implications. Magnetism was the paradigmatic occult quality, along with the medicinal properties of plants. As these examples might suggest, a quality does not count as occult simply in virtue of being unobservable. The four elemental qualities (Hot, Cold, Wet, Dry) are not observable, but they are not occult either, because they are a kind of tangible quality, and so intelligible in a way that occult qualities are not. (Although tangible, they are not observable, because they never naturally occur in isolation [§21.2].) So what more is required to make a quality occult? Christoph Scheibler offers this definition: "The tertiary or occult qualities are said to be certain hidden (*absconditae*) powers by which natural things act or are acted on by something, but whose character (*ratio*) cannot be given by primary or secondary qualities" (*Philosophia compendiosa* III.13.4). Daniel Sennert offers something similar: "Occult qualities are those that are not immediately grasped by the senses, but their power (*vis*) is apprehended mediately, from its effect, while yet that power of acting is unknown" (*Epitome* I.6, p. 74). Both definitions agree on these features of occult powers:

(i) they are powers by which a thing acts or is susceptible to being acted on;
(ii) they are hidden—that is, not themselves grasped by the senses;
(iii) the nature of the quality itself is unknown, and cannot be explained in terms of other qualities.

The first condition represents the general scholastic demand that qualities—or any entities—play a certain causal role. The second condition rules out sensible qualities, as well as intentional/spiritual qualities like light (§21.2). The third condition rules out various qualities for which we take ourselves to have a good reductive account, such as sickness or health, being a boxer or a runner. Reframing this analysis outside of its narrow scholastic context, we might say that an occult quality is one that plays a causal role, but that we can neither observe nor understand in terms of our fundamental physical theory.[20]

An important ambiguity here concerns whether the 'cannot' in (iii) is epistemic or metaphysical—that is, whether these authors suppose only that we do not presently know how to give a reductive account of magnetism and other occult phenomena, or whether they think no such reduction is possible in principle, and hence that there are various basic, occult powers in nature that go beyond the four elements and their associated qualities. Although it is often not clear which of these is meant, most discussions seem to have in mind the stronger claim. This is what one would expect. For if the category of the occult were merely epistemic, then scholastic authors would have to concede that nearly everything is occult: after all, they were quite aware of just how little they could really explain about the natural realm. (As Roger Bacon put it, "no one is so wise regarding the natural world as to know with certainty all the truths that concern the nature and properties of a single fly, or to know the proper causes of its color and why it has so many feet, neither more nor less" [*Opus maius* I.10].) This in turn helps explain why the occult qualities were so despised in the seventeenth century: the postulation of such qualities is not just an expression of humility in the face of nature's obscurity (an attitude to which one could hardly object), but the invocation of primitive, irreducible powers that could in principle never be made intelligible. As Newton would rightly put it, "occult qualities are decried not because their causes are unknown, but because the schoolmen believed that those things which were unknown to their Master Aristotle could never be known" (correspondence to Abbé Conti, as quoted in Henry, "Occult Qualities" p. 362).

So what of Newton's own forces—should they be regarded as occult? His best-known reply to this charge, from the second edition of his *Optics* (1717), goes as follows:

It seems probable to me that God in the beginning formed matter in solid, massy, hard, impenetrable particles. . . . It seems to me farther, that these particles have not only a *vis inertiae*,

---

[20] For other examples of occultness as tied to irreducibility see e.g. Aquinas, *De occultis operationibus naturae* (ed. Leonine 43:183a): "Quaecumque igitur actiones et motus elementatorum corporum sunt secundum proprietatem et virtutem elementorum, ex quibus huiusmodi corpora componuntur; huiusmodi actiones et motus habent manifestam originem, de qua nulla emergit dubitatio. Sunt autem quaedam huiusmodi corporum quae a virtutibus elementorum causari non possunt: puta quod magnes attrahit ferrum, et quod quaedam medicinae quosdam determinatos humores purgant et a determinatis corporis partibus. Oportet igitur huiusmodi actiones in aliqua altiora principia reducere"; Henry Cornelius Agrippa, *Occult Philosophy* I.10: "there are . . . virtues in things which are not from any element, as to expel poison, to drive away the noxious vapors of minerals, to attract iron, or anything else. . . . And they are called occult qualities, because their causes lie hid and man's intellect cannot in any way reach and find them out"; Chambers, *Cyclopaedia* entry on "Quality": "Occult qualities are certain latent powers arising from the specific forms of things, whereof no rational solution can be given on any principles of physics" (II:933a). See too Magirus, *Physiologia* III.8 and, at great length, Sennert, *Hypo. phys.* Bk. II (tr. *Thirteen Books* pp. 430–44), which issues a remarkable *apologia* for occult qualities, as causal powers beyond the four Aristotelian primary qualities.

Hutchison's "What Happened to Occult Qualities" contains much useful information but is quite wrong in its main thesis that seventeenth-century authors were not concerned with rejecting occult qualities. See also Hutchison's "Dormitive Virtues" and Millen, "Manifestation of Occult Qualities."

accompanied with such passive laws of motion as naturally result from the force, but also that   3
they are moved by certain active principles, such as is that of gravity, and that which causes
fermentation, and the cohesion of bodies. These principles I consider not as occult qualities,
supposed to result from the specific forms of things, but as general laws of nature, by which the   6
things themselves are formed; their truth appearing to us by phenomena, though their causes be
not yet discovered. For these are manifest qualities, and their causes only are occult. And the
Aristotelians gave the name of occult qualities only as they supposed to lie hid in bodies, and to   9
be the unknown causes of manifest effects. . . . Such occult qualities put a stop to the improve-
ment of natural philosophy, and therefore of late years have been rejected. To tell us that every
species of things is endowed with an occult specific quality by which it acts and produces   12
manifest effects is to tell us nothing: but to derive two or three general principles of motion
from phenomena, and afterwards to tell us how the properties and actions of all corporeal things
follow from those manifest principles, would be a very great step in philosophy, though the   15
causes of those principles were not yet discovered: and therefore I scruple not to propose the
principles of motion above-mentioned, they being of very general extent, and leave their causes
to be found out. (*Optics* query 31)   18

This passage is justly famed for the way it shifts away from the search for causes to the
search for "general principles" (line 13). Setting aside that issue, however, and focusing on
how Newton wants to escape the charge of occultness, it seems that he combines two
strategies. The first strategy is to identify his forces (lines 2–5) not as hidden powers but as
"general laws of nature" (line 6). Whether or not this should be regarded as Newton's
considered view is a complex scholarly question. Yet regardless of whether his forces are
to be identified with the laws of nature or with the causes behind those laws, the passage
plainly licenses the conclusion that there are such hidden causes, since it refers four times
to these "not yet discovered causes" (lines 6, 7, 16, 17). Here is where Newton needs his
second strategy, which is to distinguish between the occultness of the forces and the
occultness of the underlying causes of those forces. Even if the latter are unknown and so
occult, the former are "manifest qualities" (line 8). We are in a position to see, however,
that this strategy misses the point of the charge against him. Qualities count as occult in
the scholastic sense, as we have seen, not just because they are unobservable but also
because they cannot be reductively explained. Newton is making the point that qualities
like magnetism or gravity are perfectly observable. This is true enough. But the heart of
the scholastic doctrine—and the precise part of the doctrine that is objectionable—is the
notion that the occult qualities cannot be accounted for in terms of any broader explanatory account, and so must remain primitive and *sui generis*. In conceding that these
powers have "not yet discovered" causes, Newton is in effect leaving open the possibility
that the natural world might contain such brute forces. This is what Leibniz, from his
strict mechanistic perspective, finds so utterly objectionable.

   Newton here leaves open that anti-mechanistic possibility, and it is part of the charm
of the above passage that he simply refuses to speculate. Remarks that he makes
elsewhere, however, have led scholars to engage in such speculation. There is a case
to be made that, at least sometimes, God himself is the "not yet discovered" cause or,
alternatively, that a strictly mechanistic story might be possible. Very often, though,
Newton seems inclined to take precisely the route Leibniz finds so objectionable, and
endorse the existence of primitive causal forces to account for both gravitational and
molecular phenomena.

The heart of the dispute between Newton and Leibniz thus rests on whether it is licit to postulate non-mechanical causes as an explanation of the natural realm. According to Leibniz, "it is permissible to recognize magnetic, elastic, and other sorts of forces (*vires*), but only insofar as we understand that they are not primitive or unintelligible (ἄλογους), but arise from motions and shapes" (*Antibarbarus physicus* [*Phil. Schriften* VII:338; tr. Ariew and Garber p. 313]). Leibniz's ultimate basis for insisting on this ground-rule seems to be the Principle of Sufficient Reason. Irreducible physical forces, from Leibniz's perspective, would be unintelligible and hence unacceptable in a fully articulated physics. To this Newton's best reply is not to try to dodge the charge of occultness. It just is true that primitive physical forces are a return to scholastic occult qualities. Instead, along with continuing to stress his famous unwillingness to speculate, Newton should press Leibniz on whether the principles of the mechanistic system are ultimately any more deeply explanatory than are primitive forces. And this is precisely the approach that Newton takes in a letter from 1712 intended for Leibniz:

So then gravity and hardness go for unreasonable occult qualities unless they can be explained mechanically. And why may not the same be said of the *vis inertiae* and the extension, the duration, and mobility of bodies, and yet no man ever attempted to explain these qualities 3 mechanically, or took them for miracles or supernatural things or fictions or occult qualities. They are the natural, real, reasonable, manifest qualities of all bodies seated in them by the will of God from the beginning of the creation and perfectly incapable of being explained mechani- 6 cally, and so may the hardness of primitive particles of bodies. And therefore if any man should say that bodies attract one another by a power whose cause is unknown to us or by a power seated in the frame of nature by the will of God . . . , I know not why he should be said to 9 introduce miracles and occult qualities and fictions into the world. (In McGuire, "Force, Active Principles" pp. 202–3)

Rather than being lured into an attempt to explain the forces of gravity and hardness (line 1), Newton here challenges Leibniz as to why the basic elements of the mechanistic approach are any more intelligible. The mechanist relies on inertia, extension, duration, and mobility (lines 2–3), but what explains these? They might be said to be manifest qualities (line 5), but their causes are just as obscure as the causes behind gravity and hardness, in the sense that all are "perfectly incapable of being explained mechanically" (lines 6–7).

This is the right reply for Newton to make, and it is in a certain sense a thoroughly scholastic reply. For the scholastics, all of these features of the natural world—mechanical and otherwise—cry out for explanation. We have seen how they take seriously the need to account for phenomena such as extension and duration, generally appealing to the category of Quantity to account for the first (Ch. 14), and the theory of *entia permanentia* to account for the second (Ch. 18). The mechanistic philosophers thought that if they offered a sufficiently parsimonious ontological and causal framework, they would dispense with the need for this sort of speculative metaphysics entirely (or else, in Leibniz's case, permit a sharp distinction between the domains of physics and metaphysics). Newton's revival of forces threatens to undermine that project. To be sure, Newton himself is not aiming to revive scholastic metaphysics. The essence of his project is to find a way forward that sidesteps those issues, and it is not unreasonable to think of this method as one of the key ideas that allowed modern science to part ways with philosophy. But even while Newton found a way to sidestep metaphysical questions, his approach by no means eliminated them. On the contrary, in the wake of his work, these questions reemerged more pressing than ever.[21]

[21] On the Newton–Leibniz dispute over forces, see, e.g., Hall, *Philosophers at War* (focused mainly on the calculus dispute) and Brown, "Leibniz: Modern Philosopher?" On Newton's understanding of 'occult,' see Henry, "Occult Qualities." See Leibniz's Fifth Paper (nn. 118–23) for another version of the charge of occultness, and see also *Nouveaux essais* preface, pp. 65–8. Clarke makes Newton's appeal to the manifestness of gravity in his Fifth Reply to Leibniz (nn. 118–23). Cotes's preface to the second edition of the *Principia* makes the same maneuver, but also goes on to hint at the stronger reply that all explanations, even mechanical ones, must be grounded in something primitive.

PART VI

UNITY AND IDENTITY

24

Substantial Form

24.1. Form and Essence

There is no more notorious doctrine in scholastic metaphysics than the doctrine of substantial form. Descartes dismissively remarked that they are "a philosophical being unknown to me" (II:367). Henry Oldenburg congratulated Robert Boyle on having "driven out that drivel of substantial forms" which "has stopped the progress of true philosophy, and made the best of scholars not more knowing as to the nature of particular bodies than the meanest ploughmen" (*Correspondence* III:67). Spinoza, for his part, remarked to Oldenburg that he could hardly see why Boyle had bothered with "that childish and frivolous doctrine of substantial forms and qualities" (*Works* I:208). Very soon, 'substantial form' became a byword for all that was obscure and obsolete in scholastic Aristotelianism, and from this scorn the theory has never recovered. But what exactly were substantial forms? What are the consequences of rejecting them? This and the following six chapters will consider these questions.

The notion of a substantial form has its roots in Aristotle's physical conception of form as one of the four causes (*Phys.* II.3), along with his metaphysical conclusion that form, above all else, is substance in the primary sense (*Metaph.* VII). But this conception of form as somehow *substantial* took on new life among scholastic Aristotelians, and was developed in ways that Aristotle himself never suggested. Here, as we have seen in other domains, scholastic philosophers transformed the notion of what a form is, replacing what was for Aristotle primarily a metaphysical principle of explanation with something much more like an internal efficient cause.

As notorious as the doctrine of substantial forms was, it is not an easy doctrine to explain. Whereas earlier chapters have looked to Scotus to set the agenda for later scholastic discussions (§2.4, §10.5, §12.5, etc.), here he offers little guidance. Indeed, he seems to despair of any informative account of how substantial and accidental forms differ. In practice, according to Scotus, philosophers give various derivative (*a posteriori*) accounts of what the difference is: they point to the having of contraries, to the taking on of more or less, to being known in its own right, etc. These are all characterizations of accidental forms and not substantial ones. Still, they don't tell us about the thing in itself. It just is true that *pale* is an accident, or that *humanity* is a substantial form. Such claims are known in their own right (*per se*), and in these cases there is nothing more to be said, because nothing more can be said.[1]

This is admittedly discouraging. We should not make too much of these worries, however, because Scotus is in general unusually pessimistic about such foundational questions. He makes similar remarks elsewhere, for instance, about our ability to grasp why heat heats, or why the soul informs the body, or why in general some things have more unity than other things (§25.5). In all of these cases, moreover, Scotus does not mean that there is *nothing* that can be said that is philosophically illuminating, but only that there is no ultimate explanation; in the end, there is just the brute fact of the matter. So even while we bear in mind that at some point our explanations must run out, we still might look to find some sort of account of substantial form that offers some degree of illumination. One of the most common sayings about substantial form—closely associated with Aquinas (e.g., *Summa theol.* 1a 76.4)—is that the substantial form is what makes a thing exist *simpliciter*, whereas an accidental form makes a thing exist in some respect or another (*secundum quid*).[2] This fits with the broader scholastic conception of how a material substance is structured: as a composite of prime matter plus substantial form, in which accidental forms inhere. This in turn brings the theory of substantial form usefully into concert with the theory of prime matter as determinable stuff in need of actualization. When prime matter is so conceived, there must be *something* to play the role of substantial form, actualizing and so giving existence to that which would otherwise remain potential. In contrast, if prime matter exists on its own, as post-scholastic authors suppose, then it is easy to regard substantial form as otiose. This is one way of seeing the truth in Jean Chrysostome Magnen's remark, from back in §3.1, that one's conception of prime matter will dictate the rest of one's natural philosophy.

Still, this conception of substantial form as the actualizer of prime matter does not do full justice to the scholastic account. First, it holds only for authors who, following Averroes and especially Aquinas, subscribe to the unitarian doctrine that a single substance has just a single substantial form. Authors like Scotus who subscribe to a plurality of substantial forms cannot think that all substantial forms actualize prime matter (§25.1). Second, even for unitarians, this picture of what a substantial form does is much too thin; it raises the obvious question of why one needs substantial form as

---

[1] Scotus offers his despairing answer to this question: "Quare iste actus est per se actus, et ille per accidens? Responsio: non est causa quare ista est forma substantialis, et illa est accidens, quia propositiones per se primo modo non habent propter quid. Et sicut haec est per se primo modo 'albedo est qualitas,' similiter 'homo est substantia,' ita et haec 'humanitas, qua homo est homo, est forma substantialis' " (*In Meta.* VIII.4 [*Opera phil.* IV n. 46]). See also *Ord.* III.2.2 (Vat. IX n. 84) and *Ord.* IV.11.3 (Wadding VIII n. 44), where the reason why something is a substantial rather than an accidental form can no more be explained than we can explain why heat heats: "Et si quaeras unde potest probari quod haec forma dat esse simpliciter, illa non, si de ratione neutrius est dare illud esse quod immediate recedit a non esse, respondeo, aut tu quaeris de re in se, aut in comparatione ad cognitionem nostram. Si in se, nulla causa est quare ista dat esse simpliciter et illa secundum quid, nisi quia haec est forma substantialis, et illa accidentalis. Sicut enim nulla est causa quare calidum calefacit, quia immediata est et inter causam immediatam, et effectum non est alia causa media, ita in genere causae formalis haec est immediata: calor constituit calidum, et anima hominem, et est immediatio formae ad actum formalem." See also Cross, *Physics of Duns Scotus* pp. 103–7.

[2] For substantial form as that by which a thing has *esse simpliciter*, see also, e.g., De Soto, *In Phys.* I.10, p. 68a: "Forma autem substantialis est illa a qua sumitur esse simpliciter cuiuslibet rei." Scheibler's *Philosophia compendiosa* offers this neat formula: "Sunt autem formae substantialis officia tria: 1 Ut det esse. 2 Ut distinguat rem a re. 3 Ut sit principium operationum compositi" (I.1.5.12).

something distinct from matter, when one might instead treat matter as actualized, existent stuff (§3.2).

A richer account of the scholastic doctrine can be built upon the universally accepted connection between substantial form and essence. One classic text is Aristotle, *Physics* II.3, 194b27, which characterizes the formal cause as "the account of the essence." Averroes, too, remarks that the substantial form is what gives a thing "its name and definition" (*In Phys.* I.63), where a definition is what expresses the essence of a thing. And according to Francisco Suárez, the end of the substantial form is "to constitute and complete the essence of a natural being" (*Disp. meta.* 15.1.18). These remarks immediately raise the question, however, of just what it means to say, as Suárez does, that the substantial form "constitutes" a thing's essence. The most straightforward way to think about this—and the most common characterization among recent scholars—is to suppose that the substantial form of a thing just is its essence or the set of its essential properties.[3] This is not to identify the substantial form with all of a thing's *necessary* properties, because for an Aristotelian not all necessary properties are essential. The essential properties are those that define a thing as what it is. (To take the most familiar of examples, *rationality* is an essential property, whereas *risibility* is a merely necessary property, a so-called *proprium*.) Even when so qualified, however, such a straightforward identification of substantial form and essential properties is wrong in two respects. First, there was widespread agreement among the scholastics that the essence of a thing includes both its substantial form and its "common" matter, which is the sort of matter characteristic of a member of that species ("flesh and bones" is the standard example). Aristotle, as quoted above, might be thought to reflect this point, inasmuch as he describes the form not as the essence, but as the account (*logos, ratio*) of the essence. Glossing Aristotle's remark, the Coimbrans make it clear that the relationship between substantial form and essence is not that of identity; instead, the substantial form is "that in which the natural essence of any composite is *principally* contained, or what *completes* the essence of a thing and its definition, and distinguishes it from others" (*In Phys.* I.9.10.1).[4]

Second, the idea that a substantial form is the set of a thing's essential properties ignores the crucial and ongoing causal role that that form plays, serving as the principal internal cause of a thing's various properties and operations. To describe the substantial form as an essence suggests that the scholastics simply pick out one or more properties of the thing as somehow distinctive or definitive, and call that set of properties a form.

---

[3] For substantial form as merely a set of properties see e.g., Stump and Kretzmann, "Being and Goodness" p. 285: "On Aquinas's view, every thing has a substantial form. The substantial form of any thing is the set of characteristics that place that thing in its species and that are thus essential to it in Aquinas's sense of 'essential.'" See also Cross, *Physics of Duns Scotus* p. 12: "A substantial form, roughly speaking, is that property or set of properties in virtue of which a material substance is a substance of such-and-such a kind," and Bennett, *Learning from Six Philosophers* I:11: "The crucial explanatory fact about an organism [for Aristotle] is its 'form'. This is not a subset of the properties that the organism has, but rather a set of those that are *proper* to it, and towards which it strives or tends."

[4] On essence as substantial form plus common matter, see e.g. Aquinas, *Summa theol.* 1a 29.2 ad 3, 1a 75.4c; Scotus, *In Meta.* VII.16; Buridan, *In Meta.* VII.12; Coimbrans, *In Phys.* I.9.5; Scheibler, *Metaphys.* I.6.3.3.2 (pp. 74–5). Averroes was an exception to the standard medieval view: he thought the essence could be identified with the form alone (see *In Meta.* VII.34). Following Averroes's lead is Jandun, *In Meta.* VII.12: "dicendum est ad quaestionem quod sola forma est tota quidditas substantiae compositae sensibilis, ita quod materia non est aliqua pars quidditatis. Et hoc probatur auctoritate Commentatoris…" (f. 93C). For a searching investigation into these issues, see Amerini, "Semantics of Substantial Names."

If that were all a substantial form were, the theory would hardly have met with such virulent criticism in the seventeenth century. A just appreciation of the doctrine of substantial form, then, has to take account of two aspects of the theory: first, its *metaphysical role* in individuating a substance as a thing of a certain kind; second, its *physical role* in explaining why substances of certain kinds have properties of such and such kinds. Once these two aspects are distinguished, we will be in a position to see the many complex ways in which post-scholastic authors reject or else reformulate the theory.[5]

24.2. Form and Individuation

Substantial form is the complement, the actualizer, >of prime matter. It is that which makes a composite substance exist, and makes it exist as a thing of a certain kind. This is the beginnings of a theory, but not enough, and especially not enough in the face of post-scholastic criticisms. According to the corpuscularian alternative, prime matter needs no actualization, but rather exists on its own, as enduring particles, and comes to be a certain kind of thing when structured in a certain way. If this story is coherent, then why postulate these obscure substantial forms and an even more obscure indeterminate prime matter? The real heart of the scholastic theory lies in its answer to this question. It would take some time, however, for this question even to come into prominence. Early scholastic authors have little to say here, because the theory of substantial form had yet to be challenged. Only with the rise of a more skeptical, critical scholasticism in the mid-fourteenth century would these issues come into play, and it would not be until the sixteenth century that the theory of substantial forms was given a really sustained defense.

John Buridan provides an early example of how scholastic authors would defend the theory. In the midst of an argument for real accidents (a passage considered already in §19.5), Buridan notes that the logic of the case against accidental forms could be extended to substantial forms, leading to the view that "matter disposed in one way is fire, disposed in another way it is water, air, or stone" (*In De an.* III.11). The result, Buridan thinks, would be to deny generation and corruption:

This was the view of Democritus, Melissus, and those who claimed that everything is one in substance. For they were not so foolish as to believe that this human being is the same in number as that one, but [they did make this claim] for things that appear to be generated from one another: for instance, if from earth A comes water B, and from water B comes grass C, and from grass C comes horse D, and so on for all species of generable and corruptible things, then horse D is the same as what was grass, water, and earth, since the same matter that they claimed

---

[5] In general, students of post-scholastic thought are better informed than medievalists on the topic of substantial form. The best and most extensive recent discussion is Des Chene's *Physiologia*, which remarks that "essence, if it is identified with substantial form, is not a mere list of properties the loss of any one of which must result in the destruction of the individual" (p. 71). See also Hattab, *Descartes on Forms* pt. I; McCann, "Locke on Identity" pp. 55; Rozemond, *Descartes's Dualism* p. 104; Nadler, "Doctrines of Explanation" pp. 516–18; Ariew and Gabbey, "Scholastic Background" p. 430: "The substantial form is a determinative active principle informing and conferring essence on matter, defining the resulting substance, and locating it in its class or species. . . . Furthermore, the substantial form yields the sensible and insensible qualities (*qualitates*) possessed by the substance in question and is the immediate cause of the phenomena that are characteristic of it."

to be the whole substance of the thing was first earth, then water, grass, and horse, disposed in one way and then another. These claims are extremely obscure and dangerous, however, for in the same way a donkey was a stone, and a stone has always existed, and no horse or human   9 being has ever been generated, although matter has been made a human being or a horse. These things have been sufficiently condemned by Aristotle and others, and in no way would I want to assent to them. (ibid.)   12

Here corpuscularianism, in its ancient manifestation, is not understood as denying the synchronic individuation of material substances; one human being would be distinct from another, Buridan allows, in virtue of being composed of different matter (lines 2–3). What the corpuscularian theory cannot account for is diachronic distinctions between substances; it has no way of explaining why a sequence of material changes running through earth–water–grass–horse consists in various substances coming into and going out of existence. Such apparent cases of generation are in fact merely changes in how matter is disposed. Buridan labels the view "obscure and dangerous" (line 8), and thinks it unnecessary to say anything more against it (see also §28.2).

A fuller statement of the case in favor of substantial form appears a few years later in Marsilius of Inghen's *Generation and Corruption* commentary (prob. 1360s). Marsilius takes up the question of whether there is any need for a mixed body to have a substantial form that is something more than the four elements and their primary qualities, mixed according to a certain proportion. The first in his series of seven arguments for the affirmative makes a point much like Buridan's, that without substantial form the distinction between alteration and generation collapses. But whereas Buridan imagines the opponent of substantial form eliminating generation entirely, and treating all change as mere alteration, Marsilius supposes to the contrary that "if in the mixed body there is no other form beyond the forms of the elements, it would follow that alteration would be generation" (I.22 concl. 3). This is to say, in effect, that with no further resources beyond the elements and their qualities, any case of alteration might be counted as a case of generation. This is the opposite of the result Buridan describes, but really these are two sides of the same coin. For if the distinction between alteration and generation collapses, one could say either that all alteration is generation, or that no alteration is generation. Either substances never endure through change, but instead always become something new, or they always endure through change, and never become something new. The plausible middle ground that respects our intuitions about the individuation of material objects cannot hold. That sort of principled distinction between generation and alteration requires substantial form. Or so the scholastics argue.

As the distinction between generation and alteration goes, so go familiar distinctions between species. If *no* change is generation, then there is never a change great enough to count as a change in species. Water–grass–horse all counts as a thing of the same kind. If, in contrast, *all* change is generation, then any change to a substance, however minor, counts as a change in the species of that substance. Either there are no differences in species, then, or there are differences everywhere, at every instant. Either result is absurd. This, in effect, is Marsilius's fourth argument. Since grass and horse would be distinct only in virtue of different elemental mixtures, there would be no basis for treating them as substantially as opposed to merely numerically distinct. The obvious response is to account for specific differences in terms of the different elemental mixtures themselves: one sort of mixture yielding grass, and another yielding horse. Marsilius considers and rejects this:

Nor does it help to say that they are of distinct most specific species because of the distinct disposition of the proportions in their elemental qualities. For they are not said to differ in species through the distinct proportion and disposition in their material qualities. For if the whole substance of these mixed bodies were the elements, without any new form added on, then it would follow that their elements would not differ in species, and [so] neither would the mixed bodies that are those elements differ in virtue of their distinct qualitative dispositions or proportions. (ibid.)

There is no real argument here, just a confident assertion. Marsilius is convinced that a bare difference in how the elements and their qualities mix cannot account for specific difference, but only for the sorts of accidental differences in secondary qualities considered in previous chapters. Perhaps he thinks it enough simply to say this; perhaps he could not imagine that any reader would seriously question the need for a further substantial form. It would, indeed, take nearly 300 years for these claims to become seriously controversial among philosophers.

If we fast-forward some 200 years, to Domingo de Soto's widely read *Physics* commentary (1551), we can see the dialectic taking shape a bit more clearly. De Soto devotes an entire question to the issue of whether there are substantial forms (I.10), and offers three arguments in their favor. The first is a quick and unilluminating version of the argument that substantial form is required for specific differences. The second argues that since human beings have a substantial form, the rational soul, we should hold that all material substances have a substantial form. This too is not very helpful for our purposes: as we will see (§25.6), seventeenth-century critics would often accept that the rational soul is in some sense a substantial form, but refuse to generalize from that one case.[6] De Soto's third argument, however, is illuminating:

The conclusion is proved thirdly from substantial generation, in which some subject must necessarily be presupposed, or otherwise it would not be distinguished from creation, which is the production of a being entirely *ex nihilo*. But this form is in no way presupposed in substantial   3
generation, or at least is not presupposed as united to matter or identified with it—otherwise nothing would be made through substantial generation. Therefore beyond the matter that is the subject, which *is* presupposed by generation, there has to be given a substantial form. (ibid.)   6

De Soto begins (lines 1–3) by invoking prime matter, which must endure through all change, even substantial (§2.2). Clearly, substantial change must involve more than the endurance of prime matter; otherwise, as De Soto remarks (line 5), "nothing would be made through substantial generation." Hence something has to be added to the enduring prime matter, something that explains why that matter is now one kind of substance, whereas before it was another. This just is substantial form.

The argument is useful to consider because it is one that later corpuscularians would have to take seriously, since they all accept the picture of prime matter that it

---

[6] Suárez's mammoth discussion of substantial form puts particular weight on the same sort of strategy found in De Soto, that of arguing for substantial form in the case of the rational soul, and then generalizing the point to encompass all material substances. See *Disp. meta.* 15.1.

presupposes. One way to react to the argument would be steadfastly to deny that anything new is produced by substantial generation: there were corpuscles before, and there are the very same corpuscles now, appearing in a different guise, differently ordered, but with nothing new having been produced. To this De Soto would seem well within his rights to respond just as we saw Buridan respond earlier, by insisting that the result would be the complete elimination of substantial change. For if so-called substantial changes are nothing more than a rearrangement of corpuscles, it is hard to see what basis there would be for distinguishing between these changes and mere alteration. Consequently, it would be hard to see how we might maintain our familiar species classifications, or ever suppose that things come into or go out of existence. This is a consequence—as we will see in Chapter 28—that some post-scholastic authors found tempting. The price, however, seems extraordinarily high, and so it is natural to want to reply to De Soto's argument by granting that something new comes into existence when a substance is generated, but that this is not a substantial form. With this we return to Marsilius's fourth argument, above, and the notion that the disposition of the elements might explain substantial change and species classifications. In the present context, though, we can see the makings of a dilemma for the corpuscularian. For it seems that either this disposition is something real or it is not. If it is not, then De Soto's argument has not been answered, because it would still look as if "nothing would be made through substantial generation" (line 5), which suggests that there is no generation after all, and so no coming into or going out of existence, and so no differences between species. We would be paying the high price after all. If, instead, that disposition is something real, then it is not clear how it differs from a substantial form. It would, at any rate, apparently, be doing everything that a substantial form does.

Arguments such as these attempt to defend the doctrine of substantial form by invoking it to explain facts about diachronic identity. As we will see in Chapter 29, scholastic views in this area vary more widely than this brief sketch suggests. Even so, the standard scholastic assumption was that a material substance remains the same substance for as long as it has the same substantial form; if it changes—as it of course will, being material—those changes will be accidental to it. A material substance goes out of existence when its substantial form ceases to exist. Eliminate substantial form and the result will be either constant substantial change, or no substantial change.

A second and equally prominent line of argument for substantial form appeals to facts about synchronic identity: what makes it the case, at any given time, that one collection of matter makes one thing, whereas another collection makes another? It is notable that Buridan, in the first passage quoted in this section, lets the ancient atomists off the hook in this regard, allowing them the difference between one human being and another. Even so, such differences are highly problematic for corpuscularians. If all there are are corpuscles of various shapes and sizes, variously arranged, it is not easy to see how we might draw the boundary lines, at any given moment, between one substance and another. Scholastic authors appeal to substantial form to explain such facts. The sixth of Marsilius's arguments for substantial form, for instance, runs as follows:

Sixth, no mixed body would be one. The consequent is false, and the inference holds because there will be four elements so proportioned, and they will not be some further one thing. (*In Gen. et cor.* I.22)

This is supposed to be so obvious as to need no further explanation. For if a body is simply "four elements so proportioned," then what makes it one thing rather than a collection of uncountably many particles coming in four basic kinds? We would have no basis for regarding the parts of a tree as parts of a single substance, and no basis for regarding an individual tree as a single substance, rather than as part of a larger substance such as the whole forest, or indeed the whole material universe.[7]

A more systematic account of substantial form's unifying role can be found in the Coimbran *Physics* commentary (1592), which, in the course of considering whether substantial form and matter yield one thing, distinguishes five degrees of unity:

To do justice to the question at issue, it should initially be noted that there are five classes of unity relevant here, and from these modes of unity there are equally many ways in which something is said to be one.   3

- The first is the unity of aggregation, as with a heap of stones.
- The second is the unity of order, as with an army. This is greater than the first, since things that have order are more united than a disordered, jumbled confusion.   6
- The third is unity *per accidens*, as with an accident and the subject in which it inheres. This is greater than the second, since in the case of the second none of the things ordered dwells in another.   9
- The fourth is the *per se* unity of composite things, which results from the composition of parts that are collected in some third nature. This is seen in the case of a two-palm quantity, which is composed from two palm-length bodies joined with each another by   12 one and the same common terminus. This unity is greater than the third, since *per se* unity renders a thing absolutely (*absolute*) one, whereas unity *per accidens* renders a thing one only qualifiedly and in a certain respect (*cum adiectione et secundum quid*).   15
- The fifth is the *per se* unity of simple things and of substances free from mixture with matter. This unity is far superior to the others, since it is lies outside all composition of really discrete parts. (I.9.11.2)   18

The first three classes count as cases of unity only in a derivative sense. Things so unified are not genuinely one thing at all, but instead many things that can be said to be unified only inasmuch as they bear some special relationship to each other, whether that be (1) aggregation; (2) order; or (3) inherence. It is only with the fourth class that we arrive at unity in the proper sense, unity that is "absolute" (line 14) rather than derivative. The fifth class involves an even greater degree of unity, since here there are no real parts at all. (On the distinction between unity *per se* and *per accidens*, see §25.5. On inherence, see Ch. 11. On the *per accidens* unity of subject and accident, see §6.1.)

Substantial form yields unity of the fourth kind. The example offered in the above passage is intentionally somewhat crude: the Coimbrans here imagine a unity that results from two one-palm ($\approx$ 9-inch) bodies being in contact at a single point or surface (lines 11–13). This should not be understood as implying that two bodies can become a

---

[7] Marsilius's taxonomy of degrees of unity builds on a similar but less developed account in Albert of Saxony, *In Gen. et cor.* I.19. For a much later attempt to set out different kinds of unity, see Burgersdijk, *Inst. meta.* I.14 and I.22.

per se unity simply by touching; if that were true, then a heap might be a *per se* unity. The example seeks only to describe what intuitively would seem to be a material substance, without yet introducing substantial form. Once these five classes of unity are set out, however, the commentary immediately introduces substantial form as that which explains this unity of the fourth kind:

Something is said to be one, then, on the basis of these five different kinds of unity. So when we consider in the question whether one thing comes about from matter and form, 'one' should be understood in the fourth way described. Our conclusion is that from matter and substantial   3 form something *per se* one comes about. This is established by Aristotle [and various other authorities]..., and its truth is grasped from the fact that from the nexus of form and matter a natural composite results: a human being, fire, a heavenly body, and others of this sort, each one   6 of which is something whole that is *per se* one. (ibid.)

The union of matter and substantial form fits the profile of the fourth class of unity, because it is a case where two things—matter and substantial form—come together "in some third nature" (line 11 of the earlier passage), a "natural composite" (line 6 here). To say that this is a case of "absolute unity" is to say that the resulting "third nature" is a genuine thing, a substance rather than a mere aggregate. We get that result here not because there is something specially intimate about the inherence relationship between a form and its subject. If that were the story, then the third class of unity would also count as absolute, and the thick substance (the substance with its accidents [§6.1]) would count as a *per se* unity. It is rather the special feature of substantial form that accounts for this unity. A material substance, despite its convoluted welter of integral parts, counts as one thing in an absolute sense, one thing *per se*, because of the role substantial form plays in unifying that substance. The Coimbrans do not here explain what that role is, nor do they give any argument for supposing that substantial form plays that role, beyond citing various examples where substantial form and prime matter allegedly make something *per se unum* (lines 5–7). Just how substantial form manages to do this is what we must consider next.

24.3. Two Aspects of Substantial Form

The upshot of the previous section is that substantial forms play a crucial role in explaining the individuation of substances both over time and at a time, accounting for both substantial change and substantial unity. These are hardly surprising conclusions to reach, and certainly seventeenth-century authors were well aware of the theory's purported role in these domains. Indeed, some of the very most radical and innovative ideas of the post-scholastic era arise from an attempt to deal with such issues in a corpuscularian framework, without appealing to substantial form. Subsequent chapters will consider the various crises that arose in the seventeenth century over how, in the absence of substantial form, to explain the unity of bodies (Chs. 25–6), the reality of natural kinds (Ch. 27), and their persistence through time (Chs. 28–30).

It is not enough, however, simply to know *that* substantial form was supposed to play these various explanatory roles. A real understanding of the scholastic perspective, as well as that of its later critics, requires understanding *how* such forms were supposed to play this role. Without that, we would be left with a theory that works simply by metaphysical fiat: to account for various intuitions about what counts as substantial rather than accidental change, and what counts as genuine rather than derivative unity, we would simply postulate a thing-we-know-not-what, which as pious Aristotelians we might call a "form," and which marks off a thing as an enduring, unified substance. Criticisms along these lines led post-scholastic authors to dismiss substantial forms as hopelessly obscure, and §§27.2–3 will consider the extent to which such criticisms are valid. But even if there is undoubtedly some amount of obscurity in the scholastic doctrine, still there is much more to be said about how the theory is supposed to work, beyond simply postulating substantial forms as brute substance-makers.

The crucial first step toward a more robust account is to distinguish between two aspects of the theory, metaphysical and physical. Conceived metaphysically, forms are abstract entities. They account for the metaphysical structure of the world by being that in virtue of which it is true that this cluster of matter constitutes a genuine substance whereas another cluster is merely a heap, or that in virtue of which a substance continues to exist today and tomorrow but on Friday ceases to exist. Such metaphysical entities exercise no causal powers in the modern sense of 'cause,' but they explain the way the world is, and are the special province of the philosopher to investigate. The physical aspect of substantial form is causal in the modern sense. So conceived, forms are concrete rather than abstract; they play a causal role in the world in very much the way that motion or the four elemental qualities allegedly do. The physicist, just as much as the philosopher, must understand forms so conceived, because otherwise one could not come to a complete understanding of the forces at work in nature.

I refer to these as different "aspects" of form because I want to leave open the possibility that one might think of substantial forms in either way, or perhaps even think of them in both ways at once. Aristotle himself perhaps furnishes an example of this last kind. Although Aristotle's conception of form is notoriously open-ended, it is clear that he wanted formal explanations to hold at a higher level of abstraction than that of material or efficient causes. This is particularly striking in those passages that suggest the form of a substance just is its function. Aristotle remarks, for instance, that "if the eye were an animal, *sight* would be its soul" (*De an.* II.1, 412b18). Elsewhere, the form of a house is being "a covering for bodies and chattels" (*Meta.* VIII.2, 1043a16). In general, he holds that "what a thing is is always determined by its function: a thing really is itself when it can perform its function; an eye, for instance, when it can see" (*Meteor.* IV.12, 390a10–11). This suggests an abstract, metaphysical conception of form, according to which a cluster of matter counts as a substance in virtue of having the capacity to perform a certain function. Thus living things count as the substance they are in virtue of possessing the functions we associate with life, and houses are houses in virtue of having the function of giving shelter. The capacity to perform such a function would not be a *sign* that the thing possesses a certain substantial form; the function would instead *be* the form. Yet although this sort of metaphysical conception of form might be said to dominate Aristotle's more metaphysical writings, still there are places in Aristotle where the concrete, physical aspect of form seems paramount. This is particularly apparent in his biological writings, where the form of a thing often seems to play a straightforwardly causal role, explaining both behavior and the physical structure of an animal's body. In the *De anima*, for instance, to take a particularly straightforward example, the soul is the efficient cause of motion (e.g., *De an.* II.4, 415b8–28).

One might well wonder how, for Aristotle, the soul can be conceived of both as a function and as the efficient cause of the body's motion. In general, it is not at all obvious how forms can be viewed both as abstract metaphysical principles and as concrete causal agents. It is not my project here to understand Aristotle, but I will venture to say that no interpretive issue is more fundamental to the study of Aristotle than the question of how these two aspects of form are to be understood. Clearly, the usual modern reading of the Aristotelian doctrine is a metaphysical reading: to highlight the physical aspect of the theory threatens to wed the hylomorphic scheme to a set of empirical theses subject to disconfirmation by research into biology and chemistry. Too little attention has been paid, however, to the scholarly question of whether this metaphysical reading of form gets Aristotle's theory right.

Analogous questions arise for scholastic authors, where again we can see the doctrine of substantial form as having two aspects. Whereas Aristotle's writings have the potential to be taken in either direction, the scholastic conception of form increasingly tilts toward the physical. This claim will perhaps seem surprising in light of the previous section, where we saw substantial form being put to such wholly metaphysical purposes. It is one thing, however, to show that substantial form does metaphysical work, and another to show that it fills that role as an abstract, metaphysical principle. As the scholastic era advances, the physical aspect of substantial form becomes increasingly dominant: substantial forms explain a substance's unity and persistence, but they do so by playing a specific causal role within a substance, rather than by serving as an abstract metaphysical principle. The consequence of this approach is to open the door to corpuscularianism. For when substantial forms are so understood, the theory stands or falls with the alleged failure of any reductive account of the alleged causal role. If the physical phenomena associated with persistence and unity can be explained mechanistically, substantial forms become unnecessary. This should feel like a familiar story, because it is very much the same story I have told regarding accidental forms (§6.1, §10.5, etc.). In all of these domains, Aristotelian hylomorphism might have been given a more strictly metaphysical reading, with forms understood as abstract properties. Instead, the scholastics turned toward the concretely physical, appealing to forms as causes in natural processes, and treating the irreducibility of their role in that domain as the critical test for ontological commitment. Let us turn, then, to the physical aspect of substantial form.[8]

---

[8] Aristotle scholars vary widely in how they think about form, and do so along so many dimensions that it is hard to track the range of possibilities. For the abstract, metaphysical, see e.g. Irwin, "Metaphysical and Psychological Basis" p. 38: "A natural substance's form is its characteristic function rather than its structure or composition, which are features of its matter." Compare D. C. Williams, who remarks of the Aristotelian link between form and function that "no ties in the system are flimsier than this" ("Form and Matter" p. 309). The concrete, physical aspect of Aristotle's views is brought out nicely by Cooper, "Metaphysics in Aristotle's Embryology" p. 37: "But [the form of an animal] is directly responsible not only for its having all the tissues, organs and limbs essential to a human being, but also for many individual features of the way these are found constituted and arranged in that particular animal. Roughly, these will be all those features that, as Aristotle thinks, cannot successfully be explained as due either to environmental influences or to incidental properties of the matter that goes to constitute and sustain them" (p. 37).

If we think of souls as the paradigmatic substantial forms, then it is especially natural to think of them as being or having causal powers. See, for instance, Shields, "Aristotle's Psychology," supplement 2, which stresses the role of soul as the source of perception and thought, and as an efficient cause of motion (e.g., De an. II.4, 415b8–28). On essence in general as the cause of a substance's properties, see, e.g., De an. I.1, 402b17–25 and Gen. an. V.1, 778a29–b6.

24.4. The Physical Aspect

The strategy of metaphysical fiat responds to philosophical perplexity by invoking entities to account, in brute fashion, for whatever it is that puzzles us. Scotistic haecceities are an unabashed instance of this strategy. In response to puzzles over the individuation of qualitatively alike particulars, Scotus takes the view that nothing could serve to explain their distinctness other than a primitive difference-making feature, a thisness or haecceity. Substantial forms are today often viewed in a similar light, as obscure and nearly magical entities that play their various metaphysical roles by fiat, whose positing adds nothing to our understanding of the material world.[9] This is, however, a complete misunderstanding of the scholastic doctrine. Although it is true that scholastic authors did not take themselves to understand the particulars of any specific substantial form (§27.2), they did have a very clear general story to tell. According to this story, which was almost universally accepted in broad outlines by scholastic authors, substantial forms are something like an internal efficient cause that sustains and regulates the existence of a substance. Far from being a brute metaphysical posit, such forms in fact make a well-defined empirical assertion about the causal

Kenny has identified a "tension" in Aquinas much like the one I describe here between "two different ways of understanding the notion of form," either abstractly, as a formal cause, or as an agent, an efficient cause. He regards the two notions as "impossible to combine, without confusion, into a single notion" (*Aquinas on Mind* p. 149). Along similar lines, Bernard Williams talks of hylomorphism's "wobbling between two options," one adjectival and the other substantival ("Hylomorphism" p. 197). For reflections on these criticisms, see Gordon Barnes, "Paradoxes."

Alexander too has something like my idea about the distinction between physical and metaphysical readings of formal explanation: "The natural philosopher is concerned with *causal* explanation and the concept of real qualities is regarded by the schoolmen as a causal concept but Aristotle's use of forms in analysing change is not causal. Thus I believe that Boyle's fundamental criticism is that what for Aristotle was merely a logical analysis of change leading to the metaphysical assertion of prime matter and 'substantial' forms was mistakenly interpreted as providing the pattern for the explanation of particular natural phenomena" (*Ideas, Qualities* p. 51). I would say, however, that Boyle is equally scornful of a metaphysical interpretation of Aristotelianism (§23.2).

Maier argues for a more metaphysical understanding of the role of substantial form, on the grounds that the causal story occurs at the level of the elemental qualities: "Die Kausalerklärung aus formae subtantiales, die man der Scholastik später so zum Vorwurf gemacht hat, ist also richtig zu verstehen, und ist, richtig verstanden, gar nicht so abwegig, wie es zunächst scheint.... Das weitere Suchen nach dahinterstehenden Finalursachen einer-, substantialen Formen ander-erseits gehört in die Metaphysik und ist ein Problem anderer Art" (*Vorläufer Galileis* p. 57 [tr. Sargent p. 45]). This may be so in some cases, but I believe the overall trajectory of the scholastic debate runs toward finding a causal role for the substantial form to play. For a more recent restatement of Maier's view, see Miles, "Descartes' Mechanism." He contends that the theory of substantial form, e.g. of a stone, "belongs to the metaphysical account of why a certain compositum *is* a stone, not to the physical or dynamical explanation of any occurrence in nature" (p. 109).

Fitzpatrick suggests that the success of the mechanistic philosophy led scholastic authors to conceive of their theories in more physical terms: "Tradition, I suggest, was encouraged by what else was going on to treat its inherited distinctions as if they, too, were a kind of mechanism" ("Medieval Philosophy" p. 314). I agree on the trend, but claim that scholastics were headed in this direction well before the mechanical philosophy came into vogue.

Kit Fine, the leading modern proponent of a metaphysical hylomorphism, recognizes and then quickly sets to one side the physical aspect of the theory: "Aristotle seems to have a possible basis for the belief [in individual forms], namely that forms are real and active principles in the world, which is denied to any right-minded modern" ("Puzzle concerning Matter and Form" p. 19).

[9]   A good example of the modern dismissal of substantial form as obscurely magical is Balme, "Aristotle's Biology" p. 306: "The extraordinary later misinterpretations of Aristotle, the magical entelechies and real specific forms, must be largely due to these imported concepts—Species, Essentia, Substantia—which presided like three witches over his rebirth in the Middle Ages, but should be banished to haunt the neoplatonism from which they came." In fact, this gets the situation precisely backwards. If anyone treats form in an abstractly metaphysical way, it is Aristotle. It is the scholastics who tend to conceive of forms in highly naturalistic and empirical ways, along just the sorts of lines that Balme himself extols.

For Scotus's haecceities, see King, "Problem of Individuation."

structure of material objects, postulating that all and only substances are held together in a tight causal structure, with one form—the substantial form—producing and sustaining the various accidental forms that give a substance its particular appearances and qualities.

Descriptions of this internal causal story go back at least to Avicenna. He claims that "among accidents, there are some that occur from without and some that occur from the substance of the thing." As examples of the latter, Avicenna offers skin color, height, and the disposition to be hopeful or cheerful (*Naturalia* I.1.6, p. 61). By the middle of the thirteenth century, Latin authors were routinely ascribing this sort of role to substantial form. According to Albert the Great, "there is no reason why the matter in any natural thing should be stable in its nature, if it is not completed by a substantial form. But we see that silver is stable, and tin, and likewise other metals. Therefore they will seem to be perfected by substantial forms" (*De mineralibus* III.1.7 [tr. Wyckoff p. 173]). To be "stable in its nature" is for a thing to have a constant set of properties that are characteristic of that thing. The substantial form is not that set, but something further that explains their enduring presence. Aquinas regularly describes substantial form in a similar way. In his early treatise *De ente et essentia*, he remarks that "substance . . . must be the cause of its accidents" (ch. 6, lines 54–7), and uses one of Avicenna's examples: the black skin of an Ethiopian. More generally, Aquinas later writes that "all accidents are certain forms added onto the substance, caused by the principles of the substance" (*Summa contra gent.* IV.14.3508), where those "principles" are substantial form and matter.[10] Henry of Ghent distinguishes between two roles played by substantial form: first, to give existence to the whole composite substance (§24.1) and second to give the composite its distinctive operation, "diffusing through it its power to manifest a certain effect" (*Quod.* IV.13; f. 104v). Ockham later gives a specific example of this sort of causal role: "it is clear to the senses that hot water, if left to its own nature, reverts to coldness; this coldness cannot be caused by anything other than the substantial form of the water" (*Quod.* III.6). Later in the fourteenth century, Buridan remarks that "substantial forms, rather than the accidents conjoined to them, are the principal active principles in the changes and rests to which the forms are suited" (*In Phys.* II.5, f. 33rb). He illustrates the causal role played by the substantial form as follows: "When, in someone with a fever, the heat exceeds its correct proportion to other qualities, it is not apparent how it would be reduced to its [correct] state unless the soul were to reduce it" (ibid.). Of Marsilius of Inghen's seven arguments for substantial form (§24.2), four concern concrete physical effects that the form has on a mixed body.

Later scholastic authors, increasingly aware of the theory's vulnerability, develop this causal framework in considerable detail, as the principal argument in favor of substantial form. Near the end of what must be the most detailed treatment of the topic ever attempted, Suárez writes that "the most powerful arguments establishing substantial forms are based on the necessity, for the perfect constitution of a natural being, that all the faculties and operations of that being are rooted in one essential principle" (*Disp.*

---

[10] For further discussion of Aquinas's use of substantial form to explain a substance's accidental properties, see Wippel, *Metaphysical Thought of Thomas*, pp. 266–75, as well as my "Form, Substance, and Mechanism." Further particularly clear texts are *Quaest. de veritate* 2.7c, *Quaest. de virt. comm.* 3c, *De occultis* (ed. Leonine 43:184ab), and *In De sensu* ch. 15 (ed. Leonine 45.2, lines 229–31).

meta. 15.10.64). Suárez refers the reader back to an earlier discussion, where he had argued:

The aggregation of multiple faculties or accidental forms in a simple substantial subject is not enough for the constitution of a natural thing.... A form is required that, as it were, rules over all those faculties and accidents, and is the source of all actions and natural motions of such a being, and in which the whole variety of accidents and powers has its root and unity. (15.1.7)

A theory of material substances, as unified entities both at a time and over time, is here made to depend on something that, rather than lying beneath these attributes, "rules over" them, supplying the unity necessary for a genuine substance. Metaphysical claims are thus grounded in recognizably physical, empirical theses about what explains a substance's sensible qualities and operations. Suárez's most detailed set of arguments for this conclusion rests on the way that substances have natural states to which they gravitate: water, for instance, is naturally cold, and eventually reverts to that state even after being heated. What is the cause of this? It must be an internal principle, Suárez argues, and can be nothing other than a substantial form (15.1.8). (This is the same example that Ockham had used before, and that Boyle would attack in the seventeenth century [*Works* V:345–6; Stewart pp. 59–61].) The governing assumption behind the example is that substantial forms play a concrete, causal role in regulating the accidental properties of substances.[11]

The Coimbran commentators take much the same line. They describe how "certain proper and peculiar functions apply to individual natural things: reasoning to a human being, whinnying to a horse, heating to fire, and so on in other cases" (*In Phys.* I.9.9.2). This is obviously not a list of essential properties in the Aristotelian sense—no one would suppose that whinnying is what makes a horse be a horse. But still "the origin of such accidents must be ascribed to the substantial form, as to their source" (ibid.). Summarizing their view about the role of such forms, they write,

In all it cannot be denied that, for each and every natural thing, there is a substantial form, by which it is established, through which its degrees of excellence and perfection among physical composites is selected, on which every propagation of things depends, from which its aspect and character is stamped on each thing, which undertakes whatever task there is in nature given its power, which elicits all actions both of life and of all other functions, to which support accidents come, as if instruments, and finally, which marvelously distinguishes and furnishes the theater of this admirable world in its variety and beauty. (ibid.)

This elaborate paean to the substantial form is simply the culmination of a view that was prevalent throughout the scholastic era.

In all these texts, the dominant conception of form is decidedly physical rather than metaphysical. Substantial forms are understood as causal agents that would figure

---

[11] For a beautifully clear account of Suárez's overall argument, see Shields, "Reality of Substantial Form." He sees a larger abstract/metaphysical component in Suárez's account than I leave room for. Also very helpful is Des Chene, *Physiologia* pp. 73–5. Kronen and Reedy's translation of Disputation 15 is worth consulting for its notes alone, even for readers who do not need the translation.

Suárez in fact seems to leave room for both of these conceptions of form—concrete and abstract—when he distinguishes between the *physical form*, which is his primary focus, the *metaphysical form*, which is the thing's essence and has no causal powers, and the *logical form*, which likewise lacks causal powers and is the *differentia* that actualizes the genus (*Disp. meta.* 15.11). Only the first, on his view, is a true form.

centrally in any complete scientific account of the natural world. They explain why water is cold, gold is heavy, why horses have four legs and human beings two, and why horses merely whinny whereas human beings talk. Given this conception of form, it is no wonder that some scholastic authors contemplated describing the substantial form as a kind of *efficient* cause. Henry of Ghent contends that "every subject through its form is the active and efficient cause of its proper accidents and likewise of its common accidents, together with the initial active causes that concur with it, disposing it for this in the way described above" (*Quod.* X.9 [*Opera* XIV:223]). Henry doesn't hesitate here to describe the substantial form as an efficient cause, treating it as the internal analogue to the traditional efficient cause that comes from without. Godfrey of Fontaines, a contemporary critic, took issue with that characterization, and insisted that only the initial external causes can be referred to as efficient causes (*Quod.* VIII.2). Dispute over the proper terminology wore on for centuries. But the point does seem to be wholly terminological, inasmuch as the later scholastic conception of substantial form came to have more and more in common with an Aristotelian efficient cause.[12]

Of course, the substantial form cannot be responsible for *all* of a substance's accidental properties. Some accidents, like the cut on my left knee, clearly have an external cause. So the theory requires a distinction—as in the passage from Avicenna quoted at the start of this section—between those accidents that are intrinsic, which is to say that they arise from the essence of the substance, and those accidents that are extrinsic, and so the product of external forces. Many intrinsic accidents, though caused by the substantial form and the matter it actualizes, are distinctive of a given individual, such as eye color, the shape of one's nose, and so forth. Because both form and matter vary from individual to individual, even within the same species, numerically distinct substantial forms of the same kind can give rise to accidental forms of very different kinds. The range of possible variation just is the range of variation within a species.

The causal role of substantial form makes for an important qualification to the causal primacy of the primary qualities (§21.2). Although scholastic authors treat the four elemental primary qualities as the proximate causal agents in nature, the agency of substantial form is more fundamental, since those primary qualities act only in virtue of the substantial forms that give rise to them. So although water exerts its influence through being wet and cold, or sometimes hot, it has these qualities in virtue of either its own substantial form, or else the heat of the fire that makes it hot, which heat is itself the product of the fire's substantial form. As Daniel Sennert summarizes the doctrine in his *Epitome naturalis scientiae* (1618),

The forms of natural bodies are not active and efficacious immediately, as God is; rather, they act through the mediation of accidents and qualities. Although the form is the principle of [a substance's] primary operations, the qualities are the immediate and proximate principle of those operations, albeit less principal, and merely instrumental. Forms use those qualities as instruments in acting, whereas the operation of the qualities is by virtue of the forms from which they flow. (I.6, p. 73; tr. *Thirteen Books* p. 29)

---

[12] On the question of whether substantial forms are efficient causes, see Wippel, *Metaphysical Thought of Godfrey* pp. 176–84. Suárez, *In De an.* 3.3.6 contends that the soul is the efficient cause of a living thing's accidents. For modern assertions that the relationship should be understood as efficient causation, see Brown, *Accidental Being* pp. 74–7; Reynolds, "Properties" pp. 289–90; Adams, "Sacrament of the Altar" p. 201.

So although the primary qualities are the proximate causal agents responsible for natural change, they are not the whole story. The mechanism of Descartes or Gassendi regards an account of the mechanical primary qualities—size, shape, motion, etc.—as sufficient for a complete account of the natural world: thus Descartes boldly asserts at the end of the *Principles* that, apart from minds, "there is nothing in all of nature whose character (*ratio*) cannot be deduced through these same principles"—that is, "the shape, size, position, and motion of particles of matter" (IV.187). The scholastics, in contrast, regard even their primary qualities as merely the superficial manifestations of a deeper causal structure. The essences of material objects—substantial forms inhering in matter—are not simply the abstract truth-makers for various conceptual demarcations that we make between one thing and another. Instead, substantial forms are the primary agents in the sublunary natural world. They both determine the superficial appearance of things, and account for a thing's unity and persistence. Facts about how the world is divided into substances, and about how those substances are sorted into kinds, facts about the identity conditions of a substance at a time and its persistence conditions through time—all of this is a consequence of the physical role that substantial forms play in making a certain chunk of matter take on one set of properties rather than another.[13]

The choice to focus on the physical rather than the metaphysical aspect of substantial form would have profound consequences for the subsequent history of philosophy. To treat form as a kind of internal efficient cause is to diminish the distinctness and autonomy of formal explanations. It is one of Aristotle's most cherished ideas that material and efficient causes must be supplemented by a further level of formal analysis. Scholastic authors might be said to be sliding back toward the materialism Aristotle sought to refute, as if they could not resist the temptation to ground formal explanation on material and efficient causes at a deeper level. In turn, as the scholastic conception of form grew increasingly remote from its metaphysical roots in Aristotle, it became at the same time increasingly naturalistic. Indeed, substantial forms might well be viewed as an early step in the development of scientific essentialism. By associating essences with a definite hypothesis about the causal interrelationships within a substance, the theory provides clear criteria for distinguishing between what would later be called real and nominal essences (Ch. 27). Although the scholastics were largely pessimistic about whether we can understand the details of any particular substantial form (§27.1), the theory provides no reason to be tempted by conventionalism regarding essences. If an entity is organized by the kind of causal structure we have been considering, then the internal basis of that causal structure can be identified as the form or essence. Without such a causal structure, there is only matter insufficiently unified to count as a

---

[13] Sennert's general view of substantial form gets set out in *Epitome* I.3. His account of the instrumental role of the primary qualities has its roots in earlier scholastic discussions. See, e.g., Aquinas, *Sent.* IV.12.1.2 n. 76: "in actionibus naturalibus formae substantiales non sunt immediatum et proximum actionis principium, sed agunt mediantibus qualitatibus activis et passivis, sicut propriis instrumentis. ..." See also Giles of Orleans, *In Gen. et cor.* II.2; Buridan, *In Phys.* II.5; Oresme, *In Gen. et cor.* II.1, II.12; De Soto, *In Phys.* II.11–12; Coimbrans, *In Gen. et cor.* I.4.8. And see Maier, *An der Grenze* pp. 12–13 (tr. Sargent p. 134). Cremonini's argument that the primary qualities of the elements are their substantial forms (§7.5) rests in part on the alleged absurdity of this double causality: the substantial form acting on the qualities, which then act on the world (*De formis elementorum* ch. 11).

substance. Thus the theory of substantial form comes out as a well-defined hypothesis about the structure of material beings.[14]

24.5. Doing without Form: Descartes

According to Domingo de Soto in 1551, "it is certain that a substantial form must be acknowledged that is receivable in matter and really distinct from that matter. This conclusion is common to all" (*In Phys.* I.10, p. 68b). Post-scholastic theories of form and substance grew up in the shadow of this distinctively scholastic consensus and, as §27.6 will discuss, they did not entirely cast it off. Within 100 years, however, the consensus that De Soto describes had vanished. The leading philosophers of the seventeenth century almost all reject substantial form. What they reject, specifically, is the physical aspect of the theory. Descartes remarks that substantial forms "were introduced by philosophers solely so that through them an account could be given of the proper actions of natural things, of which this form was the principle and base" (to Regius [1642]; III:506). Boyle likewise makes a lengthy attack on the view that there is "in every natural body such a thing as a substantial form, from which all its properties and qualities immediately flow" (*Origin* [*Works* v:351; Stewart p. 67]). And Hume would later report that "the Peripatetic philosophy . . . assigns to each of these species of objects a distinct substantial form, which it supposes to be the source of all those different qualities they possess, and to be a new foundation of simplicity and identity to each particular species" (*Treatise* I.4.3). It never seems to have occurred to most post-scholastic authors that substantial form might be something other than a scientific hypothesis about why, for instance, water is cold and fire is hot. When the theory is so understood, it becomes vulnerable to replacement by an adequate corpuscular account of the various qualities of bodies. In seeing the debate in these terms, they were simply following the scholastic doctrine as they knew it.

One finds substantial form under attack in various early seventeenth-century authors. Sebastian Basso's *Philosophia naturalis adversus Aristotelem* (1621) condemns the doctrine, and Etienne de Clave and his co-conspirators reject it as absurd in their notorious broadsheet (1624). William Pemble argues at length against substantial form in his *De formarum origine* (1629), as does Joachim Jungius in the ninth of his *Hamburg Disputations* (1633), as do Gerard and Arnold Boate in their *Philosophia naturalis*

---

[14] As is so often the case, Wyclif has idiosyncratic and interesting things to say about substantial form. In *De materia et forma* ch. 3 he seems to defend an understanding of substantial form that is, by scholastic standards, radically abstract, remarking that "non negabit sapiens logicam vel metaphysicam quin tale individuum sit essentialiter et per se et non accidentaliter aer vel ferrum vel planta vel aliud huiusmodi. Ex quo patet quod ipsum esse aerem, ferrum, etc., sit substantiale; et ista veritas est forma quam ponunt philosophi. Ergo talis forma substantialis est ponenda" (p. 179). I take this to be a way of saying that the substantial form is not an entity over and above the substance, but is the fact ("ista veritas") of a substance's being a thing of a certain kind. Having said this, Wyclif immediately seems to go on to reject a more concrete, substantial conception of form: "Et patet quanto philosophi moderni difficultent iuvenes incipientes philosophari, fingendo quod forma substantialis sit una res potens per se existere coniuncta cum materia, ex quibus coextensis fit unum, sicut ex tunica et furrura. Nam certum est quod omnes homines mundi non possunt talem formam convincere; sed convincere formam datam satis est. Periculum ideo est, cum ponere plura sine evidentia sit superfluum, ubi pauciora sufficiunt. Patet quanto degenerant a philosophia, qui tales formas ponunt" (pp. 179–80).

Another idiosyncratic view worth noting is that of Auriol, whose conception of substantial form is surprisingly deflationary in its insistence on ascribing to it a kind of halfway, indeterminate existence. For some brief remarks, see Ch. 3 note 6 and Ch. 11 note 18.

reformata (1641). The same arguments appear over and over: that the scholastics lack an account of how the substantial form is generated out of prime matter (§28.1); that the view makes a form into a substance (§26.1); and that, above all, substantial forms are superfluous. Basso's discussion is particularly remarkable in this last regard. He discusses in some detail the alleged physical role of substantial form as an internal governing cause, quoting the same passage of the Coimbran *Physics* commentary quoted in §24.4. But rather than attempt to replace this story with a reductive corpuscularian account, as later seventeenth-century authors customarily would do, Basso offers what is in effect a form of occasionalism, where instead of a single internal form regulating the whole substance, it is God who immediately directs the parts of material substances so as to bring about the regular natural phenomena that we experience around us.[15]

The great exception to this pattern is Leibniz, whose views on substantial form reflect precisely the sort of pattern I have been arguing for. Viewed according to their physical aspect, forms must be rejected:

The consideration of these forms serves no purpose in the details of physics and must not be used to explain particular phenomena. That is where the Scholastics failed, as did the physicians of the past who followed their example, believing that they could account for the properties of bodies by talking about forms and qualities without taking the trouble to examine their manner of operation. (*Discourse on Metaphysics* 10 [*Phil. Schriften* IV:434; tr. Ariew and Garber p. 42])

Yet this is not to say substantial forms should be rejected, because they are in fact crucial for metaphysics:

This misunderstanding and misuse of forms must not cause us to reject something whose knowledge is so necessary in metaphysics that, I hold, without it one cannot properly know the first principles or elevate our minds sufficiently well to the knowledge of incorporeal natures and the wonders of God. (ibid.)

There is no hope of doing justice here to Leibniz's complex and changing views, and so I merely gesture toward them as a landmark just beyond our horizon.[16]

A more manageable subject for present purposes is Descartes, the most influential early example of an author who rejects substantial form. His published writings adhere

---

[15]   De Clave, Bitaud, and Villon reject substantial form in the second of the fourteen theses in their broadsheet of 1624, notably on the grounds that without prime matter it becomes unncessary: "Formae item omnes substantiales (excepta rationali) non minus absurde defenduntur ab Aristotelicis quam materia, cum per eas intelligant substantias quasdam incompletas unum per se cum materia substantiale compositum constituentes: materia enim e naturali composito sublata, et formas saltem materiales tolli necesse est" (in Kahn, "Entre atomisme" p. 246; tr. Garber, "Defending Aristotle"). For more on the 1624 broadsheet, see §19.6.

Basso's discussion of substantial form occurs mainly in the three books of his *Philosophia naturalis* devoted to form (*De forma*, pp. 130–309). *De formis* III is especially important for Basso's form of occasionalism, e.g., at p. 267: "Quid quaerunt in rebus singulis singulas formas substantiales, cum una universalis causa per omnia extensa singulis sufficiat?" and pp. 247–8: "Nos probaverimus superius res cuiusque naturalis proprias illas actiones quibus certo in finem suum collimat ac pertingit non naturae singularis quae in ipsa sit motu atque impetu elici, sed esse causae illius universalis Dei inquam ipsius operationes, qui veluti artifex res ipsas tanquam instrumenta quasque movet agitque prout ipsarum patituir aptitudo." Basso's views in this regard are discussed in Lüthy, "Thoughts and Circumstances," and in Gregory, "Sébastien Basson." For a reading of Basso on which he looks to be an occasionalist as radical as Malebranche, see Nielsen, "Seventeenth-Century Physician."

[16]   There is a large and sophisticated literature on Leibniz's views regarding substantial form. Among much else, see Levey, "On Unity"; Mercer, "Aristotelianism at the Core"; Sleigh, *Leibniz and Arnauld* and, most recently, Garber, *Leibniz*.

to a disciplined stance in this regard: he does not positively reject substantial forms, or argue against them, but simply proceeds without them, hoping to show by example that they are unnecessary. When he does mention these and other scholastic doctrines, he proceeds cautiously, as in this passage from the *Meteorology* (1637):

But to keep the peace with the philosophers, I have no wish to deny whatever they may imagine in bodies over and above what I have described, such as their "substantial forms," their "real qualities," and the like. But it seems to me that my arguments will be all the more acceptable in so far as I can make them depend on fewer things. (Discourse 1, VI:239)

Descartes's most extensive and frank remarks come in a long letter from January 1642 advising his then-disciple Henricus Regius on how to deal with attacks on their shared views. Descartes suggests that Regius make this reply to his principal critic, Gisbertus Voetius:

I wholly agree with the view of the learned Rector that those "harmless entities" called substantial forms and real qualities should not be rashly expelled from their ancient territory. Indeed, up to now we have certainly not rejected them absolutely; we merely claim that we do   3 not need them in order to explain the causes of natural things. We think, moreover, that our arguments are to be commended especially on the ground that they do not in any way depend on uncertain and obscure assumptions of this sort. Now in such matters, saying that one does   6 not wish to make use of these entities is almost the same as saying one will not accept them. Indeed, they are accepted by others only because they are thought necessary to explain the causes of natural effects. So we will be ready enough to confess that we do wholly reject them.   9 (III:500)

Descartes goes on to suggest several arguments that Regius might make against substantial forms, but this passage illustrates the heart of his view: substantial forms are not needed, hence should not be made use of, hence are in effect rejected. It is clear that he understands the theory according to its physical aspect, remarking here that others embrace them "only because they are thought necessary to explain the causes of natural effects" (lines 8–9). When substantial forms are so conceived, the only question is whether a purely corpuscularian account is sufficient to explain these "natural effects."

On Descartes's austerely corpuscularian conception of material substances, particles of various shapes and sizes, variously positioned and moved in accured with the law of nature, explain everything in the material world. Accordingly, Descartes lacks any basis for a fundamental distinction between those bodies that count as substances and those that do not. (Indeed, I will argue in §28.5 that his options are so limited in this regard that he chooses not to offer a theory of material substance at all.) So whereas scholastic authors suppose that artificial forms (e.g., the form of a chair) are accidental rather than substantial, and so hold that artifacts as such are not substances, Descartes "recognizes no difference between artifacts and natural bodies" except that it is easier to see how artifacts work (*Principles* IV.203).[17] That Descartes recognizes nothing beyond

---

[17] For Descartes on artifacts, see *Principles* IV.203: "Atque ad hoc arte facta non parum me adjuverunt: nullum enim aliud, inter ipsa et corpora naturalia, discrimen agnosco, nisi quod arte factorum operationes, ut plurimum, peraguntur instrumentis adeo magnis, ut sensu facile percipi possint: hoc enim requiritur, ut ab hominibus fabricari queant." Later scholastic discussions of artifacts are extremely interesting but have received virtually no attention. There was no dispute that artifacts, as such, should not count as substances, but there was considerable dispute over whether one should postulate accidental forms to account for why a chair, say, is a chair. For a detailed statement of the reductive view see

corpuscular explanation in the case of non-living things is obvious enough. Thus, after rejecting the alleged primacy of the four elemental qualities, he adds:

Unless I am mistaken, not only these four qualities but all the others as well, and even all the forms of inanimate bodies, can be explained without the need to suppose any other thing (*chose*) in their matter other than the motion, size, shape, and arrangement of their parts. (*Le monde* ch. 5, XI:26)

The same is clearly true for animals, since Descartes denies that their operations require any sort of soul at all: "I have seen clearly that all the motions of animals can arise from corporeal and mechanical principles" (to More [1649], V:276). Even in the case of the human body, the body's states and operations admit of their own autonomous corpuscularian explanation. Thus he tells Regius that "when we consider the body alone we perceive nothing in it on account of which it desires to be united with the soul" (III:461)—thereby announcing the body's autonomy from the soul, and rejecting Aristotle's famous dictum that "what desires the form is matter, as the female desires the male and the ugly the beautiful" (*Phys.* 192a22–23).[18]

It is not so easy, however, to dismiss the idea that Descartes's mind might count as a substantial form. Various scholars (most prominently, in recent years, Paul Hoffman) have argued forcefully that Descartes's views are in fact closer to the scholastics than is ordinarily supposed. For whereas in general Descartes can dismiss substantial forms as superfluous, he cannot take that approach in the case of the rational soul, since he of course wants to retain the mind as an entity distinct from the body. Moreover, although he prefers the term 'mind,' he also frequently uses the term 'soul,' and on multiple occasions he refers to it even as a substantial form. In his correspondence with Regius, for instance, he writes that the soul is "the true substantial form of a human being" (III:505) and that "the human soul alone is recognized as a substantial form, whereas other forms arise from the configuration and motion of the parts" (III:503). So this aspect of Descartes's view requires more careful attention.[19]

Ockham, *In Phys.* II.1.4 and Dabillon, *Physique* I.1.3. For the countervailing realistic view, see Burley, *In Phys.* II (f. 37ra) and Oresme, *In Phys.* II.4. Aquinas's views, although not as sophisticated as later treatments, have as usual received the most attention. See, recently, Rota, "Substance and Artifact."

[18] An illuminating passage regarding the limited role that soul/mind plays for Descartes in the human body occurs in the Fourth Replies, responding to Arnauld's query about how a sheep can flee the wolf without having a soul to guide it. Descartes responds: "Plurimi vero ex motibus qui in nobis fiunt nullo pacto a mente dependent: tales sunt pulsus cordis, ciborum coctio, nutritio, respiratio dormientium atque etiam in vigilantibus ambulatio, cantio et similia, cum fiunt animo non advertente. . . . Cumque hoc in nobis ipsis pro certo experiamur, quid est quod tantopere miremur si lumen e lupi corpore in ovis oculos reflexum eandem habeat vim ad motum fugae in ipsa excitandum?" (VII:229–30). On the lack of souls in animals, see also *L'homme* XI:202, and letters from 1637 (I:414–15) and 1638 (II:40–1). For general discussions of Descartes and animals, see Cottingham, "Descartes' Treatment"; Hatfield, "Animals"; Morris, "Bêtes-machines."

[19] Descartes explains his preference for 'mens' rather than 'anima' in the Fifth Replies (VII:356): "Ego vero, animadvertens principium quo nutrimur toto genere distingui ab eo quo cogitamus, dixi *animae* nomen, cum pro utroque sumitur, esse aequivocum; atque ut specialiter sumatur pro actu primo sive praecipua hominis forma, intelligendum tantum esse de principio quo cogitamus, hocque nomine *mentis* ut plurimum appellavi ad vitandam aequivocationem."

Descartes characterizes the mind as the form of the body, or as informing the body, at X:411, VII:356, IV:168, IV:346, IV:373. The original Latin text of *Principles* IV.189 says that the soul "totum corpus informet," but the subsequent French translation has the soul's being "unie à tout le corps." Voss, "End of Anthropology," contains a useful cataloguing of these and other crucial texts relating to the mind–body problem. But given that these passages extend from the *Regulae* of 1628 to correspondence in 1646, there seems little reason to accept Voss's argument that this reflects a "brief period"

Certainly, the bare fact that Descartes describes the mind as the body's form shows nothing at all. The Fifth Lateran Council (1513) had reaffirmed the Council of Vienne (1312) in holding it heretical to deny that the soul is the form of the body (§20.2). For Descartes to contravene this dictate would have made him immediately vulnerable to charges of heresy. That is not to say that his remarks in this area were disingenuous. Beyond the usual reluctance we should have to reach such a conclusion (§20.5), the charge of disingenuity is especially inappropriate here, because it presupposes a robust meaning for 'form' that simply does not exist. On the contrary, as Descartes's contemporaries recognized, the notion of *form* is so broad as to be quite platitudinous. Thus Antoine Arnauld and Pierre Nicole ask in the Port-Royal Logic (1st ed. 1662): "who can doubt that all things are composed of matter and of a certain form of this matter?" (Second Discourse, p. 33). Later they issue a harsh denunciation of "a certain bizarre kind of substances called in the School 'substantial forms'" (III.19, p. 244), than which "nothing is more badly founded" (p. 245). Yet a few pages earlier they had embraced the general notion of form: "THE FORM is what renders a thing such and distinguishes it from others, whether it is a being really distinct from the matter, according to the opinion of the School, or whether it is only the arrangement of the parts" (III.18, p. 240). So if 'form' refers to some really distinct, irreducible being, present in all material substances, then it is bizarre and unacceptable. But if 'form' is simply a way of referring to the arrangement of the parts, then the term is unproblematic. This is a standard seventeenth-century usage, and can be clearly seen even in Descartes, as when he tells Regius that "a simple alteration does not change the form of the subject (e.g., heating in wood), whereas generation changes the form (e.g., setting it on fire)" (III:461).[20]

Yet even if this notion of 'form' explains some post-scholastic usages of the term, it does not quite explain how the *mind* can be the form of the body—neither for Descartes nor for most critics of scholasticism—since these authors do not want to say that the mind in any sense "arranges" the parts of the body. Still, even in the case of mind, the platitudes can be brought to bear. The passages in the previous paragraph agree that the form of a thing is linked to its being a thing of a certain kind. Whatever a form is,

---

of scholastic thinking in Descartes's career (p. 277). This makes too little of this language, by confining it to a two-year period, and also makes too much of it, by supposing that within that period Descartes was seriously under the influence of this scholastic scheme.

The case for Descartes's mind as a substantial form has been made by Hoffman in a series of papers, beginning with "Unity of Descartes's Man," then "Descartes's Watch Analogy," and finally "Union and Interaction." See also Rodis-Lewis, "Descartes and the Unity of the Human Being." For a thorough recent statement of the negative case see Rozemond, *Descartes's Dualism* ch. 5. See too Garber, *Descartes' Metaphysical Physics* pp. 103–11.

[20] Descartes himself refers to the Fifth Lateran Council in the Synopsis to the *Meditations* (VII:3). For the importance of this decree for understanding Descartes see Rozemond, *Descartes's Dualism* pp. 163–4.

On form in the seventeenth century, see Emerton, *Scientific Reinterpretation*, who remarks that "the opponents of scholasticism ... did not usually reject the concept of form as such, and in fact the denials of the form, however vehemently stated, were more apparent than real" (p. 60; see also p. 72). I might myself rather say that *appeals* to form were often more apparent than real. It all depends on whether one is tracking form in the narrower Aristotelian sense(s), or in the wide-open platitudinous sense with which Emerton grapples. The idea of form as platitudinous endures all the way to Kant, who situates it in the context of his own thought: "Materie und Form. Dieses sind zwei Begriffe, welche aller andern Reflexion zum Grunde gelegt werden, so sehr sind sie mit jedem Gebrauch des Verstandes unzertrennlich verbunden. Der erstere bedeutet das Bestimmbare überhaupt, der zweite dessen Bestimmung" (*Critique of Pure Reason*, A266/B322).

For useful general discussions on the post-scholastic rejection of form, see Ariew and Grene, "Cartesian Destiny"; Fitzpatrick, "Medieval Philosophy"; and Mercer, "Vitality."

according to the Port-Royal Logic, it is at least that which "renders a thing such and distinguishes it from others" (as above). According to Descartes, a thing counts as wood in virtue of its form; when it ceases to have that form (say, by being burned) it ceases to be wood. There is, then, at least this much genuine content to Descartes's claim that the mind is the form of the human body: the mind, when properly joined to such a body, makes the whole be a thing of a certain kind, a human being. (I return to the details of this union in §25.6.) This, however, is not enough to make the mind count as a substantial form, unless we are to render that doctrine trivial by insisting that anyone who believes objects fall into kinds counts as a believer in substantial forms in virtue of having *something* that accounts for kind membership.

So far as I can see, there are just two plausible reasons for thinking that Descartes treats the mind as a substantial form in some more robust sense. The first is that he embraces holenmerism: the doctrine that the mind exists as a whole in each part of the body. As we have seen in some detail in Chapter 16, this is a point of similarity with scholastic authors, and Descartes's motivation is much the same as the scholastic motivation, in that it offers a way to account for the mind's location without having to treat it as truly extended. It is in this spirit that Descartes alludes to holenmerism in the Sixth Meditation, offering it to explain "the great difference between the mind and the body" (VII:85–6). Yet we can hardly regard the mind's holenmeric existence as a reason to treat the mind as the body's form, since this is how *all* spiritual substances (that is, both God and the angels) were standardly said to be present to bodies. So if an angel can be present to our body holenmerically, and God can be present everywhere holenmerically, then holenmerism shows nothing about whether Descartes's mind is the substantial form of the body.[21]

The remaining basis for treating Descartes as seriously committed to a hylomorphic understanding of the mind–body composite is a letter to the Jesuit Denis Mesland in 1645. When we speak of the human body, Descartes tells Mesland, we are referring not to a determinate quantity of matter that endorsed only briefly, but to whatever matter is united with the soul of the person in question. "And so, even though that matter changes, and its quantity increases or decreases, we still believe that it is the same body—numerically the same—so long as it remains joined and substantially united with the same soul" (IV:166). This by itself suggests something interesting about Descartes's ontology: that it admits an enduring entity that is the human body, as the counterpart of the human mind. Passages such as this point toward substance dualism of the most straightforward sort, according to which human beings are a composite of two distinct substances, an enduring mind and an enduring body (§25.4). The passage also suggests something more: that the mind is what individuates the body, making the body exist only "so long" as the two are united. If Descartes is truly committed to this view, then his mind does play one very significant role—arguably the most significant role—played by scholastic substantial forms: that of accounting for the identity through time of the

---

[21] For holenmerism as a basis for treating Descartes's mind as a genuine substantial form, see Rodis-Lewis, "Descartes and the Unity of the Human Being" p. 206 and Hoffman, "Union and Interaction" pp. 392–3. It is worth noting that although Descartes evidently does hold that the soul exists throughout the body, he does not seem to think that it acts on each part of the body, as the scholastics suppose. Instead, it acts only on the pineal gland: "l'âme ne peut avoir en tout le corps aucun autre lieu que cette glande où elle exerce immediatement ses fonctions" (*Passions* I.32). This all by itself precludes the mind from playing the *causal* role of a substantial form.

composite and its parts (§24.2, §29.1). (Indeed, to anticipate the following chapter, Descartes's conception of a human being would be surprisingly close to Thomistic unitarianism, which likewise treats the body as incapable of existing apart from the soul.) Now, all by itself, the passage just quoted does not go so far. To say that the body remains in existence only "so long" as it remains joined to the mind is to postulate only a temporal correlation, leaving open the question of what accounts for the body's ceasing to exist. A substance dualist might think that the body endures only for as long as it is joined to the mind not because the mind individuates the body, but because it is simply a law (natural or supernatural) that, whenever there is a body of a certain appropriate kind (that is, of the human kind), there must be a mind attached to it. On this sort of view, the ongoing presence of a human mind joined to a body would be a *sign* that the same human body exists, but the mind would not be the *cause* of the body's ongoing existence. Mind would not individuate body. Yet as the letter to Mesland continues, it becomes clear that Descartes really does mean to say that the mind individuates the body. This seems the only natural construal of his claim that "our bodies are numerically the same only because (*à cause que*) they are informed by the same soul" (IV:167). He reiterates this in a later letter to Mesland: "It is quite true to say that I have the same body now that I had ten years ago, although the matter of which it is composed has changed, because the numerical identity of the body of a human being depends not on its matter, but on its form, which is the soul" (IV:346). In these passages the explanatory order is just what it should be, if the mind is playing the metaphysical role of a substantial form.[22]

If these remarks to Mesland represent Descartes's considered view of the mind–body relationship, then they give us good reason to regard Descartes's mind as very much like a scholastic substantial form. There are, however, strong reasons to be doubtful. First, they are not repeated elsewhere in Descartes's work, and in particular not in any of his published writings. Second, they come in a peculiar context: as part of an attempt to explain the Eucharist. The story Descartes offers Mesland about Christ's real presence in the host requires this particular story about the metaphysics of how mind individuates body. This certainly does not show that Descartes is being disingenuous, but it does provide a motive for why he might be expressing himself in ways that are liable to mislead, if not interpreted cautiously. Third, and most importantly, what Descartes says here directly contradicts what he says in other, published works. The Synopsis to the *Meditations*, for instance, draws a distinction much like that of the letter to Mesland between body conceived of in general, as *res extensa*, and the human body, with its distinctive character. But although the human body evidently endures through its union with the mind, it is not the mind that individuates it, but its distinctive physical character: "the human body, insofar as it differs from other bodies, is made up from nothing other than a certain configuration of its organs and limbs (*membrorum*), together with other such accidents. . . . It becomes a different body merely as a result

---

[22] The importance of the Mesland correspondence is stressed in Hoffman, "Unity of Descartes's Man." Chappell, "L'homme cartésien," has argued in reply that this correspondence "contains nothing specifically Aristotelian" (p. 417). Rozemond likewise remarks, with respect to the claim that the mind individuates the body, that "I don't see how it should commit a person to a genuine sense of hylomorphism" (*Descartes's Dualism* p. 163). This, as I argue in the main text, strikes me as the wrong reply to make.

of a change in the shape of some of its parts" (VII:14). This fits quite nicely with the letters to Mesland, except that it omits the crucial part about the mind individuating the body.

Other passages similarly preclude the mind from playing this role. In the Second Replies he repeats almost verbatim the Synopsis account of the human body as a product of its organs and limbs and other accidents, and then adds that "the death of the body depends solely on some division or change to its shape" (VII:153). These claims are made even more starkly later on in *The Passions of the Soul*, his last work published during his lifetime. Here he describes "a very serious error that many have fallen into, and that I regard as the primary cause of our failure up to now to give a satisfactory explanation of the passions and of everything else belonging to the soul."

The error consists in supposing that since all dead bodies are devoid of heat and movement, it is the absence of the soul that causes this cessation of movement and heat. Thus it has been believed, without reason, that our natural heat and all the movements of our bodies depend on the soul; whereas we ought to hold, on the contrary, that the soul takes its leave when we die only because this heat ceases and the organs that bring about bodily movement decay. (*Passions* I.5)

This much, all by itself, does not conflict with the letters to Mesland. What this passage shows—and what should be no surprise—is that Descartes rejects the physical aspect of substantial form. Compare, for instance, the typical scholastic account of Franciscus Toletus:

Every accident of a living thing, as well as all its organs and temperaments and its disposition are conserved by the soul. We see this from experience, since when that soul recedes, all [these] dissolve and become corrupted. (*In De an.* II.1.1, III:40ra)

Toletus is here arguing for precisely what Descartes denies: that a living thing needs a soul as something over and above its body to sustain its various properties and functions. Inasmuch as scholastic authors universally put this at the heart of their conception of substantial form (§§24.3–4), there can be no denying that Descartes is wholly rejecting one very prominent aspect of the scholastic theory. Even so, one might insist on a metaphysical role for the mind, as the body's form. Yet this seems to be precluded by the very next article, which elaborates on how to avoid the "serious error" described above: "So as to avoid this error, let us note that death never occurs through the absence of the soul, but only because one of the principal parts of the body decays" (*Passions* I.6). If Descartes were truly committed to the view he describes to Mesland, according to which the human body continues to exist *because* it is united to the soul, it is very hard to see how he could have written this. Moreover, the article continues to undermine even the relatively uncontroversial idea from the Mesland correspondence that the body's existence is *correlated* with its union with the soul. For he compares "the difference between the body of a living man and that of a dead man" to the difference between a watch that is working and "the same watch or machine" when it is broken. This is not what Descartes should say if he takes seriously his remarks to Mesland. If a watch stands to *working* as the human body stands to *being alive*, then a broken watch should not be "the same watch."

Perhaps there is some way to read all of these passages so as to make them consistent with the claim to Mesland that the mind individuates the body. Anyone who wants to engage the difficult issue of how Descartes understands substance must make a series of contested interpretive choices. To my mind, however, this is the first and easiest of such choices. The vast preponderance of evidence favors discounting those letters, and so regarding Descartes as an unqualified opponent of the doctrine of substantial form. The following four chapters will spell out further features of Descartes's theory of substance, as I understand it.

25

Unity and Dualism

25.1. The Plurality of Forms Debate

The existence of substantial forms was common ground among Aristotelians throughout our four centuries. Mandated by Church authority in the case of the human soul
(§20.2), the doctrine was extended universally to the case of other substances and so
might well be regarded, along with real qualities, as a defining feature of scholasticism.
As usual, however, one cannot go very far in describing scholastic views before such
common ground falls away, and one enters into disputed territory. In the present
domain, those disputes arise as soon as one asks just how many substantial forms a
single substance possesses. This was one of the first and fiercest philosophical disputes
to emerge during our period. And although modern commentators have often wondered at how such an abstruse question could be philosophically significant, we will see
that it raises quite deep metaphysical questions about the unity and continuity of
substances, and sheds light on what it means to be a dualist.[1]

The unitarian position—that a single substance has just a single substantial form,
informing prime matter—is associated above all with Thomas Aquinas. No one before
him—Greek, Islamic, Jewish, or Christian—had made such systematic use out of the
idea that a material substance just is a single substantial form inhering immediately in
prime matter. One reason the idea was controversial is that it seemed to yield much too
thin a notion of substance. Although it was standard to conceive of substances thinly, as
the *per se* unity itself, apart from its accidents (§6.1), unitarians were committed to the
surprising claim, as the Thomist Giles of Lessines puts it in his *De unitate formae* (1278),

---

[1] There is a large literature on the controversy over counting substantial forms. Callus, "Two Early Oxford Masters"
p. 411, remarks that "in the thirteenth century perhaps no other problem aroused such heated controversy as the
question of plurality of forms." See also Adams, *William Ockham* ch. 15; Bazán, "Pluralisme de formes"; Biard, "Diversité
des fonctions"; Callus, "The Origins of the Problem"; Cross, *Physics of Duns Scotus* ch. 4; Michael, "Descartes and
Gassendi"; Zavalloni, *Richard de Mediavilla*. Very different assessments have been made regarding which view was more
prevalent. According to Adams, "Aquinas's 'unitarian' contention . . . was definitely a minority report" (*William Ockham*,
II:647). Michael, in contrast, looking at the later scholastic era, holds that unitarianism is "by far the majority view"
("Descartes and Gassendi" p. 143). I have no idea how one would go about conducting an accurate census, given the vast
number of texts, most never read, but as far as I can see opinion was fairly evenly divided.

For doubts over the philosophical interest of the debate see Kenny, *Aquinas on Mind*: "It is not easy to know by what
arguments, or even by the practice of what discipline, we are to settle the question of how many substantial forms there
are in, say, a living dog" (p. 26). I myself made similar remarks in *Thomas Aquinas on Human Nature* pp. 126–30, a
discussion I now think did not go nearly deep enough.

that a substance "would be composed of nothing but bare matter and an ultimate form" (p. 10 n. 3). Giles responds to this worry by stressing just how much rich content that one ultimate substantial form brings to prime matter, but even so this struck pluralists as an incredibly austere conception of what a substance is.

If all that were at issue in this debate were the question of how to individuate forms, then the whole topic really would be forbiddingly obscure. One might conceive of a substance as having a single, richly comprehensive substantial form or as having a plurality of more specialized ones—it is hard to see how we might arbitrate such a dispute, or why we would care. In fact, however, what drove the dispute were more interesting and consequential disagreements over the persistence and unity of substances. Because of the unitarians' exceptionally thin conception of substance, they had no way of accounting for partial survival: on their account, when a substance comes into existence, every part of it comes into existence anew (other than its prime matter), and when it goes out of existence, every part of it goes out of existence (other than its prime matter). This means, for instance, as we will see in §25.3, that when an animal ceases to exist, not even its body remains. The animal's corpse is not its body, but instead one or more numerically distinct substances. This seems implausible, on its face, but unitarians contended that only their view can account for the special unity of substances. Scholastic pluralists therefore needed an account of what holds their thicker, complex substances together, and their difficulties in this regard foreshadow the similar difficulties that seventeenth-century authors would have in accounting for substances without any substantial forms at all.

Unitarianism might well be regarded as Aquinas's most distinctive and influential philosophical idea, but it is not wholly unprecedented. Earlier scholastic authors routinely debated whether the nutritive, sensory, and rational powers should be conceived of in terms of three souls or one, with Albert the Great among others very clearly insisting on the one-soul solution. Even before that, Averroes can be found maintaining that "it is impossible for a single subject to have more than one form" (De substantia orbis ch. 1 [Opera f. 3vK]). But although the unitarians upheld Averroes as their champion, so did the pluralists, and both had texts to which they could appeal. It is only when one arrives at Aquinas that one finds an explicitly comprehensive statement of the doctrine, such as this:

One must say, then, that a human being has no substantial form other than the intellective soul alone, and that just as it virtually contains the sensory and nutritive souls, so it virtually contains all lower forms, and that it alone brings about whatever it is that less perfect forms bring about in other things. And the same must be said for the sensory soul in brutes, and the nutritive soul in plants, and generally for all more perfect forms with respect to the less perfect. (Summa theol. 1a 76.4c)

Aquinas here presupposes the conception of substantial form described in the last chapter, according to which it is the fundamental internal explanation for all of a thing's intrinsic features. At every level of complexity, there is just one substantial form at work. The primary qualities of elemental Earth—Cold and Dry—are explained by the element's substantial form; the qualities of a homogeneous mixed body like gold are explained by the form that dictates how the four elements combine within that mixture; the complex structure of a heterogeneous body is explained by its unique substantial form. This pattern continues all the way up to the most complex of material substances, a human being, whose rational soul explains all of its intrinsic features, from its intellective capacities all the way down to the elemental qualities on which its corporeal features supervene. At each higher level of complexity, there is just a single substantial form, responsible for everything that would be accomplished by these subsidiary forms at a lower, less complex level. Thus the rational soul "virtually contains all lower forms" in the sense that "it alone brings about whatever it is that less perfect forms bring about in other things" (lines 2–4 above).[2]

Unitarianism was condemned at Oxford in 1277 and again in 1284 by successive archbishops of Canterbury—first the Dominican Robert Kilwardby and then the Franciscan John Pecham. (The doctrine did not figure in the more famous and much lengthier Condemnation of 1277 at Paris, but was discouraged there too, as we saw in §20.5.) The Dominican order subsequently rallied around the teachings of their master, even at some cost. When Richard Knapwell held a disputation defending the unitarian position, *circa* 1285, Pecham excommunicated him. The leading scholastic figures in the fifty years after Aquinas—Henry of Ghent, Scotus, and Ockham—lined up against Aquinas's position. Yet after Aquinas's canonization in 1323, unitarianism made a comeback. It was defended not just by "all the Thomists" (as Suárez puts it [*Disp. meta.* 15.10.61]), but also by innovative and influential figures like Gregory of Rimini, John Buridan, Marsilius of Inghen, and Peter of Ailly, and later by Suárez and other Jesuits. Lined up in favor of pluralism was an equally impressive list, including John of Jandun, Nicole Oresme, Paul of Venice, Agostino Nifo, and Jacob Zabarella.[3]

---

[2] Albert the Great defends the soul's unity at *In Ethic.* I.15 (Cologne XIV n. 90): "Concedimus, quod hae tres sunt unius essentiae et sunt diversae potentiae fluentes ab una essentia, quarum quaedam sunt affixae organis et quaedam non affixae, et similiter in equo duae sunt fluentes ab una essentia, secundum sanctos et philosophiam." The same view had already been defended, just as explicitly, by Johannes Blund, *Tract. de anima* q. 4.

Averroes is quoted from the medieval Latin translation of the *De substantia orbis*. The original Arabic is not extant. Most Hebrew translations contain the inverted claim that "it is impossible for one form to have more than one subject." But the context of the passage, and its commentary tradition, suggest that the intended sense is as quoted (see Hyman's note at *De subst. orbis* p. 50n.). Other suggestive passages are *In Phys.* I.63 and *In De an.* II.2. As §4.3 discussed, Averroes treats extension as accidental to prime matter, rather than as a distinct substantial form, which is the view that would be associated with Avicenna. Further questions arise from Averroes's theory of mixture, which allows that the substantial forms of the elements remain in an attenuated state (see Wood, "Influence of Arabic Aristotelianism" and Maier, *An der Grenze* pt. I [part. tr. Sargent, ch. 6]. For later appeals to Averroes, by both unitarians and pluralists, see Michael, "Averroes and the Plurality of Forms."

Scholars disagree on the extent to which Aquinas's position is novel. Callus thinks "the question cannot have originated with him," but that he was the first to give the problem "its full significance" ("Origins of the Problem" p. 124). Zavalloni thinks a stronger conclusion can be maintained: "les scolastiques préthomistes sont tous des pluralistes, mais ce sont des pluralistes inconscients" (*Richard de Mediavilla* p. 368). This judgment has been reaffirmed more recently by Dales, *Problem of the Rational Soul* p. 2. It seems to me the stronger claim can be maintained, provided one insists on the full scope of the unitarian commitment. Although modern scholars rarely recognize the breadth of issues involved in the dispute between unitarians and pluralists, it is common for scholastic authors to list the range of possible issues that arise. Burley, for instance, lists five separate disputed issues (*De formis* p. 33), and Marsilius of Inghen offers a somewhat different list of five (*In Gen. et cor.* I.6).

[3] There are far too many scholastic discussions of the unitarian–pluralist debate to cite here. Some notable discussions on the unitarian side are Richard Knapwell, *Correctorium* aa. 32, 52, etc. and *Quaest. de unitate formae*; Giles of Orleans, *In Gen. et cor.* I.20; Gregory of Rimini, *Sent.* II.16–17.2; Marsilius of Inghen, *In Gen. et cor.* I.6; Peter of Ailly, *Tract. de an.* ch. 1, pp. 9–11; John Capreolus, *Defensiones* II.15; Pedro Fonseca, *In Meta.* VII.12.1; Coimbrans, *In Gen. et cor.* I.4.19–22.

For the pluralist side, see Henry of Ghent, esp. *Quod.* IV.13; Scotus, esp. *Ord.* IV.11.3; Ockham, *Quod.* II.10–11; Pecham, *Quod.* IV.25; William de la Mare, *Correctorium* aa. 27, 31–2, 52, 102, 114, etc.; Olivi, *Summa* II.71 (see Pasnau, "Olivi on the Metaphysics of Soul"); Marston, *Quod.* II.22; Aquasparta, *De incarnatione* q. 9, pp. 180–2; Richard of Middleton, *De gradu formarum*; Jandun, *In Phys.* VII.8, *In Meta.* II.10; Burley, *In De an.* II.1–2, *De formis* pp. 35–44; Harclay,

In a way, this lingering disagreement obscures the real story. Although Aquinas's unitarian account was bitterly attacked for centuries, even his opponents generally came to agree that such an account was preferable when available. When Henry of Ghent argued against the unitarian conception, he did so only for the special case of human beings, and even there he postulated only two substantial forms: a rational soul, including the sensory and nutritive powers, and a natural, bodily form. Scotus likewise argued only for two forms, and only in the case of living things, contending that living substances have both a soul that makes them be alive and a form that structures their body, which he called the *forma corporeitatis*. Ockham was relatively extravagant in positing three substantial forms within a human being: a rational soul, a sensory–nutritive soul, and a form of the body. All three authors agreed with Aquinas in the case of nonliving things, and they agreed that the default view should be the unitarian one, unless special considerations made it untenable. Aquinas thus succeeded in changing the terms of the debate. The kind of pluralism he attacked had posited a substantial form corresponding to each of a thing's essential properties, up and down the Porphyrian tree. This kind of promiscuous pluralism quickly went out of fashion, once Aquinas's contemporaries were won over by the elegance of the unitarian scheme. As Suárez would put it much later, in describing this promiscuous pluralism, "the view is now antiquated and rejected as utterly implausible" (*Disp. meta.* 15.10.4). After Aquinas, the main debate was not over whether to postulate a substantial form for each essential attribute, but whether to postulate one, or two, or three, and only in certain special cases (in human beings, or in living things).[4]

Yet although this represents the main line of debate, the full contours of the discussion are far more complex. Substantial forms played so many and various roles that there was conceptual space for dozens of different positions, running from the unqualified unitarianism of the Thomists to the promiscuous pluralism of Zabarella, who remarked that "if two forms at once are not contrary to reason, then neither will it be contrary for there to be four or a hundred at once in the same substance" (*De rebus nat.*, De gen. ch. 2, cols. 397–8). As we will see in the following chapter, Zabarella means this quite literally, inasmuch as he thinks that a single complete substance will contain hundreds of substantial forms for its various integral parts. In general, different theories of the soul and its powers, of extension, of elemental mixture, and of the relationship between a whole and its parts led to a wide range of alternative views, and

Quaest. ord. 8; Paul of Venice, *Summa phil. nat.* V.5; Scheibler, *Metaphys.* I.22.22; Sennert, *Hypo. phys.* I:218 (see Michael, "Sennert's Sea Change").

For good accounts of the Oxford condemnations of unitarianism, see Kelley, "Introduction" and Wippel, *Metaphysical Thought of Godfrey* pp. 314–19.

[4] The classic source for promiscuous pluralism is Avicebron (Ibn Gabirol), *Fons vitae* IV.3, V.24—see Aquinas *In De an.* II.1 (Leonine 45.1, lines 258–64). For Latin sources prior to Aquinas, see Bazán's detailed notes to Aquinas's *Quaest. de anima* q. 9 (Leonine 24.1, re. lines 55–56, 66). Aquinas attacks this view most fully in *Quaest. de spir. creat.* 3c, where he traces the view to the assumption that each intellectual conception of a thing must have some real counterpart in the thing. Hence for every way we have of describing a thing, there will be a corresponding form. Henry of Ghent, a decade or so later, describes and criticizes much the same view (*Quod.* IV.13 [ed. 1518, ff. 104r–6v]), as, later on, do Gregory of Rimini (*Sent.* II.16–17.2), Peter of Ailly (*Tract. de an.* ch. 1, p. 9), Paul of Venice (*Summa phil. nat.* V.5 concl. 2), and the Coimbrans (*In Gen. et cor.* I.4.19). The most prominent scholastic defender of this sort of link between concepts and substantial forms is John of Jandun. See, e.g., *In Phys.* VII.8, *In Meta.* II.10, and *De pluralitate formarum*: "si non esset alia forma substantialis per quam homo est animal et per quam homo est homo, non esset alius conceptus hominis ut homo est et ut animal" (in MacClintock, *Perversity and Error* p. 158 n. 27).

there was never, all the way into the seventeenth century, anything approaching consensus over these issues.

25.2. Unification Strategies I: Unitarianism

Unitarians advance a huge, baffling array of arguments. Many of these, on their face, seem too dependent on contentious principles of Thomistic metaphysics—such as the pure potentiality of prime matter—to be persuasive. Ultimately, though, the case for unitarianism rests largely on the claim that only this form of hylomorphism will yield genuine substantial unity. Zabarella, for instance, would describe this argument as "that which above all else is offered against this [pluralist] position, and that seems to have persuaded many" (*De rebus nat.*, De gen. ch. 2, col. 398). Aquinas sets the argument out with characteristic clarity and concision:

One thing *simpliciter* is produced out of many actually existing things only if there is something uniting and in some way tying them to each other. In this way, then, if Socrates were an animal and were rational in virtue of different forms, then these two, in order to be united *simpliciter*, would need something to make them one. Therefore, since nothing is available to do this, the result will be that a human being is one thing only as an aggregate, like a heap, which is one thing *secundum quid* and many things *simpliciter*. (*Quaest. de an.* 11c)

Aquinas wants to distinguish between what is one thing in the fullest sense (*unum simpliciter*) and one thing in a secondary, derivative sense (*unum secundum quid*). A heap is an egregious case of the latter; a less obvious case would be pale Socrates, which is an instance of the sort of thick substance (the substance with its accidents [§6.1]) that scholastic authors agree is not one thing in the fullest sense. So Aquinas is focusing on Socrates himself, conceived thinly, and contending that even such an entity, which is after all a paradigmatic case of a genuine unity, counts as truly one thing only if it is nothing more than a composite of prime matter and a single substantial form. If there were multiple substantial forms, the argument here goes, then there would need to be something further, above these forms, to make them one. But "nothing is available to do this" (line 4).[5]

Although this is a relatively detailed instance of the sort of argument Aquinas makes over and over for his unitarian position, it is nevertheless all too compressed to be really persuasive. To see the force of his position, two crucial issues have to be explored further. First, just how is it that a single substantial form, together with prime matter, constitutes a genuine unity? Second, why exactly could multiple substantial forms not yield this same result? I will return to this second question in §25.4. Here I consider the first question. Although the core idea is present in Aquinas, later scholastic treatments bring out the issues both more explicitly and in greater detail. By far the most detailed discussion I know of is Suárez's, whose exhaustive discussion of substantial form in the fifteenth of his *Disputationes metaphysicae* (1597) is very clear about one kind of basis for

---

[5] For further discussion of Aquinas's conception of how substantial form unifies a substance, see my *Thomas Aquinas on Human Nature* ch. 3, and "Form, Substance, and Mechanism" pp. 39–43, as well as Pegis, *St. Thomas and the Problem of the Soul* and Wippel, *Metaphysical Thought of Godfrey* pp. 327–51. Scotus criticizes Aquinas's views at *Ord.* IV.11.3 (Wadding VIII n. 25).

this argument from unity. As we should expect given the discussion of the previous chapter, Suárez focuses on the physical aspect of substantial form, and develops the argument from unity in that way. The case for unitarianism can be made, he argues, on the basis of the same considerations used to argue for substantial forms in the first place, and in particular on the notion that "all the faculties and operations of a natural being are rooted in one essential principle" (*Disp. meta.* 15.10.64—quoted at greater length in §24.4). This line of thought leads directly to unitarianism. For if a single substance were to contain multiple substantial forms, then we could not say that its various properties are "rooted" in a single source. Some features of the thing—even some essential features like corporeality and rationality—would have their root in one substantial form, and some in another, and there would be no one principle ruling over the whole. Hence he says that as soon as we accept that substantial unity requires this kind of tight connection, we can conclude that "the plurality of forms is entirely alien to the constitution of nature" (ibid.).

Physical considerations such as these interact with a more metaphysical version of the argument from unity, grounded in substantial form's role in individuating substance. We saw in §24.2 how substantial form accounts for both the synchronic and the diachronic identity of a whole substance. The theory is supposed to do more than account for the identity of the whole substance, however; it is also supposed to account for the identify of each part of a substance. All parties to the dispute agree that the substantial form of a substance informs every part of a substance, making each of those parts be a thing of a certain kind. So on the unitarian picture, since there is just a single substantial form, that form can be understood to "rule over" (Suárez's phrase) the whole substance not just as its physical cause, but as that which, by informing each part of the substance, gives that part its identity. This, for Aquinas, was one of the defining features of substantial as opposed to accidental forms: "both the whole and the parts take their species from it, and so when it leaves, neither the whole nor the parts remain the same in species. For a dead person's eye and flesh are so called only equivocally" (*Summa contra gent.* II.72.1484; see Aristotle, *De an.* 412b20–22).

This more metaphysical argument for substantial unity, already important in Aquinas, would be developed in various ways by later authors. Buridan, for instance, uses such considerations to deal with a pluralist argument for postulating a substantial form for each sub-structure within a living body. According to his opponent—advancing a line of argument we will consider more closely in the following chapter—the integral parts of a substance are themselves substances, and so require their own substantial forms. This must be so even in the case of living things, the argument goes, because the parts of an animal remain apart from the soul. Buridan replies by appealing to the functional character of terms like 'bones' and 'nerves':

These are names for offices, like 'dean' and 'prefect.' Thus Aristotle says in many places that those names are necessarily defined by the tasks (*opera*) to which they are assigned and as they require various complexions of qualities and various qualities and shapes on account of the [3] various offices to which they are assigned. . . . It can be granted, however, that in the case of dead things the names 'bone,' 'flesh,' and 'nerve' are used as substance terms, because they no longer connote a task nor are they names for offices. And so in *Metaphysics* VII [1035b22] and [6] *Meteorology* IV [389b29] those names are said to be equivocal when used for the living and the dead. Thus it is certain that if in something alive the flesh is animated and later flesh gets pointed

to in something dead, it is not true to say of the flesh in the living thing that it is the same as   9
what was pointed to in the dead thing, since what is animated will never be the same as what is
not animated. It is, to be sure, possible that the same or a similar mixture remains in something
living and in something dead, but it does not follow that therefore the same substantial form   12
remains. (*In Gen. et cor.* I.8 ad 4)

This passage is particularly useful because it makes clear just how Buridan understands
the metaphysical status of such functional parts. They do not supervene on the primary-
quality mixture that gives flesh, say, its various sensible qualities (§21.2)—this gets ruled
out when Buridan remarks that "the same or a similar mixture" might remain before
and after death (lines 11–12), and yet the part would not remain. And it of course does
not matter that we are inclined to speak in both cases of 'flesh' or 'bones.' Those usages
are equivocal, Buridan insists, appealing to Aristotle's principle of homonymy in such
cases.[6] What matters—that by which such parts are "necessarily defined" (line 2)—is
the function that these parts play in a living thing. Although bones and other parts
require a certain sort of elemental complexion in order to play their assigned role (lines
2–4), it is their playing that role within a living thing that gives them their identity.
Hence 'flesh' is equivocal in living and dead things, because "what is animated will
never be the same as what is not animated" (lines 10–11).

Based on these considerations, Buridan rejects the notion that the various integral
parts of a substance must have their own substantial forms. If that were right, then
these parts could exist independently of the whole organism, and their functional role in
the system would no longer be necessary. To the objection's claim that we grasp
substances on the basis of accidents (§7.1), and so should treat the very different
accidents of flesh versus bone as grounds for a difference in substance, Buridan grants
the methodological principle, but denies that it always requires postulating distinct
substantial forms: "a difference of accidents in the same supposit implies only that the
substantial form is organized so as to be capable of various operations requiring
different instruments of different complexions" (ibid.). Although Buridan does not
explicitly use this sort of functional argument to argue for the greater substantial
unity of the unitarian account, he is in effect making just that connection. The parts
of substances are unified, he here contends, by the sorts of functional interrelations that
make it impossible for those parts to endure without the whole. To treat a substance as
a composite of multiple substantial forms would be to violate this unity, because it
would then be possible for some parts of a substance, with their distinct substantial
forms, to exist apart from the rest of the substance.

It is an intriguing feature of this more metaphysical development of the argument
from unity that it might run independently of the physical aspect of substantial form
described in the previous chapter. One could reject that physical aspect as empirically
false—on the grounds that there is no such centralized power within a substance—and
still think that any genuine substance requires a form of some more abstract kind,
one required not for a complete physical explanation of the universe, but for a
full metaphysical understanding of how things are. This, in effect, was Leibniz's view

---

[6] See *Meteor.* IV.12, 389b31–390a19; *De an.* II.1, 412b20–22; *Metaphys.* VII.10, 1035b22–25, and the discussion in Shields, *Order in Multiplicity* ch. 5.

(§24.5), and something like it might be endorsed by the modern Aristotelian. It is not, however, how scholastic authors seem to conceive of the situation. For them, it is the physical aspect of substantial form that accounts for its metaphysical role in individuating a substance and its parts. This is apparently so even in Buridan. Although his remarks above are not perfectly clear about why a substantial form should be tied to the functional structure of a complex organism, he is elsewhere very clear about the concrete, causal role played by such forms (§24.4). I take his view here, then, to be that the substantial form holds a substance together by being responsible for the varying elemental mixtures of a thing's distinct parts, and for the way those parts are organized. In effect, then, it is *because* the substantial form plays this organizing causal role that those parts are capable of certain functions. The proper function of bone may not supervene narrowly on its elemental mixture, but such facts do supervene on the complex of elemental mixtures that constitutes the whole organic body, a structure that in turn arises from the substantial form.

Whatever the relationship between these two ways of developing the argument from unity, their conjunction makes for an extremely robust account of why substances are one thing in a special sense. For the unitarian, both the whole substance and each of its parts and intrinsic properties flow from a single physical cause, and are sustained in existence for only as long as they remain part of that substance. The parts of such an entity are, in a very strong sense, inseparable from the whole. Hence material substances, despite their complexity, are unified to a degree that justifies their traditional status as *unum per se*, or *unum simpliciter*. Indeed, short of perfectly simplicity, it is hard to conceive of a more robust form of unity.

25.3. Generation and Corruption Puzzles

Before considering the lesser sort of substantial unity attained through pluralism, it will be good to understand why these authors were driven to reject unitarianism in the first place. They too advance an overwhelming range of both philosophical and theological arguments. Almost all of these arguments, however, are variations on a single complaint: that the unitarian account makes substances *too* unified, and so results in an implausibly rigid conception of change.

Consider Scotus. He concedes that, in the absence of reasons to the contrary, the unitarian account is preferable—not because of any argument Aquinas gives, but simply because it is more parsimonious.[7] There is, however, reason to prefer pluralism: the fact that the body of a living thing can exist without the living thing. This entails that the soul of a living thing can go out of existence while the form by which the body is a

---

[7] Naturally, Ockham was not the only or even the first scholastic to make arguments from parsimony. Scotus remarks of the argument from parsimony for unitarianism that it "plus valet omnibus praecedentibus" (*Ord.* IV.11.3; Wadding VIII n. 27), where the preceding arguments were all drawn from Aquinas. Earlier still, Henry of Ghent remarks that "omnem enim operationem attribuendam composito per plures formas aeque convenienter possumus ponere per unam simplicem, etiam in homine, nisi in ipso aliud repugnaret, ut infra videbitur. Quod autem potest fieri per unum natura nunquam agit per plura, quia nihil agit frustra neque deficit in necessariis, secundum Philosophum" (*Quod.* IV.13 [ed. 1518, I:106rS]; see also ibid., I:106vY). Not everyone, however, accepted that parsimony had a role to play here. Zabarella's remark that if four then why not a hundred, as quoted earlier in the main text, seems to disavow such considerations.

body remains in existence. Applying the indiscernibility of identicals (§6.2), Scotus concludes that "if this is, and that is not, then they are not the same entity in being" (*Ordinatio* IV.11.3 [Wadding VIII n. 54]). Pluralists make this argument over and over, attacking the unitarians for their insistence that the death of a living thing entails that all its parts go out of existence. Scotus and many others regard this as absurd. How could a body that seems to have so many of the same accidental properties have undergone so thorough a substantial change that none of its parts or properties are in fact the same? Scotus simply takes it for granted that this is false, remarking without argument that "though the form of the soul does not remain, the body remains" (ibid.). Others tried to motivate this claim in various ways. Zabarella, for instance, appeals to the way that herbs and plants retain the same flavors and smells long after they are picked (*De rebus nat.*, De gen. ch. 2, col. 397). Is it really plausible to think that, in fact, these plants have numerically distinct sensible qualities, supervening on numerically distinct primary qualities, arising from a distinct substantial form? Post-scholastic authors sometimes appeal to these arguments as an indictment of substantial form in general, but their true target is the unitarian version of the theory.

Does the unitarian have a reply? Richard Cross describes the claim that a body remains the same through death as "a fairly safe empirical observation" (*Physics of Duns Scotus* p. 56). The only thing we can *observe* in such circumstances, however, is that qualitatively the same body remains through death. That is a fairly safe empirical observation, but it is not what the pluralists need. They need to establish that numerically the same body remains through death. That, however, is a metaphysical claim, and it is not clear that any observations could settle the matter. As Richard Knapwell put it very early in this debate, in his defense of Aquinas from *circa* 1283, it is reason alone that sees the need to distinguish between the body before and after corruption: "the senses, through apprehending similar accidents (these being the only things that make an impression on them), cannot go deep enough to recognize that distinction" (*Correctorium* art. 32, p. 153). This suggests a general strategy for the unitarians: they can insist that their thesis is a purely metaphysical one, and deny that any such empirical observations directly count against it. On this approach, the debate over substantial form takes on the aspect of a debate over diachronic identity. Just as no one arguing over personal identity would appeal to such things as hair color or personality traits, so the unitarian might regard as irrelevant the fact that the skin and eyes of a corpse *look* the same. What matters, according to the unitarian, are metaphysical considerations regarding substantial unity.[8]

Whether or not the advantages of such unity are worth the price is something I will try to get clearer about as this chapter progresses. There should be no mistaking, however, just how high the price is. The unitarian must hold that, for any substance,

---

[8] On numerical identity as a question for reason rather than the senses, see also Fonseca, *In Meta.* VIII.1.2.6 (IV:458bBC): "Ad septimum dices in eis quae non sensu sed ratione examinanda sunt, qualis est identitas et diversitas numeralis rerum, maxime vero similium . . . ut in duobus eiusdem galllinae ovis omnino similibus, si quis successive ea videat, neque enim ex vi visionis ea poterit numero distinguere, quae tamen diversa esse ratione demonstrabit ei, qui noverit eam gallinam bis tantum perperisse et ovum quod idem homo prius viderat ab alio comestum esse."

There was a difference of opinion regarding whether the cadaver should be thought to have just one new form of the whole or many separate substantial forms. The former was Suárez's view (*Disp. meta.* 15.10.15), the latter Zabarella's (*De rebus nat.* De gen. et int. ch. 3, col. 401E), on the grounds that a corpse is not a substance. Leibniz would later make a similar claim, in correspondence with Arnauld (*Phil. Schriften* II.75; tr. Ariew and Garber p. 78).

when it is corrupted, nothing other than its prime matter remains. My body ceases to exist when I cease to exist. If a stone goes through substantial change when it is split in half, then neither "remaining" half in fact remains. Each half, and every part of each half, is a wholly new entity. The same issues arise for the generation of substances. Whenever stuff comes together to compose a new substance, that stuff (aside from its prime matter) must cease to exist. All of this looks counterintuitive. Pedro Fonseca tries to make a virtue out of these results, remarking that the pluralist must treat a living thing's death not just as a single corruption, but as one corruption after another, such that (for instance) first the thing ceases to be rational, then it ceases to have nutritive operations, then it ceases to be a body at all. The same will be true of generation, inasmuch as, for the pluralist, "there are as many generations of substantial things as there are substantial forms introduced to denominate the whole thing" (*In Meta.* VII.12.1.2 [II:364aD]). Fonseca means this to sound odd, but it is in fact a far more intuitive way of thinking about generation and corruption, because it recognizes our inclination to say that things ordinarily come into and go out of existence piece by piece, rather than all at once. To think otherwise—to think that substances come and go as a whole without remainder (aside from prime matter)—one would have to be in the grip of some sort of powerful metaphysical thesis. And so it is. The unitarian is driven to this counterintuitive result by the idea that genuine substances must be robustly unified, in such a way that none of their parts (other than prime matter) is capable of surviving apart from the whole. This immediately entails the consequences so derided by pluralists.[9]

One way to moderate the unitarian's position here would be to delimit sharply the range of things that count as substances. This is a natural thought to have at this juncture, because once one gives a rigorous account of what substantial unity involves, it is to be expected that some traditional substance candidates fall by the wayside. Certainly, artifacts like chairs do not count (§24.5). It may be, too, that a stone is not a substance, or that an alloy like bronze is not a substance, or that at any rate not just any lump of bronze is a substance. Sometimes it is even suggested that the Aristotelian should recognize no non-living substances at all. Of course, if the end result is that *nothing* counts as a substance then the unitarian agenda will have been self-defeating. But it is clear that living things, at any rate, are supposed to be paradigmatic substances, and so the unitarian has to accept these implausible all-or-nothing results at least in those cases. Moreover, scholastic authors seem committed to the substantiality of

---

[9] Aquinas describes the sequence of generations and corruptions that lead to an animal as follows: "cum generatio unius semper sit corruptio alterius, necesse est dicere quod tam in homine quam in animalibus aliis, quando perfectior forma advenit, fit corruptio prioris: ita tamen quod sequens forma habet quidquid habebat prima, et adhuc amplius. Et sic per multas generationes et corruptiones pervenitur ad ultimam formam substantialem, tam in homine quam in aliis animalibus" (*Summa theol.* 1a 118.2 ad 2). The view was quite widespread. See also, e.g., Gregory of Rimini, *Sent.* II.16–17.2, p. 345: "sensitiva prius introducitur et deinde, facta ulteriori dispositione ad intellectivam, simul corrumpitur sensitiva et infunditur intellectiva, sicut dicendum est de aliis formis substantialibus quae praecedunt animam intellectivam, et similiter sensitivum et vegetativum in materia, quae disponitur ad intellectivam." Even pluralists would be likely to agree with these remarks, since only the most profligate pluralists postulate a distinct, overlapping substantial form for each stage of embryonic development. I discuss Aquinas's view, in the context of the modern debate over abortion, in *Thomas Aquinas on Human Nature* ch. 4.

non-living things. They take for granted that the genus *substance* divides into *living* and *non-living*, and indeed *stone* (*lapis*) is a paradigmatic example of the latter. Now perhaps '*lapis*' is merely a genus term extending to various kinds of minerals, which would leave open whether a lump of stony stuff counts as a substance, or whether instead a lump of stone is an aggregate composed of myriad micro stones. One can only speculate, or at best draw inferences from various other theoretical commitments, because—amazingly—scholastic authors made no sustained attempt to come to grips with the problem of what non-living substances there are.[10]

Whereas unitarianism invites a narrow construal of the category of Substance, pluralism looks most attractive when viewed as a broader strategy for explaining change over time. Intuitively, it seems that in many cases where a thing goes out of existence, part of that thing remains. An animal dies, but its body remains. A statue is smashed, but the clay remains. Modern philosophers are tempted to deal with these sorts of cases by holding either that there is no real substantial change (§28.4) or that in fact there were two substances overlapping for a time (the statue *and* the clay), only one of which remains. The first strategy might be tenable in some cases, such as artifacts, but seems implausible in others (such as living things). The second strategy seems to diminish the unity of substance to a degree that courts absurdity. Dogs and statues are not one substance but two? or maybe more? Pluralists are able to say something less strange: that there is only one complete substance, but that it is composed of parts capable of surviving apart from the whole. The animal is a single substance, then, and *it* goes out of existence when it dies, but nevertheless part of it endures, in virtue of its corporeal form. So whereas the unitarian collects the whole substance at a single focal point, and so makes substantial change an all-or-nothing affair, the pluralist conceives of substantial identity as turning on two axes, around one or the other of which the substance's various properties revolve. This has its appeal. There certainly are cases, like the statue and the clay, where we want to be able to say that it endures in one aspect (as clay) but not in another (as statue). The unitarian purposefully rejects the very possibility of such an analysis, insisting that true substances cannot be divided up in this way. If the clay can survive the destruction of the statue, then that shows that the statue was not a substance at all, and that its shape (or whatever it is that made it be a statue) is merely a passing accident. Inasmuch as all the scholastics are in agreement that artifacts are not substances, the statue–clay case is of merely illustrative value for

---

[10] Albert the Great makes an interesting remark about the status of stones as substances: "De formis autem quae sunt substantiales lapidum, dubitare dementis esse videtur, quoniam visus certificat de his quod coagulati sunt omnes, et materia in ipsa ad speciem certam est determinata" (*De mineralibus* I.1.6; tr. Wyckoff pp. 24–5). He goes on to contrast their status with that of clouds, rain, and snow, which evidently arise only because of "dispositiones elementorum." As for the character of these substantial forms, "sunt autem hae formae secundum plurimum innominatae, sed tamen differentiae earum innuntur diversis nominibus lapidum, cum vocantur tofus, pumices, silices, marmor, saphirus, smaragdus, et huiusmodi: quae, cum nobis occulta sunt, ideo propria diffinientia lapidum non habemus nisi circumloquendo accipiendo accidentia et signa loco diffinientium" (ibid.). This suggests that '*lapis*' refers to a class of minerals, rather than to rocky stuff of a certain shape.

The narrow conception of what counts as substances for the scholastics is taken for granted by Ayers, who treats "a piece of stone" and "a lump of lead" as accidental unities (*Locke* II:127) and suggests that for Aristotelians only living things will count as genuine substances (II:229). I have elsewhere argued that Aquinas is implicitly committed to allowing only minimal-sized bodies as substances, among non-living things, which is to say that the only piece of lead that counts as a substance is a piece so small that, if it were any smaller, it would cease to be lead (*Thomas Aquinas on Human Nature* ch. 3).

how pluralism was in fact deployed. Modern-day Aristotelians, however, might wish to deploy the view more broadly.[11]

The dispute between unitarians and pluralists lends itself to these sorts of metaphysical musings, but in practice—as I have been stressing—the debate's orientation was physical (§24.4). Viewed from this aspect, the situation for the unitarian becomes much worse than I have yet indicated. Metaphysically, the problem for the unitarian is simply to justify the implausible claim that post-corruption remnants and pre-generation ingredients, despite being qualitatively identical to the substance that was or will be, are in fact numerically distinct. Substantial forms are not, however, merely abstract metaphysical principles; they are also (or instead) the principal causal explanations of the various intrinsic accidents of a substance. Accordingly, the unitarian must account for why the corpse has accidental properties that are even *qualitatively* the same as those of the living body. If the living body's accidents were a product of its substantial form, then it seems nothing short of miraculous that, without that form, the corpse retains so many exactly similar accidents.

This further dimension of the problem is especially clear in Ockham's discussion in *Quodlibet* II.11. His principal argument for a further *forma corporeitatis* in living things, beyond a rational and sensory soul, goes as follows:

1. "Numerically the same accidents as before remain when a human being or brute animal dies."
2. "Accidents do not naturally migrate from subject to subject."
∴3. "Those accidents have numerically the same subject."
4. "That subject is not prime matter."
∴5. "Some prior form remains" [actualizing the enduring body that is the subject of these accidents].
6. "Not the sensory soul" [since the animal has died].
∴7. "The form of corporeity remains."

The inferences are unexceptionable, and most unitarians would accept all the premises but the first. Ockham knows that he has to argue at some length for that first premise, and his argument is cast entirely in terms of the impossibility of any physical explanation for the generation of numerically distinct but qualitatively identical accidents:

If the accidents are distinct [i.e., if the first premise is false], then at least they are of the same kind as the accidents of the living animal: this is clear from the fact that they are so much alike that one cannot distinguish between them. So if these accidents are new, then I ask what caused them. Not air or any other element, or a heavenly body, because then every accident of every corpse would be of the same kind, which runs contrary to what we see. [This inference holds] because, given that these are natural agents, they by nature always cause accidents of the same character in subjects (*passis*) of the same character. But matter is of the same character in every corpse. Therefore etc. (*Quod.* II.11 [*Op. theol.* IX:162–3])

[11] Zabarella provides a particularly clear example of how pluralism amounts to an alternative strategy for accounting for the multiple identities of substances—as, e.g., statue and clay. Against the Thomistic singular existence thesis (§26.5), he responds that "licet unius rei unum sit esse, per hoc tamen non stare quin eadem res sit et corpus et mistum et vivens et animal et homo, licet aliud sit esse hominem aliud sit esse corpus et caetera" (*De rebus nat.*, De gen. ch. 2, col. 398). Such distinct existences are what allow the pluralist to account for the variable identity conditions of a thing *qua* body or *qua* animal or *qua* human. Still, as Zabarella stresses, it is a single thing, under a single unifying, specifying form.

The argument continues on, ruling out other possibilities, but this is enough to get a sense of how the debate goes. Ockham wants the unitarian to give a physical explanation for why a corpse has accidents that are indistinguishable from those of the living body. If numerically the same accidents could endure, then this would not be so puzzling, but since there is no enduring subject for those accidents, the accidents cannot endure. Hence Ockham demands an explanation for the otherwise amazing coincidence that the body of a corpse looks very much like the body of a living thing. Could there be some explanation in terms of primary qualities, or a heavenly body? (lines 4–5) Nothing like that will work, because—remember—for the unitarian the only thing that endures through the corruption of the substance is prime matter. But of course "matter is of the same character in every corpse" (lines 7–8). Hence we can apply the fundamental principle that in cases of natural agency, if the agent is the same and the subject is the same (and, tacitly, the surrounding conditions are the same), then the effect will be the same (lines 6–7). The unitarian needs one cause to account for the distinctive enduring features of one corpse, and another cause to account for the distinctive enduring features of another corpse. What plausible option is there, other than to suppose that something more than prime matter endures through substantial change? This is another example of how the demand for an underlying substratum of change, first encountered in Chapter 2, becomes a kind of Trojan horse for a much more robust ontology. The considerations that support the need for an enduring substratum tend to require not just bare, indeterminate matter, but ingredients of a certain kind, suitable for bridging the gap between the thing corrupted and the thing generated. The strictest unitarians resisted all such arguments, but the pluralists thought that such "ingredients proofs" showed why something more than bare prime matter endures through substantial change.[12]

Pluralists retained an abiding animosity toward what they regarded as the absurdity of the unitarian position. Peter John Olivi, an early critic, referred to it as a "brutal error" (*Summa* II.71, II:637). Franco Burgersdijk, 350 years later, was still lambasting it as "utterly absurd" (*Collegium physicum* 20.9).[13] Even so, more temperate authors

---

[12] Adams, *William Ockham* ch. 15, provides a full account of Ockham's arguments for pluralism, including the theological arguments. See also Zavalloni, *Richard de Mediavilla*.

The text of Ockham's main argument in *Quod.* II.11 for a *forma corporeitatis* runs as follows (inserting a full stop at one crucial juncture where the editors seem to have misunderstood the logic of the argument): "mortuo homine sive bruto animali, remanent eam accidente numero quae prius; igitur habent idem subiectum numero. Consequentia patet, quia accidens naturaliter non migrat a subiecto in subiectum. Sed illud subiectum non est materia prima, quia tunc materia prima immediate reciperet accidentia absoluta, quod non videtur verum; igitur remanet aliqua forma praecedens, et non sensitiva; igitur corporeitas." The argument is discussed in more detail in Adams, *William Ockham* II:649–50.

Cajetan responds in some detail to arguments such as Ockham's at *In De ente* q. 18, contending that the agent that corrupts the old substance is what causes the new substance to have qualitatively similar features. This is perhaps plausible in some cases, but strikes me as clearly untenable in other cases, such as the corruption of living things. Adams decisively remarks of such a view that "the same agent may use the same instrument to kill a black and white cow and a brown cow, and yet the accidents of the first corpse will differ in species from those of the second" (*William Ockham* II:650).

[13] Seventeenth-century anti-scholastics sometimes latch onto the arguments against unitarianism as an argument against substantial forms in general. See, e.g., the Boate brothers (*Phil. nat. reformata* 1.3.32), although they are aware that not all scholastics are vulnerable to the objection: "Sane res haec de qua nunc agimus (nimirum unamquamque partem in cadavere esse idem, eiusdemque naturae, ac erat durante vita) adeo est clara ut multos ipsorum Peripateticorum, quibus saltem aliqua sensuum καὶ τῶν φαινομένων cura, eam negare puduerit" (p. 104). They go on to refer specifically to the pluralism of Zabarella, Ghent, and Scotus. Boyle would later use an example just like Zabarella's—he appeals to the lingering flavors of fruits plucked from a tree (*Origin of Forms* [*Works* V:348; Stewart pp. 63–4])—in arguing against

recognized the obscure and doubtful character of this debate. Ockham, for instance, prefaces the above argument with the remark that although he endorses pluralism, "this is difficult to prove through reason." The core problem is the unobservability of substantial forms, which can be grasped only inferentially, via accidents, in just the way that the thin substance as a whole can. If anything, however, this methodological observation makes things worse for the unitarian, since if we let the accidents be our guide, we should certainly be pluralists. Even Suárez has to admit that "we experience substantial form only from its effects, or accidents. But often there is no effect that evidently points to the introduction of a new form after the earlier one leaves, as with the death of a human being" (*Disp. meta.* 15.8.16). Suárez in fact considerably understates the difficulty for his side: it is not just that there is no evidence of a new substantial form after death, but also that there are many signs of the presence of the same form. The same sorts of arguments considered in §24.4 as evidence for the existence of substantial forms—based on the endurance and stability of accidents over time—point toward there being multiple such forms.

For the strict Thomist, there is no obvious way to handle these difficulties regarding substantial change. At the same time, the metaphysical advantages of unitarianism were clear. Unsurprisingly, then, many scholastics gravitated toward a non-Thomistic version of unitarianism that sidesteps these generation and corruption puzzles. To escape an argument like Ockham's, one must find a way to allow numerically the same accidents to endure through generation and corruption. This would remove the need to answer Ockham's pivotal question (lines 3–4 above): "if these accidents are new, then I ask what caused them." To retain numerically the same accidents, without abandoning unitarianism, one must deny either premise 2 or premise 4 above. One might suppose that real accidents, on their robust, later scholastic understanding, should be able to migrate from subject to subject, contrary to premise 2. I am, however, unaware of any scholastic who was willing to countenance this as a naturally occurring event. So this leaves premise 4, and the possibility that accidents might endure through substantial change by inhering in prime matter. This became an increasingly prominent position among later scholastics, embraced at first by independent fourteenth-century authors such as Peter Auriol, Gregory of Rimini, and John Buridan, and ultimately given the imprimatur of orthodoxy by Suárez and other Jesuits. As we saw in §§6.3–4, this approach faces various difficulties, but scholastics increasingly saw its advantages as outweighing its disadvantages, inasmuch as it offered a way to account for the continuity of change. Thus Rimini, after quoting Ockham above verbatim, replies that "I grant that many accidents often remain numerically the same, and in the same subject, and I say that matter alone is their subject" (*Sent.* II.16–17.2, V:352). One could be a unitarian then, like Rimini, and still allow accidents to endure through substantial change. Indeed, even a pluralist like Zabarella takes this view, because for even the pluralist there will be cases—especially substantial change involving non-living things—where none of the substantial forms endure, and yet there is some continuity in sensible qualities. From the fourteenth century forward, the strict Thomistic doctrine according to which nothing other than prime matter endures through substantial

substantial forms. Of course Boyle would not have welcomed the response that we therefore need multiple substantial forms; he seems entirely unaware of the unitarian–pluralist debate.

change is not a popular position. Here, and elsewhere, it is good to keep in mind that Thomism—contrary to what is often supposed—was always a minority view during the scholastic era.[14]

25.4. Dualism and Mind–Body Unity

The advantages of pluralism are clear enough. From a physical point of view, it better accounts for the seemingly gradual process of substantial change. From a metaphysical point of view, it offers a powerful tool to explain the seemingly multiple foci of substantial identity—being both statue and clay, human being and body. Pluralism remained controversial, however, because of its difficulties in accounting for substantial unity. The tradeoff is clear enough: either one can have robust substantial unity, at the cost of a rigidly all-or-nothing conception of substantial change, or one can have a flexible, layered conception of substantial change, but at the cost of substantial unity. The ideal solution, if it could be had, would be to find room for robust substantial unity within the pluralist framework. The following section will take up that issue, but it will be helpful first to highlight the difficulties of pluralism by considering in more detail the special case of human beings, and the way pluralism threatens to lead to one or another unacceptable version of dualism.

Let 'dualism' refer to the view that the world in general, and human composites in particular, contain two fundamentally distinct kinds of entities—material and immaterial, or corporeal and spiritual. One should be cautious in supposing that such binary distinctions are fundamental for scholastic authors in the way they plainly are for, say, Descartes, but in some sense it is surely true that almost everyone throughout our four centuries is a dualist in the sense just defined. (Hobbes is the outstanding exception [§16.2].) Although dualism so conceived is not much in dispute during this time, there are forms of dualism that were highly contested. Let 'platonic dualism' refer to theories on which human composites contain two substances, a mind and a body, each of which is in its own right a complete entity, and whose composite is a mere aggregate. In scholastic terms, the platonic dualist treats the human composite as an accidental unity—an *ens per accidens* rather than an *ens per se*. This might mean that the soul alone, rather than the soul–body composite, is the human being, the person, or the self. Alternatively, the platonic dualist might identify the human being (the person, the self) with the composite, which would imply that human beings (persons, selves) have at best derivative existence. In any case, for the platonic dualist, the fundamental entities, the *entia per se*, are soul and body.

Whether or not this "platonic" dualism is properly and truly Platonic, it was certainly the view attributed to Plato by scholastic authors, who of course generally reject it in

---

[14] The extent to which one can rightly speak of Thomism among later scholastics remains a surprisingly neglected topic. Contrary to what is often said, the Jesuits are not Thomists, and when they discuss the Thomists are not including themselves. One gets an interesting perspective on the status of Thomism in Oxford in the later fourteenth century from Wyclif's criticisms of those who blindly accept the "scripta Thomae" and assume that "si ipse sic asserit, ergo verum" (*De eucharistia* ch. 5, p. 158). Wyclif urges that in philosophical matters it is better to follow Scotus: "Nam Doctor Subtilis cui plus credendum est in speculationibus . . ." (ibid.).

favor of Aristotelianism.[15] In general, as we will see, only a few authors during our period expressly defend platonic dualism; the view looms more as a threat to be avoided than as a competing alternative. This is so partly for theological reasons: although in principle platonic dualism seems compatible with Christianity, in practice this possibility was not accepted. The Council of Vienne (1312) declared it a heresy to hold that "the rational or intellective soul is not *per se* and essentially the form of the human body" (§20.2), and this was understood to prohibit platonic dualism. Moreover, quite apart from theological considerations, the disreputability of platonic dualism is obvious enough to commonsense. We are well acquainted with the case of human beings, and it seems seriously counterintuitive to regard ourselves as merely an aggregate of two distinct substances, each of which is itself an entity in some more basic sense. To be sure, human beings have parts, integral and perhaps also metaphysical. But we regard those parts as subsumed under a larger whole, and we regard the whole as that which exists in the primary sense. Still, disreputable as it is, this form of dualism constantly looms over discussions of soul and substantial form throughout our four centuries. And among the many aspects of the mind–body problem during the seventeenth century, none is more serious than the problem of how to unify the mind–body composite without the metaphysical apparatus of scholasticism.

No scholastic author, so far as I know, embraces platonic dualism. Some views, however, are more prone to the risk than others. Least at risk are the unitarians. Although the unitarian's rational soul is a substance, capable of existing on its own, there is no corporeal substance—no body—to serve as its counterpart. Instead, for the unitarian, the counterpart of the rational soul is prime matter, which is not a body at all, but the stuff that, together with a substantial form, constitutes a body. Strictly speaking, prime matter falls into the category of Substance (§26.1), but since such matter cannot exist without form, there is no temptation to regard the human composite as a mere aggregate of complete, independent substances.[16]

Pluralism, in contrast, inevitably flirts with platonic dualism. The body informed by the rational soul not only is fully actual, but also is naturally capable of existing apart from the soul. As we have seen, this is a result that the pluralist wants, but one that

---

[15] The *locus classicus* for the early scholastic understanding of Plato's own form of dualism is Nemesius, *De natura hominis*, a work wrongly ascribed to Gregory of Nyssa: "Therefore Plato . . . did not hold that an animal is made up of soul and body, but that it is the soul using the body and (as it were) wearing the body. But this claim raises a problem: How can the soul be one with what it wears? For a shirt is not one with the person wearing it" (ch. 3, pp. 51–2). Aristotle refers in passing to the sailor–ship model of soul and body, but without ascribing it to Plato and even without clearly rejecting it (*De an.* 413a8). The Condemnations of 1277 condemns the thesis "quod intellectus non est actus corporis, nisi sicut nauta navis, nec est perfectio essentialis hominis" (n. 7).

For a detailed discussion of the "Platonic" option, see Aquinas, *Summa contra gent.* II.57. See also Arnauld's Fourth Set of Objections to the *Meditations*, which characterizes as "Platonic" the view that "nihil corporeum ad nostram essentiam pertinere, ita ut homo sit solus animus, corpus vero non nisi vehiculum animi; unde hominem definiunt animum utentem corpore" (VII:203). Notably, Arnauld acknowledges that Descartes rejects this view.

If any scholastic author approaches platonic dualism, it is perhaps Olivi, at *Summa* II.59 (II:525–6)—a text called to my attention by Calvin Normore.

[16] Although the unitarians are dualists, it is misleading to say—invoking modern terminology—that they are substance dualists. To be sure, they regard the soul as a substance, and they also regard human beings as composed of multiple substances, as the following chapter will discuss. What the unitarian crucially does not countenance is that there is any corporeal substance apart from the soul, which together with the soul constitutes a living thing. Apart from the soul, says the unitarian, no part of the human being exists. Pluralists, in contrast, clearly are substance dualists. For discussion focused on Aquinas's case, see my *Thomas Aquinas on Human Nature* pp. 65–72.

immediately raises questions about substantial unity. Pluralists invariably reject platonic dualism on the grounds that the rational soul is still a substantial form of the body,
and so gives rise to a genuinely unified whole, *unum per se* rather than *per accidens*. Yet
even if this is what the pluralist *says*, it is unclear just how much such talk explains.
There is, moreover, a class of pluralists, beginning with Ockham, who face a special
difficulty. On Scotus's less problematic version of pluralism, the rational soul is
responsible for all vital operations of the organism. In a very clear sense, then, it counts
as a form of the body, given that it actualizes the bodily organs that sustain life (heart,
lungs, eyes, brain, etc.). Pluralists who take Scotus's line can therefore make some
appeal to the physical aspect of substantial form that unitarians make so much of: that
the soul–body composite is unified in virtue of the soul's role as an internal cause.
Ockham, in contrast, postulates a distinct sensory soul, and it is this soul that bears the
responsibility for actualizing all of these animal operations. His rational soul is responsible only for the high-level cognitive and volitional operations that do not require an
organ, making its status as the form of the body especially problematic. Subsequent
pluralists split between these two kinds of view. Although Scotus's position was influential, prominent authors like Oresme and Zabarella—although disagreeing about the total
number of substantial forms to be posited—follow Ockham in limiting the rational soul
to intellectual operations. Anticipating the terminological switch that Descartes would
later bring into prominence, we might say that the rational soul, for these authors, is
simply the mind. Indeed, Zabarella himself makes this terminological switch, preferring
the term 'mind' (*mens*) rather than 'intellect' or 'rational soul' in talking about these issues.
Since such pluralists postulate both a sensory soul and a mind, I will call this view *soul-
and-mind pluralism*, in contrast to Scotus's *body-and-soul pluralism*.[17]

Ockham and other soul-and-mind pluralists stoutly insist that the rational soul
actualizes the body, and so counts as the form of the body. But given that their account
completely divorces the rational soul from its usual physical role in explaining the
body's various properties, it is quite unclear how far such an explanation goes. Such
views were commonly criticized, indeed, for their inability to preserve the hylomorphic
framework. Here, for instance, is Suárez:

> If a sensory soul were to intercede [between matter and the intellectual soul], then the
> intellective soul would be a pure principle of thought. A pure principle of thought, however,
> is not suited to inform the body. . . . Therefore for the rational soul to be a true form of the body,
> it must be the principle not only of thinking but also of the operations that are exercised by the
> body. (*Disp. meta.* 15.10.25)

Suárez is claiming that soul-and-mind pluralists cannot account for the unity of the
human composite in hylomorphic terms. This suggests that their view will inevitably

---

[17] Oresme offers his soul-and-mind pluralism at *In Phys.* I.18 and *In Gen. et cor.* I.6. The most extensive discussion is at
In De an. II.5, where he summarizes the view as follows: "Alia via est quod in homine sunt duae animae et duae formae
tantummodo ita quod, sicut in equo aut asino est unica forma materialis, ita etiam in homine, quae est corruptibilis et
generabilis de potentiae materiae, et cum hoc est in eo anima intellectiva quae non est forma materialis" (pp. 152–3).

   Zabarella ascribes to human beings three souls, vegetative, sensory, and rational—see e.g. *De rebus nat.* De facultatibus
animae chs. 9–13. Beyond that, various integral parts of the body have their own form of the mixture, which is itself a
substantial form (*De rebus nat.* De gen. et int. ch. 2, and see §26.6). For Zabarella's usage of '*mens*' to refer to the rational
soul, see *De rebus nat.* Liber de mente humana, e.g., at col. 971A: "nil aliud est anima rationalis, quae mens humana
dicitur, quam actus primus hominis, seu forma qua homo est homo."

lapse into platonic dualism—effectively, a *reductio ad absurdum*. But is this fair? To be sure, a rational soul conceived of along Ockham's lines does not perform the functions of a substantial form as envisaged by the unitarian, either metaphysically or physically. But does this mean it cannot be a substantial form at all?[18]

Such charges are difficult to resolve because—as we have seen already in so many different contexts—there is no one clear notion of what it is to be a form. It is easy, in discussing such issues, to fall into a kind of Aristotelian mysterianism, treating talk of form and matter as a magical incantation that, simply by being invoked, but in ways we cannot understand, solves various philosophical problems. The risk is especially grave in the present context, where it is tempting to suppose that postulating form–matter composition immediately solves the problem of substantial unity. Nothing is more important to the study of our four centuries than to understand that this sort of hylomorphic talk is, by itself, JUST TALK. The range of possibilities for what it might mean for the soul to be the form of the body is so vast that the bare claim by itself is literally meaningless. If this is not yet clear, then consider that it is even possible to hold that the soul is the form of the body without supposing that the two together constitute a genuine unity. Daniel Sennert's *Epitome naturalis scientiae* (1618), for instance, remarks that "no sane philosopher denies that the rational soul is the form of a human being," but then goes on to observe that one might still regard it as merely an "assisting form" joined to the body as a sailor to a ship (VIII.1, p. 513). To rule that sort of thing out, one needs to choose one from the vast number of possible theories of how soul and body relate.

Hylomorphism does not do its work, then, by some sort of primitive, ineffable magic. When unitarians claim that the rational soul is the form of the body, they have— as we have seen—a very specific and well-developed account of exactly what this means, and why it accounts for substantial unity. When pluralists offer their own accounts of substantial unity, they owe us a similar story, and of course the same is true among post-scholastic authors. To treat the soul as the form of the body is one thing. To have a theory of soul–body unity is quite another.

25.5. Unification Strategies II: Pluralism

Pluralists devoted considerable ingenuity to account for substantial unity. As ever, we might begin with Scotus, who offers a particularly forthright discussion. He accepts that substances should have a special sort of unity, remarking that "it seems absurd" for there to be "no difference between a whole that is one thing *per se* and a whole that is one thing by aggregation, like a cloud or a heap" (*Ordinatio* III.2.2; Vat. IX n. 73). Whereas unitarians treat living things as a composite of soul and prime matter, on Scotus's analysis they are a composite of soul and body—an *actual* body, actualized by another substantial form, a *forma corporeitatis*. Unitarians reject this approach, because

---

[18] Aquinas foresees the sort of difficulty that Ockham's form of pluralism encounters: "cum intellectus non habeat determinatum organum in corpore, quo mediante exerceat operationes suas; ad quid uniretur corpori nisi esset eiusdem essentiae cum anima sensitiva?" (*Quod.* XI.5c). This succinctly captures why platonic dualism would become such a risk for both soul-and-mind pluralists and for post-scholastic dualists such as Descartes. Suárez discusses the issue of a pure principle of thought's informing a body at more detail in his disputation on the angels (*Disp. meta.* 35.3.12).

the potentiality side of Scotus's composite is already too actualized to admit of any further substantial union with another form. According to Scotus's body-and-soul pluralism, however, the human composite is sufficiently unified provided that the soul stands as actuality to the body's potentiality. Scotus criticizes Henry of Ghent's version of body-and-soul pluralism for failing to unify human beings in this way, remarking that "out of two actualities, of which one is not in potentiality with respect to another, nothing can be produced that is one *per se*" (*Ordinatio* IV.11.3; Wadding VIII n. 39). Scotus, in contrast, can insist that human beings and other living things, despite their multiple substantial forms, are unified in just the way the unitarians want, by a single substantial form that actualizes and unifies the whole substance.

This is the jargon. The question is what it actually amounts to, as a theory of substantial unity. Characteristically, Scotus recognizes the question and boldly confronts it:

If you ask why there is one thing *per se* in one case more than in another, I reply that just as, according to *Metaphysics* VIII [1045a23–25], there is no question of why one thing is made from actuality and potentiality, except that this is actuality *per se* and that potentiality *per se*, so too there is no cause for why one thing *per se* is made from this actuality and that potentiality, either in things or in concepts, except that this is potentiality with respect to that, and that is actuality.... The same is likewise true for one thing *per accidens*, for this is this and that is that, and so this is actuality *per accidens* and that potentiality *per accidens*. So from this and that is made one thing *per accidens*. (*Ordinatio* IV.11.3; Wadding VIII n. 53)

This is of a piece with Scotus's broader pessimism regarding the possibility of deep philosophical explanations. In §24.1, we saw Scotus argue that the difference between substantial and accidental forms is basic and unanalyzable. Now we can see a consequence of that attitude: because Scotus thinks there is no analysis of what distinguishes substantial forms, he likewise is forced to conclude that there is no analysis of how substantial forms bring about substantial unity. That is just what substantial forms do. In support of this claim, Scotus appeals to an often-cited passage from Aristotle: "If, as we say, one is matter, the other form, one in potentiality, the other in actuality, then the question will no longer appear to be puzzling" (*Meta.* VIII.6, 1045a23–25). Aquinas and other unitarians take this to mean that hylomorphism points toward an *explanation* of what gives substantial unity to a human being. The question gets answered, for the unitarian, in terms of their robust conception of substantial unity, physical and metaphysical. For Scotus, in contrast, the question no longer poses a difficulty because there is nothing more to be said. The question is not answered, because there is no question to be legitimately asked.[19]

---

[19] Scotus's appeal to substantial unity as a primitive fact, analogous to the case of heat, appears often in his work, as at *In Meta.* VIII.4 (*Opera phil.* IV n. 54), *Ord.* III.2.2 (Vat. IX n. 84), *Sent.* II.12.1 (Wadding VI nn. 12–15 [not in *Ordinatio*]), *Lec.* II.12 (Vat. XIX nn. 50, 67).

Cross praises Scotus for his frank and principled answer, remarking that "this is perhaps indicative of the general inability of substantial form to do any genuinely explanatory work.... [I]t seems to be the only philosophically principled answer that can be given to the question of the explanatory value of a theory of substantial form" (*Physics of Duns Scotus* p. 91). I hope to have shown that substantial forms have more explanatory value than Cross allows.

Scotus discusses the detail of his pluralist conception of unity at *Ord.* IV.11.3 (Wadding VIII n. 46): "Concedo quod formale esse totius compositi est principaliter per unam formam, et illa forma est qua totum compositum est hoc ens. Ista autem est ultima adveniens omnibus praecedentibus, et hoc modo totum compositum dividitur in duas partes essentiales, actum proprium, scilicet ultimam formam, qua est illud quod est, et propriam potentiam illius actus, quae includit materiam primam cum omnibus formis praecedentibus. Et isto modo concedo quod esse illud totale est completive ab una forma, quae dat toti illud quod est: sed ex hoc non sequitur quod in toto includatur praecise una

Scotus's verdict on the prospects for a theory of substantial unity is more pessimistic, or at least more frank, than that of other pluralists. Even in Scotus's case, however, it is not exactly the case that there is *nothing* more to be said about substantial unity beyond the bare invocation of potentiality and actuality. Scotus thinks that we can no more explain why a given substantial form unifies than we can explain why the quality of heat heats. But just as there is quite a lot to be said about heat, so there is quite a lot to be said about unity. Substantial unity is not easy to talk about, however, because it is not easy to know what it involves. The standard scholastic expressions are the extensionally equivalent pair *'unum per se'* and *'ens per se.'* Although I have used these phrases several times already, I have not yet tried to give an account of what they require. Essentially, to describe something as an *ens per se* in the present context is to describe it as an individual substance. Strictly speaking, however, this way of understanding *'ens per se'* requires combining two distinct senses of that phrase. In one sense, the phrase picks out entities in the category of Substance, and so contrasts with accidents, which inasmuch as they are essentially apt to inhere in other things are conceived of as *entia per alia* (§6.1). In another sense, an *ens per se* is contrasted with a mere aggregate that fails to be an individual. Understood in this second way, an *ens per se* can be either a substance or an accident. In the present context, these two senses are effectively fused together, so that an *ens per se* is an individual substance, neither a mere aggregate of multiple substances nor an accident or mode inhering in a substance.[20]

With this terminology in mind, we can now ask what makes a human being, or any material substance, be an *ens per se*. To be sure, the answer is not that an *ens per se* is simple or indivisible. Indeed, often an *ens per se* will be composed of other substances. Strictly speaking, as we will see in the next chapter, both prime matter and substantial forms count as substances, as do the integral parts of a material body. So, although an *ens per se* is not a *mere* aggregate, it will often be an aggregate—an aggregate with the proper sort of unity to count as a substance.

What then is the proper unity? What distinguishes those aggregates that are substances from those aggregates that are mere heaps or otherwise insufficiently unified? One standard way to draw this distinction is to describe an *ens per se* as something that has its own nature or essence—something, in other words, that is a member of some

---

forma, vel quin in toto includantur plures formae, non tanquam specifice constituentes illud compositum, sed tanquam quaedam inclusa in potentiali istius compositi."

Various pluralist attempts to account for the unity of substances are discussed in Pegis, *Problem of the Soul* pp. 53–76; Zavalloni, *Richard de Mediavilla*; Adams, *William Ockham* II:647–69; Pasnau, "Olivi on the Metaphysics of Soul"; Cross, *Physics of Duns Scotus* pp. 47–93.

[20] On the two senses of *'ens per se,'* see e.g. Aquinas, *In Meta.* V.9.885 and Suárez, *Disp. meta.* 4.3.3. On these issues in general see Rozemond, *Descartes's Dualism* pp. 167–9. Olivo, "L'homme en personne," puts great weight on the distinction between these two senses, using it to contend that although Descartes treats a human being as an *ens per se* in one sense (as a unity), he does not in the other sense (as a substance). Hence "on ne peut tirer partie de ce que Descartes affirme que l'homme est *ens per se* pour en conclure, dans un sens ou dans l'autre, à propos de sa substantialité" (p. 76). But this makes no sense. For scholastic authors, anything that is an *ens per se* in the first sense is a basic entity, falling directly under the genus *being*. Such things need not be substances, but in that case they will be accidents. For Descartes, the only basic entities are substances and modes (§13.5). So the only logical space Olivo opens up here in the context of Descartes's thought is the possibility that the human composite could be a mode, a view he expressly rejects when it appears in Regius (see note 24 below). More worthy of consideration is Olivo's proposal that Descartes's human composite should be understood on the model of Christ's hypostatic union. But although such unity has interesting affinities with Descartes's conception of mind and body, there is no reason to think he himself would have wanted mind–body union to be understood in this way.

species of substance. The Coimbran catalogue of the different kinds of unity (§24.2) holds that "the *per se* unity of composite things results from the composition of parts that are collected in some third nature" (*In Phys.* I.9.11.2). Eustachius a Sancto Paulo similarly defines an *ens per se* as "what belongs to a single nature and essence" (*Summa* I.1.3b.1.3, I:48). This line of thought in effect adds to the previous characterization of an *ens per se*, ruling out not only accidents and aggregates, but also substantial parts of a whole. The part is not an *ens per se*, strictly speaking, because it does not properly have a nature of its own, but contributes to the nature of some whole. Thus, according to Christoph Scheibler, "a composite entity is *unum per se* if the partial entities that are in it are contained under one common essence" (*Metaphys.* I.4.1 n. 9). Thus water counts as *unum per se*, and so an *ens per se*, even though it is composed of various parts—matter and substantial form, and sundry portions of water—"because all those parts are contained under the one essence of water" (ibid.). In contrast, water mixed with wine is an *ens per accidens*. (The strict unitarian could hardly welcome a pool of water as an *ens per se*, unless, rather implausibly, that pool were thought to have a single substantial form, and the sundry portions of water were thought to exist only when contiguous with the whole. Scheibler, however, is no unitarian.)[21]

This appeal to natures suggests a line of argument that any pluralist, including the soul-and-mind pluralist, might deploy to avoid platonic dualism: that the mind–body composite is a single, *per se* unity because the rational soul does not have its own distinct nature, but contributes to the nature of the whole composite, the human being. Scotus, among many others, suggests this approach: "I grant that the total existence [of the composite] is completed by a single form that makes the whole be what it is. But it does not follow from this that precisely one form is contained in the whole, nor that there are not multiple forms contained in the whole" (*Ordinatio* IV.11.3 [Wadding VIII n. 46]). Multiple substantial forms do not preclude substantial unity, on this line of thought, provided that there is a story about what "makes the whole be what it is"– in other words, that gives the composite its nature.

This approach captures a defining mark of what it is to be an *ens per se*, inasmuch as every *ens per se* falls into some one species. Yet even if this points toward what makes the soul–body composite a genuine unity, it is not nearly as helpful a strategy as one might suppose, because it identifies a *consequence* of substantial unity rather than the

---

[21] For other examples of the link between *per se* unity and belonging to a natural kind, see Zabarella, *De rebus nat.*, De gen. ch. 2 (col. 398), and also Henry of Harclay, *Quaest. ord.* 8 n. 81: "quia ultima forma dat nomen et speciem, quia illa est unica, ita totum compositum unum ens et non duo entia"; Scipion Dupleix, *Métaphys.* III.2.3: "L'étant qui a cause par soi a son être réglé à l'ordre de nature. L'étant par accident a son être incertain, fortuit ou artificiel." See also Scheibler's further remarks at *Metaphys.* I.12.1 n. 13 and I.12.3 n. 57.

For the idea that an *ens per se* can be composed of parts so long as they share the same nature, see Ockham, *Quaest. var.* VI.2 (*Opera theol.* VIII:213–14): "totum per se componitur ex partibus essentialibus, quarum una est potentia essentialiter et alia actus, et neutra est per se in genere sed solum per reductionem. Totum per accidens, licet componatur ex partibus talibus quarum una est in potentia ad aliam [viz., accidens to a subject], tamen utraque pars talis entis est per se in genere, quia tam accidens quam eius subjectum"; Robert Alyngton, *In Praed.* p. 263: "Aliae tamen substantiae, scilicet materia et forma, quae sunt principia substantiarum materialium, et partes quantitativae substantiarum, sive sint minima naturalia sive maiora minimis naturalibus, ut dicit haec via, sunt per se in praedicamento substantiae sicut sunt per se entia. Verumtamen sicut sunt entia secundum partem et non complete per se, sic non sunt primo et principaliter in praedicamento substantiae, sed per se secundo." On this line of thought, a substance–accident composite (a thick substance) cannot be an *ens per se* because its parts are not even in the same category (the same highest genus), let alone in the same species.

cause of such unity. As before, it is not enough simply to stipulate that this is what the rational soul does. The problem is to *explain* the sort of union the rational soul has with the body, such that we properly categorize the whole composite as a substance in the species *human being*. To be sure, as noted earlier, common sense tells us that the soul–body composite is a single substance. But one might also follow common sense in supposing that a car (or other artifact) is a single substance, and we might imagine that its engine is analogous to the rational soul. Why is that a false analogy? Why is *car* not a species of substance, whereas *human being* is?

The closest thing to a solution I have found among scholastic pluralists rests on an appeal to teleology, which gets expressed in claims such as that soul and body are *incomplete* relative to the human composite, and that body and soul are *ordered* to one another. Versions of these ideas can be found all the way through the scholastic era, from Henry of Ghent in the late thirteenth century to Franco Burgersdijk in the early seventeenth. Burgersdijk, for instance, gives the standard pluralist account of how, when the ultimate substantial form in a substance is introduced in the process of generation, "the more imperfect form is not abolished, but ceases to be a specifying form, and becomes a disposition." Then he adds the crucial explanatory clause: "And because the imperfect form was ordered to the more perfect form, and apt to receive it, that [more perfect] posterior form, when tied to the imperfect form, does not make one thing by aggregation, but one thing *per se*" (*Collegium phys.* 20.10, pp. 206–7). This is teleological language: the less perfect is "ordered" to the more perfect, and "apt" to receive it. Even the language of the lesser form becoming a mere "disposition" for the more perfect form suggests the picture of a process working according to the intention of nature, where the lower-level substantial forms work to prepare a body that then gets perfected by the introduction of the rational soul, which is the culmination of the process of generation. This same approach is even more starkly on display in Oresme, a soul-and-mind pluralist. When he confronts the objection that on his account a human being would not be *unum per se*, he responds in a sentence: "this is denied, because the material sensory soul disposes [the body] for the intellective soul" (*In De an.* II.5, p. 155). The force of the argument is again teleological: the *purpose* of the body informed by the sensory soul is to serve as part of the composite perfected by the rational soul. Oresme allows that it would be within God's power to separate off the rational soul from this animal body, leaving the animal to roam free. What would we call such a non-rational quasi-human being? Oresme's answer is that it would belong to a new, hitherto unseen species (p. 154). Ockham, while admitting the same possibility, had denied that such a creature would count as an animal at all, except equivocally, because "it is not a complete being existing *per se* in a genus, but is naturally suited to be an essential part of something existing *per se* in a genus" (*Quodlibet* II.10 [*Opera theol.* IX:161]). For both Oresme and Ockham, facts about the natural order of things—rather than about abstract metaphysical possibilities of independence—determine the ultimate constituents in nature. Human beings count as *per se* unities because they are aimed at by nature in a way that artifacts and other *per accidens* unities are not.[22]

---

[22] The idea that unity can be given a teleological account is evident in Aristotle's initial definition of 'whole' at *Meta.* V.26: "We call a whole that from which is absent none of the parts of which it is said to be naturally (φύσει) a whole" (1023b26–27). It can be readily found in a great many scholastic discussions. Henry of Ghent, for instance, characterizes

Perhaps surprisingly, this is the first appearance of teleological reasoning in the whole course of this study. It is moreover particularly interesting that scholastic pluralists appeal to teleology here, because this is precisely the sort of context where teleology retains a foothold today: in explaining the systematic features of living organisms in terms of the functions that those systems perform. There remains something plausible in the idea that the mind–body composite should be regarded as a single organism *just because* the two are designed to function together, as a unit—even if we were to decide they are very different in nature. Even so, such explanations were generally rejected by post-scholastic authors of the seventeenth–century, who notoriously turned their back on final causes. This should lead us to wonder just what sorts of unification strategies might be deployed in the post-scholastic context, and it is to this vexed topic that I finally turn.

25.6. Unification Strategies III: Descartes

Recent scholarship has paid considerable attention to whether the mind still counts as the form of the body, in Descartes and other post-scholastic authors. This, as I have been stressing, is the wrong question. Anyone can *say* that the mind is the form of the body, and the notion of *form* is so capacious that there is bound to be some sense in which that claim comes out true. Quite regardless of whether post-scholastic authors wish to retain the vocabulary of hylomorphism, they need to account for what makes the mind–body composite one thing.

Some seventeenth-century authors, such as Pierre Gassendi and Robert Boyle, are happy to speak of the mind as the form of the body, but without gaining any

---

the pluralist view as holding that "in qualibet re naturali et individuali sunt plures formae substantiales naturales ordinem et colligantiam naturalem adinvicem habentes, simul per suam substantiam existentes in eodem, quarum illa quae est ultimo adveniens completiva est entis illius, et hoc secundum alios ex eis tanquam formalis et completiva respectu praecedentium" (*Quod.* IV.13; ed. 1518 I:104vK).

Unitarians just as much as pluralists invoke such teleological considerations (even if the pluralists have to put more weight on them). Aquinas, in the following passage, appeals both to species membership and to teleology to ward off the charge that body and rational soul make an accidental unity: "etsi possit per se subsistere non tamen habet speciem completam, sed corpus advenit ei ad complementum speciei" (*Quaest. de anima* 1 ad 1). See also *Summa theol.* 1a 75.2 ad 1 and 76.1 ad 6: "...ita anima humana manet in suo esse cum fuerit a corpore separata, habens aptitudinem et inclinationem naturalem ad corporis unionem." At *Summa contra gent.* II.56.1319, Aquinas distinguishes three possible ways of being *unum simpliciter*. "unum autem simpliciter tripliciter dicitur: vel sicut indivisibile, vel sicut continuum, vel sicut quod est ratione unum." The soul and body do not make a unity in the first way, since they are a composite, nor in the second way, since that applies only to material parts. The critical question, then, is whether soul and body make something that has a single *ratio* or nature.

The Coimbrans also appeals to the parts' aptitude for union: "quandoquidem anima et corpus sunt actus et potentia eiusdem generis, habentes inter se naturalem habitudinem et proportionem ad condendum unum quidpiam substantiale" (*In De an.* II.1.6.3). See also Suárez: "In anima vero secus res se habet, nam, etiamsi sit separata, est pars secundum positivam aptitudinem et naturam, et non tantum per non repugnantiam. Est enim pars non integralis, sed essentialis, habetque incompletam essentiam, natura sua institutam ad complendam aliam, et ideo semper est substantia incompleta" (*Disp. meta.* 33.1.11); "Cum enim neque materia neque forma per se sint entia completa et integra in suo genere, sed ad illud componendum natura sua institutae sint, merito illud quod ex eis proxime componitur, essentia et natura per se una dicitur et est" (*Disp. meta.* 4.3.8).

For a helpful general discussion of late scholastic conceptions of substantial unity, see Des Chene, *Physiologia* pp. 134–8. The importance of teleological considerations has received little attention in the secondary literature. The closest I have found is in Rozemond, who in several places describes the scholastic account of substantial unity as "teleological" (*Descartes's Dualism* pp. 160, 161). But her discussion is not as helpful as it might be, because she assimilates this way of describing the situation to the much stronger, and incorrect claim, regarding matter and soul, that "it is part of their very essence to belong to a composite" (ibid., p. 156). This is never true of scholastic conceptions of the rational soul, and for pluralists it is not true even of the human body.

explanatory advantage from so doing.[23] Others think it best to reject such Aristotelian language, and think they can avoid platonic dualism without it. Gerard and Arnold Boate, for instance, in their *Philosophia naturalis reformata* (1641), reject both substantial forms and prime matter. Yet although they insist that both body and mind are complete substances in their own right, they hold that nevertheless the two can be joined together to make a genuine unity:

We grant that the soul does not assist the body as a sailor assists a ship. . . . But it by no means follows that for this reason it ought to inform the body in the way that the peripatetic dreams it does, when other, truer modes are available for two or more distinct substances to be connected   3
so as to constitute one thing. We have innumerable examples—or, rather, models (*imita-menta*)—for this sort of thing in the case of artifacts (*artibus*). For in works of this sort distinct substances—sometimes very different from each other—are accustomed to be joined so as to   6
constitute a single body. Yet the force and industry of natural agents goes far beyond all the industry of artists, and so results in distinct substances tied together and aptly joined so as to constitute one thing—not as one thing actualizes or informs another, but as each one to itself   9
and through itself is this that it is and exhibits to the whole the complete character of the part.
(I.3.33)

The Boates here reject platonic dualism, spurning the sailor–ship analogy (line 1) and instead working toward the conclusion that soul and body stand to one another as parts of a whole (line 10). They claim to be able to get this result without appealing to hylomorphism. Resisting the temptation to treat artifacts as genuine substances, they instead refer to such cases as "models" (line 4), and contend that if an artisan can create something substance-like by (say) sticking marble eyes into the clay image of a man, then nature—which is much more powerful—ought to be able to generate true substances from equally disparate ingredients. It is, however, wholly unclear how they think nature does this. If they think that, as in artificial cases, spatial contiguity or causal connections are enough to ensure unity, then they ought to think that artifacts are genuine substances. If this is not enough, then they owe us some account of what substantial unity does amount to, and they are even farther than the pluralists from providing any answer.

Very occasionally, one finds post-scholastic authors denying that the mind–body composite is a *per se* unity. The most striking example from our period is David Gorlaeus, whose *Exercitationes philosophicae* (*circa* 1611) offers up a shockingly explicit version of platonic dualism:

---

[23] Gassendi makes it clear that the rational soul is not included in his critique of substantial form: "merito iure et substantia et substantialis forma censetur [anima rationalis seu mens]. Agimus autem de caeteris solum . . ." (*Syntagma* II.1.7.3, I:466b). Boyle makes a similar qualification: "whenever I shall speak indefinitely of substantial forms, I would always be understood to except the reasonable soul that is said to inform the human body; which declaration I here desire may be taken notice of, once for all" (*Origin of Forms* [*Works* V:300; Stewart p. 15]).

Gassendi is unusual among post-scholastic authors in being willing to postulate not just a rational but also a sensory soul. This is, in large part, just a terminological concession, in that he makes it clear that his sensory soul can be given a reductive account in atomistic terms, along the lines of other essential forms (see §27.6 for Gassendi's retention of essences). A sensory soul, according to Gassendi, "textura sit ex tenuissimis atomis." In virtue of organizing these "subtilissima" and "tenuissima" corpuscles, such a soul mediates between the body and the rational soul (*Syntagma* II.1.7.4, I:472a). This view makes its way into the preface of Charleton's *Natural History of the Passions*, as well as into various still more obscure works. For details, see Michael, "Averroes and the Plurality of Forms" p. 181; Garber, "Soul and Mind" pp. 771–2; McCracken, "Knowledge of the Soul" p. 823.

We gladly concede that there are composites, but we do not recognize any one being that should be called the composite. Instead, there are many beings. For it is indeed the composing parts that we call composites, inasmuch as they are the things composed. We hold that each part   3
has its essence before composition and also retains it afterwards, nor is any being made that is numerically one, or one being made from these parts. Instead, they are united and mixed so that one continuous thing is made, which is one being by aggregation and not by essence. Thus in a   6
human being there is a soul and also a body, and these two are united in such a way that the body is made the soul's residence, vehicle, and instrument through which the soul exercises its operations. But these two are not made into one being, called a human being. Instead, each   9
retains its complete and perfect essence, by which it is what it is. Still, the human being is not the same as the soul, nor the same as the body; rather, it is the same as the soul and the body taken together and aggregated. If, however, the human being is to be considered not as a being by   12
aggregation, but as one thing *per se*, then it will be the same as the soul existing in the body. (exerc. 12, pp. 222–3)

As we should expect, Gorlaeus stresses that the parts of the composite exist prior to the composite, each with its own independent essence (lines 3–4, 9–10). With this he rejects the unitarian conception of how a form–matter composite is unified. And whereas the scholastic pluralist insists that what results from composition is a new entity, with a new essence, Gorlaeus insists that even after composition there remain two things, continuous and so unified by aggregation (line 6), but with no new essence (line 6) and so not one thing *per se* (line 13). The point holds in general for form–matter composites (lines 1–6) and in particular for human beings (lines 6–13), which can be regarded either as nothing more than the aggregate of soul and body or—if one wants to hold onto the idea of a human being as *per se unum*—as simply the soul.

Gorlaeus argues for this sort of platonic dualism at some length, but here I will content myself simply with noting his bold claim—a claim so bold, indeed, that hardly anyone in the seventeenth–century was willing to follow him. When Descartes's disciple Henricus Regius dared to do so in 1641, he created an immediate scandal.[24] News of this quickly came to Descartes, who reproached Regius with the remark that "you could scarcely have said anything more objectionable and provocative" (III:460). It

---

[24] Regius defended the following theses in a disputation at Utrecht from December 1641: "VIII. Forma specialis est mens humana, quia per eam cum forma generali in materia corporea homo est id quod est. Haec ad formam generalem seu materialem nullo modo potest referri: quoniam ipsa (utpote substantia incorporea) nec est corpus, nec ex motu aut quiete, magnitudine, situ aut figura partium oriri potest. IX. Ex hac et corpore non fit unum per se, sed per accidens, cum singula sint substantiae perfectae seu completae. X. Cum autem dicuntur incompletae, hoc intelligendum est ratione compositi, quod ex harum unione oritur" (as quoted in Bos, *Correspondence* p. 93n.). Regius would subsequently apologize to the Utrecht theology professor Gisbertus Voetius, and offer the excuse that he had gotten the idea from Gorlaeus, without realizing how controversial it was (ibid., p. 93). In subsequent works, Regius would abandon this controversial idea for the perhaps equally controversial idea that the mind is simply a mode of the body (see Clarke, "Henricus Regius" sec. 4), a move that Descartes would later describe to him as "multo peior" (IV:250).

Voetius suggests that Gorlaeus's own source for the doctrine that a human composite is an *ens per accidens* is Nicholas Taurellus, the German Protestant whose *Philosophiae triumphus* (1573) does indeed contend that "homo non est unum per se, quod duabus immutatis constituatur formis" (axiomata f. d6r). For further information on Taurellus, as well as evidence for the link to Gorlaeus, see Lüthy, "Gorlaeus' Atomism" pp. 271 and 278–90. It is unfortunately not at all clear why Taurellus wants to deny the unity of the human composite; the above remark appears as an unargued axiom. Lüthy makes the interesting suggestion that this thesis is connected to Taurellus's overarching concern to introduce some distance between the soul and the corrupting influence of the body, as suggested in this passage: "Nos enim ex corpore et anima constituimur, sed voluntas per se considerata simplex est animae facultas, quae sine corpore intelligi atque consistere potest, qua ratione bonum quid existimanda est, licet ob corporibus affectus prae bono malum appraehendat" (*Philosophiae triumphus* p. 36).

is, however, maddeningly difficult to determine exactly what Descartes's own view is, with the result that recent scholars have variously assimilated his view to platonic dualism, scholastic pluralism, and various -isms in between. Although this and the preceding chapter are intended to help situate Descartes's thought in the proper context, his own views remain elusive. To be sure, he does not want to be read as defending platonic dualism along Gorlaeus's lines. But is this because he does not believe it to be true, or because he does not dare say it, even if he thinks it?

If one takes Descartes at his word, ingenuously, one must conclude that he rejects platonic dualism. He is quite clear about this not just in his correspondence with Regius but also in the *Meditations*: "I am present in my body not merely as a sailor is present in a ship; rather, I am so very closely joined and, as it were, intermingled with my body that with it I compose one thing" (*Med.* VI, VII:81). Throughout our period, the sailor–ship image is a shorthand image for platonic dualism, which Descartes here rejects in favor of the view that mind and body make one thing (*unum quid*). The Fourth Replies appeals to a more scholastic set of terms to reach this same conclusion:

Substances can be called incomplete in that they have nothing incomplete about them as substances, but only when referred to some other substance with which they compose something that is one *per se*. So it is that a hand is an incomplete substance when referred to the whole body of which it is a part, but it is a complete substance when considered alone. In exactly the same way the mind and the body are incomplete substances when referred to the human being that they compose, but considered alone they are complete substances. (VII:222)

The passage shows every sign of understanding *per se* unity in the scholastic sense. Such unities need not be simple, and are even, ordinarily, constituted out of other substances. (Aquinas himself had offered the hand as an example of an incomplete substance [*Summa theol.* 1a 75.2 ad 1].) The crucial point is that the parts of an *ens per se* are somehow incomplete, and dependent on the whole for their completion.

Yet granted that this is how Descartes *wants* to be understood, the question remains of whether such a conception of the mind–body composite is consistent with his broader views. Here I will focus in particular on whether he has any basis for treating mind and body as something more than an aggregate of two substances in close causal interaction. (The question of interaction is of course a further problem in its own right, but is not my concern here.) As we saw in §24.5, Descartes does sometimes describe the mind as the form of the body. It should be clear by now, however, just how little that matters. More important is Descartes's willingness to treat the mind–body composite as having a nature of its own, in the way that the sailor–ship composite does not. This underwrites the following argument, which Descartes recommends to Regius, for the human composite as an *ens per se*:

Inasmuch as a human being is considered in himself as a whole, we certainly say that he is *unum ens per se*, and not *per accidens*, because the union that joins a human body and soul to each other is not accidental to a human being, but essential, since a human being without it is not a human being. (III:508)

The point of such talk of essences, I take it, is that *human being* is a kind, and that both body and soul, as well as their union, are essential to a thing's belonging to that kind. But although this furnishes more evidence regarding the conclusion Descartes is after—

the rejection of platonic dualism—it does nothing to explain *how* soul and body are unified. As stressed in the previous section, the judgment that a certain thing is a substance, with its own nature, is a *consequence* of its having a certain sort of unity, and does nothing to *explain* that unity.[25]

As some recent commentators have observed, Descartes's position is analogous to that of the scholastic pluralists. More precisely, it is like that of the soul-and-mind pluralists, who similarly want to call the mind the form of the body, but without being able to treat the mind as a substantial form of the usual sort. One might suppose that mind and body, in Descartes, are each too complete and independent to be credibly compared with the views of any scholastic author—in effect, one might suppose that Descartes is too much of a substance dualist. This is not the case. Pluralists, especially soul-and-mind pluralists, treat both sides of the composite as genuine substances in just the way that Descartes does.[26] What makes his position trickier is not that he regards the parts as any more complete or substantial, but that he lacks any powerful explanation for the unity of the composite. This is not to say that Descartes has no explanation. On the contrary, I believe that he has two of them, but that the unity they purchase is not as strong as what scholastic authors seek.

Descartes's first strategy—his official strategy—gets set out quite explicitly in the Sixth Meditation as the reason why he "composes one thing" rather than being merely "present in my body as a sailor in a ship" (VII:81, as above). This reason is that events in the body register in the mind as "confused sensations" rather than appearing as they are, as bodily motions. So, tear a piece of paper and I register this as the mere dislocation of corpuscles; tear my skin and I register this as *pain*. There is, I think, no more to this argument than meets the eye. The point is simply that mind and body are two things that, when put together, give rise to a unique sort of phenomenon, and to

---

[25] On Descartes's mind–body composite as having its own nature, see also the Fourth Replies: "ille qui brachium hominis diceret esse substantiam realiter a reliquo eius corpore distinctam non ideo negaret illud idem ad hominis integri naturam pertinere" (VII:228). I take the Sixth Replies to be making the same point when Descartes remarks that mind and body "dicantur tantum esse unum et idem unitate compositionis, quatenus in eodem homine reperiuntur, ut ossa et carnes in eodem animali" (VII:424).

[26] Adams is clearly wrong—as the following chapter will make clear—when she writes that "medievals followed Aristotle in denying that any substance could be constituted (wholly or partially) from another substance or substances" (*William Ockham* II:634). She does seem to be right in general, however, in her claim (ibid.) that an *ens per se* cannot be composed of other *entia per se*. This principle has been used to distinguish Descartes's views from those of the scholastics, especially in Kaufman's excellent "Descartes on Composites." I agree that this is a promising line of inquiry for anyone who would deny that Descartes treats the mind–body composite as a substance, and I lack the space to investigate the issue further here. Anyone seeking more details should visit us in Boulder.
   The comparison of Descartes to the scholastic pluralists came into prominence in Hoffman, "Unity of Descartes's Man" pp. 363–64, and can found as well in Des Chene, *Physiologia* p. 65 and Rozemond, *Descartes's Dualism* p. 145, who notes the similarity to Ockham in particular. Before this flurry of interest, Gordon Wilson, "Henry of Ghent," had argued for a similar thesis.
   On Descartes's form of dualism as fundamentally distinct from the scholastics see again Kaufman, "Descartes on Composites" and also Rozemond, *Descartes's Dualism* ch. 5, who holds that "Descartes simply *never* proposes that the mind is the form of the body *as an account of their union*" (*Descartes's Dualism* p. 152). Hoffman, in contrast, has argued for the continuity between Descartes and scholastic pluralism regarding the human composite, first in "Unity of Descartes's Man," then in "Cartesian Composites," and finally in "Union and Interaction" where he writes that "it is my controversial contention that Descartes's solutions to these three problems of the union of mind and body are based on his retention of two fundamental Aristotelian metaphysical doctrines. The first doctrine is that of *hylomorphism* . . ." (p. 391). As for how hylomorphism achieves substantial unity, Hoffman embraces just the sort of mysterian strategy I wish to reject, remarking that "the relation between form and matter is a primitive and unanalyzable notion" (ibid., p. 392). Maybe so, but then instead of invoking hylomorphism we might as well say that mind stands to body as warp to weft, or as yin to yang.

that extent can be regarded as a kind of unit. Descartes subsequently reiterates this argument on many occasions. He points out to Regius, for instance, that an angelic mind, even if causally connected to a human body, would not experience the same sort of bodily sensations (III:493); it would, instead, simply observe flesh being torn, like a piece of paper. Hence an angel–body composite would not be an *ens per se*. Particularly telling is this remark to Arnauld, who had specifically accused Descartes of committing himself to a form of platonic dualism:

It seemed to me I was sufficiently careful to guard against someone's supposing that a human being is simply a soul using a body. For in that same Sixth Meditation in which I dealt with the mind's distinction from the body, I also proved at the same time that it is substantially united with the body. And the arguments that I used to prove this are as strong as any I remember having read elsewhere. (Fourth Replies, VII:227–8)

Unless one supposes that Descartes is being utterly disingenuous here, one should conclude that Descartes rejects platonic dualism (lines 1–2), that he instead thinks mind and body make a single substance (lines 3–4), and that the reason they are a substance is not that they are a hylomorphic composite, but that they yield sensations of a certain distinctive kind.[27]

Although this argument from confused sensations has been much maligned by critics, on the grounds that it does nothing to account for genuine substantial unity, it seems to me an accurate reflection of just how much unity Descartes thinks there actually could be between two substances of such wholly different natures. In *Principles* I.60 he remarks that "even if we suppose God has joined a corporeal substance to a thinking substance so closely that they could not be more closely conjoined, and so compounded these two into some one thing, they nonetheless remain really distinct." I take it that he accepts the protasis, and does so not because he envisages some sort of magical, ineffable, hylomorphic union between two very different kinds of substances, but because he thinks that not even God could produce all that much unity from two such very different things. A mind and body connected in such a way that bodily events

---

[27] As many commentators have noted, Descartes never calls the human composite a substance (e.g. Olivo, "L'homme en personne" p. 70). This is an interesting fact, inasmuch as human beings are usually treated as paradigmatic substances, throughout our four centuries. Even so, Descartes does here use the phrase "substantialiter unitam" (VII:228). And although some scholars have raised doubts about what this expression might mean for Descartes (e.g., Rozemond, *Descartes's Dualism* p. 165), it seems to me quite implausible to deny that it commits Descartes to treating the human composite as a substance. Descartes also, as discussed in §24.5, describes the soul as "vera forma substantialis hominis" (III:505), which would similarly seem to entail that a human being is a substance, no matter how attenuated Descartes's notion of substantial form.

A further notable reason not discussed in the main text for reading Descartes as a platonic dualist is that he seemingly recognizes only two kinds of substances, thinking and extended, and so has nowhere to put the human composite. (For a forceful statement of this worry see Kaufman, "Descartes on Composites.") Given the connection between being an *ens per se* and belonging to a kind, this worry is particularly serious. One reason I relegate the issue to the notes is that it is not clear this is a distinctive problem for Descartes. The scholastic Porphyrian tree for substance, after all, similarly divides substance into corporeal and incorporeal. So the scholastics too might wonder where the logical space is for human beings. (In fact, they unanimously agree that human beings are corporeal substances.) A second reason I think the issue not decisive is that although *Principles* I.48 recognizes "non plura quam duo summa genera rerum," a later passage in the *Comments on a Certain Broadsheet* (VIIIB:349–50) seems to recognize the problem and expressly leaves room for composite substances—i.e., human beings—that have two principle attributes. Olivo rightly stresses this text in "L'homme en personne" p. 79, as does Hoffman, "Cartesian Composites" p. 269.

in the latter yield thoughts of a certain unique kind in the former *are* unified in a certain sort of way, and for Descartes this is as much unity as the situation admits of.[28]

So much for the official argument. I think that Descartes also has an unofficial argument, however, one that he shares with the scholastic pluralists. This is the appeal to teleology: that soul and body constitute a substantial union because they are naturally suited to one another. This is a surprising conclusion to reach, inasmuch as Descartes is famously hostile to teleology, proclaiming in the French edition of *Principles* I.28, for instance, that "we shall entirely banish from our philosophy the search for final causes." Even so, his discussions of the workings of mind and body are full of teleological language. He speaks, for instance, of the body's organs as "designed to satisfy our natural needs" (*Principles* IV.190), and offers an account of "the true function of respiration" (*Discourse* pt. 5, VI:53). Such facts get applied to the question of unity, as when he writes that "the body is one thing, and in a way indivisible, because of the disposition of its organs, these being so related to one another that the removal of any one of them renders the whole body defective" (*Passions* I.30). Even the union of mind and body gets described in teleological terms, as in a letter that attempts to explain away Regius's embarrassing embrace of platonic dualism by insisting on the "natural aptitude" of mind and body for substantial union (to Dinet, VII:585). Indeed, his entire theory of sensation bears witness to this sort of teleological perspective on the mind–body union. The senses do not show the external world as it is, because that would not be as useful to us as what in fact they do: "properly speaking, nature has furnished sensory perceptions only so as to inform the mind of what is beneficial or harmful for the composite of which the mind is a part" (*Med.* VI, VII:83).

I do not regard these passages as an embarrassment, or as in any way inconsistent with Descartes's broader views. He does not think that appeals to final causality should play any role in his philosophy—physical, metaphysical, or otherwise. Since we cannot know what the true final causes are in nature, nothing should be built on that foundation. Still, Descartes's Christian beliefs, and even plain common sense, make it natural for him to suppose that certain parts of the created world have a special sort of functional interrelationship, by design. This cannot be any part of his official account of substantial unity. Officially, "when we consider the body alone we perceive nothing in it on account of which it desires to be united with the soul, as there is nothing in the soul on account of which it needs to be united to the body" (III:461). Hence the official argument rests on confused sensations. If we were, however, to adopt less rigorous standards for what counts as evidence, and take into account our familiar views about

---

[28] My reading of the argument from confused sensations is in effect what Margaret Wilson calls the "Natural Institution" theory, and I agree with her that this account is "philosophically resourceful and relatively intelligible" (*Descartes* p. 207). More recent interpreters are less impressed. Rozemond's exhaustive discussion of the issue concludes that "Descartes does not really explain *how* mind and body are united" (*Descartes's Dualism* p. 212) and that "I don't see in Descartes an answer to the question how mind and body are unified so that together they constitute a substance" (ibid., p. 213). For my part, I cannot see what sort of further story there could be here, and I suspect that Rozemond is looking for some kind of magic.

Kaufman dismisses the argument from confused sensations with the remark that "here, as in every text in which Descartes explicitly explains what the 'substantial union' amounts to, Descartes explains the union in terms of nothing more substantial than the fact that certain types of causal interactions between mind and body result in particular states of a mind or a body that would otherwise be absent, for instance if an angel were 'occupying' a body" ("Descartes on Composites" p. 51). He takes this as evidence that Descartes cannot suppose the mind–body composite to be a substance. I take it as evidence that his standards for what count as a substance are quite low.

how the world is supposed to be organized, then we could say that human beings, like other living things, have a special sort of unity that other aggregates lack.[29]

Yet even from this less rigorous perspective, the appeal to final causes cannot go as far in Descartes's case as it does for the scholastics. This is so specifically in human beings, and more generally for all substances. In the human case, although Descartes certainly seems to think that the mind and body are suited to be joined together, the extent of their functional interrelationship is considerably less than on scholastic views. For one thing, as stressed already (§24.5), Descartes's body does not depend on the mind, either physically or metaphysically, in the way that scholastic matter depends on substantial form. Just as importantly for present purposes, Descartes's mind does not require the body for its operations in the way that scholastic authors generally suppose. The tradition of Aristotelian empiricism insists on an intimate relationship between mind and body in the cognitive process. Suárez, for instance, appeals to "the mode of intellection in human beings" as an argument against platonic dualism—specifically, to the fact that "the intellect cannot perceive anything that was not previously supplied by the senses in some way." He concludes:

This clearly teaches that such a principle of intellection is not some whole substance altogether independent from the body in its essence; for a substance that in no way depends on a body for its being will not depend on it for its operation. (*In De an.* II.4, p. 260)

Suárez's point is that we have very good reason to treat soul and body as a single, unified substance because of the way their operations are interdependent. The human mind is *designed* to function on the basis of sensory input, and its operations will be gravely impeded without such input. Descartes famously rejects this kind of empiricist

---

[29] The best source for information on teleology in Descartes is Simmons, "Sensible Ends," to which my discussion in the main text is much indebted, though she does not directly consider the connection between teleology and substantial unity. Someone who does briefly draw that connection is Carriero, *Between Two Worlds* p. 395, though he finds traces of teleology in the confused sensation argument itself. On my view these are two distinct lines of thought. Gueroult discusses at some length the place of teleology in substantial unity (*Descartes* II:146–55). He assumes (as does Simmons, "Sensible Ends" p. 62n.) that Descartes's appeal to teleology applies only to human beings, and not to other animals. I am unpersuaded of this. Given that Descartes's occasional embrace of the language of ends occasionally gets applied to other animals, it might be thought to explain their unity as well. See also Machamer and McGuize, *Changing Mind*.

Descartes repeatedly stresses our inability to grasp the true ends of nature. See, e.g., *Med.* IV (VII:55), Fifth Replies (VII:375), *Principles* I.28, III.2–3, *Convers. with Burman* (V:158). All these passages take for granted that there are ends for which God created the world, which makes it surprising that Simmons—who cites all these passages—goes on to call into question whether Descartes accepts that God has any ends in action. The basis for her doubts is a passage in the Sixth Replies (VII:431–2), which she translates as follows: "It is inconsistent to suppose that the will of God was not indifferent from eternity concerning everything that was or will be, for one can imagine no goodness or truth, or anything worthy of belief or action or omission, whose idea was in the divine intellect prior to the decision of his will to make it so" ("Sensible Ends" pp. 65–6). This might indeed suggest, as Simmons puts it, that "God's intentions and decisions are not governed by any antecedent conception of what is good or true" (p. 66). But her translation is misleading, in numerous ways: (1) To say that God's will is *indifferentem* is merely to invoke a familiar scholastic technical term for the will's openness to contraries; (2) such openness to contraries applies not to "everything that was or will be" but to *omnia quae facta sunt aut unquam fient* (everything that has been made or ever will be made); (3) it is not that there was no idea of "goodness or truth" in God prior to God's decision to create, but that God had an idea of *nullum bonum vel verum* (no thing that is good or true); (4) it is not that, prior to creation, there was nothing "worthy of belief or action or omission," but that there was nothing that was *credendum vel faciendum vel omittendum* (no thing to be believed or to be made or not made). When the passage is so understood, it becomes clear that Descartes's point is not the bizarre one that God, prior to creation, is indifferent to everything—indifferent to himself? indifferent to goodness? indifferent to truth?— but that God is neutral between any *thing* that might or might not be made, and between any *proposition* that might or might not be made true. This is a perfectly standard scholastic theological view, routinely invoked to safeguard divine freedom (see e.g. Kretzmann, "A Particular Problem").

framework. In many ways, on his view, the body is an impediment to the mind's operations. Hence even if mind and body are suited to one another in a certain way, they also work at cross purposes, at least in some respects, which tends to undermine any appeal to teleology to explain their union.[30]

Thinking of substances more generally, Descartes faces a further obstacle to employing teleological explanations. For scholastic Aristotelians, the kinds of things there are accord with God's ideas for how things ought to be, and for every kind of material thing—dogs, cats, stones, etc.—there is a distinct substantial form (§27.3). Even if Descartes endorses the notion that the kinds of things correspond to God's ideas, he does not suppose that God executes that plan by introducing substantial forms into nature. Instead, material substances are simply bodies put into certain patterns of motion. This fundamentally changes the way Descartes thinks about the category of Substance. For the scholastics, the beginnings of an explanation of what makes substances special is that they have a substantial form. We human beings, however, do not know how to make substantial forms—at least not directly. We know only how to bring about accidental changes, which may or may not result in a new substantial form. Hence substances, on the scholastic picture, retain a special sort of connection with nature. The most we can do is make artifacts, and artifacts are not substances. For Descartes, in contrast, the sorts of processes that cause substances to come into existence are the same sorts of processes that human beings employ every day to make food, furniture, and houses. When someone constructs a bed out of a certain assembly of wood, much the same sort of story is at work as in the generation of a dog. Both are intended, and both are carried out through mechanical processes. It is no wonder, then, as we have seen (§24.5), that Descartes allows artifacts to count as substances.

For the scholastics, then, natural teleology neatly corresponds with their hylomorphic metaphysics: nature (that is, God) has designed the world a certain way, and established substantial forms to achieve that end. For Descartes, in contrast, God's means are mechanical. But since we can play that game too, there is no clear divide between what does and does not count as a substance. If a living thing is a substance, then a robot might be one too, and if a stone is a substance, then so too might a soufflé. Descartes has nothing in his ontology to distinguish between substances and non-substances, and he does not want to appeal to teleology. To the chagrin of his enthusiasts, it is not clear that he has a theory of material substance at all.

Descartes has open secrets, and I think it is natural to suspect him of having dark, closed secrets as well. Foremost among his open secrets are his rejection of substantial forms and real qualities—doctrines that he decorously avoided stating explicitly, but that everyone understood to be implicit in his work (§24.5). It is, I think, one of the dark secrets of his philosophy that he wishes to reject the significance of Substance as an ontological category. It is not that he thinks there are no substances, or that there is only one material substance, but that he thinks it a pointless relic of scholastic metaphysics to dispute over the boundaries between substances and mere aggregates. All there are are bodies and minds and their modes. Since there are no material simples

---

[30] On the independence of Descartes's mind from the senses, in contrast to Aristotelian empiricism, see e.g. Rozemond, *Descartes's Dualism* p. 160.

for Descartes (§5.4), there is no such thing as perfect unity even at the lower end. And since there is nothing in Descartes's austerely corpuscularian ontology to hold particles together at any higher level, there are simply no facts of the matter about whether or not a given cluster of *res extensa* counts as a substance. We can call a tiny particle of matter a substance; we can call a hand a substance; we can call the whole human body a substance; we can call the mind–body composite a substance. Such a composite does not have very much holding it together—just a funny sort of shared sensory operation, and our unreliable intuition that mind and body belong together. Since Descartes does not think that there is *ever* very much of a story to be had about what holds anything together, it is no wonder he finds it so easy to assert the unity of the human composite. After all, only someone with strict criteria for substancehood could be expected to be tempted by platonic dualism.

Descartes does not say these things, and so commentators have rushed to fill the void with their own preferred theories of what Descartes thinks a material substance is. I will have more to say about this in Chapter 28. For now I will just suggest that Descartes was nothing if not careful, and that we should take more seriously his silence in this domain. It was dangerous enough to call into question the category of Quality. To challenge the cogency of Substance too might have been fatal to Descartes's efforts at winning a wide audience for his views. Here, as elsewhere (§8.4), his preferred strategy was a kind of quietism. If you want it to count as a substance, count it.

26

Parts and Wholes

26.1. The Aristotelian's Dilemma

Questions about wholes and parts might plausibly be regarded as the most basic questions of metaphysics. To ask about what things are most fundamental, or what it is for a thing to change over time, or why certain things have more unity than other things—such questions demand some sort of conception of how things stand to their parts. So far this study has attempted to sort out the kinds of metaphysical parts postulated during our four centuries, and the kinds of work they were supposed to do. This chapter turns its attention primarily to integral parts, considering both their status within the whole and the problems for substantial unity that follow.

It seems on its face easy to understand the ontological status of parts for most of the earliest post-scholastic authors. For prominent figures like Gassendi and Descartes, and for a host of lesser figures as well, the parts of any whole must be as real as the whole, must be fully actual, and must be really distinct from each other. As Descartes puts it, "I conceive the two halves of a part of matter, however small it may be, as two complete substances" (III:477).[1] Gassendi endorses much the same idea, but without the "however small" clause, inasmuch as he postulates partless atoms. Either way, the appeal of this conception of the part–whole relationship is not hard to see, especially when it is combined with a strict corpuscularianism according to which the only real constituents of a substance are its integral parts. For on this sort of view, the structure of matter becomes thoroughly perspicuous. From big to small, bodies consist of entities of the same status and character. Assuming we know how to characterize bodies at one level of size and complexity, we can apply that same account to bodies of all sizes. The disadvantage of this approach, however, is that it leads directly to a host of difficult metaphysical questions regarding the unity and individuation of material substances. For if bodies have the same structure all the way up and all the way down, how do we ever draw principled lines between where one substance starts and another stops? It was largely concern over such questions that drove Descartes to his quietism on the

---

[1] Descartes continues his letter to Gibieuf with the remark that the two halves of any body are really divisible, thus refuting atomism. He makes a similar claim in *Principles* I.60: "certi tamen sumus illam [substantiam extensam] posse existere; atque, si existat, unamquamque eius partem, a nobis cogitatione definitam, realiter ab aliis eiusdem substantiae partibus esse distinctam." For brief discussion, see §5.4. For Gassendi, see §26.4.

metaphysics of substance (§25.6, §28.5), and that drove the next generation of post-scholastic authors toward their various eccentric metaphysical theses: Spinoza toward his monism,[2] for instance, and Leibniz in the opposite direction, toward his monads. Although that next generation lies outside the scope of this study, the following chapters will attempt to make clear the seriousness of the problems to which they were responding.

The focus of this chapter will mainly be on the scholastics. In contrast to that first generation of post-scholastic theories, it is not at all easy to understand the scholastic attitude toward the ontological status of parts. One reason for this is that they recognize so many different kinds of parts. This study began with the distinction between integral and metaphysical parts (§1.3), and since then it has moved systematically through the main kinds of metaphysical parts postulated by scholastic authors: prime matter, accidental forms, and substantial forms. Each of these cases raises distinct issues, as we have seen, and moreover there is considerable disagreement among scholastic authors regarding each individual case. Furthermore, the status of integral parts—bodily limbs and organs, for instance—raises distinct questions of its own, and here too scholastic authors were in considerable disagreement.

The reason there was such considerable disagreement among scholastics over the status of parts—and this is a second reason why their views are not easy to understand—is that there is a deep tension within Aristotelian thought between two ways of understanding the part–whole relationship. On one hand there is a tendency toward treating the parts of substances as themselves substances. This is true not only for integral parts, like a hand, but also for the metaphysical parts: prime matter and substantial forms. Francisco Suárez reflects this tendency when he remarks that "substance cannot be constituted *per se* from things that are altogether not substances" (*Disp. meta.* 33.1.5). The claim is carefully hedged: it leaves room for accidents (which *are* altogether not substances) to be part of the thick, *per accidens* substance. And even with respect to the thin, *per se* substance (§6.1), it may be that the parts will count as substances only in some qualified sense. But still Suárez endorses the idea that the parts of a substance must themselves, in some sense, be substances.[3]

On the other hand, the Aristotelian has a powerful incentive to resist the tendency to treat the parts of a substance as themselves substances. For inasmuch as Aristotelians want ordinary composite substances—dogs, cats, stones—to come out as genuine unities, it is natural to suppose that their parts must somehow be something less than substances. Scotus's opening argument, in a discussion of "Whether the parts of a substance are substances," makes that point:

Substance, understood as one of the [ten] most general categories, is an *ens per se*. No part of a substance is an *ens per se* when it is part of a substance, because then it would be a particular

---

[2] It is an explicit consequence of Spinoza's monism that substance is indivisible, and that the notion of a part of a substance, which would have to be a finite substance, is contradictory (*Ethics* I prop. 13).

[3] For Suárez on the parts as themselves substances, see also *In De an.* I.1 nn. 6–7. and *Disp. meta.* 13.4.4. See also Oresme, *In De an.* II.1, p. 124: "omnis pars substantiae est substantia; modo anima est pars substantiae, quia est pars animalis; [ergo anima est substantia]." And see Eustachius a Sancto Paulo, on the topic of prime matter: "Quod sit substantia patet: cum enim compositum naturale sit substantiale, non nisi ex substantiis constare potest; constat autem illud ex materia et forma" (*Summa* III.1.1.2.2, II:120).

thing (*hoc aliquid*), and one substance would be a particular thing from many particular things, which does not seem true. (*In Praed.* 15.1)

Behind the technical vocabulary in which this argument is couched is the commonsensical notion that if we want the composite substance to be the fundamental being, then its component parts had better not be independent in their own right. Ultimately, Scotus's view is not far from Suárez's, as will become clear by the end of the chapter. For although Scotus accepts the argument just quoted, he takes it to show only that the parts of a substance are not substances in one sense of the term, inasmuch as they do not fall into any general substance kind. (As suggested in §25.5, there is no substance kind either for metaphysical parts like *soul* or *matter*, or for integral parts like *hand* or *heart*.) Still, Scotus allows that in another sense the parts of a substance are substances, much as Suárez would later insist.

Although scholastic authors standardly want to draw distinctions of this sort, between one sense in which the parts count as substances and another sense in which they do not, there was considerable disagreement about how to do this. That there was such disagreement is scarcely surprising, because Aristotle himself says quite different and seemingly incompatible things in this regard. In the *Categories*, he makes it clear that he regards the parts of substances as themselves substances. Two remarks make this clear. First:

We need not be disturbed by any fear that we may be forced to say that the parts of a substance, being in a subject (the whole substance), are not substances. For when we spoke of things *in a subject* we did not mean things belonging in something as *parts*. (*Cat.* 5, 3a29–33)

It is fundamental to the scheme of the *Categories* that the things "in a subject" are accidents, not substances. But this does not show that the parts of a substance are not substances, Aristotle argues here, because parts are not in a subject in the relevant way. (They do not *inhere* in their subject.) Now Aristotle does not here indicate what sort of parts he has in mind, and he only implies without directly saying that the parts of a substance are substances. But two chapters later he discusses at some length the case of "a head or a hand or any such substance" (8b15), which makes it fairly clear both that by 'parts' he includes integral parts, and that he does indeed regard such parts as substances.

The *Metaphysics* offers a very different picture of these issues. There Aristotle remarks that "if the substance is one, it will not consist of substances present in it" (VII.13, 1039a7–8) and "no substance is composed of substances" (VII.16, 1041a4–5). Almost as if he were intending to correct the more relaxed doctrine of the *Categories*, he writes that "evidently even of the things that are thought to be substances, most are [only] potentialities, such as the parts of animals" (VII.16, 1040b5–6). Here then we seem to get quite a different story about integral parts. If they were substances in the sense in which the whole is a substance, then the whole would not be one thing, and so could not be a substance at all. The resulting picture about the structure of bodies looks very different from the standard post-scholastic picture. For here, instead of there being bodies all the way down, just as real and actual as the whole they compose, we have instead the rather murky notion of these parts being "only potentialities," as Aristotle puts it. This is what has come to be known as the doctrine of potential parts, which was often defended in some form by scholastic authors, and generally rejected in the seventeenth century. The following sections will try to come to grips with what this doctrine amounts to among scholastic authors.[4]

Before turning to that topic, however, something more should be said about the character of the dilemma that confronted the scholastic. We now read Aristotle's *Metaphysics* as a later and more sophisticated work, and so we are not surprised to find it making claims that either are not mentioned in or even contradict the *Categories*. Since scholastic authors recognized no such developmental reading, they faced an exegetical problem that we do not, and this gave them considerable incentive to develop an account on which the parts of substances both are and are not themselves substances. (For their views regarding the place of the *Categories* in Aristotle's canon, see §12.1.) This interpretive dilemma, however, is but a small part of the story. For even if we might now wish to regard the *Categories* as largely superseded by the hylomorphic framework of the *Metaphysics*, that hardly resolves the philosophical tension that drove Aristotle to these two seemingly very different views about the status of parts. What is fundamentally at stake here are the two different conceptions of substance we encountered back in §6.2. The doctrine of the *Metaphysics* rests on the idea that substances are unified, independent wholes. It was this sort of argument that we saw Scotus make above, and such considerations respond to one very central feature of Aristotelian thought about substances. The *Categories*, however, responds to another very prominent feature of the Aristotelian conception of substance, the idea that substances are the bearers of properties. Thus it takes what is "most distinctive" of substance (4a10) to be its ability to receive contrary properties: "one and the same individual human being, for instance, becomes pale at one time and dark at another, and hot and cold, and bad and good" (*Cat.* 4a18–21). If this is what defines a substance, then it seems natural to think that integral parts pass the test. One's hand becomes hot and then cold, pale and then dark, in just the way that the substance as a whole does.

When one conceives of substance along the lines of the *Categories*, then, it can look just obvious that an integral part will count. Indeed, the scheme of the *Categories* forces this conclusion upon us, because by dividing beings into substances and accidents, it offers no other place to put entities such as hands and hearts. This will be true all the way down, evidently, for as far down as we can conceive of body having parts that bear properties. It might also seem to hold all the way up, applying not just to individuals like Socrates and Fido, and not just to their integral parts, but even to aggregates of substances like flocks and herds and heaps and crowds—these too seem to be the bearers of properties, and if they are things at all, then there is no place for them other than the category of Substance. But this is to say that the conception of substance found in the *Categories* seems to be almost entirely unconcerned about issues that lie at the

---

[4] Aristotle still seems favorably disposed to the idea that the parts of a substance are substances at *Pr. An.* I.32, 47a27, and at *Phys.* I.6, 189a32–34. One might also cite *Meta.* VII.2, 1028b9: "Substance is thought to belong most obviously to bodies; and so we say that both animals and plants and their parts are substances, and so are natural bodies such as fire and water and earth and everything of the sort, and all things that are parts of these or composed of these (either of parts or of the whole bodies)." Aristotle immediately goes on to make it clear, however, that he offers this as *endoxa*, and so as a doctrine requiring critical reconsideration.

For some discussion of Aristotle's treatment of parts as potential in the *Metaphysics*, see Charleton, "Aristotle's Potential Infinites"; Koslicki, *Structure of Objects* pp. 147–8; Scaltsas, *Substances and Universals* pp. 77–90.

heart of Aristotle's mature ontology. That mature ontology takes biological organisms as its paradigm substances, and accounts for their unity in hylomorphic terms, drawing a sharp contrast between genuine substances, which have an organizing form, and mere parts and aggregates, whose identities are parasitic on the identity of substances. This will perhaps suggest that we should simply disregard the *Categories'* doctrine that the parts of substances are themselves substances. But given that this doctrine is responding to an important aspect of the Aristotelian conception of what a substance is, it is not easy to see how we are to do that.

26.2. Extreme Views

The dilemma over the parts of substances admits of various solutions, more or less compromising. First, let us consider views at either of the uncompromising extremes— views that either wholly deny that substances have parts, or else treat all the parts of a substance as having the same reality as the whole. Aristotle's *Metaphysics* suggests an extreme view of the first sort: that not only is a substance *wholly* one thing, in the sense of being a fully unified thing, but it is also *just* one thing, in the sense that there is only one thing there, inasmuch as strictly speaking none of the parts exist. Consider, for instance, the following passage:

A substance cannot consist of substances present in it actually: for things that are thus actually two are never actually one, though if they are [merely] potentially two, then they will be one. (For instance, the double line consists of two halves potentially, since their actualization divides them.) Therefore if the substance is one, it will not consist of substances present in it. This accords with the argument that Democritus states rightly: for one thing cannot come from two nor two from one. (*Meta.* VII.13, 1039a3–11)

Although I will as usual waive all questions of how best to understand Aristotle, it is certainly tempting to read this as maintaining that a genuine unity of the sort that a substance is is never genuinely composite, in the sense that it is never composed of multiple things. Although a substance may have the potential to *become* multiple things, it is in fact, actually, only one thing. This is a very strict understanding of the doctrine of potential parts. I will call it the *Simple View*, both because it is relatively simple to understand, and because the substances it postulates are, literally, simple, inasmuch as they lack all parts.

If substances are one thing in the sense of being simple, then we have identified quite a robust sense of substantial unity. Indeed, we would have gone beyond even the strongest forms of substantial unity defended by scholastic unitarians, according to which substances have a special sort of unity inasmuch as their parts are causally produced and metaphysically individuated by a single controlling form (§25.2). For what we have now arrived at is a much stronger claim: that strictly speaking a substance has no parts at all. It is not clear that this counts as progress, however, because this new conception of substantial unity seems so strict as to be inconsistent with the previous chapter's account. For if a substance literally has no parts, then it would seem to be nonsense to talk about the substantial form as what causes and individuates those parts. Rather than treating substances as unified in virtue of their substantial forms, substances would be unified in virtue of being a simple, unitary thing. Hence we need to be cautious in approaching the scholastic doctrine of potential parts. Although it is sometimes said that scholastic Aristotelians are uniformly committed to this doctrine, it is far from clear even that most of them are so committed, and indeed it is far from clear what the doctrine of potential parts is supposed to be.

One thing that is clear is that some scholastics expressly reject the doctrine of potential parts, on any substantive construal, and instead stake out an extreme position at the other end of the spectrum, according to which the parts of a substance are as real as the whole. The most prominent case is Ockham, as we have in fact seen already in discussing Ockham's reductive theory of quantity (§14.3). Ockham, like most scholastics, regards quantity as that in virtue of which a thing is extended, with *partes extra partes*. To have quantity, then, entails having integral parts. The critical move in Ockham's case against the reality of accidents in the category of Quantity is his claim that it is an intrinsic feature of a material substance that it be composed of parts that are themselves substances. If this is right, then there is no need to postulate quantity as a real accident to account for such corpuscular structure. Ockham's *Quodlibeta* devotes a whole question to assessing the critical move, and makes the following interesting argument:

When a piece of wood is divided into two halves, no substance is generated *de novo* in itself as a whole. But now that the division has been made there are two really distant substances; otherwise, the accidents in one of the halves would remain without a subject. But these two substances of wood, each of which is a determinate whole after the division, existed beforehand and made up one whole piece of wood, and they were not at that time in the same place. Therefore, at that time they were distant in position. (*Quod.* IV.19 [*Opera theol.* IX:396])

The piece of wood is understood to count as a material substance. Ockham takes it as obvious that, if one cuts that piece of wood in half, then (a) one has not generated any wholly new substance (line 1), and (b) one now has two non-overlapping ("really distant") substances (line 2). Hence those halves already existed before the cut was made.[5]

This is an interesting argument, but I do not think it counts as a good argument against the Simple View. Although it is intuitively compelling to think that cutting a piece of wood in half generates no new substance, one might simply deny this. As for the intuition itself, it may result from the choice of examples. Although the piece of wood is supposed to be an arbitrarily chosen instance of a substance, it is hardly a paradigm of the sort of strongly unified entity that the Simple View is meant to account for. A proponent of that view might just deny that a dead piece of wood is a substance at all, and claim instead that it is a heap of dead organic particles. And if one switches to a paradigm case of a genuine substance, like a mouse, and imagines performing this sort of division, it is not nearly so clear that either (a) or (b) holds.

The above argument, aimed at the Simple View, does not apply to the standard scholastic version of the potential parts doctrine, which as we will see takes a more moderate position on the reality of a thing's parts. Still, Ockham definitely does not

---

[5] Ockham's *Quod.* IV.19 argument from a piece of wood is given a more technical formulation at *Exp. Phys.* VI.13.6 [*Opera phil.* V:563–4]. That formulation begins, however, with the dubious claim that "pars potest separari a toto," which is precisely what Ockham's opponent is likely to deny, as we will see in more detail below. For a nice general discussion of this type of argument see Holden, *Architecture of Matter* pp. 114–18.

mean to defend the potential parts doctrine on any substantive construal, moderate or not. That becomes clear when we look at a different context, his discussion of the composition of the continuum. This is the place where the doctrine of potential parts received some of its most extensive discussions among scholastic authors, since one motivation for arguing that some apparent parts of bodies are merely potential is to allow one to follow Aristotle in embracing the infinite divisibility of bodies while still avoiding the paradoxes that seemingly arise from an infinity of real, actual parts. Ockham, however, thinks that those paradoxes can be disarmed without denying the actuality of parts. Hence he asserts that, within any body, however continuous and however small, there are infinitely many actual parts. Why not avoid this result by treating the apparent parts of a body as merely potential until divided? Ockham distinguishes two senses in which things might be said to exist actually: either by being actually divided from one another, or by having "true and real existence outside the soul" (*Quaest. Phys.* 68 [*Opera phil.* VI:588]). In the first sense, the parts of a continuous body are of course not actual, since they are not actually divided. This, Ockham says, is how Aristotle's talk of "potential parts" should be understood. In the second sense, however, the parts are actual: they are "in rerum natura et vere realiter exsistentia actualiter extra animam" (ibid.), a phrase that can go without translation, since it amounts to nothing more than Ockham's stringing together every Latin word for *real* that he can think of. In a sense, this is a version of the potential parts doctrine, inasmuch as Ockham is offering an interpretation of what it means to say the parts of a continuous body are merely potential. But inasmuch as this interpretation of the doctrine renders it trivially true—the parts of a continuous body are potential inasmuch as they are in fact continuous rather than actually divided—it is better to describe Ockham as rejecting the potential parts doctrine in favor of the sort of extreme view we encountered in Descartes and Gassendi at the start of the chapter. I will refer to Ockham's position in this debate as *Actualism.*[6]

---

[6] Ockham discusses the parts of the continuum in considerable detail at *Quaest. Phys.* 68–71, where he argues that "quaelibet pars continui sit in continuo actu" (q. 68), "pars . . . proprie exsistit propria exsistentia et actualitate" (q. 69), "sunt infinitae partes actu in continuo" (q. 70) and "[sunt] infinitae partes totaliter distinctae inter se" (q. 71). A very similar, apparently earlier discussion appears in *Exp. Phys.* VI.13.6. See also, more briefly, *Exp. Phys.* I.11.1 (*Opera phil.* IV:110), *Brevis summa* I.2 (*Opera phil.* VI:17–18), VI.2 (VI:102), and *In Praed.* 8.4 (*Opera phil.* II:188), where Ockham endorses without any fuss the claim of the *Categories* that the parts of a substance are themselves substances.

For two very helpful discussions of Ockham's views here, see Normore, "Ockham's Metaphysics of Parts" and, for the broader physical and mathematical context, Murdoch, "Ockham and the Logic of Infinity" pp. 184–90. I hesitantly conclude that Murdoch is wrong, however, when he writes that "to say, with Ockham, that there is an infinity of actually existing parts is not in any way to say that there is an actual infinity of parts. Indeed, his idea of the kind of infinity these actually existent parts have is that they are not so numerous but that they can be more numerous (*non tot quin plures*)." According to Murdoch, then, Ockham means 'infinite parts' only in the weaker syncategorematic sense (there can always be more), rather than the stronger categorematic sense (there are, literally, infinitely many parts). Although Ockham certainly uses phrases that suggest the syncategorematic reading, this is consistent with his accepting an actual infinity of parts in the categorematic sense too, and I see no other reason to doubt that this is his view. Indeed, I do not understand what else the view could be. The parts of a continuum are real, Ockham says. How many parts are there, right now, in actual fact? Infinitely many. This just is, so far as I can see, to embrace an actual infinity of parts, in the categorematic sense. Moreover, Ockham shows some signs of doubting the familiar scholastic principle that a real infinity is impossible (see, e.g., *Quod.* II.5 [IX:131]; but cf. *Quod.* III.1 [IX:203]).

Another well developed version of Actualism is offered by Gregory of Rimini, *Sent.* I.24.1.1 (III:17–20). E.g.: ". . . vocant ipsi partes in potentia et quae existunt in potentia et distinctas in potentia, non quidem quia huiusmodi partes non actualiter actualitate praesentiae sint, sed solum possint esse in rerum natura—hoc enim penitus falsum est, sicut patet ad sensum" (III:18). See also *Sent.* II.2.2 (IV:295–6), where Rimini argues for the theses that every continuous body contains infinitely many parts, both syncategorematically and (explicitly) categorematically. For discussion see

Actualism, as Ockham defends it, consists in three theses:

(i)   every continuous region of a continuous body actually exists as a part of that body;
(ii) each of these parts exists in virtue of its own intrinsic actuality;
(iii) every continuous body contains an infinite number of such parts.

This last thesis amounts to rejecting atomism (and so taking what would be Descartes's side against Gassendi). Ockham's treatment of the puzzles of infinity that arise from (iii) is in some ways the most complex and interesting aspect of his view. Here, however, I will set aside such issues in order to focus on the two initial, more foundational, metaphysical theses, which the remainder of this chapter will consider in turn. The first thesis amounts to rejecting the doctrine of potential parts. The second thesis goes one step further, by insisting that these parts are not only actual, but intrinsically actual. Ockham has interesting arguments for these theses, which I wish to consider. But first we must have a better grasp of the sort of view he is arguing against.[7]

(A preliminary terminological note. Aristotle distinguishes in *Physics* V.3 between bodies that are *contiguous*, inasmuch as they are touching, and bodies that are *continuous*, which is to say that they are contiguous and homogeneous. It is often hard to tell during our period whether an author is following this strict usage. Throughout, I will understand 'continuous' only in the weaker sense of *contiguous*, and expressly say so when the body is also to be conceived of as *homogeneous*. It is, however, good to keep in mind the possibility of giving 'continuous' a stronger reading.)

26.3. The Mixed View of Potential Parts

It would be astonishing if the scholastics in general were committed to the Simple View—the view that substances have no parts at all. One way to see this is to look at standard taxonomies of the different sorts of unity, such as that of the Coimbrans

---

Cross, "Infinity" pp. 96–7. Crathorn also defends Actualism (*Sent.* I.3; see Robert, "William Crathorn's Atomism"), as does Dabillon, who likewise urges the principle that the components of a substance must themselves be real and actual: "La matière et la forme sont des êtres réels, substantiels, qui existent actuellement dans la nature: car ce qui compose un être actuel, existe actuellement, ou le tout substantiel seroit composé de rien" (*Physique* I.3.2, p. 103) He gives a series of interesting arguments for this conclusion at *Physique* III.1.5, where he makes it clear that he takes the resultant infinity to be merely syncategorematic.

[7] Although the point might easily be missed, Ockham is very clear in distinguishing between theses (i) and (ii). In *Quaest. Phys.* these are treated as separate questions (qq. 68, 69). In *Exp. Phys.* VI.13.6 he offers two separate criticisms of his contemporaries: first, "multi ponentes istam distinctionem errant circa intentionem Philosophi et Commentatoris, dicentes quod partes infinitae non sunt nisi in potentia, non in actu, quasi non sint actualiter exsistentes sed in potentia tantum" (*Opera phil.* V:562); second, "a multis dicitur quod quaelibet pars est in actu, non actualitate propria, sed actualitate totius. Sed istud non valet" (V:563). It is obvious on reflection that these are distinct doctrines Ockham is criticizing, since one claims that at least some parts of a continuous body are merely *potential*, whereas the other offers an (incorrect) account of how at least some parts of a continuous body are *actual*.

For scholastic discussions of infinite divisibility, and the occasional resistance to this doctrine in the form of atomism, see Murdoch, "Infinity and Continuity" and "Atomism and Motion," and the papers in Kretzmann, *Infinity and Continuity*, and in Grellard and Robert, *Atomism*. See also the references in §5.4. Such questions of divisibility, however, need to be distinguished from questions about the ontological status of integral parts. Many scholastic authors embrace infinite divisibility without postulating infinitely many parts, as the next section makes clear. One might, conversely, embrace Actualism, including even thesis (iii), without thinking it physically possible to divide a body indefinitely far down. (This would require rejecting the assumption that a physically indivisible body is partless.) The conceptual connections between divisibility and parthood are quite intricate and cannot be sorted out without a precise account both of what 'divisibility' means and what it means for a part to be actual.

(§24.2). They describe the highest sort of unity as that of something "simple" in such a way that it "lies outside all composition of really discrete parts" (*In Phys.* I.9.11.2). But they take it for granted that this is not how material substances are unified. Material things arise from "the composition of parts that are collected in some third nature" (ibid.; see §25.5), in virtue of a substantial form. In saying this, the Coimbrans are not embracing Ockham's actualist view. They are simply taking for granted that, in some sense, material substances *of course* have parts: they are composed of metaphysical parts like form and matter, and integral parts like hands and feet.

This same conclusion can be reached by reflecting on various doctrines encountered over the course of the previous twenty-five chapters. We saw in Chapter 4, for instance, how scholastic authors were divided over whether prime matter itself should have parts. Whatever the case may be for prime matter, it is clear enough that bodies have parts, inasmuch as the standard scholastic definition of extension is the having of *partes extra partes*. Chapter 14 considered the extensive scholastic dispute over what accounts for such parts: whether bodies have their corpuscular structure intrinsically, for instance, as Ockham thinks, or in virtue of an accident in the category of Quantity. If bodies were simple, then this whole debate would make no sense whatsoever—bodies could not even satisfy the standard definition of being extended. We have also seen, in Chapter 16, how the rational soul is standardly said to be whole in each part of the body, and we have seen in Chapter 24 how substantial forms are thought to govern each part of the bodies they inform. What could these claims possibly mean, if bodies are simple? Hence despite what Aristotle might seem to suggest, the Simple View cannot be regarded as a serious possibility among scholastic authors.

So what then is the potential parts doctrine? If it is not the claim that the parts of bodies entirely fail to exist, then one might suppose that parts are being ascribed some sort of doubtful, halfway existence that falls short of full-fledged actual existence. I will have more to say about this possibility in §26.5, but for now let me just report my conviction that this is not what is being asserted. What then does that leave? One sort of view it leaves open—and this is how the doctrine is often understood today—is the view that although the parts of a body really exist, they are dependent on the whole, in such a way that they cannot exist apart from that whole. Obviously, this is an important scholastic idea. It lies at the heart of the unitarian doctrine of substance and substantial form (§25.2), and its rejection plays a prominent role in various post-scholastic developments, as we will see in subsequent chapters. But although one certainly might call this the doctrine of potential parts, this would be to use that label in a way quite different from how scholastic authors use it. When Ockham rejects the potential parts doctrine in favor of Actualism, he does not mean to be taking a position on whether the parts of a body may be individuated by their substantial form. That is a distinct issue. In general, scholastic authors who argue for the merely potential existence of parts of a continuous body are not arguing for the dependence of those parts on the whole substance. They are saying something very different and much more straightforward: that those parts do not really exist at all.

But how can this be? Have we not circled back to the Simple View, which I have already dismissed as a straw man as far as the scholastics are concerned? What seems to have gone wholly unnoticed in discussions of this topic is that proponents of the potential parts doctrine do not suppose that *every* part of a body is merely potential.

They do not even suppose that every *integral* part of a body is merely potential. Instead, every scholastic proponent of this view of whom I am aware defends a moderate, compromise version of the potential parts doctrine: that some integral parts of substances are actual, whereas others are potential. I will call this the *Mixed View*.

John of Jandun sets out a version of the Mixed View in some detail:

> There are two kinds of quantitative parts. Some are actual and some are potential. Actual parts are those that, taken in themselves and separately, can participate in the form of the whole. Potential parts are parts of exceeding smallness that, taken in themselves and separately, cannot 3
> participate in the form of the whole, but would dissolve into what contains them. (Flesh, for instance, can be divided into parts so small that if those parts were divided they would not remain flesh, but would dissolve into the air.) . . . Now then some say that a thing with quantity 6
> (*quantum*) is cognized by a cognition of its actual parts, but not by a cognition of its potential parts. For the first are [not] infinite, in any natural quantified being, and with respect to these there is no division to infinity according to the same proportion. (*In Phys.* I.15, f. 14vaF) 9

The passage is beautifully explicit. It distinguishes between two kinds of integral ("quantitative") parts: those that are large enough to be of the same kind as the whole (a piece of flesh large enough to count as flesh), and those that are too small to count (lines 1–6). Today we demarcate the first kind as those that are of molecule size or larger. On the standard scholastic terminology, the smallest pieces of the first kind are known as *minima* (e.g., the *minimum* for being a piece of flesh). On Jandun's view, then, integral parts are merely potential if and only if they fall below that minimal size. Pieces of flesh that would still count as flesh, if "taken in themselves and separately" (line 2), are "actual parts." This is just one way to develop a Mixed View regarding potential parts, but since it is the most detailed version I have found, I will focus on it in what follows.[8]

Jandun's remarks are clear not only about how to demarcate the actual–potential divide, but also about what motivates the division. By postulating actual parts, he can account for the actualist intuition that of course a body is constituted out of its parts, and that of course those parts are real. At the same time, because he identifies a stopping point, beyond which division into further actual parts is not possible, Jandun seems to escape the need to postulate an infinity of actual parts (lines 8–9). This is the essential motivation for the scholastic doctrine, as it grows out of Aristotle's discussion

---

[8] Good accounts of *minima* can be found in Burley, *In Phys.* I, f. 21rb; Jandun, *In Phys.* I.16; Buridan, *In Phys.* I.13; Pererius, *De communibus affectionibus* X.23. See also the discussions in Maier, *Vorläufer Galileis* ch.7; van Melsen, *From Atomos to Atom*; Murdoch, "Minima Naturalia."

Jandun invokes Aristotle's *De sensu* for his distinction between actual and potential parts, seemingly referring to 445b26–446a19. Perhaps there is some encouragement for Jandun's view in that text, but it is by no means clear.

The Mixed View appears explicitly, albeit briefly, in Aquinas: ". . . quantitas totius consurgit ex partibus. Sed hoc intelligendum est de partibus existentibus actu in toto, sicut caro, nervus, et os existunt in animali. . . . Et per hoc excluduntur partes totius continui, quae sunt potentia in ipso" (*In Phys.* I.9.65). For even briefer remarks along these same lines, see *In Meta.* V.21.1102. These passages suggest a somewhat different view from Jandun's, according to which none of the parts of a homogeneous body, however large, are actual, but that at least some of the parts of a heterogeneous body are actual.

A distinction like Jandun's appears also in Oresme: "Quaedam sunt partes potentes per se existere, et istae dicuntur actuales, et per consequens formales, et causa est quia forma dat esse; et etiam sunt sensibiles potentes agere per se, quia formae est agere, ideo merito dicuntur formales. Aliae sunt non potentes hoc facere propter nimiam parvitatem et insensibiles, quae vocantur ab Aristotele potentiales partes, et ideo merito dicuntur materiales" (*In Gen. et cor.* I.15, p. 130).

of how to avoid the paradoxes of an infinitely divisible continuum (see, e.g., *Phys.* 206a18–29 and 212b3–7). Given that this is the motivation, it is obviously not necessary to insist that a body has *no* actual parts; resorting to the extremes of the Simple View is quite unnecessary. One need insist only that a body does not have infinitely many actual parts. But from this motivation we can draw an important conclusion about how the scholastic doctrine must be understood. If the view is to avoid a real infinity of parts, then of course it must insist that these merely potential parts *are not real.* To say that some parts of a continuous body are merely potential, then, is not to postulate the existence of certain parts and then ascribe to them some sort of sub-actual existence, or some sort of dependence on the whole. Rather, it is to insist that, beyond a certain point, bodies simply have no parts. One goes down to some minimal level, and then must stop, because one arrives at parts that are not themselves composed of parts. This is not to say that division beyond this point is impossible. Indeed, it is the possibility of further division that makes it meaningful to speak here of there being potential parts. But it is one thing—on this view—to be divisible and another thing to have parts. A body's being divisible may involve its having a certain *potentiality*, and perhaps such potentialities and powers are themselves a kind of metaphysical part (Ch. 23). But talk of potential parts, even if it carries with it some kind of metaphysical potentiality, does not carry with it any commitment to the corpuscular structure that comes of having integral parts. So although, on this view, bodies are infinitely divisible, their corpuscular structure does not go infinitely far down.

Jandun does not make it clear that to describe a part as merely "potential" is to say that it does not exist. Ockham, however, is very clear about this:

It should be known that some claim here that the Philosopher solves the aforesaid arguments [against the possibility of motion] by claiming that it is possible to pass through an infinity that is potential but not actual. But many who advance this distinction err regarding the Philosopher's and the Commentator's intention, saying that the infinite parts exist only in potentiality, not in actuality, as if they are not actually existing (*exsistentes*) but are only in potentiality. (*Exp. Phys.* VI.13.6, *Opera phil.* V:562)

The last clause of the passage seems to capture what any non-trivial defense of the doctrine of potential parts must maintain: that although matter is infinitely divisible in principle, in fact a continuous body does not have so many parts. The infinite parts that one might suppose to exist do not in fact exist. It is against this doctrine that Ockham insists, as we have seen, that all the parts of a body really and truly exist.

In light of these remarks, we can see why the phrase 'potential parts' is so liable to mislead. For it is natural to characterize the view as holding that a continuous body is composed of parts that do not actually exist, but that could exist if the body were divided. This is wrong in two ways. First, many advocates of the potential parts doctrine resist the idea that such parts could exist if divided from the whole. On the contrary, as we have seen in some detail (§25.2), it is common to suppose that no part of a substance can exist apart from the whole. Hence the "potentiality" of these parts can hardly be a matter of their potential for actual existence apart from the whole. Second, and even more invidiously, talk of "potential parts" invites one to quantify over them, as if they exist but merely in some obscure, potential, non-actual way. As I have been stressing, this is not how the view should be understood: the view is instead that there are no such parts, only metaphysically simple stuff that has the potential to be divided up in various ways.

Now that we have a sense of what the potential parts doctrine is, we are in a position to consider how Ockham argues against it. He offers four arguments for the thesis that "every part of a continuous body actually exists in that body" (*Quaest. Phys.* 68 [*Opera phil.* VI:588–9]). The first argument holds that "every part of what actually exists is itself something truly and actually existing in reality," on the grounds that "nothing is composed from what does not exist." This argument would have to be categorically rejected by a proponent of the Simple View, who would deny that a body has parts, and so deny that it is composed of anything. Proponents of a Mixed View, however, will not be troubled by this first argument, since they allow enough actual parts—limbs, organs, *minima*, and so on—to account for a body's composition.

Ockham surely expected this sort of reply to his first argument, because his remaining three arguments are aimed at an opponent who is willing to recognize certain sorts of actual parts.[9] According to the second argument, "there is no more reason for one part of a continuous body to actually exist in reality than for another to so exist; but some part of a continuous body does actually exist; therefore each part does" (ibid.). Ockham offers an extended defense of the minor premise, along the lines we might expect: parts can be the subject of accidents; parts can be perceived; parts can act. The fact that Ockham feels the need to argue for the minor premise shows that he was worried about the Simple View. But the argument as a whole targets the Mixed View, and depends crucially on the generalizing move of the major premise: if some integral parts exist, then why not all? This aims at what is perhaps the most vulnerable aspect of the Mixed View.

One might try replying to this argument along the lines suggested by Jandun. Begin with a simple case: a homogeneous gold bar. All of the integral parts of that bar will be actual, down to the minimal bits of gold. Below that, they will be merely potential, which is to say there will be no such parts. A minimum piece of gold is not composed of any further parts. But here we arrive at the crucial issue: what could justify saying such a thing? To be sure, it is *convenient* to postulate an end to corpuscular structure at some definite point. But the question is whether we have any good reason for thinking that the parts run out at *that* specific point. Although Jandun goes no further than we have seen in defending his view, there is a plausible story that suggests itself: that the subminimal parts of the gold bar do not exist because they have no substantial form to actualize them. After all, the substantial form of the gold bar is that which makes the bar gold. The sub-minimal parts, by definition, are not gold, and so are not candidates to be actualized by that substantial form. Hence, one might conclude, such parts simply do not exist. And one might say something similar for heterogeneous bodies. Given that the substantial form of, say, a dog, is responsible for the complex organic structure

---

[9] Ockham also implies that his target is the Mixed View at *Exp. Phys.* I.11.1 (*Opera phil.* IV:110): "in omni continuo sunt partes infinitae, quia aliter continuum non esset divisibile in infinitum. . . . Nec est dicendum sicut aliqui dicunt, quod illae infinitae partes non sunt in actu sed in potentia tantum. Vere enim sunt in actu sicut caput hominis est in actu, non tamen sunt actu separatae ab invicem sicut nec caput hominis separatur a corpore, sed propter hoc non sequitur quin sint actualiter exsistentes in rerum natura. Philosophus tamen vocat eas aliquando in potentia, non quin sint vere exsistentes, sed quia non sunt actu separatae ab invicem." The passage takes for granted that of course the head of a human being is an actual part, and then urges that the parts of a continuous body are just as actual.

of that animal, this form will account for flesh, nerves, bones, and the rest, down to the minimal parts, but no lower.

Admittedly, this rationale might be resisted. Ockham might reply that, if the substantial form can actualize the diverse parts of a *heterogeneous* body, then it can also actualize the sub-minimal parts of what we (perhaps misleadingly) call a *homogeneous* body. But this then suggests a further argument for the potential parts doctrine: for if one accepts the notion that it is the substantial form that actualizes a substance and its parts, the question then arises of whether any *finite* form could actualize a body all the way down, *infinitely far*. The natural answer is No, on the grounds that any one substantial form has only so much power. In that case, however, there would come a point in any substance at which corpuscular structure runs out. Whether or not Jandun identifies the right stopping point, we would at least have an answer to Ockham's demand for some principled reason as to why not every potential part of a body is a real, actual part.

Ockham's third argument is that "an integral part of a whole really exists no less than does an essential part; but an essential part actually exists, as is clear for matter and form; therefore every integral part actually exists" (ibid.). This requires less comment, because it is clear enough how a proponent of the Mixed View would reply—by granting that form and matter actually exist, and that some integral parts do too, but not infinitely many of them.

Ockham's final argument is in some ways the most intriguing of the group: "half of a whole continuous body really exists, as is clear to the senses; therefore every half really exists, because the same reason holds for one and for all" (ibid.). This is severely enthematic. The parallel argument in the *Expositio Physicorum* is somewhat more detailed, and makes it clear that Ockham has in mind the claim that if half of the whole exists, then half of the half exists, and so on downward. Obviously, the argument applies only to a proponent who endorses a Mixed View, and so is willing to grant that half of a whole exists. As it stands, the argument is not very effective against a view like Jandun's, which offers a principled stopping point to the argument's downward trajectory. But the argument might be reframed in a way that would give the mixed theory more trouble. Instead of focusing on the infinitely diminishing halves that the *Expositio* argument picks out, consider the infinitely many equal-sized overlapping halves contained within any continuous body. Ockham himself provides the argument that such halves exist (*Quaest. Phys.* 71 concl. 6), which can be framed as follows. Take the half of a one-meter object that begins exactly at 0.5 meter. Now take the half that begins at 0.4 and ends at 0.9. Now consider that, between 0.4 and 0.5, there are infinitely many starting points for other halves. This seems to show that anyone who is prepared to recognize the reality of half a body should also recognize the reality of infinitely many equal-sized parts. For why should one recognize the reality of the half that begins at 0.5, and refuse to recognize the reality of the part that begins at 0.4, or at any arbitrary starting point in between? If one exists, they all seem to exist.

I am not sure how to reply to this fourth argument. Yet, although the argument is appalling in its ontological profligacy, it does not refute the doctrine of potential parts, because it does not force us to recognize parts at the sub-minimum level (wherever we decide that level should be set). Inasmuch as the point of the potential parts doctrine is to avoid a real infinity, the argument is perhaps an embarrassment to the Mixed View.

But proponents of the Mixed View could accept it, provided they were willing to accept an actual infinity of overlapping parts.[10]

26.4. Post-Scholastic Views

The seventeenth-century debate over the ontological status of parts recapitulates scholastic discussions, albeit it in an entirely different metaphysical framework. The banner of Actualism gets picked up by Descartes, as noted at the start of this chapter. His views in this domain are effectively Ockham's, and there seems no need to discuss them at any greater length, especially since Descartes does not argue for his view. (More interesting in Descartes's case are the ontological implications of his Actualism, an issue I began to take up in §25.6, and will explore further in §28.3 and §28.5.)

An alternative version of Actualism is Gassendi's, who accepts only the first two of Ockham's three theses, inasmuch as he endorses Actualism down to the level of the atoms, but insists that there are no parts below that level. It is, at any rate, natural to describe Gassendi as a proponent of Actualism, since his disagreement with Descartes and Ockham on the topic of atoms looks in this context like a peripheral issue. But given what we have now seen of scholastic views, we should wonder whether it is right to put Descartes and Gassendi in the same camp. After all, Gassendi is in effect defending a Mixed View, according to which bodies contain actual parts down only

---

[10] Although Ockham presents his view in considerable detail, I have been unable to find a similarly detailed scholastic statement of the mixed potential parts doctrine. Presumably more detailed discussions are extant, and a wider range of views. One place to look for further discussion is in scholastic discussions of the elements, and their survival within a mixed body. Although the details are complicated and controversial (see §22.3 for a start), the scholastics standardly hold that the elements do not actually exist within a mixed body. Although, so far as I know, recent scholars have not associated debates over the elements with the doctrine of potential parts, the two views would seem to be tightly connected. Accordingly, post-scholastic treatments of the parts of mixtures as actual are also highly relevant to the potential parts debate. See, in particular, Basso's *Philosophia naturalis*, one of whose main theses is that mixed bodies are composed of parts that are substantially distinct (e.g., I.4.6, pp. 49–52).

There is virtually no secondary literature on scholastic treatments of this topic. Most of what we know about the history of the debate over potential and actual parts comes from Holden, *Architecture of Matter*, which is full of careful and penetrating analyses, and quite impressively comprehensive for the seventeenth and eighteenth centuries. Unfortunately, the book is also a particularly clear example of how ignorance of scholastic thought leads to misunderstandings about the seventeenth century. Although Holden confidently asserts that the potential parts doctrine is "the orthodoxy of high medieval and Renaissance scholasticism" (p. 19), he offers not a single reference in support of this claim, and, accordingly, he badly misunderstands what the doctrine actually was. This shortcoming in Holden's research is understandable, because the topic is almost entirely *terra incognita* among scholars today, but it nevertheless puts his book on an extremely shaky foundation.

Even Holden's conception of what the potential parts doctrine is is highly unstable. Often he seems to think of it as merely the claim that the parts of a substance depend on the whole: "The [potential parts] doctrine is essential to orthodox scholastic natural philosophy. The basic unit of the material realm, according to this system, is an Aristotelian substance. . . . Such a substance is a genuinely unified whole, not a composite or aggregate of the parts into which it may be divided. Prior to division, these parts do not exist independently: since their identity is determined by their functional role in the whole substance, they are merely aspects or features of that whole. Only when division is carried through are the parts actualized as distinct entities" (*Architecture of Matter* p. 95). This, however, is not only not the potential parts doctrine, but it is not even a coherent position. If the identity of the parts "is determined by their functional role in the whole," then the division of these parts would cause them to go out of existence, rather than being "actualized as distinct entities." Elsewhere, Holden describes the potential parts doctrine as what I call the Simple View: "On this [potential parts] view, then, the whole is not a composite or aggregate structure, a construction from distinct actual parts. It has no particular inherent structure of distinct parts prior to division. Rather it is a metaphysically simple entity" (p. 18; see pp. 91–2). No Aristotelian could endorse this doctrine either, however, since it would require rejecting not only integral parts but also the metaphysical parts that are definitive of being an Aristotelian.

to a certain level. He differs from an author like Jandun in defining the cut-off point in terms of the physical indivisibility of atoms, rather than in terms of the hylomorphic structure of *minima*, but the consequences for the ontological status of parts are the same. Indeed, on Gassendi's view, only the atomist is in a position to defend the Mixed View. He argues that Aristotelians who insist on the infinite divisibility of bodies have no grounds for a stopping point in the enumeration of parts. Either they must say that a body has no parts, on the grounds that the body is not actually divided, or they must say that it has infinitely many parts, on the grounds that it is infinitely divisible. The Aristotelian, in short, is stuck with either Actualism or the Simple View.[11]

Gassendi's case shows how the revival of atomism yields a new basis for defending the sort of compromise middle ground that is the hallmark of Aristotelianism. One might have supposed that the diminished metaphysical resources of the post-scholastic era would drive authors toward one or another extreme regarding the status of parts, either toward Actualism or the Simple View. In fact, however, the atomist has a clear path toward the commonsensical middle: that bodies have parts, but not infinitely many parts. Gassendi gets this result, however, not simply because of his atomism. As I have stressed before (§5.4), atomism in the strict and narrow sense is a view that barely matters to broader questions of metaphysics. What Gassendi must further assume is that physical indivisibility entails the absence of parts. An atomist need not think this; indeed, an atomist could follow Ockham and Descartes in accepting (iii), that every body contains infinitely many actual parts, but that these parts can never naturally be separated from one another. Yet because Gassendi accepts the further metaphysical thesis that what is physically indivisible is simple, he is led to embrace something like the doctrine of potential parts, in its mixed form. (His view is only something like the potential parts doctrine, because strictly speaking he dislikes talk of potential parts, inasmuch as he wants to reject even the *potential* for atoms to be divided.)[12]

---

[11] Gassendi's attack on the potential parts doctrine is clearly aimed at a Mixed View: "Aristotelica evasio heic est: Non creari propterea infinitum actu ex huiusmodi partibus, quoniam tales partes non actu, sed potestate dumtaxat infinitae sunt, adeo proinde, ut creent solum infinitum potestate, quod idem sit actu finitum" (*Syntagma* II.1.3.5, I:262b).

[12] My account of Gassendi rests on his treatment of the potential parts doctrine at *Syntagma* II.1.3.5 (I:262b). There he argues, much like Ockham had, that if the test for the reality of the parts is *being actually divided*, then no continuous body would have any parts. If, however, the test is *divisibility*, then a body will have as many parts as there are possible divisions. Hence he concludes that a non-atomic body would have either no parts or infinitely many parts, each of which he, unlike Ockham, judges to be absurd. This is intended as an argument for atomism, but can be so only if Gassendi supposes that atoms, in virtue of their physical indivisibility, have no parts. There is, however, room to wonder about whether this is Gassendi's considered view, given that at the start of the same chapter he had insisted that atoms do have parts: "Adnotare autem lubet dici ἄτομον non ut vulgo putant, . . . quod partibus careat et magnitudine omni destituatur, sitque proinde aliud nihil quam punctum mathematicum . . ." (ibid., I:256b). All I can think is that here Gassendi so focused on stressing that atoms are not extensionless points that he lost sight of his need, elsewhere, to insist on their status as extended but simple. Part of what makes this tension difficult to overcome is that extension, throughout our period, just means having part outside of part (§4.1)—a notion that Gassendi himself endorses in his objections to Descartes's *Meditations* (VII:337). For this problem about extension in the context of atomism more generally, see Dutton, "Nicholas of Autrecourt" p. 81.

Autrecourt offers an argument much like Gassendi later would in favor of atomism: that the proponent of infinite divisibility is unable to make good on the idea that the parts are merely potential, and so is saddled with infinitely many real parts (*Tractatus* ch. 2, pp. 210–11).

Holden puts Gassendi on a long list of defenders of actual parts (*Architecture of Matter* p. 87), but here and elsewhere his classifications are not reliable because he does not recognize the sort of Mixed View that is in fact the most common approach during this period. Since Holden sees no middle ground between Actualism and the Simple View, he wonders why so many of the authors who defend actual parts at the same time insist that there are not infinitely many such parts, and so he catalogues many instances in which one or another author "stumbles" (p. 57) etc., simply because they are defending the standard middle ground.

One position that comes into greater prominence in the seventeenth century is the Simple View. It gets defended quite explicitly, and at some length, by Kenelm Digby in his *Two Treatises* (1644). Digby insists that in any body, homogeneous or not, the "parts" are nothing real at all until they are actually divided:

Ells, feet, inches are no more real entities in the whole that is measured by them and that make impressions of such notions in our understanding than, in our former example, colour, figure, mellowness, taste, and the like are several substances in the apple that affects our several senses   3 with such various impressions. It is but one whole that may indeed be cut into so many several parts, but those parts are not really there until by division they are parceled out: and then the whole (out of which they are made) ceases to be any longer, and the parts succeed in lieu of it,   6 and are, every one of them, a new whole. (*Treatise* I.2.3)

As the discussion continues, it becomes clear that Digby really does mean just what he seems to be saying. For he later considers the objection: "does not our eye evidently inform us, there are fingers, hands, arms, legs, feet, toes, and variety of other parts in a man's body?" (ibid. §6). His answer is No, the senses tell us no such thing, and indeed "a hand, or eye, or foot is not a distinct thing by itself, but that it is in the man, according as he has a certain virtue or power in him to distinct operations" (ibid.). Digby's position, then, lies at the opposite extreme of Actualism. He maintains there are no integral parts, ever, inasmuch as only whole bodies exist (lines 4–5).[13]

Although Digby's defense of the Simple View is commonly described as one of his most scholastic moments, in fact his position is one that, so far as I can find, scholastic authors never defended. He indeed makes it clear that he is taking a distinctive stand on what he describes as "a very great controversy in the schools" (ibid. §4). Far from treating the Simple View as the default assumption, he proceeds to argue for "the inconvenience, impossibility, and contradiction" (ibid.) of alternative options, and his discussion subsequently attacks, in turn, the two standard scholastic views, Actualism and the Mixed View. The first, he argues, inevitably leads to atomism: "if quantity were divided into all the parts into which it is divisible, it would be divided into indivisibles (for nothing divisible, and not divided, would remain in it)" (ibid.). This is Digby's main argument against an opponent, like Ockham or Descartes, who thinks that there are actual parts as far down as bodies are divisible. This leads him to take up various arguments against the possibility of indivisible atoms (ibid. §5). For present purposes, we can set atomism to one side and consider why Digby supposes that Actualism entails atomism. This is far from being clear, for Digby does not seem even to recognize the possibility that the "dividing" might just go on forever, all the way, infinitely far down. Why think it must stop at some point? The closest he comes to addressing this issue is in the parenthetical remark quoted above in defense of the key inference: that "nothing

---

[13] Digby endorses the Simple View, it should be stressed, only with respect to integral and some metaphysical parts. Since he is a realist about quantity (§14.2), he must think that this, at least, is a real part of a continuous body, albeit a metaphysical part. He also grants that the human soul is an immaterial part of a human being; this is the main conclusion of the briefer second of the two treatises. For some further remarks from Digby on divisibility, see *Two Treatises* I.14.2–3.

Thomas White, as usual, follows Digby's views closely in this area. See *Peripateticall Institutions* IV.1–2, esp. IV.1.11 and *Exclusion of Scepticks* 6.4 (p. 47).

Holden's unfamiliarity with scholastic views leads him to describe Digby as presenting "a particularly clear statement of the classic Aristotelian–scholastic arguments, and as such can serve as an archetype of the dominant system of Oxford and the Sorbonne that advocates of actual parts were rebelling against" (*Architecture of Matter* p. 118).

divisible, and not divided, would remain in it." His idea seems to be that Actualism cannot acknowledge the existence of any part that is able to be further divided. Now, to be sure, if we grant Digby this crucial tacit premise, then his argument succeeds. For what that premise in effect yields is that the only actual parts are the parts one arrives at when the "division" has been carried through all the way down to the least parts, the atoms. For Actualism, it would follow from this premise that there would be nothing actual at all: we would go downward in vain forever, looking for some stable, indivisible platform on which to rest composite reality.

This is an intriguing argument, to be sure, and one might spend some time pursuing various reasons for supposing that the crucial tacit premise holds. But if we are to let this discussion be governed by what the texts have to teach us, then this must be our stopping point, because Digby says absolutely nothing about why the actualist should suppose that only undivided bodies exist. Perhaps he thinks that bodies composed of actual parts do not have the requisite unity to exist. Perhaps he thinks that Actualism would be committed to an absurd proliferation of parts (such as the actual infinity of halves envisaged in the previous section). Perhaps Digby simply thinks that without a stopping point the whole would somehow be ungrounded. All of this is just speculation, because he does not say.

After offering this rather sketchy argument against Actualism, Digby goes on to discuss the other standard scholastic position, a Mixed View according to which only finitely many parts of a continuous body are actual. Beneath the actual parts, on this view, body would continue to be divisible and so at this level there would be only potential parts. To this Digby replies as follows:

Our answer will be to represent unto them how this is barely said, without any ground or colour of reason, merely to evade the inconvenience that the argument drives them unto. For if any parts be actually distinguished, why should not all be so? What prerogative have some that the others have not? And how came they by it? If they have their actual distinction out of their nature of being parts, then all must enjoy it alike and all be equally distinguished, as the supposition goes, and they must all be indivisibles, as we have proved. (ibid. §4)

This is precisely the sort of argument that we saw Ockham wield against the Mixed View. Either all the parts must be actual or none must be; there is no middle ground. Here the extremists—Ockham and Digby—are in league against the moderates. The previous section considered one way an Aristotelian might respond to such an argument: by appealing to metaphysical parts to actualize the body down to a certain level but no further. Thus Jandun thinks that the parts of body are actualized down to their minimal parts. Another view might treat a living body as actualized down to the level of its organs and limbs—that is, down to the functional parts of a living thing. There are many such possibilities here, at least for an Aristotelian who is prepared to acknowledge the sorts of metaphysical parts that could actualize such structure. Digby, however, is no Aristotelian—he rejects both substantial forms and real qualities. (The very first passage quoted above from Digby contends that integral parts should be rejected just as real qualities should be.) So for Digby this sort of all-or-nothing challenge has even more force than it did for Ockham. Ockham's contemporaries had the resources to draw distinctions between the actual and the potential that Digby is unwilling to grant to his opponents. Moreover, inasmuch as Digby's contemporaries are themselves increasingly unwilling to embrace metaphysical parts, the all-or-nothing principle looks much more compelling in the seventeenth century than it did in the fourteenth. The only clear way for a corpuscularian to adhere to some sort of middle ground is to embrace atomism, which is why Digby singles out that view for particular criticism.[14]

26.5. The Singular Existence Thesis

Perhaps the scholastics took a wrong turn when they allowed material substances to have actual parts that are themselves substances. Perhaps the true Aristotelian should, like Kenelm Digby, defend the Simple View, and deny that bodies have actual parts. Be that as it may, *our* Aristotelians do not choose this horn of the Aristotelian's dilemma, but instead embrace either Actualism or the Mixed View. Accordingly, they make trouble for themselves with regard to substantial unity. For if substances have real, actual parts, both metaphysical and integral, then the kinds of questions considered in the last chapter return with renewed force: why should one set of substances count as a single thing, *unum per se*, whereas another counts merely as *unum per accidens*?

When one adds that these parts themselves count as substances, that may seem to make the problem all the worse, but in fact it is only if the parts are substances that the whole even has a chance of counting as genuinely unified. Given that the category scheme exhausts the kinds of being, the real parts of a thing must go into *some* category. If they go into one of the accidental categories, however, then we are dealing with a mere *ens per accidens*, a thick substance (§6.1). Thus Suárez insists, as quoted at the start of the chapter, that "substance cannot be constituted *per se* from things that are altogether not substances" (*Disp. meta.* 33.1.5). All of this was common ground during our period.[15]

---

[14] Two further figures from our period deserve mention, and are given particularly acute treatments by Holden. The first is Hobbes, who sounds at times like a proponent of the Simple View along Digby's lines, as when he maintains in *De corpore* 7.9 that "nihil habere partem antequam dividatur, et cum divisa sit, tot solummodo eius partes esse, quoties sit divisum." But, as Holden makes quite clear (*Architecture of Matter* pp. 96–9), Hobbes's views are quite idiosyncratic, because the sort of division he has in mind is conceptual. The clearest text is *De mundo* II.1, where he attacks both the Simple View, for supposing that half a marble column is a part only if the column is broken, and the atomist, for supposing that the alleged physical indivisibility of the atom precludes its having parts. Yet Hobbes's view is not Actualism either, because—as the above *De corpore* passage makes clear—he resists the idea that the parts are actually there independently of our conceiving of them. I find it hard to see how this view can be consistent with Hobbes's fairly radical rejection of the reality of generation and corruption (§§28.4–5), but the whole issue needs further study.

A second intriguing figure is Galileo, who explicitly considers the potential parts doctrine on the first day of the *Two New Sciences*, in the course of arguing for the view that bodies are composed of infinitely many extensionless parts. In the end, Galileo seems to regard the potential–actual distinction as irrelevant to his purposes, and so he has Salviati remark to Simplicio that he can call such parts actual or potential, as he likes (ed. Favaro VIII:81; tr. p. 44). It is, however, not clear that Galileo can afford to be neutral on this issue, and Holden argues forcefully that Galileo's view requires what I call Actualism (*Architecture of Matter* pp. 162–7).

[15] The parts of a substance are sometimes said to fall into the category of Substance "per reductionem"—see e.g. Ockham, *Summula* III.2 (*Opera phil.* VI:251) and Scotus, *In Praed.* 15.10. See also this helpful passage from Eustachius a Sancto Paulo: "Denique, licet partes et differentiae substantiarum sint substantiae, non tamen per se collocantur in directa serie categoriae, eo quod sint incompleta quaedam entia, et ad integritatem ac constitutionem completorum pertineant. Neque enim sub eodem genere proprie contineri possunt, cum nihil detur commune synonymum substantiae completae et incompletae" (*Summa* I.1.3b.1.3, I:52).

The boldest strategy for uniting a composite substance is that of the Thomists. We have already seen, in the previous chapter, how their strict unitarianism unites the whole both physically and metaphysically around a single substantial form (§25.2). One might be excused for supposing that a substance, so conceived, will not have any actual parts. What the Thomists say, however, is that only the composite whole has existence (*esse*), properly speaking. All the other parts of the substance—the substantial and accidental forms, prime matter, and the integral parts—though things of a certain kind, nevertheless exist only in an improper sense, in virtue of the whole's existence. I will call this the *singular existence thesis*. This thesis might well be mistaken for a statement of the Simple View. But the singular existence thesis does not claim that the parts of a substance do not exist, or even that they are not actual. What the thesis claims, instead, is that the actuality of these parts is in some sense derived from the actuality of the whole, inasmuch as the whole substance, including all of its parts, shares in just a single existence. It was precisely this doctrine that gets rejected by tenet (ii) of Ockham's Actualism.

Aquinas states the singular existence thesis as follows:

> This existence (*esse*) is attributed to something in two ways. In one way, as to that which properly and truly has existence or exists, and in this way it is attributed only to a substance that subsists *per se*. Thus *Physics* I [186b4–8] says that a substance is what truly is. All those things, on the other hand, that do not subsist *per se*, but are in another and with another—whether they are accidents or substantial forms or any sort of parts—do not have existence in such a way that they truly exist, but existence is attributed to them in another way—that is, as that by which something is—just as whiteness is said to be not because it subsists in itself, but because by it something has existence-as-white (*esse album*). (*Quod.* IX.2.2c)

3

6

The view is not that the parts of substances do not exist, as the Simple View would have it, but that they do not exist in the same way that the whole substance exists. Rather than being things that exist in their own right, "properly and truly" (line 2), as complete substances do, they are merely principles that account for that substance's having existence-of-a-certain-sort, different parts making different sorts of contributions to the whole. We have already seen this doctrine invoked in the case of accidental forms, which exist, according to Aquinas's deflationism, only in some analogical sense (§10.2). We are now in a position to see that that is just a special case of a more general doctrine regarding the parts of substances, extending to both metaphysical and integral parts (line 5).[16]

Various later authors spell this idea out in different sorts of ways. According to Eckhart of Hochheim (Meister Eckhart) in the early fourteenth century, we should say that the whole substance is the only being (*ens*), and that its various formal parts contribute to that being in various ways, but are not themselves beings.

> The ten categories are not ten beings (*entia*) or ten things (*res*), but they are the ten first genera of things or of beings. Not that there are ten first beings. Rather, there is one being, substance, whereas the remainder are not beings, but properly of being, according to *Metaphysics* VII

3

---

[16] For other passages in Aquinas on the doctrine that only the whole substance properly exists, see *Sent.* III.6.2.2 and *Summa contra gent.* II.58.1450, as well as the discussion in §10.2. For an early, protracted discussion of the singular existence theory, see Giles of Rome, *Theoremata de esse et essentia* ths. 14–19.

[1028a18], beings only by analogy to the one absolute being, which is substance.... The reason is that only the substantial form gives existence (*esse*), whereas accidents in general do not give existence, but instead give such or so much, and others like this. Indeed, an accident finds 6 existence already in its subject, as prior by nature, and rather than give existence instead receives existence through its subject and in its subject. Thus the whole composite is one being, even if there are 10,000 accidents or accidental categories in it. For just as the whole composite is one 9 such thing by quality alone, one quantified thing by quantity alone, and so on for the other [categories], so it is a being by substance alone—that is, by the substantial form. Therefore all of these are beings or things (*res*) extrinsically, in analogy to the one that is a being and a thing, 12 namely substance. (*In Exodum* n. 54 [*Werke* II:58–9])

Even if Eckhart wants to say that only the whole substance counts as a being (lines 2–4, 8–9, 11–13), he evidently does not mean this as the Simple View would have it, since the parts of a substance do have being in a certain analogical sense (lines 4, 11), an existence that they "receive" (lines 7–8) from the substance. As with Aquinas, then, we are dealing with a more complex picture according to which the parts of a substance are beings, but only in some special sense. Contrary to Actualism, the parts lack their own proper existence. Although Eckhart's focus here is on accidents, his mention of substantial form (line 5) and "the whole composite" (line 8) invites us to extend the doctrine to other cases.[17]

An author who explicitly applies the singular existence thesis to integral parts is Domingo de Soto, the early sixteenth-century Thomist. The question arises in his discussion of the distinction between continuous and discrete quantity. When confronted with the claim that there is no real difference between one continuous body and two discrete bodies placed next to each other, De Soto offers this reply:

Discrete quantity, according to Aristotle, is not defined as every quantity divisible into multiple parts. Instead, it is that quantity alone whose parts are not joined at one common terminus— that is, a quantity whose parts are actually divided—and thus it is given a collective name. 3 Hence continuous quantity is no more discrete than discrete quantity is continuous. For it is remarkable that one stone is two feet, three feet, etc., even though it is not thereby two or three. Nor does it follow: there are two halves; therefore there are two beings (*entia*). For those 6 parts do not have distinct unities; rather those two parts are only one thing (*unum*). (*In Praed.* 6.1, p. 174H)

De Soto offers nothing like an explanation of the circumstances under which we have a single continuous body (a stone), rather than two discrete bodies in contact (two stones). But the passage does address the ontological status of the parts. In the discrete case, we of course have two things, two stones. In the case of a continuous body, we have only one thing, no matter how large that thing is (lines 4–5). And although we can talk about the right half and the left half of that thing, it does not follow that these halves are each beings in their own right (line 5). There is only one thing there, the stone. For all De Soto says—and he says nothing more—this could be taken as a statement of the Simple View. But given De Soto's Thomistic orientation, it seems more likely that he understands this along the lines described above. Bodies have parts,

---

[17] On Eckhart's theory of accidents, see Imbach, *Deus est intelligere* pp. 169–72.

parts that are in some sense real, but yet they do not exist in the same way that the whole substance exists. Properly speaking only the whole exists.[18]

All of these authors wish to reject tenet (ii) of Ockham's Actualism: that the parts of a substance have their own proper existence. Ockham is certainly aware of this line of argument: he remarks that "it is said by many that each part is in actuality not by its proper actuality, but by the actuality of the whole" (*Exp. Phys.* VI.13.6 [*Opera phil.* V:563]), and goes on to offer a highly technical objection to this notion. Rather than pursue that objection, it seems better to aim for a clearer grasp of what exactly the singular existence thesis means. It is interesting that, whereas both Eckhart and De Soto contend that the parts of a substance are not *beings*, there is another Thomistic line of thought that suggests a distinction between what counts as a being (*ens*) and what has existence (*esse*). Thus, according to John Capreolus, "it is one thing to deny a plurality of beings or realities (*entitatum vel realitatum*) and another to deny a plurality or division of existences or of existence itself (*exsistentiarum vel ipsius esse*)" (*Defensiones* II.18.1.3 [IV:152ab]). He goes on to apply the point to matter and substantial form, which "have distinct entities, but not distinct existences" (IV:152b). Is this a different claim from what we have seen in Eckhart and De Soto, or just a terminological variation on the same theory? Without a clearer understanding of what such claims mean, it is hard to know. But it is very difficult to see how we might even attempt to reach that sort of clearer understanding. What could it possibly mean to say that something is a *being* but that it does not *exist*? Or that it exists, but in a different way from how substances exist?

For the Thomist, claims such as these interact closely with the famous distinction between essence and existence. If there is a real distinction between a thing and its existence, then it is possible to say, for instance, that a substance has parts, but that these parts do not have their own proper existence. Earlier chapters have noted how this distinction might be put to interesting use in several contexts: as a way of treating accidents as in effect modes of substances (§10.2 and §13.7), and as an explanation of how a substance can be a permanent entity, even if its existence is successive (§18.5). In the present context, the payoff is a way to acknowledge the reality of the parts of a substance while still preserving a very strong sense of the unity of that substance. If this sort of strategy is even *coherent*, then the possibilities it presents are such that philosophers should devote themselves assiduously to determining whether it is *true*. I confess,

---

[18]   De Soto seems to reiterate the singular existence thesis, as applied to integral parts, a little later in his discussion: "Nam ratio magnitudinis est quod sit divisibilis in partes quae non erant actu plura, sed potentia (cum essent continuae), et per divisionem fiunt actu plura. . . . Itaque quantitas mea [*ed.* meo], quamvis in ratione continui sit divisibilis, tamen in ratione unitatis est indivisibilis" (*In Praed.* 6.2, p. 188LM). Despite his talk here of "actual" and "potential," I think this is not an instance of the potential parts doctrine, but another formulation of the view that a continuous material substance is just a single entity.

Although I speak of the Thomistic view, the singular existence thesis can be found in authors who are by no means Thomists, such as Peter Auriol: "de ratione partis in actu est quod non existat actu proprio distincto, sed actu totius tantummodo; si enim haberet actum proprium distinctum, iam esset per se, et non esset pars" (ibid., II:156bAB). It may even be that Ockham's discussion of this thesis has Auriol principally in mind rather than Aquinas, as Ockham's editors assume. There is, moreover, an intriguing suggestion in Auriol of a different sort of approach to the parts of a continuous body. He suggests that just as prime matter has being (*ens*) indeterminately (§3.1), so too the parts of a continuous body might be said to be merely indeterminate beings (*Sent* II.12.1.1, II:154aD). I find it hard to see what this means—and so I merely note the suggestion here—but it does seem to resonate with some of the issues surrounding the parts of a body, inasmuch as we intuitively want to say that these parts exist, but yet it seems indeterminate how many of them there are, and what their boundaries are.

however, that I am ultimately skeptical of whether it does make any sense to distinguish a thing from its existence, as if it is one kind of question to ask whether a thing is real, and another kind of question to ask whether it exists.

Perhaps one should not be so hasty. There is a temptation to think that we cannot make sense of the Thomistic view just because we lack the conceptual resources to do so. On this line of thought, although we no longer know how to understand talk of existence as something that a real thing might have or lack, or have properly or improperly, that is only because such concepts have fallen out of philosophical discourse, and now lie dormant, waiting to be revived. For those who study the history of philosophy in the hopes of attaining glimpses into alien lands full of conceptual terrain now lost to modern thought, this might be an exemplary instance of what there is to be gained from reading old texts.[19]

My own inclinations are more prosaic. Although modern philosophers have from time to time attempted to resurrect the idea that being is said in many ways, it seems to me they misunderstand the Thomistic view. The doctrine that only the complete substance has existence in the proper sense, and that the parts exist in some lesser, analogical sense, need not require postulating some novel sense of existence, or a class of real but non-existent things. Rather, I propose that the doctrine should be understood in light of the previous two chapters: that only complete substances have existence (*esse*) because only they have the special sort of unity described by the unitarian framework. This explains why the singular existence thesis meets with such favor from Thomists, for it functions for them as a kind of corollary to their conception of substantial form. And when the doctrine is so understood, it should not be read as denying either that the parts of substances exist, or that they are as real as the whole that they compose. To say that the complete substance exists in some special sense is to say that it alone is organized by a single governing, unifying actuality. Because the whole is unified in a special way, and because unity and existence go hand in hand, the whole has a special sort of existence. Or so the Thomists put it. We might better frame their obscure talk of proper and improper existence in the more prosaic vocabulary of identity conditions and causal structure.

This is how I would understand the singular existence thesis, but it was not obvious to scholastic authors at the time that this was the intended interpretation. The more common reaction was a sort of bafflement over what such talk could mean, and a consequent rejection of the approach. One finds this as early as Scotus, who remarks that "I have no knowledge of the fiction that existence (*esse*) is something non-composite resting on essence, even if the essence is composite. On my account, the existence of the whole composite includes the existence of all the parts, and includes the many partial existences of the many parts or forms" (*Ord.* IV.11.3 [Wadding VIII n. 46]). By the time of the Jesuit scholastics of the sixteenth century, the singular existence thesis no longer looked like the sort of *opinio communis* that the Jesuits were sworn to uphold (§20.2). Consider, first, Pedro Fonseca's late sixteenth-century *Metaphysics*

---

[19] The best-known modern attempt to distinguish between different forms of being or existing is that of Heidegger, especially in *Being and Time*. For a recent, historically informed attempt to develop such ideas, see McDaniel, "Ways of Being." For a clear-headed discussion of what "being is said in many ways" amounts to in Aristotle, see Shields, *Order in Multiplicity* ch. 9.

commentary. Confronted with the question of what sort of distinction holds between integral parts of a continuous, homogeneous body, Fonseca accepts the standard view that it is a real distinction. But he then considers the objection that it should instead be some kind of distinction of reason, since "parts of this sort are actually distinguished in their wholes only by reason or, what amounts to the same thing, by designation" (*In Meta.* V.6.6.3 [II:403]). His response is as follows:

> The integral parts of a homogeneous whole, even if they are not actually distinct as beings (*entia*) before any actual consideration or designation, still they are distinct as parts of the same being, inasmuch as in reality and apart from every operation of the intellect each is outside the   3
> others. ... I confess here that it is not easy to understand how these are actually distinguished before any operation of intellect as *parts* of the same being, whereas they are not actually distinguished as *beings*. But this is the condition of integral parts of a homogeneous or similar   6
> whole. ... (ibid.)

Fonseca wants to run the Thomistic line about singular existence: the parts are actually distinct not as beings (in their own right), but as parts of a single being (lines 1–3). But after saying this, he cannot help but admit (lines 4–6) that he does not know how to make much sense of it. How can one allow that a substance has *parts*, but not allow that those parts are *beings*?

Suárez's more adventuresome disputations of a few years later completely reject the singular existence thesis. Suárez sets the view out, without crediting it to the Thomists, as a potential explanation for the unity of an *ens per se*. But he then disavows it is an explanation:

> This account either supposes something false or explains something obscure through something else that is equally obscure. On one hand the claim might concern one simple thing without composition within it, even if it results from composition—as many say that from matter and   3
> form united one existence (*esse*) results. In this sense the claim supposes something false, since in order for a being to be *per se unum* it is not necessary for it to have this sort of simple existence. For I will show below that beings composed from matter and form do not have simple   6
> existence, but composite existence. On the other hand, the claim might concern the one composite existence (*esse*) resulting from the union of multiple partial existences (*existentiarum*). This claim is true, but regarding this existence (*esse*) the question remains of when one thing *per*   9
> *se* results from composition. (*Disp. meta.* 4.3.4)

Like Fonseca, Suárez is puzzled over what the singular existence thesis even means. If it means that substances are literally simple, then it is plainly false (lines 2–5). This would be the Simple View which, as I have stressed, no scholastic author defends. But if not this, then Suárez sees only one other option: that the parts of substances have their own "partial existences," which add up to a single "composite existence" (lines 7–8). Suárez accepts this picture, but points out that it helps not at all with explaining what makes the composite a unity (lines 9–10).

Suárez's insistence that a composite whole is made up of "partial existences" is consistent with broader trends in later scholastic thought. In place of the austere Thomistic line on prime matter as pure potentiality, later scholastics generally favor a view that gives it some kind of intrinsic actuality (§3.1). In place of the deflationary conception of accidental form common in the thirteenth century, scholastics from

Scotus forward tend to insist on real accidents as full-fledged beings—not as substances, of course, but as existing in just the same sense (§10.5). The same trend holds, we are now seeing, in the case of integral parts. Here is Suárez's explanation for why the parts of a continuous, homogeneous body are really distinct:

> The *separation* between those parts can be said to be of reason because only through reason can they be considered as if they were disjoint and as if they were [each] some kind of whole. But the *distinction* between the parts is actual and real, because these parts, even while they compose 3 some whole, have some reality. For, as Aristotle says in *Physics* I [189a32–34], "a substance is composed only from substances." Thus an integral being is composed only out of beings, albeit partial ones. Therefore such distinct entities remain, even if united. Indeed, unless they were to 6 remain distinct, they could not bring about composition, because composition arises only from distinct things. (*Disp. meta.* 7.1.23)

Suárez here ignores the singular existence thesis entirely. Integral parts are beings in their own right, even if they are parts of a larger whole (lines 3–4). If they were not, the whole could not be said to be composite (lines 6–8). As in the previous passage, Suárez insists that a substance either must be literally simple, or must be composed out of really existent parts. There is no middle ground.

Here my sympathies lie with Suárez. But since I am also sympathetic toward the Thomists, I think the singular existence thesis should be understood in a way that is consistent with Suárez's excluded middle. Either bodies have real parts or they are simple. Either parts exist or they do not. Given, then, that the scholastics insist on the reality of parts, the question returns of how to account for substantial unity. The options here are the same as they were in the previous chapter. One can, first and foremost, appeal to a unitary substantial form. This is all the Thomistic singular existence thesis amounts to, or so I have argued. This is also, as we saw (§24.4, §25.2), how Suárez accounts for substantial unity, even if he rejects the singular existence doctrine. Alternatively, as we saw (§25.5), one can appeal to teleology, stressing how the parts are not members of a separate kind, but contribute to the proper function of a complete whole. This is the principal strategy of the pluralists, with their multiple, partial existences.

Although we have now circled round to the topics of the previous chapter, there is still something further to consider. For as it became increasingly clear that the scholastics would take the real-and-actual horn of the Aristotelian's dilemma, questions accordingly arose about how to understand the actuality of those parts. This gave rise to a debate that has gone almost wholly unnoticed in modern discussions of scholasticism, but that merits serious attention: should the integral parts of a substance have their own substantial forms?[20]

---

[20] Scheibler offers a brief, clear rejection of the simple existence thesis at *Metaphys.* I.15.4.2.3 (pp. 186–7). He puts particular weight on the relationship between this thesis and the real distinction between essence and existence. Since Scheibler identifies essence and existence, and since he takes the integral parts of a substance to have their own essence, he thinks it clear that those parts must have their own existence as well.

A clear seventeenth-century rejection of the singular existence thesis appears in Malebranche, *Recherche* IV.2.4: "De même, quand Dieu anéantirait la moitié de quelque corps, il ne s'ensuivrait pas que l'autre moitié fût anéantie. Cette dernière moitié est unie avec l'autre, mais elle n'est pas une avec elle.... [S]on être, étant différent, ne peut être réduit au néant par l'anéantissement de l'autre" (tr. p. 273).

26.6. Partial Forms

The central question of later scholasticism regarding the status of integral parts is not whether or not they exist in their own right, but how to explain that distinct existence. In particular there were extensive debates over whether each of these different parts requires its own distinct substantial form. For the Thomists, given their strict unitarianism, such an idea was an abomination: for each complete substance there is just a single substantial form, informing every part of the body and unifying the whole under a single existence. But for authors not convinced by the singular existence thesis, it was very natural to suppose that the integral parts of a substance exist because they have their own substantial forms. Once again it was Scotus who gave rise to this line of thought, and who in later discussions is always credited with the doctrine, in opposition to the Thomists. Subsequent opinion splits fairly evenly on the question, and divides in unpredictable ways. Walter Burley, Paul of Venice, and Eustachius a Sancto Paulo defend partial substantial forms over the course of the next three centuries, whereas Gregory of Rimini, John Buridan, and Marsilius of Inghen reject them, as later on do Fonseca and the Coimbrans.[21]

Naturally, it was the substantial-form pluralists who were most prone to embrace partial forms. Perhaps the most influential discussion was Jacob Zabarella's. In addition to the usual pluralist distinction between one or more souls and a form of the body, Zabarella thinks that this bodily form is itself in fact many forms. The role of the bodily form is to determine how the elemental qualities mix together. But since there are different mixtures in each qualitatively distinct region of a heterogeneous body, it follows that each region requires its own distinct bodily form: "there is one form of the mixture in flesh, another in the nerves, another in the bones" (*De rebus nat.*, De gen. ch. 2, col. 396). We encountered Zabarella in the previous chapter remarking that if there can be two substantial forms in the same substance, then why not "four or a hundred" (§25.1). We can now see that he means this quite seriously.

The doctrine of potential parts was so widely endorsed that even some unitarians were inclined to accept it, most notably Suárez. This might well seem incoherent: how could someone embrace unitarianism and partial forms? Suárez's contention is that

---

[21] For Scotus's defense of partial substantial forms, see *In Meta.* VII.20: "Utrum partes organicae animalis habeant distinctas formas substantiales specie differentes." He recognizes the possibility of the composite view and rejects it at nn. 19–20 and states his own view at n. 38.

Proponents of partial substantial forms include Walter Burley, *In De an.* II.1–2 and *De formis* pp. 35–44; Paul of Venice, *Summa phil. nat.* V.5 concl. 1; Eustachius a Sancto Paulo, *Summa* III.3.1.1.8 (III:256): "Quaeritur utrum praeter illam formam totalem, nempe animam, admittendae sint aliae substantiales formae partiales pro varia partium illarum dispositione. Qua de re graviter inter Scotistas affirmantes, et Thomistas negantes paribus ferme rationum momentis controvertitur. Probabilior autem nobis videtur hac in parte Scotistarum opinio, videlicet praeter formam totalem quae est in anima, admittendas esse formas alias partiales, ut formam carnis, ossis, nervi, etc."

The opposition to partial forms is led, of course, by the unitarians, including Gregory of Rimini, *Sent.* II.16–17.2; John Buridan, *In Gen. et cor.* I.8 ad 4; Marsilius of Inghen, *In Gen. et cor.* I.6 concl. 3; Fonseca, *In Meta.* VII.16.1; Coimbrans, *In Gen. et cor.* I.4.22; John of Saint Thomas, *Cursus* III.2.1 (who accepts partial forms in the case of plants and incomplete animals such as worms). Buridan's view is particularly notable because of his contention that, since each part of an animal is informed by a whole substantial form, it follows that each part of the animal itself falls into the same species and genus as the whole. Thus, strictly speaking, each part of a human being is a human being. See *In De an.* II.7 and III.4, and the discussions in Zupko, "How Are Souls" and Kärkkäinen, "On the Semantics of 'Human Being'." Later advocates of partial substantial forms, such as Paul of Venice, would advance this as a reductio of their opponents' view.

although the integral parts of a body each have their own substantial form, these partial forms altogether compose the unitary substantial form of the complete substance:

It can readily be conceded that in distinct heterogeneous parts there are distinct heterogeneous parts of the form. For indeed in a tree the part of the form that is in the leaf is not of the same character as the part that is in the fruit, etc., but yet they are partial forms and apt to be united and made continuous with each other in such a way as to compose one complete form of the whole. Therefore it is false to imagine some total form added on top of these partial forms and again informing all those parts. (*Disp. meta.* 15.10.30)

To the Thomist, this does not look like unitarianism at all. But Suárez insists that in some robust sense there is just one substantial form for a whole substance, albeit a form that is composed of many partial forms. Even so, as a unitarian, Suárez can embrace this composite theory only in non-human cases. It was Church doctrine that, in the human case, a single rational soul informs each part of the human body (§20.2), which rules out a composite rational soul. Suárez therefore has to take the peculiar view that the metaphysical structure of the human body is completely *sui generis*, lacking the sorts of partial forms that other heterogeneous bodies have. Pluralists, in contrast, run into no such difficulty, because they distinguish the rational soul from the form of the body.

For those who embraced partial substantial forms, the composite view was a popular approach, because it avoided the need to suppose that beyond the form of bone, form of flesh, etc., there would also be a form of the whole body. Some, however, most prominently Scotus, explicitly rejected this approach, in part because they wanted to be able to treat the whole body as something distinct from the sum of its parts. This points toward one of the most important scholastic debates regarding parts and wholes: the question of whether the whole is something over and above its parts, or whether it just is identical to those parts. This debate has important implications for diachronic identity, and will be considered in §28.5.[22]

Advocates of partial forms might embrace either Actualism or the Mixed View. Indeed, partial forms go quite neatly with the Mixed View, inasmuch as they yield a clear account of what distinguishes actual from potential parts: those parts are actual that have a distinct substantial form. Actualism might be combined with partial forms, but the two views bear no particular affinity to one other. Ockham, for instance, as we have seen in earlier chapters (§4.4, §14.3), thinks that matter's infinitely deep actual corpuscular structure is intrinsic to it, prior to any form. As for the specific organic structure of any particular complex substance, that might—consistently with Ockham's theory—be explained in any number of ways, on unitarian or pluralist grounds.

---

[22] The composite view of partial forms can be found in Oresme, *In Gen. et cor.* I.7, *In De an.* II.5, and also in Albert of Saxony, *In Gen. et cor.* I.5. A very stark version of it appears in Pererius, *De communibus affectionibus* VI.4: "anima in tam diversis partibus existens non erit secundum rem una numero, sed multae numero, partialiter" (p. 354). It is not clear that Suárez sees the potential threat to his view that comes from making substantial form into a composite, but Pererius clearly does. Rather than try to account for substantial unity on the basis of a composite substantial form, he offers three alternative stories, appealing to (i) the natural union of the parts, as in the parts of a house; (ii) the dependence of the parts on one principal part, such as the heart; (iii) the relation of the parts to a single end (ibid.).

The Boates use the composite character of Suárez's soul to try to undermine his claims of substantial unity arising from a 'single' substantial form (*Philosophia naturalis reformata* 1.3.11 and 1.3.43). Boyle would later follow the scholastics in speaking of both a "total and adequate form" and various "subordinate" forms (*Origin of Forms* [*Works* V:473])—understanding such talk of "forms" in corpuscularian terms, of course.

Ockham, although a pluralist, declines to take a side on the debate over partial forms. On one side he notes the striking diversity among the properties of different integral parts; on the other side he invokes considerations of parsimony. So far as he can see, there is no way to settle the issue:

Since we do not have any experience of substances except through their accidents, and since these do not sufficiently prove that there is specific distinction or unity, it is clear that we cannot in any way sufficiently prove that there is a specific distinction or else unity between these forms. (*Quod.* III.6 [*Opera theol.* IX:227])

Ockham's epistemic modesty is salutary. The last three chapters have considered increasingly grandiose and speculative theses regarding the metaphysical and corpuscular structure of bodies, and so it is good to bear in mind (see §7.2) that scholastic authors were acutely aware of their relative ignorance in these domains. Shortly, we will leave the foggy domain of scholastic metaphysics for the clearer air of the seventeenth century (only to find revealed, as the fog recedes, a metaphysical train wreck).

Something more might yet be said, however, about how to think about the debate over partial substantial forms. In part, this debate simply rehearses by now familiar metaphysical questions about individuation. Scotus, for instance, appeals to the fact that parts of an animal can survive apart from the whole (*In Meta.* VII.20 [*Opera phil.* n. 11]), and that the heart in particular is generated before the other parts of the animal (ibid. n. 38). For pluralists who are already prepared to allow that the part can survive apart from the whole, it is natural to extend the scope of their pluralism downward so as to recognize partial substantial forms. Unitarians, of course, will deny such claims, on the grounds considered in the previous chapter.

Here too, however, the debate over substantial forms involves more than just abstract metaphysical questions. The impulse to extend pluralism downward to encompass the parts of bodies once again highlights the later scholastic trend toward conceiving of the hylomorphic framework as a physical, proto-scientific hypothesis (§6.1, §10.5, §24.3). As long as one thinks of the substantial form as a single, simple force acting on each part of a material substance, one faces the immediate objection that there simply is no such centrally organizing power within bodies. Each part of a living thing—indeed, we would now say, each and every cell—contains its own organizing instructions, instructions that allow it to carry out its operations quite independently of what happens elsewhere in the body, and so without requiring a unifying substantial form to orchestrate the whole. When that substantial form is conceived of as an abstract metaphysical principle, then such biological data are irrelevant. But when substantial forms are conceived of as, in effect, biological principles, it begins to look very implausible to postulate a central governing power. By decentralizing form in the way that Suárez and others do, the doctrine of substantial form tilts still farther away from metaphysics and toward science.

27

Real Essences

27.1. Metaphysical Chaos

This and the following three chapters describe the slow slide of post-scholastic thought toward metaphysical chaos. In place of the entrenched Aristotelian ontology of complete, individual substances, composed out of parts of various kinds organized by a governing substantial form, the seventeenth and eighteenth centuries spin off wildly in all directions. Ordinary objects are rejected as mere phenomena and replaced, variously, with world-sized substances, microscopic substances, scattered substances, or no substances at all. For those who take delight in train wrecks, such chaos can serve only to enliven the subject, and indeed this period in the history of philosophy has been the subject of massive scholarly attention. By contrast, although the Aristotelian worldview is metaphysically extravagant in its own ways—as we have seen in extensive detail—it ultimately arrives at a far less glamorous ontology, postulating substances of a sort that are both familiar and natural. Post-scholastic authors abandon the arcane metaphysical parts of scholastic thought, yet they thereby find themselves forced into theories that are, in their conclusions, every bit as extravagant.

As usual, it is beyond the scope of these chapters to consider the most spectacularly eccentric ontologies of Spinoza, Leibniz, and beyond. My focus is on what I conceive of (taking some chronological liberties with Locke [§1.1]) as an earlier stage of development, during which the implications of rejecting the scholastic framework were first being worked out. For the connoisseur, this earlier stage is in some ways the most interesting period of all. It puts on display in raw, inchoate form the tension between the allure of corpuscularianism and the need to make metaphysical sense of the world around us. No longer able to account for our commonsense ontology in any straightforward way, the first generation of post-scholastic authors faces the choice between stridently departing from common sense, or saving some vestige of it through other means.

As I will reconstruct the situation, the collapse of the Aristotelian consensus can be understood in terms of growing doubt regarding four fundamental theses:

1. We have knowledge of substances and the kinds into which they fall.
2. Our ordinary kind-distinctions carve things up according to their true essences.
3. Ordinary substances (dogs, trees, stones) are real entities.
4. Substances naturally and ordinarily come and go, in and out of existence.

There is a natural progression here from (1) to (4): one might begin with doubts about how much we know about what substances are, then decide that we are wrong about how substances divide up into kinds, then further decide that we are wrong even about what things count as substances, and then finally one might throw off the very notion that things in the world come into and go out of existence. Proceeding in this way, an author who rejects all four of these Aristotelian theses arrives at a worldview that is deeply at odds with how things seem to be. Yet, despite this orderly reconstruction of the dialectical situation, the actual course of the debate during the seventeenth century was much more complex. Different authors are tempted more or less to deny one or another of these theses, and it is often hard to say what the direction of inference is. Indeed, as we will see (§28.3), it is surprisingly common to begin by denying (4)—and even, seemingly, to treat the denial of (4) as axiomatic. Even so, it will be useful to organize the discussion around these four theses, in this order. The present chapter will consider the first two, saving the remainder for the following chapter.

27.2. The Unknown Essence of Things

One very common strand of post-scholastic thought concerns our inability to grasp the essences of things. This is a prominent theme in one of the earliest systematic attacks on scholasticism, Gianfrancesco Pico della Mirandola's *Examen vanitatis doctrinae gentium* (1520). (Gianfrancesco is the nephew of the more famous Giovanni Pico.) The fifth of this work's six long books takes up the Aristotelian doctrine of scientific demonstration, arguing first against the reliability of the senses and then against the possibility of arriving at accurate definitions—two of the fundamental bases of Aristotle's theory as presented in the *Posterior Analytics*. Since a definition states the essence of a thing, Pico is in effect challenging our grasp of real essences. He pursues at particular length the question of how to define what it is to be human, remarking that "one is able to recognize easily how uncertain definitions are, by placing before one's eyes the definition of 'human being'" (*Examen* V.8, II:1123). He then proceeds to canvass in great detail the various proposals that have been made, mocking them all for their disagreements among themselves and for their failure to get beneath the surface of what it is to be human.

More generally, Pico argues that Aristotelians are doomed to fail in their attempts to grasp the essences of things, because their approach requires working from the outside in, relying on the senses to grasp the accidents, and inferring from those accidents to a thing's essence. This is certainly fair enough as a sketch of the scholastic method. The general Aristotelian view that the senses serve as a foundation for the concepts of intellect is familiar enough, and we have seen how scholastic authors have a causal story that runs from sensory experience all the way to a thing's essence, inasmuch as sensation is produced by secondary qualities (§22.3), which are in turn, like accidents in general, a product of the substantial form (§24.4). (The substantial form [or forms], recall, is the principal constituent of the essence of a material substance, perhaps along with common matter [see §24.1].) Given this sort of causal story, the scholastics might well suppose it possible in principle to go from sensory experience all the way to the thing's essence. But Pico casts doubt on every aspect of the story. He challenges the very reliability of the senses in grasping the accidents of a thing (*Examen* V.1–6). He challenges our ability to learn anything substantive about the essence on the basis of those accidents (*Examen* V.10). And he questions whether in fact we grasp a thing's accidents before we grasp its essence, pointing to various passages where Aristotle himself suggests that substance is prior to accident even in the order of knowledge (ibid., pp. 1137–8).

The methodology Gianfrancesco Pico describes and attacks—of working from the outside in, from accidents to essence—is distinctively scholastic only in its terminology. With respect to the actual content of the view, the scholastics are saying just what anyone with an empirically minded realistic methodology must say of such inquiry: that it begins with the senses, arrives at a grasp of observable phenomena, and from there attempts to draw inferences about the underlying, unobservable nature of the thing. But although it would be well worth our time to investigate the prospects for this sort of approach, Pico himself does not afford a very attractive opportunity. Writing in the tradition of Italian humanism, his work is impressive more for its rhetoric and scholarship than for its philosophical acuity. Moreover, the criticisms that Pico is making are ones that scholastic authors themselves were well aware of, and often quite sympathetic to. One sometimes finds the scholastics under attack for being naive and overly optimistic about their grasp of essences. Locke in particular harps on "the doctrine of substantial forms, and the confidence of mistaken pretenders to a knowledge that they had not" (*Essay* III.8.2). Yet it was entirely commonplace, throughout our four centuries, to question just how much we really know of the real essences of things. Chapter 7 considered the scholastic debate in some detail, focusing on our knowledge of the thin metaphysical substance "beneath" the accidents. Inasmuch as that thin substance just is prime matter together with one or more substantial forms, to doubt our grasp of substance in effect just is to doubt our grasp of essence. (Hence it is not surprising that 'substance'—among scholastics as well as today—is often used synecdochically to refer to a thing's essence.) All of the major scholastic figures can be found acknowledging the poverty of our understanding of the essences of things, and in Franciscans like Scotus, Ockham, and Francis of Marchia such doubts turn into out-and-out skepticism, with Ockham, for instance, remarking that "we can naturally cognize no external corporeal substance in itself" (*Ordinatio* I.3.2 [*Opera theol.* II:412]). Of course, not all the scholastics were so pessimistic, and some had offered sophisticated accounts of how we might go from accidents to essences. Since this material was discussed at some length in that earlier chapter, I will not reprise it further here.[1]

---

[1] Most scholastic discussions of our knowledge of essence are couched in terms of our knowledge of substance—not because '*substantia*' is being used to mean *essence*, although that usage is common enough, but because if the substantial form is unknown, then, given that everyone agrees on the unknowability of matter (§7.2), it follows that the whole (thin) substance is unknown. Hence one can make the stronger claim.

Scholastic discussions do not generally focus on the problem of natural kinds, and whether our classification scheme is correct, though of course doubts over our knowledge of essences might well lead to doubts of this further kind. One example of such a discussion, however, is that of Blasius of Parma, who reaches a series of strikingly skeptical conclusions in this domain: "quod aliqua duo sint diversarum specierum non potest evidenter probari" (*In De an.* II.4 concl. 7, p. 93): "quod homo plus differat ab asino quam asinus ab asino non est per se notum nec deducibile ex per se notis" (ibid., concl. 8, p. 94); "quod homo formaliter et specifice distinguatur ab asino non est demonstrabile" (*In De an.* III.2, concl. 2, p. 124); "quod duo animalia, quaecumque sint, specifice ab invicem differant, non est evidens" (ibid., concl. 4, p. 125).

Doubts over our knowledge of essences have implications for a wide range of other issues in scholastic thought. Discussions of alchemy, for instance, often turn on questions over just how much we actually know about the inner

Whereas doubts over our knowledge of essences were common among scholastic authors, they become virtually *de rigueur* during the later stages of our period. Francisco Sanches's anti-Aristotelian treatise *Quod nihil scitur* (1576) begins with the charge that our names fail to map onto the true natures of things.[2] Galileo regards it as an "impossible undertaking" to "penetrate the true and internal essence of natural substances" (third letter on sunspots [ed. Flora p. 949; tr. Drake p. 123]). Marin Mersenne's *La vérité des sciences* (1625) puts into the mouth of the skeptic a withering attack on our pretenses to know the nature of things: "although the names and phrases that we use to indicate our concepts ought to signify the essence of each thing, there is in fact nothing more ridiculous. These names are indeed assigned randomly, without any rhyme or reason" (I.3, p. 38). The philosopher who serves as Mersenne's spokesman in the dialogue grants the point: names have indeed been "very badly imposed" (I.6, p. 69).[3] Pierre Gassendi too gives particular weight to this issue, as in his objections to Descartes:

Besides the color, the shape, the fact that it can melt, etc., we conceive that there is something that is the subject of the accidents and changes we observe; but what this subject is, or what sort of thing it is, we do not know. This always eludes us; and it is only a kind of conjecture that leads us to think that there must be something underneath the accidents. (Fifth Objections, VII:271)

As we will see in §27.6, Gassendi accepts our familiar ontology of material substances, including the idea of an underlying essence that gives rise to the superficial properties of the thing—all cast in corpuscularian terms, of course. But he is adamant that we lack any knowledge of this essence. As he writes in his book-length response to Descartes, the *Disquisitio metaphysica* (1644), "God has revealed to us whatever it is necessary for us to know about each thing, by giving things the properties through which they become known.... But as for the internal nature and source, as it were, from which these properties flow, since the knowledge of that is not necessary for us, God has willed it to be hidden (*occultam*)" (II.8.2).[4]

Francis Bacon might seem at first an exception to this general trend, with his rejection of "the received and inveterate opinion that the inquisition of man is not competent to find out essential forms or true differences," and his claim to the contrary "that the invention of Forms is of all other parts of knowledge the worthiest to be sought" (*Advancement of Learning* II.7.5). (Here, in 1605, skepticism regarding essences is

---

essences of things, the worry being that if we do not know what it is to be, say, gold, then we will hardly be in a position to convert other things into gold (see Newman's introduction to Paul of Taranto, *Summa perfectionis* pp. 27–9).

[2] See *Quod nihil scitur* p. 95: "A nomine rem ducamus. Mihi enim omnis nominalis definitio est, et fere omnis quaestio. Explico: rerum naturas cognoscere non possumus, ego saltem. Si dicas, te bene, non contendam. Falsum tamen est. Cur enim tu potius? Et hinc nil scimus. Quod si non cognoscamus, quo pacto demonstrabimus? Nullo. Tu tamen diffinitionem dicis esse quae rei naturam demonstrat. Da mihi unam. Non habes. Concludo ergo. Amplius, rei quam non cognoscimus quomodo nomina imponemus? Non video. Hinc circa nomina dubitatio perpetua et multa in verbis confusio et fallacia."

[3] For Mersenne, see also *La vérité des sciences* p. 212: "il ne faut pas penser que nous puissions pénétrer la nature des individus, ni ce que se passe intérieurement dans iceus, car nos sens, sans lesquels l'entendement ne peut rien connoître, ne voyent que ce qui est exterieur...." See also Dear, *Mersenne and Learning* pp. 184–5, and the selections translated by Ariew et al., *Descartes' Meditations: Background Source Materials* pp. 151–65. On Mersenne's skepticism more generally, see Popkin, *History of Skepticism* pp. 113–20.

[4] On Gassendi see also §7.1, as well as the Fifth Objections at VII:275 and VII:338 and *Disquisitio metaphysica* II.8.2–3 and VI.4.2–3. For a helpful discussion, see LoLordo, *Pierre Gassendi* pp. 213–17.

already a "received and inveterate opinion.") But Bacon immediately goes on to dismiss inquiry into the essences of substances, remarking that "to inquire the Form of a lion, of an oak, of gold; nay, of water, of air, is a vain pursuit" and that we should instead pursue an understanding of the fundamental qualities that are the building blocks of all the rest. The leading example of this is his extended inquiry into the nature of heat (§21.4). (Descartes too might seem to be an exception, with his confident talk of thought as the essence of mind, and extension the essence of body. But if the argument of §8.4 and §13.7 is correct, then these claims too should be read as going only so deep, and as leaving a great deal of room for uncertainty about the ultimate metaphysical nature of mind and body as the determinable substrata of determinate modes.)

This consensus over the unknowability of essences becomes, if anything, even more prominent in the second half of the seventeenth century, in authors such as Henry More, Robert Boyle, Newton, Locke, and a great many others. Casting his eyes over the situation at the turn of the eighteenth century, Pierre Bayle remarks that "I am quite sure there are very few good scientists of this century who are not convinced that nature is an impenetrable abyss and that its springs are known only to him who made and directs them. In this regard, then, all these philosophers are Academics and Pyrrhonists" (*Dictionnaire*, "Pyrrho" note B [XII:101a; tr. p. 195]).[5]

27.3. Damage Control: The Scholastics

Essences are utterly fundamental to most philosophical schemes during our period. They define what a thing is, and so determine its identity conditions, and they serve as a causal explanation for many of a thing's non-essential properties. So given that, as Bayle puts it, the philosophers "are all Pyrrhonists" in this regard (as above), it is surprising that such doubts did not cause more widespread damage. We might here distinguish two kinds of issues. First, there are questions concerning our grasp of natural kinds. If we cannot know the essences of things, then it might seem we cannot know what the fundamental kinds are in nature: where we have genuine differences in species, versus where we have merely accidental differences. Most immediately, this raises questions of biological taxonomy, but it also raises more general metaphysical questions about

---

[5] For Henry More see *Immortality* I.2 axiom 8: "the subject or naked essence or substance of a thing is utterly unconceivable to any of our faculties"; to Descartes, March 5, 1649: "cum radix rerum omnium ac essentia in aeternas defossa lateat tenebras, rem quamlibet necessario definiri ab habitudine aliqua" (V:299).

For Newton, see the General Scholium to the *Principia*: "Videmus tantum corporum figuras et colores, audimus tantum sonos, tangimus tantum superficies externas, olfacimus odores solos, et gustamus sapores: intimas substantias nullo sensu, nulla actione reflexa cognoscimus." The *De gravitatione* offers an interesting argument for why our knowledge in this domain is necessarily limited: that there are likely to be multiple, essentially distinct ways in which the same observable phenomena could be realized, between which we would be unable to discriminate: "Descripta extensione natura corporea ex altera parte restat explicanda. Huius autem, cum non necessario sed voluntate divina existit, explicatio erit incertior propterea quod divinae potestatis limites haud scire concessum est, scilicet an unico tantum modo materia creari potuit, vel an plures sunt quibus alia atque alia entia corporibus simillima producere licuit" (p. 105; tr. p. 27). (Boyle makes a similar argument in *The Usefulness of Natural Philosophy* [*Works* III:255–6].) For a helpful discussion of Newton's views in this regard, see Van Leeuwen, *Problem of Certainty* pp. 111–17.

See also John Tillotson: "we do not know things in their realities, but as they appear and are represented to us with all their masks and disguises" (*Works* II:538); and Samuel Parker (quoted at greater length in §9.2): "the truly wise and discerning philosophers do not endeavor after the dry and sapless knowledge of abstracted natures, but only search after the properties, qualities, virtues, and operations of natural beings" (*Free and Impartial Censure*, p. 64).

identity through change. For if we suppose that things do persist through change, then we should want some account of what sorts of changes are and are not consistent with persistence. To know this, it would seem that we have to have at least some information about the essences of things, since that will determine which properties are contingent and accidental and which are necessary.

A second issue concerns our grasp of the metaphysical structure of reality. Even the very most fundamental scholastic division among things, between the thin metaphysical substance and its accidents (§6.1), would seem to be called into question by the pervasive doubts we are considering. Most of the authors during our four centuries, however, want not only to embrace that distinction in some form but to go still further and make claims about the underlying thin substance, describing it in either hylomorphic or corpuscularian terms. One might suppose that, given the prevailing skepticism regarding our knowledge of essences, authors would be generally loath to commit themselves one way or another in this regard. As we have seen, however, this is far from being the case. Aristotelians are adamantly Aristotelian; corpuscularians are adamantly anti-Aristotelian. Whatever their view, almost all parties to this dispute seem quite certain that they are right. But if our knowledge is limited to the superficial appearances of things, what business does anyone have entering into such obscure metaphysical controversies?

With respect to natural kinds, scholastic authors employed various recourses to save the conventional taxonomy of species and genera. One approach that was enjoying its final flourishing right at the start of our period was the appeal to divine illumination. This is most notable in Henry of Ghent—the last great scholastic proponent of that venerable Augustinian theory—who distinguishes between our ability to know something true about the world (for which no special illumination is required), and our ability to grasp the "pure truth" about things:

It should be said absolutely, therefore, that there is nothing concerning which a human being can have pure truth by acquiring a grasp of it through merely natural means. Such truth can be had only through the divine light's illumination. (*Summa quaest. ord.* 1.2 [*Opera* XXI:63])

Unlike earlier, more idealistic versions of illumination theory, Ghent does not locate the pure truth solely in some incorporeal realm. Fusing Augustine's more Platonic version of the theory with thirteenth-century Aristotelianism, Ghent recognizes pure truth in the physical world around us, in the *essences* of things:

It is one thing to know of a creature what is true in respect to it, and another to know its truth.... For the senses even in brutes grasp well enough concerning a thing what is true in it... But still they do not grasp or cognize the truth of things, because they cannot judge regarding any thing what it is in actual truth—concerning a human being, for instance, that it is a true human being, or concerning a color, that it is a true color. (ibid., XXI:36)

Relying on the tacit assumption that of course we do manage to grasp the nature of what it is to be a human being, or a color, but appealing to the common doubts over how we could ever manage to get from sensory experience to essences, Ghent offers the theory of divine illumination as a solution to this Aristotelian impasse.

Ghent's attempt to find new work for a venerable old theory was much discussed but quickly fell out of fashion. Its hostile reception by Scotus ensured that even later

Franciscans—who had hitherto been the leading scholastic supporters of the theory—would no longer give the theory a prominent place in their epistemology. Consequently, the theory of divine illumination plays only the most marginal of roles during our four centuries.[6] But what then? If we cannot get from sensory inputs to a grasp of natures—as Scotus himself insisted quite forcefully (§7.3)—then what reason do we have for thinking we understand the structure of the physical world at all? One reason scholastic authors were less concerned about this than we might think they should be is that they took themselves to have supernatural guidance of another sort—not immediately from God, as the Augustinian theory had it, but mediately, through Adam's original imposition of names. According to the creation story of Genesis, even before Eve was created, Adam gave a name to all living things:

And the Lord God having formed out of the ground all the beasts of the earth, and all the fowls of the air, brought them to Adam to see what he would call them: for whatsoever Adam called any living creature, the same is its name. And Adam called all the beasts by their names, and all the fowls of the air, and all the cattle of the field. . . . (Genesis 2:19–20)

In this pre-fallen state, Adam was supposed to have possessed cognitive abilities vastly superior to us fallen human beings: hence, as Ghent puts it, Adam would have gone about his naming "as the ideal (*optimus*) metaphysician, knowing perfectly the essences and quiddities of things, imposing various names on just those species in keeping with the various essences and corresponding to those very essences of the things" (*Lectura super sacram Scripturam* ch. 2 [*Opera* XXXVI:206]). We fallen descendants of Adam have lost that talent for metaphysics, among much else, but the one legacy we retain from Adam is a language that truly cuts the world at its joints. The name that Adam gave "is its name," according to Genesis (line 3), suggesting that although we no longer speak the language of Adam we can still be confident that our vulgar tongues bear some correspondence to Adam's Ur-language.

Even if this guarantee of linguistic isomorphism was too thin, without some further illumination, to account for the sort of knowledge Ghent took us to have, still it seems to have been enough to keep at bay the sort of metaphysical chaos that would engulf the seventeenth century. Although the fourteenth century would see outbursts of doubt regarding the standard Aristotelian story regarding generation or corruption (§28.2), it would take centuries more for such doubts to take hold in any serious way. With the increased secularism and scholarly sophistication of the sixteenth century, it became possible for Sanches to remark that although Adam named all things according to their natures, that does not help *us*, given that he left no record of his efforts. And by the later seventeenth century—as we will consider in the next section—authors like

---

[6] I discuss Henry of Ghent's conception of divine illumination at length in "Twilight of Divine Illumination." For a translation of the key texts, see my *Cambridge Translations*, vol. 3. Although Ghent strikes me as distinctive in his focus on our natural inability to grasp the essences of things, one can find hints of this idea in earlier figures. See, e.g., Bonaventure, *Itinerarium mentis in Deum* 2.9: ". . . et ideo nec certitudinaliter iudicari possunt nisi per illam quae non tantum fuit forma cuncta producens, verum etiam cuncta conservans et distinguens, tanquam ens in omnibus formam tenens et regula dirigens, et per quam diiudicat mens nostra cuncta quae per sensus intrant in ipsam."

For Scotus's attack on Ghent, see *Ordinatio* I.3.1.4 (tr. *Philosophical Writings* pp. 96–132).

Boyle and Locke could express outright scorn for the received taxonomy of natural kinds.[7]

What of the metaphysical structure of substances? (This was the second way in which skepticism regarding essences threatens to infest other domains.) Here the standard scholastic approach was to treat both substantial form and prime matter as theoretical postulates. No one—not even those who are most optimistic about our grasp of the natures of things—thought that our knowledge of these metaphysical parts is anything other than highly schematic. It was a scholastic commonplace, for instance, to remark that we do not know the nature even of a fly.[8] Scotus memorably remarked that "with respect to substances we have a vocal disposition, just as someone blind is naturally able to syllogize about colors" (*In Meta.* II.2–3 [*Opera phil.* III n. 119]). The analogy is worth reflecting on, because it allows that we in fact *do* talk about the essences of things, and perhaps even do so successfully, in the way that someone blind can have quite a lot of knowledge about color. But just as the blind might be said to be inevitably ignorant about what colors essentially are, so we inevitably lack anything more than a schematic story about both prime matter and substantial form. We postulate such metaphysical entities, as explanations of phenomena that we are familiar with, but we can say almost nothing about their actual nature. Compare how the Coimbrans defend substantial form:

Natural things are not composed solely out of matter, because if the same common matter belonged to a human being, a stone, and a lion, then there would be the same essence and definition for each. Therefore beyond matter they have their own proper form, by which they differ from one another. (*In Phys.* I.9.9.2)

The argument is simple—perhaps even simplistic—but it usefully highlights the standard scholastic strategy of appealing to some evident phenomena and then invoking some metaphysical entity as the only plausible explanation. We have seen this strategy deployed over and over in previous chapters, in defense of metaphysical prime matter (Chs. 2–3), thin metaphysical substances (Chs. 6–9), real accidents (Chs. 10, 14, 15, 19), and substantial form (Chs. 24–5). In every case, such arguments proceed without anything more than the most schematic sketch of what such entities actually are. Form and matter are bare theoretical posits, known only for what they do, and in their own right unknowable.

---

[7] On Adam's naming, see Dahan, "Nommer les êtres." For another instance, see Aquinas, *Summa theol.* 1a 94.3sc: "ipse imposuit nomina animalibus, ut dicitur *Gen.* 2. Nomina autem debent naturis rerum congruere. Ergo Adam scivit naturas omnium animalium et pari ratione, habuit omnium aliorum scientiam." The idea can be found into the seventeenth century, in, e.g., the anti-skeptic Jean de Silhon, *De l'immortalité de l'ame* (1634): "Mais bien que Adam connoissant par une clarté surnaturelle des especes que Dieu lui avait infuser, l'être de toutes les bestes, et les formes essentielles qui les distinguiont l'une de l'autre . . ." (pp. 160–1). Silhon takes our own language to have been formed by this initial Edenic act of naming.

Sanches accepts Adam's knowledge of natures; he doubts only whether it has left any imprint on our own languages: "Si unam solum dicas linguam pro rerum natura impositam esse, cur non item aliae? aut quae illa? Si dicas Adami primam, verum quidem est: poterat enim, quia rerum naturas noverat, ut testatur author Pentateuchi: et tunc sane desiderandum esset ut philosophia sua, aut quam habemus, suo etiam idiomate conscripta esset" (*Quod nihil scitur* p. 120).

[8] See Roger Bacon, *Opus maius* I.10 (quoted in §23.6) and Thomas Aquinas, *In Symbolum Apostolorum* prol. (*Opusc. theol.* II n. 864).

The schematic character of these scholastic accounts is of course part of what attracted the wrath of their critics. Descartes complains over and over that the workings of substantial forms and real qualities are "unintelligible,"[9] and Locke likewise thinks the "corpuscularian hypothesis" more defensible "as that which is thought to go farthest in an intelligible explication of the qualities of bodies" (*Essay* IV.3.16). There is considerable truth in these complaints, provided that 'unintelligible' is understood not in the sense of *incoherent*, but in the sense of *unexplained*. The scholastics are in no danger of incoherence, by and large, precisely because they explain so little of the details of form and matter. Substantial forms and other metaphysical parts are simply black boxes that perform certain functions in ways that scholastic authors never even attempt to discern, seemingly treating such knowledge as impossible in principle (§19.7).

The quick Coimbran argument leverages one problematic issue regarding real essences—the individuation of natural kinds—to settle another problematic issue: that of substantial form. This was a common scholastic strategy. Scotus, for instance, considers a view on which form would be nothing over and above matter, and responds that on this view there would be no distinctions in species but only grades of matter. He takes for granted that such an outcome is unacceptable.[10] Now, to be sure, the corpuscularian might agree with Scotus and the Coimbrans that natural kinds must be saved, and might attempt to do so through strictly geometric–kinetic properties, in terms of particles variously interlocked. This was a common enough response, but what makes the seventeenth century so fascinating is that it was not the only response. Many of the most prominent critics of scholasticism are willing to concede that corpuscularianism cannot save the commonsense Aristotelian worldview, and are prepared to overthrow that worldview, beginning with our familiar taxonomy of species membership. It is remarkable how much ground such a stance yields. It effectively acknowledges that there is something right about the scholastic project: that if one wants to defend an ontology of dogs and cats and stones (a worldview that, after all, remains entrenched to this day), one needs to embrace something like the metaphysical parts of Aristotelianism. In rejecting such metaphysical commitments, corpuscularianism entails radical revisions to commonsense ontology. Thus we move, for the remainder of this chapter, to the seventeenth century, and to the second stage of metaphysical chaos.

---

[9] Descartes attacks the explanatory vacuity of the scholastic account of substantial form at *Principles* IV.198, IV.201, and in correspondence to Morin (II:199–200), to Regius (III:506), and to Voetius (VIIIB:26).

An argument just like the Coimbrans is mocked by Boyle in *Origin of Forms* (*Works* V:344; Stewart pp. 58–59).

[10] See *Lectura* II.12 n. 23: "Opinantur quod materia non est alia realitas absoluta a forma . . . "; n. 27: "si forma esset terminus intrinsecus materiae, generabilia et corruptibilia non distinguerentur specie sed isti gradus sunt essentialiter idem tertio, scilicet materiae. . . ." For discussion of this argument and related issues, see Cross, *Physics of Duns Scotus* pp. 34–41. I doubt, however, that Scotus is here responding to Richard of Middleton, as Cross, following the lead of Scotus's editors, contends.

The scholastics need essences not only for their taxonomy of species and genera, and for their hylomorphic metaphysics, but also for their account of the substantial unity of the human composite. For, as was suggested in §5.5, a crucial move in the argument for rational soul and human body as *unum per se* is to claim that the soul by itself is an incomplete, partial substance, a notion that often depends on the link between substance and species membership.

27.4. Natural Kinds

The second stage of metaphysical chaos, as described in §27.1, concerns whether our ordinary kind-distinctions carve things up according to their true essences. This stage can be usefully separated into two components: worries about the reality of our familiar kinds, and worries about the reality of the essences that supposedly ground such kinds. This section addresses the first of these concerns, leaving the remainder of the chapter to consider various forms of anti-essentialism. To worry about whether we are getting the kinds right is not the commonplace worry of §27.2, regarding our knowledge of the essences of things, but the further doubt regarding whether we are even dividing the world up according to its most natural divisions. Doubts of the first sort might naturally lead to doubts regarding the second, but this was by no means inevitable, or even usual. One might agree that we know little or nothing about what it is to be gold, or to be a fly, and yet think that surely 'gold' and 'fly' pick out natural (as opposed to purely conventional) kinds. And in practice it was usually supposed, at least tacitly, even in the seventeenth century, that our taxonomic schemes are basically correct.

In the later seventeenth century, however, serious doubts began to arise, most prominently in Boyle and Locke. Here is Boyle:

> It was not at random that I spoke, when, in the foregoing notes about the origin of qualities, I intimated, that it was very much by a kind of tacit agreement that men had distinguished the species of bodies, and that those distinctions were more arbitrary then we are wont to be aware 3
> of. For I confess that I have not yet, either in Aristotle or any other writer, met with any genuine and sufficient diagnostic and boundary for the discriminating and limiting the species of things, or to speak more plainly, I have not found that any naturalist has laid down a determinate 6
> number and sort of qualities, or other attributes, which is *sufficient* and *necessary* to constitute all portions of matter, endowed with them, distinct kinds of natural bodies. And therefore I observe that most commonly men look upon these as distinct species of bodies, that have had the luck to 9
> have distinct names found out for them; though perhaps diverse of them differ much less from one another than other bodies which (because they have been huddled up under one name) have been looked upon as but one sort of bodies. But not to lay any weight on this intimation 12
> about names, I found that for want of a true characteristic or discriminating notes, it has been, and is still, both very *uncertain* as to divers bodies, whether they are of different species or of the same, and very *difficult* to give a sufficient reason why diverse bodies, wherein nature is assisted 15
> by art, should not as well pass for distinct kinds of bodies as others that are generally reckoned to be so. (*Origin of Forms* [*Works* V:356; Stewart pp. 72–3])

It is by "tacit agreement" (line 2) rather than any "true characteristic " (line 13) that we distinguish species. Boyle certainly does not suggest that our distinctions are wholly conventional, but they are at least "more arbitrary" (line 3) than we suppose, and in part a matter of "luck" (line 9). Boyle's charge is not the unexceptional one that we cannot describe the essence itself, but the much stronger claim that we cannot even produce any "sufficient and necessary" attributes (line 7)—even in terms of accidental "qualities"—to sort things into kinds. And it is not just that he thinks the folk have been stupid about this. Implicitly relying on his extensive research into chemistry (a connection he makes explicit elsewhere), he contends the task is genuinely "difficult" (line 15). Accordingly, he is doubtful that our conventions have in fact gotten things right. It is eminently possible that various substances conventionally falling into different kinds "differ much less from one another" (lines 10–11) than do other bodies that are regarded as belonging to the same kind. The status of our conventional taxonomy is, in short, "very uncertain" (line 14).[11]

Locke follows Boyle's lead in this regard, and if anything paints a more dire picture regarding our grasp of natural kinds. His worries go back to early drafts of the *Essay* (from 1671) and become more elaborate in the first printed edition (1689), where his discussion of the "Names of Substances" (III.6) is the second longest chapter of the whole treatise. Much of it concerns the familiar idea that we are incapable of grasping the true natures of things, and he rails at length against the scholastics in this regard, as if they supposed otherwise. But Locke goes much farther than this. Coining the terminology 'real essence' and 'nominal essence,' he contends that we have hitherto classified substances only according to whatever superficial properties have been convenient for us to rely on, and so framed for each thing a merely nominal essence.[12] This would be a new idea only in its terminology, if Locke thought that these nominal essences at least tracked the underlying real essences. But he makes it quite clear that he does not. Our classifications, he holds, are "seldom adequate to the internal nature of the things they are taken from" (III.6.37). Consequently, "we find many of the individuals that are ranked into one sort, called by one common name, and so received as being of one species, have yet qualities depending on their real constitutions, as far different one from another as from others, from which they are accounted to differ specifically" (III.6.8; see III.10.20). The language here is strongly reminiscent of Boyle (lines 10–12 above), and indeed Locke goes on to invoke the experience of the chemists in support of this claim. But Locke seems often to want to go farther than Boyle in this regard. For whereas Boyle's overall position is one of hesitance and doubt regarding

---

[11] Boyle (seemingly unlike Locke) is well aware that the scholastics commonly express their own doubts about our grasp of essences—indeed, he quotes some representative passages at the head of a section of *Origin of Forms* (*Works* V:339 [printed as a footnote in Stewart p. 54]).

That Boyle's own distinctive doubts about our conventional taxonomies are grounded in his chemical research can be seen in the following passage: "And indeed by reason of the unsettled notion and almost arbitrary use of the word, *Form*, I have observed it to be so uncertainly applied to the constituting of the distinct *classes* or kinds of bodies, that I have doubted whether diverse of those forms by which such kinds are constituted be not a kind of *metaphysical conceptions*, by virtue of which bodies very differing in nature are comprised in the same denomination, because they agree in a fitness for some *use*, or in some other thing that is common to them all (as whether a bullet be silver, or brass, or lead, or cork, if it swing at the end of a string, it is enough to make it a *pendulum*), and whether a burned body be chalk, or rag-stone (which is very hard and coarse) or alabaster, which is a soft and fine stone, or an oyster-shell, or a cockle-shell, or a piece of coral; yet if it have been calcined to whiteness it is lime, rather then such true *physical forms*, as are said to make the bodies that have forms of the same denomination to be of the same specific nature. However, these forms seem to be very generical things, and more such than is commonly heeded. And I have also sometimes questioned, whether some of those things, upon whose score men constitute bodies in this or that species or classes, be so properly the true and intrinsic forms of those Bodies, as certain states of matter, wherein bodies very differing in nature may agree. As water, wine, and I know not how many other differing liquors may each of them apart be made by congelation to pass into that sort of body we call ice. And not only the tallow and grease of animals, and the expressed oils and spirits of fermented vegetables (some whereof differ exceedingly among themselves), but also (as I have tried) diverse mineral and even metalline concretes may be made (some of them without destruction of their nature) to pass into that class of body we call flame" (*Origin* [*Works* V:472; not in Stewart]).

[12] Locke signals that he is coining the terms 'real essence' and 'nominal essence' at *Essay* III.6.2, when he speaks of using "a peculiar name." See too Leibniz, *Nouveaux essais* III.3.15, who complains "il me semble que nôtre langage innove extremement dans les manières de s'exprimer. On a bien parlé jusqu'ici de definitions nominales et causales où réeles, mais non pas que je sache d'essences autres que réeles."

Locke's views about how we classify substances into kinds go back to a long discussion in the B Draft of 1671 (§§72–87), which lacks the terminology of real and nominal essences but sets out all the core ideas of what he would eventually publish. See also entries in Locke's journal from 1676 (ed. Aaron and Gibb p. 83) and 1677 (ibid. pp. 98–9).

just how well we are tracking the true natures of things, in Locke that thesis seems to have hardened into a positive conviction regarding our own ignorance:

> We in vain pretend to range things into sorts, and dispose them into certain classes, under names, by their real essences, that are so far from our discovery or comprehension. A blind man may as soon sort things by their colours, and he that has lost his smell, as well distinguish a lily and a rose by their odors, as by those internal constitutions which he knows not. (III.6.9)

The metaphors, if taken seriously, suggest that it would be a matter of blind luck if our classificatory schemes mapped onto the real divisions of nature.

Often Locke is taken to have embraced a still stronger claim: that there are no real divisions in nature or, in other words, that there are no natural kinds. This seems to me a misreading, but to get clear about the situation we need a somewhat sharper account of what a natural kind is. Since the term is a modern one, not in use during our period,[13] and since even now it is used in a range of different ways, it is important to stipulate one's precise usage. To endorse natural kinds, then, on my usage, is to maintain that material substances cluster into a small number of cohesive classes, and that there is an objective fact about what these classes are. In the context of our debate, such natural kinds are the species of things, and so the proponent of natural kinds holds that there is a unique system of species (and higher genera) that best captures the similarities and differences among individuals. So conceived, the doctrine of natural kinds is not a metaphysical doctrine: it prescinds from questions of whether individuals belong to a kind by sharing numerically the same immanent universal form, for instance, or by participating in some sort of Form or Divine Idea. An atheistic nominalist might endorse natural kinds just as much as a Christian Platonist. This doctrine of natural kinds is consistent with supposing that our current taxonomy does not capture these natural kinds, and it is also consistent with a high degree of skepticism regarding whether we can know exactly what these kinds are.

Embracing natural kinds is not all or nothing. The most extreme rejection would take material substances to be distributed along a smooth continuum so as to lack any sorts of non-random similarity clusters at all. The most extreme embrace would treat these clusters as composed of substances that exactly resemble each other with respect to their essential properties, and would suppose that all substances fall into some such well-defined cluster. Neither position is at all plausible, and so far as I know neither was defended during our period. Certainly, scholastic authors never supposed that members of a species would be exactly alike, even with respect to their essences. Given that substantial forms account for the distinctive intrinsic features of a given individual, such as size and hair color (§24.4), members of a species must differ from one another even regarding their essences. (*A fortiori*, substantial forms are not universals. Although readers sometimes take the pervasiveness of nominalism among post-scholastic authors as an important point of difference with their scholastic rivals, in fact it was rare for scholastics to depart from nominalism, if by that term we mean simply the rejection of real universals: forms or properties that exist wholly in more than one individual. [On nominalism in the broader scholastic sense, see §5.3.] For the vast majority of

---

[13] According to Hacking ("Tradition of Natural Kinds" p. 111), the term 'natural kind' arises in the nineteenth-century work of Mill, Whewell, and Venn.

scholastics, including Aquinas, Scotus, and of course Ockham, only concepts are universal, and they are so only in the sense that they stand for many things. Hence the scholastic doctrine of substantial form, or of essences, is a doctrine of property instances: non-repeatable attributes of individual substances.)[14]

Although the seventeenth century witnesses a growing suspicion of natural kinds, authors of this period do not reject them altogether—not if that means embracing the extreme position that variation among material individuals is smoothly distributed without clustering. It is fairly clear, for instance, that Boyle—even if he thinks that our standard taxonomy is highly "arbitrary" (line 3 above)—does not wish to deny that there are natural kinds. To be sure, he thinks that we have not adequately captured the real clusters that are to be found in nature, and that there are likely to be many more such clusters than we presently recognize. But this is not to deny that individuals do cluster. After describing the vast range of variables in arrangement and motion that a corpuscularian can recognize, he concludes that "it will not be hard to conceive that there may be an incomprehensible variety of associations and textures of the minute parts of bodies, and consequently a vast multitude of portions of matter endowed with store enough of differing qualities to deserve distinct appellations..." (*Origin of Forms* [*Works* V:332; Stewart p. 49]). To be deserving of "distinct appellations" is equivalent to belonging to different kinds, since throughout our period it is taken for granted that the names of things will ideally correspond to their kinds. So Boyle evidently thinks that, contrary to our relatively simple taxonomy, there is a "vast multitude" of natural kinds. Yet to say that there are a great many kinds is not to deny kinds entirely. Boyle makes this quite clear in what he immediately goes on to say: "...though for want of heedfulness and fit words men have not yet taken so much notice of their less obvious varieties as to sort them as they deserve and give them distinct and proper names." These are not the words of someone who thinks that names are inevitably imposed out of pure convention. If we take heed, there are kinds in nature on which we might impose "distinct and proper names."[15]

Locke's views in this regard are no different from Boyle's. Like Boyle, he thinks that the real nature of the material realm shows there to be a vast and bewildering variety of substances, such that our nominal essences are woefully inadequate when it comes to capturing the actual richness and complexity of nature: "we shall find everywhere that

---

[14] It is very common to suppose that Locke's rejection of universals (e.g., at *Essay* III.3.1) plays an important role in his attack on Aristotelianism, even if Locke himself does not treat that issue as part of his disagreement. See, e.g., Ayers, "Locke versus Aristotle" p. 254: "his argument hinges on the denial of real universals and on the intuitive ontological principle that everything that exists is particular. That, if accepted, is enough to refute Aristotelianism...." For a more recent example, see Leary, "How Essentialists."

For the scholastics against universals, see, e.g., this characteristic remark of Aquinas: "universalia secundum quod universalia non sunt nisi in anima" (*In De an.* II.12.144). On Aquinas's view, see Leftow, "Aquinas on Attributes." For Scotus see Noone, "Universals and Individuation" p. 111: "the community of the common nature is not at all universality in the robust sense." For an overview of scholastic views, see Klima, "Medieval Problem." Genuine realism, in the sense of a full-blooded defense of universals *in re*, can perhaps be found in Walter Burley, and in John Wyclif and some of his followers, although even then these universals are generally regarded as not really distinct from particulars (see Conti, "Realism" and "Categories and Universals").

[15] On Boyle's willingness to embrace natural kinds, see Jones, "Boyle, Classification." The earlier passage from *Origin* that Boyle alludes to in the long passage quoted in the main text occurs at *Works* V:322–3 (Stewart pp. 37–9). It focuses mainly on scholastic substantial forms, and the gap between such forms and accidents, and only hints at Boyle's conventionalism regarding our ordinary taxonomy itself.

the several species are linked together, and differ but in almost insensible degrees" (*Essay* III.6.12). This describes what has come to be known as the Great Chain of Being, an idea that was perfectly familiar to the scholastics, but that Locke advances in a strikingly bold form. Credulously accepting various dubious reports of mythical creatures at the boundaries of our recognized species, he takes the space of variations among material substances to be almost completely filled in, so that the differences between kinds are "almost insensible" (as above). But this is not to say that there are *no* kinds, if that means no clusters at all. Locke repeatedly admits that, as a purely factual matter, the natural world does admit of objective clusterings of individuals: "Nature makes many particular things, which do agree one with another in many sensible qualities, and probably too, in their internal frame and constitution" (III.6.36); "I do not deny, but nature, in the constant production of particular beings, makes them not always new and various, but very much alike and of kin one to another" (III.6.37); "those [names] of substances are not perfectly so [arbitrary], but refer to a pattern, though with some latitude" (III.4.17). Accordingly it is not out of the question that we might replace our crude taxonomic scheme with something objectively much better, if we were willing to put enough effort into this task: "it requires much time, pains, and skill, strict enquiry, and long examination, to find out what, and how many those simple ideas are, which are constantly inseparably united in nature, and are always to be found together in the same subject" (III.6.30).[16]

On my usage, then, both Boyle and Locke count as defenders of natural kinds, inasmuch as they both think that material substances fall into objectively definable clusters. If confronted with our sophisticated modern taxonomies, in either biology or chemistry, they would surely take themselves to be vindicated, judging this richly complex scheme to be precisely the sort of thing they predicted. Their complaints, then, are not with the very idea of a natural kind, but with taxonomic schemes that are insufficiently sensitive to the complexity of the natural world. Thus Locke charges his opponents with a "crude" version of the idea that material substances are ordered according to "certain regulated established essences, which are to be the models of all things to be produced" (III.6.15). This nicely situates his disagreement not only with the scholastics but also with many of his contemporaries, who hold all-too-naive conceptions regarding boundaries between species. Following Boyle, Locke thinks that reality is far more chaotic than has been commonly recognized.

Yet even if there is a clear distinction between them and their opponents, it is good to keep in mind there is no all-or-nothing question here, just a continuum of views between two indefensible (and undefended) extremes. The scholastics tend toward a more orderly picture; Boyle and Locke toward a less orderly picture, but these are simply differences of degree. One can read in Walter Charleton's *Exercitationes de differentiis et nominibus animalium* (1677) that there are nine kinds of unguiculate

---

[16] For a good discussion of Locke's views regarding natural kinds, which usefully distinguishes between the empirical question of clustering and the metaphysical question of essences, see Stuart, "Locke on Natural Kinds." See too Conn, "Locke on Natural Kinds," which similarly stresses the sense in which Locke does endorse natural kinds. For a very strong statement of the view that Locke rejects natural kinds, see Yolton, *Locke Dictionary* p. 72.

Locke's commitment to natural kinds comes out particularly clearly in the zeal he expresses for the project of refining our nominal essences in a more satisfactory way. In particular, he proposes a "Dictionary of Natural History" (III.11.25). On this see Ayers, "Locke versus Aristotle" pp. 264–5, as well as Shapiro, "Toward Perfect Collections."

viviparous wild quadrupeds: the lion, the leopard, the lynx, the tiger, the bear, the wolf, the glutton (wolverine), the hyena, and the fox (pp. 14–15). Perhaps Boyle thinks there are actually one hundred such kinds; perhaps Locke thinks there are a thousand. Perhaps Boyle thinks that 5 percent of individuals diverge significantly from their cluster; perhaps Locke thinks that 20 percent do. The differences here are merely matters of degree.

Moreover, what disagreements there are are entirely descriptive and empirical, with only an indirect bearing on metaphysics. As we will see shortly, Locke combines his guarded embrace of natural kinds with some radical and innovative metaphysical claims about essences. But his views regarding natural kinds are not, in and of themselves, metaphysical. Similarly, although scholastic authors are generally more sanguine about our success in carving nature at the joints, this has nothing to do with their metaphysics, and indeed some scholastics, such as Nicole Oresme, display a high degree of skepticism regarding whether we do succeed in making the appropriate cuts.[17] So although one might well suppose—especially after reading Locke—that it is the doctrine of substantial forms that is to blame for the scholastics' uncritical approach to taxonomy, in fact such forms have nothing to do with it. There is no reason why substantial forms might not vary continuously from individual to individual, without there being any joints to carve at all. Conversely, there is nothing in corpuscularianism that precludes supposing that nature is rigidly divided into a small number of kinds, nor is that outcome even less *likely* on corpuscularian grounds. To be sure, the quantitative character of the geometric–kinematic framework makes it is easy to *picture* how corpuscularian structure might vary smoothly over individuals without clustering. There is no reason whatsoever, however, why substantial forms could not also be smoothly distributed in this way. The debate over natural kinds engages with metaphysics only when it takes up the question of what puts an individual into a kind—that is, the question of essences. This is our next topic.[18]

---

[17] Oresme's discussion of generation and corruption is striking for its skeptical orientation: he takes seriously the worry of whether we can have any knowledge in this domain, in a way that occurs to neither earlier nor later scholastics. Even so, the skepticism is ultimately quite limited, e.g.: "licet sit certum et evidens secundo modo [viz., per experientiam] that aliqua generantur et corrumpuntur, tamen saepe dubium est de hora, sicut patet experientia de corruptione hominis, et similiter de generatione" (*In De gen. et cor.* I.1, p. 7); "Correlarium tertium: quod sunt aliqua de quibus dubium est utrum sit corruptio vel non, sicut de mutatione musti in vinum et vini in acetum, et ideo dubium est utrum ista nomina sint de genere substantiae vel accidentis" (ibid.). Marsilius of Inghen's discussion of this material (*In De gen. et cor.* I.2) follows Oresme quite closely.

[18] An interesting precursor to Boyle's and Locke's doubts about our getting species right is George Dalgarno. His *Ars signorum* (1661) attempts to construct a universal language on the basis of a logical analysis of how the things we talk about ought to be carved up. But Dalgarno refuses to extend his account down to more than a selective sample of the *infimae species*. To try to do more would be an endless task, because "quodlibet genus vel species dividi potest per infinitas differentias" (ch. 4 p. 35) and, moreover, the task would be ultimately arbitrary: "censeo tamen omnes viros vere doctos mecum in hoc consensuros: nullam harum quaestionum determinari posse sine multo arbitrii" (ch. 4 pp. 35–6).

Dalgarno offers an anti-essentialist metaphysics to go with these skeptical remarks about taxonomy: "tendendum [est] in rerum nominibus componendis non esse necessarium ut differerentia generi superaddita sit tota rei forma, quam docent philosophi esse unum aliquid simplex, occultum (ipsi nesciunt quid) latitans invisibiliter (et etiam inintelligibiliter) in rebus, ad quam inveniendam nullum acumen penetrare potest. Verum hoc est commentum absurdum: omnium enim rerum quarumcumque formae sunt inadaequate cognitae: nam quicquid cognoscimus de re aliqua est pars eius formae. Dico est pars formae: forma enim nihil est aliud quam aggregatum omnium accidentium alicuius rei. Sunt etiam formae omnes inadaequate nobis incognitae, nam multa sunt accidentia, qualitates, potentiae, respectus, etc. in rebus (etiam iis quarum naturae sunt nobis maxime notae) quae a nobis non intelliguntur. Satis igitur est si differentia superaddita generi sit tale accidens quod distinguat speciem ab omnibus aliis" (ch. 5 pp. 44–5). Dalgarno here dismisses as "absurd" the commonplace doctrine of the "philosophers" that the forms of things are hidden from us. On the contrary, whenever we

27.5. Anti-Essentialism I: Hobbes and Conway

For scholastic authors, the metaphysical doctrine underlying natural kinds is the thesis of substantial form. Bodies cluster into natural kinds inasmuch as they have similar substantial forms, and these forms in turn account for the superficial similarities that we in practice use to demarcate species and genera. To deny substantial forms—as nearly all of our seventeenth-century post-scholastic authors do—is to deny that material substances are individuated and sustained by a real physical entity, with its own causal powers, not supervening on the geometric–kinetic features of the matter it informs. Our present interest is not precisely in that issue, however, but in the broader issue of whether material substances have essences at all. This is a broader issue because having a substantial form is just one way in which a thing might have an essence. Now, to be sure, the term 'essence' gets used in many different ways. During our four centuries, however, there are two senses in particular that are of overwhelming importance: a *defining* sense and an *explanatory* sense. A defining essence, as I will use that phrase, is that which makes a thing be what it is—that in virtue of which it is a thing of a certain kind. An explanatory essence is the most basic intrinsic principle accounting for the distinctive character of the substance. Here one might want to introduce a further distinction on the side of the defining essence, between the essence as what makes a thing exist, and the essence as what makes a thing be of a certain kind. In fact, however, it is an important feature of our period that these two senses never come apart. Throughout our period, a thing's species membership is regarded as necessary to it, and so for present purposes we can lump together existence and existence as a thing of a certain kind.

Scholastic authors treat substantial forms as essences in both the defining and the explanatory sense. Although earlier chapters have considered this story in some detail, it will be important in what follows to be clear on how these two senses interact. It is, first, in virtue of having a certain substantial form that a given substance is defined as the kind of thing it is—dog, cat, stone, etc. Even if in practice we lack access to substantial forms, and so sort material substances on the basis of their accidents, still what makes it the case that a given substance is a thing of a given kind is its substantial form. Second, the reason we can use accidental properties to track the substantial forms of things is that this form serves as an explanatory essence as well, serving as the internal principle that accounts for those accidents. It is crucial to the scholastic theory that substantial forms be essences in each of these senses. Without the explanatory role, the underlying epistemic picture would be jeopardized, because there would no longer be any causal route by which we might get from accidents to essence. Also jeopardized

grasp any aspect of a thing we are grasping part of its form, inasmuch as "the form is nothing more than the aggregate of all its accidents." Given this picture, it immediately follows that there will be practically an infinite number of *infimae species*, because any difference in accidents will entail a partial difference in form. It also follows that any attempt to classify will be arbitrary, because it will require privileging one or another accident.

For further discussion of Dalgarno's views see Slaughter, *Universal Language* pp. 141–53. Although she does not recognize Dalgarno as a precursor to Boyle and Locke, her work nicely situates Dalgarno's views in the essentialist context of its time. It is particularly interesting to compare Dalgarno to the highly influential work of John Wilkins, whose own universal language is predicated on a thoroughgoing realism (see Slaughter pp. 162–3). It is very plausible to think that Locke's views about essence were written under the influence of both Dalgarno and Wilkins (see Slaughter pp. 198–9).

would be the theory's underlying realism: that there is a fact of the matter about what a thing is. The reason the defining essence of a thing is not chosen simply as a matter of convention is precisely that it is the substance's most basic intrinsic explanatory principle.

Given the close connection between these two notions of essence, there is a quick route around the scholastic account: one might simply deny that material substances have this sort of intrinsic causal principle. Without an explanatory essence, it becomes unclear what would justify belief in some defining essence, and the whole theory would collapse. This is how Thomas Hobbes argues against scholastic essentialism. As we have seen (§7.1), Hobbes categorically rejects the notion of accidents, and with it rejects the substance–accident distinction. According to Hobbes's ontology, there are only substances, some larger and some smaller. Nothing else has a place in his ontology: no forms, no accidents, no modes, and—in particular—no essences. When we use such metaphysical language to talk about bodies, we are speaking of nothing more than "the mode of conceiving a body" (De corpore 8.2). Talk of essences is simply one more manner of conception:

The accident on account of which we give a certain name to any body, or the accident that denominates its subject, is customarily called its *essence*—as rationality is the essence of a man, whiteness the essence of what is white, and extension the essence of a body. That same essence, inasmuch as it is generated, is called its *form*. Further, a body, with respect of any of its accidents, is called the *subject*, whereas with respect to the form it is called the *matter*. (De corpore 8.23)

Hobbes is systematically deconstructing scholastic terminology, as no more than various ways of conceiving of body. When we conceive of that by which a body possesses "a certain name" (line 1)—that is, as it falls under some kind—we use the term 'essence.' If we focus on that essence as something generated or corrupted (line 4), we use the term 'form.' If the body is conceived of as the possessor of the form (line 5), then we use the term 'matter.' Hobbes's point is that these are all just ways of talking about one and the same body, variously conceived. As he puts it even more starkly in his exchange with Bishop Bramhall (1668), "essence and all other abstract names are words artificial belonging to the art of logic, and signify only the manner how we consider the substance itself" (Works IV:308).[19]

Hobbes rejects essence in both the defining and explanatory sense. Because all his ontology recognizes is substance, he has no way to make sense of some intrinsic explanatory principle. The only thing an essence could be, in the explanatory sense, would be some sort of dominant corpuscle or organ, governing the whole—perhaps not an impossible view, but not one Hobbes is sympathetic to. He is equally averse to postulating any sort of defining essence. Leibniz would later criticize Hobbes for supposing that all definitions are nominal, none real.[20] It is indeed an alarming position to take, because if there is no objective fact about what a thing is, then our familiar

---

[19] Hobbes attacks the scholastic doctrine of essences at *Leviathan* 46, and at *De corpore* 3.4. See also *Six Lessons*, which refers back to *De corpore* 8.23, "where I define what it is we call essence, namely, that accident for which we give the thing its name" (*Works* VII:221).

[20] "Et hac ratione satisfit Hobbio, qui veritates volebat esse arbitrarias, quia ex definitionibus nominalibus penderent, non considerans realitatem definitionis in arbitrio non esse, nec quaslibet notiones inter se posse coniungi" (Leibniz, *Phil. Schriften* IV:425; tr. Ariew and Garber p. 26).

ontology of substances is thrown into doubt: it would no longer seem to be an objective fact that *this* is a human being, and *that* is an oak tree. These become merely ways of conceiving things. It becomes hard to see even how we can understand the notion of things going into and out of existence, since that too would seem to require some grasp of what things objectively are. Although we might conventionally speak of generation and corruption, there would seem to be no objective basis to ground such claims. Amazingly—as we will see in the following two chapters—Hobbes embraces these consequences.

Another instance of Hobbes's approach can be found in Anne Conway. Her *Principles of the Most Ancient and Moral Philosophy* (written early 1670s; publ. 1690)[21] is even more explicit than Hobbes in rejecting defining essences. Or, more precisely, she accepts just three defining essences: God, Christ, and Creature:

> The first reason is derived from the above mentioned order of things. I have already proved that there are only three such things: namely, God as the highest, Christ in the middle, and creature as the lowest order of all. This creature is just one entity or substance in respect of its nature or essence, as demonstrated above, so that it varies only according to its modes of existence. (7.1)

All creatures, then, including not only material substances but also human minds and angels, belong to the same kind, and so have the same essence. Indeed, more than that, creatures are merely modes of the "one entity or substance" (line 3) that Conway describes in the singular as "creature" (line 2). Hence there literally are only three things (*res*): God, Christ, and creature. Conway here refers back to the previous chapter, where she had set her view out in more detail:

> The second thing to be considered is whether one species of things can be changed into another. Here it must be observed as accurately as possible what accounts for the species of things being distinguished from each other. For there are many species of things, which are commonly so called, but which differ from one another not in substance or essence but only   4
> in certain modes or characteristics (*proprietatibus*). When these modes or characteristics are changed, that thing is said to have changed its species. It is not its essence or entity that so changes, however, but only its mode of being—as when water does not change but remains   7
> the same, even when the cold coagulates that which before had been fluid. When water changes into stone, there is no reason why we should suppose a change of substance to have occurred here any more than in the previous example of water changed into ice. Furthermore,   10
> when a stone is changed into softer, pliant earth, there is here too no change of substance. And so in all other changes that we are able to observe in things, the substance or essence always remains the same, and there is change only to its modes, so that a thing ceases in this mode and begins in some other mode. (6.3)   14

Conway's ontology is less austere than Hobbes's inasmuch as she accepts modes as distinct explanatory principles. But she is just as eager as Hobbes to resist giving special status to apparent differences in species. Where we take there to be a difference in essence, in fact there is only a difference in "modes or characteristics" (line 4). When

---

[21] Conway's *Principles* was written in English, probably between 1671 and 1675. It was translated into Latin (perhaps by Henry More), after which time the original English version was lost. The Latin version was published in 1690, and then retranslated back into English, in which form it was republished in 1692.

water changes to ice, or stone to earth, there is no change of substance or essence, but only a change to the mode of the enduring stuff, and according to Conway the point can be generalized to "all other changes that we are able to observe in things" (line 11).[22]

Quite strikingly, Conway applies this claim not only to bodies but also to minds. Her thesis that there is just one "creature" extends both to human minds and also to angels, because she takes both corporeity and spirituality to be modes rather than defining essences, and indeed regards the difference between them to be one of degree. Thus the first passage quoted above immediately continues with the remark that "among these modes one is corporeity, of which there are many grades, so that a thing may more or less approach to or recede from the condition and state of a body or spirit" (7.1). Aspects of reality are thus capable of becoming more bodily or more spiritual, from which Conway infers that there is no fundamental difference in kind here:

And indeed every body is a spirit, and nothing else, and differs not at all from a spirit, but in that it is darker. Therefore the grosser (*crassius*) it becomes, the more it becomes remote from the grade of spirit, so that the distinction here is only modal and gradual, not essential or substantial. (6.11)

In marked contrast to Descartes, then, who at least recognizes two essences in the created realm—thought and extension—Conway thinks of body and spirit as mere modes. As she later remarks, this aspect of her view marks her as an "anti-Cartesian" (9.2). In refusing to see any fundamental divide between mind and body, her view is again reminiscent of Hobbes (§16.2). But whereas Hobbes treats minds as bodies, Conway instead treats bodies as much more like minds. The "great error" of Cartesianism is to treat body as "a mere dead mass that not only lacks life and perception of every kind but also is entirely incapable, for all eternity, of acquiring these" (9.2). Conway—following the lead of her mentor Henry More—rejects Descartes's mechanistic approach and insists that life and perception are everywhere in the natural realm.[23]

Many interesting issues arise here regarding what it means to ascribe life and perception to all aspects of the created realm, and what it means for an aspect of creation to become "darker" or "grosser" and so less spiritual (as above). Reluctantly setting those issues aside, and focusing again on Conway's anti-essentialism, we might identify two sorts of motivations for her radical view. First, although Conway is far from being an orthodox corpuscularian, she shares that movement's suspicions regarding there being anything in the created realm that could play the role of an essence,

---

[22] Conway is aware of the close relationship between herself and Hobbes regarding essences: "I grant that all creatures are originally one substance, from the lowest to the highest, and consequently convertible or changeable from one of their natures into another. And although Hobbes says the same, that does not prejudice its truth" (9.4).

One might wonder whether Conway really maintains that the entire created realm is just a single substance. For what she says in the passage just quoted is that "all creatures are *originally* one substance," a claim that seems to imply they are no longer one substance. Since she uses this same expression elsewhere—e.g., at 8.5: "spirit and body are originally of one nature and substance"—this worry has to be taken seriously. Still, I am inclined to put more weight on the passages in the main text, which seem to be quite clear in their claims. Amazingly, so far as I can find, no one has made a detailed study of Conway's views in this area.

[23] For More's anti-mechanistic vitalism, see Gabbey, "Henry More and the Limits of Mechanism" and Jesseph, "Mechanism, Skepticism, and Witchcraft." On the relationship between More and Conway, see Hutton, *Anne Conway*.

either explanatory or defining. Just as nothing is gained or lost when water turns into ice, so nothing is gained or lost when water turns into stone (lines 7–10 above). Every body "is nothing other than an innumerable multitude of bodies"; every spirit "is likewise an innumerable multitude of spirits united together in a given body" (6.11). Although these multitudes are organized in a certain way, there is no further thing, an essence, that serves to define these aggregates. Second, Conway holds that anything in the material realm can be converted into anything else, without thereby ceasing to go out of existence. Everything is wholly mutable, and nothing ever goes out of existence, no matter how it changes. There is then no need to invoke essences to serve as the boundary markers of a thing's persistence conditions.

Conway is not denying natural kinds, no more than Hobbes is. There is nothing in their thought that requires supposing the variation among creatures to be smoothly distributed without clustering. Their interest lies elsewhere: on the metaphysical or causal underpinnings of standard natural-kind talk. What both want to insist on is that our talk of species and essences admits of no intrinsic explanation beyond the simple fact that one aspect of reality has this mode of being and another aspect of reality has another mode of being. For both, the created world is a fluid and homogeneous realm—not without variation from region to region, but without any *essential* differences from one part to another.

27.6. The Resilience of Real Essences

The anti-essentialism of Hobbes and Conway was not the dominant post-scholastic view. This might seem surprising, given the dominance of corpuscularianism. But even though seventeenth-century critics of scholasticism generally reject the reality of substantial forms, they nevertheless often hold onto the idea of essences, in very much the scholastic sense. Antoine Arnauld and Pierre Nicole, for instance, hold that "the form is what renders a thing such and distinguishes it from others, whether it is a being really distinct from the matter, according to the opinion of the School, or whether it is only the arrangement of the parts. It is by the knowledge of this form that one must explain its properties" (*Port-Royal Logic* III.18, p. 240). This passage begins by invoking form as a defining essence, and ends by alluding to its role as an explanatory essence, as that which accounts for the various properties of the thing. Both can be understood in a corpuscularian context, as the passage makes clear, as nothing above "the arrangement of the parts." Such an arrangement counts as a real essence provided it make a thing be what it is, as a thing of a certain kind (defining essence) and/or accounts for (enough of) the various further characteristics of a thing.

Gassendi is another example of a corpuscularian who takes for granted that there will be something that plays the functional role of substantial form:

the form, which through generation arises in matter and which, remaining in the generated thing, accounts for its being constituted in a certain genus of things and being denominated by that genus, for its being distinguished from other things, for its having these and not other properties, and for its eliciting these and not other actions. . . . (*Syntagma* II.1.7.3, I:466b)

For Gassendi there is no question of whether material substances have such forms, but only of whether or not they are distinct substances, over and above his atomistic framework. His answer is that only the rational soul counts as a substantial form in the non-reductive scholastic sense. Although other material substances have a form—and if they are alive this form can be referred to as a soul—such forms are merely qualities or modes that can be understood in wholly corpuscularian–mechanistic terms.

The doctrine of real essences is in Boyle, too, again in a wholly corpuscularian sense:

And so, though I shall for brevity's sake retain the word *form*, yet I would be understood to mean by it not a real *substance* distinct from matter, but only the matter itself of a natural body, considered with its peculiar manner of existence, which I think may not inconveniently be called either its *specifical* or its *denominating state*, or its *essential modification*—or, if you would have me express it in one word, its *stamp*. (*Origin* [*Works* V:324; Stewart p. 40])

Here Boyle shows himself willing to hold onto the notion of form as a defining essence, even if he prefers to give it the solidly Anglo-Saxon term 'stamp.' Elsewhere it is clear that he accepts explanatory essences as well:

And if upon further and exacter trial it appears that the whole body of the Salt-Petre, after its having been severed into very differing parts by distillation, may be adequately reunited into Salt-Petre equiponderant to its first self, this experiment will afford us a noble and (for ought we have hitherto met with) single instance to make it probable that that, which is commonly called the form of a concrete, which gives it its being and denomination, and from whence all its qualities are in the vulgar philosophy, by I know not what inexplicable ways, supposed to flow, may be in some bodies but a modification of the matter they consist of, whose parts, by being so and so disposed in relation to each other, constitute such a determinate kind of body, endowed with such and such properties; whereas if the same parts were otherwise disposed, they would constitute other bodies of very differing natures from that of the concrete whose parts they formerly were, and which may again result or be produced after its dissipation and seeming destruction, by the reunion of the same component particles, associated according to their former disposition. (*Certain Physiological Essays* [*Works* II:107–8])

Boyle rejects the "inexplicable" scholastic doctrine of substantial form, of course (lines 4–6), but he embraces the notion that there is *something* in a body that accounts for "such a determinate kind of body, endowed with such and such properties" (lines 8–9). This thing, which he elsewhere calls the "texture" of a body, is wholly corpuscularian in character—it is Boyle, after all, who coined that term (§1.3)—but nevertheless it strikingly preserves the scholastic notion of essence.[24]

---

[24] Boyle's views on essences are influenced in a distinctive way by the explanatory holism considered in §23.4, according to which explanations must take into account not only the intrinsic features of a particular substance, but also the environment of that substance. Thus he writes: "I think it is a mistake to imagine (as we are wont to do) that what is called the *nature* of this or that body is wholly comprised in its own matter and its (I say not *substantial*, but) *essential form*, as if from that or these only all its operations must flow" (*Free Enquiry* sec. 4 [*Works* X:469; Stewart p. 190; Davis and Hunter p. 39]).

Another place where Boyle invokes the explanatory and defining natures of bodies is in his *Possibility of the Resurrection*, where gold and other metals can be "disguised" in various ways "and yet retain their own nature" (*Works* VIII:305).

For Boyle's use of 'texture,' see *Origin of Forms* (*Works* V:316; Stewart p. 30): "And when many corpuscles do so convene together as to compose any distinct body, as a stone or a metal, then from their other accidents (or modes), and from these last two mentioned [viz., posture and order], there does emerge a certain disposition or contrivance of parts in the whole, which we may call the *texture* of it." A good discussion of texture in Boyle can be found in Alexander, *Ideas, Qualities* pp. 60–88. The term, in something like this sense, goes back to Lucretius (*De rerum natura* I.247, III.209, IV.657,

That seventeenth-century authors would continue to postulate explanatory essences might seem particularly surprising, but as stressed at the start of §27.5 the two notions of substance are closely connected: it is *because* bodies have an explanatory essence that we can speak of their having an objective defining essence. To be sure there might be other ways to ground the notion of a defining essence, but this was the leading strategy, throughout our four centuries. Although there were exceptional cases like Hobbes and Conway, the doctrine of real essences, in both the defining and explanatory senses, was generally taken for granted: one finds it in physicists like William Harvey,[25] chemists like Boyle, and in philosophers like Descartes[26] and Locke, who indeed coins the term 'real essence' precisely to distinguish between his theoretical commitment to genuine essences and his epistemological doubts over whether what we arrive at, nominal essences, corresponds to them in any way (see below). George Berkeley indicates that consensus on this score endured through the turn of the eighteenth century: "One great inducement to our pronouncing ourselves ignorant of the nature of things is the current opinion that everything includes within itself the cause of its properties: or that there is in each object an inward essence, which is the source whence its discernible qualities flow, and whereon they depend" (*Principles* n. 102).

Even the opponents of scholasticism, then, by and large, take themselves to need essences, and the reasons for this are clear. As the cases of Hobbes and Conway illustrate, the rejection of essences raises a host of extremely problematic metaphysical issues. For given the generally accepted linkage between a thing's essence and its identity, the rejection of essences makes a complete mess out of questions of individuation. What makes this region of the corporeal realm one thing, and that region another? Without a theory of essence, it is hard to know what to say. Supposing we do arrive at an answer to that question, we then face diachronic questions: in virtue of

VI.776, VI.1084), and reappears in Francis Bacon: "... veras corporum texturas et schematismos unde omnis occulta atque (ut vocant) specifica proprietas et virtus et rebus pendet" (*Novum organum* II.vii) and Gassendi, e.g., *Syntagma* II.1.7.4, I:472a—"textura"—and the discussion in LoLordo, *Pierre Gassendi* pp. 157–8: "thus, texture plays more or less the same role in Gassendi's atomism that form plays for Aristotelians." Compare Jones, writing about Boyle: "all the functions of form are performed by natural corpuscular structure" ("Boyle, Classification" p. 182). As I stress in my "Form, Substance, and Mechanism," Boyle uses texture not only as a defining and explanatory essence, but also as what we might call a unifying essence, inasmuch as it is meant to account for the unity and persistence of material substances (see esp. *Origin* [*Works* V:343–4, 349–51; Stewart pp. 58, 65–6]).

[25] For Harvey's commitment to explanatory essences, see his protracted discussion of when one should say that the soul comes onto the scene, in the development of egg into chick. He reasons: "si [anima] insit [ovo], proculdubio eorum omnium, quae naturaliter in ovo reperiuntur, principium et efficiens erit" (Gercitations exercitationes 47, p. 266). This presupposes that the soul will play the role of an explanatory essence.

[26] See Descartes's disparaging remarks to Regius regarding substantial forms, followed by this: "Contra autem a formis illis essentialibus, quas nos explicamus, manifestae ac mathematicae rationes redduntur actionum naturalium, ut videre est de forma salis communis in meis *Meteoris*" (III.506). What he had done in the Third Discourse of the *Meteorology* was to give a detailed account of how the microstructure of salt (and salt water) gives rise to its various sensible properties. More generally, compare how *Principles* I.53 describes the principal attributes of thought and extension: "et quidem ex quolibet attributo substantia cognoscitur; sed una tamen est cuiusque substantiae praecipua proprietas, quae ipsius naturam essentiamque constituit, et ad quam aliae omnes [proprietates] referuntur." This exactly describes both the defining and the explanatory essence. For a general discussion of Descartes on essences, in light of the scholastic background, see Secada, *Cartesian Metaphysics* ch. 3.

Chauvin, speaking generally of how the "recentiores" define 'forma,' writes: "Unde porro inferunt quod licet nullae dentur formae *substantiales*, dantur tamen *essentiales*, quibus singulis singulae corporum species praeditae sint, quibusque singulae id ipsum sint, quod sunt, et a caeteris omnibus distinguantur.... [N]on incommode eam [formam] definere liceat, per id quo unumquodque corpus in certa specie constituitur, a caeteris omnibus distinguitur, et naturae suae convenienter operatur" (*Lexicon* p. 261a).

what is this thing the same over time, and under what conditions does it cease to be the same thing? Both Hobbes and Conway reach the radical conclusion, regarding this second question, that in the strictest metaphysical sense nothing ever does cease to exist (§28.4). But that then makes all the more puzzling the initial question of synchronic individuation, because we now need to reconsider just what the basic entities are that we are trying to individuate. Conway seems again to take a very radical view, that strictly speaking there is only one created substance. Such monism does indeed make these hard questions go away, but by most people's lights that is too high a price to pay. Yet what is the alternative? The atomist might revert to his atoms, as the only true existents, but that seems an equally high price. And what if one does not postulate atoms? There is, in short, a veritable clusterfuck of problems here, and one might well say that the most interesting philosophical developments of the later seventeenth century—to be sketched over the following three chapters—revolve around the various attempts that were made to resolve them. But before moving into this further territory, we should consider in more detail the anti-essentialism of Locke, which is of particular interest because it comes supported by a particularly powerful argument.

27.7. Anti-Essentialism II: Locke

Locke's commitment to real essences is well known, and since it had to be anticipated in some detail back in Chapter 9, I will describe it only briefly here. The theory of real essences encompasses both the defining and the explanatory sense. As Locke explains, in distinguishing between real and nominal essences:

First, *essence* may be taken for the very being of any thing, whereby it is what it is. And thus the real internal, but generally in Substances, unknown constitution of things, whereon their discoverable qualities depend, may be called their *essence*. This is the proper original signification of the word. . . . (*Essay* III.3.15)

The passage specifically describes both the defining and the explanatory sense of essence. Given Locke's empiricist scruples, one might suppose it unlikely that he wants to be read as having any great confidence in the existence of such real essences (or "real constitutions," as he sometimes calls them). And, to be sure, when he presents the theory, he often stresses its status as a widely accepted hypothesis:

That men (especially such as have been bred up in the learning taught in this part of the world) do suppose certain specific essences of substances, which each individual in its several kinds is made conformable to, and partakes of, is so far from needing proof, that it will be thought strange, if any one should do otherwise. (*Essay* II.31.6)

   The particular parcel of matter which makes the ring I have on my finger is forwardly [≈ readily], by most men, supposed to have a real essence whereby it is *gold*; and from whence those qualities flow, which I find in it, *viz.* its peculiar colour, weight, hardness, fusibility, fixedness, and change of colour upon a slight touch of mercury, *etc.* (ibid.)

   I know nobody that every denied the certainty of such real essences or internal constitutions, in things that do exist. (to Stillingfleet, *Works* IV:82)

Locke appears to be quite in agreement with this consensus, never betraying any doubt that substances have such essences. He says as much to Stillingfleet: "I easily grant there is reality in them; and it was from that reality that I called them real essences" (*Works* IV:83). He says it to Molyneux: "This I do say, that there are real constitutions in things from whence those simple ideas flow, which we observed combined in them" (*Correspondence* n. 1592). And he says it even in the *Essay*: "'tis past doubt, there must be some real constitution on which any collection of simple ideas co-existing must depend" (III.3.15; cf. III.10.21).

Yet although it is clear that Locke embraces essence in the usual sense, his doing so makes for a considerable puzzle, given the radical anti-essentialism of the *Essay*. For at the same time that Locke embraces real essences, he dismisses the possibility of ascribing non-conventional essential properties to material substances. Thus, "to talk of specific differences in nature, without reference to general ideas and names, is to talk unintelligibly" (III.6.5). This is to say that we can place things in a species only according to our conventional nominal essences. The stunning consequences of that claim are brought out in this notorious passage:

That *essence*, in the ordinary use of the word, relates to *sorts*, and that it is considered in particular beings no farther than as they are ranked into *sorts*, appears from hence: that take but away the abstract ideas by which we sort individuals, and rank them under common names, and   3 then the thought of any thing *essential* to any of them instantly vanishes: we have no notion of the one without the other: which plainly shows their relation. It is necessary for me to be as I am; God and nature has made me so. But there is nothing I have, is essential to me. An   6 accident, or disease, may very much alter my colour or shape; a fever, or fall, may take away my reason or memory, or both; and an apoplexy leave neither sense nor understanding, no nor life. Other creatures of my shape may be made with more, and better, or fewer, and worse faculties   9 than I have, and others may have reason, and sense, in a shape and body very different from mine. None of these are essential to the one, or the other, or to any individual whatsoever, until the mind refers it to some sort or *species* of things; and then presently, according to the abstract   12 idea of that sort, something is found *essential*. (III.6.4)

The implications of this passage are staggering. As surely as either Hobbes's or Conway's versions of anti-essentialism, Locke's view threatens the sort of metaphysical chaos that would cause us to lose a grip on what material substances are and how they are individuated. Now it is one of the most impressive features of Locke's metaphysics that he proposes—in the second edition of the *Essay*—a bold, if not entirely original, strategy for resisting some of this chaos. I will turn to that famous account of identity in Chapter 30. In the last few pages of this chapter, however, I want to concentrate on how Locke arrives at the anti-essentialism that lies behind his theory of identity. For in contrast to so many discussions of these issues during our period—including not just essence-realists of all kinds but even anti-realists such as Hobbes and Conway—Locke has an *argument* for his view. Moreover, it is quite a powerful argument, because it takes off from premises that the essence-realist is very likely to accept.

Given that Locke embraces real essences, one might well suppose that the only sort of anti-essentialist argument Locke could make is epistemic: that we are not *justified* in ascribing essential properties to individuals because we do not grasp their real essences. Some passages suggest this sort of reading.

Fifth, the only imaginable help in this case would be, that having framed perfect complex ideas of the properties of things, flowing from their different real essences, we should thereby

distinguish them into species. But neither can this be done: for being ignorant of the real essence   3
itself, it is impossible to know all those properties that flow from it, and are so annexed to it, that
any one of them being away, we may certainly conclude that that essence is not there, and so
the thing is not of that species. We can never know what are the precise number of properties   6
depending on the real essence of *gold*, any one of which failing, the real essence of gold, and
consequently gold, would not be there, unless we knew the real essence of gold itself, and by
that determined that species. (III.6.19)   9

This passage comes at a crucial juncture. Locke has just offered a series of conditions
that would have to be satisfied—and cannot be satisfied—for our classifying substances
into species in accord with their real essence. This is the fifth and last condition: we
would have to grasp all the properties of things (lines 1–3). But, as Locke goes on to
argue, we cannot do this without grasping the real essence itself (lines 3–6). And since
we cannot do that, we cannot distinguish individuals according to their real kinds.
Evidently, this 'cannot' denotes epistemic impossibility: it is not that there is no fact of
the matter about such kinds, but only that we will never be able to grasp it.

   This seems like a perfectly straightforward reading of what Locke is up to. But it does
not seem to fit with the passages of the previous paragraph, according to which it is not
only beyond us to sort individuals into their real kinds, but positively "unintelligible,"
because outside of our conventional classifications individuals simply have no essential
properties: "there is nothing I have, is essential to me" (line 6 above). Those earlier passages
would make good sense if Locke were an anti-essentialist of the Hobbes–Conway stripe.
But given that he endorses real essences, it is hard to see what he is up to.

   Locke does seem to be committed to the claim that real essences are objectively
essential features of things. By this I mean, more precisely, that Locke endorses the
view that, necessarily, a given material substance exists if and only if its real essence
exists. It is hard to see what else he could mean when he says, as quoted above, that
"*essence* may be taken for the very being of any thing, whereby it is, what it is" (III.3.15).
If that seems insufficiently clear, consider what he says four paragraphs later:

That such abstract ideas, with names to them, as we have been speaking of, are essences, may
farther appear by what we are told concerning essences, viz. that they are all ingenerable and
incorruptible. Which cannot be true of the real constitutions of things, which begin and perish   3
with them. All things that exist, besides their author, are all liable to change; especially those
things we are acquainted with, and have ranked into bands, under distinct names or ensigns.
Thus that which was grass today is tomorrow the flesh of a sheep; and within few days after,   6
becomes part of a man: in all which, and the like changes, it is evident, their real essence, i.e. that
constitution whereon the properties of these several things depended, is destroyed, and perishes
with them. (III.3.19)   9

This is intended as an argument for treating our "abstract ideas" (line 1) as genuine,
albeit nominal, essences. The point is that they satisfy a feature that "we are told"
essences ought to satisfy: being "ingenerable and incorruptible" (lines 2–3). For our
purposes what is interesting is not this Platonic take on what an essence ought to be,
but Locke's insistence that real essences are not like this, because they "begin and
perish" (line 3) with the "things"—that is, substances—to which they belong. In a case
of change from grass to sheep-flesh to human-flesh, we have a corresponding change of
real essence as well. This commits Locke to a certain sort of realism: there are objective

facts about what the substances are in the material realm, and when they come into and go out of existence. Our grasp of those facts may be quite limited, but because of Locke's confidence in real essences, he is committed at least this far to a realistic ontology of material substances.[27]

This makes it all the harder, of course, to understand how Locke can regard it as "unintelligible" to speak of essences in any objective sense—that is, apart from our conventional scheme of nominal essences. For if the reading just offered is correct, there is a perfectly robust sense in which Locke is committed to real, non-conventional, essential properties. Here is where his interesting argument comes in. To understand that argument, one needs to keep in mind the doctrine of real essences as it was understood throughout our period. According to that doctrine, the essence of a given substance explains all of the intrinsic accidents of that thing (§24.4). This includes the *propria*, of course, which are those accidents distinctive of a given species, but it also includes accidents that are idiosyncratic to a particular individual (provided those accidents have an internal rather than external cause). It is clear that Locke understands the doctrine of real essence in this sense. For he describes real essences as the cause not just of the "properties" of a thing—by which he means the *propria*[28]—but more generally of all a thing's "discoverable qualities" (III.3.5), or "sensible qualities" (III.10.21), or "simple ideas" (III.3.15). It is not at all surprising that Locke thinks this, because—as he himself stresses—this is the absolutely standard seventeenth-century notion of what an essence is.

With this understanding of essence in mind, Locke's argument can take shape. Suppose we are skeptical in the Boyle–Locke manner about whether our actual sorting into kinds has carved the world at the joints. In that case, we cannot help ourselves to such "nominal" divisions in trying to determine what the essences of things are. We have to go individual by individual, and ask *What is the essence of that?* Locke himself puts this vividly in *Essay* III.6.19, the section quoted above where he allows that we *could* distinguish things into their true kinds if only we could grasp their real essences.

---

[27] I remarked in §27.5 that, for the entirety of our period, species membership is always treated as necessary to a thing. One might wonder whether this is so for Locke. If one thinks it is not then one would have to read him very differently from how I do. There is a passage in the correspondence with Stillingfleet that has been read as committing Locke to the possibility that a thing could continue to exist through a change in its real essence. To Stillingfleet's remark that "these real essences are unchangeable" Locke replies: "Of what, I beseech your lordship, are the internal constitutions unchangeable? Not of any thing that exists, but of God alone; for they may be changed all as easily by that hand that made them, as the internal frame of a watch" (IV:90–1). What I take Locke to mean by this is that, of course, real constitutions change: grass, e.g., changes to flesh. Locke also certainly holds that, if one conceives of a thing under a given nominal essence, then that thing-under-a-sort might endure through change to its real essence. But the correspondence with Stillingfleet does not retract the *Essay*'s claim that a thing's real essence is necessary for that thing in its own right. For a very different reading, see Ayers, *Locke* II:69–70. Even though Ayers quotes the crucial passage from III.3.19, with its talk of real essences beginning and perishing with things, he nevertheless concludes that "in reality nothing substantial is created or destroyed, just structure" (II:70).

[28] For evidence that 'property' has the technical sense of '*proprium*,' see *Essay* III.6.6: "properties belonging only to species, and not to individuals." Compare Porphyry: "species pre-subsist properties, and properties supervene on species. For there must be a man in order for there to be something laughing" (*Isagoge*, tr. Barnes, §14). The *Isagoge*, which is the *locus classicus* for the notion of a *proprium*, distinguishes four genera of *proprium*: (1) belonging to only members of that species but not all of them; (2) belonging to all but not only members of that species; (3) belonging to all and only members of that species, but only sometimes; (4) belonging to all and only members of that species, at all times. Most of what Locke describes as "properties" fall into the second genus. On Porphyry's taxonomy, accidents and *propria* are distinct. On the more common scholastic usage, however, substance and accident exhaustively divide all being, and so *propria* have to be regarded as accidents. (For the two usages, see, e.g., Aquinas, *Summa theol.* 1a 77.1 ad 5.)

Immediately after the text quoted above, he adds: "By the word *Gold* here, I must be understood to design a particular piece of matter; v.g. the last guinea that was coined." One *must* speak this way, to satisfy Locke's challenge, because otherwise one would be tacitly helping oneself to the nominal classifications that he is unwilling to depend on. So, take a particular "piece of matter." Call that 'gold,' if you like. Ask yourself: What is *its* essence? To be sure, Locke agrees that it has a real essence, and so we always have that to go on, in principle, as the defining feature of the thing, without which it would not exist. But what else can we say? Setting aside its various advening dents and scratches, so as to focus on those intrinsic features that arise from its essence, there is no ground whatsoever for focusing on some such features as essential. Every such aspect comes from its real essence, and so has an equal right to count as essential to the thing. The only way to discriminate between essential and non-essential features is by convention.

This reading of Locke's argument might seem to clash with the notorious passage from *Essay* III.6.4 quoted above, where "there is nothing I have, is essential to me" (line 6). This seems like precisely the wrong thing to say, on my account. One can see, though, as Locke goes on, that this claim is shorthand for a more complicated thought that fits nicely with my understanding of his argument. For in the next section Locke presents the full thought on which the "nothing essential" remark rests:

For I would ask anyone, what is sufficient to make an essential difference in nature, between any two particular beings, without any regard had to some abstract idea, which is looked upon as the essence and standard of a species? All such patterns and standards, being quite laid aside, particular beings, considered barely in themselves, will be found to have all their qualities equally essential, and everything, in each individual, will be essential to it, or, which is more true, nothing at all. (III.6.5)

This passage comes immediately after the sentence quoted earlier, according to which one speaks "unintelligibly" of specific differences independently of nominal essences. Here we get Locke's argument for that claim: not that things in themselves have no essential qualities, but that they have *too many* essential properties to yield any sort of intelligible story about kinds. If we have to say that "everything" is essential, then we might as well say that "nothing" is essential (line 6), because we will have completely lost a grip on what it is we are trying to do with this talk of essences, which is to sort individuals into kinds.

That this is Locke's argument is made fairly clear in III.6.39, where he offers an analogy to watches. Describing in detail the various design differences between individual watches, he remarks that, for most of us, they are all watches. Still, there are real differences here, analogous to real essences and their various derived qualities, and we might if we liked produce more fine-grained divisions:

It is certain, each of these has a real difference from the rest. But whether it be an essential, a specific difference or no, relates only to the complex idea to which the name *watch* is given.... But if anyone will make minuter divisions from differences that he knows in the internal frame of watches, and to such precise complex ideas give names that shall prevail, they will then be new species to them who have those ideas with names to them....

Locke then applies the analogy to natural substances:

Just thus, I think, it is in natural things. Nobody will doubt that the wheels or springs (if I may so say) within, are different in a rational man and a changeling, no more than that there is a difference in the frame between a drill and a changeling. But whether one or both these differences be essential, or specifical, is only to be known to us by their agreement or disagreement with the complex idea that the name *man* stands for.

The point is conceptual, not epistemic. Even if we knew the real essence of a particular drill (a baboon)—as the experts do in the watch case—there would be no non-arbitrary way to say which of its features is essential to it, unless we want to say that *all* of its intrinsic features are essential. If we go down that road—which is the only objectively defensible road to go down—then not only will baboons be different from changelings (people with profound mental disabilities, especially children), but baboons will not even be of the same kind as each other, unless we could find two baboons that were exactly alike in every respect.

This must count as one of the best arguments we have encountered in this entire study: it is a valid argument from premises that Locke's opponents ought to accept, for a stunning conclusion. The key idea is that essences explain more than just a few defining features of a thing; instead, they explain the character of a particular substance all the way down to the fine-grained, individual details. Given this background assumption, Locke's argument is devastatingly effective, because Locke is just flat-out right that—if this is what an essence does—then there is no non-arbitrary way to pick out certain of those features as essential and others as purely accidental. The distinction between *propria* and pure accidents collapses. Moreover, the key assumption is one that Locke's opponents are under considerable pressure to maintain, because—as stressed earlier—it is precisely this robust explanatory story that grounds the belief that material substances in fact have objective essences. Put in other terms, we can think of Locke's argument as a dilemma. If essences are robustly explanatory in this all-the-way down sense, then there is no way to discriminate between *propria* and pure accidents, and so the very notion of essential properties becomes incoherent or trivial. If, on the other hand, we deny that essences are robustly explanatory, and instead say that a thing's essence explains only a few select, essential features of the thing, then we need a story about why *that* should count as the essence, rather than some other aspect of the thing that explains various other, allegedly non-essential features. Again, such a decision would have to be conventional.

The dilemma does not block every possible theory of essences, only those that depend on the notion of an explanatory essence. Modern biologists, for instance, might advance quite different arguments for essentialism and species membership (such as, e.g., historical facts about reproductive communities). But for accounts based on the notion of an explanatory essence—which includes almost every author over our four centuries—the argument is devastating. The only way to resist it is to insist that our ordinary kind distinctions track the real essences of things. If—contra Locke—one supposes that this is so, then one can study what members of a species have in common and readily reach conclusions about what is and is not essential to the species—or, at least, know what the *propria* are and what the pure accidents are. Locke's genius was to see that the prevailing theory of essentialism crucially depends on confusing nominal essences with real essences. Once one sees not just that in fact our nominal essences probably do not track the real essences, but that furthermore—given the variation among individuals—they *could not* exactly track those real essences, the standard doctrine of essentialism is revealed to be merely a matter of convention.

Locke's theory is therefore an original mix of essentialism and anti-essentialism, in which the anti-essentialism emerges as a consequence of the underlying essentialism. He does believe that material substances have objective essences that serve to individuate them, even if we cannot know what those essences are. And given the existence of such essences, there are objective facts about when two individuals belong to the same real kind, or when a substance begins or ceases to exist. But the nature of those facts is such as to quash all of our pretenses to grasp the essential natures of things. The only case in which two individuals could objectively be placed in the same kind is if they were qualitatively identical. In all other cases—which is to say, at least for practical purposes, all actual cases—sameness of kind can only be conventional. Similarly, although an individual has essential features, the only objective story to be told requires treating all of an individual's features—at least its intrinsic ones—as essential. Any more selective story requires making conventional choices about which features we care about most, and how we want to categorize things. The realistic underpinnings of the theory, then, yield so little of how we take the world to be that, for all practical purposes, we can count Locke's theory as anti-essentialist. To be sure, it is anti-essentialist enough to wreak havoc on any commonsense metaphysics of material substances. That, however, is a topic for the remainder of this study.[29]

---

[29] In setting out Locke's theory, I have ignored those places (most notably, *Essay* III.6.6) in which he treats the real essence as dependent on the nominal essence. (For a very clear discussion of this, see Owen, "Locke on Real Essence.") These passages *are* important, on my understanding, because they reflect a crucial move in Locke's argument: to an opponent who wants to use the real essence to carve out kinds in our ordinary way, Locke is replying that such a usage tacitly appeals to the nominal essence in making use of the real essence. As I set the argument out, however, this move need not be made because I insist at the start that we can talk about the real essence only in the context of an individual, independently of its nominal essence. My usage of real essence—as applying only to what Owen calls "unsorted particulars"—is certainly well-attested in Locke (e.g., at III.3.15 and III.6.19–20), and is indeed probably his standard usage. For an extended discussion of this issue, see Kaufman, "Locke on Individuation" pp. 514–17.

There is a massive and quite impressive literature on real and nominal essences in Locke. It would be surprising if *no one* has understood the argument as I do, but I do not think that commentators have generally reached my interpretation, perhaps because—lacking the proper historical context—they have not entirely understood the theory of real essences. Phemister, for example, in "Real Essences in Particular," puts special weight, as I do, on the claim that real essences ground both *propria* and pure accidents, but without realizing that this is the standard notion of essence, and so without seeing the argument as a whole. Ayers sometimes comes close to my reading (and he accordingly shares my enthusiasm for Locke here). In particular, Ayers stresses that for Locke it becomes arbitrary to distinguish between *propria* and pure accidents (see, e.g., *Locke* II:73). But Ayers seems at the same time to insist, as noted above, that Locke is a complete anti-realist with regard to essences and material substances. Moreover, Ayers and others often conflate the argument I have described with an argument from what Ayers calls the "anarchy" of nature: that anti-essentialism is forced on us by the empirical fact that kinds in the natural world are far too scattered and vague to admit of essential properties (see "Locke versus Aristotle" p. 257). If this were the argument, it would be much less interesting, because it appeals to empirical claims that Locke himself has to regard as rather uncertain and that Locke's opponents would flatly reject, and probably with good reason, given that the actual extent of the anarchy is less than what Locke supposes.

Permanence and Corruption

The elaborate scholastic metaphysics of prime matter and forms, accidental and substantial, serves at the behest of common sense. It offers a theoretical framework for our ordinary way of viewing the world: as full of things undergoing changes of one and another kind, sometimes surviving those changes and sometimes not. We take ourselves to be the most familiar example of such a thing, but we suppose that the world is full of other such things—dogs and cats and stones—that likewise undergo changes that they may or may not survive.

The most radical challenge to this framework would deny the very existence of change. This is a position that no one during our period embraces. What one finds instead is the only slightly less startling claim that, barring supernatural acts of creation or annihilation, nothing comes into or goes out of existence, and that instead all change is a matter of how or where a thing is. This thesis, which I will call the *permanence thesis*, will be the principal focus of this chapter.

The permanence thesis obviously requires rethinking what the things—the substances—are. Animals cannot be substances, since they obviously do come into and go out of existence, and this means that we (supposing, as everyone does, that we exist) are not animals, which is to say we are not soul–body composites. In general, on this view, it seems that no composite body of any sort could count as a substance, inasmuch as all composite things can, and often do, dissolve. Only a few authors during our four centuries willingly embrace so thoroughgoing a rejection of commonsense ontology. But many authors, once they reject scholastic hylomorphism, are hard pressed to avoid falling into its arms. Here, as we have seen so many times already, what is most interesting about post-scholastic thought is not its rejection of scholasticism, but what comes of that rejection.

28.1. The Scholastic Framework for Substantial Change

When one thing is corrupted, another is generated. So said Aristotle (*De gen.* 318a23–25), and this notion came to be generally embraced throughout our four centuries. One way to understand the process of corruption followed by generation—substantial change—would be in terms of complete discontinuity: a thing exists, then wholly goes out of existence, at which point something wholly new comes into existence. As discussed back in Chapter 2, this possibility was universally rejected during our period, on the grounds that something has to endure through all natural change. This enduring stuff is what everyone refers to as *matter*. There was, however, no agreement on the nature of such matter, with the Thomists insisting on its status as pure potentiality (§3.1), but most viewing it as something somehow actual, whether that actuality consists simply in some sort of being, or else in indeterminate extension or perhaps even in some determinate, unchanging extension (Ch. 4). In addition to this disagreement, there was disagreement over whether anything other than matter can endure through substantial change. The Thomists again take the most austere line, insisting that every form of the corrupted substance ceases to exist with that substance. Others, however, allow that some forms endure through substantial change, inhering in the surviving matter. Some argue that accidental forms can survive in this way (§6.3), whereas others argue that both accidental and substantial forms can survive in this way (§25.3). There is indeed such a variety of views regarding the process of substantial change that one cannot speak, even in rough outline, of *the* scholastic view about substantial change. The most one can say is that there is a very broad, shared framework.

Aristotle intended his hylomorphic framework to serve as a response to the various extravagances of his predecessors: monism, atomism, Heraclitean flux, and Platonic idealism. It was intended, above all, as a realistic theory of change. No wonder, then, that when scholastic authors contemplate the rejection of hylomorphism, they forecast dire consequences. Albert the Great warns that if generation is understood as simply a new "congregation of atoms," then "many impossibilities obtain," such as that generation would be nothing more than locomotion (*In De gen.* I.1.9). John Buridan similarly warns that if substantial form is treated as just the disposition of matter, then it becomes impossible to maintain that horses, stones, and human beings come into or go out of existence (*In De an.* III.11; see §24.2). Such warnings get applied not only to the wholesale abandonment of the hylomorphic framework, but also to various disputed positions within that framework. Unitarians, for instance, charge pluralists with being unable to maintain the distinction between substantial and accidental change. Those who want to treat matter as intrinsically extended (§4.4) get accused of collapsing that same distinction. For if matter itself possesses extension, the argument goes, then it itself would seem to become the enduring substance. Changes to it, even changes in an allegedly substantial form, would in fact be merely accidental. (See also §3.3.)[1]

The most distinctive feature of the shared Aristotelian framework is the conviction that substantial change is marked by the loss and then gain of one or more substantial forms. (There might be more than one form lost or gained if a substance has multiple substantial forms, or if a single substance is corrupted into many distinct substances, or if many substances come together to make a single substance.) It is this shared conviction that guarantees the scholastics will be realists about substantial change,

---

[1] Aquinas charges the doctrine of a *forma corporeitatis* with collapsing the distinction between substantial and accidental change: "et sic rediret antiquus error, quod generatio idem est quod alteratio" (*Sent.* II.12.1.4c). On extended matter as likewise collapsing that distinction, see Peter Auriol, *Sent.* II.12.1.4 (II:163aDE); Anonymous A [see Ch. 4 note 3] (f. 61raBC); Paul of Venice, *Summa phil. nat.* VI.12 (f. 101ra). Gregory of Rimini defends himself against this sort of objection with the reply that substantial change can be distinguished as change in "nomen et definitio" (*Sent.* II.12.2.1 ad 3, V:278). This makes the fact of substantial change rest not on convention, but on species membership.

treating it as an objective fact rather than a matter of convention that certain kinds of change count as substantial whereas others count as merely accidental. On this theory, moreover, substantial change is not only a real event but also a well-defined one, inasmuch as the corruption or generation of a substance happens at an instant. In contrast to accidental change, which often takes place over time, substantial change is an all-or-nothing affair: a thing either is a dog, say, or it is not, because either it has a certain soul or it does not. Because the loss or gain of a substantial form is instantaneous, there is no vagueness regarding when a substance begins or ceases to exist.[2]

The scholastic framework is particularly vulnerable in two places. First, it requires maintaining that in generation and corruption there is something—the substantial form—that comes into existence anew, seemingly *ex nihilo*. Scholastic authors have to admit that the substantial form comes into existence anew, since otherwise the change would not count as substantial. But they cannot allow that it is truly *ex nihilo*, since that sort of coming into existence counts as *creation*, and only God can create. This led to many long discussions of various ways in which a form might or might not be "educed from the potentiality of matter"—that is, arise out of the one ingredient that all parties agree to endure through change. Among later scholastics and their critics this becomes a prominent topic of dispute, one that William Pemble refers to as "the very most vexed of questions in natural philosophy" (*De formarum origine* p. 1). The Boate brothers thought that to overthrow scholastic views in this area it is enough just to quote what they say, since "the things they say here are so absurd, and contain such evident contradictions, that setting them out before one's eyes is enough to refute them" (*Philosophia naturalis reformata* I.3.50).[3]

This debate over the origin of new substantial forms leads directly to a second vulnerable aspect of the scholastic framework, regarding just how much endures through substantial change. On one hand it is tempting to want to allow more to survive substantial change, because the more that survives—whether that be accidental or substantial forms, or simply more thoroughly actualized matter—the easier it is to explain where the new substantial form comes from (§25.3). For Thomists who think

---

[2] On generation and corruption as instantaneous, see the Coimbrans: "Deinde quod generatione pro momentanea introductione formae sit vera et realis actio ostenditur: quia generatio sic accepta est mutatio, ut in confesso est apud omnes, cum per eam materia in instanti generationis aliter se habeat secundum formam quam recipit ac sese habebat tempore generationem antecedente" (*In Gen. et cor.* I.4.12.2). They cite a great many authorities for this view. See also Oresme, *In De gen.* I.2 p. 13.

Gassendi's guarded defense of substantial change (§28.3) explicitly gives up the claim that generation and corruption are instantaneous, arguing that all natural change involves local motion, and so "cannot be instantaneous" (*Syntagma* II.1.7.4, I:473b). See too Margaret Cavendish: "both natural and artificial productions are performed by degrees, which requires time, and is not done in an instant" (*Observations* p. 67).

[3] For a standard version of the worry about how forms are generated, see Marsilius of Inghen, *In De gen. et cor.* I.2 obj. 1, which argues that only substances could be generated or corrupted, but that they cannot be, because neither prime matter nor substantial form is generated or corrupted. Marsilius's reply insists that substantial form *does* come into existence anew.

The first book of Jean Fernel's *De abditis rerum causis* contains an extensive discussion of how substantial forms arise from matter in generation. Sennert discusses the issue in detail at *Epitome* I.3 [tr. *Thirteen Books* I.3]; for discussion, see Michael, "Daniel Sennert" pp. 291–9. For a helpful discussion of this issue as it arises in Suárez, see Shields, "Reality of Substantial Form." More generally, see Des Chene, *Physiologia* pp. 139–44. On the debate over whether the rational soul is educed from matter, see Pluta, "How Matter Becomes Mind."

Basso makes a powerful argument against the eduction of forms from matter (*Phil. nat.* De formis I). Jungius likewise puts this issue at the heart of his case against substantial form (*Praelectiones phys.* assert. primae nn. 12–22; *Disp. Hamb.* 22 thes. 7). See also Gassendi, *Syntagma* II.1.7.3 (I:469a) and, at great length, Boates, *Phil. nat. reformata* I.46–64.

that only purely potential prime matter endures through substantial change, the problem of explaining the origins of the newly generated substantial form can seem well-nigh intractable. On the other hand, the Thomistic account makes it clear why generation and corruption are distinct from other sorts of change: the discontinuity of substantial change is so radical, on their approach, as to present no risk of confusion with the case of alteration. In contrast, the more one allows to survive corruption, the less clear it is how substantial change differs from accidental. If each involves no more than the coming or going of a form, then they seem not so different. To be sure, one might still say that substantial change is special because it involves the going and coming of a *substantial* form. But, as we have seen (§24.4, §27.5), the reason substantial forms are special is that they explain the accidental forms of a substance. To the extent accidental forms are allowed to endure through substantial change, independently of the substantial form, the very distinction between substantial and accidental forms comes into doubt.

Post-scholastic discussions register both of these vulnerabilities. Rejecting substantial forms (§24.5), they question whether anything really does come into or go out of existence during the process of generation and corruption. Treating the matter that endures through change as wholly actual (§3.2), they question whether there really is a fundamental distinction between substantial and accidental change. In making these challenges, they attack scholastic Aristotelianism at some of its weakest points, but leave themselves open to considerable difficulties. For if nothing comes into or goes out of existence during substantial change, then it is hard to see how there can be such a thing as substantial change at all, given that substantial change, by definition, is supposed to consist in the generation of a *new* substance. Similarly, if substantial and accidental change are different at all, it seems they must be fundamentally different, since the one kind of change is supposed to destroy the thing changed, whereas the other requires that the subject of change endure. So it is that the seventeenth-century rejection of scholasticism tends quite naturally to lead to a radical outcome: the complete rejection of all substantial change.

As we have seen over and over, however, ideas that would become famous in the seventeenth century were usually anticipated during the scholastic era. The present case is no exception. Although the scholastic framework for substantial change would remain ascendant until the middle of the seventeenth century, it had already been subject to an extensive and quite forceful attack three hundred years earlier, by Nicholas of Autrecourt. Suppressed by Church authority (§§19.4–5), Autrecourt's ideas would have little impact on the ongoing debate. They are nevertheless worth considering, both for their own sake and because they serve as the harbinger for what would come, once the floodgates of Church authority burst open.

28.2. Permanence: Autrecourt

Autrecourt's *Tractatus* (1330) offers an extended defense of an austere corpuscularian version of atomism, which simply embraces many of the radical consequences that might seem to follow from such a view. In particular, Autrecourt holds that a plausible case can be made for the thesis that nothing naturally comes into or goes out of existence. If this thesis could be established, it would undermine not only substantial but also accidental change. For if everything is eternal then not only do substantial forms not come into and go out of existence, but neither do accidental forms. This wrecks the entire hylomorphic framework, because change will no longer be a matter of matter's going from potentiality to actuality through the loss and acquisition of forms. Instead, for Autrecourt, all change consists in the motion of ingenerable and incorruptible bodies, which he characterizes as atoms. Some sorts of motions get called generation, whereas others are called corruption or alteration or growth, but in no case does anything come into or go out of existence. In general "there is only local motion, even if it receives different denominations" (*Tractatus* ch. 1, p. 204).

Autrecourt's corpuscularianism—and in particular his rejection of qualities—was the topic of §19.4. Here the focus will be his arguments for "the eternity of things," the thesis that serves as the springboard for his corpuscularianism. His strategy is not to *prove* that all things are eternal, but to show only that there is no evidence to the contrary, and that moreover there are reasons to treat such eternalism as the more plausible view. His negative attack proceeds by targeting the case where it seems we have the best evidence of things coming into and going out of existence: change in sensible qualities. This is a natural place for Autrecourt to focus, given that the theory of real qualities was as entrenched as any part of the Aristotelian framework (§§19.1–2). Moreover, Autrecourt contends that his arguments here will generalize to other cases. If he can show that, contrary to our ordinary assumptions, there is no evidence that anything begins or ceases to exist in cases of alteration, then he will also be able to use arguments of the same form against alleged cases of substantial change.[4]

How might one show that change in sensible qualities involves something's coming into or going out of existence? Not by any sort of conceptual (non-empirical) argument, Autrecourt says, because there is nothing about the *concept* of change in sensible qualities that requires the denial of eternalism. One would, then, have to establish the thesis on the basis of experience. The argument, according to Autrecourt, would have to look something like this:

---

[4] Autrecourt's clearest statement of his radical corpuscularianism occurs at *Tractatus* ch. 1, pp. 200–1, as quoted in §19.4. See also pp. 201–2: "et breviter inducendo in similibus non apparet quod alio modo fiat corruptio in rebus quam per recessum corporum." Sometimes Autrecourt restricts his claim to permanent entities (e.g., p. 201), which might suggest that he leaves room for the coming and going of successive entities, and in particular motion. He does, at this point, want to leave that as an open possibility, but eventually he offers a reductive account of successive entities (see *Tractatus* ch. 5, p. 224 and Dutton, "Nicholas of Autrecourt").

For what surprisingly little secondary literature there is on Autrecourt's eternalism, see Dutton, "Nicholas of Autrecourt" pp. 65–8 and Kaluza, "Eternité du monde."

As Kaluza's masterful study has shown (*Nicolas d'Autrécourt* pp. 160–1), Autrecourt's very complex and interesting arguments in favor of eternalism are presented out of order in the sole surviving manuscript (albeit with indications regarding the proper order). Unfortunately, both O'Donnell's edition and the translation of Kennedy et al. failed to recognize this, and as a result this part of Autrecourt's argument, in its published form, is nearly unintelligible. As Kaluza reconstructs it, ch. 1 runs as follows:

ed.	tr.
198.18–203.18	59.1–66.27
185.17–188.37	37.26–43.11
203.19–206.22	66.28–71.14 [Kaluza secludes 203.35–48/ 67.7–24 as an interpolation]
188.38–190.10	43.12–45.21
206.23–28	71.15–21
190.11–196.48	45.22–56.11

For a cut-and-pasted scan of the Kennedy et al. translation in correct order, see my Provisionalia web page.

1. "Everything that previously appeared to a sense but now does not appear, no matter where the sense turns its attention, does not exist."
2. "So it is for the whiteness that previously appeared and now does not appear."
3. "Therefore, etc." (ibid., p. 199)

Think of snow turning to a dirty grey. The idea is simply that if something appears, and then disappears, and one cannot find it anywhere—like the white of the freshly fallen snow—then one would have good reason to claim that it has gone out of existence. As crude as that may sound, it seems pretty well to capture our ordinary evidence for thinking that things go out of existence.

Autrecourt's reply is fascinating. He does not challenge the realism that underlies the argument. Like almost everyone before the seventeenth century, he takes for granted that sensible qualities exist in the world (§22.3). (Relocating the sensible qualities would not help his case, anyway, because that would just shift the problem of change to somewhere else.) Instead, Autrecourt offers three ways in which even a realist about sensible qualities might deny that they ever go out of existence. The first explanatory strategy is *Reductionism*:

It might be said that the major premise [= 1] does not have any truth, because natural forms are divisible into their minimal parts in such a way that, divided from the whole, they cannot perform their action. So even though they are seen while existing as a whole, nevertheless when dispersed and divided or separated they are not seen. (ibid.)

The idea is that whiteness might be nothing more than many microscopic parts ordered in a certain way. What we take to be whiteness's going out of existence is in fact just its being diffused in such a way that it is no longer visible.

The second explanatory strategy is *Dispositionalism*:

The second way would be to say that a motive power sometimes performs its act—that is, when it moves it appears—and sometimes is at rest, and then it does not appear. Still one does not say on this account that it has been corrupted. Something similar might be said for all other powers. . . . (pp. 199–200)

Here the idea is that whiteness might be a power or disposition that remains in existence even when it is not acting. In that case its ceasing to act would not show that it ceases to exist. Now to this one could reply that, although whiteness might be a power, and so might produce its characteristic effects only in certain circumstances, still we know what those circumstances are. So if a whiteness that was once seen cannot now be seen, even in the right lighting conditions, and to observers with properly functioning visual systems, then we have as strong evidence as anyone could hope for that the whiteness has ceased to exist. It is easy, however, to see how Autrecourt would reply to this. For as soon as one admits that the entity in question is dispositional, the quick three-step argument above becomes much more complex, because one then needs at least one further premise to rule out the possibility that the power still exists but has gone dormant. But how does one ever know in what circumstances a power might go dormant? Here is a real-world example. One sometimes sees the claim that when leaves turn bright colors in the fall, they in fact do not gain any new quality, but simply lose the greenness that they once possessed, revealing their fall colors. This is to say that the yellows and oranges are there in the spring and summer, but dormant.

Perhaps something similar should be said about the dirty snow—that it is really still white, but just not showing itself as such. Perhaps in general the "standard conditions" under which a disposition reveals itself are far more complicated than we tend to recognize, and dispositions are far less prone to go out of existence than we realize. Perhaps, indeed, the true dispositions of the world *never* cease to exist.[5]

The third explanatory strategy is *Platonism*:

> In a third way, it might be said that the nature (*ratio*) of the appearance is removed from no thing. For if you see whiteness in Socrates's face, and blackness in his hair, and a scar on his face, you will see all these after Socrates is said to be corrupted. Not that they will be where they were before; instead, they will be somewhere else—for instance, the whiteness in John, the blackness in a horse, the scar in Peter. (p. 200)

The idea is that the sensible quality itself—the whiteness, etc.—never ceases to exist, inasmuch as that thing is a universal that exists elsewhere. Autrecourt immediately confronts the objection that the whiteness of John's face is only qualitatively and not numerically the same as the whiteness of Socrates's face. To this he responds that in cases of exact similarity one has no grounds for denying numerical identity. So far, this third strategy sounds more like an *in re* theory of universals than like Platonism. But Autrecourt now shifts direction. For he immediately concedes that there is one good reason to postulate a numerical distinction between exactly similar qualities: their difference in location. Although some might deny this principle, and hold that the same thing can exist in more than one place, Autrecourt says that he at least, contrary to what some charge him with, "does not wish to proceed from premises so at odds with experience" (ibid.). Even granting that principle, however, Autrecourt thinks it cannot be shown that Socrates's whiteness is distinct from John's whiteness. For even if the first appears to your left and the second to your right, that does not prove they in fact have distinct locations. After all, he says, we are familiar with how mirrors can give the appearance of one thing's being in multiple locations. Of course it would be ridiculous to suppose that there are really mirrors everywhere, deceiving us. But it would not be ridiculous to suggest that the material world is itself a kind of mirror for the reality of the Forms:

> One might claim in this case that here below there is only the material, and that the actions of things are traced back to separate principles of the sort that Plato postulated—for instance, the action of this whiteness might be traced back to a separate Whiteness. . . . And then that material to which we attend is nothing other than a mirror, and by directing our attention to one place it naturally happens that the Whiteness is seen there. This is Plato's view. (ibid.)

If sensible qualities are Platonic Forms, then of course they do not go out of existence.

---

[5] On leaves changing colors, see this popular account: "The green chlorophyll disappears from the leaves. As the bright green fades away, we begin to see yellow and orange colors. Small amounts of these colors have been in the leaves all along. We just can't see them in the summer, because they are covered up by the green chlorophyll" (http://www. sciencemadesimple.com/leaves.html). One might well wonder about the coherence of the idea that "small amounts" of yellow and orange have been in the leaves (but not large amounts?) and that yet we "just can't see them." Autrecourt, however, needs only the *possibility* of this sort of scenario. Of course, one may wonder what Autrecourt could say about the green that "disappears." Ultimately, he might need to combine dispositionalism with reductionism or Platonism, or he might need to rethink what the true dispositions are in a much more thoroughgoing and radical way than the leaf example suggests.

It is easy to see how the first and third strategies would apply to the case of generation and corruption, although Autrecourt himself leaves this as an exercise to the reader. If we accept Reductionism, for instance, we might say that a cat is nothing more than a collection of microscopic particles, and that those particles never go out of existence. When that strategy is generalized, it follows that whatever exists always exists. Similarly, in the case of Platonism, if to be a cat is for some material to participate in the Form of Cat, then the destruction of a cat is not the destruction of anything. The Form continues to exist, and the material continues to exist. The only case whose application to substantial change is unclear is the second. Here, however, Autrecourt tells us how this will go, in the case of a human being:

On this [second] account, when the powers of a human being on which his principal operation depends are dormant, then the human being is said to have been corrupted, and when it is so in every part of some area, then the world is said to be corrupted with respect to that area. So it has been infinitely many times and so it will be if the world, with respect to its natural appearances, is said to be corrupted. (ibid.)

The idea is that what we think of as corruption is really the dormancy of one or more powers that give rise to the "principal operation" of a given thing. For a human being to die, then, presumably, is for those powers that account for its vital operations to go dormant. And for any region of matter, we think of something being corrupted there when the principal powers of that region fall quiet. In actual fact, on this account, those powers never truly go out of existence. (One might suppose that the human case would be different from that of other substances, since we have an incorruptible human soul, but in fact §29.4 will show Autrecourt to be remarkably doubtful as to whether the soul can be used to account for human persistence.)

Autrecourt takes these three scenarios to undermine any reason to believe that things come into and go out of existence. As he puts it, "each is possible; nor do I see that any of them has been sufficiently disproved by Aristotle" (ibid.). This will seem all the more true if one considers how these three options might be combined in various ways. Autrecourt himself says that he regards Reduction as the most plausible of the three. This is what one would expect, given his strict corpuscularianism, and Autrecourt is willing to pay the various prices associated with such an austere metaphysics. He is willing, in particular, to deny that anything other than atoms exists in the material realm. What his discussion shows, however, is that someone who wants to enrich a strictly corpuscularian account with other metaphysical entities has alternatives other than Aristotelian hylomorphism. One can, for instance, follow the second strategy and introduce dispositions. This is a strategy we considered already in Chapter 23, in the context both of the real powers of the scholastics and of the nominal powers of Boyle and Locke. Corpuscularians who help themselves to such powers can—at least in some contexts—offer a more plausible account of change than can strict corpuscularians. A corpuscularian willing to embrace Platonism has still more options. As I have stressed (§27.4), universals were almost never taken seriously within the scholastic tradition, or by its seventeenth-century critics, and Platonism in particular was generally regarded as wholly incredible. (One might here remember the heuristic picture of §4.1: that Platonism lies on one side of Aristotelianism, corpuscularianism on the other.) There is no reason in principle, however, why a broadly corpuscularian approach might not be supplemented by Platonic universals, so that what exists *in re* is simply particles in motion, but that these variously arranged particles might truly be said to be human, or white, in virtue of participating in Humanity and Whiteness. (Perhaps, then, the linear spectrum of §4.1 needs to be bent into a circle.)

Autrecourt does not take these various lines of argument to prove anything. (In general, as his famous letters make clear, he thinks almost nothing can be demonstrated with certainty.) So even if we were willing to grant to Autrecourt the bare possibility of one or more of the accounts he describes, we might still insist that it seems overwhelmingly more plausible to embrace the commonsense notion that things do come into and go out of existence. This was Buridan's complaint, which he seems to have aimed directly at Autrecourt's view. It is both "obscure and dangerous," Buridan charges, to contend that "a donkey was a stone, and a stone has always existed, and no horse or human being has ever been generated, although matter has been made a human being or a horse" (*In De an.* III.11; see §24.2). The "danger" to theology can perhaps be set aside, and the "obscurity" is surely part of the allure of Autrecourt's view. But isn't it all the same just an incredible picture of reality? Even if it is possible, what reason would we have for believing it?

Autrecourt sees that he needs to address these questions, if he means to do more than simply trade in the sorts of skeptical scenarios that can at best do nothing more than dislodge our prior beliefs, and that in practice never do even that much. His answer is to argue that our intuitions about the perfection of the created world favor the eternalist hypothesis. Here is his first attempt at how that argument might go:

If in each thing eternity is better than its corruption, it will then seem that the universe is more perfect if its parts—especially its permanent ones—are held to be eternal, just as its being [as a whole] is granted to be eternal. . . . Thus it might be argued as follows: [1] That should be posited in the universe that results in a greater perfection's appearing in the universe, if no impossibility follows from its being posited. [2] But in fact it is the case that, by positing that permanent natural things of the sort discussed above are eternal, a greater perfection appears in the universe—and no impossibility follows from this. [3] Therefore etc. (*Tractatus* ch. 1, p. 201)

Autrecourt is well aware that this is not demonstrative. It depends on two questionable assumptions: that this is the most perfect possible universe, and that generation and corruption is incompatible with such perfection. This second assumption gets defended in considerable detail, and it seems that Autrecourt came back to this part of the *Tractatus* repeatedly, piling new arguments on top of old ones. The core idea is that although perfection is compatible with some kinds of change, inasmuch as there might be some perfect-making features of the universe that can be instantiated only through local motion, perfection is not compatible with a thing's wholly ceasing to exist, or beginning to exist anew. Changes of that sort suggest that the world is becoming better or worse. Now inasmuch as modern readers are likely to treat it as obvious that the world *does* get better or worse, as it changes economically, politically, and environmentally, *inter alia*, it is hard to see the intuitive pull of this argument. But if one does embrace Autrecourt's initial perfect-world assumption, then one can see why he is pulled in the direction of eternalism. For there can then seem something enticingly elegant about the idea that, when God created, he created just what there ought to be in the world, with just as many things in it as its perfection requires. To be sure, things *appear* to come and go, but the underlying reality remains constant.

Although the details of Autrecourt's argument are well worth exploring, I will pass them by in order to consider how these ideas would explode onto the scene once again in the seventeenth century. It would take that long because, as with his rejection of real qualities (§19.4), Autrecourt's eternalism was quashed by Church authorities in Avignon, condemned in 1346/47 as "false, erroneous, and heretical." Hence in the later scholastic era one finds only traces of it, in Buridan, and in Nicole Oresme, Albert of Saxony, and Marsilius of Inghen, all of whom take quite seriously right at the start of their *De generatione* commentaries the question of whether generation can be proved to happen. Since they cannot talk about Autrecourt, they talk about, as Oresme puts it, "the many ancient doctors who denied that generation occurs" (*In De gen.* I.1, p. 4). Oresme readily concedes to these "ancients" that there can be no demonstrative proof in favor of generation and corruption. We think there is no fire because we no longer perceive heat, but strictly speaking the inference is not certain: our senses could be deceiving us, or the fire could be failing to produce heat for some reason we cannot perceive. Such concessions to skepticism are in themselves quite remarkable: one sees nothing like this either in earlier scholastic discussions of these issues, or even in later discussions, Autrecourt's influence having by that time apparently dried up. But even Oresme and his contemporaries are willing to bend only so far in the direction of Autrecourt's eternalism. Although it cannot be demonstratively proved that things come into and go out of existence, that hypothesis "is the most plausible of all" (ibid., p. 6). This remained the orthodox judgment—not just unchallenged but unchallenge-able—until the seventeenth century.[6]

28.3. Weak Permanence: Basso and Gassendi

One way to reject generation and corruption in favor of permanence would be from the top down, by rethinking the essences of things. If we are wrong about essences, then we may well be wrong about when things come into and go out of existence. If we are wrong enough, it might turn out that nothing comes into or goes out of existence. Yet although the previous chapter discussed how these issues are entwined in the seventeenth century, they are not connected quite so directly as this. Even if permanence *requires* rethinking the standard conception of essence, it does not usually seem to have *followed* from a critique of essences. The motivation for the permanence thesis comes, instead, through the post-scholastic critique of prime matter.

So long as prime matter is understood in metaphysical, Aristotelian terms, as halfway between nothingness and existence (as Averroes put it [§3.3]), the permanence thesis cannot even arise. If this is the only stuff that endures through all change, then other

---

[6] Oresme's measured defense of generation holds that "opinio Aristotelis inter omnes est probabilior, quamvis aliae non possint demonstrave improbari." Both Albert of Saxony and Marsilius of Inghen follow Oresme's discussion of generation closely. According to Albert, "contra istas opiniones non bene potest demonstrative argui, tamen aliqualiter potest contra eas persuaderi" (*In De gen.* I.1, f. 132rb). Marsilius similarly remarks that "non est nobis evidens evidentia summa aliquod generari vel corrumpi" (*In De gen.* I.2, f. 66vb). There is no trace of such concessions to skepticism in the early *De generatione* commentaries of Giles of Rome or Giles of Orleans.

things must come into and go out of existence. Metaphysical prime matter is too thin an enduring substratum to count as the only thing that exists. Accordingly, permanence is never a serious option for scholastic Aristotelians. Only when prime matter is conceived of as wholly actual and corpuscularian does permanence loom into view. Atomists, for instance, do not have to embrace permanence (or any particular metaphysical thesis at all, for that matter [§5.4]), but once the atoms are made to be the permanent substratum of change (§3.2) it can suddenly seem attractive to think that those atoms are the only things that really exist, and that hence there is no real generation or corruption. This was never the majority view, but it is a picture that lurks, spoken or unspoken, behind much of the seventeenth-century rebellion against scholasticism.

It is, however, far from obvious why actualized prime matter should point in this direction, given that there are at least two large and dubious assumptions lying in the way. First, one has to suppose that this actualized material substratum is itself permanent. This is the conservation thesis of §2.5, which was embraced almost universally throughout our four centuries, first under the guise of prime matter, and then as some sort of actualized, corpuscular substratum. All the way through Locke, there was a general consensus that "the dominion of man . . . can do nothing towards the making the least particle of new matter, or destroying one atom of what is already in being" (*Essay* II.2.2). Yet even if one grants the conservation thesis, one can arrive at permanence only after making a still larger leap, to the conclusion that this enduring stuff is the only stuff there is. This is the startling notion that begins to get taken seriously in the seventeenth century, and that will be the primary focus of the remainder of this chapter.

The previous section revealed one kind of argument for this further conclusion: Autrecourt's appeal to the universe's perfection. So far as I can find, no subsequent authors lit upon this argument. What one finds instead in the seventeenth century is a line of thought with a more ancient pedigree, grounded in the principle that *nothing is made from nothing*. In one sense or another this principle was accepted throughout our period. As we saw in Chapter 2, this *ex nihilo* principle underwrites the thesis of an enduring material substratum, and subsequently informs various scholastic debates over exactly what the content of that substratum is. The principle had played an important role in Epicurus and even before then among the Presocratics. Aristotle took his hylomorphic framework, and in particular the potentiality–actuality distinction, to disarm those sorts of arguments. But what one finds in the seventeenth century—as if the intervening 2000 years had not happened at all—is a renewed conviction that the *ex nihilo* principle does have radical consequences regarding change.

An early instance is Sebastian Basso. His difficult and often obscure *Philosophia naturalis* (1621)—one of the first major statements of the anti-scholastic corpuscularian movement—makes an extended case against Aristotelianism by attempting to rehabilitate the ancient authors whom Aristotle had taken himself to have buried. One of Basso's most prominent claims is that in cases of substantial change nothing is generated anew:

Here [the ancients] show how nothing is generated anew as a result of corruption, and that instead there is only the release of the same parts that had been joined together, since each of those parts is cut up into the smaller particles out of which it had been assembled. And thus fire, air, water, and earth—which before had been tied together and hidden—now appear. And whereas before they were impeded from acting, they now—impediments removed—make an impression on the senses. (De forma III, p. 243; see also p. 11)

Basso himself rejects the Aristotelian elements and primary qualities in favor of a strict atomistic corpuscularianism, but he wants to take from Aristotle's old adversaries the idea that nothing appears in generation that was not already in the thing corrupted. The target in particular is substantial form, which—as remarked in §28.1—precisely does seem to appear from nowhere in the newly generated substance:

This principle was accepted by all the philosophers: *Nothing comes from nothing.* From this they rightly inferred that nothing is made that did not preexist with respect to its parts. Otherwise would there not be something in that thing that did not preexist, at least with respect to its parts? 3
From what, then, would that something be made, if the parts out of which it was made had not existed? Obviously it is necessary that they were made from nothing—which is impossible. Now if all the parts of that thing, however minute, preexisted, then it is certain that the generation of 6
that thing is only a certain composition of the preexisting parts, as the ancients (*prisci*) held. What about Aristotle? He denies that the thing preexisted with respect to all of its parts actually, but only potentially. He claims that the thing's matter preexisted, but not its form, unless it 9
preexisted potentially. Yet he also says that this form is the principal part of a physical composite. Is this form made from nothing? He does not dare to say so. But then what? It is not the form that is made, he says, but the whole composite. What? Is not the physical 12
composite made from parts that did not exist? They existed potentially, he claims, inasmuch as the form exists potentially in the matter from which it can be derived. But the form's existing potentially in matter—is that for there to be parts of the form existing there, from which the 15
form comes about? Not at all. But then what? One can only surmise. (De forma I, p. 149)

Basso takes the *ex nihilo* principle to show that, in cases of generation, all the ingredients of a thing must already exist. What is "impossible" (line 5) is not generation, but rather something's coming into existence with some part that did not previously exist. This would violate the *ex nihilo* principle, requiring a supernatural act of creation to account for ordinary generation. From this preliminary result (lines 1–5), Basso gets two important conclusions. One is that generation is simply composition (lines 5–7). The other is that Aristotle's theory of form is incoherent, because it violates this construal of the *ex nihilo* principle (lines 8–16). And although the argument is aimed primarily at substantial form, it applies just as well to accidental form, since such forms come into and go out of existence in alteration just as substantial forms do in generation and corruption. The argument therefore attacks the hylomorphic framework at its most fundamental level.

Chapter 2 considered in some detail how the *ex nihilo* principle interacts with the conservation thesis. One conclusion of that chapter was that the *ex nihilo* principle looks intuitively compelling only on a weak construal, as the principle that nothing is made without prior ingredients, but that for purposes like Basso's it needs to be given a strong construal—as requiring that those ingredients endure in the thing newly made. So construed, the *ex nihilo* principle is equivalent to the substratum thesis of §2.2. With a few plausible further assumptions, this can be parlayed into the conservation thesis of §2.5: that this substratum of change is permanent. Basso clearly means to defend the conservation thesis, and he might seem to go even farther, all the way to the permanence thesis according to which nothing comes into or goes out of existence. After all, the first of the two above passages begins with the claim that "nothing is generated anew" (line 1). The longer passage makes it quite clear, however, that Basso does not mean to go this far, inasmuch as the critical claim there is not that nothing is made, but that "nothing is made that did not preexist with respect to its parts" (line 2). Basso thus goes only part way toward the radical permanence thesis: although he accepts a very robust version of the conservation thesis, in insisting that the parts of things must endure through all change, he does not take the further step of insisting that only those parts exist, and that therefore *everything* is permanent.[7]

Henceforth, I will refer to this halfway embrace of the permanence thesis—that the ingredients are permanent even if the wholes are not—as the *weak permanence thesis*, and refer to the full-blooded radical claim about the parts and the wholes as the *strict permanence thesis*. Given that the weak permanence thesis just is a version of the conservation thesis, it should not be surprising to find that it is common among post-scholastic authors, appearing in Descartes, Pierre Gassendi, Walter Charleton, Boyle, Locke, and many others.[8] What weak permanence adds to the conservation thesis is the idea that not only is there *a* permanent substratum of change, but that moreover, in some sense (see below), *all* the ingredients of the newly generated substance are permanent. This further claim is one that Aristotelians cannot embrace because, as we have seen (§28.1), their framework for substantial change requires the generation not just of a new whole, but of a new part—the substantial form in virtue of which the whole is indeed something new. Hence the weak permanence thesis is distinctively post-scholastic. It marks one extreme of a spectrum of views regarding how to think about the ingredients of change. At the other extreme lies the strict unitarianism of the Thomists, according to which only indeterminate, purely potential prime matter is conserved (§3.1, §25.2). Other scholastics allow more of the ingredients to endure through change (§4.3, §25.3), and by the late sixteenth century it becomes common to insist that the quantity of matter is conserved (§4.5). Weak permanence goes farthest of all down this road, insisting that *all* the ingredients of substances must endure through change.

---

[7] For Basso, Nielsen's "Seventeenth-Century Physician" remains a useful overview. A more recent and authoritative historical study is Lüthy, "Thoughts and Circumstances." See also Ariew, "Descartes, Basso, and Toletus" and *Last Scholastics* pp. 133–4; Gregory, "Sébastien Basson." Ariew and Grene, "Cartesian Destiny," suggest that Basso was an influence on Descartes in this domain.

[8] Charleton sets out the weak permanence thesis at *Physiologia* II.1.1.9: "nor is there any sober man who does not understand the common material of things to be constantly the same, through the whole flux of time, or the duration of the world, so as that from the creation therefore by the *fiat* of God, no one particle of it can perish, or vanish into nothing, until the total dissolution of nature, by the same metaphysical power, nor any one particle of new matter be superadded thereto, without miracle." That this amounts only to weak permanence is clear in the detailed discussion at IV.1.1, which begins: "That nature or the common harmony of the world is continued by changes or the vicissitudes of individuals—i.e. the *production* of some and the *destruction* of other things, determined to this or that particular species ... are positions to which all men most readily prostrate their assent."

Locke sets out the weak permanence thesis at *Essay* II.26.2: "First, when the thing is made new, so that no part thereof did ever exist before, as when a new particle of matter does begin to exist *in rerum natura*, which had before no being, and this we call *creation*. Secondly, when a thing is made up of particles which did all them before exist, but that very thing, so constituted of pre-existing particles, which considered altogether make up such a collection of simple ideas, had not any existence before, as this man, this egg, rose, or cherry, etc. And this, when referred to a substance produced in the ordinary course of nature, by an internal principle ... we call *generation*." This passage occurs almost verbatim in the B Draft of 1671 (§134).

For Descartes, Gassendi, and Boyle, see below.

As natural a development as the weak permanence thesis is, the view is not easy to state with precision. Basso writes as if *all the parts* of a thing are permanent, and others routinely speak this way. According to Boyle, for instance, it is "not that there is really any thing of substantial produced, but that those parts of matter that did indeed before preexist... are now brought together" (*Origin of Forms* [*Works* V:328; Stewart p. 45]). But this cannot be strictly right. For if it is granted that new, composite substances come into existence, then it will surely be granted that those new substances may have new parts. Weak permanence will allow not only that plants come into existence, for instance, but also that roots and leaves do. Obviously, the doctrine is not meant to block these results, but only to require that material substances are composed *at some level* of permanently enduring corpuscles. For the atomist, it is easy to spell this claim out precisely, because it will of course be at the atomic level, and presumably only there, that weak permanence holds (§3.2). Given that Basso is himself an atomist, we can understand his talk of parts in that way. But weak permanence is consistent with agnosticism toward atomism, as in the case of Boyle just above, or even with the rejection of atomism, as in Descartes's case. For figures such as these, weak permanence can be true provided just that there is some level of composition at which, in fact, the constituent parts are permanent.[9]

Unfortunately, the weak permanence thesis is often stated in terms even more misleading than Basso's, as the thesis that substance is never generated or corrupted. This saying appears most prominently in Descartes's synopsis to his *Meditations*:

Absolutely all substances, or things that must be created by God in order to exist, are by their nature incorruptible and cannot ever cease to exist unless they are reduced to nothingness by God's denying his concurrence to them. (VII:14)

On its face, this looks like an unambiguous statement of strict rather than weak permanence, and some would read Descartes in that way. But the passage is not decisive, because it is quite clear that many authors use this seemingly very strong formulation to make what is intended to be a weaker point. According to Gassendi, for instance, "it should be maintained always that in generation no substance is made anew, but instead what already exists is mingled together; and so too in corruption nothing ceases to be, but instead is separated into its remnants" (*Philosophiae Epicuri syntagma* II.1.17 p. 65; tr. Stanley, *History of Philosophy* p. 871b). And, according again to Boyle, "no new substance is in generation produced, but only that which was preexistent obtains a new modification or manner of existence" (*Origin of Forms* [*Works* V:328; Stewart p. 45]). These look for all the world like statements of strict permanence, and perhaps they reflect a certain temptation on their authors' part to embrace that more rigorous claim. We ought to be extremely suspicious in reading these passages, however, because in every case these authors offer up this doctrine without any argument at all, as if it were axiomatic. Yet if taken literally, as a statement of strict

---

[9] The no-new-part formulation of weak permanence also appears in the Boates, where again it is clearly not intended to preclude generation and corruption: "Ad quod nos respondemus, nullam (ordinaria via, creatione seposita) dari substantialem mutationem seu generationem, ita accipiendo hanc vocem quomodo ipsi accipiunt, ut nimirum substantialis mutatio seu generatio sit illa qua ipsius substantiae quae generatur aliqua pars substantialis de novo fit cum non existeret prius. In quo sane nulla est absurditas neque afferri quicquam potest cur ad substantiae generationem magis necessarium sit ut aliqua ipsius pars quam ut tota ex nihilo fiat" (*Phil. nat. reformata* 1.3.12).

permanence, then such claims would amount to the most radical of metaphysical theses, contrary not just to common sense but also to every philosophical and theological tradition from Plato onward. It would be as if these authors, without any argument or even discussion, had decided without warning to return to the monism of Parmenides, or to the most radically reductive atomism of Democritus.[10]

To be sure, one can find such radical ideas. They are in Autrecourt, as we have seen, and they reappear in the seventeenth century, as we will see shortly. But Descartes, Gassendi, and Boyle not only do not tell us that this is what they are up to, but on the contrary they in other places make it quite clear that they do not mean to go nearly so far. That this is so in Boyle's case seems clear from his overall metaphysical quietism (§23.2), which is inconsistent with such a speculative metaphysical thesis. It is also required given his embrace of real essences (§27.6). As remarked earlier, only an anti-essentialist, such as Hobbes or Conway (§27.5), can embrace strict permanence. That Descartes too means to embrace only weak permanence follows from earlier discussions of his exceptionally loose conception of substance, which includes not just living and non-living natural bodies but also artifacts (§24.5) as well as the mind–body composite (§25.6), plus all the integral parts of bodies, all the way, infinitely far down (§26.1). (I return to Descartes's case in §28.5.)[11]

---

[10]　Boyle's full statement of the no-new-substance formula is worth quoting: "These things premised, it will not now be difficult to comprise in few words such a doctrine, touching the *generation, corruption,* and *alteration* of bodies, as is suitable to our hypothesis, and the former discourse. For if in a parcel of matter there happen to be produced (it imports not much how) a concurrence of all those accidents, (whether those only, or more) that men by tacit agreement have thought *necessary* and *sufficient* to constitute any one determinate species of things corporeal, then we say that a body belonging to that species, as suppose a stone or a metal, is *generated,* or produced *de novo.* Not that there is really any thing of substantial produced, but that those parts of matter that did indeed before preexist, but were either scattered and shared among other bodies, or at least otherwise disposed of, are now brought together, and disposed of after the manner requisite to entitle the body that results from them to a new denomination, and make it appertain to such a determinate species of natural bodies, so that no new substance is in generation produced, but only that which was preexistent obtains a new modification or manner of existence" (*Origin of Forms* [*Works* V:328; Stewart pp. 44–5]).

In "Form, Substance, and Mechanism" pp. 63–4, I wrongly credited Boyle with the view I am now calling strict permanence. For other examples of that mistake, see Conn, *Locke on Essence* pp. 85–6 and Desmond Henry, *Medieval Mereology* p. 124.

[11]　Descartes repeats the no-new-substance formulation in the Second Replies: "Nec quidem etiam habemus ullum argumentum vel exemplum quod persuadeat aliquam substantiam posse interire" (VII:153), and also to Regius: "quod plane repugnat ut substantia aliqua de novo existat, nisi de novo a Deo creetur" (III:505).

It is very important to understand the meaning of the no-new-substance principle in Descartes, because otherwise it is hard to resist reading him as a material monist, committed to there being just one *res extensa.* (For recent statements, see Lennon, "The Eleatic Descartes"; Secada, *Cartesian Metaphysics* ch. 8; Sowaal, "Cartesian Bodies.") The idea is implausible on its face, given the many passages in which Descartes commits himself to ordinary, finite bodies as substances, along with the complete absence of any texts that defend monism. (For a discussion of the texts see, e.g., Slowik, "Individual Corporeal Substance" and Kaufman, "Cartesian Substances.") Still, as §28.5 will discuss, if Descartes embraces strict permanence, then monism can easily seem to be the only remaining option. But once one sees that the no-new-substance formula is a commonplace among contemporaries who clearly do not embrace strict permanence, monism becomes largely unmotivated as a reading of Descartes. One can thereby also avoid the embarrassment that faces the monist with respect to what finite bodies are. They could not be modes, despite what Gueroult rather glibly asserts (*Descartes* I:65–74), because we *know* what the modes of extension are—size, shape, motion, position, duration, number, etc. (*Principles* I.69)—and we know that a dog, say, is nothing like that. Perhaps a finite body could be a cluster of modes, but there is no reason to think Descartes would say so. What finite bodies seem to be, quite plainly, on the monist scheme, are integral parts of the one material substance. But that is an embarrassing result for the monist, because it seems clear that Descartes is an actualist about integral parts (§26.1), and that he certainly does not hold a version of the Simple View (§26.2), which denies the reality of the parts of a substance.

The case of Gassendi is clearest of all. In the extended discussion of generation and corruption in his magnum opus, the *Syntagma philosophicum* (1658), he takes up a series of objections to his strictly corpuscularian, atomistic account:

(1) the enduring matter, existing in potentiality, needs form to actualize it;
(2) without such a form, there would be no distinction between generation and alteration;
(3) without such a form, natural things would not be essentially distinct;
(4) without such a form, all composite things would be merely heaps, not entities in their own right (*entia per se*). (II.1.7.4, I:473–4)

The first objection amounts simply to stating the heart of scholastic hylomorphism. The following three objections highlight various consequences that scholastic authors constantly allege to follow from a rejection of hylomorphism. Since the issues involved in (3) and (4) have been considered elsewhere (Chs. 27 and 25), we can focus here on (2). Gassendi categorically insists that his account recognizes the distinction: "generation can always differ from alteration, inasmuch as through generation a thing is said to be made absolutely, or to come into light for the first time, whereas through alteration a thing is said to be made such, or to vary in its features while its essence persists" (ibid. I:473b). Having said this, however, Gassendi anticipates the objection that this does not count as *substantial* generation. Here his response is more guarded:

As for whether this precludes substantial generation, the question is clearly verbal. For it is precluded if you mean that something substantial is produced that did not at all preexist through either the whole or the parts. In this there is nothing absurd; on the contrary, it is entirely   3
appropriate, since otherwise a thing would be made *ex nihilo* either in whole or in part. On the other hand, substantial generation is not precluded if you mean that a composite emerges that has true subsistence, since it is the case both that its parts subsist on their own, and that they   6
cohere all together, being somehow tied to one another. (ibid.)

Gassendi claims that we should deny substantial generation if that entails violating weak permanence. But he sets out that thesis carefully, as requiring that *"either* the whole *or* the parts" preexist (line 3), which leaves room for there to be new wholes, and even new parts of wholes, so long as in every case they are composed of preexistent parts. Since this is all his version of permanence requires, he can allow that the notion of substantial generation is unproblematic if it means only that from the enduring atoms a new "composite emerges" (line 5).[12]

  Given that all of these authors commit themselves to the coming and going of substances in the world, and given that they treat the no-new-substance formula as if it were uncontroversial, we need some other way of understanding what that formula means. The most likely solution is that they intend it as a statement of weak permanence. 'Substance,' in the context of the formula, should therefore be understood as referring not to the ordinary substances that come into and go out of existence, but to the enduring substratum of change, which everyone during our period agrees to be incorruptible, but which for post-scholastic authors becomes not just an indeterminate metaphysical ingredient, but the actual physical stuff from which complex bodies

---

[12] For Gassendi on substantial change see also the protracted discussion in *Animadversiones* I:389–407.

are composed.[13] What we thus find in Gassendi, Descartes, and Boyle is a moderate position on the subject of generation and corruption. Disallowed is any conception of a metaphysical part, such as a substantial form, that would have to come into existence wholly anew—that is, without any preexisting ingredients to compose it. But this is not to say that *nothing* new can come into existence. There can be new wholes, provided they are constituted entirely (at some level) out of preexistent parts. The trouble with such a view is that it is not easy to see why we should regard these aggregates as genuinely new at all. All such aggregates are, as these authors themselves take pains to stress, is old stuff, differently mixed. Without the metaphysical resources of the scholastics to account for genuine substantial change, it is extremely tempting to deny that there ever is substantial change. So if we have not yet arrived at the radical thesis of strict permanence, we nevertheless stand right on the brink.[14]

28.4. Strict Permanence: Gorlaeus and Hobbes

The strict permanence thesis—that nothing naturally begins or ceases to exist—can be found hinted at in various early anti-scholastic treatises. One sees something like it in Giordano Bruno, who cites Ecclesiastes, and in Nicholas Hill, and even in Galileo.[15] It

---

[13] Descartes plainly uses 'substance' in the sense of the permanent substratum of change, as when he refers to the "substance of the brain" (*Treatise on Man* XI:130), the "substance of the bread" (Fourth Replies VII:250), and the "substance of the body" (*Principles* II.5). (I owe this point to Stuart, "Descartes's Extended Substance" p. 100.) In these cases, 'substance' refers not to the corporeal substance itself, but to something belonging to that substance, which in the context of Descartes's thought—barring the attribution to him of some sort of exotic ontology—can be only the integral parts that endure through change.

For a particularly clear instance of this usage see a 1692 letter from William King, regarding Locke's theory of substance: "'Tis plain when I conceive wax that I can conceive it either hard or soft, conceive the same thing turned to flame or air and after resolved into dew, then into honey and then into wax and yet there is something that still continues the *same* in it. Now that, which continues still the *same*, is that I call the *substance* of it" (Locke, *Correspondence* IV:537).

[14] I do not know where the no-new-substance formula comes from. Interestingly, it appears in Jan Baptiste van Helmont, who explicitly marks it as a new doctrine: "Whence I collect it into a new position for the schools: that no substance is to be annihilated by the force of nature or art. It has always seemed an absurd thing to me that a matter imperfect in itself, barren and impure, should after its creation be thenceforth eternal, and that forms that are to be annihilated by death should be true substances" (*Oriatrike* p. 67; see Debus, *Chemical Philosophy* II:329). Although Helmont's counts as an early statement of this principle, his works were published in Latin only posthumously, in 1648, and translated into English in 1662. Some other relevant early texts are quoted in the following note.

Leibniz endorses the no-new-substance principle but offers quite a strained pedigree for it, finding it in a pseudo-Hippocratic work and, quite absurdly, in Albert the Great, who surely thought no such thing: "j'accorde encor que toute forme substantielle ou bien toute substance est indestructible et même ingenerable, ce qui étoit aussi le sentiment d'Albert le Grand et parmi les anciens celui de l'auteur du livre *De diaeta* qu'on attribue à Hippocrate. Elle no sçauroient donc naître que par une création" (to Arnauld, 1686 [*Phil. Schriften* II:75; tr. Ariew and Garber p. 78]).

[15] Bruno suggests strict permanence at *De la causa* dial. 2, p. 53 (tr. p. 46): "non gli corpi ne l'anima deve temer la morte, perche tanto la materia quanto la forma sono principii constantissimi. . . . " He goes on to quote Ecclesiastes 1:9–10: "What is it that has been? The same thing that shall be. What is it that has been done? The same that shall be done. Nothing under the sun is new." Granada, citing *De la causa*, describes Bruno as a defender of "a rigorous ontological monism" according to which the universe is a "unique substance" and individual beings are accidents ("New Visions" p. 281).

Hill suggests strict permanence at *Philosophia epicurea* n. 117: "Entis quatenus entis non est aut causa aut ratio; omnes vero quas tuemur generationes sunt degenerationes, primorumque principiorum ab incausato et inderivato statu lapsus et deflectiones."

For Galileo on strict permanence, see *Dialogo dei massimi sistemi*, first day: "Di più, io non son mai restato ben capace di questa trasmutazione sustanziale (restando sempre dentro a i puri termini naturali), per la quale una materia venga talmente trasformata, che si deva per necessità dire, quella essersi del tutto destrutta, sì che nulla del suo primo essere vi rimanga e ch'un altro corpo, diversissimo da quella, se ne sia prodotto; ed il rappresentarmisi un corpo sotto un aspetto e di lì a poco sotto un altro differente assai, non ho per impossibile che possa seguire per una semplice trasposizione di

seems to have been given its first sustained post-scholastic defense by David Gorlaeus, whose stunningly bold *Exercitationes philosophicae* (*c.*1611; publ. 1620) rejects hylomorphism entirely, and replaces it with an atomism that insists on strict permanence. According to Gorlaeus, whatever is real is indivisible, and so the only things that exist in the material realm are atoms. Human beings are not soul–body composites, but souls alone, and the body is not part of us. Aggregates are entities only because we conceive of them as such. Accordingly, generation and corruption must be rejected:

I completely deny that any body is made, except by creation alone, when God created this world. I deny that anything has gone out of existence, or can go out of existence, unless it is brought to nothing by that same God. I deny that any body has been changed into another, or that it can be changed. (exerc. 14, p. 256)

Accordingly, in a weird but apposite inversion of the conventional wisdom, Gorlaeus denies not that things are made *ex nihilo*, but that they made *ex aliquo*: nothing, he insists, is ever made from something. Conceding that this will look ridiculous to many, he mischievously remarks nevertheless that "since we are inverting everything, we should invert this too" (exerc. 15.1, p. 278). Remarks such as these are the only reminders that this brilliant, precocious work was written by a twenty-year-old.[16]

These same ideas appear in Hobbes, who was born three years before Gorlaeus but had the good fortune of living sixty-seven years longer. We have seen intimations of Hobbes's view several times already, in his defense of the conservation of body (§2.5) and in his anti-essentialism (§27.5). In both cases, he pushes these doctrines all the way to a rejection of generation and corruption. Thus, in his *De mundo* (1642), he goes from insisting that matter cannot be corrupted to insisting in general that *ens*—being—cannot be corrupted:

If the question is whether numerically the same being (*ens*) can come back into existence, it is clear that it cannot. For in order for something that exists to come back—that is, to exist again—it must be supposed that the preceding thing has gone out of existence. But a being cannot naturally go out of existence. For even if a ship or a plank ceases to be a ship and a plank, it nonetheless never naturally ceases to be a being. For a being, unless it is annihilated, does not cease to be a being. But to annihilate is a supernatural task, for God. (12.5)

---

parti, senza corrompere o generar nulla di nuovo, perché di simili metamorfosi ne vediamo noi tutto il giorno" (ed. Flora p. 394; tr. p. 45).

[16] Gorlaeus articulates his version of strict permanence in remarks such as this: "per compositionem non fit aliquod ens, nec per dissolutionem perit" (*Exercitationes* 12, p. 230); "quodcumque est reale aliquid, id ipsum est indivisibile" (exerc. 13.1, p. 235); "asserimus animam et corpus esse duo entia, quae unum sunt per aggregationem" (exerc. 12, p. 230); "confici puto, corpus essentiae partem non esse. Essentia enim eadem numero resurrectura est, corpus idem numero resurgere non potest" (exerc. 12, p. 234); "non nego horum entium per aggregationem materiam dici entia, ex quibus aggregatae sunt, sed illa materia non est physica, quam commenti sunt Peripatetici, sed quae in logicis materia dicitur consideratione nostra" (exerc. 14, p. 266); "vulgo dici solet, nihil fieri ex nihilo. At nos, nihil fieri ex aliquo, sed quae fiunt, ex nihilo fieri; ut ita si ex hac re debeat fieri illa res, prius haec res in nihilum redigenda sit, quam illa res inde fieri possit" (exerc. 15.1, p. 278). See also Gorlaeus's *Idea physicae*, for the same ideas more briefly: "homo non est compositum per materiam et formam per se unum, quia ipsum corpus non est de essentia eius, sed anima tantum" (2.9); "omnis substantia quae facta est immediate a Deo producta est . . . Quaecumque ergo substantia fit, a Deo fit; quae perit, a Deo in nihilum redigitur; quaecumque etiam fit ex nihilo fit" (3.4).

The study of Gorlaeus is in its infancy, but good preliminary sallies can be found in Lüthy, "Gorlaeus' Atomism"; Gregory, "David Van Goorle"; and Meinel, "Early Seventeenth-Century Atomism." Lüthy argues that Gorlaeus's embrace of the permanence thesis is indebted to Nicholas Taurellus ("Gorlaeus' Atomism" p. 283), and perhaps this is suggested at *Philosophiae triumphus* pp. 120–5, but I cannot make out exactly what Taurellus's conclusion is on those pages.

The *De corpore* subsequently elaborates on this doctrine by treating generation and corruption as simply the coming and going of accidents:

When we say that an animal, a tree, or any other named body is generated or destroyed, even though these are bodies, it should not be thought that a body has been made from non-body, or non-body from body, but a non-animal from an animal, a non-tree from a tree, and so forth. That is, those accidents on account of which we name one thing an animal, another a tree, and another something else are generated and destroyed, and consequently those names that applied to them before no longer apply. (8.20)

So why do we say that now there is a tree, and now there is not? Not because anything new has come into existence, but only because there is now an accident that there was not before, which leads us to stop using "those names that applied to them before" (lines 5–6). Judging from this passage in isolation, one might at least suppose that Hobbes allows the generation and corruption of accidents (line 4). But Hobbes has no place in his ontology for any such entities (§7.1, §10.2). All he recognizes are bodies and motions: thus "bodies are things, and not generated; accidents are generated, and not things" (ibid.). Hence Hobbes can conclude in general, as in the first of the above passages, that beings never naturally go out of existence. Perhaps the most express statement of his view comes again in the *De mundo*, which offers a general theory of change. All change, Hobbes argues, consists in the motion of a thing's parts, which we detect through changes introduced in our perceptual faculties. As for the difference between accidental and substantial change, he remarks that "when a thing is changed so extensively that it deserves a new name on account of its new appearance, then we say that the thing that produced the earlier appearance has been corrupted, and that another thing, exhibiting a new appearance, has been generated" (7.1). In actual fact, "things themselves do not perish through change, but only their images and looks" (7.2)—a remark that leads Hobbes into a long discussion of how we are to think about the permanent prime matter that underlies change. His conclusion, of course, is that prime matter is simply body (§2.5).

   As similar as Gorlaeus's and Hobbes's views are, they differ in one prominent respect. According to Gorlaeus, everything that exists is simple: "we hold that no being is composite, and that whatever is is simple" (*Idea physicae* 4.7). Hobbes does not say this, and cannot say this, because his materialism, combined with his rejection of atomism (§5.4; Ch. 26 note 14), entails that in fact *nothing* is simple. This should make one wonder how Hobbes can possibly defend strict permanence: for it would seem that composite things always admit of the possibility of being broken apart, and so always admit of the possibility of ceasing to exist. The key to Hobbes's position, as I understand it, is that he rejects this inference. He believes, that is, that a body can continue to exist even after it has been broken apart and scattered. This is, indeed, precisely what he says: in considering the conditions under which a body can be regarded as persisting through time, he remarks that "a body is always the same, whether the parts of it be put together or dispersed; or whether it be congealed or dissolved" (*De corpore* 11.7; see §29.5). This means that although Gorlaeus and Hobbes start out from similar places, they arrive at quite different pictures. Gorlaeus, limited as he is to simple substances, cannot treat ordinary objects as genuine entities. Hobbes, because he allows composite bodies, can allow that dogs and cats and stones exist. But their existence is not at all what one would naturally suppose, because the body that is the dog will continue to exist forever, even after the integral parts of that body have been "dissolved" and "dispersed." Of course, we will not then call it a dog, but its being a dog was always just an accidental feature of the body.

The radically reductive character of these views makes them easy to understand, but hard to take seriously. The remainder of this chapter will consider the most prominent line of argument in favor of strict permanence. The following chapter will then consider how the implausibility of these theses might be mitigated by an explanation of what apparent cases of generation and corruption actually consist in.

28.5. The Part–Whole Identity Thesis

The two conservation theses considered in this chapter—weak and strict permanence—are part of a family of views loosely associated with one other during the seventeenth century. This family includes corpuscularianism (§1.3), the substratum thesis (§2.2), atomism (§3.2, §5.2, §5.4), the rejection of the substance–accident distinction (§7.1), actualism regarding parts (§26.1), and anti-essentialism (§27.5). None of these views, however, whether severally or jointly, entails strict permanence. It might be thought that at least anti-essentialism would yield some version of the permanence doctrine, on the grounds that if a thing has no essential properties then there can be no fact of the matter about whether it starts or stops existing. This, however, is not so. One might, for instance, think that even if none of a thing's properties is essential, still there are various combinations of properties, in various circumstances, the loss of which entails the thing's corruption. Corpuscularianism too does not entail permanence, and again not even the weak version. One might, for instance, think that all there are in the material realm are bodies variously arranged, and yet accept that the parts of a composite substance—all the way down—are individuated by that substance, with the result that when a body is corrupted it is corrupted all the way down. In principle even an atomist might think this, since physical indivisibility need not entail permanence (§5.4).

Weak permanence is entailed—or at least nearly so—by corpuscularianism in conjunction with the substratum thesis. For if something has to endure through all change, and if the only thing one lets into one's physical ontology is bodies, then it will have to be some bodies that endure through all physical change. This is not yet weak permanence: it shows only that for every physical change there is one or another persisting body, rather than the stronger conclusion that at some sufficiently minute level *all* bodies endure through change. Reflection on the motivation for the substratum thesis, however, shows why that stronger conclusion might seem justified. For, as we saw in Chapter 2, the substratum thesis depends on the intuition that nature does not make things without ingredients, and that those ingredients must exist prior to the making and after the making, as a constituent part of the new substance. For scholastic authors, there were as many ways to understand this requirement as there were theories of prime matter. Something like this intuition is still at work in Newtonian physics, with its doctrine of the conservation of mass, and remains in place in modern physics, which insists on the conservation of energy. The only way for a strict corpuscularian to honor this thesis, however, is by postulating the conservation of bodies. Without anything like matter, form, mass, or energy to endure through change, corpuscularians must invoke enduring bodies as their ingredients. In order for those ingredients to be sufficient, it seems natural to think that, at some level of composition, *all* the bodies must endure. This is why, as we saw in §28.3, many seventeenth-century authors treat weak permanence as virtually axiomatic.

This line of thought does not, however, yield *strict* permanence. For one might suppose that although the stuff of the universe endures through all change, still that stuff can make new things, when organized in one way or another. This is what scholastic authors thought (their stuff being prime matter), it is what Basso and Gassendi thought (their stuff being atoms), and it was what commonsensical modern physicists think (their stuff being energy). The proponent of strict permanence therefore needs some further premise. Gorlaeus is quite clear about this: his further premise is the doctrine that the whole is nothing over and above its parts:

We willingly grant that composites are to be posited. But we do not recognize some one being that should be called the composite. On the contrary, it is the many entities—namely, the composite parts—that we call the composite, because *they* are composed. We hold that each and every part both has its own essence before composition, and retains that essence afterwards. Neither is a being made that is numerically one, nor is one being made from these parts. On the contrary, they are united and mixed so as to make one continuum, which is one being by aggregation, not by essence. (*Exercitationes* 12, pp. 224–5)

This is in effect a statement of the strict permanence thesis, couched in terms of a refusal to postulate any further entity beyond the composed parts. The general rule, which he states over and over in various ways, is that "no composite is other than its parts" (*Idea physicae* 8.1).

This *part–whole identity thesis*, as I will call it, has a long history, first in ancient philosophy and again among the twelfth-century Nominales. Among scholastic authors, the subject was debated extensively but inconclusively.[17] Affirming the thesis

---

[17] For ancient discussions of the part–whole identity thesis, see Barnes, "Bits and Pieces." Sextus Empiricus characteristically argues against the reality of wholes by arguing on one hand that the part–whole thesis cannot be true, but on the other hand that it cannot be false (*Outlines of Skepticism* III.98–9). For the Nominales, see Normore, "Abelard and the School of the Nominales" and "Tradition of Medieval Nominalism." For Peter Abaelard in particular, see Arlig, "Medieval Mereology."

The Coimbrans cite Themistius, Philoponus, Simplicius, Alexander, and Eudemus as favoring part–whole identity, along with Durand of St. Pourçain, Giles of Rome, Gregory of Rimini and "caeteri e schola Nominalium" (*In Phys.* I.2.1.2). Oresme (*In Phys.* I.7) should be included on this list, as should William Crathorn (*Sent.* I.3), Albert of Saxony (*In Phys.* I.7), pseudo-Marsilius of Inghen (*In Phys.* I.9), and John Major (*Sent.* IV.43.2, *In Phys.* I.2.7–8). Boethius is a forerunner of the view (*In Topica Ciceronis commentaria* I [*Patr. Lat.* 64:1056; tr. Stump p. 39]), as is Averroes (*In Phys.* I.17).

The Coimbrans themselves find both sides plausible, but favor the side that denies identity, which they associate with, among others, Avicenna, Scotus and his followers, various Thomists, and Walter Burley (Coimbrans, *In Phys.* I.2.1.1). Burley does indeed insist that the whole is distinct from its parts, relying on the indiscernibility of identicals (*In Phys.* I, f. 16ra–vb). For Scotus, see *In Meta.* VIII.4 and *Ord.* III.2.2 n. 7 (Vat. IX nn. 73–7), which offers a series of characteristically powerful arguments, resulting in the doctrine that there is a form of the whole that is the essence of the whole substance, distinct from the form of the part that is the substantial form. Cross discusses Scotus's position in detail in *Physics of Duns Scotus* ch. 5. See also Normore, "Ockham's Metaphysics of Parts."

Aristotle seems to endorse part–whole identity when he remarks that "there is no whole over and above the parts" (*Phys.* IV.3, 210a17). *Metaphysics* Zeta, however, concludes with the opposite lesson, that "the syllable is not its elements" (1041b12). Rejecting both of these lines of thought, one might instead suggest that the question of part–whole identity cannot even arise for Aristotle, in light of passages where he seems to deny that a substance has actual parts (§§26.1–2). It is a further measure of the scholastic disinterest in the Simple View of §26.2 that this dismissive solution to the part–whole identity question is not in general even considered.

does not require corpuscularianism, since for an Aristotelian it will be metaphysical parts, just as much as integral parts, that make up the whole. The part–whole identity thesis also does not entail any version of permanence, since one might well think—as Aristotelians do—that substances are generated and corrupted as the parts come and go. Here again, a great deal rests on the credibility of the scholastic claim that substantial forms, unlike matter, are not conserved. Someone who rejects weak permanence on the grounds that metaphysical parts come into and go out of existence can account for generation and corruption even given part–whole identity. If, however, one insists on weak permanence, then it together with the part–whole identity thesis immediately entails strict permanence. For if all the parts (at any one level of composition) are permanent, and if those parts are identical with any whole they compose, then—by the indiscernibility of identicals—any such whole must likewise be permanent. Unsurprisingly, then, one finds the part–whole identity thesis not just in Gorlaeus, but also in Hobbes (§29.5). In contrast, authors who embrace weak but not strict permanence must, if they are to be consistent, deny the part–whole identity thesis. In §28.3 we saw that Basso and Gassendi do just this. Basso restricts the *ex nihilo* principle so as to allow something new to arise from its parts: "nothing is made that did not preexist with respect to its parts," and Gassendi allows that preexistent parts can come together in such a way that "a composite emerges that has true subsistence." To be sure, both Basso and Gassendi wish to *reduce* facts about complex bodies to facts about their integral parts, but neither wishes to *identify* the whole with its parts.

We are now in a position to see just what drives corpuscularians toward strict permanence. If they accept the substratum thesis, as they all do, then it is difficult to resist weak permanence. To go from there to strict permanence, all that is needed is the part–whole identity thesis. And although by no means everyone accepted that thesis, it is an extremely attractive view. We can see as much by looking at the quite sophisticated scholastic disputes over this subject. Although the more ontologically profligate scholastic authors—in particular Scotus and his followers, as well as some Thomists—argued that the whole is something over and above its parts, the part–whole identity thesis was widely embraced. Unsurprisingly, given his parsimonious inclinations, Ockham was among its defenders. He offers in its favor a regress argument that would be very influential on later discussions. Let the parts be *a* and *b*, and the whole be *c*. Now suppose that *c* is not identical to *a* and *b*. In that case we can ask about the whole *a, b, c*. If that whole is something further, *d*, then we are clearly off on an unacceptable infinite regress. If, however, we can deny the existence of *d*, then we should by the same reason be able to deny the existence of *c*. Hence Ockham concludes that a composite substance is nothing beyond form and matter. One finds versions of this same argument in later authors stretching from Buridan to Franciscus Toletus.[18]

Buridan contributes another influential argument. Suppose a one-pound weight is divided into two half-pound weights. The whole, which weighed one pound, would seem no longer to exist. How can it be, then, that the two parts exert the same

---

[18] Ockham sets out his regress argument as follows: "si sint ibi duae formae, aut faciunt per se unum cum materia, aut non. Si sic, aut igitur est alia entitas praeter illas tres aut nulla. Si alia, quaero de ista sicut prius, et sic erit processus in infinitum. Si nulla, igitur illae tres partes faciunt per se unum sine quarta entitate, et eadem ratione duae poterunt facere per se unum sine tertia entitate" *Summula* I.19 (*Opera phil.* VI:206). For other versions see Buridan, *In Phys.* I.9; Albert of Saxony, *In Phys.* I.7; pseudo-Marsilius of Inghen, *In Phys.* I.9; and Franciscus Toletus, *In Phys.* I.8.

influence on the scale that they did as a whole? Did the whole have no weight? The best solution, Buridan suggests, is to say that the whole just was those parts.[19]

It is by no means obvious how either of these arguments is to be answered by those who would deny the part–whole identity thesis. And if that identity thesis was attractive to scholastic authors—even to a conservative figure like Toletus—then it is no wonder that the corpuscularians would find it attractive. After all, the core motive for the view is parsimony: that there is just no need for the metaphysical extravagance of postulating some further entity—a whole—above and beyond the parts. One would expect to find post-scholastic authors lining up behind this position in droves. In a way, then, the surprise is not that authors like Gorlaeus and Hobbes embrace strict persistence, but that so many others do not. It is a testimony to their felt need to retain at least some measure of a commonsense ontology that Basso, Gassendi, and others refuse to follow the logic of their position all the way to the sort of austere version of strict permanence that would deny the generation and corruption of living things and other substances. The price of doing so is to relinquish yet again some of the austerity of the pure corpuscularian framework that the first generation of post-scholastic authors have as their ideal. Beyond positing simply particles in motion, these authors have to countenance the obscure idea of a whole that is somehow constituted from its parts, but without being identical to those parts. Scholastic authors are under no such pressure, and so many gladly embrace the part–whole thesis without suffering any radical consequences, because they can account for the ordinary coming and going of substances in terms of the coming and going of substantial forms. To reject substantial forms in favor of corpuscularianism therefore has its cost: either one must buy into an ontology of wholes as something over and above their parts, or one must let go of the possibility of generation and corruption.

Weak permanence, together with part–whole identity, entails strong permanence. This is not to say that it entails Gorlaeus's version of the theory, according to which the only things that exist are atomic simples. Another possibility, consistent with these general metaphysical constraints, is that there be no proper parts at all, but only a single, permanent whole. This old idea of monism would not come back into currency until Conway (§27.5) and Spinoza—but just as Democritus seems to have taken inspiration from the Eleatics, so in the seventeenth century that influence can be seen to have worked in the other direction. From a conception of the material realm as containing nothing more than permanent atomic simples, it is easy to form the view that in fact there is just one, global atomic simple, itself permanent.

Still another way to defend strong permanence is to go Hobbes's route, as described at the end of the previous section, and deny the link between divisibility and corruptibility. On this approach, a body continues to exist even after its parts are divided. Although Hobbes does not explain why he takes this line, the motivation is not hard to see. For if one is persuaded by strict permanence, and also persuaded that everything is

---

[19] Buridan's weight argument: "Item sequitur quod duae semilibrae totidem traherent stateram remota ab eis una libra quantum traherent cum illa libra—quod est falsum, quia tunc illa libra nihil traherent. Consequentia patet per te quia si libra divideretur in duas medietates istae duae medietates tantumdem trahunt quantum trahebant cum libra quae erat totum ipsarum et tamen ablata est illa libra cum non remaneant nisi partes quae nec sunt nec fuerunt illa libra" (*In Phys.* I.9, f. 12va). The argument is repeated by Albert of Saxony, *In Phys.* I.7, pseudo-Marsilius of Inghen, *In Phys.* I.9, and John Major, *Sent.* IV.43.2.

composite, then one must have a way of saying that those composite entities exist for as long as their constituents do, even if dissolved. The seeming absurdity of this result is part of what led Gorlaeus to deny that composites exist. But there is at least logical space to embrace the seeming absurdity, and allow that the collection of particles—the thing picked out by the word 'stone'—continues to exist even after all its various particles have been washed away down the Colorado River. This is, however, not a view that authors during our four centuries generally show much interest in. To waive all restrictions on the conditions under which parts can be said to compose a whole is to violate one of the fundamental axioms of the substance-based ontology that grounds our period: that genuine existence requires genuine unity. The link between existence and unity has animated much of the four previous chapters, and it would be highly desirable to have a better understanding of why we should insist on this link. Here, however, I have to content myself with merely highlighting its status as a virtually unchallenged axiom.

Corpuscularians committed to part–whole identity can preserve the link between existence and unity by denying, as Gorlaeus does, that there are composite substances. The many scholastic authors who are committed to part–whole identity do not want to go that route, of course, but it is not obvious what their alternative is. For if the composite whole just is its various integral and metaphysical parts, then Hobbes's scattered objects loom: the whole will continue to exist if and only if the parts continue to exist, no matter how disunified. (Scotus had raised the specter of precisely this outcome as an objection against part–whole identity.) One way in which statements of the part–whole identity thesis try to grapple with this difficulty is by stipulating that the whole is identical to the parts "taken together and unified." Yet according to opponents of part–whole identity, the need to insert this proviso shows that the parts cannot be strictly identical to the whole, and it is easy to see their point. For if the proviso is just an ontologically innocent way of saying that the whole is equal to the *collection* of the parts, then we have not blocked the absurdity of a disunified collection counting as a whole. If, on the other hand, the unity requirement imposes some more substantive constraint, then it seems we must deny strict identity: the whole would not be simply the parts, but would be the parts so arranged. Whatever 'so arranged' amounts to, it would seem to preclude strict identity.[20] The wide range of metaphysical options available to scholastic

---

[20] Proponents of the part–whole identity thesis generally insist on the proviso that the parts must be unified, in order for them to be identical to the whole. Thus Ockham, e.g., holds that "totum non est aliud a partibus simul iunctis et unitis" (*Summula* I.19; *Opera phil.* VI:205). And John Major: "totum est suae partes simul sumptae" (*Sent.* IV.43.2). That of course leads to question about what this further "unity" amounts to. For Burley, this is the critical weakness of the part–whole identity thesis, and indeed he contends that what distinguishes the whole from its parts is precisely its unity (*In Phys.* I, f. 16va). This is quite a serious objection, since most of the proponents of part–whole identity do not accept the strict unitarian theory, associated with Thomism, that provides a cost-free explanation of what such unity consists in. Ockham's most detailed discussion of these issues occurs in *Quaest. var.* 6.2 (*Opera theol.* VIII:207–19), where he contends that unified parts are those that *lack* a relation to one another, and that it is only when the parts are disunified that they stand in a relation to one another that precludes them from being a whole (VIII:210). Ockham's overall position is carefully assessed by Cross, "Ockham on Part and Whole," who pays particular attention to Scotus's claim that if the whole is just the parts, then there is no viable subject for those accidents that are properties of the whole.

It is not only the scholastics who appeal to metaphysical parts to explain the unity proviso. Gorlaeus, since he allows modes into his ontology (§13.4), is able to describe the unity of the composite parts as "tantum modum essendi" (*Exerc.* 12, pp. 226–7), an application of the theory of modes that can be found as well in Suárez (*Disp. meta.* 7.1.18) and in Scheibler (*Metaphys.* I.6.3.4, pp. 76–7).

authors ensures that the debate at this juncture is highly complex. It is worth noting, however, that proponents of the rigorous unitarian conception of substantial unity have a straightforward way of responding to this line of attack, a response not open to others. In cases where a body is simply a collection of integral parts, there is nothing about those parts that guarantees unity. Similarly, for the pluralist regarding substantial form, it is possible for the body to fragment without the parts' going out of existence—that is, indeed, the very point of the pluralist doctrine (§25.3). If, however, the parts of a hylomorphic composite are conceived along unitarian lines, then they cannot all exist apart from the whole, because they are individuated by that whole (§25.2). The unitarian version of hylomorphism thus gets restrictions on composition for free.

It is an interesting feature of recent scholarship on Descartes that all of the lines of thought just canvassed have been put forward as his theory of material substance. There are those who think he invokes hylomorphism to individuate bodies (at least in the human case), those who think he allows scattered bodies, and those who read him as a material monist—even though the textual support for any of these interpretations is thin to the point of being practically invisible.[21] What we have here is an instance of the principal occupational hazard faced by the historian of philosophy: not the oft-censured temptation to read historical texts anachronistically, but the larger and yet rarely acknowledged temptation to suppose that a great philosopher will have great answers to all the great problems of philosophy. I myself have struggled with Descartes's views in this domain for as long as I have been working on this book, and have reluctantly come to conclude—as I have suggested several times already (§24.5, §25.6)—that we should give up the idea that Descartes has a theory of material substance. To be sure, if he has one, he never tells us what it is. Many Cartesian scholars have accordingly viewed it as their professional obligation to advance one or another speculative solution. Far better, I have come to think, is simply to acknowledge that this is not an area where Descartes has a positive theory.

Since it is surely not the case that Descartes never considered the fundamental metaphysical question of what counts as a material substance, his quietism in this domain is presumably intentional. Of course, we cannot know why he made this choice, and so this is one of those places where scholarship quickly gives way to something more like gossip (§20.5). My own guess is that this is another question that Descartes regards as best left unanswered, for fear his project get bogged down in obscure scholastic metaphysics (§8.4). Still more speculatively, as suggested in §25.6, I think Descartes was strongly inclined toward anti-realism regarding material substances. This is not to say that he thinks there are no material substances. On the contrary, everything in the realm of *res extensa* is a material substance (or a mode of it), and indeed there are infinitely many such substances (§26.1). But I suspect Descartes was inclined to doubt that the difference between genuine things and mere aggregates

A characteristically heterodox discussion is Carpenter's, who argues against all sides in the debate and thus concludes that there is "no true composition" (*Phil. libera* II.9). But it is not clear what follows from this. Carpenter clearly does not embrace strict or even weak permanence. Perhaps he means to reject not the existence of wholes but the existence of parts, along Digby's lines (§26.4).

[21] For Descartes as a monist, see note 11 above. For the idea that he embraces scattered objects, see Stuart, "Descartes's Extended Substances." For his alleged embrace of hylormorphism, see §24.5.

corresponds to any very deep facts about the natural world. Rather than say as much, and provoke pointless controversy, he chose to remain silent.

It is not hard to see why Descartes would have despaired of any illuminating story about material substances. No matter whether one looks upward in the direction of increasing composition, or downward in the direction of increasing simplicity, Descartes's conception of *res extensa* lacks the resources to draw principled distinctions between what does and does not count as a substance. This is clear enough looking upward. Like any strict corpuscularian, Descartes sees all cases of material composition as simply various patterns of particles in motion. Some patterns will be stable and others fleeting, but there can be no principled distinction between those aggregates that are true unities and those that are mere heaps. To be sure, Descartes readily talks as if he endorses our commonsense metaphysics of cats and stones. Indeed, he is quite a bit more ecumenical than most during our period: the human body counts, as does the mind–body composite (§25.6); stones count, as does a piece of gold, as do bread and clothing.[22] In general, it is easy to suppose he would be willing to count any continuous region of *res extensa* as a substance. Looking downward, the story is much the same. Because Descartes rejects atomism (§5.4) and insists on the actuality of all the integral parts of any body (§26.1), infinitely far down, he has no privileged level that he might single out as uniquely real. Hence just as he lacks the resources to defend the ontology of common sense at the macro-level, so he lacks the resources to defend strict permanence at the micro-level. (Gorlaeus, in virtue of postulating metaphysically simple atoms, has such a privileged foundation. Hobbes, by allowing scattered objects [§28.4], does not need to privilege any level.)

There are, at this point, endless questions that one might ask about Descartes's view. Must a region be continuous, to count as a substance? How continuous? Must it be stable? How stable? Is Descartes committed to rejecting the part–whole identity thesis? Would the existence of wholes as something over and over their parts fit into his austere ontology? Could he instead coherently insist on part–whole identity? Can wholes be identified with their parts, in a theory that recognizes no smallest parts, meaning that every part is itself a whole, infinitely far down? (Ockham combined these views, but Ockham had metaphysical resources that Descartes eschews.) These are excellent questions to ask of someone who has a theory of substance. Descartes, however, I have come to believe, has no theory, realist or anti-realist. Here we might recall his retort to Gassendi (§8.4): "he put to me a great many questions of a kind that do not need to be answered in order to prove what I asserted in my writings, and that the most ignorant people could raise more of, in a quarter of an hour, than all the wisest people could deal with in their whole lifetimes. This is why I have not bothered to answer any of them" (IXA:213).

Having long sought and failed to find any coherent, textually supported theory of material substance in Descartes, I have come to think that he simply declines to offer

---

[22] For examples of Descartes's commitment to ordinary bodies as substances, see, e.g. Fourth Replies, VII:222 (the hand, the whole body, the mind–body composite); Third Meditation, VII:44 (a stone); to Clerselier, IV:372 (bread and gold); Sixth Replies, VII:441 (clothing). Kaufman's "Cartesian Substances" makes an extended case for taking such commitments seriously, and I am indebted to him for many discussions of this material, though his conclusions differ from my own.

one. Rather than attempt to moor the very last of the surviving Aristotelian categories onto some solid theoretical ground, Descartes chooses to let it quietly drift away. Whether this should be considered a fault depends on one's level of enthusiasm for speculative metaphysics. But Descartes is not the end of our story, and in the final two chapters I will consider various seventeenth-century attempts to salvage some vestiges of a commonsense ontology of substance, in the face of puzzles regarding change over time.

29

Identity over Time

It would be natural to suppose that the question of identity over time emerges as a philosophical problem only toward the close of our four centuries. For the scholastics, one might suppose, the hylomorphic framework resolves all such questions as soon as they arise, leaving such questions of diachronic identity to take center stage only once the Aristotelian framework is abandoned. So one might suppose, both given the existing scholarly literature on the subject, and given the sorts of conclusions reached in earlier chapters. The reality, however, is quite different. Although it is true that many scholastic authors face no problem of diachronic identity, this is not always the case. In particular, many authors associated with nominalism have to deal with extremely difficult issues regarding identity through change, to which they respond by articulating a framework that distinguishes between identity in the strict sense, which is rarely satisfied, and various looser relationships that we treat as if they amounted to identity. It is this nominalist framework, I will argue, that shapes the more famous post-scholastic discussions of identity in Hobbes and Locke.

29.1. Identity Made Easy

Debates over diachronic identity go back to Hellenistic discussions of puzzle cases such as the ship of Theseus. These questions came into renewed prominence with the rising tide of philosophical speculation in the early twelfth century. Peter Abaelard and other so-called Nominales defended the thesis that *Nulla res crescit*—"Nothing grows"—seemingly denying that material objects ever do endure through change. The only identity over time, on this view, would be absolute and complete sameness down to all of a thing's integral parts. Naturally, this claim met with considerable opposition.[1]

---

[1] The question of identity through growth is said to go back to Epicharmus in the fifth century BCE, and is briefly considered by Plato in the *Symposium* (207d–e). On the Hellenistic debates, which seem to have occurred primarily between the Academics and the Stoics, see Long and Sedley, *Hellenistic Philosophers* sec. 28, and also Sedley, "Stoic Criterion"; Eric Lewis, "Stoics on Identity"; and Sorabji, *Self* pt. II. Tellingly, the Stoics responded to Academic puzzles over identity by invoking metaphysical parts: substance and quality.

It seems unlikely to be a coincidence that the Hellenistic debate, couched in terms of whether anything grows, is taken up in exactly that same peculiar form by Abaelard. It is unclear, however, how he knew about these debates. It is also unclear precisely how to interpret the views of Abaelard and other Nominales, in part because the texts here are rather thin. See Arlig, "Abelard's Assault" and "Medieval Mereology"; Desmond Henry, *Medieval Mereology* pp. 92–139; King,

In the thirteenth century these earlier metaphysical discussions were flooded over by the Greco-Arabic Aristotelian tradition, which swept away much of twelfth-century logic and metaphysics, including these debates over diachronic identity. It is easy to see why these debates in particular might have seemed outmoded, because within an Aristotelian framework it is not obvious that there is any special problem about identity over time. In postulating a substantial form that persists for as long as the substance persists, the Aristotelian seemingly has a straightforward account of what makes a substance persist. As we saw in Chapters 24–5, the details here are complex and subject to considerable debate, but on any version the Aristotelian would seem to have a metaphysical part—the substantial form—that is ready-made to dissolve the problem of diachronic identity.

Accordingly, one finds only the most desultory discussions of identity and change among the classical authors of scholasticism, all the way through Scotus.[2] Although the debate over the plurality of substantial forms gave rise to extremely nuanced discussions of the identity conditions of a material substance and its parts (see Ch. 25), the question of how a thing endures through change was regarded as settled. One can see the rapid transformation that took place by first considering William of Auvergne's *De anima* (c.1240), written with some knowledge of the burgeoning Aristotelian movement—especially as it was manifested by Avicenna—but generally resistant to that influence. William takes up Avicenna's thoroughly Aristotelian position on diachronic identity: that what makes a human being the same over time is its soul, which endures even as the underlying matter is constantly replaced by the ordinary biological processes of nutrition and growth. According to William, "this doctrine is not only contrary to the Christian faith but also in itself impossible" (*De anima* II.1). For a body to be alive, William charges, just is for it to endure through such biological processes, and for it to die just is for it to cease to exist. Moreover, if the body were to change in this way, then the human being would change its identity, because mere identity of form would not be enough to preserve the identity of the composite. Finally, moving onto theological ground, William asks which body would be resurrected on this sort of account. Since there would be no reason for one rather than "infinitely many others" to be resurrected, they would all have to be resurrected, a monstrosity that, according to William, goes beyond the wildest of poetic fictions.

Amazingly, William says nothing at all about what makes our changing body the same over time, as it grows and decays. That debate effectively stops with him, however, because the next generation of Parisian theologians would embrace the Aristotelian model that William rejects. As a result, they have no need to worry about the body's changing over time, provided that the soul endures. Aquinas, for instance, readily admits that

---

"Metaphysics"; Martin, "Logic of Growth"; Normore, "Abelard and the School of the Nominales" and "Tradition of Medieval Nominalism."

[2] Scotus does devote a disputed question to personal identity—"An haec sit vera 'Socrates senex difffert a se ipso puero'" (*In Isagoge* q. 24)—but the discussion is technical and focused on peripheral issues. His treatment of the resurrection in *Ord.* IV.43 is not without interest, as is shown in Cross, "Identity," but does not yield a developed theory of diachronic identity.

the human body, over one's lifetime, does not always have the same parts materially, but only specifically. Materially, the parts come and go, and this does not prevent a human being from being numerically one from the beginning of his life until the end. (*Summa contra gent.* IV.81.4157)

This would be the common consensus of scholastic authors throughout our period, and it is uncontroversial enough that in the late sixteenth century the Coimbrans can cite both Aquinas and Ockham—the two bookends of the scholastic corpus—as authorities for the view that "Socrates, in continuous succession, acquires some parts and loses others" (*In Phys.* I.9.5.2). Given the presence of an enduring substantial form, such facts struck many as unproblematic, and ship-of-Theseus style worries could stay on the sideline.

This consensus regarding the changeability of underlying matter may seem surprising, inasmuch as it might seem to clash with two different aspects of scholastic Aristotelianism: first, with the doctrine that prime matter is conserved through all change (§2.5); second, with the doctrine that the parts of a material substance are individuated by its substantial form (§24.2). There is, however, no conflict between these theses. What the Coimbrans (and Aquinas, and Ockham) accept is that a material substance can gain and lose integral parts—through growth, for instance, or through a part's being forcibly removed. As we saw in Chapter 26, integral parts are themselves substances, albeit imperfect, and each such part can be understood to have its own prime matter. So what the conservation thesis predicts in such a case is that the matter will go with the part: for a substance to gain an integral part is for it to gain a certain chunk of prime matter, suitably informed, and similarly to lose an integral part is to lose a chunk of informed prime matter. With respect to the second of the above theses—the individuation of the parts by the substantial form—there is also no conflict. That thesis maintains that the integral parts of a body take their identity from their form. The implication is that when a material substance loses a part, that part loses its identity. (A severed hand is a hand in name only [Aristotle, *Meteor.* 389b31].) The thesis does not maintain that a body cannot acquire new parts—no more than it insists that a body cannot lose parts. The requirement is only that those parts that have been gained become something new, in virtue of coming to exist as part of a larger whole. To say they take on a new identity, however, is not to say that they become identical with any other part of the body, or to deny that they are indeed *new* and *distinct* parts of an enduring whole. Aristotle himself had discussed this phenomenon at some length in *Generation and Corruption* I.5, under the heading of growth, and this became one of the principal topics of discussion in commentaries on that work. Scholastic authors thus had a very vivid sense of the difficulties in accounting for diachronic identity in terms of bodily identity. Such difficulties were often thought to pose little difficulty for diachronic identity in general, however, because of course the substantial form was thought to endure. As Ockham puts it, "someone certainly is said to be numerically the same human being, because the intellective soul, which is a simple form, remains in the whole body and in each part of the body" (*Sent.* IV.13 [*Opera theol.* VII:264]). The situation is, however, much more complex than these brief remarks suggest, and the trouble in fact seems to have begun with Ockham.[3]

29.2. Identity Made Hard: Ockham

Given what I have said so far, one might have expected that diachronic identity would continue to be a non-issue throughout the scholastic era. In fact this is not the case. By the middle of the fourteenth century, in the work of John Buridan and allied figures, one finds an extremely interesting and sophisticated body of literature on these issues, which has only recently begun to receive any attention from scholars. Although the label 'nominalist' often obscures more than it clarifies (§5.3), there is a striking consensus on the topic of diachronic identity among authors associated with that movement— enough to justify our speaking of a *nominal theory of identity*.

The reason one finds this effusion of interest in diachronic identity is that these authors accept a pair of theses that make it exceptionally difficult—even for an Aristotelian—to account for endurance through change. First and foremost, they accept the *part–whole identity thesis*, according to which the whole composite material substance is nothing over and above its various parts (§28.5). This alone poses a quite severe obstacle to diachronic identity, because it—together with the indiscernibility of identicals—entails that if a thing gains or loses a part, then it is no longer the same thing. Second, these authors deny that substantial forms can ordinarily transfer from one subject to another. This *no-transfer principle*, as I will call it, means that, when the integral parts of a substance change, the substantial form must also change, at least partially. (For the vexed question of whether substantial forms have parts, see §26.6.) This no-transfer principle, when conjoined with the part–whole identity thesis, makes even more trouble for diachronic identity, for it now looks as if substances that gain or lose integral parts (as all living things presumably do) will not be the same with respect to either matter or form. It seems, in other words, as if these theses conjoined make even partial identity impossible. For the nominalists, committed as they are to these two theses, diachronic identity turns out to be surprisingly elusive.

The seeds of this predicament lie in Ockham himself, because Ockham accepts the two theses just mentioned. We have seen already his commitment to part–whole identity (§28.5). The force of that commitment emerges in his discussion of the resurrection, which is one of the few places where scholastic authors can be counted on to consider questions of diachronic identity. Taking it as an article of faith that individual human beings will live again, after death, Ockham asks whether this entails

---

[3] For a clear statement of the easy Aristotelian solution, see Burley, *De toto et parte* p. 301: "homo in iuventute et senectute est idem totum secundum formam et habet eamdem animam omnino, sed non est idem secundum materiam, quia unam materiam habet in una aetate et aliam in alia. . . ."

The easy Aristotelian solution to identity exerts a pull even on authors who are in general not very sympathetic to scholasticism. Digby, for instance, insists that "as long as the form remains the same, the thing is the same, and the matter is the same. Were it not for this, how could any body under heaven remain the same even but for a short moment's space?" (*Discourse concerning Vegetation* p. 93). But Digby is no Aristotelian: though he thinks one can say that "all bodies are composed of matter and form," he immediately adds that "I do not mean that there are two distinct entities, which being put together like meal and water do concur jointly to compose a body, as they make bread" (pp. 89–90).

that numerically the same body will be resurrected and joined with our souls. Presumably, God *might* do this if he wanted to. But would he *have* to do it, for the same human being to exist again? Ockham treats this question as equivalent to the question of whether matter belongs to the essence of a composite substance. In arguing for the affirmative, he is particularly worried about an opponent who claims that what is essential to a material substance is merely matter of the same *kind*, rather than the particular matter the substance possesses right now. Against that position Ockham deploys, in effect, the part–whole identity thesis, insisting that "that is not the same whole that does not have the same parts" (*Sent.* IV.13 [*Opera theol.* VII:260]). Hence for a thing to lose or gain a part, even if it is replaced by one of the same kind, is for that thing to become something new. Ockham spells out the consequences of this view as follows:

Having seen this, I say to the question that matter is part of the essence and quiddity of the composite, as was said. And where there is one matter in something and then another, in succession, there is in some way a real distinction between the same thing and itself at one time 3 and another, because something belongs to the essence of the one that does not belong to the essence of the other. And likewise where there is *something* entirely (*simpliciter*) the same at the start and at the end of the change, the whole can be said to be really the same, on account of 6 the identity of that [persisting part]. (ibid., VII:264)

Ockham takes the part–whole identity thesis to commit him to a form of what is now called mereological essentialism, according to which the parts of a thing are essential to it: lose a part and the thing is no longer the same. But although he commits himself to this quite expressly at lines 2–4 and elsewhere in the discussion, he is rather cagey about just what mereological essentialism implies. He clearly does not wish to understand the claim in a very radical sense, as maintaining that a whole with a new part becomes something *entirely* new. This would be an odd result, given that the rest of the parts are the same, and given that *ex hypothesi* the whole just is its parts. But in some sense the whole *is* something different from what it was. So Ockham says in the passage just quoted that in such a case there is "in some way a real distinction" (line 3) but yet "the whole can be said to be really the same" (line 6). Exactly how both of these claims can be true is not at all clear, but Ockham tells us nothing more about it.[4]

   Ockham's subsequent discussion focuses on the extent to which living things can be said to be really the same through change, in virtue of having some part that persists unchanged. He makes things easier for himself by supposing that living things of all kinds always retain some kernel of unchanging matter, from birth until death (ibid., VII:268–9). But he makes the situation much harder by endorsing the second of the complicating theses described above: that substantial forms generally depend on their material subject, and so change as that matter changes:

---

[4] Ockham's commitment to mereological essentialism appears in other contexts, without explanation or defense. See, e.g., *In Phys.* IV.18.3 (*Opera phil.* V:199): "impossibile est quod aliquid secundum se totum distinctum ab omnibus aliis sit in rerum natura nisi aliqua pars eius sit in rerum natura.... Immo impossibile est quod aliquid unum secundum se totum distinctum ab aliis sit in rerum natura nisi quaelibet pars eius sit in rerum natura. Unde si una sola pars non sit in rerum natura, nec ipsum totum est." His most detailed discussion of these issues is in *Quaest. var.* 6.2 (*Opera theol.* VIII).

   Given the ancient pedigree of the part–whole identity thesis (Ch. 28 note 17), one would expect to find a long history of interest in mereological essentialism. Indeed, Sextus Empiricus regards the view as the sort of common belief that can be legitimately taken for granted as a premise in his destructive arguments (*Outlines of Pyrrhonism* III.98).

   For a recent discussion of Ockham's views on identity very much in line with my treatment here, see Normore, "Ockham's Metaphysics of Parts."

When an animal with an extended form grows, ... just as there is growth and variation in matter, so too in the extended form. This is proved, because an extended form does not pass anew into some matter that it had not previously informed. (ibid., VII:261)

This means that hylomorphism will be surprisingly unhelpful in accounting for identity through change. When matter changes, form changes, and so a material substance can have only as much formal identity through time as it has material identity through time. Indeed, if not for the kernel of unchanging matter that Ockham postulates in living things, he would seemingly have no basis for insisting on any sort of diachronic identity for living things. *Except*, that is, in the human case. The above passage applies only to animals that have an "extended form" (lines 1, 2). For Ockham, all forms are extended, except the rational soul, which exists holenmerically throughout the body (§16.4), and persists unchanged through change to the body and even, of course, apart from the body.[5]

With these results in hand, Ockham summarizes his account of how living things persist through change:

I say, then, that in the case of growth there is not entirely (*simpliciter*) the same individual in every way before growth and after, because where there is one matter and then another, belonging to the quiddity and essence of the thing, there is in some way a real distinction,   3
because something belongs to the essence of the one that does not belong to the essence of the other, as was said. In the same way, in the case of the resurrection, it will not be in every way the same human being before resurrection and after, because according to all the doctors there   6
is not entirely the same matter numerically in the resurrected body as there was before the resurrection, nor is there the same sensory form—supposing that it is something distinct from the intellective soul and is extended—because in that case one should speak of it just as one   9
speaks of matter in growth in all cases. Still, someone certainly is said to be numerically the same human being, because the intellective soul, which is a simple form, remains in the whole and in each part. (ibid., VII:264)   12

---

[5] Ockham treats his commitment to the no-transfer principle as uncontroversial, and so later on do Buridan and other authors associated with him. For a particularly detailed discussion, see pseudo-Marsilius of Inghen, *In Phys.* I.10, who defends the no-transfer principle and holds "quod opinio ponens augmentationem in viventibus fieri per extensionem formae in plurali materia est falsa. Verbi gratia, quidam ponunt quod in augmentatione plantae anima vegetativa quae preexistebat informat materiam nutrimenti supervenientis sine generatione alicuius novae partis formae" (f. 10ra).

Paul of Venice provides a good example of an author who takes for granted the contrary view, that substantial forms are transferable: "quaelibet forma substantialis vivens per totam suam periodum maneat eadem numero primo modo [i.e., quod nec in toto nec in parte est substantialiter variatum]" (*Summa phil. nat.*, III.15, f. 44ra). If he is aware that this is a controversial thesis, he does not here show it.

By the time of Zabarella, the two positions have hardened into opposed camps, "utraque cum maximis difficultatibus coniuncta" (*De rebus nat.* De accretione ch. 13, col. 792). Zabarella in the end sides with those who favor the transferability of forms (ch. 15).

An interesting corpuscularian perspective on the no-transfer principle appears in Basso, who quotes Zabarella's discussion at length, and contends that, contrary to Zabarella's ultimate conclusion, the arguments in favor of rejecting transfer are decisive. The moral Basso derives, however, is that substantial form cannot serve its intended purpose and so should be rejected entirely (*Phil. nat.* De formis III 2.3–4).

The notion of substantial form's changing over time, along with the matter it informs, raises a host of complex questions. The situation looks relatively straightforward on views, like Oresme's, that take the whole substantial form to consist merely in the sum of the partial substantial forms (see §26.6). The situation seems more complex for authors like Buridan who deny that the integral parts of a body have their own partial substantial forms, because Buridan then needs an account of how the one substantial form of the whole partially changes, without entirely ceasing to exist. In a way, the problem of diachronic unity for the whole substance is simply recapitulated here, at the level of substantial form.

Oresme discusses change to material substantial forms in the context of his general theory of the intension and remission of forms, at *De configuratione* II.13 (p. 300).

The passage shows Ockham continuing to want it both ways. On the one hand, no living thing that endures through change will be entirely the same (lines 1–10). This is so both for the matter and for any extended—that is, non-holenmeric—substantial form that a thing has. Given Ockham's version of pluralism (§25.4), he can apply this claim even to the human sensory soul (lines 8–10). Despite this result, however, Ockham still has a way to account for the identity of a human being, even through that most radical change of death and resurrection, because of the simple, holenmeric intellective soul, which persists.

The position Ockham arrives at is unstable and perplexing. It might not be obvious that this is so: one might suppose that Ockham is stating a fairly predictable result for any hylomorphic analysis of diachronic identity: that of course a material composite changes in part, with respect to its matter, but that of course it also remains the same, with respect to its form. But the view is not nearly so straightforward. What one would expect from an Aristotelian account is an insistence that the composite wholly endures—endures *simpliciter*. One can say this, however, only if one rejects part–whole identity, in favor of the view that the composite whole is something distinct from its parts. One finds this sort of account in Scotus, for whom what is destroyed at the death of a living thing is "some positive entity that is not the material part, the formal part, or the parts [together]" (*Ord.* IV.43.1 [Wadding X n. 4]). One seems to find it in Suárez, too, who contends that in living things "the whole substance is permanent *simpliciter*," even if "the loss and gain of substantial parts is continuous or nearly so" (*Disp. meta.* 50.7.4). If, instead, the whole just is its parts, then when the parts change the whole must lose its identity. Ockham sees this quite clearly, and puts that result in the strongest way possible: that the integral parts of a body are essential to it. Hence we arrive at mereological essentialism. But what is perplexing is that Ockham refuses to follow this result to what would seem to be the inevitable conclusion: that material substances are never the same through growth and decay. Instead he thinks there is room for some sort of compromise view: that "in some way" (line 3) identity fails, but that yet so long as there is some part that endures unchanged, there is another sense in which the substance endures. This sort of partial verdict is perhaps not so odd. But what makes the whole treatment especially curious, and unstable, is that Ockham seems to think the result in the human case is not partial at all. For he ends the above passage with what seems to be the wholly unqualified conclusion that "certainly" (*bene*) the human being is numerically the same, because of its intellective soul. Why one should say that a human being certainly endures, in virtue of having one enduring essential part, rather than instead saying that it certainly does *not* endure, in virtue of losing other essential parts, is entirely unclear. So far as I have found, Ockham says nothing more to clarify the situation. The issue becomes much clearer, however, in later discussions.

29.3. Nominal Identity: Buridan and Oresme

The difficulties that Ockham's discussion inchoately raises receive an explicit and sophisticated treatment in various natural philosophers from the mid-fourteenth to early fifteenth century. Buridan seems to have been the first, in a series of discussions that runs throughout his work. One of the most extensive treatments, from his *Physics* commentary, takes up the question of "whether Socrates today is the same as he was yesterday" (I.10), supposing that today Socrates has either grown or had a part removed. After considering various ingenious arguments for one side and then the other, Buridan proceeds to offer an analysis of diachronic identity on the basis of "three ways in which we are accustomed to say that one thing is numerically the same as another" (f. 13vab). These three ways are so interesting, and would be so influential on subsequent discussions, that they are worth quoting at length:

The first way is by being totally (*totaliter*) the same—namely, because this is that and there is nothing belonging to the whole of this that does not belong to the whole of the other and vice versa. This is numerical sameness in the most proper sense. According to this way it should be said that I am not the same as I was yesterday, for yesterday there was something that belonged to my whole that has now been dissolved, and something else that yesterday did not belong to my whole which later, by nutrition, was made to belong to my whole.... 6

In a second way, however, one thing is said to be *partially* the same as another—namely, because this is part of that (and this is especially said if it is a major or principal part), or else because this and that take part in something that is a major or principal part of each.... And in this way a human being remains the same through the totality of his life because the soul remains totally the same, and the soul is a principal—indeed the most principal—part. A horse, however, does not remain the same in this way, and indeed neither does the human body. And in this way it is certainly true that you are the same one who was baptized forty years ago—especially since this holds of us principally because of the soul and not the body. It is also in this way true that I can pursue you for injuries or be required to repay you, because harmful or meritorious deeds also come principally from the soul and not from the body. So too we do not say that you were generated yesterday because we do not say that something is generated absolutely (*simpliciter*) unless it is generated as a whole or with respect to its major or principal part. 18

But in a still third way, less properly, one thing is said to be numerically the same as another according to the continuity of distinct parts, one in succession after another. In this way the Seine is said to be the same river after a thousand years, although properly speaking nothing is now a part of the Seine that was part of it ten years ago. For thus the ocean is said to be perpetual, as is this earthly world, and a horse is the same through its whole life and likewise so is the human body. (*In Phys.* I.10, f. 13vb) 24

Approached out of context, it would be quite puzzling why Buridan makes the choices he makes here. Why insist on the first, hyper-strict sense of total sameness? Why allow a human being to be the same over time only in the second, relatively weak sense of partial sameness? Why demote other animals to the third, still weaker category, making them akin to rivers? In light of Ockham's discussion, however, all of this is quite clear. Buridan reasons as he does because he shares Ockham's metaphysical commitments to the part–whole identity thesis, and to the no-transfer principle.

These motivations are made explicit in another extended discussion of this material, in Buridan's commentary on the *De generatione*, where he considers "whether something that grows remains wholly the same before and after" (I.13). His conclusions are what we should expect, given the discussion from the *Physics*: (1) a thing that grows is not totally the same as what it was; (2) a human being who grows is partially the same, in virtue of having the same intellective soul; (3) other animals are the same over time only in the way that a river is, in virtue of "the continuous succession of their parts."

Buridan's rationale for these conclusions is here made clear. Other animals can remain numerically the same only in the third and weakest sense because at most "lesser and fewer" of their parts endure through change. Not their soul (or at any rate not most of their soul), because "in the case of material forms—that is, those drawn from the potentiality of matter—the form does not pass from matter to matter" (*In Gen. et cor.* I.13, p. 190). It is then only human beings, among animals, that can be said to persist in the second way, in virtue of retaining their principal part.

Buridan is also clear about why human beings cannot be totally the same through growth and decay. To gain or lose parts would violate the indiscernibility of identicals:

Let that which yesterday was precisely Socrates be *a*, and let that which is added to it, by which it grows, be called *b*. It is obvious that now Socrates is composed of *a* and *b*. Therefore Socrates is not totally the same as *a*, and nevertheless yesterday he was totally the same as that *a*. Therefore it is clear that Socrates now is not totally the same as Socrates was yesterday. (ibid., p. 189)

This argument is sound if and only if one assumes the part–whole identity thesis. Without it, one can insist that Socrates today is not just the composite of the integral parts *a* and *b*, but that he is some further thing, *c*, which is in fact what Socrates was yesterday as well. Buridan is well aware that he needs this as a premise: the first preliminary argument of the *quaestio* had run as follows: "The whole is its parts, as is commonly said; but the parts do not remain the same—rather, they come and go; therefore the question is false" (ibid., p. 188)—that is, identity is not preserved through growth. Buridan expressly endorses this argument, and indeed the more complex argument above (in terms of *a* and *b*) is just an elaboration on this simpler template.

Given such arguments, Buridan sees no option other than to retreat to a weaker notion of sameness to account for the diachronic identity of human beings. Interestingly, however, he makes an effort to suggest that this sort of weaker identity is sufficient for our being the same over time *simpliciter*. For after spelling out his account of our partial identity in virtue of our rational soul, he adds: "from this we can conclude that, speaking unconditionally and without qualification (*simpliciter et sine addito*), a human being remains the same from the start of his life up to the end, because we are accustomed to denominate a thing unconditionally and without qualification on the basis of its most principal part" (ibid., p. 190). This is evidently not to say that we in fact remain numerically the same in the strongest sense—he had just made it quite clear that we do not. The point instead seems to be that one can truly say, without qualification, that the same human being exists from birth until death, just because *this is the way we talk*. Buridan's insistence on this point is reminiscent of Ockham's puzzling insistence, seemingly contrary to what he had just been saying, that "someone certainly is said to be numerically the same human being." Buridan, unlike Ockham, explains why he insists on this point—or, at any rate, he explains the philosophical rationale for it. What both Ockham and Buridan leave unsaid is why they feel the need to insist on the point. That reason would seem to be the shadow of 1277, when the bishop of Paris had condemned the thesis "that through nutrition a human being can be made numerically and individually distinct" (ed. Piché, n. 148). The thirteenth-century figure who defended this thesis is unknown to us now. Clearly, though, by returning to this contentious issue, Ockham and Buridan were courting controversy. To try to inoculate themselves against censure, each insists that—contrary to what their views would seem to imply—in fact it is strictly true, without qualification, that a human being remains the same through time. What Buridan's discussion makes clear, however, is that this is one of those instances where the way we talk does not correspond with the metaphysical facts on the ground (§6.4). It is perfectly legitimate to say, without qualification, that Socrates persists through change—this is legitimate, because our customary idioms allow it. From a metaphysical point of view, however, such claims are liable to mislead, if they are understood as entailing that Socrates wholly survives.[6]

So far we have seen two approaches to identity through change: either to deny part–whole identity, and postulate that the substance is something distinct from the sum of its parts, or else to concede that material substances do not totally endure through growth. Buridan's explicit discussion inspired a series of subsequent treatments of these issues that explore a wider range of options. One such option, which scholastic authors could scarcely have missed, is to treat changeable material substances as successive rather than permanent entities. As we saw in Chapter 18, permanent entities exist all at once, whereas successive entities exist in virtue of having distinct parts spread out through time. The paradigmatic examples of successive entities are motion and time. But given that many material substances consist in a sequence of parts that come and go, it is obvious, from the scholastic perspective, that such things might themselves better be understood as successive entities. What we actually have here is a range of cases, as pseudo-Marsilius of Inghen explains, in a discussion plainly inspired by Buridan:

It should be noted that one finds three *differentiae* of natural things.
- First, there are some natural things that endure (*manent*) in virtue of the permanence of all their parts at once—without any addition, change, or subtraction being made. Examples are   3
  the sun, the heavens and other such parts of the heavens.
- Then there are other beings whose parts in no way endure at once. These entities instead consist in a continuous succession of their parts, one after another. Examples are time,   6
  motion, and other things of this sort.
- Third, there are some beings in between these two, which endure in virtue of the permanence of some of their parts, while other parts succeed one another either through   9
  generation and corruption or through addition and subtraction. Examples are animals, plants, and elemental mixtures of this sort. (*In Phys.* I.10, f. 9vb)

---

[6] Buridan offers the same account, more briefly, at *In De an.* II.7 (ed. Sobol, p. 100) and *In Meta.* VII.12. *In De an.* III.6 is also relevant, and quite interesting, although the discussion there is focused narrowly on the identity of the separated soul. The preliminary objections to *In Phys.* I.10 also indicate that Buridan's position is motivated by the part–whole identity thesis.

For further discussion of Buridan see Pluta, "Buridan's Theory of Identity," which offers both extended paraphrases and a slightly revised version of some of the texts, based on the best manuscripts. (My translation of *In Phys.* I.10 follows Pluta's revisions.)

Buridan's account is followed nearly verbatim by Marsilius of Inghen, *In Gen. et cor.* I.12. For a rather different and very interesting discussion, from a leading realist opponent of nominalism, see Paul of Venice, *Summa phil. nat.* III.15. Paul follows Buridan's general approach in that he focuses on endurance in virtue of the endurance of a principal part. But because he accepts that substantial forms are transferable through material change, he is able to apply this account much more widely than Buridan is, with interesting results. Paul also takes up these issues in his *Logica magna* pt. I tr. 14, large parts of which are edited, translated, and analyzed by Desmond Henry, *Medieval Mereology* pp. 481–518.

This usefully systematizes a range of different cases. Since Aristotelians take heavenly bodies to be unchanging, they are said to endure in the first, most complete sense. We might add that the human soul also endures in this way. Why not the whole human being? For authors like Scotus and Suárez, who treat the whole as something over and above its parts (§29.2), the composite whole might aptly be put into this first class—not of course because its parts do not change, but because a change to its parts does not make *it* endure any less. This does violence to pseudo-Marsilius's way of conceiving the situation, however, because he accepts the part–whole identity thesis, and so takes it that change to the part makes for a difference in how the whole endures. Accordingly, after this passage he immediately goes on to introduce Buridan's three degrees of diachronic identity, and endorses Buridan's diagnosis of what to say about human beings and other animals. Because all animals gain and lose parts, they can at best partly survive.

The second of the above *differentiae* is of course the class of successive entities. To say that their parts are in continuous succession is evidently to say that no part ever endures. Every part has merely instantaneous existence. Whether this is the right way to think about time and motion is a difficult issue, since it is unclear what their parts are (§18.3), but this at any rate seems to be how pseudo-Marsilius thinks of *entia successiva*. This line of thought is quite explicit in Nicole Oresme, who seems to have been the source for this aspect of pseudo-Marsilius's account. (Although Oresme is not ordinarily counted as one of the nominalists, his views are often quite similar to those of Buridan and others associated with nominalism in mid-fourteenth-century Paris.) On Oresme's very brief recital of this three-way distinction, to be "successive *simpliciter*" is to be such that "nothing of it that is in one part of time was in the preceding part of time" (*In Gen. et cor.* I.13, p. 115). This makes clear why scholastic authors do not want to treat animals as successive entities. Whereas a true successive entity has nothing permanent about it, animals—no matter how quickly they gain and lose parts—do at least have some measure of permanence in those parts. The parts endure at least for a little while. Hence pseudo-Marsilius (line 8 above) positions animals halfway between being fully permanent and fully successive, as what we might call semi-permanent.

In effect, this further three-way distinction imposes on Buridan's account a more fine-grained structure. Instead of simply distinguishing between things that gain and lose parts and things that do not, we can now distinguish between things that gradually have their parts replaced and things that are wholly replaced at every instant. All our authors take animals to be of the first kind. As we saw in §18.4, however, Oresme explicitly argues that it would be *possible* for a human being to be a fully successive entity, if God were to create a human substance for just an instant, then create another instantaneous human substance, and so on for the duration of that being's life. How we know we are in fact not like that is a difficult question that Oresme, and also Albert of Saxony, show some sensitivity to. Ultimately, however, as we saw in that earlier discussion, they could not take the possibility seriously. For present purposes let us simply observe that considerations of growth are scarcely enough to justify the radical idea that animals are wholly successive entities, unless one supposes that our growth and decay is so constant and rampant that no part of us ever endures through any space of time.

Both pseudo-Marsilius and Oresme think that animals and other semi-permanent entities can be said to be the same through time. But whereas pseudo-Marsilius simply follows Buridan's account, Oresme takes a somewhat different view, by insisting that in cases of complete replacement we should not speak of identity in any sense of the term:

The first conclusion is that in the case of merely successive entities there is not the same thing today as there was before. Instead, the whole taken categorematically is a single continuum. Nor likewise [is there the same thing today as there was before] in the case of things all the parts of which are succeeded by other new parts. So there is not the same water of the Seine now that there was two years ago. (*In Gen. et cor.* I.13, p. 116)

The passage begins by ruling out diachronic identity for purely successive entities. Oresme does not thereby mean to deny that such entities exist. We can properly speak of a single motion, and use 'the whole' categorematically so that it refers to the temporally extended thing that is a continuous event. His point is just that there is nothing in that event that is the same today as it was yesterday, which is precisely why, for Oresme, it counts as a successive rather than a permanent entity. The more controversial claim of this passage is that we should also not speak of identity in semi-permanent cases where there is the complete replacement of parts. Whereas Buridan had maintained that a river counts as the same over time in virtue of its parts being replaced in continuous succession, Oresme contends that this is not enough: that some of the parts must be the same throughout the process. He illustrates this notion with the ship of Theseus (ibid., obj. 5 & ad 5). As soon as part of the ship has been replaced, we can no longer say that it is totally the same, but only that it is partly the same. As more parts are moved, it comes to be less and less the same. So far, this agrees with Buridan's account. But whereas Buridan thinks that a river or a ship can survive the complete replacement of its parts, provided the replacement occurs in continuous succession, Oresme argues that as soon as that ship loses the last of its original parts, it is no longer the same ship. Living things, however, are not like that, because Oresme adheres to the standard view of his time—seen earlier in Ockham— that some kernel of the material parts of a living things endures throughout its life.[7]

The view Oresme arrives at is in a way fairly banal: he thinks that entities display total diachronic identity if they gain or lose no parts at all, and that they display partial diachronic identity if they lose some but not all of their parts. The more parts they retain, and the more important those parts are, the more appropriate it is to say that the thing endures. Questions of identity thus become extremely easy: even easier than on the more conventional Aristotelian approach sketched in §29.1. But can it be this easy to solve the puzzle of the ship of Theseus? One cost of this approach is that it requires accepting the rather surprising result that as soon as a thing loses even the slightest part, it is no longer wholly the same as it was. But this can just look like common sense, given that Oresme—like both Ockham and Buridan—can quickly affirm that the thing is of course *mostly* the same as it was. Thus to the objection that on his account the removal of one hair of fleece from a hat would make the hat something different,

---

[7] This idea has roots in earlier theological discussions. Peter Lombard, for instance, argues that there is an enduring kernel of matter that passes from Adam into every member of the human species (*Sent.* II.30). Scotus, too, defends the idea (*Ord.* IV.44.1 [Wadding X n. 17]).

Oresme serenely replies that "this hat is not that which it was before, but it is for the most part the hat it was before, and so we are accustomed to say that it is the same but not totally" (*In Phys.* I.7).

Interestingly, and contrary to the pattern we have seen so often, Oresme, Buridan, and others can talk this way not because they invoke additional metaphysical parts in their ontology, but because they refuse to do so. For authors who postulate the whole as something over and above its parts, it is hard to make sense of this breezy insistence that the ship or the hat is partly the same and partly different. For on such a view one seems forced to give an up-or-down answer to the question of identity: either that whole that is the ship is the same or it is not. In contrast, if the whole just is its parts, then if only some of the parts endure it seems just obvious that only some of the ship endures. This is perhaps an attractive feature of the account, so long as one is thinking of ships, hats, and other artifacts. But here is another cost of the view: one has to say that the dog that grew up from a puppy, or even the man who grew up from a boy, is only partly the same thing that it was. Whereas it seems obvious, at least pre-theoretically, that your dog is the very same dog you brought home as a puppy, and your boy the very same boy you brought home as a baby, none of the authors we are considering can allow this. In strict metaphysical fact, living things can at best be only partly the same as they once were.

Perhaps it is because of this cost that, before embracing this option, Oresme considers in some detail an alternative: that, as he puts it, a single thing can be many things in succession:

> Now, as for the solution to these difficulties [regarding identity through change], there are several ways of speaking. One is that just as one thing is many things separately at the same time, so too one thing is many things successively. The first, to be sure, is possible only 3 supernaturally, in the divine, but the second is true naturally. And so Socrates, who is now certain parts, will later—he himself—be other parts, whereas before he was still other parts. It is in this way that some say that a human being who is now a body and a soul will after death be 6 only a soul. (*In Gen. et cor.* I.13, p. 113)

With this in hand, Oresme goes on to solve the sorts of puzzles that we saw Buridan consider above, regarding, for instance, how the same Socrates can gain a part, so that if yesterday Socrates was *a*, then today he is *a* and *b*. On the proposed account, the answer is simple: what was *a* just is, today, *a* and *b*. Crucially, Oresme is not saying that the whole is something over and above its parts—that there is a single, unchanging thing that is Socrates that wholly exists yesterday and today. Rather, he concedes that what we have here is "many things successively" (line 3). He *has* to say this, because he had announced at the start of the question that he would treat the part–whole identity thesis as axiomatic—a "manifest truth that everyone properly disposed grants by distinct instinct" (ibid.). (Interestingly, even while he says this, Oresme admits there are arguments against part–whole identity that he does not know how to answer.)

What does it mean for many things in succession to be just one single thing? As a model, Oresme mentions the supernatural possibility of one thing's being, at the same time, many things (lines 2–3). He does not say which supernatural case he has in mind, but the only one that would seem to serve his purposes is the Trinity, according to which God is at once three and one. (This is how Albert of Saxony later understands the example.) It is no doubt discouraging to get the Holy Trinity as an analogue to how material substances naturally persist through change, but at least this helps make clear what Oresme is offering us. The view boldly maintains the position that seems on its face to be contradictory: that what is genuinely one and the same thing can, over time, have contradictory features. Although it would be contradictory for Socrates to be *a* and *b* and *at the same time* to be just *a* (for instance, for Socrates both to have his little finger and not have it) there is in fact no contradiction in Socrates's being two and one *over time*. In effect—although Oresme does not say this—he is suggesting we reject the indiscernibility of identicals in diachronic cases. It is not contradictory for the same thing to have ten fingers and not have ten fingers, provided the having and the not-having occur at different times. Ten-fingered-Socrates can be the very same thing as nine-fingered-Socrates, over time. Socrates's fingers can be ten and nine.

This is not a proposal that we are supposed to like, or that Oresme himself likes. The comparison to the Trinity is surely *intended* to be discouraging. Oresme is telling us that we can make the problem of identity through change go away only if we suppose that the sort of mystery the faith postulates in the Godhead is one that is found all the time in the natural realm. One thing just is many things, in defiance of the apparent dictates of logic. Oresme spends some time showing how, if one does go down this road, the puzzles of change over time all disappear. But he ends on a negative note, by showing how this view threatens to prove too much. The view, he says, "cannot be generally true" (ibid., p. 115), because if it were we would have to say that a house could exist forever, through unlimited change, as could a ship. The present view would relax the conditions on identity to such a degree that we would never be in a position to deny diachronic identity: we would have to say that the house or the ship is *wholly* the same, even if *all* its parts are replaced. Although, as noted earlier, this result may seem attractive in the case of Socrates, Oresme finds it quite counterintuitive in the case of non-living things. Accordingly, although he never expressly disavows this approach to diachronic identity, he "sets it aside" at this point, and turns instead to the framework for partial identity that Buridan had articulated.[8]

[8] Oresme makes particularly clear the central role of the two complicating theses I described in the previous section. They turn up as the second and third of four preliminary principles: "... praemitto aliqua pro principiis observanda. Primum est quod idem animal manet a principio vitae usque ad finem et idem homo. Secundum est quod totum integrale est idem quod suae partes integrales nec est aliqua res superaddita.... Tertio, suppono quod forma materialis non potest esse sine materia nec potest transire de materia in materiam. Quarto, suppono quod animal est compositum ex materia et forma, scilicet ex anima et corpore" (*In De gen. et cor.* I.13, pp. 112–13). With respect to the first two of these theses, Oresme makes the remarkable observation that he accepts them without knowing how to resolve the arguments that get made against them: "tamen non propter rationes quarum non video solutiones negare presumam tam manifestas veritates, quae naturali instinctu ab omnibus bene dispositis conceduntur" (ibid.). For Oresme see also the extensive discussion in *In Phys.* I.7.

Oresme's suggestion that one thing can be many things over time is repeated in much the same terms by Albert of Saxony and, briefly, by pseudo-Marsilius (*In Phys.* I.10). Albert's two extensive discussions, although following Oresme very closely, add a few more useful details: "... possumus imaginari quod sicut supernaturaliter una res numero est plures res numero—sciliet pater, filius et spiritus sanctus—ita naturaliter una res numero potest esse successive plures res numero, quamvis non simul" (*In Gen. et cor.* I.10, f. 138rb); "... imaginor quod, sicut supernaturaliter una res numero est plures res numero, ita naturaliter una res numero est successive plures res numero, ita quod una res numero [om. *est*] corruptibilis, quamvis non simul sit plures res numero, tamen bene successive" (*In Phys.* I.8, p. 126).

29.4. Identity Made Problematic

The nominalist framework for identity remained influential through the later scholastic period. John Major's *Physics* commentary, published in Paris in 1526, at the start of the Scotsman's second term of teaching there, contains a beautifully clear defense of the nominalist view, distinguishing between identity "properly and metaphysically speaking" and identity "vulgarly speaking" (I.2.9, f. b4r). The first requires complete sameness of all the parts, a position we have been brought to expect because Major had just finished a lengthy argument for the thesis that the whole is equivalent to its parts. The second covers a range of cases running from that of a human being, where the most principal part is conserved, to a river, where nothing is conserved but there is at least continuity in its flow. Thus Major concludes that "Socrates is not metaphysically the same in his old age and in his youth . . . , because his parts in old age are distinct from his parts in his youth" (ibid., f. b4v).

Alongside this relatively moderate nominalist line, one begins to see more radical positions, and a growing sense that there is a deep problem about identity over time. As in so many other cases, these later developments are foreshadowed back in the fourteenth century by Nicholas of Autrecourt. Autrecourt's proto-corpuscularianism leads him to the permanence thesis: that naturally speaking nothing ever comes into or goes out of existence (§28.2). This is of course one way of dealing with the problem of diachronic identity, supposing one is willing to embrace one or another of the radical ontologies considered in the previous chapter. Such a theory does not inevitably lead to giving up on the existence of persisting human beings, because they can be identified with their incorruptible souls. This is the view that David Gorlaeus—another proponent of a radically revisionary account—would articulate at the start of the seventeenth century (§28.4). Autrecourt, however, is unwilling to concede even this much to commonsense ontology. He contends that although we speak as if an old man is the same as a boy, in fact this is not true at all. Without even bothering to cite the obvious sorts of changes in material composition that had concerned Ockham, Buridan, and Oresme, Autrecourt takes for granted that the only hope of accounting for human diachronic identity is in terms of something like sameness of soul, a hypothesis he then resists by showing how the various "powers" of a boy and an old man differ. Although his remarks here are quite compressed, his point seems to be that such differences in powers undermine whatever sort of psychic continuity one might want to postulate as accounting for the enduring individual. Autrecourt pays special attention to the power of memory, where one might suppose there is some sort of notable sameness over time. Even here, however, he argues against sameness: to remember is for one power to conceive of objects that had in the past been conceived of by a distinct power. What gives the illusion of sameness is the continuity of such powers: "because the change of powers is continuously toward some very close state, [the individual] is always said to be numerically the same. This would perhaps not be so if a one-year-old boy were suddenly made old" (*Tractatus* p. 252). Since we do not experience any such sudden discontinuities, we speak as if there is genuine identity in persons over time. In actual fact, however, there is none.

This conclusion leads Autrecourt into a very interesting discussion of the practical implications of his conclusion. He admits that although we punish someone for having committed a crime in the past, "from a strictly rational perspective it is true to say that he who is punished is not guilty" (ibid.). Similarly, although we fear death, we are wrong to think of death as the end of a single, persisting substance. But this is not to say that our attitudes are misguided. Our fears of punishment and death are natural to us, and beneficial, because if we had no concern for future punishments the results for society would be dire. Hence "such fear is endowed by nature so as to account for one's resisting sin" (ibid.). Likewise, although death is not what we take it to be, it is an evil: "the evil is that a well-made connection of beings is dissolved." Accordingly, "if it were not feared, many evils and many homicides would be committed" (ibid.). So although our attitudes toward the past and future are liable to push us toward a false metaphysical framework, nature has done this for a reason. Even if there is no enduring *I* that will be benefited over time, the sequence of beings that I think of as myself is benefited in just the way society as a whole is benefited.

In the later sixteenth century, such radical ideas about diachronic identity begin to be voiced in a skeptical key. Michel de Montaigne's "Apology for Raymond Sebond" (1580) quotes Plutarch at length on the changeability of all material things.[9] Francisco Sanches's *Quod nihil scitur* (1576) makes a similar point in a more philosophically rigorous context:

Between coming to be and passing away, how many changes take place? Countless. Among living things there is constant nourishment, growth, maturity, and then decline, generation, the variation among offspring, change, decay, addition, development of character, actions, work of   3
different sorts—contraries very often even within the same individual. In all, no rest. Nor is it surprising that some held the view that it cannot be said of any one human being, after one hour, that he is the same one he was an hour ago. This view should not be entirely rejected;   6
indeed, it may be true. For so indivisible is identity that if you were to add or take away from any given thing one single bit (*punctum*) of it, it would no longer be entirely (*omnino*) the same thing. ... "I know," you say, "that the individual thing is always the same for as long as the same   9
form remains; for it is from that form that the thing is said to be some one thing. ..." But what I held was that, for identity, *nothing* must be changed; otherwise the thing is not entirely the same. (pp. 126/228)   12

Although one cannot be sure who Sanches has in mind when he speaks of those who deny human diachronic identity (lines 4–6), the parallels with the nominalists are certainly striking. Like them, Sanches insists on the indiscernibility of identicals: this is what it means to remark that "for identity, *nothing* must be changed" (line 11). He moreover takes this to have just the consequences that Buridan and others had claimed: endorsing mereological essentialism (line 7–9), he contends that any change to the parts entails a change to the whole. Furthermore, again like the nominalists, he describes this as showing that the thing is not "entirely the same" (line 8), as if what one has in such cases is mere partial identity.

For present purposes there is not much more to be said about Sanches, and even less about Montaigne, because both of these authors use these remarks about diachronic identity merely to make a skeptical point: that our knowledge of the material realm is

---

[9] For Montaigne, see *Complete Essays* pp. 455–6. Another example of a skeptically inclined treatment of diachronic identity can be found in Gianfrancesco Pico's *Examen vanitatis* III.12, where a consideration of the part–whole identity thesis leads to some skeptical remarks about how we can arrive at any account of diachronic identity.

so feeble that we do not even know when things come into and go out of existence. Given that our present focus is on authors who have a positive *theory* of diachronic identity, we must move on, into the seventeenth century. Here we find a range of approaches, from the sort of atheoretical quietism I ascribe to Descartes[10] to the radically revisionary views of Gorlaeus, according to which the only things that exist are permanent. Gorlaeus's atomism later has as its counterpart the monism of Conway (§27.5) and Spinoza, whose views lie just beyond the horizon of this study. Also lying just out of sight is Leibniz's view that questions of individuation—synchronic and diachronic—can be handled only by postulating something like the metaphysical entities of the scholastics. In the remainder of this chapter and in the next I wish to consider what seems on its face to be still another sort of option, first suggested by Hobbes and then spelled out in similar terms by Locke. According to this option, the problem of diachronic identity admits of a solution (contra quietism) that preserves our commonsense ontology (contra radicalism), but without requiring any sort of quasi-scholastic metaphysical parts (contra Leibniz). What one needs to see, according to both Hobbes and Locke, is that questions of identity through time depend on how one describes the thing in question. What I will argue, however, is that this is not a new approach to identity at all, but merely another version of the familiar nominal approach to the problem, insisting on a strict and uncompromising approach to true *identity*, while offering various looser accounts of why we often speak as if two things are the same.[11]

29.5. Hobbes's Radicalism

Hobbes's *De corpore* (begun *c.*1643; publ. 1655) squarely addresses the issue of diachronic identity for material substances, describing "a great controversy among philosophers concerning the principle of individuation" that arises from "comparing the same body

---

[10] See §25.6 and §28.5. Descartes's correspondence with Mesland from February 1645 might suggest a view of identity along the lines being considered in this chapter and the next. Descartes there contends that we should think of the identity conditions of body differently depending on whether we think of it *qua* body or *qua* human (IV:166), and so regard it as subject to mereological essentialism or to being individuated by its union with the soul. Since I have already raised doubts not just about Descartes's overall interest in articulating a theory of material substance, but also about the weight that should be given to this passage in particular (§24.5), I had best leave discussion of these remarks to others.

There are also interesting questions regarding how Descartes might be able to account for the diachronic identity of the mind, as well as the synchronic individuation of one mind from another. The issues here interact with how one conceives the relation between substances and modes in his theory (see Chs. 8 and 13). For an interesting attempt to sort some of these issues out, see McCann, "Cartesian Selves."

[11] A fuller discussion of debates over diachronic identity over our period would need to take into account the many discussions of whether the same thing can go out of existence and then come back into existence. An early example can be found in Giles of Orleans, who holds that according to philosophy this is never possible, but that the faith teaches otherwise, in the case of human beings, whose bodies are resurrected after death (*In Gen. et cor.* I.22). Buridan reaches the same conclusion (*In Gen. et cor.* I.24), as does Oresme, who uses the occasion to argue for the essentiality of origins (*In Gen. et cor.* I.9–10). For discussion of these and other texts, see Caroti, "Generatio potest auferri" and Braakhuis, "Possibility of Returning." Scotus is an example of the opposing view that origins are not essential, and that there is no natural impossibility in a thing's going out of existence and coming back (*Ord.* IV.43 qq. 1 and 3, and Cross, "Identity"). The issue remains prominent in the seventeenth century, for instance in Thomas White, who argues that an individual could come back into existence only if the rest of the universe were exactly as it was when that thing first came into existence (*De mundo* pp. 108–15). It is this discussion that seems originally to have motivated Hobbes's discussion of diachronic identity. For an earlier discussion along these same lines see John Major, *Sent.* IV.43.1. Like White, he admits the possibility of recurrence, but only if the whole universe were to enter into precisely the same state for a second time, which could happen only supernaturally.

to itself at different times" (11.7). He proceeds to sketch what he takes to be the three standard views on the subject: that substances are individuated by matter; that they are individuated by form; and that they are individuated by accidents. This serves as a pretty good summary of scholastic theories of synchronic individuation: what makes this substance distinct from that one, at a particular time. Rather jarringly, however, Hobbes proceeds to consider these as three solutions to the problem of diachronic identity. This, it must be said, does considerable violence to scholastic views. Matter and accidents, after all, can only make trouble for a theory of identity through change; they cannot be part of the solution, given that these are the very things whose change needs to be accounted for. Even so, this way of setting out the debate is conducive to Hobbes's view, because he thinks that a theory of diachronic identity needs to take account of both form and matter, and that neglecting either leads to contradiction. Introducing the familiar case of the ship of Theseus, Hobbes makes an ingenious argument. On one hand, he says, it seems clear that one can replace the parts of the ship one by one, even up to the point of eventually replacing all the parts, without the ship's losing its identity. But, on the other hand, suppose one collects all the discarded pieces, and builds a ship with it. It seems clear that this too would count as the same ship of Theseus, and so "we would have two ships that are numerically the same, which is completely absurd" (ibid.). From this he concludes that "the principle of individuation should be judged to come not always from matter alone, nor always from form alone" (ibid.).

Where does that leave us? Hobbes immediately makes an extremely interesting proposal, which deserves to be quoted in full:

We must instead consider by what name anything is called, when we inquire concerning its identity. For it makes a great difference to ask concerning Socrates whether he is the same human being or whether he is the same body. For his body, when he is old, cannot be the same   3 it was when he was an infant, by reason of the difference of magnitude; for one body always has one and the same magnitude. He can, however, be the same human being.

So whenever the name by which it is asked whether a thing is the same as it was is imposed   6 on the basis of the matter only, then, if the matter is the same, it is the same individual:

- as the water that was in the sea is the same that is afterwards in the cloud;
- and a body is always the same, whether the parts of it be put together or dispersed; or   9 whether it be congealed or dissolved.

If, however, the name is imposed on the basis of such a form as is the principle of motion, then as long as that principle remains, it will be the same individual: 12

- as it will be the same human being whose actions and thoughts are all derived from one and the same principle of motion—namely, from that principle that was in his genera-tion;   15
- and that will be the same river that flows from one and the same source, whether the same water, or other water, or something other than water flows from there;
- and it will be one city, whose acts continually derive from one and the same institution,   18 whether there be the same human beings in it or different ones.

Lastly, if the name is imposed on the basis of some accident, then the identity of the thing will depend upon the matter; for, by the taking away and adding of matter, accidents are destroyed   21 and new ones are generated that are not the same numerically.

- Thus a ship, by which is signified matter so figured, will be the same if the matter is the same; but if no part of the matter is the same, then it is an entirely distinct ship, numerically; and if part of the matter remains and part is lost, then the ship will be partly the same, and partly distinct. (*De corpore* 11.7)   24

The core of Hobbes's idea is to analyze questions of diachronic identity in terms of the names under which we ask the question. If asking about Socrates's identity over time, for instance, one may ask whether he is the same human being or the same body, and arrive at two different answers (lines 2–5). In general, the sort of criterion one arrives at depends on whether the name is imposed on the basis of matter, form, or accident.

It is an initially surprising feature of Hobbes's account that the third case, accidental variation (lines 22–5), collapses into the first case, that of variation in matter. One might have thought, instead, that accidental change would pose distinct problems for dia-chronic identity. Here, however, Hobbes is very much in sync with earlier treatments of these issues. It is in fact a striking feature of discussions of identity through change, throughout almost the whole history of philosophy, that they have focused not on qualitative change—change in accidents—but on material change. From the Hellenistic era, through the Nominales of the twelfth century, the nominalists of the fourteenth, Sanches in the sixteenth, and now onto Hobbes in the seventeenth, what motivates problems of diachronic identity is the coming and going of parts. No one, in contrast, seems worried about the analogous argument from qualitative change: that today Socrates is tan, whereas last winter he was pale, and that consequently he is not the same person. On its face, this version of the argument is neither more nor less plausible than the argument from growth, but for the authors we are considering only the argument from growth and decay has any appeal. This is clearly Hobbes's view too. He maintains that the gain or loss of a part violates identity, but yet "a body is always the same, whether the parts of it be put together or dispersed; or whether it be congealed or dissolved" (lines 9–10). Since, for Hobbes, all the qualities of a thing arise from facts about how its parts are "together" or "dispersed," he is evidently committed to the doctrine that qualitative change is compatible with identity, whereas mereological change is not.

To a modern eye, this may seem baffling. On reflection, however, the reasons for it are clear. Throughout our period, accidental changes are the wrong sort of change to motivate worries about diachronic identity, because accidents are either nothing at all, as on Hobbes's view (see §7.1, §10.2), or else are extrinsic to the substance on its standard thin construal (§6.1). On the latter approach, pale Socrates is a *per accidens* composite, and it is an uninteresting fact that such composites are in constant flux. No one cares about telling a unifying story about *their* identity over time. Indeed, one of the payoffs of the substance–accident distinction, as we saw most clearly in Descartes's case (§8.2, §13.6), is that it offers a clear story about how substances persist through accidental change. The lesson of this chapter, however, is that that strategy works for only certain kinds of accidental change—the kinds that involves the gain or loss of accidental forms. Growth and decay are quite a different story, because here what is gained or lost is a part of the thin substance itself. The idea we have seen periodically surfacing from antiquity all the way to Hobbes and beyond is that in such cases, strictly speaking, there is no persisting whole.

Hobbes's similarities with the nominalist tradition grow out of three shared principles:

1. Mereological essentialism
2. The part–whole identity thesis
3. A tolerance for partial sameness.

He commits himself to the last of these in lines 25–6 above. The first and second claims are made explicit in a closely parallel discussion from his *De mundo* (1642), an unpublished response to Thomas White that looks to have served in effect as the first draft of this discussion from the *De corpore*. The *De mundo* remarks:

> Suppose it is asked of any body—for instance a ship—whether it is the same *being* or *body* that it was before. In that case, since the name 'being' and 'body' pick out nothing other than the matter, it follows that if the matter is the same as it was before, so that no part of it has been cast   3
> off, nor has any new matter been added, it will be numerically the same being and numerically the same body as it was before. If, on the other hand, some part of the prior matter has been cast off or another part has been added, then that ship will be another being or another body. For a   6
> body cannot be numerically the same whose parts are not all the same, since all the parts together are the same as the whole. (12.3)

The first six lines do not add anything to the picture of the *De corpore* passage, other than that 'being' is another of the names that trigger a focus on material sameness. The last sentence gives us something new: it both identifies a necessary condition for material sameness (sameness of parts) and provides a quick rationale for that condition (the part–whole identity thesis).

Although the similarities with the earlier nominalists are striking, Hobbes seems at first glance to have something new to say. For whereas the nominalist approach was to concede that, strictly speaking, there is no diachronic identity through mereological change, Hobbes does not seem to say that. Instead, he says that whether this is the right answer depends on how we describe the situation, and that under certain descriptions it is true to say that the thing persists. So we can talk about the same human being persisting through time as the same human being (and analogously for a river or a city), in virtue of there being the same form that is the "principle of motion" (lines 11–19 of the *De corpore* passage). Given Hobbes's strict, anti-hylomorphic corpuscularianism, it seems clear that 'form' here is being used in an extended sense that has little in common with scholastic views. Since he has no use for forms in any Aristotelian sense, he co-opts the term to refer to the *origin* of a human being, river, or city. The earlier *De mundo* discussion, in contrast, although closely parallel in many respects, understands sameness in form differently, in terms of continuity: thus a river remains the same river in virtue of the "unity of its flow, which is a single continuous motion," and a human being is the same human being "on account of the unity of the flow by which matter is expelled and reintegrated" (12.4). This is of course precisely the idea that the nominalists tried to exploit. One can perhaps see, however, why Hobbes would have shifted away from continuity toward sameness of source. Consider, for instance, a Colorado river that goes dry in the fall and runs again in the spring. Even some living things are more like that than we usually recognize: think not of an oak tree, but of, say, an iris, which survives the winter only in its rhizome, underground.

There are many such details worth investigating in Hobbes's account, but here I will confine my attention to the most general question of what it means to make questions of diachronic identity relative to the names we use. It is natural to suppose that Hobbes is committing himself here to the existence of both a human body (*corpus*) and a human being (*homo*), insisting that we make precise which one we are talking about, so that we know which identity conditions to apply. In the context of Hobbes's broader meta-physics, however, it is quite clear that nothing could be farther from what he has in mind. As we saw in §27.5, Hobbes is a fervent anti-essentialist, according to whom both accidental and essential predicates are simply names for different ways of conceiving a thing. Hence to use our different names as the basis for drawing a distinction between different things would be from Hobbes's perspective the worst sort of mistake. Indeed, he explicitly remarks in the *Leviathan*, in the context of criticizing scholastic theories of essences, that "when we say *a man is a living body*, we mean not that the *man* is one thing, the *living body* another, and the *is* or *being* a third, but that the *man* and the *living body* is the same thing, because the consequence *if he be a man, he is a living body* is a true consequence, signified by that word *is*" (46.17). Clearly, then, Hobbes does not meant to license a distinction between human beings and their bodies, as if these are two distinct coinciding entities, with distinct identity conditions.

If Hobbes draws no such distinction, then we evidently must decide which of the two criteria Hobbes offers us is the metaphysically *true* one—in the sense of being the one that holds of the thing itself. Reflection on his broader views, in light of §28.4, makes that an easy question to answer. What exist through time, for Hobbes, are what he above calls beings or bodies—a mass of material existing in any arrangement whatso-ever, united or dispersed. His commitment to the doctrine of strict permanence requires him to say that, in strict metaphysical fact, there is no such thing as a human being, river, city, or ship that endures through significant stretches of time. All of those things exist, to be sure, inasmuch as they are simply a certain collection of matter, but the way we talk about such things requires giving them persistence conditions that violate the fundamental metaphysical principle that nothing begins or ceases to exist. Indeed, his most categorical statement of strict permanence comes in the *De mundo* immediately after the discussion of diachronic identity: "a being (*ens*) cannot naturally go out of existence. For even if a ship or a plank ceases to be a ship and a plank, it nonetheless never naturally ceases to be a being" (12.5).

By insisting that questions of diachronic identity must be couched in terms of the names we use, Hobbes means to signal that he is not talking about how the world is. We have the concept of a ship, a river, a body, a human being, and we can give an analysis of the conditions under which that concept is satisfied. In actual fact, however, nothing goes into or out of existence. A ship, at a time, is a more-or-less temporary aggregation of various pieces of matter, and a human being, at a time, is another such aggregation. These are ways we construe the world, based on its appearances. Thus, in Hobbes's own words, "a body can neither be generated nor destroyed, but only appear to us in one way and then another, under different images, and conse-quently be named in one way and then another" (*De corpore* 8.20). This just is the nominal theory of identity, shorn of the substantial forms that serve to hold clusters of matter together. Without anything like a substantial form to enter into the identity conditions of bodies, Hobbes abandons any restrictions on what counts as composition, allowing a body to remain in existence "whether the parts of it be put together or dispersed; or whether it be congealed or dissolved" (lines 9–10 above). This yields that most unscholastic of results, that nothing naturally comes into or goes out of existence. Thus even while Hobbes borrows from the nominalists a theory of how to understand our ordinary ways of talking about identity through change, he abandons any vestige of a commonsense ontology.[12]

---

[12] There is little secondary literature on Hobbes's theory of diachronic identity. For some brief remarks, see Ayers, *Locke* II:212, and Thiel, "Individuation" pp. 236–7.

I do not think we can assume that a figure like Hobbes had much familiarity with the nominalist tradition, and I do not take myself to have proved that Hobbes draws on that tradition in his thinking about diachronic identity. There is, however, at least some evidence that Hobbes was interested in Ockham—see Bernhardt, "Nominalisme" pp. 239–40n.

Hobbes insists on part–whole identity in some English notes on a draft of the *De corpore*: "That which is put for all whereof it consists is called *totum*, and the singulars when from the division of the whole they are again severally considered are the parts thereof; therefore *the whole and all the parts taken together are absolutely the same*" (in Hobbes, *Critique du* De mundo appendix II, p. 451, original emphasis). That same draft contains a brief statement of his theory of diachronic identity (ibid., pp. 459–60).

The substance–accident distinction not only makes it easy to tolerate identity through accidental change over time, but even makes it conceivable that the same thing could have distinct accidental properties at the same time. John Major explores this possibility in some detail, in a discussion of whether a body can wholly exist at more than one place at the same time—that is, can exist holenmerically. Major considers a series of objections to this possibility, on the grounds that Socrates, say, might at the same time be warm in Rome but cold in Paris, or receive divine grace in Rome but not in Paris (*Sent.* IV.10.2, f. 42vab). His response is simply to hug the monster—something he can countenance because these accidents are distinct from the substance.

Locke's Nominal Substances

30.1. The Reluctant Metaphysician

As a general rule, Locke's forays into metaphysics are descriptive rather than revisionary. His project is not animated by any great radical impulse toward monism, reductive atomism, idealism, or any such thing. Indeed, Locke's concerns, first and foremost, are not with metaphysics at all, but with language and its underlying conceptual framework. Inasmuch as that framework commits us to certain conclusions about the way the world is, Locke accedes to those results. But he is, always, a reluctant metaphysician.

It is in this reluctant spirit that Locke articulates his theory of substance. Insofar as we grasp patterns of sensible qualities outside the mind, we have reason to postulate some sort of subject in which those qualities inhere. We postulate such a subject because we take it there must be something that is causally responsible for the existence of these qualities, something that serves to explain the evident fact of experience that clusters of qualities persist through time as a cohesive unity. This line of thought leads Locke, as it led nearly everyone else during our period, to the notion that dogs and cats and stones are not clusters of sensible qualities, but are rather the fundamental entities beneath those qualities, unknown but yet necessary to our conceptual framework. That theory of substance in turn points toward the notion of a real essence—the feature of the substance, presumably its microphysical structure, that explains why a given substance produces one cluster of qualities rather than another.

Although Locke's empiricist scruples impel him to hold this view at arm's length, hold it he does, even while sometimes scorning it. The resulting theory, as Chapter 9 considered in detail, positions Locke squarely in the mainstream of thought during our period. Like all of the scholastics, like Descartes, and like Robert Boyle, Locke endorses an ontology of enduring substances as the fundamental constituents of reality. Although his theory of real essences poses a challenge to our familiar taxonomy of natural kinds (§27.7), it still allows us to individuate the material realm in reasonably familiar ways. Rather than an undifferentiated space of extended stuff, bigger and smaller, the natural world is made up of substances, organized by their real essences.

So, at any rate, Locke can say about the material realm at a given instant, viewed as a snapshot. What about the world over time? This is the question that William Molyneux posed to Locke in a letter from 1693, and that Locke addressed in the famous chapter on identity and diversity that he added to the second edition (1694) of the *Essay concerning*

Human Understanding. There is perhaps no other area of seventeenth-century thought that has been subjected to so much, and so sophisticated a body of commentary, and I will not pretend to do justice to the entirety of the topic. Still, I believe that many features of Locke's account become newly perspicuous when viewed in the proper historical context, that of scholastic nominalism. Judged from within that context, Locke's project becomes at once less striking and original, but also more plausible and defensible.

According to the nominalist framework for diachronic identity, as described in the previous chapter, identity is always understood strictly. Two things are numerically the same only if they are entirely the same. Since the nominalists think that a whole just is its parts, they hold that a composite substance cannot maintain its identity over time unless it continues to have all and only the same parts. What is not entirely the same may be partly the same, in virtue of sharing parts that satisfy the strict criterion of numerical sameness. If those enduring parts are prominent enough, or if there is enough continuity in their replacement, then we might loosely say that the two not wholly identical things are the same thing. Strictly speaking, however, we would be talking about two things and not one. Accordingly, composite substances are rarely the same over time. The growth and decay of living things, or even the erosion of stones, leads to a constant succession of distinct wholes, each member of the sequence being partly the same as the last one, but partly distinct. So in the case of rivers, oceans, a horse, or the human body, we can speak of the same thing existing through time, diachronically, only in a loose sense, inasmuch as "one thing is said to be numerically the same as another according to the continuity of distinct parts, one in succession after another" (Buridan, *In Phys.* I.10; see §29.3). There is no way of knowing whether the nominalists influenced Locke directly, or perhaps indirectly, or whether he arrived at similar ideas quite independently, from common premises. Setting aside, as usual, these sorts of intractable questions of provenance, I claim only that we can arrive at a more plausible reading of Locke's theory by attending to this background.[1]

---

[1]   The previous chapter offered various examples of strict mereological identity being required of material substances, up to the late sixteenth century. For seventeenth-century examples, see Arnold Geulincx, *Metaphysica vera* II.16 and Arnauld and Nicole's *Port-Royal Logic* II.12, drawing on earlier work of Arnauld's. Citing the cases of rivers, animal bodies, and cities, Arnauld and Nicole conclude that words that purport to refer to one enduring thing in fact often refer to "plusieurs sujets distincts sous une même idée." If Locke is supposed to be doing something very different from this, I hope to know it is only because he did not write clearly enough to make himself understood.

See too Robert Boyle: "It is no such easy way, as at first it seems, to determine what is absolutely necessary and but sufficient to make a portion of matter, considered at different times or places, to be fit to be reputed the *same* body. That the generality of men do in vulgar speech allow themselves a great latitude about this affair, will be easily granted by him that observes the received forms of speaking. Thus Rome is said to be the *same* city, though it has been so often taken and ruined by the barbarians and others, that perhaps scarce any of the first houses have been left standing . . ." (*Possibility of the Resurrection*, *Works* VIII:300). The passage goes on to discuss a wide range of cases that violate mereological sameness (universities, rivers, flames, ships), and where yet we ordinarily speak of the thing remaining the same over time. Boyle does not offer a theory of diachronic identity here, and so it is not clear whether he is inclined to think these are not cases of true identity, or whether he thinks that one can somehow still truly speak of identity here. What clearly motivates the whole discussion, however, is the temptation to treat sameness as strict, mereological identity, a notion that Boyle treats as quite commonplace.

Another precedent worth mentioning is Thomas White, *Peripateticall Institutions* IV.7, who divides the problem of diachronic identity into distinct cases as Locke does, but comes to different conclusions about the proper criteria in each case.

For a sense of how thin the evidence is regarding Locke's familiarity with scholasticism, see Milton, "Scholastic Background." See also Milton, "Nominalist Tradition," which contends that "Locke was working, perhaps unconsciously, in a tradition usually known as nominalism" (p. 128)—though Milton's focus is the problem of universals.

My argument about Locke runs parallel, up to a point, with the argument I made in §29.5 regarding Hobbes. Like Hobbes, Locke insists that questions of diachronic identity are always relative to the names we use, and the ideas that lie behind those names. Like Hobbes, Locke contends that bodily sameness is subject to mereological essentialism, and that the sameness of an organism should be understood more loosely, in terms of some sort of continuity. The parallels go only so far, however, because Locke eschews the radical approach taken by Hobbes. What really exist, for Hobbes, are permanent bodies, which are never naturally generated or corrupted. The familiar entities of our commonsense conceptual scheme are merely the product of the names we impose to cope with a world of constantly changing appearances. In strict metaphysical fact, those appearances disguise a world of wholly permanent bodies, which continue to exist regardless of whether they are joined or scattered. Locke, in contrast, nowhere suggests any sympathy for this sort of radical perspective. His theory of substance, grounded in real essences, underwrites much the same sort of picture of ordinary objects that Aristotelianism takes for granted, and that we continue to take for granted today. Still, like Ockham, Buridan, and the rest of the nominalist tradition, Locke does not think such things persist for any significant amount of time.

The broadest outlines of the *Essay*'s account of diachronic identity are laid out in II.27.2, where Locke remarks that "we have the ideas but of three sorts of substances: 1. God. 2. Finite Intelligences. 3. Bodies." Locke regards the case of God as unproblematic, and the case of finite intelligences—angelic minds and human souls, assuming there are such things—as similarly straightforward. With respect to bodies, Locke distinguishes between simple and composite. Simple bodies turn out to be no more difficult to handle than were minds. In this case, as in the others, simplicity keeps the hard questions of diachronic identity at bay. It is only when Locke come to the case of composite bodies that he sees real difficulties, and accordingly he devotes almost the entirety of the chapter to explaining such cases.

The key to making a judgment of identity or diversity in composite cases, Locke says, is that "care be taken to what it is applied" (II.27.3). The first case he considers is that of a mass of atoms, which he refers to as a body. Bodies are to be individuated strictly, in accord with mereological essentialism:

If two or more atoms be joined together into the same mass, ... whilst they exist united together, the mass, consisting of the same atoms, must be the same mass or the same body, let the parts be ever so differently jumbled. But if one of these atoms be taken away, or one new one added, it is no longer the same mass or the same body. (ibid.)

Locke does not bother to explain why exact mereological sameness is the right criterion for bodily sameness, and for modern readers this passage has been a puzzle. If the Lockean project is to understand identity in terms of the different ideas we have in different cases, then it is hard to see how mereological essentialism should get into the discussion at all. It fits no one's pre-theoretical idea of sameness to suppose that a thing loses its identity when it gains or loses a single part, however small. Viewed in the proper historical context, however, there is no puzzle here at all. We can understand Locke to be taking for granted two doctrines that would have been familiar to any reader conversant with earlier discussions of this topic: first, that identity must always be understood strictly and, second, that a compound body just is its parts. With these two principles in mind, the diachronic identity of a composite body requires the identity of each and every one of its parts. Here, then, Locke's criterion for bodily sameness is motivated not by our pre-theoretical idea of what a body is, but by the logic of identity.[2]

Immediately after offering this strict criterion for bodily sameness, Locke turns to the case of composite living bodies, and remarks that they can be judged the same over time even though they violate the strict criterion, provided they display biological continuity. As Chapter 29 made clear, this is not a new idea. Buridan had clearly articulated such a view back in the fourteenth century, and generations of scholastics subsequently line up on one or the other side of this debate. Locke *would* be doing something new, to be sure, if he supposed that mere continuity yields genuine identity. This idea would be not just quite new but also seemingly contrary to the most elementary philosophical principles, since to say that a thing changes in a continuous manner would seem precisely to deny that it remains *identical*. A thing may remain wholly identical over time, it may remain partially identical over time, or it may undergo complete, continuous change. If we say the last of these, then we must give up on saying either of the first two, and indeed if we wish to express ourselves precisely we must say—even as language works against us—that there is no one thing that persists in the third case, but only a series of things, picked out by a single idea.

Although modern readers generally understand Locke to be offering such continuity as a theory of genuine identity, there are good reasons to think he appreciates the difference between identity and continuity. For after setting out his account of how biological continuity grounds our judgments of identity in the case of living things, Locke makes this crucial remark:

> It is not therefore unity of substance that comprehends all sorts of identity, or will determine it in every case. But to conceive and judge of it aright, we must consider what idea the word it is applied to stands for: it being one thing to be the same *substance*, another the same *man*, and a third the same *person*, if *Person*, *Man*, and *Substance* are three names standing for three different ideas; for such as is the idea belonging to that name, such must be the identity. (II.27.7)

By treating the strict mereological criterion as the only criterion that yields sameness of substance (lines 1, 3), Locke is implying that the other criteria do not yield genuine identity. It seems that they cannot, because in his ontology everything is either a substance or else depends on a substance (§30.3). Genuine identity requires sameness of parts, and where that is lacking the notion of identity is merely a *façon de parler*. This is by no means to say that we should not talk about the same man, or the same person existing through time. Such talk is perfectly meaningful, and it is indeed the primary burden of II.27 to explain just what that meaning is, first in terms of biological continuity, and then—most famously and innovatively—in terms of psychological continuity. But we should not suppose that such claims entail the ongoing existence of any one thing. The remainder of Locke's chapter repeats this over and over with respect to personal identity, e.g., "it being the same consciousness that makes a man be himself to himself, personal identity depends on that only, whether it be annexed solely

---

[2] I have not found Locke explaining why bodily identity requires mereological sameness. In particular, it is simply my conjecture that he embraces the part–whole identity thesis. Although *Essay* Bk. IV does repeatedly invoke the maxim that "the whole is equal to all its parts," he treats this as a tautology, true simply by virtue of the meaning of the terms (IV.7.11). So understood, it can hardly bear the sort of metaphysical weight described in §28.5.

to one individual substance, or can be continued in a succession of several substances" (II.27.10). With respect to material substances, they are always bodies, and are always individuated strictly. Locke continues this usage in his later correspondence with Stillingfleet, remarking for instance that "no body, upon removal or change of some of the particles that at any time make it up, is the same material substance or the same body" (*Works* IV:308–9). Hence although Locke wants it to come out true that an oak tree and Socrates persist through the course of their lives, this is not true in virtue of any substance's persisting. In broad outlines, and setting aside for now his bold new conception of personal identity, Locke is simply repackaging the old nominalist theory.[3]

30.2. Identity and Essence

The subject of Locke on identity is one of those vexed topics where the most scholars are able to say is that their favored interpretation is the least bad of various bad options. So far I have tried to make a *prima facie* case for a nominalist reading of Locke. I have to confess, however, that my proposal possesses its own share of badness—not as much so as other options, I believe, but nevertheless still bad. So although what I would like to do at this point is turn to some of the considerable advantages of my reading the text, what I first need to do is confront various textual difficulties for my proposal.

The heart of the problem, for me, is that the discussion of II.27 does not coordinate the theory of identity with the theory of real essences—indeed, it does not even use the word 'essence.' As I read Locke (§27.7), he accepts the usual view that an individual substance has a real essence that both defines it as what it is and explains its characteristic features. This further entails, on my reading, that a material substance is individuated by its essence, which is to say that it exists only when and only for as long as its real essence continues to exist.[4] His commitment to this doctrine leads him to observe that a thing's real essence will fix *all* of its intrinsic properties, whether they be conventionally regarded as essential or accidental. The result is that "particular beings, considered barely in themselves, will be found to have all their qualities equally essential, and everything, in each individual, will be essential to it . . ." (III.6.5). This leads Locke to a certain kind of anti-essentialism, because if *all* of a thing's properties are

---

[3] Locke distinguishes personal identity from substantial identity in nearly every section of his long discussion: secs. 7, 9, 10, 11, 12, 13, 14, 16, 17, 18, 19, 23, 24, 25, 26. It seems fair to say, indeed, that it is the principal thesis of *Essay* II.27.

There is overwhelming textual evidence that 'body' for Locke is equivalent to 'material substance,' and that such a substance is subject to mereological essentialism. *Essay* II.27.2, quoted already in the main text, says that "we have the ideas but of three sorts of substances: 1. God. 2. Finite Intelligences. 3. Bodies." *Essay* II.27.10 treats the two terms as interchangeable: "Different *substances*, by the same consciousness, . . . being united into one person, as well as different *bodies* by the same life are united into one animal, whose identity is preserved in that change of *substances* by the unity of one continued life" (emphasis added). The same pattern continues throughout Locke's later correspondence with Stillingfleet. As Kaufman remarks of one such passage, "Here, as in every other passage in the 1699 letter dealing with sameness of body, Locke equates *body* with *mass of matter* and *material substance*, and as such bodies and material substances are to be treated as having the persistence conditions of masses, i.e., mereological essentialism is true of them" ("Resurrection" p. 205). As Kaufman stresses, Locke gains no advantage from some special use of 'substance' here. On the contrary, by treating bodies, individuated strictly, as the only substances, he makes his position against Stillingfleet all the harder to defend.

[4] There is admittedly room to doubt whether the identity of real essences and their substances are yoked together as tightly as I claim. It is possible, for instance, to read Locke as holding that real essences can change even while the man or the person remains (see Kaufman, "Locke on Individuation" p. 523n.).

essential, then from a certain perspective it is as if *none* of those properties are essential—for we would lack any grounds on which to single out a subset of those properties as the ones that define the species. Hence Locke continues the passage just quoted with the remark that "or, which is more true, nothing at all"—that is, nothing will be essential, and so there will be no grounds to validate our familiar species classifications.

In the context of Locke's attack on conventional taxonomy, it is effectively the same to regard all the properties of a thing as essential or none of the properties as essential. Either way, taxonomy collapses into the limiting case where each individual is a species unto itself. From the perspective of diachronic identity, however, these two ways of talking yield utterly different results, and so one has to decide which formulation Locke takes to be literally correct. If one takes him at his word when he remarks, as above, that it is "more true" to say that *nothing* is essential to an individual, then it becomes impossible to ascribe to him any sort of absolute theory of diachronic identity. All identity would have to be relative to some conventional, nominal kind. This reading of Locke—as committed to the view that identity claims are always relative—is indeed one prominent school of interpretation among modern scholars. On this picture, whether or not there is identity over time depends on whether a thing is conceived of as, for example, a body, a man, or a person. For anyone who thinks Locke really means to deny essential properties to things, this is the natural way to understand his theory of identity.[5] Here, rather than revisit the issues discussed in §27.7, I will simply let my own interpretation stand in counterpoint. On my view, Locke has quite a strict and absolute conception of identity, according to which a substance can be numerically the same over time only if it has the same real essence and the same integral parts. The criteria for living things and persons do not stand on an equal footing with this strict criterion, but are merely ways of making sense of our conceptual scheme in the absence of genuine identity.

So far so good. Unfortunately, I cannot entirely fit these different aspects of Locke's theory together. The criterion for bodily identity, as quoted in the previous section, even while it demands that a composite body retain all and only the same parts, allows that those parts be scrambled however one likes. In Locke's words, it "must be the same mass or the same body, let the parts be ever so differently jumbled" (II.27.3). But this cannot be right in general, because structured composite bodies—in particular, living things—admit of very little jumbling before losing their identity. Jumble the cat too much, and it ceases to be a cat—it loses its real essence. Now it is fairly obvious why Locke allows unlimited jumbling in this passage. The case he has in mind is what he characterizes as a case of "the same mass," by which he evidently means to pick out nonliving, homogeneous bodies. And it is a commonplace that bodies of this kind do admit of unlimited jumbling. A pool of water, composed out of constituent water

---

[5] For the relative identity interpretation of Locke, see, e.g., Noonan, "Locke on Personal Identity" and Thiel, "Individuation." Thiel accordingly stresses that the criteria for identity track merely the nominal essences of things; see, e.g., *Lockes Theorie* p. 40: "die Hinsicht, gemäß welcher nach Locke Identität ausgesagt wird, ist vielmehr immer die *nominale Essenz* der Gegenstände." For the case against a relative identity interpretation, see e.g. Yaffe, "Locke on Ideas of Identity" pp. 198–201 and Chappell, "Locke and Relative Identity."

particles, retains its identity no matter how much those particles get jumbled.[6] This would all be fine if Locke went on to clarify how his view works in the case of structured composites. And, indeed, he immediately does remark that "in the state of living creatures, their identity depends not on a mass of the same particles, but on something else" (II.27.3). But instead of proceeding to explain how the criteria for their identity is even more strict, Locke instead turns to spelling out the biological continuity criterion as that which secures the "identity" of living things over time. There is absolutely nothing in the text to signal that at this point we have gone from genuine identity to mere nominal identity.

Now the bare fact that Locke does not signal any change of topic at this point is unfortunate but by no means decisive. As always, Locke's foremost concern is with our *ideas*, and so it is natural that, throughout the chapter, he speaks of identity, without qualification. That, after all, is the way we ordinarily think about all these cases. Moreover, as I stressed in the previous section, Locke does persistently flag the fact that it is only in the bodily case that we have genuine identity of substance over time. In particular, at the close of his initial account of how biological continuity accounts for the "identity" of living things, he offers the conclusion that "It is not therefore unity of substance that comprehends all sorts of identity" (II.27.7). Then, in introducing the notion of personal identity, he raises the problem of the many gaps in our memories, and remarks that, on this basis, "doubts are raised whether we are the same thinking thing, i.e. the same substance or no" (II.27.10). To this he makes the following remarkable response:

Which, however reasonable or unreasonable, concerns not personal identity at all. The question being what makes the same person, and not whether it be the same identical substance which always thinks in the same person, which, in this case, matters not at all: different substances, by the same consciousness (where they do partake in it) being united into one person, as well as different bodies by the same life are united into one animal, whose identity is preserved in that change of substances by the unity of one continued life. (ibid.)

This suggests quite strongly that his criteria for the "identity" of animals and persons are not intended to secure literal numerical sameness. In these cases, there is no thing, or substance, that endures.

Still, even if these remarks seems clear enough, I have to confess that the way he sets up the discussion is disastrously misleading. He gives no indication whatsoever that the unlimited jumbling criterion will not work for all composite bodies. He fails to signal that living bodies also admit of a strict, mereological essentialist criterion. Read naively, outside of its historical context, he seems to think that living things just somehow can remain identical even when nothing about them remains identical. All I can say

---

[6] For the idea that unstructured, homogeneous bodies admit of unlimited jumbling, see e.g. Aquinas, *In Meta.* V.21.1105: "Quaedam enim tota sunt in quibus diversa positio partium non facit diversitatem, sicut patet in aqua. Qualitercumque enim transponantur partes aquae, nihil different, et similiter est de aliis humidis, sicut de oleo, vino et huiusmodi." Part of what makes Hobbes's treatment extraordinary, as discussed in §29.5, is that he goes beyond unlimited jumbling to allow scattering: "a body is always the same, whether the parts of it be put together or dispersed; or whether it be congealed or dissolved" (*De corpore* 11.7). Locke makes it clear that scattering is not allowed when he describes the loss of a part as a case where "one of these atoms be taken away" (II.27.3). For Hobbes, the only way to take a part away from a whole would be to destroy it, a possibility foreclosed by his embrace of strict permanence (§28.4). Thus he gets the result that *nothing* can go out of existence.

about this, once again, is that Locke is focused on our *ideas* about identity over time. His actual metaphysical commitments are not straightforwardly displayed by the text. If they were, we would not still be arguing over what these texts mean.[7]

30.3. Persistence Candidates

Read in light of the nominalist tradition, it becomes hard to resist concluding that the criteria Locke applies to living things and persons do not yield strict identity. An oak tree and Socrates, as they exist over time, are not a single persisting substance, but a sequence of distinct substances. This interpretation not only makes better historical sense, but also resolves many of the puzzles that surround the usual modern construals of his account. One such puzzle concerns what oak trees and persons are. The text could hardly be clearer in insisting that there is no enduring substance that is an oak tree. So what then is an oak tree? What is a person? For those who want to find some enduring thing to serve as the referent of these ideas, there are only a few other possibilities, and they are all ruled out by Locke's text. First, a living thing or a person might be a mode. Although a number of commentators have made this argument, it seems both bizarre on its face and excluded by the text. Bizarre, because a mode must be a mode of something, and it is hard to see what an oak tree, say, could be a mode of, unless perhaps it is a mode of a body. But this seems to be obviously the wrong result: an oak tree is not a mode of a body, but rather it *is* a body. The proposal also seems excluded by the text, because Locke—like everyone else during our period—holds that modes are individuated by the substance they inhere in: "All other things being but modes or relations ultimately terminated in substances, the identity and diversity of each particular existence of them too will be by the same way determined" (II.27.2). So if an oak tree were a mode of a body, it would cease to exist whenever the body ceases to exist. Modes cannot leap from substance to substance. More generally, for a living thing or a person to be a mode, there would have to be some substance that endures for at least as long as the mode in question endures, and so Locke would need some further account of the diachronic identity of that substance in which the mode *man* or *person* inheres. Appealing to modes simply pushes the problem back a step.[8]

---

[7] Locke's journal contains an extremely interesting passage on unity dating from 1679: "Unity seems to me to be nothing but a capacity to be comprehended in one specific idea . . . , so that unity consists not in indivisibility but an existence comprehensible under one specific idea. Nor is the unity greater or less according as the union of it is more or less strict or lasting, or it has no parts at all. . . . What ever exists capable of any specific idea is one" (pp. 112–14). (I owe thanks to Dan Kaufman for calling this passage to my attention.)

Locke is here talking about not diachronic identity, but synchronic unity. Even so, the passage nicely displays his inclinations toward a nominalist strategy: questions of unity are best explained not by any feature of the things themselves, but simply by our ideas. Perhaps the reason this passage did not make it into the *Essay*, whereas the corresponding view about diachronic identity did, is that Locke's theory of real essences gives him a serviceable story about what gives substances their real unity.

[8] A modal interpretation of Locke is defended in Uzgalis, "Relative Identity," and in Lowe, *Locke* ch. 5, although Lowe—rather puzzlingly—both admits that there is essentially no evidence for this interpretation of Locke, and subjects the interpretation to the same sort of criticism I advance in the main text.

On modes as individuated by their subject, see also *Essay* II.12.4, which offers Locke's canonical definition of 'mode': "First, *modes* I call such complex ideas which, however compounded, contain not in them the supposition of subsisting by themselves, but are considered as dependences on or affections of substances." Admittedly, there is perhaps just barely room in this passage for allowing that a mode, while always dependent on *a* substance, need not always depend

This last passage usefully tells us that substances, modes, and relations exhaust Locke's ontology. Or almost. For he immediately goes on to consider one further special case, that of successive entities, such as motions. As we saw in §29.3, this is certainly a case worth considering, inasmuch as the variability of composite material substances makes them at least analogous to successive entities. Might they just be successive entities? Some modern commentators have urged just this, arguing that Locke's living things and persons should be understood as, in modern parlance, four-dimensional perduring entities or, in scholastic terms, *entia successiva*. This suggestion has been commonly dismissed as anachronistic, but that is quite wrong. On the contrary, Locke in fact expressly considers this possibility and rejects it:

> Only as to things whose existence is in succession, such as are the actions of finite beings, v.g. motion and thought, both which consist in a continued train of succession, concerning their diversity there can be no question: because each perishing the moment it begins, they cannot 3 exist in different times, or in different places, as permanent beings can at different times exist in distant places; and therefore no motion or thought, considered as at different times, can be the same, each part thereof having a different beginning of existence. (II.27.2)   6

Locke does not deny the reality of successive beings, but rather seems to recognize them, at least in the cases of motion and thought. (As noted in §18.1, seventeenth-century authors commonly do embrace this aspect of scholastic ontology, perhaps because their minimal ontologies impel them to hang on at least to the reality of motion.) In the context of a discussion of identity, however, Locke regards successive entities as quite irrelevant. By nature, they do not *endure* through time at all, because each of their "parts" exists at a different instant, without any overlap (lines 5–6). This is a way of existing through time, but it is not a way of being the same thing over time, as "permanent beings" are (line 4). Successive entities are therefore irrelevant to the discussion. (In §29.3, we saw Oresme exclude successive entities from his discussion of diachronic identity for just the same reason.)[9]

on the *same* substance. There is also room for an alternative reading of II.27.2, as quoted in the main text. Thiel, for instance, reads it as maintaining not that modes are individuated by substances, but that they are individuated by their existence, just as substances are ("Individuation" p. 235). This, however, strikes me both as unlikely in the context of Locke's time, and as a strained reading of the text, since it would seem to make it into a *non sequitur*. How could the fact that modes are "ultimately terminated in substances" yield the result that modes are individuated separately from substances, in terms of their own proper existence? Moreover, as Thiel himself notes, when the passage is read that way one has to conclude that Locke has nothing to say about the individuation of modes, which is odd because the passage seems in context to be intended to settle the question of the individuation of modes and relations.

Another text that insists on modes as individuated by their subject is II.27.13, where Locke considers "whether the consciousness of past actions can be transferred from one thinking substance to another." He first concedes that, "were the same consciousness the same individual action, it could not." Then he goes on to say that since it is "but a present representation of a past action" it might be transferred. Although he does not say so here, it is clear from II.19.1–2 that these acts of consciousness are modes. His point, then, is that modes cannot be transferred, and so "the same consciousness" could not be in one thinking substance and then another. But there is no obstacle in principle to one substance's having a "representation"—a memory—of a distinct conscious event had by a distinct thinking substance.

[9] For Locke as a proponent of *entia successiva*, see Conn, *Locke on Essence and Identity*, who unabashedly invokes the modern parlance of "four-dimensionalism." For worries about anachronism, see Kaufman's review. Kaufman (pp. 401–2) also notes the trouble for Conn's view posed by Locke's dismissal of successive entities in II.27.2. From a certain perspective, the view that Conn defends is similar to my own proposal, given that he holds that "a Lockean organism is thus the temporally extended aggregate of its successively existing constituent masses of matter" (p. 134). But there are crucial differences. For one thing, Conn thinks there is an entity that is the temporally extended aggregate, whereas I take Locke to be not advocating a new ontology of four-dimensional objects, but showing that our conventional ontology of

Although Locke dismisses successive entities in just a sentence, his ultimate account of composite substances is in some ways not so different. Like motion or, in general, an event, what we think of as a persisting oak tree is really just a series of distinct bodies, each existing for a brief period of time, connected by the sorts of causal relationships that Locke tries to capture with his talk of "partaking of one common life" (II.27.4). To be sure, such a sequence of bodies is not a successive entity. For one thing, Locke accepts the common scholastic characterization of a successive entity as having parts that endure for only an instant—"each perishing the moment it begins" (line 3 above; see §18.1). The temporal parts of a persisting oak tree, in contrast, are bodies, each of which endures for as long as it satisfies Locke's strict mereological constraint. More-over, motions and events exist *only* over time, as a sequence. No one part of a motion is itself a motion. In contrast, an oak tree is at every instant fully an oak tree. Indeed, this is what generates the puzzle of diachronic identity: we want to know in what sense this oak tree right here and now is the same as the oak tree on this same spot a year ago. Finally, a successive entity is indeed an entity, a thing with a distinct manner of persisting through time. Locke, in contrast, gives every sign of eschewing the idea that the series of oak-tree bodies is itself a persisting thing. It is not a substance, as he makes clear. It is also not a successive entity or a mode. What then is it? Simply a series of different bodies, causally linked together so as to yield what we take to be a "common life."

Part of the reason it is hard to see that this is Locke's view is that English lacks a term for the idea of a substance-sequence. It is, after all, Locke's very point that the idea we have of such sequences is the idea of *identity*. Still, it is easy enough to get a fix on the notion of a substance-sequence. Our idea of wood, for instance, is the idea of something that exists first in a tree, then in a lumber yard, and finally as part of a chair. We think of the wood persisting through time, first as part of one substance, and then as part of another. Perhaps there is a single substance, the wood, that endures through all these changes, but one needn't suppose so to find the notion of wood perfectly intelligible. In a Lockean spirit, I suggest we call this sort of sequence of non-identical substances a *nominal substance*. These are cases where there is no single enduring substance, but where we treat the sequence as if it were the same thing over time in the literal, numerical sense. One might in principle recognize the existence of all sorts of far-fetched, arbitrarily yoked-together nominal substances. The ones that Locke recog-nizes, however, are tied together by robust interconnections that resonate with our conceptual schemes.

In referring to these as nominal substances, I mean not only to invoke the tradition of scholastic nominalism, but also to highlight their affinities with nominal essences (and the nominal powers of Ch. 23). Just as a nominal essence is something we construct, as a rough approximation to a real essence, in an effort to organize the world around us, so a nominal substance is a construction out of the real, strictly individuated substances that are the metaphysical bedrock of the material realm. Locke's interest in the identity conditions for oak trees, men, and persons is of a piece with his broader interest in

enduring organisms and persons corresponds to no thing whatsoever (but only to a series of things). Also, Conn thinks that no substance ever persists through any period of time. On my view, we can take Locke at his word in supposing that bodies persist for as long as they retain the same parts.

reaching a clearer understanding of our language, so that it is fit not just for our relatively undemanding "civil use" in ordinary life, but for our more exacting "philosophical use" (III.9.3). The reason Locke spends so much time on the case of persons is surely that it is an idea with implications not just for philosophy, but also theology and law, a "forensic term" (II.27.26), as he famously calls it. A less pessimistically skeptical author might aim at showing his readers the true nature of the substance that is the self. Locke thinks in general that our ideas of substance are "unavoidably ... various and ... very uncertain" (III.9.13). This is true, surely, not just in respect of our efforts at assigning things to their kinds, but also with respect to our individuating things over time. The best we can hope to do is to articulate clearly the principles from which we construct nominal substances. The strictly individuated real substances that underlie them are commonly hidden from our view.[10]

30.4. Parts and Wholes Revisited

I have so far managed to say nothing about what is probably the most popular modern interpretation of Locke, according to which he endorses multiple, coinciding, material substances. In the human case, for instance, there would be a body, a man, and a person, each a distinct thing with its own criteria for individuation. This option has not yet had the chance to emerge because I have taken it as a fixed interpretive point that Locke does not treat enduring animals and persons as substances. That, after all, is what he says, over and over. Hence the puzzle of the previous section was to figure out what animals and persons could be, if not real substances, and my conclusion was that they could only be nominal substances. It is worth considering, however, whether there is some way to get a view of this sort off the ground.

Beyond the textual problem just noted, the coincidence interpretation faces the further objection that it looks quite anachronistic—far more so than the four-dimensionalist interpretation considered in the previous section. There would seem to be no historical precedent for the idea that an ordinary substance like a tree is in fact two coincident substances: a body and a living thing. This is not to say that authors from our four centuries had no interest in drawing some sort of distinction between the body of a living thing and the living thing itself. On the contrary, as we have seen, scholastic authors attempted to do just this in quite a few different ways—their theories of prime matter (Chs. 2–3), accidental quantity (Chs. 14–15), and pluralism regarding substantial forms (§25.3) were all, in part, inspired by the desire to explain how a thing's body can possess properties that the whole substance does not, or might not. One might

---

[10] An account much like the one I propose here has been considered by various other commentators. See, in particular, Winkler, "Locke on Personal Identity," who wonders whether persons and animals might be characterized as "a series of substance-stages" (p. 164). Winkler does not, however, think this view can be found in Locke's text. More recently, McCann, "Identity, Essentialism," has contended that only bodily identity "is an entirely natural or physical relation," whereas the identity of an organism "is in part a creature of our ideas or nominal essences" and is subject to "conventionalism (more or less)" (p. 189). This points in the same direction as my own view, but McCann does not supply any details. Conn, *Locke on Essence and Identity* pp. 108–11, discusses still other authors who suggest, in passing, a similar perspective. Perhaps the same reading can be found back in Edmund Law's eighteenth-century discussion, according to which the notion of a person is "solely a creature of society, an abstract consideration of man" (*Defence* p. 10) and "an artificial distinction, yet founded in the nature, but not the whole nature of man" (p. 21).

therefore contend that since Locke can avail himself of none of these strategies, he needs some device like coincident objects to account for, say, the instability of the persistence conditions of a body, versus the robustness of the persistence conditions of a living thing. Perhaps. But it is—or ought to be—very hard to take this suggestion seriously, given how clearly the texts seem to rule it out when they stress over and over that the identity of a living thing or a person does not consist in the identity of a substance.[11]

Implausible as the coincidence interpretation looks on its face, it has a powerful textual impetus behind it, in that Locke repeatedly takes human beings and other living things as his paradigmatic examples of substances. In the discussion of substance in *Essay* II.23, for instance, man and horse are two of the principal examples of ordinary, familiar substances, alongside gold, water, and stone (see, e.g., II.23.3, 4, 6). This looks on its face to be extremely strong evidence against the nominalist interpretation I am offering. For if horses and human beings are merely nominal substances, then it would seem to be seriously misleading for Locke to treat them on a par with gold and other nonliving things. Strictly speaking, a horse should not count as a substance at all.

Although this objection may look decisive, it is in fact easy to respond on behalf of the nominalist reading. The key is to recognize an equivocation in the denotation of substance terms. For as soon as one distinguishes between real and nominal substances, and treats the latter as a sequence composed of the former, an ambiguity arises in a term like 'Socrates.' That term may refer to the substance that exists here and now, or it may refer to the sequence of substances that makes up the persisting nominal substance. To mark this ambiguity, I will distinguish between *synchronic* and *diachronic* denotation. In cases where a substance endures numerically the same over time, these two denotations do not come apart. A term picks out the very same thing, regardless of whether it refers synchronically to the thing that exists right now or refers diachronically to the persisting thing. There is no room for ambiguity here, because the persisting thing, at every moment of its existence, just is the very same thing that exists right now. The notion that the diachronically denoted persistent thing is in fact a sequence of things simply has no place. For theories in the nominalist tradition, in contrast, the thing at a time is typically not numerically the same as the thing at another time, and so *a fortiori* not the same as the 'thing' that persists through time. Hence substance terms are ambiguous.

Fourteenth-century advocates of the nominalist approach to identity were aware of the problems here. A term like 'Socrates' is supposed to be a paradigmatic example of what the scholastics call an *absolute term*, picking out a thing directly, without relating it to anything else. But if 'Socrates' refers to a sequence of things, it no longer seems to function straightforwardly as an absolute term. Nicole Oresme contended that in fact it

---

[11] Chappell provides a good example of the coincidence interpretation, as does Kaufman, "Locke on Individuation," although Kaufman thinks the view is inconsistent with other aspects of Locke's account. Against the coincidence interpretation, see McCann, "Identity, Essentialism."

One kind of precedent for the coincidence view is scholastic pluralism. As noted in §25.3, the pluralist is able to use distinct substantial forms to account for the different sorts of identity conditions of a substance—*qua* human or *qua* animal or *qua* body. But scholastic pluralists always insist that these different identity conditions, although grounded in different existences, are nevertheless combined in a single unified substance, under a single governing substantial form. So this is not the coincidence view. And for Locke to approach the coincidence view from this direction, he would need a metaphysical apparatus quite alien to his thought.

is not, and that the proper analysis of diachronic identity reveals such terms to work quite differently from how scholastic logicians had always supposed.[12] Although Locke does not seem to have explicitly recognized the semantic issues that surround his conception of identity—or even that there is an ambiguity here—it seems plausible, on inspection, that his use of substance terms is ambiguous in just this way. Most often in the *Essay* these terms denote synchronically. This is true even in II.27, where the very topic of discussion gets initially framed in terms of synchronic denotation: "when considering any thing as existing at any determined time and place, we compare it with itself existing at another time, and thereon form the ideas of *identity* and *diversity*" (II.27.1). Here 'thing' is explicitly said to pick out a thing at a time and a place, and the problem of identity is the problem of whether that thing is the same as a thing at another time. The denotation must be synchronic for this problem even to make sense. In some places, though, Locke switches to the diachronic sense, as when he describes the person or the self as a temporally extended whole composed of parts: "Any thing united to it by a consciousness of former actions makes also a part of the same self, which is the same both then and now" (II.27.25). Here 'self' must denote diachronically, for the notion of a temporal 'part' to make any sense. There are, however, not many such passages. His usual usage is synchronic, and so the problem of identity is not usually that of unifying distinct parts of a diachronic whole, but of accounting for the supposed identity between distinct synchronic individuals. Even in the passage just quoted Locke needs that synchronic usage: although 'self' denotes diachronically, for the temporally extended whole, 'thing' and 'part' must denote synchronically, for a conscious thinking thing at a time. His preference for the synchronic usage is just what one would expect, if enduring persons and living things are mere nominal substances, not genuine things. And that usage explains, too, why 'horse' and 'man' serve throughout the *Essay* as paradigmatic substance terms. They do so, because they denote synchronically, for the body or compound substance that, at a given time, is a horse or a man.

But although the nominalist reading has nothing to fear from Locke's persistent talk of horses and men as substances, it seems to me nevertheless that there is a way to motivate the coincidence interpretation, and that indeed it is the most plausible alternative to my own account. The first thing that has to be done is to find some other equivocation in Locke's use of the term 'substance'—not the one just proposed, which facilitates the real–nominal distinction, but one that distinguishes between two real senses of substance, so as to allow that in one sense diachronic identity is not a matter of the same substance's surviving, whereas in another sense it is. This is not a possibility I can dismiss out of hand, given that I myself argued for an equivocation in

---

[12] Such scholastic worries about the semantics of substance terms seem to appear first in Nicole Oresme, who makes this extremely interesting, if brief, remark: "et si arguatur ulterius: igitur 'sortes' est nomen connotativum, respondetur quod non est simpliciter absolutum sicut alii termini de praedicamento substantiae, non est etiam nomen connotativum sicut nomina accidentium quae praedicantur in quid" (*In Gen. et cor.* I.13, pp. 113–14). This idea gets picked up in Albert of Saxony who repeats this remark almost verbatim, adding that 'sortes' "est unum nomen medio modo se habens" (*In Phys* I.8, p. 128; see *In Gen. et cor.* I.10). The idea is that the failure of complete identity requires a rethinking of the way absolute terms work, and allowing for some third kind of term in between absolute and connotative. See too John Major, *In Phys.* I.2.9 f. b4v.

'substance' in §28.3, between substance in the ordinary sense and substance as the enduring substratum of change. But it is not easy to see what Locke's usage could be here, if not the ordinary usage, since the chapter counts not just bodies as substances, but also God and souls. There is, however, the following passage, which offers some amount of hope to the coincidence interpretation:

Self is that conscious thinking thing (whatever substance, made up of whether spiritual or material, simple or compounded, it matters not) which is sensible or conscious of pleasure and pain, capable of happiness or misery, and so is concerned for itself, as far as that consciousness extends. (II.27.17)

Although it is hard to know how to read the first two lines, with its rather odd punctuation, it is possible to read the passage as treating the self as a "thing" that is distinct from the "substance" it is "made up of." And this suggests that we might take Locke's general point to be that horses and persons (substances both) survive even while the stuff that composes them (their underlying "substance") varies.[13]

Can Locke talk this way—in terms of enduring substances existing through changes to their underlying constituents—without embracing something like Aristotelian prime matter? He can, if he makes the move we saw Pierre Gassendi and others make in §28.3, of embracing wholes as something over and above their parts. For Locke can then distinguish between the horse and the mass of matter that constitutes it. He can treat the mass as just the aggregate of the parts, individuated strictly in just the way the nominalists claim. But since the horse is not equivalent to those parts, even though they constitute it, the horse can have distinct identity conditions, and can persist—in the strictest sense of numerical identity—even while the mass changes. Similarly, a person (or, above, the "self" that is the "conscious thinking thing") need not be regarded as identical to whatever it is that constitutes it, and so can persist, literally and strictly the same, even while its constituents change. When wholes are given their own independent reality in this way, the obstacles to strict identity through change simply melt away.

On this line of interpretation, Locke emerges not as the culmination of the nominalist tradition of diachronic identity, but as the great champion of realism, insisting against the nominalists on the possibility of strict identity in virtue of a metaphysical distinction between the whole and its parts. It is, to be sure, distressing to see that a plausible *prima facie* case can be made for either of two diamentrically opposed readings of Locke's view. Plainly, too, the fault is his, not ours. If he had meant to defend the nominal approach, he ought to have said that he was not talking about strict identity. If he had meant to defend the realist approach, he ought to have said that enduring living things and persons are substances. (Or if, improbably, he has some other ontological category in mind, he should have told us that.) As things stand, each side in this debate seemingly has equally good textual grounds for rejecting the other's view.

---

[13] For suggestions that 'substance' in II.27 has some special meaning see e.g. Alston and Bennett, "Locke on People and Substances" p. 39 and Uzgalis, "Relative Identity" p. 294: "In the Chapter on Identity, Locke adopts a new conception of substances which he does not use elsewhere in the *Essay*."

30.5. Arguments for Nominalism

Even if no reading of *Essay* II.27 is completely satisfactory, I think sufficient arguments can be mustered for some degree of confidence in a nominal reading. First, consider again his discussion of real essences. Given his skepticism in this domain, it would seem that the idea of *person* described in II.27 cannot characterize an enduring substance, just because Locke has too good an idea of what a person is, and what its identity conditions are. He famously remarks:

to find wherein personal identity consists, we must consider what person stands for; which, I think, is a thinking intelligent being that has reason and reflection, and can consider itself as itself, the same thinking thing, in different times and places. (II.27.9)

If this is what a person is, and if persons are enduring substances, then Locke would have gone a long way toward describing a real essence. In particular, he would have just sketched the necessary and sufficient conditions for the endurance of a person. But as we saw in §27.7, Locke is adamant that we cannot do this, not even in principle. This provides strong evidence for thinking that the idea of a person must be merely nominal. Unlike in substance cases, where we seek, unsuccessfully, to grasp the nature of the things themselves, we are instead constructing what Locke elsewhere calls "archetypes of the mind's own making" (*Essay* IV.4.5).

Second, consider Locke's theory of general terms. General terms, he claims, refer to "abstract and partial ideas of more complex ones, taken at first from particular existences" (III.3.9). He gives the example of going from 'Peter' to 'man' to 'animal' to 'living thing' to 'body' to 'substance' and finally to 'being' and 'thing.' Every step of the way, it is the same individual thing that gets picked out, while "leaving out something that is peculiar to each individual" and so embracing a wider range of individuals. For instance, "making a new distinct complex idea, and giving the name *animal* to it, one has a more general term that comprehends, with man, several other creatures.... By the same way the mind proceeds to *body, substance,* and at last to *being, thing* ..." (ibid.). This is what one would expect Locke to say, given that the substance just is the body, which just is the animal, which just is Peter. If the person were distinct from the man, and the man distinct from the body, then this account of general terms would make no sense. Terms of greater generality would not pick out a wider range of things, but would instead pick out entirely different things.

Third, consider Locke's theory of persons. Until now, that theory has lain in the background of this chapter, as just another case where it is unclear whether the alleged identity is merely nominal or robustly substantial. It is worth taking a moment to remark on this part of Locke's theory, however, since this is by far its most original and influential component. In this one chapter, Locke carves out the notion of a person, as something distinct from the biological human being, to be analyzed not in terms of sameness of soul but in terms of psychological continuity. Although there are historical precedents for each of the various aspects of this theory, no one before Locke had assembled all the pieces into a coherent package.[14] Yet although this is an idea worthy

---

[14] The novelty of Locke's account of persons has various dimensions, each of which perhaps has some precedent, when taken alone, but not when taken as a whole. First, there is his insistence that sameness of soul does not capture our

of celebration, modern readers have had to curb their enthusiasm, because it is very hard to see how the theory can be saved from various seemingly devastating puzzles.

It is a particularly appealing feature of the nominalist approach that it solves many of these puzzles effortlessly. Consider the oft-discussed problem of transitivity failure: the old man remembers his middle age, the middle-aged man remembered his youth, but the old man does not remember his youth. The result is that $a=b$, $b=c$, but $a\neq c$. This looks unacceptable, since identity is a transitive property. On the present interpretation, the problem dissolves. The old man is not identical to the middle-aged man, when the terms denote synchronically, nor is the middle-aged man identical to the boy. The three distinct substances may or may not be regarded as forming a nominal substance, but in any case they are not strictly identical. Transitivity may and regularly will fail.

Consider too the gappy character of our memories, which seems to make it the case on Locke's view that I, as a person, encompass very little of my past. Locke seems willing, and even glad, to embrace that result, insisting on the distinction between sameness of person and sameness of man (see, e.g., II.27.20). But could the person that is I really cover so little of the life of the biological organism? Again, on the present view, there is nothing embarrassing about this. A person (denoting diachronically) is not a thing, but a sequence of things. Given our faulty memories, it just is true that the self we conceive of is quite a thin and tenuous construction. If you tell me about something I did, but which I no longer remember, then I may be curious about whether it really happened. But even if I believe that it did happen, I cannot incorporate that into my conception of who I am. Perhaps later the memory will come back to me, and then my past action will come to be part of the person I am (denoting diachronically). Given that persons are mere nominal substances—constructs of distinct entities, tied together by memories—there seems nothing worrisome about these results.

What about false memories? If the person I construct is the sum of my current self and all the selves whose lives I remember, could that construct include conscious beings whose lives I merely take myself to remember, wrongly? It would seem not, because there might be another person who correctly remembers being that person, and then we would have $a=c$, $b=c$, but $a\neq b$—another violation of the logic of identity. Yet, on

concept. This is an issue that is obviously of great importance in considering Locke's relationship to earlier scholastic thought, even if my discussion here largely takes it for granted. (For a good discussion, see Yaffe, "Locke on Ideas of Identity" pp. 207–13.)

Second, there is the focus on psychological continuity and, specifically, on memory. One can, to be sure, find passing intimations of memory's relevance to diachronic identity in earlier authors. Sorabji, Self ch. 5, describes hints in Lucretius (De natura rerum 3.850) and Augustine (Confessions I.7.12). We have seen gestures toward it in Autrecourt (§29.4) and it can also be found, in inchoate form, in Gassendi (Philosophiae Epicuri syntagma II.1.18 p. 67 [tr. Stanley, Hist. Phil. p. 872]) and in Henry More, Psychodia Platonica, Antipsychopannychia I.8–11. Leibniz quite clearly and fully articulated the memory criterion in 1686 (Discourse on Metaphysics art. 34), but this work was published only in the nineteenth century. For a very useful discussion of the seventeenth-century background to Locke's related notion of consciousness, see Thiel, Lockes Theorie ch. 4.

Third, there is Locke's focus on the notion of a person, as something distinct from the notion of a man. This is quite a striking and unprecedented feature of his view. It seems likely that Locke was inspired by contemporary Trinitarian discussions, and specifically by William Sherlock's idea that what individuates one person of the Trinity from another is consciousness. Although in a sense this is much the same idea, Locke's distinctive contribution is to see that this idea could be applied to the notion of a human person, as something distinct from the living human organism, and that the idea could serve to articulate the idea of the same person over time, an idea that takes us into entirely new philosophical terrain. (Here I am drawing on Thiel, "Trinity," who makes clear both the similarities and the differences between Locke and Sherlock.)

the other hand, how can false memories be excluded, unless we already have an account of what it is to be the same person? Circularity looms. Again, however, the nominalist reading of Locke points toward a reply: if the diachronic identity of persons is not strict numerical identity, then we need not worry about the laws of identity. More generally, the nominalist approach makes it clear that we ought not to worry about whether a memory is true or false. If I take myself to remember doing something, then that is part of the self I construct, right or wrong, for better or worse. Just as Locke's theory can tolerate forgetting, so it can tolerate misremembering. Our conception of ourselves does not include the whole of the living organism we are, and it might include actions performed by another organism. Indeed, the selves we construct might on close inspection turn out to be riddled with error and wildly incoherent in too many respects to count. Since such persons (denoting diachronically) are merely nominal, this makes no difference. Locke is analyzing our concepts, not the way the world is, and our concepts do not have to be coherent.

On the coincidence interpretation, in contrast, all these puzzles look wholly intractable.[15]

30.6. Final Rewards

On any reading of the text, it is not easy to understand how Locke thinks about divine judgment. Reflection on this issue, however, points again toward a nominal conception of personal identity. Consider, first, this difficult passage, where Locke considers the question of what God would do about false memories:

But that which we call the *same consciousness*, not being the same individual act, why one intellectual substance may not have represented to it, as done by itself, what it never did, and was perhaps done by some other agent, why I say such a representation may not possibly be   3
without reality of matter of fact, as well as several representations in dreams are, which yet, whilst dreaming, we take for true, will be difficult to conclude from the nature of things. And yet that it never is so, will by us, till we have clearer views of the nature of thinking substances, be   6
best resolved into the goodness of God, who as far as the happiness or misery of any of his sensible creatures is concerned in it, will not by a fatal error of theirs transfer from one to another, that consciousness, which draws reward or punishment with it. (II.27.13)   9

The long first sentence raises the possibility that a person might take himself to have done something that he never did, and that in fact was "done by some other agent" (line 3). The second sentence (lines 5–9) then considers whether this would yield the result that such a person might therefore be rewarded or punished for something that he did not in fact do. Given that Locke associates personhood with moral responsibility, it would seem that he has no choice but to treat the memory as determining reward or

---

[15] For a handy summary of the main puzzles surrounding Locke's theory of personal identity, see Yaffe, "Locke on Ideas of Identity" pp. 213–29. There is a vast literature on these topics, and my remarks here amount to nothing more than a sketch of how one might go, given the line of interpretation I am offering. There is in particular still a question of whether the so-called "simple memory theory" is the right way to interpret Locke's account, even given the approach I am sketching. My main point, however, is that these sorts of issues are far less worrisome on a nominalist reading of Locke's account, making it less pressing to look for anything beyond a straightforward reading of what it means for "consciousness" to be "extended backwards" (II.27.9).

punishment. Yet, on the contrary, presumably thinking of the eternal rewards and punishments of the next life, Locke assures us that God would not let this "fatal error" (line 8) occur. It is hard to know what to make of this passage, with its seeming unwillingness to let the memory criterion count as the final word regarding personal identity. Memories can be wrong, if they represent the actions of some "other agent" (line 3), and in that case one ought not to be rewarded or punished for them. But to say this seemingly requires some other governing criterion for personal identity, a criterion that Locke seems illicitly to rely on when he speaks of distinct agents tied together falsely by consciousness.[16]

As I understand this passage, Locke happily allows that the false memories combine with true memories to construct a person. This would be a surprising outcome on the coincidence interpretation, given its realism about what a person is, but there is no reason not to allow nominal substances to be made in this way. If, however, this sort of nominal construct is all that a person is, then it is no wonder that Locke finds intolerable the idea of someone's being damned for all eternity on the basis of a false conception of the self. The same point would presumably apply to someone who has (conveniently) forgotten his past life of crime, or to someone who has (sadly) forgotten her many years of virtuous self-sacrifice. God punishes according to what we deserve, not according to what we remember. But how can this be squared with the notion that "in this personal identity is founded all the right and justice of reward and punishment" (II.27.18), so that "to punish Socrates waking for what sleeping Socrates thought, and waking Socrates was never conscious of, would be no more right than to punish one twin for what his brother-twin did, whereof he knew nothing" (II.27.19)? I take Locke's view to be that the ties in consciousness that define personhood are merely a necessary condition for just reward and punishment. The presence of such ties is not sufficient to ensure responsibility, however, because one might have false memories of things for which one bears no responsibility. Similarly, the absence of such ties is not sufficient to annul responsibility, because one might forget things for which one deserves reward or punishment.

What then are the additional necessary criteria that determine moral responsibility? What leads Locke to think that punishment on the basis of these false memories would be a "fatal error" (line 8), and that indeed they *are* false memories? Locke's position, I take it, is that he does not know, and that on the available evidence we cannot know. Thus the very question of whether false memories are possible is "difficult to conclude from the nature of things" (line 5). As for what might come of such memories, here we can only invoke "the goodness of God" (line 7), at least "till we have clearer views of the nature of thinking substances" (line 6). This is to say that *our* concept of persons is wholly inadequate to settle such questions of moral responsibility. Again, all of this suggests that our concept of person is merely a nominal one, the "workmanship of the understanding" rather than of nature (*Essay* III.3.12). God, however, as nature's author, will of course know what the right way is to resolve these issues. Apparently, God's first

---

[16] The goodness of God passage (II.27.13) has been read very differently by other commentators. Bolton, for instance, takes Locke to be contending that God will not allow false memories ("Locke on Identity" pp. 118–22). Although the text admits of this reading, I cannot believe it is what Locke means, since the phenomenon of false memories seems not just possible, but commonplace.

task will be to restore all of one's memories, and expunge any false memories. Which ones are *ours*? This is a question we cannot answer, and must leave to God to sort out; the best we can do is stick to the memory criterion. But we might speculate that if, say, we have immaterial, incorruptible souls, then God will restore a memory of all the conscious actions of that soul. If, instead, we are simply biological organisms, with no more continuity than that of an oak tree, then presumably the actions that are ours are those done by one of the temporary bodies that makes up the biologically continuous human being.

Locke does no more than hint at the view that God's judgment will be so exacting as to restore all of our memories, thereby making us responsible for everything we have ever consciously, voluntarily done. But given that memories are a necessary condition for moral responsibility, God can justly reward and punish us only for what we remember doing. To be punished or rewarded for what we cannot remember would leave us simply bewildered, at a loss, with no understanding of how the outcome was just. If Locke is right about this, then God will presumably have to restore some of the memories of some people, lest forgetting be a free get-out-of-hell card. And once God gets into the business of doing this at all, it is hard to see why he should stop halfway. What the view implies, then, is that the life to come will give us a supernaturally clear sense of the diachronic person we are, and that we will be judged on the merits of this full story. The philosophically interesting implication of this picture—setting aside the eschatological speculation—is that memory is not the ultimate, defining criterion of who we are. This single passage from §13, describing God's correction of a "fatal error," suggests that such ties in consciousness are simply the only tool we have available for articulating a conception of ourselves. It is not a bad tool, inasmuch as psychological continuity is a necessary condition for any legitimate concept of the self. But it scarcely captures the true nature of what persons are.[17]

These reflections point once again toward the implausibility of the coincidence interpretation. If the memory criterion carves out some sort of metaphysical entity, above and beyond body and soul, then one would expect such persons, so individuated, to receive their just reward in the next life. The implications of this, however, are clearly unacceptable. If persons are real substances, then for each biological human life there is, we will find in heaven each of the persons that existed over that life. Alice the old woman will be there, as will the baby version of herself that she no longer remembers, as will the partying college girl whose drunken nights have no conscious ties to anything else at all. For the one human being who is Alice, there will apparently be a horde of distinct, real, substantial persons, each of which will presumably stand in line for its own private divine judgment. Far better, clearly, is to suppose that the person we construct on the basis of memory is merely a construct, a nominal self. Only God knows a person's real essence.

---

[17]   Reason to think God will restore all and only *our* memories comes at II.27.26: "the apostle tells us that, at the great day, when everyone shall 'receive according to his doings, the secrets of all hearts shall be laid open.' The sentence shall be justified by the consciousness all persons shall have, that they themselves, in what bodies soever they appear, or what substances soever that consciousness adheres to, are the same that committed those actions, and deserve that punishment for them." To say we will be conscious of being "the same that committed those actions" is to say, I take it, that we will remember the actions.

Ultimately, the effect of Locke's views is to undermine the last place of refuge from the chaos of post-scholastic metaphysics—to undermine, that is to say, our own natures. Even though Locke eschews the sort of radically revisionary metaphysics advanced by some of his contemporaries, and even though he retains our familiar world of enduring substances and their dependent attributes, this world is not as familiar as it seems. The ideas we have of the changeable things around us turn out, on close inspection, to pick out merely nominal substances. The real substances, subject to mereological essentialism, are not something we care very much about, and Locke pays them so little attention that it is easy to ignore them altogether. These are claims that we have seen many others make before Locke. His distinctive contribution is to extend this conclusion even to our ideas of ourselves. The Lockean notion of a person requires not just a strikingly new conception of psychological continuity but also a dismantling of the prevailing conception of the self. Even while earlier figures like Descartes had deconstructed the scholastic conception of material substance, they had retained the idea of the self as an enduring thing, an immaterial mind, and so left substance intact in the case we care about most of all. Locke's signal achievement—if we can call it that—is to call into question even this limited role for the theory of substance. The final legacy of scholastic metaphysics, the category of Substance, endures in Locke's account, but it does so just barely.

ACKNOWLEDGEMENTS

My first book took me two years to write, my next one four, and this one eight. The trends are not encouraging. But at least my kids no longer scribble on my library books.

On that note, let me begin by thanking the staff at CU's Norlin Library, without whose efforts I could not have begun to write this book. In addition, I have benefited from the generosity of the Newberry Library, the vast holdings of the Bodleian Library, and above all from the growing virtual library of Latin texts made available on the internet by libraries around the world. Special thanks are due to Dana Sutton, and her indefatigable efforts at maintaining an online index of this material.

An ACLS/Mellon Fellowship contributed greatly to my research in its early stages.

My greatest debt is to my past and present colleagues in Boulder, and to the generous research support I have received from the University of Colorado. I cannot possibly give thanks to all the individuals whose comments have helped me with this project, or even to all the places where I have given talks based on this material. I would be remiss, however, not to thank the following people: Andrew Arlig, Fabrizio Amerini, Dominic Bailey, Paul Bakker, Jeffrey Brower, Chris Heathwood, Paul Hoffman, Hud Hudson, Dan Kaufman, Stefan Kirschner, Gyula Klima, DZ Korman, Henrik Lagerlund, Christian Lee, Mitzi Lee, Christoph Lüthy, Steven Marrone, Bradley Monton, Lloyd Newton, Larry Nolan, Calvin Normore, Jonathan Peeters, Sylvain Piron, David Robb, Michael Sechman, Christopher Shields, Alison Simmons, Daniel Stoljar, Michiel Streijger, Edith Sylla, Hans Thijssen, Cecilia Trifogli, Rega Wood, and Jack Zupko. Special thanks to Jorge Secada, for a set of comments on behalf of OUP that were too insightful to remain anonymous.

TABLES OF AUTHORS

Alphabetical

Authors whose careers are earlier than 1600 are ordered by first name. For cross-references between first and last names, see the Index of Names.[1]

Agostino Nifo (1469/70–1538)
Albert of Saxony (*c.*1316–1390)
Albert the Great (*c.*1200–1280)
Arnauld, Antoine (1612–1694)

Bacon, Francis (1561–1626)
Basso, Sebastian (1577/83–after 1625)
Bayle, Pierre (1647–1706)
Beeckman, Isaac (1588–1637)
Benedictus Pererius (1535–1610)
Berigard, Claude (1578–1664)
Bernardino Telesio (1509–1588)
Blasius of Parma (*c.*1345–1416)
Boate, Gerard (1604–1650) and **Arnold** (1606–1653)
Boethius of Dacia (*c.*1240–after 1277)
Bonaventure (*c.*1217–1274)
Boyle, Robert (1627–1691)
Burgersdijk, Franco (1590–1635)

Cajetan (Thomas de Vio) (1468–1534)
Campanella, Tommaso (1568–1639)
Carpenter, Nathanael (1589–1628)
Cesare Cremonini (*c.*1550–1631)
Charleton, Walter (1620–1707)
Collegium Conimbricense (fl. 1590s)
Conway, Anne (1631–1679)
Crakanthorpe, Richard (1567–1624)

Dabillon, André (d. 1664)
Descartes, René (1596–1650)

---

[1] For biographical information, see the appendices to the Cambridge Histories covering the Middle Ages (ed. Pasnau), Renaissance (ed. Schmitt and Skinner) and seventeenth century (ed. Garber and Ayers). For further information on scholastic authors, see Lohr's comprehensive guides to medieval and Renaissance Aristotle commentaries.

Dietrich of Freiburg (*c*.1250–after 1310)
Digby, Kenelm (1603–1665)
Domingo de Soto (1494/5–1560)
Durand of St. Pourçain (1270/5–1334)

Eustachius a Sancto Paulo (1573–1640)

Francesco Patrizi (1529–1597)
Francis of Marchia (1285/90–after 1344)
Francisco Sanches (1550/1–1623)
Francisco Suárez (1548–1617)
Franciscus Toletus (1532–1596)

Gabriel Biel (before 1425–1495)
Gabriel Vasquez (1549/51?–1604)
Galilei, Galileo (1564–1642)
Gassendi, Pierre (1592–1655)
Gianfrancesco Pico della Mirandola (1469–1533)
Giles of Orleans (d. after 1277)
Giles of Rome (1243/7–1316)
Giordano Bruno (1548–1600)
Giovanni Pico della Mirandola (1463–1494)
Glanvill, Joseph (1636–1680)
Godfrey of Fontaines (*c*.1250–1306/9)
Gorlaeus, David (1591–1612)
Gregory of Rimini (*c*.1300–1358)

Harvey, William (1578–1657)
Henry Cornelius Agrippa (1486–1535)
Henry of Ghent (*c*.1217–1293)
Hill, Nicholas (*c*.1570–*c*.1610)
Hobbes, Thomas (1588–1679)

Jacob Schegk (1511–1587)
Jacob Zabarella (1533–1589)
John Buridan (1295/1300–1358/61)
John Capreolus (1380–1444)
John Duns Scotus (1265/6–1308)
John of Jandun (*c*.1280s–1328)
John Major (1467/9–1550)
John of Mirecourt (fl. 1344–7)
John Wyclif (*c*.1325–1384)
Julius Caesar Scaliger (1484–1558)
Jungius, Joachim (1587–1657)

Kepler, Johannes (1571–1630)

Leibniz, Gottfried Wilhelm (1646–1716)
Locke, John (1632–1704)
Lorenzo Valla (1407–1457)

Magnen, Jean Chrysostome (1590–1679)
Malebranche, Nicolas (1638–1715)
Marsilio Ficino (1433–1499)
Marsilius of Inghen (c.1340–1396)
Mersenne, Marin (1588–1648)
More, Henry (1614–1687)

Newton, Isaac (1642–1727)
Nicholas of Autrecourt (c.1298–1369)
Nicholas of Cusa (1401–1464)
Nicole Oresme (c.1320–1382)

Paul of Venice (c.1369–1429)
Pedro Fonseca (1528–1599)
Peter of Ailly (1350–1420)
Peter Auriol (c.1280–1322)
Peter John Olivi (1247/8–1298)
Pietro Pomponazzi (1462–1525)

Radulphus Brito (c.1270–c.1320)
Richard of Middleton (c.1249–1302/3)

Scheibler, Christoph (1589–1653)
Sennert, Daniel (1572–1637)
Siger of Brabant (c.1240–1282/4)
Spinoza, Baruch (1632–1677)

Thomas Aquinas (1224/5–1274)

Vanini, Giulio Cesare (1585–1619)

Walter Burley (c.1275–c.1345)
Walter Chatton (1285/90–1343/4)
White, Thomas (1593–1676)
William of Auvergne (1180/90–1249)
William Crathorn (fl. 1330s)
William Ockham (c.1287–1347)

Chronological

William of Auvergne (1180/90–1249)
Albert the Great (*c.*1200–1280)
Bonaventure (*c.*1217–1274)
Thomas Aquinas (1224/5–1274)
  Summa theologiae (1266–73)
Henry of Ghent (*c.*1217–1293)
  Quaestiones ordinariae (1275–93)
  Quodlibeta (1275–93)
Giles of Orleans (d. after 1277)
Boethius of Dacia (*c.*1240–after 1277)
Siger of Brabant (*c.*1240–1282/4)
Giles of Rome (1243/7–1316)
Peter John Olivi (1247/8–1298)
  Summa quaestionum super Sententias (*c.*1274–95)
  Tractatus de quantitate (1282)
Richard of Middleton (*c.*1249–1302/3)
  Sentences (1280/90)
Dietrich of Freiburg (*c.*1250–after 1310)
Godfrey of Fontaines (*c.*1250–1306/9)
John Duns Scotus (1265/6–1308)
  Lectura (*c.*1298)
  Ordinatio (1300–4)
  Reportatio (1305–)
Durand of St. Pourçain (1270/5–1334)
Radulphus Brito (*c.*1270–*c.*1320)
Walter Burley (*c.*1275–*c.*1345).
  Physics commentary (after 1324)
  Ars vetus commentary (1337)
Peter Auriol (*c.*1280–1322)
  Sentences (*c.*1316)
Walter Chatton (1285/90–1343/4)
John of Jandun (*c.*1280s–1328)
William of Ockham (*c.*1287–1347)
  Sentences [*Reportatio, Ordinatio*] (1317–24)
  Summula philosophiae naturalis (*c.*1320)
  Summa logicae (*c.*1323)
  Tractatus de corpore Christi (*c.*1323)
  Quodlibeta (1321–)
Francis of Marchia (1285/90–after 1344)
  Sentences (1319–20; later revised)
William Crathorn (fl. 1330s)
Nicholas of Autrecourt (*c.*1298–1369)

Tractatus (1330s)

Letters (1335–7)

John Buridan (1295/1300–1358/61)

Questions on the De anima (1340s)

Questions on Generation and Corruption (1340s)

Questions on the Metaphysics (1340s)

Questions on the Physics (1340s)

Gregory of Rimini (*c.*1300–1358)

Sentences (1343–4)

John of Mirecourt (fl. 1344–47)

Albert of Saxony (*c.*1316–1390)

Questions on the Physics (*c.*1351)

Questions on Generation and Corruption (1350s)

Nicole Oresme (*c.*1320–1382)

De anima (*c.*1347)

De generatione et corruptione (late 1340s)

Physics (*c.*1346)

John Wyclif (*c.*1325–1384)

Tractatus de universalibus (*c.*1370)

De materia et forma (1370/5)

De eucharistia (1381)

Marsilius of Inghen (*c.*1340–1396)

Questions on Generation and Corruption (1360s?)

Blasius of Parma (*c.*1345–1416)

Peter of Ailly (1350–1420)

Paul of Venice (*c.*1369–1429)

Summa philosophiae naturalis (1408)

John Capreolus (1380–1444)

Defensiones theologiae (1411–44)

Nicholas of Cusa (1401–1464)

Lorenzo Valla (1407–1457)

Gabriel Biel (before 1425–1495)

Marsilio Ficino (1433–1499)

Pietro Pomponazzi (1462–1525)

Giovanni Pico della Mirandola (1463–1494)

John Major (1467/9–1550)

Cajetan (Thomas de Vio) (1468–1534)

Gianfrancesco Pico della Mirandola (1469–1533)

Examen vanitatis (1520)

Agostino Nifo (1469/70–1538)

Julius Caesar Scaliger (1484–1558)

Henry Cornelius Agrippa (1486–1535)

Domingo de Soto (1494/5–1560)

Bernardino Telesio (1509–1588)

De rerum natura (1565; expanded in 1586)

Jacob Schegk (1511–1587)
Pedro Fonseca (1528–1599)
  Commentarii in libros Metaphys. (1577–90)
Francesco Patrizi (1529–1597)
Franciscus Toletus (1532–1596)
Jacob Zabarella (1533–1589)
  De rebus naturalibus (1590)
Benedictus Pererius (1535–1610)
  De communibus principiis (1562)
Giordano Bruno (1548–1600)
Collegium Conimbricense
  various Aristotelian commentaries (1590s)
Francisco Suárez (1548–1617)
  Disputationes metaphysicae (1597)
Francisco Sanches (1550/1–1623)
  Quod nihil scitur (1576)
Gabriel Vasquez (1549/51?–1604)
  In Summam theologiam (1598)
Cesare Cremonini (*c.*1550–1631)
Francis Bacon (1561–1626)
  Advancement of Learning (1605)
  Instauratio Magna: Novum organum (1620)
Galileo Galilei (1564–1642)
  The Assayer (1623)
  Two Chief World Systems (1632)
Richard Crakanthorpe (1567–1624)
Tommaso Campanella (1568–1639)
Nicholas Hill (*c.*1570–*c.*1610)
  Philosophia Epicurea Democritiana (1601)
Johannes Kepler (1571–1630)
Daniel Sennert (1572–1637)
  Epitome naturalis scientiae (1618)
  Hypomnemata physica (1636)
Eustachius a Sancto Paulo (1573–1640)
  Summa philosophiae quadripartita (1609)
Sebastian Basso (1577/83–after 1625)
  Philosophiae naturalis adversus Aristotelem (1621)
Claude Berigard (1578–1664)
William Harvey (1578–1657)
Giulio Cesare Vanini (1585–1619)
Joachim Jungius (1587–1657)
Isaac Beeckman (1588–1637)
Marin Mersenne (1588–1648)
Thomas Hobbes (1588–1679)

De mundo (1642)
De corpore (begun c.1643; publ. 1655)
Leviathan (1651)

Christoph Scheibler (1589–1653)
Metaphysica (1617)

Nathanael Carpenter (1589–1628)
Philosophia libera (1621)

Jean Chrysostome Magnen (1590–1679)
Democritus reviviscens (1646)

Franco Burgersdijk (1590–1635)
Collegium physicum (1632)
Institutiones metaphysicae (1640)

David Gorlaeus (1591–1612)
Exercitationes philosophicae (c.1611; publ. 1620)
Idea physicae (c.1611; publ. 1651)

Pierre Gassendi (1592–1655)
Exercitationes paradoxicae (1624)
Objectiones quintae (1641)
Disquisitio metaphysica (1644)
Syntagma philosophicum (1658)

Thomas White (1593–1676)

René Descartes (1596–1650)
Meditations (1641)
Principles of Philosophy (1644)

Boate, Gerard (1604–1650) and **Arnold** (1606–1653)
Philosophia naturalis reformata (1641)

André Dabillon (d. 1664)

Kenelm Digby (1603–1665)
Two Treatises (1644)

Antoine Arnauld (1612–1694)
Port-Royal Logic (with Pierre Nicole) (1662)

Henry More (1614–1687)
correspondence with Descartes (1648–9)
The Immortality of the Soul (1659)
Enchiridion Metaphysicum (1671)

Walter Charleton (1620–1707)
Physiologia Epicuro-Gassendo-Charltoniana (1654)

Robert Boyle (1627–1691)
Certain Physiological Essays (1661)
Origin of Forms and Qualities (1666)

Anne Conway (1631–1679)

John Locke (1632–1704)
Essay Drafts A and B (1671)
Essay Concerning Human Understanding (1689)

Baruch Spinoza (1632–1677)
Ethics (1677)

Joseph Glanvill (1636–1680)
Vanity of Dogmatizing (1661)

Nicolas Malebranche (1638–1715)

Search after Truth (1674–5)

Isaac Newton (1642–1727)
De gravitatione (*c.*1671)
Philosophiae naturalis principia mathematica (1687)

Gottfried Wilhelm Leibniz (1646–1716)

Pierre Bayle (1647–1706)
Dictionary (1697)

BIBLIOGRAPHY

Primary Sources

Authors whose careers are earlier than 1600 are indexed by first name. Translations are listed when they serve as a starting point for my own translations. For cross-references between first and last names, see the Index of Names.

Adelard of Bath. *Quaestiones naturales*, in C. Burnett et al. (ed. and tr.) *Conversations with his Nephew: On the Same and the Different, Questions on Natural Science, and On Birds* (Cambridge: Cambridge University Press, 1998).

Albert the Great. *Opera omnia*, ed. B. Geyer et al. [Cologne] (Münster: Aschendorff, 1951–).

Albert the Great. *Opera omnia*, ed. P. Jammy (Lyon, 1651).

Albert of Orlamünde. *Philosophia pauperum sive Isagoge in libros Aristotelis*, in Albert the Great, *Opera Omnia*, ed. P. Jammy, vol. 21 (Lyon, 1651).

Albert of Saxony. *Expositio et questiones in Aristotelis libros Physicorum ad Albertum de Saxonia attributae*, ed. B. Patar (Louvain-la-Neuve: Peeters, 1999).

Albert of Saxony. *Questiones subtilissime in libros de generatione* (Venice, 1505; repr. Frankfurt: Minerva, 1970).

Alexander of Hales. *Summa theologica* (Quaracchi: Collegium S. Bonaventurae, 1924–48).

Alexander of Hales. *Quaestiones disputatae 'antequam esset frater'* (Quaracchi: Collegium S. Bonaventurae, 1960).

Anonymous. *Categoriae decem*, ed. L. Minio-Paluello (*Aristoteles Latinus* 1.1–5) (Bruges: Desclée de Brouwer, 1961).

Anonymous. *Liber sex principiorum*, ed. L. Minio-Paluello (*Aristoteles Latinus* 1.7) (Bruges: Desclée de Brouwer, 1966).

Anonymous. *Quaestiones super libros Physicorum*, in A. Zimmermann (ed.) *Ein Kommentar zur Physik des Aristoteles aus der Pariser Artistenfakultät um 1273* (Berlin: De Gruyter, 1968).

Anselm of Canterbury. *Opera omnia*, ed. F. S. Schmidt (Stuttgart: F. Frommann, 1968).

Apollinaris Offredus. *Exposito et quaestiones in libros Aristotelis De anima* (Venice, 1496).

Aristotle. *The Complete Works of Aristotle: The Revised Oxford Translation*, ed. J. Barnes (Princeton: Princeton University Press, 1984).

Aristotle. *Selections*, tr. T. Irwin and G. Fine (Indianapolis: Hackett, 1995).

Arnauld, Antoine and Pierre Nicole. *La logique ou l'art de penser*, ed. P. Clair and F. Girbal, rev. ed. (Paris: Vrin, 1981).

Arnauld, Antoine and Pierre Nicole. *Logic or the Art of Thinking* [*Port-Royal Logic*], tr. J. V. Buroker (Cambridge: Cambridge University Press, 1996).

Aubrey, John. *Lives of Eminent Men*, in J. Walker, *Letters Written by Eminent Persons in the Seventeenth and Eighteenth Centuries* (London: Longman, 1813).

Aubrey, John. *The Natural History of Wiltshire* (London: Nichols and Son, 1847; repr. New York: A. M. Kelley, 1969).

Augustine. *Opera* (Corpus Christianorum, series latina) (Turnhout: Brepols, 1954–81).

Augustine. *Opera* (Corpus scriptorum ecclesiasticorum latinorum) (Vienna: F. Tempsky, 1887–).

Averroes. *Commentarium magnum de anima*, ed. F. S. Crawford (Cambridge, MA: Mediaeval Academy of America, 1953).

Averroes. *Commentarium medium et Epitome in Aristotelis De generatione et corruptione libros*, ed. S. Kurland (Cambridge, MA: Mediaeval Academy of America, 1958).

Averroes. *Averroes' De substantia orbis: Critical Edition of the Hebrew Text with English Translation and Commentary*, ed. A. Hyman (Cambridge, MA: Mediaeval Academy of America, 1986).

Averroes. *Destructio destructionum philosophiae Algazelis in the Latin version of Calo Calonymos*, ed. B. Zedler (Milwaukee: Marquette University Press, 1961).

Averroes. *Epitome of Parva naturalia*, tr. H. Blumberg (Cambridge, MA: Mediaeval Academy of America, 1961).

Averroes. *In ea opera omnes qui ad nos pervenere Commentarii*, in Aristotle, *Omnia quae extant opera* (Venice apud Iuntas, 1552).

Avicebron. *Fons vitae*, ed. C. Baeumker (Beiträge zur Geschichte der Philosophie des Mittelalters 1.2–4) (Münster: Aschendorff, 1892–5).

Avicenna. *Liber de philosophia prima sive Scientia divina [Metaphysics]*, ed. S. van Riet (Leiden: Brill, 1977–83).

Avicenna. *Liber primus naturalium*, ed. S. Van Riet et al. (Louvain-la-Neuve: Peeters, 1992–2006).

Babin, François. *Journal ou relation fidele de tout ce qui s'est passé dans l'université d'Angers au sujet de la philosophie de Des Carthes en l'execution des ordres du Roy pendant les années 1675, 1676, 1677, et 1678* (Angers, 1679).

Bacon, Francis. *The Advancement of Learning*, ed. M. Kiernan (*The Oxford Francis Bacon* vol. 4) (Oxford: Clarendon Press, 2000).

Bacon, Francis. *The Instauratio magna part II: Novum organum and Associated Texts*, ed. and tr. G. Rees with M. Wakely (*The Oxford Francis Bacon* vol. 11) (Oxford: Clarendon, 2004).

Bacon, Francis. *Philosophical Studies c.1611–c.1619*, ed. G. Rees (*The Oxford Francis Bacon* vol. 6) (Oxford: Clarendon, 1996).

Barrow, Isaac. *Lectiones mathematicae XXIII* (London: J. Playford, 1685).

Barrow, Isaac. *The Usefulness of Mathematical Learning*, tr. J. Kirkby (London: Stephen Austen, 1734).

Basso, Sebastian. *Philosophiae naturalis adversus Aristotelem Libri XII* (Geneva, 1621).

Bayle, Pierre. *Dictionnaire historique et critique*, nouvelle édition, 16 vols. (Paris: Desoer, 1820).

Bayle, Pierre. *Historical and Critical Dictionary: Selections*, tr. R. Popkin (Indianapolis: Hackett, 1991).

Beeckman, Isaac. *Journal tenu par Isaac Beeckman de 1604 à 1634*, ed. C. de Waard, 4 vols. (The Hague: Nijhoff, 1939–53).

Benedictus Pererius. *De communibus omnium rerum naturalium principiis et affectionibus* (Paris, 1579).

Berigard, Claude. *Circulus Pisanus de veteri et peripatetica philosophia* (Padua: P. Frambotto, 1661).

Berkeley, George. *Works*, ed. A. A. Luce and T. E. Jessop, 9 vols. (London: Nelson, 1948–57).

Bernardino Telesio. *De rerum natura iuxta propria principia libri IX* (Naples, 1586; repr. Hildesheim: Olms, 1971).

Blasius of Parma. *Quaestio de intensione et remissione formarum*, in G. Federici Vescovini (ed.) "La Quaestio de intensione et remissione formarum de Biagio Pelacani da Parma," *Physis: Rivista internazionale di storia della scienza* 31 (1994) 433–535.

Blasius of Parma. *Les quaestiones de anima*, ed. G. Federici Vescovini (Florence: Olschki, 1974).

Blasius of Parma. *Questiones super Tractatus logice Magistri Petri Hispani*, ed. J. Biard and G. Federici Vescovini (Paris: Vrin, 2001).

Boate, Gerard and Arnold. *Philosophia naturalis reformata: id est, philosophiae Aristotelicae accurata examinatio ac solida confutatio et novae ac verioris introductio* (Dublin, 1641).

Boethius. *In Categorias Aristotelis libri quatuor [In Praed.]*, in J. P. Migne (ed.) *Patrologiae Cursus Completus, Series Latina* (Paris, 1847) vol. 64.

Boethius. *In Ciceronis Topica*, tr. E. Stump (Ithaca: Cornell University Press, 1988).

Boethius. *Philosophiae consolatio*, ed. L. Bieler (Corpus Christianorum, Series Latina, 94) (Turnholt: Brepols, 1957).

Boethius. *The Theological Tractates and the Consolation of Philosophy*, ed. and tr. H. F. Stewart and E. K. Rand (Cambridge, MA: Harvard University Press, 1918).

Boethius. *In Topica Ciceronis commentaria*, in J. P. Migne (ed.) *Patrologiae Cursus Completus, Series Latina* (Paris, 1847) vol. 64.

Boethius of Dacia. *Opera*, ed. J. Pinborg et al. (Copenhagen: DSL/Gad, 1969–).

Bonaventure. *Itinerarium mentis in Deum*, tr. P. Boehner (St. Bonaventure, NY: Franciscan Institute, 1956).

Bonaventure. *Libri IV Sententiarum*, ed. L. M. Bello (Quaracchi: Collegium S. Bonaventurae, 1938).

Bostocke, Robert. *The Difference betwene the Auncient Physicke . . . and the Latter Phisicke* (London: R. Walley, 1585).

Boyle, Robert. *A Free Enquiry into the Vulgarly Received Notion of Nature*, ed. E. B. Davis and M. Hunter (Cambridge: Cambridge University Press, 1996).

Boyle, Robert. *Selected Philosophical Papers of Robert Boyle*, ed. M. A. Stewart (Manchester: Manchester University Press, 1979).

Boyle, Robert. *The Works of Robert Boyle*, ed. M. Hunter and E. B. Davis (London: Pickering & Chatto, 1999–2000).

Burgersdijk, Franco. *Collegium physicum, disputationibus XXXII absolutum*, 3rd ed. (Cambridge, 1650).

Burgersdijk, Franco. *Institutiones logicae* (Cambridge: Ex Academiae celeberrimae typrographeo, 1637).

Burgersdijk, Franco. *Institutiones metaphysicae* (London: Crook and Baker, 1653).

Cajetan (Tommaso de Vio). *Commentaria in partem primam Summae theologiae*, in *S. Thomae Aquinatis Doctoris Angelici opera omnia* (Rome: Commissio Leonina, 1882–) vol. 5.

Cajetan (Tommaso de Vio). *In De ente et essentia d. Thomae Aquinatis commentaria*, ed. M.-H. Laurent (Turin: Marietti, 1934).

Cajetan of Thiene. *Recollecte super octo libros Physicorum* (Venice, 1496).

Carpenter, Nathanael. *Philosophia libera*, 2nd ed. (Oxford, 1622).

Cavendish, Margaret. *Observations upon Experimental Philosophy*, ed. E. O'Neill (Cambridge: Cambridge University Press, 2001).

Chambers, Ephraim. *Cyclopaedia, or, An Universal Dictionary of Arts and Sciences*, 2 vols. (London, 1728).

Charleton, Walter. *Epicurus' Morals* (London: W. Wilson for H. Herringman, 1656).

Charleton, Walter. *Exercitationes de differentiis et nominibus animalium* (Oxford, 1677).

Charleton, Walter. *The Immortality of the Human Soul* (London: William Wilson for Henry Herringman, 1657).

Charleton, Walter. *Natural History of the Passions* (London: J. Magnes, 1674).

Charleton, Walter. *Physiologia Epicuro-Gassendo-Charltoniana* (London, 1654; repr. New York: Johnson, 1966).

Chauvin, Stephanus. *Lexicon philosophicum*, 2nd ed. (Leeuwarden: F. Halma, 1713; repr. Düsseldorf: Stern-Verlag Janssen, 1967).

Chillingworth, William. *The Religion of the Protestants A Safe Way to Salvation* (Oxford: Leonard Lichfield, 1638).

Collegium Conimbricense. *Commentarii Collegii Conimbricensis in octo libros Physicorum Aristotelis* (Lyon, 1594; repr. Hildesheim: Olms, 1984).

Collegium Conimbricense. *Commentarii Collegii Conimbricensis in libros de generatione et corruptione Aristotelis* (Cologne, 1606; repr. Hildesheim: Olms, 2003).

Collegium Conimbricense. *Commentarii Collegii Conimbricensis in universam dialecticam Aristotelis* (Cologne, 1607; repr. Hildesheim: Olms, 1976).

Conway, Anne. *The Principles of the Most Ancient and Modern Philosophy*, ed. P. Loptson (The Hague: M. Nijhoff, 1982).

Conway, Anne. *The Principles of the Most Ancient and Modern Philosophy*, tr. A. P. Coudert and T. Corse (Cambridge: Cambridge University Press, 1996).

Crakanthorpe, Richard. *Introductio in metaphysicam* (Oxford: Lichfield & Short, 1619).

Cremonini. Cesare, *De formis quattuor corporum simplicium quae vocantur elementa disputatio* (Venice, 1605).

Cudworth, Ralph. *The True Intellectual System of the Universe* (London: R. Royston, 1678; repr. Stuttgart Frommann, 1964).

Dabillon, André. *La physique des bons esprits* (Paris: Sebastien Piquet, 1643).

Dalgarno, George. *Ars signorum, vulgo character universalis et lingua philosophica* (London: J. Hayes, 1661).

d'Espagnet, Jean. *Summary of Physics Restored (Enchyridion physicae restitute)*, tr. E. Ashmole, ed. T. Willard (New York: Garland, 1999).

de Launoy, Jean. *De varia Aristotelis in academia Parisiensi fortuna*, 3rd ed. (Paris, 1662).

Descartes, René. *Correspondance avec Arnaud et Morus*, tr. G. Rodis-Lewis (Paris: Vrin, 1953).

Descartes, René. *Oeuvres de Descartes*, ed. C. Adam and P. Tannery (Paris: Cerf, 1897; repr. Paris: Vrin, 1996).

Descartes, René. *The Philosophical Writings of Descartes*, tr. J. Cottingham, R. Stoothoff, D. Murdoch, 2 vols. (Cambridge: Cambridge University Press, 1984).

Descartes, René. *The Philosophical Writings of Descartes*, tr. J. Cottingham, R. Stoothoff, D. Murdoch, A. Kenny, vol. 3. (Cambridge: Cambridge University Press, 1991).

Desiderius Erasmus. *Colloquies*, tr. C. Thompson (Toronto: University of Toronto Press, 1997).

Desiderius Erasmus. *Opera omnia*, ed. J. Le Clerc (Lyon, 1703–6; repr. London: Gregg Press, 1962).

Dietrich of Freiberg. *Opera omnia*, 4 vols. (Hamburg: Felix Meiner, 1977–84).

Digby, Kenelm. *A Discourse concerning the Vegetation of Plants* (London, 1661).

Digby, Kenelm. *Two Treatises* (Paris: G. Blaizot, 1644).

Diogenes Laertius. *Lives of Eminent Philosophers*, tr. H. D. Hicks (Loeb Classical Library), 2 vols. (London: Heinemann, 1925).

Domingo Bàñez. *Scholastica commentaria in primam partem Summae theologicae S. Thomae Aquinatis*, ed. L. Urbano (Madrid: Editorial F.E.D.A., 1934).

Domingo de Soto. *Commentaria in octo libros Physicorum Aristotelis* (Burgos, 1665).

Domingo de Soto. *In Porphyrii Isagogen, Aristotelis Categorias, librosque De demonstratione absolutissima commentaria* (Venice, 1587; repr. Frankfurt: Minerva, 1967).

Duchesne, Joseph. *De priscorum philosophorum verae medicinae materia* (Orleans, 1603).

Dupleix, Scipion. *La métaphysique*, ed. R. Ariew (Paris: Fayard, 1992).

Dupleix, Scipion. *La physique, ou science des choses naturelles*, ed. R. Ariew (Paris: Fayard, 1990).

Durand of St. Pourçain. *In Petri Lombardi Sententias theologicas commentarium libri quatuor* (Venice: ex typographia Guerraea, 1571; repr. Ridgewood, NJ: Gregg, 1964).

Eckhart of Hochheim. *Die deutschen und lateinischen Werke* (Stuttgart: Kohlhammer, 1936–).

Euclid. *The Thirteen Books of Euclid's Elements*, tr. T. Heath, 2nd ed. (New York: Dover, 1956).

Eustachius a Sancto Paulo. *Summa philosophiae quadripartita* (Cambridge, 1648).

Francesco Patrizi. *Discussionum peripateticarum tomi IV* (Basel, 1581).

Francesco Patrizi. *Nova de universes philosophia* (Ferrara, 1591).

Francesco Petrarch. *Invectives*, ed. and tr. D. Marsh (Cambridge, MA: Harvard University Press, 2003).

Francesco Petrarch. *Petrarch, the First Modern Scholar and Man of Letters: A Selection from His Correspondence with Boccaccio and Other Friends, Designed to Illustrate the Beginnings of the Renaissance*, ed. and tr. J. H. Robinson (New York: Putnam's, 1898).

Francisco Sanches. *That Nothing Is Known (Quod Nihil Scitur)*, ed. and tr. E. Limbrick and D. F. S. Thomson (Cambridge: Cambridge University Press, 1988).

Francisco Suárez. *De anima: Commentaria una cum quaestionibus in libros Aristotelis De anima*, ed. S. Castellote (Madrid: Sociedad de Estudios y Publicaciones, 1978).

Francisco Suárez. *Disputationes metaphysicae* (Paris: Vivès, 1866; repr. Hildesheim: Olms, 1965).

Francisco Suárez. *Metaphysicae disputationes*, 2 vols. (Salamanca, 1597).

Francisco Suárez. *On the Formal Cause of Substance: Metaphysical Disputation XV*, tr. J. Kronen and J. Reedy (Milwaukee: Marquette University Press, 2000).

Francisco Suárez. *Opera omnia*, ed. D. M. André and C. Berton, 28 vols. (Paris: Vivès, 1856–78).

Franciscus de Prato. *La logica di Francesco da Prato: con l'edizione critica della Loyca e del Tractatus de voce univoca*, ed. F. Amerini (Florence: SISMEL, Edizioni del Galluzzo, 2005).

Franciscus de Sylvestris Ferrariensis. *Commentaria in libros quatuor contra gentiles s. Thomae de Aquino*, in *S. Thomae Aquinatis Doctoris Angelici Opera omnia* (Rome: Commissio Leonina, 1918–30) vols. 13–15.

Franciscus Toletus. *Opera omnia philosophica* (Cologne: Birckmann, 1615–16; repr. Hildesheim: Olms, 1985).

Francis of Marchia. *Commentarius in IV libros Sententiarum Petri Lombardi. Distinctiones primi libri prima ad decimam*, ed. N. Mariani (Grottaferrata: Editiones Collegii S. Bonaventurae, 2006).

Froidmont, Libert. *Labyrinthus sive de compositione continui liber unus* (Antwerp, 1631).

Gabriel Biel. *Canonis misse expositio*, ed. H. A. Oberman et al. (Wiesbaden: F. Steiner, 1963–76).

Gabriel Biel. *Collectorium circa quattuor libros Sententiarum*, ed. H. Rückert et al. (Tübingen: J. C. B. Mohr, 1973–92).

Gabriel Vasquez. *Commentariorum ac disputationum in primam [-tertiam] partem Sancti Thomae*, 8 vols. (Antwerp: Belleros, 1621).

Galilei, Galileo. *Discoveries and Opinions of Galileo*, tr. S. Drake (Garden City, NY: Doubleday Anchor, 1957).

Galilei, Galileo. *Le opere di Galileo Galilei*, ed. A. Favaro, 20 vols. (Florence: G. Barbèra, 1890–1909).

Galilei, Galileo. *Opere*, ed. F. Flora (Milan: R. Ricciardi, 1953).

Galilei, Galileo. *Two New Sciences*, tr. S. Drake, 2nd ed. (Toronto: Wall & Emerson, 1989).

Gassendi, Pierre. *Animadversiones in decimum librum Diogenis Laertii, qui est De vita, moribus, placitisque Epicuri* (Lyon: G. Barbier, 1649).

Gassendi, Pierre. *Dissertations en forme de paradoxes contre les Aristotéliciens (Exercitationes paradoxicae adversus Aristoteleos) Livres I et II*, ed. B. Rochot (Paris: Vrin, 1959).

Gassendi, Pierre. *Philosophiae Epicuri syntagma* (London: R. Daniel, 1660).

Gassendi, Pierre. *Syntagmatis philosophici*, in *Opera omnia* (Lyon, 1658; repr. Stuttgart-Bad Cannstatt: Frommann-Holzboog, 1964).

Geulincx, Arnold. *Metaphysics*, tr. M. Wilson (Wisbech, Cambridgeshire: Christoffel Press, 1999).

Geulincx, Arnold. *Opera philosophica*, ed. J. P. N. Land, 3 vols. (The Hague: Nijhoff, 1891–3; repr. Stuttgart-Bad Cannstatt: Frommann-Holzboog, 1968).

Gianfrancesco Pico della Mirandola. *Examen vanitatis doctrinae gentium, et veritatis Christianae doctrinae*, in Giovanni Pico della Mirandola, *Opera omnia* (Basel, 1557; repr. Hildesheim: Olms, 1969) II:710–1264.

Gibbon, Edward. *Essai sur l'étude de la littérature* (London: Becket & De Hondt, 1761).

Giles of Lessines. *De unitate formae*, ed. M. De Wulf (*Les Philosophes Belges* vol. 1) (Leuven: Institut Supérieur de Philosophie de l'Université, 1901).

Giles of Orleans. *Quaestiones super De generatione et corruptione*, ed. Z. Kuksewicz (Amsterdam: B. R. Grüner, 1993).

Giles of Rome (?). *Errores philosophorum*, ed. J. Koch; tr. J. Riedl (Milwaukee: Marquette University Press, 1944).

Giles of Rome. *Expositio super libros de generatione et corruptione* (Venice: Otinus de Luna, 1500).

Giles of Rome. *In libros de Physico auditu Aristotelis commentaria accuratissime emendata . . . Questio de gradibus formarum* (Venice, 1502).

Giles of Rome. *Metaphysicales Quaestiones* (Venice, 1552).

Giles of Rome. *Reportatio lecturae super libros I–IV Sententiarum, Reportatio monacensis*, ed. C. Luna (Florence, 2003).

Giles of Rome. *Theoremata de corpore Christi* (Rome, 1554); repr. in *Opera Exegetica Opuscula I* (Frankfurt: Minerva, 1968).

Giles of Rome. *Theoremata de esse et essentia*, ed. E. Hocedez (Leuven: Museum Lessianum, 1930).

Giordano Bruno. *De la causa, principio, et uno* (Venice [London], 1584).

Giordano Bruno. *Cause, Principle and Unity and Essays on Magic*, ed. R. J. Blackwell and R. de Lucca (Cambridge: Cambridge University Press, 1998).

Giovanni Pico della Mirandola. *Opera omnia* (Basel, 1557; repr. Hildesheim: Olms, 1969).

Glanvill, Joseph. *Scepsis scientifica: or, Confest Ignorance, the Way of Science* (London, 1665).

Glanvill, Joseph. *Scire tuum nihil est: or, the Authors Defence of the Vanity of Dogmatizing* (London, 1665).

Glanvill, Joseph. *The Vanity of Dogmatizing* (London, 1661).

Goclenius, Rudolphus. *Lexicon philosophicum quo tanquam clave philosophiae fores aperiuntur* (Frankfurt, 1613; repr. Hildesheim: Olms, 1964).

Godfrey of Fontaines. *Le huitième Quodlibet de Godfroid de Fontaines*, ed. J. Hoffmans (*Philosophes Belges* vol. 4) (Leuven: Institut supérieur de philosophie de l'Université, 1924).

Godfrey of Fontaines. *Les quatre premiers Quodlibets*, ed. M. De Wulf and A. Pelzer (*Philosophes Belges* vol. 2) (Leuven: Institut supérieur de Philosophie de l'Université, 1904).

Godfrey of Fontaines. *Les quodlibet cinq, six, et sept*, ed. M. De Wulf and J. Hoffmans (*Philosophes Belges* vol. 3) (Leuven: Institut Supérieur de Philosophie, 1914).

Godfrey of Fontaines. *Les quodlibets onze et douze, les quodlibets treize et quatorze*, ed. J. Hoffmans (*Philosophes Belges* vol. 5) (Leuven: Institut supérieur de Philosophie de l'Université, 1932–5).

Goodman, Godfrey. *The Fall of Man or the Corruption of Nature, Proved by the Light of Our Naturall Reason* (London: F. Kyngston, 1616).

Gorlaeus, David. *Exercitationes philosophicae* (Leiden, 1620).

Gorlaeus, David. *Idea physicae* (Utrecht, 1651).

Grassi, Orazio. *Ratio ponderum librae et simbellae . . . auctore Lothario Sarsio . . . *(Lutetiae Parisiorum: S. Cramoisy, 1626).

Gregory of Rimini. *Lectura super primum et secundum Sententiarum*, ed. D. Trapp et al. (Berlin: De Gruyter, 1979–84).

Hakewill, George. *An Apologie of the Power And Providence Of God in the Government of the World, or, An Examination and Censure of the Common Errour Touching Natures Perpetuall and Universall Decay* (Oxford, 1627).

Harvey, William. *Exercitationes de generatione animalium* (Amsterdam: Elzevier, 1651).

Helmont, Jean Baptiste van. *Oriatrike, or, Physick Refined* (London: L. Loyd, 1662).

Henry Cornelius Agrippa. *Of the Vanity and Uncertainty of Arts and Sciences* (London, 1569).

Henry Cornelius Agrippa. *Three Books of Occult Philosophy*, tr. J. French (London, 1651).

Henry of Ghent. *Opera omnia* (Leiden: Brill, 1979–).

Henry of Ghent. *Quodlibeta* (Paris, 1518; repr. Leuven: Bibliotheque S.J., 1961).

Henry of Ghent. *Summa quaestionum ordinariarum* (Paris, 1520; repr. St. Bonaventure: Franciscan Institute, 1953).

Henry of Harclay. *Ordinary Questions*, ed. M. G. Henninger, 2 vols. (Oxford: Oxford University Press, 2008).

Hervaeus Natalis. *In quatuor libros Sententiarum commentaria* (Paris, 1647; repr. Farnborough: Gregg, 1966).

Hieronymus Fracastorius. *De contagione et contagiosis morbis et eorum curatione libri III*, ed. W. C. Wright (New York: Putnam, 1930).

Hill, Nicholas. *Philosophia Epicurea, Democritiana, Theophrastica proposita simpliciter, non edocta* (Cologne, 1619) [orig. publ. 1601].

Hobbes, Thomas. *The Correspondence of Thomas Hobbes*, ed. N. Malcolm, 2 vols. (Oxford: Oxford University Press, 1994).

Hobbes, Thomas. *Critique du De mundo de Thomas White*, ed. J. Jacquot and H. W. Jones (Paris: Vrin, 1973).

Hobbes, Thomas. *Elements of Law*, ed. F. Tönnies (London: Simpkin & Marshall, 1889).

Hobbes, Thomas. *The English Works of Thomas Hobbes of Malmesbury*, ed. W. Molesworth, 11 vols. (London: J. Bohn, 1839–45).

Hobbes, Thomas. *Leviathan*, ed. E. Curley (Indianapolis: Hackett, 1994).

Hobbes, Thomas. *Of Liberty and Necessity*, in V. Chappell (ed.) *Hobbes and Bramhall on Liberty and Necessity* (Cambridge: Cambridge University Press, 1999) 15–42.

Hobbes, Thomas. *Opera latina* (London: John Bohn, 1845).

Hooke, Robert. *Micrographia* (London, 1665).

Hume, David. *A Treatise of Human Nature*, ed. P. H. Nidditch, 2nd ed. (Oxford: Clarendon, 1978).

Ignatius of Loyola. *The Constitutions of the Society of Jesus*, tr. G. E. Ganss (St. Louis: Institute of Jesuit Sources, 1970).

Jacob Schegk. *Commentaria in Organi Aristotelis libros* (Tübingen, 1570).

Jacob Zabarella. *In III Aristotelis libros de anima* (Frankfurt, 1606; repr. Frankfurt: Minerva, 1966).

Jacob Zabarella. *De rebus naturalibus libri xxx* (Frankfurt, 1607; repr. Frankfurt: Minerva, 1966).

James of Viterbo. *Disputatio secunda de quolibet*, ed. E. Ypma (Würzburg: Augustinus Verlag, 1969).

Jean Fernel. *De abditis rerum causis libri duo* (Venice, 1550).

Johannes Blund. *Tractatus de anima*, ed. D. A. Callus and R. W. Hunt (London: British Academy, 1970).

Johannes Magirus. *Physiologiae peripateticae libri sex* (Cambridge, 1642) [orig. publ. 1597].

John Buridan. *In Metaphysicam Aristotelis quaestiones* (Paris, 1588; repr. Frankfurt: Minerva, 1964).

John Buridan. *Questiones in Aristotelis tres libros de anima*, ed. G. Lokert (Paris, 1516; repr. in *Le traité de l'âme*, ed. B. Patar [Leuven: Éditions de l'Institut Supérieur de Philosophie, 1991]).

John Buridan. *Quaestiones in duos Aristotilis libros Posteriorum Analyticorum*, ed. H. Hubien (unpublished).

John Buridan, *Quaestiones in Praedicamenta*, ed. J. Schneider (Munich: Beck, 1983).

John Buridan. *Quaestiones in primum librum Analyticorum Posteriorum*, ed. H. Hubien (unpublished).

John Buridan. *Quaestiones in Aristotelis De anima liber secundus*, in P. G. Sobol (ed.) "John Buridan on the Soul and Sensation, with an Edition of the Quaestiones in Aristotelis De anima liber secundus, de tertia lectura" (Ph.D. dissertation, Indiana University, 1984).

John Buridan. *Quaestiones in Aristotelis De anima liber tertius*, in J. Zupko (ed.) "John Buridan's Philosophy of Mind: An Edition and Translation of Book III of his 'Questions on Aristotle's De Anima' (Third Redaction)" (Ph.D. dissertation, Cornell University, 1989).

John Buridan. *Quaestiones super De generatione et corruptione*, ed. M. Streijger (Leiden: Brill, forthcoming).

John Buridan. *Quaestiones super octo physicorum libros Aristotelis* (Paris, 1509; repr. Frankfurt: Minerva, 1964).

John Buridan. *Summulae de dialectica*, tr. G. Klima (New Haven: Yale University Press, 2001).

John Buridan (?). *Le traité de l'âme de Jean Buridan (De prima lectura)*, ed. B. Patar (Leuven: Éditions de l'Institut Supérieur de Philosophie, 1991).

John Capreolus. *Defensiones theologiae divi Thomae Aquinatis*, ed. C. Paban and T. Pègues (Turin: A. Cattier, 1900–8; repr. Frankfurt: Minerva, 1967).

John of Damascus. *De fide orthodoxa: Versions of Burgundio and Cerbanus*, ed. E. M. Buytaert (St. Bonaventure, NY: Franciscan Institute, 1955).

John Dumbleton. *Summa logicae et philosophiae naturalis* (manuscript: Cambridge, Peterhouse 272).

John Duns Scotus. *Cuestiones Cuodlibetales*, ed. F. Alluntis (Madrid: Biblioteca de Auctores Cristianos, 1968).

John Duns Scotus. *Opera omnia*, ed. L. Wadding (Lyon, 1639).

John Duns Scotus. *Opera omnia*, ed. C. Balić et al. (Vatican: Scotistic Commission, 1950–).

John Duns Scotus. *Opera philosophica*, ed. T. Noone et al. (St. Bonaventure, NY: Franciscan Institute, 1997–2006).

John Duns Scotus. *Philosophical Writings*, tr. A. Wolter (Edinburgh: Nelson, 1962; repr. Indianapolis: Hackett, 1987).

John Duns Scotus. *Reportatio I-A*, ed. A. B. Wolter and O.V. Bychkov, 2 vols. (St. Bonaventure, NY: Franciscan Institute, 2004–8).

John Gerson. *Oeuvres complètes*, ed. P. Glorieux (Paris: Desclée de Brouwer, 1960–73).

John of Jandun (?). *Quaestiones super De substantia orbis*, in *In libros Aristotelis De coelo et mundo quae extant quaestiones subtilissimae* (Venice, 1552).

John of Jandun. *Quaestiones in duodecim libros metaphysicae* (Venice: H. Scotus, 1553; repr. Frankfurt: Minerva, 1966).

John of Jandun. *Super libros Aristotelis de anima subtilissimae quaestiones* (Venice, 1587; repr. Frankfurt: Minerva, 1966).

John Major. *In secundum Sententiarum* (Paris, 1510).

John Major. *Octo libri Physicorum cum naturali philosophia atque metaphysica* (Paris, 1526).

John Major. *Quartus Sententiarum* (Paris: Ponset le Preux, 1509).

John of Mirecourt. *Quaestiones in librum primum Sententiarum*, qq. 2–6, in A. Franzinelli (ed.) "Questioni inedite di Giovanni di Mirecourt sulla conoscenza," *Rivista critica di storia della filosofia* 13 (1958) 319–40, 415–49.

John of Mirecourt. *Quaestiones in librum primum Sententiarum*, qq. 13–16, in M. Parodi (ed.) "Questioni inedite tratte dal I libro del commento alle Sentenze di Giovanni di Mirecourt (qq. 13–16)," *Medioevo* 3 (1978) 237–84; 4 (1978) 59–92.

John Paul Pernumia. *Philosophia naturalis ordine definitivo tradita* (Padua, 1570).

John Pecham. *Quodlibeta quatuor*, ed. G. Etzkorn and F. Delorme (Quaracchi: Collegium S. Bonaventurae, 1989).

John of Saint Thomas. *Cursus philosophicus thomisticus* (Turin: Marietti, 1930–7).

John of Salisbury. *Metalogicon*, ed. J. B. Hall and K. S. B. Keats-Rohan (Turnhout: Brepols, 1991).

John Wyclif. *De actibus animae*, in M. H. Dziewicki (ed.) *Myscellanea philosophica* (London: Trübner, 1902).

John Wyclif. *De ente praedicamentali*, in R. Beer (ed.) *Latin Works* (London: Trübner, 1891) vol. 11.

John Wyclif. *De eucharistia*, in J. Loserth (ed.) *Latin Works* (London: Trübner, 1892) vol. 12.

John Wyclif. *De materia et forma* in M. H. Dziewicki (ed.) *Myscellanea philosophica* (London: Trübner, 1902).

John Wyclif. *Tractatus de logica*, ed. M. H. Dziewicki, 3 vols. (London: Trübner, 1893–9).

John Wyclif. *Tractatus de universalibus*, ed. I. J. Mueller (Oxford: Clarendon, 1985).

Jungius, Joachim. *Disputationes Hamburgenses*, ed. C. Müller-Glauser (Göttingen: Vandenhoeck & Ruprecht, 1988).

Jungius, Joachim. *Praelectiones physicae: historisch-kritische Edition*, ed. C. Meinel (Göttingen: Vandenhoeck & Ruprecht, 1982).

Kant, Immanuel. *Critique of Pure Reason*, tr. P. Guyer and A. Wood (Cambridge: Cambridge University Press, 1998).

Kant, Immanuel. *Kritik der reinen Vernunft*, ed. R. Schmidt (Hamburg: F. Meiner, 1956).

Keckermann, Bartholomew. *Opera omnia* (Cologne, 1614).

Keill, John. *Introductio ad veram physicam seu lectiones physicae habitae in schola naturalis philosophiae Academiae Oxoniensis, quibus accedunt Christiani* (Oxford, 1702).

Kepler, Johannes. *Gesammelte Werke*, ed. W. von Dyck and M. Caspar (Munich: C. H. Beck'sche Verlagsbuchhandlung, 1937–).

Law, Edmund. *A Defence of Mr. Locke's Opinion Concerning Personal Identity* (Cambridge, 1769).

Leibniz, Gottfried Wilhelm. *The Leibniz–Clarke Correspondence*, ed. H. G. Alexander (Manchester: Manchester University Press, 1956).

Leibniz, Gottfried Wilhelm. *New Essays on Human Understanding*, tr. P. Remnant and J. Bennett (Cambridge: Cambridge University Press, 1996).

Leibniz, Gottfried Wilhelm. *Nouveaux essais sur l'entendement humain*, ed. A. Robinet and H. Schepers (Berlin: Akademie-Verlag, 1962).

Leibniz, Gottfried Wilhelm. *Philosophical Essays*, tr. R. Ariew and D. Garber (Indianapolis: Hackett, 1989).

Leibniz, Gottfried Wilhelm. *Philosophical Papers and Letters*, ed. L. E. Loemker, 2nd ed. (Dordrecht: Reidel, 1969).

Leibniz, Gottfried Wilhelm. *Die philosophischen Schriften*, ed. C. I. Gerhardt (Berlin: Wiedmann, 1875–90; repr. Hildesheim: Olms, 1965).

Locke, John. *The Correspondence of John Locke*, ed. E. S. de Beer, 9 vols. (Oxford: Clarendon, 1976–).

Locke, John. *An Early Draft of Locke's Essay together with Excerpts from His Journals*, ed. R. Aaron and J. Gibb (Oxford: Clarendon, 1936).

Locke, John. *An Essay concerning Human Understanding*, ed. P. H. Nidditch (Oxford: Clarendon, 1975).

Locke, John. *The Works of John Locke*, 11th ed. (London: W. Otrige, 1812).

Lorenzo Valla. *On Pleasure: De voluptate*, tr. A. K. Hieatt and M. Lorch (New York: Abaris Books, 1977).

Lorenzo Valla. *Repastinatio dialectice et philosophie [et Retractio]*, ed. G. Zippel, 2 vols. (Padua: Antenore, 1982).

Louis Le Roy. *De la vicissitude ou varieté des choses en l'univers*, ed. P. Desan (Paris: Fayard, 1988).

Louis Le Roy. *Of the Interchangeable Course or Variety of Things in the Whole World*, tr. R. Ashley (London: C. Yetsweirt, 1594).

Lucretius. *De natura rerum*, tr. T. Creech (Oxford: L. Lichfield, 1682).

Lucretius. *De rerum natura*, ed. M. F. Smith, tr. W. H. D. Rouse (Cambridge, MA: Harvard University Press, 1982).

Magnen, Jean Chrysostome. *Democritus reviviscens, sive vita et philosophia Democriti* (Leiden: A. Wyngaerden, 1648).

Malebranche, Nicolas. *De la recherche de la vérité*, ed. J.-C. Bardout (Paris: Vrin, 2006).

Malebranche, Nicolas. *The Search after Truth*, tr. T. M. Lennon and P. J. Olscamp (Cambridge: Cambridge University Press, 1997).

Marsilio Ficino. *Platonic Theology*, ed. J. Hankins and W. Bowen; tr. M. Allen and J. Warden (Cambridge, MA: Harvard University Press, 2001–6).

Marsilius of Inghen. *Abbreviationes libri Physicorum* (Venice, 1521).

Marsilius of Inghen. *Quaestiones de generatione et corruptione* (Venice, 1505; repr. Frankfurt: Minerva, 1970).

Martin of Dacia. *Opera*, ed. H. Roos (Copenhagen: Det Danske Sprogog Litteraturselskab [Gad], 1961).

Matthew of Aquasparta. *Quaestiones disputatae de incarnatione et de lapsu* (Quaracchi: Collegium S. Bonaventurae, 1957).

Matthew Paris. *Chronica majora*, ed. H. R. Luard, 7 vols. (London: Longman, 1872–83; repr. Wiesbaden: Kraus, 1964).

Mersenne, Marin. *L'impieté des déistes, athées et libertins de ce temps* (Paris, 1624; repr. Stuttgart-Bad Cannstatt: Frommann, 1975).

Mersenne, Marin. *Quaestiones celeberrimae in Genesim* (Paris: S. Cramoisy, 1623).

Mersenne, Marin. *La vérité des sciences: contre les sceptiques ou pyrrhoniens* (Paris, 1625; repr. Stuttgart-Bad Cannstatt: Frommann, 1969).

Michel de Montaigne. *The Complete Essays of Montaigne*, tr. D. M. Frame (Stanford: Stanford University Press, 1958).

Micraelius, Johann. *Lexicon philosophicum terminorum philosophis usitatorum* (Düsseldorf: Stern-Verlag Janssen, 1966).

Milton, John. *Areopagitica* (Oxford: Oxford University Press, 1875).

More, Henry. *An Antidote against Atheism*, in *A Collection of Several Philosophical Writings* (London: James Flesher, 1662; repr. New York: Garland, 1978).

More, Henry. *A Collection of Several Philosophical Writings* (London: James Flesher, 1662; repr. New York: Garland, 1978).

More, Henry. *Democritus Platonissans; or, An Essay upon the Infinity of Worlds out of Platonick Principles* (Cambridge, 1646; repr. Los Angeles, CA: William Andrews Clark Memory Library, University of California, 1968).

More, Henry. *Divine Dialogues* (London, 1668).

More, Henry. *Enchiridion metaphysicum, sive, De rebus incorporeis succincta et luculenta dissertatio* (London, 1671).

More, Henry. *The Immortality of the Soul*, ed. A. Jacob (Dordrecht: Martinus Nijhoff, 1987).

More, Henry. *Psychodia platonica, or A Platonicall Song of the Soul Consisting of Foure Severall Poems* (Cambridge: R. Daniel, 1642).

Morin, Jean-Baptiste. *Refutation des theses erronées d'Anthoine Villon dit le soldat Philosophe, & Estienne de Claves Medecin Chymiste* (Paris, 1624).

Moses Maimonides. *The Guide for the Perplexed*, tr. M. Friedländer, 2nd ed. (London: Routledge, 1904; repr. New York: Dover, 1956).

Nemesius. *De natura hominis*, ed. G. Verbeke and J. R. Moncho (Leiden: Brill, 1975).

Newton, Isaac. *Certain Philosophical Questions: Newton's Trinity Notebook*, ed. J. E. McGuire and M. Tamny (Cambridge: Cambridge University Press, 1983).

Newton, Isaac. *De gravitatione et aequipondio fluidorum*, in A. R. Hall and M. B. Hall (eds.) *Unpublished Scientific Papers of Isaac Newton: A Selection from the Portsmouth Collection in the University Library, Cambridge* (Cambridge: Cambridge University Press, 1962) 89–156.

Newton, Isaac. *Philosophiae naturalis principia mathematica*, 2 vols. (Glasgow: Tegg and Griffin, 1833).

Newton, Isaac. *Philosophical Writings*, ed. A. Janiak (Cambridge: Cambridge University Press, 2004).

Newton, Isaac. *The Principia: Mathematical Principles of Natural Philosophy*, tr. I. B. Cohen and A. Whitman (Berkeley: University of California Press, 1999).

Nicholas of Autrecourt. *Correspondence with Master Giles and Bernard of Arezzo*, ed. and tr. L. M. de Rijk (Leiden: Brill, 1994).

Nicholas of Autrecourt. *Tractatus utilis ad videndum an sermones peripateticorum fuerint demonstrativi*, in J. R. O'Donnell (ed.), "Nicholas of Autrecourt," *Mediaeval Studies* 1 (1939) 179–267.

Nicholas of Autrecourt. *The Universal Treatise*, tr. L. A. Kennedy, R. E. Arnold, A. E. Millward (Milwaukee: Marquette University Press, 1971).

Nicholas of Cusa. *Opera omnia*, ed. E. Hoffmann et al. (Leipzig: F. Meiner, 1932–).

Nicholas Eymerich. *Directorium inquisitorum* (Barcelona, 1503).

Nicholas Taurellus. *Philosophiae triumphus, hoc est, metaphysica philosophandi methodus* (Basel, 1573).

Nicole Oresme. *De causis mirabilium* in *Nicole Oresme and the Marvels of Nature: A Study of his* De causis mirabilium *with Critical Edition, Translation and Commentary* (Toronto: Pontifical Institute of Mediaeval Philosophy, 1985).

Nicole Oresme. *Expositio et quaestiones in Aristotelis De anima*, ed. B. Patar (Leuven: Peeters, 1995).

Nicole Oresme. *Nicole Oresme and the Medieval Geometry of Qualities and Motions: A Treatise on the Uniformity and Difformity of Intensities known as* Tractatus de configurationibus qualitatum et motuum, ed. and tr. M. Clagett (Madison: University of Wisconsin Press, 1968).

Nicole Oresme. *Quaestiones super libros Physicorum*, ed. S. Caroti et al. (forthcoming).

Oldenburg, Henry. *Correspondence*, ed. A. R. Hall and M. B. Hall (Madison: University of Wisconsin Press, 1965).

Paracelsus. *Essential Readings*, tr. N. Goodrick-Clarke (Wellingborough, Northamptonshire: Crucible, 1990).

Parker, Samuel. *A Free and Impartial Censure of the Platonick Philosophy* (Oxford: Hall and Davis, 1666).

Paul of Taranto. *Liber tam theoricae quam practicae veritatis in arte alkimica*, ed. W. R. Newman, in "The *Summa Perfectionis* and Late Medieval Alchemy: A Study of Chemical Traditions, Techniques, and Theories in Thirteenth-Century Italy" (Ph.D. dissertation: Harvard University, 1986).

Paul of Taranto. *Summa perfectionis*, ed. and tr. W. Newman (Leiden: Brill, 1991).

Paul of Venice. *Sententia super Metaphysicam* Bk. VII, ed. F. Amerini (manuscript).

Paul of Venice. *Summa philosophiae naturalis* (Venice, 1503; repr. Hildesheim: Olms, 1974).

Pedro Fonseca. *Commentariorum in libros Metaphysicorum Aristotelis Stagiritae* (Cologne, 1615; repr. Hildesheim: Olms, 1964).

Pemble, William. *De formarum origine* (London: Young and Bartlet, 1629).

Peter Abaelard. *Glossae in Categorias*, in M. Dal Pra (ed.) *Pietro Abelardo: Scritti di logica*, 2nd ed. (Florence: La Nuova Italia Editrice, 1969).

Peter of Ailly. *Quaestiones super libros Sententiarum cum quibusdam in fine adjunctis* (Strassburg, 1490; repr. Frankfurt: Minerva, 1968).

Peter of Ailly. *Tractatus de anima* in O. Pluta (ed.) *Die philosophische Psychologie des Peter von Ailly* (Amsterdam: B. R. Grüner, 1987).

Peter Auriol. *Commentariorum in primum[-quartum] librum Sententiarum* (Rome, 1596–1605).

Peter John Olivi. "Epistola ad fratrem R.," ed. S. Piron et al. *Archivum Franciscanum Historicum* 91 (1998) 33–64.

Peter John Olivi. *Quaestiones in secundum librum Sententiarum* [= *Summa*], ed. B. Jansen (Quaracchi: Collegium S. Bonaventurae, 1922–6).

Peter John Olivi. *Quodlibeta quinque*, ed. S. Defraia (Grottaferrata: Editiones Collegii S. Bonaventurae ad Claras Aquas, 2002).

Peter John Olivi. *Tractatus de quantitate*, in *Quodlibeta* (Venice, 1509) ff. 49vb–53ra.

Peter Lombard. *Sententiae in IV libris distinctae* (Quaracchi: Collegium S. Bonaventurae, 1971–81).

Peter of Spain. *Syncategoreumata*, ed. L. M. de Rijk, tr. J. Spruyt (Leiden: Brill, 1992).

Pietro Pomponazzi. *Corsi inediti dell'insegnamento padovano*, ed. A. Poppi, 2 vols. (Padua: Antenore, 1966–70).

Pietro Pomponazzi. *Dubitationes in quartum meteorologicorum Aristotelis librum* (Venice: Franciscus de Franciscis, 1563).

Pietro Pomponazzi. *Super libello de substantia orbis expositio et quaestiones quattuor*, in A. Poppi (ed.) *Corsi inediti dell'insegnamento padovano*, ed. A. Poppi, vol. 1 (Padua: Antenore, 1966).

Plato. *Complete Works*, ed. J. M. Cooper (Indianapolis: Hackett, 1997).

Plotinus. *Enneads*, tr. A. H. Armstrong (Cambridge, MA: Harvard University Press, 1984).

Plotinus. *Opera*, ed. P. Henry and H.-R. Schwyzer (Paris: Desclée de Brouwer, 1959).

Porphyry. *Introduction*, tr. J. Barnes (Oxford: Clarendon, 2003).

Pseudo-Aquinas. *De tempore*, in Thomas Aquinas, *Opera Omnia* (Parma: Fiaccadori, 1864).

Pseudo-Avicenna. *Liber celi et mundi: A Critical Edition with Introduction*, ed. O. Gutman (Leiden: Brill, 2003).

Pseudo-Campsall. *Logica*, in Richard of Campsall, *Works*, ed. E. A. Synan (Toronto: Pontifical Institute of Mediaeval Studies, 1982).

Pseudo-Marsilius of Inghen. *Quaestiones subtilissimae super octo libros Physicorum secundum nominalium viam* (Lyon: J. Marion, 1518; repr. Frankfurt: Minerva, 1964).

Radulphus Brito. *Quaestiones super librum Praedicamentorum* [quest. 8], in W. McMahon, "Radulphus Brito on the Sufficiency of the Categories," *Cahiers de l'Institut du Moyen-âge Grec et Latin* 39 (1981) 81–96.

Reid, Thomas. *Essays on the Intellectual Powers of Man*, ed. D. R. Brookes (University Park: Pennsylvania State University Press, 2002).

Reid, Thomas. *Works*, ed. W. Hamilton, 6th ed. (Edinburgh: Maclachlan and Stewart, 1863).

Richard Knapwell. *Les premières polémiques Thomistes: le* Correctorium Corruptorii "Quare", ed. P. Glorieux (Kain: Le Saulchoir, 1927).

Richard Knapwell. *Quaestio disputata de unitate formae*, ed. F. E. Kelley (Paris: Vrin, 1982).

Richard of Middleton. *Quodlibeta quaestiones octuaginta* (Brescia, 1590; repr. Frankfurt: Minerva, 1963).

Richard of Middleton. *Super IV libros Sententiarum Petri Lombardi quaestiones subtilissimae* (Brescia, 1591; repr. Frankfurt: Minerva, 1963).

Richard Rufus of Cornwall. *Scriptum in Metaphysicam Aristotelis*, ed. R. Wood (forthcoming).

Robert Alyngton. *Litteralis sententia super Praedicamenta Aristotelis* (excerpts) in A. Conti (ed.) "Linguaggio e realtà nel commento alle *Categorie* di Robert Alyngton," *Documenti e studi sulla tradizione filosofica medievale* 4 (1993) 179–306.

Robert Grosseteste. *Commentarius in Posteriorum analyticorum libros*, ed. P. Rossi (Florence: L. S. Olschki, 1981).

Robert Grosseteste. *Die philosophischen Werke des Robert Grosseteste*, ed. L. Baur (Münster: Aschendorff, 1912).

Robert Orford (?). *De natura materiae*, in Thomas Aquinas, *Opuscula philosophica*, ed. R. M. Spiazzi (Rome: Marietti, 1954) 131–45.

Roger Bacon. *Opus maius*, ed. J. H. Bridges (Oxford: Clarendon, 1897–1900; repr. Frankfurt: Minerva, 1964).

Roger Marston. *Quodlibeta quatuor*, ed. G. Etzkorn and I. Brady, 2nd ed. (Grottaferrata: Collegii S. Bonaventurae, 1994).

Sanderson, Robert. *Logicae artis compendium* (Oxford, 1640).

Sarasin, Jean-François. *Oeuvres*, ed. P. Festugière, 2 vols. (Paris: E. Champion, 1926).

Scheibler, Christoph. *Metaphysica duobus libris* (Oxford, 1665).

Scheibler, Christoph. *Philosophia compendiosa*, 6th ed. (Oxford, 1639).

Sennert, Daniel. *Epitome naturalis scientiae*, editio ultima (Oxford: Hall and West, 1664).

Sennert, Daniel. *Hypomnemata physica* (Frankfurt, 1636).

Sennert, Daniel. *Thirteen Books of Natural Philosophy* (London: Peter and Edward Cole, 1661).

Sextus Empiricus. *Opera*, ed. H. Hutschmann (Leipzig, 1914; repr. 1984).

Sextus Empiricus. *Outlines of Skepticism*, tr. J. Annas and J. Barnes (Cambridge: Cambridge University Press, 2000).

Siger of Brabant. *Quaestiones in Metaphysicam: texte inédit de la reportation de Cambridge; édition revue de la reportation de Paris*, ed. A. Maurer (Louvain-la-Neuve: Éditions de l'Institut Supérieur de Philosophie, 1983).

Silhon, Jean de. *De l'immortalité de l'ame* (Paris, 1634).

Simon of Faversham. *Opera omnia*, ed. P. Mazzarella (Padua: CEDAM, 1957).

Spinoza, Baruch. *The Collected Works of Spinoza*, tr. E. Curley (Princeton: Princeton University Press, 1985).

Sprat, Thomas. *The History of the Royal Society of London, for the Improving of Natural Knowledge* (London: J. Martyn, 1667).

Stanley, Thomas. *The History of Philosophy*, 2nd ed. (London: T. Bassett, 1687).

Stillingfleet, Edward. *Origines sacrae, or, A Rational Account of the Grounds of the Christian Faith* (London, 1662).

Theodoricus de Magdeburg. *Quaestiones super "De substantia orbis,"* ed. Z. Kuksewicz (Wroclaw: Polska Akademia Nauk, 1985).

Thomas Aquinas. *In duodecim libros Metaphysicorum Aristotelis expositio*, ed. M. R. Cathala and R. M. Spiazzi (Rome: Marietti, 1971).

Thomas Aquinas. *In octo libros Physicorum Aristotelis expositio*, ed. P. M. Maggiòlo (Turin: Marietti, 1965).

Thomas Aquinas. *Liber de veritate Catholicae fidei contra errores infidelium, seu Summa contra gentiles*, ed. C. Pera, P. Marc, and P. Carmello (Rome: Marietti, 1961–7).

Thomas Aquinas. *Opera omnia*, ed. Leonine Commission (Rome: Commissio Leonina, 1882–).

Thomas Aquinas. *Scriptum super libros Sententiarum*, ed. P. Mandonnet and M. F. Moos (Paris: P. Lethielleux, 1929–56).

Thomas of Sutton. *Quodlibeta*, ed. M. Schmaus and M. Gonzalez-Haba (Munich: Bayerische Akademie der Wissenschaften, 1969).

Tillotson, John. *The Works of the Most Reverend Dr. John Tillotson*, ed. R. Barker, 4th ed. (London, 1728).

Vanini, Giulio Cesare. *Amphitheatrum aeternae providentiae divino-magicum, christiano-physicum, nec non astrologo-catholicum* (Lyon, 1615).

Vanini, Giulio Cesare. *De admirandis naturae reginae deaque mortalium arcanis* (Paris: A. Périer, 1616).

Walter Burley. *De formis*, ed. F. Scott (Munich: Verlag der Bayerischen Akademie der Wissenschaften, 1970).

Walter Burley. *De primo et ultimo instanti*, in H. Shapiro and C. Shapiro (eds.) "De primo et ultimo instanti des Walter Burley," *Archiv für Geschichte der Philosophie* 47 (1966) 157–73.

Walter Burley. *De toto et parte*, ed. H. Shapiro and F. Scott, *Archives d'histoire doctrinale et littéraire du moyen age* 33 (1966) 299–303.

Walter Burley. *Expositio in libros octo Physicorum Aristotelis* (Venice, 1501; repr. Hildesheim: Olms, 1972).

Walter Burley. *Expositio super artem veterem Porphyrii et Aristotelis* (Venice, 1509).

Walter Burley. *Quaestiones super de anima*, ed. P. Bakker (unpublished partial transcription of Vat. lat. 2151).

Walter Chatton. *Reportatio super Sententias*, ed. J. C. Wey and G. J. Etzkorn (Toronto: Pontifical Institute of Mediaeval Studies, 2002–5).

Walter Map. *De nugis curialium*, ed. and tr. M. R. James; rev. C. N. L. Brooke and R. A. B. Mynors (Oxford: Clarendon, 1983).

Webster, John. *Academiarum Examen, or the Examination of Academies* (London: Giles Calvert, 1654).

White, Thomas. *De mundo dialogi tres* (Paris: D. Moreau, 1642).

White, Thomas. *An Exclusion of Scepticks from All Title to Dispute: Being an Answer to the Vanity of Dogmatizing* (London: J. Williams, 1665).

White, Thomas. *Peripateticall Institutions in the Way of that Eminent Person and Excellent Philosopher, Sir Kenelm Digby* (London, 1656).

Wilkins, John. *An Essay towards a Real Character and a Philosophical Language* (London, 1668).

William of Auvergne. *Tractatus de anima*, in *Opera Omnia* (Paris, 1674; repr. Frankfurt: Minerva, 1963).

William Crathorn. *Quästionen zum ersten Sentenzenbuch*, ed. F. Hoffmann (Münster: Aschendorff, 1988).

William de la Mare. *Correctivum fratris Thomae*, in *Les premières polémiques Thomistes: le Correctorium Corruptorii "Quare"*, ed. P. Glorieux (Kain: Le Saulchoir, 1927).

William Ockham. *Dialogus*, ed. and tr. J. Kilcullen et al. at http://www.britac.ac.uk/pubs/dialogus/ockdial.html.

William Ockham. *Opera philosophica et theologica* (St. Bonaventure: Franciscan Institute, 1967–89).

William of Sherwood. *Syncategoremata*, in J. R. O'Donnell (ed.) "The Syncategoremata of William of Sherwood," *Mediaeval Studies* 3 (1941) 46–93.

William of Sherwood. *Treatise on Syncategorematic Words*, tr. N. Kretzmann (Minneapolis, University of Minnesota Press, 1968).

Secondary Sources

Aaron, Richard I. *John Locke*, 3rd ed. (Oxford: Clarendon, 1971).

Adams, Marilyn McCord. "Aristotle and the Sacrament of the Altar: A Crisis in Medieval Aristotelianism," in R. Bosley and M. Tweedale (eds.) *Aristotle and His Medieval Interpreters* [*Canadian Journal of Philosophy*, supp. vol. 17] (Calgary: University of Calgary Press, 1992) 195–249.

Adams, Marilyn McCord. "Things versus 'Hows', or Ockham on Predication and Ontology," in J. Bogen and J. E. McGuire (eds.) *How Things Are: Studies in Predication and the History of Philosophy and Science* (Dordrecht: Reidel, 1985) 175–88.

Adams, Marilyn McCord. *William Ockham* (Notre Dame: University of Notre Dame Press, 1987).

Adams, Robert M. "Flavors, Colors, and God," in *The Virtue of Faith and Other Essays in Philosophical Theology* (New York: Oxford University Press, 1987) 243–62.

Adams, Robert M. *Leibniz: Determinist, Theist, Idealist* (New York: Oxford University Press, 1994).

Adams, Robert M. "Middle Knowledge and the Problem of Evil," in *The Virtue of Faith and Other Essays in Philosophical Theology* (New York: Oxford University Press, 1987) 77–93.

Alexander, H. G. *The Leibniz–Clarke Correspondence* (Manchester: Manchester University Press, 1956).

Alexander, Peter. *Ideas, Qualities and Corpuscles: Locke and Boyle on the External World* (Cambridge: Cambridge University Press, 1985).

Alquié, Fernand. "Experience ontologique et deduction systématique dans la constitution de la métaphysique de Descartes," in *Descartes: cahiers de Royaumont Philosophie* n. II (Paris: Éditions de Minuit, 1957) 10–71.

Alston, William P. and Jonathan Bennett. "Locke on People and Substances," *Philosophical Review* 97 (1988) 25–46.

Amerini, Fabrizio. "The Semantics of Substantial Names: The Tradition of the Commentaries on Aristotle's *Metaphysics*," *Recherches de théologie et philosophie médiévales* 75 (2008) 395–440.

Amerini, Fabrizio. "*Utrum inhaerentia sit de essentia accidentis*. Francis of Marchia and the Debate on the Nature of Accidents," *Vivarium* 44 (2006) 96–150.

Andrews, Robert. "Anonymus Matritensis. *Quaestiones super librum Praedicamentorum*: An Edition," *Cahiers de l'Institut du Moyen Age Grec et Latin* 56 (1988) 117–92.

Andrews, Robert. "Thomas Maulevelt's Denial of Substance," in L. A. Newton (ed.) *Medieval Commentaries on Aristotle's* Categories (Leiden: Brill, 2008) 347–68.

Anscombe, G. E. M. "Substance," *Proceedings of the Aristotelian Society* supp. vol. 38 (1964) 69–78.

Anstey, Peter. *The Philosophy of Robert Boyle* (London: Routledge, 2000).

Anstey, Peter. "Robert Boyle and the Heuristic Value of Mechanism," *Studies in the History of Philosophy and Science* 33 (2002) 161–74.

Ariew, Roger. "Descartes and the Jesuits of La Flèche: The Eucharist," in *Descartes and the Last Scholastics* (Ithaca: Cornell University Press, 1999) 140–54.

Ariew, Roger. "Descartes, Basso, and Toletus: Three Kinds of Corpuscularians," in *Descartes and the Last Scholastics* (Ithaca: Cornell University Press, 1999) 123–39.

Ariew, Roger. *Descartes and the Last Scholastics* (Ithaca: Cornell University Press, 1999).

Ariew, Roger. "Descartes and Scholasticism: The Intellectual Background to Descartes' Thought," in J. Cottingham (ed.) *The Cambridge Companion to Descartes* (Cambridge: Cambridge University Press, 1992) 58–90.

Ariew, Roger. "Modernity," in R. Pasnau (ed.) *Cambridge History of Medieval Philosophy* (Cambridge: Cambridge University Press, 2010) 114–26.

Ariew, Roger, John Cottingham, and Tom Sorell (eds.). *Descartes' Mediations: Background Source Materials* (Cambridge: Cambridge University Press, 1998).

Ariew, Roger and Alan Gabbey. "The Scholastic Background," in D. Garber and M. Ayers (eds.) *The Cambridge History of Seventeenth-Century Philosophy* (Cambridge: Cambridge University Press, 1998) 425–53.

Ariew, Roger and Marjorie Grene. "The Cartesian Destiny of Form and Matter," in *Descartes and the Last Scholastics* (Ithaca: Cornell University Press, 1999) 77–96.

Arlig, Andrew. "Abelard's Assault on Everyday Objects," *American Catholic Philosophical Quarterly* 81 (2007) 209–27.

Arlig, Andrew. "Medieval Mereology," in E. Zalta (ed.) *The Stanford Encyclopedia of Philosophy* (Summer 2006 Edition) http://plato.stanford.edu/archives/sum2006/entries/mereology-medieval/.

Ayers, Michael. "The Ideas of Power and Substance in Locke's Philosophy," *Philosophical Quarterly* 25 (1975) 1–27.

Ayers, Michael. *Locke: Epistemology and Ontology* (London: Routledge, 1991).

Ayers, Michael. "Locke, John," in E. Craig (ed.) *Routledge Encyclopedia of Philosophy* (London: Routledge, 1998) V:665–87.

Ayers, Michael. "Locke versus Aristotle on Natural Kinds," *Journal of Philosophy* 78 (1981) 47–72.

Ayers, Michael. "Primary and Secondary Qualities in Locke's *Essay*," in L. Nolan (ed.) *Primary and Secondary Qualities: The Historical and Ongoing Debate* (Oxford: Oxford University Press, forthcoming).

Bakker, Paul J. J. M. "Aristotelian Metaphysics and Eucharistic Theology: John Buridan and Marsilius of Inghen on the Ontological Status of Accidental Being," in J. Thijssen and J. Zupko (eds.) *The Metaphysics and Natural Philosophy of John Buridan* (Leiden: Brill, 2001) 247–64.

Bakker, Paul J. J. M. *La raison et le miracle: les doctrines eucharistiques (c.1250–c.1400). Contribution à l'étude des rapports entre philosophie et théologie* (Nijmegen: Katholieke Universiteit Nijmegen, 1999).

Balme, David. "Aristotle's Biology Was Not Essentialist," in A. Gotthelf and J. G. Lennox (eds.) *Philosophical Issues in Aristotle's Biology* (Cambridge: Cambridge University Press, 1987) 291–312.

Barbour, Julian B. *The Discovery of Dynamics: A Study from a Machian Point of View of the Discovery and the Structure of Dynamical Theories* (Oxford: Oxford University Press, 2001).

Barker, Peter and Bernard R. Goldstein. "Theological Foundations of Kepler's Astronomy," *Osiris* 16 (2001) 88–113.

Barnes, Gordon P. "The Paradoxes of Hylomorphism," *Review of Metaphysics* 56 (2003) 501–23.

Barnes, Jonathan. "Bits and Pieces," in J. Barnes and M. Mignucci (eds.) *Matter and Metaphysics: Fourth Symposium Hellenisticum* (Naples: Bibliopolis, 1988) 223–94.

Barnes, Jonathan. "Les catégories et les *Catégories*," in O. Bruun and L. Corti (eds.) *Les Catégories et leur histoire* (Paris: Vrin, 2005) 11–80.

Bazán, Bernardo Carlos. "Pluralisme de formes ou dualisme de substances?" *Revue philosophique de Louvain* 67 (1969) 30–73.

Barzun, Jacques. *From Dawn to Decadence: 500 Years of Cultural Life, 1500 to the Present* (New York: Harper Collins, 2000).

Beck, L. J. *The Metaphysics of Descartes: A Study of the Meditations* (Oxford: Clarendon, 1965).

Bellosta, Hélène. "Burning Instruments: From Diocles to Ibn Sahl," *Arabic Sciences and Philosophy* 12 (2002) 285–303.

Bennett, Jonathan. *Learning from Six Philosophers: Descartes, Spinoza, Leibniz, Locke, Berkeley, Hume* (Oxford: Clarendon, 2001).

Bennett, Jonathan. *A Study of Spinoza's Ethics* (Indianapolis: Hackett, 1984).

Bennett, Jonathan. "Substratum," *History of Philosophy Quarterly* 4 (1987) 197–215.

Bernhardt, Jean. "Nominalisme et mécanisme dans la pensée de Hobbes," *Archives de philosophie* 48 (1985) 235–49.

Berthold, Gerhard. *Rumford und die mechanische Wärmetheorie: Versuch einer Forgeschichte der mechanischen Theorie der Wärme* (Heidelberg: Carl Winter, 1875).

Bianchi, Luca. "1277: A Turning Point in Medieval Philosophy?" in J. A. Aertsen and A. Speer (eds.) *Was ist Philosophie im Mittelalter?* (Miscellanea Mediaevalia 26) (Berlin: De Gruyter, 1998) 90–110.

Bianchi, Luca. *Censure et liberté intellectuelle à l'Université de Paris: XIIIe–XIVe siècles* (Paris: Belles lettres, 1999).

Bianchi, Luca. "Continuity and Change in the Aristotelian Tradition," in J. Hankins (ed.) *The Cambridge Companion to Renaissance Philosophy* (Cambridge: Cambridge University Press, 2007) 49–71.

Biard, Joël. "La conception Cartésienne de l'étendue et les débats médiévaux sur la quantité," in J. Biard and R. Rashed (eds.) *Descartes et le Moyen Age* (Paris: Vrin, 1997) 349–61.

Biard, Joël. "Les controverses sur l'objet du savoir et les 'complexe significabilia' à Paris au XIVe siècle," in S. Caroti (ed.) *Quia inter doctores est magna dissensio: les débats de philosophie naturelle à Paris au XIVe siècle* (Florence: Olschki, 2004) 1–31.

Biard, Joël. "Diversité des fonctions et unité de l'âme dans la psychologie péripatéticienne (XIVe–XVIe siècle)," *Vivarium* 46 (2008) 342–67.

Biard, Joël. "Nominalism in the Later Middle Ages," in R. Pasnau (ed.) *Cambridge History of Medieval Philosophy* (Cambridge: Cambridge University Press, 2010) 661–73.

Biard, Joël. "Le statut du mouvement dans la philosophie naturelle buridanienne," in S. Caroti and P. Souffrin (eds.) *La nouvelle physique du XIVe siècle* (Florence: Olschki, 1997) 141–59.

Biard, Joël and Irène Rosier-Catach. *La tradition médiévale des catégories, XIIe–XVe siècles* (Louvain: Peeters, 2003).

Blackwell, Richard. "Descartes' Concept of Matter," in E. McMullin (ed.) *The Concept of Matter in Modern Philosophy* (Notre Dame: University of Notre Dame Press, 1963) 59–75.

Bloom, Harold. *The Anxiety of Influence: A Theory of Poetry*, 2nd ed. (New York: Oxford University Press, 1997).

Blum, Paul. "Benedictus Pererius: Renaissance Culture at the Origins of Jesuit Science," *Science and Education* 15 (2006) 279–304.

Boas Hall, Marie. "The Establishment of the Mechanical Philosophy," *Isis* 10 (1952) 412–541.

Boas Hall, Marie. "Matter in Seventeenth-Century Science," in E. McMullin (ed.) *The Concept of Matter in Modern Philosophy* (Notre Dame: University of Notre Dame Press, 1963) 76–99.

Bolton, Martha Brandt. "Locke on Identity: The Scheme of Simple and Compounded Things," in K. F. Barber and J. J. E. Gracia (eds.) *Individuation and Identity in Early Modern Philosophy: Descartes to Kant* (Albany, NY: SUNY Press, 1994) 103–31.

Bolton, Martha Brandt. "Substances, Substrata, and Names of Substances in Locke's *Essay*," *Philosophical Review* 85 (1976) 488–513.

Bos, E. P. "Petrus Thomae's *De distinctione praedicamentorum* (with a Working Edition)," in M. Kardaun and J. Spruyt (eds.) *The Winged Chariot: Collected Essays on Plato and Platonism in Honour of L. M. de Rijk* (Leiden: Brill, 2000) 277–312.

Bos, E. P. and H. A. Krop (eds.). *Franco Burgersdijk (1590–1635): Neo-Aristotelianism in Leiden* (Amsterdam: Rodopi, 1993).

Bos, E. P. and A. C. van der Helm. "The Division of Being over the Categories According to Albert the Great, Thomas Aquinas and Duns Scotus," in E. P. Bos (ed.) *John Duns Scotus: Renewal of Philosophy: Acts of the Third Symposium Organized by the Dutch Society for Medieval Philosophy* (Elementa: Schriften zur Philosophie und ihrer Problemgeschichte 72) (Amsterdam: Rodopi, 1998) 183–96.

Bos, Erik-Jan. *The Correspondence between Descartes and Henricus Regius* (Utrecht: The Leiden-Utrecht Research Institute of Philosophy, 2002).

Bouillon, Dominique. "Un discourse inédit de Iacopo Zabarella préliminaire à l'exposition de la 'Physique' d'Aristote (Padoue 1568)," *Atti e memorie dell'Accademia galileiana di scienze lettere ed arti in Padova* 111 (1998/9) 119–27.

Boureau, Alain. "Le concept de relation chez Pierre de Jean Olivi," in A. Boureau and S. Piron (eds.) *Pierre de Jean Olivi (1248–1298): pensée scolastique, dissidence spirituelle et société* (Paris: Vrin, 1999) 41–55.

Braakhuis, H. A. G. "John Buridan and the 'Parisian School' on the Possibility of Returning as Numerically the Same. A Note on a Chapter in the History of the Relationship between Faith and Natural Science," in S. Caroti and P. Souffrin (eds.) *La nouvelle physique du XIVe siècle* (Florence: Olschki, 1997) 111–40.

Broackes, Justin. "Substance," *Proceedings of the Aristotelian Society* 106 (2006) 131–66.

Brockliss, Laurence. "The Moment of No Return: The University of Paris and the Death of Aristotelianism," *Science and Education* 15 (2006) 259–78.

Broughton, Janet. *Descartes's Method of Doubt* (Princeton: Princeton University Press, 2002).

Brower, Jeffrey and Susan Brower-Toland. "Aquinas on Mental Representation," *Philosophical Review* 117 (2008) 193–243.

Brower-Toland, Susan. "Instantaneous Change and the Physics of Sanctification: Quasi-Aristotelianism in Henry of Ghent's *Quodlibet* XV q. 13," *Journal of the History of Philosophy* 40 (2002) 19–46.

Brown, Barry F. *Accidental Being: A Study in the Metaphysics of St. Thomas Aquinas* (Lanham, MD: University Press of America, 1985).

Brown, Stuart. "Leibniz: Modern, Scholastic, or Renaissance Philosopher?" in T. Sorell (ed.) *The Rise of Modern Philosophy* (Oxford: Clarendon, 1993) 213–30.

Burr, David. "Olivi and the Limits of Intellectual Freedom," in G. H. Shriver (ed.) *Contemporary Reflections on the Medieval Christian Tradition: Essays in Honor of Ray C. Petry* (Durham, NC: Duke University Press, 1974) 185–99.

Burr, David. "The Persecution of Peter Olivi," *Transactions of the American Philosophical Society* 66 (1976) 3–98.

Burr, David. "Quantity and Eucharistic Presence: The Debate from Olivi through Ockham," *Collectanea Franciscana* 44 (1974) 5–44.

Burtt, Edwin A. *The Metaphysical Foundations of Modern Physical Science* (Garden City, NY: Doubleday, 1954).

Callus, D. A. "The Origins of the Problem of the Unity of Form," in J. A. Weisheipl (ed.) *The Dignity of Science: Studies in Philosophy of Science Presented to William Hubert Kane, O.P.* (Washington, DC: Thomist Press, 1961) 121–49.

Callus, D. A. "Two Early Oxford Masters on the Plurality of Forms: Adam of Buckfield – Richard Rufus of Cornwall," *Revue neo-scholastique de philosophie* 42 (1939) 411–45.

Caroti, Stefano. "'*Generatio potest auferri, non differri*.' Causal Order and Natural Necessity in Nicole Oresme's 'Questiones super De generatione et corruptione'," in J. M. M. H. Thijssen and H. A. G. Braakhuis (eds.) *The Commentary Tradition on Aristotle's "De generatione et corruptione": Ancient, Medieval and Early Modern* (Turnhout: Brepols, 1999) 183–205.

Caroti, Stefano. "La position de Nicole Oresme sur la nature du mouvement (*Questiones super Physicam* III, 1–8): Problèmes gnoséologiques, ontologiques et sémantiques," *Archives d'histoire doctrinale et littéraire du Moyen Age* 61 (1994) 303–85.

Caroti, Stefano. "*Modi rerum* and Materialism: A Note on a Quotation of a Condemned *Articulus* in Some Fourteenth-Century Parisian *De anima* Commentaries," *Traditio* 55 (2000) 211–34.

Caroti, Stefano. "Nicole Oresme et les *modi rerum*," *Oriens–Occidens: Sciences, mathématiques et philosophie de l'Antiquité à l'Âge classique* 3 (2000) 115–44.

Caroti, Stefano. "Les *modi rerum* . . . Encore une fois. Une source possible de Nicole Oresme: Le commentaire sur le livre 1er des *Sentences* de Jean de Mirecourt," in S. Caroti and J. Celeyrette (eds.) *Quia inter doctores est magna dissensio: les débats de philosophie naturelle à Paris au XIVe siècle* (Florence: Olschki, 2004) 195–222.

Caroti, Stefano and Jean Celeyrette (eds.). *Quia inter doctores est magna dissensio: les débats de philosophie naturelle à Paris au XIVe siècle* (Florence: Olschki, 2004).

Caroti, Stefano and P. Souffrin (eds.). *La nouvelle physique du XIVe siècle* (Florence: Olschki, 1997).

Carriero, John. *Between Two Worlds: A Reading of Descartes's* Meditations (Princeton: Princeton University Press, 2009).

Catto, J. I. (ed.) *The History of the University of Oxford*, vol. 1: *The Early Oxford Schools* (Oxford: Oxford University Press, 1984).

Celenza, Christopher. "The Revival of Platonic Philosophy," in J. Hankins (ed.) *The Cambridge Companion to Renaissance Philosophy* (Cambridge: Cambridge University Press, 2007) 72–96.

Cesalli, Laurent. "Le réalisme propositionnel de Walter Burley," *Archives d'histoire doctrinale et littéraire du Moyen Age* 68 (2001) 155–221.

Chalmers, Alan. "The Lack of Excellency of Boyle's Mechanical Philosophy," *Studies in History and Philosophy of Science* 24 (1993) 541–64.

Chappell, Vere. "Descartes on Substance," in J. Broughton and J. Carriero (eds.) *A Companion to Descartes* (Oxford: Blackwell, 2008) 251–70.

Chappell, Vere. "L'homme cartésien," in J.-M. Beyssade and J.-L. Marion (eds.) *Descartes: objecter et répondre* (Paris: Presses Universitaires de France, 1994) 403–26.

Chappell, Vere. "Locke and Relative Identity," *History of Philosophy Quarterly* 6 (1989) 69–83.

Charlton, William. "Aristotle's Potential Infinities," in L. Judson (ed.) *Aristotle's* Physics: *A Collection of Essays* (Oxford: Clarendon, 1991) 129–49.

Chisholm, Roderick. *Person and Object: A Metaphysical Study* (La Salle, IL: Open Court, 1976).

Clarke, Desmond. *Descartes's Theory of Mind* (Oxford: Clarendon, 2003).

Clarke, Desmond. "Henricus Regius," in E. N. Zalta (ed.) *The Stanford Encyclopedia of Philosophy (Fall 2008 Edition)* at http://plato.stanford.edu/archives/fall2008/entries/henricus-regius/.

Clemenson, David. *Descartes' Theory of Ideas* (London: Continuum, 2007).

Clericuzio, Antonio. *Elements, Principles and Corpuscles: A Study of Atomism and Chemistry in the Seventeenth Century* (Dordrecht: Kluwer, 2000).

Clericuzio, Antonio. "Gassendi, Charleton and Boyle on Matter and Motion," in C. Lüthy et al. (eds.) *Late Medieval and Early Modern Corpuscular Matter Theories* (Leiden: Brill, 2001) 467–82.

Clucas, Stephen. "Corpuscular Matter Theory in the Northumberland Circle," in C. Lüthy et al. (eds.) *Late Medieval and Early Modern Corpuscular Matter Theories* (Leiden: Brill, 2001) 181–207.

Clucas, Stephen. "'The Infinite Variety of Forms and Magnitudes': 16th- and 17th-Century English Corpuscular Philosophy and Aristotelian Theories of Matter and Form," *Early Science and Medicine* 2 (1997) 251–71.

Conn, Christopher Hughes. *Locke on Essence and Identity* (Dordrecht: Kluwer, 2003).

Conn, Christopher Hughes. "Locke on Natural Kinds and Essential Properties," *Journal of Philosophical Research* 27 (2002) 475–97.

Conti, Alessandro D. "Categories and Universals in the Later Middle Ages," in L. A. Newton (ed.) *Medieval Commentaries on Aristotle's* Categories (Leiden: Brill, 2008) 369–409.

Conti, Alessandro D. "Ontology in Walter Burley's Last Commentary on the *Ars Vetus*," *Franciscan Studies* 50 (1990) 121–76.

Conti, Alessandro D. "Realism," in R. Pasnau (ed.) *Cambridge History of Medieval Philosophy* (Cambridge: Cambridge University Press, 2010) 647–60.

Conti, Alessandro D. "A Realist Interpretation of the *Categories* in the Fourteenth Century: The *Litteralis sententia super Praedicamenta Aristotelis* of Robert Alyngton," in L. A. Newton (ed.) *Medieval Commentaries on Aristotle's* Categories (Leiden: Brill, 2008) 317–46.

Conti, Alessandro D. "Thomas Sutton's Commentary on the 'Categories' according to Ms Oxford, Merton College 289," in P. O. Lewry (ed.) *The Rise of British Logic* (Toronto: Pontifical Institute of Mediaeval Studies, 1985) 173–213.

Conti, Alessandro D. "Walter Burley," in Edward N. Zalta (ed.) *The Stanford Encyclopedia of Philosophy (Fall 2004 Edition)* at http://plato.stanford.edu/archives/fall2004/entries/burley/.

Conti, Alessandro D. "Wyclif's Logic and Metaphysics," in I. C. Levy (ed.) *A Companion to John Wyclif: Late Medieval Theologian* (Leiden: Brill, 2006) 67–125.

Cooper, John. "Metaphysics in Aristotle's Embryology," *Proceedings of the Cambridge Philological Society* 214 (1988) 14–41.

Copenhaver, Brian P. and Charles B. Schmitt. *Renaissance Philosophy* (Oxford: Oxford University Press, 1992).

Côté, Antoine. "Siger of Brabant and Thomas Aquinas on Divine Power and the Separability of Accidents," *British Journal for the History of Philosophy* 16 (2008) 681–700.

Cottingham, John. "A Brute to the Brutes? Descartes' Treatment of Animals," *Philosophy* 53 (1978) 551–9.

Cottingham, John. "A New Start? Cartesian Metaphysics and the Emergence of Modern Philosophy," in T. Sorell (ed.) *The Rise of Modern Philosophy* (Oxford: Clarendon, 1993) 145–66.

Cottingham, John. "Descartes on Colour," *Proceedings of the Aristotelian Society* 90 (1989–90) 231–46.

Courtenay, William J. "*Antiqui* and *Moderni* in Late Medieval Thought," *Journal of the History of Ideas* 48 (1987) 3–10.

Courtenay, William J. "The Categories, Michael de Massa, and Natural Philosophy at Paris, 1335–1340," in J. Biard and I. Rosier-Catach (eds.) *La tradition médiévale des Catégories XIIe–XIVe siècles* (Louvain: Peeters, 2003) 243–59.

Courtenay, William J. "Erfurt CA 2 127 and the Censured Articles of Mirecourt and Autrecourt," in A. Speer (ed.) *Die Bibliotheca Amploniana: ihre Bedeutung im Spannungsfeld von Aristotelismus, Nominalismus und Humanismus* (Berlin: de Gruyter, 1995) 341–52.

Courtenay, William J. "Inquiry and Inquisition: Academic Freedom in Medieval Universities," *Church History* 58 (1989) 168–81.

Courtenay, William J. "John of Mirecourt's Condemnation: Its Original Form," *Recherches de théologie ancienne et médiévale* 53 (1986) 190–1.

Courtenay, William J. "The Preservation and Dissemination of Academic Condemnations at the University of Paris in the Middle Ages," in B. Bazán et al. (eds.) *Les philosophies morales et politiques au Moyen Âge* (New York: Legas, 1995) III:1659–67.

Courtenay, William J. "The Reception of Ockham's Thought at the University of Paris," in Z. Kaluza and P. Vignaux (eds.) *Preuve et raisons à l'Université de Paris: Logique, ontologie et théologie au XIVe siècle* (Paris: Vrin, 1984) 43–64.

Courtenay, William J. "The Reception of Ockham's Thought in Fourteenth-Century England," in A. Hudson and M. Wilks (eds.) *From Ockham to Wyclif* (Oxford: Blackwell, 1987) 89–107.

Courtenay, William J. "Was There an Ockhamist School?," in M. Hoenen, J. Schneider, and G. Wieland (eds.) *Philosophy and Learning: Universities in the Middle Ages* (Leiden: Brill, 1995) 263–92.

Crombie, A. C. *Robert Grosseteste and the Origins of Experimental Science, 1100–1700* (Oxford: Clarendon, 1953).

Cross, Richard. *Duns Scotus* (Great Medieval Thinkers) (Oxford: Oxford University Press, 1999).

Cross, Richard. "Four-Dimensionalism and Identity Across Time: Henry of Ghent vs. Bonaventure," *Journal of the History of Philosophy* 37 (1999) 393–414.

Cross, Richard. "Identity, Origin, and Persistence in Duns Scotus's Physics," *History of Philosophy Quarterly* 16 (1999) 1–18.

Cross, Richard. "Infinity, Continuity, and Composition: The Contribution of Gregory of Rimini," *Medieval Philosophy and Theology* 7 (1998) 89–110.

Cross, Richard. "Ockham on Part and Whole," *Vivarium* 37 (1999) 143–67.

Cross, Richard. *The Physics of Duns Scotus: The Scientific Context of a Theological Vision* (Oxford: Clarendon, 1998).

Curley, Edwin. "Hobbes versus Descartes," in R. Ariew and M. Grene (eds.) *Descartes and His Contemporaries* (Chicago: University of Chicago Press, 1995) 97–109.

Curley, Edwin. "Locke, Boyle and the Distinction between Primary and Secondary Qualities," *Philosophical Review* 81 (1972) 438–64.

Curtis, Mark H. *Oxford and Cambridge in Transition 1558–1642: An Essay on Changing Relations between the English University and English Society* (Oxford: Clarendon, 1959).

Dahan, Gilbert. "Nommer les êtres: exégèse et théories du langage dans les commentaires médiévaux de Genèse 2, 19–20," in S. Ebbesen (ed.) *Sprachtheorien in Spätantike und Mittelalter* (Tübingen: G. Narr, 1995) 55–74.

Dales, Richard C. *The Problem of the Rational Soul in the Thirteenth Century* (Leiden: Brill, 1995).

Daston, Lorraine and Michael Stolleis. *Natural Law and Laws of Nature in Early Modern Europe: Jurisprudence, Theology, Moral and Natural Philosophy* (Farnham, UK: Ashgate, 2008).

de Libera, Alain. "Le traité *De appellatione* de Lambert de Lagny (Lambert d'Auxerre)," *Archives d'histoire doctrinale et littéraire du Moyen Age* 48 (1981) 227–85.

de Libera, Alain. *Penser au Moyen Âge* (Paris: Seuil, 1991).

de Libera, Alain. *La référence vide: théories de la proposition* (Paris: Seuil, 2002).

de Rijk, L. M. "On Buridan's View of Accidental Being," in E. P. Bos and H. Krop (eds.) *John Buridan: A Master of Arts: Some Aspects of His Philosophy* (Nijmegen: Ingenium, 1993) 41–51.

de Rochemonteix, Camille. *Un collège des Jesuites au XVIIe et XVIIIe siècles: le Collège Henri IV de la Flèche*, 4 vols. (Le Mans: Leguicheux, 1889).

De Wulf, Maurice. *Histoire de la philosophie médiévale*, 2 vols., 5th ed. (Louvain: Institut supérieure de Philosophie, 1924).

Debus, Allen G. *The Chemical Philosophy: Paracelsian Science and Medicine in the Sixteenth and Seventeenth Centuries*, 2 vols. (New York: Science History Publications, 1977).

Deitz, Luc. "'Falsissima est ergo haec de triplici substantia Aristotelis doctrina.' A Sixteenth-Century Critic of Aristotle—Francesco Patrizi da Cherso on Privation, Form, and Matter," *Early Science and Medicine* 2 (1997) 227–49.

Dekker, Dirk-Jan. "Buridan's Concept of Time: Time, Motion and the Soul in John Buridan's Questions on Aristotle's *Physics*," in J. Thijssen and J. Zupko (eds.) *The Metaphysics and Natural Philosophy of John Buridan* (Leiden: Brill, 2001) 151–63.

Denifle, Henri and Émile Châtelain. *Chartularium Universitatis Parisiensis* (Paris: Delalain, 1889–97).

Denzinger, Heinrich (ed.). *Enchiridion symbolorum*, 34th ed. (Herder: Freiburg, 1967).

Des Chene, Dennis. "Descartes and the Natural Philosophy of the Coimbra Commentaries," in S. Gaukroger et al. (eds.) *Descartes' Natural Philosophy* (London: Routledge, 2000) 29–45.

Des Chene, Dennis. *Physiologia: Natural Philosophy in Late Aristotelian and Cartesian Thought* (Ithaca, NY: Cornell University Press, 1996).

Des Chene, Dennis. "Wine and Water: Honoré Fabri on Mixtures," in C. Lüthy et al. (eds.) *Late Medieval and Early Modern Corpuscular Matter Theories* (Leiden: Brill, 2001) 363–79.

Dewender, Thomas, "Einige Bemerkungen zur Authentizität der Physikkommentare die Marsilius von Inghen zugeschrieben werden," in S. Wielgus (ed.) *Marsilius von Inghen: Werk und Wirkung* (Lublin: Redakcja Wydawnictw, 1993) 245–69.

Dhanani, Alnoor. *The Physical Theory of Kalām: Atoms, Space, and Void in Basrian Mu'tazilī Cosmology* (Leiden: Brill, 1994).

Diels, Hermann and Walther Kranz. *Die Fragmente der Vorsokratiker*, 2 vols. (Dublin: Weidmann, 1966).

Dobbs, B. J. T. "Stoic and Epicurean Doctrines in Newton's System of the World," in M. J. Osler (ed.) *Atoms, Pneuma, and Tranquillity: Epicurean and Stoic Themes in European Thought* (Cambridge: Cambridge University Press, 1991) 221–38.

Donati, Silvia. "La dottrina delle dimensioni indeterminate in Egidio Romano," *Medioevo* 14 (1988) 149–233.

Donati, Silvia. "The Notion of '*Dimensiones indeterminatae*' in the Commentary Tradition of the 'Physics' in the Thirteenth and Early Fourteenth Century," in C. H. Leijenhorst et al. (eds.) *The Dynamics of Aristotelian Natural Philosophy from Antiquity to the Seventeenth Century* (Leiden: Brill, 2002) 189–223.

Donati, Silvia. "*Utrum accidens possit existere sine subiecto*: aristotelische Metaphysik und christliche Theologie in den Physikkommentaren des 13. Jahrhunderts," in J. Aertsen et al. (eds.) *Nach der Verurteilung von 1277: Philosophie und Theologie an der Universität von Paris im letzten Viertel des 13. Jahrhunderts. Studien und Texte* (Berlin: de Gruyter, 2001) 577–617.

Doncoeur, Paul. "La théorie de la matière et de la forme chez Guill. Occam," *Revue des sciences philosophiques et théologiques* 10 (1921) 21–51.

Downing, Lisa. "The Uses of Mechanism: Corpuscularianism in Drafts A and B of Locke's *Essay*, in C. Lüthy et al. (eds.) *Late Medieval and Early Modern Corpuscular Matter Theories* (Leiden: Brill, 2001) 515–34.

Downing, Lisa. "Sensible Qualities and Material Bodies in Descartes and Boyle," in L. Nolan (ed.) *Primary and Secondary Qualities: The Historical and Ongoing Debate* (Oxford: Oxford University Press, forthcoming).

Doyle, John P. "Suárez, Francisco," in E. Craig (ed.) *Routledge Encyclopedia of Philosophy* (London: Routledge) IX:189–96.

Drake, Stillman. "Galileo: A Biographical Sketch," in E. McMullin (ed.) *Galileo: Man of Science* (New York: Basic Books, 1967) 52–66.

Dumont, Stephen D. "The Univocity of the Concept of Being in the Fourteenth Century: John Duns Scotus and William Alnwick," *Mediaeval Studies* 49 (1987) 1–75.

Dutton, Blake D. "Nicholas of Autrecourt and William of Ockham on Atomism, Nominalism, and the Ontology of Motion," *Medieval Philosophy and Theology* 5 (1996) 63–85.

Ebbesen, Sten. "Les *Catégories* au Moyen Age et au début de la modernité," in O. Bruun and L. Corti (eds.) *Les* Catégories *et leur histoire* (Paris: Vrin, 2005) 245–74.

Ebbesen, Sten. "Concrete Accidental Terms: Late Thirteenth-Century Debates about Problems Relating to Such Terms as 'Album'," in N. Kretzmann (ed.) *Meaning and Inference in Medieval Philosophy* (Dordrecht: Kluwer, 1988) 107–74.

Ebbesen, Sten. "Radulphus Brito on the 'Metaphysics'," in J. Aertsen et al. (ed.) *Nach der Verurteilung von 1277: Philosophie und Theologie an der Universität von Paris im letzen Viertel des 13. Jahrhunderts: Studien und Texte* (Berlin: de Gruyter, 2001) 456–92.

Ebbesen, Sten. "Termini accidentales concreti: Texts from the Late 13th Century," *Cahiers de l'Institut du Moyen Age Grec et Latin* 53 (1986) 37–150.

Ehrle, Franz. *Die Ehrentitel der scholastischen Lehrer des Mittelalters* (Munich: Bayerischen Akademie der Wissenschaften, 1919).

Ehrle, Franz. *Der Sentenzenkommentar Peters von Candia des Pisaner Papstes Alexanders V: ein Beitrag zur Scheidung der Schulen in der Scholastik des 14. Jahrhunderts und zur Geschichte des Wegestreites* (Münster: Aschendorff, 1925).

Elderidge, Laurence. "Changing Concepts of Church Authority in the Later Fourteenth Century: Pierre Ceffons of Clairvaux and William of Woodford, OFM," *Revue de l'Université d'Ottawa* 48 (1978) 170–8.

Emerton, Norma E. *The Scientific Reinterpretation of Form* (Ithaca, NY: Cornell University Press, 1984).

Feingold, Mordechai. *The Newtonian Moment: Isaac Newton and the Making of Modern Culture* (New York: New York Public Library, 2004).

Fernández García, Mariano. *Lexicon scholasticum philosophico-theologicum* (Quaracchi: Collegium S. Bonaventurae, 1910).

Fine, Kit. "A Puzzle concerning Matter and Form," in T. Scaltsas, D. Charles and M. L. Gill (eds.) *Unity, Identity, and Explanation in Aristotle's Metaphysics* (Oxford: Clarendon, 1994) 13–40.

Finocchiaro, Maurice A. *The Galileo Affair: A Documentary History* (Berkeley: University of California Press, 1989).

Fisher, Saul. *Pierre Gassendi's Philosophy and Science: Atomism for Empiricists* (Leiden: Brill, 2005).

Fitzpatrick, P. J. and John Haldane. "Medieval Philosophy in Later Thought," in A. S. McGrade (ed.) *The Cambridge Companion to Medieval Philosophy* (Cambridge: Cambridge University Press, 2003) 300–27.

Foucault, Didier. "Fondaments d'une ontologie matérialiste dans l'*Amphitheatrum* et le *De admirandis* de Vanini," *Kairos* 12 (1998) 39–69.

Fox, Robert. *The Caloric Theory of Gases: From Lavoisier to Regnault* (Oxford: Clarendon, 1971)

Fox, Robert. *The Culture of Science in France, 1700–1900* (Aldershot: Variorum, 1992).

Funkenstein, Amos. *Theology and the Scientific Imagination from the Middle Ages to the Seventeenth Century* (Princeton: Princeton University Press, 1986).

Furley, David. "Democritus and Epicurus on Sensible Qualities," in J. Brunschwig and M. Nussbaum (eds.) *Passions and Perceptions: Studies in Hellenistic Philosophy of Mind* (Cambridge: Cambridge University Press, 1993) 72–94.

Fussenegger, Gerold. "'Littera septem sigillorum' contra doctrinam Petri Ioannis Olivi edita," *Archivum franciscanum historicum* 47 (1954) 45–53.

Gabbey, Alan. "Force and Inertia in the 17th century: Descartes and Newton," in S. Gaukroger (ed.) *Descartes: Philosophy, Mathematics and Physics* (Brighton: Harvester, 1980) 230–320.

Gabbey, Alan. "Henry More and the Limits of Mechanism," in S. Hutton (ed.) *Henry More (1614–1687): Tercentenary Studies* (Dordrecht: Kluwer, 1990) 19–35.

Gabbey, Alan. "Philosophia Cartesiana Triumphata: Henry More (1646–1671)," in T. M. Lennon et al. (eds.) *Problems of Cartesianism* (Kingston: McGill-Queen's University Press, 1982) 171–250.

Gabbey, Alan. "The Mechanical Philosophy and Its Problems: Mechanical Explanations, Impenetrability, and Perpetual Motion," in J. C. Pitt (ed.) *Change and Progress in Modern Science* (Dordrecht: Reidel, 1985) 9–84.

Gabriel, Astrik. "'Via antiqua' and 'Via moderna' and the Migration of Paris Students and Masters to the German Universities in the Fifteenth Century," in A. Zimmermann (ed.) *Antiqui und Moderni: Traditionsbewusstsein und Fortschrittsbewusstsein im späten Mittelalter* (Berlin: De Gruyter, 1974) 439–83.

Ganson, Todd S. "On the Origins of Philosophical Inquiry concerning the Secondary Qualities" (Ph.D. dissertation, Cornell University, 1998).

Garber, Daniel. "Defending Aristotle/Defending Society in the Early 17th Century Paris," in W. Detel and C. Zittel (eds.) *Wissensideale und Wissenskulturen in der freuhen Neuzeit: Ideals and Cultures of Knowledge in Early Modern Europe* (Frankfurt: Akademie Verlag, 2002) 135–60.

Garber, Daniel. "Descartes, the Aristotelians, and the Revolution that Did Not Happen in 1637," *Monist* 71 (1988) 471–86.

Garber, Daniel. *Descartes' Metaphysical Physics* (Chicago: University of Chicago Press, 1992).

Garber, Daniel. *Leibniz: Body, Substance, Monad* (Oxford: Oxford University Press, 2009).

Garber, Daniel. "Leibniz and the Foundations of Physics: The Middle Years," in K. Okruhlik (ed.) *The Natural Philosophy of Leibniz* (Dordrecht: Reidel, 1985) 27–130.

Garber, Daniel. "Leibniz on Form and Matter," *Early Science and Medicine* 2 (1997) 326–52.

Garber, Daniel. "On the Frontlines of the Scientific Revolution: How Mersenne Learned to Love Galileo," *Perspectives on Science* 12 (2004) 135–63.

Garber, Daniel. "Soul and Mind: Life and Thought in the Seventeenth Century," in D. Garber and M. Ayers (eds.) *The Cambridge History of Seventeenth-Century Philosophy* (Cambridge: Cambridge University Press, 1998) 759–95.

Garber, Daniel. "Voetius and Other Voids," *Times Literary Supplement* (Sept. 8, 2006) 8–9.

Garber, Daniel and Michael Ayers (eds.). *The Cambridge History of Seventeenth-Century Philosophy* (Cambridge: Cambridge University Press, 1998).

Garber, Daniel, John Henry, Lynn Joy, and Alan Gabbey. "New Doctrines of Body and its Power, Places, and Space," in D. Garber and M. Ayers (eds.) *The Cambridge History of Seventeenth-Century Philosophy* (Cambridge: Cambridge University Press, 1998) 553–623.

Garin, Eugenio. *La cultura filosofica del Rinascimento italiano. Ricerche e documenti* (Florence: Sansoni, 1961).

Gaukroger, Stephen. *The Emergence of a Scientific Culture: Science and the Shaping of Modernity 1210–1685* (Oxford: Oxford University Press, 2006).

Gibson, James. *Locke's Theory of Knowledge and Its Historical Relations* (Cambridge: Cambridge University Press, 1917).

Gilbert, Neil Ward, "Ockham, Wyclif, and the 'Via Moderna'," in A. Zimmermann (ed.) *Antiqui und Moderni: Traditionsbewusstsein und Fortschrittsbewusstsein im späten Mittelalter* (Berlin: De Gruyter, 1974) 85–125.

Gilson, Etienne. *The Unity of Philosophical Experience* (New York: Scribner's, 1937).

Ginzburg, Carlo. "High and Low: The Theme of Forbidden Knowledge in the Sixteenth and Seventeenth Centuries," *Past and Present* 73 (1976) 28–41.

Goddu, André. "William of Ockham's Arguments for Action at a Distance," *Franciscan Studies* 44 (1984) 227–44.

Goering, Joseph. "The Invention of Transubstantiation," *Traditio* 46 (1991) 147–70.

Gómez Rodeles, Cecilio et al. (eds.). *Monumenta paedagogica Societatis Jesu, quae primam Rationem studiorum 1586 editam praecessere* (Madrid: A. Avrial, 1901).

Gorham, Geoffrey. "Cartesian Causation: Continuous, Instantaneous, Overdetermined," *Journal of the History of Philosophy* 42 (2004) 389–423.

Gorham, Geoffrey. "Descartes on Persistence and Temporal Parts," in J. Campbell et al. (eds.) *Time and Identity* (Cambridge, MA: MIT Press, 2010) 165–82.

Gorman, Michael and Jonathan Sanford (eds.). *Categories: Historical and Systematic Essays* (Washington: Catholic University of America Press, 2004).

Gousset, Thomas Marie Joseph. *Les actes de la province ecclésiastique de Reims*, 4 vols. (Reims: L. Jacquet, 1842–4).

Gracia, Jorge (ed.). *Individuation in Scholasticism: The Later Middle Ages and the Counter-Reformation, 1150–1160* (Albany: State University of New York Press, 1994).

Gracia, Jorge and Lloyd Newton. "Medieval Theories of the Categories," in E. Zalta (ed.) *The Stanford Encyclopedia of Philosophy (Summer 2006 Edition)* at http://plato.stanford.edu/archives/sum2006/entries/medieval-categories/.

Granada, Miguel A. "New Visions of the Cosmos," in J. Hankins (ed.) *Cambridge Companion to Renaissance Philosophy* (Cambridge: Cambridge University Press, 2007) 270–86.

Grant, Edward. *Much Ado about Nothing: Theories of Space and Vacuum from the Middle Ages to the Scientific Revolution* (Cambridge: Cambridge University Press, 1981).

Grant, Edward. "The Principle of Impenetrability of Bodies in the History of Concepts of Separate Space from the Middle Ages to the Seventeenth Century," *Isis* 69 (1978) 551–71.

Grant, Edward (ed.). *A Source Book in Medieval Science* (Cambridge, MA: Harvard University Press, 1974).

Gregory, Tullio. "David Van Goorle et Daniel Sennert," in M. Raiola (tr.) *Genèse de la raison classique de Charron à Descartes* (Paris: Presses Universitaires de France, 2000) 235–67.

Gregory, Tullio. "Ralph Cudworth," in M. Raiola (tr.) *Genèse de la raison classique de Charron à Descartes* (Paris: Presses Universitaires de France, 2000) 269–90.

Gregory, Tullio. "Sébastien Basson," in M. Raiola (tr.) *Genèse de la raison classique de Charron à Descartes* (Paris: Presses Universitaires de France, 2000) 191–234.

Grellard, Christophe. *Croire et savoir: les principes de la connaissance selon Nicolas d'Autrécourt* (Paris: Vrin, 2005).

Grellard, Christophe. "Nicholas of Autrecourt's Atomistic Physics," in C. Grellard and A. Robert (eds.) *Atomism in Late Medieval Philosophy and Theology* (Leiden: Brill, 2009) 107–26.

Grellard, Christophe and Aurélien Robert (eds.). *Atomism in Late Medieval Philosophy and Theology* (Leiden: Brill, 2009).

Grene, Marjorie. *Descartes among the Scholastics* (The Aquinas Lecture 1991) (Milwaukee: Marquette University Press, 1991).

Guerlac, Henry. "Amicus Plato and Other Friends," *Journal of the History of Ideas* 39 (1978) 627–33.

Guerlac, Henry. "Can There Be Colours in the Dark? Physical Color Theory before Newton," *Journal of the History of Ideas* 47 (1986) 3–20.

Gueroult, Martial. *Descartes' Philosophy Interpreted According to the Order of Reasons*, tr. R. Ariew, 2 vols. (Minneapolis: University of Minnesota Press, 1984).

Hacker, P. M. S. *Appearance and Reality: A Philosophical Investigation into Perception and Perceptual Qualities* (Oxford: Blackwell, 1987).

Hacking, Ian. "A Tradition of Natural Kinds," *Philosophical Studies* 61 (1991) 109–26.

Hall, A. Rupert. *Philosophers at War: The Quarrel between Newton and Leibniz* (Cambridge: Cambridge University Press, 1980).

Hankins, James. "Humanism, Scholasticism, and Renaissance Philosophy," in J. Hankins (ed.) *The Cambridge Companion to Renaissance Philosophy* (Cambridge: Cambridge University Press, 2007) 30–48.

Haskins, Charles Homer. *The Rise of the Universities* (Ithaca, NY: Great Seal Books, 1957).

Hatfield, Gary. "Animals," in J. Broughton and J. Carriero (eds.) *A Companion to Descartes* (Oxford: Blackwell, 2008) 404–25.

Hatfield, Gary. *Descartes and the Meditations* (London: Routledge, 2003).

Hatfield, Gary. "Force (God) in Descartes' Physics," in J. Cottingham (ed.) *Descartes* (Oxford: Oxford University Press, 1998) 281–310 [orig. publ. 1979].

Hattab, Helen. *Descartes on Forms and Mechanisms* (Cambridge: Cambridge University Press, 2009).

Haydn, Hiram. *The Counter-Renaissance* (New York: Harcourt, Brace & World, 1950).

Hedley, Douglas and Sarah Hutton. *Platonism at the Origins of Modernity: Studies on Platonism and Early Modern Philosophy* (Dordrecht: Springer, 2008).

Heidegger, Martin. *Sein und Zeit* (Halle: M. Niemeyer, 1929).

Heil, John. "Dispositions," *Synthese* 144 (2005) 343–56.

Henninger, Mark G. *Relations: Medieval Theories 1250–1325* (Oxford: Clarendon, 1989).

Henry, Desmond Paul. *Medieval Mereology* (Amsterdam: B. R. Grüner, 1991).

Henry, John. "Metaphysics and the Origins of Modern Science: Descartes and the Importance of Laws of Nature," *Early Science and Medicine* 9 (2004) 73–114.

Henry, John. "Occult Qualities and the Experimental Philosophy: Active Principles in Pre-Newtonian Matter Theory," *History of Science* 24 (1986) 335–81.

Hill, Christopher. *The World Turned Upside Down: Radical Ideas during the English Revolution* (London: Temple Smith, 1972).

Hill, James. "Locke's Account of Cohesion and its Philosophical Significance," *British Journal for the History of Philosophy* 12 (2004) 611–30.

Himmelfarb, Gertrude. *The Roads to Modernity: The British, French, and American Enlightenments* (New York: Knopf, 2004).

Hissette, Roland. *Enquête sur les 219 articles condamnés à Paris le 7 mars 1277* (Louvain: Publications universitaires, 1977).

Hobsbawm, Eric. *The Age of Extremes: A History of the World, 1914-1991* (New York: Pantheon, 1994).

Hoenen, Maarten J. F. M. "Fifteenth Century: Doctrinal, Institutional, and Church Political Factors in the *Wegestreit*," in R. Friedman and L. Nielsen (eds.) *The Medieval Heritage in Early Modern Metaphysics and Modal Theory, 1400–1700* (Dordrecht: Kluwer, 2003) 9–36.

Hoffman, Paul. "Cartesian Composites," *Journal of the History of Philosophy* 37 (1999) 251–70.

Hoffman, Paul. "Descartes's Watch Analogy," *British Journal for the History of Philosophy* 15 (2007) 561–7.

Hoffman, Paul. "St. Thomas Aquinas on the Halfway State of Sensible Being," *Philosophical Review* 99 (1990) 73–92.

Hoffman, Paul. "The Union and Interaction of Mind and Body," in J. Broughton and J. Carriero (eds.) *A Companion to Descartes* (Oxford: Blackwell, 2008) 390–403.

Hoffman, Paul. "The Unity of Descartes's Man," *Philosophical Review* 95 (1986) 339–70.

Holden, Thomas. *The Architecture of Matter: Galileo to Kant* (Oxford: Clarendon, 2004).

Honnefelder, Ludger. "Scotus und der Scotismus: ein Beitrag zur Bedeutung der Schulbildung in der Mittelalterlichen Philosophie," in M. Hoenen, J. Schneider, and G. Wieland (eds.) *Philosophy and Learning: Universities in the Middle Ages* (Leiden: Brill, 1995) 249–62.

Hudson, Hud. "Omnipresence," in T. P. Flint and M. C. Rea (eds.) *The Oxford Handbook of Philosophical Theology* (Oxford: Oxford University Press, 2008) 199–216.

Hutchison, Keith. "Dormitive Virtues, Scholastic Qualities, and the New Philosophies," *History of Science* 29 (1991) 245–78.

Hutchison, Keith. "What Happened to Occult Qualities in the Scientific Revolution?," *Isis* 73 (1982) 233–53.

Hutton, Sarah. *Anne Conway: A Woman Philosopher* (Cambridge: Cambridge University Press, 2004).

Hutton, Sarah. "Aristotle and the Cambridge Platonists: The Case of Cudworth," in C. Blackwell and S. Kusukawa (eds.) *Philosophy in the Sixteenth and Seventeenth Centuries: Conversations with Aristotle* (Aldershot: Ashgate, 1999) 337–49.

Hyman, Arthur. "Aristotle's 'First Matter' and Avicenna's and Averroes' 'Corporeal Form'," in S. Lieberman et al. (eds.) *Harry Austryn Wolfson Jubilee Volume* (Jerusalem: American Academy for Jewish Research, 1965) 385–406.

Imbach, Ruedi. *Deus est intelligere: das Verhältnis von Sein und Denken in seiner Bedeutung für das Gottesverständnis bei Thomas von Aquin und in den Pariser Quaestionen Meister Eckharts* (Freiburg: Universitätsverlag, 1976).

Imbach, Ruedi. "Metaphysik, Theologie und Politik: zur Diskussion zwischen Nikolaus von Strassburg und Dietrich von Freiberg über die Abtrennbarkeit der Akzidentien," *Theologie und Philosophie* 61 (1986) 359–95.

Imbach, Ruedi. "Pourquoi Thierry de Freiberg a-t-il critiqué Thomas d'Aquin? Remarques sur le *De accidentibus*," *Freiburger Zeitschrift für Philosophie une Theologie* 45 (1998) 116–29.

Imbach, Ruedi. "Le traité de l'eucharistie de Thomas d'Aquin et les averroïstes," *Revue des sciences philosophiques et théologiques* 77 (1993) 175–94.

Imbach, Ruedi and François-Xavier Putallaz. "Olivi et le temps," in A. Boureau and S. Piron (eds.) *Pierre de Jean Olivi (1248–1298): pensée scolastique, dissidence spirituelle et société* (Paris: Vrin, 1999) 27–39.

Irwin, Terence. "The Metaphysical and Psychological Basis of Aristotle's Ethics," in A. O. Rorty (ed.) *Essays on Aristotle's Ethics* (Berkeley: University of California Press, 1980) 35–53.

Jackson, Reginald. "Locke's Distinction between Primary and Secondary Qualities," in C. B. Martin and D. M. Armstrong (eds.) *Locke and Berkeley: A Collection of Critical Essays* (Notre Dame: University of Notre Dame Press, 1968) 53–77 [orig. publ. 1929].

Jacovides, Michael. "Epistemology under Locke's Corpuscularianism," *Archiv für Geschichte der Philosophie* 84 (2002) 161–89.

Jacovides, Michael. "Locke on the Propria of Body," *British Journal for the History of Philosophy* 15 (2007) 485–511.

Jacovides, Michael. "Locke's Distinctions between Primary and Secondary Qualities," in L. Newman (ed.) *The Cambridge Companion to Locke's "Essay concerning Human Understanding"* (Cambridge: Cambridge University Press, 2007) 101–29.

Jeauneau, Édouard. "Nains et géants," in É. Jeauneau and M. de Gandillac (eds.) *Entretiens sur la renaissance du 12e siècle* (Paris: Mouton, 1968) 21–52.

Jeck, Udo. *Aristoteles contra Augustinum: zur Frage nach dem Verhältnis von Zeit und Seele bei den antiken Aristoteleskommentatoren, im arabischen Aristotelismus und im 13. Jahrhundert* (Amsterdam: Grüner, 1994).

Jenkins, John I. "Aquinas on the Veracity of the Intellect," *Journal of Philosophy* 88 (1991) 623–32.

Jesseph, Douglas. "Mechanism, Skepticism, and Witchcraft: More and Glanvill on the Failures of the Cartesian Philosophy," in T. M. Schmaltz (ed.) *Receptions of Descartes: Cartesianism and Anti-Cartesianism in Early Modern Europe* (London: Routledge, 2005) 199–217.

Johnson, Paul. *The Birth of the Modern: World Society, 1815–1830* (New York: HarperCollins, 1991).

Johnston, Mark. "How to Speak of the Colors," *Philosophical Studies* 68 (1992) 221–63.

Jolley, Nicholas. *Leibniz and Locke: A Study of the New Essays on Human Understanding* (Oxford: Clarendon, 1984).

Jolley, Nicholas. *The Light of the Soul: Theories of Ideas in Leibniz, Malebranche, and Descartes* (New York: Oxford University Press, 1990).

Jones, Howard. *The Epicurean Tradition* (London: Routledge, 1989).

Jones, Jan-Erik. "Boyle, Classification and the Workmanship of the Understanding Thesis," *Journal of the History of Philosophy* 43 (2005) 171–83.

Jones, Richard F. *Ancients and Moderns: A Study of the Rise of the Scientific Movement in Seventeenth-Century England*, 2nd ed. (St. Louis: Washington University Studies, 1961).

Joy, Lynn Sumida. *Gassendi the Atomist: Advocate of History in an Age of Science* (Cambridge: Cambridge University Press, 1987).

Kahn, Didier. "Entre atomisme, alchimie, et théologie: la reception des theses d'Antoine de Villon et Éstienne de Clave contre Aristote, Paracelse et les 'cabalistes' (24–25 août 1624)," *Annals of Science* 58 (2001) 241–86.

Kaluza, Zénon. "Les catégories dans *L'Exigit ordo*: étude de l'ontologie formelle de Nicolas d'Autrécourt," *Studia Mediewistyczne* 33 (1998) 97–124.

Kaluza, Zénon. "La crise des années 1474–1482: l'interdiction du nominalisme par Louis XI," in M. Hoenen, J. Schneider, and G. Wieland (eds.) *Philosophy and Learning: Universities in the Middle Ages* (Leiden: Brill, 1995) 293–327.

Kaluza, Zénon. "Les débuts de l'albertisme tardif (Paris et Cologne)," in M. Hoenen and A. de Libera (eds.) *Albertus Magnus und der Albertismus: deutsche philosophische Kultur des Mittelalters* (Leiden: Brill, 1995) 207–302.

Kaluza, Zénon. "Eternité du monde et incorruptibilité des choses dans l'*Exigit ordo* de Nicolas d'Autrécourt," in G. Alliney and L. Cova (eds.) *Tempus, aevum, aeternitas: la concettualizzazione del tempo nel pensiero tardomedievale* (Florence: Olschki, 2000) 207–40.

Kaluza, Zénon. "Nicolas d'Autrécourt, ami de la vérité," *Histoire littéraire de la France* 42 (1995) 1–232.

Kaluza, Zénon. *Les querelles doctrinales à Paris: nominalistes et réalistes aux confins du XIVe et du XVe siècles* (Bergamo: Lubrina, 1988).

Kärkkäinen, Pekka. "On the Semantics of 'Human Being' and 'Animal' in Early 16th Century Erfurt," *Vivarium* 42 (2004) 237–56.

Kaufman, Dan. "Cartesian Substances, Individual Bodies, and Corruptibility" (forthcoming).

Kaufman, Dan. "Descartes on Composites, Incomplete Substances, and Kinds of Unity," *Archiv für Geschichte der Philosophie* 90 (2008) 39–73.

Kaufman, Dan. "Locks, Schlocks, and Poisoned Peas: Boyle on Actual and Dispositive Qualities," *Oxford Studies in Early Modern Philosophy* 3 (2006) 153–98.

Kaufman, Dan. "The Resurrection of the Same Body and the Ontological Status of Organisms: What Locke Should Have (and Could Have) Told Stillingfleet," in P. Hoffman, D. Owen, and G. Yaffe (eds.) *Contemporary Perspectives on Early Modern Philosophy* (Peterborough, Ont.: Broadview, 2008) 191–214.

Kaufman, Dan. Review of Christopher Hughes Conn, *Locke on Essence and Identity*, in *British Journal for the History of Philosophy* 13 (2005) 397–402.

Keating, Laura. "Un-Locke-ing Boyle: Boyle on Primary and Secondary Qualities," *History of Philosophy Quarterly* 10 (1993) 305–23.

Kelley, Francis E. "Introduction," in Richard Knapwell, *Quaestio disputata de unitate formae* (Paris: Vrin, 1982) 9–44.

Kenny, Anthony. *Aquinas on Being* (Oxford: Clarendon, 2002).

Kenny, Anthony. *Aquinas on Mind* (New York: Routledge, 1993).

Kenny, Anthony. *Wyclif* (Oxford: Oxford University Press, 1985).

Kessler, Eckhard. "The Transformation of Aristotelianism during the Renaissance," in J. Henry and S. Hutton (eds.) *New Perspectives on Renaissance Thought: Essays in the History of Science, Education, and Philosophy in Memory of Charles B. Schmitt* (London: Duckworth, 1990) 137–47.

Khalidi, Muhammad Ali (tr.). *Medieval Islamic Philosophical Writings* (Cambridge: Cambridge University Press, 2005).

King, Peter. "The Inner Cathedral: Mental Architecture in High Scholasticism," *Vivarium* 46 (2008) 253–74.

King, Peter. "Metaphysics," in J. Brower and K. Guilfoy (eds.) *The Cambridge Companion to Abelard* (Cambridge: Cambridge University Press, 2004) 65–125.

King, Peter. "The Problem of Individuation in the Middle Ages," *Theoria* 66 (2000) 159–184.

King, Peter. "Scotus on Metaphysics," in T. Williams (ed.) *The Cambridge Companion to Duns Scotus* (Cambridge: Cambridge University Press, 2003) 15–68.

King, Peter. "Why Isn't the Mind–Body Problem Medieval?" in H. Lagerlund (ed.) *Forming the Mind: Essays on the Internal Senses and the Mind/Body Problem from Avicenna to the Medical Enlightenment* (Dordrecht: Springer, 2007) 187–205.

Kirschner, Stefan. *Nicolaus Oresmes Kommentar zur Physik des Aristoteles: Kommentar mit Edition der Quaestionen zu Buch 3 und 4 der Aristotelischen Physik sowie von vier Quaestionen zu Buch 5* (Stuttgart: F. Steiner, 1997).

Kleineidam, Erich. *Das Problem der hylomorphen Zusammensetzung der geistigen Substanzen im 13. Jahrhundert, behandelt bis Thomas von Aquin* (Breslau: G. Tesch, 1930).

Klima, Gyula. "Buridan's Logic and the Ontology of Modes," in S. Ebbesen and R. L. Friedman (eds.) *Medieval Analyses in Language and Cognition* (Copenhagen: The Royal Danish Academy of Sciences and Letters, 1999) 473–95.

Klima, Gyula. "The Medieval Problem of Universals," in E. Zalta (ed.) *The Stanford Encyclopedia of Philosophy (Winter 2008 Edition)* at http://plato.stanford.edu/archives/win2008/entries/universals-medieval/.

Klima, Gyula. "Nominalist Semantics," in R. Pasnau (ed.) *Cambridge History of Medieval Philosophy* (Cambridge: Cambridge University Press, 2010) 159–72.

Klima, Gyula. "Peter of Spain," in J. J. E. Gracia and T. B. Noone (eds.) *A Companion to Philosophy in the Middle Ages* (Malden, MA: Blackwell, 2003) 526–31.

Klima, Gyula. "Substance, Accident and Modes," in H. Lagerlund (ed.) *Encyclopedia of Medieval Philosophy* (Dordrecht: Springer, forthcoming).

Klima, Gyula. "Thomistic 'Monism' vs. Cartesian 'Dualism'," *Logical Analysis and History of Philosophy* 10 (2007) 92–112.

Koch, Josef. *Durandus de S. Porciano, O.P.: Forschungen zum Streit um Thomas von Aquin zu Beginn des 14. Jahrhunderts* (Münster: Aschendorff, 1927).

Koch, Josef. "Neue Aktenstücke zu dem gegen Wilhelm Ockham in Avignon geführten Prozess," *Recherches de théologie ancienne et médiévale* 7 (1935) 353–80; 8 (1936) 79–93, 168–97.

Korman, Daniel Z. "Locke on Substratum: A Deflationary Interpretation," *Locke Studies* (forthcoming).

Koslicki, Kathrin. *The Structure of Objects* (Oxford: Oxford University Press, 2008).

Kovach, Francis J. "The Enduring Question of Action at a Distance in Saint Albert the Great," in F. J. Kovach and R.W. Shahan (eds.) *Albert the Great: Commemorative Essays* (Norman, OK: University of Oklahoma, 1990) 161–235.

Koyré, Alexandre. *From the Closed World to the Infinite Universe* (Baltimore: Johns Hopkins University Press, 1957).

Kretzmann, Norman. "Incipit/Desinit," in P. Machamer and R. Turnbull (eds.) *Motion and Time, Space and Matter: Interrelations in the History of Philosophy and Science* (Columbus, OH: Ohio State University Press, 1976) 101–36.

Kretzmann, Norman. "Infallibility, Error, and Ignorance," in *Aristotle and His Medieval Interpreters*, ed. R. Bosley and M. Tweedale (*Canadian Journal of Philosophy* supp. vol. 17 [1991]) (Calgary: University of Calgary Press, 1992) 159–94.

Kretzmann, Norman (ed.). *Infinity and Continuity in Ancient and Medieval Thought* (Ithaca: Cornell University Press, 1982).

Kretzmann, Norman. "A Particular Problem of Creation: Why Would God Create This World," in S. MacDonald (ed.) *Being and Goodness: The Concept of the Good in Metaphysics and Philosophical Theology* (Ithaca, NY: Cornell University Press, 1991) 229–49.

Kubbinga, H. H. "Les premières théories 'moléculaires': Isaac Beeckman (1620) et Sébastien Basson (1621)," *Revue d'histoire des sciences* 37 (1984) 215–33.

Kuhn, Heinrich. *Venetischer Aristotelismus am Ende der aristotelischen Welt: Aspekte der Welt und des Denkens des Cesare Cremonini (1550–1631)* (Frankfurt: Peter Lang, 1996).

Kuhn, Thomas S. "Robert Boyle and Structural Chemistry in the Seventeenth Century," *Isis* 43 (1952) 12–36.

Laberge, Damascus. "Fr. Petri Ioannis Olivi, O.F.M., tria scripta sui ipsius apologetica annorum 1283 et 1285," *Archivum Franciscanum Historicum* 28 (1935) 115–55, 374–407.

Lambert, Malcolm. *Medieval Heresy: Popular Movements from the Gregorian Reform to the Reformation*, 3rd ed. (Oxford: Blackwell, 2002).

Lange, Marc. "How Can Instantaneous Velocity Fulfill Its Causal Role?" *Philosophical Review* 114 (2005) 433–68.

Larsen, R. E. "The Aristotelianism of Bacon's *Novum Organum*," *Journal of the History of Ideas* 23 (1962) 435–50.

Lasswitz, Kurd. *Geschichte der Atomistik vom Mittelalter bis Newton*, 2 vols. (Hamburg: Voss, 1890).

Laymon, Ronald. "Transubstantiation: Test Case for Descartes's Theory of Space," in T. M. Lennon et al. (eds.) *Problems of Cartesianism* (Kingston: McGill-Queen's University Press, 1982) 149–70.

Lea, H. C. *A History of the Inquisition of the Middle Ages* (New York: Harper & Brothers, 1887).

Leary, Nigel. "How Essentialists Misunderstand Locke," *History of Philosophy Quarterly* 26 (2009) 273–92.

Leftow, Brian. "Aquinas on Attributes," *Medieval Philosophy and Theology* 11 (2003) 1–41.

Leijenhorst, Cees. "Hobbes, Heresy, and Corporeal Deity," in J. Brooke and I. Maclean (eds.) *Heterodoxy in Early Modern Science and Religion* (Oxford: Oxford University Press, 2005).

Leijenhorst, Cees. *The Mechanisation of Aristotelianism: The Late Aristotelian Setting of Thomas Hobbes's Natural Philosophy* (Leiden: Brill, 2002).

Lennon, Thomas. "The Eleatic Descartes," *Journal of the History of Philosophy* 45 (2007) 29–47.

Levey, Samuel. "On Unity: Leibniz-Arnauld Revisited," *Philosophical Topics* 31 (2003) 245–75.

Levy, Ian Christopher. *John Wyclif: Scriptural Logic, Real Presence, and the Parameters of Orthodoxy* (Milwaukee: Marquette University Press, 2003).

Lewis, Eric. "The Stoics on Identity and Individuation," *Phronesis* 40 (1995) 89–108.

Lewis, Frank A. *Substance and Predication in Aristotle* (Cambridge: Cambridge University Press, 1991).

Link, Perry. "Chinese Shadows," *New York Review of Books* (November 16, 2006) 33–5.

Loeb, Louis. *From Descartes to Hume: Continental Metaphysics and the Development of Modern Philosophy* (Ithaca, NY: Cornell University Press, 1981).

Lohr, Charles H. "Medieval Latin Aristotle Commentaries," *Traditio* 23–30 (1967–74).

Lohr, Charles H. "Jesuit Aristotelianism and Sixteenth-Century Metaphysics," in *Paradosis: Studies in Memory of Edwin A. Quain* (New York: Fordham University Press, 1976) 203–20.

Lohr, Charles H. *Latin Aristotle Commentaries, II: Renaissance Authors* (Florence: Olschki, 1988).

Lohr, Charles H. "Metaphysics and Natural Philosophy as Sciences: The Catholic and the Protestant Views in the Sixteenth and Seventeenth Centuries," in C. Blackwell and

S. Kusukawa (eds.) *Philosophy in the Sixteenth and Seventeenth Centuries: Conversations with Aristotle* (Aldershot: Ashgate, 1999) 280–95.

LoLordo, Antonia. "Gassendi and the Seventeenth-Century Atomists on Primary and Secondary Qualities," in L. Nolan (ed.) *Primary and Secondary Qualities: The Historical and Ongoing Debate* (Oxford: Oxford University Press, forthcoming).

LoLordo, Antonia. *Pierre Gassendi and the Birth of Early Modern Philosophy* (New York: Cambridge University Press, 2007).

Long, A. A. and Sedley, D. N. *The Hellenistic Philosophers* (Cambridge: Cambridge University Press, 1987).

Long, R. James. "Of Angels and Pinheads: The Contributions of the Early Oxford Masters to the Doctrine of Spiritual Matter," *Franciscan Studies* 56 (1998) 239–54.

Lottin, Odon. *Psychologie et morale aux XIIe et XIIIe siècles*, 6 vols. (Louvain: Abbaye du Mont Ceésar, 1942–60).

Lowe, E. J. *Locke on Human Understanding* (Routledge Philosophy Guidebooks) (London: Routledge, 1995).

Löwenheim, Louis. *Die Wissenschaft Demokrits und ihr Einfluß auf die moderne Naturwissenschaft* (Berlin: Simion, 1913).

Lüthy, Christoph. "An Aristotelian Watchdog as Avant-Garde Physicist: Julius Caesar Scaliger," *Monist* 84 (2001) 542–61.

Lüthy, Christoph. "David Gorlaeus' Atomism, or: The Marriage of Protestant Metaphysics with Italian Natural Philosophy," in C. Lüthy et al. (eds.) *Late Medieval and Early Modern Corpuscular Matter Theories* (Leiden: Brill, 2001) 245–90.

Lüthy, Christoph. "The Fourfold Democritus on the Stage of Early Modern Science," *Isis* 91 (2000) 443–79.

Lüthy, Christoph. "Thoughts and Circumstances of Sébastien Basson: Analysis, Micro-History, Questions," *Early Science and Medicine* 2 (1997) 1–73.

Lüthy, Christoph and William Newman. "'Matter' and 'Form': By Way of a Preface," *Early Modern Science* 2 (1997) 215–25.

Lüthy, Christoph, John Murdoch, and William Newman (eds.). *Late Medieval and Early Modern Corpuscular Matter Theories* (Leiden: Brill, 2001).

McCann, Edwin. "Cartesian Selves and Lockean Substances," *Monist* 69 (1986) 458–82.

McCann, Edwin. "Identity, Essentialism, and the Substance of Body in Locke," in P. Hoffman, D. Owen, and G. Yaffe (eds.) *Contemporary Perspectives on Early Modern Philosophy* (Peterborough, Ont.: Broadview, 2008) 173–90.

McCann, Edwin. "Locke on Identity: Matter, Life, and Consciousness," *Archiv für Geschichte der Philosophie* 69 (1987) 54–77.

McCann, Edwin. "Locke's Philosophy of Body," in V. Chappell (ed.) *The Cambridge Companion to Locke* (Cambridge: Cambridge University Press, 1994) 56–88.

McCann, Edwin. "Locke's Theory of Substance Under Attack!," *Philosophical Studies* 106 (2001) 87–105.

McClaughlin, Trevor. "Censorship and Defenders of the Cartesian Faith in Mid-Seventeenth Century France," *Journal of the History of Ideas* 40 (1979) 563–81.

MacClintock, Stuart. *Perversity and Error: Studies on the "Averroist" John of Jandun* (Bloomington: Indiana University Press, 1956).

McCormick, John F. "Quaestiones Disputandae," *New Scholasticism* 13 (1939) 368–74.

McCracken, Charles. "Knowledge of the Soul," in D. Garber and M. Ayers (eds.) *The Cambridge History of Seventeenth-Century Philosophy* (Cambridge: Cambridge University Press, 1998) 796–832.

McCue, James F. "The Doctrine of Transubstantiation from Berenger through Trent: The Point at Issue," *Harvard Theological Review* 61 (1968) 385–430.

McDaniel, Kris. "Ways of Being" in D. Chalmers et al. (eds.) *Metametaphysics: New Essays on the Foundations of Ontology* (Oxford: Oxford University Press, 2009) 290–319.

McDowell, John. "Singular Thought and the Extent of Inner Space," in J. McDowell and P. Pettit (eds.) *Subject, Thought and Context* (Oxford: Clarendon, 1986) 137-68.

McGinn, Bernard (tr.). *Three Treatises on Man: A Cistercian Anthropology* (Kalamazoo, MI: Cistercian Publications, 1977).

McGuire, J. E. "Existence, Actuality and Necessity: Newton on Space and Time," *Annals of Science* 25 (1978) 463–508.

McGuire, J. E. "Force, Active Principles, and Newton's Invisible Realm," *Ambix* 15 (1968) 154–208.

McGuire, J. E. "Neoplatonism and Active Principles: Newton and the *Corpus Hermeticum*, in R. S. Westman and J. E. McGuire (eds.) *Hermeticism and the Scientific Revolution* (Los Angeles: Clark Memorial Library, University of California, 1977) 93–142.

McGuire, J. E. "Transmutation and Immutability: Newton's Doctrine of Physical Qualities," *Ambix* 14 (1967) 69–95.

Machamar, Peter and J. E. McGuire. *Descartes's Changing Mind* (Princeton: Princeton University Press 2009).

Mackie, J. L. *Problems from Locke* (Oxford: Clarendon, 1976).

McLaughlin, Mary Martin. *Intellectual Freedom and Its Limitations in the University of Paris in the Thirteenth and Fourteenth Centuries* (New York: Arno Press, 1977) [orig. publ. 1952].

McMahon, William. "Some Non-Standard Views of the Categories," in J. Biard and I. Rosier-Catach (eds.) *La tradition médiévale des Catégories XIIᵉ–XIVᵉ siècles* (Louvain: Peeters, 2003) 53–67.

McMahon, William. "Reflections on Some Thirteenth- and Fourteenth-Century Views of the Categories," in M. Gorman and J. Sanford (eds.) *Categories: Historical and Systematic Essays* (Washington, DC: Catholic University of America Press, 2004) 45–57.

McMullin, Ernan. "Introduction," in E. McMullin (ed.) *The Concept of Matter in Modern Philosophy* (Notre Dame: University of Notre Dame Press, 1963) 1–55.

McMullin, Ernan. "Matter as Principle," in E. McMullin (ed.) *The Concept of Matter in Greek and Medieval Philosophy* (Notre Dame: University of Notre Dame Press, 1963) 173–212.

McMullin, Ernan. *Newton on Matter and Activity* (Notre Dame: University of Notre Dame Press, 1978).

Machamer, Peter and J.E. McGuire, *Descartes's Changing Mind* (Princeton: Princeton University Press, 2009).

Macy, Gary. "The Dogma of Transubstantiation in the Middle Ages," *Journal of Ecclesiastical History* 45 (1994) 11–41.

Maier, Anneliese. *An der Grenze von Scholastik und Naturwissenschaft*, 2nd ed. (Rome: Edizioni di Storia e Letteratura, 1952).

Maier, Anneliese. "An der Schwelle der exakten Naturwissenschaft," in *Metaphysische Hintergründe der spätscholastischen Naturphilosophie* (Rome: Edizioni di Storia e Letteratura, 1955) 339–402.

Maier, Anneliese. "Bewegung ohne Ursache," in *Zwischen Philosophie und Mechanik: Studien zur Naturphilosophie der Spätscholastik* (Rome: Edizioni di Storia e Letteratura, 1958) 289–339.

Maier, Anneliese. "Galilei und die scholastische Impetustheorie," in *Ausgehendes Mittelalter: gesammelte Aufsätze zur Geistesgeschichte des 14. Jahrhunderts* (Rome: Edizioni di Storia e Letteratura, 1967) II:465–90.

Maier, Anneliese. "Die Mechanisierung des Weltbilds im 17. Jahrhundert," in *Zwei Untersuchungen zur nachscholastischen Philosophie* (Rome: Edizioni di Storia e Letteratura, 1968) 13–67.

Maier, Anneliese. "Das Problem der Quantität oder räumlichen Ausdehnung," in *Metaphysische Hintergründe der spätscholastischen Naturphilosophie* (Rome: Edizioni di Storia e Letteratura, 1955) 141–223.

Maier, Anneliese. "Das Problem der 'Species Sensibiles in Medio' und die neue Naturphilosophie des 14. Jahrhunderts," *Freiburger Zeitschrift für Philosophie und Theologie* 10 (1963) 3–32.

Maier, Anneliese. "Die naturphilosophische Bedeutung der scholastischen Impetustheorie," in *Ausgehendes Mittelalter: gesammelte Aufsätze zur Geistesgeschichte des 14. Jahrhunderts* (Rome: Edizioni di Storia e Letteratura, 1964) I:353–79.

Maier, Anneliese. *On the Threshold of Exact Science: Selected Writings of Anneliese Maier on Late Medieval Natural Philosophy*, tr. S. Sargent (Philadelphia: University of Pennsylvania Press, 1982).

Maier, Anneliese. "Das Zeitproblem," in *Metaphysische Hintergründe der spätscholastischen Naturphilosophie* (Rome: Edizioni di Storia e Letteratura, 1955) 45–137.

Maier, Anneliese. *Die Vorläufer Galileis im 14. Jahrhundert. Studien zur Naturphilosophie der Spätscholastik* (Rome: Edizioni di Storia e Letteratura, 1949).

Malherbe, Michel. "Bacon's Method of Science," in M. Peltonen (ed.) *The Cambridge Companion to Bacon* (Cambridge: Cambridge University Press, 1996) 75–98.

Malherbe, Michel. "Hobbes et la doctrine de l'accident," *Hobbes Studies* 1 (1988) 45–62.

Malherbe, Michel and Jean-Marie Pousser (eds.). *Francis Bacon, science et méthode* (Paris: Vrin, 1985).

Mandelbaum, Maurice. "Locke's Realism," in *Philosophy, Science, and Sense Perception* (Baltimore: Johns Hopkins University Press, 1964) 1–60.

Marion, Jean-Luc. *On Descartes' Metaphysical Prism: The Constitution and the Limits of Onto-theo-logy in Cartesian Thought*, tr. J. L. Kosky (Chicago: University of Chicago Press, 1999).

Markie, Peter. "Descartes's Concepts of Substance," in J. Cottingham (ed.) *Reason, Will, and Sensation: Studies in Descartes's Metaphysics* (Oxford: Clarendon, 1994) 63–87.

Martin, Christopher J. "The Logic of Growth: Twelfth-Century Nominalists and the Development of Theories of the Incarnation," *Medieval Philosophy and Theology* 7 (1998) 1–15.

Maurer, Armand. "Ockham's Razor and Chatton's Anti-Razor," in *Being and Knowing* (Toronto: Pontifical Institute of Mediaeval Philosophy, 1990) 431–43.

Mayo, Thomas Franklin. *Epicurus in England (1650–1725)* (Dallas: Southwest Press, 1934).

Meinel, Christoph. "Early Seventeenth-Century Atomism," *Isis* 79 (1988) 68–103.

Meinel, Christoph. *In physicis futurum saeculum respicio: Joachim Jungius und die Naturwissenschaftliche Revolution des 17. Jahrhunderts* (Göttingen: Vandenhoeck & Ruprecht, 1984).

Menn, Stephen. "The Greatest Stumbling Block: Descartes' Denial of Real Qualities," in R. Ariew and M. Grene (eds.) *Descartes and His Contemporaries: Meditations, Objections, and Replies* (Chicago: University of Chicago Press, 1995) 182–207.

Menn, Stephen. "Suárez, Nominalism, and Modes," in K. White (ed.) *Hispanic Philosophy in the Age of Discovery* (Washington, DC: Catholic University of America Press, 1997) 226–56.

Mercer, Christia. "The Aristotelianism at the Core of Leibniz's Philosophy," in C. Leijenhorst et al. (eds.) *The Dynamics of Aristotelian Natural Philosophy from Antiquity to the Seventeenth Century* (Leiden: Brill, 2002) 413–40.

Mercer, Christia. *Leibniz's Metaphysics: Its Origins and Development* (Cambridge: Cambridge University Press, 2001).

Mercer, Christia. "The Platonism at the Core of Leibniz's Philosophy," in D. Hedley and S. Hutton (eds.) *Platonism at the Origins of Modernity: Studies on Platonism and Early Modern Philosophy* (Dordrecht: Springer, 2008) 225–38.

Mercer, Christia. "The Vitality and Importance of Early Modern Aristotelianism," in T. Sorell (ed.) *The Rise of Modern Philosophy* (Oxford: Clarendon, 1993) 33–67.

Merton, Robert King. *On the Shoulders of Giants: A Shandean Postscript* (New York: Free Press, 1965).

Methuen, Charlotte. "The Teaching of Aristotle in Late Sixteenth-Century Tübingen," in C. Blackwell and S. Kusukawa (eds.) *Philosophy in the Sixteenth and Seventeenth Centuries: Conversations with Aristotle* (Aldershot: Ashgate, 1999) 189–205.

Michael, Bernd. "Johannes Buridan: Studien zu seinem Leben, seinen Werken und zu Rezeption seiner Theorien im Europa des späten Mittelalters," 2 vols. (Ph.D. dissertation: University of Berlin, 1985).

Michael, Emily. "Averroes and the Plurality of Forms," *Franciscan Studies* 52 (1992) 155–82.

Michael, Emily. "Daniel Sennert on Matter and Form: At the Juncture of the Old and the New," *Early Science and Medicine* 2 (1997) 272–99.

Michael, Emily. "Descartes and Gassendi on Matter and Mind: From Aristotelian Pluralism to Early Modern Dualism," in S. F. Brown (ed.) *Meeting of the Minds* (Turnhout: Brepols, 1998) 145–66.

Michael, Emily. "John Wyclif's Atomism," in C. Grellard and A. Robert (eds.) *Atomism in Late Medieval Philosophy and Theology* (Leiden: Brill, 2009) 183–220.

Michael, Emily. "Sennert's Sea Change: Atoms and Causes," in C. Lüthy et al. (eds.) *Late Medieval and Early Modern Corpuscular Matter Theories* (Leiden: Brill, 2001) 331–62.

Miethke, Jürgen. "Bildungsstand und Freiheitsforderung (12. bis 14. Jahrhundert)," in J. Fried (ed.) *Die Abendländische Freiheit vom 10. zum 14. Jahrhundert: der Wirkungszusammenhang von Idee und Wirklichkeit im Europäischen Vergleich* (Sigmaringen: Thorbecke, 1991) 221–47.

Miles, Murray. "Descartes' Mechanicism and the Medieval Doctrine of Causes, Qualities, and Forms," *Modern Schoolman* 65 (1988) 97–117.

Millen, Ron. "The Manifestation of Occult Qualities in the Scientific Revolution," in M. J. Osler and P. L. Farber (eds.) *Religion, Science, and Worldview: Essays in Honor of Richard S. Westfall* (Cambridge: Cambridge University Press, 1985) 185–216.

Millington, E. C. "Theories of Cohesion in the Seventeenth Century" *Annals of Science* 5 (1945) 253–69.

Miłosz, Czesław. *The Captive Mind*, tr. J. Ziolonko (New York: Knopf, 1953).

Milton, J. R. "John Locke and the Nominalist Tradition," in R. Brandt (ed.) *John Locke: Symposium Wolfenbüttel 1979* (Berlin: de Gruyter, 1981) 128–45.

Milton, J. R. "Laws of Nature," in D. Garber and M. Ayers (eds.) *Cambridge History of Seventeenth-Century Philosophy* (Cambridge: Cambridge University Press, 1998) 680–701.

Milton, J. R. "The Scholastic Background to Locke's Thought," *Locke Newsletter* 15 (1984) 25–34.

Mintz, Samuel. *The Hunting of Leviathan: Seventeenth-Century Reactions to the Materialism and Moral Philosophy of Thomas Hobbes* (Cambridge: Cambridge University Press, 1962).

Molland, A. G. "Medieval Ideas of Scientific Progress," *Journal of the History of Ideas* 39 (1978) 561–77.

Moody, Ernest A. "Galileo and His Precursors," in *Studies in Medieval Philosophy, Science, and Logic: Collected Papers 1933–1969* (Berkeley: University of California Press, 1975) 393–408.

Moody, Ernest A. "Ockham and Aegidius of Rome," in *Studies in Medieval Philosophy, Science, and Logic: Collected Papers 1933–1969* (Berkeley: University of California Press, 1975) 161–88 [orig. publ. 1949].

Moody, Ernest A. "Ockham, Buridan, and Nicholas of Autrecourt: The Parisian Statutes of 1339 and 1340," in *Studies in Medieval Philosophy, Science, and Logic: Collected Papers 1933–1969* (Berkeley: University of California Press, 1975) 127–60.

Moore, R. I. *The Formation of a Persecuting Society: Authority and Deviance in Western Europe, 950–1250* (Malden, MA: Blackwell, 2007).

Moran, Bruce T. *Distilling Knowledge: Alchemy, Chemistry, and the Scientific Revolution* (Cambridge, MA: Harvard University Press, 2005).

Moran, Dermot. "Nicholas of Cusa and Modern Philosophy," in J. Hankins (ed.) *The Cambridge Companion to Renaissance Philosophy* (Cambridge: Cambridge University Press, 2007) 173–92.

Morris, Katherine. *"Bêtes-machines,"* in S. Gaukroger et al. (eds.) *Descartes' Natural Philosophy* (London: Routledge, 2000) 401–19.

Muralt, André de. *L'enjeu de la philosophie médiévale: études thomistes, scotistes, occamiennes et grégoriennes* (Leiden: Brill, 1991).

Murdoch, John E. "Atomism and Motion in the Fourteenth Century," in E. Mendelsohn (ed.) *Transformation and Tradition in the Sciences: Essays in Honor of I. Bernard Cohen* (Cambridge: Cambridge University Press, 1984) 45–66.

Murdoch, John E. "Infinity and Continuity," in N. Kretzmann et al. (eds.) *Cambridge History of Later Medieval Philosophy* (Cambridge: Cambridge University Press, 1982) 564–91.

Murdoch, John E. "The Medieval and Renaissance Tradition of *Minima Naturalia*," in C. Lüthy et al. (eds.) *Late Medieval and Early Modern Corpuscular Matter Theories* (Leiden: Brill, 2001) 91–131.

Murdoch, John E. "Naissance et développement de l'atomisme au bas moyen âge Latin," *Cahiers d'études médiévales* 2 (1974) 11–32.

Murdoch, John E. "William of Ockham and the Logic of Infinity and Continuity," in N. Kretzmann (ed.) *Infinity and Continuity in Ancient and Medieval Thought* (Ithaca: Cornell University Press, 1982) 165–206.

Nadler, Steven. "Doctrines of Explanation in Late Scholasticism and in the Mechanical Philosophy," in D. Garber and M. Ayers (eds.) *Cambridge History of Seventeenth-Century Philosophy* (Cambridge: Cambridge University Press, 1998) 513–52.

Nason, John W. "Leibniz's Attack on the Cartesian Doctrine of Extension," *Journal of the History of Ideas* 7 (1946) 447–83.

Nauta, Lodi. *In Defense of Common Sense: Lorenzo Valla's Humanist Critique of Scholastic Philosophy* (Cambridge, MA: Harvard University Press, 2009).

Nederman, Cary J. "Individual Autonomy," in R. Pasnau (ed.) *Cambridge History of Medieval Philosophy* (Cambridge: Cambridge University Press, 2010) 551–64.

Nelson, Alan. "Introduction: Descartes's Ontology," *Topoi* 16 (1997) 103–9.

Newman, William R. *Atoms and Alchemy: Chymistry and the Experimental Origins of the Scientific Revolution* (Chicago: University of Chicago Press, 2006).

Newman, William R. "Experimental Corpuscular Theory in Aristotelian Alchemy: From Geber to Sennert," in C. Lüthy et al. (eds.) *Late Medieval and Early Modern Corpuscular Matter Theories* (Leiden: Brill, 2001) 291–329.

Newman, William R. "New Light on the Identity of Geber," *Sudhoffs Archiv* 69 (1985) 76–90.

Newton, Lloyd (ed.). *Medieval Commentaries on Aristotle's* Categories (Leiden: Brill, 2008).

Nielsen, Lauge Olaf. "A Seventeenth-Century Physician on God and Atoms: Sebastian Basso," in N. Kretzmann (ed.) *Meaning and Inference in Medieval Philosophy: Studies in Memory of Jan Pinborg* (Dordrecht: Kluwer, 1988) 297–369.

Nolan, Larry. "Descartes on 'What We Call Colour'," in L. Nolan (ed.) *Primary and Secondary Qualities: The Historical and Ongoing Debate* (Oxford: Oxford University Press, forthcoming).

Nolan, Larry. "Reductionism and Nominalism in Descartes's Theory of Attributes," *Topoi* 16 (1997) 129–40.

Nolan, Larry and John Whipple. "Self-Knowledge in Descartes and Malebranche," *Journal of the History of Philosophy* 43 (2005) 55–81.

Nolan, Larry and John Whipple. "The Dustbin Theory of the Mind: A Cartesian Legacy?" *Oxford Studies in Early Modern Philosophy* 3 (2006) 33–55.

Noonan, Harold. "Locke on Personal Identity," *Philosophy* 53 (1978) 343–53.

Noone, Timothy. "Universals and Individuation," in T. Williams (ed.) *The Cambridge Companion to Duns Scotus* (Cambridge: Cambridge University Press, 2003) 100–28.

Normore, Calvin G. "Abelard and the School of the Nominales," *Vivarium* 30 (1992) 80–96.

Normore, Calvin G. "Accidents and Modes," in R. Pasnau (ed.) *Cambridge History of Medieval Philosophy* (Cambridge: Cambridge University Press, 2010) 674–85.

Normore, Calvin G. "Buridan's Ontology," in J. Bogen and J. E. McGuire (eds.) *How Things Are: Studies in Predication and the History and Philosophy of Science* (Dordrecht: Reidel, 1985) 189–203.

Normore, Calvin G. "Cartesian Modes" (manuscript).

Normore, Calvin G. "Ockham's Metaphysics of Parts," *Journal of Philosophy* 103 (2006) 737–54.

Nuchelmans, Gabriel. *Theories of the Proposition: Ancient and Medieval Conceptions of the Bearers of Truth and Falsity* (Amsterdam: North-Holland, 1973).

Oderberg, David. "Introduction," in D. Oderberg (ed.) *Form and Matter: Themes in Contemporary Metaphysics* (Oxford: Blackwell, 1999) vii–xi.

Olivo, Gilles. "L'homme en personne," in T. Verbeek (ed.) *Descartes et Regius: autour de l'explication de l'esprit humain* (Amsterdam: Rodopi, 1993) 69–91.

O'Toole, Frederick J. "Qualities and Powers in the Corpuscular Philosophy of Robert Boyle," *Journal of the History of Philosophy* 12 (1974) 295–315.

Ott, Walter. *Causation and Laws of Nature in Early Modern Philosophy* (Oxford: Oxford University Press, 2009).

Owen, David. "Locke on Real Essence," *History of Philosophy Quarterly* 8 (1991) 105–18.

Pabst, Bernhard. *Atomtheorien des lateinischen Mittelalters* (Darmstadt: Wissenschaftliche Buchgesellschaft, 1994).

Partington, J. R. *A History of Chemistry*, 4 vols. (London: Macmillan, 1961–).

Pasnau, Robert (tr.). *Cambridge Translations of Medieval Philosophical Texts*, vol. 3: *Mind and Knowledge* (New York: Cambridge University Press, 2002).

Pasnau, Robert. "Democritus and Secondary Qualities," *Archiv für Geschichte der Philosophie* 89 (2007) 99–121.

Pasnau, Robert. "The Event of Color," *Philosophical Studies* 142 (2009) 353–69.

Pasnau, Robert. "Final Causes and Intentionality," in D. Perler (ed.) *Ancient and Medieval Theories of Intentionality* (Leiden: Brill, 2001) 301–23.

Pasnau, Robert. "Form, Substance, and Mechanism," *Philosophical Review* 113 (2004) 31–88.

Pasnau, Robert. "Henry of Ghent and the Twilight of Divine Illumination," *Review of Metaphysics* 49 (1995) 49–75.

Pasnau, Robert. "The Mind-Soul Problem," in P. J. J. M. Bakker and J. M. M. H. Thijssen (eds.) *Mind, Cognition, and Representation: The Tradition of Commentaries on Aristotle's* De anima (Aldershot: Ashgate, 2008) 3–19.

Pasnau, Robert. "Olivi on the Metaphysics of Soul," *Medieval Philosophy and Theology* 6 (1997) 109–32.

Pasnau, Robert. "Science and Certainty," in R. Pasnau (ed.) *Cambridge History of Medieval Philosophy* (Cambridge: Cambridge University Press, 2010) 357–68.

Pasnau, Robert. "Sensible Qualities: The Case of Sound," *Journal of the History of Philosophy* 38 (2000) 27–40.

Pasnau, Robert. *Theories of Cognition in the Later Middle Ages* (New York: Cambridge University Press, 1997).

Pasnau, Robert. *Thomas Aquinas on Human Nature: A Philosophical Study of* Summa theologiae 1a 75–89 (New York: Cambridge University Press, 2002).

Paulus, Jean. *Henri de Gand: essai sur les tendances de sa métaphysique* (Paris: Vrin, 1938).

Pegis, Anton C. *St. Thomas and the Problem of the Soul in the Thirteenth Century* (Toronto: Pontifical Institute of Mediaeval Studies, 1934).

Penn, Stephen. "Wyclif and the Sacraments," in I. C. Levy (ed.) *A Companion to John Wyclif: Late Medieval Theologian* (Leiden: Brill, 2006) 241–91.

Perler, Dominik. "Introduction," *Vivarium* 46 (2008) 223–31.

Perler, Dominik. "Sind die Gegenstände farbig?" *Archiv für Geschichte der Philosophie* 80 (1998) 182–210.

Perler, Dominik. "Skepticism," in R. Pasnau (ed.) *The Cambridge History of Medieval Philosophy* (Cambridge: Cambridge University Press, 2010) 384–96.

Perler, Dominik. *Zweifel und Gewissheit: skeptische Debatten im Mittelalter* (Frankfurt: Klostermann, 2006).

Perler, Dominik and Ulrich Rudolph. *Occasionalismus: Theorien der Kausalität im arabisch-islamischen und im europäischen Denken* (Göttingen: Vandenhoeck & Ruprecht, 2000).

Peters, Edward. *Inquisition* (New York: Free Press, 1988).

Peters, Edward. "*Libertas Inquirendi* and the *Vitium Curiositas* in Medieval Thought," in G. Makdisi et al. (eds.) *La notion de liberté au Moyen Age Islam, Byzance, Occident* (Paris: Les Belles Lettres, 1985) 89–98.

Phemister, Pauline. "Real Essences in Particular," *Locke Newsletter* 21 (1990) 27–55.

Piché, David (ed.). *La condamnation parisienne de 1277* (Paris: Vrin, 1999).

Pickavé, Martin. "Simon of Faversham on Aristotle's *Categories* and the *Scientia Praedicamentorum*," in L. A. Newton (ed.) *Medieval Commentaries on Aristotle's* Categories (Leiden: Brill, 2008) 183–220.

Pinborg, Jan. "Speculative Grammar," in N. Kretzmann et al. (eds.) *The Cambridge History of Later Medieval Philosophy* (Cambridge: Cambridge University Press, 1982) 254–69.

Pines, Schlomo. *Studies in Islamic Atomism*, tr. M. Schwarz, ed. T. Langermann (Jerusalem: Magnes Press, 1997).

Pini, Giorgio. *Categories and Logic in Duns Scotus: An Interpretation of Aristotle's Categories in the Late Thirteenth Century* (Leiden: Brill, 2002).

Pini, Giorgio. "Scotus on Deducing Aristotle's *Categories*," in J. Biard and I. Rosier-Catach (eds.) *La tradition médiévale des Catégories XIIe–XIVe siècles* (Louvain: Peeters, 2003) 23–35.

Pini, Giorgio. "Scotus on Doing Metaphysics *in statu isto*," *Archa Verbi: Subsidia* 3 (2009) 29–53.

Pini, Giorgio. "Scotus on Knowing and Naming Natural Kinds," *History of Philosophy Quarterly* 26 (2009) 255–72.

Pini, Giorgio. "Scotus's Realist Conception of the Categories: His Legacy to Late Medieval Debates," *Vivarium* 43 (2005) 63–110.

Pini, Giorgio. "Substance, Accident, and Inherence: Scotus and the Paris Debate on the Metaphysics of the Eucharist," in O. Boulnois (ed.) *Duns Scot à Paris 1302–2002: Actes du colloque de Paris 2–4 septembre 2002* (Turnhout: Brepols, 2004) 273–311.

Piron, Sylvain. *Parcours d'un intellectuel franciscain: d'une théologie vers une pensée sociale: l'oeuvre de Pierre de Jean Olivi (ca. 1248–1298) et son traité "De contractibus"* (Paris: Ecole des Hautes Etudes en Sciences Sociales, 1999).

Pluta, Olaf. "Ailly, Pierre d'," in E. Craig (ed.) *Routledge Encyclopedia of Philosophy* (London: Routledge, 1998).

Pluta, Olaf. "Buridan's Theory of Identity," in J. Thijssen and J. Zupko (eds.) *The Metaphysics and Natural Philosophy of John Buridan* (Leiden: Brill, 2001) 49–64.

Pluta, Olaf. "How Matter Becomes Mind: Late-Medieval Theories of Emergence," in H. Lagerlund (ed.) *Forming the Mind: Essays on the Internal Senses and the Mind/Body Problem from Avicenna to the Medical Enlightenment* (Dordrecht: Springer, 2007) 149–67.

Pluta, Olaf. "Persecution and the Art of Writing: The Parisian Statute of April 1, 1272, and Its Philosophical Consequences," in P. J. J. M. Bakker (ed.) *Chemins de la pensée médiévale: études offertes à Zénon Kaluza* (Turnhout: Brepols, 2002) 563–85.

Popkin, Richard H. *The History of Scepticism from Savonarola to Bayle*, rev. ed. (Oxford: Oxford University Press, 2003).

Poppi, Antonino. "Zabarella, or Aristotelianism as a Rigorous Science," in R. Pozzo (ed.) *The Impact of Aristotelianism on Modern Philosophy* (Washington: Catholic University of America Press, 2004) 35–63.

Porro, Pasquale (ed.). *The Medieval Concept of Time: Studies on the Scholastic Debate and Its Reception in Early Modern Philosophy* (Leiden: Brill, 2001).

Proust, Jacques. *L'encyclopédisme dans le bas-languedoc au XVIIIe siècle* (Montpellier: Faculté des Lettres et Sciences Humaines de Montpellier, 1968).

Putallaz, François-Xavier. "Censorship," in R. Pasnau (ed.) *The Cambridge History of Medieval Philosophy* (Cambridge: Cambridge University Press, 2010) 99–113.

Putallaz, François-Xavier. *Insolente liberté: controverses et condamnations au XIIIe siècle* (Paris: Cerf, 1995).

Pyle, Andrew. *Atomism and Its Critics: Problem Areas Associated with the Development of the Atomic Theory of Matter from Democritus to Newton* (Bristol: Thoemmes Press, 1995).

Quinto, Riccardo. *Scholastica: storia di un concetto* (Padua: Il poligrafo, 2001).

Redondi, Pietro. *Galileo Eretico* (Turin: G. Einaudi, 1983).

Redondi, Pietro. *Galileo Heretic*, tr. R. Rosenthal (Princeton: Princeton University Press, 1987).

Reid, Jasper. "The Evolution of Henry More's Theory of Divine Absolute Space," *Journal of the History of Philosophy* 45 (2007) 79–102.

Reid, Jasper. "The Spatial Presence of Spirits among the Cartesians," *Journal of the History of Philosophy* 46 (2008) 91–118.

Reif, Patricia. "The Textbook Tradition in Natural Philosophy, 1600–1650," *Journal of the History of Ideas* 30 (1969) 17–32.

Reynolds, Philip. "*Per se* Accidents, Accidental Being and the Theology of the Eucharist in Thomas Aquinas," *Documenti e studi sulla tradizione filosofica medievale* 13 (2002) 193–230.

Reynolds, Philip. "Properties, Causality, and Epistemic Optimism in Thomas Aquinas," *Recherches de théologie et philosophie médiévales* 68 (2001) 270–309.

Rickless, Samuel C. "Locke on Primary and Secondary Qualities," *Pacific Philosophical Quarterly* 78 (1997) 297–319.

Riondato, Ezio and Antonino Poppi (eds.). *Cesare Cremonini: aspetti del pensiero e scritti*, 2 vols. (Padua: Accademia Galileiana di Scienze, Lettere e Arti in Padova, 2000).

Robert, Aurélien. "William Crathorn's Mereotopological Atomism," in C. Grellard and A. Robert (eds.) *Atomism in Late Medieval Philosophy and Theology* (Leiden: Brill, 2009) 127–62.

Rodis-Lewis, Geneviève. *Descartes: His Life and Thought* (Ithaca: Cornell University Press, 1998).

Rodis-Lewis, Geneviève. "Descartes and the Unity of the Human Being," in J. Cottingham (ed.) *Descartes* (Oxford Readings in Philosophy) (Oxford: Oxford University Press, 1998) 197–210.

Rogers, G. A. J. "Locke, Plato and Platonism," in D. Hedley and S. Hutton (eds.) *Platonism at the Origins of Modernity: Studies on Platonism and Early Modern Philosophy* (Dordrecht: Springer, 2008) 193–205.

Rossi, Paolo. *Francis Bacon: From Magic to Science*, tr. S. Rabinovitch (London: Routledge and Kegan Paul, 1968).

Rossi, Paolo. "The Idea of Scientific Progress," in S. Attanasio (tr.) and B. Nelson (ed.) *Philosophy, Technology, and the Arts in the Early Modern Era* (New York: Harper & Row, 1970) 63–99.

Rota, Michael. "Substance and Artifact in Thomas Aquinas," *History of Philosophy Quarterly* 21 (2004) 241–59.

Rozemond, Marleen. *Descartes's Dualism* (Cambridge, MA: Harvard University Press, 1998).

Rozemond, Marleen. "Descartes, Mind–Body Union, and Holenmerism," *Philosophical Topics* 31 (2003) 343–67.

Rozemond, Marleen and Gideon Yaffe. "Peach Trees, Gravity and God: Mechanism in Locke," *British Journal for the History of Philosophy* 12 (2004) 387–412.

Ruby, Jane. "The Origins of Scientific Law," *Journal of the History of Ideas* 47 (1986) 341–59.

Russell, Paul. *The Riddle of Hume's Treatise: Skepticism, Naturalism, and Irreligion* (Oxford: Oxford University Press, 2008).

Rutherford, Donald. "Universal Language," in E. Craig (ed.) *Routledge Encyclopedia of Philosophy* (London: Routledge, 1998) IX:533–5.

Sarasohn, Lisa. *Gassendi's Ethics: Freedom in a Mechanistic Universe* (Ithaca: Cornell University Press, 1996).

Scaltsas, Theodore. *Substance and Universals in Aristotle's Metaphysics* (Ithaca: Cornell University Press, 1994).

Schabel, Christopher. "Francis of Marchia's *Virtus derelicta* and the Context of Its Development," *Vivarium* 44 (2006) 60–80.

Schmaltz, Tad M. *Descartes on Causation* (New York: Oxford University Press, 2008).

Schmaltz, Tad M. *Malebranche's Theory of the Soul: A Cartesian Interpretation* (New York: Oxford University Press, 1996).

Schmaus, Michael. *Der Liber Propugnatorius des Thomas Anglicus und die Lehrunterschiede zwischen Thomas von Aquin und Duns Scotus* (Münster: Aschendorff, 1930).

Schmitt, Charles B. *Aristotle and the Renaissance* (Cambridge, MA: Harvard University Press, 1983).

Schmitt, Charles B. "Cesare Cremonini: un Aristotelico al tempo di Galilei," in *The Aristotelian Tradition and Renaissance Universities* (London: Variorum, 1984) XI.

Schmitt, Charles B. "Galilei and the Seventeenth-Century Text-Book Tradition," in C. Webster (ed.) *Reappraisals in Renaissance Thought* (London: Variorum, 1989) XI.

Schmitt, Charles B. *Gianfrancesco Pico della Mirandola (1469–1533) and His Critique of Aristotle* (The Hague: Martinus Nijhoff, 1967).

Schmitt, Charles B. "L'introduction de la philosophie Platonicienne dans l'enseignement des universités à la Renaissance," in *Studies in Renaissance Philosophy and Science* (London: Variorum, 1981) III.

Schmitt, Charles B. "Recent Trends in the Study of Medieval and Renaissance Science," in C. Webster (ed.) *Reappraisals in Renaissance Thought* (London: Variorum, 1989) XII.

Schmitt, Charles B. "Towards a History of Renaissance Philosophy," in C. Webster (ed.) *Reappraisals in Renaissance Thought* (London: Variorum, 1989) XV.

Schmitt, Charles B. and Quentin Skinner (eds.). *The Cambridge History of Renaissance Philosophy* (Cambridge: Cambridge University Press, 1988).

Schröder, Winfried. *Ursprünge des Atheismus: Untersuchungen zur Metaphysik- und Religionskritik des 17. und 18. Jahrhunderts* (Stuttgart-Bad Cannstatt: Frommann-Holzboog, 1998).

Schüssler, Rudolf. "Jean Gerson, Moral Certainty and the Renaissance of Ancient Skepticism," *Renaissance Studies* 23 (2009) 445–62.

Secada, Jorge. *Cartesian Metaphysics: The Late Scholastic Origins of Modern Philosophy* (Cambridge: Cambridge University Press, 2000).

Sedley, David. "Epicurean Anti-Reductionism," in J. Barnes and M. Mignucci (eds.) *Matter and Metaphysics: Fourth Symposium Hellenisticum* (Naples: Bibliopolis, 1988) 295–327.

Sedley, David. "The Stoic Criterion of Identity," *Phronesis* 27 (1982) 255–75.

Shapiro, Herman. *Motion, Time and Place according to William Ockham* (St. Bonaventure, NY: Franciscan Institute, 1957).

Shapiro, Lionel. "Toward 'Perfect Collections of Properties': Locke on the Constitution of Substantial Sorts," *Canadian Journal of Philosophy* 29 (1999) 551–92.

Shields, Christopher. "Aristotle's Psychology," in E. Zalta (ed.) *The Stanford Encyclopedia of Philosophy (Summer 2003 Edition)* at http://plato.stanford.edu/archives/sum2003/entries/aristotle-psychology/.

Shields, Christopher. *Order in Multiplicity: Homonymy in the Philosophy of Aristotle* (Oxford: Clarendon, 1999).

Shields, Christopher. "The Reality of Substantial Form: Suárez, Metaphysical Disputations XV," in D. Schwartz and J. South (eds.) *Interpreting Suárez: Critical Readings* (Cambridge: Cambridge University Press, forthcoming).

Shields, Christopher. "The Unity of the Soul in Francisco Suárez" (forthcoming).

Shogimen, Takashi. "From Disobedience to Toleration: William of Ockham and the Medieval Discourse of Fraternal Correction," *Journal of Ecclesiastical History* 52 (2001) 599–622.

Simmons, Alison. "Are Cartesian Sensations Representational?" *Nous* 33 (1999) 347–69.

Simmons, Alison. "Sensible Ends: Latent Teleology in Descartes' Account of Sensation," *Journal of the History of Philosophy* 39 (2001) 49–75.

Singer, Charles Joseph. *A Short History of Anatomy from the Greeks to Harvey*, 2nd ed. (New York: Dover, 1957).

Slaughter, Mary M. *Universal Language and Scientific Taxonomy in the Seventeenth Century* (Cambridge: Cambridge University Press, 1982).

Sleigh, Robert C. *Leibniz and Arnauld: A Commentary on their Correspondence* (New Haven: Yale University Press, 1990).

Slowik, Edward. "Descartes and Individual Corporeal Substance," *British Journal for the History of Philosophy* 9 (2001) 1–15.

Smalley, Beryl. "Ecclesiastical Attitudes to Novelty c. 1100–c. 1250," *Studies in Church History* 13 (1975) 113–31.

Solère, Jean-Luc. "Postérité d'Ockham. Temps cartésien et temps newtonien au regard de l'apport nominaliste," in E. Alliez et al. (eds.) *Metamorphosen der Zeit* (Munich: W. Fink, 1999) 293–322.

Sorabji, Richard. *Matter, Space and Motion: Theories in Antiquity and Their Sequel* (Ithaca, NY: Cornell University Press, 1988).

Sorabji, Richard. *Self: Ancient and Modern Insights about Individuality, Life, and Death* (Chicago: University of Chicago Press, 2006).

Sorell, Tom. "Descartes's Modernity," in J. Cottingham (ed.) *Reason, Will, and Sensation: Studies in Descartes's Metaphysics* (Oxford: Clarendon, 1994) 29–45.

Sowaal, Alice. "Cartesian Bodies," *Canadian Journal of Philosophy* 34 (2004) 217–40.

Spade, Paul Vincent (ed.). *The Cambridge Companion to Ockham* (Cambridge: Cambridge University Press, 1999).

Spade, Paul Vincent. "Introduction," in P. V. Spade (ed.) *The Cambridge Companion to Ockham* (Cambridge: Cambridge University Press, 1999) 1–16.

Spade, Paul Vincent. "Ockham, Adams and Connotation: A Critical Notice of Marilyn Adams, William Ockham," *Philosophical Review* 99 (1990) 593–612.

Spade, Paul Vincent. "Ockham's Nominalist Metaphysics: Some Main Themes," in P. V. Spade (ed.) *The Cambridge Companion to Ockham* (Cambridge: Cambridge University Press, 1999) 100–17.

Spade, Paul Vincent. *Thoughts, Words and Things*, version 1.1 (2002) at http://www.pvspade.com/Logic/docs/thoughts1_1a.pdf.

Spade, Paul Vincent. "Three Versions of Ockham's Reductionist Program," *Franciscan Studies* 56 (1998) 335–46.

Stegmüller, Friedrich. "Die zwei Apologien des Jean de Mirecourt," *Recherches de théologie ancienne et médiévale* 5 (1933) 40–78, 192–204.

Stimson, Dorothy. "Ballad of Gresham Colledge," *Isis* 18 (1932) 103–17.

Stone, Abraham D. "Simplicius and Avicenna on the Essential Corporeity of Material Substance," in R. Wisnovsky (ed.) *Aspects of Avicenna* (Princeton: Markus Wiener, 2001) 73–130.

Stuart, Matthew. "Descartes's Extended Substances," in R. Gennaro and C. Huenemann (eds.) *New Essays on the Rationalists* (Oxford: Oxford University Press, 1999) 82–104.

Stuart, Matthew. "Locke on Natural Kinds," *History of Philosophy Quarterly* 16 (1999) 277–96.

Stuart, Matthew. "Locke's Colors," *Philosophical Review* 112 (2003) 57–96.

Stump, Eleonore. *Aquinas* (Arguments of the Philosophers) (London: Routledge, 2003).

Stump, Eleonore and Norman Kretzmann. "Being and Goodness," in T. V. Morris (ed.) *Divine and Human Action: Essays in the Metaphysics of Theism* (Ithaca, NY: Cornell University Press, 1988) 281–312.

Sylla, Edith Dudley. "Autonomous and Handmaiden Science: St. Thomas Aquinas and William of Ockham on the Physics of the Eucharist," in J. E. Murdoch and E. D. Sylla (eds.) *The Cultural Context of Medieval Learning: Proceedings of the First International Colloquium on Philosophy, Science, and Theology in the Middle Ages—September 1973* (Dordrecht: Reidel, 1975) 349–96.

Sylla, Edith Dudley. "Space and Spirit in the Transition from Aristotelian to Newtonian Science," in C. Leijenhorst et al. (eds.) *The Dynamics of Aristotelian Natural Philosophy from Antiquity to the Seventeenth Century* (Leiden: Brill, 2002) 249–87.

Tabarroni, Andrea. "'Utrum Deus Sit in Praedicamento': Ontological Simplicity and Categorial Inclusion," in J. Biard and I. Rosier-Catach (eds.) *La tradition médiévale des catégories, XIIe–XVe siècles* (Louvain: Peeters, 2003) 271–87.

Thackray, Arnold. *Atoms and Powers: An Essay on Newtonian Matter-Theory and the Development of Chemistry* (Cambridge, MA: Harvard University Press, 1970).

Thiel, Udo. "Individuation," in D. Garber and M. Ayers (eds.) *The Cambridge History of Seventeenth-Century Philosophy* (Cambridge: Cambridge University, 1998) 212–62.

Thiel, Udo. *Lockes Theorie der personalen Identität* (Bonn: Bouvier, 1983).

Thiel, Udo. "The Trinity and Human Personal Identity," in M. A. Stewart (ed.) *English Philosophy in the Age of Locke* (Oxford: Clarendon, 2000) 217–43.

Thijssen, J. M. M. H. "The Buridan School Reassessed: John Buridan and Albert of Saxony," *Vivarium* 42 (2004) 18–42.

Thijssen, J. M. M. H. *Censure and Heresy at the University of Paris, 1200–1400* (Philadelphia: University of Pennsylvania Press, 1998).

Thomasson, Amie. "Categories," in E. Zalta (ed.) *The Stanford Encyclopedia of Philosophy (Fall 2004 Edition)* at http://plato.stanford.edu/archives/fall2004/entries/categories/.

Thorndike, Lynn. "Censorship by the Sorbonne of Science and Superstition in the First Half of the Seventeenth Century," *Journal of the History of Ideas* 16 (1955) 119–25.

Thorndike, Lynn. *University Records and Life in the Middle Ages* (New York: Columbia University Press, 1944).

Trapp, Damasus. "Aegidii Romani de doctrina modorum," *Angelicum* 12 (1935) 449–501.

Trapp, Damasus. "Peter Ceffons of Clairvaux," *Recherches de théologie ancienne et médiévale* 24 (1957) 101–54.

Trifogli, Cecilia. "Change, Time, and Place" in R. Pasnau (ed.) *The Cambridge History of Medieval Philosophy* (Cambridge: Cambridge University Press, 2010) 267–78.

Trifogli, Cecilia. *Oxford Physics in the Thirteenth Century (ca. 1250–1270): Motion, Infinity, Place and Time* (Leiden: Brill, 2000).

Uzgalis, William L. "Relative Identity and Locke's Principle of Individuation," *History of Philosophy Quarterly* 7 (1990) 283–97.

van Leeuwen, Henry. *The Problem of Certainty in English Thought: 1630–1690* (The Hague: Martinus Nijhoff, 1970).

van Melsen, A. G. M. *From Atomos to Atom: The History of the Concept Atom*, tr. H. J. Koren (Pittsburgh: Duquesne University Press, 1952).

Verbeke, Gerard. "Philosophy and Heresy: Some Conflicts between Reason and Faith," in W. Lourdaux and D. Verhelst (eds.) *The Concept of Heresy in the Middle Ages (11ᵗʰ–13ᵗʰ C.)* (Leuven: Leuven University Press, 1976) 172–97.

Voss, Stephen. "Descartes: The End of Anthropology," in J. Cottingham (ed.) *Reason, Will, and Sensation: Studies in Descartes's Metaphysics* (Oxford: Clarendon, 1994) 273–306.

Voss, Stephen. "Descartes: Heart and Soul," in J. P. Wright and P. Potter (eds.) *Psyche and Soma: Physicians and Metaphysicians on the Mind–Body Problem from Antiquity to Enlightenment* (Oxford: Clarendon, 2000) 173–96.

Wakefield, Walter L. and Austin P. Evans. *Heresies of the High Middle Ages* (New York: Columbia University Press, 1969).

Wald, Berthold. *"Accidens est Formaliter Ens*: Duns Scotus on Inherence in his *Quaestiones Subtilissimae* on Aristotle's *Metaphysics*," in J. Marenbon (ed.) *Aristotle in Britain during the Middle Ages* (Turnhout: Brepols, 1996) 177–93.

Walmsley, J. C. "Locke's Natural Philosophy in Draft A of the *Essay*," *Journal of the History of Ideas* 65 (2004) 15–37.

Ward, G. R. M. *Oxford University Statutes*, 2 vols. (London: W. Pickering, 1845–51).

Wéber, Édouard-Henri. "L'incidence du traité de l'eucharistie sur la métaphysique de S. Thomas d'Aquin," *Revue des sciences philosophiques et théologiques* 77 (1993) 195–218.

Wedin, Michael V. *Aristotle's Theory of Substance: The* Categories *and* Metaphysics Zeta (Oxford: Oxford University Press, 2000).

Weinberg, Julius Rudolph. *Nicolaus of Autrecourt: A Study in 14th Century Thought* (Princeton: Princeton University Press, 1948; repr. New York: Greenwood Press, 1969).

Weisheipl, James A. "Comment," in E. McMullin (ed.) *The Concept of Matter in Modern Philosophy* (Notre Dame: University of Notre Dame Press, 1963) 100–3.

Weisheipl, James A. "The Concept of Matter in Fourteenth-Century Science," in E. McMullin (ed.) *The Concept of Matter in Greek and Medieval Philosophy* (Notre Dame: University of Notre Dame Press, 1963) 147–69.

Weisheipl, James A. "Ockham and the Mertonians," in *The History of the University of Oxford: Volume 1. The Early Oxford Schools*, ed. J. I. Catto (Oxford: Oxford University Press, 1984) 607–58.

Weisheipl, James A. "The Place of John Dumbleton in the Merton School," *Isis* 50 (1959) 439–54.

Wells, Norman J. "Suarez, Historian and Critic of the Modal Distinction between Essential Being and Existential Being," *New Scholasticism* 36 (1962) 419–44.

Westerhoff, Jan. *Ontological Categories: Their Nature and Significance* (Oxford: Oxford University Press, 2005).

Westfall, Richard S. *The Construction of Modern Science: Mechanisms and Mechanics* (Cambridge: Cambridge University Press, 1977).

Westfall, Richard S. *Force in Newton's Physics* (London: MacDonald, 1971).

Wieland, Georg. *Untersuchungen zum Seinsbegriff im Metaphysikkommentar Alberts des Grossen* (Münster: Aschendorff, 1972).

Wierenga, Edward. "Omnipresence," in E. Zalta (ed.) *The Stanford Encyclopedia of Philosophy (Fall 2009 Edition)* at http://plato.stanford.edu/archives/fall2009/entries/omnipresence

Wiggins, David. "Substance," in A. C. Grayling (ed.) *Philosophy: A Guide through the Subject* (Oxford: Oxford University Press, 1995) 214–46.

Williams, Bernard. *Descartes: The Project of Pure Enquiry* (London: Penguin, 1978).

Williams, Bernard. "Hylomorphism," *Oxford Studies in Ancient Philosophy* 4 (1986) 189–99.

Williams, D. C. "Form and Matter," *Philosophical Review* 67 (1958) 291–312, 499–521.

Wilson, Catherine. *Epicureanism at the Origins of Modernity* (Oxford: Clarendon, 2008).

Wilson, Gordon. "Henry of Ghent and René Descartes on the Unity of Man," *Franziskanische Studien* 64 (1982) 97–110.

Wilson, Margaret Dauler. *Descartes* (The Arguments of the Philosophers) (London: Routledge, 1978).

Wilson, Margaret Dauler. "History of Philosophy in Philosophy Today and the Case of the Sensible Qualities," *Philosophical Review* 101 (1992) 191–243.

Wilson, Robert A. "Locke's Primary Qualities," *Journal of the History of Philosophy* 40 (2002) 201–28.

Winkler, Kenneth. "Locke on Personal Identity," in V. Chappell (ed.) *Locke* (Oxford: Oxford University Press, 1998) 149–74 [orig. publ. 1991].

Wippel, John F. "Essence and Existence," in R. Pasnau (ed.) *Cambridge History of Medieval Philosophy* (Cambridge: Cambridge University Press, 2010) 622–34.

Wippel, John F. *The Metaphysical Thought of Godfrey of Fontaines: A Study in Late Thirteenth-Century Philosophy* (Washington, DC: Catholic University of America Press, 1981).

Wippel, John F. *The Metaphysical Thought of Thomas Aquinas: From Finite Being to Uncreated Being* (Washington, DC: Catholic University of America Press, 2000).

Wood, Rega. "The Influence of Arabic Aristotelianism on Scholastic Natural Philosophy: Projectile Motion, The Place of the Universe, and Elemental Composition," in R. Pasnau (ed.) *Cambridge History of Medieval Philosophy* (Cambridge: Cambridge University Press, 2010) 247–66.

Wood, Rega. "Introduction," in Adam Wodeham, *Tractatus de indivisibilibus* (Dordrecht: Reidel, 1987).

Wood, Rega and Michael Weisberg. "Interpreting Aristotle on Mixture: Problems about Elemental Composition from Philoponus to Cooper," *Studies in History and Philosophy of Science* 35 (2004) 681–706.

Woolhouse, R. S. *Descartes, Spinoza, Leibniz: The Concept of Substance in Seventeenth-Century Metaphysics* (London: Routledge, 1993).

Wuellner, Bernard. *A Dictionary of Scholastic Philosophy* (Milwaukee: Bruce, 1966).

Yaffe, Gideon. "Locke on Ideas of Identity and Diversity," in L. Newman (ed.) *The Cambridge Companion to Locke's "Essay concerning Human Understanding"* (Cambridge: Cambridge University Press, 2007) 192–230.

Yolton, John W. *Locke and the Compass of Human Understanding: A Selective Commentary on the Essay* (Cambridge: Cambridge University Press, 1970).

Yolton, John W. *A Locke Dictionary* (Oxford: Blackwell, 1993).

Yolton, John W. *Thinking Matter: Materialism in Eighteenth-Century Britain* (Minneapolis: University of Minnesota Press, 1983).

Zagorin, Perez. *Francis Bacon* (Princeton: Princeton University Press, 1998).

Zavalloni, Roberto. *Richard de Mediavilla et la controverse sur la pluralité des formes* (Louvain: Éditions de l'Institut Supérieur de Philosophie, 1951).

Zilsel, Edgar. "The Genesis of the Concept of Scientific Progress," in P. Wiener and A. Noland (eds.) *Roots of Scientific Thought: A Cultural Perspective* (New York: Basic Books, 1957) 251–75.

Zimmermann, Ivana. "Kommentare zu der Schrift des Averroes 'De substantia orbis' in der Bibliotheca Amploniana," in A. Speer (ed.) *Die Bibliotheca Amploniana: ihre Bedeutung im Spannungsfeld von Aristotelismus, Nominalismus und Humanismus* (Berlin: de Gruyter, 1995) 122–6.

Zupko, Jack. "How Are Souls Related to Bodies? A Study of John Buridan," *Review of Metaphysics* 46 (1993) 575–601.

Zupko, Jack. *John Buridan: Portrait of a Fourteenth-Century Arts Master* (Notre Dame: University of Notre Dame Press, 2003).

INDEX OF NAMES

Authors whose careers predate 1600 are indexed by first name.

SUBJECT INDEX

www.ingramcontent.com/pod-product-compliance
Lightning Source LLC
Chambersburg PA
CBHW080853050725
29159CB00028B/523